Dedication

To Chailin and Debbie, still the loves of our lives
And to our wonderful children, Catherine Cummings
and Sarah, Hannah, and Samuel Worley

In Memory of the Fallen

Larry Greiner
Richard Hackman
Tony Raia
Edie Seashore
Charlie Seashore

In Loving Memory

Jessica Joan Worley

Brief Contents

Preface xvi

About the Authors xxii

CHAPTER 1
General Introduction to Organization Development 1

PART 1 Overview of Organization Development 20

CHAPTER 2
The Nature of Planned Change 21

CHAPTER 3
The Organization Development Practitioner 45

PART 2 The Process of Organization Development 74

CHAPTER 4
Entering and Contracting 75

CHAPTER 5
Diagnosing 89

CHAPTER 6
Collecting, Analyzing, and Feeding Back Diagnostic Information 123

CHAPTER 7
Designing Interventions 157

CHAPTER 8
Managing Change 179

CHAPTER 9
Evaluating and Institutionalizing Organization Development Interventions 207

PART 3 Human Process Interventions 264

CHAPTER 10
Interpersonal and Group Process Approaches 265

CHAPTER 11
Organization Process Approaches 297

PART 4 Technostructural Interventions 338

CHAPTER 12
Restructuring Organizations 339

CHAPTER 13
Employee Involvement 375

CHAPTER 14
Work Design 403

PART 5 Human Resource Interventions 438

CHAPTER 15
Performance Management 439

CHAPTER 16
Talent Management 473

CHAPTER 17
Workforce Diversity and Wellness 497

PART 6 Strategic Change Interventions 528

CHAPTER 18
Transformational Change 529

CHAPTER 19
Continuous Change 569

CHAPTER 20
Transorganizational Change 605

PART 7 Special Applications of Organization Development 658

CHAPTER 21
Organization Development for Economic, Ecological, and Social Outcomes 659

CHAPTER 22
Organization Development in Nonindustrial Settings: Health Care, School Systems, the Public Sector, and Family–Owned 685

CHAPTER 23
Future Directions in Organization Development 731

Glossary 784

Name Index 793

Subject Index 797

Contents

Preface xvi
About the Authors xxii

CHAPTER 1 General Introduction to Organization Development 1

1-1 **Organization Development Defined 1**
1-2 **The Growth and Relevance of Organization Development 4**
1-3 **A Short History of Organization Development 7**
1-3a Laboratory Training Background 8
1-3b Action Research and Survey-Feedback Background 8
1-3c Normative Background 9
1-3d Productivity and Quality-of-Work-Life Background 11
1-3e Strategic Change Background 13
1-4 **Evolution in Organization Development 13**
1-5 **Overview of the Book 15**
Summary 17
Notes 17

PART 1 Overview of Organization Development 20

CHAPTER 2 The Nature of Planned Change 21

2-1 **Theories of Planned Change 22**
2-1a Lewin's Change Model 22
2-1b Action Research Model 24
2-1c The Positive Model 26
2-1d Comparisons of Change Models 27
2-2 **General Model of Planned Change 28**
2-2a Entering and Contracting 28
2-2b Diagnosing 29
2-2c Planning and Implementing Change 29
2-2d Evaluating and Institutionalizing Change 30
2-3 **Different Types of Planned Change 30**
2-3a Magnitude of Change 30
Application 2.1 *Planned Change at the San Diego County Regional Airport Authority 31*
2-3b Degree of Organization 34
2-3c Domestic versus International Settings 35
Application 2.2 *Planned Change in an Underorganized System 36*
2-4 **Critique of Planned Change 40**
2-4a Conceptualization of Planned Change 40
2-4b Practice of Planned Change 41

Summary 42
Notes 42

CHAPTER 3 The Organization Development Practitioner 45

3-1 **Who Is the Organization Development Practitioner? 46**
3-2 **Competencies of an Effective Organization Development Practitioner 47**
3-2a Intrapersonal Skills or "Self-Management" Competence 48
3-2b Interpersonal Skills 51
3-2c General Consultation Skills 51
3-2d Organization Development Theory 52
3-3 **The Professional Organization Development Practitioner 52**
3-3a Role of Organization Development Professional Positions 52
Application 3.1 *Personal Views of the Internal and External Consulting Positions 55*
3-3b Careers of Organization Development Professionals 59
3-4 **Professional Values 60**
3-5 **Professional Ethics 61**
3-5a Ethical Guidelines 61
3-5b Ethical Dilemmas 62
Application 3.2 *Kindred Todd and the Ethics of OD 65*
Summary 66
Notes 67
Appendix 70

PART 2 The Process of Organization Development 74

CHAPTER 4 Entering and Contracting 75

4-1 **Entering into an OD Relationship 76**
4-1a Clarifying the Organizational Issue 76
4-1b Determining the Relevant Client 77
4-1c Selecting an OD Practitioner 78
4-2 **Developing a Contract 79**
Application 4.1 *Entering Alegent Health 80*
4-2a Mutual Expectations 81
4-2b Time and Resources 81
4-2c Ground Rules 82
4-3 **Interpersonal Process Issues in Entering and Contracting 82**
Application 4.2 *Contracting with Alegent Health 83*
Summary 87
Notes 87

CHAPTER 5 Diagnosing 89

5-1 **What Is Diagnosis? 90**
5-2 **The Need for Diagnostic Models 91**
5-3 **Open-Systems Model 92**
5-3a Organizations as Open Systems 92
5-3b Diagnosing Organizational Systems 94

5-4 **Organization-Level Diagnosis 96**
5-4a Inputs 96
5-4b Design Components 98
5-4c Outputs 100
5-4d Alignment 100
5-4e Analysis 101

Application 5.1 *Steinway & Sons 102*

5-5 **Group-Level Diagnosis 106**
5-5a Inputs 106
5-5b Design Components 107
5-5c Outputs 108
5-5d Alignment 108
5-5e Analysis 109

Application 5.2 *Top-Management Team at Ortiv Glass Corporation 110*

5-6 **Individual-Level Diagnosis 112**
5-6a Inputs 112
5-6b Design Components 113
5-6c Outputs 113
5-6d Alignment 114
5-6e Analysis 114

Application 5.3 *Job Design at Pepperdine University 115*

Summary 119

Notes 119

CHAPTER 6 Collecting, Analyzing, and Feeding Back Diagnostic Information 123

6-1 **The Diagnostic Relationship 123**

6-2 **Collecting Data 126**
6-2a Questionnaires 127
6-2b Interviews 129
6-2c Observations 130
6-2d Unobtrusive Measures 131

6-3 **Sampling 132**

6-4 **Analyzing Data 133**
6-4a Qualitative Tools 133
6-4b Quantitative Tools 135

Application 6.1 *Collecting and Analyzing Diagnostic Data at Alegent Health 136*

6-5 **Feeding Back Data 142**
6-5a Content of Feedback 142
6-5b Process of Feedback 144

6-6 **Survey Feedback 145**
6-6a What Are the Steps? 145

Application 6.2 *Training OD Practitioners in Data Feedback 146*
6-6b Survey Feedback and Organizational Dependencies 148

Application 6.3 *Survey Feedback and Planned Change at Cambia Health Solutions 149*
6-6c Limitations of Survey Feedback 152
6-6d Results of Survey Feedback 152

Summary 154

Notes 154

CHAPTER 7 Designing Interventions 157

7-1 **Overview of Interventions 157**
7-1a Human Process Interventions 157
7-1b Technostructural Interventions 159
7-1c Human Resources Management Interventions 160
7-1d Strategic Change Interventions 161

7-2 **What Are Effective Interventions? 162**

7-3 **How to Design Effective Interventions 163**
7-3a Contingencies Related to the Change Situation 164
7-3b Contingencies Related to the Target of Change 171

Summary 173

Notes 175

CHAPTER 8 Managing Change 179

8-1 **Overview of Change Activities 179**

8-2 **Motivating Change 181**
8-2a Creating Readiness for Change 181
8-2b Overcoming Resistance to Change 183

8-3 **Creating a Vision 184**

Application 8.1 *Motivating Change in the Sexual Violence Prevention Unit of Minnesota's Health Department 185*
8-3a Describing the Core Ideology 186
8-3b Constructing the Envisioned Future 187

8-4 **Developing Political Support 188**

Application 8.2 *Creating a Vision at Premier 189*
8-4a Assessing Change Agent Power 192
8-4b Identifying Key Stakeholders 192
8-4c Influencing Stakeholders 192

8-5 **Managing the Transition 193**

Application 8.3 *Developing Political Support for the Strategic Planning Project in the Sexual Violence Prevention Unit 194*
8-5a Activity Planning 196
8-5b Commitment Planning 196
8-5c Change-Management Structures 196
8-5d Learning Processes 196

8-6 **Sustaining Momentum 197**

Application 8.4 *Transition Management in the HP–Compaq Acquisition 198*
8-6a Providing Resources for Change 200
8-6b Building a Support System for Change Agents 200
8-6c Developing New Competencies and Skills 200
8-6d Reinforcing New Behaviors 201
8-6e Staying the Course 201

Application 8.5 *Sustaining Change at RMIT University Library in Melbourne, Australia 202*

Summary 204

Notes 205

CHAPTER 9 Evaluating and Institutionalizing Organization Development Interventions 207

9-1 **Evaluating Organization Development Interventions 207**
- 9-1a Implementation and Evaluation Feedback 208
- 9-1b Measurement 211
- 9-1c Research Design 216

Application 9.1 *Evaluating Change at Alegent Health 219*

9-2 **Institutionalizing Organizational Changes 221**
- 9-2a Institutionalization Framework 222
- 9-2b Organization Characteristics 222
- 9-2c Intervention Characteristics 223
- 9-2d Institutionalization Processes 224
- 9-2e Indicators of Institutionalization 226

Application 9.2 *Institutionalizing Structural Change at Hewlett-Packard 227*

Summary 229

Notes 229

Selected Cases 232
- Sunflower Incorporated 232
- Kenworth Motors 234
- Peppercorn Dining 238
- Diagnosis and Feedback at Adhikar 257
- Managing Change: Action Planning for the Vélo V Project in Lyon, France 262

PART 3 Human Process Interventions 264

CHAPTER 10 Interpersonal and Group Process Approaches 265

10-1 **Diagnostic Issues in Interpersonal and Group Process Interventions 266**

10-2 **Process Consultation 267**
- 10-2a Basic Process Interventions 268

Application 10.1 *Process Consultation at Christian Caring Homes, Inc. 271*
- 10-2b Results of Process Consultation 273

10-3 **Third-Party Interventions 274**
- 10-3a An Episodic Model of Conflict 275
- 10-3b Facilitating the Conflict Resolution Process 276

10-4 **Team Building 277**

Application 10.2 *Conflict Management at Ross & Sherwin 278*
- 10-4a Team-Building Activities 282
- 10-4b Interventions Relevant to Individual Behavior 285
- 10-4c Interventions Relevant to the Group's Behavior 285
- 10-4d Interventions Affecting the Group's Integration with the Rest of the Organization 286

Application 10.3 *Aligning Senior Teams at Vaycot Products 287*
- 10-4e The Manager's Role in Team Building 291
- 10-4f The Results of Team Building 292

Summary 293

Notes 294

CHAPTER 11 Organization Process Approaches 297

11-1 **Diagnostic Issues in Organization Process Interventions 298**

11-2 **Organization Confrontation Meeting 298**

11-2a Application Stages 299

Application 11.1 *A Work-Out Meeting at General Electric Medical Systems Business 300*

11-2b Results of Confrontation Meetings 301

11-3 **Intergroup Relations Interventions 301**

11-3a Microcosm Groups 301

11-3b Resolving Intergroup Conflict 304

Application 11.2 *Improving Intergroup Relationships in Johnson & Johnson's Drug Evaluation Department 307*

11-4 **Large Group Interventions 309**

11-4a Application Stages 310

Application 11.3 *Using the Decision Accelerator to Generate Innovative Strategies in Alegent's Women's and Children's Service Line 314*

11-4b Results of Large Group Interventions 318

Summary 319

Notes 320

Selected Cases 322

Lincoln Hospital: Third-Party Intervention 322

Large Group Interventions at Airbus' ICT Organization 329

PART 4 Technostructural Interventions 338

CHAPTER 12 Restructuring Organizations 339

12-1 **Structural Design 339**

12-1a The Functional Structure 340

12-1b The Divisional Structure 342

12-1c The Matrix Structure 344

12-1d The Process Structure 346

12-1e The Customer-Centric Structure 349

Application 12.1 *Healthways' Process Structure 350*

12-1f The Network Structure 353

12-2 **Downsizing 356**

Application 12.2 *Amazon.com's Network Structure 357*

12-2a Application Stages 359

Application 12.3 *Downsizing in Menlo Park, California 362*

12-2b Results of Downsizing 363

12-3 **Reengineering 364**

12-3a Application Stages 365

12-3b Results from Reengineering 368

Application 12.4 *Honeywell IAC's TotalPlant™ Reengineering Process 369*

Summary 371

Notes 371

CHAPTER 13 Employee Involvement 375

13-1 **Employee Involvement: What Is It? 376**

13-1a A Working Definition of Employee Involvement 376

13-1b The Diffusion of Employee Involvement Practices 377
13-1c How Employee Involvement Affects Productivity 377

13-2 **Employee Involvement Interventions 379**
13-2a Parallel Structures 379

Application 13.1 *Using the AI Summit to Build Union–Management Relations at Roadway Express 382*
13-2b Total Quality Management 385

Application 13.2 *TQM at the Ritz-Carlton 391*
13-2c High-Involvement Organizations 392

Application 13.3 *Building a High-Involvement Organization at Air Products and Chemicals, Inc. 396*

Summary 399

Notes 399

CHAPTER 14 Work Design 403

14-1 **The Engineering Approach 404**

14-2 **The Motivational Approach 405**
14-2a The Core Dimensions of Jobs 405
14-2b Individual Differences 407
14-2c Application Stages 407

Application 14.1 *Enriching Jobs at the Hartford's Employee Relations Consulting Services Group 410*
14-2d Barriers to Job Enrichment 412
14-2e Results of Job Enrichment 413

14-3 **The Sociotechnical Systems Approach 414**
14-3a Conceptual Background 414
14-3b Self-Managed Work Teams 415
14-3c Application Stages 419

Application 14.2 *Developing Self-Managed Teams at WI, Inc. 421*
14-3d Results of Self-Managed Teams 423

14-4 **Designing Work for Technical and Personal Needs 425**
14-4a Technical Factors 425
14-4b Personal-Need Factors 426
14-4c Meeting Both Technical and Personal Needs 428

Summary 429

Notes 429

Selected Cases 433
City of Carlsbad, California: Restructuring the Public Works Department (A) 433
The Sullivan Hospital System 435

PART 5 Human Resource Interventions 438

CHAPTER 15 Performance Management 439

15-1 **A Model of Performance Management 440**

15-2 **Goal Setting 442**
15-2a Characteristics of Goal Setting 442
15-2b Application Stages 443

15-2c Management by Objectives 444
15-2d Effects of Goal Setting and MBO 445

Application 15.1 *Changing the Human Capital Management Practices at Cambia Health Solutions 446*

15-3 **Performance Appraisal 448**
15-3a The Performance Appraisal Process 449
15-3b Application Stages 451
15-3c Effects of Performance Appraisal 452

15-4 **Reward Systems 452**

Application 15.2 *Adapting the Appraisal Process at Capital One Financial 453*
15-4a Structural and Motivational Features of Reward Systems 455
15-4b Reward System Design Features 457
15-4c Skill- and Knowledge-Based Pay Systems 458
15-4d Performance-Based Pay Systems 460
15-4e Gain-Sharing Systems 462
15-4f Promotion Systems 464
15-4g Reward-System Process Issues 464

Application 15.3 *Revising the Reward System at Lands' End 465*

Summary 468

Notes 468

CHAPTER 16 Talent Management 473

16-1 **Coaching and Mentoring 474**
16-1a What Are the Goals? 474
16-1b Application Stages 475
16-1c The Results of Coaching and Mentoring 476

16-2 **Management and Leadership Development Interventions 476**
16-2a What Are the Goals? 477
16-2b Application Stages 477

Application 16.1 *Leading Your Business at Microsoft Corporation 479*
16-2c The Results of Development Interventions 480

16-3 **Career Planning and Development Interventions 480**
16-3a What Are the Goals? 481
16-3b Application Stages 482

Application 16.2 *PepsiCo's Career Planning and Development Framework 491*
16-3c The Results of Career Planning and Development 493

Summary 493

Notes 494

CHAPTER 17 Workforce Diversity and Wellness 497

17-1 **Workforce Diversity Interventions 497**
17-1a What Are the Goals? 498
17-1b Application Stages 499
17-1c The Results for Diversity Interventions 503

17-2 **Employee Stress and Wellness Interventions 504**
17-2a What Are the Goals? 504

Application 17.1 *Aligning Strategy and Diversity at L'Oréal 505*
17-2b Application Stages 507
17-2c The Results of Stress Management and Wellness Interventions 513

Application 17.2 *Johnson & Johnson's Health and Wellness Program* 514
Summary 516
Notes 516
Selected Cases 519
Employee Benefits at HealthCo 519
Designing and Implementing a Reward System at Disk Drives, Inc. 523

PART 6 Strategic Change Interventions 528

CHAPTER 18 Transformational Change 529

18-1 **Characteristics of Transformational Change 530**
18-1a Change Is Triggered by Environmental and Internal Disruptions 530
18-1b Change Is Initiated by Senior Executives and Line Managers 531
18-1c Change Involves Multiple Stakeholders 532
18-1d Change Is Systemic and Revolutionary 532
18-1e Change Involves Significant Learning and a New Paradigm 533
18-2 **Organization Design 534**
18-2a Conceptual Framework 534
18-2b Basic Design Alternatives 535
18-2c Worldwide Organization Design Alternatives 537
Application 18.1 *Organization Design at Deere & Company* 538
Application 18.2 *Implementing the Global Strategy: Changing the Culture of Work in Western China* 542
18-2d Application Stages 546
18-3 **Integrated Strategic Change 548**
18-3a Key Features 549
18-3b Implementing the ISC Process 549
18-4 **Culture Change 552**
18-4a Defining and Diagnosing Organization Culture 552
Application 18.3 *Managing Strategic Change at Microsoft Canada* 553
18-4b Implementing the Culture Change Process 558
Application 18.4 *Culture Change at IBM* 561
Summary 563
Notes 563

CHAPTER 19 Continuous Change 569

19-1 **Dynamic Strategy Making 570**
19-1a Conceptual Framework 571
19-1b Application Stages 573
19-2 **Self-Designing Organizations 576**
19-2a The Demands of Turbulent Environments 576
Application 19.1 *Dynamic Strategy Making at Whitbread PLC* 577
19-2b Application Stages 579
19-3 **Learning Organizations 582**
Application 19.2 *Self-Design at Healthways Corporation* 583
19-3a Conceptual Framework 584
19-3b Organization Learning Interventions 586
19-4 **Built-to-Change Organizations 593**
19-4a Design Guidelines 593

Application 19.3 *Dialogue and Organization Learning at DMT 594*
19-4b Application Stages 597
Application 19.4 *Creating a Built-to-Change Organization at Capital One Financial 599*
Summary 601
Notes 602

CHAPTER 20 Transorganizational Change 605
20-1 **Transorganizational Rationale 606**
20-2 **Mergers and Acquisitions 607**
20-2a Application Stages 608
Application 20.1 *Planning the United–Continental Merger 613*
20-3 **Strategic Alliance Interventions 616**
20-3a Application Stages 616
Application 20.2 *Building Alliance Relationships 618*
20-4 **Network Interventions 620**
20-4a Creating the Network 621
20-4b Managing Network Change 624
Application 20.3 *The Alaska Workforce Coalition 627*
Summary 631
Notes 632
Selected Cases 636
Global Mobile Corporation 636
Leading Strategic Change at DaVita: The Integration of the Gambro Acquisition 645

PART 7 **Special Applications of Organization Development 658**

CHAPTER 21 Organization Development for Economic, Ecological, and Social Outcomes 659
21-1 **Sustainable Management Organizations 659**
21-1a Design Guidelines 660
21-1b Application Stages 667
21-2 **Global Social Change 670**
21-2a Global Social Change Organizations 670
Application 21.1 *Interface Carpet's Transformation to Sustainability 671*
21-2b Application Stages 674
21-2c Change-Agent Roles and Skills 677
Application 21.2 *Social and Environmental Change at LDI Africa 678*
Summary 681
Notes 682

CHAPTER 22 Organization Development in Nonindustrial Settings: Health Care, School Systems, the Public Sector, and Family–Owned 685
22-1 **Organization Development in Health Care 686**
22-1a The Health Care Industry—A Snapshot 686
22-1b Trends in Health Care 687

22-1c Opportunities for Organization Development Practice 690
22-1d Conclusions 693

22-2 **Organization Development in Public School Systems 693**
22-2a A Complex, Diverse, and Evolving K-12 Educational System 693
22-2b Change Forces 694
22-2c Disappointing Reform Efforts 696
22-2d Considerations for OD Practitioners 699
22-2e Conclusions 702

22-3 **Organization Development in the Public Sector 703**
22-3a Comparing Public- and Private-Sector Organizations 705
22-3b Recent Research and Innovations in Public-Sector Organization Development 710
22-3c Conclusions 711

22-4 **Organization Development in Family-Owned Businesses 711**
22-4a The Family Business System 712
22-4b Business, Ownership, and Family Systems 714
22-4c Family Business Developmental Stages 715
22-4d A Parallel Planning Process 716
22-4e Values 716
22-4f Critical Issues in Family Business 719

Summary 725

Notes 726

CHAPTER 23 Future Directions in Organization Development 731

23-1 **Trends Within Organization Development 732**
23-1a Traditional Trend 732
23-1b Pragmatic Trend 733
23-1c Scholarly Trend 733
23-1d Implications for OD's Future 734

23-2 **Trends in the Context of Organization Development 735**
23-2a The Economy 735
23-2b The Workforce 738
23-2c Technology 739
23-2d Organizations 740
23-2e Implications for OD's Future 741

Summary 747

Notes 747

Integrative Cases 750
B. R. Richardson Timber Products Corporation 750
Building the Cuyahoga River Valley Organization 764
The Transformation of Meck Insurance 774

Glossary 784

Name Index 793

Subject Index 797

Preface

What a difference an edition makes. We need look no farther than this text to get a sense of the pace and consequences of change. Compared to the promise of hope and change that accompanied Barack Obama's first election while we were finishing the ninth edition, finishing this tenth edition in 2013 brings daily reminders that things are moving far more quickly and unpredictably than we could ever have imagined. As a global society, we are still living with the enormous personal, social, and economic consequences of the financial turmoil brought on by the mortgage-lending crisis and the subsequent recession that enveloped the world's economies; still coping with the distressing aftermath of man-made and natural calamities such as the BP/Macondo/Deepwater Horizon disaster in the Gulf of Mexico and the earthquake and tsunami that devastated Japan; and still apprehensive about the spreading strife and seemingly intractable unrest in the Middle East, the angry rhetoric from the Korean peninsula, and the ever present threat of terrorist attacks almost anywhere, any time. We are reminded almost daily that global climate change, nuclear weapons proliferation, and disease pandemics can actually happen in our lifetime, businesses are not too big to fail, and almost no industry or sector of society is free of ethical breeches, illegal practices, or mismanagement. From a more optimistic perspective, more and more of the world's population is taking advantage of the rapid advances in information technology that are transforming how we do business, communicate and relate with each other, deliver and access information, and educate and entertain ourselves. Add to this the enormous advances in medicine and health care that are offering promising new treatments for many of the maladies that plague us.

For organizations existing in these times, life can be extremely challenging. Businesses increasingly face global markets in which competition is intense, and economic, political, and cultural conditions are diverse and can change unexpectedly. Sources of competitive advantage, such as technical, product, or resource superiority, can quickly erode as can a firm's storehouse of human capital and knowledge. Government agencies encounter more and more demands to operate more efficiently, offering faster, cheaper, and better service at lower cost. Yet funding is scarcer and tied unpredictably to shifting economic conditions, political whims, and public mandates. Educational institutions increasingly are being asked to keep pace with the changing needs of a global society by delivering more knowledge to larger numbers of more diverse students at lower costs in ways that transcend the physical classroom. At the same time, budgets for public education have been falling, advances in information technology have far exceeded the willingness and capability of educators to apply them to student learning, and the bureaucracy surrounding curriculum change remains well in place.

In times like these, organization development (OD) and change has never been more relevant and necessary. For our part, this is the tenth edition of the market-leading text in the field. OD is an applied field of change that uses behavioral science knowledge to improve organizations' functioning and performance and to increase their capability to change. OD is more than change management, however, and goes well beyond the mechanistic, programmatic assumptions that organization change can simply be scripted by various methods of "involving" people and "enrolling" them in the change. OD is not concerned about change for change's sake, a way to implement the latest fad, or a pawn for doing management's bidding. It is about learning and improving in ways that make individuals, groups, organizations, and ultimately societies better off and more capable of managing change in the future. Moreover, OD is more than a set of tools and techniques. It is not a bunch of "interventions" looking to be applied in whatever organization that comes along. It is an integrated theory and practice aimed at increasing an organization's effectiveness. Finally, OD is more than a set of values. It is not a front for the promulgation of humanistic and spiritual beliefs or a set of interventions that boil down to "holding hands and singing Kumbaya." It is a set of evidence-based ideas and practices about how organizations can produce sustainable high performance and human fulfillment.

The original edition of this text, authored by OD pioneer Edgar Huse in 1975, became a market leader because it faced the relevance issue. It took an objective, research perspective and placed OD practice on a strong theoretical footing. Ed showed that, in some cases, OD did produce meaningful results but that additional work was still needed. Sadly, Ed passed away following the publication of the second edition. His wife, Mary Huse, asked Tom Cummings to revise the book for subsequent editions. With the fifth edition, Tom asked Chris Worley to join him in writing the text.

The most recent editions have had an important influence on the perception of OD. While maintaining the book's strengths of even treatment and unbiased reporting, the newer editions made even larger strides in placing OD on a strong empirical foundation. They broadened the scope and increased the relevance of OD by including interventions that had a content component, including work design, employee involvement, organization design, and transorganization change. They took another step toward relevance and suggested that OD had begun to incorporate a strategic perspective. This strategic orientation proposed that OD could be as concerned with performance issues as it was with human potential. Effective OD, from this newer perspective, relied as much on knowledge about organization theory and economics as it did on the more "micro" behavioral sciences. The most recent additions describe how OD has become more global. This global orientation includes the growing application of OD in cross-cultural settings. It also shows how OD can help organizations design their global structures and operations. It is our greatest hope that the current edition continues this tradition of rigor and relevance.

Revisions to the Tenth Edition

Our goal in the tenth edition is to update the field again. We take our role as the authors of the leading textbook in OD seriously and, we hope, responsibly. Although we have retained several features of the prior editions, we have made some important changes.

Integration and Flow

The chapter sequence from previous editions has been maintained, but we have reduced the number of chapters from 25 to 23 and worked hard to better integrate the content. For example, we achieved a more integrated presentation of the diagnostic process by combining two chapters into one. Similarly, we combined chapters on data collection, analysis, and feedback into one, more tightly integrated description. Finally, we have tried to use a consistent organization design framework in the diagnosis, structural design, and strategic change sections.

Global Integration

We have also improved the integration and flow of material by making a concerted attempt to address global issues and global perspectives throughout the text. We began the internationalization of the text in the sixth edition with the addition of a chapter on "global issues in OD." However, in the past, the text could be criticized, and rightfully so, for being "North America centric." The examples, applications, and cases came almost exclusively from U.S.-based companies. In the tenth edition, we have tried—ultimately the reader will be the judge of our effectiveness—to dramatically reduce the North American bias and to cite European, Asian, Australian, South American, and where possible, African examples.

Strategic Emphasis Continued

Reflecting on where we think OD is headed, we completely rewrote Part 6 on strategic change interventions. While we kept the chapter titles, we added dynamic strategy making, completely revised the section on organization design, leveraged the design section to more deeply explore integrated strategic change, and completely revised the sections on organization learning, built to change, and culture change.

Sustainability

We have added a new chapter (Chapter 21) focusing on OD practices intended to improve and balance organizations' economic, social, and ecological outcomes. This topic is a growing area of OD practice and one that we believe will continue to expand.

Key Chapter Revisions

Other chapters have received important updates and improvements. Chapter 7's description of designing interventions, in keeping with the global integration described above, has been rewritten to account for cross-cultural values in interventions. In Chapter 22, the sections on OD in Healthcare, Education, Government, and Family Businesses have been completely rewritten by new and familiar guest authors. Finally, Chapter 23—Future Directions in Organization Development—has received a thorough revision based on the authors' recent research.

Distinguishing Pedagogical Features

The text is designed to facilitate the learning of OD theory and practice. Based on feedback from reviewers, this format more closely matches the OD process. Instructors can teach the process and then link OD practice to the interventions.

Organization

The tenth edition is organized into seven parts. Following an introductory chapter that describes the definition and history of OD, Part 1 provides an overview of organization development. It discusses the fundamental theories that underlie planned change (Chapter 2) and describes the people who practice it (Chapter 3). Part 2 is a six-chapter description of the OD process. It describes how OD practitioners enter and contract with organizations (Chapter 4); diagnose organizations, groups, and jobs (Chapter 5); collect, analyze, and feed back diagnostic data (Chapter 6); design interventions (Chapter 7); lead and manage change (Chapter 8); and evaluate and institutionalize change (Chapter 9). In this manner, instructors can focus on the OD process without distraction. Parts 3, 4, 5, and 6 then cover the major OD interventions used today according the same classification scheme used in previous editions of the text. Part 3 covers human process interventions; Part 4 describes technostructural approaches; Part 5 presents interventions in human resource management; and Part 6 addresses strategic change interventions. In the final section, Part 7, we cover special applications of OD, including

OD for economic, social, and environmental outcomes (Chapter 21); OD in health care, family businesses, schools, and the public sector (Chapter 22); and the future of OD (Chapter 23). We believe this ordering provides instructors with more flexibility in teaching OD.

Applications

Within each chapter, we describe actual situations in which different OD techniques or interventions were used. These applications provide students with a chance to see how OD is actually practiced in organizations. In the tenth edition, about 30 percent of the applications are new and many others have been updated to maintain the text's currency and relevance. In response to feedback from reviewers, all of the applications describe a real situation in a real organization (although sometimes we felt it necessary to use disguised names). In many cases, the organizations are large public companies that should be readily recognizable. We have endeavored to write applications based on our own OD practice or that have appeared in the popular literature. In addition, we have asked several of our colleagues to submit descriptions of their own practice and these applications appear throughout the text. The time and effort to produce these vignettes of OD practice for others is gratefully acknowledged.

Cases

At the end of each major part in the book, we have included cases to permit a more in-depth discussion of the OD process. Seven of the 16 cases are new to the tenth edition. We have kept some cases that have been favorites over the years but have also replaced some of the favorites with newer ones. Also in response to feedback from users of the text, we have endeavored to provide cases that vary in levels of detail, complexity, and sophistication to allow the instructor some flexibility in teaching the material to either undergraduate or graduate students.

Audience

This book can be used in a number of different ways and by a variety of people. First, it serves as a primary textbook in organization development for students at both the undergraduate and graduate levels. Second, the book can also serve as an independent study guide for individuals wishing to learn more about how organization development can improve productivity and human satisfaction. Third, the book is intended to be of value to OD professionals, executives and administrators, specialists in such fields as training, occupational stress, and human resource management, and anyone interested in the complex process known as organization development.

Acknowledgments

The Grateful Dead's lyric, "What a long strange trip it's been" seems particularly apropos in writing this edition. Reflecting the global world we live in, we revised this text virtually. Tom and Chris never once saw each other face-to-face once the work began. Tom wrote from his office in Los Angeles and his view in Palos Verdes while trying to run the Department of Management and Organization at the Marshall School of Business; Chris wrote from his sabbatical home in Lyon, France while trying to adopt the French lifestyle. However, we think it is safe to say that after collaborating on five editions of the text, we finally have figured out how to do this effectively. This revision has gone very smoothly. That is not to say that we haven't lived in the VUCA world. Volatility, uncertainty, complexity, and ambiguity certainly affected our lives in strange and tragic ways, but after five editions, we've learned to roll with the punches, adapt and adjust schedules, and cover each other's back. Sometimes our writing is so bad, we want to throw up; sometimes it's so good it brings tears to our eyes. We hope this edition will, at times, at least make you feel good.

We'd like to thank those who supported us in this effort. We are grateful to and for our families: Chailin and Catherine Cummings and the Worley clan, Debbie, Sarah, Hannah, and Sam. We would like to thank our students for their comments on the previous editions, for contributing many of the applications, and for helping us to try out new ideas and perspectives. A particular word of thanks go to our colleagues at USC's Center for Effective Organizations—Ed Lawler, Sue Mohrman, John Boudreau, Alec Levenson, Gerry Ledford, Theresa Welbourne, Jim O'Toole, Jay Conger, and Jay Galbraith. They have been consistent sources of support and intellectual inquiry. We also extend thanks to Tom Williams at Booz&Co. for his patience, support, and partnership. To our friends at Pepperdine University's MSOD program (Ann Feyerherm, Miriam Lacey, Terri Egan, Julie Chesley, Gary Mangiofico, and Kent Rhodes) we send our appreciation for their dedication to maintaining the "long grey line." As well, the following individuals reviewed the text and influenced our thinking with their honest and constructive feedback:

Jack Cox, Amberton University
Stacy Ball-Elias, Southwest Minnesota State University
Bruce Gillies, California Lutheran University
Jim Maddox, Friends University
Shannon Reilly, George Brown College

We also would like to express our appreciation to members of the staff at Cengage Learning for their aid and encouragement. Special thanks go to Scott Person, Sarah Blasco, and Jennifer King for their help and guidance throughout the development of this revision. And Jerusha Govindakrishnan patiently made sure that the editing and producing of our book went smoothly.

Thomas G. Cummings
Palos Verdes Estates, California

Christopher G. Worley
San Juan Capistrano, California
Lyon, France

August, 2013

Pixmann/Imagezoo/Getty Images

About the Authors

Thomas G. Cummings, professor, chair of the Department of Management and Organization, received his B.S. and MBA from Cornell University, and his Ph.D. from the University of California at Los Angeles. He has authored over 70 articles and 22 books and was formerly President of the Western Academy of Management, Chair of the Organization Development and Change Division of the Academy of Management, and Founding Editor of the *Journal of Management Inquiry*. Dr. Cummings was the 61st President of the Academy of Management, the largest professional association of management scholars in the world with a total membership of over 19,000. He is listed in *American Men and Women of Science* and *Who's Who in America*. His major research and consulting interests include designing high-performing organizations and strategic change management. He has conducted several large-scale organization design and change projects, and has consulted to a variety of private and public-sector organizations in the United States, Europe, Mexico, and Scandinavia.

Christopher G. Worley is a Senior Research Scientist at the Center for Effective Organizations (USC's Marshall School of Business) and professor of management in Pepperdine University's Master of Science in Organization (MSOD) program. He received B.S. from Westminster College, master's degrees from Colorado State University and Pepperdine University, and his doctorate from the University of Southern California. He served as Chair of the Organization Development and Change Division of the Academy of Management, received the Luckman Teaching Fellowship at Pepperdine University, and the Douglas McGregor Award for best paper in the *Journal of Applied Behavioral Science*. His most recent books are *Management Reset* and *Built to Change*, and he is completing a book on organization agility. His articles on agility and strategic organization design have appeared in the *Journal of Applied Behavioral Science*, *Journal of Organization Behavior*, *Sloan Management Review*, *Strategy+Business*, and *Organizational Dynamics*. He and his family live in San Juan Capistrano, CA.

1

General Introduction to Organization Development

learning objectives

- Define and describe the practice and study of organization development (OD).
- Describe the history and relevance of OD.
- Distinguish OD and planned change from other forms of organization change.

This is a book about organization development (OD)—a process that applies a broad range of behavioral science knowledge and practices to help organizations build their capability to change and to achieve greater effectiveness, including increased financial performance, employee satisfaction, and environmental sustainability. Organization development differs from other planned change efforts, such as project management or product innovation, because the focus is on building the organization's ability to assess its current functioning and to make necessary changes to achieve its goals. Moreover, OD is oriented to improving the total system—the organization and its parts in the context of the larger environment that affects them.

This book reviews the broad background of OD and examines assumptions, strategies and models, intervention techniques, and other aspects of OD. This chapter provides an introduction to OD, describing first the concept of OD itself. Second, it explains why OD has expanded rapidly in the past 60 years, both in terms of people's need to work with and through others in organizations and in terms of organizations' need to adapt in a complex and changing world. Third, it reviews briefly the history of OD, and fourth, it describes the evolution of OD into its current state. This introduction to OD is followed by an overview of the rest of the book.

1-1 Organization Development Defined

Organization development is both a professional field of social action and an area of scientific inquiry. The practice of OD covers a wide spectrum of activities, with seemingly endless variations upon them. Team building with top corporate management, structural change in a municipality, and job enrichment in a manufacturing firm are all examples of OD. Similarly, the study of OD addresses a broad range of topics, including the effects of change, the methods of organizational change, and the factors influencing OD success.

A number of definitions of OD exist and are presented in Table 1.1. Each definition has a slightly different emphasis. For example, Burke's description focuses attention on culture as the target of change; French's definition is concerned with OD's long-term focus and the use of consultants; and Beckhard's and Beer's definitions address the process of OD. More recently, Burke and Bradford's definition broadens the range and interests of OD. Worley and Feyerherm suggested that for a process to be called organization development, (1) it must focus on or result in the change of some aspect of the organizational system; (2) there must be learning or the transfer of knowledge or skill to the organization; and (3) there must be evidence of improvement in or an intention to improve the effectiveness of the organization.[1] The following definition incorporates most of these views and is used in this book:

> *Organization development is a system-wide application and transfer of behavioral science knowledge to the planned development, improvement, and reinforcement of the strategies, structures, and processes that lead to organization effectiveness.*

This definition emphasizes several features that differentiate OD from other approaches to organizational change and improvement, such as management consulting, project management, and operations management. The definition also helps to distinguish

TABLE 1.1

Definitions of Organization Development

Definitions of Organization Development
Organization development is a planned process of change in an organization's culture through the utilization of behavioral science technology, research, and theory. (Warner Burke)[2]
Organization development refers to a long-range effort to improve an organization's problem-solving capabilities and its ability to cope with changes in its external environment with the help of external or internal behavioral-scientist consultants, or change agents, as they are sometimes called. (Wendell French)[3]
Organization development is an effort (1) planned, (2) organization-wide, and (3) managed from the top, to (4) increase organization effectiveness and health through (5) planned interventions in the organization's "processes," using behavioral science knowledge. (Richard Beckhard)[4]
Organization development is a system-wide process of data collection, diagnosis, action planning, intervention, and evaluation aimed at (1) enhancing congruence among organizational structure, process, strategy, people, and culture; (2) developing new and creative organizational solutions; and (3) developing the organization's self-renewing capacity. It occurs through the collaboration of organizational members working with a change agent using behavioral science theory, research, and technology. (Michael Beer)[5]
Based on (1) a set of values, largely humanistic; (2) application of the behavioral sciences; and (3) open-systems theory, organization development is a system-wide process of planned change aimed toward improving overall organization effectiveness by way of enhanced congruence of such key organization dimensions as external environment, mission, strategy, leadership, culture, structure, information and reward systems, and work policies and procedures. (Warner Burke and David Bradford)[6]

OD from two related subjects, *change management* and *organization change*, that also are addressed in this book.

First, OD applies to changes in the strategy, structure, and/or processes of an entire system, such as an organization, a single plant of a multiplant firm, a department or work group, or individual role or job. A change program aimed at modifying an organization's strategy, for example, might focus on how the organization relates to a wider environment and on how those relationships can be improved. It might include changes both in the grouping of people to perform tasks (structure) and in methods of communicating and solving problems (process) to support the changes in strategy. Similarly, an OD program directed at helping a top-management team become more effective might focus on social processes and task coordination within the group. This focus might result in the improved ability of top management to solve company problems in strategy and structure. This contrasts with approaches focusing on one or only a few aspects of a system, such as technological innovation or quality control. In these approaches, attention is narrowed to improvement of particular products or processes, or to development of production or service delivery functions.

Second, OD is based on the application and transfer of behavioral science knowledge and practice, including microconcepts, such as leadership, group dynamics, and work design, and macroapproaches, such as strategy, organization design, and culture change. These subjects distinguish OD from such applications as management consulting, technological innovation, or operations management that emphasize the economic, financial, and technical aspects of organizations. These approaches tend to neglect the personal and social characteristics of a system. Moreover, OD is distinguished by its intent to transfer behavioral science knowledge and skill so that the organizational system is more capable of carrying out planned change in the future.

Third, OD is concerned with managing planned change, but not in the formal sense typically associated with management consulting or project management, which tends to comprise programmatic and expert-driven approaches to change. Rather, OD is more an adaptive process for planning and implementing change than a blueprint for how things should be done. It involves planning to diagnose and solve organizational problems, but such plans are flexible and often revised as new information is gathered as the change process progresses. If, for example, there was concern about the performance of a set of international subsidiaries, a reorganization process might begin with plans to assess the current relationships between the international divisions and the corporate headquarters and to redesign them if necessary. These plans would be modified if the assessment discovered that most of the senior management teams in the subsidiaries were not given adequate cross-cultural training prior to their international assignments.

Fourth, OD involves the design, implementation, and subsequent reinforcement of change. It moves beyond the initial efforts to implement a change program to a longer-term concern for making sure the new activities sustain within the organization. For example, implementing self-managed work teams might focus on ways in which supervisors could give workers more control over work methods. After workers had more control, attention would shift to ensuring that supervisors continued to provide that freedom. That assurance might include rewarding supervisors for managing in a participative style. This attention to reinforcement is similar to training and development approaches that address maintenance of new skills or behaviors, but it differs from other change perspectives that do not address how a change can be sustained over time.

Finally, OD is oriented to improving organizational effectiveness. Effectiveness is best measured along three dimensions. First, OD affirms that an effective organization is able to solve its own problems and to continually improve itself. OD helps organization members gain the skills and knowledge necessary to conduct these activities by involving them in the change process. Second, an effective organization has high financial and technical performance, including sales growth, acceptable profits, quality products and services, and high productivity. OD helps organizations achieve these ends by leveraging social science practices to lower costs, improve products and services, and increase productivity. Finally, an effective organization has an engaged, satisfied, and learning workforce as well as satisfied and loyal customers or other external stakeholders. The organization's performance responds to the needs of external groups, such as stockholders, customers, suppliers, and government agencies, which provide the organization with resources and legitimacy. Moreover, it is able to attract and motivate effective employees, who then perform at higher levels. Other forms of organizational change clearly differ from OD in their focus. Management consulting, for example, primarily addresses financial performance, whereas operations management or industrial engineering focuses on productivity.

Organization development can be distinguished from change management and organizational change. OD and change management both address the effective implementation of planned change. They are both concerned with the sequence of activities, the processes, and the leadership that produce organization improvements. They differ, however, in their underlying value orientation. OD's behavioral science foundation supports values of human potential, participation, and development in addition to performance and competitive advantage. Change management focuses more narrowly on values of cost, quality, and schedule.[7] As a result, OD's distinguishing feature is its concern with the transfer of knowledge and skill so that the organization is more able to manage change in the future. Change management does not necessarily require the transfer of these skills. In short, all OD involves change management, but change management may not involve OD.

Similarly, organizational change is a broader concept than OD. As discussed above, organization development can be applied to managing organizational change. However, it is primarily concerned with managing change in such a way that knowledge and skills are transferred to build the organization's capability to achieve goals and solve problems. It is intended to change the organization in a particular direction, toward improved problem solving, responsiveness, and effectiveness. Organizational change, in contrast, is more broadly focused and can apply to any kind of change, including technical and managerial innovations, organization decline, or the evolution of a system over time. These changes may or may not be directed at making the organization more developed in the sense implied by OD.

The behavioral sciences have developed useful concepts and methods for helping organizations to deal with changing environments, competitor initiatives, technological innovation, globalization, or restructuring. They help managers and administrators to manage the change process. Many of these concepts and techniques are described in this book, particularly in relation to managing change.

1-2 The Growth and Relevance of Organization Development

In each of the previous editions of this book, we argued that organizations must adapt to increasingly complex and uncertain technological, economic, political, and cultural changes. We also argued that OD could help an organization to create effective responses to these changes and, in many cases, to proactively influence the strategic direction of the firm. The rapidly changing conditions of the past few years confirm our arguments and accentuate their relevance. According to several observers, organizations are in the midst of unprecedented uncertainty and chaos, and nothing short of a management revolution will save them.[8] Three major trends are shaping change in organizations: globalization, information technology, and managerial innovation.

First, *globalization* is changing the markets and environments in which organizations operate as well as the way they function.[9] The world is rapidly becoming smaller and more tightly interconnected economically, socially, and ecologically. Significant movements of goods and services, technology, human resources, and capital across international borders have intensified the economic interdependence among nations and organizations. This globalization opens new markets and sources of innovation and capital for organizations, but at the risk of economic problems in one sector of the world spreading rapidly to other sectors. The United States' 2007–2008 fiscal crisis quickly evolved into a "global recession" that sent the European Economic Union into a financial tailspin while negatively impacting the economies of nations in almost every region of the globe. Similarly, social differences along cultural, political, and religious lines have rendered global markets increasingly uncertain, complex, and conflictive. Persistent tensions in the Middle East have had repercussions for firms throughout the globe making them more vulnerable to terrorist attacks, escalating diplomatic and military conflicts, and disrupting energy supplies. Globalization also affects organizations ecologically, expanding their access to natural resources yet making the planet more susceptible to abuse by organizations with questionable environmental practices and governments with loose environmental regulations. Growing international debates about climate change and calls for more responsible and sustainable organizational practices underscore the ecological consequences of globalization.

Second, *information technology* is redefining the traditional business model by changing how work is performed, how knowledge is used, and how the cost of doing business is calculated.[10] The way an organization collects, stores, manipulates, uses, and transmits information can lower costs and increase the value and quality of products and services. Information technology is at the heart of emerging e-commerce strategies and organizations. Amazon.com and eBay are among the survivors of a busted dot-com bubble; Facebook, LinkedIn, and Twitter are revolutionizing the way that we converse and interact with each other both personally and professionally. Google has emerged as a major competitor to Microsoft, and the amount of business being conducted on the Internet is projected to grow at double-digit rates. Moreover, the underlying rate of innovation is not expected to decline. Cloud computing—a state-of-the-art technology application a few years ago—is now considered routine business practice. Digital publishing and online courses are transforming how we deliver knowledge and education. The ability to move information easily and inexpensively throughout and among organizations has fueled the downsizing, delayering, and restructuring of firms. The Internet has enabled new forms of work such as virtual teams and telecommuting; it has enabled many companies to outsource customer-service functions to global regions where labor is relatively inexpensive. Finally, information technology is changing how organizations create and use knowledge. Enormous data sets, so-called "big data," are being analyzed to discover underlying trends and patterns that can inform strategic decision making. Information is also being widely shared throughout the organization. This reduces the concentration of power at the top of the organization as employees now share the same key information that senior managers once used to control decision making.

Third, *managerial innovation* has responded to the globalization and information technology trends and has accelerated their impact on organizations. New organizational forms, such as networks, strategic alliances, and virtual corporations, provide organizations with new ways of thinking about how to manufacture goods and deliver services. The strategic alliance, for example, has emerged as one of the indispensable tools in strategy implementation. No single organization, not even IBM, Toyota, or General Electric, can control the environmental and market uncertainty it faces. In addition, change innovations, such as downsizing or reengineering, have radically reduced the size of organizations and increased their flexibility; new large group interventions, such as the search conference and open space, have increased the speed with which organizational change can take place; and organization learning interventions have leveraged knowledge as a critical organizational resource.[11] Managers, OD practitioners, and researchers argue that these globalization and information technology forces not only are powerful in their own right but are interrelated. Their interaction makes for a highly uncertain and complex environment for all kinds of organizations, including manufacturing and service firms and those in the public and private sectors. Fortunately, a growing number of organizations are undertaking the kinds of organizational changes needed to survive and prosper in today's environment. They are making themselves more streamlined and agile, more responsive to external demands, and more ecologically and socially sustainable. They are involving employees in key decisions and paying for performance rather than for time. They are taking the initiative in innovating and managing change, rather than simply responding to what has already happened.

Organization development plays a key role in helping organizations change themselves. It helps organizations assess themselves and their environments and revitalize and rebuild their strategies, structures, and processes. OD helps organization members gain the skills and knowledge needed to continuously improve and change the organization. It helps members go beyond surface changes to transform the underlying assumptions and values governing their behaviors. The different concepts and methods discussed in this book increasingly are finding their way into government agencies, manufacturing firms, multinational corporations, service industries, educational and health care institutions, and not-for-profit organizations. Perhaps at no other time has OD been more responsive and practically relevant to organizations' needs to operate effectively in a highly complex and changing world.

OD is obviously important to those who plan a professional career in the field, either as an internal consultant employed by an organization or as an external consultant practicing in many organizations. A career in OD can be highly rewarding, providing challenging and interesting assignments working with managers and employees to improve their organizations and their work lives. In today's environment, the demand for OD professionals is rising rapidly. For example, large professional services firms must have effective "change management" practices to be competitive. Career opportunities in OD should continue to expand in the United States and abroad.

Organization development also is important to those who have no aspirations to become professional practitioners. All managers and administrators are responsible for supervising and developing subordinates and for improving their departments' performance. Similarly, all staff specialists, such as financial analysts, engineers, accountants, information technologists, or market researchers, are responsible for offering advice and counsel to managers and for introducing new methods and practices. Finally, OD is important to general managers and other senior executives because OD can help the whole organization be more innovative, adaptable, and effective.

Organization development can also help managers and staff personnel perform their tasks more effectively. It can provide the skills and knowledge necessary for establishing effective interpersonal relationships and building productive teams. It can show personnel how to work effectively with others in diagnosing complex problems and in devising appropriate solutions. It can help others become committed to the solutions, thereby increasing chances for their successful implementation. In short, OD is highly relevant to anyone having to work with and through others in organizations.

1-3 A Short History of Organization Development

A brief history of OD will help to clarify the evolution of the term as well as some of the problems and confusion that have surrounded it. As currently practiced, OD emerged from five major backgrounds or stems, as shown in Figure 1.1. The first was the growth of the National Training Laboratories (NTL) and the development of training groups, otherwise known as sensitivity training or T-groups. The second stem of OD was the classic work on action research conducted by social scientists interested in applying research to managing change. An important feature of action research was a technique known as survey feedback. Kurt Lewin, a prolific theorist, researcher, and practitioner in group dynamics and social change, was instrumental in the development of T-groups, survey feedback, and action research. His work led to the creation of OD and still serves as a major source of its concepts and methods. The third stem reflects a normative view of OD. Rensis Likert's participative management framework and Blake and Mouton's Grid® OD suggest a "one best way" to design and operate organizations. The fourth background is the approach focusing on productivity and the quality of work life. The fifth stem of OD, and the most recent influence on current practice, involves strategic change and organization transformation.

FIGURE 1.1

The Five Stems of OD Practice

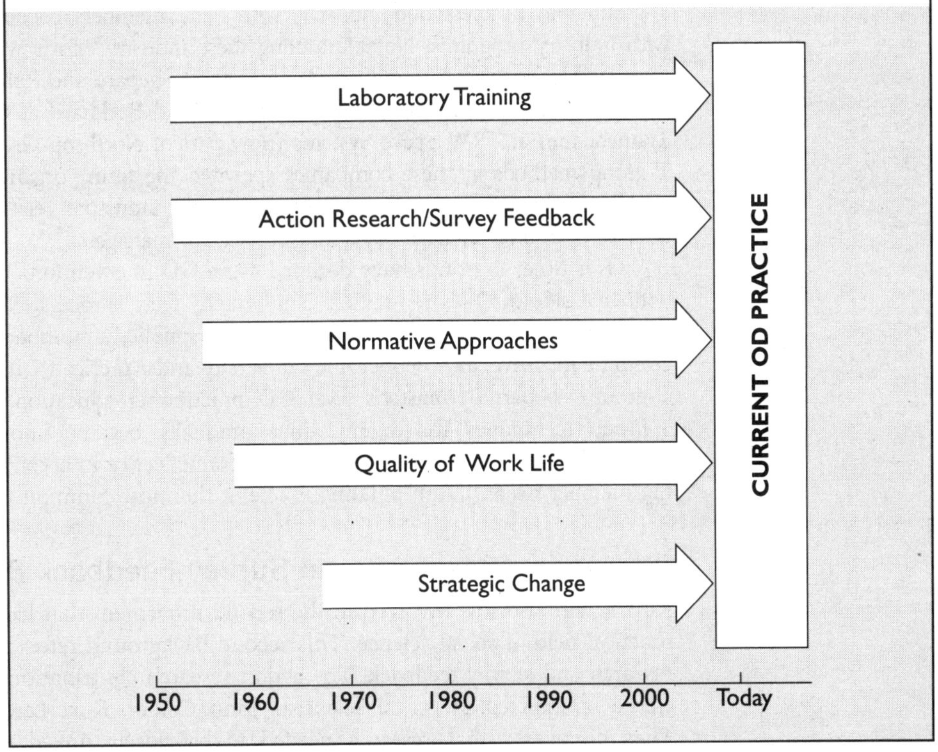

1-3a Laboratory Training Background

This stem of OD pioneered laboratory training, or the T-group—a small, unstructured group in which participants learn from their own interactions and evolving group processes about such issues as interpersonal relations, personal growth, leadership, and group dynamics. Essentially, laboratory training began in the summer of 1946, when Kurt Lewin and his staff at the Research Center for Group Dynamics at the Massachusetts Institute of Technology (MIT) were asked by the Connecticut Interracial Commission and the Committee on Community Interrelations of the American Jewish Congress for help in research on training community leaders. A workshop was developed, and the community leaders were brought together to learn about leadership and to discuss problems. At the end of each day, the researchers discussed privately what behaviors and group dynamics they had observed. The community leaders asked permission to sit in on these feedback sessions. Reluctant at first, the researchers finally agreed. Thus, the first T-group was formed in which people reacted to data about their own behavior. The researchers drew two conclusions about this first T-group experiment: (1) feedback about group interaction was a rich learning experience and (2) the process of "group building" had potential for learning that could be transferred to "back-home" situations.[12]

As a result of this experience, the Office of Naval Research and the National Education Association provided financial backing to form the National Training Laboratories, and Gould Academy in Bethel, Maine, was selected as a site for further work (since then, Bethel has played an important part in NTL). The first Basic Skill Groups were offered in the summer of 1947. The program was so successful that the Carnegie Foundation provided support for programs in 1948 and 1949. This led to a permanent program for NTL within the National Education Association.

In the 1950s, three trends emerged: (1) the emergence of regional laboratories, (2) the expansion of summer program sessions to year-round sessions, and (3) the expansion of the T-group into business and industry, with NTL members becoming increasingly involved with industry programs. Notable among these industry efforts was the pioneering work of Douglas McGregor at Union Carbide, of Herbert Shepard and Robert Blake at Esso Standard Oil (now ExxonMobil), of McGregor and Richard Beckhard at General Mills, and of Bob Tannenbaum at TRW Space Systems (now part of Northrop Grumman).[13] Applications of T-group methods at these companies spawned the term "organization development" and, equally important, led corporate personnel and industrial relations specialists to expand their roles to offer internal consulting services to managers.[14]

Over time, T-groups have declined as an OD intervention. They are closely associated with that side of OD's reputation as a "touchy-feely" process. NTL, as well as UCLA and Stanford, continues to offer T-groups to the public, a number of proprietary programs continue to thrive, and Pepperdine University and American University continue to utilize T-groups as part of master's level OD practitioner education. The practical aspects of T-group techniques for organizations gradually became known as team building—a process for helping work groups become more effective in accomplishing tasks and satisfying member needs. Team building is one of the most common OD interventions today.

1-3b Action Research and Survey-Feedback Background

Kurt Lewin also was involved in the second movement that led to OD's emergence as a practical field of social science. This second background refers to the processes of action research and survey feedback. The action research contribution began in the 1940s with studies conducted by social scientists John Collier, Kurt Lewin, and William Whyte. They discovered that research needed to be closely linked to action if organization members were to use it to manage change. A collaborative effort was initiated between organization members and social scientists to collect research data about an organization's functioning, to analyze it for causes of problems, and to devise and implement solutions. After implementation, further data were collected to assess the results, and the cycle of data collection and action often continued. The results of action research were twofold: Members of organizations were able to use research on themselves to guide action and change, and social scientists were able to study that process to derive new knowledge that could be used elsewhere.

Among the pioneering action research studies were the work of Lewin and his students at the Harwood Manufacturing Company[15] and the classic research by Lester Coch and John French on overcoming resistance to change.[16] The latter study led to the development of participative management as a means of getting employees involved in planning and managing change. Other notable action research contributions included Whyte and Edith Hamilton's famous study of Chicago's Tremont Hotel[17] and Collier's efforts to apply action research techniques to improving race relations when he was commissioner of Indian affairs from 1933 to 1945.[18] These studies did much to establish action research as integral to organization change. Today, it is the backbone of many OD applications.

A key component of most action research studies was the systematic collection of survey data that were fed back to the client organization. Following Lewin's death in 1947, his Research Center for Group Dynamics at MIT moved to Michigan and joined with the Survey Research Center as part of the Institute for Social Research. The institute was headed by Rensis Likert, a pioneer in developing scientific approaches to attitude surveys. His doctoral dissertation at Columbia University developed the widely used 5-point "Likert Scale."[19]

In an early study by the institute, Likert and Floyd Mann administered a companywide survey of management and employee attitudes at Detroit Edison.[20] The feedback process that evolved was an "interlocking chain of conferences." The major findings of the survey were first reported to the top management and then transmitted throughout the organization. The feedback sessions were conducted in task groups, with supervisors and their immediate subordinates discussing the data together. Although there was little substantial research evidence, the researchers intuitively felt that this was a powerful process for change.

In 1950, eight accounting departments asked for a repeat of the survey, thus generating a new cycle of feedback meetings. In four departments, feedback approaches were used, but the method varied; two departments received feedback only at the departmental level; and because of changes in key personnel, nothing was done in the remaining two departments.

A third follow-up study indicated that more significant and positive changes, such as job satisfaction, had occurred in the departments receiving feedback than in the two departments that did not participate. From those findings, Likert and Mann derived several conclusions about the effects of survey feedback on organization change. This led to extensive applications of survey-feedback methods in a variety of settings. The common pattern of data collection, data feedback, action planning, implementation, and follow-up data collection in both action research and survey feedback can be seen in these examples.

1-3c Normative Background

The intellectual and practical advances from the laboratory training stem and the action research and survey-feedback stem were followed closely by the belief that a human relations approach represented a "one best way" to manage organizations. This normative belief was exemplified in Likert's *Participative Management Program* and Blake and Mouton's *Grid Organization Development* approaches to organization improvement.[21]

Likert's Participative Management Program characterized organizations as having one of four types of management systems:[22]

- **Exploitive authoritative systems** (System 1) exhibit an autocratic, top-down approach to leadership. Employee motivation is based on punishment and occasional rewards. Communication is primarily downward, and there is little lateral interaction or teamwork. Decision making and control reside primarily at the top of the organization. System 1 results in mediocre performance.
- **Benevolent authoritative systems** (System 2) are similar to System 1, except that management is more paternalistic. Employees are allowed a little more interaction, communication, and decision making but within boundaries defined by management.
- **Consultative systems** (System 3) increase employee interaction, communication, and decision making. Although employees are consulted about problems and decisions, management still makes the final decisions. Productivity is good, and employees are moderately satisfied with the organization.
- **Participative group systems** (System 4) are almost the opposite of System 1. Designed around group methods of decision making and supervision, this system fosters high degrees of member involvement and participation. Work groups are highly involved in setting goals, making decisions, improving methods, and appraising results. Communication occurs both laterally and vertically, and decisions are linked throughout the organization by overlapping group membership. System 4 achieves high levels of productivity, quality, and member satisfaction.

Likert applied System 4 management to organizations using a survey-feedback process. The intervention generally started with organization members completing the Profile of Organizational Characteristics.[23] The survey asked members for their opinions about both the present and ideal conditions of six organizational features: leadership, motivation, communication, decisions, goals, and control. In the second stage, the data were fed back to different work groups within the organization. Group members examined the discrepancy between their present situation and their ideal, generally using System 4 as the ideal benchmark, and generated action plans to move the organization toward System 4 conditions.

Blake and Mouton's Grid Organization Development originated from research about managerial and organizational effectiveness.[24] Data gathered on organizational excellence from 198 organizations located in the United States, Japan, and Great Britain showed that the two foremost barriers to excellence were planning and communications.[25] Each of these barriers was researched further to understand its roots, and the research resulted in a normative model of leadership—the Managerial Grid.

According to the Managerial Grid, an individual's style can be described according to his or her concern for production and concern for people.[26] A concern for production covers a range of behaviors, such as accomplishing productive tasks, developing creative ideas, making quality policy decisions, establishing thorough and high-quality staff services, or creating efficient workload measurements. Concern for production is not limited to things but also may involve human accomplishment within the organization, regardless of the assigned tasks or activities. A concern for people encompasses a variety of issues, including concern for the individual's personal worth, good working conditions, a degree of involvement or commitment to completing the job, security, a fair salary structure and fringe benefits, and good social and other relationships. Each dimension is measured on a nine-point scale and results in 81 possible leadership styles, ranging from 1,1 to 9,9.

For example, 1,9 managers have a low concern for production and a high concern for people: They view people's feelings, attitudes, and needs as valuable in their own right. This type of manager strives to provide subordinates with work conditions that provide ease, security, and comfort. On the other hand, 9,1 managers have a high concern for production but a low concern for people: They minimize the attitudes and feelings of subordinates and give little attention to individual creativity, conflict, and commitment. As a result, the focus is on the work organization.

Blake and Mouton proposed that the 9,9 managerial style is the most effective in overcoming the communications barrier to corporate excellence. The basic assumptions behind this managerial style differ qualitatively and quantitatively from those underlying the other managerial styles, which assume there is an inherent conflict between the needs of the organization and the needs of people. By showing a high concern for both people and production, managers allow employees to think and to influence the organization, thus promoting active support for organizational plans. Employee participation means that better communication is critical; therefore, necessary information is shared by all relevant parties. Moreover, better communication means self-direction and self-control, rather than unquestioning, blind obedience. Organizational commitment arises out of discussion, deliberation, and debate over major organizational issues.

One of the most structured interventions in OD, Blake and Mouton's Grid Organization Development has two key objectives: to improve planning by developing a strategy for organizational excellence based on clear logic, and to help managers gain the necessary knowledge and skills to supervise effectively. It consists of six phases designed to analyze an entire business and to overcome the planning and communications barriers to corporate excellence. The first phase is the Grid Seminar, a one-week program where participants analyze their personal style and learn methods of problem solving. Phase 2 consists of team development and Phase 3 involves intergroup development. In Phase 4, an ideal model of organizational excellence is developed and in Phase 5, the model is implemented. The final phase consists of an evaluation of the organization.

Despite some research support, the normative approach to change has given way to a contingency view that acknowledges the influence of the external environment, technology, and other forces in determining the appropriate organization design and management practices. Still, Likert's participative management and Blake and Mouton's Grid OD frameworks are both used in organizations today.

1-3d Productivity and Quality-of-Work-Life Background

The contribution of the productivity and quality-of-work-life (QWL) background to OD can be described in two phases. The first phase included the original projects developed in Europe in the 1950s and their emergence in the United States during the 1960s. Based on the research of Eric Trist and his colleagues at the Tavistock Institute of Human Relations in London, early practitioners in Great Britain, Ireland, Norway, and Sweden developed work designs aimed at better integrating technology and people.[27] Referred to as "sociotechnical systems," these QWL programs generally involved joint participation by unions and management in the design of work and resulted in work designs giving employees high levels of discretion, task variety, and feedback about results. Perhaps the most distinguishing characteristic of these QWL programs was the discovery of self-managing work groups as a form of work design. These groups were composed of multiskilled workers who were given the necessary autonomy and information to design and manage their own task performances.

As these programs migrated to America, a variety of concepts and techniques were adopted and the approach tended to be more mixed than in European practice. For example, two definitions of QWL emerged during its initial development.[28] QWL was first defined in terms of people's reaction to work, particularly individual outcomes related to job satisfaction and mental health. Using this definition, QWL focused primarily on the personal consequences of the work experience and how to improve work to satisfy personal needs.

A second definition of QWL defined it as an approach or method.[29] People defined QWL in terms of specific techniques and approaches used for improving work.[30] It was viewed as synonymous with methods such as job enrichment, self-managed teams, and labor-management committees. This technique orientation derived mainly from the growing publicity surrounding QWL projects, such as the General Motors–United Auto Workers project at Tarrytown and the Gaines Pet Food plant project. These pioneering projects drew attention to specific approaches for improving work.

The excitement and popularity of this first phase of QWL in the United States lasted until the mid-1970s, when other more pressing issues, such as inflation and energy costs, diverted national attention. However, starting in 1979, a second phase of QWL activity emerged. A major factor contributing to the resurgence of QWL was growing international competition faced by the United States in markets at home and abroad. It became increasingly clear that the relatively low cost and high quality of foreign-made goods resulted partially from the management practices used abroad, especially in Japan. Books extolling the virtues of Japanese management, such as Ouchi's *Theory Z*,[31] made best-seller lists.

As a result, QWL programs expanded beyond their initial focus on work design to include other features of the workplace that can affect employee productivity and satisfaction, such as reward systems, work flows, management styles, and the physical work environment. This expanded focus resulted in larger-scale and longer-term projects than had the early job enrichment programs and shifted attention beyond the individual worker to work groups and the larger work context. Equally important, it added the critical dimension of organizational efficiency to what had been up to that time a primary concern for the human dimension.

At one point, the productivity and QWL approach became so popular that it was called an ideological movement. This was particularly evident in the spread of quality circles within many companies. Popularized in Japan, quality circles are groups of employees trained in problem-solving methods that meet regularly to resolve work environment, productivity, and quality-control concerns and to develop more efficient ways of working. At the same time, many of the QWL programs started in the early 1970s were achieving success. Highly visible corporations, such as General Motors, Ford, and Honeywell, and unions, such as the United Automobile Workers, the Oil, Chemical, and Atomic Workers, the Communications Workers of America, and the Steelworkers, were more willing to publicize their QWL efforts. In 1980, for example, more than 1,800 people attended an international QWL conference in Toronto, Canada. Unlike previous conferences, which were dominated by academics, the presenters at Toronto were mainly managers, workers, and unionists from private and public corporations.

Today, this second phase of QWL activity continues primarily under the banner of "employee involvement" (EI) as well as total quality management and Six Sigma programs, rather than of QWL. For many OD practitioners, the term EI signifies, more than the name QWL, the growing emphasis on how employees can contribute more to running the organization so it can be more flexible, productive, and competitive. Recently, the term "employee empowerment" has been used interchangeably with the term EI, the former suggesting the power inherent in moving decision making downward in the organization.[32] Employee empowerment may be too restrictive, however. Because it draws attention to the power aspects of these interventions, it may lead practitioners to neglect other important elements needed for success, such as information, skills, and rewards. Consequently, EI seems broader and less restrictive than does employee empowerment as a banner for these approaches to organizational improvement.

1-3e Strategic Change Background

The strategic change background is a recent influence on OD's evolution. As organizations have become more global and information intensive and their environments have become more complex and uncertain, the scale and intricacies of organizational change have increased. These trends have produced the need for a strategic perspective on OD and encouraged planned change processes at the organization and multiorganization levels.[33]

Strategic change involves improving the alignment among an organization's design, strategy, and environment.[34] Strategic change interventions seek to improve both the organization's relationship to its environment and the fit among its technical, structural, informational, human resource, and cultural components.[35] The need for strategic change is usually triggered by some major disruption to the organization, such as the lifting of regulatory requirements, a technological breakthrough, or a new chief executive officer coming in from outside the organization.[36]

One of the first applications of strategic change was Richard Beckhard's use of open-systems planning.[37] He focused on an organization's environment and strategy. Based on the organization's core mission, the differences between what the environment demanded and how the organization responded could be reduced and performance improved. Since then, change agents have proposed a variety of large-scale or strategic-change models;[38] each of these approaches recognizes that strategic change is often driven from the top by powerful executives, involves multiple levels of the organization and a change in its culture, and has important effects on performance. More recently, strategic approaches to OD have been extended beyond the boundaries of a single organization to include mergers and acquisitions, strategic alliances among firms, and network development.[39]

The strategic change background has significantly influenced OD practice. For example, implementing strategic change requires OD practitioners to be familiar with competitive strategy, finance, and marketing, as well as team building, action research, and survey feedback. Together, these skills have improved OD's relevance to organizations and their managers.

1-4 Evolution in Organization Development

Current practice in organization development is strongly influenced by these five backgrounds as well as by the trends shaping change in organizations. The laboratory training, action research and survey feedback, normative, and QWL roots of OD are evident in the strong humanistic focus that underlies its practice. The more recent influence of the strategic change background has greatly improved the relevance and rigor of OD practice. They have added financial and economic indicators of effectiveness to OD's traditional measures of work satisfaction and personal growth. All of the backgrounds support the transfer of knowledge and skill to the organization so it can better manage change in the future.

Today, the field increasingly is being influenced by the globalization and information technology trends described earlier. OD is being carried out in many more countries and in many more organizations operating on a worldwide basis. This is generating a whole new set of interventions as well as modifications to traditional OD practice.[40] In addition, OD is adapting its methods to the technologies being used in organizations. As information technology continues to influence organizations and their environments, OD is managing change processes in cyberspace as well as face-to-face. The diversity of this evolving discipline has led to tremendous growth in the number of professional OD practitioners, in the kinds of organizations involved with OD, in the range of countries within which OD is practiced, and in the kinds of interventions used to change and improve organizations.

The expansion of the OD Network (www.odnetwork.org), which began in 1964, is one indication of this growth. It has grown from 200 members in 1970 to 1,554 in 2012. At the same time, Division 14 of the American Psychological Association, formerly known as the Division of Industrial Psychology, changed its title to the Society for Industrial and Organizational Psychology (www.siop.org) in 1982. In 2012, the Society had over 8,000 members worldwide. In 1968, the American Society for Training & Development (www.astd.org) set up an OD division, which currently operates as the Human Capital Community of Practice with more than 2,000 members. In 1971, the Academy of Management established an Organization Development and Change Division (http://division.aomonline.org/odc), which currently has more than 2,300 members. Pepperdine University (www.pepperdine.edu), Bowling Green State University (www.bgsu.edu), and Case Western Reserve University (www.cwru.edu) offered the first master's degree programs in OD in 1975, and Case Western Reserve University began the first doctoral program in OD. Organization development now is being taught at the graduate and undergraduate levels in a large number of universities.[41]

Many different organizations have undertaken a wide variety of OD efforts. In many cases, organizations have been at the forefront of innovating new change techniques and methods as well as new organizational forms. Larger corporations that have engaged in organization development include General Electric, Boeing, Kaiser Permanente, Texas Instruments, American Airlines, DuPont, Intel, Hewlett-Packard, Microsoft, General Foods, Procter & Gamble, IBM, Raytheon, Wells Fargo Bank, the Hartford Financial Services, and Limited Brands. Traditionally, much of the work was considered confidential and was not publicized. Today, however, organizations increasingly are going public with their OD efforts, sharing the lessons with others.

OD work also is being done in schools, communities, and local, state, and federal governments. Several reviews of OD projects have been directed at OD in public administration.[42] Extensive OD work was done in the armed services, including the army, navy, air force, and coast guard, although OD activity and research activities have ebbed and flowed with changes in the size and scope of the military. Public schools began using both group training and survey feedback relatively early in the history of OD.[43] Usually, the projects took place in suburban middle-class schools, where stresses and strains of an urban environment were not prominent and ethnic and socioeconomic differences between consultants and clients were not high. In more recent years, OD methods have been extended to urban schools and to colleges and universities.

Organization development is increasingly international. It has been applied in nearly every country in the world. These efforts have involved such organizations as Saab (Sweden), Imperial Chemical Industries (England), Orrefors (Sweden), Akzo-Nobel (The Netherlands), the Beijing Arbitration Commission and Neusoft Corporation (China), Air New Zealand, and Vitro (Mexico).

Although it is evident that OD has expanded vastly in recent years, relatively few of the total number of organizations in the United States are actively involved in formal OD programs. However, many organizations are applying OD approaches and techniques without using that term explicitly.

1-5 Overview of the Book

This book presents the process and practice of organization development in a logical flow, as shown in Figure 1.2. Part 1 provides an overview of OD that describes the process of planned change and those who perform the work. It consists of two chapters. Chapter 2

FIGURE 1.2

Overview of the Book

Part 1: Overview of Organization Development

The Nature of Planned Change (Chapter 2)

The Organization Development Practitioner (Chapter 3)

Part 2: The Process of Organization Development

Entering and Contracting (Chapter 4)

Diagnosing (Chapter 5)

Collecting, Analyzing, and Feeding Back Diagnostic Information (Chapter 6)

Designing Interventions (Chapter 7)

Managing Change (Chapter 8)

Evaluating and Institutionalizing OD Interventions (Chapter 9)

Part 3: Human Process Interventions

Interpersonal and Group Process Approaches (Chapter 10)

Organization Process Approaches (Chapter 11)

Part 4: Technostructural Interventions

Restructuring Organizations (Chapter 12)

Employee Involvement (Chapter 13)

Work Design (Chapter 14)

Part 5: Human Resource Management Interventions

Performance Management (Chapter 15)

Talent Management (Chapter 16)

Workforce Diversity and Wellness (Chapter 17)

Part 6: Strategic Change Interventions

Transformational Change (Chapter 18)

Continuous Change (Chapter 19)

Transorganizational Change (Chapter 20)

Part 7: Special Applications of Organization Development

Organization Development for Economic, Ecological and Social Outcomes (Chapter 21)

OD in Health Care, School Systems, the Public Sector, and Family-Owned Businesses (Chapter 22)

Future Directions in Organization Development (Chapter 23)

discusses the nature of planned change and presents some models describing the change process. Planned change is viewed as an ongoing cycle of four activities: entering and contracting, diagnosing, planning and implementing, and evaluating and institutionalizing. Chapter 3 describes the OD practitioner and provides insight into the knowledge and skills needed to practice OD and the kinds of career issues that can be expected.

Part 2 is composed of six chapters that describe the process of organization development. Chapter 4 characterizes the first activity in this process: entering an organizational system and contracting with it for organization development work. Chapters 5 and 6 present the steps associated with the next major activity of the OD process: diagnosing. This involves helping the organization understand its current functioning and discover areas for improvement. Chapter 5 presents an open-systems model to guide diagnosis at three levels of analysis: the total organization, the group or department, and the individual job or position. Chapter 6 reviews methods for collecting, analyzing, and feeding back diagnostic data. Chapters 7 and 8 address issues concerned with the third activity: designing OD interventions and implementing change. Chapter 7 presents an overview of the intervention design process. Major kinds of interventions are identified, and the specific approaches that make up the next four parts of the book are introduced. Chapter 8 discusses the process of leading and managing change. It identifies key factors contributing to the successful implementation of change programs. Chapter 9 describes the final activity of the planned change process: evaluating OD interventions and establishing them as a permanent part of organizational functioning.

Parts 3 through 6 present the major interventions used in OD today. Part 3 (Chapters 10 and 11) is concerned with human process interventions aimed at the social processes occurring within organizations. These are the oldest and most traditional interventions in OD. Chapter 10 describes interpersonal and group process approaches, such as process consultation, third-party interventions, and team building. Chapter 11 presents more system-wide process approaches, such as organizational confrontation meetings, intergroup relations, and large group interventions.

Part 4 (Chapters 12, 13, and 14) reviews technostructural interventions that are aimed at organization structure and at better integrating people and technology. Chapter 12 is about restructuring organizations; it describes the alternative methods of organizing work activities as well as processes for downsizing and reengineering the organization. Chapter 13 presents interventions for improving employee involvement. These change programs increase employee knowledge, power, information, and rewards through parallel structures, total quality management, and high-involvement organizations. Chapter 14 describes change programs directed at work design, both of individual jobs and of work groups, for greater employee satisfaction and productivity.

Part 5 (Chapters 15, 16, and 17) presents human resource management interventions that are directed at integrating people into the organization. These interventions are associated traditionally with the human resource function in the organization and increasingly have become a part of OD activities. Chapter 15 concerns the process of performance management. This is a cycle of activities that helps groups and individuals to set goals, appraise work, and reward performance. Chapter 16 discusses interventions that manage human talent in the organization, including coaching, career planning and development, and management and leadership development. Chapter 17 presents two interventions that address and leverage workforce diversity and improve employee wellness.

Part 6 (Chapters 18, 19, and 20) concerns strategic interventions that focus on organizing the firm's resources to gain a competitive advantage in the environment. These change programs generally are managed from the top of the organization and take considerable time, effort, and resources. Chapter 18 presents three interventions having to do with organization transformation, including organization design, integrated strategic change, and culture change. Chapter 19 describes continuous change interventions, including dynamic strategy making, self-design, organization learning, and creating built-to-change organizations. Finally, Chapter 20 describes three transorganizational interventions: merger-and-acquisition integration processes, alliance formation and management, and network development and change.

Part 7 (Chapters 21, 22, and 23) is concerned with special topics in OD. Chapter 21 describes the growing application of OD to building sustainable management organizations and global social change organizations. Chapter 22 presents broad applications of OD in different kinds of organizations, including educational, government, family-owned, and health care agencies. Finally, Chapter 23 examines the future of organization development, including the trends affecting the field and the prospects for its influence on organization effectiveness.

SUMMARY

This chapter introduced OD as a planned change discipline concerned with applying behavioral science knowledge and practices to help organizations achieve greater effectiveness. Managers and staff specialists must work with and through people to achieve organizational objectives, and OD can help them form effective relationships with others. Organizations are faced with rapidly accelerating change, and OD can help them cope with the consequences of change. The concept of OD has multiple meanings. The definition provided here resolved some of the problems with earlier definitions. The history of OD reveals its five roots: laboratory training, action research and survey feedback, normative approaches, productivity and quality of work life, and strategic change. The current practice of OD goes far beyond its humanistic origins by incorporating concepts from organization strategy and design that complement the early emphasis on social processes. The continued growth in the number and diversity of OD approaches, practitioners, and involved organizations attests to the health of the discipline and offers a favorable prospect for the future.

NOTES

1. C. Worley and A. Feyerherm, "Reflections on the Future of OD," *Journal of Applied Behavioral Science* 39 (2003): 97–115.
2. W. Burke, *Organization Development: Principles and Practices* (Boston: Little, Brown, 1982).
3. W. French, "Organization Development: Objectives, Assumptions, and Strategies," *California Management Review* 12, no. 2 (1969): 23–34.
4. R. Beckhard, *Organization Development: Strategies and Models* (Reading, MA: Addison-Wesley, 1969).
5. M. Beer, *Organization Change and Development: A Systems View* (Santa Monica, CA: Goodyear Publishing, 1980).
6. W. Burke and D. Bradford, "The Crisis in OD," in *Reinventing Organization Development*, ed. D. Bradford and W. Burke (San Francisco: John Wiley & Sons, 2005): 1–14.
7. R. Paton and J. McCalman, *Change Management*, 3rd ed. (Thousand Oaks, CA: Sage Publications, 2010); N. Worren, K. Ruddle, and K. Moore, "From Organization Development to Change Management: The Emergence of a New Profession," *Journal of Applied Behavioral Science* 35 (1999): 273–86; J. Hayes, *The Theory and Practice of Change Management* (New York: Palgrave, 2002).
8. G. Hamel, *The Future of Management* (Boston: Harvard Business School Press, 2007); W. Burke, *Organization*

Change (Newbury Park, CA: Sage Publications, 2002); D. Watts, *Six Degrees* (New York: W. W. Norton, 2003); S. Chowdhury, ed., *Organization 21C* (Upper Saddle River, NJ: Financial Times Prentice Hall, 2002); B. Jones and M. Brazzel, eds., *The NTL Handbook of Organization Development and Change* (San Francisco: John Wiley & Sons, 2006).

9. T. Friedman, *The World Is Flat* (New York: Farrar, Straus, and Giroux, 2006); J. Perkins, *Confessions of an Economic Hit Man* (San Francisco: Berrett-Koehler, 2005); A. Chua, *World on Fire* (New York: Doubleday, 2002); International Forum on Globalization, *Alternatives to Economic Globalization* (San Francisco: Berrett-Koehler, 2002).
10. E. Brynjolfsson and A. McAfee, *Race Against the Machine: How the Digital Revolution is Accelerating Innovation, Driving Productivity, and Irreversibly Transforming Employment and the Economy* (New York: Digital Frontier Press, 2012); A. McAffee, *Enterprise 2.0: New Collaborative Tools for Your Organization's Toughest Challenges* (Cambridge, MA: Harvard Business School Press, 2009).
11. M. Anderson, ed., *Fast Cycle Organization Development* (Cincinnati: South-Western College Publishing, 2000); M. Hammer and J. Champy, *Reengineering the Corporation* (New York: HarperCollins, 1993); P. Senge, *The Fifth Discipline* (New York: Doubleday, 1990).
12. A. Kleiner, *The Age of Heretics* (New York: Doubleday, 1996); A. Freedman, "The History of Organization Development and the NTL Institute: What We Have Learned, Forgotten, and Rewritten," *Psychologist-Manager Journal* 3 (1999): 125–41; L. Bradford, "Biography of an Institution," *Journal of Applied Behavioral Science* 3 (1967): 127; A. Marrow, "Events Leading to the Establishment of the National Training Laboratories," *Journal of Applied Behavioral Science* 3 (1967): 145–50.
13. Kleiner, *Age of Heretics*; M. Mortara, "Organization Development and Change at TRW Space Technology Laboratories" (unpublished master's thesis, Pepperdine University, 2003).
14. W. French, "The Emergence and Early History of Organization Development with Reference to Influences upon and Interactions among Some of the Key Actors," in *Contemporary Organization Development: Current Thinking and Applications*, ed. D. Warrick (Glenview, IL: Scott, Foresman, 1985): 12–27.
15. A. Marrow, D. Bowers, and S. Seashore, *Management by Participation* (New York: Harper & Row, 1967).
16. L. Coch and J. French, "Overcoming Resistance to Change," *Human Relations* 1 (1948): 512–32.
17. W. Whyte and E. Hamilton, *Action Research for Management* (Homewood, IL: Irwin-Dorsey, 1964).
18. J. Collier, "United States Indian Administration as a Laboratory of Ethnic Relations," *Social Research* 12 (May 1945): 275–76.
19. French, "Emergence and Early History," 19–20.
20. F. Mann, "Studying and Creating Change," in *The Planning of Change: Readings in the Applied Behavioral Sciences*, ed. W. Bennis, K. Benne, and R. Chin (New York: Holt, Rinehart, & Winston, 1962), 605–15.
21. R. Likert, *The Human Organization* (New York: McGraw-Hill, 1967); S. Seashore and D. Bowers, "Durability of Organizational Change," *American Psychologist* 25 (1970): 227–33; D. Mosley, "System Four Revisited: Some New Insights," *Organization Development Journal* 5 (Spring 1987): 19–24; R. Blake and J. Mouton, *The Managerial Grid* (Houston: Gulf, 1964); R. Blake and J. Mouton, *Corporate Excellence Through Grid Organization Development: A Systems Approach* (Houston: Gulf, 1968); R. Blake and J. Mouton, *Building a Dynamic Corporation Through Grid Organization Development* (Reading, MA: Addison-Wesley, 1969).
22. Likert, *Human Organization.*
23. Ibid.
24. Blake and Mouton, *The Managerial Grid*; Blake and Mouton, *Corporate Excellence;* Blake and Mouton, *Building a Dynamic Corporation;* R. Blake and A. McCanse, *Leadership Dilemmas—Grid Solutions* (Houston: Gulf, 1991).
25. Blake and Mouton, *Corporate Excellence.*
26. Blake and Mouton, *Managerial Grid.*
27. A. Rice, *Productivity and Social Organization: The Ahmedabad Experiment* (London: Tavistock Publications, 1958); E. Trist and K. Bamforth, "Some Social and Psychological Consequences of the Longwall Method of Coal-Getting," *Human Relations* 4 (January 1951): 1–38; P. Gyllenhamer, *People at Work* (Reading, MA: Addison-Wesley, 1977); E. Thorsrud, B. Sorensen, and B. Gustavsen, "Sociotechnical Approach to Industrial Democracy in Norway," in *Handbook of Work Organization and Society*, ed. R. Dubin (Chicago: Rand McNally, 1976): 648–87; *Work in America: Report of a Special Task Force to the Secretary of Health, Education, and Welfare* (Cambridge, MA: MIT Press, 1973); L. Davis and A. Cherns, eds., *The Quality of Working Life*, 2 vols. (New York: Free Press, 1975).
28. D. Nadler and E. Lawler III, "Quality of Work Life: Perspectives and Directions" (working paper, Center for Effective Organizations, University of Southern California, Los Angeles, 1982); L. Davis, "Enhancing the Quality of Work Life: Developments in the United States," *International Labour Review* 116 (July–August 1977): 53–65; L. Davis, "Job Design and Productivity: A New Approach," *Personnel* 33 (1957): 418–30.
29. Ibid.

30. R. Ford, "Job Enrichment Lessons from AT&T," *Harvard Business Review* 51 (January–February 1973): 96–106; J. Taylor, J. Landy, M. Levine, and D. Kamath, *Quality of Working Life: An Annotated Bibliography, 1957–1972* (Center for Organizational Studies, Graduate School of Management, University of California at Los Angeles, 1972); J. Taylor, "Experiments in Work System Design: Economic and Human Results," *Personnel Review* 6 (1977): 28–37; J. Taylor, "Job Satisfaction and Quality of Working Life: A Reassessment," *Journal of Occupational Psychology* 50 (December 1977): 243–52.

31. W. Ouchi, *Theory Z* (Reading, MA: Addison-Wesley, 1981).

32. J. Vogt and K. Murrell, *Empowerment in Organizations* (San Diego: University Associates, 1990).

33. M. Jelinek and J. Litterer, "Why OD Must Become Strategic," in *Research in Organizational Change and Development*, vol. 2, ed. W. Pasmore and R. Woodman (Greenwich, CT: JAI Press, 1988), 135–62; P. Buller, "For Successful Strategic Change: Blend OD Practices with Strategic Management," *Organizational Dynamics* (Winter 1988): 42–55; C. Worley, D. Hitchin, and W. Ross, *Integrated Strategic Change* (Reading, MA: Addison-Wesley, 1996).

34. Worley, Hitchin, and Ross, *Integrated Strategic Change*; N. Rajagopalan and G. Spreitzer, "Toward a Theory of Strategic Change: A Multi-Lens Perspective and Integrative Framework," *Academy of Management Review* 22 (1997): 48–79.

35. R. Beckhard and R. Harris, *Organizational Transitions: Managing Complex Change*, 2nd ed. (Reading, MA: Addison-Wesley, 1987); N. Tichy, *Managing Strategic Change* (New York: John Wiley & Sons, 1983); E. Schein, *Organizational Culture and Leadership* (San Francisco: Jossey-Bass, 1985); C. Lundberg, "Working with Culture," *Journal of Organization Change Management* 1 (1988): 38–47.

36. D. Miller and P. Freisen, "Momentum and Revolution in Organization Adaptation," *Academy of Management Journal* 23 (1980): 591–614; M. Tushman and E. Romanelli, "Organizational Evolution: A Metamorphosis Model of Convergence and Reorientation," in *Research in Organizational Behavior*, vol. 7, ed. L. Cummings and B. Staw (Greenwich, CT: JAI Press, 1985), 171–222.

37. Beckhard and Harris, *Organizational Transitions*.

38. T. Covin and R. Kilmann, "Critical Issues in Large-Scale Organization Change," *Journal of Organization Change Management* 1 (1988): 59–72; A. Mohrman, S. Mohrman, G. Ledford Jr., T. Cummings, and E. Lawler, eds., *Large-Scale Organization Change* (San Francisco: Jossey-Bass, 1989); W. Torbert, "Leading Organizational Transformation," in *Research in Organizational Change and Development*, vol. 3, ed. R. Woodman and W. Pasmore (Greenwich, CT: JAI Press, 1989), 83–116; J. Bartunek and M. Louis, "The Interplay of Organization Development and Organization Transformation," in *Research in Organizational Change and Development*, vol. 2, ed. W. Pasmore and R. Woodman (Greenwich, CT: JAI Press, 1988), 97–134; A. Levy and U. Merry, *Organizational Transformation: Approaches, Strategies, Theories* (New York: Praeger, 1986).

39. M. Marks and P. Mirvis, *Joining Forces* (San Francisco: Jossey-Bass, 1998).

40. A. Jaeger, "Organization Development and National Culture: Where's the Fit?" *Academy of Management Review* 11 (1986): 178; G. Hofstede, *Culture's Consequences: International Differences in Work-Related Values* (London: Sage, 1980); P. Sorensen Jr., T. Head, N. Mathys, J. Preston, and D. Cooperrider, *Global and International Organization Development* (Champaign, IL: Stipes, 1995); A. Chin (with C. Chin), *Internationalizing OD: Cross-Cultural Experiences of NTL Members* (Alexandria, VA: NTL Institute, 1997).

41. G. Varney and A. Darrow, "Market Position of Master-Level Graduate Programs in OD," *OD Practitioner* 27 (1995): 39–43; OD Institute, *International Registry of O.D. Professionals and O.D. Handbook* (Cleveland: OD Institute, 1995); G. Varney and A. Darrow, "Name Recognition of Master's Level Graduate Programs in Organization Development and Change," *OD Practitioner* 30 (1998): 36–40.

42. R. Golembiewski and G. Brewer, "The Status of OD in Public Administration: Another Case of Practice Being Ahead of Theory," in *Handbook of Organization Development*, ed. T. Cummings (Los Angeles: Sage Publications, 2008): 541–51; R. Golembiewski, C. Proehl, and D. Sink, "Success of OD Applications in the Public Sector, Toting Up the Score for a Decade, More or Less," *Public Administration Review* 41 (1981): 679–82; R. Golembiewski, *Humanizing Public Organizations* (Mt. Airy, MD: Lomond, 1985); P. Robertson and S. Seneviratne, "Outcomes of Planned Organization Change in the Public Sector: A Meta-Analytic Comparison to the Private," *Public Administration Review* 55 (1995): 547–61.

43. R. Shmuck and M. Miles, *Organizational Development in Schools* (Palo Alto, CA: National Press Books, 1971); R. Havelock, *The Change Agent's Guide to Innovation in Education* (Englewood Cliffs, NJ: Educational Technology, 1973); R. Schmuck and P. Runkel, "Organization Development in Schools," *Consultation* 4 (Fall 1985): 236–57; S. Mohrman and E. Lawler, "Motivation for School Reform" (working paper, Center for Effective Organizations, University of Southern California, Los Angeles, 1995).

PART 1

OVERVIEW OF ORGANIZATION DEVELOPMENT

2 The Nature of Planned Change

3 The Organization Development Practitioner

2

The Nature of Planned Change

learning objectives

- Describe and compare three major theories of planned change.
- Introduce a general model of planned change that will be used to organize the material presented in the book.
- Explain how planned change can be adopted to fit different contexts.
- Critique the practice of planned change.

The pace of global, economic, and technological development makes change an inevitable feature of organizational life. However, change that happens to an organization can be distinguished from change that is planned by its members. In this book, the term *change* will refer to planned change. Organization development (OD) is directed at bringing about planned change to increase an organization's effectiveness and capability to change itself. It is generally initiated and implemented by managers, often with the help of an OD practitioner from either inside or outside of the organization. Organizations can use planned change to solve problems, to learn from experience, to reframe shared perceptions, to adapt to external environmental changes, to improve performance, and to influence future changes.

All approaches to OD rely on some theory about planned change. The theories describe the different stages through which planned change may be effected in organizations and explain the temporal process of applying OD methods to help organization members manage change. In this chapter, we first describe and compare three major theories of organization change that have received considerable attention in the field: Lewin's change model, the action research model, and the positive model. Next, we present a general model of planned change that integrates the earlier models and incorporates recent conceptual advances in OD. The general model has broad applicability to many types of planned change efforts and serves to organize the chapters in this book. We then discuss different types of change and how the process can vary depending on the change situation. Finally, we present several critiques of planned change.

2-1 Theories of Planned Change

Conceptions of planned change have tended to focus on how change can be implemented in organizations.[1] Called "theories of changing," these frameworks describe the activities that must take place to initiate and carry out successful organizational change. In this section, we describe and compare three theories of changing: Lewin's change model, the action research model, and the positive model. These frameworks have received widespread attention in OD and serve as the primary basis for a general model of planned change.

2-1a Lewin's Change Model

One of the earliest models of planned change was provided by Kurt Lewin.[2] He conceived of change as modification of those forces keeping a system's behavior stable. Specifically, a particular set of behaviors at any moment in time is the result of two groups of forces: those striving to maintain the status quo and those pushing for change. When both sets of forces are about equal, current behaviors are maintained in what Lewin termed a state of "quasi-stationary equilibrium." To change that state, one can increase those forces pushing for change, decrease those forces maintaining the current state, or apply some combination of both. For example, the level of performance of a work group might be stable because group norms maintaining that level are equivalent to the supervisor's pressures for change to higher levels. This level can be increased either by changing the group norms to support higher levels of performance or by increasing supervisor pressures to produce at higher levels. Lewin suggested that decreasing those forces maintaining the status quo produces less tension and resistance than increasing forces for change and consequently is a more effective change strategy.

Lewin viewed this change process as consisting of the following three steps, which are shown in Figure 2.1(A):

1. **Unfreezing.** This step usually involves reducing those forces maintaining the organization's behavior at its present level. Unfreezing is sometimes accomplished through a process of "psychological disconfirmation." By introducing information that shows discrepancies between behaviors desired by organization members and those behaviors currently exhibited, members can be motivated to engage in change activities.[3]
2. **Moving.** This step shifts the behavior of the organization, department, or individual to a new level. It involves intervening in the system to develop new behaviors, values, and attitudes through changes in organizational structures and processes.
3. **Refreezing.** This step stabilizes the organization at a new state of equilibrium. It is frequently accomplished through the use of supporting mechanisms that reinforce the new organizational state, such as organizational culture, rewards, and structures.

Lewin's model provides a general framework for understanding organizational change. Because the three steps of change are relatively broad, considerable effort has gone into elaborating them. For example, the planning model developed by Lippitt, Watson, and Westley arranges Lewin's model into seven steps: scouting, entry, diagnosis (unfreezing), planning, action (moving), stabilization and evaluation, and termination (refreezing).[4] Similarly, Kotter's eight-stage process can be mapped onto Lewin's phases: establishing a sense of urgency, creating the guiding coalition, developing a vision and strategy, and communicating the change vision (unfreezing); empowering broad-based action, generating short-term wins (moving); and consolidating gains and producing

FIGURE 2.1

Comparison of Planned Change Models

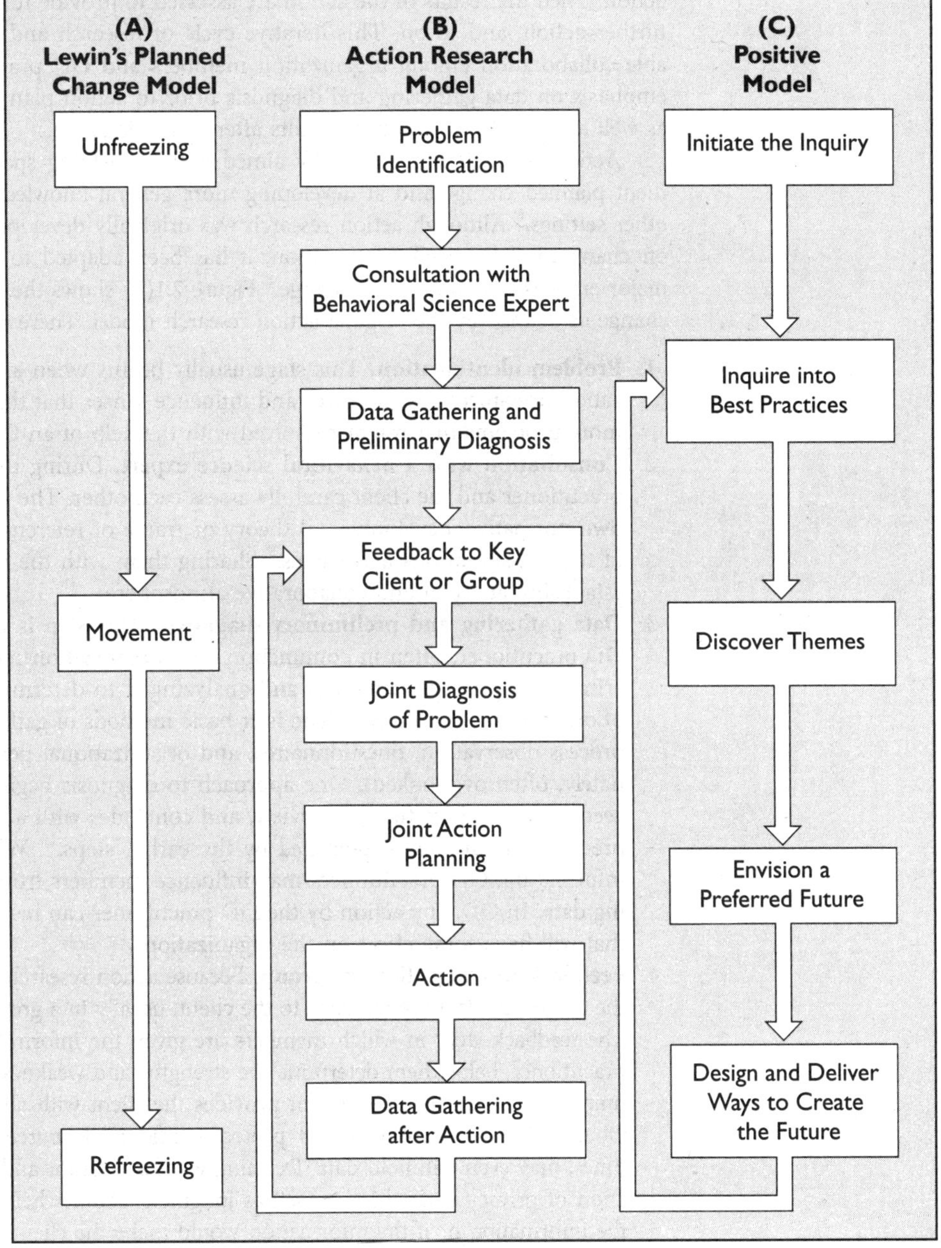

more change, and anchoring new approaches in the culture (refreezing).[5] Lewin's model remains closely identified with the field of OD, however, and is used to illustrate how other types of change can be implemented. For example, Lewin's three-step model has been used to explain how information technologies can be implemented more effectively.[6]

2-1b Action Research Model

The classic action research model focuses on planned change as a cyclical process in which initial research about the organization provides information to guide subsequent action. Then the results of the action are assessed to provide further information to guide further action, and so on. This iterative cycle of research and action involves considerable collaboration among organization members and OD practitioners. It places heavy emphasis on data gathering and diagnosis prior to action planning and implementation, as well as careful evaluation of results after action is taken.

Action research is traditionally aimed both at helping specific organizations implement planned change and at developing more general knowledge that can be applied to other settings.[7] Although action research was originally developed to have this dual focus on change and knowledge generation, it has been adapted to OD efforts in which the major emphasis is on planned change.[8] Figure 2.1(B) shows the cyclical phases of planned change as defined by the original action research model. There are eight main steps.

1. **Problem identification.** This stage usually begins when an executive in the organization or someone with power and influence senses that the organization has one or more problems that might be solved with the help of an OD practitioner.
2. **Consultation with a behavioral science expert.** During the initial contact, the OD practitioner and the client carefully assess each other. The practitioner has his or her own normative, developmental theory or frame of reference and must be conscious of those assumptions and values.[9] Sharing them with the client from the beginning establishes an open and collaborative atmosphere.
3. **Data gathering and preliminary diagnosis.** This step is usually completed by the OD practitioner, often in conjunction with organization members. It involves gathering appropriate information and analyzing it to determine the underlying causes of organizational problems. The four basic methods of gathering data are interviews, process observation, questionnaires, and organizational performance data (unfortunately, often overlooked). One approach to diagnosis begins with observation, proceeds to a semistructured interview, and concludes with a questionnaire to measure precisely the problems identified by the earlier steps.[10] When gathering diagnostic information, OD practitioners may influence members from whom they are collecting data. In OD, any action by the OD practitioner can be viewed as an intervention that will have some effect on the organization.[11]
4. **Feedback to a key client or group.** Because action research is a collaborative activity, the diagnostic data are fed back to the client, usually in a group or work-team meeting. The feedback step, in which members are given the information gathered by the OD practitioner, helps them determine the strengths and weaknesses of the organization or unit under study. The consultant provides the client with all relevant and useful data. Obviously, the practitioner will protect confidential sources of information and, at times, may even withhold data. Defining what is relevant and useful involves consideration of privacy and ethics as well as judgment about whether the group is ready for the information or if the information would make the client overly defensive.
5. **Joint diagnosis of the problem.** At this point, members discuss the feedback and explore with the OD practitioner whether they want to work on identified problems. A close interrelationship exists among data gathering, feedback, and diagnosis because the consultant summarizes the basic data from the client members and presents the data to them for validation and further diagnosis. An important point to remember, as Schein suggests, is that the action research process is very different from the doctor–patient model, in which the consultant comes in, makes a diagnosis, and

prescribes a solution. Schein notes that the failure to establish a common frame of reference in the client–consultant relationship may lead to a faulty diagnosis or to a communication gap whereby the client is sometimes "unwilling to believe the diagnosis or accept the prescription." He believes that "most companies have drawers full of reports by consultants, each loaded with diagnoses and recommendations which are either not understood or not accepted by the 'patient.'"[12]

6. **Joint action planning.** Next, the OD practitioner and the client members jointly agree on further actions to be taken. This is the beginning of the moving process (described in Lewin's change model), as the organization decides how best to reach a different quasi-stationary equilibrium. At this stage, the specific action to be taken depends on the culture, technology, and environment of the organization; the diagnosis of the problem; and the time and expense of the intervention.
7. **Action.** This stage involves the actual change from one organizational state to another. It may include installing new methods and procedures, reorganizing structures and work designs, and reinforcing new behaviors. Such actions typically cannot be implemented immediately but require a transition period as the organization moves from the present to a desired future state.[13]
8. **Data gathering after action.** Because action research is a cyclical process, data must also be gathered after the action has been taken to measure and determine the effects of the action and to feed the results back to the organization. This, in turn, may lead to rediagnosis and new action.

The action research model underlies most current approaches to planned change and is often considered synonymous with OD. Recently, it has been refined and extended to new settings and applications, and consequently, researchers and practitioners have made requisite adaptations of its basic framework.[14]

Trends in the application of action research include movement from smaller subunits of organizations to total systems and communities.[15] In these larger contexts, action research is more complex and political than in smaller settings. Therefore, the action research cycle is coordinated across multiple change processes and includes a diversity of stakeholders who have an interest in the organization. (We describe these applications more thoroughly in Chapters 18, 19, and 20.) Action research also is applied increasingly in international settings, particularly in developing nations in the Southern Hemisphere.[16] Embedded within the action research model, however, are "Northern Hemisphere" assumptions about change. For example, action research traditionally views change more linearly than do Asian cultures, and it treats the change process more collaboratively than do Latin American and African nations. To achieve success in these settings, action research is tailored to fit cultural assumptions. (See section "2–3 Different Types of Planned Change.") Finally, action research is applied increasingly to promote social change and innovation, as demonstrated most clearly in community development and global social change projects.[17] These applications are heavily value laden and seek to redress imbalances in power and resource allocations across different groups. Action researchers tend to play an activist role in the change process, which is often chaotic and conflictual. (Chapter 21 reviews global social change processes.)

In light of these general trends, contemporary applications of action research have substantially increased the degree of member involvement in the change process. This contrasts with traditional approaches to planned change, whereby consultants carried out most of the change activities, with the agreement and collaboration of management.[18] Although consultant-dominated change still persists in OD, there is a growing tendency to involve organization members in learning about their organization and how to change it. Referred to as "participatory action research," "action learning," "action science," or "self-design," this approach to planned change emphasizes the need for organization members to learn firsthand about planned change if they are to gain the knowledge and skills needed to change the organization.[19] In today's complex and changing environment, some argue that OD must go beyond solving particular problems to helping members gain the competence needed to change and improve the organization continually.[20]

In this modification of action research, the role of OD consultants is to work with members to facilitate the learning process. Both parties are "colearners" in diagnosing the organization, designing changes, and implementing and assessing them.[21] Neither party dominates the change process. Rather, each participant brings unique information and expertise to the situation, and they combine their resources to learn how to change the organization. Consultants, for example, know how to design diagnostic instruments and OD interventions, and organization members have "local knowledge" about the organization and how it functions. Each participant learns from the change process. Organization members learn how to change their organization and how to refine and improve it. OD consultants learn how to facilitate complex organizational change and learning.

The action research model will continue to be the dominant methodological basis for planned change in the near future. But the basic philosophy of science on which traditional action research operates is also evolving and is described below.

2-1c The Positive Model

The third model of change, the positive model, represents an important departure from Lewin's model and the action research process. Those models are primarily deficit based; they focus on the organization's problems and how they can be solved so it functions better. The positive model focuses on what the organization is doing right. It helps members understand their organization when it is working at its best and builds off those capabilities to achieve even better results. This positive approach to change is consistent with a growing movement in the social sciences called "positive organizational scholarship," which focuses on positive dynamics in organizations that give rise to extraordinary outcomes.[22] Considerable research on expectation effects also supports this model of planned change.[23] It shows that people tend to act in ways that make their expectations occur. Thus, positive expectations about the organization can create an anticipation that energizes and directs behavior toward making those beliefs happen.

The positive model has been applied to planned change primarily through a process called appreciative inquiry (AI).[24] As a "reformist and rebellious" form of social constructionism, AI explicitly infuses a positive value orientation into analyzing and changing organizations.[25] Social constructionism assumes that organization members' shared experiences and interactions influence how they perceive the organization and behave in it.[26] Because such shared meaning can determine how members approach planned change, AI encourages a positive orientation to how change is conceived and managed. It promotes broad member involvement in creating a shared vision about the organization's positive potential. That shared appreciation provides a powerful and guiding image of what the organization could be.

Drawing heavily on AI, the positive model of planned change involves five phases that are depicted in Figure 2.1(C).[27]

1. **Initiate the inquiry.** This first phase determines the subject of change. It emphasizes member involvement to identify the organizational issue they have the most energy to address. For example, members can choose to look for successful male–female

collaboration (as opposed to sexual discrimination), instances of customer satisfaction (as opposed to customer dissatisfaction), particularly effective work teams, or product development processes that brought new ideas to market especially fast. If the focus of inquiry is real and vital to organization members, the change process itself will take on these positive attributes.

2. **Inquire into best practices.** This phase involves gathering information about the "best of what is" in the organization. If the topic is organizational innovation, then members help to develop an interview protocol that collects stories of new ideas that were developed and implemented in the organization. The interviews are conducted by organization members; they interview each other and tell stories of innovation in which they have personally been involved. These stories are pulled together to create a pool of information describing the organization as an innovative system.
3. **Discover the themes.** In this third phase, members examine the stories, both large and small, to identify a set of themes representing the common dimensions of people's experiences. For example, the stories of innovation may contain themes about how managers gave people the freedom to explore a new idea, the support organization members received from their coworkers, or how the exposure to customers sparked creative thinking. No theme is too small to be represented; it is important that all of the underlying mechanisms that helped to generate and support the themes be described. The themes represent the basis for moving from "what is" to "what could be."
4. **Envision a preferred future.** Members then examine the identified themes, challenge the status quo, and describe a compelling future. Based on the organization's successful past, members collectively visualize the organization's future and develop "possibility propositions"—statements that bridge the organization's current best practices with ideal possibilities for future organizing. These propositions should present a truly exciting, provocative, and possible picture of the future. Based on these possibilities, members identify the relevant stakeholders and critical organization processes that must be aligned to support the emergence of the envisioned future. The vision becomes a statement of "what should be."
5. **Design and deliver ways to create the future.** The final phase involves the design and delivery of ways to create the future. It describes the activities and creates the plans necessary to bring about the vision. It proceeds to action and assessment phases similar to those of action research described previously. Members make changes, assess the results, make necessary adjustments, and so on as they move the organization toward the vision and sustain "what will be." The process is continued by renewing the conversations about the best of what is.

2-1d Comparisons of Change Models

All three models—Lewin's change model, the action research model, and the positive model—describe the phases by which planned change occurs in organizations. As shown in Figure 2.1, the models overlap in that their emphasis on action to implement organizational change is preceded by a preliminary stage (unfreezing, diagnosis, or initiate the inquiry) and is followed by a closing stage (refreezing or evaluation). Moreover, all three approaches emphasize the application of behavioral science knowledge, involve organization members in the change process to varying degrees, and recognize that any interaction between an OD practitioner and an organization constitutes an intervention that may affect the organization. However, Lewin's change model differs from the other two in that it focuses on the general process of planned change, rather than on specific OD activities.

Lewin's model and the action research model differ from the positive approach in terms of the level of involvement of the participants and the focus of change. Lewin's model and traditional action research emphasize the role of the OD practitioner with relatively limited member involvement in the change process. Contemporary applications of action research and the positive model, on the other hand, treat both OD consultants and participants as colearners who are heavily involved in planned change. In addition, Lewin's model and action research are more concerned with fixing problems than with focusing on what the organization does well and leveraging those strengths.

2-2 General Model of Planned Change

The three models of planned change suggest a general framework for planned change as shown in Figure 2.2. The framework describes the four basic activities that practitioners and organization members jointly carry out in organization development. The arrows connecting the different activities in the model show the typical sequence of events, from entering and contracting, to diagnosing, to planning and implementing change, to evaluating and institutionalizing change. The lines connecting the activities emphasize that organizational change is not a straightforward, linear process but involves considerable overlap and feedback among the activities. Because the model serves to organize the remaining parts of this book, Figure 2.2 also shows which specific chapters apply to the four major change activities.

2-2a Entering and Contracting

The first set of activities in planned change concerns entering and contracting (described in Chapter 4). Those events help managers decide whether they want to engage further in a planned change program and to commit resources to such a process. Entering an organization involves gathering initial data to understand the problems facing the organization or to determine the positive areas for inquiry. Once this information is collected, the problems or opportunities are discussed with managers and other organization members to develop a contract or agreement to engage in planned change. The contract spells out future change activities, the resources that will be committed to the

FIGURE 2.2

A General Model of Planned Change

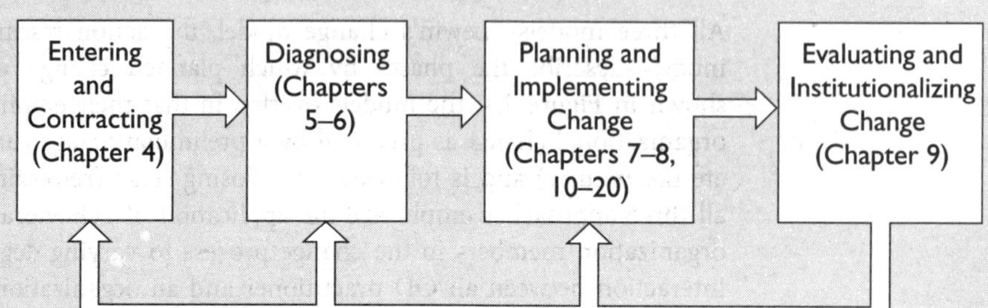

process, and how OD practitioners and organization members will be involved. In many cases, organizations do not get beyond this early stage of planned change because one or more situations arise: Disagreements about the need for change surface, resource constraints are encountered, or other methods for change appear more feasible. When OD is used in nontraditional and international settings, the entering and contracting process must be sensitive to the context in which the change is taking place.

2-2b Diagnosing

In this stage of planned change, the client system is carefully studied. Diagnosis can focus on understanding organizational problems, including their causes and consequences, or on collecting stories about the organization's positive attributes. The diagnostic process is one of the most important activities in OD. It includes choosing an appropriate model for understanding the organization and gathering, analyzing, and feeding back information to managers and organization members about the problems or opportunities that exist.

Diagnostic models for analyzing problems (described in Chapter 5) explore three levels of activities. Organization issues represent the most complex level of analysis and involve the total system. Group-level issues are associated with department and group effectiveness. Individual-level issues involve the way jobs are designed and performed.

Gathering, analyzing, and feeding back data are the central change activities in diagnosis. Chapter 6 describes how data can be gathered through interviews, observations, survey instruments, or such archival sources as meeting minutes and organization charts. It explains how data can be reviewed and analyzed. Chapter 6 also describes the process of feeding back diagnostic data. Organization members, often in collaboration with an OD practitioner, jointly discuss the data and their implications for change.

2-2c Planning and Implementing Change

In this stage, organization members and practitioners jointly plan and implement OD interventions. They design interventions to achieve the organization's vision or goals and make action plans to implement them. There are several criteria for designing interventions, including the organization's readiness for change, its current change capability, its culture and power distributions, and the change agent's skills and abilities (discussed in Chapter 7). Depending on the outcomes of diagnosis, there are four major types of interventions in OD:

1. Human process interventions at the individual, group, and total system levels (Chapters 10 and 11)
2. Interventions that modify an organization's structure and technology (Chapters 12, 13, and 14)
3. Human resources interventions that seek to improve member performance and wellness (Chapters 15, 16, and 17)
4. Strategic interventions that involve managing the organization's relationship to its external environment and the internal structure and process necessary to support a business strategy (Chapters 18, 19, and 20).

Chapter 21 presents specialized information for carrying out OD in organizations seeking sustainable results and in organizations trying to implement global social change. Chapter 22 describes special applications of OD in such nontraditional organizations as schools, health care institutions, family-owned businesses, and the public sector.

Implementing interventions is concerned with leading and managing the change process. As discussed in Chapter 8, it includes motivating change, creating a desired future vision of the organization, developing political support, managing the transition toward the vision, and sustaining momentum for change.

2-2d Evaluating and Institutionalizing Change

The final stage in planned change involves evaluating the effects of the intervention and managing the institutionalization of successful change programs so they persist. (Those two activities are described in Chapter 9.) Feedback to organization members about the intervention's results provides information about whether the changes should be continued, modified, or suspended. Institutionalizing successful changes involves reinforcing them through feedback, rewards, and training.

Application 2.1 describes the initiation of a planned change process in a government organization. It provides especially rich detail on the planning and implementing phase of change, and on how people can be involved in the process.[28]

2-3 Different Types of Planned Change

The general model of planned change describes how the OD process typically unfolds in organizations. In actual practice, the different phases are not nearly as orderly as the model implies. OD practitioners tend to modify or adjust the stages to fit the needs of the situation. Steps in planned change may be implemented in a variety of ways, depending on the client's needs and goals, the change agent's skills and values, and the organization's context. Thus, planned change can vary enormously from one situation to another.

To understand the differences better, planned change can be contrasted across situations on three key dimensions: the magnitude of organizational change, the degree to which the client system is organized, and whether the setting is domestic or international.

2-3a Magnitude of Change

Planned change efforts can be characterized as falling along a continuum ranging from incremental changes that involve fine-tuning the organization to fundamental changes that entail radically altering how it operates.[29] Incremental changes tend to involve limited dimensions and levels of the organization, such as the decision-making processes of work groups. They occur within the context of the organization's existing business strategy, structure, and culture and are aimed at improving the status quo. Fundamental changes, on the other hand, are directed at significantly altering how the organization operates. They tend to involve several organizational dimensions, including structure, culture, reward systems, information processes, and work design. They also involve changing multiple levels of the organization, from top-level management through departments and work groups to individual jobs.

Planned change traditionally has been applied in situations involving incremental change. Organizations in the 1960s and 1970s were concerned mainly with fine-tuning their bureaucratic structures by resolving many of the social problems that emerged with increasing size and formalization. In those situations, planned change involves a relatively bounded set of problem-solving activities. OD practitioners are typically contracted by managers to help solve specific problems in particular organizational systems, such as poor communication among members of a work team or low customer-satisfaction scores in a department store. Diagnostic and change activities tend to be

application 2.1

PLANNED CHANGE AT THE SAN DIEGO COUNTY REGIONAL AIRPORT AUTHORITY

The San Diego County Regional Airport Authority (SDCRAA) was created by a California state law in October 2001; this gave it the responsibility to establish and operate airports within San Diego County. Most importantly, from Thella Bowens's perspective, the law required the San Diego Unified Port District (Port of San Diego) to transfer operation of San Diego's international airport to the SDCRAA by January 2003. Bowens was the current senior director of the Aviation Division within the Port of San Diego that was responsible for operating the San Diego International Airport. When the law was passed, she was named Interim Executive Director of the SDCRAA, and assigned an interim advisory board to help manage the transition.

Bowens's tenure with the organization gave her an important understanding of the organization's operations and its history. For example, the San Diego International Airport accounted for about $4.3 billion or roughly 4% of San Diego's regional economy. Forecasts called for air travel to more than double to 35 million passengers by 2030, and contribute up to $8 billion to the regional economy. In addition, Bowens had participated in the Aviation Division's strategic planning process in 2001. She was well positioned to lead this effort.

As she thought about managing the start-up of the SDCRAA, two broad but interdependent categories of initial activity emerged: developing the transition plan and dealing with the legal and regulatory issues.

DEVELOPING THE TRANSITION PLAN

In April 2002, Bowens took the senior team from the old Aviation Division to an off-site workshop to discuss the creation and management of an effective transition process. This group understood the importance of SDCRAA quickly becoming a stand-alone agency and the need to be seen differently in the marketplace. The group recommended revising the existing strategic plan, to hire staff to research, discuss, and create a transition plan, and to conduct retreats with employees from multiple organizational levels. In response, Bowens chartered the Airport Transition Team to ensure the smooth and seamless transfer of operations and public services provided by the airport without regard to which agency was responsible for their provision.

In May 2002, seven employees were hand-picked from the Aviation Division to become members of the Airport Transition Team and relieved of their day-to-day job responsibilities so they could focus on the transition. The selection criteria included the ability to work within a process yet think outside of the box, to communicate well with others in a team, and to influence directors and managers without having formal authority. A one-and-a-half-day kick-off meeting was held to set expectations, to communicate goals and responsibilities, and to initiate the team. A "war room" was established for the team to keep records, hold meetings, and serve as a communication hub. The team named themselves the "Metamorphs."

Many Metamorph members came from different parts of the organization and, having never worked together, needed to rely on each other to effectively design the transition process. Senior team member Angela Shafer-Payne, then director of Airport Business and Administration, worked closely with the Metamorphs and led formal team-building activities throughout the year. Through their work together, the Metamorphs discovered how large and daunting the organizational change was and yet appreciated the unique, once-in-a-lifetime opportunity to make an impact. As one member put it, "How many times in your life can you say that you helped put together a brand-new organization?"

The Metamorphs decided that to meet their charter, any transition plan had to be designed specifically to minimize disruption to customers and service, minimize airport and nonairport financial impacts, and properly address and resolve all legal and regulatory matters. These criteria guided the creation of 12 functional teams (which expanded later to 19). Responsibility for the teams was divided among the transition team members, and each team was composed of employees from the old Aviation Division and other Port of San Diego departments. Their mission was to collect data, establish new or parallel functions for the SDCRAA, and highlight any issues related to the start-up of that particular function. Once the teams were in place, they were given tools to use and questions that needed to be addressed. Each team set aside time to review all of the records in each functional area. For example, the human resources functional team consisted of Aviation Division employees, HR professionals from the Port of San Diego, and Port attorneys; it was charged with developing the actual transition mechanism, HR operations, and HR organizational structure. Another team focused on the environmental issues involved in the transition. They examined over 100 different environmental permits held by the Port of San Diego to understand if SDCRAA needed a similar permit, needed to be a copermittee with the Port of San Diego, or if the SDCRAA could stand alone. If it were a stand-alone situation, then documentation would be prepared to transfer the permit.

To ensure that no issues fell through the cracks, three distinct peer reviews were held in the summer and fall of 2002. The peer review panels were staffed by professionals within the aviation industry, people who had experienced a transition of some type within an organization, or those who were integral to the start-up of the organization. The first peer review panel examined the transition plan and offered advice on whether to add any other critical and/or missing components. The second peer review panel, consisting of mostly human resources professionals, examined the proposed organizational structure. The final peer review panel focused on the IT systems portion of the transition plan because of technology's critical role in the overall success of many of the internal processes.

DEALING WITH THE LEGAL AND REGULATORY ISSUES

By January 2002, the SDCRAA was not yet a full agency and had only one employee, Thella Bowens. Despite all the work of the Metamorphs and the functional teams, and sometimes because of it, Bowens also had to interface with the California legislature. The original legislation (California Senate Bill AB93 [2001–2002]) provided a framework for setting up the new agency but left many questions unanswered, including issues relating to property transfer (SDCRAA would lease land from the Port on a 66-year lease) and the transitioning of employees from one public agency to another. To provide clarity and another layer of understanding, "clean-up" legislation (SB 1896) was passed in mid-2002. Together with the original bill, the legislation protected employees to ensure no loss of jobs or benefits. This gave the Metamorphs additional information and guidance to deal with employee contract issues. For example, in the middle of the transition planning process, the Port District had to renegotiate its union contract. The Metamorphs had to work closely with the airport's external counsel, the Port of San Diego counsel, and state senators to ensure a smooth negotiation.

Finally, Bowens and the Metamorphs had to address changes to federal security regulations outlined in the Aviation and Transportation Security Act that resulted from the September 11, 2001, attacks. Those events caused a number of disruptions for many stakeholders in the air transportation industry. They required the transition plan to include a component that focused on keeping costs contained to enable aviation partners, the airlines, the gate gourmets, and tenants, to weather the storm.

IMPLEMENTATION AND EVALUATION

The final transition plan was presented to the interim board and then to the Board of Port Commissioners for approval in October 2002. The approved plan was comprised of several components, including an IT conversion plan and the process for formally transferring responsibility to the SDCRAA, but the key elements were human resources and communication plans.

The human resources plan specified the transition of 145 budgeted Aviation Division employees to 52 vacancies plus the 90 other positions identified by the Metamorphs to make the organization whole. The plan called for all of the positions to be filled by mid-2005. The human resources plan also provided for the purchase of services, like the Harbor Police, from the Port of San Diego until mid-2005.

The communication plan was critical to the implementation phase. The Metamorphs regularly carried information about their progress to coworkers in their respective departments. In addition, communication meetings with the entire organization, called "all hands meetings," were held to provide information about the transition. The Airport Transition Plan contained a special emphasis on the needs of the employee. Bowens understood the sociotechnical nature of change and did not want the human factor to be forgotten in the midst of all the legal, technical, and other transitions. She included a number of change-management education sessions for all employees. The change-management education sessions were developed to reassure employees; to encourage genuine, candid, frequent, high-quality communications; and to neutralize anxiety and fears.

During the sessions, employees were (1) updated on the progress of the transition; (2) introduced to change theories, models, and concepts; and (3) encouraged to share their issues, fears, anxieties, concerns, and creative ideas. Employee input was organized into themes, then documented and communicated to Bowens and her direct reports. The leadership team was committed to answering questions and addressing concerns that emerged from the change-management sessions. Airport managers met regularly to select and answer questions for publication in the organization newsletter or live communication at "all hands meetings." In addition, the employee satisfaction survey was updated with questions to learn about transition concerns.

Thella Bowens was named President and CEO of the SDCRAA on January 1, 2003. By June 2003, the SDCRAA had received awards based on superb customer service and outstanding levels of performance. The SDCRAA, based on all available metrics, is successfully operating San Diego's international airport and serving over 15.2 million passengers on 620 daily flights in and out of the airport. Part of the success is due to the way the transition plan was developed. Because of the broad participation in its creation, many employees understood the plan. When issues arose, identifying the personnel to become part of an ad hoc problem-solving group already familiar with the topic was easy.

"Ms. Bowens accomplished the extraordinary job of leading a successful transition of the airport from the Unified Port of San Diego to the Authority," said Joseph W. Craver, Authority (SDCRAA) Chairman. "She is highly regarded and respected for both her breadth of knowledge of aviation management issues and her visionary leadership." Thella Bowens added, "Fortunately, we've been supported by very dedicated professional employees who have exhibited great resolve and sheer hard work through the transition process, and continue to do so as we create a 'world-class' organization."

limited to the defined issues, although additional problems may be uncovered and may need to be addressed. Similarly, the change process tends to focus on those organizational systems having specific problems, and it generally terminates when the problems are resolved. Of course, the OD practitioner may contract to help solve additional problems.

In recent years, OD has been increasingly concerned with fundamental change. As described in Chapter 1, the greater competitiveness and uncertainty of today's environment have led a growing number of organizations to alter drastically the way in which they operate. In such situations, planned change is more complex, extensive, and long term than when applied to incremental change.[30] Because fundamental change involves most features and levels of the organization, it is typically driven from the top, where corporate strategy and values are set. OD practitioners help senior executives create a vision of a desired future organization and energize movement in that direction. They also help them develop structures for managing the transition from the present to the future organization and may include, for example, a program management office and a variety of overlapping steering committees and redesign teams. Staff experts also may redesign many features of the firm, such as performance measures, rewards, planning processes, work designs, and information systems.

Because of the complexity and extensiveness of fundamental change, OD professionals often work in teams comprising members with different yet complementary areas of expertise. The consulting relationship persists over relatively long time periods and includes a great deal of renegotiation and experimentation among consultants and managers. The boundaries of the change effort are more uncertain and diffuse than those in incremental change, thus making diagnosis and change seem more like discovery than like problem solving. (We describe complex strategic and transformational types of change in more detail in Chapters 18, 19, and 20.)

It is important to emphasize that fundamental change may or may not be developmental in nature. Organizations may drastically alter their strategic direction and way of operating without significantly developing their capacity to solve problems, to make future changes, and to achieve both high performance and quality of work life. For example, firms may simply change their marketing mix, dropping or adding products, services, or customers; they may drastically downsize by cutting out marginal businesses and laying off managers and workers; or they may tighten managerial and financial controls and attempt to squeeze more out of the labor force. On the other hand, organizations may undertake fundamental change from a developmental perspective. They may seek to make themselves more competitive by developing their human resources; by getting managers and employees more involved in problem solving and innovation; and by promoting flexibility and direct, open communication. The OD approach to fundamental change is particularly relevant in today's rapidly changing and competitive environment. To succeed in this setting, firms such as General Electric, Kimberly-Clark, Asea Brown Boveri, IBM, and Banca Intesa are transforming themselves from control-oriented bureaucracies to high-involvement organizations capable of changing and improving themselves continually.

2-3b Degree of Organization

Planned change efforts also can vary depending on the degree to which the organization or client system is organized. In overorganized situations, such as in highly mechanistic, bureaucratic organizations, various dimensions such as leadership styles, job designs, organization structure, and policies and procedures are too rigid and overly defined for effective task performance. Communication between management and employees is typically suppressed, conflicts are avoided, and employees are apathetic. In underorganized organizations, on the other hand, there is too little constraint or regulation for effective task performance. Leadership, structure, job design, and policy are poorly defined and fail to direct task behaviors effectively. Communication is fragmented, job responsibilities are ambiguous, and employees' energies are dissipated because they lack direction. Underorganized situations are typically found in such areas as product development, project management, and community development, where relationships among diverse groups and participants must be coordinated around complex, uncertain tasks.

In overorganized situations, where much of OD practice has historically taken place, planned change is generally aimed at loosening constraints on behavior. Changes in leadership, job design, structure, and other features are designed to liberate suppressed energy, to increase the flow of relevant information between employees and managers, and to promote effective conflict resolution. The typical steps of planned change—entry, diagnosis, intervention, and evaluation—are intended to penetrate a relatively closed organization or department and make it increasingly open to self-diagnosis and revitalization. The relationship between the OD practitioner and the management team attempts to model this loosening process. The consultant shares leadership of the change process with management, encourages open communications and confrontation of conflict, and maintains flexibility in relating to the organization.

When applied to organizations facing problems in being underorganized, planned change is aimed at increasing organization by clarifying leadership roles, structuring communication between managers and employees, and specifying job and departmental responsibilities. These activities require a modification of the traditional phases of planned change and include the following four steps:[31]

1. **Identification.** This step identifies the relevant people or groups who need to be involved in the change program. In many underorganized situations, people and departments can be so disconnected that there is ambiguity about who should be included in the problem-solving process. For example, when managers of different departments have only limited interaction with each other, they may disagree or be confused about which departments should be involved in developing a new product or service.
2. **Convention.** In this step, the relevant people or departments in the company are brought together to begin organizing for task performance. For example, department managers might be asked to attend a series of organizing meetings to discuss the division of labor and the coordination required to introduce a new product.
3. **Organization.** Different organizing mechanisms are created to structure the newly required interactions among people and departments. This might include creating new leadership positions, establishing communication channels, and specifying appropriate plans and policies.
4. **Evaluation.** In this final step, the outcomes of the organization step are assessed. The evaluation might signal the need for adjustments in the organizing process or for further identification, convention, and organization activities.

In carrying out these four steps of planned change in underorganized situations, the relationship between the OD practitioner and the client system attempts to reinforce the organizing process. The consultant develops a well-defined leadership role, which might be directive during the early stages of the change program. Similarly, the consulting relationship is clearly defined and tightly specified. In effect, the interaction between the consultant and the client system supports the larger process of bringing order to the situation.

Application 2.2 is an example of planned change in an underorganized situation. In this case, the change agent is a person from industry who identifies a multifaceted problem: University research that should be helpful to manufacturing organizations is not being shaped, coordinated, or transferred. In response, he forms an organization to tighten up the relationships between the two parties.[32]

2-3c Domestic versus International Settings

Planned change efforts have traditionally been applied in North American and European settings, but they are increasingly used outside of these regions.[33] Developed in Western societies, OD reflects the underlying values and assumptions of these cultural settings, including equality, involvement, and short-term time horizons. Under these conditions, it works quite well. In other societies, a different set of cultural values and assumptions can be operating and make the application of OD problematic.

PLANNED CHANGE IN AN UNDERORGANIZED SYSTEM

application 2.2

The Institute for Manufacturing and Automation Research (IMAR) was founded in 1987 in Los Angeles by a group of manufacturing industry members. In its earliest stages of development, one person who had a clear picture of the obstacles to manufacturing excellence was Dale Hartman, IMAR's executive director and former director for manufacturing at Hughes Aircraft Company. He and several other industry associates pinpointed the predominant reasons for flagging competitiveness: needless duplication of effort among manufacturing innovators; difficulties in transferring technological breakthroughs from university to industry; frequent irrelevance of university research to the needs of industry; and the inability of individual industry members to commit the time and funds to research projects needed for continued technological advances.

Hartman and his colleagues determined that organizations should create a pool of funds for research and concluded that the research would most efficiently be carried out in existing university facilities. They worked through at least several plans before they arrived at the idea of the IMAR consortium. The U.S. Navy had been interested in joint efforts for innovations in artificial intelligence, but its constraints and interests were judged to be too narrow to address the problems that Hartman and the others identified.

Networking with other industry members—TRW, Hughes, Northrop, and Rockwell—and two universities with which Hughes had been engaging in ongoing research—the University of Southern California (USC) and University of California, Los Angeles (UCLA)—this original group formed a steering committee to investigate the viability of a joint research and development consortium. Each of the six early planners contributed $5,000 as seed money for basic expenses. The steering committee, based on experience in cooperative research, determined that a full-time person was needed to assume leadership of the consortium. Members of the committee persuaded Dale Hartman to retire early from Hughes and take on IMAR's leadership full-time. Hartman brought with him a wealth of knowledge about barriers to innovation and technology transfer, and a solid reputation in both industry and academia that was crucial for the success of multiple-sector partnerships. As a former Hughes networker, he knew how to lobby state and federal government sources for funds and legislation that promoted industry innovation. He also knew a host of talented people in Southern California whom he would persuade to become IMAR members.

In his 30 years in manufacturing, Hartman found that university-driven research had not produced a respectable yield of usable information. University research was frequently irrelevant to industry needs and seldom provided for transfer of usable innovation to the plant floor. Industry was only tangentially involved in what the university was doing and Hartman saw little opportunity for the two sectors to benefit from a partnership. Therefore, it was determined that IMAR would be user-driven. Industry would set the agenda by choosing projects from among university proposals that promised to be of generic use to industry members, and it would benefit by influencing the direction of research and receiving early information about research results.

In the next several months, the steering committee and Hartman met regularly to define common research needs and locate funding sources. They sought industry sponsors from high-technology companies with an understanding of the problems in manufacturing research and a desire to do more than merely supply money. They wanted members who would be willing to get involved in IMAR's programs. Furthermore, they wanted all members to be able to use the results of IMAR's generic research while not competing directly with each other. Finally, they decided that they wanted a relatively small membership. If the membership grew too large, it might become unwieldy and thus obstruct efforts to get things done.

IMAR's industrial advisory board was formed with six industrial organizations represented—Xerox, Hughes, TRW, Northrop, IBM, and Rockwell—in addition to USC and

UCLA. Members were to pay $100,000 each and make a three-year commitment to IMAR. With initial objectives in place and a committed membership, Hartman was already searching for additional funding sources. He was successful in getting a bill introduced in California's state legislature, later signed by the governor, that authorized the state department of commerce to fund IMAR $200,000. Moreover, IMAR was able to tie into the Industry–University Cooperative Research Center Program (IUCRCP) of the National Science Foundation (NSF) by forming an industry–university consortium called the Center for Manufacturing and Automation Research (CMAR). NSF funded CMAR with a $2 million grant and a five-year commitment. NSF funding in particular was sought because of the instant credibility that NSF sponsorship gives to such an institute.

NSF requested that several more universities be added to the consortium. In addition, an NSF evaluator was to be present at all IMAR meetings and conduct ongoing evaluation of CMAR's progress. IMAR already had UCLA and USC among its members and now added four university affiliates to work on research projects: the University of California, Irvine; University of California, Santa Barbara; Caltech; and Arizona State University. The IMAR steering committee then voted to fund research projects at an affiliated university only if it involved cooperation with either USC or UCLA. Each of the four university affiliates was paired with either USC or UCLA. Each affiliate university was selected because it provided expertise in an area of interest to IMAR's industrial membership. Arizona State, for example, had expertise in knowledge-based simulation systems in industrial engineering, a field of special concern to IMAR's membership. IMAR funded a number of projects, including projects between the affiliated universities, between joint investigators at USC and UCLA, and independent projects at USC and UCLA. Figure 2.3 shows IMAR's structure.

CMAR operated under the auspices of IMAR with the same board of directors serving both consortia. There are two codirectors of CMAR: Dr. George Bekey, chairman of the Computer Science Department at USC, and Dr. Michel Melkanoff, director of UCLA's Center for Integrated Manufacturing. As codirectors they had an indirect reporting relationship to Dale Hartman. Their responsibilities included distributing the research funds and serving as the focal point on their respective campuses. Questions from project team members are directed to one or the other codirector, depending on the project. Each of the codirectors takes responsibility for managing project team members and providing rewards, such as reduced course loads, to research professors wherever possible.

The codirectors further work to encourage informal ties with industry members. For example, Dr. Bekey initiated efforts to have IMAR representatives regularly visit others' facilities to encourage them to cooperate and share ideas. That practice further deepens each industrial member's commitment to IMAR because the representatives were associating with one another and other colleagues in the workplace. In the event that an industry or university representative left, an associate was more likely to be there to take his or her place. Further, Bekey noted that the association between industry and university helped industry to overcome its short-term orientation and helped university people appreciate applied problems and manufacturing needs.

IMAR's board of directors set the research agenda at annual reviews in which it made recommendations for topics to be funded. IMAR took these recommendations and translated them into "requests for proposals" that were circulated among the participating university members. CMAR's codirectors then solicited proposals from the university membership. Researchers' proposals were evaluated and ranked by industry representatives and then passed back to the industry advisory board, which made final determinations on which projects would be funded.

Not only did IMAR engage in research projects, such as microelectronics, digital computers, lasers, and fiber optics, it worked to resolve critical problems for manufacturing innovation research. One area of study was technology transfer. IMAR established a pilot production facility that Hartman called "a halfway house for manufacturing." The facility permitted basic research to be brought to maturity and was capable of producing deliverable parts. The facility also engaged in systems-level research in such areas as management and systems software, and provided an excellent training ground for students.

FIGURE 2.3

Organizational Structure of the Institute for Manufacturing and Automation Research (IMAR)

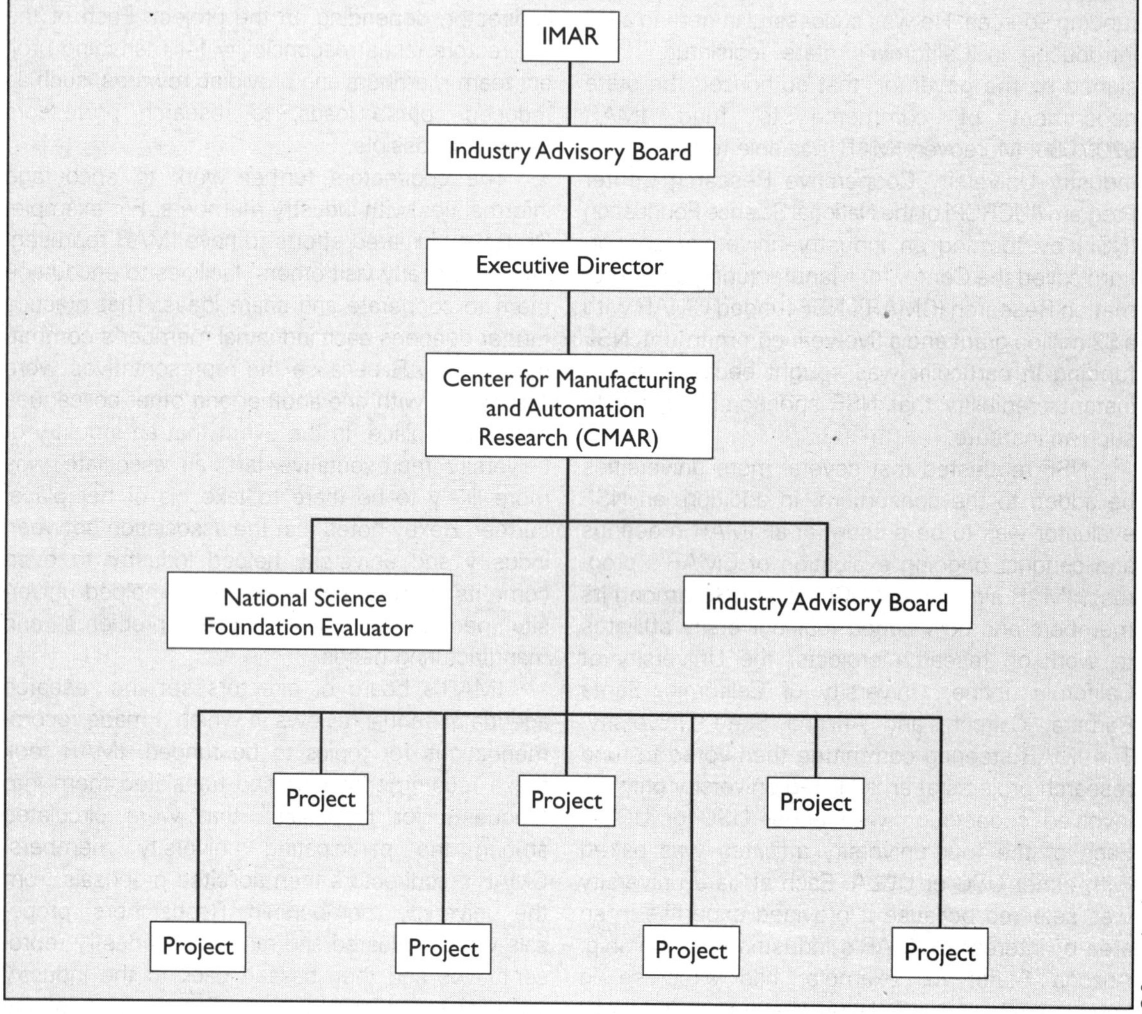

Another strength of IMAR was its affiliation with an NSF evaluator who was appointed to follow the progress of the industry–university cooperative research center. Dr. Ann Marczak was IMAR's initial NSF evaluator. NSF conducted regular audits of the 39 IUCRCPs it sponsored and made information available about survey results, others' reports of what works, and so forth. Dr. Marczak served a valuable function to IMAR as an objective source of feedback. After her first evaluation, for example, Marczak recommended that a project team be formed to conduct ongoing progress assessment for each of the research projects IMAR sponsored. The evaluator's findings also served as NSF's means of determining how well each of the funded centers was performing. A center was judged successful if after five years it could exist without NSF funds. NSF also evaluated each center in terms of how much industry money its projects generated, how much additional money the center generated in research projects, the number of patents granted, products produced, and the satisfaction of faculty and industry participants.

After two years of operation, IMAR had dealt with many of the problems that so frequently plague collaborative research and development efforts among organizations. It had a well-defined purpose that was strongly supported by its members. It was well structured and had a good balance of resources and needs among its membership. Formal and informal communication networks were established. It had strong leadership. Members of IMAR respected Hartman for his technological expertise and skills as a networker. Hartman had a strong sense of IMAR's mission. After a discussion with him, one got the sense that there was not an obstacle he would not overcome. His vision continued to inspire commitment among the IMAR membership. As one member put it, "You end up wanting to see what you can do for the cause."

Not only did IMAR have the commitment of a full-time leader and strong feedback from its NSF evaluator, it involved user-driven research. Although the research was basic, it was chosen by the users themselves to benefit all members of the consortium. If the research had been applied, it would have been more difficult for members to find projects yielding information that all of them could use. The involvement of multiple universities further provided the talent of top researchers in diverse areas of technological expertise. Finally, NSF was furnishing a large proportion of the funding for the first five years as well as regular evaluations.

In contrast to Western societies, for example, the cultures of most Asian countries are more hierarchical and status conscious, less open to discussing personal issues, more concerned with "saving face," and have a longer time horizon for results. These cultural differences can make OD more difficult to implement, especially for North American or European practitioners; they may simply be unaware of the cultural norms and values that permeate the society.

The cultural values that guide OD practice in the United States, for example, include a tolerance for ambiguity, equality among people, individuality, and achievement motives. An OD process that encourages openness among individuals, high levels of participation, and actions that promote increased effectiveness is viewed favorably. The OD practitioner is also assumed to hold these values and to model them in the conduct of planned change. Many reported cases of OD involve Western-based organizations using practitioners trained in the traditional model and raised and experienced in Western society.

When OD is applied outside of North America or Europe (and sometimes even within these settings), the action research process must be adapted to fit the cultural context. For example, the diagnostic phase, which is aimed at understanding how the organization currently functions, can be modified in a variety of ways. Diagnosis can involve many organization members or include only senior executives; be directed from the top, conducted by an outside consultant, or performed by internal consultants; or involve face-to-face interviews or organizational documents. Each step in the general model of planned change must be carefully mapped against the cultural context.

Conducting OD in international settings can be highly stressful on OD practitioners. To be successful, they must develop a keen awareness of their own cultural biases, be open to seeing a variety of issues from another perspective, be fluent in the values and assumptions of the host country, and understand the economic and political context of business in the host country. Most OD practitioners are not able to meet all of those criteria and partner with a "cultural guide," often a member of the client organization, to help navigate the cultural, operational, and political nuances of change in that society.

2-4 Critique of Planned Change

Despite their continued refinement, the models and practice of planned change are still in a formative stage of development, and there is considerable room for improvement. Critics of OD have pointed out several problems with the way planned change has been conceptualized and practiced.

2-4a Conceptualization of Planned Change

Planned change has typically been characterized as involving a series of activities for carrying out effective organization development. Although current models outline a general set of steps to be followed, considerably more information is needed to guide how those steps should be performed in specific situations. In an extensive review and critique of planned change theory, Porras and Robertson argued that planned change activities should be guided by information about (1) the organizational features that can be changed, (2) the intended outcomes from making those changes, (3) the causal mechanisms by which those outcomes are achieved, and (4) the contingencies upon which successful change depends.[34] In particular, they noted that the key to organizational change is change in the behavior of each member and that the information available about the causal mechanisms that produce individual change is lacking. Overall, Porras and Robertson concluded that the information necessary to guide change is only partially available and that a good deal more research and thinking are needed to fill the gaps. Chapters 10 through 22 on OD interventions review what is currently known about change features, outcomes, causal mechanisms, and contingencies.

A related area where current thinking about planned change is deficient is knowledge about how the stages of planned change differ across situations. Most models specify a general set of steps that are intended to be applicable to most change efforts. However, the previous section of this chapter showed how change activities can vary depending on such factors as the magnitude of change, the degree to which the client system is organized, and whether the change is being conducted in a domestic or an international setting. Considerably more effort needs to be expended identifying situational factors that may require modifying the general stages of planned change. That would likely lead to a rich array of planned change models, each geared to a specific set of situational conditions. Such contingency thinking is greatly needed in planned change.

Planned change also tends to be described as a rationally controlled, orderly process. Critics have argued that although this view may be comforting, it is seriously misleading.[35] They point out that planned change has a more chaotic quality, often involving shifting goals, discontinuous activities, surprising events, and unexpected combinations of changes. For example, executives often initiate changes without plans that clarify their strategies and goals. As change unfolds, new stakeholders may emerge and demand modifications reflecting previously unknown or unvoiced needs. Those emergent conditions make planned change a far more disorderly and dynamic process than is customarily portrayed, and conceptions need to capture that reality.

Most descriptions of planned change typically describe a beginning, middle, and end to the process. Critics have argued that planned change models that advocate evaluation and institutionalization processes reinforce the belief that the organization will "refreeze" into some form of equilibrium following change.[36] In the face of increasing globalization and technological change, it is unlikely that change will ever *be over*. Executives, managers, and organization members must be prepared for constant change in a variety of organizational features that are not obvious in most models of planned change.

Finally, the relationship between planned change and organizational performance and effectiveness is not well understood. OD traditionally has had problems assessing whether interventions are producing observed results. The complexity of the change situation, the lack of sophisticated analyses, and the long time periods for producing results have contributed to weak evaluation of OD efforts. Moreover, managers have often accounted for OD efforts with post hoc testimonials, reports of possible future benefits, and calls to support OD as the right thing to do. In the absence of rigorous assessment and measurement, it is difficult to make resource allocation decisions about change programs and to know which interventions are most effective in certain situations.

2-4b Practice of Planned Change

Critics have suggested several problems with the way planned change is carried out.[37] Their concerns are not with the planned change model itself but with how change takes place and with the qualifications and activities of OD practitioners.

A growing number of OD practitioners have acquired skills in a specific technique, such as team building, total quality management, appreciative inquiry, large group interventions, or gain sharing, and have chosen to specialize in that method. Although such specialization may be necessary, it can lead to a certain myopia given the complex array of techniques that define OD. Some OD practitioners favor particular techniques and ignore other strategies that might be more appropriate, tending to interpret organizational problems as requiring the favored technique. Thus, for example, it is not unusual to see consultants pushing such methods as diversity training, reengineering, organization learning, or self-managing work teams as solutions to most organizational problems.

Effective change depends on a careful diagnosis of how the organization is functioning. Diagnosis identifies the underlying causes of organizational problems, such as poor product quality and employee dissatisfaction, or determines the positive opportunities that need to be promoted. It requires both time and money, and some organizations are not willing to make the necessary investment. Rather, they rely on preconceptions about what the problem is and hire consultants with skills appropriate to solve that problem. Managers may think, for example, that work design is the problem, so they hire an expert in job enrichment to implement a change program. The problem may be caused by other factors such as poor reward practices, however, and job enrichment would be inappropriate. Careful diagnosis can help to avoid such mistakes.

In situations requiring complex organizational changes, planned change is a long-term process involving considerable innovation and learning on-site. It requires a good deal of time and commitment and a willingness to modify and refine changes as the circumstances require. Some organizations demand more rapid solutions to their problems and seek quick fixes from experts. Unfortunately, some OD consultants are more than willing to provide quick solutions.[38] They sell prepackaged programs for organizations to adopt. Those programs appeal to managers because they typically include an explicit recipe to be followed, standard training materials, and clear time and cost boundaries. The quick fixes have trouble gaining wide organizational support and commitment, however, and seldom produce the positive results that have been advertised.

Other organizations have not recognized the systemic nature of change. Too often, they believe that intervention into one aspect or subpart of the organization will be sufficient to ameliorate the problems, and they are unprepared for the other changes that may be necessary to support a particular intervention. For example, at Verizon, the positive benefits of an employee involvement program did not begin to appear until after the organization redesigned its reward system to support the cross-functional collaboration necessary to solve highly complex problems. Changing any one part or feature of an organization often requires adjustments in the other parts to maintain an appropriate alignment. Thus, although quick fixes and change programs that focus on only one part or aspect of the organization may resolve some specific problems, they generally do not lead to complex organizational change or increase members' capability to carry out change.[39]

SUMMARY

Theories of planned change describe the activities necessary to modify strategies, structures, and processes to increase an organization's effectiveness. Lewin's change model, the action research model, and the positive model offer different views of the phases through which planned change occurs in organizations. Lewin's change model views planned change as a three-step process of unfreezing, moving, and refreezing. It provides a general description of the process of planned change. The action research model focuses on planned change as a cyclical process involving joint activities between organization members and OD practitioners. It involves multiple steps that overlap and interact in practice: problem identification, consultation with a behavioral science expert, data gathering and preliminary diagnosis, feedback to a key client or group, joint diagnosis of the problem, joint action planning, action, and data gathering after action. The action research model places heavy emphasis on data gathering and diagnosis prior to action planning and implementation, and on assessment of results after action is taken. In addition, change strategies often are modified on the basis of continued diagnosis, and termination of one OD program may lead to further work in other areas of the firm. The positive model is oriented to what the organization is doing right. It seeks to build on positive opportunities that can lead to extraordinary performance.

Planned change theories can be integrated into a general model. Four sets of activities—entering and contracting, diagnosing, planning and implementing, and evaluating and institutionalizing—can be used to describe how change is accomplished in organizations. These four sets of activities also describe the general structure of the chapters in this book. The general model has broad applicability to planned change. It identifies the steps an organization typically moves through to implement change and specifies the OD activities needed to effect change. Although the planned change models describe general stages of how the OD process unfolds, there are different types of change depending on the situation. Planned change efforts can vary in terms of the magnitude of the change, the degree to which the client system is organized, and whether the setting is domestic or international. When situations differ on those dimensions, planned change can vary greatly. Critics of OD have pointed out several problems with the way planned change has been conceptualized and practiced, and specific areas where planned change can be improved.

NOTES

1. W. Bennis, *Changing Organizations* (New York: McGraw-Hill, 1966); J. Porras and P. Robertson, "Organization Development Theory: A Typology and Evaluation," in *Research in Organizational Change and Development*, vol. 1, ed. R. Woodman and W. Pasmore (Greenwich, CT: JAI Press, 1987), 1–57.
2. K. Lewin, *Field Theory in Social Science* (New York: Harper & Row, 1951).
3. E. Schein, *Process Consultation*, vols. 1 and 2 (Reading, MA: Addison-Wesley, 1987).
4. R. Lippitt, J. Watson, and B. Westley, *The Dynamics of Planned Change* (New York: Harcourt, Brace and World, 1958).
5. J. Kotter, *Leading Change* (Boston: Harvard Business School Press, 1996, 2012).

6. R. Benjamin and E. Levinson, "A Framework for Managing IT-Enabled Change," *Sloan Management Review* 35 (Summer 1993): 23–33.

7. K. McArdle and P. Reason, "Action Research and Organization Development," in *Handbook of Organization Development*, ed. T. Cummings (Los Angeles, Sage Publications, 2008): 123–36; A. Shani and G. Bushe, "Visionary Action Research: A Consultation Process Perspective," *Consultation* 6 (Spring 1987): 3–19; G. Sussman and R. Evered, "An Assessment of the Scientific Merit of Action Research," *Administrative Science Quarterly* 12 (1978): 582–603.

8. W. French, "Organization Development: Objectives, Assumptions, and Strategies," *California Management Review* 12 (1969): 23–34; A. Frohman, M. Sashkin, and M. Kavanagh, "Action Research as Applied to Organization Development," *Organization and Administrative Sciences* 7 (1976): 129–42; E. Schein, *Organizational Psychology*, 3rd ed. (Englewood Cliffs, NJ: Prentice Hall, 1980).

9. D. Jamieson and C. Worley, "The Practice of Organization Development," in *Handbook of Organization Development*, ed. T. Cummings (Thousand Oaks, CA: Sage Publications, 2008): 99–121; N. Tichy, "Agents of Planned Change: Congruence of Values, Cognitions, and Actions," *Administrative Science Quarterly* 19 (1974): 163–82.

10. M. Beer, "The Technology of Organization Development," in *Handbook of Industrial and Organizational Psychology*, ed. M. Dunnette (Chicago: Rand McNally, 1976), 945.

11. E. Schein, *Process Consultation Revisited: Building the Helping Relationship* (Reading, MA: Addison-Wesley, 1998).

12. E. Schein, *Process Consultation: Its Role in Organization Development* (Reading, MA: Addison-Wesley, 1969), 6.

13. R. Beckhard and R. Harris, *Organizational Transitions*, 2nd ed. (Reading, MA: Addison-Wesley, 1987).

14. McArdle and Reason, "Action Research and Organization Development;" P. Reason and H. Bradbury, eds., *Handbook of Action Research: Participative Inquiry and Practice*, 2nd ed. (Thousand Oaks, CA: Sage Publications, 2007).

15. A. Shani, S. Mohrman, W. Pasmore, B. Stymne, and N. Adler, eds., *Handbook of Collaborative Management Research* (Thousand Oaks, CA: Sage Publications, 2007).

16. M. Swantz, E. Ndedya, and M. Saiddy Masaiganah, "Participatory Action Research in Southern Tanzania, with Special Reference to Women," in *Handbook of Action Research*, ed. P. Reason and H. Bradbury (Thousand Oaks, CA: Sage Publications, 2001); K. Murrell, "Evaluation as Action Research: The Case of the Management Development Institute in Gambia, West Africa," *International Journal of Public Administration* 16, no. 3 (1993): 341–56; J. Preston and L. DuToit, "Endemic Violence in South Africa: An OD Solution Applied to Two Educational Settings," *International Journal of Public Administration* 16 (1993): 1767–91.

17. L. D. Brown, M. Leach, and J. Covey, "Organization Development for Social Change," in *Handbook of Organization Development*, ed. T. Cummings (Los Angeles: Sage Publications, 2008): 593–613; R. Tandon, "Organization Development in Nongovernmental Organizations," in *Handbook of Organization Development*, ed. T. Cummings (Los Angeles: Sage Publications, 2008): 615–28; D. Brown, "Participatory Action Research for Social Change: Collective Reflections with Asian Nongovernmental Development Organizations," *Human Relations* 46, no. 2 (1993): 208–27; D. Cooperrider and J. Dutton, eds., *Organizational Dimensions of Global Change: No Limits to Cooperation* (Newbury Park, CA: Corwin Press, 1999); D. Bornstein, *How to Change the World: Social Entrepreneurs and the Power of New Ideas* (New York: Oxford University Press, 2004).

18. W. Burke, *Organization Development: A Normative View* (Reading, MA: Addison-Wesley, 1987); J. Heron and P. Reason, "The Practice of Cooperative Inquiry: Research 'with' rather than 'on' People," in *Handbook of Action Research*, ed. P. Reason and H. Bradbury (Thousand Oaks, CA: Sage Publications, 2001).

19. D. Greenwood, W. Whyte, and I. Harkavy, "Participatory Action Research as Process and as Goal," *Human Relations* 46, no. 2 (1993): 175–92; G. Morgan and R. Ramirez, "Action Learning: A Holographic Metaphor for Guiding Social Change," *Human Relations* 37 (1984): 1–28; C. Argyris, R. Putnam, and D. Smith, *Action Science* (San Francisco: Jossey-Bass, 1985); S. Mohrman and T. Cummings, *Self-Designing Organizations: Learning How to Create High Performance* (Reading, MA: Addison-Wesley, 1989).

20. T. Fredberg, F. Norrgren, and A. Shani, "Change Capability via Learning Mechanisms: A Longitudinal Perspective on Transformation," in *Research in Organizational Change and Development*, vol. 19, ed. W. Pasmore and R. Woodman (Greenwich, CT: JAI Press, 2011): 117–61; P. Senge, *The Fifth Discipline* (New York: Doubleday, 1990).

21. M. Weisbord, *Productive Workplaces* (San Francisco: Jossey-Bass, 1987).

22. K. Cameron, J. Dutton, and R. Quinn, eds., *Positive Organizational Scholarship: Foundations of a New Discipline* (New York: Berrett-Kohler, 2003).

23. D. Eden, "Creating Expectation Effects in OD: Applying Self-Fulfilling Prophecy," in *Research in Organizational Change and Development*, vol. 2, ed. W. Pasmore and R. Woodman (Greenwich, CT: JAI Press, 1988); D. Cooperrider, "Positive Image, Positive Action: The

Affirmative Basis for Organizing," in *Appreciative Management and Leadership*, ed. S. Srivastva, D. Cooperrider, and Associates (San Francisco: Jossey-Bass, 1990).

24. D. Cooperrider and D. Whitney, *Appreciative Inquiry: A Positive Revolution in Change* (San Francisco: Berrett-Koehler, 2005); D. Cooperrider, P. Sorensen, D. Whitney, and T. Yaeger, *Appreciative Inquiry: Rethinking Human Organization Toward a Positive Theory of Change* (Champaign, IL: Stipes Publishing, 2000); J. Watkins and B. Mohr, *Appreciative Inquiry* (San Francisco: Jossey-Bass, 2001).
25. I. Hacking, *The Social Construction of What?* (Cambridge, MA: Harvard University Press, 1999).
26. P. Berger and T. Luckman, *The Social Construction of Reality* (New York: Anchor Books, 1967); K. Gergen, "The Social Constructionist Movement in Modern Psychology," *American Psychologist* 40 (1985): 266–75; V. Burr, *An Introduction to Social Constructionism* (London: Routledge, 1995).
27. D. Whitney and A. Trosten-Bloom, *The Power of Appreciative Inquiry: A Practical Guide to Positive Change* (San Francisco: Berrett-Koehler, 2010); D. Cooperrider, D. Whitney, and J. Stavros, *Appreciative Inquiry Handbook: For Leaders of Change*, 2nd ed. (Brunswick, OH: Crown Custom Publishing, 2008).
28. This application was submitted by Dr. Evelyn D. Robertson, who participated in the airport's transition. The following documents were used in developing the case: *Air Transportation and the Future of the San Diego Region: The Impact of Constrained Air Transportation Capacity on the San Diego Regional Economy. Airport Economic Analysis* (Fall 2000), Port of San Diego, San Diego Association of Governments, 2–3, http://www.san.org/sdcraa/documents/sandag/publicationid_374_507.pdf; *The Impacts of Constrained Air Transportation Capacity on the San Diego Regional Economy, Final Report*, January 5, 2000, Hamilton, Rabinovitz & Alschuler, Inc., p. 1, http://www.san.org/sdcraa/documents/sandag/publicationid_227_546.pdf; San Diego International Airport, http://www.san.org/sdcraa/planning.asp; California Senate Bill AB93, California State Session 2000–2001, introduced by Assembly Member Wayne (coauthors: Assembly Members Kehoe and Vargas) (Principal coauthor: Senator Peace) (Coauthor: Senator Alpert), http://gillespiepilots.org/ab93.htm; San Diego Port District, Internal Document, COMPASS, 2002; San Diego County Regional Airport Authority, live interview teleconference, Angela Shafer-Payne, Vice President, Strategic Planning.
29. D. Nadler, "Organizational Frame-Bending: Types of Change in the Complex Organization," in *Corporate Transformation*, ed. R. Kilmann and T. Covin (San Francisco: Jossey-Bass, 1988), 66–83; P. Watzlawick, J. Weakland, and R. Fisch, *Change* (New York: W. W. Norton, 1974); R. Golembiewski, K. Billingsley, and S. Yeager, "Measuring Change and Persistence in Human Affairs: Types of Change Generated by OD Designs," *Journal of Applied Behavioral Science* 12 (1975): 133–57; A. Meyer, G. Brooks, and J. Goes, "Environmental Jolts and Industry Revolutions: Organizational Responses to Discontinuous Change," *Strategic Management Journal* 11 (1990): 93–110.
30. A. Mohrman, G. Ledford Jr., S. Mohrman, E. Lawler III, and T. Cummings, *Large-Scale Organization Change* (San Francisco: Jossey-Bass, 1989).
31. L. D. Brown, "Planned Change in Under-organized Systems," in *Systems Theory for Organization Development*, ed. T. Cummings (Chichester, England: John Wiley & Sons, 1980), 181–203.
32. T. Cummings and M. Nathan, "Fostering New University–Industry Relationships," in *Making Organizations Competitive*, ed. R. Kilman (San Francisco: Jossey-Bass, 1991).
33. T. Yaeger, T. Head, and P. Sorensen, eds., *Global Organization Development: Managing Unprecedented Change* (Charlotte, NC: Information Age Publishing, 2006); P. Sorensen, *International Organization Development* (Champaign, IL: Stipes Publishing, 1991).
34. Porras and Robertson, "Organization Development Theory"; J. Porras and P. Robertson, "Organization Development: Theory, Practice, and Research," in *Handbook of Industrial and Organizational Psychology*, 2nd ed., vol. 3, ed. M. Dunnette and M. Hough (Palo Alto, CA: Consulting Psychologists Press, 1992).
35. T. Cummings, S. Mohrman, A. Mohrman, and G. Ledford, "Organization Design for the Future: A Collaborative Research Approach," in *Doing Research That Is Useful for Theory and Practice*, ed. E. Lawler III, A. Mohrman, S. Mohrman, G. Ledford, and T. Cummings (San Francisco: Jossey-Bass, 1985), 275–305.
36. E. Lawler and C. Worley, *Built to Change* (San Francisco: Jossey-Bass, 2006).
37. Jamieson and Worley, "The Practice of Organization Development"; Frohman, Sashkin, and Kavanagh, "Action Research"; Mohrman and Cummings, *Self-Designing Organizations*; M. Beer, R. Eisenstat, and B. Spector, "Why Change Programs Don't Produce Change," *Harvard Business Review* 6 (November–December 1990): 158–66.
38. C. Worley and R. Patchett, "Myth and Hope Meet Reality: The Fallacy of and Opportunities for Reducing Cycle Time in Strategic Change," in *Fast Cycle Organization Development*, ed. M. Anderson (Cincinnati: South-Western College Publishing, 2000).
39. Beer, Eisenstat, and Spector, "Change Programs."

3

The Organization Development Practitioner

learning objectives

- Discuss the roles and characteristics of OD practitioners.
- Describe the competencies required of effective OD practitioners.
- Compare the internal versus external OD practitioner.
- Understand the values and ethics guiding the practice of OD.

Chapters 1 and 2 provided an overview of the field of organization development and a description of the nature of planned change. This chapter extends that introduction by examining the people who perform organization development (OD). A closer look at OD practitioners can provide a more personal perspective on the field and can help us understand how and why OD relies so heavily on personal relationships between practitioners and organization members.

Much of the literature about OD practitioners views them as internal or external consultants providing professional services—diagnosing systems, developing interventions, and helping to implement them. Perspectives that are more recent expand the practice scope to include professionals in related disciplines, such as industrial psychology, human resource management, and strategic management, as well as line managers who have learned how to carry out OD to change and develop their organizations.

A great deal of opinion and some research studies have focused on the necessary skills and knowledge of an effective OD practitioner. Studies of the profession provide a comprehensive list of basic skills and knowledge that all effective OD practitioners must possess.

Most of the relevant literature focuses on people specializing in OD as a profession and addresses their roles and careers. The OD practitioner's role can be described in relation to its position: internal to the organization, external to it, or in a team comprising both internal and external consultants. The OD practitioner's role can also be examined in terms of its marginality in organizations, of the emotional demands made on the practitioner, and of where it fits along a continuum from client-centered to consultant-centered functioning. Finally, organization development is an emerging profession providing alternative opportunities for gaining competence and developing a career. The stressful nature of helping professions, however, suggests that OD practitioners must cope with the possibility of professional burnout.

As in other helping professions, such as medicine and law, values and ethics play an important role in guiding OD practice and in minimizing the chances that clients will be neglected or abused.

3-1 Who Is the Organization Development Practitioner?

Throughout this text, the term *organization development practitioner* refers to at least three sets of people. The most obvious group of OD practitioners are those people specializing in OD as a profession. They may be internal or external consultants who offer professional services to organizations, including their top managers, functional department heads, and staff groups. OD professionals traditionally have shared a common set of humanistic values promoting open communications, employee involvement, and personal growth and development. They tend to have common training, skills, and experience in the social processes of organizations (for example, group dynamics, decision making, and communications). In recent years, OD professionals have expanded those traditional values and skill sets to include more concern for organizational effectiveness, competitiveness, and bottom-line results, and greater attention to the technical, structural, and strategic parts of organizations. That expansion, mainly in response to the highly competitive demands facing modern organizations, has resulted in a more diverse set of OD professionals geared to helping organizations cope with those pressures.[1]

The second set of people to whom the term OD practitioner applies are those specializing in fields related to OD, such as human resource management, organization design, quality control, information technology, and business strategy. These content-oriented fields increasingly are becoming integrated with OD's process orientation, particularly as OD projects have become more comprehensive, involving multiple features and varying parts of organizations. For example, the integrated strategic change intervention described in Chapter 18 and the dynamic strategy-making intervention presented in Chapter 21 are the result of marrying OD with business strategy.[2] A growing number of professionals in these related fields are gaining experience and competence in OD, mainly through working with OD professionals on large-scale projects and through attending OD training sessions. Most of the large accounting firms, for example, diversified into management consulting and change management.[3] In most cases, professionals in these related fields do not subscribe fully to traditional OD values, nor do they have extensive OD training and experience. Rather, they have formal training and experience in their respective specialties, such as industrial engineering, information systems, or corporate strategy. They are OD practitioners in the sense that they apply their special competence within an OD-like process, typically by engaging OD professionals and managers to design and implement change programs. They also practice OD when they apply their OD competence to their own specialties, thus spreading an OD perspective into such areas as compensation practices, work design, labor relations, and strategic planning.

The third set of people to whom the term OD practitioner applies are the increasing number of managers and administrators who have gained competence in OD and who apply it to their own work areas. Studies and recent articles argue that OD increasingly is applied by managers rather than by OD professionals.[4] Such studies suggest that the faster pace of change affecting organizations today is highlighting the centrality of the manager in managing change. Consequently, OD must become a general management skill. Along those lines, Kanter studied a growing number of firms, such as General Electric, Hewlett-Packard, and 3M, where managers and employees have become "change masters."[5] They have gained the expertise to introduce change and innovation into the organization.

Managers tend to gain competence in OD through interacting with OD professionals in actual change programs. This on-the-job training frequently is supplemented with more formal OD training, such as the various workshops offered by the National Training Laboratories (NTL), USC's Center for Effective Organizations, the Center for Creative Leadership, the Gestalt Institute, UCLA's Extension Service, the Tavistock Institute, the Institute for Socio-Economic Enterprises (ISEOR), and others. Line managers increasingly are attending such external programs. Moreover, a growing number of organizations, including Capital One, Disney, and General Electric, have instituted in-house training programs for managers to learn how to develop and change their work units. As managers gain OD competence, they become its most basic practitioners.

In practice, the distinctions among the three sets of OD practitioners are blurring. A growing number of managers have transferred, either temporarily or permanently, into the OD profession. For example, companies such as Procter & Gamble have trained and rotated managers into full-time OD roles so that they can gain skills and experience needed for higher-level management positions. Also, it is increasingly common to find managers and staff specialists using their experience in OD to become external consultants. More OD practitioners are gaining professional competence in related specialties, such as business process reengineering, reward systems, and strategic planning. Conversely, many specialists in those related areas are achieving professional competence in OD. Cross-training and integration are producing a more comprehensive and complex kind of OD practitioner—one with a greater diversity of values, skills, and experience than a traditional practitioner.

3-2 Competencies of an Effective Organization Development Practitioner

The literature about OD competencies reveals a mixture of personality traits, experiences, knowledge, and skills presumed to lead to effective practice. For example, research on the characteristics of successful change practitioners yields the following list of attributes and abilities: diagnostic ability, basic knowledge of behavioral science techniques, empathy, knowledge of the theories and methods within the consultant's own discipline, goal-setting ability, problem-solving ability, ability to perform self-assessment, ability to see things objectively, imagination, flexibility, honesty, consistency, and trust.[6] Although these qualities and skills are laudable, there has been relatively little consensus or research about their importance to effective OD practice.

Two projects have sought to define, categorize, and prioritize the skills and knowledge required of OD practitioners. In the first effort, a broad group of well-known practitioners and researchers were asked to review and update a list of professional competencies. This survey resulted in a list of 187 statements in nine areas of OD practice, including entry, start-up, assessment and feedback, action planning, intervention, evaluation, adoption, separation, and general competencies.[7] The statements ranged from "staying centered in the present, focusing on the ongoing process" and "understanding and explaining how diversity will affect the diagnosis of the culture" to "basing change on business strategy and business needs" and "being comfortable with quantum leaps, radical shifts, and paradigm changes." Other items added to the list relate to international OD, large group interventions, and transorganization skills.

To understand the relative importance of this long list, Worley and his colleagues collected data from 364 OD practitioners.[8] The average respondent had about eight years of OD experience, a master's degree, and came from the United States. The results suggested an underlying structure to the list. Twenty-three competencies were generated that reflected both the skills and knowledge necessary to conduct planned change processes and the individual characteristics necessary to be an effective OD practitioner. Similar to other lists, the competencies included the ability to evaluate change, work with large-scale change efforts, create implementation plans, and manage diversity. One of the more surprising results, however, was the emergence of "self mastery" as the most important competence. The results supported the long-held belief that good OD practitioners know themselves and that such knowledge forms the basis of effective practice.

The second project, sponsored by the Organization Development and Change Division of the Academy of Management,[9] sought to develop a list of competencies to guide curriculum development in graduate OD programs. More than 40 OD practitioners and researchers worked to develop the two competency lists shown in Table 3.1. First, foundation competencies are oriented toward descriptions of an existing system. They include knowledge from organization behavior, psychology, group dynamics, management and organization theory, research methods, and business practices. Second, core competencies are aimed at how systems change over time. They include knowledge of organization design, organization research, system dynamics, OD history, and theories and models for change; they also involve the skills needed to manage the consulting process, to analyze and diagnose systems, to design and choose interventions, to facilitate processes, to develop clients' capability to manage their own change, and to evaluate organization change.

The information in Table 3.1 applies primarily to people specializing in OD as a profession. For them, possessing the listed knowledge and skills seems reasonable, especially in light of the growing diversity and complexity of interventions in OD. Gaining competence in those areas may take considerable time and effort, and it is questionable whether the other two types of OD practitioners—managers and specialists in related fields—also need that full range of skills and knowledge. It seems more reasonable to suggest that some subset of the items listed in Table 3.1 should apply to all OD practitioners, whether they are OD professionals, managers, or related specialists. Those items would constitute the practitioner's basic skills and knowledge. Beyond that background, the three types of OD practitioners likely would differ in areas of concentration. OD professionals would extend their breadth of skills across the remaining categories in Table 3.1; managers would focus on the functional knowledge of business areas; and related specialists would concentrate on skills in their respective areas.

Based on the data in Table 3.1 and the other studies available, all OD practitioners should have the following basic skills and knowledge to be effective.

3-2a Intrapersonal Skills or "Self-Management" Competence

Despite the growing knowledge base and sophistication of the field, organization development is still a human craft. As the primary instrument of diagnosis and change, practitioners often must process complex, ambiguous information and make informed judgments about its relevance to organizational issues.

The core competency of analysis and diagnosis listed in Table 3.1 includes the ability to inquire into one's self, and as noted above, it remains one of the cornerstone skills in OD.[10] Practitioners must have the personal centering to know their own values, feelings, and purposes as well as the integrity to behave responsibly in a helping relationship with others. Bob Tannenbaum, one of the founders of OD, argued that self-knowledge is the most central ingredient in OD practice and suggested that practitioners are becoming too enamored with skills and techniques.[11] There are data to support his view. A study of 416 OD practitioners found that 47% agreed with the statement, "Many of the new entrants into the field have little understanding of or appreciation for the history or values underlying the field."[12] Because OD is a highly uncertain process requiring

TABLE 3.1

Knowledge and Skill Requirements of OD Practitioners

	Foundation Competencies	Core Competencies
Knowledge	1. Organization behavior A. Organization culture B. Work design C. Interpersonal relations D. Power and politics E. Leadership F. Goal setting G. Conflict H. Ethics 2. Individual psychology A. Learning theory B. Motivation theory C. Perception theory 3. Group dynamics A. Roles B. Communication processes C. Decision-making process D. Stages of group development E. Leadership 4. Management and organization theory A. Planning, organizing, leading, and controlling B. Problem solving and decision making C. Systems theory D. Contingency theory E. Organization structure F. Characteristics of environment and technology G. Models of organization and system 5. Research methods/statistics A. Measures of central tendency B. Measures of dispersion C. Basic sampling theory D. Basic experimental design E. Sample inferential statistics	1. Organization design: the decision process associated with formulating and aligning the elements of an organizational system, including but not limited to structural systems, human resource systems, information systems, reward systems, work design, political systems, and organization culture A. The concept of fit and alignment B. Diagnostic and design model for various subsystems that make up an organization at any level of analysis, including the structure of work, human resources, information systems, reward systems, work design, political systems, and so on C. Key thought leaders in organization design 2. Organization research: field research methods; interviewing; content analysis; design of questionnaires and interview protocol; designing change evaluation processes; longitudinal data collection and analysis; understanding and detecting alpha, beta, and gamma change; and a host of quantitative and qualitative methods 3. System dynamics: the description and understanding of how systems evolve and develop over time, how systems respond to exogenous and endogenous disruption as well as planned interventions (e.g., evolution and revolution, punctuated equilibrium theory, chaos theory, catastrophe theory, incremental vs. quantum change, transformation theory, and so on) 4. History of organization development and change: an understanding of the social, political, economic, and personal forces that led to the emergence and development of organization development and change, including the key thought leaders, the values underlying their writings and actions, the key events and writings, and related documentation A. Human relations movement B. NTL/T-groups/sensitivity training C. Survey research D. Quality of work life E. Tavistock Institute F. Key thought leaders G. Humanistic values H. Statement of ethics

continued

TABLE 3.1

Knowledge and Skill Requirements of OD Practitioners, (*continued*)

	Foundation Competencies	Core Competencies
	6. Comparative cultural perspectives A. Dimensions of natural culture B. Dimensions of industry culture C. Systems implications 7. Functional knowledge of business A. Interpersonal communication (listening, feedback, and articulation) B. Collaboration/working together C. Problem solving D. Using new technology E. Conceptualizing F. Project management G. Present/education/coach	5. Theories and models for change: the basic action research model, participatory action research model, planning model, change typologies (e.g., fast, slow, incremental, quantum, revolutionary), Lewin's model, transition models, and so on
Skills		1. Managing the consulting process: the ability to enter, contract, diagnose, design appropriate interventions, implement those interventions, manage unprogrammed events, and evaluate change process 2. Analysis/diagnosis: the abilities to conduct an inquiry into a system's effectiveness, to see the root cause(s) of a system's current level of effectiveness; the core skill is interpreted to include all systems—individual, group, organization, and multiorganization—as well as the ability to understand and inquire into one's self 3. Designing/choosing appropriate, relevant interventions: understanding how to select, modify, or design effective interventions that will move the organization from its current state to its desired future state 4. Facilitation and process consultation: the ability to assist an individual or group toward a goal; the ability to conduct an inquiry into individual and group processes such that the client system maintains ownership of the issue, increases its capacity for reflection on the consequences of its behaviors and actions, and develops a sense of increased control and ability

TABLE 3.1

Knowledge and Skill Requirements of OD Practitioners, (*continued*)

Foundation Competencies	Core Competencies
	5. Developing client capability: the ability to conduct a change process in such a way that the client is better able to plan and implement a successful change process in the future, using technologies of planned change in a values-based and ethical manner
	6. Evaluating organization change: the ability to design and implement a process to evaluate the impact and effects of change intervention, including control of alternative explanations and interpretation of performance outcomes

constant adjustment and innovation, practitioners must have active learning skills and a reasonable balance between their rational and emotional sides. Finally, OD practice can be highly stressful and can lead to early burnout, so practitioners need to know how to manage their own stress.

3-2b Interpersonal Skills

Practitioners must create and maintain effective relationships with individuals and groups within the organization and help them gain the competence necessary to solve their own problems. Table 3.1 identifies group dynamics, comparative cultural perspectives, and business functions as foundation knowledge, and managing the consulting process and facilitation as core skills. All of these interpersonal competencies promote effective helping relationships. Such relationships start with a grasp of the organization's perspective and require listening to members' perceptions and feelings to understand how they see themselves and the organization—a process called "active listening." This understanding provides a starting point for joint diagnosis and problem solving. Practitioners must establish trust and rapport with organization members so that they can share pertinent information and work effectively together. This requires being able to converse in members' own language and to give and receive feedback about how the relationship is progressing.

To help members learn new skills and behaviors, practitioners must serve as role models of what is expected. They must act in ways that are credible to organization members and provide them with the counseling and coaching necessary to develop and change. Because the helping relationship is jointly determined, practitioners need to be able to negotiate an acceptable role and to manage changing expectations and demands.

3-2c General Consultation Skills

Table 3.1 identifies the ability to manage the consulting process and the ability to design interventions as core competencies that all OD practitioners should possess. OD starts with diagnosing an organization or department to understand its current functioning and to discover areas for further development. OD practitioners need to know how to carry out an effective diagnosis, at least at a rudimentary level. They should know how to engage organization members in diagnosis, how to help them ask the right questions, and how to collect and analyze information. A manager, for example, should be able to work with subordinates to determine jointly the organization's or department's strengths or problems. The manager should know basic diagnostic questions (see Chapter 5), some methods for gathering information, such as interviews or surveys, and some techniques for analyzing it, such as force-field analysis or statistical means and distributions (see Chapter 6).

In addition to diagnosis, OD practitioners should know how to design and execute an intervention. They need to be able to define an action plan and to gain commitment to the program. They also need to know how to tailor the intervention to the situation, using information about how the change is progressing to guide implementation (see Chapter 9). For example, managers should be able to develop action steps for an intervention with subordinates. They should be able to gain their commitment to the program (usually through participation), sit down with them, assess how it is progressing, and make modifications if necessary.

3-2d Organization Development Theory

The last basic tool OD practitioners should have is a general knowledge of organization development, such as is presented in this book. They should have some appreciation for planned change, the action research model, and the positive approaches to managing change. They should be familiar with the range of available interventions and the need for evaluating change programs. Perhaps most important is that OD practitioners should understand their own role in the emerging field of organization development, whether it is as an OD professional, a manager, or a specialist in a related area.

3-3 The Professional Organization Development Practitioner

Most of the literature about OD practitioners has focused on people specializing in OD as a profession. In this section, we discuss the role and typical career paths of OD professionals.

3-3a Role of Organization Development Professional Positions

Organization development professionals have positions that are either internal or external to the organization. Internal consultants are members of the organization and may be located in the human resources department or report directly to a line manager. They may perform the OD role exclusively, or they may combine it with other tasks, such as compensation practices, training, or employee relations.[13] Many large organizations, such as Boeing, Raytheon, Disney, Microsoft, Philip Morris, Procter & Gamble, Weyerhaeuser, Kimberly-Clark, and Citigroup, have created specialized OD consulting groups. These internal consultants typically have a variety of clients within the organization, serving both line and staff departments.

External consultants are not members of the client organization; they typically work for a consulting firm, a university, or themselves. Organizations generally hire external consultants to provide a particular expertise that is unavailable internally, to bring a different and potentially more objective perspective into the organization development process, or to signal shifts in power.[14] Table 3.2 describes the differences between these two roles at each stage of the action research process.[15]

TABLE 3.2

The Differences between External and Internal Consulting

Stage of Change	External Consultants	Internal Consultants
Entering	• Source clients • Build relationships • Learn company jargon • "Presenting problem" challenge • Time-consuming • Stressful phase • Select project/client according to own criteria • Unpredictable outcome	• Ready access to clients • Ready relationships • Knows company jargon • Understands root causes • Time efficient • Congenial phase • Obligated to work with everyone • Steady pay
Contracting	• Formal documents • Can terminate project at will • Guard against out-of-pocket expenses • Information confidential • Loss of contract at stake • Maintain third-party role	• Informal agreements • Must complete projects assigned • No out-of-pocket expenses • Information can be open or confidential • Risk of client retaliation and loss of job at stake • Acts as third party, driver (on behalf of client), or pair of hands
Diagnosing	• Meet most organization members for the first time • Prestige from being external • Build trust quickly • Confidential data can increase political sensitivities	• Has relationships with many organization members • Prestige determined by job rank and client stature • Sustain reputation as trustworthy over time • Data openly shared can reduce political intrigue
Intervening	• Insist on valid information, free and informed choice, and internal commitment • Confine activities within boundaries of client organization	• Insist on valid information, free and informed choice, and internal commitment • Run interference for client across organizational lines to align support
Evaluating	• Rely on repeat business and customer referral as key measures of project success • Seldom see long-term results	• Rely on repeat business, pay raise, and promotion as key measures of success • Can see change become institutionalized • Little recognition for job well done

SOURCE: M. Lacey, "Internal Consulting: Perspectives on the Process of Planned Change," *Journal of Organizational Change Management* 8 (1995): 76, © 1995. Reprinted with permission of the publisher. All rights reserved.

During the entry process, internal consultants have clear advantages. They have ready access to and relationships with clients, know the language of the organization, and have insights about the root cause of many of its problems. This allows internal consultants to save time in identifying the organization's culture, informal practices, and sources of power. They have access to a variety of information, including rumors, company reports, and direct observations. In addition, entry is more efficient and congenial, and their pay is not at risk. External consultants, however, have the advantage of being able to select the clients they want to work with according to their own criteria. The contracting phase is less formal for internal consultants and there is less worry about expenses, but there is less choice about whether to complete the assignment. Both types of consultants must address issues of confidentiality, risk project termination (and other negative consequences) by the client, and fill a third-party role.

During the diagnosis process, internal consultants already know many organization members and enjoy a basic level of rapport and trust. But external consultants often have higher status than internal consultants, which enables them to probe difficult issues and assess the organization more objectively. In the intervention phase, both types of consultants must rely on valid information, free and informed choice, and internal commitment for their success.[16] However, internal consultants' strong ties to the organization may make them overly cautious, particularly when powerful others can affect a career. Internal consultants also may lack certain skills and experience in facilitating organizational change. Insiders may have some small advantages in being able to move around the system and cross key organizational boundaries. Finally, the measures of success and reward differ from those of the external practitioner in the evaluation process.

A promising approach to having the advantages of both internal and external OD consultants is to include them both as members of an internal–external consulting team.[17] External consultants can combine their special expertise and objectivity with the inside knowledge and acceptance of internal consultants. The two parties can use complementary consulting skills while sharing the workload and possibly accomplishing more than either would by operating alone. Internal consultants, for example, can provide almost continuous contact with the client, and their external counterparts can provide specialized services periodically, such as two or three days each month. External consultants also can help train their organization partners, thus transferring OD skills and knowledge to the organization.

Although little has been written on internal–external consulting teams, studies suggest that the effectiveness of such teams depends on members developing strong, supportive, collegial relationships. They need to take time to develop the consulting team, confronting individual differences and establishing appropriate roles and relationships. Members need to provide each other with continuous feedback and also make a commitment to learn from each other. In the absence of these team-building and learning activities, internal–external consulting teams can be more troublesome and less effective than either internal or external consultants working alone.

Application 3.1 provides a personal, first-person account of the internal and external consulting positions as well as interactions between them.[18]

Marginality A promising line of research on the professional OD role centers on the issue of marginality.[19] The marginal person is one who successfully straddles the boundary between two or more groups with differing goals, value systems, and behavior patterns. Whereas in the past, the marginal role always was seen as dysfunctional, marginality now is seen in a more positive light. There are many examples of marginal roles in organizations: the salesperson, the buyer, the first-line supervisor, the integrator, and the project manager.

Evidence is mounting that some people are better at taking marginal roles than are others. Those who are good at it seem to have personal qualities of low dogmatism, neutrality, open-mindedness, objectivity, flexibility, and adaptable information-processing

application 3.1

PERSONAL VIEWS OF THE INTERNAL AND EXTERNAL CONSULTING POSITIONS

THE INTERNAL CONSULTANT'S VIEW

I am an agent of change. I am also a member of this organization. I was hired for my OD skills, but also for the fact that I was seen as a "cultural fit." Sometimes I struggle between my dual roles of "team member" and "free radical." After all, it is my job to disrupt the status quo around here, helping leaders to find ways to make the organization more effective.

I have the great advantage of knowing and understanding how my organization works—its processes, policies, norms, and areas of resistance. I can usually anticipate how difficult a given change will be for members of the organization, and where the resistance will come from. Because I believe in the mission of my organization, I am able to cope with the inevitable challenges of the change process. Still, I am frequently a magnet for resistance and a receptacle of institutional anxiety. While I understand how people can be frustrated and frightened by change, it can still be difficult for me to bear the disruption I help to create.

To keep myself sharp and healthy, I breathe, run, meditate, and read. I take every learning opportunity that comes my way, and work diligently to create and maintain a network of colleagues who can support me through the rough patches. I find that my best support comes not from friends, but from people who know and understand the hard work of planned change.

As an internal consultant, I have exposure to many of the same people over time—executives, managers, and employees get to know who I am and what I do. I get to know who they are and what they do. I have the opportunity to leverage my executive relationships from project to project; over time the executives here have come to understand my work and trust my skills as a consultant. This understanding and trust saves us time and energy each time we work together. Of course, I realize that if I fail one of my executive clients, my life in this organization could become less pleasant. That can stress me out when I'm working on a messy or unpopular project. After all, my performance review is affected by client feedback, and my compensation is tied to people's perceptions of my performance. This can make it difficult to press forward with risky interventions. I am proud of my reputation around here—proud of the fact that I have built solid relationships at the executive level, that managers respect my work, and that employees value having me in the organization. Still, I am ever aware that I must walk the fine line between "respected insider" and "paid agitator."

Sometimes I'm lonely—often I'm the only OD person working in an organization; sometimes there are two or more of us, but we're always spread so thin that connecting is difficult and truly supporting one another is virtually impossible. I may work with other staff people—HR for instance—but they don't always understand my role and can't really relate to my challenges. Sometimes they can be resentful of my relationship with the client, which makes me feel alienated. I enjoy my client groups, but I must be careful not to over-identify with them; the greatest value I bring to my clients is a clean "outsider" perspective. I can't do hard change efforts with them if I'm worried about them liking me. Being a lone ranger can be thrilling, but being an outsider can get tiring.

Occasionally I bring in an external consultant to work on a specific project or problem in my organization. This can be both challenging and rewarding for me. It is time-consuming to bring an outsider up to speed on my organization's business, processes, and politics. I seek external consultants who will fit in our culture, while helping us see our issues more clearly and realistically. I enjoy the process of partnering with people who have exposure to other organizations, who possess different skills and strengths from mine, and who understand the inherent discomfort of the change process. Still, this can be risky, because my reputation will be affected by this person's work and the outcomes we are able to achieve. When it works best, my partnership with the external consultant leads to improved effectiveness for my organization, while affording me a valued learning opportunity and professional support.

The best thing to me about being an internal consultant is knowing that I am contributing to the mission of my organization with every client I work with, every day.

THE EXTERNAL CONSULTANT'S VIEW

I am an agent of change. I work for many different organizations of varying sizes with different missions and goals. I spend most of my time helping managers, HR people, and internal consultants initiate and manage change—both planned and unplanned. I enjoy the variety in my work and the learning that comes from seeing the way change happens in different organizations and contexts.

But it is hard being an "outsider." I must work quickly to understand each new organization I work with. As an outsider it can be frustrating to navigate the inner workings of the organization—its politics, pecking order, and culture—and to root out what's important and what's not. In my role, I'm not around while the unglamorous, time-consuming, and important work of nurturing a change along is being done. So, although I experience the risk and excitement of some part of the change, I do not always get to experience the whole change process from start to finish. I rarely get to see the project bear fruit and the organization become more effective as a result of the work I've done. Sometimes the process feels incomplete, and I almost always wonder how much I've actually helped.

Being an external consultant is both rewarding and risky work. On the one hand, I am seen as an expert. I am appreciated for my assistance, applauded for my knowledge, and liked for my interpersonal skills. I have the benefit of many revenue sources, so I'm never overly dependent on one client. I am often rewarded handsomely for my time and effort, although most people mistake "daily fee" as actual income and forget about self-employment taxes and the health benefits I have to pay myself. The other truth is that I am always at risk—economic crises, budget cuts, personnel changes, executive shake ups, organizational politics, and the occasional hostile HR person are but a few of the land mines an external consultant faces. For the most part, I feel pleased and rewarded for my work as a consultant. But I always know that my situation is dependent on my client's situation, and I can never afford to get too comfortable.

When I'm hired by an executive or manager, sometimes the HR person or internal consultant may be resistant, feeling threatened by my presence. When this happens, I have to find ways to address their concern, partner with them, and still do the important work of organizational change. Sometimes just creating space for the conversation by using simple probes—"You seem very concerned about this situation" or "You must feel pretty unsupported right now"—help me uncover their discomfort so we can move forward. Sometimes these relationships are difficult throughout the engagement. It's the downside of being brought in as an "expert."

I am asked by clients to perform a wide variety of tasks ranging from content expert to process expert to personal coach. Regardless of the request, however, I am frequently aware of an unspoken need on the part of the client—manager, HR person, or internal consultant—to have me support his or her project, position, or person. When the request is to support a project, it is usually clear. When the request is to support a position, it is less clear but typically surfaces during the course of our work together. However, when the request is to support the individual personally, the request is almost never overt. This is where my self-as-instrument work serves me best, helping me to understand the unspoken—the question behind the question. While my goal is always to help my client organizations become more effective, I never forget that change can happen many different ways and at multiple levels of the system. It is my work to be aware of opportunities to intervene, and to have the skill and courage to do so as an outsider.

ability. Rather than being upset by conflict, ambiguity, and stress, they thrive on it. Individuals with marginal orientations are more likely than others to develop integrative decisions that bring together and reconcile viewpoints among opposing organizational groups and are more likely to remain neutral in controversial situations. Thus, research suggests that the marginal role can have positive effects when it is filled by a person with a marginal orientation. Such a person can be more objective and better able to perform successfully in linking, integrative, or conflict-laden roles.[20]

A study of both external and internal OD practitioners showed that external professionals were more comfortable with the marginal role than were internal professionals. Internal consultants with more years of experience were more marginally oriented than were those with less experience.[21] These findings, combined with other research on marginal roles, suggest the importance of maintaining the OD practitioner's marginality, with its flexibility, independence, and boundary-spanning characteristics.

Emotional Demands The OD practitioner role is emotionally demanding. Research and practice support the importance of understanding emotions and their impact on the practitioner's effectiveness.[22] The research on "emotional intelligence" in organizations suggests a set of abilities that can aid OD practitioners in conducting successful change efforts. Emotional intelligence refers to the ability to recognize and express emotions appropriately, to use emotions in thought and decisions, and to regulate emotion in one's self and in others.[23] It is, therefore, a different kind of intelligence from problem-solving ability, engineering aptitude, or the knowledge of concepts. In tandem with traditional knowledge and skill, emotional intelligence affects and supplements rational thought; emotions help prioritize thinking by directing attention to important information not addressed in models and theories. In that sense, some researchers argue that emotional intelligence is as important as cognitive intelligence.[24]

Reports from OD practitioners support the importance of emotional intelligence in practice. From the client's perspective, OD practitioners must understand emotions well enough to relate to and help organization members address resistance, commitment, and ambiguity at each stage of planned change. Despite the predominant focus on rationality and efficiency, almost any change process must address important and difficult issues that raise emotions such as the fear of failure and of the unknown, rejection, anxiety, and anger.[25] OD practitioners can provide psychological support, model appropriate emotional expression, reframe client perspectives, and provide resources. OD practitioners must also understand their own emotions. Ambiguity, unfamiliarity, or denial of emotions can lead to inaccurate and untimely interventions. For example, a practitioner who is uncomfortable with conflict may intervene to defuse an argument between two managers because of the discomfort he or she feels, not because the conflict is destructive. In such a case, the practitioner is acting to address a personal need rather than intervening to improve the system's effectiveness.

Evidence suggests that emotional intelligence increases with age and experience.[26] Research also supports the conclusion that competence with emotions can be developed through personal growth processes such as sensitivity training, counseling, and therapy. It seems reasonable to suggest that professional OD practitioners dedicate themselves to a long-term regimen of development that includes acquiring both cognitive learning and emotional intelligence.

Use of Knowledge and Experience The professional OD role has been described in terms of a continuum ranging from client-centered (using the client's knowledge and experience) to consultant-centered (using the consultant's knowledge and experience),

FIGURE 3.1

Use of Consultant's Versus Client's Knowledge and Experience

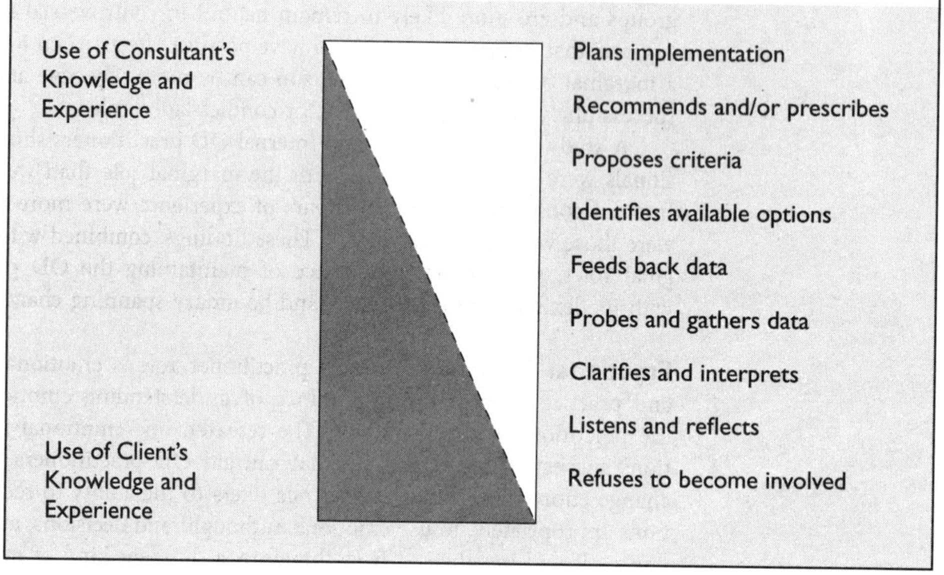

SOURCE: Adapted by permission of the authors from W. Schmidt and A. Johnson, "A Continuum of Consultancy Styles" (unpublished manuscript, July 1970), p. 1.

as shown in Figure 3.1. Traditionally, OD consultants have worked at the client-centered end of the continuum. Organization development professionals, relying mainly on process consultation and team building (see Chapter 10), have been expected to remain neutral, refusing to offer expert advice on organizational problems. Rather than contracting to solve specific problems, the consultant has tended to work with organization members to identify problems and potential solutions, to help them study what they are doing now and consider alternative behaviors and solutions, and to help them discover whether, in fact, the consultant and they can learn to do things better. In doing that, the OD professional has generally listened and reflected upon members' perceptions and ideas and helped clarify and interpret their communications and behaviors.

The recent proliferation of OD interventions in the structural, human resource management, and strategy areas has expanded that limited definition of the professional OD role to include the consultant-centered end of the continuum. In many of the newer approaches, the consultant may have to take on a modified role of expert, with the consent and collaboration of organization members. For example, managers trying to bring about a major structural redesign (see Chapter 12) may not have the appropriate knowledge and expertise to create and manage the change and need the help of an OD practitioner with experience in this area. The consultant's role might be to present the basic concepts and ideas and then to work jointly with the managers to select an approach that might be useful to the organization and to decide how it might best be implemented. In this situation, the OD professional recommends or prescribes particular changes and is active in planning how to implement them. This expertise, however, is always shared rather than imposed.

With the development of new and varied intervention approaches, the OD professional's role needs to be seen as falling along the entire continuum from client-centered to consultant-centered. At times, the consultant will rely mainly on organization members' knowledge and experiences to identify and solve problems. At other times, it will be more appropriate to take on the role of an expert, withdrawing from that role as managers gain more knowledge and experience.

3-3b Careers of Organization Development Professionals

In contrast to such long-standing occupations as medicine and law, organization development is an emerging practice, still developing the characteristics of an established profession: a common body of knowledge, educational requirements, a recognized code of ethics, and rules and methods for governing conduct. People enter professional OD careers from various educational and work backgrounds. Because they do not have to follow an established career path, they have some choice about when to enter or leave an OD career and whether to be an internal or external consultant.[27]

Despite the looseness or flexibility of the field, most professionals have had specific training in OD. That training can include relatively short courses (one day to two weeks), programs, and workshops conducted within organizations or at outside institutions (such as NTL, USC, University Associates, Columbia University, the University of Michigan, Stanford University, and UCLA). OD training also can be more formal and lengthy, including master's programs (for example, at Pepperdine University, American University, Benedictine University, Bowling Green State University, Case Western Reserve University, Loyola University, and the Fielding Institute) and doctoral training (for example, at Benedictine University, Case Western Reserve University, Columbia University Teachers College, the Fielding Institute, and George Washington University).

As might be expected, career choices widen as people gain training and experience in OD. Those with rudimentary training tend to be internal consultants, often taking on OD roles as temporary assignments on the way to higher managerial or staff positions. Holders of master's degrees generally are evenly split between internal and external consultants. Those with doctorates may join a university faculty and do consulting part-time, join a consulting firm, or seek a position as a relatively high-level internal consultant.

External consultants tend to be older, to have more managerial experience, and to spend more of their time in OD than do internal practitioners. However, one study suggested there were no differences between internal and external consultants in pay or years of consulting experience.[28] Perhaps the most common career path is to begin as an internal consultant, gain experience and visibility through successful interventions or publishing, and then become an external consultant. A field study found that internal consultants acquired greater competence by working with external consultants who purposely helped develop them. This development took place through a tutorial arrangement of joint diagnosis and intervention in the organization, which gave the internal consultants a chance to observe and learn from the model furnished by the external consultants.[29]

There is increasing evidence that an OD career can be stressful, sometimes leading to burnout.[30] Burnout comes from taking on too many jobs, becoming overcommitted, and generally working too hard. The number one complaint of OD practitioners is constant traveling.[31] OD work often requires six-day work weeks, with some days running as long as 15 hours. Consultants may spend a week working with one organization or department and then spend the weekend preparing for the next client. They may spend 50%–75% of their time on the road, living in planes, cars, hotels, meetings, and restaurants. Indeed, one practitioner has suggested that the majority of OD consultants would repeat the phrase "quality of work life for consultants" this way: "Quality of work life? For consultants?"[32]

OD professionals increasingly are taking steps to cope with burnout. They may shift jobs, moving from external to internal roles to gain more predictable hours or avoid travel. They may learn to pace themselves better and to avoid taking on too much work. Many are engaging in fitness and health programs and are using stress-management techniques, such as those described in Chapter 17.

3-4 Professional Values

Values have played an important role in organization development from its beginning. Traditionally, OD professionals have promoted a set of humanistic values, including a concern for open inquiry, democratic principles, and personal well-being.[33] They have sought to help organizations build trust and collaboration among members, an open, problem-solving climate, and member self-control. More recently, OD practitioners have added to those humanistic values a concern for improving organizational effectiveness (for example, to increase productivity or to reduce turnover) and environmental sustainability (for example, to reduce the organization's carbon imprint). They have shown an increasing desire to promote human, economic, and ecological values in practicing OD.[34]

The values of humanizing organizations, improving their effectiveness, and sustaining the environment have received widespread support in the OD profession as well as increasing encouragement from executives, employees, labor leaders, government officials, and global organizations such as NATO. Indeed, it would be difficult not to support those joint concerns. However, in practice, OD professionals face serious challenges in simultaneously promoting human, economic, and ecological values.[35] More practitioners are experiencing situations in which there is conflict between employees' needs for greater meaning and the organization's need for more effective and efficient use of its resources. For example, expensive capital equipment may run most efficiently if it is highly programmed and routinized, but people may not derive satisfaction from working with such technology. Should efficiency be maximized at the expense of people's satisfaction? Can technology be changed to make it more humanly satisfying while remaining efficient? What compromises are possible? How do these trade-offs shift when they are applied in different regional cultures? These value dilemmas are inherent in trying to optimize human benefits, organizational effectiveness, and environmental sustainability.

In addition to value issues within organizations, OD practitioners are dealing more and more with value conflicts with powerful outside groups. Organizations are open systems and exist within increasingly turbulent environments. For example, hospitals are facing complex and changing task environments. This has led to a proliferation of external stakeholders with interests in the organization's functioning, including patients, suppliers, medical groups, insurance companies, employers, the government, stockholders, unions, the press, and various interest groups. Those external groups often have different and competing values for judging the organization's effectiveness. For example, stockholders may judge the firm in terms of earnings per share, the government in terms of compliance with equal employment opportunity legislation, patients in terms of quality of care, and ecology groups in terms of hazardous waste disposal. Because organizations must rely on these external groups for resources and legitimacy, they cannot simply ignore these competing values. They must somehow respond to them and try to reconcile the different interests.

Recent attempts to help firms manage external relationships suggest the need for new interventions and competence in OD.[36] Practitioners must have not only social skills like those proposed in Table 3.1 but also political skills. They must understand the distribution of power, conflicts of interest, and value dilemmas inherent in managing external relationships, and be able to manage their own role and values with respect to those dynamics. Research suggests this is especially true in interorganizational and international applications of OD.[37] Interventions promoting collaboration and trust may be ineffective in this larger arena, especially when there are power and dominance relationships among organizations and competition for scarce resources. Under those conditions, OD practitioners may need more power-oriented interventions, such as bargaining, coalition forming, and pressure tactics, which traditionally have not been associated with OD.

For example, organizations are coming under increasing pressure to align their practices with ecologically sound principles. Popular and scientific concerns over global warming, toxic waste, and natural resource depletion each have formidable nonprofit groups, citizen action committees, and professional lobbyists representing them. In addition, an increasing number of consulting firms are marketing services to help organizations achieve a more sustainable relationship with the environment. In response, more and more firms have "gone green," announced contributions to environmental funds, and created alliances with environmental, nongovernmental groups. Critics argue that these changes are more window-dressing than real, more political than operational, and more public relations than substantive. To be fair, a growing number of organizations are making important changes in their business practices, strategies, and resource allocations. As a result, the relationships between organizations and environmental groups range from benign to hostile to collaborative. OD practitioners increasingly may need to help organizations manage these relationships and implement strategies to manage their constituencies effectively. That effort will require political skills and greater attention to how the OD practitioner's own values fit with those of the organization.

3-5 Professional Ethics

Ethical issues in OD are concerned with how practitioners perform their helping relationship with organization members. Inherent in any helping relationship is the potential for misconduct and client abuse. OD practitioners can let personal values stand in the way of good practice, use the power inherent in their professional role to abuse (often unintentionally) organization members, or favor one group of stakeholders at the expense of other stakeholders.

3-5a Ethical Guidelines

To its credit, the field of OD always has shown concern for the ethical conduct of its practitioners. There have been several articles and symposia about ethics in OD.[38] In addition, statements of ethics governing OD practice have been sponsored by the American Society for Training & Development (www.astd.org), Organization Development International (www.theodinstitute.org/od-library/code_of_ethics.htm), and a consortium of professional associations in OD. The consortium has sponsored an ethical code derived from a large-scale project conducted at the Center for the Study of Ethics in the Professions at the Illinois Institute of Technology. The project's purposes included preparing critical incidents describing ethical dilemmas and using that material for preprofessional and continuing education in OD; providing an empirical basis for a statement of values and ethics for OD professionals; and initiating a process for making the ethics of OD practice explicit on a continuing basis.[39] The ethical guidelines from that project appear in the appendix to this chapter.

3-5b Ethical Dilemmas

Although adherence to statements of ethics helps prevent the occurrence of ethical problems, OD practitioners still encounter ethical dilemmas. Figure 3.2 is a process model that explains how ethical dilemmas can occur in OD. The antecedent conditions include an OD practitioner and a client system with different goals, values, needs, skills, and abilities. The entry and contracting phase of planned change is intended to address and clarify these differences. As a practical matter, however, it is unreasonable to assume that all of the differences will be identified and resolved. Under such circumstances, the subsequent intervention process or role episode is almost certainly subject to role conflict and role ambiguity. Neither the client nor the OD practitioner is clear about respective responsibilities. Each party is pursuing different goals, and each is using different skills and values to achieve those goals. The role conflict and ambiguity may produce five types of ethical dilemmas: misrepresentation, misuse of data, coercion, value and goal conflict, and technical ineptness.

Misrepresentation Misrepresentation occurs when OD practitioners claim that an intervention will produce results that are unreasonable for the change program or the situation. The client can contribute to the problem by portraying inaccurate goals and needs. In either case, one or both parties are operating under false pretenses and an ethical dilemma exists. For example, in an infamous case called "The Undercover Change Agent," an attempt was made to use sensitivity training in an organization whose top management did not understand it and was not ready for it. The OD consultant sold this interpersonally intense intervention as the activity that would solve the problems facing the organization. After the president of the firm made a surprise visit to the site where the training was being held, the consultant was fired because the

FIGURE 3.2

A Role Episodic Model of Ethical Dilemmas

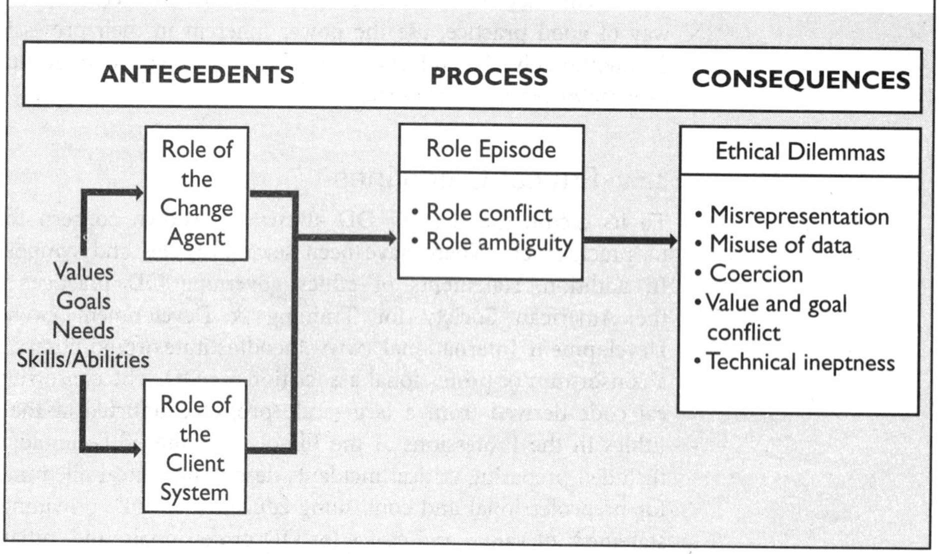

SOURCE: Wooten, K. C. and White, L P.: 1983, "Ethical Problems in the Practice of Organization Development," *Training and Development Journal* 37(4), p. 19.

nature and style of the sensitivity training was in direct contradiction to the president's concepts about leadership.[40] Misrepresentation is likely to occur in the entering and contracting phases of planned change when the initial consulting relationship is being established. To prevent misrepresentation, OD practitioners need to gain clarity about the goals of the change effort, and to explore openly with the client its expected effects, its relevance to the client system, and the practitioner's competence in executing the intervention.

Misuse of Data Misuse of data occurs when information gathered during the OD process is used punitively. Large amounts of information are invariably obtained during the entry and diagnostic phases of OD. Although most OD practitioners value openness and trust, it is important that they be aware of how such data are going to be used. It is a human tendency to use data to enhance a power position. Openness is one thing, but leaking inappropriate information can be harmful to individuals and to the organization. It is easy for a consultant, under the guise of obtaining information, to gather data about whether a particular manager is good or bad. When, how, or if this information can be used is an ethical dilemma not easily resolved. To minimize misuse of data, practitioners should reach agreement up front with organization members about how data collected during the change process will be used. This agreement should be reviewed periodically in light of changing circumstances.

Coercion Coercion occurs when organization members are forced to participate in an OD intervention. People should have the freedom to choose whether to participate in a change program if they are to gain self-reliance to solve their own problems. In team building, for example, team members should have the option of deciding not to become involved in the intervention. Management should not decide unilaterally that team building is good for members. However, freedom to make a choice requires knowledge about OD. Many organization members have little information about OD interventions, what they involve, and the nature and consequences of becoming involved with them. This makes it imperative for OD practitioners to educate clients about interventions before choices are made for implementing them.

Coercion also can pose ethical dilemmas for the helping relationship between OD practitioners and organization members. Inherent in any helping relationship are possibilities for excessive manipulation and dependency, two facets of coercion. Kelman pointed out that behavior change "inevitably involves some degree of manipulation and control, and at least an implicit imposition of the change agent's values on the client or the person he [or she] is influencing."[41] This places the practitioner on two horns of a dilemma: (1) Any attempt to change is in itself a change and thereby a manipulation, no matter how slight and (2) there exists no formula or method to structure a change situation so that such manipulation can be totally avoided. To attack the first aspect of the dilemma, Kelman stressed freedom of choice, seeing any action that limits freedom of choice as being ethically ambiguous or worse. To address the second aspect, Kelman argued that the OD practitioner must remain keenly aware of her or his own value system and alert to the possibility that those values are being imposed on a client. In other words, an effective way to resolve this dilemma is to make the change effort as open as possible, with the free consent and knowledge of the individuals involved.

The second facet of coercion that can pose ethical dilemmas for the helping relationship involves dependency. Helping relationships invariably create dependency between those who need help and those who provide it.[42] A major goal in OD is to lessen clients' dependency on consultants by helping clients gain the knowledge and skills to address organizational problems and manage change themselves. In some cases, however, achieving independence from OD practitioners can result in clients being either counterdependent or overdependent, especially in the early stages of the relationship. To resolve dependency issues, consultants can openly and explicitly discuss with the client how to handle the dependency problem, especially what the client and consultant expect of one another. Another approach is to focus on problem finding. Usually, the client is looking for a solution to a perceived problem. The consultant can redirect the energy to improved joint diagnosis so that both are working on problem identification and problem solving. Such action moves the energy of the client away from dependency. Finally, dependency can be reduced by changing the client's expectation from being helped or controlled by the practitioner to a greater focus on the need to manage the problem. Such a refocusing can reinforce the understanding that the consultant is working for the client and offering assistance that is at the client's discretion.

Value and Goal Conflict This ethical conflict occurs when the purpose of the change effort is not clear or when the client and the practitioner disagree over how to achieve the goals. The important practical issue for OD consultants is whether it is justifiable to withhold services unilaterally from an organization that does not agree with their values or methods. OD pioneer Gordon Lippitt suggested that the real question is the following: Assuming that some kind of change is going to occur anyway, doesn't the consultant have a responsibility to try to guide the change in the most constructive fashion possible?[43] That question may be of greater importance and relevance to an internal consultant or to a consultant who already has an ongoing relationship with the client.

Argyris takes an even stronger stand, maintaining that the responsibilities of professional OD practitioners to clients are comparable to those of lawyers or physicians, who, in principle, may not refuse to perform their services. He suggests that the very least the consultant can do is to provide "first aid" to the organization, as long as the assistance does not compromise the consultant's values. Argyris suggests that if the Ku Klux Klan asked for assistance and the consultant could at least determine whether the KKK was genuinely interested in assessing itself and willing to commit itself to all that a valid assessment would entail concerning both itself and other groups, the consultant should be willing to help. If later the Klan's objectives proved to be less than honestly stated, the consultant would be free to withdraw without being compromised.[44]

Technical Ineptness This final ethical dilemma occurs when OD practitioners try to implement interventions for which they are not skilled or when the client attempts a change for which it is not ready. Critical to the success of any OD program is the selection of an appropriate intervention, which depends, in turn, on careful diagnosis of the organization. Selecting an intervention is closely related to the practitioner's own values, skills, and abilities. In solving organizational problems, many OD consultants emphasize a favorite intervention or technique, such as team building, total quality management, or self-managed teams. They let their own values and beliefs dictate the change method.[45] Technical ineptness dilemmas also can occur when interventions do not align with the ability of the organization to implement them. Again, careful diagnosis can reveal the extent to which the organization is ready to make a change and possesses the skills and knowledge to implement it.

Application 3.2 presents an ethical dilemma that arises frequently in OD consulting.[46] What points in the process represent practical opportunities to intervene? Do you agree with Todd's resolution to the problem? What other options did she have?

application 3.2

KINDRED TODD AND THE ETHICS OF OD

Kindred Todd had just finished her master's degree in organization development and had landed her first consulting position with a small consulting company in Edmonton, Alberta, Canada. The president, Larry Stepchuck, convinced Todd that his growing organization offered her a great opportunity to learn the business. He had a large number of contacts, an impressive executive career, and several years of consulting experience behind him.

In fact, the firm was growing; adding new clients and projects as fast as its president could hire consultants. A few weeks after Todd was hired, Stepchuck assigned her to a new client, a small oil and gas company. "I've met with the client for several hours," he told her. "They are an important and potentially large opportunity for our firm. They're looking to us to help them address some long-range planning issues. From the way they talk, they could also use some continuous quality improvement work as well."

As Todd prepared for her initial meeting with the client, she reviewed financial data from the firm's annual report, examined trends in the client's industry, and thought about the issues that young firms face. Stepchuck indicated that Todd would first meet with the president of the firm to discuss initial issues and next steps.

When Todd walked into the president's office, she was greeted by the firm's entire senior management team. Team members expressed eagerness to get to work on the important issues of how to improve the organization's key business processes. They believed that an expert in continuous quality improvement (CQI), such as Todd, was exactly the kind of help they needed to increase efficiency and cut costs in the core business. Members began to ask direct questions about technical details of CQI, the likely timeframe within which they might expect results, how to map key processes, and how to form quality-improvement teams to identify and implement process improvements.

Todd was stunned and overwhelmed. Nothing that Stepchuck said about the issues facing this company was being discussed and, worse, it was clear that he had sold her to the client as an "expert" in CQI. Her immediate response was to suggest that all of their questions were good ones, but that they needed to be answered in the context of the long-range goals and strategies of the firm. Todd proposed that the best way to begin was for team members to provide her with some history about the organization. In doing so, she was able to avert disaster and embarrassment for herself and her company, and to appear to be doing all the things necessary to begin a CQI project. The meeting ended with Todd and the management team agreeing to meet again the following week.

Immediately the next day, Todd sought out the president of her firm. She reported on the results of the meeting and her surprise at being sold to this client as an expert on CQI. Todd suggested that her own competencies did not fit the needs of the client and requested that another consultant—one with expertise in CQI—be assigned to the project.

Larry Stepchuck responded to Todd's concerns: "I've known these people for over ten years. They don't know exactly what they need. CQI is an important buzzword. It's the flavor of the month and if that's what they want, that's what we'll give them." He also told her that there were no other consultants available for this project. "Besides," he said, "the president of the client firm just called to say how much he enjoyed meeting with you and was looking forward to getting started on the project right away."

Kindred Todd felt that Stepchuck's response to her concerns included a strong, inferred ultimatum: If you want to stay with this company, you had better take this job. "I knew I had to sink or swim with this job and this client," she later reported.

As Todd reflected on her options, she pondered the following questions:

- How can I be honest with this client and thus not jeopardize my values of openness and honesty?
- How can I be helpful to this client?

- How much do I know about quality-improvement processes?
- How do I satisfy the requirements of my employer?
- What obligations do I have?
- Who's going to know if I do or don't have the credentials to perform this work?
- What if I fail?

After thinking about those issues, Todd summarized her position in terms of three dilemmas: a dilemma of self (who is Kindred Todd?), a dilemma of competence (what can I do?), and a dilemma of confidence (do I like who I work for?). Based on the issues, Todd made the following tactical decisions. She spent two days at the library reading about and studying total quality management and CQI. She also contacted several of her friends and former classmates who had experience with quality-improvement efforts. Eventually, she contracted with one of them to be her "shadow" consultant—to work with her behind the scenes on formulating and implementing an intervention for the client.

Based on her preparation in the library and the discussions with her shadow consultant, Kindred Todd was able to facilitate an appropriate and effective intervention for the client. Shortly after her assignment was completed, she resigned from the consulting organization.

SUMMARY

This chapter has examined the role of the organization development practitioner. The term OD practitioner applies to three sets of people: individuals specializing in OD as a profession, people from related fields who have gained some competence in OD, and managers having the OD skills necessary to change and develop their organizations or departments. Comprehensive lists enumerate core and advanced skills and knowledge that an effective OD professional should possess, but a smaller set of basic skills and knowledge is applicable for all practitioners at all levels. These include four kinds of background: intrapersonal skills, interpersonal skills, general consultation skills, and knowledge of OD theory.

The professional OD role can apply to internal consultants who belong to the organization undergoing change, to external consultants who are members of universities and consulting firms or are self-employed, and to members of internal–external consulting teams. The OD practitioner's role may be described aptly in terms of marginality and emotional demands. People with a tolerance for marginal roles seem especially suited for OD practice because they are able to maintain neutrality and objectivity and to develop integrative solutions that reconcile viewpoints among opposing organizational departments. Similarly, the OD practitioner's emotional intelligence and awareness are keys to implementing the role successfully. Whereas in the past the OD practitioner's role has been described as standing at the client end of the continuum from client-centered to consultant-centered functioning, the development of new and varied interventions has shifted the role of the OD professional to cover the entire range of that continuum.

Although OD is still an emerging field, most practitioners have specific training that ranges from short courses and workshops to graduate and doctoral education. No single career path exists, but internal consulting is often a stepping-stone to becoming an external consultant. Because of the hectic pace of OD practice, specialists should be prepared to cope with high levels of stress and the possibility of career burnout.

Values have played a key role in OD, and traditional values promoting trust, collaboration, and openness have been supplemented recently with concerns for improving organizational effectiveness and environmental sustainability. OD specialists may face value dilemmas in trying to optimize human benefits, organization performance, and sound environmental practices. They also may encounter value conflicts when dealing with powerful external stakeholders, such as the government, stockholders, and customers. Dealing with those outside groups may take political skills, as well as the more traditional social skills.

Ethical issues in OD involve how practitioners perform their helping role with clients. As a profession, OD always has shown a concern for the ethical conduct and several ethical codes for OD practice have been developed by various professional associations. Ethical dilemmas in OD arise around misrepresentation, misuse of data, coercion, value and goal conflict, and technical ineptness.

NOTES

1. A. Church and W. Burke, "Practitioner Attitudes about the Field of Organization Development," in *Research in Organization Change and Development*, ed. W. Pasmore and R. Woodman (Greenwich, CT: JAI Press, 1995).
2. L. Greiner and T. Cummings, *Dynamic Strategy Making: A Real-Time Approach for the 21st Century Leader* (San Francisco: Jossey-Bass, 2009); C. Worley, D. Hitchin, and W. Ross, *Integrated Strategic Change* (Reading, MA: Addison-Wesley, 1996).
3. L. Greiner and F. Poulfelt, *Management Consulting Today and Tomorrow* (New York: Routledge, 2010); N. Worren, K. Ruddle, and K. Moore, "From Organization Development to Change Management: The Emergence of a New Profession," *Journal of Applied Behavioral Science* 35 (1999): 273–86.
4. M. Beer and E. Walton, "Organization Change and Development," *Annual Review of Psychology* 38 (1987): 229–72; S. Sherman, "Wanted: Company Change Agents," *Fortune*, December 11, 1999, 197–98.
5. R. Kanter, *The Change Masters* (New York: Simon & Schuster, 1983).
6. R. Lippitt, "Dimensions of the Consultant's Job," in *The Planning of Change*, ed. W. Bennis, K. Benne, and R. Chin (New York: Holt, Rinehart, & Winston, 1961), 156–61; C. Rogers, *On Becoming a Person* (Boston: Houghton Mifflin, 1971); "OD Experts Reflect on the Major Skills Needed by Consultants: With Comments from Edgar Schein," *Academy of Management OD Newsletter* (Spring 1979): 1–4; K. Shepard and A. Raia, "The OD Training Challenge," *Training and Development Journal* 35 (April 1981): 90–96; E. Neilsen, *Becoming an OD Practitioner* (Englewood Cliffs, NJ: Prentice Hall, 1984); S. Eisen, J. Cherbeneau, and C. Worley, "A Future-Responsive Perspective for Competent Practice in OD," in *Practicing Organization Development*, 2nd ed., ed. W. Rothwell and R. Sullivan (San Diego: Pfeiffer, 2005); A. Church, "The Professionalization of Organization Development," in *Research in Organization Change and Development*, ed. R. Woodman and W. Pasmore (Oxford: JAI Press, 2001); A. Freedman and R. Zackrison, *Finding Your Way in the Consulting Jungle* (San Francisco: Jossey-Bass, 2001).
7. R. Sullivan and K. Quade, "Essential Competencies for Internal and External OD Consultants," in *Practicing Organization Development*, ed. W. Rothwell, R. Sullivan, and G. McLean (San Diego: Pfeiffer, 1995).
8. C. Worley, W. Rothwell, and R. Sullivan, "Competencies of OD Practitioners," in *Practicing Organization Development*, 2nd ed., ed. W. Rothwell and R. Sullivan (San Diego: Pfeiffer, 2005).
9. C. Worley and G. Varney, "A Search for a Common Body of Knowledge for Master's Level Organization Development and Change Programs—An Invitation to Join the Discussion," *Academy of Management ODC Newsletter* (Winter 1998): 1–4.
10. C. Worley and A. Feyerherm, "Reflections on the Future of Organization Development," *Journal of Applied Behavioral Science* 39 (2003): 97–115; Worley, Rothwell, and Sullivan, "Competencies of OD Practitioners."
11. B. Tannenbaum, "Letter to the Editor," *Consulting Practice Communique, Academy of Management Managerial Consultation Division* 21, no. 3 (1993): 16–17; B. Tannenbaum, "Self-Awareness: An Essential Element Underlying Consultant Effectiveness," *Journal of Organizational Change Management* 8, no. 3 (1995): 85–86.
12. A. Church and W. Burke, "Practitioner Attitudes about the Field of Organization Development," in *Research in Organizational Change and Development*, ed. W. Pasmore and R. Woodman (Greenwich, CT: JAI Press, 1995).
13. M. Lacey, "Internal Consulting: Perspectives on the Process of Planned Change," *Journal of Organizational Change Management* 8, no. 3 (1995): 75–84.
14. M. Kaarst-Brown, "Five Symbolic Roles of the External Consultant–Integrating Change, Power, and Symbolism," *Journal of Organizational Change Management* 12 (1999): 540–61.
15. Lacey, "Internal Consulting."
16. C. Argyris, *Intervention Theory and Method* (Reading, MA: Addison-Wesley, 1973).
17. A. Foss, D. Lipsky, A. Orr, B. Scott, T. Seamon, J. Smendzuik-O'Brien, A. Tavis, D. Wissman, and C. Woods, "Practicing Internal OD," in *Practicing Organization Development*, 2nd ed., ed. W. Rothwell and R. Sullivan (San Diego: Pfeiffer, 2005); E. Kirkhart and T. Isgar, "Quality of Work Life for Consultants: The Internal–External Relationship," *Consultation* 5 (Spring 1986): 5–23.

18. This application was developed by Kimberly McKenna based on her experiences as both an external and internal OD practitioner and on Kirkhart and Isgar, "Quality of Work Life for Consultants."
19. R. Ziller, *The Social Self* (Elmsford, NY: Pergamon, 1973).
20. W. Liddell, "Marginality and Integrative Decisions," *Academy of Management Journal* 16 (March 1973): 154–56; P. Brown and C. Cotton, "Marginality, A Force for the OD Practitioner," *Training and Development Journal* 29 (April 1975): 14–18; H. Aldrich and D. Gerker, "Boundary Spanning Roles and Organizational Structure," *Academy of Management Review* 2 (April 1977): 217–30; C. Cotton, "Marginality—A Neglected Dimension in the Design of Work," *Academy of Management Review* 2 (January 1977): 133–38; N. Margulies, "Perspectives on the Marginality of the Consultant's Role," in *The Cutting Edge*, ed. W. Burke (La Jolla, CA: University Associates, 1978), 60–79.
21. P. Brown, C. Cotton, and R. Golembiewski, "Marginality and the OD Practitioner," *Journal of Applied Behavioral Science* 13 (1977): 493–506.
22. C. Lundberg and C. Young, "A Note on Emotions and Consultancy," *Journal of Organizational Change Management* 14 (2001): 530–38; A. Carr, "Understanding Emotion and Emotionality in a Process of Change," *Journal of Organizational Change Management* 14 (2001): 421–36.
23. D. Goleman, *Emotional Intelligence* (New York: Bantam Books, 1995); R. Cooper and A. Sawaf, *Executive EQ: Emotional Intelligence in Leadership and Organizations* (New York: Grosset/Putnum, 1997); P. Salovey and D. Sluyter, eds., *Emotional Development and Emotional Intelligence* (New York: Basic Books, 1997); J. Allen, *Emotional Intelligence: The Emotional Intelligence Book* (Charleston, SC: CreateSpace Independent Publishing Platform, 2013).
24. Goleman, *Emotional Intelligence.*
25. J. Sanford, *Fritz Kunkel: Selected Writings* (Mahwah, NJ: Paulist Press, 1984); Lundberg and Young, "Note on Emotions"; Carr, "Understanding Emotion."
26. J. Ciarrochi, J. Forgas, and J. Mayer, *Emotional Intelligence in Everyday Life: A Scientific Inquiry* (New York: Psychology Press, 2001).
27. D. Kegan, "Organization Development as OD Network Members See It," *Group and Organization Studies* 7 (March 1982): 5–11.
28. D. Griffin and P. Griffin, "The Consulting Survey," *Consulting Today*, Special Issue (Fall 1998): 1–11.
29. J. Lewis III, "Growth of Internal Change Agents in Organizations" (Ph.D. Diss., Case Western Reserve University, 1970).
30. G. Edelwich and A. Brodsky, *Burn-Out Stages of Disillusionment in the Helping Professions* (New York: Human Science, 1980); M. Weisbord, "The Wizard of OD: Or, What Have Magic Slippers to Do with Burnout, Evaluation, Resistance, Planned Change, and Action Research?" *OD Practitioner* 10 (Summer 1978): 1–14; M. Mitchell, "Consultant Burnout," in *The 1977 Annual Handbook for Group Facilitators*, ed. J. Jones and W. Pfeiffer (La Jolla, CA: University Associates, 1977), 145–56.
31. Griffin and Griffin, "Consulting Survey."
32. T. Isgar, "Quality of Work Life of Consultants," *Academy of Management OD Newsletter* (Winter 1983): 2–4.
33. P. Hanson and B. Lubin, *Answers to Questions Most Frequently Asked about Organization Development* (Newbury Park, CA: Sage Publications, 1995).
34. Church and Burke, "Practitioner Attitudes."
35. D. Jamieson and C. Worley, "The Practice of Organization Development," in *Handbook of Organization Development*, ed. T. Cummings (Thousand Oaks, CA: Sage Publications, 2008); M. Wheatley, R. Tannenbaum, P. Griffin, and K. Quade, *Organization Development at Work* (San Francisco: Pfeiffer, 2003).
36. Church, "Professionalization of Organization Development"; S. Guastello, *Chaos, Catastrophe, and Human Affairs* (Mahwah, NJ: LEA Publishers, 1995); R. Stacey, D. Griffin, and P. Shaw, *Complexity and Management* (London: Routledge, 2000); R. Garud, A. Kumaraswamy, and R. Langlois, *Managing in the Modular Age* (Malden, MA: Blackwell Publishing, 2003); A. Shani and P. Docherty, *Learning by Design* (Malden, MA: Blackwell Publishing, 2003).
37. R. Saner and L. Yiu, "Porous Boundary and Power Politics: Contextual Constraints of Organization Development Change Projects in the United Nations Organizations," *Gestalt Review* 6 (2002): 84–94.
38. D. Jamieson and W. Gellermann, "Values, Ethics, and OD Practice," in *The NTL Handbook of Organization Development and Change*, ed. B. Jones and M. Brazzel (San Francisco: Pfeiffer, 2006); T. Egan and W. Gellermann, "Values, Ethics, and Practice in the Field of Organization Development," in *Practicing Organization Development*, 2nd ed., ed. W. Rothwell and R. Sullivan (San Francisco: Pfeifer, 2005); D. Coghlan and A. Shani, "Roles, Politics, and Ethics in Action Research Design," *Systemic Practice and Action Research* 18 (2005): 533–51; D. Bowen, "Value Dilemmas in Organization Development," *Journal of Applied Behavioral Science* 13 (1977): 545–55; L. White and K. Wooten, "Ethical Dilemmas in Various Stages of Organization Development," *Academy of Management Review* 8 (1963): 690–97; K. Scalzo, "When Ethics and Consulting Collide" (unpublished master's thesis, Pepperdine University, Graziadio School of Business and Management, Los Angeles, CA, 1994); L. White and M. Rhodeback, "Ethical Dilemmas in Organization Development: A Cross-Cultural Analysis," *Journal of Business Ethics* 11, no. 9 (1992): 663–70; M. Page, "Ethical dilemmas

in organization development consulting practice" (unpublished master's thesis, Pepperdine University, Graziadio School of Business and Management, Los Angeles, CA, 1998).

39. W. Gellerman, M. Frankel, and R. Ladenson, *Values and Ethics in Organization and Human System Development: Responding to Dilemmas in Professional Life* (San Francisco: Jossey-Bass, 1990).
40. W. Bennis, *Organization Development: Its Nature, Origins, and Prospects* (Reading, MA: Addison-Wesley, 1969).
41. H. Kelman, "Manipulation of Human Behavior: An Ethical Dilemma for the Social Scientist," in *The Planning of Change*, 2nd ed., ed. W. Bennis, K. Benne, and R. Chin (New York: Holt, Rinehart, & Winston, 1969), 584.
42. E. Schein, *Process Consultation Revisited* (Reading, MA: Addison-Wesley, 1999); R. Beckhard, "The Dependency Dilemma," *Consultants' Communique* 6 (July–September 1978): 1–3.
43. G. Lippitt, *Organization Renewal* (Englewood Cliffs, NJ: Prentice Hall, 1969).
44. C. Argyris, "Explorations in Consulting–Client Relationships," *Human Organizations* 20 (Fall 1961): 121–33.
45. J. Slocum Jr., "Does Cognitive Style Affect Diagnosis and Intervention Strategies?" *Group and Organization Studies* 3 (June 1978): 199–210.
46. This application was submitted by Kathy Scalzo, an OD consultant in western Canada. It is based on an actual case from her interviews with OD consultants on how they resolve ethical dilemmas. The names and places have been changed to preserve anonymity.

APPENDIX

Ethical Guidelines for an Organization Development/Human Systems Development (OD/HSD) Professional

Sponsored by the Human Systems Development Consortium (HSDC), a significant integrative effort by Bill Gellermann has been under way to develop "A Statement of Values and Ethics for Professionals in Organization and Human System Development." HSDC is an informal collection of the leaders of most of the professional associations related to the application of the behavioral and social sciences. A series of drafts based on extensive contributions, comments, and discussions involving many professionals and organizations has led to the following version of this statement.

As an OD/HSD Professional, I commit to supporting and acting in accordance with the following guidelines:

I. Responsibility for Professional Development and Competence

A. Accept responsibility for the consequences of my acts and make every effort to ensure that my services are properly used.

B. Recognize the limits of my competence, culture, and experience in providing services and using techniques; neither seek nor accept assignments outside those limits without clear understanding by the client when exploration at the edge of my competence is reasonable; refer client to other professionals when appropriate.

C. Strive to attain and maintain a professional level of competence in the field, including

1. broad knowledge of theory and practice in
    a. applied behavioral science generally.
    b. management, administration, organizational behavior, and system behavior specifically.
    c. multicultural issues including issues of color and gender.
    d. other relevant fields of knowledge and practice.
2. ability to
    a. relate effectively with individuals and groups.
    b. relate effectively to the dynamics of large, complex systems.
    c. provide consultation using theory and methods of the applied behavioral sciences.
    d. articulate theory and direct its application, including creation of learning experiences for individuals, small and large groups, and for whole systems.

D. Strive continually for self-knowledge and personal growth; be aware that "what is in me" (my perceptions of myself in my world) and "what is outside me" (the realities that exist apart from me) are not the same; be aware that my values, beliefs, and aspirations can both limit and empower me and that they are primary determinants of my perceptions, my behavior, and my personal and professional effectiveness.

E. Recognize my own personal needs and desires and deal with them responsibly in the performance of my professional roles.

F. Obtain consultation from OD/HSD professionals who are native to and aware of the specific cultures within which I work when those cultures are different from my own.

II. Responsibility to Clients and Significant Others

A. Serve the short- and long-term welfare, interests, and development of the client system and all its stakeholders; maintain balance in the timing, pace, and magnitude of planned change so as to support a mutually beneficial relationship between the system and its environment.

B. Discuss candidly and fully goals, costs, risks, limitations, and anticipated outcomes of any program or other professional relationship under consideration; seek to avoid automatic confirmation of predetermined conclusions, either the client's or my own; seek optimum involvement by client system members in every step of the process, including managers and workers' representatives; fully inform client system members about my role, contribution, and strategy in working with them.

C. Fully inform participants in any activity or procedure as to its sponsorship, nature, purpose, implications, and any significant risk associated with it so that they can freely choose their participation in any activity initiated by me; acknowledge that their choice may be limited with activity initiated by recognized authorities; be particularly sensitive to implications and risks when I work with people from cultures other than my own.

D. Be aware of my own personal values, my values as an OD/HSD professional, the values of my native culture, the values of the people with whom I am working, and the values of their cultures; involve the client system in making relevant cultural differences explicit and exploring the possible implications of any OD/HSD intervention for all the stakeholders involved; be prepared to make explicit my assumptions, values, and standards as an OD/HSD professional.

E. Help all stakeholders while developing OD/HSD approaches, programs, and the like, if they wish such help; for example, this could include workers' representatives as well as managers in the case of work with a business organization.

F. Work collaboratively with other internal and external consultants serving the same client system and resolve conflicts in terms of the balanced best interests of the client system and all its stakeholders; make appropriate arrangements with other internal and external consultants about how responsibilities will be shared.

G. Encourage and enable my clients to provide for themselves the services I provide rather than foster continued reliance on me; encourage, foster, and support self-education and self-development by individuals, groups, and all other human systems.

H. Cease work with a client when it is clear that the client is not benefiting or the contract has been completed; do not accept an assignment if its scope is so limited that the client will not benefit or it would involve serious conflict with the values and ethics outlined in this statement.

I. Avoid conflicts of interest.

  1. Fully inform the client of my opinion about serving similar or competing organizations; be clear with myself, my clients, and other concerned stakeholders about my loyalties and responsibilities when conflicts of interest arise; keep parties informed of these conflicts; cease work with the client if the conflicts cannot be adequately resolved.
  2. Seek to act impartially when involved in conflicts between parties in the client system; help them resolve their conflicts themselves, without taking sides; if necessary to change my role from serving as impartial consultant, do so explicitly; cease work with the client, if necessary.
  3. Identify and respond to any major differences in professionally relevant values or ethics between myself and my clients with the understanding that conditions may require ceasing work with the client.
  4. Accept differences in the expectations and interests of different stakeholders and realize that those differences cannot be reconciled all the time.

J. Seek consultation and feedback from neutral third parties in case of conflict between myself and my client.

K. Define and protect the confidentiality of my client–professional relationships.

  1. Make limits of confidentiality clear to clients/participants.
  2. Reveal information accepted in confidence only to appropriate or agreed-upon recipients or authorities.
  3. Use information obtained during professional work in writings, lectures, or other public forums only with prior consent or when disguised so that it is impossible from my presentations alone to identify the individuals or systems with whom I have worked.
  4. Make adequate provisions for maintaining confidentiality in the storage and disposal of records; make provisions for responsibly preserving records in the event of my retirement or disability.

L. Establish mutual agreement on a contract covering services and remuneration.

  1. Ensure a clear understanding of and mutual agreement on the services to be performed; do not shift from that agreement without both a clearly defined professional rationale for making the shift and the informed consent of the clients/participants; withdraw from the agreement if circumstances beyond my control prevent proper fulfillment.
  2. Ensure mutual understanding and agreement by putting the contract in writing to the extent feasible, yet recognize that
     a. the spirit of professional responsibility encompasses more than the letter of the contract.
     b. some contracts are necessarily incomplete because complete information is not available at the outset.

c. putting the contract in writing may be neither necessary nor desirable.

3. Safeguard the best interests of the client, the profession, and the public by making sure that financial arrangements-are fair and in keeping with appropriate statutes, regulations, and professional standards.

M. Provide for my own accountability by evaluating and assessing the effects of my work.

1. Make all reasonable efforts to determine if my activities have accomplished the agreed-upon goals and have not had other undesirable consequences; seek to undo any undesirable consequences, and do not attempt to cover up these situations.
2. Actively solicit and respond with an open mind to feedback regarding my work and seek to improve.
3. Develop, publish, and use assessment techniques that promote the welfare and best interests of clients/participants; guard against the misuse of assessment results.

N. Make public statements of all kinds accurately, including promotion and advertising, and give service as advertised.

1. Base public statements providing professional opinions or information on scientifically acceptable findings and techniques as much as possible, with full recognition of the limits and uncertainties of such evidence.
2. Seek to help people make informed choices when making statements as part of promotion or advertising.
3. Deliver services as advertised and do not shift without a clear professional rationale and the informed consent of the participants/clients.

III. Responsibility to the Profession

A. Act with due regard for the needs, special competencies and obligations of my colleagues in OD/HSD and other professions; respect the prerogatives and obligations of the institutions or organizations with which these other colleagues are associated.

B. Be aware of the possible impact of my public behavior upon the ability of colleagues to perform their professional work; perform professional activity in a way that will bring credit to the profession.

C. Work actively for ethical practice by individuals and organizations engaged in OD/HSD activities and, in case of questionable practice, use appropriate channels for confronting it, including

1. direct discussion when feasible.
2. joint consultation and feedback, using other professionals as third parties.
3. enforcement procedures of existing professional organizations.
4. public confrontation.

D. Contribute to continuing professional development by

1. supporting the development of other professionals, including mentoring with less-experienced professionals.
2. contributing ideas, methods, findings, and other useful information to the body of OD/HSD knowledge and skill.

E. Promote the sharing of OD/HSD knowledge and skill by various means including

1. granting use of my copyrighted material as freely as possible, subject to a minimum of conditions, including a reasonable price defined on the basis of professional as well as commercial values.
2. giving credit for the ideas and products of others.

IV. Social Responsibility

A. Strive for the preservation and protection of fundamental human rights and the promotion of social justice.

B. Be aware that I bear a heavy social responsibility because my recommendations and professional actions may alter the lives and well-being of individuals within my client systems, the systems themselves, and the larger systems of which they are subsystems.

C. Contribute knowledge, skill, and other resources in support of organizations, programs, and activities that seek to improve human welfare; be prepared to accept clients who do not have sufficient resources to pay my full fees at reduced fees or no charge.

D. Respect the cultures of the organization, community, country, or other human system within which I work (including the cultures' traditions, values, and moral and ethical expectations and their implications), yet recognize and constructively confront the counterproductive aspects of those cultures whenever feasible; be sensitive to cross-cultural differences and their implications; be aware of the cultural filters which bias my view of the world.

E. Recognize that accepting this statement as a guide for my behavior involves holding myself to a standard that may be more exacting than the laws of any country in which I practice.

F. Contribute to the quality of life in human society at large; work toward and support a culture based on mutual respect for each other's rights as human beings; encourage the development of love, trust, openness, mutual responsibility, authentic and harmonious relationships, empowerment, participation, and involvement in a spirit of freedom and self-discipline as elements of this culture.

G. Engage in self-generated or collaborative endeavor to develop means for helping across cultures.

H. Serve the welfare of all the people of Earth, all living things, and their environment.

PART 2

THE PROCESS OF ORGANIZATION DEVELOPMENT

4 Entering and Contracting

5 Diagnosing

6 Collecting, Analyzing, and Feeding Back Diagnostic Information

7 Designing Interventions

8 Managing Change

9 Evaluating and Institutionalizing Organization Development Interventions

SELECTED CASES

Sunflower Incorporated

Kenworth Motors

Peppercorn Dining

Diagnosis and Feedback at Adhikar

Managing Change: Action Planning for the Vélo V Project in Lyon, France

4

Entering and Contracting

learning objectives

Describe the issues associated with entering into an OD process.
Describe the issues associated with contracting for an OD process.

The planned change process described in Chapter 2 generally starts when one or more managers or administrators sense an opportunity for their organization, department, or group, believe that new capabilities need to be developed, or decide that performance could be improved through organization development (OD). The organization might be successful yet have room for improvement. It might be facing impending environmental conditions that necessitate a change in how it operates. The organization could be experiencing particular problems, such as poor product quality, high rates of absenteeism, or dysfunctional conflicts among departments. Conversely, the problems might appear more diffuse and consist simply of feelings that the organization should be "more innovative," "more competitive," or "more effective."

Entering and contracting are the initial steps in the OD process. They involve defining in a preliminary manner the organization's problems or opportunities for development and establishing a collaborative relationship between the OD practitioner and members of the client system about how to work on those issues. Entering and contracting set the initial parameters for carrying out the subsequent phases of OD: diagnosing, planning and implementing changes, and evaluating and institutionalizing them. They help to define what issues will be addressed by those activities, who will carry them out, and how they will be accomplished.

Entering and contracting can vary in complexity and formality depending on the situation. In those cases where the manager of a work group or department serves as his or her own OD practitioner, entering and contracting typically involve the manager and group members meeting to discuss what issues to work on and how they will jointly meet the goals they set. Here, entering and contracting are relatively simple and informal. They involve all relevant members directly in the process—with a minimum of formal procedures. In situations where managers and administrators are considering the use of professional OD practitioners, either from inside or from outside the organization, entering and contracting tend to be more complex and formal.[1] OD practitioners may need to collect preliminary information to help define the problematic or development issues. They may need to meet with representatives of the client organization rather than with the total membership; they may need to formalize their respective roles and how the change process will unfold. In cases where the anticipated changes are strategic and large in scale, formal proposals from multiple consulting firms may be requested and legal contracts drawn up.

This chapter first discusses the activities and content-oriented issues involved in entering into and contracting for an OD initiative. We will focus our attention on complex processes involving OD professionals and client organizations. Similar entering and contracting issues, however, need to be addressed in even the simplest OD efforts, where managers serve as OD practitioners for their own work units. Unless there is clarity and agreement about what issues to work on, who will address them, how that will be accomplished, and what timetable will be followed, subsequent stages of the OD process are likely to be confusing and ineffective. The chapter concludes with a discussion of the interpersonal process issues involved in entering and contracting for OD work.

4-1 Entering into an OD Relationship

An OD process generally starts when a member of an organization or unit contacts an OD practitioner about potential help in addressing an organizational issue.[2] The organization member may be a manager, staff specialist, or some other key participant; the practitioner may be an OD professional from inside or outside of the organization. Determining whether the two parties should enter into an OD relationship typically involves clarifying the nature of the organization's current functioning and the issue(s) to be addressed, the relevant client system for that issue, and the appropriateness of the particular OD practitioner.[3] In helping assess these issues, the OD practitioner may need to collect preliminary data about the organization. Similarly, the organization may need to gather information about the practitioner's competence and experience.[4] This knowledge will help both parties determine whether they should proceed to develop a contract for working together.

This section describes the activities involved in entering an OD relationship: clarifying the organizational issue, determining the relevant client, and selecting the appropriate OD practitioner.

4-1a Clarifying the Organizational Issue

When seeking help from OD practitioners, organizations typically start with a *presenting problem*—the issue that has caused them to consider an OD process. It may be specific (decreased market share, increased absenteeism) or general ("we're growing too fast," "we need to prepare for rapid changes"). The presenting problem often has an implied or stated solution. For example, managers may believe that because costs are high, laying off members of their department is the obvious answer. They may even state the presenting problem in the form of a solution: "We need to downsize our organization."

In many cases, however, the presenting problem is only a symptom of an underlying problem. For example, high costs may result from several deeper causes, including ineffective new-product development or manufacturing processes, inappropriate customer-service policies and procedures, or conflict between two interdependent groups. The issue facing the organization or department must be clarified early in the OD process so that subsequent diagnostic and intervention activities are focused correctly.[5]

Gaining a clearer perspective on the organizational issue may require collecting preliminary data.[6] OD practitioners often examine company records and interview a few key members to gain an introductory understanding of the organization, its context, and the nature of the presenting problem. Those data are gathered in a relatively short period of time—typically over a few hours to one or two days. They are intended to provide enough rudimentary knowledge of the organizational issue to enable the two parties to make informed choices about proceeding with the contracting process.

The diagnostic phase of OD involves a far more extensive assessment of the problematic or development issue than occurs during the entering and contracting stage. The diagnosis also might discover other issues that need to be addressed, or it might lead to redefining the initial issue that was identified during the entering and contracting stage. This is a prime example of the emergent nature of the OD process: Things may change as new information is gathered and new events occur.

4-1b Determining the Relevant Client

A second activity in entering an OD relationship is defining the relevant client for addressing the organizational issue.[7] Generally, the relevant client includes those organization members who can directly impact the change issue, whether it is solving a particular problem or improving an already successful organization or department. Unless these members are identified and included in the entering and contracting process, they may withhold their support for and commitment to the OD process. In trying to improve the productivity of a unionized manufacturing plant, for example, the relevant client may need to include union officials as well as managers and staff personnel. It is not unusual for an OD project to fail because the relevant client was inappropriately defined.

Determining the relevant client can vary in complexity depending on the situation. In those cases where the organizational issue can be addressed in a specific organization unit, client definition is relatively straightforward. Members of that unit constitute the relevant client. They or their representatives must be included in the entering and contracting process. For example, if a manager asked for help in improving the decision-making process of his or her team, the manager and team members would be the relevant client. Unless they are actively involved in choosing an OD practitioner and defining the subsequent change process, there is little likelihood that OD will improve team decision making.

Determining the relevant client is more complex when the organizational issue cannot readily be addressed in a single unit. Here, it may be necessary to expand the definition of the client to include members from multiple units, from different hierarchical levels, and even from outside of the organization. For example, the manager of a production department may seek help in resolving conflicts between his or her unit and other departments in the organization. The relevant client would extend beyond the boundaries of the production department because that department alone cannot resolve the issue. The client might include members from all departments involved in the conflict as well as the executive to whom all of the departments report. If that interdepartmental conflict also involved key suppliers and customers from outside of the firm, the relevant client might include members of those groups.

In such complex situations, OD practitioners need to gather additional information about the organization to determine the relevant client, generally as part of the preliminary data collection that typically occurs when clarifying the issue to be addressed. When examining company records or interviewing personnel, practitioners can seek to identify the key members and organizational units that need to be involved. For example, they can ask organization members questions such as these: Who can directly influence the organizational issue? Who has a vested interest in it? Who has the power to approve or reject the OD effort? Answers to those questions can help determine who is the relevant client for the entering and contracting stage. However, the client may change during the later stages of the OD process as new data are gathered and changes occur. If so, participants may have to return to and modify this initial stage of the OD effort.

4-1c Selecting an OD Practitioner

The last activity involved in entering an OD relationship is selecting an OD practitioner who has the expertise and experience to work with members on the organizational issue. Unfortunately, little systematic advice is available on how to choose a competent OD professional, whether from inside or outside of the organization.[8] To help lower the uncertainty of choosing from among external OD practitioners, organizations may request that formal proposals be submitted. In these cases, the OD practitioner must take all of the information gathered in the prior steps and create an outline of how the process might unfold. Table 4.1 provides one view of the key elements of such a proposal. It suggests that a written proposal include project objectives, outlines of proposed processes, a list of roles and responsibilities, recommended interventions, and proposed fees and expenses.

For less formal and structured selection processes, the late Gordon Lippitt, a pioneering practitioner in the field, suggested several criteria for selecting, evaluating, and developing OD practitioners.[9] Lippitt listed areas that managers should consider before selecting a practitioner—including their ability to form sound interpersonal relationships, the degree of focus on the problem, the skills of the practitioner relative to the problem, the extent that the consultant clearly informs the client as to his or her role and contribution, and whether the practitioner belongs to a professional association. References from other clients are highly important. A client may not like the consultant's work, but it is critical to know the reasons for both pleasure and displeasure. One important consideration is whether the consultant approaches the organization with openness and an insistence on diagnosis or whether the practitioner appears to have a fixed program that is applicable to almost any problem or organization.

TABLE 4.1

Essentials of an Effective OD Proposal

Elements	Description
Objectives of proposed project	A statement of the goals in clear and concise terms, including measurable results, if any.
Proposed process or action plan	Provide an overview of the process to be used. Usually includes a diagnosis (including how the data will be collected), feedback process, and action-planning or implementation process.
Roles and responsibilities	A list of key stakeholders in the process, including the OD practitioner, and the specific responsibilities for which they will be held accountable.
Recommended interventions	A description of the proposed change strategies, including training, off-site meetings, systems or processes to be redesigned, and other activities.
Fees, terms, and conditions	Provide an outline of the fees and expenses associated with project.

SOURCE: Adapted from A. Freedman and R. Zackrison, *Finding Your Way in the Consulting Jungle*, 141–47. San Francisco: Jossey-Bass/Pfeiffer. © 2001.

Certainly, OD consulting is as much a person specialization as it is a task specialization. The OD professional needs not only a repertoire of technical skills but also the personality and interpersonal competence to use himself or herself as an instrument of change. Regardless of technical training, the consultant must be able to maintain a boundary position, coordinating among various units and departments and mixing disciplines, theories, technology, and research findings in an organic rather than in a mechanical way. The practitioner is potentially the most important OD technology available.

Thus, in selecting an OD practitioner perhaps the most important issue is the fundamental question, "How effective has the person been in the past, with what kinds of organizations, using what kinds of techniques?" In other words, references must be checked. Interpersonal relationships are tremendously important, but even con artists have excellent interpersonal relationships and skills.

The burden of choosing an effective OD practitioner should not rest entirely with the client organization.[10] As described in the Ethical Dilemmas section of Chapter 3, consultants also bear a heavy responsibility in finding whether there is a match between their skills and knowledge and what the organization or department needs. Few managers are sophisticated enough to detect or to understand subtle differences in expertise among OD professionals, and they often do not understand the difference between intervention specialties. Thus, practitioners should help educate potential clients, being explicit about their strengths and weaknesses and their range of competence. If OD professionals realize that a good match does not exist, they should inform the client and help them find more suitable help.

Application 4.1 describes the entering process at Alegent Health, a large health care system in Nebraska and western Iowa. The entry process was largely "virtual" in that the researchers worked through two consultants who were conducting OD interventions on a regular basis. The case highlights how OD work can come in different forms and through different channels. It also reflects how quickly the "entry" process can occur. This is the first in a series of applications based on the Alegent project that will be used throughout the text.

4-2 Developing a Contract

The activities of entering an OD relationship are a necessary prelude to developing an OD contract. They define the major focus for contracting, including the relevant parties. Contracting is a natural extension of the entering process and clarifies how the OD process will proceed. It typically establishes the expectations of the parties, the time and resources that will be expended, and the ground rules under which the parties will operate.

The goal of contracting is to make a good decision about how to carry out the OD process.[11] It can be relatively informal and involve only a verbal agreement between the client and the OD practitioner. A team leader with OD skills, for example, may voice his or her concerns to members about how the team is functioning. After some discussion, they might agree to devote one hour of future meeting time to diagnosing the team with the help of the leader. Here, entering and contracting are done together, informally. In other cases, contracting can be more protracted and result in a formal document. That typically occurs when organizations employ outside OD practitioners. Government agencies, for example, generally have procurement regulations that apply to contracting with outside consultants.[12]

application 4.1

ENTERING ALEGENT HEALTH

Alegent Health (AH) is a five-hospital system that serves the greater Omaha, Nebraska, and western Iowa region. Alegent was formed when two religious-sponsored health care systems merged to leverage health care industry changes and to bargain more powerfully with physicians and insurance providers. The system had its own managed care insurance program, was implementing a consumer-directed health care program for its employees, and had about 100 employed physicians in addition to the physicians with privileges at its hospitals.

Two well-known OD consultants had been working with AH for about two years, doing a variety of OD work. By far, the largest project was the design and delivery of large group interventions known as decision accelerators (DAs) to create strategies for the major clinical service areas, such as orthopedics, cardiology, and women's and children's services. [Note: Large group interventions are multistakeholder meetings of over 50 people—see Chapter 11 for more information.]

At an organization design conference in April, one of the consultants was talking with researchers from the Center for Effective Organizations at USC. The conversation turned to a discussion of the work at AH and the possibility of evaluating the change effort. The researchers were excited about the organization development and large group intervention work in the health care context. The consultant agreed to pitch the idea to AH's Chief Innovation Officer (CIO).

Following some additional background conversations with the researchers and the CIO, the consultant sent the following email in June:

> Dear CIO,
>
> I would like to introduce you to the Center for Effective Organization researchers. As we discussed, the researchers are very interested in the work being done at AH and will be calling you early next week to discuss the possibility of doing a research project on the Decision Accelerator effort. The form of research is typically action research, meaning the data will be valuable for Alegent in not only assessing the impact and effectiveness of the DA intervention but learning how to position this capability for improved Alegent organizational effectiveness. This can be quite valuable as Alegent moves into the next round of change and transformation.
>
> Thanks all.

The researchers spent the next few days talking to the two consultants about AH, its history, strategy, structure, and culture, as well as the motivation for the large-group, decision accelerator process. They also collected data on AH through the Internet. Alegent was indeed a unique organization. It was highly successful from a financial point of view, had a new CEO who had been brought in from Florida, and had a strong faith-based mission.

In the first phone call with the CIO, the researchers introduced themselves, described the mission of the research center, and their interest in doing a case study of change at Alegent. The CIO talked about the history of change at AH and asked questions about the value the project would have for them. He saw several benefits, including the opportunity to generate a history of the change, to learn about the impacts of the change process on the organization's culture and members, and to build a database that could be used to advance AH's objective of "changing the face of health care." The call ended with the agreement that the CIO would talk with others in the organization, including the CEO, and that the researchers should begin to put together a project purpose, cost estimate, and schedule.

In the second call, the researchers presented their understanding of the project as a case study assessment of how innovation was created and implemented at Alegent. They described a way of working with organizations—the establishment of a "study team" composed of several key stakeholders in the organization. The study team would meet, before the project officially began, to review the objectives of the study and ensure that the work was relevant to the organization. There was some conversation about who might be on that team, including the CEO, CFO, the hospital presidents, and the VPs of the clinical service areas.

Subsequent email exchanges among the consultants, the CIO, and the researchers led to a verbal agreement that the project should begin in October. The CIO believed there was much to gain from the project, and asked the Director of the Right Track office (this was the internal name AH had given to the decision accelerator) to lead the contracting process and to help the researchers schedule meetings and interviews.

Regardless of the level of formality, all OD processes require some form of explicit contracting that results in either a verbal or a written agreement. Such contracting clarifies the client's and the practitioner's expectations about how the OD process will take place. Unless there is mutual understanding and agreement about the process, there is considerable risk that someone's expectations will be unfulfilled.[13] That can lead to reduced commitment and support, to misplaced action, or to premature termination of the process.

The contracting step in OD generally addresses three key areas:[14] setting mutual expectations or what each party expects to gain from the OD process; the time and resources that will be devoted to it; and the ground rules for working together.

4-2a Mutual Expectations

This part of the contracting process focuses on the expectations of the client and the OD practitioner. The client states the services and outcomes to be provided by the OD practitioner and describes what the organization expects from the process and the consultant. Clients usually can describe the desired outcomes, such as lower costs or higher job satisfaction. Encouraging them to state their wants in the form of outcomes, working relationships, and personal accomplishments can facilitate the development of a good contract.[15]

The OD practitioner also should state what he or she expects to gain from the OD process. This can include opportunities to try new interventions, report the results to other potential clients, and receive appropriate compensation or recognition.

4-2b Time and Resources

To accomplish change, the organization and the OD practitioner must commit time and resources to the effort. Each must be clear about how much energy and how many resources will be dedicated to the change process. Failure to make explicit the necessary requirements of a change process can quickly ruin an OD effort. For example, a client may clearly state that the assignment involves diagnosing the causes of poor productivity in a work group. However, the client may expect the practitioner to complete the assignment without talking to the workers. Typically, clients want to know how much time will be necessary to complete the assignment, who needs to be involved, how much it will cost, and so on.

Peter Block has suggested that resources can be divided into two parts.[16] Essential requirements are things that are absolutely necessary if the change process is to be successful. From the practitioner's perspective, they can include access to key people or information, enough time to do the job, and commitment from certain stakeholder groups. The organization's essential requirements might include a speedy diagnosis or assurances that the project will be conducted at the lowest price. Being clear about the constraints on carrying out the assignment will facilitate the contracting process and improve the chances for success. Desirable requirements are those things that would be nice to have but are not absolutely necessary, such as access to special resources or written rather than verbal reports.

4-2c Ground Rules

The final part of the contracting process involves specifying how the client and the OD practitioner will work together. The parameters established may include such issues as confidentiality, if and how the OD practitioner will become involved in personal or interpersonal issues, how to terminate the relationship, and whether the practitioner is supposed to make expert recommendations or help the manager make decisions. For internal consultants, organizational politics make it especially important to clarify issues of how to handle sensitive information and how to deliver "bad news."[17] Such process issues are as important as the needed substantive changes. Failure to address the concerns may mean that the client or the practitioner has inappropriate assumptions about how the process will unfold.

Application 4.2 describes the contracting process for the evaluation project at Alegent Health. In this case, the contracting process was much more complicated than the entry process. What would you list as the strengths and weaknesses of this example?

4-3 Interpersonal Process Issues in Entering and Contracting

The previous sections on entering and contracting addressed the activities and content-oriented issues associated with beginning an OD project. In this final section, we discuss the interpersonal issues an OD practitioner must be aware of to produce a successful agreement. In most cases, the client's expectations, resources, and working relationship requirements will not fit perfectly with the OD practitioner's essential and desirable requirements. Negotiating the differences to improve the likelihood of success can be personally and interpersonally challenging.[18]

Entering and contracting are the first exchanges between a client and an OD practitioner. Establishing a healthy relationship at the outset makes it more likely that the client's desired outcomes will be achieved and that the OD practitioner will be able to improve the organization's capacity to manage change in the future. As shown in Figure 4.1, this initial stage is full of uncertainty and ambiguity. On the one hand, the client is likely to feel exposed, inadequate, or vulnerable. The organization's current effectiveness and the request for help may seem to the client like an admission that the organization is incapable of solving the problem or providing the leadership necessary to achieve a set of results. Moreover, clients are entering into a relationship where they may feel unable to control the activities of the OD practitioner. As a result, they feel vulnerable because of their dependency on the practitioner to provide assistance. Consciously or unconsciously, feelings of exposure, inadequacy, or vulnerability may lead clients to resist coming to closure on the contract. The OD practitioner must be alert to the signs of resistance, such as asking for extraordinary amounts of detail, and be able to address them skillfully.

application 4.2

CONTRACTING WITH ALEGENT HEALTH

Following the verbal approval of the CIO to begin the work, the researchers began working with the Right Track director and the consultants to formulate an agreement on how to proceed with the case study and assessment. The contracting process proceeded on two parallel paths. One path was the specification of the formal contract—who, what, how much, and why—and the second path was the project scheduling—who, when, and where.

FORMAL CONTRACTING PROCESS

The formal contracting process required the researchers to propose a purpose, cost estimate, and schedule for the case study. The researchers' initial proposal looked like this:

Work Stream	September	October	November	December	January
DA archives	• Collect DA materials • Create coding scheme	• Coding	• Write up archival data		
Interviews	• Finalize interview questions • Arrange interview schedule	• First round of interviews • Develop coding scheme	• Second round of interviews • Coding • Begin analysis of interviews		
Governance		• Meet with "study team"	• Feedback meeting	• Transfer learning to organization	• Article writing

The first work stream was the DA archives. The researchers had learned, through the consultants and the Right Track director, that the Right Track staff kept nearly verbatim transcripts and descriptions of each of the decision accelerator meetings that took place. Thus, the researchers proposed an analysis of those documents as an important work stream in the process. The second work stream, representing the bulk of the data collection, would be two rounds of interviews with executives, managers, and staff involved in the change process. Finally, the project would be governed by a study team that would work to frame project objectives, receive the feedback and assist in data interpretation, and help to transfer the learning back to the organization.

In addition to the timeline, the research proposal outlined the purpose of the project; the likely benefits to Alegent; the estimated costs for interviews, data analysis, and direct expenses; the support resources expected from AH, including the establishment of the study team; a statement about data confidentiality; and some suggested publication outlets. The Right Track director reviewed the document and asked for some additional detail. As described in the "Project Scheduling Process" section below, the start date had slipped to early November.

> Dear Right Track Director,
>
> We got a message from the consultants that you need a little extra "drill down detail" on the case study assessment project. We've taken a stab at such a document and it is attached.
>
> The document includes a one-page description of proposed dates, activities, and information to be gathered. Please let me know if this meets your needs.

The document also lists a set of potential questions for the initial round of interviews. There are two issues we could use your guidance on. First, what is the appropriate time frame for questions about strategy? Second, we've listed a couple of options for using a survey during the interview to collect information that would take too long to collect through just interview questions. Your counsel would be appreciated.

Thanks.

DATA COLLECTION PLAN—RIGHT TRACK ASSESSMENT PROJECT

Date	Activity	Data to Be Collected
Day 1 during the week of November 6th	• Meet with study team members to verify objectives and methods and refine them in order to incorporate sponsor concerns • Initial interviews with senior executives* to understand broad strategic context of organization and Right Track process	• Executive sense of business strategy, organization design, and Right Track impact on organization • Broad scoping of the post-RT implementation/refinement activities germane to planning remainder of interviews/data gathering • (Initial draft of questions attached)
Day 2 during the week of November 6th	• Initial interviews with senior executives* to understand broad strategic context of organization and Right Track process	• Executive sense of business strategy, organization design, and Right Track impact on organization • Broad scoping of the post-RT implementation/refinement activities germane to planning remainder of interviews/data gathering • (Initial draft of questions attached)
Prior to next visit	• Finalize detailed interview questions for different stakeholders • Validate questions and sampling approach with study team	• Work with Right Track office to schedule interviews
Potential dates: November 27, 28 December 4, 5 December 7, 8 December 13, 14	• Detailed interviews with RT participants, nonparticipants, service-line managers, and other related managers**	• Details about perceptions of RT process, service-line strategies, implementation processes, and implementation success
Ongoing	• Telephone interviews with key personnel unavailable during visits to Omaha	
January, 2007 (date to be mutually determined)	• Meeting with study team and/or extended stakeholder group to review and discuss implications of findings	
February	• Work with Alegent sponsors to determine a publication strategy	

*Initial interview sample includes as many of the following as possible: [List of executives and physicians.]

**Interview sample for detailed background information includes: [List of executives, managers, and other roles expected to be important.]

Shortly thereafter, the Right Track director sent the following email:

> Center for Effective Organization Researchers,
>
> Thanks for this added info. I, along with one of my staff members, have taken this along with all the documentation you have sent me to date and have attempted to create one cohesive document that can serve as the contract, statement of work, action plan, cost estimate, etc ... This document is attached for your review.
>
> I have also tried to answer some of the outstanding questions we have had in this document and have tried to further narrow the onsite dates and activities to include the interview list and the two questions you mentioned below. On your questions I think the two-year window is appropriate and I preferred option 2 which is incorporated in the attached.
>
> Please review this latest document and provide any feedback and/or changes you might have to us all. I will be out of town for a few days but my staff can keep the process moving through Legal and the CIO's office in my absence. I can also be reached via cell phone through the rest of the week as needed.
>
> Thanks.

The attachment referred to in the Right Track director's email was a standard, corporate consulting contract, with the researchers' proposal and revised schedule attached as the scope of work. Within the standard contract was a paragraph noting that all surveys, data, and documents created during the project would become the exclusive property of the Alegent Health corporation. The paragraph directly contradicted the confidentiality statement in the researchers' proposal. A number of conversations among the consultants, the researchers, and the different Alegent departments ensued. Eventually, a paragraph was written that was satisfactory to all parties and allowed for the researchers to use the data in their publications, but also gave Alegent the right to review, edit, and approve any articles, chapters, or descriptions of the organization change effort.

PROJECT SCHEDULING PROCESS

The project scheduling process—which was done in parallel with the formal contracting process described above—involved working with the Right Track office to pick dates, schedule interviews, communicate with interviewees, and set up other logistical requirements to begin the study. Following a few introductory emails, and based on the CIO's interest in beginning in October, the researchers sent the following message in early September:

> Hi Right Track Director,
>
> With the CIO's approval, we're ready to begin the Right Track assessment project. The consultants and the researchers are very excited about the effort. We need your help to set up the first couple of days in October, ideally on the 17th and 18th.
>
> On the 17th, we'd like to have a meeting of the "study team." This can be in the morning or afternoon, whichever best fits into the CIO's schedule.
>
> The balance of the 17th and all day on the 18th should be 60-minute interviews with the senior leadership of Alegent. Based on our discussions with the consultants and the CIO, the list for the initial round of interviews would be 10 to 12 of the following people:
>
> [List of top 15 executives and 7 key physicians]
>
> Thanks for your help.

In response, the Right Track director sent back the following email:

> Center for Effective Organizations Researchers,
>
> Welcome aboard and looking forward to working with you on this effort. Is there a specific reason you are targeting 10/17 & 18? I ask because there is a DA scheduled those two days that some of these folks are supposed to be in and that I will be helping to support. It is actually an external group, namely the Boy Scouts. Are you planning to come that week because of that or is this just a coincidence? My contact info is enclosed.
>
> Thanks.

Thus, there was some initial confusion on the start date of the project, and subsequent phone calls and emails clarified that starting the project in November would be a better fit for the Alegent organization. Some initial dates that fit in the researchers' schedule were not good for the AH executives and physicians, while dates that were good for AH didn't fit with the researchers' schedule.

Eventually, the beginning of the project was pushed back to early December, and the researchers flew to Omaha to begin the interviewing process. In the rush to schedule interviews, make travel arrangements, and finalize the interview questions and survey items, the meeting of the "study team" was overlooked.

FIGURE 4.1

Factors Affecting Client-Practitioner Dynamics

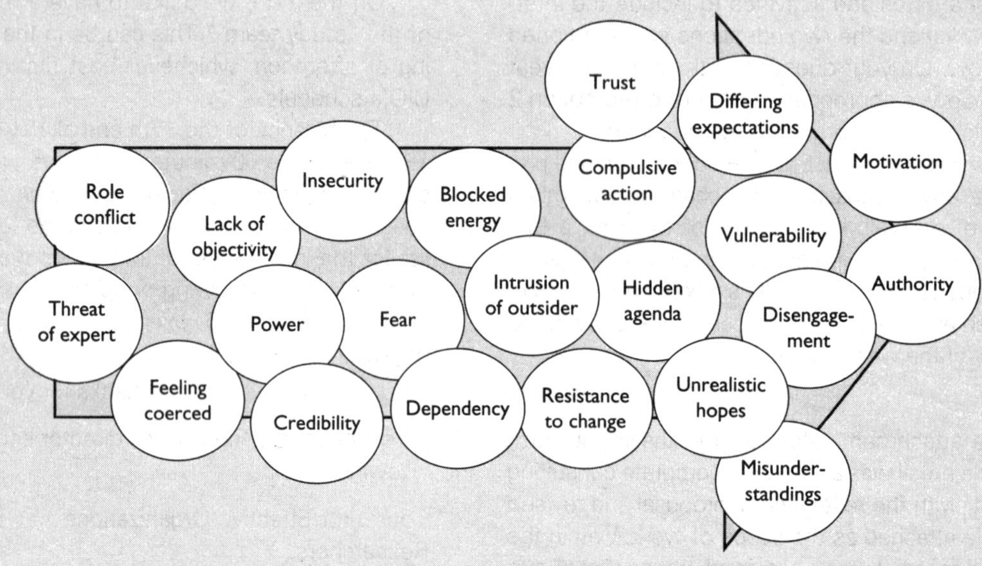

SOURCE: B. Jones and M. Brazzel (editors), *The NTL Handbook of Organization Development & Change*, Pfeiffer, 2006, Figure 10.2, pp. 177–91. Reproduced with permission of John Wiley & Sons Inc.

On the other hand, the OD practitioner may have feelings of empathy, unworthiness, and dependency. The practitioner may over-identify with the client's issues and want to be so helpful that he or she agrees to unreasonable deadlines or inadequate resources. The practitioner's desire to be seen as competent and worthy may lead to an agreement on a project for which the practitioner has few skills or experience. Finally, in response to reasonable client requests, the practitioner may challenge the client's motivation and become defensive. Schein noted that OD practitioners too often underestimate or ignore the power and impact of entry and contracting as an intervention in their own right.[19] With even the simplest request for help, there are a myriad of things the OD practitioner, entering a system for the first time, does not know. Establishing a relationship with a client must be approached carefully; the initial contacts and conversations must represent a model of how the OD process will be conducted. As a result, actually coming to agreement during the contracting phase can be difficult and intense. A number of complex emotional and psychological issues are in play, and OD practitioners must be mindful of their own as well as the client's perspectives. Attending to those issues as well as to the content of the contract will help increase the likelihood of success.

SUMMARY

Entering and contracting constitute the initial activities of the OD process. They set the parameters for the phases of planned change that follow: diagnosing, planning and implementing change, and evaluating and institutionalizing it. Organizational entry involves clarifying the organizational issue or presenting problem, determining the relevant client, and selecting an OD practitioner. Developing an OD contract focuses on making a good decision about whether to proceed and allows both the client and the OD practitioner to clarify expectations about how the change process will unfold. Contracting involves setting mutual expectations, negotiating time and resources, and developing ground rules for working together.

NOTES

1. M. Lacey, "Internal Consulting: Perspectives on the Process of Planned Change," *Journal of Organization Change Management* 8, no. 3 (1995): 75–84; J. Geirland and M. Maniker-Leiter, "Five Lessons for Internal Organization Development Consultants," *OD Practitioner* 27 (1995): 44–48; A. Freedman and R. Zackrison, *Finding Your Way in the Consulting Jungle* (San Francisco: Jossey-Bass/Pfeiffer, 2001).
2. P. Block, *Flawless Consulting: A Guide to Getting Your Expertise Used*, 3rd ed. (San Francisco: Jossey-Bass, 2011); C. Margerison, "Consulting Activities in Organizational Change," *Journal of Organizational Change Management* 1 (1988): 60–67; R. Harrison, "Choosing the Depth of Organizational Intervention," *Journal of Applied Behavioral Science* 6 (1970): 182–202.
3. S. Gallant and D. Rios, "Entry and Contracting Phase," in *The NTL Handbook of Organization Development and Change*, ed. B. Jones and M. Brazzel (San Francisco: Pfeiffer, 2006); M. Beer, *Organization Change and Development: A Systems View* (Santa Monica, CA: Goodyear, 1980); G. Lippitt and R. Lippitt, *The Consulting Process in Action*, 2nd ed. (San Diego: University Associates, 1986).
4. L. Greiner and F. Poulfelt, *Management Consulting Today and Tomorrow* (New York: Routledge, 2010); L. Greiner and R. Metzger, *Consulting to Management* (Englewood Cliffs, NJ: Prentice Hall, 1983), 251–58; Beer, *Organization Change and Development*, 81–83.
5. Block, *Flawless Consulting*.
6. D. Jamieson, "Pre-Launch," in *Practicing Organization Development*, 2nd ed., ed. W. Rothwell and R. Sullivan (San Francisco: Pfeiffer, 2005); J. Fordyce and R. Weil, *Managing WITH People*, 2nd ed. (Reading, MA: Addison-Wesley, 1979).
7. Beer, *Organization Change and Development*; Fordyce and Weil, *Managing WITH People*.
8. L. Forcella, "Marketing Competency and Consulting Competency for External OD Practitioners" (unpublished master's thesis, Pepperdine University, Malibu, CA, 2003).
9. G. Lippitt, "Criteria for Selecting, Evaluating, and Developing Consultants," *Training and Development Journal* 28 (August 1972): 10–15.
10. Greiner and Metzger, *Consulting to Management*.
11. Block, *Flawless Consulting*; Gallant and Rios, "Entry and Contracting Phase," in *The NTL Handbook of Organization Development and Change*; Beer, *Organization Change and Development*.
12. T. Cody, *Management Consulting: A Game Without Chips* (Fitzwilliam, NH: Kennedy and Kennedy, 1986), 108–16; H. Holtz, *How to Succeed as an Independent Consultant*, 2nd ed. (New York: John Wiley & Sons, 1988), 145–61.
13. G. Bellman, *The Consultant's Calling* (San Francisco: Jossey-Bass, 1990).

14. M. Weisbord, "The Organization Development Contract," *Organization Development Practitioner* 5 (1973): 1–4; M. Weisbord, "The Organization Contract Revisited," *Consultation* 4 (Winter 1985): 305–15; D. Nadler, *Feedback and Organization Development: Using Data-Based Methods* (Reading, MA: Addison-Wesley, 1977), 110–14.
15. Block, *Flawless Consulting.*
16. Ibid.
17. Lacey, "Internal Consulting."
18. S. Pellegrinelli, "Managing the Interplay and Tensions of Consulting Interventions. The Consultant-Client Relationship as Mediation and Reconciliation," *Journal of Management Development* 21 (2002): 343–65.
19. E. Schein, "Taking Culture Seriously in Organization Development: A New Role for OD" (working paper no. 4287-03, MIT Sloan School of Management, Cambridge, Mass, 2003).

5

Diagnosing

learning objectives

- Discuss the philosophy and purpose of diagnosis in organization development (OD).
- Explain the role of diagnostic models in OD, especially the open-systems model.
- Describe and apply organization-level diagnostic processes.
- Describe and apply group-level diagnostic processes.
- Describe and apply individual-level diagnostic processes.

Diagnosing is the second major phase in the general model of planned change described in Chapter 2 (Figure 2.2). It follows the entering and contracting stage (Chapter 4) and precedes the planning and implementation phase. When done well, diagnosis clearly points the organization and the organization development (OD) practitioner toward a set of appropriate intervention activities that will improve organization effectiveness.

Diagnosis is the process of understanding a system's current functioning. It involves collecting pertinent information about existing operations as well as analyzing those data and drawing conclusions about the reasons for current performance and the potential for change and improvement. Effective diagnosis provides the systematic knowledge of the organization needed to design appropriate interventions. Thus, OD interventions derive from diagnosis and include specific actions intended to improve organizational functioning. (Chapters 10–20 present the major interventions used in OD today.)

This and the next chapter describe different aspects of the diagnostic process. This chapter presents a general definition of diagnosis and discusses the need for diagnostic models in guiding the process. Diagnostic models derive from conceptions about how organizations function, and they tell OD practitioners what to look for in diagnosing organizations, groups, or jobs. They serve as a road map for discovering current functioning. A general, comprehensive diagnostic model is presented based on open-systems theory. We then describe and apply the model to diagnostic situations at the organization, group, and job levels. Chapter 6 completes the diagnostic phase by discussing processes of data collection, analysis, and feedback.

5-1 What Is Diagnosis?

Diagnosis is the process of understanding how the organization is currently functioning, and it provides the information necessary to design change interventions.[1] It generally follows from successful entry and contracting, which set the stage for successful diagnosis. Those processes help OD practitioners and client members jointly determine which organizational issues to focus on, how to collect and analyze data to understand them, and how to work together to develop action steps from the diagnosis. In another sense, diagnosis is happening all the time. Managers, organization members, and OD practitioners are always trying to understand the drivers of organization effectiveness as well as how and why changes are proceeding in a particular way.

Unfortunately, the term diagnosis can be misleading when applied to organizations. It suggests a model of organization change analogous to the medical model of diagnosis: An organization (patient) experiencing problems seeks help from an OD practitioner (doctor); the practitioner examines the organization, finds the causes of the problems, and prescribes a solution. Diagnosis in organization development, however, is much more collaborative than such a medical perspective implies and does not accept the implicit assumption that something is wrong with the organization.

First, the values and ethical beliefs that underlie OD suggest that both organization members and OD practitioners should be involved in discovering the determinants of current organization effectiveness. Similarly, both should be involved actively in developing appropriate interventions and implementing them. For example, a manager might seek an OD practitioner's help to reduce absenteeism in his or her department. The manager and an OD consultant jointly might decide to diagnose the cause of the problem by examining company absenteeism records and by interviewing selected employees about possible reasons for absenteeism. Alternatively, they might examine employee loyalty and discover the organizational elements that encourage people to stay. Analysis of those data could uncover determinants of absenteeism or loyalty in the department, thus helping the manager and the OD practitioner jointly to develop an appropriate intervention to address the issue.

Second, the medical model of diagnosis also implies that something is wrong with the patient and that one needs to uncover the cause of the illness. In those cases where organizations do have specific problems, diagnosis can be problem oriented, seeking reasons for the problems. On the other hand, as suggested by the absenteeism example above, the OD practitioner and the client may choose one of the newer views of organization change and frame the issue positively. Additionally, the client and the OD practitioner may be looking for ways to enhance the organization's existing functioning. Many managers involved with OD are not experiencing specific organizational problems. Here, diagnosis is development oriented. It assesses the current functioning of the organization to discover areas for future development. For example, a manager might be interested in using OD to improve a department that already seems to be functioning well. Diagnosis might include an overall assessment of both the task performance capabilities of the department and the impact of the department on its individual members. This process seeks to uncover specific areas for future development of the department's effectiveness.

In organization development, diagnosis is used more broadly than a medical definition would suggest. It is a collaborative process between organization members and the OD practitioner to collect pertinent information, analyze it, and draw conclusions for action planning and intervention. Diagnosis may be aimed at uncovering the causes of specific problems, focused on understanding effective processes, or directed at assessing the overall functioning of the organization or department to discover areas for future development. Diagnosis provides a systematic understanding of organizations so that appropriate interventions may be developed for solving problems and enhancing effectiveness.

5-2 The Need for Diagnostic Models

Entry and contracting processes can result in a need to understand either a whole system or some part, process, or feature of the organization. To diagnose an organization, OD practitioners and organization members need to have an idea about what information to collect and analyze. Choices about what to look for invariably depend on how organizations are conceived. Such conceptions can vary from intuitive hunches to scientific explanations of how organizations function. Conceptual frameworks that OD practitioners use to understand organizations are referred to as "diagnostic models." They describe the relationships among different features of the organization, as well as its environment and its effectiveness. As a result, diagnostic models point out what areas to examine and what questions to ask in assessing how an organization is functioning.

However, all models represent simplifications of reality and therefore emphasize certain organizational features as critical while ignoring other features. Focusing attention on particular features, often to the exclusion of others, can result in a biased diagnosis. For example, a diagnostic model that relates team effectiveness to the handling of interpersonal conflict would lead an OD practitioner to ask questions about relationships among members, decision-making processes, and conflict resolution methods. Although relevant, those questions ignore other group issues such as member skills and knowledge, the complexity of the tasks performed by the group, and task interdependencies. Thus, OD practitioners must choose diagnostic models and processes carefully to address the organization's presenting problems as well as to ensure comprehensiveness.

Potential diagnostic models are everywhere. Any collection of concepts and relationships that attempts to represent a system or explain its effectiveness can potentially qualify as a diagnostic model. Major sources of diagnostic models in OD are the thousands of articles and books that discuss, describe, and analyze how organizations function. They provide information about how and why certain organizational systems, processes, or functions are effective. The studies often concern a specific facet of organizational behavior, such as employee stress, leadership, motivation, problem solving, group dynamics, job design, and career development. They also can involve the larger organization and its context, including the environment, strategy, structure, and culture. Diagnostic models can be derived from that information by noting the dimensions or variables that are associated with an organization's effectiveness.

Another source of diagnostic models is OD practitioners' experience in organizations. So-called "field knowledge" offers a wealth of practical information about how organizations operate. Unfortunately, only a small part of that vast experience has been translated into diagnostic models that represent the professional judgments of people with years of experience in organizational diagnosis. The models generally link diagnosis with specific organizational processes, such as group problem solving, employee motivation, or communication between managers and employees. The models list specific questions for diagnosing such processes.

This chapter presents a general framework for diagnosing organizations rather than trying to cover the range of OD diagnostic models. The framework describes the systems perspective prevalent in OD today and integrates several of the more popular diagnostic models. The systems model provides a useful starting point for diagnosing organizations, groups, and individual jobs. (Chapters 10–20 present additional diagnostic models that are linked to specific OD interventions.)

5-3 Open-Systems Model

This section introduces systems theory, a set of concepts and relationships describing the properties and behaviors of things called systems—organizations, groups, and jobs, for example. Systems are viewed as unitary wholes composed of parts or subsystems; the system serves to integrate the parts into a functioning unit. For example, organization systems are composed of groups or departments, such as sales, operations, and finance. The organization serves to coordinate behaviors of its departments so that they function together in service of an organization goal or strategy. The general framework that underlies most of the diagnosing in OD is called the "open-systems model."

5-3a Organizations as Open Systems

As shown in Figure 5.1, the open-systems model recognizes that organizations exist in the context of a larger *environment* that affects how the organization performs, and, in turn, is affected by how the organization interacts with it. The model suggests that organizations acquire specific *inputs* from the environment and *transform* them using social and technical processes. The *outputs* of the transformation process are returned to the environment and information about the consequences of those outputs serve as *feedback* to the organization's functioning.

The open-systems model also suggests that organizations and their subsystems—groups and individual jobs—share a number of common features that explain how they are organized and how they function. For example, open systems display a hierarchical ordering. Each higher level of system is composed of lower-level systems: Systems at the level of society are comprised of organizations; organizations are comprised of groups; and groups are comprised of individual jobs. Although systems at different levels vary in many ways—in size and complexity, for example—they have a number of common characteristics by virtue of being open systems. The following open-systems properties are described below: environments; inputs, transformations, and outputs; boundaries; feedback; and alignment.

FIGURE 5.1

The Open-Systems Model

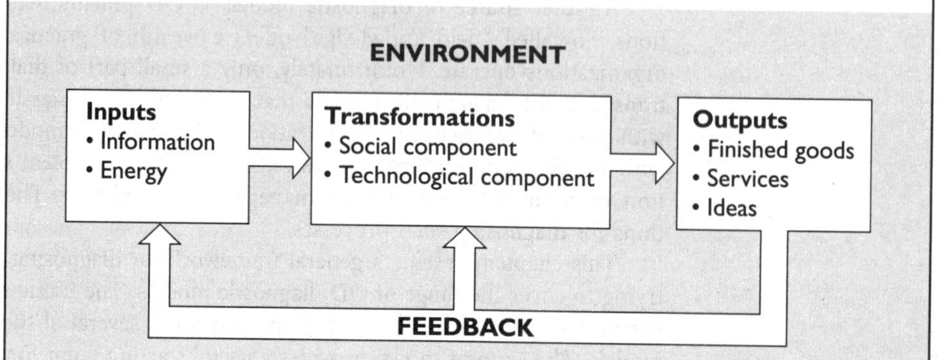

Environments Environments are everything outside of the system that can directly or indirectly affect its outputs. Open systems, such as organizations and groups, exchange information and resources with their environments. Because these external forces influence the system, organizations cannot completely control their own behavior. Organizations, for example, are affected by such environmental conditions as the availability of labor and human capital, raw material, customer demands, competition, and government regulations. Understanding how these external forces affect the organization can help to explain some of its internal behavior.

Inputs, Transformations, and Outputs Organizational systems are composed of three related properties: inputs, transformations, and outputs. Inputs consist of human capital or other resources, such as information, energy, and materials, coming into the system from the environment. For example, a manufacturing organization acquires raw materials from an outside supplier. Similarly, a hospital nursing unit acquires information concerning a patient's condition from the attending physician. In each case, the system (organization or nursing unit) obtains resources (raw materials or information) from its environment.

Transformations are the processes of converting inputs into outputs. In organizations, a production or operations function composed of both social and technological components generally carries out transformations. The social component consists of people and their work relationships, whereas the technological component involves tools, techniques, and methods of production or service delivery. Organizations have developed elaborate mechanisms for transforming incoming resources into goods and services. Banks, for example, transform deposits into mortgage loans and interest income. Schools attempt to transform students into more educated people. Transformation processes also can take place at the group and individual levels. For example, research and development departments can transform the latest scientific advances into new product ideas, and bank tellers can transform customer requests into valued services.

Outputs are the results of what is transformed by the system and sent to the environment. Thus, inputs that have been transformed represent outputs that leave the system. Group health insurance companies receive premiums and medical bills, transform them through record keeping, and export payments to hospitals and physicians.

Boundaries The idea of boundaries helps to distinguish between organizational systems and their environments. Boundaries—the borders or limits of the system—help to protect or buffer the organization's transformation process from external disruptions; they also assure that the right inputs enter the organization and the relevant outputs leave it. An organizational system's boundaries can vary in permeability, with some systems, such as a highly cohesive work team on the shop floor, being relatively closed to the environment and other systems, such as a field sales force, being open to external forces. Organizational boundaries are determined not only by physical location, but also can be defined for managerial, technical, or social purposes. For example, to facilitate managerial control, a department's boundaries could encompass all members reporting to a common administrator; to promote a smooth workflow, the department's boundaries might include suppliers, employees, and customers located along a common supply chain; or to foster cohesion among members, the department's boundaries could embrace those members sharing particular social connections and attitudes. Because organizational boundaries can serve different purposes, OD practitioners may need to determine early in the OD process if the client system's boundaries are appropriate for the intended purpose of the change effort. This may result in redefining or changing the client's boundaries before diagnosing begins. For example, the boundaries that identify a particular client system on an organization chart might be well suited for addressing leadership issues in that unit. However, the client system's boundaries might have to be enlarged to include other related departments if the intent of OD is to improve coordination among interdependent work groups.

Feedback As shown in Figure 5.1, feedback is information regarding the actual performance or the outputs of the system. Not all such information is feedback, however. Only information used to control the future functioning of the system is considered feedback. Feedback can be used to maintain the system in a steady state (for example, keeping an assembly line running at a certain speed) or to help the organization adapt to changing circumstances. McDonald's, for example, has strict feedback processes to ensure that a meal in one outlet is as similar as possible to a meal in any other outlet. On the other hand, a salesperson in the field may report that sales are not going well and may insist on some organizational change to improve sales. A market-research study may lead the marketing department to recommend a change to the organization's advertising campaign.

Alignment How well a system's different parts and elements align with each other partly determines its overall effectiveness. This alignment or fit concerns the relationships between the organization and its environment as well as among the components that comprise the design of the organization. Alignment represents the extent to which the features and operations of one component support the effectiveness of another component. Just as the teeth in the wheels of a watch must mesh perfectly for the watch to keep time, so do the parts of an organizational system need to mesh for it to be effective. Diagnosing environmental relationships and the interactions among the various components of an organizational system requires taking "a systemic perspective." This view suggests that diagnosing often involves the search for misalignments among the various parts of an organizational system.

5-3b Diagnosing Organizational Systems

When viewed as open systems, organizations can be diagnosed at three levels. The highest level is the overall organization and includes the company's strategy, structure, and processes. Large organization units, such as divisions, subsidiaries, or strategic business units, also can be diagnosed at that level. The next lowest level is the group or department, which includes group design and methods for structuring interactions among members, such as norms and work schedules. The lowest level is the individual position or job. This includes ways in which jobs are designed to elicit required task behaviors.

Diagnosis can occur at all three organizational levels, or it may be limited to issues occurring at a particular level. The key to effective diagnosis is knowing what to look for at each level as well as how the levels affect each other.[2] For example, diagnosing a work group requires knowledge of the variables important for group functioning and how the larger organization design affects the group. In fact, a basic understanding of organization-level issues is important in almost any diagnosis because they serve as critical inputs to understanding groups and jobs.

Figure 5.2 presents a comprehensive model for diagnosing these different organizational systems. For each level, it shows (1) the inputs that the system has to work with, (2) the key components for designing the system to create, and (3) the system's outputs. The relationships shown in Figure 5.2 illustrate how each organization level affects the lower levels.

FIGURE 5.2

Comprehensive Model for Diagnosing Organizational Systems

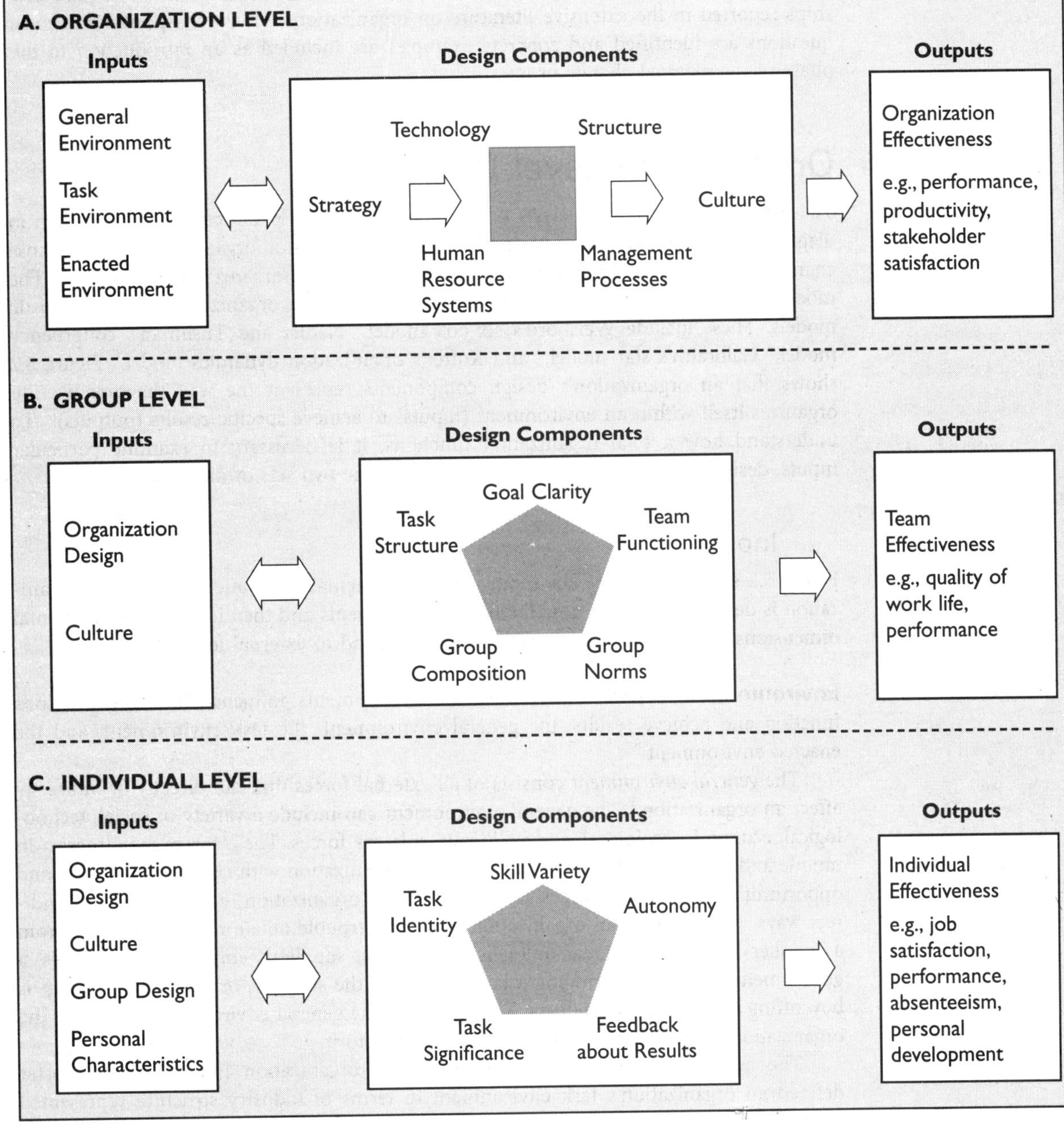

The environment is the key input to organization design dècisions. Organization design is an input to group design, which in turn serves as an input to job design. These cross-level relationships emphasize that organizational levels must fit with each other if the organization is to operate effectively. For example, organization structure must fit with and support group task design, which in turn must fit with individual-job design.

The following sections of this chapter address diagnosing at each of the three levels—organization, group, and individual job. General overviews of the dimensions (and their relationships) that need to be understood at each level are presented. It is beyond the scope of this chapter to describe in detail the many variables and relationships reported in the extensive literature on organizations. However, specific diagnostic questions are identified and concrete examples are included as an introduction to this phase of the planned change process.

5-4 Organization-Level Diagnosis

The organization level of analysis is the broadest systems perspective typically taken in diagnostic activities. (In some cases, OD is applied to a multiorganization system; those change processes are discussed in Chapter 20 on Transorganizational Change.) The model shown in Figure 5.2 is similar to other popular organization-level diagnostic models. These include Weisbord's six-box model,[3] Nadler and Tushman's congruency model,[4] Galbraith's star model,[5] and Kotter's organization dynamics model.[6] Figure 5.2 shows that an organization's design components represent the way the organization organizes itself within an environment (inputs) to achieve specific results (outputs).[7] To understand how a total organization functions, it is necessary to examine particular inputs, design components, and the alignment of the two sets of dimensions.

5-4a Inputs

Figure 5.2 shows that three key inputs or environmental types affect the way an organization is designed. We first describe these environments and then identify environmental dimensions that influence how organizations respond to external forces.

Environmental Types Three classes of environments influence how organizations function and achieve results: the general environment, the task environment, and the enacted environment.[8]

The *general environment* consists of all external forces that can directly or indirectly affect an organization.[9] The general environment can include a variety of social, technological, economic, ecological, and political/regulatory forces. These forces may interact in unique and unpredictable ways, presenting the organization with challenging threats and opportunities. Each of the forces also can affect the organization in both direct and indirect ways. For example, an organization may have trouble obtaining raw materials from a supplier because a national union is grieving the supplier's employment practices, a government regulator is bringing a lawsuit against the supplier, or a consumer group is boycotting the supplier's products. Thus, parts of the general environment can affect the organization without having any direct connection to it.

The *task environment* is another important organization input. Michael Porter defined an organization's task environment in terms of industry structure represented by five forces: supplier power, buyer power, threats of substitutes, threats of entry, and rivalry among competitors.[10] First, an organization must be sensitive to powerful suppliers who can increase prices (and therefore lower profits) or force the organization to pay more attention to the supplier's needs than to its own needs. For example, unions represent powerful suppliers of labor that can affect the costs of any organization within an industry. Second, a firm must respond to powerful buyers. Powerful retailers, such as Walmart and Costco, can force Procter & Gamble, Johnson & Johnson, or other suppliers to lower prices or deliver their products in particular ways. Third, an organization must be sensitive to the threat of new firms entering into competition. Profits in the restaurant business tend to be low because of the ease of starting a new restaurant. Fourth, a company must respond to the threat of new products or services that can replace existing offerings. Ice cream producers must carefully monitor their costs and prices because it is easy for a consumer to purchase frozen yogurt or other types of desserts instead. Finally, an organization must be sensitive to rivalry among existing competitors. If many organizations are competing for the same customers, then the organization must be responsive to product offerings, costs, and structures if it is to survive and prosper. Together, these five forces play an important role in determining an organization's success, whether it is a manufacturing or service firm, a nonprofit organization, or a government agency.

While the general environment and the task environment describe the objective pressures an organization faces, the organization must first recognize those forces. The *enacted environment* consists of organization members' perception and representation of the general and task environments. Environments must be perceived before they can influence decisions about how to respond to them.[11] Organization members must actively observe, register, and make sense of the environment before it can affect their decisions about what actions to take. Thus, only the enacted environment can affect which organizational responses are chosen. The general and task environments, however, influence whether those responses are successful or ineffective. For example, members may perceive customers as relatively satisfied with their products and may decide to make only token efforts at developing new products. If those perceptions are wrong and customers are dissatisfied with existing products, the meager product development efforts can have disastrous organizational consequences. As a result, an organization's enacted environment should accurately reflect its general and task environments if members' decisions and actions are to be effective.[12]

Environmental Dimensions In addition to understanding what inputs are at work, the environment can be understood in terms of its rate of change and complexity.[13] The *rate of change* in an organization's general environment or task environment can be characterized along a dynamic–static continuum. Dynamic environments change rapidly and unpredictably while static environments change more slowly and expectedly. The *complexity* of the environment refers to the number of different elements in the general and task environments that can significantly affect the organization. Some organizations, such as software development firms, face dynamic and complex environments. Not only do technologies, regulations, customers, and suppliers change rapidly, but also all of them are important to the firm's survival. On the other hand, other organizations, such as manufacturers of glass containers, face more stable and less complex environments.

A useful way to understand how the rate of change and complexity of environments influence organizations is to view environments as information flows that organizations need to process to discover how to relate to their environments.[14] The key dimension of the environment affecting information processing is *information uncertainty*, or the degree to which environmental information is ambiguous. Organizations seek to remove uncertainty from the environment so that they know how to transact with it. For example, organizations may try to discern customer needs through focus groups and surveys and attempt to understand competitor strategies through press releases, sales force behaviors, and knowledge of key personnel. The greater an organization environment's rate of change and complexity, the more information uncertainty the organization faces, and consequently, the more information the organization must process to learn about the environment.[15] Thus, dynamic and complex environments pose difficult information-processing problems for organizations. For example, global competition, technological change, and financial markets have created highly uncertain environments for many multinational firms and have severely strained their information-processing capacity.

5-4b Design Components

Figure 5.2 shows that an organization's design is composed of four components—technology, structure, management processes, and human resources systems. It is surrounded by an intermediate input—*strategy*—and an intermediate output—*culture*—that need to be considered along with the organization's design. Effective organizations align their strategy to environmental inputs and then fit the design components to each other to support the strategy and to jointly promote strategic behaviors. (Chapter 18 describes strategy and organization design interventions.)

A *strategy* represents the way an organization uses its resources (human, economic, or technical) to achieve its goals and to gain a competitive advantage in a particular environment.[16] Because strategy defines how an organization positions itself to compete in an environment, it is shown in Figure 5.2 as an intermediate input between the environment and the four design components. A complete statement of strategy includes the organization's mission, goals and objectives, strategic intent, and functional policies.[17] An organization's mission defines the long-term purpose of the organization, the range of products or services offered, the markets served, and the societal needs addressed. Goals and objectives include specific targets for achieving strategic success. They provide explicit direction, set organization priorities, provide guidelines for management decisions, and serve as the cornerstone for organizing activities and setting standards of achievement. "Strategic intent" is a succinct label or metaphor that describes how the organization intends to leverage three resource dimensions—breadth, aggressiveness, and differentiation—to achieve its goals and objectives. For example, in 2013, a turnaround strategic intent drove Nokia's goals of restoring financial confidence. That turnaround can be characterized by a narrower (as opposed to broader) focus on specific markets and products, increased aggressiveness demonstrated by its marketing expenditures and internal cost reductions, and improved differentiation through its alliance with Microsoft and its Windows 8 operating system. Finally, functional policies are the methods, procedures, rules, or administrative practices that guide decision making and convert strategic plans into actions. In the semiconductor business, for example, Intel had a policy of allocating about 30% of revenues to research and development to maintain its lead in microprocessors production.[18] (Chapters 18 and 19 describe strategy interventions.)

Technology is concerned with the way an organization converts inputs into products and services. It represents the core transformation process and includes production methods, workflow, and equipment. Two features of the technological core have been shown to influence other design components: technical interdependence and technical uncertainty.[19] Technical interdependence involves the extent to which the different parts of a technological system are related. High interdependence requires considerable coordination among tasks, such as might occur when departments must work together to bring out a new product. Technical uncertainty refers to the amount of information processing and decision making required during task performance. Generally, when tasks require high amounts of information processing and decision making, they are difficult to plan and routinize. The technology of car manufacturing is relatively certain and moderately interdependent. As a result, automobile manufacturers can specify in advance the behaviors workers should exhibit and how their work should be coordinated.

Structure is the basic organizing mode for (1) dividing the overall work of an organization into subunits that can assign tasks to groups or individuals and (2) coordinating these subunits for completion of the overall work.[20] Structure, therefore, needs to be closely aligned with the organization's technology. Organization structure can divide work by function (e.g., accounting, sales, or production), by product or service (e.g., Chevrolet, GMC, or Cadillac), by customer (e.g., large, medium, or small enterprise), or by some combination of both (e.g., a matrix composed of functional departments and product groupings). Structures can coordinate work across subunits through the managerial hierarchy or a variety of lateral mechanisms, such as plans and schedules, budgets, project managers, liaison positions, integrators, cross-departmental task forces, and matrix relationships. The amount of coordination required in a structure is a function of (1) the amount of uncertainty in the environment, (2) the degree to which subunits differ from each other, and (3) the amount of interdependence among subunits.[21] As uncertainty, subunit difference, and interdependence increase, more sophisticated coordinating devices are required.[22] (Chapter 12 discusses structural interventions.) *Management processes* are methods for processing information, making decisions, and controlling the operation of the organization. They help the organization to understand how well it is performing, to detect and control deviations from goals, to make relevant decisions, and to communicate the results. Closely related to structural coordination, management processes monitor organizational operations and feed data about work activities to managers and members so that they can better understand current performance, make relevant decisions, and coordinate work. Effective information, decision making, and control systems are linked closely to strategic objectives; provide accurate, understandable, and timely information; are accepted as legitimate by organization members; and produce benefits in excess of their cost.

Human resources systems include mechanisms for selecting, developing, appraising, and rewarding organization members. These influence the mix of skills, personal characteristics, and behaviors of organization members. An organization's strategy and technology provide important information about the skills and knowledge required if the organization is to be successful. Appraisal processes identify whether those skills and knowledge are being applied to the work, and reward systems complete the cycle by recognizing performance that contributes to goal achievement. Reward systems may be tied to measurement systems so that rewards are allocated based on measured results. (Chapters 15, 16, and 17 discuss specific human resources systems, such as rewards and career development.)

Organization *culture* represents the basic assumptions, values, and norms shared by organization members.[23] Those cultural elements are generally taken for granted and serve to guide members' perceptions, thoughts, and actions. For example, McDonald's culture emphasizes efficiency, speed, and consistency. It orients employees to company goals and suggests the kinds of behaviors necessary for success. In Figure 5.2, culture is shown as an intermediate output from the four design components because it represents both an outcome and a constraint. Culture initially derives from an organization founder's values and is reinforced and sustained through organization selection and socialization processes. It is also an outcome of the organization's history and environment as well as of prior choices made about the strategy, technology, structure, management processes, and human resources systems. Because organization culture is personally internalized, it can be difficult to change and can restrict an organization's ability to change its strategy and organization design components.[24] In that sense, culture can either hinder or facilitate organization change. In diagnosing organizations, the culture needs to be understood well enough to determine its alignment with the organization's strategy and the four design components. (Chapter 18 discusses culture change in more detail.)

5-4c Outputs

The outputs of organization design are measures of how well the design contributes to *organization effectiveness*. This can include three kinds of outcomes. First, organization performance refers to financial outcomes, such as sales, profits, return on investment (ROI), or earnings per share (EPS). For nonprofit and government agencies, performance often refers to the extent to which costs were lowered or budgets met. Second, productivity concerns internal measurements of efficiency, such as sales per employee, waste, error rates, quality, or units produced per hour. Third, stakeholder satisfaction reflects how well the organization has met the expectations of different groups having an interest in the organization. For example, customer loyalty can be measured in terms of market share or focus-group data; employee engagement can be measured in terms of an opinion survey; investor satisfaction can be measured in terms of stock price or analyst opinions; and environmental sustainability can be measured by the organization's carbon footprint.

5-4d Alignment

Diagnosing the effectiveness of an organization requires knowledge of the above elements to determine the alignment or fit among them.

1. **Does the organization's strategy fit with the inputs?** To be effective, an organization's strategy needs to be responsive to the general and task environments. They include external forces, threats, and opportunities that need to be considered in making strategic choices about mission, goals and objectives, strategic intent, and functional policies. The organization makes those choices based on members' perceptions of the environment (the enacted environment). Thus, the organization's information-processing and strategy-making capabilities must match the information uncertainty of the general and task environments if the organization's perceptions and strategic choices are to accurately reflect external realities. Environments that change rapidly and are complex are highly uncertain. In these situations, organizations need to constantly process information and monitor wide segments of their environments; their strategy-making process needs to be flexible resulting in strategic choices that can quickly be adapted to changing external conditions. (Chapter 19 describes dynamic strategy-making interventions.) Conversely, organizations can periodically assess selected parts of the environment and make strategic choices that are stable over moderate to long periods of time when the information uncertainty of their general and task environments is relatively low.
2. **Do the organization design components fit with each other to jointly support the strategy?** For example, if the organization's strategy is highly flexible and responsive to environmental change, then the design components must mutually support and reinforce agile and adaptable organizational behaviors. Successful firms in Silicon Valley, such as Apple and Oracle, tend to have flexible strategies that promote innovation and change. Their organization design components include leading-edge technologies that are complex and uncertain; flexible structures that emphasize agility and fast responses; management processes that provide rapid information and feedback and promote employee decision making; human resource policies that select, develop, and reward talented employees. These flexible and agile firms have organization cultures that value technical sophistication, member commitment, invention, and customer loyalty.

5-4e Analysis

Application 5.1 describes the Steinway organization and provides an opportunity to perform an organization-level analysis.[25] A useful starting point is to examine *outputs* and to ask about the organization's current effectiveness. Steinway has excellent market share in the high-quality segment of the grand piano market, a string of improving financial measures, and strong customer loyalty. However, the data on employee satisfaction are mixed; there are both long-tenured people and an indication that some workers are leaving for other jobs. Financial improvements appear modest when contrasted with industry averages. Understanding the underlying causes of these effectiveness issues begins with an assessment of the inputs and organization design and then proceeds to an evaluation of the alignments among the different parts.

In diagnosing the inputs, two questions are important.

1. **What is the company's general environment?** Steinway's external environment is only moderately uncertain and not very complex. Socially, Steinway is an important part of a country's artistic culture and the fine arts. It must be aware of fickle trends in music and display an appropriate sensitivity to them. Politically, the organization operates on a global basis and its distribution and sales networks must be attuned to different governmental and country requirements. The manufacturing plant in Hamburg, Germany, suggests an important political dependency that must be monitored. Technologically, Steinway appears reasonably concerned about the latest breakthroughs in piano design, materials, and construction. They are aware of alternative technologies, such as the assembly-line process at Yamaha, but prefer the classic methods they have always used. Ecologically, Steinway must be mindful. Their product requires lumber and they are very selective (some would say wasteful) about the choices, rejecting many pieces. It is likely that environmentalists would express concern over how Steinway uses this natural resource. Together, these environmental forces paint a relatively moderate level of uncertainty. Most of these issues are knowable and can be forecast with some confidence. In addition, while there are several environmental elements that need to be addressed, not all of them are vitally important. The environment is not very complex.
2. **What is the company's task environment?** Steinway's industry is moderately competitive and profit pressures can be mapped by looking at five key forces. First, the threat of entry is fairly low. There are some important barriers to cross if an organization wanted to get into the piano business. For example, Steinway, Yamaha, and Baldwin have very strong brands and dealer networks. Any new entrant would need to overcome these strong images to get people to buy their product. Second, the threat of substitute products is moderate. On the one hand, electronic keyboards have made important advances and represent an inexpensive alternative to grand and upright pianos. On the other hand, the sophisticated nature of many of the artists and audiences suggests that there are not many substitutes for a concert grand piano. Third, the bargaining power of suppliers, such as providers of labor and raw materials, is high. The labor union has effective control over the much-sought-after craft workers who manufacture and assemble grand pianos. Given the relatively difficult time that most high-end piano manufacturers have in holding onto these highly trained employees, the organization must expend considerable resources to retain them. Similarly, given the critical nature of wood to the final product, lumber suppliers can probably exert significant influence. Fourth, the bargaining power of buyers varies by segment. In the high-end segment, the number of buyers is relatively small and sophisticated, and the small number of high-quality

STEINWAY & SONS

application 5.1

Steinway & Sons, which turned 160 years old in April 2013, is generally regarded as the finest piano maker in the world. Founded in 1853 by the Steinway family, the firm was sold to CBS in 1972, taken private in 1985 by John and Robert Birmingham, and sold again in 1995 to Dana Messina and Kyle Kirkland, who took it public in 1996. Steinway & Sons is the piano division of the Steinway Musical Instruments Company that also owns Selmer Instruments and other manufacturers of band instruments (www.steinwaymusical.com). Piano sales in 2002 were $169 million, down 7.6% from the prior year and mirroring the general economic downturn. Since going public, Steinway's corporate revenues have grown a compounded 6–7% a year, while earnings per share have advanced, on average, a compounded 11%. The financial performance for the overall company in 2002 was slightly below industry averages.

The Steinway brand remains one of the company's most valuable assets. The company's president notes that despite only 2% of all keyboard unit sales in the United States, they have 25% of the sales dollars and 35% of the profits. Their market share in the high-end grand piano segment is consistently over 80%. For example, 98% of the piano soloists at 30 of the world's major symphony orchestras chose a Steinway grand during the 2000/2001 concert season. Over 1,300 of the world's top pianists, all of whom own Steinways and perform solely on Steinways, endorse the brand without financial compensation.

Workers at Steinway & Sons manufacturing plants in New York and Germany have been with the company for an average of 15 years, often over 20 or 30 years. Many of Steinway's employees are descendants of parents and grandparents who worked for the company.

THE ENVIRONMENT

The piano market is typically segmented into grand pianos and upright pianos, with the former being a smaller but higher-priced segment. In 1995, about 550,000 upright pianos and 50,000 grand pianos were sold. Piano customers can also be segmented into professional artists, amateur pianists, and institutions such as concert halls, universities, and music schools. The private (home) market accounts for about 90% of the upright piano sales and 80% of the grand piano sales, with the balance being sold to institutional customers. New markets in Asia represent important new growth opportunities.

The piano industry has experienced several important and dramatic changes for such a traditional product. Industry sales, for example, dropped 40% between 1980 and 1995. Whether the decline was the result of increased electronic keyboard sales, a real decline in the total market, or some temporary decline was a matter of debate in the industry. Since then, sales growth has tended to reflect the ups and downs of the global economy.

Competition in the piano industry has also changed. In the United States, several hundred piano makers at the turn of the century had consolidated to eight by 1992. The Baldwin Piano and Organ Company is Steinway's primary U.S. competitor. It offers a full line of pianos under the Baldwin and Wurlitzer brand names through a network of over 700 dealers. In addition to relatively inexpensive upright pianos produced in high-volume plants, Baldwin also makes handcrafted grand pianos that are well-respected and endorsed by such artists as Dave Brubeck and Stephen Sondheim, and by the Boston, Chicago, and Philadelphia orchestras. Annual sales are in the $100 million range; Baldwin was recently sold to the Gibson Guitar Company. The European story is similar. Only Bösendorfer of Austria and Fazioli of Italy remain as legitimate Steinway competitors.

Several Asian companies have emerged as important competitors. Yamaha, Kawai, Young Chang, and Samick collectively held about 35% of the vertical piano market and 80% of the grand piano market in terms of units and 75% of global sales in 1995. Yamaha is the world's largest piano manufacturer with sales of over $1 billion and a global market share of about 35%. Yamaha's strategy has been to produce consistent piano quality through continuous improvement. A separate handcrafted concert grand piano operation has also tried to use continuous improvement methods to create consistently high-quality instruments. More than any other high-quality piano manufacturer, Yamaha has been able to emulate and compete with Steinway.

THE STEINWAY ORGANIZATION

Steinway & Sons offers several different pianos, including two brands (Steinway and the less expensive Boston brand) and both upright and grand piano models. The company handcrafts its grand pianos in New York and Germany, and sells them through more than 200 independent dealers. About half of the dealers are in North and South America and approximately 85% of all Steinway pianos are sold through this network. The company also owns retail outlets in New York, New Jersey, London, Munich, Hamburg, and Berlin.

The dealer network is an important part of Steinway's strategy because of its role in the "concert bank" program. Once artists achieve a certain status, they are invited to become part of this elite group. The performer can go to any local dealer, try out different pianos, and pick the one they want to use at a performance for only the cost of bringing the piano to the concert hall. The concert bank contains over 300 pianos in more than 160 cities. In return for the service, Steinway is given exclusive use of the performer's name for publicity purposes.

Creating a Steinway concert grand piano is an art, an intricate and timeless operation (although alternate methods have been created and improved, the basic process hasn't changed much). It requires more than 12,000 mostly handcrafted parts and more than a little magic. The tone, touch, and sound of each instrument is unique, and 120 technical patents and innovations contribute to the Steinway sound. Two years are required to make a Steinway grand as opposed to a mass-produced piano that takes only about 20 days. There are three major steps in the production process: wood-drying (which takes about a year), parts-making, and piano-making.

Wood-drying operations convert moisture-rich lumber into usable raw material through air-drying and computer-controlled kilns. Time is a critical element in this process because slow and natural drying is necessary to ensure the best sound-producing qualities of the wood. Even after all the care of the drying process, the workers reject approximately 50% of the lumber.

After drying, the parts-making operations begin. The first of these operations involves bending of the piano rim (the curved side giving a grand piano its familiar shape). These rims are formed of multiple layers of specially selected maple that are manually forced into a unified shape, held in presses for several hours, and then seasoned for 10 weeks before being joined to other wooden parts. During this time, the sounding board (a specially tapered Alaska Sitka spruce panel placed inside the rim to amplify the sound) and many other case parts are made. The final critical operation with parts-making involves the fabrication of the 88 individual piano action sets that exist inside a piano. Piano "actions" are the intricate mechanical assemblies—made almost completely of wood and some felt, metal, and leather—that transmit finger pressure on the piano keys into the force that propels the hammers that strike the strings. The action is a particularly important part of a piano because this mechanical linkage gives Steinways their distinctive feel. In the action department, each operator is responsible for inspecting his or her own work, with all assembled actions further subject to 100% inspection.

Piano-making operations include "bellying," finishing, and tone regulating. The bellying process involves the precise and careful fitting of the soundboard, iron piano plate, and rim to each other. It requires workers to lean their stomachs against the rim of the piano to complete this task. Because of individual variations in material and the high degree of precision required, bellying takes considerable skill and requires several hours per piano. After the bellying operations, pianos are strung and moved to the finishing department. During finishing, actions and keyboards are individually fit to each instrument to accommodate differences in materials and tolerances to produce a working instrument. The final piano-making step involves tone regulating. Here, the pianos are "voiced" for Steinway sound. Unlike tuning, which involves the loosening and tightening of strings, voicing requires careful adjustments to the felt surrounding the hammers that strike the strings. This operation is extremely delicate and is performed by only a small handful of tone regulators. The tone regulators at Steinway are widely considered to be among the most skilled artisans in the factory. Their voicing of a concert grand can take as much as 20 to 30 hours. All tone regulators at Steinway have worked for the company in various other positions before reaching their present posts, and several have more than 20 years with the firm. Finally, after tone regulation, all pianos are polished, cleaned, and inspected one last time before packing and shipment.

Steinway produced more than 3,500 pianos in 2002 at its New York and Hamburg, Germany, plants. Almost 430 people work in the New York plant and all but about 100 of them work in production. They are represented by the United Furniture Worker's union. Seventy-five percent of the workers are paid on a straight-time basis; the others, primarily artisans, are paid on piece rates. Retaining workers has proved increasingly difficult as well-trained Steinway craftspeople are coveted by other manufacturers, and many of the workers could easily set up their own shop to repair or rebuild older Steinway pianos. Excess inventories due to weak sales both pre and post September 11 forced Steinway to adjust its production schedule; rather than lay off highly skilled workers needed to build its pianos, workers in the New York plant reported to work every other week.

pianos means that customers can put pressure on prices, although they are clearly willing and able to pay more for quality. In the middle and lower segments, the number of buyers is much larger and fragmented. It is unlikely that they could collectively exert influence over price. Finally, the rivalry among firms is severe. A number of well-known and well-funded domestic and international competitors exist. Almost all of them have adopted marketing and manufacturing tactics similar to Steinway's in the high-end segment, and they are competing for the same customers. The extensive resources available to Yamaha as a member of their *keiretsu*, for example, suggest that it is a strong and long-term competitor that will work hard to unseat Steinway from its position. Thus, powerful buyers and suppliers as well as keen competition make the piano industry only moderately attractive and represent the key sources of uncertainty that Steinway faces. Overall, Steinway executives' perceptions of the general and task environments seem to be accurate.

The following questions are important in assessing Steinway's strategy and organization design:

1. **What is the company's strategy?** Steinway's primary strategy is a sophisticated niche and differentiation strategy. It attempts to meet its financial and other objectives by offering a unique and high-quality product to sophisticated artists. However, its product line does blur the strategy's focus. With both Boston and Steinway brands and both upright and grand models, a question about Steinway's commitment to the niche strategy could be raised. No formal mission or goals are mentioned in the case, and this makes it somewhat difficult to judge the effectiveness of the strategy. Nevertheless, it seems reasonable to assume a clear intent to maintain its dominance in the high-end segment. However, with new owners in 1995, it is also reasonable to question whether goals of profitability or revenue growth, implying very different tactics, have been sorted out.
2. **What are the company's technology, structure, management processes, human resources systems, and culture?** First, Steinway's core technology is highly uncertain and moderately interdependent. The manufacturing process is craft-based and

dependent on the nature of the materials. Each piano is built and adjusted with the specific characteristics of the wood in mind. So much so that each piano has a different sound that is produced as a result of the manufacturing process. The technology is moderately interdependent because the major steps in the process are not closely linked in time. Making the "action sets" is independent of the "bellying" process, for example. Similarly, the key marketing program, the concert bank, is independent of manufacturing. Second, the corporate structure is divisional (pianos and band instruments), while the piano subsidiary appears to have a functional structure. The key functions are manufacturing, distribution, and sales. A procurement, finance, and human resources group is also reasonable to assume. Third, management processes are focused on the production system. There are specific mentions of inspections by both the worker and the organization. For example, 100% inspection (as opposed to statistical sampling) costs time and manpower and no doubt is seen as critical to quality. In addition, there must be some system of keeping track of work-in-progress, finished goods, and concert bank inventories. Fourth, the human resources system is highly developed. It includes a reward system that is both hourly and piece rate; a unionized employee relationship; worker retention programs; and global hiring, compensation, benefits, and training programs. Fifth, while there is little specific information, Steinway's culture can be inferred. The dominant focus on the high-end segment, the craft nature of the production process, the importance of the concert bank program, and the long history of family influence all point to a culture of quality, craftsmanship, and responsiveness. These values are manifest in the way the organization chooses its raw materials, the way it caters to its prized customers, the care in the production process, and the image it works to retain.

Now that the organization inputs, design components, and outputs have been assessed, it is time to ask the crucial question about how well they fit together. The first concern is the fit between the environmental inputs and the strategy. The moderate complexity and uncertainty in the general and task environments argue for a strategy that is flexible enough to address the few critical dependencies but formal enough to control a sophisticated production process. Steinway's focus on the high-end segment of the industry and the moderate breadth in its product line support this flexibility. It clearly intends to differentiate its product by serving the high-end segment with unique high-quality pianos. However, the market for higher-priced and more specialized concert grands is much smaller than the market for lower-priced uprights and limits the growth potential of sales unless Steinway wants to compete vigorously in the emerging Asian markets where the Asian companies have a proximity advantage. Steinway's lack of clear strategic goals in general and policies that support neither growth nor profitability also would make entry into new markets difficult. Steinway's flexible and responsive manufacturing process supports and defends its preeminence as the top grand piano maker in the world. It also mitigates the powerful buyer forces in this segment. Steinway's moderate product line breadth gives it some flexibility and efficiency as well. It can achieve some production efficiencies in the upright and medium-market grand piano segments, and its brand image helps in marketing these products. Steinway must be careful not to broaden its product line too much, however, as this could dilute its strategic focus on the high-end market. Overall, the alignment between Steinway's environment and its strategy appears sound.

The second concern is the alignment of the design components to support the strategy. There appears to be a good fit between Steinway's strategy and the organization design components. The differentiated strategic intent requires technologies, structures, and systems that focus on creating sophisticated and unique products, specialized marketing and distribution, and the concert bank program. The flexible structure, formal inspection systems, and responsive culture seem well suited for that purpose. Steinway's technology appears aligned with its structure. The production process is craft-based and deliberately not standardized. The functional structure promotes specialization and professionalization of skills and knowledge. Specific tasks that require flexibility and adaptability from the organization are given a wide berth. Although a divisional structure overlays Steinway's corporate activities, the piano division's structure is functional but not rigid and appears to be responsive to the craft and the artists it serves. In addition, the concert bank program is important for two reasons. First, it builds customer loyalty and ensures future demand. Second, it is a natural source of feedback on the instruments themselves, keeping the organization close to the artist's demands and emerging trends in sound preferences. The well-developed human resources system supports the responsive production and marketing functions as well as the global nature of the enterprise. Finally, Steinway's culture of quality and responsiveness promotes coordination among the production tasks, serves to socialize and develop people, and establishes methods for moving information throughout the organization. Clearly, any change effort at Steinway will have to acknowledge its long-established culture and design an intervention accordingly. The strong culture will either sabotage or facilitate change depending on how the change process aligns with the culture's values and norms.

Based on this diagnosis of the Steinway organization, at least two OD interventions seem relevant. First, in collaboration with the client, the OD practitioner could suggest increasing the clarity of Steinway's strategy. In this intervention, the practitioner would want to talk about formalizing—rather than changing—Steinway's strategy because the culture would likely resist strategy change. However, there are obvious advantages to be gained from a clearer sense of Steinway's future goals, its businesses, and the relationships among them. Second, Steinway could focus on better coordinating its structure, measurement systems, and human resources systems. The difficulty of retaining key production personnel warrants continuously improved retention systems as well as efforts to codify and retain key production knowledge in case workers do leave. This would apply to the marketing and distribution functions as well, since they control an important interface with the customer.

5-5 Group-Level Diagnosis

Work groups are prevalent in all types and sizes of organizations. They generally consist of a relatively small number of people working together on a shared task either face-to-face or virtually via electronic communication. Work groups can be relatively permanent and perform an ongoing function, or they can be temporary and exist only to perform a certain task or to make a specific decision. Figure 5.2 shows the inputs, design components, outputs, and relational fits for group-level diagnosis. The model is similar to other popular group-level diagnostic models such as Hackman and Morris's task group design model,[26] McCaskey's framework for analyzing groups,[27] and Ledford, Lawler, and Mohrman's participation group design model.[28]

5-5a Inputs

Organization design and *culture* are the major inputs to group design. They consist of the design components characterizing the larger organization within which the group is embedded—technology, structure, management processes, and human resources systems—and organization culture. Technology can determine the characteristics of the group's task; structural systems can specify the level of coordination required among groups. Management processes can determine how much information the group receives and how much decision making and self-control it can exercise. The human resources and measurement systems, such as performance appraisal and reward systems, play an important role in determining team functioning.[29] For example, individual-based, forced-ranking performance appraisal and reward systems tend to interfere with team functioning because members may be concerned with maximizing their individual performance to the detriment of team performance. Organization culture can influence the norms that groups develop to control member behavior. Collecting information about the group's organization design context can greatly improve the accuracy of diagnosis.

5-5b Design Components

Figure 5.2 shows that group designs have five major components: goal clarity, task structure, group composition, team functioning, and performance norms.

Goal clarity involves how well the group understands its objectives. In general, goals should be moderately challenging; there should be a method for measuring, monitoring, and feeding back information about goal achievement; and the goals should be clearly understood by all members.

Task structure is concerned with how the group's work is designed. Task structures can vary along two key dimensions: coordination of members' efforts and regulation of their task behaviors.[30] The coordination dimension involves the degree to which group tasks are structured to promote effective interaction among group members. Coordination is important in groups performing interdependent tasks, such as surgical teams and problem-solving groups. It is relatively unimportant, however, in groups composed of members who perform independent tasks, such as a group of call center specialists or salespeople. The regulation dimension involves the degree to which members can control their own task behaviors and be relatively free from external controls such as supervision, plans, and programs. Self-regulation generally occurs when members can decide on such issues as task assignments, work methods, production goals, and membership. (Chapter 14 discusses OD interventions for designing group task structure.)

Group composition concerns the membership of groups. Members can differ on a number of dimensions having relevance to group behavior. Demographic variables, such as age, education, experience, and skills and abilities can affect how people behave and relate to each other in groups. Demographics can determine whether the group is composed of people having task-relevant skills and knowledge, including interpersonal skills. People's internal needs and personal traits also can influence group behaviors. Individual differences in social needs can determine whether group membership is likely to be satisfying or stressful.[31]

Team functioning is the underlying basis of group life. It involves group processes having to do with how members relate to each other, which is important in work groups because the quality of relationships can affect task performance. In some groups, for example, interpersonal competition and conflict among members result in their providing little support and help for each other. Conversely, groups may become too concerned about sharing good feelings and spend too little time on task performance. In OD, considerable effort has been invested in helping work-group members develop healthy interpersonal relations, including an ability and a willingness to share feelings and perceptions about members' behaviors so that interpersonal problems and task difficulties can be worked through and resolved.[32] Group functioning, therefore, involves task-related activities, such as advocacy and inquiry; coordinating and evaluating activities; and the group-maintenance function, which is directed toward holding the group together as a cohesive team and includes encouraging, harmonizing, compromising, setting standards, and observing.[33] (Chapter 10 presents interpersonal and group process interventions.)

Performance norms are member beliefs about how the group should perform its task and what levels of performance are acceptable.[34] Norms derive from interactions among members and serve as guides to group behavior. Once members agree on performance norms, either implicitly or explicitly, then members routinely perform tasks according to those norms. For example, members of problem-solving groups often decide early in the life of the group that decisions will be made through voting; voting then becomes a routine part of group task behavior. (Chapter 10 discusses interventions aimed at helping groups to develop appropriate performance norms.)

5-5c Outputs

Team effectiveness has two dimensions: performance and quality of work life. Performance is measured in terms of the group's ability to control or reduce costs, increase productivity, or improve quality. It is a "hard" measure of effectiveness. In addition, effectiveness is indicated by group members' quality of work life. It concerns work satisfaction, team cohesion, and organizational commitment.

5-5d Alignment

Diagnosing team effectiveness requires assessment of how well the group elements described above fit with each other.

1. **Does the group design fit with the inputs?** As shown in Figure 5.2, the key inputs into group design are the larger organization's design and culture. Organization designs and cultures that are highly flexible and promote agile and adaptive organizational behaviors generally fit with work groups composed of highly skilled and experienced members performing highly interdependent tasks. Conversely, organization designs and cultures that are bureaucratic and support standardized behaviors generally align with work groups that have clear, quantitative goals and norms and structures that support routine task behaviors and interactions. Although there is little direct research on these fits, the underlying rationale is that congruence between organization design and culture and group design supports overall integration of task behaviors within the organization. When group designs are not compatible with organization designs and cultures, groups often conflict with the organization.[35] They may develop norms that run counter to organizational effectiveness, such as occurs in groups supportive of horseplay, goldbricking, and other counterproductive behaviors.
2. **Do the group design components fit with each other?** The nature of a group's task determines how the design components should align with each other. When the task is highly interdependent and requires coordination among group members, goal clarity, task structure, group composition, performance norms, and team functioning all need to promote effective task interaction among members. For example, task structure might physically locate related tasks together; group composition might include members with similar interpersonal skills and social needs; performance norms would support task-relevant interactions; and healthy interpersonal relationships would be developed. Conversely, when a group's task

is independent, the design components should promote individual task performance.[36] The other relevant task dimension concerns task uncertainty, which has to do with the amount of information processing and decision making that need to occur during task performance. When a work group has an uncertain task, then task structure, group composition, performance norms, and team functioning should promote self-regulation. Members should have the necessary freedom, information, and skills to assign members to appropriate tasks, to decide on production methods, and to set performance goals.[37] For example, when self-regulation is needed, task structure might be relatively flexible and allow the interchange of members across group tasks; composition might include members with multiple skills, interpersonal competencies, and social needs; performance norms would support complex problem solving; and efforts would be made to develop healthy interpersonal relations. On the other hand, when technology is relatively certain, group designs should promote standardization of behavior and groups should be externally controlled by supervisors, schedules, and plans.[38]

5-5e Analysis

Application 5.2 presents an example of applying group-level diagnosis to a top-management team engaged in problem solving.

Examination of the group's *outputs* shows that it is ineffective at problem solving. Members report a backlog of unresolved issues, poor use of meeting time, lack of follow-through and decision implementation, and a general dissatisfaction with the team meetings. Examining group inputs and design components and assessing the fit among them can uncover the causes of those group problems.

The key inputs into a work group are the design and culture of the larger organization. The Ortiv Glass Corporation's decentralized philosophy allows each plant to set up its own organization design. Freedom to innovate in the manufacturing plants is probably an outgrowth of the firm's OD activities and culture, which promote participation and innovation. Although little specific data are given about the new plant's organization design, tasks are structured into functional departments that must work together to produce plate glass. The team's problem-solving activities reflect this interdependence among the departments as coordination among team members is needed to resolve plantwide issues. The team meetings also seem to involve many issues that are complex and not easily solved, so there is probably uncertainty in the technology or work process. This ambiguity is typical in a new plant and makes it difficult for a problem-solving team to determine the causes of problems or to find acceptable solutions. Consequently, members of the top-management team must process considerable information during problem solving.

Diagnosis of the team's design components answers the following questions:

1. **How clear are the group's goals?** The team's goals seem relatively clear: they are to solve problems. There appears to be no clear agreement, however, on the specific problems to be addressed. As a result, members come late because they have "more pressing" problems needing attention.
2. **What is the group's task structure?** The team's task structure includes face-to-face interaction during the weekly meetings. This structure allows members from different functional departments to come together physically to share information and to solve problems mutually affecting them. It facilitates coordination of problem

TOP-MANAGEMENT TEAM AT ORTIV GLASS CORPORATION

application 5.2

The Ortiv Glass Corporation produces and markets plate glass for use primarily in the construction and automotive industries. The multiplant company has been involved in OD for several years and actively supports participative management practices and employee involvement programs. Ortiv's organization design is relatively flexible, and the manufacturing plants are given freedom and encouragement to develop their own organization designs and approaches to participative management. It recently put together a problem-solving group made up of the top-management team at its newest plant.

The team consisted of the plant manager and the managers of the five functional departments reporting to him: engineering (maintenance), administration, human resources, production, and quality control. In recruiting managers for the new plant, the company selected people with good technical skills and experience in their respective functions. It also chose people with some managerial experience and a desire to solve problems collaboratively, a hallmark of participative management. The team was relatively new, and members had been working together for only about five months.

The team met formally for two hours each week to share pertinent information and to deal with plantwide issues affecting all of the departments, such as safety procedures, interdepartmental relations, and personnel practices. Members described these meetings as informative but often chaotic in terms of decision making. The meetings typically started late as members straggled in at different times. The latecomers generally offered excuses about more pressing problems occurring elsewhere in the plant. Once started, the meetings were often interrupted by "urgent" phone messages for various members, including the plant manager, and in most cases, the recipient would leave the meeting hurriedly to respond to the call.

The group had problems arriving at clear decisions on particular issues. Discussions often rambled from topic to topic, and members tended to postpone the resolution of problems to future meetings. This led to a backlog of unresolved issues, and meetings often lasted far beyond the two-hour limit. When group decisions were made, members often reported problems in their implementation. Members typically failed to follow through on agreements, and there was often confusion about what had actually been agreed upon. Everyone expressed dissatisfaction with the team meetings and their results.

Relationships among team members were cordial yet somewhat strained, especially when the team was dealing with complex issues in which members had varying opinions and interests. Although the plant manager publicly stated that he wanted to hear all sides of the issues, he often interrupted the discussion or attempted to change the topic when members openly disagreed in their views of the problem. This interruption was typically followed by an awkward silence in the group. In many instances, when a solution to a pressing problem did not appear forthcoming, members either moved on to another issue or they informally voted on proposed options, letting majority rule decide the outcome. Members rarely discussed the need to move on or vote; rather, these behaviors emerged informally over time and became acceptable ways of dealing with difficult issues.

solving among the departments in the plant. The structure also seems to provide team members with the freedom necessary to regulate their task behaviors in the meetings. They can adjust their behaviors and interactions to suit the flow of the discussion and problem-solving process.

3. **What is the composition of the group?** The team is composed of the plant manager and the heads of the five functional departments. All members appear to have task-relevant skills and experience, both in their respective functions and in their managerial roles. They also seem to be interested in solving problems collaboratively. That shared interest suggests that members have job-related social needs and should feel relatively comfortable participating in group problem-solving situations.
4. **What are the group's performance norms?** Group norms cannot be observed directly but must be inferred from group behaviors. The norms involve member beliefs about how the group should perform its task, including acceptable levels of performance. A useful way to describe norms is to list specific behaviors that complete the sentences "A good group member should ..." and "It's okay to ...." Examination of the team's problem-solving behaviors suggests the following performance norms:
   - It's okay to come late to team meetings.
   - It's okay to interrupt meetings with phone messages.
   - It's okay to leave meetings to respond to phone messages.
   - It's okay to hold meetings longer than two hours.
   - A good group member should not openly disagree with others' views.
   - It's okay to vote on decisions.
   - A good group member should be cordial to other members.
   - It's okay to postpone solutions to immediate problems.
   - It's okay not to follow through on previous agreements.
5. **What is the nature of team functioning in the group?** The case strongly suggests that interpersonal relations are not healthy on the management team. Members do not seem to confront differences openly. Indeed, the plant manager purposely deflects issues when conflicts emerge. Members feel dissatisfied with the meetings but spend little time talking about those feelings. Relationships are strained, but members fail to examine the underlying causes.

The problems facing the team can now be explained by assessing how well the group design fits the inputs. The plant's organization design requires coordinated problem solving among functional departments. The newness of the plant and the uncertainty of the technology result in complex, plantwide issues that require considerable information processing to resolve. The weekly team meetings are an attempt to address and resolve these interdependent and complex problems. The plant's culture promotes participation in problem solving and the team meetings are a reflection of that involvement. Although it is too early to tell whether the team will succeed, there does not appear to be significant incongruity between the plant's organization design and culture and what the team is trying to do.

Next, alignment among the group design components is assessed to determine how well they fit together to promote interdependent and complex problem solving. The team's task structure and composition appear to fit the type of issues that the team is supposed to address. The face-to-face meetings help to coordinate problem solving among the department managers, and except for interpersonal and group problem-solving skills, members seem to have the necessary task-relevant expertise to address the plantwide problems. There appears, however, to be a conflict in the priority between the problems to be solved by the team and the problems faced by individual managers. Moreover, there seems to be a mismatch between the demands of the problem-solving task and the team's performance norms and interpersonal relations. Complex, interdependent problems require performance norms that support sharing of diverse and often conflicting kinds of information. The norms must encourage members to generate novel solutions and to assess the relevance of problem-solving strategies in light of new issues. Members need to address explicitly how they are using their knowledge and skills and how they are weighing and combining members' individual contributions. The team's performance norms fail to support complex problem solving; rather, they promote a problem-solving method that is often superficial, haphazard, and subject to external disruptions. Members' interpersonal relationships reinforce adherence to the ineffective norms. Members do not confront personal differences or dissatisfactions with the group process. They fail to examine the very norms contributing to their problems. In this case, diagnosis suggests the need for group interventions aimed at improving performance norms and developing healthy interpersonal relationships. (Chapter 10 describes interpersonal and group process interventions.)

5-6 Individual-Level Diagnosis

The final level of organizational diagnosis is the individual job or position. An organization consists of numerous groups; a group, in turn, is composed of several individual jobs. This section discusses the inputs, design components, and relational fits needed for diagnosing jobs. The model shown in Figure 5.2 is similar to other popular job diagnostic frameworks, such as Hackman and Oldham's job diagnostic survey and Herzberg's job enrichment model.[39]

5-6a Inputs

Four major inputs affect job design: organization design, culture, group design, and the personal characteristics of jobholders.

Organization design is concerned with the larger organization within which the individual job is the smallest unit. Organization design is a key part of the larger context surrounding jobs. An organization's technology, structure, management processes, and human resources systems can have a powerful impact on the way jobs are designed and on people's experiences in them. For example, company reward systems can orient employees to particular job behaviors and influence whether people see job performance as fairly rewarded. In general, technology characterized by relatively uncertain tasks is likely to support job designs allowing employees flexibility and discretion in performing tasks. Conversely, low-uncertainty tasks are likely to promote standardized job designs requiring routinized task behaviors.[40]

Culture represents the values and norms shared by organization members. Because they are generally taken for granted, they guide members' perceptions, thoughts, and actions. Culture can influence the kinds of work designs that organizations consider and that members perceive as legitimate. The more an organization culture promotes member participation and innovation, the more likely job designs will be highly flexible and involve member decision making.

Group design concerns the work group containing the individual job. Like organization design, group design is an essential part of the job context. Task structure, goal clarity, group composition, performance norms, and team functioning serve as inputs to job design. They typically have a more immediate impact on jobs than do the larger, organization design components. For example, group task structure can determine how individual jobs are grouped together—as in groups requiring coordination among jobs or in ones comprising collections of independent jobs. Group composition can influence the kinds of people who are available to fill jobs. Group performance norms can affect the kinds of job designs that are considered acceptable, including the level of jobholders' performances. Goal clarity helps members to prioritize work, and group functioning can affect how powerfully the group influences individual-job behaviors. When members maintain close relationships and the group is cohesive, group norms are more likely to be enforced and followed.[41]

Personal characteristics of individuals occupying jobs include age, education, experience, skills, and abilities. All of these can affect how people react to job designs and perform. Individual needs and expectations also can affect employee job responses. For example, individual differences in growth needs—the need for self-direction, learning, and personal accomplishment—can determine how much people are satisfied by jobs with high levels of skill variety, autonomy, and feedback about results.[42] Similarly, work motivation can be influenced by people's expectations that they can perform a job well and that good job performance will result in valued outcomes.[43]

5-6b Design Components

Figure 5.2 shows that individual jobs have five key dimensions: skill variety, task identity, task significance, autonomy, and feedback about results.[44]

Skill variety is the degree to which a job requires a range of activities and abilities to perform the work. Assembly-line jobs, for example, generally have limited skill variety because employees perform a small number of repetitive activities. On the other hand, most professional jobs include a great deal of skill variety because people engage in diverse activities and employ several different skills in performing their work.

Task identity measures the degree to which a job requires the completion of a relatively whole, identifiable piece of work. Skilled craftspeople, such as tool-and-die makers and carpenters, generally have jobs with high levels of task identity. They are able to see a job through from beginning to end. Assembly-line jobs involve only a limited piece of work and score low on task identity.

Task significance identifies the degree to which a job has a significant impact on other people's lives. Custodial jobs in a hospital are likely to have more task significance than similar jobs in a toy factory because hospital custodians are likely to see their jobs as affecting someone else's health and welfare.

Autonomy indicates the degree to which a job provides freedom and discretion in scheduling the work and determining work methods. Assembly-line jobs generally have little autonomy; the work pace is scheduled and people perform preprogrammed tasks. College teaching positions have more autonomy. Professors usually can determine how a course is taught, even though they may have limited say over class scheduling.

Feedback about results involves the degree to which a job provides employees with direct and clear information about the effectiveness of task performance. Assembly-line jobs often provide high levels of feedback about results, whereas college professors must often contend with indirect and ambiguous feedback about how they are performing in the classroom.

Those five job dimensions can be combined into an overall measure of job enrichment. Enriched jobs have high levels of skill variety, task identity, task significance, autonomy, and feedback about results. They provide opportunities for self-direction, learning, and personal accomplishment at work. Many people find enriched jobs internally motivating and satisfying. (Chapter 14 discusses job enrichment more fully.)

5-6c Outputs

Individual-job effectiveness includes two kinds of outputs, those related to how well the job is performed and those having to do with how people experience their job. Performance is measured in terms of the quantity, quality, time, and cost of producing a particular job outcome such as a product or service. Indicators of an individual's experience of the job include job satisfaction, absenteeism, and personal development.

5-6d Alignment

The diagnostic model in Figure 5.2 suggests that the job-design elements just described must align with each other to produce effective job outputs, such as high quality and quantity of individual performance, low absenteeism, and high job satisfaction.

1. **Does the job design fit with the inputs?** Job design should be congruent with the larger organization design, culture, and group design within which the job is embedded.[45] Both the organization and the group serve as powerful contexts for individual jobs or positions. They support and reinforce particular job designs. Highly flexible organization designs, participative cultures, and work groups that permit members to self-regulate their behavior align with enriched jobs. These organization and group inputs promote autonomy, flexibility, and innovation at the individual-job level. Conversely, bureaucratic organizations and cultures and groups relying on external controls are congruent with job designs scoring low on the five design components. These organization and group inputs reinforce standardized, routine jobs. As suggested earlier, congruence across different levels of organizational design promotes integration of the organization, group, and job levels. Whenever the levels do not fit each other, conflict is likely to emerge.

   Job design also should fit jobholders' personal characteristics if they are to perform effectively and derive satisfaction from work. Generally, enriched jobs fit people with strong growth needs.[46] These people derive satisfaction and accomplishment from performing jobs involving skill variety, autonomy, and feedback about results. Enriched jobs also fit people possessing moderate-to-high levels of task-relevant skills, abilities, and knowledge. Enriched jobs generally require complex information processing and decision making; people must have comparable skills and abilities to perform effectively. Jobs scoring low on the five job-design components generally fit people with rudimentary skills and abilities and with low growth needs. Simpler, more routinized jobs requiring limited skills and experience fit better with people who place a low value on opportunities for self-direction and learning. However, because people can develop growth needs and expertise through education, training, and experience, job design must be monitored and adjusted from time to time to fit jobholders' changing needs and enhanced knowledge and skills.
2. **Do the job-design components fit with each other?** The five job-design components must align with each other to provide a clear and consistent direction to how the job should be performed. Enriched job designs that score high on skill variety, task identity, task significance, autonomy, and feedback of results signal the need for flexibility, active engagement, and decision making to perform the job. Conversely, traditional job designs that score low on the design components indicate the need for routine and standardized job performances.

5-6e Analysis

Application 5.3 presents an example of individual-level diagnosing. As part of a larger cost-cutting initiative, the university is considering a change in the job design of a program administrator. The application provides information about the administrator's current job. Diagnosing the individual-level elements and the alignment among them can help to address whether or not the proposed change makes sense.

application 5.3

JOB DESIGN AT PEPPERDINE UNIVERSITY

The Graziadio School of Business and Management (GSBM) at Pepperdine University is one of the largest business schools in the country and has the third largest part-time MBA program. The school also provides graduate education aimed at different markets including an executive MBA (EMBA), a presidential/key executive MBA (PKE), and a specialized master's degree in organization development (MSOD). The MSOD program's curriculum consists of 10 four-unit classes over 22 months. Eight of the classes are conducted off-site during eight-day sessions at both domestic and international locations. The MSOD program office consists of a faculty director, a program administrator, and an administrative assistant. In response to cost-cutting initiatives at the university level, a proposal was being considered to alter the job designs of the MSOD program staff.

The MSOD Program Administrator, the focus of this application, was responsible for marketing and recruiting new students, managing the delivery logistics of the off-site program, managing the students' registration and financial relationships with the university, and maintaining relationships with the MSOD alumni. The marketing and recruiting duties involved working with the Program Director and the Director of Marketing for GSBM to develop marketing tactics including advertisements, brochures, conference marketing and support, and other market development activities. The recruiting process involved explaining the curriculum to prospective applicants, overseeing the application process for each applicant, working with the faculty to have qualified applicants interviewed, and managing the admissions process. This too had to be coordinated with the director and the administrative assistant. Once a class was admitted, the Program Administrator worked with various off-site facilities to establish room and board rates and catering services; managed the faculty's travel and teaching requirements; managed various intersession activities including the final exam; managed the students' enrollment and graduation processes including their interface with the university's registrar and finance office and the school's financial aid office; and coached students through the program. After graduation, the Program Administrator served as an unofficial placement service, hooking up eligible graduates with prospective employers who called looking for MSOD talent, provided career guidance, and worked with the program's alumni organization to sponsor conferences and other alumni activities.

Each of the above activities was somewhat programmable; they occurred at specific times of the year and could be scheduled. However, because each applicant, student, class, or graduate was somewhat unique, the specific tasks or actions could not always be specified in advance and there were a number of exceptions and unique situations that arose during each day, month, or year.

The MSOD Program Administrator has worked with the MSOD program for over 15 years and was a fixture in both the MSOD and the general OD communities. Year over year, the Program Administrator delivered qualified applicants in excess of available space although that task had become increasingly difficult in the face of tuition increases, increasingly restrictive corporate policies on tuition reimbursement, and the ups and downs of the economy. He handled both routine and nonroutine administrative details professionally, displays and reports a high level of job satisfaction and commitment to the program, and has been complimented formally and informally by the students in the program. In fact, each cohort develops its own relationship with the administrator and he becomes a de facto member of almost every class. The alumni considered the Program Administrator a key and integral part of the MSOD program. The set of duties described above has evolved considerably over the Program Administrator's tenure. In particular, he has become more involved and responsible for marketing and recruiting activities, and the alumni relations duties have been added in response to alumni requests that cannot be filled by traditional university departments.

In an effort to improve efficiencies, and in recognition of the MSOD Program Administrator's outstanding productivity, a proposal was being considered by GSBM administration to change the design of his job. The proposal suggested that the MSOD Program Administrator continue to perform all of the current duties of the position and, in addition, provide administrative support to two PKE classes from their initial class to graduation. The duties of administrating the PKE program would be similar in nature to the delivery aspects of the MSOD program, including working with faculty to support their teaching efforts, managing textbook ordering processes, and providing different facilities logistics activities. It would not include marketing, recruiting, and alumni development activities. The Program Administrator would receive additional compensation for the increased responsibilities and a title change. The new position would include joint supervision, with the EMBA program administrator, of an assistant program administrator, who would in turn manage a pool of administrative assistants. In addition, the new program administrator job would report to both the MSOD program director and the director of EMBA/PKE programs.

Diagnosis of individual-level inputs answers the following questions:

1. **What are the design and culture of the organization within which the individual job is embedded?** Although the example says little about the organization's design and culture, a number of inferences are possible. The business school's administration was attempting to reward the Program Administrator with a more enriched job. This suggests that the culture of the organization was supportive of employee involvement. However, the proposed change also was being considered as part of an efficiency drive. The school is large, hosting the third largest part-time MBA program in the United States. This helps to explain why a specialized master's degree in OD has been paired with two EMBA programs and differentiated from the large, part-time MBA program. To the extent that the MSOD program has different students or different marketing, delivery, and alumni relations processes than the EMBA programs, there may be difficult points of integration between the two types of programs.
2. **What is the design of the group containing the individual job?** Three individual jobs were grouped together according to the type of program. In this case, a faculty director, program administrator, and administrative assistant comprise the program office. The office is clearly dependent on other university and school functions, such as the registrar's office, financial aid, and the teaching faculty. Each of the three jobs has specific duties, but there is a clear sense that all three jobs are highly interdependent. The Program Administrator must coordinate with the faculty director on marketing, admissions, and curriculum decisions and with the administrative assistant on recruiting, program delivery, and routine administrative processes. Interaction during task performance is thus intense, and although partly scheduled, the work involves a high number of exceptions.
3. **What are the personal characteristics of the jobholder?** The application provides some clues about the Program Administrator's personal characteristics. First, he has stayed in the position for more than 15 years; this speaks to a loyalty or commitment to the OD program. Second, his job has evolved considerably and suggests at least a moderate amount of growth needs strength.

Diagnosing individual jobs involves the following design components:

1. **How much skill variety is included in the job?** The program administrator job involves a wide variety of tasks, including recruiting students; advising prospective and current students on career opportunities; making input into marketing strategies and tactics; handling routine and nonroutine administrative matters such as registration, grade changes, and graduation processes; supervision of an administrative assistant; coordination with other functions and departments within the school and university; traveling to several class sessions and handling logistics details; negotiating with a variety of resort properties on rooming costs, menus, meal costs, and room setup; working with alumni; and a variety of ancillary tasks.
2. **How much task identity does the job contain?** The program administrator job is "all of a piece." It involves following individuals through an entire process, as applicants, students, and alumni. It engages them as individuals, as professionals, and as members of a family or other community.
3. **How much task significance is involved in the job?** The program administrator job scores high on task significance. It includes bringing potential students into a well-respected program, working with them during their matriculation, advising them on their experiences in the program, and taking an important hand in their personal and professional development. The job is an integral part of a transformational educational process, which also contributes to its task significance.
4. **How much autonomy is included in the job?** There is a moderate-to-high amount of autonomy included in the program administrator job. It involves considerable discretionary decision making without much supervision or external controls.
5. **How much feedback about results does the job contain?** The program administrator job receives a lot of feedback. It comes from the faculty director on job performance; from program evaluations about service quality; and from students on the amount of support and guidance received.

Assessing individual-level *outputs* involves measures of job satisfaction, performance, absenteeism, and personal development. The Program Administrator performs his job well and seems to be very satisfied with it and the personal development opportunities it affords. Although there is no information on his level of absenteeism, it seems safe to assume that it is negligible.

These positive outcomes suggest that currently there is a good fit between the job design and the inputs and among the job-design components. When the job components are examined together, the program administrator job contains high levels of enrichment. Task variety, task identity, task significance, autonomy, and feedback about results are all high and mutually contribute to an enriched job experience. Over time, the level of enrichment appears to have increased because skill variety and autonomy have increased. The fit between the job design and the organization design is mixed, however. The business school's technology of recruiting and educating students and managing alumni is at least moderately, if not highly, uncertain. Tasks that are uncertain require considerable information processing and decision making. Enriched jobs fit such tasks, and the program administrator job has gradually evolved to fit the high levels of task uncertainty. Structurally, as a specialized master's degree that is different from an EMBA program, the MSOD program office, and the administrator job in particular, have evolved to be somewhat independent of the business school's other programs. There does not appear to be much sharing or coordination of tasks across these different MBA programs, despite obvious opportunities such as student registration, graduation, book ordering, and others. Either the MSOD program is sufficiently different from the

EMBA programs that it warrants such independence, or there are some important opportunities for improved efficiencies from the proposed change. There also seems to be only a partial fit between Graziadio School of Business and Management's culture and the administrator's job design. The culture includes values that promote both employee involvement and efficiency, with the former supporting an enriched job and the latter potentially impeding enrichment. The program administrator job and the other jobs in the program office closely interact with each other to form a team that is cohesive and mostly self-managed. This suggests a good fit between the enriched program administrator job and the design of the office team. Finally, the design of the program administrator job aligns well with the personal characteristics of the Program Administrator.

In the current context, the proposed change to the program administrator job needs to be considered very carefully. Will the change likely improve productivity, enhance quality, or increase job satisfaction? In general, the answer appears to be "no." For example, the proposed change argues that adding new responsibilities will increase task variety, task identity, and task significance. However, the additional administrative tasks of the EMBA classes do not increase the skill variety of the existing program administrator job. There are, in fact, no new skills required to administer those classes, and adding these responsibilities may actually unbalance the existing skill mix. That is, under the proposed new job, the program delivery component of the job will increase dramatically with respect to the other job components and more or less dominate the mix. This could actually result in decreased task variety.

The proposed change also contends that task significance will increase because the program administrator job will be able to affect the lives of both the MSOD program participants and the EMBA students. There is some merit to this idea, but it must be tempered with the chance that task identity might decrease. The task identity of the program administrator job, as described in the application, is high while the task identity for the EMBA program is relatively low. In the EMBA program, the program administrator job would interact with the students only during the program; it would have little involvement with them in the recruiting process and later as alumni. Thus, any increase in the number of people the proposed new job affects (task significance) is likely to be offset by the reduced involvement it would have with about half of these people (task identity).

Finally, the proposed change claims that the Program Administrator is being given more responsibility, which is true, but he will have less autonomy. The new program administrator job will report to two bosses: the MSOD program director and the EMBA/PKE director. Thus, the Program Administrator will probably have more, not less, supervision as the MSOD program director ensures that the MSOD program objectives are addressed, and the EMBA/PKE program director ensures that his or her program objectives are being addressed.

Examining the proposed changes in relation to the design components of the program administrator job suggests an intervention dilemma in this case. Should the business school's administration continue with the proposed change? The hoped-for efficiencies may or may not materialize. The Program Administrator's extensive skills and knowledge may in fact be applied to improve productivity. However, will it do so at a cost to his work satisfaction? Over time, such a solution may not be sustainable. If the change is implemented, OD interventions probably should be aimed at mitigating the negative effects on task identity, task significance, and autonomy. The MSOD director and the EMBA/PKE director need to work with the Program Administrator to set out clear expectations for his new job. They need to figure out methods to allow the Program

Administrator to perform certain tasks that he finds most rewarding. (Chapter 14 describes interventions for matching people, technology, and job design.) If the proposed changes are not implemented, alternative structural arrangements within the EMBA programs organization may need to be examined.

SUMMARY

This chapter presented information for diagnosing organizations, groups, and individual jobs. Diagnosis is a collaborative process, involving both organization members and OD practitioners in collecting pertinent data, analyzing them, and drawing conclusions for action planning and intervention. Diagnosis may be aimed at discovering the causes of specific problems, or it may be directed at assessing the organization or department to find areas for future development. Diagnosis provides the necessary practical understanding to devise interventions for solving problems and improving organization effectiveness.

Diagnosis is based on conceptual frameworks about how organizations function. Such diagnostic models serve as road maps by identifying areas to examine and questions to ask in determining how an organization or department is operating.

The model presented here views organizations as open systems. The organization serves to coordinate the behaviors of its departments. It is open to exchanges with the larger environment and is influenced by external forces. As open systems, organizations are hierarchically ordered; that is, they are composed of groups, which in turn are composed of individual jobs. Organizations also display five key open-systems properties: environments; inputs, transformations, and outputs; boundaries; feedback; and alignment.

A comprehensive model for diagnosing organizational systems was described and applied to three organizational levels—organization, group, and individual job. It consists of inputs; a set of design components; and a variety of outputs, such as performance, productivity, and stakeholder satisfaction. For each organizational level, diagnosing involves understanding each of the parts in the model and then assessing how the design components align with each other and with the inputs. Effective outputs are likely to result from good alignment.

NOTES

1. C. Lundberg, "Organization Development Diagnosis," in *Handbook of Organization Development*, ed. T. Cummings (Los Angeles: Sage Publications, 2008), 137–50; D. Nadler, "Role of Models in Organizational Assessment," in *Organizational Assessment*, ed. E. Lawler III, D. Nadler, and C. Cammann (New York: John Wiley & Sons, 1980), 119–31; R. Burton, B. Obel, H. Starling, M. Sondergaard, and D. Dojbak, *Strategic Organizational Diagnosis and Design: Developing Theory for Application*, 2nd ed. (Dordrecht, The Netherlands: Kluwer Academic Publishers, 2001).
2. M. Poole and A. Van de Ven, eds., *Handbook of Organizational Change and Innovation* (New York: Cambridge University Press, 2004); D. Coghlan, "Organization Development through Interlevel Dynamics," *International Journal of Organizational Analysis* 2 (1994): 264–79.
3. M. Weisbord, "Organizational Diagnosis: Six Places to Look for Trouble with or without a Theory," *Group and Organizational Studies* 1 (1976): 430–37.
4. D. Nadler and M. Tushman, *Competing by Design: The Power of Organizational Architecture* (New York: Oxford University Press, 1997).
5. J. Galbraith, *Designing Organizations* (San Francisco: Jossey-Bass, 2002).
6. J. Kotter, *Organizational Dynamics: Diagnosis and Intervention* (Reading, MA: Addison-Wesley, 1978).
7. M. Tushman and E. Romanelli, "Organization Evolution: A Metamorphosis Model of Convergence and Reorientation," in *Research in Organizational Behavior*, vol. 7, ed. L. Cummings and B. Staw (Greenwich, CT: JAI Press, 1985); C. Worley, D. Hitchin, and W. Ross, *Integrated*

Strategic Change: How OD Builds Competitive Advantage (Reading, MA: Addison-Wesley, 1996).

8. R. Daft, *Organization Theory and Design*, 11th ed. (Cincinnati, OH: South-Western College Publishing, 2013); R. Miles, *Macro Organization Behavior* (Santa Monica, CA: Goodyear, 1980).
9. M. Porter, *Competitive Strategy* (New York: Free Press, 1980).
10. Ibid.
11. K. Weick, *The Social Psychology of Organizing*, 2nd ed. (Reading, MA: Addison-Wesley, 1979).
12. J. Pfeffer and G. Salancik, *The External Control of Organizations: A Resource Dependence Perspective* (New York: Harper & Row, 1978); H. Aldrich, *Organizations and Environments* (New York: Prentice Hall, 1979); L. Hrebiniak and W. Joyce, "Organizational Adaptation: Strategic Choice and Environmental Determinism," *Administrative Science Quarterly* 30 (1985): 336–49.
13. F. Emery and E. Trist, "The Causal Texture of Organizational Environments," *Human Relations* 18 (1965): 21–32; H. Aldrich, *Organizations and Environments* (Englewood Cliffs, NJ: Prentice Hall, 1979).
14. J. Galbraith, *Competing with Flexible Lateral Organizations*, 2nd ed. (Reading, MA: Addison-Wesley, 1994); P. Evans and T. Wurster, "Strategy and the New Economics of Information," *Harvard Business Review* 75 (1997): 70–83.
15. M. Tushman and D. Nadler, "Information Processing as an Integrating Concept in Organizational Design," *Academy of Management Review* 3 (1978): 613–24.
16. M. Porter, *Competitive Advantage* (New York: Free Press, 1985); M. Hitt, R. D. Ireland, and R. Hoskisson, *Strategic Management* (Mason, OH: South-Western College Publishing, 2006).
17. C. Hofer and D. Schendel, *Strategy Formulation: Analytical Concepts* (St. Paul, MN: West Publishing, 1978).
18. E. Lawler and C. Worley, *Built to Change* (San Francisco: Jossey-Bass, 2006).
19. J. Thompson, *Organizations in Action* (New York: McGraw-Hill, 1967); D. Gerwin, "Relationships between Structure and Technology," in *Handbook of Organizational Design*, vol. 2, ed. P. Nystrom and W. Starbuck (Oxford: Oxford University Press, 1981), 3–38.
20. Galbraith, *Designing Organizations*; Daft, *Organization Theory and Design*.
21. P. Lawrence and J. Lorsch, *Organization and Environment* (Cambridge, MA: Harvard University Press, 1967).
22. Galbraith, *Competing with Flexible Lateral Organizations*.
23. J. Martin, *Organizational Culture: Mapping the Terrain* (Newbury Park, CA: Sage Publishing, 2002); E. Schein, *Organizational Culture and Leadership*, 2nd ed. (San Francisco: Jossey-Bass, 1990).
24. E. Abrahamson and C. Fombrun, "Macrocultures: Determinants and Consequences," *Academy of Management Review* 19 (1994): 728–56.
25. Adapted from material in R. Brammer, "Sizing Up Small Caps: Stay Tuned," *Barrons* (April 19, 2002); A. Serwer, "Happy Birthday, Steinway," *Fortune*, March 17, 2003, 96–98; D. Garvin, "Steinway & Sons," *Harvard Business School Case 628-025* (Boston: Harvard Business School, 1981); J. Gourville and J. Lassiter, *Steinway & Sons: Buying a Legend* (Boston: Harvard Business School, 1999).
26. J. Hackman and C. Morris, "Group Tasks, Group Interaction Process, and Group Performance Effectiveness: A Review and Proposed Integration," in *Advances in Experimental Social Psychology*, vol. 9, ed. L. Berkowitz (New York: Academic Press, 1975), 45–99; J. Hackman, ed., *Groups That Work (and Those That Don't): Creating Conditions for Effective Teamwork* (San Francisco: Jossey-Bass, 1989).
27. M. McCaskey, "Framework for Analyzing Work Groups," *Harvard Business School Case 9-480-009* (Boston: Harvard Business School, 1997).
28. G. Ledford, E. Lawler, and S. Mohrman, "The Quality Circle and Its Variations," in *Productivity in Organizations: New Perspectives from Industrial and Organizational Psychology*, ed. J. Campbell, R. Campbell, and Associates (San Francisco: Jossey-Bass, 1988), 255–94.
29. D. Ancona and H. Bresman, *X-teams: How to Build Teams that Lead, Innovate, and Succeed* (Boston: Harvard Business School Press, 2007); S. Mohrman, S. Cohen, and A. Mohrman, *Designing Team-Based Organizations* (San Francisco: Jossey-Bass, 1995).
30. G. Susman, *Autonomy at Work* (New York: Praeger, 1976); T. Cummings, "Self-Regulating Work Groups: A Socio-Technical Synthesis," *Academy of Management Review* 3 (1978): 625–34; J. Slocum and H. Sims, "A Typology for Integrating Technology, Organization, and Job Design," *Human Relations* 33 (1980): 193–212.
31. J. R. Hackman and G. Oldham, *Work Redesign* (Reading, MA: Addison-Wesley, 1980).
32. E. Schein, *Process Consultation*, vols. 1–2 (Reading, MA: Addison-Wesley, 1987).
33. W. Dyer, *Team Building*, 3rd ed. (Reading, MA: Addison-Wesley, 1994).
34. Hackman and Morris, "Group Tasks"; T. Cummings, "Designing Effective Work Groups," in *Handbook of Organizational Design*, vol. 2, ed. P. Nystrom and W. Starbuck (Oxford: Oxford University Press, 1981), 250–71.
35. Cummings, "Designing Effective Work Groups."
36. Susman, *Autonomy at Work*; Cummings, "Self-Regulating Work Groups"; Slocum and Sims, "Typology."
37. Cummings, "Self-Regulating Work Groups"; Slocum and Sims, "Typology."

38. Ibid.

39. Hackman and Oldham, *Work Redesign*; F. Herzberg, "One More Time: How Do You Motivate Employees?" *Harvard Business Review* 46 (1968): 53–62.

40. J. Pierce, R. Dunham, and R. Blackburn, "Social Systems Structure, Job Design, and Growth Need Strength: A Test of a Congruence Model," *Academy of Management Journal* 22 (1979): 223–40.

41. Susman, *Autonomy at Work*; Cummings, "Self-Regulating Work Groups"; Slocum and Sims, "Typology."

42. Hackman and Oldham, *Work Redesign*; Pierce, Dunham, and Blackburn, "Social Systems Structure."

43. E. Lawler III, *Motivation in Work Organizations* (Monterey, CA: Brooks/Cole, 1973).

44. Hackman and Oldham, *Work Redesign*.

45. Pierce, Dunham, and Blackburn, "Social Systems Structure"; Susman, *Autonomy at Work*; Cummings, "Self-Regulating Work Groups"; Slocum and Sims, "Typology."

46. Hackman and Oldham, *Work Redesign*; Pierce, Dunham, and Blackburn, "Social Systems Structure."

6

Collecting, Analyzing, and Feeding Back Diagnostic Information

learning objectives

- Understand the importance of the diagnostic relationship in the organization development (OD) process.
- Describe the methods for collecting diagnostic data.
- Understand the primary techniques used to analyze diagnostic data.
- Outline the process issues associated with data feedback.
- Describe and evaluate the survey feedback intervention.

Organization development is vitally dependent on collecting diagnostic information that will be shared with the client in jointly assessing how the organization is functioning and determining the best change intervention. The quality of the information gathered and the effectiveness of the feedback process, therefore, are critical parts of the OD process. In this chapter, we discuss several key issues associated with collecting, analyzing, and feeding back diagnostic data on how an organization or department functions.

Data collection involves gathering information on specific organizational features, such as the inputs, design components, and outputs presented in Chapter 5. The process begins by establishing an effective relationship between the organization development (OD) practitioner and those from whom data will be collected and then choosing data collection techniques. Four methods can be used to collect data: questionnaires, interviews, observations, and unobtrusive measures. Data analysis organizes and examines the information to make clear the underlying causes of an organizational problem or to identify areas for future development. Data feedback presents diagnostic information to organizational members so they can understand it and draw action implications from it. Effective feedback involves attention to both the content and the process of data feedback. A popular technique for feeding back questionnaire data is called *survey feedback*. Its central role in many large-scale OD efforts warrants a special look. The overall process of data collection, analysis, and feedback is shown in Figure 6.1.

6-1 The Diagnostic Relationship

In most cases of planned change, OD practitioners play an active role in gathering data from organization members for diagnostic purposes. For example, they might interview members of a work team about causes of conflict among members; they might survey

FIGURE 6.1

The Cycle of Data Collection and Feedback

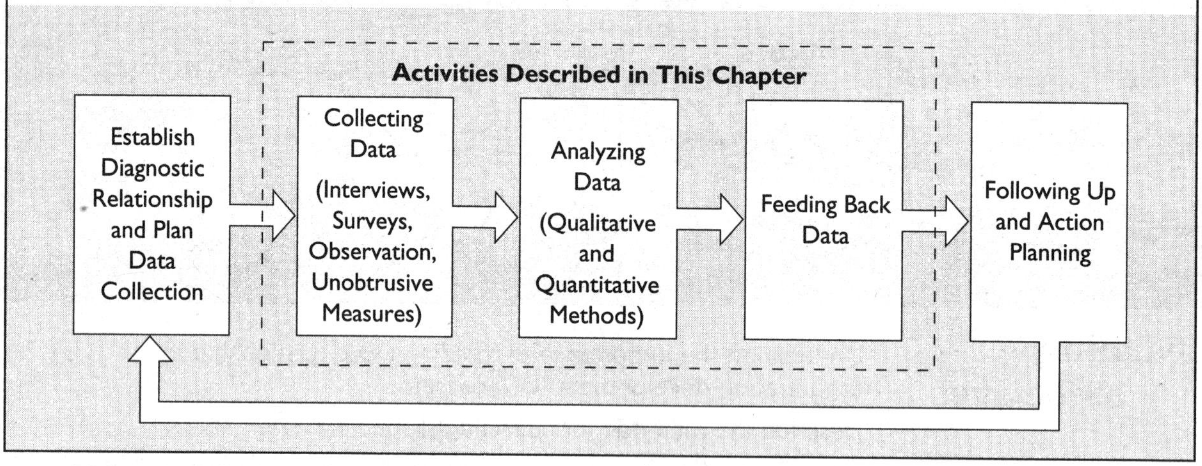

SOURCE: Figure adapted from D. Nadler, *Feedback and Organization Development,* 1977, Pearson Education, Upper Saddle River, NJ.

employees at a large industrial plant about factors contributing to poor product quality. Before collecting diagnostic information, practitioners need to establish a relationship with those who will provide and subsequently use it. Because the nature of that relationship affects the quality and usefulness of the data collected, it is vital that OD practitioners clarify for organization members who they are, why the data are being collected, what the data gathering will involve, and how the data will be used.[1] That information can help allay people's natural fears that the data might be used against them and gain members' participation and support, which are essential to developing successful interventions.

Establishing the diagnostic relationship between the OD practitioner and relevant organization members is similar to forming a contract. It is meant to clarify expectations and to specify the conditions of the relationship. In those cases where members have been directly involved in the entering and contracting process described in Chapter 4, the diagnostic contract will typically be part of the initial contracting step. In situations where data will be collected from members who have not been directly involved in entering and contracting, however, OD practitioners will need to establish a diagnostic contract as a prelude to diagnosis. The answers to the following questions provide the substance of the diagnostic contract:[2]

1. **Who am I?** The answer to this question introduces the OD practitioner to the organization, particularly to those members who do not know the consultant and yet will be asked to provide diagnostic data.
2. **Why am I here, and what am I doing?** These answers are aimed at defining the goals of the diagnosis and data-gathering activities. The consultant needs to present the objectives of the action research process and to describe how the diagnostic activities fit into the overall developmental strategy.
3. **Who do I work for?** This answer clarifies who has hired the OD practitioner, whether it be a manager, a group of managers, or a group of employees and managers. One way to build trust and support for the diagnosis is to have those people directly involved in establishing the diagnostic contract. Thus, for example, if the

consultant works for a joint labor–management committee, representatives from both sides of that group could help the consultant build the proper relationship with those from whom data will be gathered.

4. **What do I want from you, and why?** Here, the OD practitioner needs to specify how much time and effort people will need to give to provide valid data and subsequently to work with these data in solving problems. Because some people may not want to participate in the diagnosis, it is important to specify that such involvement is voluntary.
5. **How will I protect your confidentiality?** This answer addresses member concerns about who will see their responses and in what form. This is especially critical when employees are asked to provide information about their attitudes or perceptions. Either OD practitioners can ensure confidentiality or state that full participation in the change process requires open information sharing. In the first case, employees are frequently concerned about privacy and the possibility of being punished for their responses. To alleviate concern and to increase the likelihood of obtaining honest responses, the consultant may need to assure employees of the confidentiality of their information, perhaps through explicit guarantees of response anonymity. In the second case, full involvement of the participants in their own diagnosis may be a vital ingredient of the change process. If sensitive issues arise, assurances of confidentiality can coopt the OD practitioner and thwart meaningful diagnosis. The consultant is bound to keep confidential the issues that are most critical for the group or organization to understand.[3] OD practitioners must think carefully about how they want to handle confidentiality issues.
6. **Who will have access to the data?** Respondents typically want to know whether they will have access to their data and who else in the organization will have similar access. The OD practitioner needs to clarify access issues and, in most cases, should agree to provide respondents with their own results. Indeed, the collaborative nature of diagnosis means that organization members will work with their own data to discover causes of problems and to devise relevant interventions.
7. **What is in it for you?** This answer is aimed at providing organization members with a clear delineation of the benefits they can expect from the diagnosis. This usually entails describing the feedback process and how they can use the data to improve the organization.
8. **Can I be trusted?** The diagnostic relationship ultimately rests on the trust established between the OD practitioner and those providing the data. An open and honest exchange of information depends on such trust, and the practitioner should provide ample time and face-to-face contact during the contracting process to build this trust. This requires the consultant to listen actively and discuss openly all questions raised by participants.

Careful attention to establishing the diagnostic relationship helps to promote the three goals of data collection.[4] The first and most immediate objective is to obtain valid information about organizational functioning. Building a data collection contract can ensure that organization members provide honest, reliable, and complete information.

Data collection also can rally energy for constructive organizational change. A good diagnostic relationship helps organization members start thinking about issues that concern them, and it creates expectations that change is possible. When members trust the OD practitioner, they are likely to participate in the diagnostic process and to generate energy and commitment for organizational change.

Finally, data collection helps to develop the collaborative relationship necessary for effecting organizational change. The diagnostic stage of action research is probably the first time that most organization members meet the OD practitioner, and it can be the basis for building a longer-term relationship. The data collection contract and subsequent data-gathering and feedback activities provide members with opportunities for seeing the consultant in action and for knowing him or her personally. If the consultant can show employees that he or she is trustworthy, is willing to work with them, and is able to help improve the organization, then the data collection process will contribute to the longer-term collaborative relationship so necessary for carrying out organizational changes.

6-2 Collecting Data

The four major techniques for gathering diagnostic data are questionnaires, interviews, observations, and unobtrusive measures. Table 6.1 briefly compares the methods and lists their major advantages and problems. No single method can fully measure the kinds of diagnostic variables important to OD because each has certain strengths and weaknesses.[5] For example, perceptual measures, such as questionnaires and surveys, are open to self-report biases, such as respondents' tendency to give socially desirable answers rather than honest opinions. Observations, on the other hand, are susceptible to observer biases, such as seeing what one wants to see rather than what is really there. Because of the biases inherent in any data collection method, more than one method should be used when collecting diagnostic data. If data from the different methods are compared and found to be consistent, it is likely that the variables are being

TABLE 6.1

Strengths and Weaknesses of Different Data Collection Methods

Data Collection Method	Primary Strengths	Primary Weaknesses
Surveys and questionnaires	Member beliefs and attitudes can be quantified easily Can gather large amount of data from many people Inexpensive on a per-person basis	Relatively impersonal Mechanistic and rigid—assumes all the right questions are asked Easy to "over interpret" the data Response bias
Interviews	Very flexible—can adapt to interviewee and data collection subject Data is "rich" Interview process builds rapport and empathy	Relatively expensive Interviewer responses can be biased Difficult to code and interpret Self-report bias
Observations	Collects data on actual behavior, rather than reports of behavior Real time, not retrospective Adaptive and objective	Difficult to code and interpret Sampling may be inconsistent Observer bias and reliability can be questioned Can be expensive
Unobtrusive measures	No response bias High face validity Easily quantified	Privacy, access, and retrieval difficulties Validity concerns Difficult to code and interpret

measured validly. For example, questionnaire measures of job discretion could be supplemented with observations of the number and kinds of decisions employees are making. If the two kinds of data support each other, job discretion is probably being assessed accurately. If the two kinds of data conflict, the validity of the measures should be examined further—perhaps by using a third method, such as interviews.

6-2a Questionnaires

One of the most efficient ways to collect data is through questionnaires. Because they typically contain fixed-response queries about various features of an organization, these measures can be administered to large numbers of people simultaneously. Also, they can be analyzed quickly, especially with the use of computers, thus permitting quantitative comparison and evaluation. As a result, data can easily be fed back to employees. Numerous basic resource books on survey methodology and questionnaire development are available.[6]

Questionnaires can vary in scope, some measuring selected aspects of organizations and others assessing more comprehensive organizational characteristics. They also can vary in the extent to which they are either standardized or tailored to a specific organization. Standardized instruments generally are based on an explicit model of organization, group, or individual effectiveness and contain a predetermined set of questions that have been developed and refined over time. For example, Table 6.2 presents a standardized questionnaire for measuring the job-design dimensions identified in Chapter 5: skill variety, task identity, task significance, autonomy, and feedback about results. The questionnaire includes three items or questions for each dimension, and a total score for each job dimension is computed simply by adding the responses for the three relevant items and arriving at a total score from 3 (low) to 21 (high). The questionnaire has wide applicability. It has been used in a variety of organizations with employees in both blue-collar and white-collar jobs.

Several research organizations have been highly instrumental in developing and refining surveys. The Institute for Social Research at the University of Michigan (http://home.isr.umich.edu) and the Center for Effective Organizations at the University of Southern California (http://ceo.usc.edu) are two prominent examples. Two of the Institute's most popular measures of organizational dimensions are the *Survey of Organizations* and the *Michigan Organizational Assessment Questionnaire.* Few other instruments are supported by such substantial reliability and validity data.[7] Other examples of packaged instruments include Weisbord's *Organizational Diagnostic Questionnaire*, Dyer's *Team Development Survey*, Cameron and Quinn's *Organizational Culture Assessment Instrument*, and Hackman and Oldham's *Job Diagnostic Survey.*[8] In fact, so many questionnaires are available that rarely would an organization have to create a totally new one. However, because every organization has unique problems and special jargon for referring to them, almost any standardized instrument will need to have organization-specific additions, modifications, or omissions.

On the other hand, customized questionnaires are tailored to the needs of a particular organization. Typically, they include questions composed by OD practitioners or organization members, receive limited use, and do not undergo longer-term development. They can be combined with standardized instruments to provide valid and reliable data focused toward the particular issues facing an organization.

Questionnaires, however, have a number of drawbacks that need to be taken into account in choosing whether to employ them for data collection. First, responses are limited to the questions asked in the instrument. They provide little opportunity to probe for additional data or to ask for points of clarification. Second, questionnaires tend to be impersonal, and

TABLE 6.2

Job-Design Questionnaire

Here are some statements about your job. How much do you agree or disagree with each?

My Job:	Strongly Disagree	Disagree	Slightly Disagree	Undecided	Slightly Agree	Agree	Strongly Agree
1. provides much variety …	[1]	[2]	[3]	[4]	[5]	[6]	[7]
2. permits me to be left on my own to do my own work …	[1]	[2]	[3]	[4]	[5]	[6]	[7]
3. is arranged so that I often have the opportunity to see jobs or projects through to completion …	[1]	[2]	[3]	[4]	[5]	[6]	[7]
4. provides feedback on how well I am doing as I am working …	[1]	[2]	[3]	[4]	[5]	[6]	[7]
5. is relatively significant in our organization …	[1]	[2]	[3]	[4]	[5]	[6]	[7]
6. gives me considerable opportunity for independence and freedom in how I do my work …	[1]	[2]	[3]	[4]	[5]	[6]	[7]
7. gives me the opportunity to do a number of different things …	[1]	[2]	[3]	[4]	[5]	[6]	[7]
8. provides me an opportunity to find out how well I am doing …	[1]	[2]	[3]	[4]	[5]	[6]	[7]
9. is very significant or important in the broader scheme of things …	[1]	[2]	[3]	[4]	[5]	[6]	[7]
10. provides an opportunity for independent thought and action …	[1]	[2]	[3]	[4]	[5]	[6]	[7]
11. provides me with a great deal of variety at work …	[1]	[2]	[3]	[4]	[5]	[6]	[7]
12. is arranged so that I have the opportunity to complete the work I start …	[1]	[2]	[3]	[4]	[5]	[6]	[7]
13. provides me with the feeling that I know whether I am performing well or poorly …	[1]	[2]	[3]	[4]	[5]	[6]	[7]
14. is arranged so that I have the chance to do a job from the beginning to the end (i.e., a chance to do the whole job) …	[1]	[2]	[3]	[4]	[5]	[6]	[7]
15. is one where a lot of other people can be affected by how well the work gets done …	[1]	[2]	[3]	[4]	[5]	[6]	[7]

Scoring:

Skill variety	questions 1, 7, 11
Task identity	questions 3, 12, 14
Task significance	questions 5, 9, 15
Autonomy	questions 2, 6, 10
Feedback about results	questions 4, 8, 13

SOURCE: Reproduced by permission of E. Lawler, S. Mohrman, and T. Cummings, Center for Effective Organizations, University of Southern California.

employees may not be willing to provide honest answers. Third, questionnaires often elicit response biases, such as the tendency to answer questions in a socially acceptable manner. This makes it difficult to draw valid conclusions from employees' self-reports.

6-2b Interviews

A second important measurement technique is the *individual* or *group interview.* Interviews are probably the most widely used technique for collecting data in OD. They permit the interviewer to ask the respondent direct questions. Further probing and clarification is, therefore, possible as the interview proceeds. This flexibility is invaluable for gaining private views and feelings about the organization and for exploring new issues that emerge during the interview.

Interviews may be highly structured—resembling questionnaires—or highly unstructured—starting with general questions that allow the respondent to lead the way. Structured interviews typically derive from a conceptual model of organization functioning; the model guides the types of questions that are asked. For example, a structured interview based on the organization-level design components identified in Chapter 5 would ask managers specific questions about strategy, technology, organization structure, management processes, human resources systems, and organization culture.

Unstructured interviews are more general and include the following broad questions about organizational functioning:

- What are the major goals or objectives of the organization or department?
- How does the organization currently perform with respect to these purposes?
- What are the strengths and weaknesses of the organization or department?
- What barriers stand in the way of good performance?

Although interviewing typically involves one-to-one interaction between an OD practitioner and an employee, it can be carried out in a group context. Group interviews save time and allow people to build on others' responses. A major drawback, however, is that group settings may inhibit some people from responding freely.

A popular type of group interview is the *focus group* or *sensing meeting.*[9] These are unstructured meetings conducted by a manager or a consultant. A small group of 10 to 15 employees is selected to represent a cross section of functional areas and hierarchical levels or a homogeneous grouping, such as minorities or engineers. Group discussion is frequently started by asking general questions about organizational features and functioning, an OD intervention's progress, or current performance. Group members are then encouraged to discuss their answers more fully. Consequently, focus groups and sensing meetings are an economical way to obtain interview data and are especially effective in understanding particular issues in greater depth. The richness and validity of the information gathered will depend on the extent to which the manager or the OD practitioner develops a trusting relationship with the group and listens to member opinions.

Another popular unstructured group interview involves assessing the current state of an intact work group. The manager or the consultant generally directs a question to the group, calling its attention to some part of group functioning. For example, group members may be asked how they feel the group is progressing on its stated task. The group might respond and then come up with its own series of questions about barriers to task performance. This unstructured interview is a fast, simple way to collect data about group behavior. It enables members to discuss issues of immediate concern and to engage actively in the questioning and answering process. This technique is limited, however, to relatively small groups and to settings where there is trust among employees and managers and a commitment to assessing group processes.

Interviews are an effective method for collecting data in OD. They are adaptive, allowing the interviewer to modify questions and to probe emergent issues during the interview process. They also permit the interviewer to develop an empathetic relationship with employees, frequently resulting in frank disclosure of pertinent information.

A major drawback of interviews is the amount of time required to conduct and analyze them. Interviews can consume a great deal of time, especially if interviewers take full advantage of the opportunity to hear respondents out and change their questions accordingly. Personal biases also can distort the data. Like questionnaires, interviews are subject to the self-report biases of respondents and, perhaps more important, to the biases of the interviewer. For example, the nature of the questions and the interactions between the interviewer and the respondent may discourage or encourage certain kinds of responses. These problems suggest that interviewing takes considerable skill to gather valid data. Interviewers must be able to understand their own biases, to listen and establish empathy with respondents, and to change questions to pursue issues that develop during the course of the interview.

6-2c Observations

One of the more direct ways of collecting data is simply to *observe* organizational behaviors in their functional settings. The OD practitioner may do this by walking casually through a work area and looking around or by simply counting the occurrences of specific kinds of behaviors (e.g., the number of times a phone call is answered after three rings in a service department). Observation can range from complete participant observation, in which the OD practitioner becomes a member of the group under study, to more detached observation, in which the observer is clearly not part of the group or situation itself and may use film, videotape, and other methods to record behaviors.

Observations have a number of advantages. They are free of the biases inherent in self-report data. They put the OD practitioner directly in touch with the behaviors in question, without having to rely on others' perceptions. Observations also involve real-time data, describing behavior occurring in the present rather than the past. This avoids the distortions that invariably arise when people are asked to recollect their behaviors. Finally, observations are adaptive in that the consultant can modify what he or she chooses to observe, depending on the circumstances.

Among the problems with observations are difficulties interpreting the meaning underlying the observations. OD practitioners may need to devise a coding scheme to make sense out of observations, and this can be expensive, take time, and introduce biases into the data. When the observer is the data collection instrument, the data can be biased and subjective unless the observer is trained and skilled in knowing what to look for; how, where, and when to observe; and how to record data systematically. Another problem concerns sampling: Observers not only must decide which people to observe, but they also must choose the time periods, territory, and events in which to make those observations. Failure to attend to these sampling issues can result in highly biased samples of observational data.

When used correctly, observations provide insightful data about organization and group functioning, intervention success, and performance. For example, observations are particularly helpful in diagnosing the interpersonal relations of members of work groups. As discussed in Chapter 5, interpersonal relationships are a key component of work groups; observing member interactions in a group setting can provide direct information about the nature of those relationships.

6-2d Unobtrusive Measures

Unobtrusive data are not collected directly from respondents but from secondary sources, such as company records and archives. These data are generally available in organizations and include records of absenteeism or tardiness; grievances; quantity and quality of production or service; financial performance; meeting minutes; and correspondence with key customers, suppliers, or governmental agencies.

Unobtrusive measures are especially helpful in diagnosing the organization, group, and individual outputs presented in Chapter 5. At the organization level, for example, market share and return on investment usually can be obtained from company reports. Similarly, organizations typically measure the quantity and quality of the outputs of work groups and individual employees. Unobtrusive measures also can help to diagnose organization-level design components—structure, management processes, and human resources systems. A company's organization chart, for example, can provide useful information about organization structure. Information about management processes usually can be obtained by examining the firm's management information system, operating procedures, and accounting practices. Data about human resources systems often are included in a company's employee manual.

Unobtrusive measures provide a relatively objective view of organizational functioning. They are free from respondent and consultant biases and are perceived as being "real" by many organization members. Moreover, unobtrusive measures tend to be quantified and reported at periodic intervals, permitting statistical analysis of behaviors occurring over time. Examining monthly absenteeism rates, for example, might reveal trends in employee withdrawal behavior.

The major problems with unobtrusive measures occur in collecting such information and drawing valid conclusions from it. Company records may not include data in a form that is usable by the OD practitioner. If, for example, individual performance data are needed, the consultant may find that many firms only record production information at the group or department level. Unobtrusive data also may have their own built-in biases. Changes in accounting procedures and in methods of recording data are common in organizations, and such changes can affect company records independently of what is actually happening in the organization. For example, observed changes in productivity over time might be caused by modifications in methods of recording production rather than by actual changes in organizational functioning.

Despite these drawbacks, unobtrusive data serve as a valuable adjunct to other diagnostic measures, such as interviews and questionnaires. Archival data can be used in preliminary diagnosis, identifying those organizational units with absenteeism, grievance, or production problems. Then, interviews might be conducted or observations made in those units to discover the underlying causes of the problems. Conversely, unobtrusive data can be used to cross-check other forms of information. For example, if questionnaires reveal that employees in a department are dissatisfied with their jobs, company records might show whether that discontent is manifested in heightened withdrawal behaviors, in lowered quality work, or in similar counterproductive behaviors.

6-3 Sampling

Before discussing how to analyze data, the issue of *sampling* needs to be emphasized. Application of the different data collection techniques invariably raises the following questions: "How many people should be interviewed and who should they be?" "What events should be observed and how many?" "How many records should be inspected and which ones?"[10]

Sampling is not an issue in many OD cases. Because OD practitioners collect interview or questionnaire data from all members of the organization or department in question, they do not have to worry about whether the information is representative of the organization or unit.

Sampling becomes an issue in OD, however, when data are collected from selected members, behaviors, or records. This is often the case when diagnosing organization-level issues or large systems. In these cases, it may be important to ensure that the sample of people, behaviors, or records adequately represents the characteristics of the total population. For example, a sample of 50 employees might be used to assess the perceptions of all 300 members of a department. A sample of production data might be used to evaluate the total production of a work group. OD practitioners often find that it is more economical and quicker to gather a sampling of diagnostic data than to collect all possible information. If done correctly, the sample can provide useful and valid information about the entire organization or unit.

Sampling design involves considerable technical detail, and consultants may need to become familiar with basic references in this area or to obtain professional help.[11] The first issue to address is *sample size*, or how many people, events, or records are needed to carry out the diagnosis or evaluation. This question has no simple answer: The necessary sample size is a function of population size, the confidence desired in the quality of the data, and the resources (money and time) available for data collection.

First, the larger the population (for example, the number of organization members or total number of work outcomes) or the more complex the client system (e.g., the number of salary levels that must be sampled or the number of different functions), the more difficult it is to establish a "right" sample size. As the population increases in size and complexity, simple measures, such as an overall average score on a questionnaire item, are less meaningful. Because the population comprises such different types of people or events, more data are needed to ensure an accurate representation of the potentially different subgroups. Second, the larger the proportion of the population that is selected, the more confidence one can have about the quality of the sample. If the diagnosis concerns an issue of great importance to the organization, then extreme confidence may be needed, indicative of a very large sample size. Third, limited resources constrain sample size. If resources are limited but the required confidence is high, then questionnaires will be preferred over interviews because more information can be collected per member per dollar.

The second issue to address is *sample selection*. Probably the most common approach to sampling diagnostic data in OD is a simple *random sample*, in which each member, behavior, or record has an equal chance of being selected. For example, assume that an OD practitioner would like to select 50 people randomly out of the 300 employees at a manufacturing plant. Using a complete list of all 300 employees, the consultant can generate a random sample in one of two ways. The first method is to use a random number table printed in the back of almost any statistics text; the consultant would pick out the employees corresponding to the first 50 numbers under 300 beginning anywhere in the table. The second method is to pick every sixth name (300/50 = 6) starting anywhere in the list.

If the population is complex, or many subgroups need to be represented in the sample, a *stratified sample* may be more appropriate than a random one. In a stratified sample, the population of members, events, or records is segregated into a number of mutually exclusive subpopulations and a random sample is taken from each subpopulation. For example, members of an organization might be divided into three groups (managers, white-collar workers, and blue-collar workers), and a random sample of members, behaviors, or records could be selected from each grouping to reach diagnostic conclusions about each of the groups.

Adequate sampling is critical to gathering valid diagnostic data, and the OD literature has paid little attention to this issue. OD practitioners should gain rudimentary knowledge in this area and use professional help if necessary.

6-4 Analyzing Data

Data analysis techniques fall into two broad classes: qualitative and quantitative. Qualitative techniques generally are easier to use because they do not rely on numerical data. That fact also makes them more open to subjective biases but also easier to understand and interpret. Quantitative techniques, on the other hand, can provide more accurate readings of the organizational problem.

6-4a Qualitative Tools

Of the several methods for summarizing diagnostic data in qualitative terms, two of the most important are content analysis and force-field analysis.

Content Analysis A popular technique for assessing qualitative data, especially interview data, is *content analysis*, which attempts to summarize comments into meaningful categories. When done well, a content analysis can reduce hundreds of interview comments into a few themes that effectively summarize the issues or attitudes of a group of respondents. The process of content analysis can be quite formal, and specialized references describe this technique in detail.[12] In general, however, the process can be broken down into three major steps. First, responses to a particular question are read to gain familiarity with the range of comments made and to determine whether some answers are occurring over and over again. Second, based on this sampling of comments, themes are generated that capture recurring comments. Themes consolidate different responses that say essentially the same thing. For example, in answering the question "What do you like most about your job?," different respondents might list their coworkers, their supervisors, the new machinery, and a good supply of tools. The first two answers concern the social aspects of work, and the second two address the resources available for doing the work. Third, the respondents' answers to a question are then placed into one of the categories. The categories with the most responses represent those themes that are most often mentioned.

Force-Field Analysis A second method for analyzing qualitative data in OD derives from Kurt Lewin's three-step model of change described in Chapter 2. Called *force-field analysis*, this method organizes information pertaining to organizational change into two major categories: forces for change and forces for maintaining the status quo or resisting change.[13] Using data collected through interviews, observations, or unobtrusive measures, the first step in conducting a force-field analysis is to develop a list of all the forces promoting change and all those resisting it. Then, based either on the OD practitioner's personal belief or perhaps on input from several organization members, the most powerful positive and negative forces are determined. One can either rank the order or rate the strength of the different forces.

Figure 6.2 illustrates a force-field analysis of the performance of a work group. The arrows represent the forces, and the length of the arrows corresponds to the strength of the forces. The information could have been collected in a group interview in which members were asked to list those factors maintaining the current level of group performance and those factors pushing for a higher level. Members also could have been asked to judge the strength of each force, with the average judgment shown by the length of the arrows.

This analysis reveals two strong forces pushing for higher performance: pressures from the supervisor of the group and competition from other work groups performing similar work. These forces for change are offset by two strong forces for maintaining the status quo: group norms supporting present levels of performance and well-learned skills that are resistant to change. According to Lewin, efforts to change to a higher level of group performance, shown by the darker band in Figure 6.2, should focus on reducing the forces maintaining the status quo. This might entail changing the group's performance norms and helping members to learn new skills. The reduction of forces maintaining the status quo is likely to result in organizational change with little of the tension or conflict typically accompanying change caused by increasing the forces for change.

Application 6.1 describes another installment in the change evaluation process at Alegent Health. (The introduction of this longitudinal case began in Chapter 4.) In this application, the research team collected data from interviews and questionnaires, but also used observation and unobtrusive measures. The analysis used a combination of

FIGURE 6.2

Force-Field Analysis of Work-Group Performance

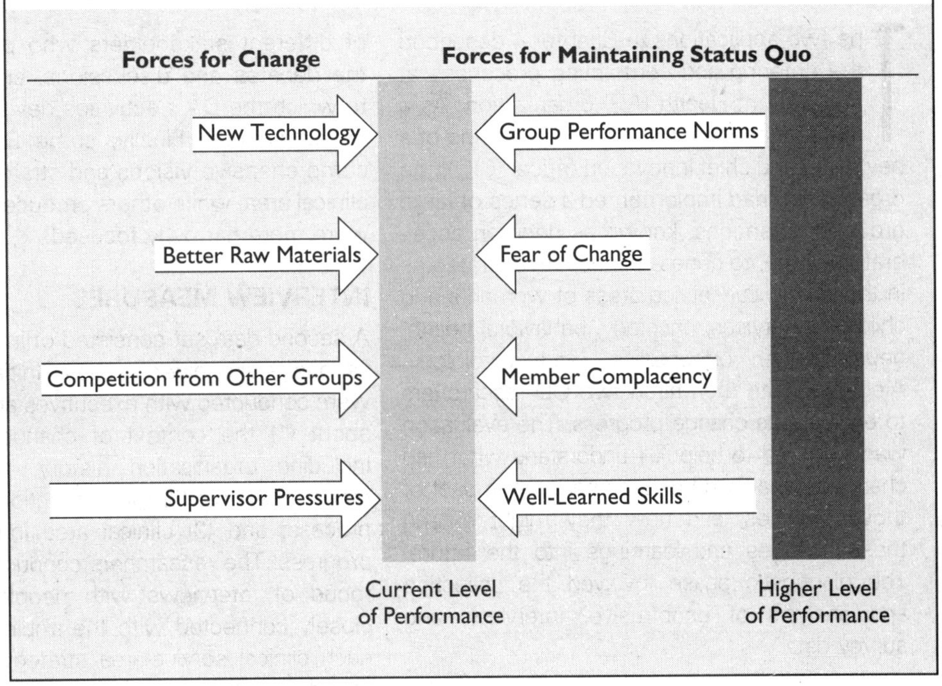

qualitative and quantitative techniques. What do you see as the strengths and weaknesses of the data collection and analysis process at Alegent?

6-4b Quantitative Tools

Methods for analyzing quantitative data range from simple descriptive statistics of items or scales from standard instruments to more sophisticated, multivariate analysis of the underlying instrument properties and relationships among measured variables.[14] The most common quantitative tools are means, standard deviations, and frequency distributions; scattergrams and correlation coefficients; and difference tests. These measures are routinely produced by most statistical computer software packages. Therefore, mathematical calculations are not discussed here.

Means, Standard Deviations, and Frequency Distributions One of the most economical and straightforward ways to summarize quantitative data is to compute a *mean* and *standard deviation* for each item or variable measured. These represent the respondents' average score and the spread or variability of the responses, respectively. These two numbers easily can be compared across different measures or subgroups. For example, Table 6.3 shows the means and standard deviations for six questions asked of 100 employees concerning the value of different kinds of organizational rewards. Based on the 5-point scale ranging from 1 (*very low value*) to 5 (*very high value*),

application 6.1

COLLECTING AND ANALYZING DIAGNOSTIC DATA AT ALEGENT HEALTH

The two applications in Chapter 4 described the entering and contracting processes at the Alegent Health (AH) organization. As a result of a recent merger and the hiring of a new CEO and chief innovation officer (CIO), the organization had implemented a series of large group interventions, known as decision accelerators (DAs), to generate innovative strategies in the six clinical service areas of women's and children's services, oncology, behavioral health, neuroscience, orthopedics, and cardiology. Alegent Health then hired two OD researchers to evaluate its change progress. The evaluation was intended to help AH understand what had changed, what had been learned, the impact of those changes, and how they might extend those changes and learnings into the future. The diagnostic phase involved the collection and analysis of unobtrusive, interview, and survey data.

UNOBTRUSIVE MEASURES

Immediately following each DA, the Right Track office (a group set up to manage the DA experience) compiled a report listing participant names and affiliations, an agenda, instructions and elapsed times for each activity and process, photographs of different activities and all small-group outputs, and nearly verbatim transcripts of the large-group report-outs, activity debriefings, and discussions.

These reports were analyzed to understand the process and outcomes associated with each DA. The researchers created a coding scheme and process to capture the characteristics of the participants, the nature of the process, and a description of the DA outputs. Two coders analyzed the data to ensure the reliability of the analysis.

First, the results suggested that the DAs varied in their composition. For example, some DAs were composed of higher percentages of physicians or community members than other DAs. Second, some DAs were more "intense" than others as indicated by the amount of debate over decisions or issues, the number of different stakeholders who participated in the debates and discussions, and the extent to which the DA's activities deviated from the preset agenda. Finally, some DAs produced comprehensive visions and strategies for their clinical area, while others produced visions that were more narrowly focused.

INTERVIEW MEASURES

A second data set consisted of interviews with various stakeholder groups. Initial interviews were conducted with executives and physicians about (1) the context of change at Alegent, including organization history, strategy, and recent changes; (2) their reflections on the DA process; and (3) clinical area implementation progress. The researchers conducted a second round of interviews with people who were closely connected with the implementation of each clinical service-area strategy. They were asked questions about the clarity of action plans, the level of involvement of different people, and implementation progress. Finally, a third set of interviews were conducted with a sample of staff nurses who had not participated in the original DAs or been directly involved in implementation activities, such as steering committees or design teams.

Each set of interview data was content analyzed for key themes and perspectives. A few of the summary results from the initial interviews are presented here.

When asked, "How clear were the action plans coming out of the DA?," the executives were evenly split in their beliefs that the action plans were clear as opposed to the plans being essentially absent. Executives were also asked, "What is going well/not so well in implementation of the different service line strategies?" About 20% of executives believed that the strategies were aligned with the mission/vision of the health system and that the DAs had provided a clear vision to guide change. However, more than half of executives expressed concern that the organization lacked a real change capability. Executives were also concerned about being overwhelmed by change, insufficient communication, and the need to involve stakeholders more.

When asked, "What would you list as the 'high points' or 'best success stories' of the DA process?" and "What have been some of the least successful activities/concerns?," the answers were more positive than negative. Nearly all of the interviewees noted the improved relationships with physicians, and more than a third of executives said there had been some good learning on how to increase the speed of decision making. Both of these results reflected cultural changes in the organization that were among the purposes for conducting the DAs. On the negative side, a small percentage of executives noted the continued difficulties associated with coordinating the operations of a multihospital system.

Another area of interview data concerned executive perceptions of how the DA might evolve in the future. There was a strong belief that the DA needed to evolve to fit the changed organizational conditions and a widespread perception that this should include a more explicit focus on execution, better change governance, and better follow-up and communication.

In addition to these initial interview results, data from the second round of implementation interviews were used to develop six cases studies, one for each clinical service area. They described the initial DA event and the subsequent decisions, activities, and events for the 18 months following the formation of the clinical strategies. Importantly, the case studies listed the organizational changes that most people agreed had been implemented in the first 18 months. Each case study was given to the VP in charge of the clinical area for validation.

SURVEY MEASURES

The researchers also collected two sets of survey data. The first survey, administered during the initial round of executive and physician interviews, asked them to rate several dimensions of clinical area strategy and progress. The second survey was administered to people who attended a "review DA" for three of the six clinical areas. It too measured perceptions of clinical strategy and progress.

The survey data were organized into three categories and analyzed by a statistical program. The first category measured five dimensions of strategy for each clinical area: comprehensiveness, innovativeness, aggressiveness, congruence with Alegent's strategy, and business focus. Both executives and managers rated the clinical strategies highest on comprehensiveness and lowest on congruence with Alegent's mission. Executives also rated the strategies lower on innovativeness. In all dimensions and for each clinical area, managers rated the five dimensions higher than executives did.

The second category measured how well the implementation process was being managed. Executives "somewhat agreed" that the clinical area strategies were associated with a clear action plan; however, there was considerable variance, suggesting that some clinical areas had better action plans than others. Similarly, managers "somewhat agreed" that change governance systems exist and that change was coordinated.

The third category assessed implementation success. As with the strategy dimensions, managers rated overall implementation progress higher than executives did, but both groups were somewhat guarded (between neutral and agree) in their responses. Managers were asked a more detailed set of questions about implementation. There was more agreement that the clinical strategies were the "right thing to do" and had helped to "build social capital" in the organization, but they were neutral with respect to whether "people feel involved" in the change.

the data suggest that challenging work and respect from peers are the two most highly valued rewards. Monetary rewards, such as pay and fringe benefits, are not as highly valued.

However, the mean can be a misleading statistic. It only describes the average value and thus provides no information on the distribution of the responses.

TABLE 6.3

Descriptive Statistics of Value of Organizational Rewards

Organizational Rewards	Mean	Standard Deviation
Challenging work	4.6	0.76
Respect from peers	4.4	0.81
Pay	4.0	0.71
Praise from supervisor	4.0	1.55
Promotion	3.3	0.95
Fringe benefits	2.7	1.14

Number of respondents = 100
1 = very low value; 5 = very high value

Different patterns of responses can produce the same mean score. Therefore, it is important to use the standard deviation along with the frequency distribution to gain a clearer understanding of the data. The *frequency distribution* is a graphical method for displaying data that shows the number of times a particular response was given. For example, the data in Table 6.3 suggest that both pay and praise from the supervisor are equally valued with a mean of 4.0. However, the standard deviations for these two measures are very different at 0.71 and 1.55, respectively. Table 6.4 shows the frequency distributions of the responses to the questions about pay and praise from the supervisor. Employees' responses to the value of pay are distributed toward the higher end of the scale, with no one rating it of low or very low value. In contrast, responses about the value of praise from the supervisor fall into two distinct groupings: Twenty-five employees felt that supervisor praise has a low or very low value, whereas 75 people rated it high or very high. Although both rewards have the same mean value, their standard deviations and frequency distributions suggest different interpretations of the data.

In general, when the standard deviation for a set of data is high, there is considerable disagreement over the issue posed by the question. If the standard deviation is small, the data are similar on a particular measure. In the example described above, there is disagreement over the value of supervisory praise (some people think it is important, but others do not), but there is fairly good agreement that pay is a reward with high value.

Scattergrams and Correlation Coefficients In addition to describing data, quantitative techniques also permit OD practitioners to make inferences about the relationships between variables. Scattergrams and correlation coefficients are measures of the strength of a relationship between two variables. For example, suppose the problem being faced by an organization is increased conflict between the manufacturing department and the engineering design department. During the data collection phase, information about the number of conflicts and change orders per month over the past year is collected. The data are shown in Table 6.5 and plotted in a scattergram in Figure 6.3.

TABLE 6.4

Frequency Distributions of Responses to "Pay" and "Praise from Supervisor" Items

Pay (Mean = 4.0)		
Response	**Number Checking Each Response**	**Graph***
(1) Very low value	0	
(2) Low value	0	
(3) Moderate value	25	XXXXX
(4) High value	50	XXXXXXXXXX
(5) Very high value	25	XXXXX
Praise from Supervisor (Mean = 4.0)		
Response	**Number Checking Each Response**	**Graph***
(1) Very low value	15	XXX
(2) Low value	10	XX
(3) Moderate value	0	
(4) High value	10	XX
(5) Very high value	65	XXXXXXXXXXXXX

*Each X = five people checking the response

A *scattergram* is a diagram that visually displays the relationship between two variables. It is constructed by locating each case (person or event) at the intersection of its value for each of the two variables being compared. For example, in the month of August, there were eight change orders and three conflicts, whose intersection is shown in Figure 6.3 as an ×.

Three basic patterns can emerge from a scattergram, as shown in Figure 6.4. The first pattern is called a positive relationship because as the values of x increase, so do the values of y. The second pattern is called a negative relationship because as the values of x increase, the values of y decrease. Finally, there is the "shotgun" pattern wherein no relationship between the two variables is apparent. In the example shown in Figure 6.3, an apparently strong positive relationship exists between the number of change orders and the number of conflicts between the engineering design department and the manufacturing department. This suggests that change orders may contribute to the observed conflict between the two departments.

The *correlation coefficient* is simply a number that summarizes data in a scattergram. Its value ranges between +1.0 and −1.0. A correlation coefficient of +1.0 means that there is a perfectly positive relationship between two variables, whereas a correlation

TABLE 6.5

Relationship between Change Orders and Conflicts

Month	Number of Change Orders	Number of Conflicts
April	5	2
May	12	4
June	14	3
July	6	2
August	8	3
September	20	5
October	10	2
November	2	1
December	15	4
January	8	3
February	18	4
March	10	5

of −1.0 signifies a perfectly negative relationship. A correlation of 0 implies a "shotgun" scattergram where there is no relationship between two variables.

Difference Tests The final technique for analyzing quantitative data is the *difference test.* It can be used to compare a sample group against some standard or norm to determine whether the group is above or below that standard. It also can be used to determine whether two samples are significantly different from each other. In the first case, such comparisons provide a broader context for understanding the meaning of diagnostic data. They serve as a "basis for determining 'how good is good or how bad is bad.'"[15] Many standardized questionnaires have standardized scores based on the responses of large groups of people. It is critical, however, to choose a comparison group that is similar to the organization being diagnosed. For example, if 100 engineers take a standardized attitude survey, it makes little sense to compare their scores against standard scores representing married males from across the country. On the other hand, if industry-specific data are available, a comparison of sales per employee (as a measure of productivity) against the industry average would be valid and useful.

The second use of difference tests involves assessing whether two or more groups differ from one another on a particular variable, such as job satisfaction or absenteeism. For example, job satisfaction differences between an accounting department and a sales department can be determined with this tool. Given that each group took the same questionnaire, their means and standard deviations can be used to compute a difference score (*t*-score or *z*-score) indicating whether the two groups are statistically different.

FIGURE 6.3

Scattergram of Change Order versus Conflict

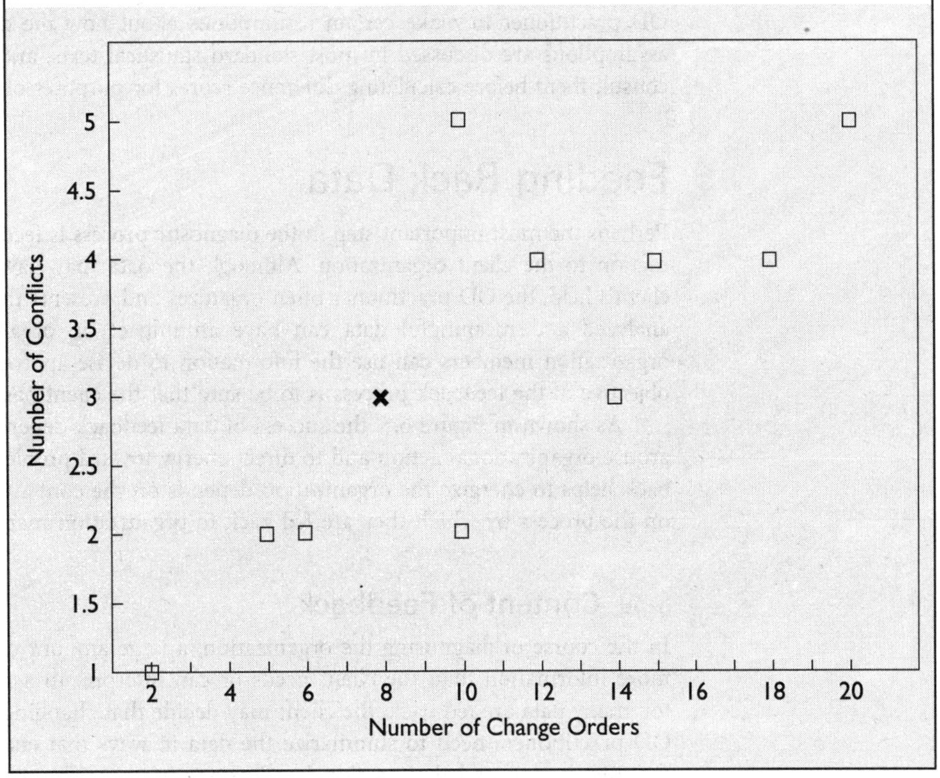

FIGURE 6.4

Basic Scattergram Patterns

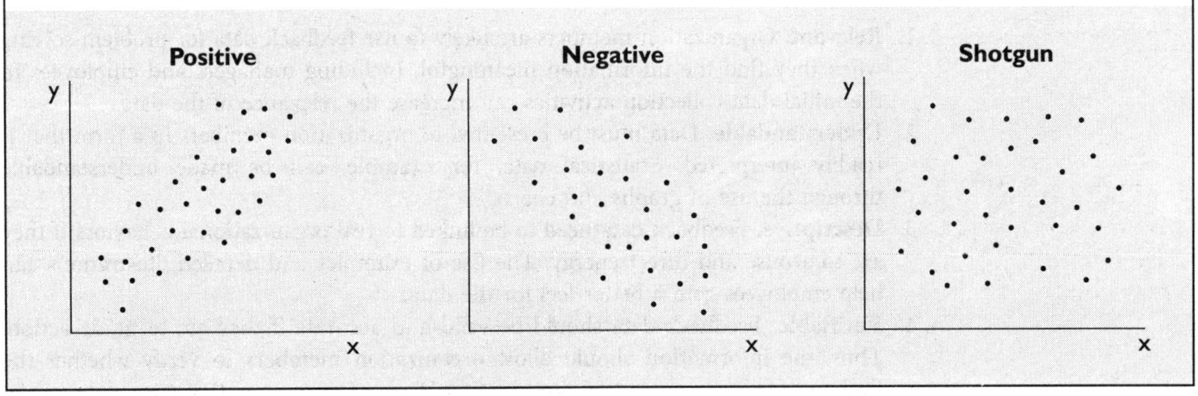

The larger the difference score relative to the sample size and standard deviation for each group, the more likely that one group is more satisfied than the other.

Difference tests also can be used to determine whether a group has changed its score on job satisfaction or some other variable over time. The same questionnaire can be given to the same group at two points in time. Based on the group's means and standard deviations at each point in time, a difference score can be calculated. The larger the score, the more likely the group actually changed its job satisfaction level.

The calculation of difference scores can be very helpful for diagnosis but requires the OD practitioner to make certain assumptions about how the data were collected. These assumptions are discussed in most standard statistical texts, and OD practitioners should consult them before calculating difference scores for purposes of diagnosis or evaluation.[16]

6-5 Feeding Back Data

Perhaps the most important step in the diagnostic process is feeding back diagnostic information to the client organization. Although the data may have been collected with the client's help, the OD practitioner often organizes and presents them to the client. Properly analyzed and meaningful data can have an impact on organizational change only if organization members can use the information to devise appropriate action plans. A key objective of the feedback process is to be sure that the client has ownership of the data.

As shown in Figure 6.5, the success of data feedback depends largely on its ability to arouse organizational action and to direct energy toward problem solving. Whether feedback helps to energize the organization depends on the content of the feedback data and on the process by which they are fed back to organization members.

6-5a Content of Feedback

In the course of diagnosing the organization, a large amount of data is collected—often, more information than the client needs or can interpret in a realistic period of time. If too many data are fed back, the client may decide that changing is impossible. Therefore, OD practitioners need to summarize the data in ways that enable clients to understand the information and draw action implications from it. The techniques for data analysis described earlier in this chapter can inform this task. Additional criteria for determining the content of diagnostic feedback are described below.

Several characteristics of effective feedback data have been described in the literature.[17] They include the following nine properties:

1. **Relevant.** Organization members are likely to use feedback data for problem solving when they find the information meaningful. Including managers and employees in the initial data collection activities can increase the relevance of the data.
2. **Understandable.** Data must be presented to organization members in a form that is readily interpreted. Statistical data, for example, can be made understandable through the use of graphs and charts.
3. **Descriptive.** Feedback data need to be linked to real organizational behaviors if they are to arouse and direct energy. The use of examples and detailed illustrations can help employees gain a better feel for the data.
4. **Verifiable.** Feedback data should be valid and accurate if they are to guide action. Thus, the information should allow organization members to verify whether the findings really describe the organization. For example, questionnaire data might include information about the sample of respondents as well as frequency distributions for each item or measure. Such information can help members verify whether the feedback data accurately represent organizational events or attitudes.
5. **Timely.** Data should be fed back to members as quickly as possible after being collected and analyzed. This will help ensure that the information is still valid and is linked to members' motivations to examine it.

FIGURE 6.5

Possible Effects of Feedback

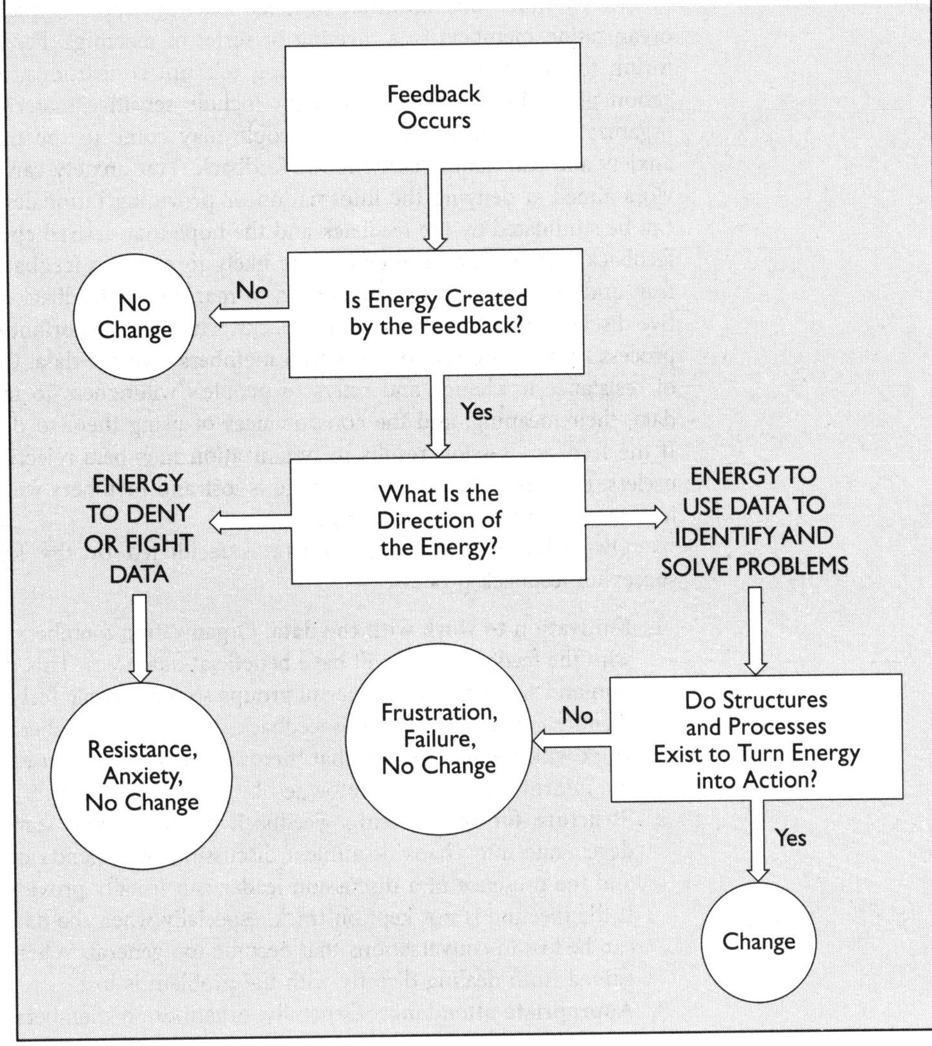

6. **Limited.** Because people can easily become overloaded with too much information, feedback data should be limited to what employees can realistically process at one time.
7. **Significant.** Feedback should be limited to those problems that organization members can do something about because it will energize them and help direct their efforts toward realistic changes.
8. **Comparative.** Feedback data can be ambiguous without some benchmark as a reference. Whenever possible, data from comparative groups should be provided to give organization members a better idea of how their group fits into a broader context.
9. **Unfinalized.** Feedback is primarily a stimulus for action and thus should spur further diagnosis and problem solving. Members should be encouraged, for example, to use the data as a starting point for more in-depth discussion of organizational issues.

6-5b Process of Feedback

In addition to providing effective feedback data, it is equally important to attend to the process by which that information is fed back to people. Typically, data are provided to organization members in a meeting or series of meetings. Feedback meetings provide a forum for discussing the data, drawing relevant conclusions, and devising preliminary action plans. Because the data might include sensitive material and evaluations about organization members' behaviors, people may come to the meeting with considerable anxiety and fear about receiving the feedback. This anxiety can result in defensive behaviors aimed at denying the information or providing rationales. More positively, people can be stimulated by the feedback and the hope that desired changes will result from the feedback meeting. Because people are likely to come to feedback meetings with anxiety, fear, and hope, OD practitioners need to manage the feedback process so that constructive discussion and problem solving occur. The most important objective of the feedback process is to ensure that organization members own the data. Ownership is the opposite of resistance to change and refers to people's willingness to take responsibility for the data, their meaning, and the consequences of using them to devise a change strategy.[18] If the feedback session results in organization members rejecting the data as invalid or useless, then the motivation to change is lost and members will have difficulty engaging in a meaningful process of change.

Ownership of the feedback data is facilitated by the following five features of successful feedback processes:[19]

1. **Motivation to work with the data.** Organization members need to feel that working with the feedback data will have beneficial outcomes. This may require explicit sanction and support from powerful groups so that people feel free to raise issues and to identify concerns during the feedback sessions. If members have little motivation to work with the data or feel that there is little chance to use the data for change, then the information will not be owned by the client system.
2. **Structure for the meeting.** Feedback meetings need some structure or they may degenerate into chaos or aimless discussion. An agenda or outline for the meeting and the presence of a discussion leader can usually provide the necessary direction. If the meeting is not kept on track, especially when the data are negative, ownership can be lost in conversations that become too general. When this happens, the energy gained from dealing directly with the problem is lost.
3. **Appropriate attendance.** Generally, organization members who have common problems and can benefit from working together should be included in the feedback meeting. This may involve a fully intact work team or groups comprising members from different functional areas or hierarchical levels. Without proper representation in the meeting, ownership of the data is lost because participants cannot address the problem(s) suggested by the feedback.
4. **Appropriate power.** It is important to clarify the power possessed by the group receiving the feedback data. Members need to know on which issues they can make necessary changes, on which they can only recommend changes, and over which they have no control. Unless there are clear boundaries, members are likely to have some hesitation about using the feedback data for generating action plans. Moreover, if the group has no power to make changes, the feedback meeting will become an empty exercise rather than a real problem-solving session. Without the power to address change, there will be little ownership of the data.
5. **Process help.** People in feedback meetings require assistance in working together as a group. When the data are negative, there is a natural tendency to resist the

implications, deflect the conversation onto safer subjects, and the like. An OD practitioner with group process skills can help members stay focused on the subject and improve feedback discussion, problem solving, and ownership.

When combined with effective feedback data, these features of successful feedback meetings enhance member ownership of the data. They help to ensure that organization members fully discuss the implications of the diagnostic information and that their conclusions are directed toward relevant and feasible organizational changes.

Application 6.2 presents excerpts from some training materials that were delivered to a group of internal OD facilitators at a *Fortune* 100 telecommunications company.[20] It describes how the facilitators were trained to deliver the results of a survey concerning problem solving, team functioning, and perceived effectiveness.

6-6 Survey Feedback

Survey feedback is a process of collecting and feeding back data from an organization or department through the use of a questionnaire or survey. The data are analyzed, fed back to organization members, and used by them to diagnose the organization and to develop interventions to improve it. Because questionnaires often are used in organization diagnosis, particularly in OD efforts involving large numbers of participants, and because it is a powerful intervention in its own right, survey feedback is discussed here as a special case of data feedback.

As discussed in Chapter 1, survey feedback is a major technique in the history and development of OD. Originally, this intervention included only data from questionnaires about members' attitudes. However, attitudinal data can be supplemented with interview data and more objective measures, such as productivity, turnover, and absenteeism.[21] Another trend has been to combine survey feedback with other OD interventions, including work design, structural change, large group interventions, and intergroup relations. These change methods are the outcome of the planning and implementation phase following from survey feedback and are described fully in Chapters 10–20.

6-6a What Are the Steps?

Survey feedback generally involves the following five steps:[22]

1. Members of the organization, including those at the top, are involved in preliminary planning of the survey. In this step, all parties must be clear about the level of analysis (organization, group, or job) and the objectives of the survey. Because most surveys derive from a model about organization or group functioning, organization members must, in effect, approve that diagnostic framework. This is an important initial step in gaining ownership of the data and in ensuring that the right problems and issues are addressed by the survey.

   Once the objectives are determined, the organization can use one of the standardized questionnaires described earlier in this chapter, or it can develop its own survey instrument. If the survey is developed internally, pretesting the questionnaire is essential to ensure that it has been constructed properly. In either case, the survey items need to reflect the objectives established for the survey and the diagnostic issues being addressed.
2. The survey instrument is administered to all members of the organization or work group. This breadth of data collection is ideal, but it may be appropriate to administer

TRAINING OD PRACTITIONERS IN DATA FEEDBACK

application 6.2

As part of a large-scale, employee involvement (EI) program, a large telecommunications company and the Communications Workers of America union were working to build an internal organization development consulting capability. This involved the hiring and training of several union and management employees to work with managers, facilitate EI problem-solving team meetings, and assist in the implementation of recommended changes. The implementation process included an evaluation component and the EI facilitators were expected to collect and feed back data to the organization.

The data collected included observation of various work processes and problem-solving meetings; unobtrusive measures such as minutes from all meetings, quarterly income statements, operational reports, and communications; and questionnaire and interview data. A three-page questionnaire was administered every three months and it asked participants on EI problem-solving teams for their perceptions of team functioning and performance. Internal EI facilitators were appointed from both management and union employees, and part of their work required them to feed back the results of the quarterly surveys.

To provide timely feedback to the problem-solving teams, the EI facilitators were trained to deliver survey feedback. Some of the material developed for that training is summarized below.

I. PLANNING FOR A SURVEY-FEEDBACK SESSION

The success of a survey-feedback meeting often has more to do with the level of preparation for the meeting than with anything else. There are several things to do in preparing for a survey-feedback meeting.

A. *Distribute copies of the feedback report in advance.* This enables people to devote more time at the meeting to problem solving and less to just digesting the data. This is especially important when a large quantity of data is being presented.

B. *Think about substantive issues in advance.* Formulate your own view of what the data suggest about the strengths and weaknesses of the group. Does the general picture appear to be positive or problematic? Do the data fit the experience of the group as you know it? What issues do the data suggest need group attention? Is the group likely to avoid any of these issues? If so, how will you help the group confront the difficult issues?

C. *Make sure you can answer likely technical questions about the data.* Survey data have particular strengths and weaknesses. Be able to acknowledge that the data are not perfect, but that a lot of effort has gone into ensuring that they are reliable and valid.

D. *Plan your introduction to the survey-feedback portion of the meeting.* Make the introduction brief and to the point. Remind the group of why it is considering the data, set the stage for problem solving by pointing out that many groups find such data helpful in tracking their progress, and be prepared to run through an example that shows how to understand the feedback data.

II. PROBLEM SOLVING WITH SURVEY-FEEDBACK DATA

A. *Chunk the feedback.* If a lot of data are being fed back, use your knowledge of the group and the data to present small portions of data. Stop periodically to see if there are questions or comments about each section or "chunk" of data.

B. *Stimulate discussion on the data.* What follows are various ways to help get the discussion going.

1. Help clarify the meaning of the data by asking
   - What questions do you have about what the data mean?

- What does [a specific number] mean?
- Does anything in the data surprise you?
- What do the data tell you about how we're doing as a group?

2. Help develop a shared diagnosis about the meaning of the data by commenting
   - What I hear people saying is... Does everyone agree with that?
   - Several people are saying that... is a problem. Do we agree that this is something the group needs to address?
   - Some people seem to be saying... while other comments suggest... Can you help me understand how the group sees this?
   - The group has really been struggling with [specific issue that the facilitator is familiar with], but the data say that we are strong on this. Can someone explain this?
3. Help generate action alternatives by asking
   - What are some of the things we can do to resolve... ?
   - Do we want to brainstorm some action steps to deal with... ?

C. *Focus the group on its own data.* The major benefit of survey feedback for EI teams will be in learning about the group's own behavior and outcomes. Often, however, groups will avoid dealing with issues concerning their own group in favor of broader and less helpful discussions about what other groups are doing right and wrong. Comments you might use to help get the group on track include:
   1. What do the data say about how we are doing as a group?
   2. There isn't a lot we can do about what other groups are doing. What can we do about the things that are under our control?
   3. The problem you are mentioning sounds like one this group also is facing [explain]. Is that so?

D. *Be prepared for problem-solving discussions that are only loosely connected to the data.* It is more important for the group to use the data to understand itself better and to solve problems than it is to follow any particular steps in analyzing the data. Groups often are not very systematic in how they analyze survey-feedback data. They may ignore issues that seem obvious to them and instead focus on one or two issues that have meaning for them.

E. *Hot issues and how to deal with them.* Survey data can be particularly helpful in addressing some hot issues within the group that might otherwise be overlooked. For example, a group often will prefer to portray itself as very effective even though group members privately acknowledge that such is not the case. If the data show problems that are not being addressed, you can raise this issue as a point for discussion. If someone denies that group members feel there is a problem, you can point out that the data come from the group and that group members reported such-and-such on the survey. Be careful not to use a parental tone; if you sound like you're wagging your finger at or lecturing the group, you're likely to get a negative reaction. Use the data to raise issues for discussion in a less emotional way.

Ultimately, the group must take responsibility for its own use of the data. There will be times when the OD practitioner sees the issues differently from the way group members see them or times when it appears certain to the practitioner that the group has a serious problem that it refuses to acknowledge. A facilitator cannot push a group to do something it's not ready to do, but he or she can poke the group at times to find out if it is ready to deal with tough issues. "A little irritation is what makes a pearl in the oyster."

the instrument to only a sample of members because of cost or time constraints. If so, the size of the sample should be as large as possible to improve the motivational basis for participation in the feedback sessions.

3. The OD practitioner usually analyzes the survey data, tabulates the results, suggests approaches to diagnosis, and trains client members to lead the feedback process.
4. Data feedback usually begins at the top of the organization and cascades downward to groups reporting to managers at successively lower levels. This waterfall approach ensures that all groups at all organizational levels involved in the survey receive appropriate feedback. Most often, members of each organization group at each level discuss and deal with only that portion of the data involving their particular group. They, in turn, prepare to introduce data to groups at the next lower organizational level if appropriate.

   Data feedback also can occur in a "bottom-up" approach. Initially, the data for specific work groups or departments are fed back and action items proposed. At this point, the group addresses problems and issues within its control. The group notes any issues that are beyond its authority and suggests actions. That information is combined with information from groups reporting to the same manager, and the combined data are fed back to the managers who review the data and the recommended actions. Problems that can be solved at this level are addressed. In turn, their analyses and suggestions regarding problems of a broader nature are combined, and feedback and action sessions proceed up the hierarchy. In such a way, the people who most likely will carry out recommended action get the first chance to propose suggestions.
5. Feedback meetings provide an opportunity to work with the data. At each meeting, members discuss and interpret their data, diagnose problem areas, and develop action plans. OD practitioners can play an important role during these meetings,[23] facilitating group discussion to produce accurate understanding, focusing the group on its strengths and weaknesses, and helping to develop effective action plans.

Although the preceding steps can have a number of variations, they generally reflect the most common survey-feedback design. Application 6.3 presents a contemporary example of how the survey-feedback methodology can be adapted to serve strategic purposes. The application describes how Cambia Health Solutions used a survey and survey feedback process to initiate a strategic change effort.

6-6b Survey Feedback and Organizational Dependencies

Traditionally, the steps of survey feedback have been applied to work groups and organizational units with little attention to dependencies among them. Research suggests, however, that the design of survey feedback should vary depending on how closely the participating units are linked with one another.[24] When the units are relatively independent and have little need to interact, survey feedback can focus on the dynamics occurring within each group and can be applied to the groups separately. When there is greater dependency among units and they need to coordinate their efforts, survey feedback must take into account relationships among the units, paying particular attention to the possibility of intergroup conflict. In these situations, the survey-feedback process needs to be coordinated across the interdependent groups. The process will typically be managed by special committees and task forces representing the groups. They will facilitate the intergroup confrontation and conflict resolution generally needed when relations across groups are diagnosed.

application 6.3

SURVEY FEEDBACK AND PLANNED CHANGE AT CAMBIA HEALTH SOLUTIONS

Cambia Health Solutions (www.cambiahealth.com) is a nonprofit total health solutions company dedicated to transforming the way people experience the health care system. Located in the Pacific Northwest and intermountain region of the United States, Cambia's portfolio of companies spans health care information technology and software development; retail health care; health insurance plans; pharmacy benefit management; life, disability, dental, vision, and other lines of protection; alternative solutions to health care access; and freestanding health and wellness solutions. The largest business in the portfolio is Regence Health, a health insurance plan associated with the Blue Cross and Blue Shield brands. Regence Health is over 90 years old and operates in Washington, Oregon, Idaho, and Utah.

To support this increasingly broad portfolio, Cambia had restructured itself into two divisions: Regence Insurance Holding Company and Direct Health Solutions. All of the start-up, alternative health care products and services were housed in the direct health solutions division. In 2009, the organization was concerned about the health care reform initiatives taking place in Washington, D.C. and more specifically the implications of the recently passed "Obamacare" legislation. What were the implications of establishing regional health exchanges and accountable care organizations? How would the organization have to change? In particular, was the organization's culture "fit for the future?"

As corporate sponsors of USC's Center for Effective Organizations, the vice president of human resources and the director of organization development called the Center to talk about the latest thinking in organization culture and how they might go about managing cultural change. After several conversations about different approaches and the research being done at the Center regarding organization design, change, and agility, the researchers proposed an assessment process of Cambia's current organization in terms of how people saw the strategies, structures, systems, and culture. A design team composed of the executive vice president of corporate services, the VP of HR, the director of OD, and an internal HR business partner worked with the researcher to make the assessment relevant.

In early 2011, a three-page diagnostic survey was administered to all managers with titles of assistant director or above, a population of about 150 people. In addition, 16 senior leaders were interviewed from the headquarters and regional organizations. The leaders represented a good mix of functions and tenure with the organization.

The survey consisted of about 50 items to be rated on a scale of 1 to 5 where 1 = "Not at all" and a 5 = "To a great extent." These pretested items fell into 14 dimensions, including the extent to which the organization formulated "robust strategies," engaged in future focused environmental scanning, had flat and responsive structures, rewarded performance and change, leveraged information systems, developed its talent well, and managed resources flexibly. In addition, the survey asked several questions about the organization's cultural values and how members perceived leaders spending their time. The hour-long interviews asked questions addressing similar issues in terms of strategies, processes, and culture but were focused more on gathering rich stories and examples that might help the survey data "come alive."

The results of the survey were placed into a spreadsheet and analyzed with statistical programs that generated summary tables and charts of the data. The interview data was summarized using content analysis procedures and preliminary themes were discussed with design team members to ensure that the interview responses and categories had meaning for the organization.

The summary results were then placed into three categories: "Positive issues," "Areas of Concern," and "Problems." Compared to the overall scores from other firms, Cambia's scores were generally below the overall average of other firms but were similar to other financial services firms. The economic recession and financial crises of the time had affected the culture of many of these firms and it was not surprising that the financial services sector scores were lower.

The key "positive issue" was that people reported a strong sense of shared purpose in the organization. Captured by "The Cause," a statement announced in early 2004 stating that the Cambia organization wanted to be a "catalyst for change" in health care, there was broad support for this clear direction. The Cause and the organization's history also supported a clear "member-focused" culture. People liked working for a not-for-profit insurer and believed that such a corporate form was an important differentiator in the way the organization did business. This belief was reflected in the survey data as a very healthy balance between driving for results and taking care of people.

In the areas of concern category, and despite the strong shared sense of purpose scores, people struggled with what The Cause meant to their day-to-day behaviors. It was one thing to be clear about "being a catalyst for change" in health care, but how did that translate into how organization members were supposed to treat customers? In this sense, people were concerned about "who we are" as an organization and did not see how the Cause helped them have a real "voice" in making day-to-day decisions.

The recent reorganization into a health care business and a set of entrepreneurial "start-up" businesses that were intended to explore the future of the health care industry clearly reflected The Cause. However, people were concerned about what it meant for the culture. A lot of senior management's attention was focused on the innovative nature of these new businesses, and some people in the insurance division felt left out. The culture of Cambia was clearly changing, but was the Regence culture expected to change as well and if so in what direction? The Cause helped people understand where the organization was headed, but it didn't really help people answer the question "who are we?" and how to make decisions. People were frustrated by this.

In general, people were also concerned about how well the new direction was being supported by different organizational systems. They believed that recent structural and reward systems changes were heading in the right direction, but other comments raised questions over other features, such as the way organizational and individual goals were set, how the organization responded to opportunities, and the way information and communication moved throughout the organization. These systems were not changing and did not necessarily align with the new direction. The IT systems, in particular, had a very bad reputation. A complex systems changeover was generally regarded as an example of poor execution, and was producing a number of headaches around the organization.

Finally, two big problems loomed. First, there was widespread agreement that the organization did not have the change and learning capabilities to execute a change of this magnitude. As a 90-year-old organization in a slow-moving and regulated industry, there was little expertise in the organization regarding how to manage change. Second, in a related way, the organization was relying on innovation in both the new start-up businesses and the traditional health care business as part of The Cause. However, the organization lacked the resources, processes, and experience to generate new product/service ideas or identify and implement process improvements. The processes that had helped them to adapt in the past were unlikely to be effective in the future.

The summary data were fed back in multiple forums. The first forum was an all-day meeting of the design team. A PowerPoint deck provided both detailed summaries and analyses of the data as well as charts that made interpretation more intuitive. For example, the 14 scales regarding strategy, structure, and processes were presented as bar charts that allowed the design team to "see" how their data compared to other organizations and overall averages.

The data presentation was broken up by categories. First, the "good news" was presented and discussed. The organization had important strengths that any change process would naturally want to leverage or reinforce. The strong sense of shared purpose in the organization would provide an important base. The discussion among design team members centered on the acknowledgement that a strong history in the different regions had created a "members first" culture. While it was acknowledged as a strength, the design team also wondered whether such a legacy orientation would be strength or a weakness if change was necessary.

The areas of concern and problems were presented next. The group spent quite a bit of time discussing their implications. There was ready agreement on the problems. Design team members believed that the organization needed (and lacked) change, learning, and innovation capabilities. But they also believed that just building these capabilities was not enough and might be a waste of time. They needed to be focused on changing and innovating the right things.

Much of the conversation then centered around the implication that there was a distinction to be made between the clear direction provided by The Cause and the concern that there was no guidance for decision making. The interviews clearly pointed to a frustration about how hard it was to "get things done" in the organization. There was a perception that too many decisions were pushed up to the top for resolution and that silos in the organization prevented the required cross-group collaboration.

From here, the diagnostic conversation turned to a broader subject. The design team members were concerned that not being able to "get stuff done" and pushing decisions up the hierarchy was indicative of a more basic problem. People generally did not have clear goals ("it's hard to get stuff done when you don't know where you are going") and were not held accountable ("it's not my decision"). The culture of "Northwest Nice" was working against such culture change objectives. The design team believed that if change and innovation capability building could be focused on helping the organization more effectively execute specific strategies and goals, then that would represent an important impetus for culture change.

Before the meeting ended, the design team believed it was important to share the data and their conclusions with the CEO to gauge his level of interest in moving a change process forward. The team spent a considerable amount of time sorting through the data to find the most central and most influential data points to tell a story. The CEO's summary was only two pages long and consisted of the high-level summary of positives, concerns, and negatives as well as a summary of the survey scale scores compared to other firms.

The CEO and the VP of HR met with the researcher. After a few brief comments about the data, the CEO began by inquiring about the diagnostic process. He wanted to know if the data he was looking at was "good" data or not. Once satisfied that a sound process had been followed in terms of sampling and analysis, he turned his attention to the actual data. Like the design team, he asked some clarifying questions about the distinction between strategic direction and cultural influences. He also asked some insightful questions about specific words that had been chosen to capture the design team's "sense" of the data.

His attention was mostly on the concerned and negative themes. Many of the issues (both positive and negative) raised were familiar to him and he doubted that the organization could fulfill the promise of The Cause with this set of weaknesses. On the spot, he commissioned the HR vice president with leading the design team to formulate a change strategy to address the issues raised in the assessment.

The HR vice president and the researcher reconvened the design team and added members from other departments, such as IT and the regional organizations, to better represent the overall enterprise. They began to develop an action plan for the change. It began with feedback of the assessment data to other parts of the organization. This happened in two primary ways. First, the results were fed back to the existing senior leadership team. They were tasked with committing to the change and formulating statements that would represent an organizational future state. Second, the data were fed back to the top 150 leaders at the organization's annual leadership summit. This group had been the primary group sampled in the survey and they were given a chance to review the data, ask questions, and provide guidance on a proposed action plan.

The design team also formally commissioned four initiative task forces to address specific issues in the assessment. One team took on the challenge of revising the human capital management process (see Application 15.1 for a summary of this effort). A second task force was charted to diagnose and explore in more detail the issues surrounding people's beliefs that it was hard to "get stuff done" at Cambia. A third team addressed the related issue of strategic planning and corporate communication. Was there a clear, well-understood, and shared process for setting organization objectives that were relevant to the managers and departments in the organization and how were those objectives communicated? Finally, a fourth team was given the task of creating and implementing an organization-wide change-management process.

The design team and VP of HR worked on a variety of organization changes. These included a realignment of the senior leadership group, supporting key leadership changes, changes in the leadership development programs, and the reorganization of several functional groups, including HR, and a complete redesign of the performance management process.

After one year of implementation, the design team commissioned a midpoint review to gauge progress on the action plan. Interviews with the design team members, a sample of managers who had participated on the task forces, and a sample of managers and executives who had not been directly involved in the change effort were conducted. In general, the interview data supported that the change was heading in the right direction. Many people believed that, in fact, the culture was changing and that the work of the design team was an important contributor to that change. The interviewees also made a variety of suggestions for continuing different initiatives as well as suggestions for "next steps."

6-6c Limitations of Survey Feedback

Although the use of survey feedback is widespread in contemporary organizations, the following limits and risks have been identified:[25]

1. **Ambiguity of purpose.** Managers and staff groups responsible for the survey-feedback process may have difficulty reaching sufficient consensus about the purposes of the survey, its content, and how it will be fed back to participants. Such confusion can lead to considerable disagreement over the data collected and paralysis about doing anything with them.
2. **Distrust.** High levels of distrust in the organization can render the survey feedback ineffective. Employees need to trust that their responses will remain anonymous and that management is serious about sharing the data and solving problems jointly.
3. **Unacceptable topics.** Most organizations have certain topics that they do not want examined. This can severely constrain the scope of the survey process, particularly if the neglected topics are important to employees.
4. **Organizational disturbance.** The survey-feedback process can unduly disturb organizational functioning. Data collection and feedback typically infringe on employee work time. Moreover, administration of a survey can call attention to issues with which management is unwilling to deal, and can create unrealistic expectations about organizational improvement.

6-6d Results of Survey Feedback

Survey feedback has been used widely in business organizations, schools, hospitals, federal and state governments, and the military. The navy has used survey feedback in more than 500 navy commands. More than 150,000 individual surveys were completed, and a large bank of computerized research data was generated. Promising results were noted among survey indices on nonjudicial punishment rates, incidence of drug abuse reports, and performance of ships undergoing refresher training (a post overhaul training and evaluation period).[26] Positive results have been reported in such diverse areas as an industrial organization in Sweden and the Israeli Army.[27]

One of the most important studies of survey feedback was done by Bowers, who conducted a five-year longitudinal study (the Intercompany Longitudinal Study) of 23 organizations in 15 companies involving more than 14,000 people in both white-collar and blue-collar positions.[28] In each of the 23 organizations studied, repeat measurements were taken. The study compared survey feedback with three other OD interventions: interpersonal process consultation, task process consultation, and laboratory training. The study reported that survey feedback was the most effective of the four interventions and the only one "associated with large across-the-board positive changes in organization climate."[29] Although these findings have been questioned on a number of methodological grounds,[30] the original conclusion that survey feedback is effective in achieving organizational change was supported. The study suggested that any conclusions to be drawn from action research and survey-feedback studies should be based, at least in part, on objective operating data.

Comprehensive reviews of the literature reveal differing perspectives on the effects of survey feedback. In one review, survey feedback's biggest impact was on attitudes and perceptions of the work situation. The study suggested that survey feedback might best be viewed as a bridge between the diagnosis of organizational problems and the implementation of problem-solving methods because little evidence suggests that survey feedback alone will result in changes in individual behavior or organizational output.[31] This view is supported by research suggesting that the more the data were used to solve problems between initial surveys and later surveys, the more the data improved.[32] Similarly, Church and his colleagues, based on a longitudinal evaluation of a survey feedback process in a large multinational corporation, found that groups that shared feedback data and acted on that data were more likely to report positive attitudes about the company, their manager, job training, and support for work-life balance.[33] The authors stated, "Put another way, the impact of sharing and acting on survey data on overall employee attitudes is (a) significant and pronounced, (b) replicable over time, (c) applies across different employee groups/levels, and (d) applies across content areas and overall rating tendencies. If there was ever a reason to decide to take action from an organizational survey effort, this is a clear mandate."

Another study suggested that survey feedback has positive effects on both outcome variables (for example, productivity, costs, and absenteeism) and process variables (for example, employee openness, decision making, and motivation) in 53% and 48%, respectively, of the studies measuring those variables. When compared with other OD approaches, survey feedback was only bettered by interventions using several approaches together—for example, change programs involving a combination of survey feedback, process consultation, and team building.[34] On the other hand, another review found that, in contrast to laboratory training and team building, survey feedback was least effective, with only 33% of the studies that measured hard outcomes reporting success. The success rate increased to 45%, however, when survey feedback was combined with team building.[35] Finally, a meta-analysis of OD process interventions and individual attitudes suggested that survey feedback was not significantly associated with overall satisfaction or attitudes about coworkers, the job, or the organization. Survey feedback was able to account for only about 11% of the variance in satisfaction and other attitudes.[36]

Studies of specific survey-feedback interventions identify conditions that improve the success of this technique. One study in an urban school district reported difficulties with survey feedback and suggested that its effectiveness depends partly on the quality of those leading the change effort, members' understanding of the process, the extent to which the survey focuses on issues important to participants, and the degree to which the values expressed by the survey are congruent with those of the respondents.[37] Another study in the military concluded that survey feedback works best when supervisors play an active role in feeding back data to employees and helping them to work with the data.[38] Similarly, a field study of funeral cooperative societies concluded that the use and dissemination of survey results increased when organization members were closely involved in developing and carrying out the project and when the consultant provided technical assistance in the form of data analysis and interpretation.[39] Finally, a long-term study of survey feedback in an underground mining operation suggested that continued, periodic use of survey feedback can produce significant changes in organizations.[40]

SUMMARY

This chapter described methods for collecting, analyzing, and feeding back diagnostic data. Because diagnosing is an important step that occurs frequently in the planned change process, a working familiarity with these techniques is essential. Methods of data collection include questionnaires, interviews, observation, and unobtrusive measures. Methods of analysis include qualitative techniques, such as content analysis and force-field analysis, and quantitative techniques, such as the determination of mean, standard deviation, and frequency distributions; scattergrams and correlation coefficients; as well as difference tests. Feeding back data to a client system is concerned with identifying the content of the data to be fed back and designing a feedback process that ensures ownership of the data. If members own the data, they will be motivated to solve organizational problems. A special application of the data collection and feedback process is called survey feedback, which enables OD practitioners to collect diagnostic data from a large number of organization members and to feed back that information for purposes of problem solving.

NOTES

1. S. Mohrman, T. Cummings, and E. Lawler III, "Creating Useful Knowledge with Organizations: Relationship and Process Issues," in *Producing Useful Knowledge for Organizations*, ed. R. Kilmann and K. Thomas (New York: Praeger, 1983): 613–24; C. Argyris, R. Putnam, and D. Smith, eds., *Action Science* (San Francisco: Jossey-Bass, 1985); E. Lawler III, A. Mohrman, S. Mohrman, G. Ledford Jr., and T. Cummings, *Doing Research That Is Useful for Theory and Practice* (San Francisco: Jossey-Bass, 1985).
2. D. Nadler, *Feedback and Organization Development: Using Data-Based Methods* (Reading, MA: Addison-Wesley, 1977): 110–14.
3. W. Nielsen, N. Nykodym, and D. Brown, "Ethics and Organizational Change," *Asia Pacific Journal of Human Resources* 29 (1991).
4. Nadler, *Feedback*, 105–7.
5. W. Wymer and J. Carsten, "Alternative Ways to Gather Opinion," *HR Magazine*, April 1992, 71–78.
6. Examples of basic resource books on survey methodology include L. Rea and R. Parker, *Designing and Conducting Survey Research: A Comprehensive Guide* (San Francisco: Jossey-Bass, 2012); W. Saris and I. Gallhofer, *Design, Evaluation, and Analysis for Survey Research* (New York: Wiley-Interscience, 2007); S. Seashore, E. Lawler III, P. Mirvis, and C. Cammann, *Assessing Organizational Change* (New York: Wiley-Interscience, 1983); E. Lawler III, D. Nadler, and C. Cammann, *Organizational Assessment: Perspectives on the Measurement of Organizational Behavior and the Quality of Work Life* (New York: Wiley-Interscience, 1980).
7. J. Taylor and D. Bowers, *Survey of Organizations: A Machine-Scored Standardized Questionnaire Instrument* (Ann Arbor: Institute for Social Research, University of Michigan, 1972); C. Cammann, M. Fichman, G. Jenkins, and J. Klesh, "Assessing the Attitudes and Perceptions of Organizational Members," in *Assessing Organizational Change: A Guide to Methods, Measures, and Practices*, ed. S. Seashore, E. Lawler III, P. Mirvis, and C. Cammann (New York: Wiley-Interscience, 1983), 71–138.
8. M. Weisbord, "Organizational Diagnosis: Six Places to Look for Trouble with or without a Theory," *Group and Organization Studies* 1 (1976): 430–37; R. Preziosi, "Organizational Diagnosis Questionnaire," in *The 1980 Handbook for Group*

Facilitators, ed. J. Pfeiffer (San Diego: University Associates, 1980); W. Dyer, *Team Building: Issues and Alternatives* (Reading, MA: Addison-Wesley, 1977); J. Hackman and G. Oldham, *Work Redesign* (Reading, MA: Addison-Wesley, 1980); K. Cameron and R. Quinn, *Diagnosing and Changing Organizational Culture* (Reading, MA: Addison-Wesley, 1999).

9. J. Fordyce and R. Weil, *Managing WITH People*, 2nd ed. (Reading, MA: Addison-Wesley, 1979); R. Krueger and M. Casey, *Focus Groups: A Practical Guide for Applied Research*, 4th ed. (Thousand Oaks, CA: Sage Publications, 2009).
10. J. Daniel, *Sampling Essentials: Practical Guidelines for Making Sampling Choices* (Thousand Oaks, CA: Sage Publications, 2012).
11. Daniel, *Sampling Essentials*; W. Deming, *Sampling Design* (New York: John Wiley & Sons, 1960).
12. K. Krippendorf, *Content Analysis: An Introduction to Its Methodology*, 3rd ed. (Thousand Oaks, CA: Sage Publications, 2013).
13. K. Lewin, *Field Theory in Social Science* (New York: Harper & Row, 1951).
14. A simple explanation on quantitative issues in OD can be found in: S. Wagner, N. Martin, and C. Hammond, "A Brief Primer on Quantitative Measurement for the OD Professional," *OD Practitioner* 34 (2002): 53–57. More sophisticated methods of quantitative analysis are found in the following sources: W. Hays, *Statistics* (New York: Holt, Rinehart, & Winston, 1963); J. Nunnally and I. Bernstein, *Psychometric Theory*, 3rd ed. (New York: McGraw-Hill, 1994); F. Kerlinger, *Foundations of Behavioral Research*, 2nd ed. (New York: Holt, Rinehart, & Winston, 1973); J. Cohen, P. Cohen, S. West, and L. Aiken, *Applied Multiple Regression/Correlation Analysis for the Behavioral Sciences*, 3rd ed. (Hillsdale, NJ: Routledge Academic, 2002); E. Pedhazur, *Multiple Regression in Behavioral Research* (New York: Harcourt Brace, 1997).
15. A. Armenakis and H. Field, "The Development of Organizational Diagnostic Norms: An Application of Client Involvement," *Consultation* 6 (Spring 1987): 20–31.
16. Cohen, Cohen, West, and Aiken, *Applied Multiple Regression*.
17. J. Folkman, *The Power of Feedback: 35 Principles for Turning Feedback from Others into Personal and Professional Change* (New York: John Wiley & Sons, 2006); S. Mohrman, T. Cummings, and E. Lawler III, "Creating Useful Knowledge with Organizations: Relationship and Process Issues," in *Producing Useful Knowledge for Organizations*, ed. R. Kilmann and K. Thomas (New York: Praeger, 1983), 613–24.
18. C. Argyris, *Intervention Theory and Method: A Behavioral Science View* (Reading, MA: Addison-Wesley, 1970); P. Block, *Flawless Consulting: A Guide to Getting Your Expertise Used*, 3rd ed. (San Francisco: Jossey-Bass, 2011).
19. D. Nadler, *Feedback and Organization Development: Using Data-Based Methods* (Reading, MA: Addison-Wesley, 1977), 156–58.
20. G. Ledford and C. Worley, "Some Guidelines for Effective Survey Feedback" (working paper, Center for Effective Organizations, University of Southern California, Los Angeles, 1987).
21. D. Nadler, P. Mirvis, and C. Cammann, "The Ongoing Feedback System: Experimenting with a New Managerial Tool," *Organizational Dynamics* 4 (Spring 1976): 63–80.
22. F. Mann, "Studying and Creating Change," in *The Planning of Change*, ed. W. Bennis, K. Benne, and R. Chin (New York: Holt, Rinehart, & Winston, 1964), 605–15; Nadler, *Feedback*; A. Church, A. Margiloff, and C. Coruzzi, "Using Surveys for Change: An Applied Example in a Pharmaceuticals Organization," *Leadership and Organization Development Journal* 16 (1995): 3–12; J. Folkman and J. Zenger, *Employee Surveys That Make a Difference: Using Customized Feedback Tools to Transform Your Organization* (New York: Executive Excellence, 1999).
23. Ledford and Worley, "Effective Survey Feedback."
24. M. Sashkin and R. Cooke, "Organizational Structure as a Moderator of the Effects of Data-Based Change Programs" (paper delivered at the thirty-sixth annual meeting of the Academy of Management, Kansas City, 1976); D. Nadler, "Alternative Data-Feedback Designs for Organizational Intervention," *The 1979 Annual Handbook for Group Facilitators*, ed. J. Jones and J. Pfeiffer (La Jolla, CA: University Associates, 1979), 78–92.
25. S. Seashore, "Surveys in Organizations," in *Handbook of Organizational Behavior*, ed. J. Lorsch (Englewood Cliffs, NJ: Prentice Hall, 1987), 142.
26. R. Forbes, "Quo Vadis: The Navy and Organization Development" (paper delivered at the Fifth Psychology in the Air Force Symposium, United States Air Force Academy, Colorado Springs, CO, April 8, 1976).
27. S. Rubenowitz, Gottenburg, Sweden: Göteborg Universitet, personal communication, 1988; D. Eden and S. Shlomo, "Survey-Based OD in the Israel Defense Forces: A Field Experiment" (undated manuscript, Tel Aviv University).
28. D. Bowers, "OD Techniques and Their Result in 23 Organizations: The Michigan ICL Study," *Journal of Applied Behavioral Science* 9 (January–March 1973): 21–43.
29. Ibid., 42.
30. W. Pasmore, "Backfeed, The Michigan ICL Study Revisited: An Alternative Explanation of the Results," *Journal of Applied Behavioral Science* 12 (April–June 1976): 245–51; W. Pasmore and D. King, "The Michigan ICL Study Revisited: A Critical Review" (working paper no. 548, Krannert Graduate School of Industrial Administration, West Lafayette, IN, 1976).

31. F. Friedlander and L. Brown, "Organization Development," in *Annual Review of Psychology*, ed. M. Rosenzweig and L. Porter (Palo Alto, CA: Annual Reviews, 1974).
32. D. Born and J. Mathieu, "Differential Effects of Survey-Guided Feedback: The Rich Get Richer and the Poor Get Poorer," *Group and Organization Management* 21 (1996): 388–404.
33. A. Church, L. Golay, C. Rotolo, M. Tuller, A. Shull, and E. Desrosiers, "Without Effort there can be no Change: Reexamining the Impact of Survey Feedback and Action Planning on Employee Attitudes," in *Research in Organizational Change and Development, vol.* 20 (Emerald Group Publishing Limited, 2012), 223–64.
34. J. Porras and P. O. Berg, "The Impact of Organization Development," *Academy of Management Review* 3 (April 1978): 249–66.
35. J. Nicholas, "The Comparative Impact of Organization Development Interventions on Hard Criteria Measures," *Academy of Management Review* 7 (October 1982): 531–42.
36. G. Neuman, J. Edwards, and N. Raju, "Organizational Development Interventions: A Meta-Analysis of Their Effects on Satisfaction and Other Attitudes," *Personnel Psychology* 42 (1989): 461–83.
37. S. Mohrman, A. Mohrman, R. Cooke, and R. Duncan, "Survey Feedback and Problem-Solving Intervention in a School District: 'We'll Take the Survey But You Can Keep the Feedback,'" in *Failures in Organization Development and Change*, ed. P. Mirvis and D. Berg (New York: John Wiley & Sons, 1977), 149–90.
38. F. Conlon and L. Short, "An Empirical Examination of Survey Feedback as an Organizational Change Device," *Academy of Management Proceedings* (1983): 225–29.
39. R. Sommer, "An Experimental Investigation of the Action Research Approach," *Journal of Applied Behavioral Science* 23 (1987): 185–99.
40. J. Gavin, "Observation from a Long-Term Survey-Guided Consultation with a Mining Company," *Journal of Applied Behavioral Science* 21 (1985): 201–20.

Designing Interventions

learning objectives

- Describe the interventions presented in the text.
- Discuss how contingencies related to the change situation affect the design of effective organization development (OD) interventions.
- Discuss how contingencies related to the target of change affect the design of effective OD interventions.

An organization development intervention is a sequence of activities, actions, and events intended to help an organization improve its performance and effectiveness. Designing interventions, or action planning, derives from careful diagnosis and is meant to resolve specific problems and to improve particular areas of organizational functioning identified in the diagnosis. Organization development (OD) interventions vary from standardized programs that have been developed and used in many organizations to relatively unique programs tailored to a specific organization or department.

This chapter serves as an overview of the intervention design process. It briefly describes the various types of OD interventions presented in this book. Parts 3–6 of this text describe fully the major interventions used in OD today. Criteria that define effective OD interventions are discussed and contingencies that guide successful intervention design are identified.

7-1 Overview of Interventions

The OD interventions described here represent the major organization change methods used in OD today. They include four major types of planned change: human process interventions, technostructural interventions, human resource management interventions, and strategic change interventions.

7-1a Human Process Interventions

Part 3 of the book presents interventions focusing on people within organizations and the processes through which they accomplish organizational goals. These processes include communication, problem solving, group decision making, and leadership. This type of intervention is deeply rooted in OD's history and represents the earliest change programs characterizing the field. Human process interventions derive mainly from the disciplines of psychology and social psychology and the applied fields of group dynamics and human relations. Practitioners applying these interventions generally value human fulfillment and expect that organizational effectiveness follows from improved functioning of people and organizational processes.[1]

Chapter 10 discusses human process interventions related to interpersonal relationships and group dynamics. They are among the oldest and most applied interventions in OD and include the following three change programs:

1. **Process consultation.** This intervention focuses on interpersonal relations and social dynamics occurring in work groups. Typically, a process consultant helps group members diagnose group functioning and devise appropriate solutions to process problems, such as dysfunctional conflict, poor communication, and ineffective norms. The aim is to help members gain the skills and understanding necessary to identify and solve interpersonal and group problems themselves.
2. **Third-party intervention.** This change method is a form of process consultation aimed at dysfunctional interpersonal relations in organizations. Interpersonal conflict may derive from substantive issues, such as disputes over work methods, or from interpersonal issues, such as miscommunication. The third-party intervener helps people resolve conflicts through such methods as problem solving, bargaining, and conciliation.
3. **Team building.** This intervention helps work groups become more effective in accomplishing tasks. Like process consultation, team building helps members diagnose group processes and devise solutions to problems. It goes beyond group processes, however, to include examination of the group's task, member roles, and strategies for performing tasks. The OD practitioner also may function as a resource person offering expertise related to the group's task.

Chapter 11 presents human process interventions that are more system-wide than those described in Chapter 10. They typically focus on the total organization or an entire department, as well as on relations between groups. They include three interventions:

1. **Organization confrontation meeting.** This change method mobilizes organization members to identify problems, set action targets, and begin working on problems. It is usually applied when organizations are experiencing stress and when management needs to organize resources for immediate problem solving. The intervention generally includes various groupings of employees in identifying and solving problems.
2. **Intergroup relations.** These interventions are designed to improve interactions among different groups or departments in organizations. The microcosm group intervention involves a small group of people whose backgrounds closely match the organizational problems being addressed. This group addresses the problems and develops means to solve them. The intergroup conflict model typically involves an OD practitioner helping two groups understand the causes of their conflict and choosing appropriate solutions.
3. **Large group interventions.** These interventions involve getting a broad variety of stakeholders into a large meeting to clarify important values, to develop new ways of working, to articulate a new vision for the organization, or to solve pressing organizational problems. Such meetings are powerful tools for creating awareness of organizational problems and opportunities for specifying valued directions for future action.

7-1b Technostructural Interventions

Part 4 of the book presents interventions focusing on an organization's technology (e.g., task methods and job design) and structure (e.g., division of labor and hierarchy). These change methods are receiving increasing attention in OD, especially in light of current concerns about productivity and organizational effectiveness. They include approaches to employee involvement, as well as methods for structuring organizations, groups, and jobs. Technostructural interventions are rooted in the disciplines of engineering, sociology, and psychology and in the applied fields of sociotechnical systems and organization design. Practitioners generally stress both productivity and human fulfillment and expect that organization effectiveness will result from appropriate work designs and organization structures.[2]

In Chapter 12, we discuss the following three technostructural interventions concerned with restructuring organizations:

1. **Structural design.** This change process concerns the organization's division of labor—how tasks are subdivided into work units and how those units are coordinated for task completion. Interventions aimed at structural design include moving from more traditional ways of dividing the organization's overall work (such as functional, self-contained unit, and matrix structures) to more integrative and flexible forms (such as process-based, customer-centric, and network-based structures). Diagnostic guidelines exist to determine which structure is appropriate for particular organizational environments, technologies, and conditions.
2. **Downsizing.** This intervention reduces costs and bureaucracy by decreasing the size of the organization through personnel layoffs, organization redesign, and outsourcing. Each of these downsizing methods must be planned with a clear understanding of the organization's strategy.
3. **Reengineering.** This intervention radically redesigns the organization's core work processes to create tighter linkage and coordination among the different tasks. This workflow integration results in faster, more responsive task performance. Reengineering is often accomplished with new information technology that permits employees to control and coordinate work processes more effectively. Reengineering often fails if it ignores the basic principles and processes of OD.

Chapter 13 is concerned with methods for involving employees in decision making. These generally attempt to move knowledge, power, information, and rewards downward in the organization. They include the following three interventions:

1. **Parallel structures.** This intervention involves organization members in resolving ill-defined, complex problems. Parallel structures, such as cooperative union-management projects and quality circles, operate in conjunction with the formal organization and provide members with an alternative setting in which to address problems and propose solutions.
2. **Total quality management.** This intervention involves organization members in continuously improving quality as part of normal work operations. It includes extensive training in total quality management knowledge and skills and the constant application of that expertise to improve quality at work.
3. **High-involvement organizations.** This comprehensive intervention designs almost all features of the organization to promote high levels of employee involvement. Changes in structure, work design, information and control systems, and human resource practices jointly support member involvement in relevant decision making throughout the firm.

Chapter 14 discusses designing work for individual jobs and interactive groups. These change programs involve engineering, motivational, and sociotechnical systems approaches to work design. They include two OD interventions:

1. **Job enrichment**. Based on motivational principles, this intervention creates jobs that employees are likely to experience as meaningful with high levels of autonomy and feedback from performing the work. Job enrichment results in high job satisfaction and performance quality, especially for those individuals who have needs for growth and learning at work.
2. **Self-managed work teams**. This intervention designs work for teams performing highly interrelated tasks that require real-time decision making. Self-managed work teams are typically responsible for a complete product or service and members are able to make decisions and control their own task behaviors without a lot of external controls.

7-1c Human Resources Management Interventions

Part 5 of the book focuses on interventions used to select, reward, develop, and support people in organizations. These practices traditionally have been associated with the human resources function in organizations. In recent years, interest has grown in integrating human resources management with OD. Human resources management interventions are rooted in labor relations and in the applied practices of compensation and benefits, employee selection and placement, performance appraisal, career development, and employee diversity and wellness. Practitioners in this area typically focus on the people in organizations, believing that organizational effectiveness results from improved practices for integrating employees into organizations.

Chapter 15 discusses interventions concerning performance management, including the following change programs:

1. **Goal setting.** This change program involves setting clear and challenging goals. It attempts to improve organization effectiveness by establishing a better fit between personal and organizational objectives. Managers and subordinates periodically meet to plan work, review accomplishments, and solve problems in achieving goals. Management by Objectives, a special case of the goal-setting intervention, is also discussed.
2. **Performance appraisal.** This intervention is a systematic process of jointly assessing work-related achievements, strengths, and weaknesses. It is the primary human resources management intervention for providing performance feedback to individuals and work groups. Performance appraisal represents an important link between goal-setting and reward systems.
3. **Reward systems.** This intervention involves the design of organizational rewards to improve employee satisfaction and performance. It includes innovative approaches to pay, promotions, and fringe benefits.

Chapter 16 focuses on these change methods for managing, developing, and retaining organizational talent:

1. **Coaching and mentoring.** This intervention helps executives and employees to clarify their goals, deal with potential stumbling blocks, and improve their performance. It often involves a one-on-one relationship between the OD practitioner and the client and focuses on personal learning that gets transferred into organizational results and more effective leadership skills.

2. **Management and leadership development.** Among the oldest strategies for organizational change, training and development interventions increase organization members' skills and knowledge. The focus of these interventions is on building the competencies needed to lead the organization in the future and includes traditional classroom lectures as well as simulations, action learning, and case studies.
3. **Career planning and development.** This intervention helps people choose organizations and career paths and attain career objectives. It generally focuses on managers and professional staff and is seen as a way to increase the retention of valuable employees and to improve the quality of work life.

Chapter 17 describes interventions for supporting organization members:

1. **Managing workforce diversity.** This change program makes human resources practices more responsive to a variety of individual needs. Important trends, such as the increasing number of women, ethnic minorities, and physically and mentally challenged people in the workforce, require a more flexible set of policies and practices.
2. **Employee stress and wellness.** These interventions include employee assistance programs (EAPs) and stress management. EAPs are counseling programs that help employees deal with substance abuse and mental health, marital, and financial problems that often are associated with poor work performance. Stress-management programs help employees cope with the negative consequences of stress at work. They help people reduce specific sources of stress, such as role conflict and ambiguity, and provide methods for reducing such stress symptoms as hypertension and anxiety.

7-1d Strategic Change Interventions

Part 6 of the book considers interventions that link the internal functioning of the organization to the larger environment and transform the organization to keep pace with changing conditions. These change programs are among the newest additions to OD. They are implemented organization-wide and bring about a fit between business strategy, organization design, and the larger environment. The interventions derive from the disciplines of strategic management, organization theory, economics, and anthropology.

In Chapter 18, we describe the characteristics of transformational change and discuss interventions that transform the way the organization relates to its environment or operates internally:

1. **Organization design.** Organization design interventions address the different elements that comprise the "architecture" of the organization, including structure, work design, human resources practices, and management processes. In either domestic or worldwide settings, organization design aligns these components with the organization's strategy and with each other so they mutually direct behavior to execute the strategy.
2. **Integrated strategic change.** This comprehensive OD intervention describes how planned change can make a value-added contribution to strategic management. It argues that business strategies and organizational systems must be changed together in response to external and internal disruptions. A strategic change plan helps members manage the transition between a current strategy and organization design and the desired future strategy and design.
3. **Culture change.** This intervention helps an organization develop a culture (behaviors, values, beliefs, and norms) appropriate to its strategy and competitive environment. It focuses on developing a strong organization culture to keep organization members pulling in the same direction.

Chapter 19 addresses the increasing need for organizations to change continuously in response to rapidly changing environments. These interventions are designed to support continuous organizational change:

1. **Dynamic strategy making.** This intervention helps organizations build a strategic system that can adapt continually to changing conditions. It involves both the content (the "what") of strategy formulation and the process (the "how" and "who") of strategy implementation.
2. **Self-designing organizations.** This change program helps organizations gain the capacity to alter themselves fundamentally. It is a highly participative process involving multiple stakeholders in setting strategic directions and designing and implementing appropriate structures and systems. Organizations learn how to design and implement their own strategic changes.
3. **Learning organizations.** This intervention involves increasing the organization's capability to acquire and develop new knowledge, including how that knowledge can be organized and used to improve organization performance. These changes enable organizations to move beyond solving existing problems to learn how to improve themselves continuously.
4. **Built-to-change organizations.** This approach to continuous change challenges the traditional assumption that stability is the key to organizational success. Built-to-change organizations, on the other hand, assume that the source of effectiveness is the ability to change continuously. The features, skills and knowledge, and processes of leading and managing these adaptable organizations are described.

In the final chapter of Part 6, Chapter 20, we describe strategic interventions that shape how organizations collaborate with each other:

1. **Mergers and acquisitions.** This intervention describes how OD practitioners can assist two or more organizations to form a new entity. Addressing key strategic, leadership, and cultural issues prior to the legal and financial transaction helps to smooth subsequent operational integration of the organizations.
2. **Alliances.** This collaborative intervention helps two organizations pursue common goals through the sharing of resources, including intellectual property, people, capital, technology, capabilities, or physical assets. Effective alliance development generally follows a process of strategy formulation, partner selection, alliance structuring and start-up, and alliance operation and adjustment.
3. **Networks.** This intervention helps to develop relationships among three or more organizations to perform tasks or solve problems that are too complex for single organizations to resolve. It helps organizations recognize the need for partnerships and develop appropriate structures for implementing them. It also addresses how to manage change within existing networks.

7-2 What Are Effective Interventions?

OD interventions involve a set of sequenced and planned actions or events intended to help an organization increase its effectiveness. Interventions purposely disrupt the status quo; they are deliberate attempts to change an organization or subunit toward a different and more effective state. Three major criteria define an effective OD intervention: (1) the extent to which it fits the needs of the organization; (2) the degree to which it is based on causal knowledge of intended outcomes; and (3) the extent to which it transfers change management competence to organization members.

The first criterion concerns the extent to which the intervention is relevant to the organization and its members. Effective interventions are based on valid information about the organization's functioning; they provide organization members with opportunities to make free and informed choices; and they gain members' internal commitment to those choices.[3]

Valid information is the result of an accurate diagnosis of the organization's functioning. It must reflect fairly what organization members perceive and feel about their primary concerns and issues. *Free and informed choice* suggests that members are actively involved in making decisions about the changes that will affect them. This principle also means that they can choose not to participate and that interventions will not be imposed on them. This is an important distinction between change management—where a change legitimately can be imposed on people—and OD—where the intent of the change process is to build capacity for change *and* increase effectiveness. *Internal commitment* means that organization members accept ownership of the intervention and take responsibility for implementing it. If interventions are to result in meaningful changes, management, staff, and other relevant members must be committed to carrying them out.

The second criterion of an effective intervention involves knowledge of outcomes. Because interventions are intended to produce specific results, they must be based on valid knowledge that those outcomes actually can be produced. Otherwise, there is no scientific basis for designing an effective OD intervention. Unfortunately—and in contrast to other applied disciplines, such as medicine and engineering—knowledge of intervention effects is in a rudimentary stage of development in OD. Much of the evaluation research lacks sufficient rigor to make strong causal inferences about the success or failure of change programs. (Chapter 9 discusses how to evaluate OD programs rigorously.) Moreover, few attempts have been made to examine the comparative effects of different OD techniques. All of these factors make it difficult to know whether one method is more effective than another.

Despite these problems, more attempts are being made to assess systematically the strengths and weaknesses of OD interventions and to compare the impact of different techniques on organization effectiveness.[4] Many of the OD interventions that are discussed in Parts 3–6 have been subjected to evaluative research, and the chapters explore the research appropriate to them.

The third criterion of an effective intervention involves the extent to which it enhances the organization's capacity to manage change. The values underlying OD suggest that following an intervention, organization members should be better able to carry out planned change activities on their own. From active participation in designing and implementing the intervention, they should gain knowledge and skill in managing change. Competence in change management is essential in today's environment, where technological, social, economic, and political changes are rapid and persistent. Many organizations, such as Capital One, The Hartford, Limited Brands, and Microsoft, recognize this need and are systematically building their change management capabilities.

7-3 How to Design Effective Interventions

Designing OD interventions requires paying careful attention to the needs and dynamics of the change situation and crafting a change program that will be consistent with the previously described criteria of effective interventions. Current knowledge of OD interventions provides only general prescriptions for change. There is scant precise information or research about how to design interventions or how they can be expected to interact with organizational conditions to achieve specific results.[5] Moreover, because the ability to implement most OD interventions is highly dependent on the skills and knowledge of the change agent, the design of an intervention will depend to some extent on the expertise of the practitioner.

Two major sets of contingencies that can affect intervention success have been discussed in the OD literature: those having to do with the change situation and those related to the target of change. Both kinds of contingencies need to be considered in designing interventions.

7-3a Contingencies Related to the Change Situation

Researchers have identified a number of contingencies present in the change situation that can affect intervention success. These include individual differences among organization members (e.g., needs for autonomy), organizational factors (e.g., management style and technical uncertainty), and dimensions of the change process itself (e.g., degree of top-management support). Unless these factors are taken into account, designing an intervention will have little impact on organizational functioning or, worse, it may produce negative results. For example, to resolve motivational problems among blue-collar workers in an oil refinery, it is important to know whether interventions intended to improve motivation (e.g., job enrichment) will succeed with the kinds of people who work there. In many cases, knowledge of these contingencies results in modifying or adjusting the change program to fit the setting. In applying a reward-system intervention to an organization, the changes might have to be modified depending on whether the firm wants to reinforce individual or team performance.

Although knowledge of contingencies is still at a rudimentary stage of development in OD, researchers have discovered several situational factors that can affect intervention success.[6] These include specific contingencies for many of the interventions reviewed in this book, and they will be discussed in respective chapters describing the change programs. Two additional and generic contingencies related to the country or region's national culture and stage of economic development are presented here.

National Culture The applicability and effectiveness of OD in countries outside of the United States is the subject of intense debate.[7] Because OD was developed predominantly by American and Western European practitioners, its practices and methods are heavily influenced by the values and assumptions of these Western industrialized cultures. Thus, traditional approaches to planned change may promote management practices that conflict with the values and assumptions of other societies. Will Chinese cultural values, for example, be preserved or defended as an increasing number of European and American organizations establish operations in that country? How should OD be conducted in an Indian firm operating in the United States? On the other hand, some practitioners believe that OD can result in organizational improvements in any culture.

Researchers have proposed that applying OD in different countries requires a "context-based" approach to designing interventions.[8] This involves fitting the change process to the organization's cultural context, including the values held by members in the particular country or region. These beliefs inform people about behaviors that are important and acceptable in their culture. Cultural values play a major role in shaping the customs and practices that occur within organizations as well, and influencing how members react to phenomena having to do with power, conflict, ambiguity, time, and change.

There is a growing body of knowledge about cultural diversity and its effect on organizational and management practices.[9] As shown in Table 7.1, researchers have

TABLE 7.1

Cultural Values and Organization Customs

Value	Definition	Organization Customs When the Value Is at One Extreme	Representative Countries
Context	The extent to which words carry the meaning of a message; how time is viewed	Ceremony and routines are common Structure is less formal; fewer written policies exist People are often late for appointments	*High:* Asian and Latin American countries *Low:* Scandinavian countries, United States
Power distance	The extent to which members of a society accept that power is distributed unequally in an organization	Decision making is autocratic Superiors consider subordinates as part of a different class Subordinates are closely supervised Employees are not likely to disagree Powerful people are entitled to privileges	*High:* Latin American and Eastern European countries *Low:* Scandinavian countries
Uncertainty avoidance	The extent to which members of an organization tolerate the unfamiliar and unpredictable	Experts have status/authority Clear roles are preferred Conflict is undesirable Change is resisted Conservative practices are preferred	*High:* Asian countries *Low:* European countries
Achievement orientation	The extent to which organization members value assertiveness and the acquisition of material goods	Achievement is reflected in wealth and recognition Decisiveness is valued Larger and faster are better Gender roles are clearly differentiated	*High:* Asian and Latin American countries, South Africa *Low:* Scandinavian countries
Individualism	The extent to which people believe they should be responsible for themselves and their immediate families	Personal initiative is encouraged Time is valuable to individuals Competitiveness is accepted Autonomy is highly valued	*High:* United States *Low:* Latin American and Eastern European countries

identified five key values that describe national cultures and influence organizational customs:

1. **Context orientation.** This value describes how information is conveyed and time is valued in a culture. In low-context cultures, such as Scandinavia and the United States, people communicate directly in words and phrases. The more specific the word, the more meaning is expressed. In addition, time is viewed as discrete and linear—as something that can be spent, used, saved, or wasted. In high-context cultures, on the other hand, the communication medium reflects the message more

than the words, and time is a fluid and flexible concept. For example, social cues in Japan and Venezuela provide as much, if not more, information about a particular situation than do words alone. Business practices in high-context cultures emphasize ceremony and ritual. For example, knowing how to exchange business cards, participate in a reception, or conduct a banquet in China honors the client and facilitates the business relationship. How one behaves is an important signal of support and compliance with the way things are done. Structures are less formal in high-context cultures; there are few written policies and procedures to guide behavior. Because high-context cultures view time as fluid, punctuality for appointments is less a priority than is maintaining relationships.

2. **Power distance.** This value concerns the way people view authority, status differences, and influence patterns. People in high power-distance regions, such as Latin America and Eastern Europe, tend to accept unequal distributions of power and influence, and consequently autocratic and paternalistic decision-making practices are the norm. Organizations in high power-distance cultures tend to be centralized, with several hierarchical levels and a large proportion of supervisory personnel. Subordinates in these organizations represent a lower social class. They expect to be supervised closely and believe that power holders are entitled to special privileges. Such practices would be inappropriate in low power-distance regions, such as Scandinavia, where participative decision making and egalitarian methods prevail.
3. **Uncertainty avoidance.** This value reflects a preference for conservative practices and familiar and predictable situations. People in high uncertainty-avoidance regions, such as Asia, prefer stable routines over change and act to maintain the status quo. They do not like conflict and believe that company rules should not be broken. In regions where uncertainty avoidance is low, such as in many European countries, ambiguity is less threatening. Organizations in these cultures tend to favor fewer rules, higher levels of participation in decision making, more organic structures, and more risk taking.
4. **Achievement orientation.** This value concerns the extent to which the culture favors the acquisition of power and resources. Employees from achievement-oriented cultures, such as Asia and Latin America, place a high value on career advancement, freedom, and salary growth. Organizations in these cultures pursue aggressive goals and can have high levels of stress and conflict. Organizational success is measured in terms of size, growth, and speed. On the other hand, workers in cultures where achievement is less of a driving value, such as those in Scandinavia, prize the social aspects of work, including working conditions and supervision, and typically favor opportunities to learn and grow at work.
5. **Individualism.** This value is concerned with looking out for oneself as opposed to one's group or organization. In high-individualism cultures, such as the United States and Australia, personal initiative and competitiveness are valued strongly. Organizations in individualistic cultures often have high turnover rates and individual rather than group decision-making processes. Employee empowerment is supported when members believe that it improves the probability of personal gain. These cultures encourage personal initiative, competitiveness, and individual autonomy. Conversely, in low individualism countries, such as China, Japan, and Mexico, allegiance to one's group is paramount. Organizations operating in these cultures tend to favor cooperation among employees and loyalty to the company.

Economic Development In addition to cultural context, an important situational contingency affecting OD success is a country's level of industrial and economic development.[10] For example, although long considered an industrial economy, Russia's political and economic transformation, and the concomitant increases in uncertainties over infrastructure, corruption, cash flow, and exchange rates, has radically altered assumptions underlying business practices. Thus, economic development can be judged from social, economic, and political perspectives.[11] For example, a country's development level can be reflected in its information systems and skills; decision-making and action-taking capabilities; project planning and organizing abilities; evaluation and control technologies; leadership, motivational, and reward systems; and human selection, placement, and development levels. The United Nations' Human Development Programme has created a Human Development Index that assesses a country's economic development in terms of life expectancy, educational attainment, and adjusted real income.

Researchers have identified three broad stages of economic development:

1. **Subsistence economies.** Countries such as Pakistan, Nepal, Nigeria, Uganda, and Rwanda have relatively low degrees of development and their economies are primarily agriculture-based. Their populations consume most of what they produce, and any surplus is used to barter for other needed goods and services. A large proportion of the population is unfamiliar with the concept of "employment." Working for someone else in exchange for wages is not common or understood, and consequently few large organizations exist outside of the government. In subsistence economies, OD interventions emphasize global social change and focus on creating conditions for sustainable social and economic progress. These change methods are described in Chapter 21.
2. **Industrializing economies.** Malaysia, Venezuela, India, Turkey, the Philippines, Iran, and the People's Republic of China are moderately developed and tend to be rich in natural resources. An expanding manufacturing base that accounts for increasing amounts of the country's gross domestic product fuels economic growth. The rise of manufacturing also contributes to the formation of a class system including upper-, middle-, and low-income groups. Organizations operating in these nations generally focus on efficiency of operations and revenue growth. Consequently, OD interventions address strategic, structural, and work design issues.[12] They help organizations identify domestic and international markets, develop clear and appropriate goals, and structure themselves to achieve efficient performance and market growth.
3. **Industrial economies.** Highly developed countries, such as Sweden, Japan, France, and the United States, emphasize nonagricultural industry. In these economies, manufactured goods are exported and traded with other industrialized countries; investment funds are available both internally and externally; the workforce is educated and skilled; and technology is often substituted for labor. Because the OD interventions described in this book were developed primarily in industrial economies, they can be expected to have their strongest effects in those contexts. Their continued success cannot be ensured, however, because these countries are advancing rapidly to postindustrial conditions. Here, OD interventions will need to fit into economies driven by information and knowledge, where service outpaces manufacturing, and where national and organizational boundaries are more open and flexible.

How National Culture and Economic Development Affect OD Interventions The situational contingencies of national culture and economic development can have powerful effects on the way OD interventions are designed and implemented in various countries.[13] They can determine whether change proceeds slowly or quickly; involves few or many members; is directed by hierarchical authority or by consensus; and focuses on business, organizational, or human process issues. When the two situational contingencies are considered together, they reveal four different international settings for

FIGURE 7.1

The Cultural and Economic Contexts of International OD Practice

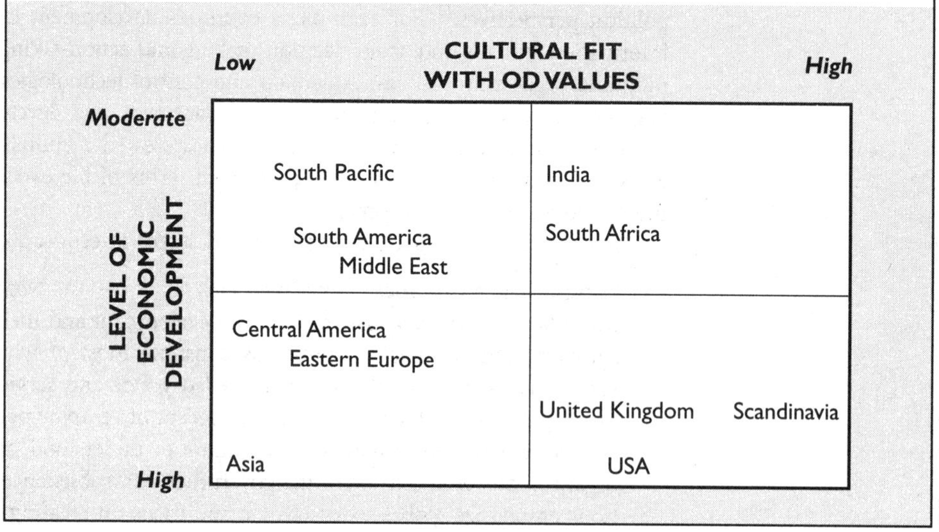

OD practice, as shown in Figure 7.1. These different situations reflect the extent to which a country's culture fits with traditional OD values of direct and honest communication, sharing power, and improving their effectiveness and the degree to which the country is economically developed.[14] When the country's culture supports traditional OD values, OD interventions can be applied to organizational and human process issues with only small adjustments.[15] The more the cultural context differs from OD's traditional values profile, the more the interventions will need to be modified to fit the situation.

In Figure 7.1, the degree of economic development is restricted to industrializing and highly industrialized regions. Subsistence economies are not included because they afford little opportunity to practice traditional OD; in those contexts, a more appropriate strategy is global social change, discussed later in Chapter 21. In general, however, the more developed the economy, the more OD is applied to the organizational and human process issues described in this book. In less-developed situations, OD focuses on business issues, such as procuring raw materials, producing efficiently, and marketing successfully.[16] As shown in Figure 7.1, the four international settings include the following:

1. **Low cultural fit, moderate industrialization.** This context is least suited to traditional OD practice. It includes industrializing economies with some cultural values that align poorly with traditional OD values, including many Middle East nations, such as Iraq, Iran, and the United Arab Emirates; the South Pacific region, including Malaysia and the Philippines; and certain Central and South American countries, such as Brazil, Ecuador, Guatemala, and Nicaragua. These regions are highly dependent on their natural resources and have a relatively small manufacturing base. They tend to be high-context cultures with values of high power-distance and achievement orientation and of moderate uncertainty avoidance, but they also tend toward moderate or high levels of collectivism, especially in relation to family.

   These settings require OD interventions that fit local customs and that address business issues. Cultural values of high power-distance and achievement are inconsistent with traditional OD activities emphasizing openness, collaboration, and empowerment. Moreover, executives in industrializing economies frequently equate OD with human process interventions, such as team building, training, and conflict management. They often perceive OD as too soft to meet their business needs. For example, Egyptian and Filipino managers tend to be autocratic, engage in protracted decision making, and focus on economic and business problems. Consequently, organizational change is slow paced, centrally controlled, and aimed at achieving technical rationality and efficiency.[17]

These contextual forces do not influence all organizations in the same way. A recent study of 20 large group interventions in Mexico suggests that culture may not be as constraining as has been hypothesized.[18] Similarly, in an apparent exception to the rule, the president of Semco S/A (Brazil), Ricardo Semler, designed a highly participative organization.[19] Most Semco employees set their own working hours and approve hires and promotions. Information flows downward through a relatively flat hierarchy, and strategic decisions are made participatively by companywide vote. Brazil's cultural values are not as strong on power distance and masculinity as in other Latin American countries, and that may explain the apparent success of this high-involvement organization. It suggests that OD interventions can be implemented within this cultural context when strongly supported by senior management.

2. **High cultural fit, moderate industrialization.** This international context includes industrializing economies with cultures that align with traditional OD values. Such settings support the kinds of OD processes described in this book, especially technostructural and strategic interventions that focus on business development. According to data on economic development and cultural values, relatively few countries fit this context. India's industrial base and democratic society are growing rapidly and may fit this contingency. Similarly, South Africa's recent political and cultural changes make it one of the most interesting settings in which to practice OD.[20]

   A study of large South African corporations suggests the directions that OD is likely to take in that setting.[21] The study interviewed internal OD practitioners about key organizational responses to the political changes in the country, such as the free election of Nelson Mandela, abolishment of apartheid, and the Reconstruction and Development Program. Change initiatives at Spoornet, Eskom, and Telkom, for example, centered around two strategic and organizational issues. First, the political changes opened up new international markets, provided access to new technologies, and exposed these organizations to global competition. Consequently, these firms initiated planned change efforts to create corporate visions and to identify strategies for entering new markets and acquiring new technologies. Second, the political changes forced corporations to modify specific human resources and organizational practices. The most compelling change was mandated affirmative action quotas. At Spoornet, Eskom, and Telkom, apartheid was thoroughly embedded in the organizations' structures, policies, and physical arrangements. Thus, planned change focused on revising human resources policies and practices. Similarly, organizational structures that had fit well within the stable environment of apartheid were outmoded and too rigid to meet the competitive challenges of international markets. Planned changes for restructuring these firms were implemented as part of longer-term strategies to change corporate culture toward more egalitarian and market-driven values.

3. **Low cultural fit, high industrialization.** This international setting includes industrialized countries with cultures that fit poorly with traditional OD values. Many countries in Central America, Eastern Asia, and Eastern Europe fit this description. Reviews of OD practice in those regions suggest that planned change includes all four types of interventions described in this book, although the change process itself

is adapted to local conditions.[22] For example, Mexico, Venezuela, China, Japan, and Korea are high-context cultures where knowledge of local mannerisms, customs, and rituals is required to understand the meaning of communicated information. To function in such settings, OD practitioners must know not only the language but the social customs as well. Similarly, cultural values emphasizing high levels of power distance, uncertainty avoidance, and achievement orientation foster organizations where roles, status differences, and working conditions are clear; where autocratic and paternalistic decisions are expected; and where the acquisition of wealth and influence by the powerful is accepted. OD interventions that focus on social processes and employee empowerment are not favored naturally in this cultural context and consequently need to be modified to fit the situations.

Japanese and Korean organizations, such as Matsushita, Nissan, Toyota, Fujitsu, NEC, and Hyundai, provide good examples of how OD interventions can be tailored to this global setting. These firms are famous for continuous improvement and quality management practices, and they adapt these interventions to fit the culture. In Asia, OD is an orderly process, driven by consensus and challenging performance goals. Organizational changes are implemented slowly and methodically, roles and behaviors are highly specified so trust builds and change-related uncertainty is reduced. Teamwork and consensus decision-making practices associated with quality-improvement projects also help to manage uncertainty. When large numbers of employees are involved, information is spread quickly and members are kept informed about the changes taking place. Management controls the change process by regulating the implementation of suggestions made by the problem-solving groups. Because these interventions focus on work processes, teamwork and employee involvement do not threaten the power structure. Moreover, continuous improvement interventions do not alter the organization radically but produce small, incremental changes that can add up to impressive gains in long-term productivity and cost reduction. Because Asian values promote a cautious culture that prizes consensus, dignity, and respect, OD tends to be less personal and to focus mainly on workflow improvements. Human process issues are rarely addressed because people are expected to act in ways that do not cause others to "lose face" or to bring shame to the group.

In these cultures, OD practitioners also tailor the change process itself to fit local conditions. Mexican companies, for example, expect OD practitioners to act as experts and to offer concrete advice on how to improve the organization. To be successful, OD practitioners need sufficient status and legitimacy to work with senior management and to act in expert roles.[23] Status typically is associated with academic credentials, senior management experience, high-level titles, or recommendations by highly placed executives and administrators. As might be expected, the change process in Latin America is autocratic and driven downward from the top of the organization. Subordinates or lower-status people generally are not included in diagnostic or implementation activities because inclusion might equalize power differences and threaten the status quo. Moreover, cultural norms discourage employees from speaking out or openly criticizing management. There is relatively little resistance to change because employees readily accept changes dictated by management.

4. **High cultural fit, high industrialization.** This last setting includes industrialized countries with cultural contexts that fit well with traditional OD values. Much of the OD practice described in this book was developed in these situations, particularly in the United States and the United Kingdom,[24] and so we focus here on how OD is practiced in Scandinavian countries—Sweden, Norway, Finland, and Denmark.

Scandinavians enjoy a high standard of living and strong economic development. Because their cultural values most closely match those traditionally espoused in OD, organizational practices are highly participative and egalitarian. It is not surprising, then, that Scandinavian companies, including Saab and Volvo, pioneered sociotechnical interventions to improve productivity and quality of work life. Multiple stakeholders, such as governments, managers, unionists, and staff personnel, actively are involved in all stages of the change process, from entry and diagnosis to intervention and evaluation. The Norwegian government, for example, was instrumental in introducing industrial democracy to that nation's companies. It helped union and management in selected industries implement pilot projects to enhance productivity and quality of work life. This level of involvement is much higher than that typically occurring in the United States. It results in a change process that is heavily oriented to the needs of all organization members. Norwegian labor laws, for example, give unionists the right to participate in technological innovations that can affect their work lives. Such laws also mandate that all employees in the country have the right to enriched forms of work.

7-3b Contingencies Related to the Target of Change

OD interventions often seek to change specific features or parts of organizations. These targets of change are the main focus of many interventions, and researchers have identified two key contingencies related to change targets that can affect intervention success: the organizational issues that the intervention is intended to resolve and the level of organizational system at which the intervention is expected to have a primary impact.

Organizational Issues Organizations need to address certain issues to operate effectively. Figure 7.2 lists these issues along with the OD interventions that are intended to resolve them. (The parts and chapters of this book that describe the specific interventions are also identified in the figure.) It shows the following four interrelated issues that are key targets of OD interventions:

1. **Strategic issues.** Organizations need to decide what products or services they will provide and the markets in which they will compete, as well as how to relate to their environments and how to transform themselves to keep pace with changing conditions. These strategic issues are among the most critical ones facing organizations in today's changing and highly complex environments. Strategic change interventions address these issues.
2. **Technological and structural issues**. Organizations must decide how to divide work into departments and then how to coordinate among those departments to support strategic directions. They also must make decisions about how to deliver products or services and how to link people to tasks. Technostructural interventions deal with these structural and technological issues.
3. **Human resources issues.** These issues are concerned with attracting talented people to the organization, setting goals for them, appraising and rewarding their performance, and ensuring that they develop their careers and sustain their wellness. Human resources management interventions attend to these issues.
4. **Human process issues.** These issues have to do with social processes occurring among organization members, such as communication, decision making, leadership, and group dynamics. Human process interventions focus on these kinds of issues.

FIGURE 7.2

Types of OD Interventions and Organizational Issues

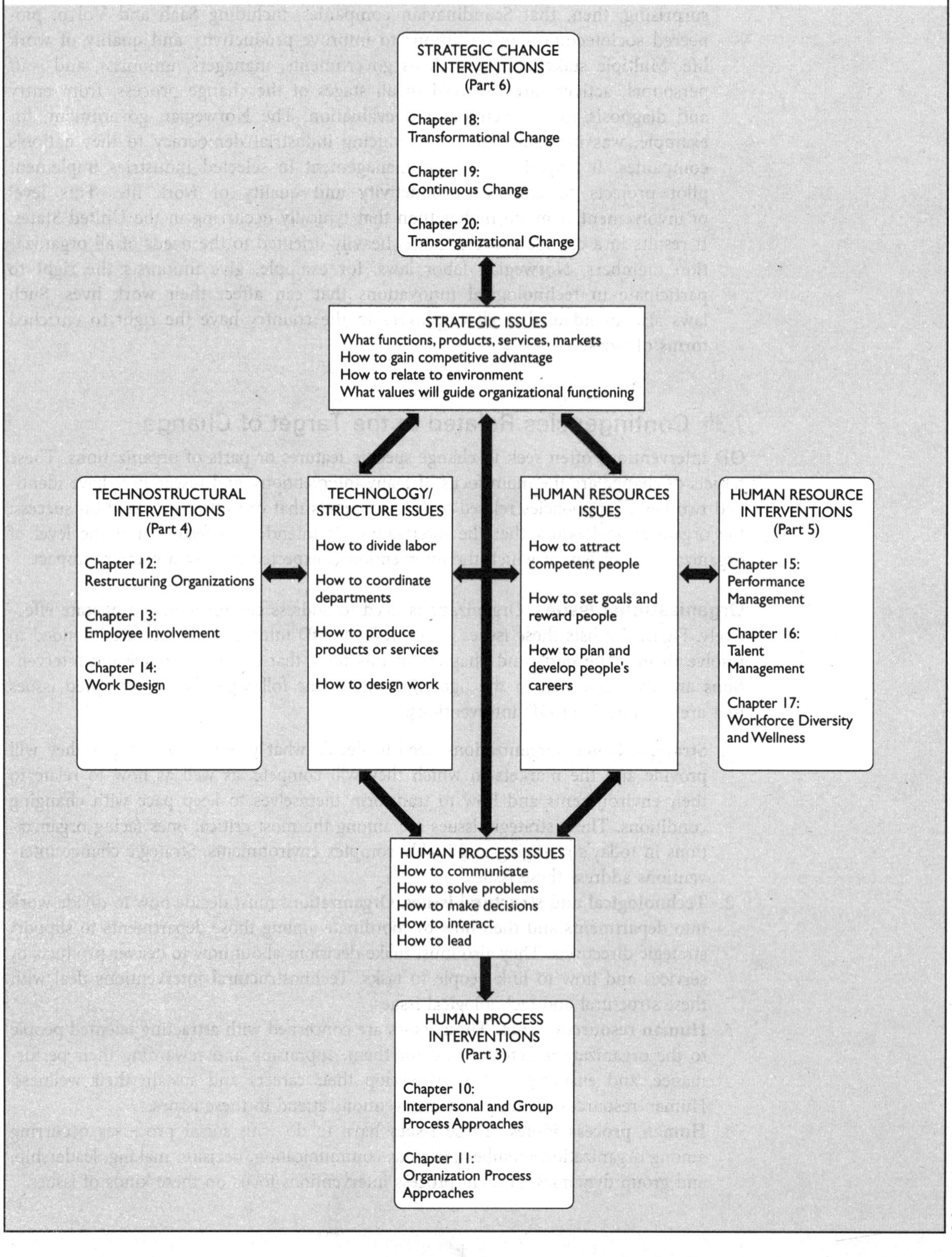

Consistent with systems theory as described in Chapter 5, these organizational issues are interrelated and need to be integrated with one another. The double-headed arrows connecting the different issues in Figure 7.2 represent the fits or linkages among them. Organizations need to match answers to one set of questions with answers to other sets of questions to achieve high levels of effectiveness. For example, decisions about gaining competitive advantage need to fit with choices about organization structure, setting goals for and rewarding people, communication, and problem solving.

The interventions presented in this book are intended to resolve these different concerns. As shown in Figure 7.2, particular OD interventions apply to specific issues. Thus, intervention design must create change methods appropriate to the organizational issues identified in diagnosis. Moreover, because the organizational issues are themselves linked together, OD interventions similarly need to be integrated with one another. For example, a goal-setting intervention that tries to establish motivating goals may need to be integrated with supporting interventions, such as a reward system that links pay to goal achievement.

The key point is to think systemically.[25] Interventions aimed at one kind of organizational issue will invariably have repercussions on other kinds of issues. Careful thinking about how OD interventions affect the different kinds of issues and how different change programs might be integrated to bring about a broader and more coherent impact on organizational functioning is critical to effective OD intervention.

Organizational Levels In addition to facing interrelated issues, organizations function at different levels: individual, group, organization, and transorganization. Thus, organizational levels are targets of change in OD. Table 7.2 lists OD interventions in terms of the level of organization that they primarily affect. For example, some technostructural interventions affect mainly individual jobs and groups (e.g., work design), whereas others impact primarily the total organization (e.g., structural design).

It is important to emphasize that only the primary level affected by the intervention is identified in Table 7.2. Many OD interventions also have a secondary impact on the other levels. For example, structural design affects mainly the organization level, but it can have an indirect effect on groups and individual jobs because it sets the broad parameters for designing work groups and jobs. Again, practitioners need to think systemically. They must design interventions to apply to specific organizational levels, address the possibility of cross-level effects, and integrate interventions affecting different levels to achieve overall success.[26] For example, an intervention to create self-managed work teams may need to be linked to organization-level changes in measurement and reward systems to promote team-based work.

SUMMARY

This chapter discussed designing OD interventions including the four major types of interventions that are presented in this book: (1) human process interventions aimed at people within organizations and their interaction processes; (2) technostructural interventions directed at organization technology and structures for linking people and technology; (3) human resource management interventions focused at integrating people into the organization successfully; and (4) strategic change interventions targeted at how the organization uses its resources to gain a competitive advantage in the larger environment. Designing OD interventions is based on a thorough diagnosis of the organization or subunit. Effective interventions are designed to fit the needs of the organization, are based on causal knowledge of intended outcomes, and transfer competence to manage change to

TABLE 7.2

Types of Interventions and Organization Levels

Interventions	Primary Organization Level Affected		
	Individual	Group	Organization
Human Process (Part 3)			
Process consultation		X	
Third-party interventions	X	X	
Team building		X	
Organization confrontation meeting		X	X
Intergroup relations interventions		X	X
Large group interventions			X
Technostructural (Part 4)			
Structural design			X
Downsizing			X
Reengineering		X	X
Parallel structures		X	X
Total quality management		X	X
High-involvement organizations	X	X	X
Work design	X	X	
Human Resources Management (Part 5)			
Goal setting	X	X	
Performance appraisal	X	X	
Reward systems	X	X	X
Coaching and mentoring	X		
Management and leadership development	X		
Career planning and development interventions	X		
Workforce diversity interventions	X	X	X
Employee stress and wellness interventions	X		
Strategic (Part 6)			
Organization design			X
Integrated strategic change			X
Culture change			X
Dynamic strategy making			X
Self-designing organizations		X	X
Organization learning and knowledge management		X	X
Built-to-change			X
Merger-and-acquisition integration			X
Strategic alliance interventions			X
Network interventions			X

organization members. Researchers have identified two kinds of contingencies on which the success of OD interventions depends. One type of contingency involves the change situation and includes the national culture and stage of economic development of the country within which the intervention is applied. The other kind of contingency has to do with the target of change and includes the organizational issue that the intervention is intended to resolve and the organizational level at which the intervention is expected to have a primary impact. OD interventions need to be designed to fit these contingencies to achieve expected outcomes.

NOTES

1. B. Burnes and B. Cooke, "The Past, Present, and Future of Organization Development: Taking the Long View," *Human Relations* 65 (2012): 1395–1429; F. Friedlander and L. D. Brown, "Organization Development," *Annual Review of Psychology* 25 (1974): 313–41.
2. E. Lawler III, *The Ultimate Advantage* (San Francisco: Jossey-Bass, 1992); F. van Eijnatten, A.B. Shani, and M. Leary, "Socio-Technical Systems: Designing and Managing Sustainable Organizations," in *Handbook of Organization Development*, ed. T. Cummings (Thousand Oaks, CA: Sage Publications, 2008), 277–309.
3. C. Argyris, *Intervention Theory and Method: A Behavioral Science View* (Reading, MA: Addison-Wesley, 1970).
4. M. Higg and D. Rowland, "All Changes Great and Small: Exploring Approaches to Change and its Leadership," *Journal of Change Management* 5 (2005): 121–51; A. Armenakis and A. Bedeian, "Organization Change: A Review of Theory and Research in the 1990s," *Journal of Management* 25 (1999): 293–315; C. Worley, S. Mohrman, and J. Nevitt, "Large Group Interventions: An Empirical Field Study of Their Composition, Process, and Outcomes," *Journal of Applied Behavioral Science* 47 (2011): 404–31; R. Woodman, J. Bingham, and F. Yuan, "Assessing Organization Development and Change Interventions," in *Handbook of Organization Development*, ed. T. Cummings (Thousand Oaks, CA: Sage Publications, 2008), 187–215; T. Cummings, E. Molloy, and R. Glen, "A Methodological Critique of 58 Selected Work Experiments," *Human Relations* 30 (1977): 675–708; J. Nicholas, "The Comparative Impact of Organization Development Interventions on Hard Criteria Measures," *Academy of Management Review* 7 (1982): 531–42; K. Weick and R. Quinn, "Organizational Change and Development," *Annual Review of Psychology* 50 (1999): 361–86; M. Beer, "Developing an Effective Organization: Intervention Method, Empirical Evidence, and Theory," in *Research in Organizational Development and Change*, vol. 19, ed. W. Pasmore, A. B. Shani, and R. Woodman (Howard House: Emerald Publishing, 2011), 1–54.
5. D. Warrick, "Action Planning," in *Practicing Organization Development*, ed. W. Rothwell, R. Sullivan, and G. McClean (San Diego: Pfeiffer, 1995); J. Bartunek, J. Austin and M. Seo, "The Conceptual Underpinnings of Intervening in Organizations," in *Handbook of Organization Development*, ed. T. Cummings (Thousand Oaks, CA: Sage Publications, 2008).
6. W. Pasmore, "Tipping the Balance: Overcoming Persistent Problems in Organizational Change," in *Research in Organizational Change and Development*, vol. 19, ed. W. Pasmore, A. B. Shani, and R. Woodman (Howard House: Emerald Publishing, 2011), 259–92; J. Porras and P. Robertson, "Organization Development Theory: A Typology and Evaluation," in *Research in Organizational Change and Development*, vol. 1, ed. R. Woodman and W. Pasmore (Greenwich, CT: JAI Press, 1987), 1–57; G. Schwarz, "Elephant on a Treadmill: An Evaluation of Thematic Narrowness in Organizational Change Research," in *Research in Organizational Change and Development*, vol. 17, ed. W. Pasmore, A. B. Shani, and R. Woodman (Howard House: Emerald Publishing, 2009), 301–48.
7. J. Neumann, M. Chung, and C. Worley, "Ready for Consideration: International Organizational Development and Change as an Emerging Field of Practice," *Journal of Applied Behavioral Science* 45 (2009): 171–85; S. Camden-Anders and T. Knott, "Contrasts in Culture: Practicing OD Globally," in *Global and International Organization Development*, ed. P. Sorensen, T. Head, T. Yaeger, and D. Cooperrider (Chicago: Stipes Publishing, 2001); L. Bourgeois and M. Boltvinik, "OD in Cross-Cultural Settings: Latin America," *California Management Review* 23 (Spring 1981): 75–81; L. Brown, "Is Organization Development Culture Bound?" *Academy of Management Newsletter* (Winter 1982); P. Evans, "Organization Development in the Transnational Enterprise," in *Research in Organizational Change and Development*, vol. 3, ed. R. Woodman and W. Pasmore (Greenwich, CT: JAI Press, 1989), 1–38; R. Marshak, "Lewin Meets Confucius: A Review of the OD Model of Change," *Journal of Applied Behavioral Science* 29 (1997): 400–2; A. Chin and C. Chin, *Internationalizing OD: Cross-Cultural Experiences of NTL Members* (Alexandria, VA: NTL Institute, 1997); A. Shevat, "Practicing OD with a Technology-driven Global Company," *OD Practitioner* 33 (2001): 28–35; T. Yaeger, T. Head, and P. Sorensen, *Global Organization Development: Managing Unprecedented*

Change (Greenwich, CT: IAP, 2006); B. Spector, H. Lane, and D. Shaughnessy, "Developing Innovation Transfer Capacity in a Cross-National Firm," *Journal of Applied Behavioral Science* 45 (2009): 261–79.

8. E. Schein, *Organization Culture and Leadership*, 2nd ed. (San Francisco: Jossey-Bass, 1992); P. Evans, "Organization Development in the Transnational Enterprise," in *Research in Organizational Change and Development*, vol. 3, ed. R. Woodman and W. Pasmore (Greenwich, CT: JAI Press, 1989), 1–38.
9. G. Hofstede, *Culture's Consequences* (Beverly Hills, CA: Sage Publications, 1980); A. Jaeger, "Organization Development and National Culture: Where's the Fit?" *Academy of Management Journal* 11 (1986): 178–90; A. Francesco and B. Gold, *International Organizational Behavior*, 2nd ed. (Upper Saddle River, NJ: Prentice Hall, 2004); R. Hodgetts, F. Luthans, and J. Doh, *International Management: Culture, Strategy, and Behavior*, 6th ed. (New York: McGraw-Hill, 2005); E. Hall and M. Hall, "Key Concepts: Understanding Structures of Culture," in *International Management Behavior*, 3rd ed., ed. H. Lane, J. DiStefano, and M. Maznevski (Cambridge, MA: Blackwell, 2000); F. Kluckhohn and F. Strodtbeck, *Variations in Value Orientations* (Evanston, IL: Peterson, 1961); F. Trompenaars, *Riding the Waves of Culture* (London: Economist Press, 1993).
10. T. Head and J. Cicarelli, "The Role of a Country's Economic Development in Organization Development Implementation," in *Global and International Organization Development*, ed. Sorensen et al., 25–34.
11. J. Sachs, *The End of Poverty* (New York: Penguin Books, 2005); A. Sen, *Development as Freedom* (New York: Anchor Books, 1999); K. Murrell, "Management Infrastructure in the Third World," in *Global Business Management in the 1990s*, ed. R. Moran (New York: Beacham, 1990); S. Fukuda-Parr, N. Woods, and N. Birdsall, *Human Development Report 2002* (New York: United Nations Development Program, 2002) (http://www.undp.org).
12. B. Webster, "Organization Development: An International Perspective" (unpublished master's thesis, Pepperdine University, 1995).
13. Jaeger, "Organization Development and National Culture."
14. The dearth of published empirical descriptions of OD in particular countries and organizations necessitates a regional focus. The risk is that these descriptions may generalize too much. Practitioners should take great care in applying these observations to specific situations.
15. K. Johnson, "Estimating National Culture and O.D. Values," in *Global and International Organization Development*, ed. Sorensen et al., 329–44; Jaeger, "Organization Development and National Culture."
16. W. Woodworth, "Privatization in Belarussia: Organizational Change in the Former USSR," *Organization Development Journal* 3 (1993): 53–59.
17. A. Shevat, "The Practice of Organizational Development in Israel," in *Global and International Organization Development*, ed. Sorensen et al., 237–41; W. Fisher, "Organization Development in Egypt," in *Global and International Organization Development*, 3rd ed., ed. Sorensen et al., 241–49.
18. M. Manning and J. Delacerda, "Building Organization Change in an Emerging Economy: Whole Systems Change Using Large Group Methods in Mexico," in *Research in Organization Change and Development*, vol. 14, ed. W. Pasmore and R. Woodman (Oxford: JAI Press, 2003), 51–97.
19. R. Semler, *Maverick* (New York: Random House, 2001); R. Semler, *The Seven Day Weekend: Changing the Way Work Works* (New York: Penguin Books, 2004).
20. J. Preston, L. DuToit, and I. Barber, "A Potential Model of Transformational Change Applied to South Africa," in *Research in Organizational Change and Development*, vol. 9, ed. R. Woodman and W. Pasmore (Greenwich, CT: JAI Press, 1998); G. Sigmund, "Current Issues in South African Corporations: An Internal OD Perspective" (unpublished master's thesis, Pepperdine University, 1996).
21. Sigmund, "Current Issues."
22. Webster, "Organization Development"; I. Perlaki, "Organization Development in Eastern Europe," *Journal of Applied Behavioral Science* 30 (1994): 297–312; J. Putti, "Organization Development Scene in Asia: The Case of Singapore," in *Global and International Organization Development*, ed. Sorensen et al., 275–84; I. Nonaka, "Creating Organizational Order Out of Chaos: Self-Renewal in Japanese Firms," *California Management Review* (Spring 1988): 57–73; K. Johnson, "Organizational Development in Venezuela," in *Global and International Organization Development*, ed. Sorensen et al., 305–10; Fuchs, "Organizational Development"; R. Babcock and T. Head, "Organization Development in the Republic of China (Taiwan)," in *Global and International Organization Development*, 3rd ed., ed. Sorensen et al., 285–92; R. Marshak, "Training and Consulting in Korea," *OD Practitioner* 25 (Summer 1993): 16–21; R. Nyberg and T. Jensen, "Honoring the Kun Lun Way: Cross-Cultural Organization Development Consulting to a Hospitality Company in Datong, China," *Journal of Applied Behavioral Science* 45 (2009): 305–37.
23. Johnson, "Organizational Development"; A. Mueller, "Successful and Unsuccessful OD Interventions in a Venezuelan Banking Organization: The Role of Culture" (unpublished master's thesis, Pepperdine University, 1995).
24. Webster, "Organization Development"; B. Gustavsen, "The LOM Program: A Network-based Strategy for

Organization Development in Sweden," in *Research in Organizational Change and Development*, vol. 5, ed. R. Woodman and W. Pasmore (Greenwich, CT: JAI Press, 1991), 285–316; P. Sorensen Jr., H. Larsen, T. Head, and H. Scoggins, "Organization Development in Denmark," in *Global and International Organization Development*, ed. Sorensen et al., 95–112; A. Derefeldt, "Organization Development in Sweden," in *Global and International Organization Development*, ed. Sorensen et al., 113–22.

25. R. Stacey, D. Griffin, and P. Shaw, *Complexity and Management* (New York: Routledge, 2000).

26. D. Coghlan, "Rediscovering Organizational Levels for OD Interventions," *Organization Development Journal* 13 (1995): 19–27.

© Pixmann/Imagezoo/Getty Images

8

Managing Change

learning objectives

Understand the five key elements of successful change management.

Explore the processes of change associated with each element.

After diagnosing reveals the causes of problems or identifies opportunities for development, organization members begin planning and subsequently implementing the changes necessary to improve organization effectiveness and performance. A large part of organization development (OD) is concerned with interventions for improving organizations. The previous chapter discussed the design of interventions and introduced the major ones currently used in OD. Chapters 10–20 describe those interventions in detail. This chapter addresses the key activities associated with successfully managing organizational changes.

Change can vary in complexity from the introduction of relatively simple processes into a small work group to transforming the strategies and design features of the whole organization. Although change management differs across situations, in this chapter we discuss activities that must be performed in managing any kind of organizational change. (Tasks applicable to specific kinds of changes are examined in the chapters on intervention in Parts 3–6.)

8-1 Overview of Change Activities

The OD literature has directed considerable attention at managing change. Much of the material is highly prescriptive, advising managers about how to plan and implement organizational changes. For example, one study suggested that successful managers in continuously changing organizations (1) provide employees with clear responsibility and priorities, including extensive communication and freedom to improvise; (2) explore the future by experimenting with a wide variety of low-cost probes; and (3) link current projects to the future with predictable (time-paced rather than event-paced) intervals and choreographed transition procedures.[1] Traditionally, change management has focused on identifying sources of resistance to change and offering ways to overcome them.[2] Other contributions have challenged the focus on resistance and have been aimed at creating visions and desired futures, gaining political support for them, and managing the transition of the organization toward them.[3] Still others have described the learning practices and leader behaviors that accelerate complex change.[4]

FIGURE 8.1

Activities Contributing to Effective Change Management

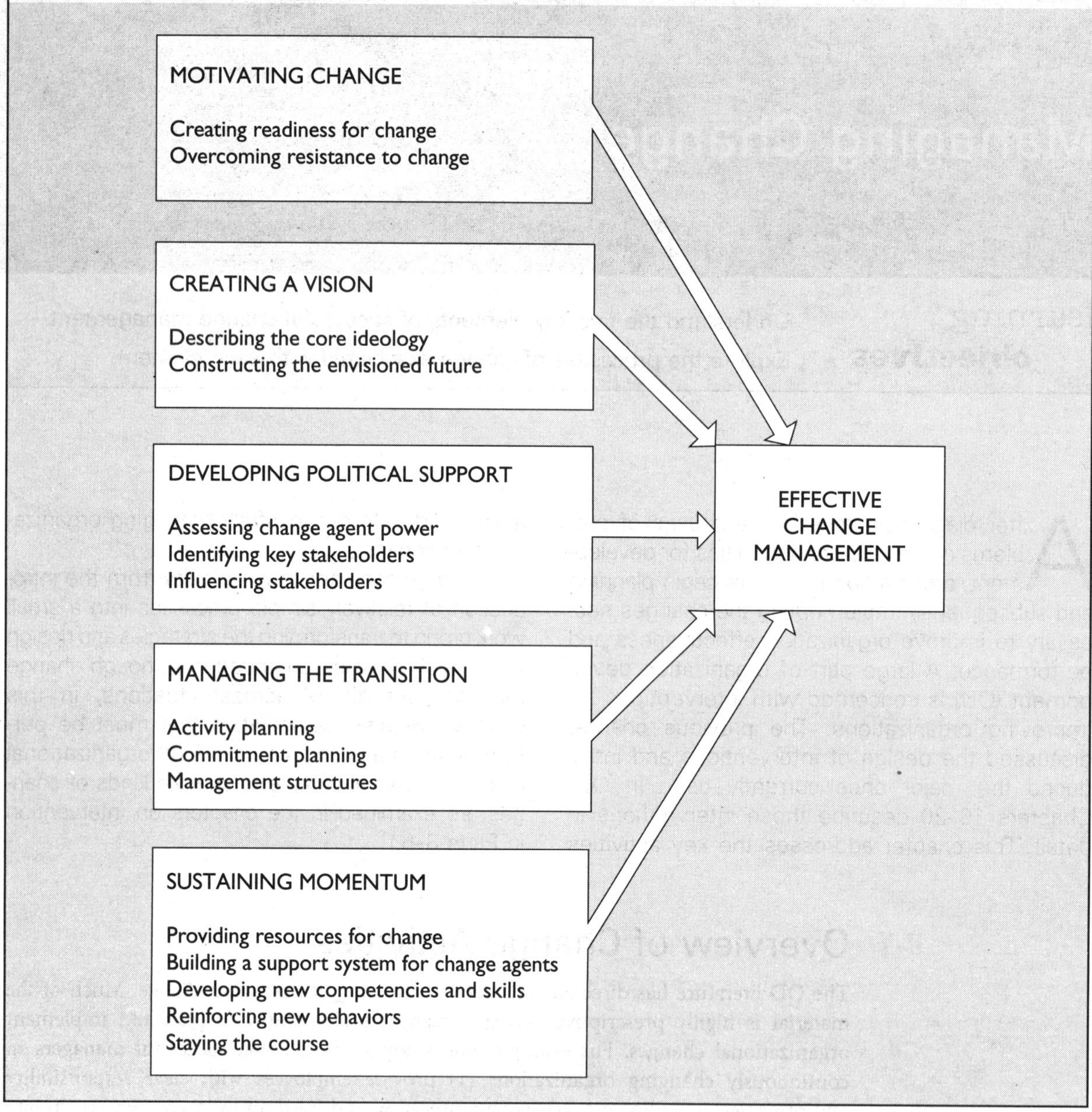

The diversity of practical advice for managing change can be organized into five major activities, as shown in Figure 8.1. The activities contribute to effective change management and are listed roughly in the order in which they typically are performed. Each activity represents a key element in change leadership.[5] The first activity involves *motivating change* and includes creating a readiness for change among organization members and helping them address resistance to change. Leadership must create an environment in which people accept the need for change and commit physical and psychological energy to it. Motivation is a critical issue in starting change because ample evidence indicates that people and organizations seek to preserve the status quo and are willing to change only when there are compelling reasons to do so. The second activity is concerned with *creating a vision* and is closely aligned with leadership activities. The vision provides a purpose and reason for change and describes the desired future state. Together, they provide the "why" and "what" of planned change. The third activity involves *developing political support* for change. Organizations are composed of powerful individuals and groups that can either block or promote change, and leaders and change agents need to gain their support to implement changes. The fourth activity is concerned with *managing the transition* from the current state to the desired future state. It involves creating a plan for managing the change activities as well as planning special management structures for operating the organization during the transition. The fifth activity involves *sustaining momentum* for change so that it will be carried to completion. This includes providing resources for implementing the changes, building a support system for change agents, developing new competencies and skills, and reinforcing the new behaviors needed to implement the changes.

Each of the activities shown in Figure 8.1 is important for managing change. Although little research has been conducted on their relative contributions, leaders must give careful attention to each activity when planning and implementing organizational change. Unless individuals are motivated and committed to change, getting movement on the desired change will be extremely difficult. In the absence of vision, change is likely to be disorganized and diffuse. Without the support of powerful individuals and groups, change may be blocked and possibly sabotaged. Unless the transition process is managed carefully, the organization will have difficulty functioning while it moves from the current state to the future state. Without efforts to sustain momentum for change, the organization will have problems carrying the changes through to completion. Thus, all five activities must be managed effectively to realize success.

In the following sections of this chapter, we discuss more fully each of these change activities, directing attention to how leaders contribute to planning and implementing organizational change.

8-2 Motivating Change

Organizational change involves moving from the known to the unknown. Because the future is uncertain and may adversely affect people's competencies, worth, and coping abilities, organization members generally do not support change unless compelling reasons convince them to do so. Similarly, organizations tend to be heavily invested in the status quo, and they resist changing it in the face of uncertain future benefits. Consequently, a key issue in planning for action is how to motivate commitment to organizational change. As shown in Figure 8.1, this requires attention to two related tasks: creating readiness for change and overcoming resistance to change.

8-2a Creating Readiness for Change

One of the more fundamental axioms of OD is that people's readiness for change depends on creating a felt need for change. This involves making people so dissatisfied with the status quo that they are motivated to try new work processes, technologies, or ways of behaving. Creating such dissatisfaction can be difficult, as anyone knows who has tried to lose weight, stop smoking, or change some other habitual behavior.

Generally, people and organizations need to experience deep levels of hurt before they will seriously undertake meaningful change. For example, IBM, Harley-Davidson, and Sears experienced threats to their very survival before they undertook significant change programs. The following three methods can help generate sufficient dissatisfaction to produce change:

1. **Sensitize organizations to pressures for change.** Innumerable pressures for change operate both externally and internally to organizations. As described in Chapter 1, modern organizations face unprecedented environmental pressures to change themselves, including heavy foreign competition, rapidly changing technology, and volatile global economies. Internal pressures to change include new leadership, poor product quality, high production costs, and excessive employee absenteeism and turnover. Before these pressures can serve as triggers for change, however, organizations must be sensitive to them. The pressures must pass beyond an organization's threshold of awareness if managers are to respond to them. Many organizations, such as Kodak, Polaroid, and Northwest Airlines, set their thresholds of awareness too high and neglected pressures for change until those pressures reached disastrous levels.[6]

   Organizations can make themselves more sensitive to pressures for change by encouraging leaders to surround themselves with devil's advocates; by cultivating external networks that comprise people or organizations with different perspectives and views; by visiting other organizations to gain exposure to new ideas and methods; and by using external standards of performance, such as competitors' progress or benchmarks, rather than the organization's own past standards of performance.[7] At Wesley Long Community Hospital, in Greensboro, North Carolina, for example, managers visited the Ritz-Carlton Hotel, Marconi Commerce Systems' high-involvement plant, and other hospitals known for high quality to gain insights about revitalizing their own organization.
2. **Reveal discrepancies between current and desired states.** In this approach to generating a felt need for change, information about the organization's current functioning is gathered and compared with desired states of operation. (See Section 8-3 "Creating a Vision," on page 184, for more information about desired future states.) These desired states may include organizational goals and standards, as well as a vision of a more desirable future state.[8] Significant discrepancies between actual and ideal states can motivate organization members to initiate corrective changes, particularly when members are committed to achieving those ideals. A major goal of diagnosing, as described in Chapter 5, is to provide members with feedback about current organizational functioning so that the information can be compared with goals or with desired future states. Such feedback can energize action to improve the organization. At Waste Management, Sunbeam, and Banker's Trust, for example, financial statements had reached the point at which it was painfully obvious that drastic renewal was needed.[9]
3. **Convey credible positive expectations for the change.** Organization members invariably have expectations about the results of organizational changes. The positive approaches to planned change described in Chapter 2 suggest that these expectations can play an important role in generating motivation for change.[10] Expectations can serve as a self-fulfilling prophecy, leading members to invest energy in change programs that they expect will succeed. When members expect success, they are likely to develop greater commitment to the change process and to direct more energy into the constructive behaviors needed to implement it.[11] The key to achieving these positive effects is to communicate realistic, positive expectations about the organizational changes. Research suggests that information about why the change is occurring, how it

will benefit the organization, and how people will be involved in the design and implementation of the change was most helpful.[12] Organization members also can be taught about the benefits of positive expectations and be encouraged to set credible positive expectations for the change program.

8-2b Overcoming Resistance to Change

Change can generate deep resistance in people and in organizations, thus making it difficult, if not impossible, to implement organizational improvements.[13] At a personal level, change can arouse considerable anxiety about letting go of the known and moving to an uncertain future.[14] People may be unsure whether their existing skills and contributions will be valued in the future, or may have significant questions about whether they can learn to function effectively and to achieve benefits in the new situation. At the organization level, resistance to change can come from three sources.[15] *Technical resistance* comes from the habit of following common procedures and the consideration of sunk costs invested in the status quo. *Political resistance* can arise when organizational changes threaten powerful stakeholders, such as top executive or staff personnel, or call into question the past decisions of leaders.[16] Organization change often implies a different allocation of already scarce resources, such as capital, training budgets, and talented people. Finally, *cultural resistance* takes the form of systems and procedures that reinforce the status quo, promoting conformity to existing values, norms, and assumptions about how things should operate.

There are at least three major strategies for positively dealing with resistance to change:[17]

1. **Empathy and support.** A first step in overcoming resistance is learning how people are experiencing change. This strategy can identify people who are having trouble accepting the changes, the nature of their resistance, and possible ways to overcome it, but it requires a great deal of empathy and support. It demands a willingness to suspend judgment and to see the situation from another's perspective, a process called *active listening*. When people feel that those people who are responsible for managing change are genuinely interested in their feelings and perceptions, they are likely to be less defensive and more willing to share their concerns and fears. This more open relationship not only provides useful information about resistance, but also helps establish the basis for the kind of joint problem solving needed to overcome barriers to change.
2. **Communication.** People resist change when they are uncertain about its consequences. Lack of adequate information fuels rumors and gossip and adds to the anxiety generally associated with change. Effective communication about changes and their likely results can reduce this speculation and allay unfounded fears. It can help members realistically prepare for change. However, communication is also one of the most frustrating aspects of managing change. Organization members constantly receive data about current operations and future plans as well as informal rumors about people, changes, and politics. Managers and OD practitioners must think seriously about how to break through this stream of information. One strategy is to make change information more salient by communicating through a new or different channel. If most information is delivered through memos and emails, then change information can be delivered through meetings and presentations. Another method that can be effective during large-scale change is to deliberately substitute change information for normal operating information. This sends a message that changing one's activities is a critical part of one's job.

3. **Participation and involvement.** One of the oldest and most effective strategies for overcoming resistance is to involve organization members directly in planning and implementing change. Participation can lead both to designing high-quality changes and to overcoming resistance to implementing them.[18] Members can provide a diversity of information and ideas, which can contribute to making the innovations effective and appropriate to the situation. They also can identify pitfalls and barriers to implementation. Involvement in planning the changes increases the likelihood that members' interests and needs will be accounted for during the intervention. Consequently, participants will be committed to implementing the changes because doing so will suit their interests and meet their needs. Moreover, for people having strong needs for involvement, the act of participation itself can be motivating, leading to greater effort to make the changes work.[19]

Application 8.1 describes how an OD consultant helped the sexual violence prevention unit of the Minnesota Department of Health generate commitment to a change process when the unit's leader left shortly after the change process began.[20]

8-3 Creating a Vision

The second activity in managing change involves creating a vision of what members want the organization to look like or become. It is one of the most popular yet least understood practices in management.[21] Generally, a vision describes the core values and purpose that guide the organization as well as an envisioned future toward which change is directed. It provides a valued direction for designing, implementing, and assessing organizational changes. The vision also can energize commitment to change by providing members with a common goal and a compelling rationale for why change is necessary and worth the effort. However, if the vision is seen as impossible or promotes changes that the organization cannot implement, it actually can depress member motivation. For example, George H. W. Bush's unfulfilled "thousand points of light" vision was emotionally appealing, but it was too vague and contained little inherent benefit. In contrast, John Kennedy's vision of "putting a man on the moon and returning him safely to the earth" was just beyond engineering and technical feasibility. In the context of the 1960s, it was bold, alluring, and vivid; it provided not only a purpose but a valued direction for the country. Recent research suggests that corporations with carefully crafted visions can significantly outperform the stock market over long periods of time.[22]

Creating a vision is considered a key element in most leadership frameworks.[23] Organization or subunit leaders are responsible for effectiveness, and they must take an active role in describing a desired future and energizing commitment to it. In the best cases, leaders encourage participation in developing the vision to gain wider input and support. For example, they involve subordinates and others who have a stake in the changes. The popular media frequently offer accounts of executives who have helped to mobilize and direct organizational change, including Sergio Marchionne at Fiat and Louis Gerstner at IBM. Describing a desired future is no less important for people leading change in small departments and work groups than for senior executives. At lower organizational levels, there are ample opportunities to involve employees directly in the visioning process.

Developing a vision is heavily driven by people's values and preferences for what the organization should look like and how it should function. The envisioned future represents people's ideals or dreams of what they would like the organization to look like or become. Unfortunately, dreaming about the future is discouraged in most organizations

application 8.1

MOTIVATING CHANGE IN THE SEXUAL VIOLENCE PREVENTION UNIT OF MINNESOTA'S HEALTH DEPARTMENT

Addressing the prevention of sexual violence is a complex challenge. Unlike cigarette smoking or automobile accidents, sexual violence is not only a health issue, but also a social issue connected to people's attitudes, beliefs, norms, and taboos. The sexual violence prevention unit of Minnesota's health department decided to undertake a five-year strategic planning effort to address the "primary prevention" of sexual violence. Primary prevention is defined as activities that focus on preventing sexual violence *before* it occurs. While there have been numerous successful programs focused on dealing with victims or addressing what happens after an assault, there was a clear need for primary prevention.

There were two driving forces for the plan. First, the U.S. Centers for Disease Control had identified sexual violence as a key health issue and was providing grants to states for the development of primary prevention plans. Second, Minnesota was a recognized leader in sexual violence prevention. The health department worked closely with the Minnesota Coalition Against Sexual Violence (MNCASA), a primary recipient of state funding, and other stakeholders who were working on sexual violence prevention. This coalition had been meeting for several years to develop education in primary prevention and to engage in a cross-sector dialogue on the issue.

The two primary objectives of the project were to:

- Create a strategic plan for the primary prevention of sexual violence in the state of Minnesota.
- Mobilize a broad range of individuals and organizations to take action in the primary prevention of sexual violence.

This application describes the activities involved with motivating change within the sexual violence prevention unit to create the strategic planning process. Application 8.3 describes the activities associated with managing the various stakeholders involved with this change and the large group intervention that kicked off the strategic planning and implementation effort.

BEGINNING THE PROJECT

The sexual violence prevention unit hired a local OD consulting firm to facilitate the strategic planning process. Everyone in the unit believed that strategic planning was the next right step. Community members wanted action. In fact, they had stopped meeting in a dialogue forum because they felt they were not making progress in addressing the issue systemically or strategically.

The project got off to a rough start. The day after the OD consultants began working with the unit, the unit director resigned. She had been a major force in bringing the project to fruition, and her departure represented a key challenge for the consultants. In the interim, the unit's program director and administrator stepped in to provide content leadership with the help of the director of MNCASA. Her departure also created a strong need to mobilize the members of the unit and to recruit the necessary external stakeholders with content knowledge and community reputation to galvanize action in the community.

To focus the key stakeholders on the change effort, the OD consultants met with the departing director to identify a range of community stakeholders to interview. The interviews were critical in building the consultants' knowledge of the issue and quickly establishing relationships with key stakeholders. They also helped identify community members who could provide leadership on the project.

MOTIVATING COMMITMENT

As part of the effort to reinforce commitment to the change process, a steering committee was formed. It consisted of project leaders from the health department, the OD consultants, and six community members. This committee was responsible for identifying and recruiting other internal and external stakeholders to participate in the planning process. They also served as advisors to the OD consultants on selecting the best forum to conduct the planning, reviewing draft agendas, and providing feedback on plan drafts. They were asked to convene for two meetings as well as provide input on plans and written reports virtually.

All of the steering committee members were volunteers recruited by the project leaders and OD consultants after the initial interviews. The OD consultants were part of the identification and recruitment process because they had formed relationships with several of the members through previous work and had established strong rapport through their interviews. The community members of the committee were chosen not only because of their expertise and history in the field, locally and nationally, but also because they had good process skills. Another criterion for participation was diversity. It was important that this group include members who could speak for underrepresented groups, such as Native American, Hispanic, African American, and youth segments. Everyone who was asked to participate wanted to be part of this effort.

Despite this high level of commitment to the project, time was a big constraint. To use time well, the consultants asked for two meetings. In between meetings, they drafted proposals for the group to react to, rather than asking members to decide on the work to be done by the group. When members could not be at a meeting, the consultants got their input individually, both before and after the meeting. Because of their commitment to prevention, all of the steering committee members stayed in close contact with the consultants and responded promptly to all requests.

because it requires creative and intuitive thought processes that tend to conflict with the rational, analytical methods prevalent there.[24] Consequently, leaders may need to create special conditions in which to describe a desired future, such as off-site workshops or exercises that stimulate creative thinking.

Research suggests that compelling visions are composed of two parts: (1) a core ideology or relatively stable identity that describes the organization's core values and purpose and (2) an envisioned future with bold goals and a vivid description of the desired future state that reflects the specific change under consideration.[25]

8-3a Describing the Core Ideology

The fundamental basis of a vision for change is the organization's core ideology. It describes the organization's core values and purpose and is relatively stable over time. *Core values* typically include three to five basic principles or beliefs that have stood the test of time and best represent what the organization stands for. Although the vision ultimately describes a desired future, it must acknowledge the organization's historical roots—the intrinsically meaningful core values and principles that have guided and will guide the organization over time. Core values are not "espoused values"; they are the "values-in-use" that actually inform members what is important in the organization. The retailer Nordstrom, for example, has clear values around the importance of customer service; toymaker Lego has distinct values around the importance of families; and the Disney companies have explicit values around wholesomeness and imagination. These values define the true nature of these firms and cannot be separated from them. Thus, core values are not determined or designed; they are discovered and described through a process of inquiry.

Members can spend considerable time and energy discovering their organization's core values through long discussions about organizational history, key events, founder's beliefs, the work people actually do, and the "glue" that holds the organization together.[26] In many cases, organizations want the core values to be something they are not. For example, many U.S. firms want "teamwork" to be a core value despite strong cultural norms and organizational practices that promote individuality.

The organization's *core purpose* is its reason for being, the idealistic motivation that brings people to work each day and gives work meaning.[27] A core purpose is not a strategy. Purpose describes why the organization exists and the organization's understanding of its image, brand, and reputation; strategy describes how an objective will be achieved. Research suggests that organization purposes may fall into one of four categories and that organizations often create a slogan or metaphor that captures the real reason they are in business.[28] Heroism refers to a purpose that exhorts members to do great things. Dell Computer, Microsoft, and Ford were all founded to change the world for the better. Henry Ford wanted to "build a machine to improve the world." Discovery, a core purpose for Apple, Sony, and 3M, refers to an innate desire to learn new things. A third purpose, altruism, infers a belief in serving others. Disney's return to prominence in the late 1980s and 1990s was guided by the essential purpose of "making people happy" and Whole Foods, Ben and Jerry's, and The Body Shop all take on the responsibility of serving the greater good. Tata Corporation's purpose of "what India needs next" has supported their growth for over 100 years. Finally, Berkshire Hathaway and Toyota reflect the purpose of excellence.

Hatch's concept of organization identity is similar to purpose and core ideology.[29] Identity—the way core values, purpose, brand, and reputation are integrated—provides guidelines for the strategic choices that will work and can be implemented versus those that will not work because they contradict the true nature of the organization. Lawler and Worley suggested that the real power of an organization's identity was its ability to consistently support and encourage change even though identity itself remained fairly stable.[30] An envisioned future can be compelling and emotionally powerful to members only if it aligns with and supports the organization's core values, purpose, and identity.[31]

8-3b Constructing the Envisioned Future

The core ideology provides the context for the envisioned future. Unlike core values and purpose, which are stable aspects of the organization and must be discovered, the envisioned future is specific to the change project at hand and must be created. The envisioned future varies in complexity and scope depending on the changes being considered. A relatively simple upgrading of a work group's word-processing software requires a less complex envisioned future than the transformation of a government bureaucracy.

The envisioned future typically includes the following two elements that can be communicated to organization members:[32]

1. **Bold and valued outcomes.** Descriptions of envisioned futures often include specific performance and human outcomes that the organization or unit would like to achieve. These valued outcomes can serve as goals for the change process and standards for assessing progress. For example, BHAGs (Big, Hairy, Audacious Goals) are clear, tangible, energizing targets that serve as rallying points for organization action. They can challenge members to meet clear target levels of sales growth or customer satisfaction, to overcome key competitors, to achieve role-model status in the industry,

or to transform the organization in some meaningful way. For example, in 1990, Wal-Mart Stores made a statement of intent "to become a $125 billion company by the year 2000." (Revenue in 2012 exceeded $445 billion.) Following the downsizing of the U.S. military budget, Rockwell proposed the following bold outcome for its change efforts: "Transform this company from a defense contractor into the best diversified high-technology company in the world."

2. **Desired future state.** This element of the envisioned future specifies, in vivid detail, what the organization should look like to achieve bold and valued outcomes. It is a passionate and engaging statement intended to draw organization members into the future. The organizational features described in the statement help define a desired future state toward which change activities should move. This aspect of the visioning process is exciting and compelling. It seeks to create a word picture that is emotionally powerful to members and motivates them to change.

Application 8.2 describes how Premier recognized the need for change and built a vision of the future for their organization.[33]

8-4 Developing Political Support

From a political perspective, organizations can be seen as loosely structured coalitions of individuals and groups having different preferences and interests.[34] For example, shop-floor workers may want secure, high-paying jobs, and top executives may be interested in diversifying the organization into new businesses. The marketing department might be interested in developing new products and markets, and the production department may want to manufacture standard products in the most efficient ways. These different groups or coalitions compete with one another for scarce resources and influence. They act to preserve or enhance their self-interests while managing to arrive at a sufficient balance of power to sustain commitment to the organization and achieve overall effectiveness.

Given this political view, attempts to change the organization often threaten the balance of power among groups, thus resulting in political conflicts and struggles.[35] Individuals and groups will be concerned with how the changes affect their own power and influence, and they will act accordingly. Some groups will become less powerful; others will gain influence. Those whose power is threatened by the change will act defensively and seek to preserve the status quo. For example, they may try to present compelling evidence that change is unnecessary or that only minor modifications are needed. On the other hand, those participants who will gain power from the changes will push heavily for them, perhaps bringing in seemingly impartial consultants to legitimize the need for change. Consequently, significant organizational changes are frequently accompanied by conflicting interests, distorted information, and political turmoil.

Methods for managing the political dynamics of organizational change are relatively recent additions to OD. Traditionally, OD has neglected political issues mainly because its humanistic roots promoted collaboration and power sharing among individuals and groups.[36] Today, change agents are paying increased attention to power and political activity, particularly as they engage in strategic change involving most parts and features of organizations. Some practitioners are concerned, however, about whether power and OD are compatible.

A growing number of advocates suggest that OD practitioners can use power in positive ways.[37] They can build their own power base to gain access to other power holders within the organization. Without such access, those who influence or make decisions

application 8.2

CREATING A VISION AT PREMIER

Premier (www.premierinc.com) is a leading health care alliance collectively owned by more than 200 independent hospitals and health care systems in the United States. Together, the owners operate or are affiliated with nearly 1,500 hospitals and other health care sites. Premier resulted from the 1995 merger of Chicago-based Premier Health Alliance, San Diego-based American Healthcare Systems, and The SunHealth Alliance of Charlotte, North Carolina. Premier offers a comprehensive array of services and products through its companies and business units, including group purchasing, consulting services, technology management services, insurance services, benchmarking and market intelligence services, and legislative advocacy.

Two and a half years after the organization's formation, a comprehensive organizational assessment suggested that Premier had not been successful in establishing a common organizational culture. Many of its services and employees continued to operate in a fractured or isolated fashion relating largely to their prior organization and its geographic location. As a result, Premier's strategy and business model were poorly understood, and more importantly, not well implemented. The assessment pointed to a growing lack of trust in the organization. Premier executives conceded that the organization was culturally adrift and without a well-understood or widely accepted sense of direction.

Another key finding of the assessment concerned the organization's vision. Shortly after the merger, a new set of values, mission, and vision statements had been developed. The statements themselves were clear and compelling; however, they had been developed by a relatively small group of executives. At best, most employees did not feel much ownership of the values; at worst, they saw the failure of top management to behave consistently with the values as evidence that they were not trusted, supported, or important.

In the fall of 1997, Premier hired Richard Norling as COO. Norling had been a chief executive at one of the health care systems that owned Premier, and his arrival signaled the potential for change and new possibilities. At his former organization, Norling had initiated and sustained a comprehensive OD effort, based on identifying core organizational values and the behaviors that supported them. The experience of that health care system had demonstrated that core values shaped and accepted by an organization's employees could build a deep sense of community in the organization, and lead to greater levels of trust and commitment that could be harnessed to enhance organization performance and effectiveness. Given Premier's emerging problem, a similar approach made sense.

In the spring of 1998, Premier executives determined to address these issues by building on the values and mission statements that had been developed earlier. Their intent was to involve a large number of employees in validating Premier's values, specifying the behaviors that supported them, and identifying ways in which the values could be integrated into the routines and processes of the organization—all of which would (they hoped) infect the organization with a renewed sense of identity and enthusiasm.

The first step in Premier's change process was planning and conducting a three-day values conference with over 200 employees. The conference was designed by a team of employees representing a diagonal slice of the organization and assisted by an OD practitioner. At the conference, employees examined Premier's business model and their organizational culture; developed and recommended a set of core organizational values for the organization; crafted an envisioned future; and identified and proposed strategies for employee involvement, integration, and organization transformation companywide.

Following the conference, the team of Premier employees who had planned the meeting was asked to become a permanent committee, charged with refining and implementing plans and recommendations that the conference participants had generated.

Ultimately, input was obtained from over 60% of the workforce and 16 actions were recommended and approved by senior management. Some of those actions included:

- Incorporating the values into Premier's performance management/performance appraisal system
- Incorporating the values into the recruitment and selection process by developing sample interview questions for use by hiring managers aimed at helping them learn whether prospective employees would be a good match to Premier's organizational culture
- Instituting an annual meeting of approximately 200 employees from all parts of Premier modeled after the 1998 values conference. The agenda would be focused on business issues, strategy, and organizational culture and values. Rotate those invited so that every Premier employee has an opportunity to attend every three to five years.

The outcome of the vision and values effort follows:

PREMIER

FOUNDATION STATEMENTS

Core Ideology

Core Values

- Integrity of the individual and the enterprise
- A passion for performance and a bias for action, creating real value for all stakeholders, and leading the pace
- Innovation: seeking breakthrough opportunities, taking risks, and initiating meaningful change
- Focus on people: showing concern and respect for all with whom we work, building collaborative relationships with the community, our customers, coworkers, and business associates

Core Purpose

To improve the health of communities

Core Roles of the Enterprise

- Improve quality, reduce costs
- Improve financial health
- Create value for owners
- Improve organizational health
- Facilitate knowledge transfer
- Grow the enterprise

Envisioned Future

10–30 Year Goal

Premier's owners will be the leading health care systems in their markets, and, with them, Premier will be the major influence in reshaping health care

Vivid Description

By the year 2020, we will have changed the world's view of U.S. health care to "the best and most cost-effective" at sustaining the good health of populations. In the United States, the health care industry will be considered the best managed and most innovative of all the economic sectors.

Across the nation, our owners, physicians, and other allies will lead the local transformations that are the building blocks of a reshaped health care system. These transformations will begin to make *public health and health services* indistinguishable, engaging citizens and civic resources in endeavors that attack the causes of illness and injury. Through efforts that go far beyond providing treatment, people will have a sense of responsibility for their own personal health and the health of their communities.

Together in Premier, we will invent new and superior models of delivering health services, and we will leverage the size, linkages, and resources of Premier to deliver those services to more people, at a lower cost and higher quality, than any others will. Our owners will operate at costs in the lowest quarter among all similar organizations at quality levels in the highest quarter. We will research and use the most effective and seamless clinical approaches to achieve superior health outcomes and increased values. Our competitive edge will be the unmatched ability to transfer and act on our collective experience and innovation.

Our owners will earn recognition as the most valued community resource for health. As a result of their efforts, "Premier" will be viewed as the hallmark of quality and value that all others seek to emulate. When people see our emblem, they will associate it with health care improvement and advances in health status.

Demonstrating a better way and supported by our constituencies, we will build consensus for national policy directions that stimulate and reward health and healthy communities.

We will indeed be *premier.*

may not have the advantage of an OD perspective. OD practitioners can use power strategies that are open and aboveboard to get those in power to consider OD applications. They can facilitate processes for examining the uses of power in organizations and help power holders devise more creative and positive strategies than political bargaining, deceit, and the like. They can help power holders confront the need for change and can help ensure that the interests and concerns of those with less power are considered. Although OD professionals can use power constructively in organizations, they probably will continue to be ambivalent and tense about whether such uses promote OD values and ethics or whether they represent the destructive, negative side of power. That tension seems healthy, and we hope that it will guide the wise use of power in OD.

As shown in Figure 8.2, managing the political dynamics of change includes the following activities: assessing the change agent's power, identifying key stakeholders, and influencing stakeholders.

FIGURE 8.2

Sources of Power and Power Strategies

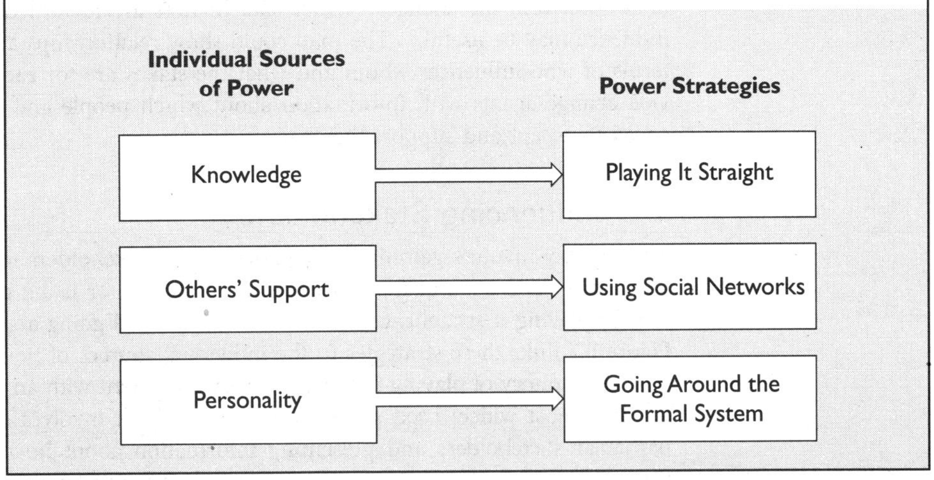

SOURCE: *Power and Organization Development: Mobilizing Power to Implement Change* (Prentice Hall Organizational Development Series), 1st Ed. By Greiner, Larry E.; Schein, Virginia E., ISBN 0201121859. © 1988 Addison-Wesley Publishing Company Inc.

8-4a Assessing Change Agent Power

The first task is to evaluate the change agent's own sources of power. This agent may be the leader of the organization or department undergoing change, or he or she may be the OD practitioner if professional help is being used. By assessing their own power base, change agents can determine how to use it to influence others to support changes. They also can identify areas in which they need to enhance their sources of power.

Greiner and Schein, in the first OD book written entirely from a power perspective, identified three key sources of personal power in organizations (in addition to one's formal position): knowledge, personality, and others' support.[38] Knowledge bases of power include having expertise that is valued by others and controlling important information. OD professionals typically gain power through their expertise in organizational change. Personality sources of power can derive from change agents' charisma, reputation, and professional credibility. Charismatic leaders can inspire devotion and enthusiasm for change from subordinates. OD consultants with strong reputations and professional credibility can wield considerable power during organizational change. Others' support can contribute to individual power by providing access to information and resource networks. Others also may use their power on behalf of the change agent. For example, leaders in organizational units undergoing change can call on their informal networks for resources and support, and encourage subordinates to exercise power in support of the change.

8-4b Identifying Key Stakeholders

Having assessed their own power bases, change agents should identify powerful individuals and groups with an interest in the changes, such as staff groups, unions, departmental managers, and top-level executives. These key stakeholders can thwart or support change, and it is important to gain broad-based support to minimize the risk that a single interest group will block the changes. As organizations have become more global, networked, and customer-focused, and change has become more strategic, it is also important to identity key external stakeholders. Key customers, regulatory agencies, suppliers, and the local community, for example, can exert considerable influence over change.

Identifying key stakeholders can start with the simple question, "Who stands to gain or to lose from the changes?" Once stakeholders are identified, creating a map of their influence may be useful.[39] The map could show relationships among the stakeholders in terms of who influences whom and what the stakes are for each party. This would provide change agents with information about which people and groups need to be influenced to accept and support the changes.

8-4c Influencing Stakeholders

This activity involves gaining the support of key stakeholders to motivate a critical mass for change. There are at least three major strategies for using power to influence others in OD: playing it straight, using social networks, and going around the formal system.[40] Figure 8.2 links these strategies to the individual sources of power discussed above.

The strategy of playing it straight is very consistent with an OD perspective, and thus it is the most widely used power strategy in OD. It involves determining the needs of particular stakeholders and presenting information about how the changes can benefit them. This relatively straightforward approach is based on the premise that information and knowledge can persuade people about the need and direction for change. The success of this strategy relies heavily on the change agent's knowledge base. He or she must have the expertise and information to persuade stakeholders that the changes are a logical way to meet their needs. For example, a change agent might present diagnostic data, such as company reports on productivity and absenteeism or surveys of members' perceptions of problems, to generate a felt need for change among specific stakeholders. Other persuasive evidence might include educational material and expert testimony, such as case studies and research reports, demonstrating how organizational changes can address pertinent issues.

The second power strategy, using social networks, is more foreign to OD and involves forming alliances and coalitions with other powerful individuals and groups, dealing directly with key decision makers, and using formal and informal contacts to gain information. In this strategy, change agents attempt to use their social relationships to gain support for changes. As shown in Figure 8.2, they use the individual power base of others' support to gain the resources, commitment, and political momentum needed to implement change. This social networking might include, for example, meeting with other powerful groups and forming alliances to support specific changes. This would likely involve ensuring that the interests of the different parties—labor and management, for example—are considered in the change process. Many union and management cooperative efforts to improve performance and reduce costs involve forming such alliances. This strategy also might include using informal contacts to discover key roadblocks to change and to gain access to major decision makers who need to sanction the changes.

The power strategy of going around the formal system is probably least used in OD and involves purposely circumventing organizational structures and procedures to get the changes made. Existing organizational arrangements can be roadblocks to change, and working around the barriers may be more expedient and effective than taking the time and energy to remove them. As shown in Figure 8.2, this strategy relies on a strong personality base of power. The change agent's charisma, reputation, or professional credibility lend legitimacy to going around the system and can reduce the likelihood of negative reprisals. For example, managers with reputations as winners often can bend the rules to implement organizational changes. Their judgment is trusted by those whose support they need to enact the changes. This power strategy is relatively easy to abuse, however, and OD practitioners should consider carefully the ethical issues and possible unintended consequences of circumventing formal policies and practices.

Application 8.3 shows how Minnesota's sexual violence prevention unit recruited external and internal stakeholders into the strategic planning process. They used the social networks of people with clear interests in the subject to support the planning and implementation of change.

8-5 Managing the Transition

Implementing organization change involves moving from an existing organization state to a desired future state. Such movement does not occur immediately but, as shown in Figure 8.3, instead requires a transition period during which the organization learns how to implement the conditions needed to reach the desired future. Beckhard and Harris pointed out that the transition may be quite different from the present state of the organization and consequently may require special management structures and activities.[41] They identified three major activities and structures to facilitate organizational transition: activity planning, commitment planning, and change-management structures. A fourth set of activities involves managing the learning process during change.

application 8.3

DEVELOPING POLITICAL SUPPORT FOR THE STRATEGIC PLANNING PROJECT IN THE SEXUAL VIOLENCE PREVENTION UNIT

Application 8.1 described the beginning of the sexual violence prevention unit's project to develop a five-year plan for primary prevention. The plan's unique purpose was to mobilize statewide efforts to prevent sexual violence before it occurs. In this application, the process that the committee used to identify and manage the political stakeholders—both internal and external—is described.

IDENTIFYING AND RECRUITING STAKEHOLDER PARTICIPATION

The steering committee interviewed representatives from various stakeholder groups, coalitions, and state agencies. The results of the interviews suggested (1) a need for broad involvement, especially from underrepresented groups, such as communities of color, immigrant communities, gay and lesbian groups, and youth and (2) a desire among those involved to move from dialogue and education toward taking collective action.

In response to these data, the OD consultant proposed a two-day strategic planning retreat for a large group of stakeholders. This format was selected because of the strong desire voiced in the interviews to get to action. The steering committee confirmed that this approach was preferable to stretching the planning over weeks of shorter meetings.

The unit administrator was essential in pulling together the list of stakeholders who were invited to participate. The goal was to get as many stakeholders as possible involved, and she knew the majority of people who were active in sexual violence prevention work in Minnesota. The steering committee reviewed and augmented the initial list to create a diverse group of 80 stakeholders to invite to the retreat. This group included people from the many groups, coalitions, state agencies, and underrepresented communities across the state.

Invitations to attend the retreat were sent out via email. The OD consultants crafted the invitation and the Health Unit Director sent them out. The steering committee members also contacted personally any invitees they knew and encouraged them to attend. The Health Unit Administrator was instrumental in communicating with those invited. Follow-up reminders and phone calls were made to ensure that an RSVP was received from everyone invited to attend. In addition, there were regular communications on the progress of the planning effort in newsletters, meetings, and conferences, communication channels that were already in place. An important constraint to this process was the nature of the physical facility that was to hold the meeting (see below). The steering committee had to balance the need for broad participation with the limits of the meeting space. One tool they used was to limit participation to the first 50 people who signed up. This encouraged people to sign up early to secure their space at the retreat.

Because primary sexual violence prevention was a central concern to most of these stakeholders, there was little resistance in terms of interest in participating. Other hurdles, however, had to be addressed, including the costs associated with attending the conference, travel issues, and the time to attend. The health department was able to secure funding to cover participants' costs. However, the steering committee had to work hard to find a meeting site that was within commuting distance from many cities and able to provide rooms for those traveling from afar. In the end, a Catholic retreat center fit many of the requirements of the conference, but presented another set of challenges. For a few stakeholder groups, there were negative perceptions about the perceived role of the church in sexual violence; the location lacked air conditioning; and there was no handicap access.

The planners of the project were also able to build on several efforts that the health department had previously used to gain stakeholder involvement. For several years, the department hosted a forum called the Sexual Violence Prevention Action Council. This group had been engaged in education and dialogue on the issue. Diverse stakeholders were already coming together around the issues and had adopted a framework developed by the Prevention Institute called the "Spectrum of Prevention." Without this foundational work, it would have been risky to attempt to get stakeholders aligned around a strategic plan in a two-day meeting.

Finally, another tool the steering committee initiated for gaining involvement was an online survey. This survey was sent to all invitees so that even those who could not attend the retreat would have a voice in the planning. The survey was also sent to others who were not invited to the retreat. They were encouraged to pass the survey on to other stakeholders who might be interested in this plan. Close to 100 people responded to the survey. A majority of respondents provided contact information and volunteered to help with the plan implementation.

CONDUCTING THE MEETING

Fifty invitees were able to attend the planning retreat. Using a large-group OD process over two days, participants worked together to create the framework of a strategic plan. Part of the planned agenda was to have stakeholders sign up for an action team toward the end of the two days. The dilemma faced during the session was in trying to get both focused strategies *and* a very diverse group of stakeholders to take action. Actions would need to occur both at the state level and within individual communities. Going into the meeting, the steering committee was not sure that the team sign-up process would work. They agreed to meet during lunch on the second day to review the work and to determine how to move the group toward action.

During the lunch meeting, the steering committee decided that the strategies were not clear enough to create teams at the meeting. While the group was concerned about losing people's action commitment, they believed it was more important to have teams that made strategic sense and utilized limited resources well. After lunch, the strategies and success indicators were posted on the wall. Consultants then used a multivoting process to identify six priorities for action.

Following the retreat, the OD consultants developed a proposed structure for action around these six priorities and sent this to the steering committee members for review. Their feedback was incorporated into an action structure that was included in the written strategic plan. Health department staff members then took over the planning and launching of these teams.

SUSTAINING MOMENTUM

When the strategic planning project had begun, the head of the sexual violence prevention unit had left the organization, and the position had gone unfilled throughout the project. Just prior to the retreat, a well-known state leader in sexual violence work, Patty Wetterling, agreed to fill the position. Seventeen years earlier, Wetterling's young son had been abducted in their small Minnesota town and was never found. Her work in establishing new laws regarding abductions as an advocate and state legislator, as well as a run for the U.S. Senate, made Wetterling a perfect choice to provide statewide leadership in implementing the strategic plan.

FIGURE 8.3

Organization Change as a Transition

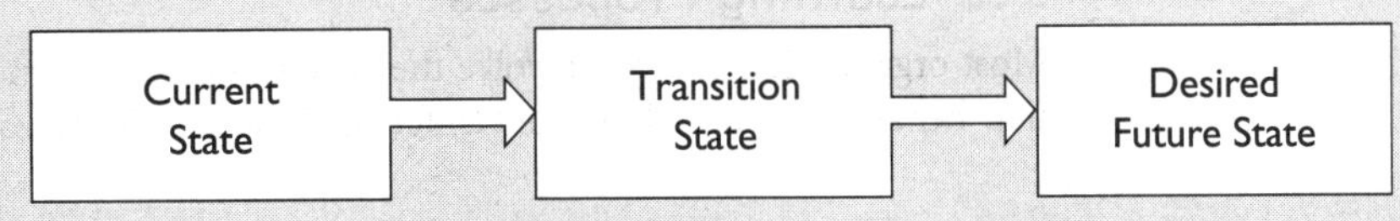

8-5a Activity Planning

Activity planning involves making a road map for change, citing specific activities and events that must occur if the transition is to be successful. It should clearly identify, temporally orient, and integrate discrete change tasks, and it should explicitly link these tasks to the organization's change goals and priorities. Activity planning also should gain top-management approval, be cost-effective, and remain adaptable as feedback is received during the change process.

An important feature of activity planning is that visions and desired future states can be quite general when compared with the realities of implementing change. As a result, it may be necessary to supplement them with midpoint goals as part of the activity plan.[42] Such goals represent desirable organizational conditions between the current state and the desired future state. For example, if the organization is implementing continuous improvement processes, an important midpoint goal can be the establishment of a certain number of improvement teams focused on understanding and controlling key work processes. Midpoint goals are clearer and more detailed than desired future states, and thus they provide more concrete and manageable steps and benchmarks for change. Activity plans can use midpoint goals to provide members with the direction and security they need to work toward the desired future.

8-5b Commitment Planning

This activity involves identifying key people and groups whose commitment is needed for change to occur and formulating a strategy for gaining their support. Although commitment planning is generally a part of developing political support, discussed above, specific plans for identifying key stakeholders and obtaining their commitment to change need to be made early in the change process.

8-5c Change-Management Structures

Because organizational transitions tend to be ambiguous and to need direction, special structures for managing the change process need to be created. These management structures should include people who have the power to mobilize resources to promote change, the respect of the existing leadership and change advocates, and the interpersonal and political skills to guide the change process. Alternative management structures include the following:[43]

- The chief executive or head person manages the change effort.
- A project manager temporarily is assigned to coordinate the transition.
- A steering committee of representatives from the major constituencies involved in the change jointly manages the project.
- Natural leaders who have the confidence and trust of large numbers of affected employees are selected to manage the transition.
- A cross section of people representing different organizational functions and levels manages the change.
- A "kitchen cabinet" representing people whom the chief executive consults with and confides in manages the change effort.

8-5d Learning Processes

Most organization changes involve the acquisition of new knowledge and skills that support new behaviors. Research at the Center for Effective Organizations suggests that change can be implemented more quickly when leaders consciously design learning processes into the transition.[44] Four practices, supported by a continuous dialogue and conversation process, were associated with accelerated transitions. The first learning practice, creating a systems view of the organization, involves creating a model of work and change that allows individual organizational members to see how their efforts contribute to organizational functioning and performance. When people can see how their efforts support change, it is easier for them to pick up new skills and knowledge; there is a context created that demands new behaviors.

The second learning practice, creating shared meaning, describes the use of models, language, tools, and processes that provide people with a way to making sense of the change. Most organization change is accompanied by considerable anxiety as the organization begins moving from the known to the unknown. By creating common ways of viewing the change, work, customers, and the new organization, people develop a shared view of the new reality. This shared view lowers anxiety and allows organization members to learn new skills and behaviors more quickly.

Engaging in "after-action reviews" or other processes that reflect on change experience is the third learning practice. In this activity, initial attempts to try out new activities, new processes, or new behaviors are assessed and reviewed. Organization members get to ask, "how well did we do?" and "what can we learn from that?" The answers to these questions are then used to redesign or redefine correct behavior. When people get timely and supportive feedback on new behaviors, their ability to learn more quickly increases.

The final learning practice involves decentralizing implementation processes and decisions to the lowest levels possible in the organization, what the researchers called "local self-design." Complex organization change contains too many variables, uncertainties, and local contingencies to be completely programmed from the top of the organization. By allowing organizational units in the lower organization levels to be responsible for the implementation of change, the overall change is accelerated. It is important in this process of local self-design to ensure that the organizational units have a clear understanding of their boundaries. That is, senior leaders in the organization need to be clear about what resources are available for change, the timeline within which the change must occur, and the things that cannot be changed in achieving the change goals.

These four learning practices are held together by conversation and dialogue. More than any other single practice, it is the opportunity to discuss the organization change—to create shared meaning, to understand how each individual fits into the change, to reflect on experience, and to discuss the change at local levels—that integrates the practices and accelerates implementation. Leading change, therefore, is largely a function of creating opportunities for organization members to discuss change activities.

Application 8.4 shows how Hewlett-Packard and Compaq used all of these techniques to manage the integration activities associated with this acquisition. Despite research indications of a high proportion of failed acquisition processes, the extraordinary detail used in this process, and the bank of institutionalized knowledge (see Application 9.2), the HP–Compaq integration process received positive reviews.[45]

8-6 Sustaining Momentum

Once organizational changes are under way, explicit attention must be directed to sustaining energy and commitment for implementing them. The initial excitement and activity of changing often dissipate in the face of practical problems of trying to learn

application 8.4

TRANSITION MANAGEMENT IN THE HP–COMPAQ ACQUISITION

In the Fall of 2001, Carly Fiorina announced HP's intent to acquire Compaq Corporation. Over the next nine months, a proxy fight ensued as many shareholders and employees challenged the wisdom of the proposed change. Wall Street analysts and organization researchers too debated whether or not the acquisition made sense, especially given the size of the change and the rather dismal history of performance in acquisition cases. Scott McNealy, chief executive of rival Sun Microsystems Inc., predicted "a slow-motion collision of two garbage trucks."

Within days of the initial announcement, however, Fiorina and Michael Capellas, then CEO of Compaq, met with Webb McKinney, a 19-year HP veteran, and Jeff Clarke, Compaq's CFO and survivor of Compaq's acquisition of Digital Equipment Corporation. These two men were named to lead the transition process, one that would involve redeploying a combined 145,000 workers in 160 countries including more than 15,000 layoffs, untangling 163 overlapping product lines, and producing $2.5 billion dollars in promised cost reductions.

It was no accident that McKinney and Clarke were asked to lead the integration team. Both were senior managers with substantial followings and excellent reputations. Days after their initial meeting, they began recruiting managers in equal numbers; Clarke rounded up Compaq talent and McKinney lined up their HP matches. Within weeks of the merger's announcement, the integration group, called the "clean team," had 500 members; by March 2002, more than 900. Even after the merger closed in May 2002, it kept growing, peaking at more than 1,000 full-time employees. By establishing such a huge body of outstanding managers and reassuring them that their jobs would be safe even if the merger failed, Clarke and McKinney were able to coax them to share in confidence everything they knew. It also kept most of them motivated to stay—another critical benchmark.

In addition to getting the right people on board, McKinney and Clarke set up an assembly line for decision making. Their research on successful and unsuccessful acquisitions and Clarke's experience with the Digital acquisition convinced them that slow decision making and the lack of a clear decision-making process was like a cancer in the transition process. In response, they created the "adopt and go" strategy: Get cross-company pairs of managers to meet daily to determine the best choice or best course of action on any particular issue. Weekly meetings kept the pace fast. If any issues couldn't be resolved by the teams, McKinney and Clarke would jump in. If those two couldn't resolve the impasse, they'd pass it to a committee chaired by Fiorina.

In addition to getting the right people on board and setting up a decision process built for speed, the transition team created activity plans for the key issues facing the integration, including people, products, culture, Day-one activities, and day-to-day operations. Excerpts and examples from some of those plans are reviewed below.

- The "adopt and go" process was used to decide which products to keep and which to discontinue. At weekly presentations with McKinney and Clarke, managers had to offer up one for elimination. In contrast to Compaq's merger with Digital, HP executives made quick product decisions and every week pored over progress charts with red, green, and yellow markers to review how each product exit was proceeding. Red and yellow markers indicated a task was troubled; green signaled a task going well. In four months, a road map for product lines emerged and helped to close redundant warehouses and factories, ultimately saving $500 million in procurement costs. In the end, while many Compaq products beat out HP's, such as Compaq's iPac over HP's Jornada, the HP brand survived.
- The "adopt and go" process also helped HP make the hard decisions about personnel appointments. HP appointed its top

three tiers of executives before the acquisition was finalized and made new levels of appointments every few weeks. While not perfect—rumors that Compaq people were favored in the sales organization—Clarke contends that all decisions were made "by the book."

- HP created a team to deal specifically with melding the corporate cultures and hired consultants to document the differences. To address perceptions that Compaq employees were "shoot from the hip cowboys" and that HP staff members were "bureaucrats," the team created a series of cultural workshops. They were designed to identify the various cultures and subcultures, and then integrate them. For example, key sales managers and about two dozen salespeople from both HP and Compaq held a workshop designed to address sales integration and transition issues. Many attendees first looked at each other suspiciously. Following some ice-breaker exercises, however, an HP representative talked about how HP had been working with key customer SBC, the telecommunications company. That was followed by a Compaq rep discussing how it sold to SBC. Then the big group drew up a 100-day work plan for selling to SBC in the future, including a weekly conference call for the team every Friday. The progress from these sessions was tracked by a team of 650 part-time internal "cultural consultants," who also continued in their normal jobs at the company.
- The cultural workshops delivered in the first quarter after the deal was signed set the stage for further cultural integration. The workshops welcomed everyone to the new team, described the HP business, HP's values and operating models, the roles and objectives of different groups, and how people were expected to work together. All of this material was pushed out into the HP market before the launch, inviting a few thousand of the top HP managers to an orientation and education session on what to do, how to communicate, and the details of the new HP and their roles in it.
- The clean team also made extensive "Day-one" plans. Day-one readiness included plans to address customers, issues of leadership and structure, and internal administrative issues. The new HP was launched with everyone on the same email, not a paycheck missed, and every sign changed the morning of launch day. Customers participated heavily in the transition process. Customer councils, interviews, research, information sessions, education, and other data were included in the knowledge transfer to groups that faced the customer. The go-to-market plans were detailed, with playbooks given to each group manager who touched the customers, so that on launch day they knew what to do, what to say to a customer, where to get information. Each customer was given an HP buddy from the same level so that he or she could contact that person and get whatever information the customer needed. There was an enormous amount of detail, down to the script of what to say, what answers to give to specific questions, where to get further information, and how to transition an inquiry to the right person.

By most measures, this transition work paid off: HP met the integration goals that Chairman and Chief Executive Carleton S. Fiorina set for the merged company. The biggest of these was cost savings, which surpassed expectations. By mid-2003, HP said it saved $734 million—14% more than projected—from payroll cuts and better terms with its suppliers.

new ways of operating. A strong tendency exists among organization members to return to old behaviors and well-known processes unless they receive sustained support and reinforcement for carrying the changes through to completion. In this section, we present approaches for sustaining momentum for change. The subsequent tasks of assessing and stabilizing changes are discussed in Chapter 9. The following five activities can help to sustain momentum for carrying change through to completion: providing resources for change, building a support system for change agents, developing new competencies and skills, reinforcing new behaviors, and staying the course.

8-6a Providing Resources for Change

Implementing organization change generally requires additional financial and human resources, particularly if the organization continues day-to-day operations while trying to change itself. These extra resources are needed for such change activities as training, consultation, data collection and feedback, and special meetings. Extra resources also are helpful to provide a buffer as performance may drop during the transition period. Organizations can underestimate seriously the need for special resources devoted to the change process. Significant organizational change invariably requires considerable management time and energy, as well as the help of OD consultants. A separate "change budget" that exists along with capital and operating budgets can earmark the resources needed for training members in how to behave differently and for assessing progress and making necessary modifications in the change program.[46] Unless these extra resources are planned for and provided, meaningful change is less likely to occur.

8-6b Building a Support System for Change Agents

Organization change can be difficult and filled with tension not only for participants but also for change agents as well.[47] They often must give members emotional support, but they may receive little support themselves. They often must maintain "psychological distance" from others to gain the perspective needed to lead the change process. This separation can produce considerable tension and isolation, and change agents may need to create their own support system to help them cope with such problems. A support system typically consists of a network of people with whom the change agent has close personal relationships—people who can give emotional support, serve as a sounding board for ideas and problems, and challenge untested assumptions. For example, OD professionals often use trusted colleagues as "shadow consultants" to help them think through difficult issues with clients and to offer conceptual and emotional support. Similarly, a growing number of companies, such as Procter & Gamble, The Hartford, and Kaiser Permanente, are forming internal networks of change agents to provide mutual learning and support.

8-6c Developing New Competencies and Skills

Organizational changes frequently demand new knowledge, skills, and behaviors from organization members. In many cases, the changes cannot be implemented unless members gain new competencies. For example, employee involvement programs often require managers to learn new leadership styles and new approaches to problem solving. Change agents must ensure that such learning occurs. They need to provide multiple learning opportunities, such as traditional training programs, on-the-job counseling and coaching, and experiential simulations, covering both technical and social skills. Because it is easy to overlook the social component, change agents may need to devote special time and resources to helping members gain the social skills required to implement changes.

As part of McKesson's commitment to quality, the corporation identified specially selected high performers to become Six Sigma black belts and then promoted them accordingly to signal the importance of these skills and knowledge in career planning. In addition, senior managers in all of the divisions are required to attend training that builds new problem-solving skills, team behaviors, and a commitment to the quality philosophy.[48]

8-6d Reinforcing New Behaviors

In organizations, people generally do those things that bring them rewards. Consequently, one of the most effective ways to sustain momentum for change is to reinforce the kinds of behaviors needed to implement the changes. This can be accomplished by linking formal rewards directly to the desired behaviors. For example, Integra Financial encouraged more teamwork by designing a rewards and recognition program in which the best team players got both financial rewards and management attention, and a variety of behaviors aimed at promoting self-interest were directly discouraged.[49] (Chapter 15 discusses several reward-system interventions.) In addition, desired behaviors can be reinforced more frequently through informal recognition, encouragement, and praise. Perhaps equally important are the intrinsic rewards that people can experience through early success in the change effort. Achieving identifiable early successes can make participants feel good about themselves and their behaviors, and thus reinforce the drive to change.

8-6e Staying the Course

Change requires time, and many of the expected financial and organizational benefits from change lag behind its implementation. If the organization changes again too quickly or abandons the change before it is fully implemented, the desired results may never materialize. There are two primary reasons that managers do not keep a steady focus on change implementation. First, many managers fail to anticipate the decline in performance, productivity, or satisfaction as change is implemented. Organization members need time to practice, develop, and learn new behaviors; they do not abandon old ways of doing things and adopt a new set of behaviors overnight. Moreover, change activities, such as training, extra meetings, and consulting assistance, are extra expenses added onto current operating expenditures. There should be little surprise, therefore, that effectiveness declines before it gets better. However, perfectly good change projects often are abandoned when questions are raised about short-term performance declines. Patience and trust in the diagnosis and intervention design are necessary.

Second, many managers do not keep focused on a change because they want to implement the next big idea that comes along. When organizations change before they have to, in response to the latest management fad, a "flavor-of-the-month" cynicism can develop. As a result, organization members provide only token support to a change under the (accurate) notion that the current change won't last. Successful organizational change requires persistent leadership that does not waver unnecessarily.

Application 8.5 describes the implementation of an engagement and innovation process at the RMIT University Library in Australia. After initial interventions were made, a midterm review suggested additional changes that were designed to sustain the change process's momentum.[50]

application 8.5

SUSTAINING CHANGE AT RMIT UNIVERSITY LIBRARY IN MELBOURNE, AUSTRALIA

RMIT University is a large tertiary educational institution located in Melbourne Australia. The university has more than 75,000 students, including approximately 16,000 students attending an off-shore campus or studying with partner institutions. Australian education is undergoing rapid change in response to various government initiatives, the change to a "demand-driven" system, and a general tightening of funding. These pressures have resulted in the need for more innovation in the education process and increased leadership capacity to support these changes.

In addition to the changes in the broader education environment, the large amount of technological change in the information industry provided the library management and staff an important context and encouragement to innovate and change. The most direct and obvious indicator of the changing role of the library was the steady drop in its traditional form of service—loaning out books. Despite a 33% increase in students between 2000 and 2010, the number of book loans per student declined from 10.8 to 5.7. Other indicators of library use also changed, including a shift from long, in-depth reference questions from faculty and students to shorter and more specific inquiries.

Engaged staff and confident leaders were needed to adapt to changed patterns of use, to meet changing user expectations, and to envisage and implement new approaches to service. However, input from a broad leadership group formed inside the library and an organization-wide climate survey, which provided results at unit level, indicated that library staff engagement levels were below desirable levels.

Over the last five years, the RMIT University Library has adopted strategies that were designed to increase and sustain employee engagement and levels of innovation. The library's initial approach involved four interventions: leadership development, specific purpose working groups, cross unit work experiences, and increased involvement in professional associations.

LEADERSHIP DEVELOPMENT

As part of a broader University-level leadership development program—leadRMIT—the RMIT University Library worked to strengthen its leadership capacity. Since 2008, the library has recognized 18 to 20 staff as a "leadership" group. The group identified the positive and negative elements of the library's existing culture. Desirable changes to the culture were then identified and a variety of leadership development activities were provided to equip managers to support the agreed direction. This included participating in the leadRMIT courses which involved several full-day sessions with expert external facilitators over a few months. In addition, survey instruments that identified the leadership skills and emotional competencies of the managers provided insights into the approaches and leadership styles that supported staff engagement. The library arranged sessions to address specific people management skill needs. After the initial batch of training, a round table was formed as an ongoing opportunity to share insights gained from professional reading, conferences, and other sources, and to discuss leadership and management issues.

THE CUE PROGRAM

As in any large library, there was a tendency towards a culture of specialization in the workplace. Staff in the loans area, for example, had little knowledge or experience in the technical service areas, and those in technical service areas tended not to have experience working with library users. To overcome this "silo effect" and build a more flexible workforce, cross unit work experience opportunities (called "CUEs") were instituted in 2008. Under this system, managers were invited to create training opportunities that were then placed on an internal register. A CUE was initiated by a librarian expressing interest in an opportunity that was mediated by the staff development librarian. Four categories of CUEs were defined, including:

1. Short, half-day opportunities over a three-day period were primarily aimed at staff in their first two years of employment to enhance cross unit cooperation.
2. A shadowing assignment provided a short-term opportunity to gain insight into another's work, often where actually doing the work was not feasible.
3. Longer one-day/week for six months opportunities promoted multiskilling and workforce flexibility.
4. Full-time immersion experiences over four to eight weeks provided an opportunity to deepen and enhance multiskilling and workforce flexibility.

SPECIFIC PURPOSE WORKING GROUPS

A variety of specific working groups were created to encourage more open and innovative approaches to the changing environment. For example, the New Professionals Group was created with the intention of entrenching a positive organizational culture and developing organizational savvy and capability. It was hoped that the formation of this group would support the less-experienced professionals to act as change agents. Similarly, the Innovative Librarians or "Innovatives" group focused on exploring new technologies, communicating these to staff, and making recommendations as to how these might be used. One of the challenges in terms of the impact of this group was that the members were in relatively low-influence positions in terms of traditional hierarchy and they often lacked strong advocacy skills and confidence.

INVOLVEMENT IN PROFESSIONAL ASSOCIATIONS

To maximize innovative activity requires buy-in which extends beyond leaders and select individuals. As a result, the university librarian promoted involvement in professional associations and led by example. Library staff were encouraged and supported to participate in professional activities, including attending and presenting at meetings and conferences, writing news items and articles, and undertaking study tours.

Although every intervention ideally should receive a separate and formal assessment, several indicators were used to sense implementation success and suggest follow-on activities. For example, a management skills audit undertaken in late 2010 and early 2011 affirmed significant progress in the overall confidence levels of managers regarding their people management skills. Anecdotal evidence, evaluation forms provided by participants in the CUE program, and the ongoing commitment of managers to create and support the scheme indicated that the experience was valuable for the staff member and productive from the manager's perspective. Finally, the impact of participation in cross unit projects and the specific purpose groups had clearly had positive impact on participants.

To sustain the staff's engagement and to encourage additional innovation at the library, a simple innovation process was created and was supported by an individual and team development program.

A MODEL OF INNOVATION

The RMIT University Library innovation process was modeled after popular processes developed by IDEO as well as library specific processes located through benchmarking efforts. In itself the model was far from novel, but its simple "generate, develop and deploy" labels provided a common language for units and staff across the library and served as a basis for skill development in support of innovation.

For example, a short-term specific-purpose working group was formed to select and describe idea generation techniques considered appropriate to the RMIT University Library. This group also developed approaches for strengthening ideas. They wanted to avoid "idea assassination" where ideas were recommended without adequate thought and to ensure that good ideas were as well presented as possible before formal approvals were sought. This necessitated clarifying criteria used to decide whether or not to accept and implement suggestions, and reaching agreement on a template for making suggestions and providing feedback. To ensure this work was not isolated from reality, techniques were piloted on current library projects.

INDIVIDUAL AND TEAM DEVELOPMENT

To support broader individual and team skill development, the library adopted a team management profile process. Staff members completed an online survey and then participated in workshops to understand the sources of team effectiveness, to gain insights into and appreciation of diverse approaches to work, to assess team strengths weaknesses and priorities, and to take steps to enhance effectiveness. While the workshops did not place a major focus on the link between team effectiveness and innovation, the team management profiles and workshop experiences laid an important foundation for improving innovation levels by identifying individual work preferences, affirming the value of each person's unique contribution, increasing understanding between individuals which may increase levels of trust, and opening up conversations on new ways of thinking about work.

The RMIT University Library used initial interventions and an informal midterm assessment to track the progress of the change and then crafted additional interventions to sustain the change. The initial interventions of leadership development to enhance the knowledge, motivation, and skills of managers to engage staff; cross unit work experiences to build a more flexible workforce; specific purpose working groups to address particular issues; and the promotion of involvement in professional associations helped start the change. Subsequently, adoption of a common innovation process model and the provision of practical team effectiveness techniques helped to sustain innovation and engagement in the organization. A repeat organizational climate survey in the future will help to determine whether the engagement levels have risen among library staff.

SUMMARY

In this chapter, we described five kinds of activities that change agents must carry out when planning and implementing changes. The first activity is motivating change, which involves creating a readiness for change among organization members and overcoming their resistance. The second activity concerns creating a vision that builds on an organization's core ideology. It describes an envisioned future that includes a bold and valued outcome and a vividly described desired future state. The core ideology and envisioned future articulate a compelling reason for implementing change. The third task for change agents is developing political support for the changes. Change agents first must assess their own sources of power, then identify key stakeholders whose support is needed for change and devise strategies for gaining their support. The fourth activity concerns managing the transition of the organization from its current state to the desired future state. This requires planning a road map for the change activities, as well as planning how to gain commitment for the changes. It also may involve creating special change-management structures and a set of learning processes that accelerate the transition. The fifth change task is sustaining momentum for the changes so that they are carried to completion. This includes providing resources for the change program, creating a support system for change agents, developing new competencies and skills, reinforcing the new behaviors required to implement the changes, and staying the course.

NOTES

1. K. Brown and M. Eisenhardt, "The Art of Continuous Change: Linking Complexity Theory and Time-Paced Evolution in Relentlessly Shifting Organizations," *Administrative Science Quarterly* 42 (1997): 1–34.
2. J. Kotter and L. Schlesinger, "Choosing Strategies for Change," *Harvard Business Review* 57 (1979): 106–14; R. Ricardo, "Overcoming Resistance to Change," *National Productivity Review* 14 (1995): 28–39; A. Armenakis, S. Harris, and K. Mossholder, "Creating Readiness for Organizational Change," *Human Relations* 46 (1993): 681–704.
3. E. Dent and S. Goldberg, "Challenging 'Resistance to Change,'" *Journal of Applied Behavioral Science* 35 (March 1999): 25; M. Weisbord, *Productive Workplaces* (San Francisco: Jossey-Bass, 1987); R. Beckhard and R. Harris, *Organizational Transitions: Managing Complex Change*, 2nd ed. (Reading, MA: Addison-Wesley, 1987); R. Beckhard and W. Pritchard, *Changing the Essence* (San Francisco: Jossey-Bass, 1991); J. Collins and J. Porras, *Built to Last* (New York: Harper Business, 1994); J. Conger, G. Spreitzer, and E. Lawler, *The Leader's Change Handbook* (San Francisco: Jossey-Bass, 1999).
4. R. Tenkasi, S. Mohrman, and A. Mohrman, "Accelerated Learning during Organizational Transition," in *Tomorrow's Organization*, ed. S. Mohrman, J. Galbraith, E. Lawler, and Associates (San Francisco: Jossey-Bass, 1998).
5. Conger, Spreitzer, and Lawler, *Change Handbook.*
6. N. Tichy and M. Devanna, *The Transformational Leader* (New York: John Wiley & Sons, 1986); Armenakis, Harris, and Mossholder, "Creating Readiness."
7. R. Cosier and C. Schwenk, "Agreement and Thinking Alike: Ingredients for Poor Decisions," *Academy of Management Executive* 4 (1990): 69–74; S. Walleck, D. O'Halloran, and C. Leader, "Benchmarking World-Class Performance," *McKinsey Quarterly* 1 (1991).
8. W. Burke, *Organization Development: A Normative View* (Reading, MA: Addison-Wesley, 1987); Collins and Porras, *Built to Last.*
9. R. Charan and G. Colvin, "Why CEOs Fail," *Fortune*, June 21, 1999, 69–78.
10. D. Eden, "OD and Self-Fulfilling Prophecy: Boosting Productivity by Raising Expectations," *Journal of Applied Behavioral Science* 22 (1986): 1–13; D. Cooperrider, "Positive Image, Positive Action: The Affirmative Basis of Organizing," in *Appreciative Management and Leadership: The Power of Positive Thought and Actions in Organizations*, ed. S. Srivastva, D. Cooperrider, and Associates (San Francisco: Jossey-Bass, 1990).
11. Eden, "OD and Self-Fulfilling Prophecy," 8; M. Choi and W. Ruona, "Individual Readiness for Organizational Change and its Implications for Human Resource and Organization Development," *Human Resource Development Review* 10 (2011): 46–73.
12. L. Szamosi and L. Duxbury, "Development of a Measure to Assess Organizational Change," *Journal of Organizational Change* 15 (2002): 184–201.
13. R. van Dijk and R. van Dick, "Navigating Organizational Change: Change Leaders, Employee Resistance and Work-based Identities," *Journal of Change Management* 9 (2009): 143–63; Kotter and Schlesinger, "Choosing Strategies"; P. Block, *Flawless Consulting: A Guide to Getting Your Expertise Used* (Austin, TX: Learning Concepts, 1981); P. Strebel, "Why Do Employees Resist Change?" *Harvard Business Review* (May–June 1996): 86–93; S. Piderit, "Rethinking Resistance and Recognizing Ambivalence: A Multidimensional View of Attitudes Toward an Organizational Change," *Academy of Management Review* (2000): 783–95; K. Trader-Leigh, "Case Study: Identifying Resistance in Managing Change," *Journal of Organizational Change Management* 15 (2002): 138–56; S. Ijaz and A. Vitalis, "Resistance to Organizational Change: Putting the Jigsaw Together," *International Review of Business Research Papers* 7 (2011): 112–21.
14. C. Neck, "Thought Self-leadership: A Self-regulatory Approach Towards Overcoming Resistance to Organizational Change," *International Journal of Organizational Analysis* 4 (1996): 202–16; J. Wolfram Cox, "Manufacturing the Past: Loss and Absence in Organizational Change," *Organization Studies* 18 (1996): 623–54.
15. N. Tichy, "Revolutionize Your Company," *Fortune*, December 13, 1993, 114–18.
16. D. Macri, M. Tagliaventi, and F. Bertolotti, "A Grounded Theory for Resistance to Change in a Small Organization," *Journal of Organizational Change Management* 15 (2002): 292–311.
17. D. Kirkpatrick, ed., *How to Manage Change Effectively* (San Francisco: Jossey-Bass, 1985); J. Ford and L. Ford, "Stop Blaming Resistance and Start Using It," *Organizational Dynamics* 39 (2009): 24–36.
18. V. Vroom and P. Yetton, *Leadership and Decision Making* (Pittsburgh: University of Pittsburgh Press, 1973); D. Dunphy, "Organizational Change in Corporate Settings," *Human Relations* 49 (1996): 541–52; P. Nutt, "Tactics of Implementation," *Academy of Management Journal* 29 (1986): 230–61; J. O'Toole and E. Lawler,

The New American Workplace (New York: Palgrave Macmillan, 2006).

19. T. Cummings and E. Molloy, *Improving Productivity and the Quality of Work Life* (New York: Praeger, 1977).
20. Applications 8.1 and 8.3 were developed and submitted by Ms. Ginny Belden-Charles, Founding Partner, Waterline Consulting. The authors gratefully acknowledge her contribution.
21. Collins and Porras, *Built to Last*; T. Stewart, "A Refreshing Change: Vision Statements That Make Sense," *Fortune*, September 30, 1996, 195–96; T. Stewart, "Why Value Statements Don't Work," *Fortune*, June 10, 1996, 137–38.
22. Collins and Porras, *Built to Last*.
23. J. Kotter, *Leading Change* (Boston: Harvard Business School Press, 1994); W. Bennis and B. Nanus, *Leadership* (New York: Harper & Row, 1985); J. O'Toole, *Leading Change: Overcoming the Ideology of Comfort and the Tyranny of Custom* (San Francisco: Jossey-Bass, 1995); F. Hesselbein, M. Goldsmith, and R. Beckhard, ed., *The Leader of the Future* (San Francisco: Jossey-Bass, 1995).
24. Tichy and Devanna, *Transformational Leader*; E. Lawler and C. Worley, *Built to Change* (San Francisco: Jossey-Bass, 2006).
25. Collins and Porras, *Built to Last*; Lawler and Worley, *Built to Change*; M. Hatch and M. Schultz, "The Dynamics of Organizational Identity," *Human Relations* 55 (2002): 989–1018.
26. T. Stewart, "Company Values That Add Value," *Fortune*, July 8, 1996, 145–47; E. Schein, *Organization Culture and Leadership*, 2nd ed. (San Francisco: Jossey-Bass, 1992).
27. G. Bains, *Meaning Inc.* (London: Profile Books, 2007).
28. N. Mourkogiannis, *Purpose: The Starting Point of Great Companies* (New York: Palgrave Macmillan, 2006).
29. Hatch and Schultz, "The Dynamics of Organizational Identity."
30. Lawler and Worley, *Built to Change*.
31. J. Amis, T. Slack, and C. Hinings, "Values and Organization Change," *Journal of Applied Behavioral Science* 38 (2002): 436–65.
32. Collins and Porras, *Built to Last*.
33. This application was adapted from R. Barnett and J. Scott, "Partnership in Organizational Culture Transformation" (a paper presented to the 14th annual conference of the Society for Industrial and Organizational Psychology, Atlanta, Ga., May 1999).
34. J. Pfeffer, *Power in Organizations* (New York: Pitman, 1982).
35. D. Nadler, "The Effective Management of Change," in *Handbook of Organizational Behavior*, ed. J. Lorsch (Englewood Cliffs, NJ: Prentice Hall, 1987), 358–69.
36. C. Alderfer, "Organization Development," *Annual Review of Psychology* 28 (1977): 197–223.
37. T. Bateman, "Organizational Change and the Politics of Success," *Group and Organization Studies* 5 (June 1980): 198–209; A. Cobb and N. Margulies, "Organization Development: A Political Perspective," *Academy of Management Review* 6 (1981): 49–59; A. Cobb, "Political Diagnosis: Applications in Organization Development," *Academy of Management Review* 11 (1986): 482–96; L. Greiner and V. Schein, *Power and Organization Development: Mobilizing Power to Implement Change* (Reading, MA: Addison-Wesley, 1988); D. Buchanan and R. Badham, "Politics and Organizational Change: The Lived Experience," *Human Relations* 52 (1999): 609–11.
38. Greiner and Schein, *Power and Organization Development*.
39. Nadler, "Effective Management"; Beckhard and Pritchard, *Changing the Essence*.
40. Greiner and Schein, *Power and Organization Development*.
41. Beckhard and Harris, *Organizational Transitions*.
42. Ibid.
43. Ibid.
44. R. Tenkasi, S. Mohrman, and A. Mohrman, "Accelerated Learning during Organizational Transition," in *Tomorrow's Organization*, ed. S. Mohrman, J. Galbraith, E. Lawler and Associates (San Francisco: Jossey-Bass, 1998).
45. This application was derived from the following articles: B. Caulfield, "Saving $3 Billion the HP Way," *Business 2.0*, 4 (2003): 52–57; P. Tam, "Elaborate Planning Helps Keep HP Union on Target," *Wall Street Journal*, April 23, 2003, A1; L. Segil, "Why the HP/Compaq Merger Will Go Down in History as the Best Ever," *Wall Street Journal*, April 28, 2003; D. Takahashi and T. Poletti, "Combined Company Is Faring Better Than Some Rivals," *San Jose Mercury News*, April 12, 2003, 1F. The kind assistance of Emily Horn and Jenny Galitz from Hill and Knowlton, and Sarah Peterson and Cathy Fitzgerald from HP is gratefully acknowledged.
46. C. Worley, D. Hitchin, and W. Ross, *Integrated Strategic Change: How OD Helps to Build Competitive Advantage* (Reading, MA: Addison-Wesley, 1996).
47. M. Beer, *Organization Change and Development: A Systems View* (Santa Monica, CA: Goodyear, 1980).
48. S. Gale, "Building Frameworks for Six Sigma Success," *Workforce* 82 (2003): 64–69.
49. A. Fisher, "Making Change Stick," *Fortune*, April 17, 1995, 121–31.
50. This application was adapted from J. Leong and C. Anderson, "Fostering Innovation through Cultural Change," *Library Management* 33 (2012): 490–97.

9

Evaluating and Institutionalizing Organization Development Interventions

learning objectives

- **Illustrate the research design and measurement issues associated with evaluating organization development (OD) interventions.**
- **Explain the key elements in the process of institutionalizing OD interventions.**

This chapter focuses on the final stage of the organization development cycle—evaluation and institutionalization. *Evaluation* is concerned with providing feedback to practitioners and organization members about the progress and impact of interventions. Such information may suggest the need for further diagnosis and modification of the change program, or it may show that the intervention is successful. *Institutionalization* is a process for maintaining a particular change for an appropriate period of time. It ensures that the results of successful change programs persist over time.

Evaluation processes consider both the implementation success of the intended intervention and the long-term results it produces. Two key aspects of effective evaluation are measurement and research design. The persistence of intervention effects is examined in a framework showing the organization characteristics, intervention dimensions, and processes contributing to institutionalization of OD interventions in organizations.

9-1 Evaluating Organization Development Interventions

Assessing OD interventions involves judgments about whether an intervention has been implemented as intended and, if so, whether it is having desired results. Managers investing resources in OD efforts increasingly are being held accountable for results—being asked to justify the expenditures in terms of hard, bottom-line outcomes. More and more, managers are asking for rigorous assessment of OD interventions and are using the results to make important resource allocation decisions about OD, such as whether to continue to support the change program, to modify or alter it, or to terminate it and try something else.

Traditionally, OD evaluation has been discussed as something that occurs after the intervention. Chapters 10 through 20, for example, present evaluative research about the interventions after discussions of the respective change programs. That view can be misleading, however. Decisions about the measurement of relevant variables and the design of the evaluation process should be made early in the OD cycle so that evaluation choices can be integrated with intervention decisions.

There are two distinct types of OD evaluation: one intended to guide the implementation of interventions and another to assess their overall impact. The key issues in evaluation are measurement and research design.

9-1a Implementation and Evaluation Feedback

Most discussions and applications of OD evaluation imply that evaluation is something done after intervention. It is typically argued that once the intervention is implemented, it should be evaluated to discover whether it is producing the intended effects. For example, it might be expected that a job enrichment program would lead to higher employee satisfaction and performance. After implementing job enrichment, evaluation would involve assessing whether these positive results indeed did occur. This after-implementation view of evaluation is only partially correct. It assumes that interventions have been implemented as intended and that the key purpose of evaluation is to assess their effects. However, in many, if not most, organization development programs, implementing interventions cannot be taken for granted.[1] Most OD interventions require significant changes in people's behaviors and ways of thinking about organizations, but they typically offer only broad prescriptions for how such changes are to occur. For example, job enrichment (see Chapter 14) calls for adding discretion, variety, and meaningful feedback to people's jobs. Implementing such changes requires considerable learning and experimentation as employees and managers discover how to translate these general prescriptions into specific behaviors and procedures. This learning process involves much trial and error and needs to be guided by information about whether behaviors and procedures are being changed as intended.[2] Consequently, we should expand our view of evaluation to include both *during-implementation* assessments about if and how well changes are actually being implemented and *after-implementation* evaluation of whether they are producing expected results.

Both kinds of evaluation provide organization members with feedback about interventions. Evaluation aimed at guiding implementation may be called *implementation feedback,* and assessment intended to discover intervention outcomes may be called *evaluation feedback.* Figure 9.1 shows how the two kinds of feedback fit with the diagnostic and intervention stages of OD. The application of OD to a particular organization starts with a thorough diagnosis of the situation (Chapters 5 and 6), which helps identify particular organizational problems, areas for improvement, or strengths to leverage as well as the likely drivers underlying them. Next, from an array of possible interventions (Chapters 10 through 20), one or some set is chosen as a means of improving the organization. The choice is based on knowledge linking interventions to diagnosis (Chapter 7) and change management (Chapter 8).

In most cases, the chosen intervention provides only general guidelines for organizational change, leaving managers and employees with the task of translating those guidelines into specific behaviors and procedures. Implementation feedback informs this process by supplying data about the different features of the intervention itself, perceptions of the people involved, and data about the immediate effects of the intervention. These data, collected repeatedly and at short intervals, provide a series of snapshots about how the intervention is progressing. Organization members can use this information, first, to gain a clearer understanding of the intervention (the kinds of behaviors and procedures required to implement it) and, second, to plan for the next implementation

FIGURE 9.1

Implementation and Evaluation Feedback

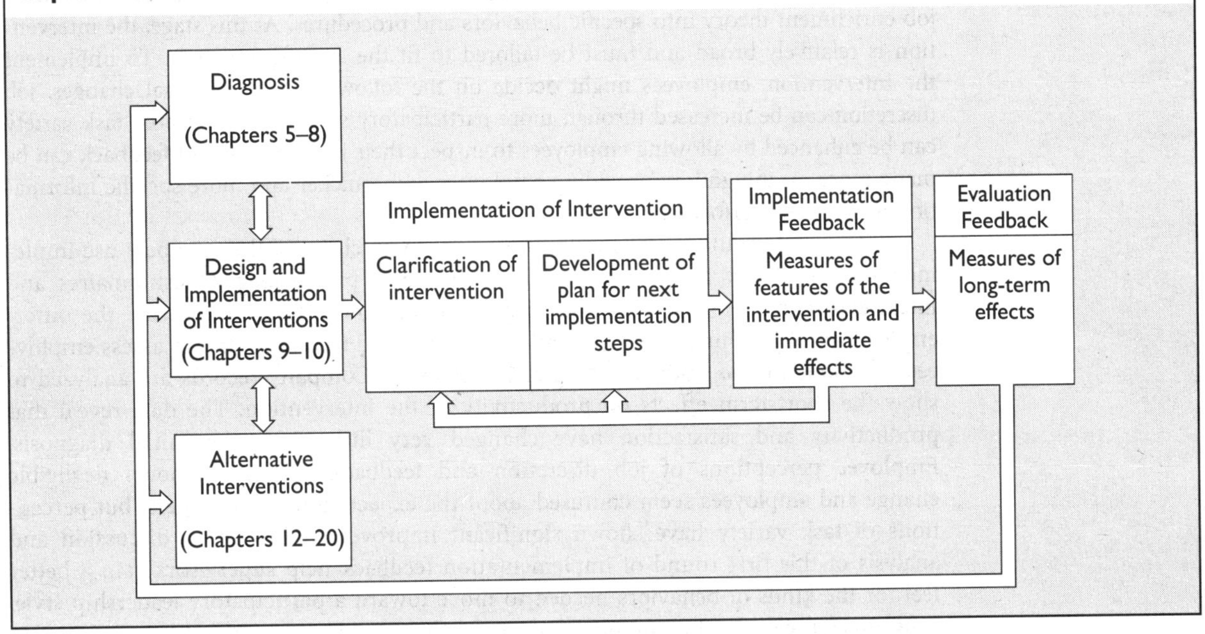

steps. This feedback cycle might proceed for several rounds, with each round providing members with knowledge about the intervention and ideas for the next stage of implementation.

Once implementation feedback informs organization members that the intervention is sufficiently in place and accepted, evaluation feedback begins. In contrast to implementation feedback, it is concerned with the overall impact of the intervention and with whether resources should continue to be allocated to it or to other possible interventions. Evaluation feedback takes longer to gather and interpret than does implementation feedback. It typically includes a broad array of outcome measures, such as performance, job satisfaction, productivity, and turnover. Negative results on these measures tell members either that the initial diagnosis was seriously flawed or that the wrong intervention was chosen. Such feedback might prompt additional diagnosis and a search for a more effective intervention. Positive results, on the other hand, tell members that the intervention produced expected outcomes and might prompt a search for ways to institutionalize the changes, making them a permanent part of the organization's normal functioning.

An example of a job enrichment intervention helps to clarify the OD stages and feedback linkages shown in Figure 9.1. Suppose the initial diagnosis reveals that employee performance and satisfaction are low and that jobs being overly structured and routinized are an underlying cause of this problem. An inspection of alternative interventions to improve productivity and satisfaction suggests that job enrichment might be applicable for this situation. Existing job enrichment theory proposes that increasing employee discretion, task variety, and feedback can lead to improvements in work quality and attitudes and that this job design and outcome linkage is especially strong for employees who have growth needs—needs for challenge, autonomy, and development. Initial diagnosis suggests that most of the employees have high growth needs and that the existing job designs prevent the fulfillment of these needs. Therefore, job enrichment seems particularly suited to this situation.

Managers and employees now start to translate the general prescriptions offered by job enrichment theory into specific behaviors and procedures. At this stage, the intervention is relatively broad and must be tailored to fit the specific situation. To implement the intervention, employees might decide on the following organizational changes: job discretion can be increased through more participatory styles of supervision; task variety can be enhanced by allowing employees to inspect their job outputs; and feedback can be made more meaningful by providing employees with quicker and more specific information about their performances.

After three months of trying to implement these changes, the members use implementation feedback to see how the intervention is progressing. Questionnaires and interviews (similar to those used in diagnosis) are administered to measure the different features of job enrichment (discretion, variety, and feedback) and to assess employees' reactions to and understanding of the changes. Company records are analyzed to show the short-term effects on productivity of the intervention. The data reveal that productivity and satisfaction have changed very little since the initial diagnosis. Employee perceptions of job discretion and feedback also have shown negligible change and employees seem confused about the expectations of managers, but perceptions of task variety have shown significant improvement. In-depth discussion and analysis of this first round of implementation feedback help supervisors gain a better feel for the kinds of behaviors needed to move toward a participatory leadership style. This greater clarification of one feature of the intervention leads to a decision to involve the supervisors in leadership training to develop the skills and knowledge needed to lead participatively. A decision also is made to make job feedback more meaningful by translating such data into simple bar graphs, rather than continuing to provide voluminous statistical reports.

After these modifications have been in effect for about three months, members gather a second round of implementation feedback to see how the intervention is progressing. The data now show that productivity and satisfaction have moved moderately higher than in the first round of feedback and that employee perceptions of task variety and feedback are both high. Employee perceptions of discretion, however, remain relatively low. Members conclude that the variety and feedback dimensions of job enrichment are sufficiently implemented but that the discretion component needs further improvement. They decide to put more effort into supervisory training and to ask OD practitioners to provide counseling and coaching to supervisors about their leadership styles.

After four more months, a third round of implementation feedback is sought. The data now show that satisfaction and performance are significantly higher than in the first round of feedback and moderately higher than in the second round. The data also show that discretion, variety, and feedback are all high, suggesting that the job enrichment intervention has been successfully implemented. Now evaluation feedback is used to assess the overall effectiveness of the program.

The evaluation feedback includes all the data from the satisfaction and performance measures used in the implementation feedback. Because both the immediate and broader effects of the intervention are being evaluated, additional outcomes are examined, such as employee absenteeism, maintenance costs, and reactions of other organizational units not included in job enrichment. The full array of evaluation data might suggest that after one year from the start of implementation, the job enrichment program is having the expected effects and thus should be continued and made more permanent.

9-1b Measurement

Providing useful implementation and evaluation feedback involves two activities: selecting the appropriate variables and designing good measures of them.

Selecting Appropriate Variables Ideally, the variables measured in OD evaluation should derive from the theory or conceptual model underlying the intervention. The model should incorporate the key features of the intervention as well as its expected results. The general diagnostic models described in Chapter 5 meet this criterion, as do the more specific models introduced in Chapters 10 through 20. For example, the job-level diagnostic model described in Chapter 5 proposes several major features of work: task variety, feedback, and autonomy. The theory argues that high levels of these elements can be expected to result in high levels of work quality and satisfaction. In addition, as we shall see in Chapter 14, the strength of this relationship varies with the degree of employee growth needs: the higher the need, the more that job enrichment produces positive results.

The job-level diagnostic model suggests a number of measurement variables for implementation and evaluation feedback. Whether the intervention is being implemented could be assessed by determining how many job descriptions have been rewritten to include more responsibility or how many organization members have received cross-training in other job skills. Evaluation of the immediate and long-term impact of job enrichment would include measures of employee performance and satisfaction over time. Again, these measures would likely be included in the initial diagnosis, when the company's problems or areas for improvement are discovered.

Measuring both intervention and outcome variables is necessary for implementation and evaluation feedback. Unfortunately, there has been a tendency in OD to measure only outcome variables while neglecting intervention variables altogether.[3] It generally is assumed that the intervention has been implemented, and attention, therefore, is directed to its impact on such organizational outcomes as performance, absenteeism, and satisfaction. As argued earlier, implementing OD interventions generally takes considerable time and learning. It must be empirically determined that the intervention has been implemented; it cannot simply be assumed. Implementation feedback serves this purpose, guiding the implementation process and helping to interpret outcome data. Outcome measures are ambiguous without knowledge of how well the intervention has been implemented. For example, a negligible change in measures of performance and satisfaction could mean that the wrong intervention has been chosen, that the correct intervention has not been implemented effectively, or that the wrong variables have been measured. Measurement of the intervention variables helps determine the correct interpretation of outcome measures.

As suggested above, the selection of intervention variables to be measured should derive from the conceptual framework underlying the OD intervention. OD research and theory increasingly have come to identify specific organizational changes needed to implement particular interventions (much of that information is discussed in Chapters 10 through 20). These variables should guide not only implementation of the intervention but also choices about what change variables to measure for evaluative purposes. Additional sources of knowledge about intervention variables can be found in the numerous references at the end of each of the chapters on intervention in this book and in several of the books in the Wiley Series on Organizational Assessment and Change.[4]

The choice of what outcome variables to measure also should be dictated by intervention theory, which specifies the kinds of results that can be expected from particular change programs. Again, the material in this book and elsewhere identifies numerous outcome measures, such as job satisfaction, intrinsic motivation, organizational commitment, absenteeism, turnover, and productivity.

Historically, OD assessment has focused on attitudinal outcomes, such as job satisfaction, while neglecting hard measures, such as performance. Increasingly, however, managers and researchers are calling for development of behavioral measures of OD outcomes. Managers are interested primarily in applying OD to change work-related behaviors that involve joining, remaining, and producing at work, and are assessing OD more frequently in terms of such bottom-line results. Macy and Mirvis have done extensive research to develop a standardized set of behavioral outcomes for assessing and comparing intervention results.[5] Table 9.1 lists 11 outcomes, including their behavioral definitions and recording categories. The outcomes are in two broad categories: participation-membership, including absenteeism, tardiness, turnover, internal employment stability, and strikes and work stoppages; and performance on the job, including productivity, quality, grievances, accidents, unscheduled machine downtime and repair, material and supply overuse, and inventory shrinkage. All of the outcomes should be important to most managers, and they represent generic descriptions that can be adapted to both industrial and service organizations.

Designing Good Measures Each of the measurement methods described in Chapter 6—questionnaires, interviews, observations, and unobtrusive measures—has advantages and disadvantages. Many of these characteristics are linked to the extent to which a measurement is operationally defined, reliable, and valid. These assessment characteristics are discussed below.

Operational Definition. A good measure is operationally defined; that is, it specifies the empirical data needed, how they will be collected and, most important, how they will be converted from data to information. For example, Macy and Mirvis developed operational definitions for the behavioral outcomes listed in Table 9.1 (see Table 9.2).[6] They consist of specific computational rules that can be used to construct measures for each of the behaviors. Most of the behaviors are reported as rates adjusted for the number of employees in the organization and for the possible incidents of behavior. These adjustments make it possible to compare the measures across different situations and time periods. These operational definitions should have wide applicability across both industrial and service organizations, although some modifications, deletions, and additions may be necessary for a particular application.

Operational definitions are extremely important in measurement because they provide precise guidelines about what characteristics of the situation are to be observed and how they are to be used. They tell OD practitioners and organization members exactly how diagnostic, intervention, and outcome variables will be measured.

Reliability. Reliability concerns the extent to which a measure represents the "true" value of a variable—that is, how accurately the operational definition translates data into information. For example, there is little doubt about the accuracy of the number of cars leaving an assembly line as a measure of plant productivity. Although it is possible to miscount, there can be a high degree of confidence in the measurement. On the other hand, when people are asked to rate their level of job satisfaction on a scale of 1 to 5, there is considerable room for variation in their response. They may just have had an argument with their supervisor, suffered an accident on the job, been rewarded for high levels of productivity, or been given new responsibilities. Each of these events can sway the response to the question on any given day. The individuals' "true" satisfaction score is difficult to discern from this one question and the measure lacks reliability.[7]

TABLE 9.1

Behavioral Outcomes for Measuring OD Interventions: Definitions and Recording Categories

Behavioral Definitions	Recording Categories
Absenteeism: each absence or illness over four hours	*Voluntary:* short-term illness (less than three consecutive days), personal business, family illness *Involuntary:* long-term illness (more than three consecutive days), funerals, out-of-plant accidents, lack of work (temporary layoff), presanctioned days off *Leaves:* medical, personal, maternity, military, and other (e.g., jury duty)
Tardiness: each absence or illness under four hours	*Voluntary:* same as absenteeism *Involuntary:* same as absenteeism
Turnover: each movement beyond the organizational boundary	*Voluntary:* resignation *Involuntary:* termination, disqualification, requested resignation, permanent layoff, retirement, disability, death
Internal employment stability: each movement within the organizational boundary	*Internal movement:* transfer, promotion, promotion with transfer *Internal stability:* new hires, layoffs, rehires
Strikes and work stoppages: each day lost as a result of strike or work stoppage	*Sanctioned:* union-authorized strike, company-authorized lockout *Unsanctioned:* work slowdown, walkout, sitdown
Accidents and work-related illness: each recordable injury, illness, or death from a work-related accident or from exposure to the work environment	*Major:* OSHA accident, illness, or death which results in medical treatment by a physician or registered professional person understanding orders from a physician *Minor:* non-OSHA accident or illness which results in one-time treatment and subsequent observation not requiring professional care *Revisits:* OSHA and non-OSHA accident or illness which requires subsequent treatment and observation
Grievances: written grievance in accordance with labor–management contract	*Stage:* recorded by step (first through arbitration)
Productivity:* resources used in production of acceptable outputs (comparison of inputs with outputs)	*Output:* product or service quantity (units or $) *Input:* direct and/or indirect (labor in hours or $)
Production quality: resources used in production of unacceptable outputs	*Resource utilized:* scrap (unacceptable in-plant products in units or $); customer returns (unacceptable out-of-plant products in units or $); recoveries (salvageable products in units or $); rework (additional direct and/or indirect labor in hours or $)
Downtime: unscheduled breakdown of machinery	*Downtime:* duration of breakdown (hours or $) *Machine repair:* nonpreventive maintenance ($)
Inventory, material, and supply variance: unscheduled resource utilization	*Variance:* over- or under-utilization of supplies, materials, inventory (resulting from theft, inefficiency, and so on)

*Reports only labor inputs.

SOURCE: B. Macy and P. Mirvis, "Organizational Change Efforts: Methodologies for Assessing Organizational Effectiveness and Program Costs Versus Benefits," *Evaluation Review* 6, pp. 306–10. © 1982 by Sage Publications, Inc. Reprinted by permission of Sage Publications, Inc.

TABLE 9.2

Behavioral Outcomes for Measuring OD Interventions: Measures and Computational Formula

Behavioral Measure*	Computational Formula
Absenteeism rate** (monthly)	$\frac{\Sigma \text{ Absence days}}{\text{Average workforce size} \times \text{Working days}}$
Tardiness rate** (monthly)	$\frac{\Sigma \text{ Tardiness incidents}}{\text{Average workforce size} \times \text{Working days}}$
Turnover rate (monthly)	$\frac{\Sigma \text{ Turnover incidents}}{\text{Average workforce size}}$
Internal stability rate (monthly)	$\frac{\Sigma \text{ Internal movement incidents}}{\text{Average workforce size}}$
Strike rate (yearly)	$\frac{\Sigma \text{ Striking Workers} \times \text{Strike days}}{\text{Average workforce size} \times \text{Working days}}$
Accident rate (yearly)	$\frac{\Sigma \text{ of Accidents, illnesses}}{\text{Total yearly hours worked}} \times 200{,}000$***
Grievance rate (yearly)	$\frac{\Sigma \text{ Grievance incidents}}{\text{Plant: Average workforce size}}$
	Individual: $\frac{\Sigma \text{ Aggrieved individuals}}{\text{Average workforce size}}$
Productivity:****	
Total	$\frac{\text{Output of goods or services (units or \\$)}}{\text{Direct and/or indirect labor (hours or \\$)}}$
Below standard	Actual versus engineered standard
Below budget	Actual versus budgeted standard
Variance	Actual versus budgeted variance
Per employee	Output/average workforce size
Quality:****	
Total	Scrap + Customer returns + Rework − Recoveries ($, units, or hours)
Below standard	Actual versus engineered standard
Below budget	Actual versus budgeted standard
Variance	Actual versus budgeted variance
Per employee	Total/average workforce size
Downtime	Labor ($) + Repair costs or dollar value of replaced equipment ($)
Inventory, supply, and material usage	Variance (actual versus standard utilization) ($)

*All measures reflect the number of incidents divided by an exposure factor that represents the number of employees in the organization and the possible incidents of behavior (e.g., for absenteeism, the average workforce size × the number of working days). Mean monthly rates (i.e., absences per workday) are computed and averaged for absenteeism, leaves, and tardiness for a yearly figure and summed for turnover, grievances, and internal employment stability for a yearly figure. The term rate refers to the number of incidents per unit of employee exposure to the risk of such incidences during the analysis interval.

**Sometimes combined as number of hours missing/average workforce size × working days.

***Base for 100 full-time equivalent workers (40 hours × 50 weeks).

****Monetary valuations can be expressed in labor dollars, actual dollar costs, sales dollars; overtime dollar valuations can be adjusted to base year dollars to control for salary, raw material, and price increases.

SOURCE: B. Macy and P. Mirvis, "Organizational Change Efforts: Methodologies for Assessing Organizational Effectiveness and Program Costs Versus Benefits," *Evaluation Review* 6, pp. 306–10. © 1982 by Sage Publications, Inc. Reprinted by permission of Sage Publications, Inc.

OD practitioners can improve the reliability of their measures in four ways. First, rigorously and operationally define the chosen variables. Clearly specified operational definitions contribute to reliability by explicitly describing how collected data will be converted into information about a variable. An explicit description helps to allay the organization's concerns about how the information was collected and coded.

Second, use multiple methods to measure a particular variable. As discussed in Chapter 6, the use of questionnaires, interviews, observations, and unobtrusive measures can improve reliability and result in a more comprehensive understanding of the organization. Because each method contains inherent biases, several different methods can be used to triangulate on dimensions of organizational issues. If the independent measures converge or show consistent results, the dimensions or problems likely have been diagnosed accurately.[8]

Third, use multiple items to measure the same variable on a questionnaire. For example, in Hackman and Oldham's Job Diagnostic Survey for measuring job characteristics (Chapter 14), the intervention variable "autonomy" is operationally defined by the average of respondents' answers to the following three questions (measured on a 7-point scale):[9]

1. The job permits me to decide *on my own* how to go about doing the work.
2. The job denies me any chance to use my personal initiative or judgment in carrying out the work. [reverse scored]
3. The job gives me considerable opportunity for independence and freedom in how I do the work.

By asking more than one question about "autonomy," the survey increases the accuracy of its measurement of this variable. Statistical analyses (called *psychometric tests*) are readily available for assessing the reliability of perceptual measures, and OD practitioners should apply these methods or seek assistance from those who can apply them.[10] Similarly, there are methods for analyzing the content of interview and observational data, and OD evaluators can use these methods to categorize such information so that it can be understood and replicated.[11]

Fourth, use standardized instruments. A growing number of standardized questionnaires are available for measuring OD intervention and outcome variables. For example, the Center for Effective Organizations at the University of Southern California (http://ceo.usc.edu) and the Institute for Social Research at the University of Michigan (http://home.isr.umich.edu) have developed comprehensive survey instruments to measure the features of many of the OD interventions described in this book, as well as their attitudinal outcomes.[12] Considerable research and testing have gone into establishing measures that are reliable and valid. These survey instruments can be used for initial diagnosis, for guiding implementation of interventions, and for evaluating immediate and long-term outcomes.

Validity. Validity concerns the extent to which a measure actually reflects the variable it is intended to measure. For example, the number of cars leaving an assembly line might be a reliable measure of plant productivity, but it may not be a valid measure. The number of cars is only one aspect of productivity; they may have been produced at an unacceptably high cost or at exceptionally low quality. Because the number of cars does not account for cost and quality, it is not a completely valid measure of plant productivity.

OD practitioners can increase the validity of their measures in several ways. First, ask colleagues and organization members if a proposed measure actually represents a particular variable. This is called *face validity* or *content validity*. If experts and members agree that the measure reflects the variable of interest, then there is increased confidence in the measure's validity. Second, use multiple measures of the same variable, as described in the section about reliability, to make preliminary assessments of the measure's *criterion* or *convergent validity.* That is, if several different measures of the same variable correlate highly with each other, especially if one or more of the other measures have been validated in prior research, then there is increased confidence in the measure's validity. A special case of criterion validity, called *discriminant validity,* exists when the proposed measure does not correlate with measures that it is not supposed to correlate with. For example, there is no good reason for daily measures of assembly line productivity to correlate with daily air temperature. The lack of a correlation would be one indicator that the number of cars is measuring productivity and not some other variable. Finally, *predictive validity* is demonstrated when the variable of interest accurately forecasts another variable over time. For example, a measure of team cohesion can be said to be valid if it accurately predicts improvements in team performance in the future.

It is difficult, however, to establish the validity of a measure until it has been used. To address this concern, OD practitioners should make heavy use of content validity processes and use measures that already have been validated. For example, presenting proposed measures to colleagues and organization members for evaluation prior to measurement has several positive effects: It builds ownership and commitment to the data collection process and improves the likelihood that the client system will find the data meaningful. Using measures that have been validated through prior research improves confidence in the results and provides a standard that can be used to validate any new measures used in collecting the data.

9-1c Research Design

In addition to measurement, OD practitioners must make choices about how to design the evaluation to achieve valid results. The key issue is how to design the assessment to show whether the intervention did in fact produce the observed results. This is called *internal validity.* The secondary question of whether the intervention would work similarly in other situations is referred to as *external validity.* External validity is irrelevant without first establishing an intervention's primary effectiveness, so internal validity is the essential minimum requirement for assessing OD interventions. Unless managers can have confidence that the outcomes are the result of the intervention, they have no rational basis for making decisions about accountability and resource allocation.

Assessing the internal validity of an intervention is, in effect, testing a hypothesis—namely, that specific organizational changes lead to certain outcomes. Moreover, testing the validity of an intervention hypothesis means that alternative hypotheses or explanations of the results must be rejected. That is, to claim that an intervention is successful, it is necessary to demonstrate that other explanations—in the form of rival hypotheses—do not account for the observed results. For example, if a job enrichment program appears to increase employee performance, such other possible explanations as new technology, improved raw materials, or new employees must be eliminated.

Accounting for rival explanations is not a precise, controlled, experimental process such as might be found in a research laboratory.[13] OD interventions often have a number of features that make it difficult to determine whether they produced the observed results. They are complex and often involve several interrelated changes that obscure whether individual features or combinations of features are accounting for the results. Many OD interventions are long-term projects and take considerable time to produce desired outcomes. The longer the time period of the change program, the greater are the chances that other factors, such as technology improvements, will emerge to affect the results. Finally, OD interventions usually are applied to existing work units rather than to randomized groups of organization members. Ruling out alternative explanations associated with randomly selected intervention and comparison groups is, therefore, difficult.

Given the problems inherent in assessing OD interventions, practitioners have turned to *quasi-experimental research designs*.[14] These designs are not as rigorous and controlled as are randomized experimental designs, but they allow evaluators to rule out many rival explanations for OD results other than the intervention itself. Although several quasi-experimental designs are available, those with the following three features are particularly powerful for assessing changes:

1. **Longitudinal measurement.** This involves measuring results repeatedly over relatively long time periods. Ideally, the data collection should start before the change program is implemented and continue for a period considered reasonable for producing expected results.
2. **Comparison unit.** It is always desirable to compare results in the intervention situation with those in another situation where no such change has taken place. Although it is never possible to get a matching group identical to the intervention group, most organizations include a number of similar work units that can be used for comparison purposes.
3. **Statistical analysis.** Whenever possible, statistical methods should be used to rule out the possibility that the results are caused by random error or chance. Various statistical techniques are applicable to quasi-experimental designs, and OD practitioners should apply these methods or seek help from those who can apply them.

Table 9.3 provides an example of a quasi-experimental design having these three features. The intervention is intended to reduce employee absenteeism. Measures of absenteeism are taken from company monthly records for both the intervention and comparison groups. The two groups are similar yet geographically separate subsidiaries of a multiplant company. Table 9.3 shows each plant's monthly absenteeism rate for four consecutive months both before and after the start of the intervention. The plant receiving the intervention shows a marked decrease in absenteeism in the months following the intervention, whereas the control plant shows comparable levels of absenteeism in both time periods. Statistical analyses of these data suggest that the abrupt downward shift in absenteeism following the intervention was not attributable to chance variation. This research design and the data provide relatively strong evidence that the intervention was successful.

Quasi-experimental research designs using longitudinal data, comparison groups, and statistical analysis permit reasonable assessments of intervention effectiveness. Repeated measures often can be collected from company records without directly involving members of the experimental and comparison groups. These unobtrusive measures are especially useful in OD assessment because they do not interact with the intervention

TABLE 9.3

Quasi-Experimental Research Design

	Monthly Absenteeism (%)								
	Sept.	Oct.	Nov.	Dec.		Jan.	Feb.	Mar.	Apr.
Intervention group	5.1	5.3	5.0	5.1	Start of intervention	4.6	4.0	3.9	3.5
Comparison group	2.5	2.6	2.4	2.5		2.6	2.4	2.5	2.5

and affect the results. Measures that are more obtrusive, such as questionnaires and interviews, are reactive and can sensitize people to the intervention. When this happens, it is difficult to know whether the observed findings are the result of the intervention, the measuring methods, or some combination of both.

Multiple measures of intervention and outcome variables should be applied to minimize measurement and intervention interactions. For example, obtrusive measures such as questionnaires could be used sparingly, perhaps once before and once after the intervention. Unobtrusive measures, such as the behavioral outcomes shown in Tables 9.1 and 9.2, could be used repeatedly, thus providing a more extensive time series than the questionnaires. When used together, the two kinds of measures should produce accurate and nonreactive evaluations of the intervention.

The use of multiple measures also is important in assessing perceptual changes resulting from interventions. Considerable research has identified three types of change—alpha, beta, and gamma—that occur when using self-report, perceptual measures.[15]

Alpha change refers to movement along a measure that reflects stable dimensions of reality. For example, comparative measures of perceived employee discretion might show an increase after a job enrichment program. If this increase represents alpha change, it can be assumed that the job enrichment program actually increased employee perceptions of discretion.

Beta change involves the recalibration of the intervals along some constant measure of reality. For example, before-and-after measures of perceived employee discretion can decrease after a job enrichment program. If beta change is involved, it can explain this apparent failure of the intervention to increase discretion. The first measure of discretion may accurately reflect the individual's belief about the ability to move around and talk to fellow workers in the immediate work area. During implementation of the job enrichment intervention, however, the employee may learn that the ability to move around is not limited to the immediate work area. At a second measurement of discretion, the employee, using this new and recalibrated understanding, may rate the current level of discretion as lower than before.

Gamma change involves fundamentally redefining the measure as a result of an OD intervention. In essence, the framework within which a phenomenon is viewed changes. For example, the presence of gamma change would make it difficult to compare measures of employee discretion taken before and after a job enrichment program. The measure taken after the intervention might use the same words, but they represent an entirely different concept. As described above, the term "discretion" may originally refer to the ability to move about the department and interact with other workers. After the intervention, discretion might be defined in terms of the ability to make decisions about work rules, work schedules, and productivity levels. In sum, the job enrichment intervention changed the way discretion is perceived and how it is evaluated.

These three types of change apply to perceptual measures. When changes other than alpha ones occur, interpreting measurement changes becomes far more difficult. Potent OD interventions may produce both beta and gamma changes, and this severely complicates interpretations of findings reporting change or no change. Further, the distinctions among the three different types of change suggest that the heavy reliance on questionnaires, so often cited in the literature, should be balanced by using other measures, such as interviews and unobtrusive records. Analytical methods have been developed to assess the three kinds of change, and OD practitioners should gain familiarity with these recent techniques.[16]

Application 9.1 describes the implementation and evaluation feedback that were developed for the Alegent Health project. It is a good example of how data can be used

application 9.1

EVALUATING CHANGE AT ALEGENT HEALTH

In July and August of 2005, Alegent Health (AH) conducted six large group interventions or "decision accelerators" (DAs) to generate innovative strategies for its six clinical service areas. Researchers at USC's Center for Effective Organizations contracted with AH to assess the impact of the interventions and to help the organization learn how to leverage further change. The applications in Chapter 4 described how the researchers entered and contracted with the organization, and Application 6.1 described the data collection and analysis process. In this application, we describe the implementation and evaluation feedback the researchers generated.

In terms of implementation feedback, the collected data described perceptions of change progress and employee involvement. For example, executive interviews and surveys from people who participated in "review DAs" to reflect on implementation progress and plan future changes supported a positive assessment of overall progress. People generally agreed that the implementation of the clinical strategies was going well. They were positive about the social capital that had been created by the DAs, especially between administrators and physicians, as well as the evidence of culture change. Nearly everyone in the organization believed that the clinical strategies were the "right thing to do." In contrast to these positive findings, there was some concern about feeling involved in the change.

That is, the DAs were a great energizer for the organization, generated comprehensive strategies, and catalyzed important changes. However, the data also contained some reservations about the organization's ability to leverage the changes. As described in Application 6.1, the implementation approaches were mostly informal; the organization was afraid that too many dedicated change processes and systems might slow down the change process. The data revealed a more complex set of issues.

First, executives and some physicians understood the roles, decisions, and processes related to implementation more than operational managers and other physicians. The six clinical services areas studied described an intense period of business planning following the DAs. Senior management, all of whom had participated in the original six DAs, drove this process and were quite clear about the resulting priorities and initiatives. This clarity, however, was not widely shared by the hospital COOs, many physicians, and many operational managers. This resulted in a perception of a strong connection between strategy formulation and implementation at the top of the organization, but a weak perception in the middle of the organization. Managers and nurses felt overwhelmed—they heard about change with little context, and believed that the speed of change was slower rather than faster because "everything was important." Similarly, many physicians who were energized by the DAs wanted to know "where's the change?" While exceptions to this observation did exist, there was a general sense that senior managers were more involved and saw more change than others saw.

Second, the absence of formal change-management processes made important resource allocation decisions, trade-offs on technology, and coordination of quality processes across the system more difficult. There was no visible mechanism, for example, to decide how quality programs should be rolled out or where to pilot electronic medical record systems. The lack of formal change-management systems (action plans, governance mechanisms, learning practices) following the DAs was related to some feelings among all stakeholder groups that change was slow in coming and overwhelming when it did come. Most people correctly viewed the strategies created by the DAs as high-level plans providing general direction. However, the process for developing action plans and implementation activities was not visible to many people. Ad hoc change systems emerged based on the nature of the strategy implementation activities and these helped to focus attention and resources. Interestingly, these systems all started to emerge about one year after the original DAs.

Based on these implementation data, and the data presented in Application 6.1 about how the DA needed to evolve, the researchers recommended (1) creating different versions of the DA to address different issues and (2) formalizing some change processes so that the resourcing, execution, and communication of change were more coordinated. However, their overall recommendation was to continue using the DA for strategy formulation and visioning, as well as tactical and implementation-oriented issues.

In terms of evaluation feedback, the analysis of the activities described in the DA reports provided some important conclusions. For example, the composition of the DAs, or the mix of AH managers and staff, physicians, community members, and other stakeholders, affected the processes and outcomes. First, in DAs where there was a higher proportion of physicians, there was a narrower range of stakeholder participation and an increased likelihood that the group would deviate from the agenda. In addition, there was a weak relationship between higher percentages of community participants and all DA processes. That is, when the DA had more community participants, there was broader participation in the discussions, the debates were more intense, and the DA stayed on track.

Second, the composition of the DA had differential impacts on the outcomes of meeting. When the DA had a high percentage of physicians, the resulting vision was less comprehensive. On the other hand, when the DA had a high concentration of community participants, the vision was more comprehensive. These results were reflected in the survey data as well. The percentage of community participants was positively related to perceptions that the strategy was more innovative but less aggressive and business oriented. The concentration of physicians in the DA tended to have opposite relationships with the strategy dimensions.

When these data were fed back to the organization, the researchers specifically pointed out that these findings did not suggest that it was wrong to involve physicians or that a higher percentage of community members was better. To the contrary, the fundamental assumption of DA interventions was that a broader mix of stakeholders contributes to a better solution. These data did suggest that not all stakeholder groups are created equal. Too many of any type of stakeholder group may lead to lopsided discussions and sway the agenda. In several of the DAs, for example, almost half of the participants were physicians, making it likely that this constituency would disproportionately impact the flow of the meeting.

The table below summarizes many of the findings from the Alegent project.

Evaluation Question	Data
• Does Alegent's strategy, purpose, and organization support change?	– Yes—Many powerful internal and external forces are pushing for and supporting change
• How effective were the original six DAs in achieving intended outcomes?	– Very effective—The DAs generated a lot of energy for change, healed physician relationships, and utilized good thinking
• What DA characteristics made a difference?	– The DA's composition was an important influence on its processes and outcomes
• How do executives and managers characterize the service-line strategies?	– Comprehensive, somewhat innovative, and business-oriented
• Are they similar or different?	– Managers are more positive than executives
• How is the implementation process being orchestrated?	– Informally—As a result, people feel overwhelmed by change
• What processes, structure, and roles have been put in place to make the strategies a reality?	– Few—People agree there is change capacity but want more involvement and action
• How is the implementation going?	– Generally positive attributions
• Is there evidence that implementation is likely to produce desired outcomes?	– While uncertainty exists, there are many shared suggestions for moving forward and commitment is high

Overall, the researchers concluded that:

1. There was a demonstrable and palpable change in a variety of organization features that if not directly tied to the DA were certainly hastened by it. A large number of specific strategic, operational, and practice-oriented changes connected with each clinical area had been implemented relatively quickly. In addition, there was substantial agreement that the culture was changing, as evidenced by new language, regular and extensive use of DAs, collaborative decision making, openness to innovation, confidence in leadership, and openness to joint ventures with the physicians. Finally, there was broad agreement that the DA process represented a visible and tangible effort to address physician relationships and clearly moved those relationships in a positive direction.
2. The organization's initial use of the DA process as a strategic visioning intervention persists in the minds of most organization members. Alegent Health can productively apply the technology and principles to other, more implementation-oriented issues. On the other hand, DAs cannot do everything, and complementary governance and implementation processes are necessary.

to guide current implementation and evaluate the effectiveness of an intervention. But the evaluation is not perfect. What are the strengths and weaknesses of the assessment? How could it have been improved? How much confidence do you have in the lessons learned from this organization?

9-2 Institutionalizing Organizational Changes

Once it is determined that changes have been implemented and are effective, attention is directed at institutionalizing the changes—maintaining them as a normal part of the organization's functioning for an appropriate period of time.[17] In complex and uncertain environments, some changes are only part of a long journey of organization adaptation. Innovating new products is not a one-time change but a continuous process that must be implemented over and over again. Other changes, such as the process for appraising performance, need to persist. For example, there is little to be gained from making front-line supervisors learn a new performance rating system every year.

Lewin described change as occurring in three stages: unfreezing, moving, and refreezing. Institutionalizing an OD intervention concerns refreezing. It involves the long-term persistence of organizational changes: To the extent that changes persist, they can be said to be institutionalized. Such changes are not dependent on any one person but exist as a part of the culture of an organization. This means that numerous others share norms about the appropriateness of the changes.

How planned changes become institutionalized has not received much attention in the OD literature. Rapidly changing environments have led to admonitions from consultants and practitioners to "change constantly," to "change before you have to," and "if it's not broke, fix it anyway." Such a context has challenged the utility of the institutionalization concept. Why endeavor to make any change permanent given that it may require changing again soon? However, the admonitions also have resulted in institutionalization concepts being applied in new ways. Change itself has become the focus of institutionalization. Dynamic strategy making, self-design, organization learning, and built-to-change interventions described in Chapter 19 all are aimed at enhancing the organization's change capability.[18] In this vein, processes of institutionalization take on increased utility. This section presents a framework for identifying factors and processes that contribute to the institutionalization of OD interventions, including the process of change itself.

9-2a Institutionalization Framework

Figure 9.2 presents a framework that identifies organization and intervention characteristics and institutionalization processes affecting the degree to which change programs are institutionalized.[19] The model shows that two key antecedents—organization and intervention characteristics—affect different institutionalization processes operating in organizations. These processes, in turn, affect various indicators of institutionalization. The model also shows that organization characteristics can influence intervention characteristics. For example, organizations having powerful unions may have trouble gaining internal support for OD interventions.

9-2b Organization Characteristics

Figure 9.2 shows that the following three dimensions of an organization can affect intervention characteristics and institutionalization processes:

1. **Congruence.** This is the degree to which an intervention is perceived as being in harmony with the organization's managerial philosophy, strategy, and structure; its current environment; and other changes taking place.[20] When an intervention is congruent with these dimensions, the probability is improved that it will be supported and sustained. Congruence can facilitate persistence by making it easier to gain member commitment to the intervention and to diffuse it to wider segments of the organization. The converse also is true: Many OD interventions promote employee

FIGURE 9.2

Institutionalization Framework

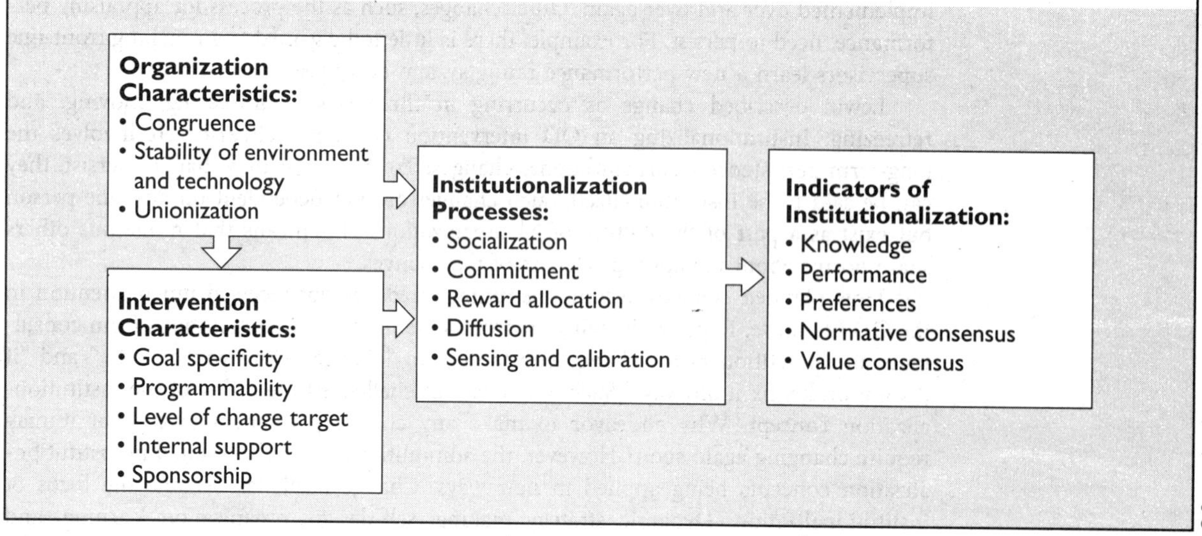

participation and growth. When applied in highly bureaucratic organizations with formalized structures and autocratic managerial styles, participative interventions are not perceived as congruent with the organization's managerial philosophy.

2. **Stability of environment and technology.** This involves the degree to which the organization's environment and technology are changing. The persistence of change is favored when environments are stable. Under these conditions, it makes sense to embed the change in an organization's culture and organization design processes. On the other hand, volatile demand for the firm's products or services can lead to reductions in personnel that may change the composition of the groups involved in the intervention or bring new members on board at a rate faster than they can be socialized effectively.
3. **Unionization.** Diffusion of interventions may be more difficult in unionized settings, especially if the changes affect union contract issues, such as salary and fringe benefits, job design, and employee flexibility. For example, a rigid union contract can make it difficult to merge several job classifications into one, as might be required to increase task variety in a job enrichment program. It is important to emphasize, however, that unions can be a powerful force for promoting change, particularly when a good relationship exists between union and management.

9-2c Intervention Characteristics

Figure 9.2 shows that the following five features of OD interventions can affect institutionalization processes:

1. **Goal specificity.** This involves the extent to which intervention goals are specific rather than broad. Specificity of goals helps direct socializing activities (for example, training and orienting new members) to particular behaviors required to implement the intervention. It also helps operationalize the new behaviors so that rewards can be linked clearly to them. For example, an intervention aimed only at increasing product quality is likely to be more focused and readily put into operation than a change program intended to improve quality, quantity, safety, absenteeism, and employee development.
2. **Programmability.** This involves the degree to which the changes can be programmed or the extent to which the different intervention characteristics can be specified clearly in advance to enable socialization, commitment, and reward allocation. For example, job enrichment specifies three targets of change: employee discretion, task variety, and feedback. The change program can be planned and designed to promote those specific features.
3. **Level of change target.** This concerns the extent to which the change target is the total organization, rather than a department or small work group. Each level of the organization has facilitators and inhibitors of persistence. Department and group change are susceptible to countervailing forces from others in the organization. These can reduce the diffusion of the intervention and lower its ability to impact organization effectiveness. However, this does not preclude institutionalizing the change within a department that successfully insulates itself from the rest of the organization. Such insulation often manifests itself as a subculture within the organization.[21]

   Targeting the intervention toward wider segments of the organization, on the other hand, can also help or hinder change persistence. A shared belief about the intervention's value can be a powerful incentive to maintain the change, and promoting a consensus across organization departments exposed to the change can facilitate institutionalization. However, targeting the larger system also can inhibit institutionalization. The intervention can become mired in political resistance because of the "not invented here" syndrome or because powerful constituencies oppose it.

4. **Internal support.** This refers to the degree to which there is an internal support system to guide the change process. Internal support, typically provided by an internal OD practitioner, can gain commitment for the changes and help organization members implement them. External consultants also can provide support, especially on a temporary basis during the early stages of implementation. For example, in many interventions aimed at implementing high-involvement organizations (see Chapter 13), both external and internal OD practitioners provide change support. The external consultant typically brings expertise on organizational design and trains members to implement the design. The internal consultant generally helps members relate to other organizational units, resolve conflicts, and legitimize the change activities within the organization.
5. **Sponsorship.** This concerns the presence of a powerful sponsor who can initiate, allocate, and legitimize resources for the intervention. Sponsors must come from levels in the organization high enough to control appropriate resources, and they must have the visibility and power to nurture the intervention and see that it remains viable. There are many examples of OD interventions that persisted for several years and then collapsed abruptly when the sponsor, usually a top administrator, left the organization. There also are numerous examples of middle managers withdrawing support for interventions because top management did not include them in the change program.

9-2d Institutionalization Processes

The framework depicted in Figure 9.2 shows the following five institutionalization processes that can directly affect the degree to which OD interventions are institutionalized:

1. **Socialization.** This concerns the transmission of information about beliefs, preferences, norms, and values with respect to the intervention. Because implementation of OD interventions generally involves considerable learning and experimentation, a continual process of socialization is necessary to promote persistence of the change program. Organization members must focus attention on the evolving nature of the intervention and its ongoing meaning. They must communicate this information to other employees, especially new members of the organization. Transmission of information about the intervention helps bring new members onboard and allows participants to reaffirm the beliefs, norms, and values underlying the intervention.[22] For example, employee involvement programs often include initial transmission of information about the intervention, as well as retraining of existing participants and training of new members. Such processes are intended to promote persistence of the program as new behaviors are learned and new members introduced.
2. **Commitment.** This binds people to behaviors associated with the intervention. It includes initial commitment to the program, as well as recommitment over time. Opportunities for commitment should allow people to select the necessary behaviors freely, explicitly, and publicly. These conditions favor high commitment and can

promote stability of the new behaviors. Commitment should derive from several organizational levels, including the employees directly involved and the middle and upper managers who can support or thwart the intervention. In many early employee involvement programs, for example, attention was directed at gaining workers' commitment to such programs. Unfortunately, middle managers were often ignored and considerable management resistance to the interventions resulted.

3. **Reward allocation.** This involves linking rewards to the new behaviors required by an intervention. Organizational rewards can enhance the persistence of changes in at least two ways. First, a combination of intrinsic and extrinsic rewards can reinforce new behaviors. Intrinsic rewards are internal to people and derive from the opportunities for challenge, development, and accomplishment found in the work. When interventions provide these opportunities, motivation to perform should persist. This behavior can be further reinforced by providing extrinsic rewards, such as money, for increased contributions. Because the value of extrinsic rewards tends to diminish over time, it may be necessary to revise the reward system to maintain high levels of desired behaviors.

   Second, new behaviors will persist to the extent that rewards are perceived as equitable by employees. When new behaviors are fairly compensated, people are likely to develop preferences for those behaviors. Over time, those preferences should lead to normative and value consensus about the appropriateness of the intervention. For example, many employee involvement programs fail to persist because employees feel that their increased contributions to organizational improvements are unfairly rewarded. This is especially true for interventions relying exclusively on intrinsic rewards. People argue that an intervention that provides opportunities for intrinsic rewards also should provide greater pay or extrinsic rewards for higher levels of contribution to the organization.
4. **Diffusion.** This refers to the process of transferring changes from one system to another. Diffusion facilitates institutionalization by providing a wider organizational base to support the new behaviors. Many interventions fail to persist because they run counter to the values, purpose, or identity of the larger organization. Rather than support the intervention, the larger organization rejects the changes and often puts pressure on the change target to revert to old behaviors. Diffusion of a change to other organizational units reduces this counter-implementation force. It tends to lock in behaviors by providing normative consensus from other parts of the organization. Moreover, the act of transmitting institutionalized behaviors to other systems reinforces commitment to the changes.
5. **Sensing and calibration.** This involves detecting deviations from desired intervention behaviors and taking corrective action. Institutionalized behaviors invariably encounter destabilizing forces, such as changes in the environment, new technologies, and pressures from other departments to nullify changes. These factors cause some variation in performances, preferences, norms, and values. To detect this variation and take corrective actions, organizations must have some sensing mechanism. Sensing mechanisms, such as implementation feedback, provide information about the occurrence of deviations. This knowledge can then initiate corrective actions to ensure that behaviors are more in line with the intervention. For example, if a high level of job discretion associated with a job enrichment intervention does not persist, information about this problem might initiate corrective actions, such as renewed attempts to socialize people or to gain commitment to the intervention.

9-2e Indicators of Institutionalization

Institutionalization is not an all-or-nothing concept but reflects degrees of persistence in a change. Figure 9.2 shows five indicators of the extent of an intervention's persistence. The extent to which the following factors are present or absent indicates the degree of institutionalization:

1. **Knowledge.** This involves the extent to which organization members have knowledge of the behaviors associated with an intervention. It is concerned with whether members know enough to perform the behaviors and to recognize the consequences of that performance. For example, job enrichment includes a number of new behaviors, such as performing a greater variety of tasks, analyzing information about task performance, and making decisions about work methods and plans.
2. **Performance.** This is concerned with the degree to which intervention behaviors are actually performed. It may be measured by counting the proportion of relevant people performing the behaviors. For example, 60% of the employees in a particular work unit might be performing the job enrichment behaviors described above. Another measure of performance is the frequency with which the new behaviors are performed. In assessing frequency, it is important to account for different variations of the same essential behavior, as well as highly institutionalized behaviors that need to be performed only infrequently.
3. **Preferences.** This involves the degree to which organization members privately accept the organizational changes. This contrasts with acceptance based primarily on organizational sanctions or group pressures. Private acceptance usually is reflected in people's positive attitudes toward the changes and can be measured by the direction and intensity of those attitudes across the members of the work unit receiving the intervention. For example, a questionnaire assessing members' perceptions of a job enrichment program might show that most employees have a strong positive attitude toward making decisions, analyzing feedback, and performing a variety of tasks.
4. **Normative consensus.** This focuses on the extent to which people agree about the appropriateness of the organizational changes. This indicator of institutionalization reflects how fully changes have become part of the normative structure of the organization. Changes persist to the degree members feel that they should support them. For example, a job enrichment program would become institutionalized to the extent that employees support it and see it as appropriate to organizational functioning.
5. **Value consensus.** This is concerned with social consensus on values relevant to the organizational changes. Values are beliefs about how people ought or ought not to behave. They are abstractions from more specific norms. Job enrichment, for example, is based on values promoting employee self-control and responsibility. Different behaviors associated with job enrichment, such as making decisions and performing a variety of tasks, would persist to the extent that employees widely share values of self-control and responsibility.

These five indicators can be used to assess the level of change persistence. The more the indicators are present in a situation, the higher will be the degree of institutionalization. Further, these factors seem to follow a specific development order: knowledge, performance, preferences, norms, and values. People must first understand new behaviors or changes before they can perform them effectively. Such performance generates rewards and punishments, which in time affect people's preferences. As many individuals come to prefer the changes, normative consensus about their appropriateness develops. Finally, if

application 9.2

INSTITUTIONALIZING STRUCTURAL CHANGE AT HEWLETT-PACKARD

In May 2002, the hotly contested acquisition of Compaq by Hewlett-Packard (www.hp.com) was finalized. Unlike the major organization changes before it, the acquisition challenged the abilities of this perennial "most admired company" to execute a complex structural change. The success of the integration process described in Application 8.4 is partly due to a store of institutionalized knowledge and capability within the HP organization. This application describes a number of large-scale structural changes at HP. The company's repeated ability to carry out such change speaks to its institutionalized capability to manage change.

Since its founding in 1939, HP has implemented successfully no fewer than a dozen major organizational changes, including the transition from a high-tech entrepreneurial start-up to a professionally managed company; from a small instruments business to a leading computer company; from a company oriented around complex-instruction-set computing technology to reduced-instruction-set computing technology; from a technology/engineering-based company to a market/brand-driven company; and, from a "pure products" company to a services company.

HP's electronics and computer business was characterized by highly volatile technological and market change. It had to quickly adopt, innovate, and implement a variety of technological and organizational changes just to survive. HP's traditional and current strategies were built on innovation, differentiation, and high quality. Another important feature of HP, and one of its more enduring characteristics, is the "HP Way"—a cultural artifact that supports a participative management style and emphasizes commonness of purpose and teamwork on one hand and individual freedom and initiative on the other. Over time, however, the HP Way has been both a constraint to and a facilitator of change.

For example, the HP Way has been at the root of the company's difficulties in institutionalizing structural and behavioral changes to bring about more cooperation among the computer divisions. The initial structural change occurred in 1982 when HP transformed itself from a producer of high-quality electronic measuring instruments into a computer company. At the time, computers and computer-related equipment accounted for only about one-third of revenues and HP was structured into more than 50 highly autonomous and decentralized product divisions focused on specialized niche markets. Individual engineers came up with innovative ideas and "bootstrapped" new products any way they could. Organization members were encouraged to work with other engineers in other departments within the same division, but there was little incentive to coordinate the development of technologies across divisions. This focus on the individual was supported by a performance management system that measured and rewarded "sustained contributions;" the key to success for an individual was working with many people in the division. HP prospered by maximizing each of its parts.

Former CEO John Young's decision to focus on computers fundamentally shifted the keys to success. Computer production required a coordinated effort among the different component divisions and market shares large enough to encourage software vendors to write programs for their machines. In a culture that supported individual contributions over divisional cooperation, Young placed all the instruments divisions into one group and all the computer divisions into another group, a basic design that persisted until the spin-off of the Agilent instruments business in 1999. In addition, he centralized research, marketing, and manufacturing, which had previously been assigned to the divisions. Problems quickly arose. In one case, the company's new and highly touted graphics printer would not work with its HP3000 minicomputer. The operating software, made by a third HP division, would not allow the two pieces of hardware to interface.

In response, the computer group formed committees to figure out what new technologies to pursue, which to ignore, which of HP's products should be saved, and which would be shelved. As the committees came up with recommendations, the committees themselves kept multiplying. The company's entrenched culture, built around the HP Way's philosophy of egalitarianism and mutual respect, promoted consensus: Everyone had to have a hand in making a decision.

By 1988, the organization chart still showed a predominantly decentralized divisional structure. What it didn't show was the overwhelming number of committees that slowed decision making and product development. In one case, it took seven months and nearly a hundred people on nine committees to name the company's new software product. This web of committees, originally designed to foster communication among HP's operating divisions, had pushed up costs and slowed development. In the rapidly changing world of software, personal computers, minicomputers, and printers, the HP Way was hamstringing the organization's success. The ethic of individual freedom balanced by teamwork had produced an unwieldy bureaucracy.

After a series of delays of important new products, John Young reorganized the computer group. In late 1990, he eliminated most of the committees and removed layers of management by dividing the computer business into two groups: one to handle personal computers and peripherals sold through dealers, and the other to handle sales of workstations and minicomputers to big customers. To match the organization structure, the previously centralized corporate sales force was split and assigned to particular divisions. This change focused HP's computer systems on the market and restored much of the autonomy to the divisions. The balance between individuality and common purpose that characterized the original HP Way was unleashed, leading to several years of strong revenue and profit growth.

In 1993, and before he was officially installed as the new CEO, Lewis Platt announced that HP would pursue the convergence of several base technologies, such as wireless communication, printing, and measurement, to create whole new products for the converging computer, communication, and consumer electronics markets. Implementing such a strategy again depended on strong coordination among HP's product divisions. To ensure that the gains in cooperation were not lost as HP embarked on its new strategy, CEO Platt tied division managers' incentive compensation to working cooperatively with other divisions to create new products that used multiple-division technologies.

The new structure was a big success. Growth in the printer and PC markets drove revenues from $13.2 billion in 1990 to $38.4 billion in 1996, with profits growing in the same proportions. In 1996, they were the fifth-most-admired company in the United States. In the Internet world, however, their success was short-lived, and critics argued that Platt's subsequent attention to "soft" issues such as work/life balance and promoting diversity, rather than launching an Internet strategy, resulted in stalled growth. For 1997 and 1998, and aided by the Asian financial crisis, growth rates slipped to single digits. In the summer of 1998, Platt believed that HP had simply become too big and complex. In March 1999, he announced and implemented the spin-off of HP's $7.6 billion instruments division, the business on which the company had been founded.

Shortly after being named HP's fourth CEO in 1999, and the first to come from outside the company, Carly Fiorina laid out her agenda: create a compelling vision for HP, implement a structure to support the vision, and launch a marketing campaign to build the HP brand. The vision called for a shift from a stand-alone products company to a services company. The structural change involved merging the four major product divisions into a group focused on computing and a group focused on printing. This structure for the first time united HP's laser and ink-jet printing divisions and furthered the opportunities for computer products to coordinate their activities. Fiorina also announced a major marketing campaign focused on the HP Way's value of innovation. Then, in the fall of 2001, Fiorina announced the intended acquisition of Compaq computers.

The lessons of history had not been lost on the CEO. The acquisition process pulled knowledge from the experiences of other mergers and other changes within HP; it acknowledged the strengths and weaknesses of the HP Way; and structural changes were backed up with changes in the compensation system. Few organizations implemented as many major changes and still maintained both strong financial performance and corporate reputation during this decisive period in the computer industry. HP's history of seeing the need for, implementing, and reaping the benefits of structural change was a testament to its ability to institutionalize change, as these examples demonstrate.

there is normative agreement about the changes reflecting a particular set of values, over time there should be some consensus on those values among organization members.

Given this developmental view of institutionalization, it is implicit that whenever one of the last indicators is present, all the previous ones are automatically included as well. For example, if employees normatively agree with the behaviors associated with job enrichment, then they also have knowledge about the behaviors, can perform them effectively, and prefer them. An OD intervention is fully institutionalized only when all five factors are present.

Application 9.2 describes Hewlett-Packard's successful history of institutionalizing a new set of behaviors through structural change. It describes how culture and reward systems can play a strong role in both supporting and constraining change.[23]

SUMMARY

We discussed in this chapter the final two stages of planned change—evaluating interventions and institutionalizing them. Evaluation was discussed in terms of two kinds of necessary feedback: implementation feedback, concerned with whether the intervention is being implemented as intended, and evaluation feedback, indicating whether the intervention is producing expected results. The former comprises collected data about features of the intervention, perceptions of the people involved, and its immediate effects, which are fed back repeatedly and at short intervals. The latter comprises data about the long-term effects of the intervention, which are fed back at long intervals.

Evaluation of interventions also involves decisions about measurement and research design. Measurement issues focus on selecting variables and designing good measures. Ideally, measurement decisions should derive from the theory underlying the intervention and should include measures of the features of the intervention and its immediate and long-term consequences. Further, these measures should be operationally defined, reliable, and valid and should involve multiple methods, such as a combination of questionnaires, interviews, and company records.

Research design focuses on setting up the conditions for making valid assessments of an intervention's effects. This involves ruling out explanations for the observed results other than the intervention. Although randomized experimental designs are rarely feasible in OD, quasi-experimental designs exist for eliminating alternative explanations.

OD interventions are institutionalized when the change program persists and becomes part of the organization's normal functioning. A framework for understanding and improving the institutionalization of interventions identified organization characteristics (congruence, stability of environment and technology, and unionization) and intervention characteristics (goal specificity, programmability, level of change target, internal support, and sponsorship) that affect institutionalization processes. The framework also described specific institutionalization processes (socialization, commitment, reward allocation, diffusion, and sensing and calibration) that directly affect indicators of intervention persistence (knowledge, performance, preferences, normative consensus, and value consensus).

NOTES

1. T. Cummings and E. Molloy, *Strategies for Improving Productivity and the Quality of Work Life* (New York: Praeger, 1977); J. Whitfield, W. Anthony, and K. Kacmar, "Evaluation of Team-Based Management: A Case Study," *Journal of Organizational Change Management* 8, no. 2 (1995): 17–28.
2. T. Cummings and S. Mohrman, "Self-Designing Organizations: Towards Implementing Quality-of-Work-Life

Innovations," in *Research in Organizational Change and Development*, vol. 1, ed., R. Woodman and W. Pasmore (Greenwich, CT: JAI Press, 1987), 275–310.

3. Cummings and Molloy, *Strategies for Improving Productivity and the Quality of Work Life*.
4. P. Goodman, *Assessing Organizational Change: The Rushton Quality of Work Experiment* (New York: John Wiley & Sons, 1979); A. Van de Ven and D. Ferry, eds., *Measuring and Assessing Organizations* (New York: John Wiley & Sons, 1985); E. Lawler III, D. Nadler, and C. Cammann, eds., *Organizational Assessment: Perspectives on the Measurement of Organizational Behavior and Quality of Work Life* (New York: John Wiley & Sons, 1980); A. Van de Ven and W. Joyce, eds., *Perspectives on Organizational Design and Behavior* (New York: John Wiley & Sons, 1981); S. Seashore, E. Lawler III, P. Mirvis, and C. Cammann, eds., *Assessing Organizational Change: A Guide to Methods, Measures, and Practices* (New York: Wiley-Interscience, 1983).
5. B. Macy and P. Mirvis, "Organizational Change Efforts: Methodologies for Assessing Organizational Effectiveness and Program Costs Versus Benefits," *Evaluation Review* 6 (1982): 301–72.
6. Ibid.
7. J. Nunnally, *Psychometric Theory*, 2nd ed. (New York: McGraw-Hill, 1978); J. Kirk and M. Miller, *Reliability and Validity in Qualitative Research* (Beverly Hills, CA: Sage Publications, 1985).
8. J. Corbin and A. Strauss, *Basics of Qualitative Research*, 4th ed. (Thousand Oaks, CA: Sage Publications, 2013); D. Miller, *Handbook of Research Design and Social Measurement* (Thousand Oaks, CA: Sage Publications, 1991); N. Denzin and Y. Lincoln, eds., *Handbook of Qualitative Research* (Thousand Oaks, CA: Sage Publications, 1994).
9. R. Hackman and G. Oldham, *Work Redesign* (Reading, MA: Addison-Wesley, 1980).
10. Nunnally, *Psychometric Theory*.
11. M. Huberman and M. Miles, *Qualitative Data Analysis: An Expanded Sourcebook*, 2nd ed. (Newbury Park, CA: Sage Publications, 1994); K. Neuendorf, *The Content Analysis Guidebook*, 2nd ed. (Thousand Oaks, CA: Sage Publications, 2013).
12. J. Taylor and D. Bowers, *Survey of Organizations: A Machine-Scored Standardized Questionnaire Instrument* (Ann Arbor: Institute for Social Research, University of Michigan, 1972); G. Ledford and S. Mohrman, *Comprehensive Quality-of-Work-Life Survey* (Los Angeles: Center for Effective Organizations, University of Southern California, 1981); C. Cammann, M. Fichman, G. D. Jenkins, and J. Klesh, "Assessing the Attitudes and Perceptions of Organizational Members," in *Assessing Organizational Change: A Guide to Methods, Measures, and Practices*, ed. S. Seashore, E. Lawler III, P. Mirvis, and C. Cammann (New York: Wiley-Interscience, 1983), 71–119.
13. R. Woodman, J. Bingham, and F. Yuan, "Assessing Organization Development and Change Interventions," in *Handbook of Organization Development*, ed. T. Cummings (Thousand Oaks, CA: Sage Publications, 2008): 187–216; R. Bullock and D. Svyantek, "The Impossibility of Using Random Strategies to Study the Organization Development Process," *Journal of Applied Behavioral Science* 23 (1987): 255–62.
14. D. Campbell and J. Stanley, *Experimental and Quasi-Experimental Design for Research* (Chicago: Rand McNally, 1966); T. Cook and D. Campbell, *Quasi-Experimentation: Design and Analysis Issues for Field Settings* (Chicago: Rand McNally, 1979); Woodman, Bingham, and Yuan, "Assessing Organization Development and Change Interventions."
15. R. Golembiewski and R. Munzenrider, "Measuring Change by OD Designs," *Journal of Applied Behavioral Science* 12 (April–June 1976): 133–57.
16. W. Randolph and R. Edwards, "Assessment of Alpha, Beta and Gamma Changes in a University-Setting OD Intervention," *Academy of Management Proceedings* (1978): 313–17; J. Terborg, G. Howard, and S. Maxwell, "Evaluating Planned Organizational Change: A Method for Assessing Alpha, Beta, and Gamma Change," *Academy of Management Review* 7 (1982): 292–95; R. Millsap and S. Hartog, "Alpha, Beta, and Gamma Change in Evaluation Research: A Structural Equation Approach," *Journal of Applied Psychology* 73 (1988): 574–84; R. Thompson and J. Hunt, "Inside the Black Box of Alpha, Beta, and Gamma Change: Using a Cognitive-Processing Model to Assess Attitude Structure," *Academy of Management Review* 21 (1996): 655–91.
17. D. Buchanan, L. Fitzgerald, D. Ketley, R. Gollop, J. Jones, S. Lamont, A. Neath, and E. Whitby, "No Going Back: A Review of the Literature on Sustaining Organization Change," *International Journal of Management Reviews* 7 (2005): 189–205.
18. E. Lawler and C. Worley, *Built to Change* (San Francisco: Jossey-Bass, 2006); P. Senge, *The Fifth Discipline* (New York: Doubleday, 1990); Cummings and Mohrman, "Self-Designing Organizations"; L. Greiner and T. Cummings, *Dynamic Strategy Making: A Real-Time Approach for the 21st Century Leader* (San Francisco: Jossey-Bass, 2009).
19. This section is based on the work of P. Goodman and J. Dean, "Creating Long-Term Organizational Change," in *Change in Organizations*, ed. P. Goodman (San Francisco: Jossey-Bass, 1982), 226–79. To date, the framework is largely untested and unchallenged. Other than a few case studies with inducted principles, Ledford's process model of persistence (see note 20) is the only other model

proposed to explain institutionalization. The empirical support for either model, however, is small but growing slowly as described in Buchanan, "No going back."

20. G. Ledford, "The Persistence of Planned Organizational Change: A Process Theory Perspective" (Ph.D. diss., University of Michigan, 1984).

21. J. Martin and C. Siehl, "Organizational Cultures and Counterculture: An Uneasy Symbiosis," *Organizational Dynamics* (1983): 52–64; D. Meyerson and J. Martin, "Cultural Change: An Integration of Three Different Views," *Journal of Management Studies* 24 (1987): 623–47.

22. L. Zucker, "The Role of Institutionalization in Cultural Persistence," *American Sociological Review* 42 (1977): 726–43; R. Jacobs, "Institutionalizing Organization Change Through Cascade Training," *Journal of European Industrial Training* 26 (2002): 177–83.

23. R. Von Werssowetz and M. Beer, "Human Resources at Hewlett-Packard," *Harvard Business School Case 9-482-125* (Boston: Harvard Business School, 1982); B. Buell and R. Hof, "Hewlett-Packard Rethinks Itself," *BusinessWeek*, April 1, 1991, 76–79; R. Hof, "Suddenly, Hewlett-Packard Is Doing Everything Right," *BusinessWeek*, March 23, 1992, 88–89; "Can John Young Redesign Hewlett-Packard," *BusinessWeek*, December 6, 1982, 72–78; J. Levine, "Mild-Mannered Hewlett-Packard Is Making Like Superman," *BusinessWeek*, March 7, 1988, 110–14; R. Hof, "Hewlett-Packard Digs Deep for a Digital Future," *BusinessWeek*, October 18, 1993, 72–75; A. Fisher, "America's Most Admired Corporations," *Fortune*, March 4, 1996, 90–98; P. Burrows and P. Elstrom, "The Boss," *BusinessWeek*, August 2, 1999, 76–83; D. Hamilton, "H-P to Relaunch Its Brand, Adopt New Logo," *Wall Street Journal*, November 16, 1999, B6; D. Hamilton and S. Thurm, "H-P to Spin Off Its Measurement Operations," *Wall Street Journal*, March 3, 1999, A3; E. Nee, "Lew Platt: Why I Dismembered HP," *Fortune*, March 29, 1999, 167–69.

SUNFLOWER INCORPORATED*

Sunflower Incorporated is a large distribution company with over 5,000 employees and gross sales of over $700 million (1991). The company purchases and distributes salty snack foods and liquor to independent retail stores throughout the United States and Canada. Salty snack foods include corn chips, potato chips, cheese curls, tortilla chips, and peanuts. The United States and Canada are divided into 22 regions, each with its own central warehouse, salespeople, finance department, and purchasing department. The company distributes national as well as local brands and packages some items under private labels. The head office encourages each region to be autonomous because of local tastes and practices. The northeast United States, for example, consumes a greater percentage of Canadian whisky and American bourbon, while the West consumes more light liquors, such as vodka, gin, and rum. Snack foods in the Southwest are often seasoned to reflect Mexican tastes.

Early in 1989, Sunflower began using a financial reporting system that compared sales, costs, and profits across regions. Management was surprised to learn that profits varied widely. By 1990, the differences were so great that management decided some standardization was necessary. They believed that highly profitable regions were sometimes using lower-quality items, even seconds, to boost profit margins. This practice could hurt Sunflower's image. Other regions were facing intense price competition in order to hold market share. National distributors were pushing hard to increase their market share. Frito-Lay, Bordens, Nabisco, Procter & Gamble (Pringles), and Standard Brands (Planter's peanuts) were pushing hard to increase market share by cutting prices and launching new products.

As these problems accumulated, Mr. Steelman, president of Sunflower, decided to create a new position to monitor pricing and purchasing practices. Agnes Albanese was hired from the finance department of a competing organization. Her new title was director of pricing and purchasing, and she reported to the vice president of finance, Mr. Mobley. Steelman and Mobley gave Albanese great latitude in organizing her job and encouraged her to establish whatever rules and procedures were necessary. She was also encouraged to gather information from each region. Each region was notified of her appointment by an official memo sent to the regional managers. A copy of the memo was posted on each warehouse bulletin board. The announcement was also made in the company newspaper.

After three weeks on the job, Albanese decided that pricing and purchasing decisions should be standardized across regions. As a first step, she wanted the financial executive in each region to notify her of any change in local prices of more than 3%. She also decided that all new contracts for local purchases of more than $5,000 should be cleared through her office. (Approximately 60% of items distributed in the regions was purchased in large quantities and supplied from the home office. The other 40% was purchased and distributed within the region.) Albanese believed that the only way to standardize operations was for each region to notify the home office in advance of any change in prices or purchases. Albanese discussed the proposed policy with Mobley. He agreed, so they submitted a formal proposal to the president and board of directors, who approved the plan. Sunflower was moving into the peak holiday season, so Albanese wanted to implement the new procedures right away. She decided to send an email to the financial and purchasing executives in each region notifying them of the new procedures. The change would be inserted in all policy and procedure manuals throughout Sunflower within four months.

Albanese showed a draft of the email to Mobley and invited his comments. Mobley said the Internet was an excellent idea but wondered if it was sufficient. The regions handle hundreds of items and were used to decentralized decision

*Adapted from R. Daft, Organization Theory and Design (St. Paul: West, 1983), pp. 334–36.

making. Mobley suggested that Albanese ought to visit the regions and discuss purchasing and pricing policies with the executives. Albanese refused, saying that the trips would be expensive and time-consuming. She had so many things to do at headquarters that a trip was impossible. Mobley also suggested waiting to implement the procedures until after the annual company meeting in three months. Albanese said this would take too long because the procedures would not take effect until after the peak sales season. She believed the procedures were needed now. The email went out the next day.

During the next few days, replies came in from most of the regions. The executives were in agreement with the email and said they would be happy to cooperate.

Eight weeks later, Albanese had not received notices from any regions about local price or purchase changes. Other executives who had visited regional warehouses indicated to her that the regions were busy as usual. Regional executives seemed to be following usual procedures for that time of year.

Questions

1. How well did Albanese manage the pricing and purchasing changes at Sunflower? Were the changes implemented successfully? How would you find this out?
2. What might Albanese have done differently? What should she do now?

KENWORTH MOTORS*

It began with a telephone call, as did so many of my engagements. The person calling identified himself as Robert Denton, the plant manager of Kenworth Motors' Seattle truck manufacturing operations. Denton said he'd gotten my name from Charles Wright, a client of mine in Seattle. Charlie is the OD manager for a major timber products company. I'd been doing several projects with Charlie's group of internal consultants for the past three years and occasionally served as the OD group's consultant. Denton noted that Charlie and he were members of the same sailing club. He went on to say that when, as someone relatively new to Seattle, he'd asked Charlie if he knew any consultants, Charlie had spoken highly of me. I remember thinking that Charlie probably wouldn't have mentioned me unless he thought I could be useful to Denton. My trust in Charlie's competence and judgment was very high.

Denton went on to explain that he'd been the plant manager for only eight months, that things seemed to be going well, but that he had a gnawing sense that things could be better. I must have murmured something appropriate because Denton invited me to visit him and become acquainted with his operation.

I was both flattered by and interested in Denton's invitation. After all, I thought to myself, it's nice to be wanted, a consulting engagement might come out of it, I always wanted to get behind the gate of the Kenworth plant, and Denton sounded like a basically smart guy and nice besides. However, reality intruded into my thoughts, as it often does.

THOUGHTS ON THE ROAD

I reminded Denton that I lived across the state in Spokane and added that I had limited time available in the short run. I noted that I had plans to visit Seattle in three weeks and could see him then, otherwise it might not be for a month. Denton sounded almost eager as he agreed to a 10 A.M. appointment on April 11.

The drive westward from Spokane across the state of Washington on Interstate 90 begins with several hours of boring highway. I had purposely put off thinking about my appointment with Robert Denton until I was on the road. As the interstate stretched out over the rolling sagebrush hills and checkered wheat fields, I turned my thoughts to Kenworth Motors and Denton. Uppermost in my mind was that I was about to talk with a man I knew little about, consult with a firm I knew very little about, and I had no focused agenda. What should I say and do?

As the miles went by, I envisioned several alternative scenarios for my upcoming appointment with Robert Denton, the plant manager of the truck manufacturing division of Kenworth Motors Corporation. I saw his office in several possible ways. It could be spartan and centrally located to the production floor. It could be conventionally furnished but of a fair size. It could be large. It might even be opulent. It could be personalized with mementos of career, hobbies, or family. It might be far from the production floor, or even in a separate building. The more I tried to envision Denton's office, the more alternatives came to mind. So I focused on Denton, trying to imagine him from the voice cues on the telephone—not old, probably fit, probably clean shaven. Again the futility of trying to imagine came home to me.

What did I think I knew? I didn't know much beyond a handful of facts about his title and his job tenure, the fact that he knew Charlie, believed things were generally going OK at the plant, and had some vague notion something wasn't quite right. I also had the distinct impression he had been fairly eager to talk with me—after all, he'd initiated calling me and had quickly settled for an appointment convenient to me.

What did I really want to accomplish when I met with Denton? The more I considered this question, the more I pared down my answers. At minimum, it seemed for me a low-cost situation—a couple of hours of my time, perhaps some impressions of me that would be communicated to Charlie (though I believed Charlie and I had a relationship of mutual

*Craig C. Lundberg, *Cornell University*.

respect and trust based on a lot of shared work). On the other hand, there was potentially a lot to gain—perhaps another consulting job, perhaps more visibility and reputation in Seattle, which would be good for my business.

I decided I couldn't plan for our meeting in much detail; about all I could reasonably do was to be true to the posture I found to be useful in situations like this. I had to be myself, be as real as possible. I see myself as a curious, friendly person who basically likes others. I also know I can be bold and thought I might have to be to get the conversation going, to help Denton become clear as to why we were talking together, and to clarify my role.

I also wanted to leave our meeting with a decision to either go forward or not. While I didn't mind investing a little time, my time was valuable. I also felt strongly, as I always do, that I didn't want to work with anyone who I didn't basically like as a person or who didn't seem to genuinely want to do some real work. Seeing the Cascade mountains on the horizon, I began to feel easier. I'd be myself, whatever happened. Only one question nagged: Could Denton and I connect swiftly enough so there would be time to push for clarity in our possible work relationship?

MAKING CONTACT

At the Kenworth plant, the uniformed guard at the plant gate checked his clipboard, slipped around my car, and copied down my license plate number. Returning to my open window, he pointed ahead to a one-story brick building attached to the multi-storied plant and told me I could park in the space in front and then go inside and identify myself to the receptionist.

The floor of the wide hallway inside the double glass doors of the office building was freshly waxed. Framed photographs of trucks and large buildings lined the walls. A middle-aged woman in a suit looked up from her desk and smiled. After I identified myself, she led me down a side corridor to an alcove and informed the secretary there who I was and that I was there to see Mr. Denton. She then turned to me, smiled again, and wished me a good day. The seated secretary told me Mr. Denton was expecting me, but was on the telephone. She gestured toward a bank of chairs and asked me to wait. As I sat down, I observed the corridor traffic, busy but quiet. I settled back to wait.

About ten minutes later, a man of medium height and build wearing a sports jacket over an open-collared shirt came through the door behind the secretary and walked directly to me. He extended his hand, smiled, introduced himself as Bob Denton and motioned me into his office.

The office was larger than I expected. It was paneled and a large Persian rug was centered on the floor. At one end were a clean desk with side chairs and a table full of papers behind it. At the other side of the office were a couch and two stuffed chairs around a low coffee table. Drapes framed one large window that looked out on the parking lot. Denton asked if I wanted coffee, and I said I did. He went to the door and asked the secretary to bring us both coffee and added we were not to be disturbed. While waiting for the coffee, we sat on the two stuffed chairs and made small talk. He asked about my drive across the state; I asked about the framed sailing prints on the wall and whether he'd been sailing lately. We chatted about the Sonics, the Kingdome, and the coming World's Fair in Vancouver. After our coffee arrived, I asked him to tell me about his plant and products.

Denton spoke excitedly for 10 or 12 minutes on a wide range of topics—the daily production rate of 23 trucks, the cost of a truck, the sales order backlog, some equipment updating just finished, his coming to this job from a plant in the Midwest, his spending a lot of time lately with the next year's budget, and so forth. My impression of Denton was that he was highly involved in his work. He spoke rapidly but clearly with enthusiasm. Finally, he leaned back, smiled, and said, "Well, I've been going on, haven't I?" I remember thinking I liked Denton's ease and his willingness to talk about his plant and himself. I'd already learned a lot about the plant and his job without more than looking interested. Denton certainly did seem likable, and he was younger and more casual than I expected.

GETTING DOWN TO BUSINESS

I clearly recall my response to Denton's question. "Actually, I've appreciated your sharing all this background with me. I've always been curious about this plant. Years ago, I had a part-time job when I was in college and used to deliver some industrial supplies in this end of town and always wanted to know what happened in this plant. All I could see from the road were those lines of big shiny trucks. It's nice to know they're built with care. But you asked for this meeting, Bob. Remember you told me that while things were going well here you sensed something wasn't quite right. Can you tell me a little more now?"

"Not really. I know the plant is doing fine. I feel pretty much on top of my job. I like what I'm doing here very much. My department heads—all nine of them—are all good people. All but two have been here quite a while. They're dependable, damn good at what they do, get along fine, and basically are good managers," he said.

"I get along good with everyone. I go out in the plant every day and circulate around. Things are moving smoothly. My two newer managers—one runs our purchasing and inventory, the other is in personnel—couldn't be working out better. Yet some things nag at me that I can't put my finger on. I guess it boils down to some crazy notion I have that while we get along fine and work together well, we haven't jelled together as a team quite like I'd hoped."

I bombarded Denton with questions, trying to find something that didn't hang together or might indicate a problem. No matter what I asked about—from union relations to accounts receivable, from engineering-production relations to turnover figures—Denton's responses were consistently factual and full, and everything seemed to be in remarkably good shape.

I caught myself from going on with more questions. Instead I said, "Bob, everything I've been asking about tells me you're OK. Maybe things here really are OK. Maybe you've just got some apprehension that things couldn't be that good. After all, you've been here long enough to really know. While there is some chance that you're not well informed, and some things aren't so hot, the odds are against it. About all I can suggest is whether you might want someone like me to independently confirm how things are going." Denton smiled as if to himself and replied, "Hmm, maybe, what would you suggest?"

"What's usually done in situations like this, if there is the interest and if there is the money to pay for it, is to engage someone like me to spend a few days interviewing a sample of managers and other key staff people to see what might turn up."

"From what you've heard so far, do you think that makes sense here?" Denton asked.

"Frankly, I don't know. It might be worth it to you just to learn things really are OK. What usually happens, however, is that I do find out about something that could be improved. After all that's what I'm supposed to be good at, finding problems. One way or another, Bob, the mere fact I was here would have some impact. The word would spread pretty fast that some outsider was snooping around. What impact that might have I can't say. If things really are OK, my presence might mean little. If there are real problems, my being here would probably create some tensions, it could raise expectations that something would be done about them, and it could even cause problems."

Denton nodded, "I see what you mean. If you came in, it would cost me some bucks, it would have some risks in how my people reacted; one way or another I'd have to do something." He paused and then went on. "Well, to tell the truth, I don't want to upset things if they're OK, but just finding out whether they are or not appeals to me. Isn't there some other way to do this?"

Bob Denton seemed to me to be open to some minimal work by me. He'd responded as I'd hoped to my candidness about the risks of some conventional diagnostic snooping. He'd really seemed to pay attention to what I'd said, and I was beginning to like him and was intrigued with the situation. At times like this, my thought processes seem to jump into high gear. After all, a careful response was called for and there were a number of considerations to factor in. The things I recall noting to myself went like this: apparently some minimal motivation on Bob's part; my real lack of information about the Kenworth situation; my own schedule for the coming months—which was pretty full; my intuition that probably nothing major was wrong with Bob and his managers; and that whatever I proposed had to be of modest cost.

LET'S HAVE A RETREAT

I said to Bob: "Let me sketch out one idea that comes to mind. We could do a modest retreat. You, your department managers, and I could meet away from here for a couple of days, say on a weekend, to jointly explore how things are going. At minimum, I see several probable outcomes from such a meeting: everyone would get somewhat better acquainted with one another; we'd know better if there were serious issues to tackle; we'd have the experience of jointly going through problem identification; and you'd get a sense of whether or not your team was open to working with an outsider like myself."

I paused and went on: "Such a meeting would be relatively efficient. It wouldn't take time away from work, and it wouldn't cost an arm and a leg." Bob nodded, sipped his coffee and looked at me intently. "OK," he said, "I can see your points. Just what would we be doing?"

Seeing Bob's interest as well as warming to the idea myself, I went on to outline a retreat. I suggested doing it at a country club or lodge within a few hours' drive of Seattle. This setting was to provide a symbolic break from the customary business environment, and because it would cost everyone weekend time and the company the expense of travel, food, and lodging, it would show Bob's seriousness about the event. I then suggested we begin with cocktails and dinner on a Friday evening, work all day Saturday with appropriate breaks, and conclude by noon Sunday. Again, Bob nodded. He then asked, "But what would we do? What would you charge?"

I did some quick calculations and responded, "As for my fee, I'd have to bill you for a minimum of three days at my daily rate of $___ per day, and travel expenses—assuming Kenworth would provide food and lodging. As for what we'd actually do, that's more difficult to say exactly. Frankly, while I have several ways to get us started, I'd need to play it by ear. In general, it would be my responsibility to see we talked straight and a lot with one another to surface our concerns both big and small. I'm afraid you'd have to trust me on this." I said this last couple of sentences with some trepidation, knowing from my experience that most managers would want much more clarity, but I needed to know how Bob was viewing me.

I was surprised at what happened next. Denton quickly agreed to have a retreat weekend as I'd outlined. We also selected a weekend a month-and-a-half away. He would find a site and let me know. In addition, we agreed he would use the phrase "a communications workshop" when he informed participants. Glancing at my watch as I left Denton's office, I saw it was just 11:30.

Questions

1. How well did the OD consultant prepare for the meeting with Denton? Would you have done anything differently?
2. In the discussion between the OD consultant and Denton, what was effective and ineffective about the consultant's behavior?
3. How effective was the contracting process described in the last part of the case? What is the scope and clarity of the agreement?
4. How would you design the upcoming retreat?

PEPPERCORN DINING*

The partners of Square One Consulting were having lunch at Peppercorn Dining on the campus of All-American University. Although Square One was headquartered nearby, most of the consultants' business was conducted in other cities. The partners were enjoying having the opportunity to attend a seminar on a campus in their hometown. By chance, Drew Randall, the manager of Peppercorn, noticed the trio and recognized Erica, who had worked her way through college as a student manager at the dining unit. Drew pulled up a chair and started to catch up on the two years that had transpired since she had graduated. The other consultants, Roger and Lynn, listened as they began to reminisce about the "good old days" at Peppercorn.

Erica recalled the time a swim test coincided with her first shift at the dining hall. She called to let the unit know she would be detained, and she finally arrived about an hour late. When Erica entered the unit, she was greeted by a supervisor who took her downstairs to change into the uniform of blue pants, blue-and-white-checkered shirt, a hair net, and a name tag, an outfit similar to what was being worn by the current employees. Erica was then taken to the dish room and informed she was receiving a verbal warning for being late. As the group laughed, the consultants chided Erica further by commenting that her sense of timing hadn't changed. Drew, however, suggested that times had changed.

DEVELOPING A CONTRACT

The consultants were eager to learn about Peppercorn, and Erica, eager to learn about the changes Drew had alluded to, asked about current operations at the unit. Drew, sipping on his coffee, commented, "Staffing is a nightmare. We can't find qualified people anywhere; recruiting and retention has become a constant challenge." Drew went on to explain that the labor market in the county had become tight due to the prosperous Reagan years. Garden County had become a boomtown and, as a result, the university was having difficulty gaining employees. Roger wondered aloud about the general steps Peppercorn had taken to offset the current labor shortage.

Drew, sensing the consultant's interest, openly discussed his perceptions of the dining unit. He stated:

> I would like to make Peppercorn a more pleasant place for everyone to work. I get great productivity out of these guys and they really care. It's just that there needs to be something more. Maybe morale is a little low. There's not much creativity involved in most of the tasks, but the cooks feel great when they sell out of stuff. However, when we sell out, it's probably because the forecast was incorrect rather than as a response to a good product. I take a humanistic management approach, maybe they just need some kind of support. On the other hand, I may give them too much autonomy since I let them manage themselves to a large degree.
>
> I believe that scheduling is management's right. I base my scheduling on operational need. Ultimately, the manager is responsible for the success or failure of the operation, therefore, I should have the right to put the people where I deem best. You know, niche management. Although, I did inherit a lot of the schedule.

As Erica tentatively nodded her head in response to Drew's comments, Roger and Lynn caught each other's gaze and shrugged inquisitively. By the consultants' behavior, it was apparent they were wondering about the meaning behind Drew's words. However, because he was obviously in the mood to talk, the consultants did not interrupt.

Warming up to his listeners, Drew continued, "Some employees have been at Peppercorn, working in the same position, for 20 plus years. Bob, the day cook, has been working here for 28 years. Can you believe that Doug, the night cook, has been here for 10 years and is waiting for Bob to retire so that he can

---

*JoAnn Carmin, *Cornell University;* Todd Comen, *Cornell University;* Yariels Kerr, *Cornell University.*

transfer to the day shift? Doug may have to wait a long time since Bob won't be retiring for at least 15 years. It's hard for me to believe that Doug looks forward to that time and that he refuses to transfer to another dining unit."

"That's amazing," said Roger. "You seem to have loyal employees. It must be easy to manage people who know their job so well."

Drew responded:

> It's not that simple. The union contract forms a second set of rules and operating parameters. The contract deals with turnover, sick leave, pay, promotion, and all of the other usual stuff. It seems that there is no reward for non-sickness, but there is a reward for sickness. Now people get one and a half times the pay for sick days if they are on overtime. If they are on overtime, absenteeism is more of a contractual issue than a workplace issue.
>
> Frankly, I believe that staffing affects attitudes and attitudes affect quality; both of which affect productivity. Increased productivity means making better use of time. Perhaps I should structure the tasks in a better way, but managing and working behind the lines makes it difficult for me to see the trees through the forest. There's no time for anyone to stand back and see what's happening.

Drew paused and, as if speaking more to himself than to the consultants, said, "Since I've been so busy, maybe I've lost track of some of my priorities." Turning to the consultants, Drew inquired about their experience with situations of this type and what advice they might offer.

The partners explained they are usually contacted by organizations when management believes an external opinion could provide a fresh outlook on operations. They went on to state they normally begin their work by performing an operations audit, the results of which are presented to management. Additionally, when the situation warrants, strategic interventions are designed to facilitate the achievement of management objectives. The partners further indicated they believe it is essential to become familiar with an organization before appropriate suggestions can be made.

Without hesitation, Drew said to the consultants, "The situation here at Peppercorn has been concerning me for quite some time. I know that you must be very busy, but perhaps you could find the time to work with me. Erica already knows a lot about the operation, and it wouldn't take long for her to become reacquainted."

Because the consultants were planning to be in the area for several days to attend the seminar and to complete some paperwork, Erica suggested they observe operations at Peppercorn. The group, discussing Erica's suggestion, agreed that the first stage should be a preliminary evaluation of the unit, followed by a feedback session with management. Then, based on the outcome, management could conduct an in-depth operations audit. Drew concurred that evaluation and feedback could be useful first steps in achieving his goals. He restated that his goals for Peppercorn were to increase productivity and to improve morale among the workers.

The consultants concluded their discussion by telling Drew they would drop off a written contract by the following afternoon. The contract would include their fee structure as well as a schedule of the dates and times they would like to be on the premises.

REVIEWING BACKGROUND INFORMATION

Two days later, the team gathered around the table in Roger's office to discuss the Peppercorn consultation. Roger and Lynn initiated the discussion by reintroducing the subject of Erica's objectivity. It became obvious that all three of the partners were concerned about how Erica's past experiences would bias her view of the operation. The partners also discussed the fact that Erica's views would influence Roger and Lynn's perceptions of the dining unit. Although Erica believed she could recognize and work with her bias, she suggested she focus on gathering current managerial data. Because their time was limited, Lynn recommended that Erica also conduct a few on-site interviews with people who would be more candid with an old friend than with strangers.

As he was reaching for a notepad, Roger asked Erica about the general operating procedures and the key personnel at Peppercorn. Erica began outlining the operation:

> Peppercorn's hours are 11 A.M. to 7:30 P.M., Monday through Friday. When I first started, we served about 1,500 to 1,600 lunches

and 900 to 1,000 dinners daily. By the time I graduated, the counts were down by about 30 percent at lunch and approximately 50 percent at dinner.

When I was a student worker at Peppercorn, there were full-time employees, all of whom were union members. There were also student workers, and we had our own student management staff. When I first started working, there were more student workers than when I graduated. Some of the gaps were filled by full-time temporary workers.

Lynn pointed out that it would be important to determine if these changes were affecting the operation. Erica agreed and indicated that by the time she had graduated, minor conflicts were arising between student and temporary workers at Peppercorn. Erica continued her briefing by providing an overview of the key personnel during her tenure with All-American Dining, the parent organization of Peppercorn.

Erica stated:

> Drew is obviously the manager of Peppercorn. He was also the manager of the Salt Mill over at the "B"-School. He was responsible to Stan O'Malley, one of the assistant directors of All-American Dining. Stan supervised Drew and Beth Clarkson, the manager of food service in the student union.
>
> John Cerrano was the receiving clerk. He always worked closely with Drew. There never seemed to be any problems with his work; he always knew where everything was because he received the goods and then put them in storage. John, or "Bo-bo" as we called him, was the shop steward. He had a close relationship with most of the employees and a bunch of us used to go out drinking with him regularly.
>
> Matt Copperfield was definitely a key player. Matt was the professional supervisor who handled inventory, purchasing, scheduling, and other administrative tasks. It always seemed as if he was at the heart of the operation. I can't remember her name, but there was a secretary who was also in a pivotal position. She had access to a lot of information and she was the source and respondent of all official Peppercorn communication.
>
> The student supervisors were the only other key players that I can think of at this point, and they had extensive responsibilities which included daily management, scheduling, and hiring of the student workers.

The partners' conversation shifted to the amount of time available for the investigation. Lynn asked her partners how much time they thought was necessary for conducting the initial investigation. "Well, Lynn," replied Roger, "based on the information we have so far, it's possible that the longtime employees may not be as open as we might like. They may be protective of their turf." Lynn agreed but added that they shouldn't jump to any conclusions. She noted that often it was the old-time employees who were most interested in talking about their work.

The consultants agreed that three days should be an ample amount of time to gather the necessary data and to develop a presentation for the management of Peppercorn Dining. The consultants concluded the meeting by agreeing that Lynn would concentrate on the production areas of the unit while Roger would survey front-of-house operations.

DAY ONE: INTERVIEWS AND OBSERVATIONS

Lynn was the first to arrive at Peppercorn the following morning. As she approached the facility, she noticed that three female employees were smoking cigarettes on the loading dock, joking around with a purveyor. Lynn introduced herself and lingered with the workers for a few minutes.

Back of House

Entering the kitchen from the loading dock, Lynn noticed it was clean and most of the equipment looked relatively new. The kitchen had fairly good fluorescent lighting, and natural lighting was provided by windows in the pot washing and food preparation areas.

As Lynn placed her coat and briefcase on a rack in the storage area, she observed that the dry goods were neatly arranged, although the supplies were not plentiful. From the storeroom doorway, she could see that the workers were busy, but not rushed. The members of the kitchen staff chatted as they worked and they appeared to know what tasks to perform without needing direction.

The kitchen was divided into five areas (as shown in Figure 1). After introducing herself to the workers and taking a brief tour of the kitchen, Lynn positioned herself near the walk-in cooler where she could easily see most of the kitchen operations. She noticed that the walk-in cooler and freezer were clean and were stocked with a moderate amount of supplies. She also observed that the workers' uniforms were clean. However, some of the workers were wearing aprons and some were not. As if reading her thoughts, a student worker passing through the room commented to no one in particular, "We're out of aprons again. Oh well, it's no big deal." Lynn wondered what else might not be a "big deal" to the workers.

The doors to the dining facility were opened at 10:55 A.M. at which time the pantry workers took a break.

Bob, the day chef, was grilling sandwiches in the tilt brazier while Robert, the day cook, was breading pork. Robert moved between food preparation, the fryer, and the steamer. During lunch service, the kitchen staff appeared to be relaxed. Although there was not much talking, they did joke with each other from time to time.

Shortly after 11:00 A.M., a man wearing a chefs uniform entered the kitchen and greeted the other workers. He then took a clipboard and a stack of computer printouts to a table near where Lynn was

FIGURE 1

Floor Plan of Peppercorn Dining

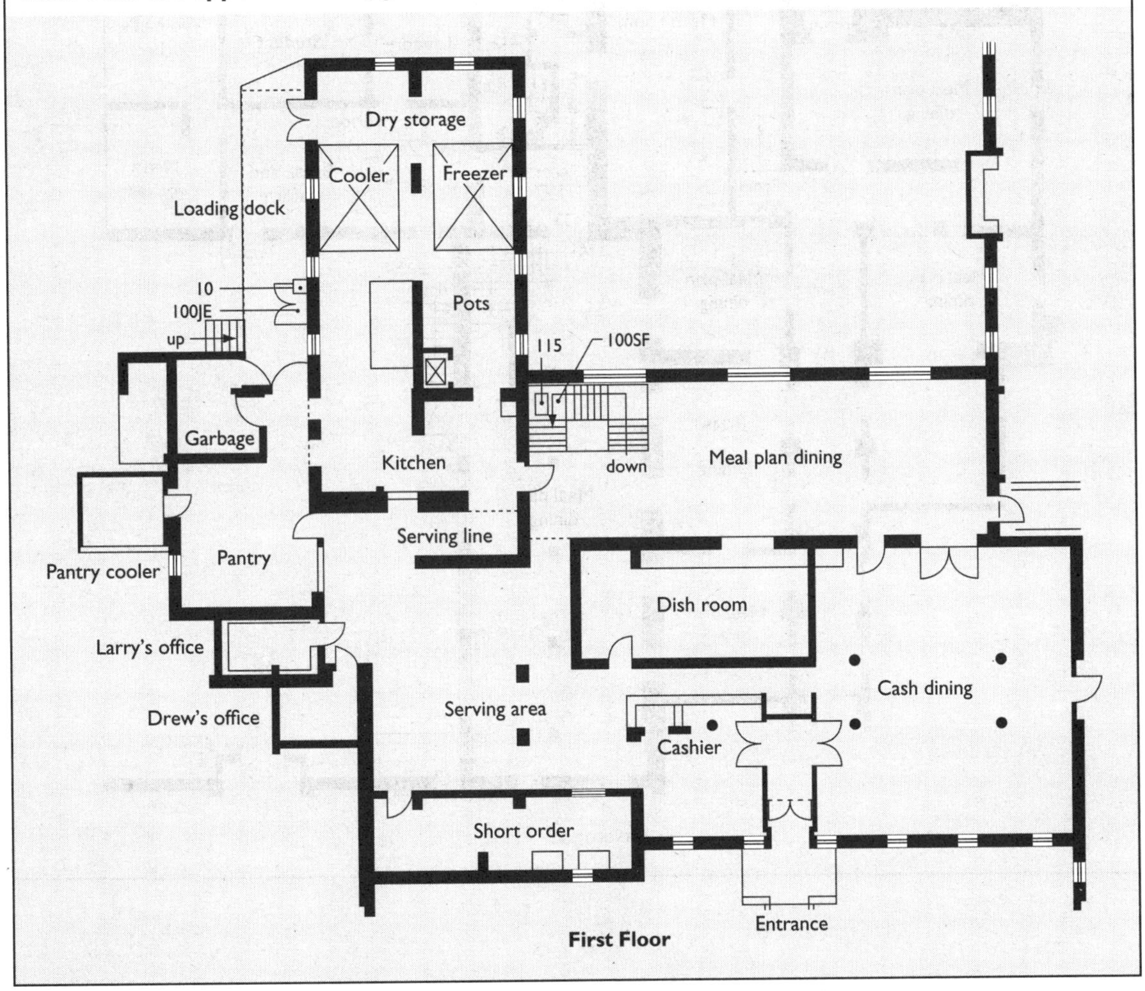

FIGURE 1

Floor Plan of Peppercorn Dining, (*continued*)

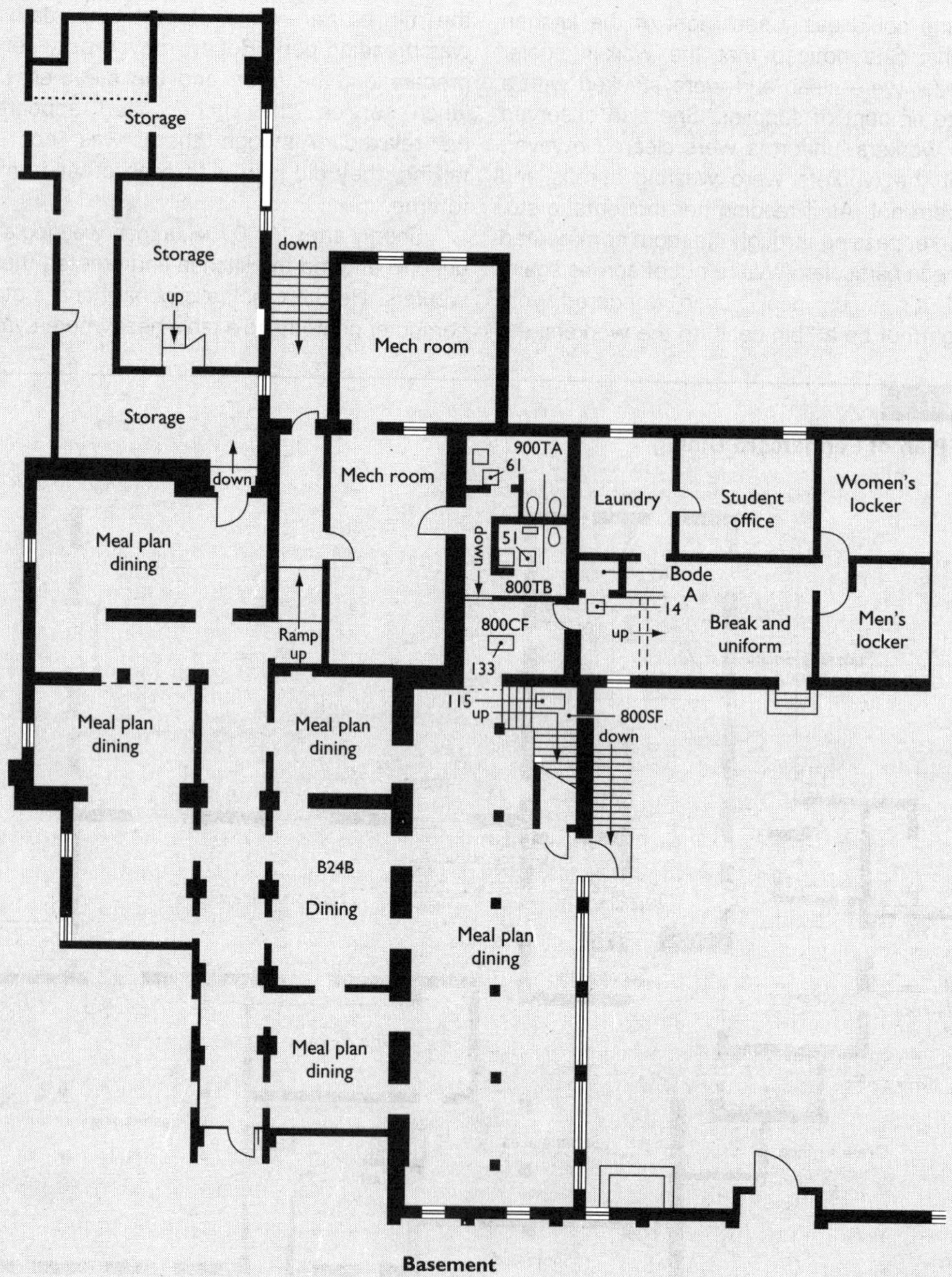

standing. Lynn felt a bit awkward until he introduced himself as Doug, the dinner chef.

Lynn explained she was observing the facility in order to become familiar with the operation. Doug showed interest in Lynn's curiosity and stated:

> I want the kitchen to run as smoothly as possible. I believe that it takes organization, morale, communication, and a system to have an efficient operation. Communication is important. I ask the servers how things are working out so that I know if I should change anything. I try to maintain a routine system so there won't be many questions during service. I train all of my workers and I enjoy having the opportunity to teach. I've been in food service for 25 years and at Peppercorn for 10 years. I started working in the food service industry when I was about 11.
>
> I think that Peppercorn has the best food on campus. Some of my own recipes have been accepted by management and are now a part of the menu database. I've also developed ideas that have been adopted here and at other campus dining facilities. For example, I started the trend of keeping plastic tasting spoons by the steam kettles. I'm also the person who started using a yellow marker to highlight important items on the computer printouts.

As Lynn and Doug were talking, a man came over and listened to their conversation. Doug's speech became hesitant in this man's presence. After only a few minutes, the man left. Lynn wondered who the man was and why he had such an effect on Doug. From the way he was dressed, there was no way to determine if he worked at Peppercorn, was from the union, or was part of the All-American management staff.

Coincidentally, Doug explained to Lynn that the man was Larry, the professional supervisor. He went on to say Larry plans the menus and tries to balance the use of ovens and kettles so the equipment is not overloaded. According to Doug, Larry prints out the menus from a computer located in the office. Doug added that the system does not always work the way it should. It is supposed to print menus, compile order lists, and check the inventory. Doug commented, "Sometimes it works well, and sometimes not. Sometimes the menus have to be changed at the last minute because of short stock. We haven't had any salt all semester. This is mostly a result of computer errors."

Doug went on to talk about some of his coworkers. Bob, the lunch chef, has been at Peppercorn for 28 years. Chris, the assistant dinner chef, has been with the unit for about three years. Chris, who moved to the kitchen from the short-order station, was trained by Doug. They enjoy sharing ideas and they always try to prepare the food a day in advance.

While Lynn was talking with Doug, she could see the cafeteria line by way of a pass-through window. She noticed that a steady flow of diners was entering the facility. Realizing that Doug enjoyed talking about the unit and being curious about Doug's responses, Lynn felt comfortable continuing the conversation. Observing a student supervisor restocking the hot food line, Lynn asked Doug how he felt about working with students.

He replied, "Some student workers are reliable, while others are less committed." Lynn asked Doug about the role of the student supervisor and in response Doug called the student over. The student seemed unhurried and went on to explain that student supervisors do not have any power over the regular workers; only over temps and other students. Students have their own management structure that includes a student coordinator, managers, and pay clerk. The student personnel coordinator handles complaints. Temps and regular workers take complaints to the regular personnel worker. More temps have been needed recently since there are less student workers at Peppercorn than in previous years.

As Lynn, Doug, and the student were talking, Larry entered the kitchen again. When the student noticed him, he quickly went back to work restocking the food line.

The activity in the kitchen seemed to be getting busier, and Lynn decided she should move to another position so Doug could continue his work. Before she left, Doug commented about the union. He stated, "Skilled workers are on the same union contract as unskilled workers. I think that this arrangement holds back the skilled workers and helps the unskilled to get ahead. It doesn't work well, and we don't even have a shop steward. The only way that I can move up in the organization is to become part of management."

Lynn bid Doug farewell and went into the service area to get some lunch. As she went through the cafeteria line, she noticed Roger observing the cafeteria service. Lynn invited him to join her for lunch, but Roger declined, saying he had just begun his observation and he wanted to spend some time watching service during the busiest hours.

Service Areas

Roger immediately noticed the line servers interacted a great deal with the customers. He also noted there was no portion control. The students would ask the line servers for "a little more spaghetti, just meatballs, no corn, more sauce, or a small cup of soup." Each customer wanted the standard portions or combinations of food items altered to meet their personal needs, and they were accommodated.

The first line server plates the entrees and the second worker serves the side dishes (see Figure 2). The workers must communicate in order to properly fill each order. The overall atmosphere in the serving area was relaxed. Roger timed the service and discovered it took two to four minutes for a customer to enter the line and be served during a busy period.

As the flow of customers slowed, Roger initiated a conversation with a line worker who introduced herself as Carrie. She told Roger she had been at Peppercorn for 10 years and was a door checker for 9½ of those years. She explained the door checker made sure that only diners on the university meal plan were allowed in the noncash dining area. She went on to say she had become bored with her position. She was also dissatisfied with her former hours, which were from 11 A.M. to 7:30 P.M. Carrie attained her new position with Drew's help. He facilitated a trade between her and a line server. Now that the swap is final, Carrie believes the other woman, who is now the door checker, may not think the trade was equitable.

During his conversation with Carrie, Roger saw the chef come out of the kitchen and pick up an empty pan. The chef lingered for a minute. He appeared to be watching the line service. Roger returned his attention to Carrie and continued the conversation by asking her about line staffing. Carrie explained, "Usually there are three main workers on the line, two full-timers at one station and one student or temp at the other. We choose our own positions on the line and we usually stick to the same spots. When it gets busy, additional student workers fill in. Today one full-timer is sick, so a temp from another area filled the position. Sometimes they can't find substitutes, so we just have to work that much harder."

Roger stepped aside as a student worker carrying a tray of soup cups began to restock the service line. Roger apologized for any inconvenience and explained he was a member of a group learning about the operations at Peppercorn. Roger asked the student if he could take a moment to tell him about the relationship between student and nonstudent workers.

The student explained that Peppercorn is supposed to be staffed primarily by students. The students are grouped into three segments: student managers, student supervisors, and student workers. However, he said, "Since the supply of students has been diminishing over the years, more temps have had to fill the positions. There's a lot of tension between students and temps as well as between students and full-timers. This isn't surprising since the students supervise the operation. They call us 'students' as opposed to 'supervisors' and we seem to be stereotyped."

FIGURE 2

Line Servers Setup

Starch	Vegetable	Backup	Entree	Entree
Soup	Vegetable	Entree	Entree	Entree

Server 2 — Server I

He clarified his statement, saying, "There's a discrepancy with age, economic status, and experience in many cases. Only the full-timers and the professional managers are not under the supervision of students. Students have a difficult time supervising older people, and older people have a difficult time taking orders from young people who they probably consider similar to their own children."

The student went back to work, leaving Roger to his thoughts. He was reminded of the conversation that he had with his partners about the conflicts between student and nonstudent workers. It was becoming clear to Roger that this was an important issue.

Just as Roger was beginning to consider the problems that can arise from role conflict and role ambiguity, he was startled by the sound of shattering glass. Roger turned in time to notice a student stepping away from a broken glass, acting as if nothing had happened. Several dishwashers, on their way to the drink station, also saw the broken glass as they walked by. Roger was curious to see how long it would take for someone to clean up the mess. Two minutes later, a dishwasher returned and swept up the glass. During this time, a student supervisor was informed of the problem. Roger noted she never returned to make sure the situation was corrected.

Roger followed the dishwasher toward the dish room. As he rounded the corner of the serving area, Roger heard the sound of blaring music. He had to weave his way through a narrow passage that was blocked with customers at the cashier's station.

As he entered the dish room through an open doorway, Roger was greeted by a mixture of machinery noise, loud music, and a hot, humid atmosphere. The machinery was arranged in a pattern that allowed many people to perform different tasks simultaneously. The five workers gave Roger a cursory glance and continued with their tasks.

Roger, feeling a bit out of place and self-conscious, stood to one side of the work area and watched the activity. There was a lot of joking, talking, and interacting as the workers sorted and cleaned dishes, silverware, glasses, and trays. Full dish trays were stacked at the rinse station. Each rack was rinsed and then sent through the dishwashing machine. When the dishes completed their cycle, a worker sorted the dishes. Roger noted the worker put several freshly washed dishes into racks with dirty dishes. He also noticed the silverware was run through the dishwasher twice.

Roger wanted to know why the silverware had to go through the wash cycle two times, so he asked the dish sorter who was positioned at the end of the line. The sorter said, "We're concerned that plates and especially the silver are clean. We wouldn't want people catching something from someone else."

The sorter asked Roger what he was doing in the dish room. Roger explained and then asked the worker how long he had been at Peppercorn. The worker said he had been at Peppercorn for a year. Further discussion revealed the worker is on a split shift. He works from noon to 4 P.M. and then from 6 P.M. until 10 P.M. He said he likes having a midday break in order to get things done in his personal life. He explained that he knew three of the other workers before he started the job. Because he was the newest employee in the dish room, he was stationed at the hottest position. He pointed out that the two full timers he worked with had held their positions for four and two years, respectively. The other three workers, including him, were temps.

The worker finished sorting and left the dish room to get his coworkers a cold drink. Roger went over to the area where workers were scraping and sorting dirty plates. The dishes and filled racks were piling up. Roger noted the dish machine was not able to keep up with the demand. He also saw that the paper items were shredded with the food scraps and that Styrofoam was sorted separately.

The oldest woman in the dish room yelled out from time to time, "Come on, keep it movin'." Roger spent a few more minutes observing. As he recalled Erica's story about her first day at Peppercorn, Roger wondered why there were no students working in the dish room. As he was leaving, a student supervisor came in to get trays for the service area.

Roger proceeded to the cashier station where he found the dish sorter chatting with the cashier. After a minute, the sorter returned to the dish room. Roger struck up a conversation with the cashier. After briefing her about his project, the cashier proceeded to tell Roger about some of her observations and experiences at Peppercorn.

She explained that the cashier's job is a full-time, nonunion position she has held for two years. She replaced the person who is currently the secretary. She enjoys having the opportunity to meet people and getting to know the regulars, but she has found that some of the students are rude.

The cashier stated, "I usually get along well with management. Everyone has their good and bad days. I was a manager in my previous job, so I understand what Drew has to deal with. I also understand the problems that the student supervisors have." Roger wondered what the cashier meant by this statement. What does Drew have to deal with and what problems do the student supervisors really have to deal with? Thus far, he had noted that the operation appeared effective, although some communication problems were evident.

The cashier, seeing Drew passing by, stopped him and asked him for more change and small bills. Roger asked if it was standard procedure for her to ask managers for more money, or if she was able to get it herself. She replied she is authorized to get cash, but it is difficult for her to leave her station.

While the cashier was waiting for Drew to return, Roger asked her about work conditions. The cashier replied:

> I get cold in the winter because I'm so close to the entrance and the wind blows in. It's ironic because the rest of the workers complain about it being too hot at their stations. Peppercorn is built over heating ducts, so it's very hot everywhere except at my station. People's biggest complaint is the heat. There isn't adequate ventilation or air flow. Another common complaint is that there's not enough room in the dining, kitchen, and service areas. This is because Peppercorn used to be a riding stable.
>
> In the winter I get sick easily, but I only miss about five days per year. I've learned to live with not feeling well on the job. I have a sore back every night because I sit on a bar stool all day.

Before Roger could inquire if she had ever talked to management about her work conditions, she stated, "I'm the only cashier. I have to call on the secretary when it's really busy, but I know she has a lot of work to do. I also restock silverware. This entails shutting down the register, running to the dish room, and then restocking before the register line gets too long. Our job descriptions say that if someone sees something that needs doing, they are supposed to do it. Therefore, during slow periods I help clean tables, do the menu board, and look around for other things to do."

Roger asked the cashier about her plans for the future, and she explained she would like to have a secretarial job so she could get away from food service for a while. The cashier went on to say there are temps and students that make more money than she does as a full-timer and this disparity makes her resentful. The wages seem to be based on job position or union membership. Only four positions are nonunion. These positions include the cashier, secretary, supervisor, and manager. The rest of the workers at Peppercorn are temporary, union members, or students. The cashier added there are only five single people on the staff.

When Roger asked the cashier about the relationship between student and full-time workers, she replied there is a lot of pressure in the dish room. She believes the pressure builds up because the student supervisors never send student workers in to help. The supervisors' excuse is that they are short of help elsewhere. Drew returned with the cash, and Roger went to see if he could find his partners.

Administrative Information

Roger found Lynn and Erica sitting in the dining area. Erica was telling Lynn she had arranged for them to have dinner with some students that evening. Roger sat down with his partners and asked Erica if she could clarify some details about the organizational structure.

Erica responded, "There are three tiers of management at Peppercorn (Figure 3). There is the professional management staff, which consists of Drew and Larry. They oversee the full-time workers. There are also student managers and student supervisors. The student managers oversee student supervisors as well as the student workers. The student supervisors are responsible for daily operations. The student workers and the temporary employees report to them. It seems, however, that the temporary workers also report to, and are trained by, the professional managers."

Roger and Lynn interjected that they had noticed difficulties between the students and the other workers at Peppercorn. Lynn asked Erica if she would clarify the distinction between the

FIGURE 3

Peppercorn Dining Organizational Chart

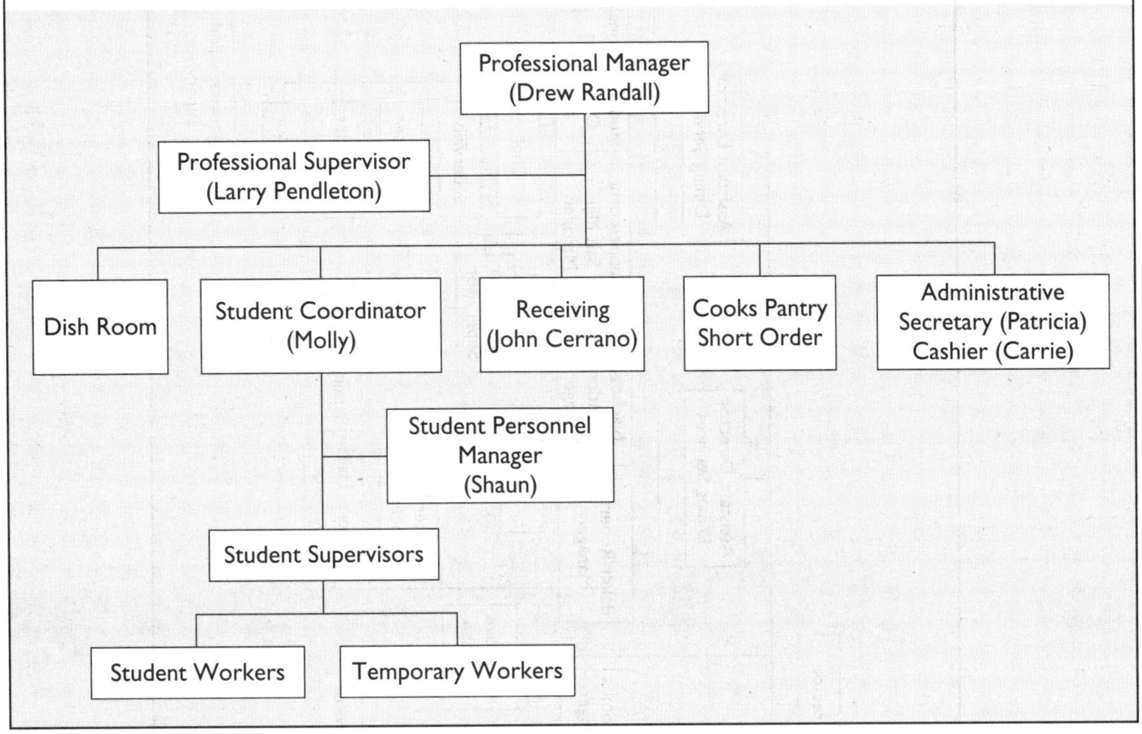

different levels of employees. Erica clarified the organizational structure stating:

> There are full-time union employees, full-time nonunion temporary employees, and student labor. Full-time employees hold the positions of cooks, short order chefs, pantry workers, and cashiers. In past years, students filled all the other supplementary positions, including dishwashers, servers, cooks, helpers, short order helpers, pantry helpers, beverage servers, and serving area floaters. For the past four to five years, fewer students have wanted jobs at Peppercorn. This phenomena has resulted in the addition of the third type of employee, the full-time temporary worker.

Erica went on to tell her partners that she had gathered enough information to update them on the key players at All-American Dining. She explained that Larry Pendleton is the new professional supervisor, replacing Matt Copperfield at Peppercorn. In the central office, Nancy Lawrence is still the director of All-American Dining (Figure 4). She has been spending a great deal of time traveling to different universities in order to analyze their food service operations. Stan O'Malley is still an assistant director of All-American Dining. Although there is a central office, each unit is independently operated.

Roger asked Erica is she had the opportunity to speak with any employees and if she had been able to uncover any information about management-employee relations. Erica told her partners she had spoken with John Cerrano and some of the pantry workers.

Erica went on to say she and John spoke about changes that had occurred at Peppercorn since she had left. John told Erica the lack of student help has hurt operations at the unit. For example, a special dining event that Peppercorn sponsored last night was difficult for the workers. There were virtually no students on the staff. As a result, the full-time workers and temps had to pick up the slack.

John also commented that Larry doesn't listen to his advice about ordering food. John spends a

FIGURE 4
Department of Dining Services

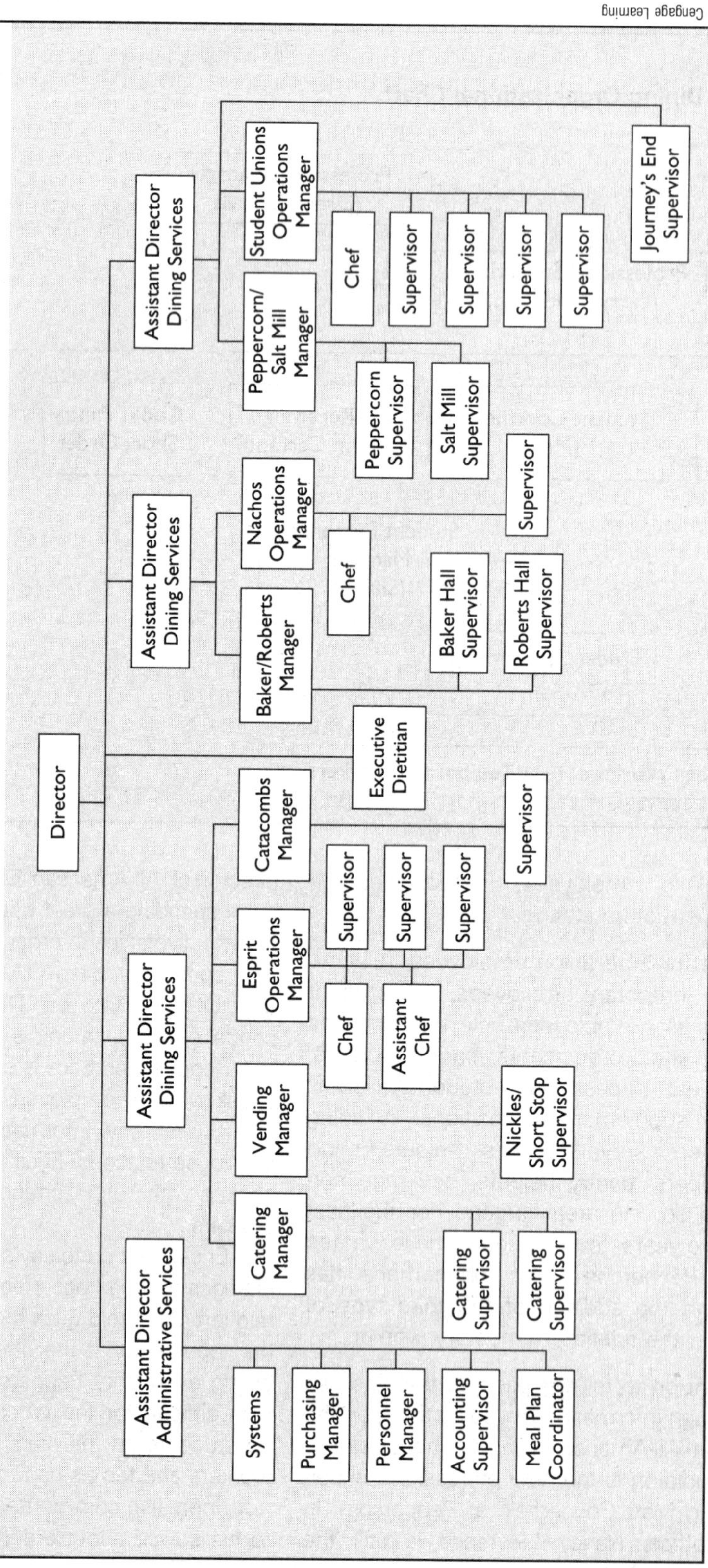

lot of his time getting food items that should have come in from the suppliers from the other units on campus. According to John, Larry doesn't have the respect of the staff. He doesn't take anyone's advice and acts like a know-it-all. The situation is made worse because Larry doesn't do his job very well.

Erica went on to discuss the pantry workers stating:

> The workers seemed to indicate a general belief that the management of All-American Dining, as well as the management at Peppercorn, doesn't really care about them. They mentioned how All-American's previous personnel director used to visit the different dining units at least once a month and talk with the full-time employees. During that time, the workers felt that someone cared about them. They said that the new personnel director doesn't come around at all and probably doesn't even know who the full-time employees are.
>
> The workers also told me that there is minimal union representation for food service employees. According to the workers, food service members are a minority faction of the union and aren't considered important unless a strike is in progress. Apparently, the union's primary concern is with maintenance workers, groundskeepers, janitors, and bus drivers. There's no shop steward and union officials don't come to Peppercorn unless there is an official grievance.

Lynn added that Doug had also commented on the union. She stated, "Based on what we have heard so far, no one is thrilled with the union. Workers and management alike seem to find the union a burden."

Roger asked Erica about how each unit on the campus was staffed. Erica explained that the units were independently staffed and at the beginning of each semester, the different units held recruitment campaigns.

Erica became quite excited as she stated, "OK, enough of the routine stuff. One thing that I found out today is that the university is building a new 400-seat dining facility. Also, a privately funded food service operation that will include a variety of dining concepts is opening nearby. Of course, these things will impact Peppercorn, but the scoop is that Drew will be the manager of the new facility!"

Erica, acting quite pleased, sat back, smiled, and waited for her partners to respond. Lynn paused only for a moment and then, turning to Erica, said, "This isn't making much sense, but, before I ask the obvious, why don't you tell us the rest of the facts?"

Erica, a little disappointed at the response her comment evoked, went on to explain that Drew would be leaving Peppercorn in about five months and that Eric Weston, the current vending manager, would take charge of the unit as soon as Drew left.

As Lynn and Erica began to engage in an intense discussion about the future of Peppercorn dining, Roger, in true form, looked at his watch and stated, "Well, not only do we have a contract, we also have a dinner engagement in 20 minutes. Let's get some fresh air before we meet with the students!" The partners began laughing and, recognizing the sanity of Roger's comment, decided a break was in order.

Dinner with Student Managers

After freshening up, the trio returned to Peppercorn to meet the students for dinner. Molly, the student coordinator, and Shaun, the student personnel manager, were waiting for the consultants at Peppercorn's main entrance. The five of them went through the cafeteria line and then entered the dining room, where they found a quiet table to have their dinner.

Shaun seemed to know why the consultants had asked them to dinner and began to tell them about his tenure at Peppercorn. Shaun explained that when he had started at Peppercorn four years ago, there were two to three times the number of student workers. He went on to say more students made the work fun and the operation ran more efficiently. Shaun explained it is hard for the students who have been at Peppercorn for a long time because they know how it used to be.

Molly agreed with Shaun, saying students would work at Peppercorn because it had a reputation for being social. "To attract student workers," Molly said, "Peppercorn must become special, more conducive to meeting students' needs. In the early days, students were proud to be Peppies and looked forward to seeing their coworkers." She proceeded to say they have to treat students well because they can't risk alienating anyone. They can't afford to fire students or give them too many warnings.

Erica asked the students to comment on working with the temporary workers. Shaun said, "The temp-student relationship is not great. Temps are under the student supervisors' authority, but it doesn't really work that way. Temps are less efficient than students, but they are needed to fill the vacant positions. They are probably not as efficient because they have less loyalty to Peppercorn than the students."

Molly interjected, "This year, no students and temps work in the same areas except for emergencies. Temps are trained by the professional management but are supervised by students. Last year, it was unclear who was in charge of the temps. This year it is better. Most things are written in manuals."

"The regular and temporary workers don't talk much to the students," continued Molly. "Temps and full-timers think students are stupid; they have an attitude toward students. It's hard for the students to get cooperation and respect from the temps."

Lynn asked the students about their relationships with Drew. Shaun and Molly explained that while most students don't interact with Drew frequently, they, as supervisors, meet with him regularly. Most of the students think Drew is rude and cold and unapproachable, but they have found he can be very patient. Additionally, many students don't believe Drew is knowledgeable about food service operations. Molly and Shaun have discovered that he is, in fact, an astute person. They attributed his reputation to a lack of accessibility, noting that Drew is generally more accessible to the full-time and temporary workers than to the students.

Lynn further inquired about the students' reactions to the forthcoming management changes. Molly replied, "Since most of the students don't work closely with Drew, we really can't foresee the change having much of an effect on them. Most students don't have any preconceived ideas about the new management."

Shaun disagreed with Molly stating, "It's going to be hard for a new manager to come in mid-year. The transition will cause problems since the new manager won't have the experience. I think that the new manager should change things quickly. New student workers are recruited by us in the spring and meet their supervisors when they begin working in the fall. They immediately have some respect for their supervisor. I think that the new manager will be in a bind."

Molly said she believed the change would have a greater effect on the full-time and temporary workers than on the students. She has heard some workers mention they are concerned because Peppercorn's future is unclear. Many of the full-time workers are loyal to Drew; they have become comfortable with his management style.

Roger, addressing Molly, asked about communication at Peppercorn. Molly responded:

> Communication has been a major problem. The students thought that if they left me notes, things would get done. I would take the notes to management, but important things were not noted as being important. Mostly, the problems were repair and maintenance issues. People brooded that things didn't get done quickly. They didn't realize that most things have to go through a lot of channels, which takes time. There is so much paperwork involved. Now the students make special notations when issues are urgent so that I can establish priorities.
>
> An area that is related to communication is ordering. There are a lot of problems with Larry. Last year, we had a problem with the person who filled a similar job but the job description has changed. Last year, the kitchen workers were getting burnt out. Larry revised the menus and for a while the kitchen seemed better. Larry just doesn't do his job well and we constantly run out of things.

Roger asked about the student pay structure at Peppercorn. Molly told him the pay rate has been changed twice. The effect is that workers are kept on the same pay grade because the raises push people back to level one. The only workers who benefit from the changes are the student managers.

Shaun noted that one of the most frustrating situations at Peppercorn was the lack of student interest, something that could not be controlled. Even when the wages were raised, no one applied for jobs. Shaun added that the student supervisors are upset about paying for their meal plan tickets because many of them worked their way through school.

It was getting late and the students had to attend classes the next morning. The consultants thanked the students for being so candid with them. After the students left, the consultants discussed their impressions of Peppercorn.

Roger commented that their earlier concerns about the willingness of employees to speak with them were unfounded. Lynn agreed, noting that although most of the workers seemed to be quite open, Doug was an exception. He was eager to talk, but the discussion seemed contrived. He seemed to be conveying information that he thought she should know and was careful to portray himself and the operation in a favorable light. Lynn said she thought he was concerned about possible repercussions from his responses.

Lynn went on to recount the interactions she had observed earlier in the day between Larry, Doug, and the student supervisor. She then commented, "Larry is an interesting player. All of the workers mention him. He seems to have a lot of power over the other workers, yet he seems to govern by fear. The workers become timid in his presence, nonetheless, they don't appear to have much respect for him."

Picking up on Lynn's train of thought, Roger noted that in his conversations and observations throughout the day, he had begun to wonder about the social system at the unit. He commented, "Although the organization was highly stratified, operations still seem to run smoothly. While workers may be timid around Larry and even fear Drew, the fact that operations are smooth and that the workers appear to be loyal indicates that personality conflicts and role ambiguity are symptoms of a larger problem."

"That's true," said Erica. "The unit always had a reputation for being a social environment. In the past, we were able to overlook personality and role conflicts because there was a strong culture at the unit."

Noticing that the cleaning crew was beginning to break down the dining room, the partners decided to call it a night.

DAY TWO: INTERVIEWS AND OBSERVATIONS

Erica arrived at the dining hall at 10:30 A.M. As she climbed the stairs beside the loading dock, she noticed a worker was in the car wash, hosing down the trash cans. As she entered the kitchen, Erica spotted Drew helping out in the pantry. They greeted each other cordially and chatted for a few minutes. Drew, taking off his lab coat, said he was due at a meeting on the other side of the campus.

Erica left the kitchen and went into the office to gather more information on the structure and operations of Peppercorn. When she entered through the open office door, she found Larry working at the computer, placing orders with the central purchasing system. Larry explained to Erica that the computer system had not been working properly. It is supposed to generate order lists and inventories based on the menus that he inputs. He indicated, however, there must be some problem with the system because the orders are not coming in, and when they do, they frequently are late. After providing Erica with some literature such as employee handbooks, Larry suggested she talk to Patricia, the secretary at the main office.

Erica followed Larry's suggestion and on her way out of the unit she met Roger. She explained she was planning to visit the main office and said she would meet her partners in the late afternoon to discuss her findings.

Roger wandered around the unit for over an hour, observing the lunch service. During the first hour, the cafeteria was packed with customers. Roger noticed the student supervisors were busy refilling the salad and beverage stations. Shaun helped by restocking glasses and trays. The cafeteria line became long and at one point, Drew, having returned from his meeting, helped serve food. Roger noted that by the end of the lunch period, the cafeteria was short on silverware.

As the lunch service slowed, Roger decided to take a look at the student office. As he entered the downstairs dining room, he immediately noticed it was very hot, that a large percentage of the tables were dirty, and that many of the light bulbs in the dining room needed replacement. Roger located the student office and what appeared to be a small gathering or meeting area.

From the open office doorway, Roger could see a bank of time cards on the wall. Roger also noted the office contained a suggestion box. As he peered in the door, he was greeted by the sound of a woman's voice. Roger entered and introduced himself. In response, the woman identified herself as Sarah Lange. Roger asked Sarah if she would be willing to discuss her work experiences at Peppercorn.

Sarah began by saying she had worked at Peppercorn for three years and had been a student supervisor two years. Sarah stated, "Working at Peppercorn is not as much fun as it used to be. Although the job was never easy, it has become increasingly difficult. As supervisors, we don't really manage any more, and the upper-level student managers like Shaun don't work and don't care. He won't even help out when we are short staffed."

Sarah described an incident when Naomi, another student supervisor, was working a snack shift that was understaffed. Shaun, aware of the problem, stayed downstairs at his desk. When Naomi went downstairs to ask him for help, he acted ambivalent. Shaun finally helped in the dining room for about 20 minutes.

"In contrast to Shaun," Sarah commented, "Molly is willing to pitch in when we are short staffed, but this has caused her to become burnt out. Molly has a hard time dealing with problems that arise among the student supervisors. A few days ago, she called a meeting and told us there was a new policy restricting the snacks that we were allowed to eat. She also told us that we were scheduled to work on special dining programs, which are always at dinnertime. The whole time that Molly spoke with us, she was really curt and acted like she was annoyed. We don't even have a student rep to complain to anymore. At least Molly is leaving at the end of the school year."

Sarah said that although she is not very happy working at Peppercorn, she does not want to quit. She has loyalty to both her fellow workers and to the unit. Sarah said she would definitely quit if some of her friends, who are also supervisors at Peppercorn, stopped working at the unit.

Roger thanked Sarah for talking with him and wished her luck in the future. As he walked up the stairs to the service area, Roger made a mental note to talk to his partners about information flow and to further discuss coalitions within the unit.

While Roger had been observing service, Lynn, who arrived at 12:30, had entered the unit from the loading dock. Hoping the workers would be less self-conscious if she was undetected, Lynn quietly observed operations for almost an hour. During that time, Lynn noticed the steam kettles were draining, and much like the previous day, the kitchen workers appeared unhurried but attentive to their tasks. The manner in which they worked seemed highly professional and reflective of the long years the employees had worked together.

When Doug finally noticed Lynn, he greeted her warmly and began to chat with her. As Doug and Lynn were talking, a man who Doug said was a short-order cook walked through the kitchen. He stopped and stared at Lynn for a moment and then asked, "Are you with the health department or the union?" Lynn introduced herself and explained the nature of her project. The man stared at her again briefly and then walked away.

Doug excused himself and Lynn, left to her thoughts, wondered if the man had accurately stated the paranoia she had perceived in Doug the previous day. Doug returned a few minutes later with a cup of soup and offered it to Lynn, saying he thought she should have the opportunity to taste Peppercorn's good food. As Lynn was finishing the soup, she saw two students walk through the kitchen carrying tacos. They proceeded to the loading dock and began to eat their meal. Lynn, wanting some fresh air, went out to the dock and began to converse with the students.

The students told Lynn they had worked at Peppercorn for three years. One of the students said, "Peppercorn used to be a better place to work. We used to have more students working here. The unit always used to be cheerful, and they used to buy beer and have parties on Friday nights."

Lynn asked what had caused the situation to change and the second student replied, "Drew is much tighter about things. The management is only concerned about customers and not about workers. When I first started working here, we had to mop the floor, but there were a lot of students so it was more fun. Then they didn't make us mop any more. Now we have to mop again, but there is not as much camaraderie among the workers."

The worker continued, "What makes the situation worse is that we can't even mop properly because we are always short of supplies. We haven't had any bleach for a week."

Doug came out to the loading dock and said he was going on break. He wanted the students to come inside so he could give them instructions before he left. Doug told the students that because there was not much work to be done, they could work at a slow pace or even sweep the floor so they could work their full shift.

Lynn followed Doug and the students back into the kitchen. Bob and Robert were finishing the lunch cleanup, and Chris was looking at the dinner menu while eating a snack. When Chris saw Lynn standing alone, he approached her and immediately began to tell her about his work experiences and views of Peppercorn.

Chris told Lynn he likes working at Peppercorn. In the same breath, he said he had recently seen ads for positions at a hotel and plans on applying for jobs. Chris said, "I think the food service industry is hard. We're always working when other people are off, and it's hard to get good financial compensation."

Chris went on to explain that the management at Peppercorn does not give the kitchen staff feedback. He believes this is because management does not eat at Peppercorn often. He also said the management is very cost oriented and won't bring in the best quality products.

Chris went on to state:

> Dining used to pay for us to attend professional culinary classes. Now they don't want to spend the money, so they present lectures by campus chefs. It doesn't accomplish much since we are usually taught things that we already know how to make or things that are not within the budget constraints. It doesn't make sense that they are willing to shell out bucks for things like unit specials and management classes and not spend any money on us.
>
> It's hard to get new recipes on the menu. I've tried, but I'm usually met with resistance. I guess that in large quantities they can't afford mistakes. Once, they let us try to test market a new recipe by putting out small chaffing dishes in the meal plan dining room and then asking students for comments on the product. It worked out fairly well and we've used the recipe several times.

As Lynn was wondering about Drew's comment on being a participatory manager, Erica entered the kitchen and came over to tell her she was able to gather some information from the main office. Lynn thanked Chris for speaking with her, and she and Erica went into the service area to find Roger. Roger was chatting with some customers near the salad bar. When he saw his partners approaching, he concluded his conversation.

The consultants each purchased a beverage and on their way to the dining room, Roger told his partners that customers generally had a favorable impression of Peppercorn. They like the food but thought the service was too slow. The only other comment the customers made was that the dining areas were too warm. Erica added that when she had worked at Peppercorn there were rarely any complaints about the food, but they constantly received negative feedback about the heat.

After the consultants were seated, Roger asked Erica what she was able to discover about the structure of the All-American Dining organization. Erica showed her partners copies of the organizational chart, mission statement (Figure 5), and goals and objectives (Figure 6). Erica went on to describe a few of the things she had discovered that day. For example, menu and staffing changes had to be approved by the central office. She also found out that managers are frequently transferred between units.

FIGURE 5

Mission

The mission of All-American Dining is to meet the nutritional, social, aesthetic, and economic needs of the university community with varied and innovative dining services. By meeting these needs we:

- Exert a strong and positive influence on community life.
- Provide educational opportunities for students, staff, and faculty.
- Create a living environment that will help maintain All-American's position as an outstanding center of learning.

The challenge is to accomplish all this within the framework of the enterprise concept.

FIGURE 6

Goals and Objectives

The goals of All-American Dining are closely interwoven with those of the Division of Campus Living and the University. These goals and related objectives are outlined below.

I. Customer Satisfaction. The primary goal is to provide the All-American community with a nutritious, economical, and quality dining program. The objectives are to:

- Provide high-quality cuisine at an affordable price.
- Conduct surveys to determine customer satisfaction and provide guidelines for change.
- Maintain a variety of quality dining services, including: cafeterias, professional catering, vending, and retail food outlets.
- Offer special dining experiences such as gourmet cuisines, unit specials, and community dining events.
- Create flexible and cost-effective meal plans and options that give customers a wide choice of dining times and locations.
- Maintain the highest standards of health and safety.

II. Excellent Facilities. The department's goal is to maintain dining facilities in superior condition. The objective is to continually assess and maintain the functional and aesthetic design of facilities in the comprehensive context of the following:

- An ever-changing and varied customer market.
- The need to assure that production and service areas are clean, safe, efficient, and comfortable.
- Budgetary constraints.
- Department and university master facilities planning processes.
- Energy conservation goals.

III. Professional Management. Recruit and maintain a professional management staff that can meet the challenges of a dynamic food service enterprise. The objectives are to:

- Encourage a participatory, decentralized management style.
- Recruit exceptional talent and support internal promotions.
- Provide a stimulating work environment through interunit transfers, challenging staff assignments, and intradepartmental competition of programs and services.
- Maintain a compensation program that attracts and motivates an innovative, skilled staff.
- Maintain open and positive lines of communication among management, staff, and customers.
- Provide and encourage education and training opportunities that promote professional and personal growth.
- Conduct regular performance evaluations that are based on predetermined goals and objectives.
- Maintain policy and procedural manuals that will ensure consistent and efficient administration.

FIGURE 6

Goals and Objectives, (*continued*)

IV. Sound Financial Management. Develop and maintain effective financial accounting and reporting systems that facilitate effective planning, decision making, and accountability. The objectives are to:

- Be financially self-sufficient.
- Encourage financial responsibility by providing timely, accurate statements, emphasizing the management budget process and requiring managers to be financially accountable.
- Maintain an effective system of internal controls.
- Control labor costs through efficient use of employee time and control the costs of goods with purchasing, menuing, forecasting, and precosting policies and procedures.
- Protect the department against fluctuation in meat costs through hedging in the commodities market.
- Evaluate and budget effectively for future facilities and equipment replacement needs.
- Conduct thorough cost-benefit analyses of potential programs and products.
- Cut costs with a comprehensive energy conservation program.
- Use resources in a reasonable manner.
- Evaluate short-term possibilities with long-range perspective.

V. Contribution to the University Mission. Dining's program must contribute to the educational, economic, and community service goals of the University. The objectives are to:

- Support the educational goals of the University through staff teaching and lecturing.
- Provide educational opportunities for the students.
- Use the diverse dining facilities as laboratories for student research and job training.
- Contribute professional time in support of the community.
- Encourage staff participation in University committees and projects.

VI. Industry Leadership. Maintain Dining's position as a leader through continual educational and professional contributions to the food service industry. The objectives are to:

- Develop active and creative food service leaders.
- Participate in professional organizations and committees.
- Communicate our ideas and problem-solving techniques to others in the industry.

Erica then asked her partners what their thoughts were on the structure of All-American Dining and what effect it had at the unit level. Roger suggested that from the information that Erica had gathered, the organization seemed highly centralized. However, workers at the unit level are interested in making their own decisions. He added that the structure of the organization could be contributing to the problems that Drew perceived with productivity and morale.

Lynn, looking over the mission and goal statements that Erica had collected, commented, "All-American professes to be decentralized. Also, Drew believes he is a participatory manager. It seems as if this organization doesn't play by its own rules. I haven't seen any indication of participation, let alone adequate communication between management and line employees."

The consultants continued to talk for a while about the tension they had noticed at the unit. Since Drew was leaving, they wondered if their presence at the unit would have any affect and if the feedback session would really serve its purpose. The consultants decided they would spend several hours the following morning reviewing the information they had gathered. In order to facilitate their meeting, they quickly constructed a partial list of the individuals they had encountered during their observations. This list included characteristics the consultants believed might be important to their analysis (Figure 7).

FIGURE 7

All-American Dining and Peppercorn Dining Personnel Chart (partial)

Name	Job Title	Education	Seniority	Age	Full-time	Part-time Student	Management
Peppercorn							
Drew	Manager	A.S.-Restaurant	8 yrs.	37			X
Bob	Day chef		28 yrs.	48	X		
Robert	Day cook	Navy cook	11 yrs.	44	X		
Doug	Night chef	Navy cook	10 yrs.	36	X		
Chris	Night cook		3 yrs.	31	X		
Carrie	Server		10 yrs.	28	X		
Larry	Supervisor	A.S.-Mgmt.	1 mo.	32			X
John	Receiving		11 yrs.	35	X		
Bonnie	Cashier		2 yrs.	28	X		
Molly	Coordinator	Senior-A&S	4 yrs.	21		X	
Shaun	H.R. manager	Senior-E.E.	4 yrs.	21		X	
Sarah	Supervisor	Senior-Gov't.	4 yrs.	21		X	
All-American Dining							
Nancy	Director	A.S.-Restaurant	12 yrs.	41			X
Stan	Asst. director	B.S.-Hotel	9 yrs.	32			X
Larry	Supervisor	A.S.-Mgmt.	6 yrs.	32			X
Eric	Vending manager	B.A.-English	8 yrs.	34			X

As the consultants sat at the table, several of the employees came over to speak with them. The workers seemed relaxed and joked with the consultants. Doug commented he was working on putting his résumé together, and Chris told the partners about some new recipes he was developing. The pantry workers and dish room workers made small talk until the consultants said they had to depart. Roger, Lynn, and Erica thanked the workers for being so cooperative and said they hoped to see them sometime soon.

Questions

1. How effective was the OD consultants' data gathering? The content of the data? The process of how the data were collected?
2. What concepts or models might help you analyze the data? What conclusions would you draw from the analysis?
3. How should the feedback session be designed?

Selected Cases

DIAGNOSIS AND FEEDBACK AT ADHIKAR*

Adhikar[†] is a human rights-based, non-governmental organization (NGO). Headquartered in Jharkhand, India, it was founded in 1985 to empower society's poor and marginalized populations. It has worked from within socially marginalized communities to organize against the unjust distribution of wealth, resources, or power. Rajan Mishra founded the organization and demonstrated the importance of self-determination by organizing people into unions and other collectives. The organization has grown from a handful of people inspired by Mishra's vision during its early days to over 200 employees.

Adhikar's scope of work and involvement are outlined in Figure 1. Under the umbrella of the Adivasi Sangathan unit, Adhikar organizes regional laborers into unions. Adhikar also works in the area of budgetary analysis and expenditure monitoring of the state government through its financial education unit called Arthik Siksha. In addition, Adhikar administers a scholarship program that seeks to fund and train local level leaders and an emergency response program that delivers relief services in times of natural disasters.

INITIATING A CHANGE PROCESS—ENTRY AND CONTRACTING

The Adhikar engagement began with contact between Ms. Pia Mishra, an Adhikar regional coordinator and an OD practitioner with whom she had worked previously, to discuss the possibility of an intervention. The organization had grown substantially, and its founder had recently joined the central government, necessitating his withdrawal from day-to-day management. A second meeting was arranged to explain the nature of the intended engagement and seek formal permission to enter the organization, gather information, and report back on the analysis and recommendations for action.

Together, Pia and the OD practitioners agreed to one- to two-hour interviews with each coordinator concerning their views of the organization, its culture, and any concerns or suggestions. All the respondents were to be assured of the confidentiality of their responses. In addition, the OD practitioner would visit a field location in Ghatsila to interact with the workers and interview the regional coordinator, Mr. Dubey. During this visit, she would sit in on one of the regional meetings and interview the field workers in small groups of four or five. This was done to understand the organization from the view of the fieldworkers and gain insight into its issues through their lens.

Finally, the OD practitioner would make systematic observations of nonverbal behaviors, patterns of interaction, and descriptions of the relationships among members during interviews, focus groups, and the meetings she attended. This would provide indications of the organization's climate.

Following the data collection, a session would be held with all the coordinators to present the findings. This would serve as both a mirroring (feedback) activity as well as a forum for initiating dialogue and communication across the various units and members of the organization.

Prior to the interviews, the OD practitioner familiarized herself with Adhikar and its activities through a study of various reports and publications, including annual reports, budget analysis reports of Arthik Siksha, newspaper clippings, and other documents relating to the organization. The OD practitioner then met each of the coordinators of Adhikar, starting with Pia, who served as the point of contact throughout. Most of the issues and concerns described below surfaced through these sessions. She observed that while most coordinators opened up freely to discuss their concerns, others, like Ms. Devi (the Chaibasa Regional Coordinator), were less open and did

*This case was abridged and adapted from N. Nair and N. Vohra, "The case of OD in an NGO in India," *Journal of Management Development*, 30 (2011): 148–59.

[†]The names of the organization, its location, and the various individuals have been disguised to maintain confidentiality.

FIGURE 1

Adhikar's Scope of Work

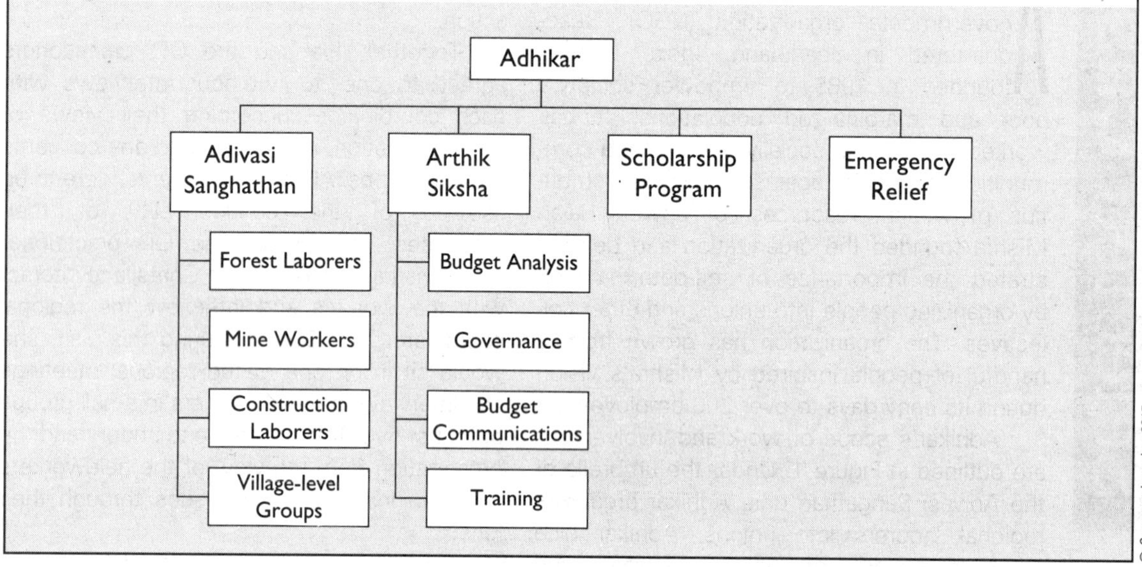

not share much about their views on Adhikar and its functioning.

Most coordinators had been with the organization since its inception. All of them echoed a strong sense of organizational identification and commitment. There was high regard for the founder, Mr. Mishra. However, Pia has had to prove herself in the organization, although she is professionally qualified and has been actively working in the field. Interestingly, during meetings with Pia, she never mentioned that she was the daughter of the founder. The OD practitioner came to know this only during the course of her later interviews.

DIAGNOSTIC DATA

The data from the interviews were categorized using Weisbord's six-box model (Figure 2) and are described below.

Issues Related to Purpose

There was considerable agreement on the organization's objective: facilitating social change through rights-based mobilization and advocacy. However, some coordinators believed that the organization needed to work more towards the *capacity building development* of the tribal/regional unions and not just their formation. The vision and future direction of Adhikar as either rights-based or developmental or a combination of both did not have a consensus among all the coordinators. The view posed by some was that it was time for Adhikar to move into developmental work, given that much of the rights-based work had been successful and the future lay in the area of capacity building.

Issues Related to Structure

There appeared to be a lack of clarity regarding Adhikar's structure. As the organization had grown, its structure had evolved. Adhikar was currently structured along both geographic and program dimensions (Figure 3). The various unions and programs were managed by different coordinators that all reported directly to the Managing Trustee, Mr. Mishra. In addition, location coordinators in Chaibasa, Ghatsila, and Saraikela worked to see that the programs were implemented locally and also reported to the Managing Trustee.

The structural confusion existed primarily because of considerable overlap in reporting relationships and responsibilities between programs and regions. Interviewees cited instances when this caused conflict regarding reporting relationships or precedence of command.

FIGURE 2

Weisbord's Six-Box Model

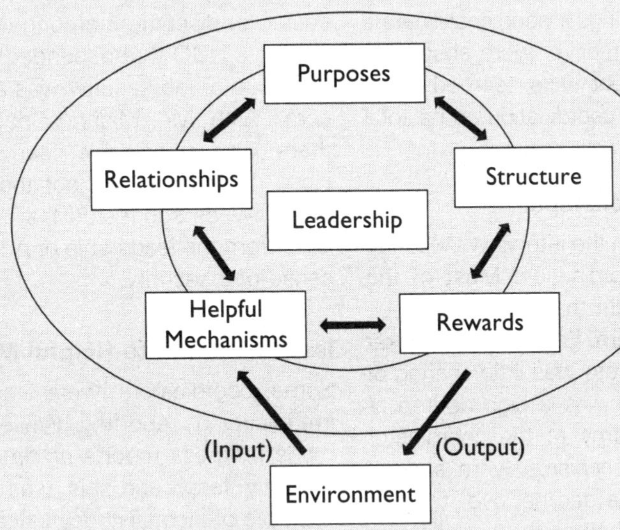

FIGURE 3

Adhikar Reporting Structure

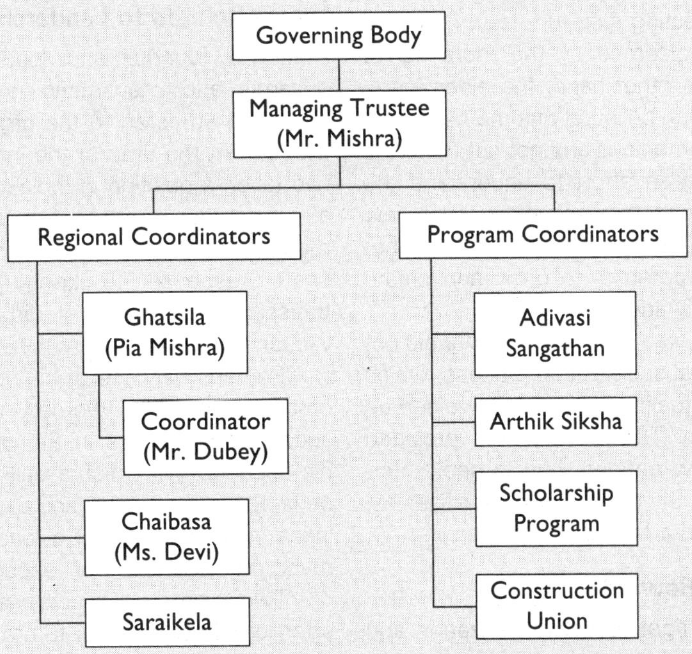

Coordinators had considerable autonomy. However, some felt that the sense of responsibility and accountability that comes with empowerment was lacking in Adhikar. Various coordinating mechanisms, such as periodic meetings among coordinators to make decentralization effective, were absent. In such a scenario, the different units seemed to be operating in silos with little coordination and a total absence of centralization at any level.

Issues Related to Relationships

The most common theme in the interviews was the concern over a lack of coordination. Most of the program coordinators thought that there should be more integration among them. Each unit of Adhikar was performing well, but there was little sharing of information. Although there was a high degree of decentralization and autonomy at the coordinator level, the coordinating mechanisms were absent. There had been a noticeable decline, over time, in the number of meetings when all the coordinators met, and many cited this as a reason for the disconnect they felt with Adhikar as a whole.

In talking with old versus new coordinators, the data supported the conclusion that there was little trust between the two groups. The new coordinators felt their professional growth and program initiatives were stymied by the old guard who appeared to be protecting their turf. New coordinators did not feel welcomed by the more senior coordinators. On the other hand, the older members in the organization believed that the new coordinators were over-ambitious and got right into the field without making an effort to understand the organization. This concern was voiced by a few but not all coordinators, but the OD practitioner believed it had the potential to grow and create conflict if not properly addressed.

A related theme was that new entrants did not go through any formal socialization process, which also manifested in a feeling of not being welcomed into the organization. The interviewees provided examples where new entrants had to seek information and figure things out for themselves, which further created a feeling of isolation.

Issues Related to Rewards

Adhikar began as a rights-based organization and most of the older employees chose to work there because of their dedication to the original cause. The newer employees (some better qualified professionally) were getting paid higher wages, which was perceived to be discriminatory and was a source of discontent among the older members.

As a NGO that depended on external funding, the issue of job security was also a matter of concern. With Mr. Mishra's declining involvement, there was a palpable fear that Adhikar might close its doors in the not too distant future. The interviewees suggested that some form of assurance from the leadership of Adhikar might ease the sense of insecurity.

Issues Related to Helpful Mechanisms

Some coordinators were concerned about the irregularity of reporting. While some coordinators made progress reports on time, others were consistently tardy and this was pointed out as an example of inconsistency in leadership and authority. Most coordinators in the past had reported verbally on a regular basis to Mr. Mishra, who was able to fill in gaps of information whenever required for other coordinators. Thus, the formal system of submitting and reading others' reports had never been emphasized.

Issues Related to Leadership

Adhikar's founder and leader was considered dynamic and charismatic—a number of people had been attracted to the organization by his personality. At the time of the interviews, Mr. Mishra had taken a position in India's central government and was moving away from day-to-day management. This behavior was interpreted as an appropriate response to keep political alignments transparent. However, it did create a leadership vacuum.

Perhaps because of his absence, many in the organization were worried about a dearth of second-level leaders in the organization. Even in his absence, Mr. Mishra still appeared to be the de facto leader. The organization seemed to be facing a crisis in terms of a leader who could command the same level of respect and following.

Two women, Ms. Devi and Pia, were most often cited as potential future leaders of Adhikar. The Chaibasa coordinator, Ms. Devi, had been with the organization since its founding and was supported by the people in her region. In the eyes of some others, however, Ms. Devi was a shadow of Mr. Mishra and a surrogate leader for Pia. Ms. Devi was viewed consistently as a good worker, but lacked the vision needed to lead a highly motivated team. Ms. Devi had not been very forthcoming in the interview.

In the absence of her father, Pia appeared to be the chief decision maker. She had been with the organization for five years as the Program Director of Ghatsila, and operated from the headquarters while Ms. Devi preferred to work from her Chaibasa location.

Both women, independently, echoed reservations as potential next leaders and mentioned their gender as one of the reasons. They felt that the other male coordinators and the community they served might not be ready for a female leader. In discussions with most of the other coordinators, however, the OD practitioner got the sense that they were open to having a woman leader. Some of the coordination issues were expected to be addressed if a new leader was appointed.

Questions

1. Based on the data provided in the case, what's your *analysis* of the situation at Adhikar? Is the organization in trouble? If so, how big is the problem? Is the organization "doing fine?" That is, are all the data presented just symptoms of an organization that is young and growing?
2. Design the feedback meeting. What's the purpose of the meeting, what's the agenda, how will you present the data?
3. What activities do you believe the Adhikar organization should take? What problems do you think these actions would solve?

MANAGING CHANGE: ACTION PLANNING FOR THE VÉLO V PROJECT IN LYON, FRANCE

The city of Lyon is located in the central part of France, about two hours south of Paris via TGV. It has a long and rich history as the capital of Gaul in the Roman Empire, a worldwide center of silk production, and a stronghold of the French resistance during World War II. Today, Lyon is the third largest city in France, has a thriving high tech and pharmaceutical industry, and is considered the gastronomical capital of a country known for its cuisine and wine. Unfortunately, with size and industry came pollution, overcrowding, and traffic jams. In the mid-1990s, only 18% of its citizens had easy access to public transportation versus 30% in other towns of equivalent size.

By 2000, Lyon's city government had constructed an above-ground light rail system to complement the existing underground metro and bus network in an effort to extend public transportation to more people. However, the outdoor station's stops needed shelters to protect waiting passengers from the wind, rain, and snow. In an innovative program, the marketing and advertising firm, JCDecaux, in cooperation with Lyon's development office, created "street furniture" to house the benches, ticket vending machines, route maps, and time tables. JCDecaux constructed and maintained the sites in exchange for the revenue from advertisements placed on the shelters. The program was a win–win for both organizations.

The success of the cooperative tram and bus shelter project, and the city's continued interest in easing pollution and traffic jams in the commercial center of the city, led them to seek out additional change. They asked JCDecaux for input. JCDecaux had been testing the idea of a self-service bicycle program in Vienna, Austria and Córdobo and Gijon, Spain and they proposed adopting and implementing a "bike exchange" network in and around Lyon in mid-2002. For Lyon and its neighboring city of Villeurbanne, it was a risky and large-scale proposal.

The vision—common now in many European cities, but completely novel at the time—was that commuters and pedestrians could pick up a bicycle at installations around the city—near metro stops, businesses, or large public venues—and use it to shop, go to work, or simply get from one part of town to the other more conveniently than a car or the bus, metro, or light-rail system. The original idea was that the bike could be used for free for less than an hour and at very low prices if used for longer periods. (To get a picture of the system and its different parts today, go to www.velov.grandlyon.com.) "It is our intent to turn bicycles into a mode of daily travel for workers in the city," said one government official.

An initial budget of €2 million per year was estimated to invest in bikes, registration systems, installations, and support operations until about 2007. To support the project, the city also envisioned construction or remodeling of several parking garages to encourage people to park their cars on the outskirts of town and then pick up a bike to finish the commute. Two parking garages in the downtown area had already begun offering free bicycles for those who parked their vehicle there.

The project—named Vélo V—was presented by the city's mayor before the second annual "day without a car" festival. Vélo V would be managed by JCDecaux. They would own and maintain the bikes and finance operations through advertising receipts. The head of the city's development function suggested that it was a bold attempt to "effect a radical change in the philosophy" of the urban community. At the time, less than 3% of the people in Lyon used a bicycle, against 10% in Strasbourg and other cities. The proposal was supported by *Les Verts,* France's Green political party, but the president of the local nongovernmental transportation union was upset that there had been little dialogue with various concerned organizations.

The goal was to launch a 24 hours/day operation in May 2005 with 1,200 bicycles in 120 stations. According to a JCDecaux regional manager, they expected 2,000 bikes in 180 stations by October and projected 3,000 bikes in 2006 and 4,000 bikes in 2007.

Questions

1. Assume you are a project manager at JCDecaux and have been assigned to work with the City of Lyon to implement this physical, organizational, and social change. What are the practical and philosophical implications of this work?
2. Using the tools, methods, and processes described in Chapter 8, construct a comprehensive "action plan" for this project. Where would you start? Who are the key stakeholders and how will you manage them? What are the practical categories of activities that need to be addressed? What are the sequences of change that have to happen? What do you see as the key activities and initiatives?

PART 3

HUMAN PROCESS INTERVENTIONS

10 Interpersonal and Group Process Approaches

11 Organization Process Approaches

SELECTED CASES

Lincoln Hospital: Third-Party Intervention

Large Group Interventions at Airbus' ICT Organization

10

Interpersonal and Group Process Approaches

learning objectives

- Understand the diagnostic issues associated with interpersonal relations and group dynamics interventions.
- Illustrate the principles of the process consultation intervention.
- Describe the process of third-party conflict resolution.
- Discuss and evaluate the core organization development (OD) intervention of team building.

This chapter discusses change programs related to interpersonal relations and group dynamics. They are among the earliest interventions devised in OD, they remain very popular, and they have been adapted for use in a variety of worldwide and cross-cultural settings. Interpersonal and group process approaches are aimed at helping group members assess their interactions and devise more effective ways of working. These change programs represent a basic skill requirement for an OD practitioner.

Interpersonal and group process approaches, including process consultation, third-party interventions, and team building, are among the most enduring OD interventions. Process consultation helps group members understand, diagnose, and improve their behaviors. Through process consultation, the group should become better able to use its own resources to identify and solve the interpersonal problems that often block work-related problem solving. Third-party interventions focus directly on dysfunctional interpersonal conflict. This approach is used only in special circumstances and only when both parties are willing to engage in the process of direct confrontation. Team building is aimed both at helping a team perform its tasks better and at satisfying individual needs. Through team-building activities, group goals and norms become clearer. In addition, team members become better able to confront difficulties and problems and to understand the roles of individuals within the team. Among the specialized team-building approaches presented are interventions with ongoing teams and temporary teams such as project teams and task forces.

As the economy has globalized and as organizations in other countries have developed, OD practitioners are applying these fundamental OD interventions more and more. Like other social innovations, however, process consultation, third-party interventions, and team building must be adapted to fit with local cultural values. Traditional OD values, rooted in North American and European cultures, favor openness, directness, and participation. Other country and organization cultures may not favor these same values, requiring adjustments in these interpersonal and group process interventions. For example, third-party interventions are less likely in Asia given the "saving face" norms prevalent in that region. Similarly, team-building processes must account for norms of uncertainty, avoidance, and deference to authority during problem-solving activities or interventions intended to alter group processes.

10-1 Diagnostic Issues in Interpersonal and Group Process Interventions

Chapter 5 introduced the diagnostic issues associated with OD interventions. With respect to interpersonal and group process issues, we draw mostly from the concepts involved in group-level diagnosis. The primary inputs to understanding group effectiveness are the organization's design—its strategy, structure, and culture. For example, if the organization is pursuing an aggressive growth strategy with a functional structure, moderate-to-high levels of conflict may be quite acceptable. As described in Chapter 12, the high levels of expertise that are a strength of functional structures also produce a tendency for conflict. The OD practitioner must diagnose whether the aggressive objectives are exacerbating that tendency. Client concerns over the levels of conflict and requests for conflict resolution interventions may be inappropriate. The organization's design may be a more important driver of conflict than individual skill levels or group functioning problems.

The primary design components of group effectiveness are goal clarity, task structure, composition, group functioning, and performance norms. Each of these design components must be considered in interpersonal and group process interventions. For example, if a group's goals are not clear, improving their decision-making processes may only allow them to be more effective at solving the wrong problems.

In general, however, individual and group process interventions address the task structures, group functioning, and performance norm elements of the model, and their current characteristics must be diagnosed. Such social processes directly and indirectly affect how work is accomplished. When group process promotes effective interactions, groups are likely to perform tasks successfully.[1] Group process includes:

- **Communications.** One area of interest in all of these interventions is the nature and style of communication, or the process of transmitting and receiving thoughts, facts, and feelings. Communication can be overt—who talks to whom, about what, for how long, and how often. It can include body language, including facial expressions, fidgeting, posture, and hand gestures.[2] Communication can also be covert, as when a manager says, "I'm not embarrassed" as his or her face turns scarlet. Covert communication is "hidden" and the process consultant often seeks to find the best way to make the message more explicit.
- **The functional roles of group members.** The OD practitioner must be keenly aware of the different roles individual members take on in a group. Both upon entering and while remaining in a group, individuals must address and understand the self-identity, influence, and power issues that will satisfy personal needs while working to accomplish group goals. In addition, group members must take on roles that enhance: (a) task-related activities, such as giving and seeking information, elaborating work processes, and coordinating and evaluating activities; and (b) group-maintenance actions, directed toward holding the group together as a cohesive team, including encouraging, harmonizing, compromising, setting standards, and observing. Many ineffective groups perform little group maintenance, and this is a primary reason for bringing in an OD consultant.

- **Group problem solving and decision making.** To be effective, a group must be able to identify problems, examine alternatives, and make decisions. For example, one way of making decisions is to ignore a suggestion, as when one person makes a suggestion and someone else offers another before the first has been discussed. A second method is to give decision-making power to the person in authority. Sometimes decisions are made by minority rule—the leader arrives at a decision and turns for agreement to several people who will comply. Frequently, silence is regarded as consent. Decisions can also be made by majority rule, consensus, or unanimous consent. The OD consultant can help the group understand how it makes decisions and the consequences of each decision process, as well as help diagnose which type of decision process may be the most effective in a given situation. Decision by unanimous consent or consensus, for example, may be ideal in some circumstances but too time-consuming or costly in other situations.
- **Group norms.** Especially if a group of people works together over a period of time, it develops group norms or standards of behavior about what is good or bad, allowed or forbidden, right or wrong. The OD consultant can be very helpful in assisting the group to understand and articulate its own norms and to determine whether those norms are helpful or dysfunctional. By understanding its norms and recognizing which ones are helpful, the group can grow and deal realistically with its environment, make optimum use of its own resources, and learn from its own experiences.[3]
- **The use of leadership and authority.** An OD practitioner needs to understand processes of leadership and how different leadership styles can help or hinder a group's functioning. In addition, the consultant can help the leader adjust his or her style to fit the situation.

Each interpersonal and group process intervention includes diagnosis as an essential ingredient and is guided by the client's objectives and understanding of these processes.

10-2 Process Consultation

Process consultation (PC) is a general framework for carrying out helping relationships.[4] Schein defines process consultation as "the creation of a relationship that permits the client to perceive, understand, and act on the process events that occur in [his or her] internal and external environment in order to improve the situation as defined by the client."[5] The process consultant does not offer expert help in the form of solutions to problems, as in the doctor–patient model. Rather, the process consultant works to help managers, employees, and groups assess and improve *human processes*, such as communication, interpersonal relations, decision making, and task performance. Schein argues that effective consultants and managers should be good helpers, aiding others in getting things done and in achieving the goals they have set.[6] Thus, PC is as much a philosophy as a set of techniques aimed at performing this helping relationship. The philosophy ensures that those who are receiving the help own their problems, gain the skills and expertise to diagnose them, and solve them themselves. PC is an approach to helping people and groups help themselves.

As a philosophy of helping relationships, Schein proposes ten principles to guide the process consultant's actions.[7]

- **Always try to be helpful.** Process consultants must be mindful of their intentions, and each interaction must be oriented toward being helpful.

- **Always stay in touch with the current reality.** Each interaction should produce diagnostic information about the current situation. It includes data about the client's opinions, beliefs, and emotions; the system's current functioning; and the practitioner's reactions, thoughts, and feelings.
- **Access your ignorance.** An important source of information about current reality is the practitioner's understanding of what is known, what is assumed, and what is not known. Process consultants must use themselves as instruments of change.
- **Everything you do is an intervention.** Any interaction in a consultative relationship generates information as well as consequences. Simply conducting preliminary interviews with group members, for example, can raise members' awareness of a situation and help them see it in a new light.
- **The client owns the problem and the solution.** This is a key principle in all OD practice. Practitioners help clients solve their own problems and learn to manage future change.
- **Go with the flow.** When process consultants access their own ignorance, they often realize that there is much about the client system and its culture that they do not know. Thus, practitioners must work to understand the client's motivations and perceptions.
- **Timing is crucial.** Observations, comments, questions, and other interventions intended to be helpful may work in some circumstances and fail in others. Process consultants must be vigilant to occasions when the client is open (or not open) to suggestions.
- **Be constructively opportunistic with confrontive interventions.** Although process consultants must be willing to go with the flow, they also must be willing to take appropriate risks. From time to time and in their best judgment, practitioners must learn to take advantage of "teachable moments." A well-crafted process observation or piece of feedback can provide a group or individual with great insight into their behavior.
- **Everything is information; errors will always occur and are the prime source for learning.** Process consultants never can know fully the client's reality and invariably will make mistakes. The consequences of these mistakes, the unexpected and surprising reactions, are important data that must be used in the ongoing development of the relationship.
- **When in doubt, share the problem.** The default intervention in a helping relationship is to model openness by sharing the dilemma of what to do next.

10-2a Basic Process Interventions

For each of the interpersonal and group processes described above, a variety of interventions may be used. In broad terms, these are aimed at making individuals and groups more effective.[8]

Individual Interventions These interventions are designed primarily to help people be more effective in their communication with others. For example, the process consultant can provide feedback to one or more individuals about their overt behaviors during meetings. At the covert or hidden level of communication, feedback can be more personal and is aimed at increasing the individual's awareness of how their behavior affects others. A useful model for this process has been developed by Luft in what is called the *Johari Window*.[9] Figure 10.1, a diagram of the Johari Window, shows that some personal issues are perceived by both the individual and others. This is the "open" window. In the

FIGURE 10.1

The Johari Window

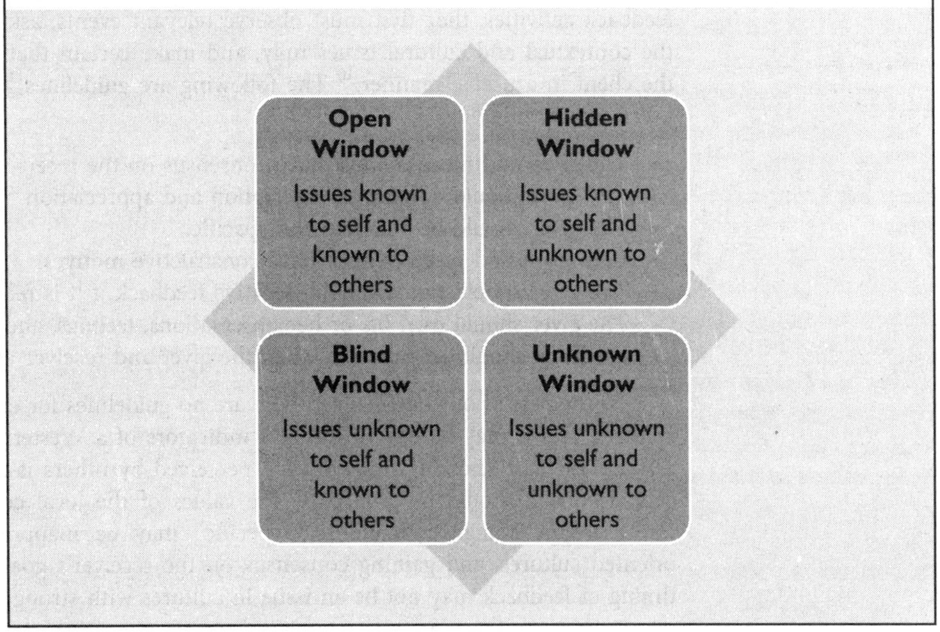

SOURCE: Adapted from "The Johari Window," *Human Relations Training News* 5 (1961): 6–7.

"hidden" window, people are aware of their behavior, motives, and issues, but they conceal them from others. People with certain feelings about themselves or others in the work group may not share with others unless they feel safe and protected; by not revealing reactions they feel might be hurtful or impolite, they lessen the degree of communication.

The "blind" window comprises personal issues that are unknown to the individual but that are communicated clearly to others. For example, one manager who made frequent business trips invariably told his staff to function as a team and to make decisions in his absence. The staff, however, consistently refused to do this because it was clear to them, and to the process consultant, that the manager was really saying, "Go ahead as a team and make decisions in my absence, but be absolutely certain they are the exact decisions I would make if I were here." Only after the manager participated in several meetings in which he received feedback was he able to understand that he was sending a double message. Thereafter, he tried both to accept decisions made by others and to use management by objectives (described in Chapter 12) with his staff and with individual managers. Finally, the "unknown" window represents those personal aspects that are unknown to either the individual or others. Because such areas are outside the realm of the process consultant and the group, focus is typically on the other three cells.

The individual interventions described in practice encourage people to be more open with others and to disclose their views, opinions, concerns, and emotions, thus reducing the size of the hidden window. Further, the consultant can help individuals give feedback to others, thus reducing the size of the blind window. Reducing the size of these two windows helps improve the communication process by enlarging the open window, the "self" that is open to both the individual and others. This is a very North American and

European notion and using the Johari window in this way may not be appropriate in different cultural and cross-cultural settings.

Before OD practitioners give individual feedback or encourage others to engage in feedback activities, they first must observe relevant events, ask questions to understand the contextual and cultural issues fully, and make certain that the feedback is given to the client in a usable manner.[10] The following are guidelines[11] for effective feedback in a Western setting:

- The giver and receiver must have consensus on the receiver's goals.
- The giver should emphasize description and appreciation.
- The giver should be concrete and specific.
- Both giver and receiver must have constructive motives.
- The giver should not withhold negative feedback if it is relevant.
- The giver should own his or her observations, feelings, and judgments.
- Feedback should be timed to when the giver and receiver are ready.

To the best of our knowledge, there are no guidelines for effective feedback in other cultures, and it may be one of the best indicators of a Western bias in OD. Under the assumption that knowing how you are perceived by others is a generally positive concept, feedback should be guided by the values of the local country and organization. For example, being "concrete and specific" may be inappropriate for relationship-oriented cultures, and gaining consensus on the receiver's goals or worrying about the timing of feedback may not be an issue in cultures with strong authoritarian values.

Group Interventions These interventions are aimed at the process, content, or structure of the group. *Process interventions* sensitize the group to its own internal processes and generate interest in analyzing them. Interventions include comments, questions, or observations about relationships between and among group members; problem solving and decision making; and the identity and purpose of the group. For example, process consultants can help by suggesting that some part of each meeting be reserved for examining how these decisions are made and periodically assessing the feelings of the group's members. As Schein points out, however, the basic purpose of the process consultant is not to take on the role of expert but to help the group share in its own diagnosis and do a better job in learning to diagnose its own processes: "It is important that the process consultant encourage the group not only to allocate time for diagnosis but to take the lead itself in trying to articulate and understand its own processes."[12] This sound advice helps to make process consultation relevant in different cultural contexts.

Content interventions help the group determine what it works on. They include comments, questions, or observations about group membership; agenda setting, review, and testing procedures; interpersonal issues; and conceptual inputs on task-related topics.

Finally, *structural interventions* help the group examine the stable and recurring methods it uses to accomplish tasks and deal with external issues. They include comments, questions, or observations about inputs, resources, and customers; methods for determining goals, developing strategies, accomplishing work, assigning responsibility, monitoring progress, and addressing problems; and relationships to authority, formal rules, and levels of intimacy.

Application 10.1 presents an example of process consultation at Christian Caring Homes. The focus of the application is the relationship between two senior executives during a succession process but also involves relationships with the organization's board and top-management team.[13]

application 10.1

PROCESS CONSULTATION AT CHRISTIAN CARING HOMES, INC.

Christian Caring Homes, Inc. (CCH or "The Homes") is among the largest multilocation, nonprofit senior care providers. The organization comprises four facilities spread across two states with a strong community reputation dating back 40 years. After 35 years at the helm, the CEO, Winston, decided to retire at age 62. The CCH Board decided that before conducting an external search for Winston's successor, they would explore the qualifications of three internal candidates. The Board chose CCH's young CFO, Paul, as Winston's successor. Paul had several years' experience as an external auditor and three years within the organization. The Board announced that Winston was "CEO and President" and Paul would be "CEO and President-Elect."

The Board wanted to ensure that Paul had the proper support to make the transition and that Winston's well-earned value and respect would be preserved and leveraged. As a result, the Board created a three-member "Transition Steering Committee" consisting of the Board president and two long time board members with experience in management and recruiting. The Committee suggested that the two leaders might benefit from a consultant's advice over the agreed-upon one-year transition period.

The Steering Committee located and vetted a semi-retired, locally based OD consultant, Simon. They introduced him to the leaders for consideration.

In the "get-acquainted" meeting of the steering committee and the two leaders, Simon noted that Winston and Paul appeared congenial. They approved of Simon's experience and his history of commitments to the region and social service organizations. Simon asked the two leaders what was rewarding about their jobs and what Winston valued about his contribution to the Homes. Winston responded with pride about past accomplishments and was supported by his designated successor and the committee. He then took the lead in describing the ongoing challenges that would coincide with the transition.

After the meeting, each leader emailed Simon expressing thanks for his attendance and copied the other. Over the next month, communication between Simon, Paul, and Winston consisted of three exploratory email exchanges and two conference calls (always with both leaders) to address the question: How might Simon be of help?

The two leaders then suggested that Simon make a proposal. They wanted their senior leadership team (SLT) to review any possible working arrangement. Simon wrote a short proposal for a four-month "transition process consultation" to explore and advance the handoff between Winston and Paul and the transition of their roles, responsibilities, and relationships with the board and the SLT. At the end of that time, the two leaders could assess the value from the consultation. Simon further recommended a retainer arrangement, obviating the concern for open-ended consultant expense.

The SLT discussed the proposal at their next monthly meeting. Winston and Paul together called Simon to report that the SLT had agreed they could proceed with the engagement.

Simon reflected on the work to date. It had taken more than two months to agree to work together. He felt impatient with what appeared to be extreme caution on the part of the top leadership of CCH. He also noted that the two leaders were never apart. They always appeared together at SLT meetings, on calls, or in emails. However, the process seemed interesting and at this point, he "went with the flow," slow as it was.

Simon attended the next two monthly day-long SLT meetings. He did not participate except when asked for his view. Invariably, he responded with a group process observation that tended to relate to one of three themes that emerged during the meetings:

1. The operations leaders formed subgroups based on the geography where their facilities were located.

2. Routine HR issues absorbed a big chunk of the agenda.
3. Paul often made statements intended to bring a "corporate" point of view.

Simon followed up each meeting with a one-page review of what appeared to be the key issues regarding roles, relationships, and responsibilities related to the transition. In follow-up discussions with Winston and Paul, they expressed different interests. Winston focused on individual facility issues while Paul wondered how he could get the SLT members to take a high-level view of issues facing The Homes as an organizational entity. Simon frequently commented on this difference in approach. He was aware that successfully navigating a transition would involve the whole organization, not just the two top roles, and he shared that awareness.

After two more months, there appeared to be no actions or plans regarding the transition. Simon was surprised when the Board president called him and asked if anything was being done about the "organization structure." Despite his curiosity about where the subject of organization structure had come from, Simon responded that he saw his agreement as exclusively with the two principals and that they were in the best place to communicate progress to the Board and to her. The Board president immediately agreed and was happy to respect the client/consultant boundary.

In his next conference call with Paul and Winston, Simon inquired if there "were any issues around organization structure."

The question appeared to open up a huge trove of information. As CEO, Winston had 14 direct reports and no Chief Operating Officer role. Simon was told the story of Pinkerton, the previous COO, who had attempted (with the support of an external consultant) to implement a coup through which he would replace Winston. The Board had intervened to fire the autocratic and "conniving" Pinkerton. The position had not been filled for two years. The story supported the conclusion that the CCH executives were reluctant to take strong, independent action and feared being manipulated by consultants. This story of organizational intrigue and power dynamics seemed to explain the caution and politeness that Simon had originally observed.

Simon considered three possible choices for what to do next:

1. Explore directly the lack of substantive action regarding the transition of executive responsibilities. Was the implication of the Pinkerton story that the organization did not trust consultants? Did they not trust him?
2. Explore the subject of a structural change. Did the leaders see "structure" as a solution and if so, what problem was being solved by a structural change?
3. Explore his observations that the organization had a congenial and compliant attitude and culture. Did the Pinkerton experience result in an organization style that devalued consensus and transparency and favored risk-avoidance?

Simon chose the second option with the following hypothesis: If the leaders felt a problem existed because of structure, then following that path of inquiry might reveal obstacles to redistribution of leadership responsibilities—likely necessary following Winston's departure. It might also expose doubts or distrust in the SLT executive group regarding Paul's, Winston's, and Simon's motivation. Simon concluded that because of their experience with the authoritarian Pinkerton, the SLT members did not raise issues of doubt or distrust. They appeared so tyrannized that Simon later joked that they had been "Pinkerton-ized."

Following disclosure of the painful history, and while Winston was away at conference, Paul arranged a business dinner with the SLT. He floated the possibility of creating an organization for the Homes that *would not* include a new COO. He found some support for the idea and shared it with Winston when he returned. The two leaders asked Simon for his reaction and inquired whether he could help with such a change.

Simon was quite surprised at Paul's move. Paul had openly challenged the assumption that Winston's laissez-faire style would be continued during the transition period and beyond. For his part, Winston was skeptical that "collective leadership from the SLT" would render the COO role unnecessary but accepted it as a way that Paul could "learn the ropes."

Simon's first reaction was to jump at the chance to work with structure but realized that such a move could have unknown implications for a smooth transition. Instead, he chose the opportunity to readdress and possibly advance the transition process by offering an observation and a confronting intervention.

The observation was that the transition between Winston and Paul would necessarily require changes throughout the organization. Working with the proposed structure was one way (an experiment) to anticipate and work through the changes in responsibilities that might bring clarity for the executives constituting the SLT. Simon could help them learn from their work.

The confronting intervention was to send Winston and Paul an email with an attachment entitled "The Leader's First 90 Days," and a single question: "When does Paul's first 90 days begin?"

The email generated numerous intense conversations between Paul and Winston. The concept of "When does the transition of power take place" surfaced the assumptions of the two men. Several differences in philosophy and expectations also surfaced. Winston thought the change would take place in nine months. Paul thought he should have full authority in three months! They also faced choices about what the future CCH organization would look like structurally and stylistically.

Simon saw the two as behaving kindly with each other but not managing the differences. He chose to speak individually with each to help them clarify their concerns and to get their suggestions for moving forward. Winston was not clear that the legal transition could take place so soon and had no proposal for what his role would be after the "official turnover." Paul was anxious to make some changes and did not want Winston to influence decisions he would have to live with in the long term. Meeting again with the two, Simon asked them to share their concerns and suggest ways for moving forward. They concluded they should describe their situation with the Transition Steering Committee.

Subsequently, Paul, Winston, and Simon met with the Board's Transition Steering Committee. Simon limited his role to encouraging openness on the part of the two leaders as they shared their thoughts with the committee. Led by the Board president, the committee started to shift from a neutral position to that of supporting Paul's position, the person they would be working with in determining the future of CCH.

The committee's dialogue resulted in Paul's ability to move forward with his own vision and at the same time create a role for Winston as outgoing CEO. The committee supported a decision whereby Winston would relinquish the title of "CEO and President" four months earlier than planned. He would take the title of "CEO and President-Emeritus" and serve as mentor to Paul, reporting only to him.

Simon's four-month "transition process consultation" was coming to an end. He requested a review of his engagement. As a result, Paul (in his new CEO role) asked Simon to reengage for another four months. Significantly, Paul took this decision independent of Winston or the SLT, consulting only with the Board president. Simon saw this as a vote of confidence, evidence of a new set of operating assumptions emerging, and an opportunity to support Paul as he took on his broader CEO responsibilities, including building a stronger relationship with the CCH Board and the Board president.

10-2b Results of Process Consultation

Although process consultation is an important part of organization development and has been widely practiced over the past 45 years, a number of difficulties arise in trying to measure performance improvements as a result of process consultation. One problem is that most process consultation is conducted with groups performing mental tasks (e.g., decision making); the outcomes of such tasks are difficult to evaluate. A second difficulty with measuring PC's effects occurs because in many cases process consultation is combined with other interventions in an ongoing OD program. Isolating the impact of process consultation from other interventions is challenging.

Kaplan's review of process-consultation studies underscored the problems of measuring performance effects.[14] It examined published studies in three categories: (1) reports in which process intervention is the causal variable but performance is measured inadequately or not at all, (2) reports in which performance is measured but process consultation is not isolated as the independent variable (the case in many instances), and (3) research in which process consultation is isolated as the causal variable and performance is adequately measured. The review suggests that process consultation has positive effects on participants, according to self-reports of greater personal involvement, higher mutual influence, group effectiveness, and similar variables. However, very little, if any, research clearly demonstrates that objective task effectiveness was increased. In most cases, either the field studies did not directly measure performance or the effect of process intervention was confounded with other variables.

A third problem with assessing the performance effects of process consultation is that much of the relevant research has used people's perceptions rather than hard performance measures as the index of success.[15] Although much of this research shows positive results, these findings should be interpreted carefully until further research is done using more concrete measures of performance.

10-3 Third-Party Interventions

Third-party interventions focus on conflicts arising between two or more people within the same organization. Conflict is inherent in groups and organizations and can arise from a variety of sources, including differences in personality, task orientation, goal interdependence, and perceptions among group members, as well as competition for scarce resources. Tjosvold notes that too little consensus on the definition of conflict has contributed to the perception that conflict is bad. Moreover, when it is defined as opposing interests or divergent goals, it narrows the range of potentially productive interventions. He suggests that conflict is best viewed as "incompatible activities." Such a definition opens up options for resolution, places responsibility for the conflict with the individuals involved, and allows conflict to be seen in a positive way.[16]

To emphasize that conflict is neither good nor bad per se is important.[17] Conflict can enhance motivation and innovation and lead to greater understanding of ideas and views. On the other hand, it can prevent people from working together constructively, destroying necessary task interactions among group members. Consequently, third-party interventions are used primarily in situations in which conflict significantly disrupts necessary task interactions and work relationships among members.

Third-party interventions vary considerably depending on the kind of issues underlying the conflict. Conflict can arise over substantive issues, such as work methods, pay rates, and conditions of employment, or it can emerge from interpersonal issues, such as personalities and misperceptions. When applied to substantive issues, conflict resolution interventions often involve resolving labor–management disputes through arbitration and mediation. The methods used in such substantive interventions require considerable training and expertise in law and labor relations and generally are not considered part of OD practice. For example, when union and management representatives cannot resolve a joint problem, they can call upon the Federal Mediation and Conciliation Service to help them resolve the conflict. In addition, "alternative dispute resolution" (ADR) practices increasingly are offered in lieu of more expensive and time-consuming court trials[18] and can provide a more structured process of conflict resolution in cultures where direct confrontation is inappropriate. Conflicts also may arise at the boundaries of the organization, such as between suppliers and the company, between a company and a public-policy agency, or between multiple organizations or groups.[19]

When conflict involves interpersonal issues in developed, Western organizations, however, OD has developed approaches that help control and resolve it. These third-party interventions help the parties interact with each other directly, recognize the personal choices each party is making, and facilitate their diagnosis of the conflict and its resolution. The ability to facilitate conflict resolution is a basic skill in OD and applies to all of the process interventions discussed in this chapter. Consultants, for example, frequently coach clients through a conflict or help organization members resolve interpersonal conflicts that invariably arise during process consultation and team building.

Third-party interventions cannot resolve all interpersonal conflicts in organizations, nor should they. Many times, interpersonal conflicts are not severe or disruptive enough to warrant attention. At other times, they simply may burn themselves out. Evidence also suggests that other methods may be more appropriate under certain conditions. For example, managers tend to control the process and outcomes of conflict resolution actively when they are under heavy time pressures, when the disputants are not expected to work together in the future, and when the resolution of the dispute has a broad impact on the organization.[20] Under those conditions, the third party may resolve the conflict unilaterally with little input from the conflicting parties.

10-3a An Episodic Model of Conflict

Interpersonal conflict often occurs in iterative, cyclical stages known as "episodes." An episodic model is shown in Figure 10.2. At times, issues underlying a conflict are latent and do not present any manifest problems for the parties. Then something triggers the conflict and brings it into the open. For example, reports identifying cost overruns or a dissatisfied customer can trigger a violent disagreement or frank confrontation. Because the focus is on resolving the expense or customer problem, the interpersonal conflict remains unresolved and again becomes latent. And again, something triggers the conflict, making it overt, and so the cycle continues with the next conflict episode.

FIGURE 10.2

A Cyclical Model of Interpersonal Conflict

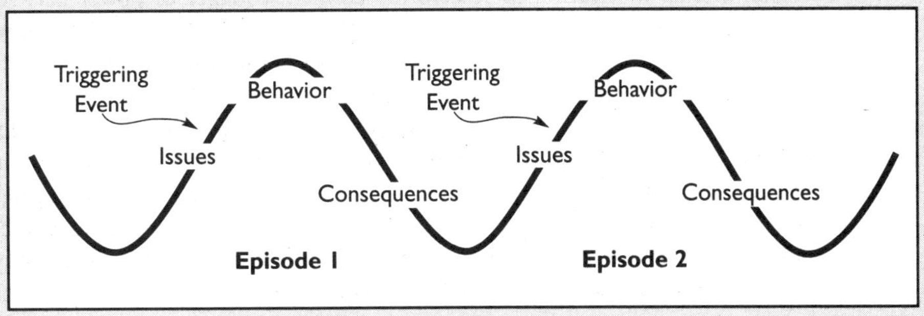

SOURCE: *Managing Conflict: Interpersonal Dialogue and Third-Party Roles* (Prentice Hall Organizational Development Series), 2nd ed. by Walton, Richard E., ISBN 0201088592. © 1987 Addison-Wesley.

Conflict has both costs and benefits to the antagonists and to those in contact with them. Unresolved conflict can proliferate and expand. An interpersonal conflict may be concealed under a cause or issue that serves to make the conflict appear more legitimate. Frequently, the overt conflict is only a symptom of a deeper problem.

The episodic model identifies four strategies for conflict resolution. The first three attempt to control the conflict and may be appropriate under a variety of organizational and cultural conditions. Only the last approach tries to change the basic issues underlying it.[21] The first strategy is to prevent the ignition of conflict by arriving at a clear understanding of the triggering factors and thereafter avoiding or blunting them when the symptoms occur. For example, if conflict between the research and production managers is always triggered by new-product introductions, then senior executives can warn them that conflict will not be tolerated during the introduction of the latest new product. However, this approach may not always be functional and may merely drive the conflict underground until it explodes. As a control strategy, however, this method may help to achieve a temporary cooling-off period.

The second control strategy is to set limits on the form of the conflict. Conflict can be constrained by informal gatherings before a formal meeting or by exploration of other options. It also can be limited by setting rules and procedures specifying the conditions under which the parties can interact. For example, a rule can be instituted that union officials can attempt to resolve grievances with management only at weekly grievance meetings.

The third control strategy is to help the parties cope differently with the consequences of the conflict. The third-party consultant may work with the people involved to devise coping techniques, such as reducing their dependence on the relationship, ventilating their feelings to friends, and developing additional sources of emotional support. These methods can reduce the costs of the conflict without resolving the underlying issues.

The fourth method is an attempt to eliminate or to resolve the basic issues causing the conflict. Although this objective seems the most direct and obvious approach, it is often the most difficult to bring about.

10-3b Facilitating the Conflict Resolution Process

Walton has identified a number of factors and tactical choices that can facilitate the use of the episodic model in resolving the underlying causes of conflict.[22] The following ingredients can help third-party consultants achieve productive dialogue between the disputants so that they examine their differences and change their perceptions and behaviors: mutual motivation to resolve the conflict; equality of power between the parties; coordinated attempts to confront the conflict; relevant phasing of the stages of identifying differences and of searching for integrative solutions; open and clear forms of communication; and productive levels of tension and stress.

Among the tactical choices identified by Walton are those having to do with diagnosis, the context of the third-party intervention, and the role of the consultant. One of the tactics in third-party intervention is the gathering of data, usually through preliminary interviewing. Group process observations can also be used. Data gathering provides some understanding of the nature and the type of conflict, the personality and conflict styles of the individuals involved, the issues and attendant pressures, and the participants' readiness to work together to resolve the conflict.

The context in which the intervention occurs is also important. Consideration of the neutrality of the meeting area, the formality of the setting, the appropriateness of the time for the meeting (that is, a meeting should not be started until a time has been agreed on to conclude or adjourn), and the careful selection of those who should attend the meeting are all elements of this context.

In addition, the third-party consultant must decide on an appropriate role to assume in resolving conflict. The specific tactic chosen will depend on the diagnosis of the situation. For example, facilitating dialogue of interpersonal issues might include initiating the agenda for the meeting, acting as a referee during the meeting, reflecting and restating the issues and the differing perceptions of the individuals involved, giving feedback and receiving comments on the feedback, helping the individuals diagnose the issues in the conflict, providing suggestions or recommendations, and helping the parties do a better job of diagnosing the underlying problem.

Third-party consultants must develop considerable skill at diagnosis, intervention, and follow-up, and be highly sensitive to their own feelings and to those of others. They must recognize that some tension and conflict are inevitable and that although there can be an optimum amount and degree of conflict, too much conflict can be dysfunctional for both the people involved and the larger organization. The third-party consultant must be sensitive to the situation and able to use a number of different intervention strategies and tactics when intervention appears to be useful. Finally, he or she must have professional expertise in third-party intervention and must be seen by the parties as neutral or unbiased regarding the issues and outcomes of the conflict resolution.

Application 10.2 describes a third-party intervention at a law firm. The OD consultant was brought in by another consultant to help rescue a struggling strategic planning process. The OD consultant initially used structural interventions to simply help the partners get work done but eventually had to utilize more interpersonal process interventions to address the personality conflicts.[23]

10-4 Team Building

Team building refers to a broad range of planned activities that help groups improve the way they accomplish tasks, help members enhance their interpersonal and problem-solving skills, and increase team performance.[24] Organizations comprise many different types of groups including permanent work groups, temporary project teams, and virtual teams. Team building is an effective approach to improving teamwork and task accomplishment in such environments. It can help problem-solving groups make maximum use of members' resources and contributions. It can help members develop a high level of motivation to implement group decisions. Team building also can help groups overcome specific problems, such as apathy and general lack of member interest; loss of productivity; increasing complaints within the group; confusion about assignments; low participation in meetings; lack of innovation and initiation; increasing complaints from those outside the group about the quality, timeliness, and effectiveness of services and products; and hostility or conflicts among members.

Team building also can facilitate other OD interventions, such as employee involvement, work design, restructuring, and strategic change. Those change programs typically are designed by management teams, implemented through various committees and work groups, and result in new teams that need to operate at a high level of effectiveness quickly. Team building can help the groups design high-quality change programs and ensure that the programs are accepted and implemented by organization members. Indeed, most technostructural, human resource management, and strategic interventions depend on some form of team building for effective implementation.

application 10.2

CONFLICT MANAGEMENT AT ROSS & SHERWIN

Ross and Sherwin (R&S) is a 40-year-old, Chicago-based law firm with 65 lawyers and one of the largest specialty intellectual property (IP) firms in the country. Since the firm's founding, a single Managing Partner has run the partnership meetings and worked with the firm's operations director to make administrative decisions about staff and lawyers. Its clear niche and consistently strong results meant that the Managing Partner could spend most of his/her time continuing their law practice. In fact, it was easy to keep your head down and "just practice law" at R&S.

Beginning in 2008, changes in the firm's strategy and pressure from clients and competitors began to challenge the easy-going style of the organization. For example, the recently added IP litigation services required new lawyers with different skill sets. In addition, clients were pressuring the firm to lower hourly rates for basic transactional work, such as trademark and patent applications, and to increase the number of litigation cases under a "contingency" arrangement. That is, R&S's fees would depend on the court's findings and significantly increase the firm's risks compared to the bill-by-the-hour arrangement that had worked for years.

Most of the transactional lawyers had reservations about the contingency work. Although the payoff could be good for the victorious inventor and the law firm who represented him, the possibility of sinking a million dollars of billable time into a case with potentially no return was terrifying to some. As a result, the firm's Managing Partner began calling for regular meetings to discuss whether to invest in contingency cases and how steeply to discount transactional work. In 2009, the firm lost two partners to competitors and partner income dipped in 2009 and 2010.

By the end of 2010, the partners had agreed on two things: they needed to think more about firm strategy and they needed a new leadership structure. The R&S partners believed that a single managing partner could no longer lead the firm because the two very different businesses, IP litigation (increasingly contingency work) and IP transactions (hourly work with significant rate pressure) required representation at the highest level. Moreover, Andrew, the Managing Partner since 2000, was eager to retire and fully endorsed the need for new leadership.

In 2011, R&S named its first-ever "Comanaging Partners," Brad and Ron. Brad is conservative in every way. He is slow to delegate and even slower to endorse the litigation group's growth through contingency work. Ron, on the other hand, is a risk taker in terms of the work he will take on, and in terms of his willingness to pass responsibilities to other lawyers early in their careers.

Brad and Ron also share certain characteristics, however. While they are effective at navigating thorny conversations with clients and adversaries, they have little patience for working through the firm's internal differences. Both of them will say what people want to hear and then go off and do things as they see fit.

The downside of this common trait showed up in their first action as Comanaging Partners. They agreed to lead the firm through a strategic planning process and hired an external consultant familiar with law firm strategy to assist. Brad believed that Ron was eager to have a discussion about expansion, including contingency litigation but believed that he was so focused on his own group's success that he might jeopardize the core business and push risk-averse lawyers into uncomfortable situations. Ron believed that Brad's primary interest was in stabilizing the firm and "protecting" the hourly work that "paid the bills," and worried that Brad saw litigation as a dispensable part of the firm.

However, instead of engaging in a thorough discussion and exchanging views about the merits of the different options, they chose to gather input from others. They argued publicly that this was the right thing to do. Privately, they weren't so much gathering data as they were avoiding one another and an uncomfortable conflict. They walked into their initial all-partners planning meeting as Comanaging Partners with different agendas and considerable distrust for one another.

Twenty minutes into the meeting, Dan, the firm's leading transactional practice partner and enemy of any planning process that was unrelated to supporting his work, began his cross-examination of the two new leaders. While Dan had some good questions about where Ron and Brad thought the planning process would lead, he quickly attached his remarks to the supremacy of his own practice, his potential new clients, and that any other investment represented a threat to him and his team. The questions carried a hostile tone and were met with defensiveness by Ron and Brad. Ron was feeling alone and needing to defend the idea of expanding contingency work, and Brad felt attacked by an influential partner in one of his first efforts at firm-wide leadership. The meeting limped along but ended with everyone feeling that nothing was accomplished and wondering how or if Ron and Brad were going to be able to effectively lead the firm.

Ron and Brad each blamed the other for not having a clearer plan and structure for the meeting. They each believed that the others' misplaced agenda created the opening for Dan to torpedo the proceedings. Again, however, rather than looking at and dealing with one another, they turned away from each other and pointed at Dan.

The strategy consultant had seen enough. She could see the conflict derailing the strategy formulation process and recommended an OD consultant with conflict resolution experience.

As the OD consultant entered the system, Ron and Brad presented their recommendation: "fix" Dan and everything would be ok. Each of them agreed that Dan was a trouble-maker and would remain a challenging presence as they tried to lead the firm. When they did finally drop the subject of Dan and compare visions for the firm, Ron would waive the banner about the importance of growth and balancing hourly work with the potential for big victories, and Brad would dig into his position that too much risk scared transactional lawyers and threatened the stability of the firm. They would quickly get frustrated, shorten the meeting, and go back to what they each did so well—practicing law.

The most detrimental aspect of the unresolved tension between them was the conversations that took place behind each other's backs. Ron would worry aloud that Brad did not see an important role for litigation going forward. He described Brad as chummy with his old friends and unwelcoming of anything that threatened his conservative view of the firm. Brad would describe litigation as Ron's pet project and motivated by their inability to develop hourly work. He told his partners that he didn't trust that Ron provided all relevant information about the cases he wanted the firm to invest in. They said they talked more about their conflict to their other partners than they did to one another.

To make the recommendation palatable for Dan, Ron and Brad proposed that the three partners work together in a leadership development process. Initially, Dan pretended to be on board with the plan. Soon thereafter, however, it was clear that Dan wanted nothing to do with coaching, leadership development, or help of any kind. Ron and Brad were left looking at each other. Realizing that the firm was, indeed, at a precarious juncture and needed strong leadership from them, the OD consultant proposed, and Ron and Brad agreed to engage in a process designed to help the two of them manage their conflict so that they could develop and implement a strategy for the firm.

The OD consultant's initial impression was that these two brilliant lawyers rarely, if ever, stopped to think about the impact of their style on others in the firm. Before they could have a constructive dialogue about working together more effectively, Ron and Brad needed some understanding of their own roles in the dysfunctional dynamic. The first step was to gather feedback and help them see how others perceived them.

Ron and Brad each went through a full day of meetings with the consultant to discuss the feedback, to articulate a vision for the firm, and to describe a collaborative relationship with the other. Over the course of the day, they were each quite articulate about what they wanted to help the firm accomplish, where they found themselves frustrated, and how each of them viewed the other.

For the first time since their appointment as managing partners, each of them drafted bullet points describing a vision for the firm. The premise of this exercise was that there might be a good amount of common ground; and, if all of the key items were laid out on the table, it might be possible to work through the various interests, see what was attainable, and what they could agree on. Each of the partners also created a set of steps that the two of them could take to develop a more trusting, coordinated relationship as Comanaging Partners.

After the one-on-one meetings, the OD consultant asked that they share with each other their visions for the firm and their own action steps to create collaborative leadership. They were genuinely surprised by the similarities on the lists. Brad, to Ron's surprise, did want to expand the firm. He had a different timeline and his view included satellite offices, but he wanted to build. Ron was pleased to see that Brad was not "hunkering down" and riding things out until his retirement. Ron, to Brad's relief, never envisioned the contingency work consuming more that 20% of the firm's billable time. This was still a bigger number than Brad would like, but it was a meaningful, reasonable limitation that Ron put forth.

Walking through these and other concrete items on their respective bullet lists, they saw that they were largely wrong in their assumptions about what the other person did or did not want to accomplish as Comanaging Partner. Similarly, walking together through their respective "better collaboration" lists, they saw that they both knew they needed more time with just the two of them together communicating (the norm had been to include the COO, third member of the Executive Committee, in all of their meetings). They realized that they both tended to posture and take exaggerated positions in front of an audience. They also agreed to be more open and quicker to raise issues and concerns with one another.

The OD consultant had follow-up calls with each of them over the next six months to follow up on commitments that they made to each other based on the two lists. They made significant progress. For example, they developed a contingency work strategy that created a portfolio of cases with different levels of investment. The portfolio would ramp up only as positive verdicts and rewards materialized. This allowed Ron to see that growth was possible depending on the success of his group, and it allowed Brad to see that there were manageable limitations on the risk. They also were successful in carving out some meeting time for just the two of them. However, they were not successful in being open with one another and speaking up when they had a concern about how they were working together or what the other person was up to.

Despite the forward progress and excellent financial results in six months since engaging in the process, both Ron and Brad remained "worn out," "exhausted," "stressed," and believed they were on thin ice as leaders and with one another. For example, Ron and Brad presided over a partnership meeting that Dan hijacked in the first 15 minutes. Dan asked pointed questions about a new contingency case. In Ron's mind, this should have been an easy distraction to dismiss. He and Brad were aligned on the plan related to the intake of contingency work and the partners had signed on. If Brad, the transactional partner of the duo, had simply and clearly told Dan that the new case was accepted pursuant to the agreed-upon system, the discussion would have ended. However, Brad said nothing and left Ron to defend (with the potential appearance of self-interest) the decision to take the case. Ron felt hung out to dry.

Despite some excellent progress together, the partnership meeting and other similar events triggered old patterns and familiar flare-ups. Feeling frustrated, Ron and Brad described the hijacked partnership meeting in their next session with the OD consultant. The consultant reminded them of the important steps that they had taken together over the previous months and that they had jointly steered the firm out of a difficult business cycle for many law firms in the country. He assured them that a "conflict-free" partnership was not possible and not even the goal. They had gotten to the point where they could remain focused on joint business goals and related tasks despite the occasional flare-ups; however, their relationship needed more resilience. They were too quick to doubt one another and to doubt themselves as an effective unit.

Any "team building" to date had been done through the work of managing the firm. Ron and Brad, both doers, related easily to the task-orientation of making lists and checking items off of the list. The consultant had remained focused on structural interventions as well. However, seeing the frustration in both of them, he believed it was time to take a chance and introduce a more explicit relationship-building component to the meetings.

The OD consultant proposed that the partners join him on a stand-up paddle-board outing on the ocean. They had not seen one another looking quite so foolish and despite a couple of mishaps getting out through the surf, they had never before shared much laughter.

The freeing, shared experience created a very different tone for the meeting that followed and the most direct discussion of trust between them. Ron talked about Brad's silence at the partners meeting and Brad talked about his feeling that Ron was less than completely forthcoming about all material facts related to contingency cases he brought into the firm. Brad's concerns were about the timing of the information and the level of detail. The comments from each of them came across as confronting, but rather than the usual defensiveness or steering the conversation to Dan or something else; they both owned up to what they could and should have done differently. The conflict resolution intervention followed a traditional OD process. It began with diagnosis, working with the energy of the client, and initially focused on structural and behavioral changes that helped the partners get work done. As trust was developed, the consultant was able to suggest other interventions that helped the two partners begin building trust at deeper levels of their relationship.

The importance of team building is well established, and its high use is expected to continue in the coming years. Management teams are encountering issues of greater complexity and uncertainty, especially in such fast-paced industries as software and hardware development, entertainment, and health and financial services. Team building can provide the kind of teamwork and problem-solving skills needed to tackle such issues. When the team represents the senior management of an organization, team building can be an important part of establishing a coherent corporate strategy, and can promote the kind of close cooperation needed to implement complex strategies and new forms of governance.[25] As manufacturing and service technologies continue to develop—for example, just-in-time inventory systems, lean manufacturing, and service quality concepts—there is increasing pressure on organizations to implement team-based work designs. Team building can assist in the development of group goals and norms that support high productivity and quality of work life.

The globalization of work and organizations implies that people from different cultures and geographic locations will increasingly interact over complex management and operational tasks using a variety of information and communication technologies. Team-building activities for these "virtual" and cross-cultural teams have increased substantially over the past several years.[26] Most team-building processes are based on assumptions of face-to-face interaction and relationships are built partially on the basis of visual cues. In virtual teams, research suggests that closeness between team members is created through proactive offers of help and support on task-related issues, and maintained through frequent, short, and task-focused communications (often technology mediated). Thus, team-building can help virtual teams to examine cross-cultural issues and their impact on decision making and problem solving, facilitate communication processes where tone and body language clues are absent, and build trust.

Finally, mergers and acquisitions, restructurings, and strategic alliances continue to proliferate. The success of these endeavors depends partly on getting members from different organizations to work together effectively. Team building can facilitate the formation of a unified team with common goals and procedures.

In the OD literature, team building is not clearly differentiated from process consultation and group facilitation. This confusion exists because most team building includes process consultation—helping the group diagnose and understand its own internal processes—and facilitation—providing structure to a group's interactions so that it can focus on an agenda and exchange information. However, process consultation is a more general approach to helping relationships than is team building. Team building focuses explicitly on helping groups perform tasks and solve problems more effectively. Process consultation, on the other hand, is concerned with establishing effective helping relationships in organizations while facilitation often represents a substitute for group process. It is seen as key to effective management and consultation and can be applied to any helping relationship, from subordinate development to interpersonal relationships to group development. Thus, team building consists of process consultation plus other, more task-oriented interventions.

Team building is applicable in a large number of situations, from starting a new team, to resolving conflicts among members, to revitalizing a complacent team. Dyer has developed a checklist for identifying whether a team-building program is needed and whether the organization is ready to start such a program (Table 10.1).[27] If the problem is a structural or technical one, an intergroup issue, an administrative mistake, or a conflict between only two people, team building would not be an appropriate change strategy.

10-4a Team-Building Activities

A team is a group of interdependent people who share a common purpose, have common work methods, and hold each other accountable.[28] The nature of that interdependence varies, creating the following types of teams: groups reporting to the same supervisor, manager, or executive; groups involving people with common organizational goals; temporary groups formed to do a specific, one-time task; groups consisting of people whose work roles are interdependent; and groups whose members have no formal links in the organization but whose collective purpose is to achieve tasks they cannot accomplish alone. Another important variable in teams is location. When team members are in close proximity, a traditional team exists; when members are geographically dispersed and their interaction is mediated by information technology, a virtual team exists.

Several factors can affect the outcomes of any specific team-building activity: the length of time allocated to the activity, the team's willingness to look at its processes, the length of time the team has been working together, the cultural backgrounds of team members, and the team's permanence. Consequently, the results of team-building activities can range from comparatively modest changes in the team's operating mechanisms (e.g., meeting more frequently or gathering agenda items from more sources) to much deeper changes (e.g., modifying team members' behavior patterns or the nature and style of the group's management, or developing greater openness and trust).

Hackman has proposed that effective teams produce outputs that satisfy external stakeholders, constantly improve their team functioning, and have members that are learning.[29] As a result, team-building interventions can be categorized according to their purpose and focus (see Table 10.2). Team-building activities can be oriented toward (1) individual behavior, (2) group behavior, or (3) the group's integration with its organizational context. They also can be classified according to whether their purpose is (1) diagnostic or (2) improvement. A particular team-building activity can overlap these categories, and, on occasion, a change in one area will have negative results in other areas. For example, a very cohesive team may increase its isolation from other groups, leading to intergroup conflict or other dysfunctional results, which in turn can have a negative impact on the total organization unless the team develops sufficient diagnostic skills to recognize and deal with such problems.

TABLE 10.1

Team-Building Checklist

I. Problem identification: To what extent is there evidence of the following problems in your work unit?

	Low Evidence		Some Evidence	High Evidence	
1. Loss of production or work-unit output	1	2	3	4	5
2. Grievances or complaints within the work unit	1	2	3	4	5
3. Conflicts or hostility between unit members	1	2	3	4	5
4. Confusion about assignments or unclear relationships between people	1	2	3	4	5
5. Lack of clear goals or low commitment to goals	1	2	3	4	5
6. Apathy or general lack of interest or involvement of unit members	1	2	3	4	5
7. Lack of innovation, risk taking, imagination, or taking initiative	1	2	3	4	5
8. Ineffective staff meetings	1	2	3	4	5
9. Problems in working with the boss	1	2	3	4	5
10. Poor communications: people afraid to speak up, not listening to each other, or not talking together	1	2	3	4	5
11. Lack of trust between boss and members or between members	1	2	3	4	5
12. Decisions are made that people do not understand or agree with	1	2	3	4	5
13. Good work is not recognized or rewarded	1	2	3	4	5
14. Lack of encouragement for working together in a better team effort	1	2	3	4	5

Scoring: Add the scores for the 14 items. If your score is between 14 and 28, there is little evidence your unit needs team building. If your score is between 29 and 42, there is some evidence but no immediate pressure, unless two or three items are very high. If your score is between 43 and 56, you should think seriously about planning the team-building program. If your score is over 56, team building should be top priority for your work unit.

II. Are you (or your manager) prepared to start a team-building program? Consider the following statements. To what extent do they apply to you or your department?

	Low		Medium	High	
1. You are comfortable in sharing organizational leadership and decision making with subordinates and prefer to work in a participative atmosphere.	1	2	3	4	5

continued

TABLE 10.1

Team-Building Checklist, (*continued*)

	Low		Medium	High	
2. You see a high degree of interdependence as necessary among functions and workers in order to achieve your goals.	1	2	3	4	5
3. The external environment is highly variable or changing rapidly, and you need the best thinking of all your staff to plan for these conditions.	1	2	3	4	5
4. You feel you need the input of your staff to plan major changes or develop new operating policies and procedures.	1	2	3	4	5
5. You feel that broad consultation among your people as a group in goals, decisions, and problems is necessary on a continuing basis.	1	2	3	4	5
6. Members of your management team are (or can become) compatible with each other and are able to create a collaborative rather than a competitive environment.	1	2	3	4	5
7. Members of your team are located close enough to meet together as needed.	1	2	3	4	5
8. You feel you need to rely on the ability and willingness of subordinates to resolve critical operating problems directly and in the best interest of the company or organization.	1	2	3	4	5
9. Formal communication channels are not sufficient for the timely exchange of essential information, views, and decisions among your team members.	1	2	3	4	5
10. Organization adaptation requires the use of such devices as project management, task forces, or ad hoc problem-solving groups to augment conventional organization structure.	1	2	3	4	5
11. You feel it is important to bring out and deal with critical, albeit sensitive, issues that exist in your team.	1	2	3	4	5
12. You are prepared to look at your own role and performance with your team.	1	2	3	4	5
13. You feel there are operating or interpersonal problems that have remained unsolved too long and need the input from all group members.	1	2	3	4	5
14. You need an opportunity to meet with your people to set goals and develop commitment to these goals.	1	2	3	4	5

Scoring: If your total score is between 50 and 70, you probably are ready to go ahead with the team-building program. If your score is between 35 and 49, you probably should talk the situation over with your team and others to see what would need to be done to get ready for team building. If your score is between 14 and 34, you probably are not prepared to start team building.

SOURCE: W. G. Dyer, *Team Building: Issues and Alternatives*, 42–46. © 1987. Reprinted by permission of the Estate of W. G. Dyer.

TABLE 10.2

Categories of Team-Building Interventions

Purpose of Intervention	Focus of Intervention	Individual Behavior	Group Behavior	Integration with Organization
	Diagnosis	Assessment instruments and interview data to understand personal style and motivation	Team surveys, interviews, and observations to understand group operations	Interviews and surveys from internal customers and other group stakeholders to understand group's role and effectiveness
	Improvement	Individual coaching and feedback 360-degree feedback Third-party conflict resolution	Group vision, mission, purpose development Role clarification and decision rights	Strategic planning and stakeholder mapping Large group intervention Intergroup conflict resolution

SOURCE: Adapted from W.G. Dyer, *Team Building: Issues and Alternatives*, 1987.

10-4b Interventions Relevant to Individual Behavior

People come into groups and organizations with varying needs for achievement, inclusion, influence, and belonging. These needs can be supported and nurtured by the team's structure and process or they can be discouraged. Diagnostic interviews and personal-style instruments can help members to better understand their motivations, preferences, or emotions in the group context. It results in one or more of the members gaining a better understanding of the way inclusion, emotions, control, and power affect problem solving and other group processes, and provide choices about their degree of involvement and commitment. Such activities provide information so that people have a clearer sense of how their needs and wants can or will be supported.

Improvement activities that address an individual's behavior in a group include coaching, 360-degree feedback, and assistance with conflict. These interventions attempt to alter the group's ongoing processes by focusing on the behaviors and attitudes of individual members. For example, one team's typical decision-making process included the leader having several agenda items for discussion. Each of the items, however, had a predetermined set of actions that she wanted the group to take. Most members were frustrated by their inability to influence the conclusions. The team-building process consisted of coaching the team leader and group members about ways to change this process. The leader received feedback about specific examples of her not-so-subtle manipulation to arrive at preconceived decisions and how group members felt about it. At the next meeting, the leader acknowledged the feedback and indicated her willingness to be challenged about such preconceived decisions. Team members expressed their increased willingness to engage in problem-solving discussions, their trust in the leader, and their ability to make the challenge without fear of reprisal.

10-4c Interventions Relevant to the Group's Behavior

The most common focus of team-building activities is behavior related to task performance and group process. In an effective team, task behavior and group process must be integrated with each other as well as with the needs and wants of the people making up the group. Diagnostic activities involve gathering data through the use of team surveys or, more commonly, through interviews. The nature of the data gathered will vary depending on the purpose of the team-building program, the consultant's knowledge about the organization and its culture, and the people involved. The consultant already may have obtained a great deal of data by sitting in as a process observer at staff and other meetings. The data gathered also will depend on what other OD efforts have taken place in the organization. By whatever method obtained, however, the data usually include information on leadership styles and behavior; goals, objectives, and decision-making processes; organizational culture, communication patterns, and interpersonal relationships and processes; barriers to effective group functioning; and task and related technical problems. Diagnostic activities often establish a framework within which further work can be done.

Improvement activities aim to improve the group's process and functioning. A variety of exercises have been described by different authors.[30] They include role clarification, improving goal clarity and member commitment, modifying or clarifying the decision-making or problem-solving process, changing norms, increasing risk taking and trust, and improving communication.

Application 10.3 presents an example of a team-building meeting involving a top-management team.[31] Ask yourself the following questions as you read this case.

- Do you agree with Ted's and the executive committee's decision to make the workshop's focus task-oriented vs. more interpersonally oriented on the relationships? What do you think of Ted's choices during the workshop?
- Could an external consultant have followed Ted's approach and gotten a similar result? What other choices, as an internal consultant, did Ted have?
- What were the benefits and risks associated with Ted's decision to start working with the directors before engaging the executive committee first?

10-4d Interventions Affecting the Group's Integration with the Rest of the Organization

As a team gains a better understanding of itself and becomes better able to diagnose and solve its own problems, it focuses on its role within the organization. A group's relationship to the larger organizational context is an important aspect of group effectiveness.[32] Diagnostic activities usually focus on understanding the group's organizational role, how its goals support the larger organization, or how the group interacts with other groups by interviewing internal customers and other stakeholders.

Improvement activities involve strategic planning and stakeholder mapping interventions to modify the group's contribution to the organization, how it acquires resources, or alters its outputs in terms of cost, quality, and quantity. Sometimes, the team may recognize a need for more collaboration with other parts of the organization and may try to establish a project team that crosses the boundaries of existing teams.

As the team becomes more cohesive, it usually exerts a stronger influence on other groups within the organization. This can lead to intergroup conflict and the need for large group interventions or intergroup conflict resolution interventions (Chapter 11). Because that is one area in which team building can have negative effects, the process consultant must help the group understand its role within the larger organization, develop its own diagnostic skills, and examine alternative action plans so that intergroup tensions and conflicts do not expand.

application 10.3

ALIGNING SENIOR TEAMS AT VAYCOT PRODUCTS

Vaycot Products (a disguised name) is a publicly traded, 28-year-old $750 million medical equipment manufacturer and marketer. Their products include MRI, ultrasound, and X-ray machines. Corporate performance in 2011 had been dismal, and the organization was under a great deal of pressure to improve results. The organization had missed sales and earnings targets for seven consecutive quarters, revenues were down 7%, and growth rates were half the industry average. Vaycot's board, industry analysts, and a well-known corporate raider were vocal with their concerns.

People described Vaycot's culture as "strong and toxic." Forty-eight percent of employees were disengaged and 58% were considering leaving the company. A recent survey asked employees to describe the culture, and more than 35% of employees used the terms angry, disrespectful, fear-based, paralyzed, penalizing, risk-averse, or untrusting. Employees often felt pressured to cut corners or engage in unethical practices to get work done and achieve overly aggressive goals.

The organization was managed by two teams: the executive committee and the operating committee. The executive committee consisted of Oscar (the CEO) and eight functional vice presidents. The broader operating committee consisted of the executive team plus the directors who reported to them. Decision making in these groups was slow to nonexistent because the directors and vice presidents feared being derided in public by the CEO over a wrong decision. Despite being very capable, the vice presidents had learned how to deal with Oscar's autocratic, volatile, and intimidating leadership style. Most of their time was spent in meetings being told how to do their job or making course corrections to adjust to Oscar's ever-changing mind.

Not surprisingly, the vice presidents were distracted, demotivated, and disengaged, and the negativity flowed down directly to the directors. The directors were under constant pressure and usually in crisis mode. A small group of directors asked the internal OD consultant, Ted, for help. Ted knew most of the directors primarily through one-on-one coaching over the years, and he guided a subgroup of the operating committee through a process to increase trust, collaboration, and team effectiveness.

ENTRY AND CONTRACTING

After hearing from several of the directors about how well the process worked, and seeing firsthand the directors' improved relationships and results, the CFO and the vice presidents of sales and operations approached Ted to see if he would work with the executive committee.

Ted was candid. "I'm hesitant to do it because of Oscar. Based on my interactions with him, I'm concerned that his need for control and resistance to getting feedback will keep him from being a constructive participant." The vice presidents agreed with Ted's assessment and asked if he'd work with just them. Ted was reluctant on this point as well. He explained that team building works best when the leader actively participates and is willing to deal with any emergent issues. That left the ball in the vice presidents' court. They needed to convince their boss to participate and that would require giving Oscar feedback on why they believed a team-based intervention was needed.

As Ted continued the conversations, he came to the conclusion that the only way that the vice presidents could actually influence Oscar was with hard data. He offered to interview the vice presidents and then facilitate a meeting where *they* would deliver the feedback to Oscar. When the interviews were complete, he walked the group through about a dozen findings and insights. After some brief discussion and a few minor revisions, the group confirmed that the conclusions were valid and they agreed unanimously that it was finally time to meet with Oscar.

Ted asked how the feedback meeting should be structured. No one spoke. Despite their promise to follow through and talk to

Oscar, no one wanted to be in the room when Oscar heard *their* feedback. Despite Ted's frustration, he offered to meet with Oscar on their behalf. They still hesitated because they feared the repercussions if Oscar were to know who said what. Ted promised anonymity and then got the go ahead to talk to Oscar.

This was a pivot point for Ted. On one hand, he didn't want to make a career-limiting move by angering Oscar. On the other hand, he feared that all of the good work and progress made by the directors would die on the vine unless someone could convince Oscar to come along. Ted scheduled a time to meet with Oscar and prepared himself for a difficult conversation. Not wanting to overwhelm Oscar, Ted focused on three key messages:

1. *Trust your team.* Let go of the day-to-day, even if things start to go in the wrong direction. Avoid the temptation to jump in and do your people's jobs.
2. *Facilitate, don't dominate.* Continue to use your style of direct communication to ensure that the right issues are put on the table, but then back off more often to allow your team to add value.
3. *Let go and take issues offline when appropriate.* Know when to let go of an issue and when to include fewer people in the discussion. Especially when you have an issue with a single individual—no one likes to get yelled at in front of others.

Oscar was clearly irritated by the data and he vented for a few minutes. Ted listened without interrupting. Eventually, they got back on track when Oscar asked what to do next. Ted suggested a team-building process to align members of the executive committee. He described the process he used with the operating committee and suggested that the executive committee could go through a similar process. At this point, Oscar was still fuming from the feedback but he asked Ted several detailed questions about how the process would work, what he'd need to do, and what outcomes to expect. Ted answered each question.

Then Oscar asked how much time an off-site would take. Ted knew he'd be pushing it too far if he asked for the full three days he thought were needed. So he proposed two days and Oscar agreed. Though the feedback session was uncomfortable for both Oscar and Ted, it ended on a high note.

DATA FEEDBACK AND INTERVENTION DESIGN

Ted's review of the business strategy, organization design (structures, processes, systems, and controls), engagement surveys, customer surveys, and exit interviews identified a variety of misfits that could drive the team building. For example, even though customers rated Vaycot high in innovation, engagement surveys rated it low. In addition, bonuses were supposed to be tied to performance, yet 94% of people got the full target bonus amount. This didn't make sense given the organization's poor financial performance. Another misfit was that leadership effectiveness was highly rated in the engagement survey but it was consistently disclosed in the exit surveys as a reason people resigned. Ted viewed this as a symptom of a fear-based culture. As a final step he interviewed the vice presidents again individually and asked them to rate the following statements, on a scale of 1 to 5 with 5 being "totally agree":

- Current roles and accountabilities of all members of the team are clear.
- The decision-making process is effective and appropriate to the task.
- Team members openly speak their mind with each other.
- The team is effective at resolving conflicts.
- Team meetings are productive.

Ted analyzed and organized the data. The interview responses were low, ranging between 1.5–2.25; it was clear that these critical operating factors needed work.

Ted shared the data and his assessment with Oscar and the vice presidents. They were not surprised by the low ratings; they had been living in the system every day and were well aware of its poor condition. They validated Ted's assessment and agreed that they owned the data.

Ted used the data to design a two-day workshop. He knew designing a set of activities would be a challenge. The relationships among the executive committee members were fragile, and he knew from experience that this group would not tolerate a more personal approach. Oscar had famously referred to highly interpersonal processes as "touchy feely flavor-of-the-month garbage." As a result, he decided that the design needed to be task-oriented and focused on getting things done.

He reviewed the objectives and workshop agenda with the full executive committee. To keep the group focused on tasks, much of the design addressed the team's data related to working together to avoid personal grudges and fear from getting in the way. The executive team approved the design and expressed optimism that the off-site would be productive.

WORKSHOP IMPLEMENTATION

The workshop opened with a recap of how the executive committee got to this point. Ted asked everyone to tell a short story about their experience with the process so far. It was a lively conversation—very positive in tone—and everyone spoke. Oscar thanked the group for their hard work and dedication so far in the process. He assured them that he was going to be an active participant in the session.

Next, Ted proposed a set of ground rules, such as "what's said in the room stays in the room," "attack issues not people," and "don't speak for others." Everyone agreed to abide by them. Ted reiterated that the objective of the meeting was to address the team's ability to get work done. "The data show that this team has some significant interpersonal challenges that need to be addressed, but these are outside of the scope of this workshop." Most participants expressed a sense of relief and no one objected.

Ted then divided the group into two subgroups and asked one group to list its hopes for the session on a flipchart. The second group was instructed to list its fears for the session on another flipchart. Each group presented its list and the top three hopes and top three fears were recorded on a new piece of paper and taped to the wall. Ted's intention in this exercise was to set a baseline of how safe the group members were going to play. This would serve as a point of comparison later to see if people became more trusting and open as the workshop progressed.

The next exercise facilitated the development of a group purpose statement. Ted asked everyone to write a sentence that described why they thought the executive committee existed. Then each member read their sentence. Most sentences and statements addressed achieving results, allocating resources, and making strategic decisions. Only two statements, however, mentioned employee or human capital issues, and Ted commented on that output. The group debated whether their role involved employees or not and agreed that there needed to be more consideration given to the workforce. The statement of purpose eventually evolved to the point where it included the idea that part of the executive team's purpose was to help people understand how their work contributes to driving the strategy and assure that recognition and rewards were tied to contributions.

The rest of the first day was spent working on the interview data. They discussed the data associated with each statement and developed actions to improve the ratings. The discussions were tense and strained at first, but they evolved. Initially, there was a lot of finger pointing and pouting. Ted facilitated these discussions away from the interpersonal issues toward a more productive problem-solving approach based on data and behaviors. Over time, the team developed a productive rhythm. The day ended with the executive committee agreeing to the following positive statements and to working on the items required to deliver those results.

The current roles/accountabilities of all members of the team are very clear.

- As a group, we need to work better across functions, clarify the roles of sales vs. market development vs. marketing, and be more deliberate in setting and communicating top priorities by function

The decision-making process on this team is effective and appropriate to the task.

- As a group, we need to take the emotion out of decision making, create more collaboration around issues and engage in less unilateral decision making, and be clearer about our decision-making process. Who is the decision maker (e.g., function lead, team, CEO) and what style of decision making is appropriate (consensus, majority, unilateral)?

Team members are very candid and openly speak their mind with each other.

- As a group, we need to increase trust, allow more time for dialogue to develop, and ask Oscar to play a facilitator role more often

This team is very effective at resolving conflicts.

- As a group, we need to use an objective, fact-based approach to analyze and resolve issues, reduce emotion, and decrease the number of CEO overrides and decreed solutions

Team meetings are very productive.

- As a group, we need to do less venting and going over the same issues time and time again, give more respect and credence to subject-matter experts, and limit attendance to the people who need to be there

The second day started with a brief recap of Day 1 and a discussion of the hopes and fears posted on the wall. There was consensus that the group had "played it safe" and identified hopes and fears that were shallow and noncontroversial. For example one of the top three fears was "not getting enough done." The conversation that ensued was animated; executive team members were more at ease in sharing their deeper hopes and fears.

Oscar was pretty quiet during the exercise until the end. "It seems like dealing with these fears would increase performance significantly, and I have to admit that it appears I am the source of much of it," said Oscar. As the conversation around Oscar's role expanded, Ted dropped an activity and introduced the dialogue technique. He described the importance of suspending assumptions, actively listening, asking and reflecting, and advocating during conversations. The participants took turns practicing dialogue skills and developed a deeper understanding of theirs and Oscar's roles.

After a period of time, Ted decided to look for common themes and asked, "How did this exercise go, and what topics were covered?" Everyone agreed that the hardest part of dialoging was to listen intently and to not interrupt when another person was speaking. Common topics included that the functions needed to better collaborate and support each other, and that training on conflict resolution and negotiation would be beneficial. The group agreed they had gotten a lot out of the dialogue module.

The next exercise, "give and get," was intended to build awareness of interdependencies. Going around the group two at a time, each pair of executives took turns saying what he or she specifically needed from the other person to be more effective. Then the other person would repeat the request. Together, they either committed to actions or said why they could not. The exercise continued until everyone had gotten/made commitments from/to everyone else. The output of the exercise neatly summarized and operationalized the actions listed under the positive statements of group operation from Day 1.

The agenda then called for the development of a short list of enterprise projects to move the organization forward and drive performance. Despite the progress made so far, there was still some risk that Oscar would strong arm the project selection process. At Ted's urging, Oscar excluded himself from the exercise. He didn't want him to influence or limit what the vice presidents came up with. Next Ted asked everyone to come up with a headline to describe what the team needed to do immediately to improve organizational effectiveness.

Topping the list was:

- Shared ownership of common goals, and goal alignment throughout organization
- More collaboration between functions
- Increased employee engagement and productivity

Ted then asked the team to identify two or three large-scale change projects to drive sustainable high performance. The session concluded with the executive committee endorsing the following enterprise projects:

- Cascade goals to link every employee's daily work to the strategy
- Conduct cross-function "give and get" round-robins to increase trust and collaboration
- Deploy an enterprise change program to improve the culture and increase engagement

At the end of Day 2, Ted wrapped up the session just as he started it. He asked each participant to tell a story about their workshop experience. Again, it was a lively conversation—very positive in tone—and everyone spoke. Oscar thanked the group for their commitment and work during the two days. He told them that they could count on him to help drive and complete the initiatives that were selected.

After Oscar left to go to another meeting, the vice presidents lingered to discuss the events of the past two days. They felt relieved and optimistic that things, and most importantly Oscar, would be different going forward. Ted believed that the group was grateful for the outcomes, committed to implementing the initiatives, and thoroughly exhausted. All signs of a good two days' work by a team of executives that stepped up and changed its mindset and behaviors to commit to making significant changes in how the business would be run in the future.

RESULTS AND REFLECTION

Following the workshop, teams were formed and chartered, and work began immediately on the three enterprise projects. The executive committee asked Ted to work with them throughout the year and to design and facilitate structured workshops every six months. Gradually, the operating committee, then the managers, and then the rest of the workforce felt the positive impacts of the executive committee's increased team effectiveness.

Three years later, the numbers told the story of Vaycot's turn around:

- Beat sales and earnings targets five quarters in a row, and year-to-year sales were up 9%
- Engagement index was up 21 points
- Turnover was in line with industry averages

Being a realist, Ted knew that Oscar had not undergone an overall personal transformation—he was still basically the same guy. Oscar's few key behavior changes were mostly motivated by the realization that he could get a lot more performance out of his team, and the whole organization, if he changed the way he led. In the end, Oscar became a better leader and, in part, that led to an organizational transformation.

Looking back, Ted would have preferred working with the executive committee first and then the operating committee. However, based on his organizational knowledge and his relationships with stakeholders, he had decided that there was no harm to be done by building cohesion and momentum with the directors. He had trusting relationships built up through coaching, the subgroup of directors was less encumbered by the fear that held back the vice presidents, and the directors were closer to the workforce and customers and were in a better position to impact the business. Oscar would have surely shut things down before any progress had been made if they started with the executive committee.

The whole experience reminded Ted of his mentor's advice. "Follow the energy and start where the client is, not where you want them to be."

10-4e The Manager's Role in Team Building

Ultimately, the manager is responsible for team functioning, although this responsibility obviously must be shared by the group itself. Therefore, it is management's task to develop a work group that can regularly analyze and diagnose its own effectiveness and work process. With the team's involvement, the manager must diagnose the group's effectiveness and take appropriate actions if it shows signs of operating difficulty or stress.

Boss and McConkie surveyed over 3,500 team-building participants and found that 92% identified the team's leader as the single most important role in successful team building.[33] Many managers, however, have not been trained to perform the data gathering, diagnosis, planning, and action necessary to maintain and improve their teams continually. Thus, the issue of who should lead a team-building session is a function of managerial capability. The initial use of an OD consultant usually is advisable if a manager is aware of problems, feels that he or she may be part of the problem, and believes that some positive action is needed to improve the operation of the team, but is not sure how to go about it.[34]

Basically, the role of the OD consultant is to work closely with the manager (and members of the team) to a point at which the manager is capable of engaging in team development activities as a regular and ongoing part of overall managerial responsibilities. Assuming that the manager wants and needs a consultant, the two should work together in developing the initial program, keeping in mind that (1) the manager ultimately is responsible for all team-building activities, even though the consultant's resources are available; and (2) the goal of the consultant's presence is to help the manager learn to continue team development processes with minimum consultant help or without the ongoing help of the consultant.

Thus, in the first stages, the consultant might be much more active in data gathering, diagnosis, and action planning, particularly if a one- to three-day off-site workshop is considered. In later stages, the consultant takes a much less active role, with the manager becoming more active and serving as both manager and team developer.

10-4f The Results of Team Building

The early research on team building's effectiveness produced inconsistent, but generally positive, results. Several studies reported positive results across a range of variables including feelings, attitudes, and measures of performance.[35] Other studies produced less positive outcomes.[36]

Less powerful research designs, short time frames, and the confounding impact of other interventions occurring in conjunction with team building were the most important explanation for the lack of consistent results.[37] For example, one review of 30 studies found that only ten tried to measure changes in performance. Buller and Bell attempted to differentiate the effects of team building from the effects of other interventions that occur along with team building.[38] Specifically, they tried to separate the effects of team building from the effects of goal setting, an intervention aimed at setting realistic performance goals and developing action plans for achieving them. In a rigorous field experiment, Buller and Bell examined the differential effects of team building and goal setting on productivity measures of underground miners. Their results showed that team building affected the quality of performance and goal setting affected the quantity of performance. This differential impact was explained in terms of the nature of the mining task. The task of improving the quality of performance was more complex, unstructured, and interdependent than was the task of achieving quantity. This suggests that team building can improve group performance, particularly on tasks that are complex, unstructured, and interdependent.

More recently, a 2009 meta-analysis of 20 studies representing 579 teams found positive and moderate overall effect sizes; there was a significant tendency for team building to positively influence team outcomes.[39] Four team-building activities—goal setting, interpersonal relations, problem solving, and role clarification—and four team outcomes—cognitive, affective, process, and performance—were examined more closely. Goal-setting and role clarification interventions were the most powerful, while affective and process outcomes registered the largest improvements.

Team building, like OD at the organization level, is a process over time, and OD practitioners need to be aware of the full range of reasons teams are effective. Research by Hackman and his colleagues have suggested that too much time may be spent trying to help teams that were designed and launched incorrectly. They argue that one of the most important tasks of the OD practitioner is to be sure that any team gets chartered and started correctly.[40] In a related study where the teams' launching was held constant, Woolley found that task-focused (as opposed to process-focused) interventions given at the midpoint of a team's lifecycle had the biggest impact on team performance.[41]

The results of team building in virtual teams is still emerging, but shows that many of the lessons learned from face-to-face team-building practice can be transferred. For example, one lab study found that when communications technologies were augmented to include goal-setting processes, team functioning and team performance improved[42] while another lab study of Chinese undergraduates found that a dialogue intervention intended to improve shared mental models among team members was as effective in face-to-face teams as it was in video-conferenced teams.[43] Because virtual teams are usually geographically dispersed, they can also take advantage of a variety of asychnronous facilitation tools, such as wikis, shared portals, or other groupware.[44] Hart and Mcleod found that interpersonal closeness between members of a virtual team is created when one member proactively helps another member to solve a problem or address a concern, and that the closeness is maintained by frequent, short, but content-oriented (as opposed to process-oriented) messages.[45] Gibson and Cohen found that team performance was enhanced by initial face-to-face team-building meetings in the start-up stage of a team's work.[46]

Finally, Boss has presented considerable evidence to support the effectiveness of personal management interviews (PMIs) in sustaining the long-term effects of off-site team building.[47] A PMI is a follow-up intervention that arrests the potential fade-out effects of off-site team building.[48] A team leader negotiates roles with each member and then holds regular meetings with each team member to resolve problems and increase personal accountability. Boss and his colleagues have amassed a large, longitudinal data set, mostly in public administration, hospital, and health care settings. When team-building interventions have included PMI activities (compared to those that have not included PMI follow-ups), they have found consistent and sustained improvement in measures of team functioning and operational performance.

SUMMARY

In this chapter, we presented human process interventions aimed at interpersonal relations and group dynamics. Among the earliest interventions in OD, these change programs help people gain interpersonal competence, work through interpersonal conflicts, and develop effective groups.

Process consultation is used not only as a way of helping groups become effective but also as a means whereby groups learn to diagnose and solve their own problems and continue to develop their competence and maturity. Important areas of activity include communications, roles of group members, difficulties with problem-solving and decision-making norms, and leadership and authority. The basic difference between process consultation and third-party intervention is that the latter focuses on interpersonal dysfunctions in social relationships between two or more individuals within the same organization and is targeted toward resolving direct conflict between those individuals.

Team building is directed toward improving group effectiveness and the ways in which members of teams work together. Teams may be permanent or temporary or traditional or virtual, but their members have either common organizational aims or work activities. The general process of team building, like process consultation, tries to equip a team to handle its own ongoing problem solving.

NOTES

1. M. Marks, J. Mathieu, and S. Zaccaro, "A Temporally Based Framework and Taxonomy of Team Processes," *Academy of Management Review* 26 (2001): 356–78.
2. J. Fast, *Body Language* (Philadelphia: Lippincott, M. Evans, 1970).
3. D. Levi, *Group Dynamics for Teams* (Thousand Oaks, CA: Sage Publications, 2011); N. Clapp, "Work Group Norms: Leverage for Organizational Change, Theory and Application" (undated working paper, Block Petrella Weisbord, Plainfield, NJ); R. Allen and S. Pilnick, "Confronting the Shadow Organization: How to Detect and Defeat Negative Norms," *Organizational Dynamics* (Spring 1973): 3–18.
4. E. Schein, *Process Consultation Volume II: Lessons for Managers and Consultants* (Reading, MA: Addison-Wesley, 1987).
5. E. Schein, *Process Consultation Revisited* (Reading, MA: Addison-Wesley, 1998), 20.
6. Schein, *Process Consultation Volume II*, 5–17.
7. Schein, *Process Consultation Revisited.*
8. Schein, *Process Consultation Revisited*, 147.
9. J. Luft, "The Johari Window," *Human Relations Training News* 5 (1961): 6–7.
10. C. Seashore, E. Seashore, and G. Weinberg, *What Did You Say? The Art of Giving and Receiving Feedback* (Columbia, MD: Bingham House Books, 2001).
11. J. Gibb, "Defensive Communication," *Journal of Communication* 11 (1961): 141–48; Schein, *Process Consultation Revisited*; Seashore, Seashore, and Weinberg, *What Did You Say?*
12. E. Schein, *Process Consultation: Its Role in Organization Development* (Reading, MA: Addison-Wesley, 1969), 44.
13. This application was authored and submitted by Charles Hathorn, Principal, Hathorn.org, and his contribution is gratefully acknowledged.
14. R. Kaplan, "The Conspicuous Absence of Evidence That Process Consultation Enhances Task Performance," *Journal of Applied Behavioral Science* 15 (1979): 346–60.
15. G. Lippitt, *Organizational Renewal* (New York: Appleton-Century-Crofts, 1969); C. Argyris, *Organization and Innovation* (Homewood, IL: Richard D. Irwin, 1965).
16. D. Tjosvold, "Defining Conflict and Making Choices About Its Management," *International Journal of Conflict Management* 17 (2006): 87–95.
17. C. K. DeDreu and L. Weingart, "Task versus Relationship Conflict, Team Performance, and Team Member Satisfaction: A Meta-analysis," *Journal of Applied Psychology* 88 (2003): 741–49.
18. People interested in finding assistance might want to contact the Society of Professionals in Dispute Resolution (SPIDR) at http://www.acrnet.org, or the Straus Institute of Dispute Resolution at http://law.pepperdine.edu/straus.
19. D. Kolb and Associates, *When Talk Works: Profiles of Mediators* (San Francisco: Jossey-Bass, 1994); R. Saner and L. Yiu, "External Stakeholder Impacts on Third-Party Interventions in Resolving Malignant Conflicts: The Case of a Failed Third-Party Intervention in Cyprus," *International Negotiation* 6 (2001): 387–416.
20. H. Prein, "Strategies for Third-Party Intervention," *Human Relations* 40 (1987): 699–720; P. Nugent, "Managing Conflict: Third-Party Interventions for Managers," *Academy of Management Executive* 16 (2002): 139–54.
21. R. Walton, *Managing Conflict: Interpersonal Dialogue and Third-Party Roles*, 2nd ed. (Reading, MA: Addison-Wesley, 1987); Nugent, "Managing Conflict."
22. Walton, *Managing Conflict*, 83–110.
23. This application was developed by John Childers, President, Childers and Partners LLC. His contribution is gratefully acknowledged.
24. W. Dyer, W. Dyer, and J. Dyer, *Team Building*, 4th ed. (San Francisco: Jossey-Bass, 2007).
25. T. Patten, *Organizational Development Through Team Building* (New York: John Wiley & Sons, 1981), 2; D. Stepchuck, "Strategies for Improving the Effectiveness of Geographically Distributed Work Teams" (unpublished master's thesis, Pepperdine University, 1994).
26. C. Gibson and S. Cohen, eds., *Virtual Teams That Work: Creating Conditions for Virtual Team Effectiveness* (San Francisco: Jossey-Bass, 2003); R. Hart and P. Mcleod, "Rethinking Team Building in Geographically Dispersed Teams," *Organizational Dynamics* 31 (2003): 352–61; W. Huang, K Wei, R. Watson, and B. Tan, "Supporting Virtual Team-building with a GSS: An Empirical Investigation," *Decision Support Systems* 34 (2002): 359–67; D. Mancini, "Building Organizational Trust in Virtual Teams," *Journal of Behavioral Studies in Business* 2 (May 2010): 1–15; R. Lepsinger and D. DeRosa, *Virtual Team Success* (San Francisco: Pfeiffer, 2011).
27. W. Dyer, *Team Building: Issues and Alternatives*, 2nd ed. (Reading, MA: Addison-Wesley, 1987).
28. J. Katzenbach and D. Smith, *The Wisdom of Teams* (Boston: Harvard Business School Press, 1993).
29. J. Hackman, "The Design of Work Teams," in *The Handbook of Organizational Behavior*, ed. J. Lorsch (Englewood Cliffs, NJ: Prentice Hall, 1987): 315–42.
30. Dyer, *Team Building*; Katzenbach and Smith, *Wisdom of Teams*; C. Torres, D. Fairbanks, and R. Roe, eds.,

Teambuilding: The ASTD Trainer's Sourcebook (New York: McGraw-Hill, 1996); L. Offermann and R. Spiros, "The Science and Practice of Team Development: Improving the Link," *Academy of Management Journal* 44 (2001): 376–93; P. Lencioni, *Overcoming the Five Dysfunctions of a Team* (San Francisco: Jossey-Bass, 2005).

31. This application was developed by David Jardin. His contribution is gratefully acknowledged.
32. D. Ancona and D. Caldwell, "Bridging the Boundary: External Activity and Performance in Organizational Teams," *Administrative Science Quarterly* 37 (1992): 634–65; S. Cohen, "Designing Effective Self-Managing Work Teams" (paper presented at the Theory Symposium on Self-Managed Work Teams, Denton, TX, June 4–5, 1993).
33. R. W. Boss and M. McConkie, "Team Building" in *Handbook of Organization Development*, ed. T. Cummings (Thousand Oaks, CA: Sage Publications, 2007).
34. Dyer, *Team Building.*
35. K. De Meuse and S. Liebowitz, "An Empirical Analysis of Team-building Research," *Group & Organizational Studies* 6 (1981): 357–78; S. Tannenbaum, R. Beard, and E. Salas, "Team Building and Its Influence on Team Effectiveness: An Examination of Conceptual and Empirical Developments," in *Issues, Theory, and Research in Industrial/Organizational Psychology*, ed. K. Kelley (Amsterdam: Elsevier, 1992); G. Neuman, J. Edwards, and N. Raju, "Organizational Development Interventions: A Meta-Analysis of Their Effects on Satisfaction and Other Attitudes," *Personnel Psychology* 42 (1989): 461–89; R. Guzzo and M. Dickson, "Teams in Organizations: Recent Research on Performance and Effectiveness," in *Annual Review of Psychology*, vol. 47, ed. J. Spence, J. Darley, and J. Foss (Palo Alto, CA: Annual Reviews, 1996): 307–38; J. Porras and P. O. Berg, "The Impact of Organization Development," *Academy of Management Review* 3 (April 1978): 249–66; J. Nicholas, "The Comparative Impact of Organization Development Interventions on Hard Criteria Measures," *Academy of Management Review* 7 (October 1982): 531–42.
36. D. Eden, "Team Development: A True Field Experiment at Three Levels of Rigor," *Journal of Applied Psychology* 70 (1985): 94–100.
37. De Meuse and Liebowitz, "An Empirical Analysis of Team-building Research"; R. Woodman and J. Sherwood, "The Role of Team Development in Organizational Effectiveness: A Critical Review," *Psychological Bulletin* 88 (July–Nov. 1980); Eden, "Team Development."
38. R. Buller and C. Bell Jr., "Effects of Team Building and Goal Setting: A Field Experiment," *Academy of Management Journal* 29 (1986): 305–28.
39. C. Klein, D. DiazGranados, E. Salas, H. Le, C. Burke, R. Lyons, and G. Goodwin, "Does Team Building Work?" *Small Group Research* 40 (2009): 181–222.
40. Hackman, "The Design of Work Teams"; R. Hackman and R. Wageman, "A Theory of Team Coaching," *Academy of Management Review* 30 (2005): 269–87.
41. A. Woolley, "Effects of Intervention Content and Timing on Group Task Performance," *Journal of Applied Behavioral Science* 34 (1998): 30–46.
42. Huang, Wei, Watson, and Tan, "Supporting Virtual Team-building with a GSS."
43. Z. Guo, J. D'Ambra, T. Turner, and H. Zhang, "Improving the Effectiveness of Virtual Teams: A Comparison of Video-Conferencing and Face-to-Face Communication in China," *IEEE Transaction on Professional Communication* 52 (March 2009): 1–16.
44. N. Rangarajan and J. Rohrbaugh, "Multiple Roles of Online Facilitation: An Example in Any-Time, Any-Place Meetings," *Group Facilitation* 5 (2003): 26–36.
45. Hart and Mcleod, "Rethinking Team Building in Geographically Dispersed Teams."
46. C. Gibson and S. Cohen, eds., *Virtual Teams That Work: Creating Conditions for Virtual Team Effectiveness* (San Francisco: Jossey-Bass, 2003).
47. R. W. Boss, "Team Building and the Problem of Regression: The Personal Management Interview as an Intervention," *Journal of Applied Behavioral Science* 19 (1983): 67–83; R. Boss and M. McConkie, "Creating High Performance Work Teams: Team Building Results from 3,679 Participants," paper presented at the Eleventh International Conference on Advances in Management, Orlando, FL, March 2004.
48. Ibid.

11

Organization Process Approaches

learning objectives

- Understand the diagnostic issues associated with organization-wide process interventions.
- Demonstrate the organization confrontation meeting.
- Compare the intergroup relations interventions of microcosm groups and intergroup conflict.
- Describe and evaluate the effectiveness of large-group interventions.

In Chapter 10, we presented interventions aimed at improving interpersonal and group processes. This chapter describes system-wide process interventions—change programs directed at increasing the effectiveness of organizational problem solving, visioning and strategy making, and collaboration—for a major subsystem or for an entire organization.

The first type of intervention, the organization confrontation meeting, is among the earliest organization-wide process approaches developed by organization development (OD) practitioners. It helps mobilize the problem-solving resources of a major subsystem or whole organization by encouraging members to identify and confront pressing issues.

The second organization process approach is called intergroup relations. It consists of two interventions: microcosm groups and the intergroup conflict resolution meeting. Both interventions are aimed at diagnosing and addressing important organization-level processes, such as conflict, the coordination of organizational units, and innovation. The intergroup conflict intervention is specifically oriented toward conflict processes, whereas the microcosm group is a more generic system-wide change strategy.

The third and final system-wide process approach, the large group intervention, has received considerable attention recently and is one of the fastest-growing areas in OD. Large group interventions get a "whole system into the room"[1] and create processes that allow a variety of stakeholders to interact simultaneously. A large group intervention can be used to articulate a new organization vision, develop a new strategy, solve cross-functional problems, develop a change strategy, or redesign work, structures, and systems. It is a powerful tool for addressing organizational problems and opportunities and for accelerating the pace of organizational change.

11-1 Diagnostic Issues in Organization Process Interventions

Organization process approaches are driven by diagnostic data collected at the organization level. In particular, these interventions address issues, problems, and opportunities that occur between or among groups as they try to implement the organization's strategy. The key contextual inputs to the diagnosis are the organization's environment, in terms of information uncertainty, complexity, resource dependency, and industry structure. The need for organization process interventions often has its genesis in some environmental change. For example, if there is considerable environmental uncertainty arising from the defection of a number of customers to competitors or, in a nonprofit case, if funding has become more difficult to come by, organization process interventions could be used to understand why these problems are occurring and how to address them. Effective OD practitioners closely watch the organization's external environment for change pressures.

With respect to the design components of strategy, structure, technology, management systems, and human resource systems, organization process approaches can be driven by diagnostic data from any of these issues. A broad and aggressive strategy may put pressure on scarce resources, such as specialized talent or specific organization units, or there may be unanticipated problems in establishing key product or service differentiators. These issues could be handled by organization process interventions. Alternatively, diagnostic data may suggest considerable inefficiency with respect to productivity in the organization (technology design component) as compared to benchmark organizations in the industry. An organization confrontation meeting might be convened to generate new work process innovations or a large group intervention might be designed to involve union leaders, technology vendors, front-line employees, and managers to diagnose current value-added processes and recommend changes. Increasingly, as organizations see themselves as whole systems, these interventions are being used to address all of these diagnostic categories in broad organization design solutions.

In sum, good OD practitioners link the use of organization process interventions to sound diagnostic data. OD practitioners should be able to clearly articulate a sound business case as to how the environmental pressures or organization design features constraining current effectiveness will be addressed by these interventions.

11-2 Organization Confrontation Meeting

The *confrontation meeting* is an intervention designed to mobilize the resources of the entire organization to identify problems, to set priorities and action targets, and to begin working on identified problems. Originally developed by Beckhard,[2] the intervention can be used at any time but is particularly useful when the organization is under stress and when there is a gap between the top and the rest of the organization (such as when a new top manager joins the organization). General Electric's "Work-Out" program is an example of how the confrontation meeting has been adapted to fit today's organizations.[3] Although the original model involved only managerial and professional people, it has since been used successfully with technicians, clerical personnel, and assembly workers. It has also been applied in a variety of domestic and international settings. The process as described helps organizations, even those with conflict avoidance or uncertainty-avoidance values, to address relevant organizational concerns.

11-2a Application Stages

When the diagnosis of the system's current situation suggests that the organization is facing several unprioritized problems that will require broad coordination, the organization confrontation meeting typically involves the following steps:

1. A group meeting of all those involved is scheduled and held in an appropriate place. Usually the task is to identify problems related to the work environment and the effectiveness of the organization.
2. Groups are appointed representing all departments of the organization. Thus, each group might have one or more members from sales, purchasing, finance, operations, and quality assurance. For obvious reasons, a subordinate should not be in the same group as his or her boss, and top management should form its own group. Group size can vary from 5 to 15 members, depending on such factors as the size of the organization and available meeting places.
3. The point is stressed that the groups are to be open and honest and to work hard at identifying problems they see in the organization. No one will be criticized for bringing up problems and, in fact, the groups will be judged on their ability to do so.
4. The groups are given an hour or two to identify organization problems. Generally, an OD practitioner goes from group to group, encouraging openness and assisting the groups with their tasks.
5. The groups then reconvene in a central meeting place. Each group reports the problems it has identified and sometimes offers solutions. Because each group hears the reports of all the others, a maximum amount of information is shared.
6. At this point, a master list of problems is created and then broken down into categories. This can be done by the participants, by the person leading the session, or by the manager and his or her staff. It can also be done at the end of a day with the group reconvening at another time, although it is important to maintain momentum. This process eliminates duplication and overlap and allows the problems to be separated according to functional or other appropriate areas.
7. Following problem categorization, participants are divided into problem-solving groups whose composition may, and usually does, differ from that of the original problem-identification groups. For example, all operations problems may be handled by people in that subunit. Or task forces representing appropriate cross sections of the organization may be formed.
8. Each group ranks the problems, develops a tactical action plan, and determines an appropriate timetable for completing this phase of the process.
9. Each group then periodically reports its list of priorities and tactical plans of action to management or to the larger group.
10. Schedules for periodic (frequently monthly) follow-up meetings are established and project management resources may be necessary to monitor and support progress. At these sessions, the team leaders report either to top management, to the other team leaders, or to the group as a whole regarding their team's progress and plans for future action. The formal establishment of such follow-up meetings ensures both continuing action and the modification of priorities and timetables as needed.

Application 11.1 presents the Work-Out process at General Electric Medical Systems business. It shows how the basic framework of a confrontation meeting can be adapted to address organizational problems, such as productivity and employee involvement.[4]

A WORK-OUT MEETING AT GENERAL ELECTRIC MEDICAL SYSTEMS BUSINESS

application 11.1

As part of the large-scale change effort, former CEO Jack Welch and several managers at General Electric devised a method for involving many organization members in the change process. Work-Out is a process for gathering the relevant people to discuss important issues and develop a clear action plan. The program has four goals: to use employees' knowledge and energy to improve work, to eliminate unnecessary work, to build trust through a process that allows and encourages employees to speak out without being fearful, and to engage in the construction of an organization that is ready to deal with the future.

At GE Medical Systems (GEMS), internal consultants conducted extensive interviews with managers throughout the organization. The interviews revealed considerable dissatisfaction with existing systems, including performance management (too many measurement processes, not enough focus on customers, unfair reward systems, and unrealistic goals), career development, and organizational climate. Managers were quoted as saying that

> I'm frustrated. I simply can't do the quality of work that I want to do and know how to do. I feel my hands are tied. I have no time. I need help on how to delegate and operate in this new culture.
>
> The goal of downsizing and delayering is correct. The execution stinks. The concept is to drop a lot of "less important" work. This just didn't happen. We still have to know all the details, still have to follow all the old policies and systems.

In addition to the interviews, Jack Welch spent some time at GEMS headquarters listening to and trying to understand the issues facing the organization.

Based on the information compiled, about 50 GEMS employees and managers gathered for a five-day Work-Out session. The participants included the group executive who oversaw the GEMS business, his staff, employee relations managers, and informal leaders from the key functional areas who were thought to be risk takers and who would challenge the status quo. Most of the work during the week was spent unravelling, evaluating, and reconsidering the structures and processes that governed work at GEMS. Teams of managers and employees addressed business problems. Functional groups developed visions of where their operations were headed. An important part of the teams' work was to engage in "bureaucracy busting" by identifying CRAP (Critical Review APpraisals) in the organization. Groups were asked to list needless approvals, policies, meetings, and reports that stifled productivity. In an effort to increase the intensity of the work and to encourage free thinking, senior managers were not a part of these discussions.

At the end of the week, the senior management team listened to the concerns, proposals, and action plans from the different teams. During the presentations, senior GEMS managers worked hard to understand the issues, communicate with the organization members, and build trust by sharing information and discussing constraints and opportunities. Most of the proposals focused on ways to reorganize work and improve returns to the organization. According to traditional Work-Out methods, managers must make instant, on-the-spot decisions about each idea in front of the whole group. The three decision choices are (1) approval; (2) rejection with clear reasons; and (3) need more data, with a decision to be made within a month.

The five-day GEMS session ended with individuals and functional teams signing close to a hundred written contracts to implement the new processes and procedures or drop unnecessary work. The contracts were between people, between functional groups, and between levels of management. Other organizational contracts affected all GEMS members. One important outcome of the Work-Out effort at GEMS was a decision to involve suppliers in its internal email network. Through that interaction, GEMS and a key supplier eventually agreed to build new-product prototypes together, and their joint efforts have led to further identification of ways to reduce costs, improve design quality, or decrease cycle times.

Work-Out at GE has been very successful but hard to measure in dollar terms. Since 1988, hundreds of Work-Outs have been held, and the concept has continued to evolve into best-practice investigations, process mapping, and change-acceleration programs. The Work-Out process, however, clearly is based on the confrontation meeting model, where a large group of people gather to identify issues and plan actions to address problems.

11-2b Results of Confrontation Meetings

Because organization confrontation meetings often are combined with other approaches, such as survey feedback, determining specific results is difficult. In many cases, the results appear dramatic in mobilizing the total resources of the organization for problem identification and solution. Beckhard cites a number of specific examples in such different organizations as a food products manufacturer, a military products manufacturer, and a hotel.[5] Positive results also were found in a confrontation meeting with 40 professionals in a research and development firm.[6]

The organization confrontation meeting is a classic and robust approach for mobilizing organizational problem solving, especially in times of low performance. Although the results of its use appear impressive, little systematic study of this intervention has been done. For example, although a variety of anecdotal descriptions exist, there has been no published large-sample evaluation of the Work-Out process. There is a clear need for evaluative research.

11-3 Intergroup Relations Interventions

The ability to diagnose and understand intergroup relations is important for OD practitioners because (1) groups often must work with and through other groups to accomplish their goals; (2) groups within the organization often create problems and place demands on each other; and (3) the quality of the relationships between groups can affect the degree of organizational effectiveness. Two OD interventions—microcosm groups and intergroup conflict resolution—are described here. A microcosm group uses members from several groups to help solve organization-wide problems. Intergroup issues are explored in this context, and then solutions are implemented in the larger organization. Intergroup conflict resolution helps two groups work out dysfunctional relationships. Together, these approaches help improve intergroup processes and lead to organizational effectiveness.

11-3a Microcosm Groups

A microcosm group consists of a small number of individuals who are chosen to reflect and represent the issue being addressed.[7] For example, a medium-sized investment firm whose reputation was damaged during the economic crisis was interested in learning about how the firm's culture may have been a factor. A microcosm group composed of members representing different functions and levels in the organizations was created, and the group was tasked with diagnosing the organization's values-in-use and the organization design features that might have contributed to the firm's behavior. In addition to addressing organization design and culture problems, microcosm groups have been used to solve communications problems, facilitate merger integration, explore diversity issues, smooth the transition to a new structure, and address dysfunctional political processes.

Microcosm groups work through "parallel processes," which are the unconscious changes that take place in individuals when two or more groups interact.[8] After members from different groups interact, they often find that the role and interaction patterns in their group begin to reflect the roles and dynamics of the larger system they came from. Put simply, groups seem to "infect" and become "infected" by the other groups. The following example given by Alderfer[9] helps to clarify how parallel processes work:

> An organizational diagnosis team had assigned its members to each of five departments in a small manufacturing company. Members of the team had interviewed each department head and several department members, and had observed department meetings. The team was preparing to observe their first meeting of department heads and were trying to anticipate the group's behavior. At first they seemed to have no "rational" basis for predicting the top group's behavior because they "had no data" from direct observation. They decided to role-play the group meeting they had never seen. Diagnostic team members behaved as they thought the department heads would, and the result was uncanny. Team members found that they easily became engaged with one another in the simulated department-head meeting; emotional involvement occurred quickly for all participants. When the team actually was able to observe a department-head meeting, they were amazed at how closely the simulated meeting had approximated the actual session.

In another example, one of the key diagnostic findings from a culture survey at Cambia Health Solutions in Portland, OR, was the ineffectiveness of cross-functional work processes and decision making. As part of the intervention to increase the organization's agility, cross-functional project teams were set up to design and recommend change processes for four different systems. The cross-functional teams began to display all the dysfunctions of the larger organization, and so helping the teams to work cross-functionally helped to create change processes for the larger organization. The "parallel processes" idea suggests that if a small and representative group can intimately understand and solve a complex organizational problem for themselves, they are in a good position to recommend action to address the problem in the larger system.

This example also suggests that organizations use microcosm groups frequently as design teams, task forces, or temporary project teams. However, these groups often are not identified as such and cannot take advantage of the knowledge about parallel processes that could make them more effective.

Application Stages The process of using a microcosm group to address organization-wide issues involves the following five steps:

1. **Identify an issue.** This step involves finding a system-wide problem to be addressed. This may result from an organizational diagnosis or may be an idea generated by an organization member or task force. For example, one microcosm group charged with improving organizational communications was started by a division manager. He was concerned that the information provided by those reporting directly to him

differed from the data he received from informal conversations with people throughout the division.

2. **Convene the group.** Once an issue is identified, the microcosm group can be formed. The most important convening principle is that group membership needs to reflect the appropriate mix of stakeholders related to the issue. If the issue is organizational diversity, then the group should reflect the issue in terms of race, gender, age, disability, sexual orientation, culture, or other dimension. If the issue is integrating two corporate cultures following a merger, the microcosm group should contain people from both organizations who understand their respective cultures. Building a microcosm group with the right people can be a challenge in worldwide organizations where the problem's scope crosses business unit or country boundaries. A virtual microcosm team may need to be formed, and their work may need to be facilitated through computer-mediated communication technologies, such as teleconferencing. Following the initial setup, the group itself becomes responsible for determining its membership. It will decide whether to add new members and how to fill vacant positions.

   Convening the group also draws attention to the issue and gives the group status. Members need to be perceived as credible representatives of the problem. This will increase the likelihood that organization members will listen to and follow the suggestions they make.

3. **Provide group training.** Once the microcosm group is established, training is provided in group problem solving and decision making. Team-building interventions also may be appropriate. Group training focuses on establishing a group mission or charter, working relationships among members, group decision-making norms, and definitions of the problem to be addressed.

   From a group process perspective, OD practitioners may need to observe and comment on how the group develops. Because the group is a microcosm of the organization, it will tend, through its own behavior and attitudes, to reflect the problem in the larger organization. For example, if the group is addressing diversity issues in the organization, it is likely to manifest the particular dynamics that raised the issues in the first place. That is, the group may exhibit difficulty communicating across cultures or decision making may exclude or downplay certain group's inputs. Recognizing, within the group, the problem or issue it was formed to address is the first step toward solving the problem in the larger system.

4. **Address the issue.** This step involves solving the problem and implementing solutions. OD practitioners may help the group diagnose, design, implement, and evaluate changes. A key issue is gaining commitment in the wider organization to implementing the group's solutions. Several factors can facilitate such ownership. First, a communication plan should link group activities to the organization. This may include publishing minutes from team meetings; inviting organization members, such as middle managers, union representatives, or hourly workers, into the meetings; and making presentations to different organizational groups. Second, group members need to be visible and accessible to management and labor. This can ensure that the appropriate support and resources are developed for the recommendations. Third, problem-solving processes should include an appropriate level of participation by organization members. Different data collection methods can be used to gain member input and to produce ownership of the problem and solutions.

5. **Dissolve the group.** The microcosm group can be disbanded following successful implementation of changes. This typically involves writing a final report or holding a final meeting.

Results of Microcosm Groups The microcosm group intervention derives from an intergroup relations theory developed by Alderfer, who has applied it to communications and race-relations problems. A microcosm group that addressed communications issues improved the way meetings were conducted; developed a job posting, career development, and promotion program; and conducted new-employee orientations.[10] In addition, the group assisted in the development, administration, and feedback of an organization-wide employee opinion survey. Alderfer also reported seven years of longitudinal data on a race-relations advisory group in a large organization.[11] Over time, white members showed significant improvements in their race-relations perceptions; African Americans consistently perceived more evidence of racism in the organization; and attendance at the meetings varied both over time and by race. In addition to the intragroup data, the case documented several changes in the organization, including the development of a race-relations competency document, the implementation of a race-relations workshop, and the creation of an upward-mobility policy.

The dearth of research on microcosm groups reflects how difficult it is to measure parallel processes and associate them with measures of organizational processes. Given their prevalence in organizations, however, more research on this intervention would be welcome.

11-3b Resolving Intergroup Conflict

Unlike the interpersonal conflict interventions discussed in Chapter 10, the intergroup conflict intervention is designed specifically to help two groups or departments within an organization resolve dysfunctional conflicts. Intergroup conflict is neither good nor bad in itself, and in some cases, conflict among departments is necessary and productive for organizations.[12] This applies where there is little interdependence among departments and conflict or competition among them can spur higher levels of productivity. For example, organizations structured around different product lines might want to promote competition among the product groups. This might increase each group's productivity and add to the overall effectiveness of the firm.

In other organizations, especially those with highly interdependent departments, conflict may become dysfunctional.[13] Two or more groups may grow polarized, and their continued conflict may result in the development of defensiveness and negative stereotypes of the other group. Polarization can be revealed in such statements as: "Any solution they come up with is wrong," "We find that nobody in that group will cooperate with us," or "What do you expect of those idiots?" Particularly when intergroup communication is necessary, the amount and quality of communication usually drops off. Groups begin seeing the others as "the enemy" rather than in positive or even neutral terms. As the amount of communication decreases, the amount of mutual problem solving falls off as well. The tendency increases for one group to sabotage the efforts of the other group, either consciously or unconsciously. The diagnostic process should be oriented to understanding the history of relationships between the two groups.

Application Stages A basic strategy for improving interdepartmental or intergroup relationships is to change the perceptions (perhaps, more accurately, misperceptions) that the two groups have of each other. One formal approach for accomplishing this, originally described by Blake and his associates, consists of a ten-step procedure.[14]

1. A consultant external to the two groups obtains their agreement to work directly on improving intergroup relationships. (The use of an outside consultant is highly recommended because without the moderating influence of such a neutral third party, it is almost impossible for the two groups to interact without becoming deadlocked and polarized in defensive positions.)
2. A time is set for the two groups to meet—preferably away from their normal work situations.
3. The consultant, together with the managers of the two groups, describes the purpose and objectives of the meeting: to develop better mutual relationships, explore the perceptions the groups have of each other, and formulate plans for improving the relationship. The two groups are presented the following or similar questions: "What qualities or attributes best describe our group?" "What qualities or attributes best describe the other group?" and "How do we think the other group will describe us?" Then, the two groups are encouraged to establish norms of openness for feedback and discussion.
4. The two groups are assigned to separate rooms and asked to write their answers to the three questions. Usually, an outside consultant works with each group to help the members become more open and to encourage them to develop lists that accurately reflect their perceptions, both of their own image and of the other group.
5. After completing their lists, the two groups reconvene. A representative from each group presents the written statements. Only the two representatives are allowed to speak. The primary objective at this stage is to make certain that the images, perceptions, and attitudes are presented as accurately as possible and to avoid the arguments that might arise if the two groups openly confront each other. Questions, however, are allowed to ensure that both groups clearly understand the written lists. Justifications, accusations, or other statements are not permitted.
6. When it is clear that the two groups thoroughly understand the content of the lists, they separate again. By this point, a great number of misperceptions and discrepancies have been brought to light.
7. The task of the two groups (almost always with a consultant as a process observer) is to analyze and review the reasons for the discrepancies. The emphasis is on solving the problems and reducing the misperceptions. The actual or implicit question is not whether the perception of the other group is right or wrong but rather "How did these perceptions occur? What actions on the part of our group may have contributed to this set of perceptions?"
8. When the two groups have worked through the discrepancies, as well as the areas of common agreement, they meet to share both the identified discrepancies and their problem-solving approaches to those discrepancies. Because the primary focus is on the behavior underlying the perceptions, free, open discussion is encouraged between the two groups, and their joint aim is to develop an overall list of remaining and possible sources of friction and isolation.
9. The two groups are asked to develop specific plans of action for solving specific problems and for improving their relationships.
10. When the two groups have gone as far as possible in formulating action plans, at least one follow-up meeting is scheduled so that the groups can report on actions that have been implemented, identify any further problems that have emerged, and, where necessary, formulate additional action plans.

In addition, to this formal approach to improving interdepartmental or intergroup relationships there are a number of more informal procedures. Beckhard asks each of the two groups to develop a list of what irritates or exasperates them about the other group and to predict what they think the other group will say about them.[15] Similarly, based on their experience at TRW Systems, Fordyce and Weil developed a modified approach whereby each group builds three lists—one containing "positive feedback" items (those things the group values and likes about the other group), a "bug" list (those things the group dislikes about the other group), and an "empathy" list (predictions about what the other group's list contains).[16] When the groups come together, they build a master list of major concerns and unresolved problems, which are assigned priorities and developed into an agenda. When they have completed the task, the subgroups report the results of their discussions to the total group, which then develops a series of action steps for improving the relations between the groups and commits itself to following through. For each action step, specific responsibilities are assigned, and an overall schedule is developed for prompt completion of the action steps.

These different approaches to resolving intergroup conflict form a continuum from behavioral solutions to attitudinal change solutions.[17] Behavioral methods are oriented to keeping the relevant parties physically separate and specifying the limited conditions under which interaction will occur. Little attempt is made to understand or change how members of each group see the other. Conversely, attitudinal methods, such as exchanging group members or requiring intense interaction with important rewards or opportunities clearly tied to coordination, are directed at changing how each group perceives the other. Here, it is assumed that perceptual distortions and stereotyping underlie the conflict and need to be changed to resolve it.

Most of the OD solutions to intergroup conflict reviewed in this section favor attitudinal change strategies. However, such interventions typically require considerably more skill and time than do the behavioral solutions. Changing attitudes is difficult in conflict situations, especially if the attitudes are deep-seated and form an integral part of people's personalities. Attitudinal change interventions should be reserved for those situations in which behavioral solutions might not work.

Behavioral interventions seem most applicable in situations in which task interdependence between the conflicting groups is relatively low and predictable. For example, the task interaction between the production and the maintenance departments might be limited to scheduled periodic maintenance of machines. Here, higher management can physically separate the departments and specify the limited conditions under which they should interact. Where the shared task requires only limited interaction, that interaction can be programmed and standardized.

Attitudinal change interventions seem necessary when task interdependence between the conflicting groups is high and unpredictable, such as might be found between the research and the production departments during a new-product introduction. Here, the two departments need to work together closely, often at unpredictable times and with novel, complex issues. When conflicts arise because of misperceptions, they must be worked through in terms of people's perceptions and attitudes. The shared task does not permit physical separation or limited, specific interaction. It is in these highly interdependent and unpredictable task situations that the conflict resolution interventions discussed in this section are most appropriate.

Application 11.2 presents an example of intergroup conflict resolved by an attitudinal change intervention.[18] The method reflects a variation on the traditional process described above and also places the intervention in a planned change context.

application 11.2

IMPROVING INTERGROUP RELATIONSHIPS IN JOHNSON & JOHNSON'S DRUG EVALUATION DEPARTMENT

Johnson & Johnson (J&J) is one of the world's largest manufacturers of health care products. The fundamental objective of the company is to provide scientifically sound, high-quality products and services to help heal the sick, cure disease, and improve the quality of life. In mid-2000, J&J made a strategic decision to merge two research and development organizations in the Pharmaceuticals Group. Departments in the Robert Wood Johnson Pharmaceutical Research Institute, headquartered in New Jersey, and the Janssen Research Foundation, headquartered in Belgium, were integrated to create a leading-edge global function called the Drug Evaluation (DE) organization. DE's purpose is to rapidly generate data that allows J&J to make the best investment decisions about the drug portfolio. In the overall R&D process, the group is the bridge between discovery of new compounds and full development of a new drug. As a group, they are responsible for investigating all compounds that may be potential new products and making data-driven decisions in collaboration with the discovery and full-development groups. The highest-quality and highest-potential discovery compounds are quickly and efficiently moved through preclinical development and into initial human trials. DE employees experience a genuine and unique opportunity to shape the R&D pipeline in J&J and ultimately influence patient well-being. It is an exciting and challenging place to be in.

Most of the first half of 2001 was spent in merger and integration activity with the groups, while moving compounds through the pipeline. The DE management team has overall responsibility for the organization and consists of the global head of DE and seven direct reports representing chemical pharmaceuticals, clinical drug evaluation, clinical operations, and portfolio planning and resource management (PPRM), among others.

One of the groups, the PPRM group was a new function created to improve the efficiency of DE processes. They allowed the DE management team to accurately track compounds as they moved through the process and provided information in a consistent manner across the organization. The group consisted of project champions, portfolio planners, resource managers, and support staff. Project champions were the core of the PPRM group. When a compound is accepted into DE, the project champion leads a project team consisting of representatives from the different functions. This team is responsible for planning and executing the DE plan for their compound. The project champion works closely with all of the functions to ensure the compound progresses on schedule through the different stages of the process and ultimately on the handoff to full development.

The Clinical Drug Evaluation group was responsible for developing clinical plans that would take the new drug compound into human trials. The group consisted primarily of clinical scientists, M.D.s who were responsible for focusing on the key questions to be identified to achieve DE deliverables. Clinical scientists were also responsible for communicating these questions and the results from the clinical aspects of the project to the rest of the project team. The quality of the data depends on asking the right questions, so this role is critical to delivering business benefits of the compound.

In the fall of 2001, the DE management team expressed concern that there were many issues surfacing about the nature of the work, roles and responsibilities, and the general cohesion within DE. This was particularly true with the clinical scientists and the project champions. They worried that a conflict between the schedule-oriented project champions and the quality-oriented clinical specialists was hurting department morale. The DE management team asked an OD practitioner to help with understanding and addressing these issues. As part of the process, the practitioner conducted diagnostic interviews with various members of the PPRM and Clinical Drug Evaluation groups. She found that opinions varied widely as to the nature of the problem and its characteristics. For example, some people did not perceive a problem, some believed it had nothing to do with the interaction of the project champions and the clinical scientists, and others believed it was a lack of clear roles and responsibilities. Overall, seven different themes emerged from the data, although no single issue dominated. Faced with this lack of agreement on the issue and its causes, the practitioner, in collaboration with the different groups, proposed a three-day off-site meeting to work through the data and concerns.

The meeting was held in January 2002 in Villars, Switzerland (selected for its neutrality), and consisted of exercises to improve communications and a process to address intergroup conflict. Members of the PPRM and Clinical Drug Evaluation groups were asked to address the following questions:

- What do we want from you?
- What we don't want from you?
- What do we offer/give you?
- What we don't offer/give you?

Each group was asked to discuss and come to consensus about their perceptions of the other group. Reflecting the diagnostic data, there was a lively discussion within each group as perceptions were shared, discussed, and resolved.

When each group presented their results, typical responses included the following: "We want your expertise;" "We want everyone to be a part of the team;" "We want input, support and agreement, adequate time, and frequent interaction." The groups did not want surprise decisions, delayed or filtered information, and responsibility for another's job. These themes were consistent across both groups.

The practitioner then opened the floor for a large group discussion of the presentations. Although a variety of issues were discussed and clarified, the groups noticed that they were in 90% agreement. The key issue that needed to be resolved was the decision-making process. The practitioner then facilitated a discussion of how the two groups should make decisions and they agreed on a method to do so.

As a result of the meeting, the two groups reported improved relations and increased trust because of an increased understanding of each other's perspectives. They developed positive, cooperative attitudes toward the other group, understood how different cultural backgrounds and working styles were contributing to the strained decision-making process, and were able to reach agreement on a variety of important roles and responsibilities. In addition, a few weeks after the meeting, the participants said they realized the importance of setting the time aside to work through the issues. They gained an appreciation for a need to have consistency in methods and tools for the teams. The DE management team was pleased with the results.

Results of Intergroup Conflict Interventions Early OD practitioners reported on a number of studies concerning the effects of intergroup conflict resolution. Several researchers have reported positive results in a variety of settings, including union–management relations, an Indian tribal council, government organizations, and for-profit firms.[19] The results include attitudinal changes, such as improved perceptions, increased trust, and less stereotyping in addition to improved operational results. For example, Huse found that bringing representatives of different groups together to work on common work-related problems had a marked effect, not only on relationships among a number of different manufacturing groups but also on the quality of the product, which increased 62%.[20]

The technology for improving intergroup relations is promising. A greater distinction between attitudinal and behavioral changes needs to be made in planning effective intergroup interventions. A greater variety of interventions that address the practical difficulties of bringing two groups together is also necessary. Finally, more knowledge is needed about how culture affects intergroup conflict and how interventions need to be adjusted in cross-cultural situations.[21] Growing knowledge and theory suggest that conflict can be either functional or dysfunctional, depending on the circumstances. Further research is needed to identify when conflict should be intensified and when it should be reduced.

11-4 Large Group Interventions

The third system-wide process intervention is called large group intervention. Such change programs have been referred to variously as "search conferences," "open-space meetings," "open-systems planning," "world cafés," "future searches," "decision accelerators," and "Appreciative Inquiry Summits."[22] They focus on issues that affect the whole organization or large segments of it, such as developing new products or services, responding to environmental change, redesigning the organization, or introducing new technology. The defining feature of large group interventions, what differentiates them from confrontation meetings, is the bringing together of large numbers of organization members, often more than a hundred, and a broader range of other stakeholders for a two- to four-day meeting or conference. Here, conference attendees work together to identify and resolve organization-wide problems, to design new approaches to structuring and managing the firm, or to propose future directions for the organization. Large group interventions are among the fastest-growing OD applications. They reflect the core values of OD (inclusion, participation, and learning), have been used successfully in large and small organizations, and have been successfully adapted to a variety of cultural contexts.[23]

Large group interventions can vary on several dimensions, including purpose, size, length, structure, and number. The purpose of these change methods can include creating the future plan and setting direction, redefining work, organization structures, and systems, and planning or solving particular organizational problems.[24] Large group interventions have been run with groups of less than 50 to more than 2,000 participants and have lasted between one and five days. Some large group processes are relatively planned and structured; others are more informal. Some interventions involve a single large-group meeting; others include a succession of meetings to accomplish system-wide change in a short period of time.

Despite these differences, most large group interventions have similar conceptual foundations and methods.[25] These interventions have evolved over the past 30 years and represent a combination of open-systems thinking, participation and social construction, and self-management. Open-systems thinking, as outlined in Chapter 5, directs attention to how organizations interact with and are shaped by their environments. Proponents of large group interventions suggest that an organization's current state is the result of the intentional and unintentional interaction among many groups and individuals both inside and outside the organization. Changing the organization's vision, structure, strategy, or work therefore requires the deliberate, face-to-face coordination of these groups.

The participation and social construction assumptions support this open-systems view. The participation assumption suggests that a variety of organization stakeholders must be involved to create an accurate view of the environment and organization. The social construction assumption suggests that only by developing a shared understanding of the environment and the organization among these stakeholders can "common ground" be found and coordinated action be possible. Without a broad and shared view, conflicts can arise about what parts of the environment or what actions are most important. Such perceptual disagreements make planning and implementing a coherent strategy difficult.[26]

Finally, the self-management assumption proposes that large group processes must create the conditions for ownership and commitment. All large group methods attempt to create a rhythm of large group presentations balanced against small-group discussions, exercises, tasks, and dialogues. Through the small-group work, participants work with a variety of stakeholders, build perspective, and become committed to action.

11-4a Application Stages

Conducting a large group intervention generally involves preparing for the meeting, conducting it, and following up on outcomes. These activities are described below.

Preparing for the Large Group Meeting A design team/microcosm group comprising OD practitioners and organization members reflecting the general theme of the conference is formed to plan and organize the intervention. The team generally addresses four key ingredients for successful large group interventions: a compelling meeting theme, appropriate participants, relevant tasks to address the theme, and postmeeting follow-through.

1. **Compelling meeting theme.** Large group interventions require a compelling reason or focal point for change. Although "people problems" can be an important focus, more powerful reasons for large group efforts include managing impending mergers or reorganizations, responding to environmental threats and opportunities, or proposing radical organizational changes.[27] Drawing on diagnostic data regarding the organization's current state and the forces pressing for change, senior leaders must communicate and make clear to others the purpose of the large group meeting. Ambiguity about the reason for the intervention can dissipate participants' energy and commitment to change. For example, a large group meeting that successfully envisioned a hospital's future organization design was viewed as a failure by a few key managers who thought that the purpose was to cut costs from the hospital's budget. Their subsequent lack of support stalled the change effort.
2. **Appropriate participants.** A fundamental goal of large group interventions is to "get the whole system in the room." This involves inviting as many people as possible who have a stake in the conference theme and who are energized and committed to conceiving and initiating change. Senior managers, suppliers, union leaders, internal and external customers, trade-group representatives, government and regulatory officials, and organization members from a variety of jobs, genders, races, and ages are potential participants.

   Recent research on large group interventions suggest that simple representation from different stakeholder groups is not enough to achieve the advantages of having the "whole system in the room."[28] If only one customer attends the meeting, and customers are critical to the conference theme, it is unlikely that the customer "voice" will be fully represented in the meeting deliberations. Planners must ensure that each important stakeholder group has sufficient representation.
3. **Relevant tasks to address the conference theme.** As described below, a successful large group intervention is dependent on the sequence of tasks performed by the group. These tasks typically are assigned to subgroups that examine the theme and

draw conclusions for action. Generally, participants rely on their own experience and expertise to address system-wide issues, rather than drawing on resources from outside of the large group meeting. However, newer forms of large group interventions, such as the decision accelerator, relax this assumption and provide a means for the group to access information on the Internet or other sources. This ensures that the meeting can be completed within the allotted time and that members can participate fully as important sources of information.

The design team must think clearly about the conference objectives, the expected deliverables, and the sequence of activities, exercises, and conversations that will produce those results. The three generic models described in the next section are a good starting point. However, with the help of an OD practitioner experienced in large group meeting design, a team can be very creative and innovative with respect to the activities performed during the meeting.

Finally, design teams and practitioners must give appropriate attention to the logistics and support required to manage a large group of people. This includes technological issues, such as audio/visual needs, microphones, and other communications concerns, logistical issues, such as moving people from table to table or room to room, note takers, and small-group facilitators, and facilities issues, such as meals, the size of the room, and noise. Many large group interventions do not meet their objectives because of poor planning in this area.

4. **Postmeeting follow-through.** Abundant evidence suggests that without a clear plan for taking the outputs, action plans, and recommendations from a large group intervention, the meeting will just be an "event." There is little likelihood that change will occur. Given the high expectations that are often generated by this intervention, it is imperative that the design team specify how the outputs from the meeting will be used. This could include clarifying how senior leaders will make decisions about which recommendations to support and fund, how action plans from the conference will be integrated with other ongoing strategic initiatives, or how particular changes will be implemented.

Conducting the Meeting The flow of events in a large group meeting can vary greatly, depending on its purpose and the framework adopted. Most large group processes, however, fit within three primary frameworks: open-systems methods, open-space methods, and positive methods. These various methods reflect different strategies for dealing with the four key dilemmas of large group interventions:[29]

1. The dilemma of voice refers to the problem of encouraging participation on the one hand and being overwhelmed if each individual wants to speak. Even when a large group event is relatively small in terms of participants, time would quickly run out if everyone wanted to speak up in the large group.
2. The dilemma of structure refers to how tightly or loosely the meeting should be organized. Some methods, like the open-systems processes described below, can be tightly controlled while others, like the open-space methods, are almost unstructured. The dilemma is not knowing how much structure a particular group prefers, how much they want, or how much anxiety they are experiencing.
3. The egocentric dilemma refers to the problem of people holding on to their own personal views of right or wrong, better or worse. When individuals hold on too tightly, it makes large-group decision making difficult. Similarly, when a large group event overly represents one stakeholder group, that group can dominate the conversation and be less open to alternative points of view.

4. The dilemma of emotional contagion refers to a group dynamic where many people take on the frustrations or excitement of others. When emotional contagion happens, people unconsciously give up their ownership of a problem, action, or solution and get swept up in the moment. It represents a large group version of "groupthink" and can result in solutions that people, upon reflection, cannot support.

Open-Systems Methods. A variety of large group approaches, such as search conferences, open-systems planning, decision accelerators, and real-time strategic change, have their basis in open-systems methods and are among the more structured large group processes. These approaches help organizations assess their environments systematically and develop strategic responses to them. They help organization members develop a strategic mission for relating to the environment and influencing it in favorable directions. Open-systems methods begin with a diagnosis of the existing environment and how the organization relates to it. They proceed to develop possible future environments and action plans to bring them about.[30] These steps are described below.

1. **Map the current environment surrounding the organization.** In this step, the different domains or parts of the environment are identified and prioritized. This involves listing all external groups directly interacting with the organization, such as customers, suppliers, or government agencies, and ranking them in importance. Participants then are asked to describe each domain's expectations for the organization's behavior.
2. **Assess the organization's responses to environmental expectations.** This step asks participants to describe how the organization currently addresses the environmental expectations identified in step 1.
3. **Identify the core mission of the organization.** This step helps to identify the underlying purpose or core mission of the organization, as derived from how it responds to external demands. Attention is directed at discovering the mission as it is revealed in the organization's behavior, not as it is pronounced in the organization's official statement of purpose. This is accomplished by examining the organization and environment transactions identified in steps 1 and 2 and then assessing the values that seem to underlie those interactions. These values provide clues about the actual identity or mission of the organization.
4. **Create a realistic future scenario of environmental expectations and organization responses.** This step asks members to project the organization and its environment into the near future, assuming no real changes in the organization. It asks participants to address the question, "What will happen if the organization continues to operate as it does at present?" Participant responses are combined to develop a likely organization future under the assumption of no change.
5. **Create an ideal future scenario of environmental expectations and organization responses.** Members are asked to create alternative, desirable futures. This involves going back to steps 1, 2, and 3 and asking what members ideally would like to see happen in the near future in both the environment and the organization. People are encouraged to fantasize about desired futures without worrying about possible constraints.
6. **Compare the present with the ideal future and prepare an action plan for reducing the discrepancy.** This last step identifies specific actions that will move both the environment and the organization toward the desired future. Planning for appropriate interventions typically occurs in three timeframes: tomorrow, six months from now, and two years from now. Participants also decide on a follow-up schedule for sharing the flow of actions and updating the planning process.

There are a number of variations on this basic model, each of which follows a similar pattern of creating common ground, discussing the issues, and devising an agenda for change. For example, search conferences begin with an exercise called "appreciating the past," which asks participants to examine the significant events, milestones, and highlights of the organization's previous 30 years (or less, in the case of newer organizations).[31] It demonstrates that participants share a common history, although they may come from different organizations, departments, age groups, or hierarchical levels.

Once common ground is established, members can discuss the system-wide issue or theme. To promote widespread participation, members typically organize into subgroups of eight to ten people representing as many stakeholder viewpoints as possible. The subgroups may address a general question (for example, "What are the opportunities for new business in our global market?") or focus on a specific issue (for example, "How can we improve quality and cut costs on a particular product line?"). Subgroup members brainstorm answers to these questions, record them on flipchart paper, and share them with the larger group. The whole group compares responses from the subgroups and identifies common themes. Other methods, such as presentations to the large group, small-group meetings on particular aspects of the conference theme, or spontaneous meetings of interest to the participants, are used to discuss the conference theme and distribute information to members.

The final task of large group meetings based on open-systems methods is creating an agenda for change. Participants are asked to reflect on what they have learned at the meeting and to suggest changes for themselves, their department, and the whole organization. Members from the same department often are grouped together to discuss their proposals and decide on action plans, timetables, and accountabilities. Action items for the total organization are referred to a steering committee that addresses organization-wide policy issues and action plans. At the conclusion of the large group meeting, the departmental subgroups and the steering committee report their conclusions to all participants and seek initial commitment to change.

Application 11.3 describes the large group decision accelerator process at Alegent Health. The decision accelerator model was used to generate an innovative vision and strategy for the key clinical areas within the health care system. It followed an open-systems model to design and implement its large group meeting.

Open-Space Methods. The second approach to large group interventions attempts to address the four dilemmas by imposing a minimal level of formal structure. Open-space methods temporarily restructure or "self-organize" participants around interests and topics associated with the conference theme. They generally follow these steps:[32]

1. **Set the conditions for self-organizing.** In the first step, the OD practitioner or manager responsible for the large group intervention sets the stage by announcing the theme of the session and the norms that will govern it. In addition, participants are informed that the meeting will consist of small-group discussions convened by the participants and addressing any topic they believe critical to the theme of the conference. Two sets of norms govern how open-space methods are applied, and although the norms may sound ambiguous, they are critical to establishing the conditions for a successful meeting.

   The first set of norms concerns the "Law of Two Feet." It encourages people to take responsibility for their own behavior—to go to meetings and discussions where they are learning, contributing, or in some way remaining interested. Moving from group to group is legitimized by the roles of "butterflies" and "bumblebees." Butterflies attract others into spontaneous conversations and, in fact, may never attend a formal meeting. Bumblebees go from group to group and sprinkle knowledge, information, or new ideas into different meetings.

USING THE DECISION ACCELERATOR TO GENERATE INNOVATIVE STRATEGIES IN ALEGENT'S WOMEN'S AND CHILDREN'S SERVICE LINE

application 11.3

The applications in Chapters 4, 6, and 9 described the process of entry, contracting, data collection, and evaluation in a large group intervention at Alegent Health. In this application, we describe the Women's and Children's Right Track Decision Accelerator workshop. It was one of the initial six DAs intended to set a vision and strategy for the clinical service areas within the health system.

The Alegent Health (AH) organization is a large health care system in eastern Nebraska and western Iowa. It has five large hospitals and a variety of outpatient clinics. As part of the change agenda from the new CEO, Wayne Sensor, a Chief Innovation Officer, Ted Schwab, was hired to lead in the development of a transformed health care system. Under a corporate vision that included achieving "world-class leadership in compassionate, faith-based health services that measurably enriches the lives of families we serve through an exceptional commitment to quality," Schwab engaged two OD consultants from California, Joel Fadem and Stu Winby. Fadem was a professor at UCLA who specialized in health care organizations, and Winby was a former internal OD consultant at Hewlett-Packard, where he had innovated on large group interventions during the HP–Compaq merger (see Application 8.4). Together, Schwab, Fadem, and Winby worked with other members of AH to decide on the use of large group interventions as a way to generate innovative thinking, strategies, and decision making in the organization.

The strategic innovation process was kicked off in June 2005, with six large group "decision accelerators," one for each of the clinical service lines. A decision accelerator is similar to other large group interventions, especially those based on open-systems thinking. It has two unique attributes that distinguish it from the others. First, a DA is more than a process; it is a physical space. Alegent Health not only committed to the large group intervention as a method for innovation, it committed physical resources to maximizing the impact of the work. The organization leased half a floor of an office building in Omaha, gutted the offices, and built a completely flexible facility to support the DA process (see figure here). Each DA space is designed to fit the situation and organization needs, but has several things in common. The primary working space is completely flexible with moveable white boards where small groups record their outputs and discussions, moveable chairs, and so on. Alegent's DA space had a unique feature that proved to be a favorite among the participants. All of the walls in the space could be written on with erasable markers. That is, the walls of the room—and there was a lot of wall space—could host planned or impromptu meetings where the group members could draw what they were thinking.

Second, the DA, like other large group interventions, assumes that by getting the "whole system in the room," a richer, more complete conversation and better decisions ensue. However, the DA does not assume that "all" of the necessary or available information is in the room and so most DA spaces include some kind of library with Internet-enabled computer terminals and other source documentation (e.g., white papers, articles, books) that might inform the discussion during the DA.

The Women's and Children's (W&C) DA was the fourth one conducted at AH. The agenda for the W&C DA was similar to others, but Fadem and Winby worked with the VP in charge of the clinical area, Joan Neuhaus, to modify some of the activities to fit with the challenges, opportunities, and existing features of the W&C service line. For example, Joan wanted the group to address the handling of high-risk pregnancies and deliveries as well as thinking about women's health issues more broadly. Also as part of the preparation, Steve Houston, who directed the facility, put together

Flexible Facility Layout for DA

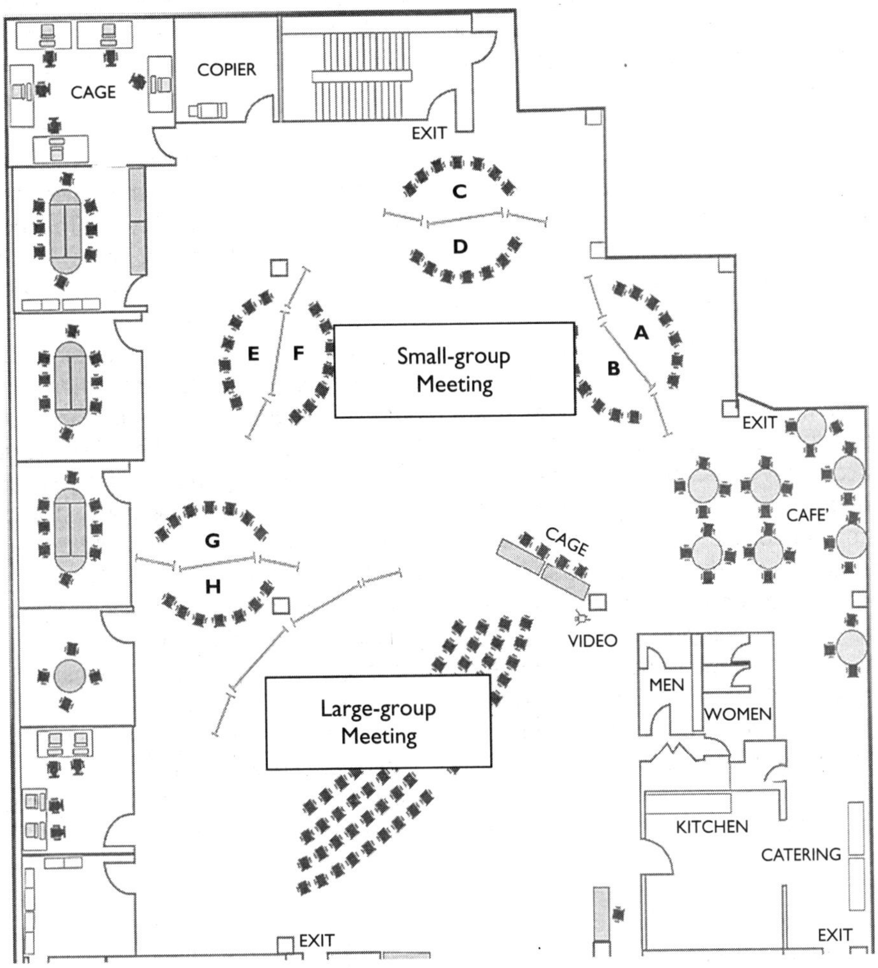

his team of support staff, including note takers who transcribed large group discussions and report-outs, photographers who captured all small-group outputs, a graphic facilitator who recorded the large group conversations in a visual format, and catering for the meeting. The support staff played a critical role in the success of a DA by knowing the agenda well enough to position the physical facility in advance of any activity so that the participants needed only to focus on the content of the meeting. This included having handouts, instructions, surveys, and other documents prepared in advance, which made it possible to handle any immediate requests from the facilitators.

On Day 1, the participants arrived to a light breakfast and were immediately given a task. Using the white boards that were in front of the large group meeting space, called the theater, each participant in the workshop was to find a marker and to write down the events, forces, trends, and innovations that they knew of or heard about in seven different categories (e.g., technology, medicine/health care, society, the economy, globally, ecologically, and in education). The white boards had been prepared in advance by Houston's team with the seven categories and with each white board representing a particular time period: 1975–1990, 1991–2005, and 2006–2020. After about 15 minutes, the participants were asked to find two people they didn't know and the trio had to share the things they had written down.

Following the environmental scanning activity, an introduction and overview of the agenda took place. The CEO welcomed the participants and encouraged them to talk about the things that would make Alegent Health a "world-class" organization. He referred the group to the corporate vision, expressed his commitment to the effort, and said he would be back on the last day to hear their ideas for creating a world-class W&C service line.

The next few activities asked participants, in small groups first and then in large group report-outs, to think about the implications of the environmental events on the W&C service line by 2015, what was implied by the "world class" part of the Alegent Health vision, and the implications "world class" had for the W&C clinical area. For each activity, a relevant organizing structure was used. For example, for discussing the implications of "world class" on the W&C clinical area, the groups were broken down into stakeholder categories. How might, for example, patients, the community, or physicians view a world-class W&C service? In each activity, the small groups were composed of multiple stakeholders, including physicians, managers/executives from Alegent, patients and families, community members, and other stakeholders.

Before the day ended, Winby asked the group a question: "If there was one thing that you really want to make sure gets addressed at this meeting to make it a success for you, what would that be?" He had people write their questions on a piece of paper and put it into a box as they were leaving.

During the debrief after the first day, the facilitators and support team reviewed what went well and any processes that needed to be improved, discussed the energy and interests of the participants, and sorted the "what's most important" questions into similar themes in preparation for an activity on Day 2.

Day 2 began with a welcome from Neuhaus and then the group went to work. The first activity was to take the work from the Day 1 W&C visioning activities and prioritize the different elements. The group was questioned as to what, for them, were the most important dimensions of a world-class W&C service line? In addition, the group was led through an exercise to determine if there were any technologies or regulatory events that would fundamentally alter the way health care was delivered in this area. The group discussed, for example, the implications of being able to deliver a child that was less than 20 weeks old.

In the next exercise, the facilitators asked the group to address the questions they had asked at the end of Day 1. The questions had been categorized into six areas, including gaps in the community's health care, women's health service offerings, and obstetrics among others. The participants were allowed to sign up to discuss whatever subject interested them. In the report-out of the groups, an important issue that had been simmering throughout Day 1 was surfaced. That is, should high-risk pregnancies and deliveries be centralized to one hospital and what would that imply? The large group debated this subject from a variety of perspectives. In the end, it was agreed that such a move made sense from the world-class perspective, but that it would be difficult to implement and would face much resistance.

The final activity asked the participants to synthesize their discussions and activities into a high-level "horizons map." That is, for each of the major categories that had been discussed, including women's health, obstetrics, child/adolescent medicine, and community health, the group was to lay out the key decisions, milestones, and events that would need to take place over the next 18 months, by 2010, and by 2015 to realize their vision of a world-class W&C clinical area.

On Day 3, the senior leadership team from Alegent Health joined the group and listened to a presentation of the horizon map. The graphic facilitator drew the final horizons map with pictures, words, and symbols, and this was used as the outline for the presenters. Following the presentations, the executives asked questions and discussed some of the group's decisions. In addition, they laid out the "next steps" of the process, including gathering the data from all of the clinical area DAs in order to resource the strategies appropriately.

The second set of norms is labeled the "Four Principles." The first principle is "whoever comes is the right people." It is intended to free people to begin conversations with anyone at any time. It also signals that the quality of a conversation is what's most important, not who's involved. The second principle, "Whatever happens is the only thing that could have," infuses the group with responsibility, encourages participants to be flexible, and prepares them to be surprised. "Whenever it starts is the right time" is the third principle and is aimed at encouraging creativity and following the natural energy in the group. The final principle, "When it's over, it's over," allows people to move on and not feel like they have to meet for a certain time period or satisfy someone else's requirements.

2. **Create the agenda.** The second step in open-space interventions is to develop a road map for the remainder of the conference. This is accomplished by asking participants to describe a topic related to the conference theme that they have passion for and interest in discussing. This topic is written on a large note card or "sticky note," announced to the group, and then posted on the community bulletin board where meeting topics, times, and locations are displayed.[33] The person announcing the topic agrees to convene the meeting at the posted time and place and to prepare a short summary of the meeting. This process continues until everyone who wants to define a topic has been given the chance to speak. The final activity in this step asks participants to sign up for as many of the sessions as they have interest in. The open-space meeting begins with the first scheduled sessions.
3. **Coordinate activity through information.** During an open-space session, there are two ways to coordinate activities. First, each morning and evening a community meeting is held to announce new topics that have emerged for which meeting dates and times have been assigned, or to share observations and learnings. Second, as the different meetings occur, the conveners produce one-page summaries of what happened, who attended, what subjects were discussed, and what recommendations or actions were proposed. Typically, this is done on computer in a room dedicated for this purpose. These summaries are posted near the community bulletin board in an area often labeled "newsroom." Participants are encouraged to visit the newsroom and become familiar with what other groups have been discussing. The summaries also can be printed and copied for conference participants.

Positive Methods. The final large group intervention represents a hybrid approach to the four dilemmas. It is distinguished from the other two methods by its use of the positive approach to change described in Chapter 2. In fact, many of the futuring and visioning exercises in the open-systems approaches that help guide members in creating "images of potential" toward which the organization can grow and develop are drawn from this approach.[34] These methods can increase members' energy for change and build a broad consensus toward a new future. Like other large group methods, these approaches can help look at a variety of organizational issues; however, their distinguishing feature is the "appreciative" framing of issues and the leveraging of the organization's positive core attributes. The Appreciative Inquiry (AI) Summit approach suggests that human organizing and change should be a relational process of inquiry, grounded in affirmation and appreciation.[35] The four steps in an AI summit are as follows:

1. **Discover the organization's positive core.** With respect to the purpose of the summit, participants first pair up with another person and conduct an appreciative interview. If the summit is organized to take advantage of a new market opportunity, the questions would generate stories about experiences where a group or organization was most

successful in being entrepreneurial and swift. If the summit were about addressing poor organization coordination, the questions and stories would be personal experiences where two or more groups worked well together.

Following the interviews, the pairs join up with three other pairs to discuss their answers to the questions. What is it that is common among all these stories? What are the elements of successful entrepreneurship or collaboration, for example? These small-group conversations are then aggregated to create a broad and inclusive list of success factors and other themes associated with these successful experiences.

2. **Dream about and envision a more desired and fulfilling future.** In this step, participants use the themes and success factors from the first activity to develop compelling images of the future. In this visioning exercise, participants are encouraged to make bold and provocative propositions about what could be in the future. To arrive at a bold vision, small groups share their greatest hopes or act out skits and presentations that convey what they believe is possible. Unlike open system or open-space methods, there is very little prioritizing or culling out of the best or more compelling themes. The positive approach believes that breadth and inclusiveness are the most important way to galvanize organization change.
3. **Design the structural and systems arrangements that will best reflect and support the vision or dream.** Members of the summit identify the design features (strategies, structures, systems, processes) that will need to be in place to make the vision a reality. This step allows participants to articulate the dream in concrete terms.
4. **Create the specific action plans that will fulfill the organization's destiny.** The primary task of the destiny step is to identify the projects, initiatives, and action plans required to implement the design criteria. Task forces are formed, teams volunteer to take on projects, and any governance mechanisms needed to coordinate the effort are created.

Following Up on Meeting Outcomes Follow-up efforts are vital to implementing the action plans from large-scale interventions. These efforts involve communicating the results of the meeting to the rest of the organization, gaining wider commitment to the changes, and structuring the change process. In those cases where all the members of the organization were involved in the large group meeting, implementation can proceed immediately according to the timetable included in the action plans.

11-4b Results of Large Group Interventions

The number of case studies describing the methods and results of large group interventions has increased dramatically. Such interventions have been conducted at for-profit firms like Allstate Insurance, Hewlett-Packard, Toyota, Boeing, Microsoft, Motorola, Marriott, and Rockport, and at such governmental and nongovernmental organizations as Save the Children, World Vision, the City of Carlsbad, California, and the U.S. Department of Agriculture. Large group interventions are increasingly common in other countries, including Pakistan, South Africa, China, Australia, England, Mexico, and India.[36] Despite the proliferation of practice, however, Purser and Griffin lament that "empirical research, such as longitudinal studies, quasi-experimental field studies, and studies of large sample sizes across a wide variety of large-group interventions are severely lacking. Data that is available tends to be anecdotal or single case studies from practitioners and consultants who have a commercial stake in promoting their own methods."[37] Yaeger, Sorensen, and Bengtsson's review of AI supports this criticism. Of the 34 reported empirical evaluations of the AI Summit approach, all of them were case studies.[38]

In response to some of these concerns, Worley, Mohrman, and Nevitt analyzed six large group interventions conducted at Alegent Health in Omaha, Nebraska.[39] The six "decision accelerators" were nearly identical in purpose—to develop a new strategy and vision—and in design. They varied only in the composition of the group and the specific theme (e.g., cardiology versus women's and children's health) being addressed. The study's methods—a naturally occurring field experiment and independent measures—allowed the researchers to isolate the relationships among group composition, process, and outcomes and rule out various alternative explanations for the results.

Two conclusions were particularly important. First, the study supported the popular assertion that group composition or "getting the whole system in the room" affected group process, but as noted earlier, the data showed that it was "balanced representation" that was important. When the decision accelerators were populated with relatively equal numbers of organization members, physicians, and community representatives (e.g., patients, government officials, regulatory representatives, and vendors), the large group process was more likely to consider the views of the different stakeholders and consider a wider variety of strategy, vision, and change options. Second, although the study did not support a relationship between group composition and outcomes, it did support the hypothesis that characteristics of the group's process had important influences on the decision accelerator's outcomes. In particular, the more "intense" the debate and discussion of different issues in the meeting, the more comprehensive, aggressive, and innovative was the strategy and vision as described by the participants.

Because large group interventions often set the stage for subsequent OD interventions, it is difficult to isolate their specific results from those of the other changes. Anecdotal evidence from practitioners and case studies suggest that benefits can include increased energy toward organizational change, improved feelings of community, ability to see "outside the box," increased speed of change, and improved relationships with stakeholders.[40] In addition, several case studies have documented improved business outcomes, such as decreased turnover, absenteeism, and costs.[41] Clearly, more systematic research is needed on this important system-wide process intervention.

SUMMARY

This chapter described three types of system-wide process interventions: confrontation meetings, intergroup interventions, and large group interventions. The organization confrontation meeting is a way of mobilizing resources for organizational problem solving and seems especially relevant for organizations undergoing stress. The intergroup relations approaches are designed to help solve a variety of organizational problems. Microcosm groups can be formed to address particular issues and use parallel processes to diffuse group solutions to the organization. The intergroup conflict resolution approach involves a method for mitigating dysfunctional conflicts between groups or departments. Conflict can be dysfunctional in situations in which groups must work together. It may, however, promote organizational effectiveness when departments are relatively independent of each other. Large group interventions are designed to focus the energy and attention of a "whole system" around organizational processes such as a vision, strategy, organization design, or culture. It is best used when the organization is about to begin a large-scale change effort or is facing a new situation. These three process interventions represent important, time-honored, and successful methods of introducing change in organizations.

NOTES

1. M. Weisbord, *Productive Workplaces* (San Francisco: Jossey-Bass, 1987).
2. R. Beckhard, "The Confrontation Meeting," *Harvard Business Review* 4 (1967): 149–55.
3. B. B. Bunker and B. Alban, *Large Group Interventions* (San Francisco: Jossey-Bass, 1997); N. Tichy and S. Sherman, *Control Your Destiny or Someone Else Will* (New York: HarperCollins, 1993).
4. This application was adapted from material in Bunker and Alban, *Large Group Interventions*; and Tichy and Sherman, *Control Your Destiny or Someone Else Will.*
5. R. Beckhard, *Organization Development: Strategies and Models* (Reading, MA: Addison-Wesley, 1969).
6. W. Bennis, *Organization Development: Its Nature, Origins, and Prospects* (Reading, MA: Addison-Wesley, 1969), 7.
7. C. Alderfer, "An Intergroup Perspective on Group Dynamics," in *Handbook of Organizational Behavior*, ed. J. Lorsch (Englewood Cliffs, NJ: Prentice Hall, 1987), 190–222; C. Alderfer, "Improving Organizational Communication Through Long-Term Intergroup Intervention," *Journal of Applied Behavioral Science* 13 (1977): 193–210; C. Alderfer, R. Tucker, C. Alderfer, and L. Tucker, "The Race Relations Advisory Group: An Intergroup Intervention," in *Organizational Change and Development*, vol. 2, ed. W. Pasmore and R. Woodman (Greenwich, CT: JAI Press, 1988), 269–321.
8. Alderfer, "Intergroup Perspective."
9. Ibid., 210.
10. Alderfer, "Improving Organizational Communication."
11. Alderfer et al., "The Race Relations Advisory Group."
12. K. Jehn, "A Multimethod Examination of the Benefits and Detriments of Intragroup Conflict," *Administrative Science Quarterly* 40 (1995): 256–83.
13. D. Tjosvold, "Cooperation Theory and Organizations," *Human Relations* 37 (1984): 743–67.
14. R. Blake, H. Shepard, and J. Mouton, *Managing Intergroup Conflict in Industry* (Houston, TX: Gulf, 1954).
15. Beckhard, *Organization Development.*
16. J. Fordyce and R. Weil, *Managing WITH People* (Reading, MA: Addison-Wesley, 1971).
17. E. Neilson, "Understanding and Managing Intergroup Conflict," in *Organizational Behavior and Administration*, ed. P. Lawrence, L. Barnes, and J. Lorsch (Homewood, IL: Richard D. Irwin, 1976), 291–305.
18. This application was written and submitted by Marianne Tracy, who served as the OD practitioner in this case.
19. Blake, Shepard, and Mouton, *Managing Intergroup Conflict in Industry*; Bennis, *Organization Development*; R. Golembiewski and A. Blumberg, "Confrontation as a Training Design in Complex Organizations: Attitudinal Changes in a Diversified Population of Managers," *Journal of Applied Behavioral Science* 3 (1967): 525–47; W. French and C. Bell, *Organization Development: Behavioral Science Interventions for Organization Improvement* (Englewood Cliffs, NJ: Prentice Hall, 1978); E. Huse and M. Beer, "Eclectic Approach to Organizational Development," *Harvard Business Review* 49 (1971): 103–13; E. Huse, "The Behavioral Scientist in the Shop," *Personnel* 44 (May–June 1965): 8–16.
20. Huse, "The Behavioral Scientist in the Shop."
21. A. Hubbard, "Cultural and Status Differences in Intergroup Conflict Resolution: A Longitudinal Study of a Middle East Dialogue Group in the United States," *Human Relations* 52 (1999): 303–23.
22. Weisbord, *Productive Workplaces*; M. Weisbord, *Discovering Common Ground* (San Francisco: Berrett-Koehler, 1993); Bunker and Alban, *Large Group Interventions*; H. Owen, *Open Space Technology: A User's Guide* (Potomac, MD: Abbott, 1992); J. Brown, D. Isaacs, and the World Café Community, *The World Cafe: Shaping Our Futures Through Conversations That Matter* (San Francisco: Berrett-Koehler Publishers, 2005); J. Ludema, D. Whitney, B. Mohr, and T. Griffin, *The Appreciative Inquiry Summit* (San Francisco: Berrett-Koehler, 2003).
23. P. Holman, T. Devane, and S. Cady, *The Change Handbook*, 2nd ed. (San Francisco: Berrett-Kohler, 2007); R. Axelrod, *Terms of Engagement: New Ways of Leading and Changing Organizations*, 2nd ed. (San Francisco: Berrett-Koehler, 2010); R. Purser and T. Griffin, "Large-group Interventions: Whole Systems Approaches to Organizational Change," in *Handbook of Organization Development*, ed. T. Cummings (Thousand Oaks, CA: Sage Publications, 2007); Bunker and Alban, *Large Group Interventions.*
24. B. Bunker and B. Alban, *The Handbook of Large Group Methods* (San Francisco: Jossey-Bass, 2006); P. Holman and T. Devane, eds., *The Change Handbook: Group Methods for Shaping the Future* (San Francisco: Berrett-Koehler, 1999).
25. J. Bartunek, J. Balogun, and B. Do, "Considering Planned Change Anew: Stretching Large Group Interventions Strategically, Emotionally, and Meaningfully," *The Academy of Management Annals* 5 (2011): 1–52; Purser and Griffin, "Large Group Interventions."
26. L. Bourgeois, "Strategic Goals, Perceived Uncertainty, and Economic Performance in Volatile Environments,"

Academy of Management Journal 28 (1985): 548–73; C. West Jr. and C. Schwenk, "Top Management Team Strategic Consensus, Demographic Homogeneity, and Firm Performance: A Report of Resounding Nonfindings," *Academy of Management Journal* 17 (1996): 571–76.

27. Weisbord, *Productive Workplaces.*
28. C. Worley, S. Mohrman, and J. Nevitt, "Large Group Interventions: An Empirical Field Study of Their Composition, Process, and Outcomes," *Journal of Applied Behavioral Science* 47 (2011): 404–31.
29. Bunker and Alban, *Large Group Interventions*; Purser and Griffin, "Large Group Interventions."
30. C. Krone, "Open Systems Redesign," in *Theory and Method in Organization Development: An Evolutionary Process*, ed. J. Adams (Arlington, VA: NTL Institute for Applied Behavioral Science, 1974), 364–91; G. Jayaram, "Open Systems Planning," in *The Planning of Change*, 3rd ed., ed. W. Bennis, K. Benne, R. Chin, and K. Corey (New York: Holt, Rinehart and Winston, 1976), 275–83; R. Beckhard and R. Harris, *Organizational Transitions: Managing Complex Change*, 2nd ed. (Reading, MA: Addison-Wesley, 1987); Cummings and Srivastva, *Management of Work.*
31. Weisbord, *Productive Workplaces.*
32. Bunker and Alban, *Large Group Interventions*; Owen, *Open Space Technology*; V. Prewitt, "Working in the Café: Lessons in Group Dialogue," *The Learning Organization* 18 (2011): 189–202.
33. Owen, *Open Space Technology.*
34. F. Emery and E. Trist, *Towards a Social Ecology* (New York: Plenum Publishing, 1973); R. Beckhard and R. Harris, *Organizational Transitions: Managing Complex Change*, 2nd ed. (Reading, MA: Addison-Wesley, 1987); R. Lippitt, "Future Before You Plan," in *The NTL Manager's Handbook* (Arlington, VA: NTL Institute, 1983), 38–41.
35. Ludema et al., *The Appreciative Inquiry Summit.*
36. Weisbord, *Discovering Common Ground*; Owen, *Open Space Technology*; M. Manning and J. DelaCerda, "Building Organizational Change in an Emerging Economy: Whole Systems Change Using Large Group Interventions in Mexico," in *Research in Organization Change and Development*, ed. W. Pasmore and R. Woodman (Oxford: JAI Press, 2003), 51–98.
37. Purser and Griffin, "Large Group Interventions."
38. T. Yaeger, P. Sorensen, and U. Bengtsson, "Assessment of the State of Appreciative Inquiry: Past, Present, and Future," in *Research in Organization Change and Development*, ed. R. Woodman and W. Pasmore (Oxford: Elsevier, 2005), 297–319.
39. Worley, Mohrman, and Nevitt, "Large Group Interventions."
40. R. Purser, S. Cabana, M. Emery, and F. Emery, "Search Conferencing: Accelerating Large-Scale Strategic Planning," in *Fast Cycle Organization Development*, ed. M. Anderson (Cincinnati, OH: South-Western College Publishing, 2000); D. Coghlan, "The Process of Change through Interlevel Dynamics in a Large-Group Intervention for a Religious Organization," *Journal of Applied Behavioral Science* 34 (1998): 105–20.
41. See, for example, the case studies on the AI Commons website: http://appreciativeinquiry.case.edu.

LINCOLN HOSPITAL: THIRD-PARTY INTERVENTION*

Soon after the election of a new chief of surgery, the president of Lincoln Hospital faced a crisis. Lincoln, a 400-bed for-profit hospital in the southwestern United States, was experiencing severe problems in its operating room (OR). Forty percent of the OR nurses had quit during the previous eight months. Their replacements were significantly less experienced, especially in the specialty areas. Furthermore, not all could be replaced; when the crisis came to a head, the OR was short seven surgical nurses.

Also, needed equipment often was not available. On several occasions, orthopedic surgeons had already begun surgery before they realized the necessary prosthesis (for example, an artificial hip, finger joint, or knee joint) was not ready, or was the wrong size, or had not even been ordered. Surgery then had to be delayed while equipment was borrowed from a neighboring hospital. Other serious problems also plagued the OR. For example, scheduling problems made life extremely difficult for everyone involved. Anesthesiologists often were unavailable when they were needed, and habitually tardy surgeons delayed everyone scheduled after them. The nursing shortage exacerbated these difficulties by requiring impossibly tight scheduling; even when the doctors were ready to begin, the scheduled nurses might still be occupied in one of the other ORs.

The surgeons were at odds among themselves. Over 30 of them were widely regarded as prima donnas who considered their own time more valuable than anyone else's and would even create emergencies in order to get "prime time" OR slots—for which, as often as not, they were late. Worst of all, however, the doctors and nurses were virtually at war. Specifically, Don, the new chief of surgery, was at war with Mary, the veteran OR director; indeed, he had campaigned on a promise to get her fired.

Lincoln's president was faced with a difficult choice. On the one hand, he needed to satisfy the physicians, who during the tenure of his predecessor had become accustomed to getting their way in personnel matters by threatening to take their patients elsewhere. The market was, as the physicians knew, increasingly competitive, and the hospital was also faced with escalating costs, changes in government regulations, and strict Joint Commission on Accreditation of Hospitals standards. Could the president afford to alienate the surgeons by opposing their newly chosen representative—who had a large practice of his own?

On the other hand, could he afford to sacrifice Mary? She had been OR director for 13 years, and he was generally satisfied with her. As he later explained,

> Mary is a tough lady, and she can be hard to get along with at times. She also doesn't smile all that much. But she does a lot of things right. She consistently stays within her budget ....

Furthermore, whereas Don had long been an outspoken critic of the hospital and was generally distrusted by its administrators, Mary was loyal, a strict constructionist who adhered firmly to hospital policies and procedures:

> She is supportive of me, of the hospital, and of our interests. She doesn't let the doctors get away with much. She has been an almost faultless employee for years, in the sense that she comes to work, gets the job done, never complains, and doesn't make any waves. I really don't understand the reason for the recent problems. I trust her and want to keep her. It would be extremely difficult to replace her.

The last point was a key one; a sister hospital had spent almost three years unsuccessfully trying to recruit an OR director.

After talking with both nurses and doctors, the president decided not to fire Mary. Instead, he told both Mary and Don that they must resolve their differences. They were to begin

---

*R. Wayne Boss, *University of Colorado*; Leslee S. Boss, *Organization Research and Development Associates*; Mark W. Dundon, *Sisters of Providence Hospital*.

meeting right away and keep on meeting, however long it took, until they got the OR straightened out.

The results were predictable. Neither party wanted to meet with the other. Mary thought the whole exercise was pointless, and Don saw it as a power struggle that he could not afford to lose. The president, who wanted an observer present, chose Terry, the new executive vice president and chief operating officer. Mary didn't know Terry very well so she asked that her boss, the vice president of patient services, sit in. Don, who "didn't trust either Mary or her boss as far as he could throw them," countered with a request for a second of his own, the vice president for medical services. When the meeting finally occurred, it quickly degenerated into a free-for-all, as Don and Mary exchanged accusations, hotly defended themselves, and interpreted any interventions by the three "observers" as " taking sides."

DIAGNOSIS

At this point, Lincoln's president called me. We negotiated a psychological contract, where the president shared the above historical information, described the problem as he saw it, and identified his expectations of me and for the project. I, in turn, articulated my expectations of the president. We then agreed to take no steps until I had interviewed both Don and Mary.

Later that afternoon, Don expressed his anger and frustration with the hospital administration and, most of all, with Mary:

> I don't want to have anything to do with this lady. She is a lousy manager. Her people can't stand to work with her. We don't have the equipment or the supplies that we need. The turnover in the OR is outrageous. The best nurses have quit, and their replacements don't know enough to come in out of the rain.... All we want is to provide quality patient care, and she refuses to let us do that. She doesn't follow through on things.

He particularly resented Mary's lack of deference.

> Mary's behavior is so disgraceful it is almost laughable. She shows no respect whatsoever for the physicians.... She thinks she can tell us what to do and order us around; and I am not going to put up with it any longer. When I agreed to take this job as chief of surgery, I promised my colleagues that I would clean up the mess that has plagued the OR for years. I have a mandate from them to do whatever is necessary to accomplish that. The docs are sick and tired of being abused, and I am going to deal with this lady head on. If we got rid of her, 95% of our problems would go away. She has just gone too far this time.

In his cooler moments, Don admitted that Mary was only partly to blame for the OR's problems, but he still insisted she must be fired, if only to prove to the doctors that the hospital administration was concerned about those problems, and that something was being done.

> *Observation:* I am always a bit suspicious about the objectivity of someone who has reached the conclusion that someone must be fired. There is almost always something else that is going on that requires more investigation.

Mary was both angry and bewildered. She saw herself as fair and consistent in dealing with doctors and nurses:

> Things had gone relatively well until six months ago. At that time, some of the ortho-pods started scheduling surgeries and then canceling them at the last minute, which, in turn, fouled up the schedule for the rest of the doctors. When I called them on it, Don went on a rampage. He is the leader of the pack, and now he has blood in his eyes. I have tried to talk with him about it, but he won't listen.

And just as Don's assessment echoed, in an exaggerated form, the doctors' perception of Mary as an exceptionally strong-willed woman, Mary's assessment of Don echoed his reputation among the orthopedic nurses and hospital administrators, who feared and distrusted his quick temper and sharp tongue:

> Not only that, but I find his filthy mouth very offensive. I am not going to cooperate with

> him when he behaves like that. Nobody else talks to me that way and gets away with it. Nobody, I won't put up with it. As long as he behaves that way, it is a waste of time to meet with him. I am sure that I am doing things that bother him, and I want the OR to run as smoothly as possible. But there is no way we can deal with these problems unless we can sit down and talk about them without being abusive.

Clearly, both Mary and Don had strong needs to control other people's behavior, while remaining free of control themselves. It is significant that each used the word *abuse* to describe the other's behavior. They did respect each other's technical abilities, but morally, Mary saw Don as "an egotistical jerk," and he saw her as a "rigid, petty tyrant." Neither trusted the other, thus, each was inclined to misconstrue even unintentionally negative comments—an especially disastrous state of affairs in the gossipy environment at Lincoln, where surgeons, nurses, and administrators were quick to relay, and amplify, the signals of hostility.

It was obvious from these initial interviews that Don and Mary were largely contributing to the OR problems; but it was also obvious that many others had a stake in the outcome of their battle. I therefore went on to interview the surgical head nurses, the vice presidents for patient services and medical services, the executive vice president, the president, and 25 physicians.

The vice presidents and the surgical head nurses agreed with the president: Mary might not be the hospital's most personable manager, but she was a good one. Her conservative, tenacious, no-nonsense style had earned the trust of administrators and the respect of OR nurses, as well as some physicians. As one nurse asserted: "Good OR managers are hard to find and certainly Lincoln is far better off with Mary than without her."

The doctors, in general, supported Don, though some of them had reservations. At one extreme, an anesthesiologist began with a classic disclaimer:

> Now, I want you to know that I don't have any problems with Mary, personally. In fact, I really like her. We have been friends for years, and we get along just great.

Nevertheless, he was convinced the OR problems were "100% Mary's fault. I have no doubt about that." Furthermore, although he claimed to be, as an anesthesiologist, "a completely neutral third party in this whole business," he clearly shared Don's assumption that Mary's job as an OR manager was to keep the surgeons happy:

> Her people hate her. She is a lousy manager. She just can't work with the MDs. Surgeons are a rare breed, and there is no changing them. You have got to get someone in there who can work with them and give them what they want.

His conclusion echoed Don's: "She ought to be fired, if for no other reason than to prove that something is being done to address the problems in the OR."

> *Observation:* I am always leery of someone who says, "It is all her fault." When someone is blamed for 100% of the problem, it usually evidences either denial or a coverup. There may be a completely innocent party in an emotionally charged conflict, but I have never met one. Emotionally charged conflicts are always power struggles, and it takes two parties to play that game.

A less enthusiastic partisan, a surgeon who was a ten-year veteran of the Lincoln OR, was very conscious of the way expectations such as those expressed by Don and the anesthesiologist were apt to be viewed by others in the medical community:

> Quite frankly, I am embarrassed to admit that I am a surgeon in this town; by doing so, I am automatically branded as an egotistical dimwit. With only a few exceptions, those guys are a group of conceited, narcissistic technicians who are so caught up with themselves that they have no clue about what is going on around them. Some of them are bullies, and they push the rest of us around because we don't have the patient census they do.

His assessment of blame was correspondingly more moderate than the anesthesiologist's: "A lot of people would like you to think that this problem is one sided, and that Mary is totally responsible for this mess. But that isn't true." And while he supported Don, whom he described as reasonable and willing to listen to logic, his principal wish was to avoid personal involvement: "I am glad he is fighting this battle. I won't. The thought of getting caught between him and Mary scares me to death."

This last wish was vividly elaborated by another surgeon, who also highlighted the general perception of Mary as a strong personality:

> I don't mess with Mary at all. I'm not stupid. It's true that I don't like some of the things that she does. Sometimes she is just plain ornery. But I also am not willing to take her on. In fact, at this point, I will do whatever she wants, whenever she wants it. If the other docs are smart, they won't mess with her either. They can talk big in their meetings, but if they have any sense, they won't mess with that lady. She controls too many of the resources I need to do my job. So far she has been very helpful, and she has gone out of her way to do me some favors. I don't want to mess that up. I think it is great that Don is willing to take her on, and I wish him success. That way, if she wins, it will be him that gets beat up, not me.

The high turnover among OR nurses was a particularly sore point among the surgeons in general, whose frustration was explained by Don:

> I don't think the administration has a clue as to how urgent this matter really is. It takes at least five years for a surgical nurse to gain the necessary skills to be useful. In the last two months, we have lost some of the best nurses I have ever worked with in my life. As a result, I had to start the training process all over again. It has seemed like I've been working with a group of student nurses! This turnover has cut my productivity by more than 50%.

Most of the doctors blamed the high turnover on the nursing managers' inability to retain qualified personnel, whereas the managers blamed it on the doctors' verbal abuse. And in fact, a significant number of doctors were widely regarded by some of their peers as well as by the nurses as impatient, intolerant perfectionists who demanded far more of others than they did of themselves.

From the extended interviews, it was obvious that while Mary had greater credibility with the hospital administration and Don had more backing from the doctors, each had a certain amount of power over the other's constituency: Mary controlled the surgeons' working conditions, while Don controlled a significant portion of the hospital's patient flow. The OR problems could not be resolved without genuine cooperation from both of them—especially from Don, who was outside the formal hierarchy of the hospital and could not be coerced by the president.

I met again privately with each of them to determine whether they were honestly committed to improving their working relationship. Both were skeptical about the possibility of real change but said they were willing to do everything they could to help, as long as their own basic values were not violated. Each defined the kind of help he or she was willing to accept from me and the circumstances under which that help was to be given.

INTERVENTION

Only at this point did actual third-party facilitation intervention begin. I used a design that included perception sharing, problem identification, contracting, and follow-up meetings. At their first formal meeting together with me and the three vice presidents who acted as observers, Mary and Don began by writing answers to three questions:

1. What does he or she do well?
2. What do I think I do that bugs him or her?
3. What does he or she do that bugs me?

The very process of writing things down was helpful. It gave them time to get used to this explicitly confrontational situation before either of them had a chance to "pop off" at the other, and it forced an element of rationality into an emotionally charged situation. Also, the questions required specific answers concerning behaviors, not subjective generalizations about personalities. Listing specific behaviors made each of them realize that at least some of the things they disliked about the other could be changed.

They then explained these responses orally, in the order shown in Figure 1. Because of their

FIGURE 1

Participant Responses to Three Questions in the Third-Party Facilitation Model

1. **What does Mary admire about Don and think he does well?**
   - He is very concerned about patient care.
   - I admire him for his skills as a surgeon. I would have no problem sending a member of my family to him.
   - He is interested and wants to work out issues that we have with each other.
   - He can be very gentle and considerate at times.
   - He is well respected for his skills by his peers and by the OR nursing staff.
2. **What does Don admire about Mary and think that she does well?**
   - She is honest in her work.
   - She has met my needs in orthopedics in getting us the instruments and equipment we need.
   - She has a lot of external pressures on her and she has handled them well.
   - She deals well with the various groups that are pulling at her: patients, staff, administration, physicians.
   - She manages the overall picture very well in the OR.
3. **What does Don think he does that bugs Mary?**
   - I am impatient. (Mary agrees)
   - I am demanding of personnel in surgery, but everyone can't always get what they want, when they want it. (Mary disagrees)
   - She is uncertain as to how much I am willing to support her this coming year. (Mary agrees)
   - I am not the best listener. (Mary agrees)
4. **What does Mary think she does that bugs Don?**
   - I don't listen to him. (Don agrees)
   - I appear defensive at times. (Don agrees)
   - I respond to some directives in a very detailed manner. (Don agrees)
5. **What does Mary do that bugs Don?**
   - She is difficult to communicate with. I can talk to her, but I am not sure that she is listening.
   - She doesn't assume the responsibility for some specific problems, such as not being able to do an operation without a full set of prosthesis available.
   - She doesn't effectively manage the personnel that she supervises in OR. Specifically, there is a great deal of disruption going on. And there are also morale problems, particularly as they relate to their trust of her and her trust of them in the OR.
6. **What does Don do that bugs Mary?**
   - He generalizes and is not very specific with examples, even when questioned.
   - The staff labels him as a whiner, in terms of "nothing is ever right," his complaining, etc. This also relates to laying out problems and then walking away.
   - He sometimes says one thing but means another—and gives mixed messages. An explanation of this is my asking him how things are going, he says fine, but then I find out that he has problems later in the day.
   - I do not feel a full measure of support from him, and that bugs me.
   - He doesn't always listen to my concerns.

mutual hostility, I thought it safer to require that at first they address their remarks only to the third party, not to each other. Each, however, was required to hear the other's presentation so each would understand the other's perceptions. And because both were guaranteed an uninterrupted speech, each was more likely to listen to the other. Taking up the positive perceptions first helped. As Don later explained:

> I was stunned to hear her say those positive things, particularly the part about me taking care of her family. For a long time, I had seen her as my enemy, and I expected only the worst. I was amazed that she had so much respect for me. As a result, many of my negative feelings for her began to leave. It is really tough to stay angry at someone who says so many nice things about you. I also found that I was much more willing to listen to what I do that bugs her. Somehow, criticism is always easier to take when it is accompanied by something positive.

It also helped that before making any accusations against each other, they were required to examine their own behavior. As Mary acknowledged, neither had ever taken the time to figure out specifically how he or she might be causing problems for the other:

> It had never really occurred to me that I may be doing something that caused Don to react that way. Vaguely, I suspected that I may be doing something that he didn't like, but I was hard pressed to identify what it was. I really had to stand back and say to myself, "What is it that I am doing that is making this working relationship go sour?" I had spent so much time concentrating on what he was doing that bugged me that I hadn't looked at myself.

The oral discussion of this question made it obvious that neither was intentionally causing problems for the other, making both parties less hypersensitive to imaginary insults. Also, because both were much harder on themselves than they were on each other, the milder criticisms they did subsequently direct at each other were not nearly as offensive as they would otherwise have been.

The next step was to identify specific problems for Mary and Don to address. They wrote their responses to question three on a sheet of newsprint, assigning vectors to represent the relative seriousness of the problem. Some of the most serious problems could be resolved immediately; others were going to take longer, but at least Don and Mary now knew what their priorities had to be.

Finally, it became possible for them to agree on specific behavioral changes that might help. Don and Mary each defined what they wanted from the other and negotiated what they themselves were willing to undertake; I moderated the meeting and wrote down the decisions. (At the end of the meeting, Don, Mary, and the three observers each received a copy of these commitments.) Because Mary and Don were interdependent, either could easily have sabotaged the other's efforts. Therefore, in defining each action item, I reminded them to specify responsibilities for both parties:

- What will Don (Mary) do to resolve this problem?
- What will Mary (Don) do to help the other succeed?

This technique made both parties jointly responsible for resolving each problem and thus changed the whole dynamic of the relationship—from mutual isolation to collaboration, from denial of responsibility to acceptance of responsibility, and from a focus on problems to a focus on solutions.

During the next year, I had four more meetings with Don, Mary, and the three vice presidents. Before each meeting, I interviewed each participant privately. At the beginning of each meeting, the participants gave general reports on what was going on, between Mary and Don and in the OR in general. In particular, I asked the two to list positive events and specific behaviors on each other's part that they appreciated. They then reviewed the commitments they had made during the previous meeting. In almost every case, both Mary and Don had kept these commitments, thus building a basis of trust for further commitments during the latter part of the meeting. Where they had not kept the commitments, plans were made to ensure follow-through before the next meeting.

Questions

1. If you had been called by Lincoln's president to help resolve the problems described in the case, how would you have carried out the contracting and diagnosis stages? What would you have done differently than what the OD consultant did?
2. Is third-party intervention an appropriate intervention in this case? Other possible OD interventions?
3. How effective was the third-party intervention? Next steps?

Selected Cases

LARGE GROUP INTERVENTIONS AT AIRBUS' ICT ORGANIZATION*

Airbus, an EADS company, is one of the leading aircraft manufacturers in the world. Its customer focus, commercial know-how, technological leadership, and manufacturing efficiency have propelled it to the forefront of the industry. With revenues of over €38 billion in 2012 and an industry record backlog of 4,682 aircraft valued at over €523 billion, Airbus today consistently captures about half of all commercial airliner orders.

Headquartered in Toulouse, France, Airbus is a truly global enterprise of some 55,000 employees, with fully owned subsidiaries in the United States, China, Japan, and the Middle East; spare parts centers in Hamburg, Frankfurt, Washington, Beijing, Dubai, and Singapore; training centers in Toulouse, Miami, Hamburg, Bangalore, and Beijing; and more than 150 field service offices around the world round out its physical footprint. Airbus also relies on industrial cooperation and partnerships with major companies all over the world, and a network of some 1,600 suppliers in 30 countries.

This case describes the launch of a transformation process that has taken root in Airbus' Information and Communication Technology (ICT) function. ICT is a transnational group of around 1,300 information system professionals located wherever Airbus operates. ICT develops, maintains, and operates—24 hours a day, 365 days a year—every facet of the information systems that enable Airbus' core business processes.

THE CHANGE CHALLENGE

Guus Dekkers joined Airbus as Chief Information Officer in June 2008. The organization he inherited had been split, integrated, and split again in a series of reorganizations over the previous seven years. Not surprisingly, he faced a change-fatigued and cynical ICT workforce. Moreover, the reorganizations had not produced the results that Airbus top management was expecting with respect to time, cost, and quality objectives in projects or improved productivity in service delivery.

At the same time, the continuing global financial and economic crisis along with the intense competition in the aircraft manufacturing industry resulted in increasing budget pressures, growing business demands, changing business models, and increasingly disenchanted internal customers. The performance of his function needed to improve significantly and fast.

In his first year, Dekkers formed a new executive team with a mix of experienced internal managers, newcomers from outside Airbus, and others from outside the aviation industry. He worked with his new team and a core group of middle managers to define ICT's new vision, mission, and customer-facing transnational organization (Figure 1). However, he knew that these changes were only the beginning. It could take months, or even years, to formulate and implement the necessary changes.

Dekkers asked Susan Donnan to guide the implementation process as his internal change agent. She had the right background, education, and experience to facilitate large-scale change in organizations. She joined Dekker's team in July 2009.

THE CHANGE STRATEGY

Working from her belief that high performance results when all parts of an organization's design are aligned, Donnan searched for a change methodology that would simultaneously reconfigure design features and engage a critical mass of organizational members at all levels. She had studied large group interventions during her Masters of Science in Organization Development (MSOD) degree program at Pepperdine University. In addition, through her consulting work, she had experienced a variety of large group interactive events as a participant, a member of a design team, and a member of a logistics team that supported an event. She was convinced that such an intervention should be

*Susan Donnan, Airbus; Roland L. Sullivan, Sullivan Transformation Agents Pte. Ltd.

FIGURE 1

The New ICT Organization (~2009)

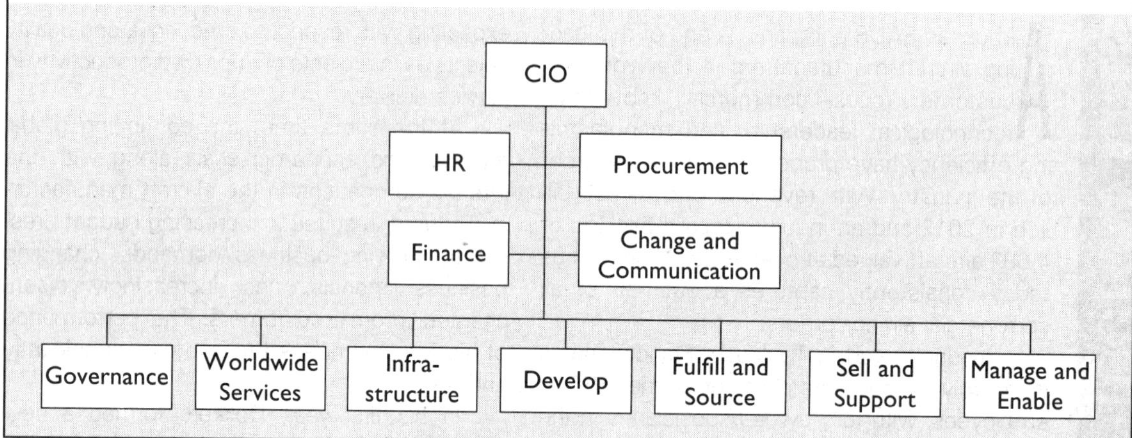

a central element of the change methodology. She considered a variety of these large group methods, including the Appreciative Inquiry Summit and Future Search, but was concerned that the current culture would not support such approaches.

In the end, she selected a process known as Whole Systems Transformation (WST), a process developed and refined by Roland Sullivan. Like other large group interventions, it is designed to help leaders engage a large, critical, and representative segment of the organization. It combines best practices in action research, small group dynamics, and large group dynamics. Unlike other large group interventions, it leads with alignment and transformation of the executive team, then transforms a critical mass of the organization, and follows up with efforts to sustain the transformation. In her experience, Donnan knew too well that an aligned leadership team was a critical success factor for transformation. She contracted with Sullivan to provide external consulting support.

INITIATING CHANGE AT ICT

Phase 1: Contracting with the Leadership Team

Like most large organizations, Airbus had adopted a traditional change management approach—top management announced the change and facilitated it through extensive communication. To implement a change strategy that was clearly outside the organization's norm, Donnan needed to convince Dekkers and his team that the traditional approach would be too slow and produce incremental change at best.

Her process began by securing executive commitment one-step-at-a-time while painting the picture for the whole journey. For example, Donnan presented a roadmap (Figure 2) that outlined the different milestones for the WST process.

She emphasized that transforming the executive team into a group with "one brain, one heart" would be a critical pre-requisite for launching the "transform the ICT critical mass" phase. Committing ICT to such a radically different approach was a leap of faith and a courageous act for the executive team, especially for Dekkers. The executive team knew that they would need to learn and become different leaders to lead the transformation but they were willing to trust Donnan and Sullivan to guide them through the process.

She also recommended—because she knew from previous experience—that the organization needed to put an infrastructure in place to drive and support the transformation process. Figure 3 describes the ICT transformation infrastructure that was agreed to by the ICT executive team to support the change. Finally, she paid special attention to ICT's Human Resource Business Partners. She was convinced that the HR organization needed to be fully on board if the change was to be successful.

FIGURE 2

ICT Transformation Roadmap

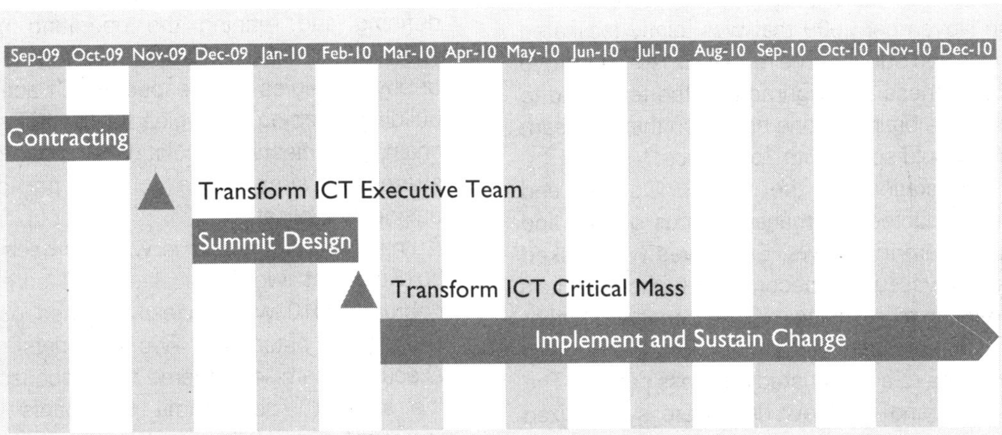

FIGURE 3

Whole System Transformation Team Organization

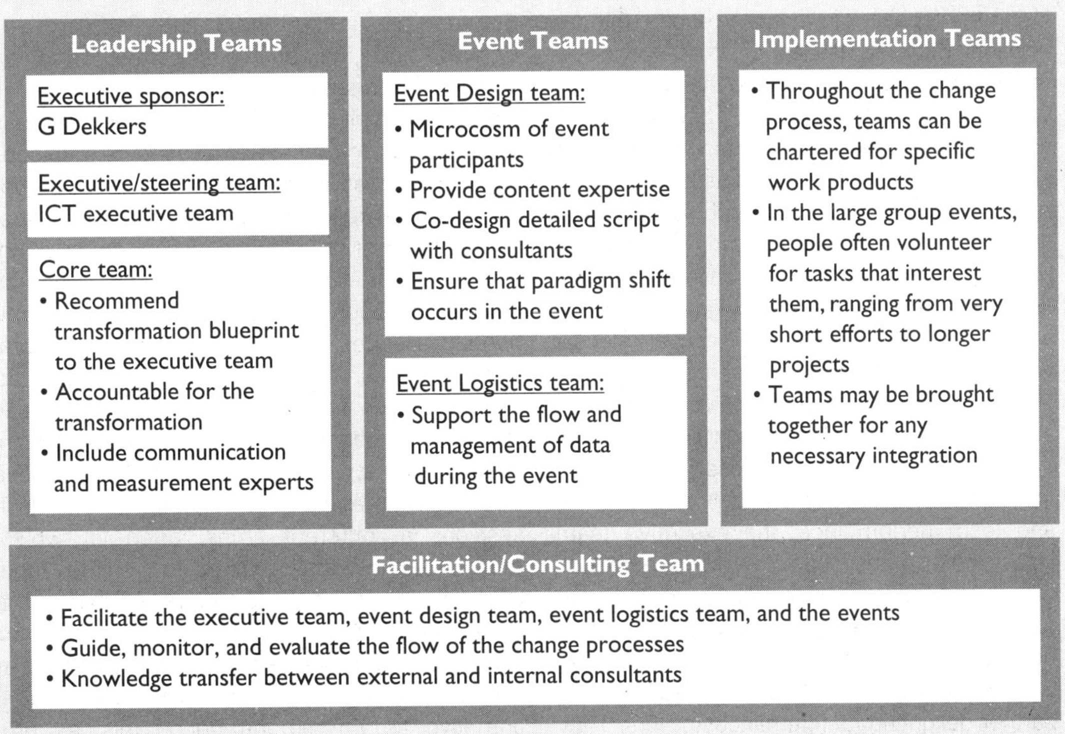

Phase 2: Transform the Leadership Team

ICT's transformation process began with a two-and-a-half-day leadership retreat for the executive team in November 2009 that was jointly facilitated by Donnan and Sullivan. The retreat aimed to improve the effectiveness and alignment of the team and to develop "one brain and one heart" so that the team members could speak with "one voice."

In preparation for the retreat, Donnan and Sullivan conducted ICT manager focus groups and executive team interviews. Executives were asked about the key issues in becoming a higher performing leadership team, helping ICT to become a higher performing function, thrilling internal customers, and deserving the role of a trusted business partner. The focus group and interview data were synthesized into data reports that were shared with the entire team prior to the retreat. Dekkers saw the data as reliable, valid, and rich, and it was used to ensure that the retreat addressed the right topics. Two members of the executive team worked with Donnan and Sullivan to co-design the event, acting as sounding board and providing valuable feedback.

Three important outcomes were achieved during the retreat:

1. Using the feedback in the data reports, the participants explored issues of trust within the team and worked on improving their relationship with Dekkers and each other. They exchanged appreciation for each other's strengths, provided suggestions for improvements, and made requests and offers with each other. As a recently formed executive team, an important practical outcome of this conversation was new team norms and meeting ground rules. In addition, they developed a new annual calendar with dedicated meetings for operational reviews and strategic topics. Together, these deliverables had an important and positive impact on the team's process effectiveness.
2. In addition to working on their relationships and team performance, the executive team visualized and described how ICT would look when its vision, mission, and strategy were fully achieved. They identified the priorities to be addressed to take ICT from where it was to where they wanted it to be: a trusted business partner delighting its internal customers. They agreed on actions and commitments that they would either personally or collectively perform to implement the ICT strategy. These included defining and refining the operating model, specifying ICT career paths, developing make or buy strategies with respect to ICT activities, building sourcing strategies for the ICT supply chain, and clearly articulating a convergence strategy to simplify the complex portfolio of business applications.
3. A final important outcome was the decision to hold the first two-and-a-half-day ICT summit in February 2010 with a clearly defined purpose and set of outcomes. Two members of the executive team volunteered to be sponsors for the summit. The summit participants would represent a carefully selected, diagonal cross-section or microcosm of ICT with all subfunctions, all locations, and all levels involved. The executive team nominated and empowered a design team of 13 members, representative of the summit participants, to design the event.

Phase 3: Transform a Critical Mass of ICT Members

Between November 2009 and February 2010, Donnan and Sullivan co-facilitated three two-and-a-half-day sessions with the design team to plan the summit. In the beginning, the consultants intentionally allowed the process to be ambiguous. At times, it was a messy and disruptive process, an emotional roller coaster for the team's members. However, it was necessary to creating a safe environment where design team members could speak openly and directly about the organization's challenges, their fears about the transformation's success, and their hopes for the future. Several design team members were skeptical of the need for change and did not believe that they would be empowered. To address this issue, executive team members participated in the design sessions at different times, often in two's or three's, to show their support, to give their inputs, to answer questions, and to give feedback on the emerging summit design. The design team was surprised and impressed by the alignment in the executive team and how much they acted as one. Over the three-month period, this new group formed into a high-performing team. They were motivated and committed to creating an impactful, memorable, and transformative experience for the participants.

With Donnan and Sullivan's guidance, the team used the following principles to guide the design of the summit:

- The participants should represent a critical mass of the ICT organization, including believers and skeptics of change.
- The design should create a safe place for people to speak openly and truthfully by ensuring that all small group discussions involved a maximum mix ("max-mix") of people from different levels and sub-functions, and by ensuring no one in the group was from the same hierarchy or chain of command. All report-outs would come from the table as a whole so no individual would be exposed.
- Table activities, breakout groups, and plenary sessions should engage each participant's "whole brain," both rational and emotional.
- The purpose and outcomes for each activity should be defined clearly for participants.
- Allow the large group to alternate between divergent and convergent activities and report-outs.
- Diverse perspectives and the awareness of multiple realities should be generated through divergent activities, such as generating ideas, creating multiple views of today's frustrations, or visioning tomorrow's hopes and dreams.
- Make effective, collective, and integrated decisions through convergent activities, such as "preferring" (i.e., a voting process) to identify priorities and expert panels to share views from customers or senior management.
- Leverage Beckhard's change formula to drive change activities in the summit: change is more likely to occur when the *dissatisfaction with the status quo*, multiplied by the *vision of the future*, multiplied by the *clarification of first steps* is greater than the *resistance to change*.

The design team worked long and hard to define the purpose and outcomes (Figure 4) for the summit. They debated and deliberated until everyone on the team was satisfied. Whenever the team could not agree, they referred back to the summit's purpose and outcomes and used those as "tiebreakers."

Eventually, the team designed the summit to take the participants through a process that

FIGURE 4

ICT Summit 2010 Purpose and Outcomes

Purpose:

- The purpose of the summit is to accelerate the continued implementation of our ICT vision and mission by creating a single team with **one mind and one voice**, fully engaged and committed to change—enabling the success of Airbus.

Tangible Outcomes:

- Identified improvement and concrete actions.
- Personal commitment to change (measurable) things.
- Communication and involvement plans to involve and engage the rest of the ICT organization.
- Formal mechanisms to ensure execution/implementation and measurement of success.

Intangible Outcomes:

- Clear understanding and buy-in of the Vision, Mission and Strategy of ICT.
- System wide understanding of operational activities and how we each contribute.
- Increased respect and trust.
- Change in attitude and mindset.
- Commitment to being ICT ambassadors.

FIGURE 5

ICT Summit 2010 High-level Agenda

Day 1	Day 2	Day 3
• Powerful opening • Purpose and outcomes • Building table teams • Achievements • Vision, Mission and Strategy • Whole system working and not working • Customer view • Elephant questions generated • CIO reflections	• Feedback from Day 1 • Elephant questions answered • Articulation of success • Barry Oshry's top/middle/bottom • Intergroup breakouts—(Exec/Mgrs/Non-mgrs) • Whole system action planning • Breakouts—Transversal action planning • Elephant questions answered • CIO reflections	• Feedback from Day 2 • Elephant questions answered • Breakouts—How to engage rest of ICT • System-wide communication • Appreciative feedback • Personal commitments • CIO inspirational sendoff

mirrored the roller coaster they had experienced in the event design process. Figure 5 shows the high-level agenda.

The first day of the summit began with a dramatic video that was edited just for this event, featuring the maiden flight of the A380 aircraft. Following the video, Fernando Alonso, who was the leader of the flight crew for the maiden voyage, spoke about the importance of trust. He talked passionately about the confidence he had in the A380 aircraft and its expected performance on that first flight. He described what it was like having the world's attention on them but knowing that the flight crew would not decide to take off unless every team member was ready. He shared that ultimately his trust extended beyond the flight crew to the entire Airbus organization. No one, at any Airbus meeting, had ever spoken about emotions, like trust, as the key to success. Immediately, the participants knew that the summit was to be unlike any other meeting they had ever attended.

At the max-mix tables, participants reflected on the meaning and the implications of Alonso's talk on trust. They reflected on and celebrated personal, team, and ICT achievements over the last 12 to 18 months. Then, after listening to ICT executive team members describe the vision, mission, and strategy, participants were encouraged to ask clarifying questions.

For the first time in their history, participants found themselves having deep and meaningful conversations sitting face-to-face with their colleagues, middle managers, and senior managers. The executive team, who were equally distributed among the tables, were coached by the design team to "trust the process." They were encouraged to listen, be supportive of diverse ideas, and answer questions directly.

Participants then discussed what was working well and what was not working well, focusing on ICT's mission, operating model, customers, and people. These strengths and weaknesses were posted around the room and each participant was given green and red dots to identify his/her top three "working" and "not working" focus areas. The top issues for the group quickly emerged and "dotting" has since become a favorite means to arrive at consensus at ICT.

As the last activity of the day, participants were given the opportunity to pose "elephant" questions—something that they had always wanted to ask but were afraid to ask. Next, participants were invited to write down their feedback for the day. Finally, Dekkers closed the day with his reflections. He spontaneously asked participants to use their green "thumbs up" or red "thumbs down" signs to indicate how they felt the summit was going, and he was rewarded with a sea of green and a few red dots sprinkled around.

Participants continued to socialize and network in the evening over drinks and dinner with old friends and new colleagues. Because many of the participants came from around the world and worked virtually, the time for personal interaction was appreciated.

The second day of the summit began with the ICT executive team answering honestly some of the "elephant" questions developed by the participants the day before. The participants were both surprised and satisfied with the openness and willingness of the executives to answer in a spirit of vulnerability, honesty, and sensitivity.

Working at their tables, participants visualized what success would look like in five years' time. The sharing of their creative presentations of the "future" was one of the high points of the summit. With vivid pictures of success and knowledge of the top issues, they identified actions needed from the individual, sub-function, and ICT levels to move ICT to where they would like it to be. This was breakthrough work. The day ended with Dekkers' reflections and participants' feedback, followed by social activities and more networking.

The third day of the summit also began with answering additional "elephant" questions from the first day. This was followed by activities to define ways to engage the rest of the ICT organization after the summit. The participants agree on ways to communicate to the rest of the ICT community going forward. After rounds of appreciative feedback at the tables, the summit closed with the ICT executive team making personal commitments on stage in front of all, for which they received a standing ovation.

Phase 4: Implement and Sustain the Change

Immediately after the summit, the 300 participants returned to their offices and acted as ambassadors for change. At the top of the list was the wish to communicate the process and the results of the summit to the rest of the organization. Supported by communication kits and a web-based e-journal with photos and videos provided by Donnan, this occurred in all sub-functions and all locations.

In addition to communication, summit actions were translated into projects and personal objectives. Examples of projects included: harmonization and standardization of ICT activities using industry best practices; understanding these activities' drivers and costs and measuring their performance; fighting bureaucracy and streamlining processes; working with its business partners to drive improvements on demand management and prioritization; and developing the competencies and careers of ICT employees.

ICT Executive Team members drove cross-functional or within function transformation in their respective groups. The design team volunteered to stay on as the transformation network. Together with Donnan, they monitored progress and supported the executives in driving implementation of summit actions in their respective functions. Donnan met monthly with the transformation network to share insights and best practices.

For the next 12 months, ICT Transformation remained a priority for the executive team.

Many of the transformation projects delivered bottom-line savings and enabled company objectives. The ICT organization got measurably better at delivering on its projects, services, and cost promises. Communication up, down, and across ICT improved appreciably.

Last but not least, the collaborative approach to change sent a clear message that transformation could not be successful without the engagement of ICT employees. Grass roots initiatives and volunteerism were actively encouraged. People at all levels felt greater empowerment. For example, in multiple locations, people chose to become local change agents and organized local transformation and social events, some of which continue today.

MAINTAINING THE CHANGE MOMENTUM

Following the success of the first ICT summit, the (1) align and transform the executive team, (2) assess and plan the next cycle of change, (3) align and transform a critical mass of organization members, and (4) implement and sustain change process became institutionalized and has occurred every year since. A new design team and a compelling focus from the leadership team underpins the annual cycle of the process.

For example, the focus for the 2010–2011 cycle was cross-unit or cross-functional breakthroughs involving the leadership population of about 200 ICT managers. The theme of the summit was "Leading as ONE." The focus of the 2011–2012 cycle was creating an ICT environment that actively encourages agility, innovation, and leadership. Unlike previous summits, the third summit did not focus on what was not working or broken; rather it focused on new way of thinking and working. Participants learned about design thinking through a simulated innovation project, explored psychological concepts that contribute to innovative thinking, and applied those concepts to four dynamics in the organization: agility and stability; anticipation and reaction; customization and standardization; and innovation and standardization.

During the months that followed the 2011–2012 summit, ICT dealt with a difficult business challenge using a collaborative approach that most people agreed would not have been possible three years earlier. It received, together with its customers, five 2012 Awards for Excellence, three of which were in the "Drive Improvement and Innovation" category and one of these won the Top Award of the Year.

In addition, ICT has made the greatest improvement in employee engagement in the company over a three-year period as measured by the Gallup Q12. Through productivity improvements, ICT also succeeded in handling 25% in volume growth while maintaining a flat budget in the same period.

ICT's efforts have made important contributions to implementing its vision, mission, and strategy. It has achieved operational excellence, a critical foundation or prerequisite for becoming a trusted business partner. Going forward, the executive team would like to evolve ICT's way of working: to be better immersed in the business strategy and business processes of its customers, to better anticipate their business needs, to focus sharply on value for Airbus, and to quickly propose and provide right-sized solutions. The journey continues.

LEARNING

Ever since her MSOD days at Pepperdine, Donnan had been searching for ways to facilitate system-wide alignment and to accelerate change. For her, the WST process has been the most effective methodology for achieving both. She reflected on her learning.

- **The importance of aligned leadership.** Breakthroughs in the ICT executive team enabled breakthroughs in ICT as a whole. When leaders speak with one voice, provide a unified direction in vision and strategy, demonstrate a sense of urgency, and walk their talk, it gives organization members the confidence to act in alignment for the health of the whole. On the other hand, when leaders are not aligned and give conflicting directions, this causes conflicts and confusion that cascades all the way down the organization.
- **The critical roles of the event design team.** The ICT case would not have been a success without the effective use of the event design team. In addition to bringing in data from across the ICT organization and mirroring the organization's current state as part of the design process, the event design team members took an active role in facilitating different modules in the summit, listening to the participants during the summit, synthesizing the participants' daily feedback, and refining the summit design based on their feedback. The teamwork within the team was critical for the smooth execution of the summit.
- **The real work of transformation occurs between large group interventions.** While many people focus on how a large group event "releases the magic" of a paradigm shift, the real work of transformation occurs after the event or between events in the "implement and sustain change" phase. ICT is part of a global organization that has experienced and continues to experience tremendous growth and challenge. Managers are typically overloaded just running and delivering today's business; requests to transform the business for the future are often overwhelming. Moreover, saying "no" to lesser priorities remains difficult for the organization. As a result, finding the resources and time for transformation remains a challenge. ICT's experiments with a mix of structured and emergent approaches yielded two major lessons. First, do not launch more actions than the organization can handle, and second, focus more on cross-functional improvements that optimize overall results rather than local maximization.
- **The lead and lag indicators of success.** Organization change is a journey that takes time and requires incredible patience. Following a large group interactive event, the lead indicators of success are team spirit, confidence, commitment, relationships, energy,

trust, inclusiveness, transparency, and alignment. These are difficult to measure but can be felt, observed, and captured in anecdotal stories. Later, improvement projects lead to more tangible results, such as behavioral and engagement changes. However, only when the improvement projects are successfully implemented can improved business results be seen. These are the lag indictors of success. Executives and managers must understand that the easy-to-measure lag indicators of success will come if they recognize, support, and nurture the difficult-to-measure but equally valuable lead indicators of success. Many change initiatives fail because executives insist on instant results, give up too soon and move onto the next change.

- **Transforming how the organization deals with change.** The ultimate measure of organization development is the degree to which the ability to change again is enhanced or diminished. Without any doubt, the WST process has helped people in ICT build a change capability. Realizing that transformation is a journey and not a destination, ICT people are no longer paralyzed by change and are more likely to embrace change as an opportunity rather than a threat. They have developed greater capacity and capability to act in aligned ways. In reflecting on the organization's journey, Dekkers said, "Today, our ICT community is better mobilized and motivated to change."
- **WST needs to be repeated regularly.** In today's complex, chaotic, and uncertain world, an organization's ability to learn and innovate at the individual, team, and organizational levels allows the organization to adapt. Change is a constant and the days of returning to stability or business-as-usual are gone. To ensure a sustained long-term journey, the WST process must be repeated to regularly restore whole system alignment while adapting to internal and external drivers for change.

In conclusion, each year that the ICT has used the WST process, it became more and more competent to self-direct and master its own change process. The organization is becoming better at doing what it says it will do, more respected by its customers, and more agile. ICT people is learning how to learn in real time as an entire function.

Questions

1. What is your analysis and evaluation of the design of this intervention? What large-group intervention theories and models were applied in this case? Do you believe that the interventions made a difference in this organization?
    - If your analysis is positive, what do you think were the critical intervention features that led to success?
    - If your analysis is negative, what changes would you make in the intervention's design or implementation?
2. What do you think of the summit's agenda and flow? Do you think the right activities were planned and executed given the objectives of the intervention?

PART 4

TECHNOSTRUCTURAL INTERVENTIONS

12 Restructuring Organizations

13 Employee Involvement

14 Work Design

SELECTED CASES

City of Carlsbad, California: Restructuring the Public Works Department (A)

The Sullivan Hospital System

12

Restructuring Organizations

learning objectives

- Describe the most common organization structures used today and understand their strengths and weaknesses.
- Present the process of downsizing.
- Describe and evaluate the reengineering intervention.

In this chapter, we begin to examine techno-structural interventions—change programs focusing on the technology and structure of organizations. Increasing global competition and rapid technological and environmental changes are forcing organizations to restructure themselves from rigid bureaucracies to leaner, more flexible designs. These new forms of organizing are highly adaptive and innovative, but require more sophisticated managerial capabilities to operate successfully. They often result in fewer managers and employees and in streamlined work flows that break down functional barriers.

Interventions aimed at structural design include moving from more traditional ways of dividing the organization's overall work, such as functional, divisional, and matrix structures, to more integrative and flexible forms, such as process, customer-centric, and network structures. Diagnostic guidelines help determine which structure is appropriate for particular organizational environments, technologies, and conditions.

Downsizing seeks to reduce costs and bureaucracy by decreasing the size of the organization. This reduction in personnel can be accomplished through layoffs, organization redesign, and outsourcing, which involves moving functions that are not part of the organization's core competence to outside contractors. Successful downsizing is closely aligned with the organization's strategy.

Reengineering radically redesigns the organization's core work processes to give tighter linkage and coordination among the different tasks. This workflow integration results in faster, more responsive task performance. Reengineering often is accomplished with new information technology that permits employees to control and coordinate work processes more effectively.

12-1 Structural Design

Organization structure describes how the overall work of the organization is divided into subunits and how these subunits are coordinated for task completion. Based on a contingency perspective shown in Figure 12.1, organization structures should be designed to fit with at least four factors: the environment, organization size, technology, and

FIGURE 12.1

Contingencies Influencing Structural Choices

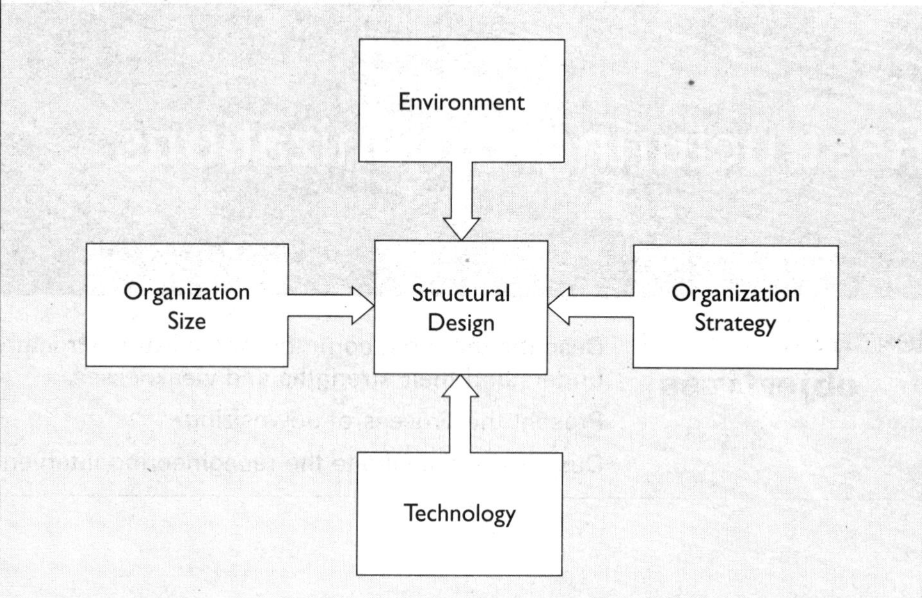

organization strategy. Organization effectiveness depends on the extent to which its structure is responsive to these contingencies.[1]

Organizations traditionally have structured themselves into one of three forms: functional departments that are task specialized; self-contained divisional units that are oriented to specific products, customers, or regions; or matrix structures that combine both functional specialization and self-containment. Faced with accelerating changes in competitive environments and technologies, however, organizations increasingly have redesigned their structures into more integrative and flexible forms. These more recent innovations include process structures that design subunits around the organization's core work processes, customer-centric structures that focus attention and resources on specific customers or customer segments, and network-based structures that link the organization to other, interdependent organizations. The advantages, disadvantages, and contingencies of the different structures are described below.

12-1a The Functional Structure

The most widely used organizational structure in the world today is the basic *functional structure*, depicted in Figure 12.2. The organization usually is divided into functional units, such as marketing, operations, research and development, human resources, and finance. This structure is based on early management theories regarding specialization, line and staff relations, span of control, authority, and responsibility.[2] The major functional units are staffed by specialists from those functions. It is considered easier to manage specialists if they are grouped together under the same head and if the head of the department has been trained and has experience in that particular function.

Table 12.1 lists the advantages and disadvantages of functional structures. On the positive side, functional structures promote specialization of skills and resources by

FIGURE 12.2

The Functional Structure

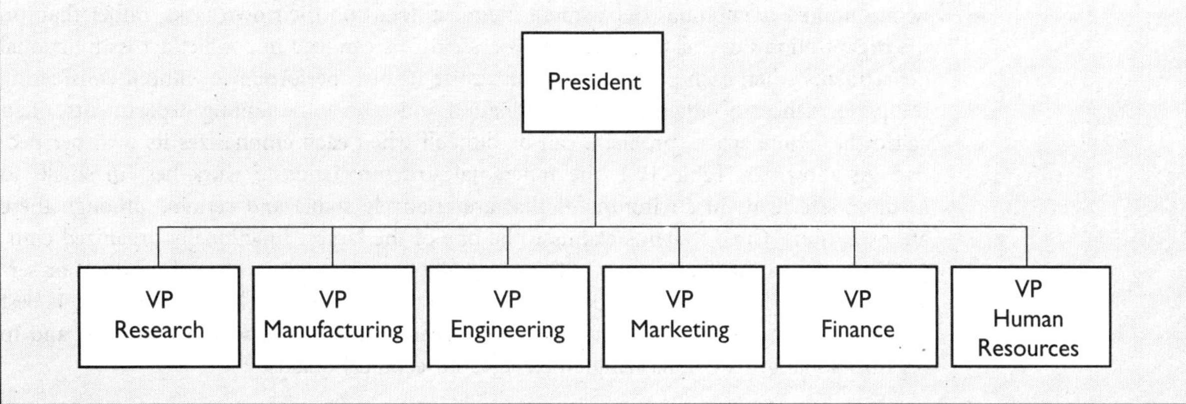

TABLE 12.1

Advantages, Disadvantages, and Contingencies of the Functional Structure

ADVANTAGES

- Promotes and develops technical specialization
- Supports flexibility of deployment and reduces duplication of scarce resources
- Enhances career development for specialists within large departments
- Facilitates communication and performance because superiors share expertise with their subordinates
- Supports the development of common processes

DISADVANTAGES

- Emphasizes routine tasks, which encourages short time horizons
- Fosters narrow perspectives by managers, not business metrics and broader criteria for decision making
- Processes cut across functions, which can make coordination and scheduling difficult (the "white space" problem)
- Obscures accountability for overall outcomes; managers and employees may not have a line of sight to the business
- Difficulty developing general management capability

CONTINGENCIES

- Stable and certain environment
- Small- to medium-size
- Routine technology, interdependence within functions
- Goals of efficiency and technical quality

grouping people who perform similar work and face similar problems. This grouping facilitates communication within departments and allows specialists to share their expertise through standardized processes. It also enhances career development within the specialty, whether it is accounting, finance, engineering, or sales. The functional structure reduces duplication of services because it makes the best use of people and resources.

On the negative side, functional structures tend to promote routine tasks behaviors with a limited orientation. Department members focus on their own tasks, rather than on the organization's overall value-added processes. This can lead to conflict across functional departments when each group tries to maximize its own performance without considering the performances of other units. Coordination and scheduling among departments, often called the "white space" problem, can be difficult when each emphasizes its own perspective. As shown in Table 12.1, the functional structure tends to work best in small- to medium-size firms in environments that are relatively stable and certain, although there are exceptions. Cisco Systems claims to be one of the largest functionally organized companies in the world. These organizations typically have a small number of products or services, and coordination across specialized units is relatively easy. This structure also is best suited to routine technologies in which there is interdependence within functions, and to organizational goals emphasizing efficiency and technical quality.

12-1b The Divisional Structure

The *divisional structure* represents a fundamentally different way of organizing. Also known as a product or self-contained-unit structure, it was developed at about the same time by General Motors, Sears, Standard Oil of New Jersey (now ExxonMobil), and DuPont.[3] It groups organizational activities on the basis of products, services, customers, or geography. All or most of the resources and functions necessary to accomplish a specific objective are set up as a division headed by a product or division manager. For example, General Electric has plants that specialize in making jet engines and others that produce household appliances. Each plant manager reports to a particular division or product vice president, rather than to a manufacturing vice president. In effect, a large organization may set up smaller (sometimes temporary) special-purpose organizations, each geared to a specific product, service, customer, or region. Many organizations use the divisional structure to expand globally. Samsung Electronics, for example, structures self-contained business units around particular product groups that are responsible for their respective products worldwide. Colgate-Palmolive forms self-contained units around geographic regions with each region responsible for the firm's products in that area. A typical division structure is shown in Figure 12.3. It is interesting to note that the formal structure within a self-contained unit often is functional in nature.

Table 12.2 lists the advantages and disadvantages of divisional structures. These organizations recognize key interdependencies and coordinate resources toward an overall outcome. This strong outcome orientation ensures accountability and promotes cohesion among those contributing to the self-contained unit. These structures provide employees with opportunities for learning new skills and expanding knowledge because workers can move more easily among the different specialties within the unit. As a result, divisional structures are well suited for developing general managers.

Divisional structures do have certain problems. They may not have enough specialized work to use people's skills and abilities fully. Specialists may feel isolated from their professional colleagues and may fail to advance in their career specialty. The structures may promote allegiance to a specific product, service, customer, or region rather than to the organization's objectives. They also place multiple demands on people, thereby creating stress.

The divisional structure works best in conditions almost the opposite of those favoring a functional organization, as shown in Table 12.2. The organization needs to be relatively large to support the duplication of resources assigned to the units. Because each unit is

FIGURE 12.3

The Divisional Structure

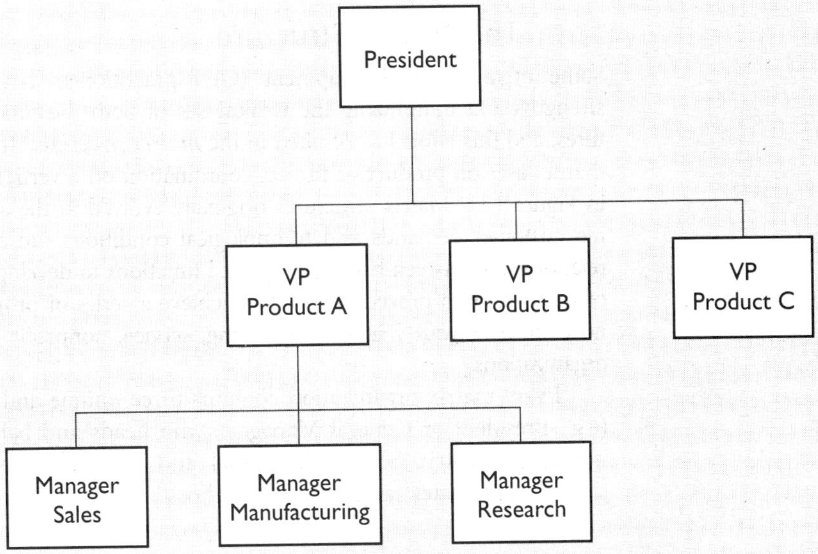

TABLE 12.2

Advantages, Disadvantages, and Contingencies of the Divisional Structure

ADVANTAGES

- Recognizes sources of interdepartmental dependencies, reduces complexity
- Fosters an orientation toward divisional outcomes and clients
- Allows diversification and expansion of skills and training
- Ensures accountability by departmental managers and so promotes delegation of authority and responsibility
- Heightens departmental cohesion and involvement in work

DISADVANTAGES

- May use skills and resources inefficiently: coordination, sharing, and learning across divisions is difficult
- Limits career advancement by specialists to movements out of their departments
- Impedes specialists' exposure to others within the same specialties; hard to create common processes
- Puts multiple-role demands on people and so creates stress
- Line of sight is to business and may promote divisional objectives over organization objectives

CONTINGENCIES

- Unstable and uncertain environments
- Large-size
- Technological interdependence across functions
- Goals of product specialization and innovation

designed to fit a particular niche, the structure adapts well to uncertain conditions. Divisional units also help to coordinate technical interdependencies falling across functions and are suited to goals promoting product or service specialization and innovation.

12-1c The Matrix Structure

Some organization development (OD) practitioners have focused on maximizing the strengths and minimizing the weaknesses of both the functional and the divisional structures, and this effort has resulted in the *matrix structure*.[4] It superimposes a lateral structure that focuses on product or project coordination on a vertical functional structure, as shown in Figure 12.4. Matrix structures originally evolved in the aerospace industry where changing customer demands and technological conditions caused managers to focus on lateral relationships between highly specialized functions to develop a flexible and adaptable system of resources and procedures, and to achieve a series of project objectives. Matrix structures now are used widely in manufacturing, service, nonprofit, governmental, and professional organizations.[5]

Every matrix organization contains three unique and critical roles: the top manager (e.g., President or General Manager), who heads and balances the dual chains of command; the matrix bosses (functional and product or program vice presidents), who share subordinates; and a few "two-boss" managers, who report to the two different

FIGURE 12.4

The Matrix Structure

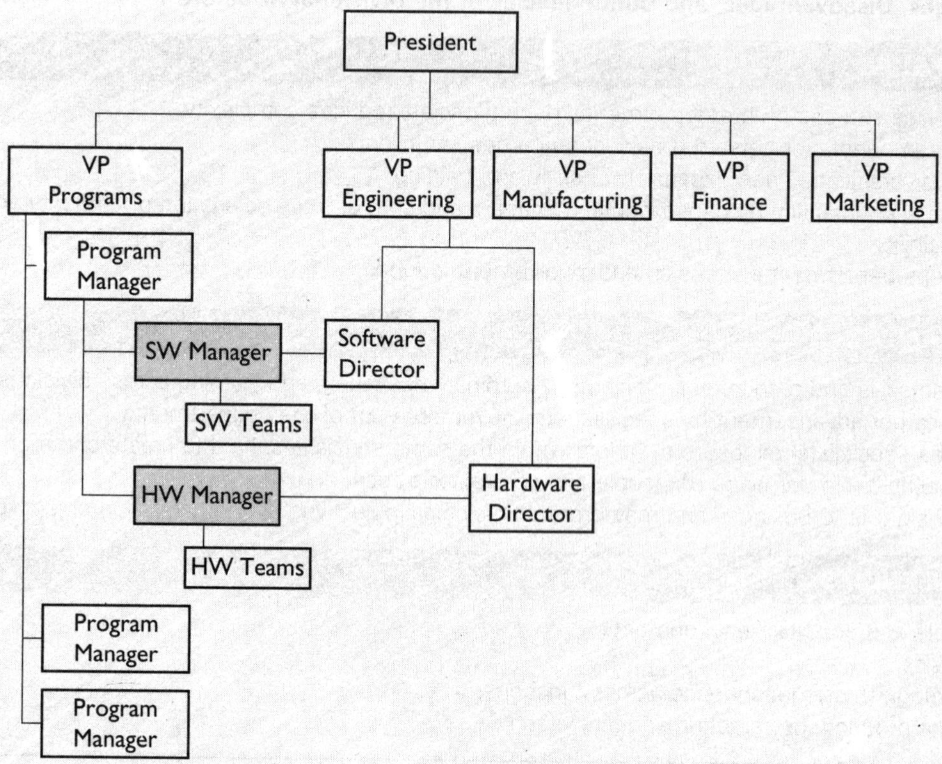

matrix leaders and manage workers deployed to the specific product or program. In Figure 12.4, only the Software (SW) Manager and Hardware (HW) Manager have two bosses. The SW and HW team members take their day-to-day direction from the software and hardware managers but belong to the Engineering function.

Each of these roles has its own unique requirements. For example, functional matrix leaders are expected to maximize their respective technical expertise within constraints posed by market realities. Two-boss managers, however, must accomplish work within the demands of supervisors who want to achieve technical sophistication on the one hand, and to meet customer expectations on the other. Thus, a matrix organization has more than its matrix structure. It also must be reinforced by matrix performance management systems that get input from both functional and project bosses, by matrix leadership behavior that operates comfortably with lateral decision making, and by a matrix culture that fosters open conflict management and a balance of power.[6]

Matrix structures, like all organization structures, have both advantages and disadvantages, as shown in Table 12.3. On the positive side, they enable multiple orientations. Specialized, functional knowledge is integrated with a focus on a particular business or project. New products or projects can be implemented quickly by using people flexibly and by moving between product and functional orientations as circumstances demand. Matrix structures allow functional expertise learned in one business or program to be transferred to another product, program, or business. For many people, matrix structures are motivating and exciting.

TABLE 12.3

Advantages, Disadvantages, and Contingencies of the Matrix Structure

ADVANTAGES
• Emphasizes cross-functional product or program focus and integration of functional excellence
• Uses people flexibly, because departments maintain reservoirs of specialists
• Permits functional learning to be carried between projects or programs
• Recognizes and provides mechanisms for dealing with legitimate, multiple sources of power in the organization
• Can adapt to environmental changes by shifting emphasis between project and functional aspects
DISADVANTAGES
• Can be very difficult to introduce without a preexisting supportive management climate
• Conflicts between businesses and functions over methods, resources, priorities is always present
• Increases role ambiguity, stress, and anxiety by assigning people to more than one department
• Without power balancing between product and functional forms, lowers overall performance
• Makes inconsistent demands, which may result in unproductive conflicts and short-term crisis management
• May reward political skills as opposed to technical skills
CONTINGENCIES
• Dual focus on unique product demands and technical specialization
• Pressure for high information-processing capacity
• Pressure for shared resources

On the negative side, these structures can be difficult to manage. To implement and maintain them requires heavy managerial costs and support. IT managers must deal with the often conflicting tensions between technical excellence and customer responsiveness. When people are assigned to more than one department, there may be role ambiguity and conflict, and overall performance may be sacrificed if there are power conflicts between functional departments and project structures. People can get confused about how the matrix operates, and that can lead to chaos and inefficiencies. To make matrix structures work, organization members need interpersonal and conflict management skills as well as some tolerance for ambiguity.

As shown in Table 12.3, matrix structures are appropriate under three important conditions.[7] First, there must be real outside pressures for a dual focus. For example, a matrix structure works well when there are many customers with unique demands, on the one hand, and strong requirements for technical sophistication, on the other. The OD practitioner must work with management to determine whether there is real pressure for a dual focus. Managers often agree, without carefully testing the assumption, that both functional and product orientations are important. Second, a matrix organization is appropriate when the organization must process a large amount of information. Circumstances requiring such capacity are few and include the following: when external environmental demands change unpredictably; when the organization produces a broad range of products or services, or offers those outputs to a large number of different markets; when the relevant technologies evolve quickly; and when there is reciprocal interdependence among the tasks in the organization's technical core. In each case, there is considerable complexity in decision making and pressure on communication and coordination systems. Third, there must be pressures for shared resources. When customer demands vary greatly and technological requirements are strict, valuable human and physical resources are likely to be scarce. The matrix works well under those conditions because it facilitates the sharing of scarce resources. If any one of the foregoing conditions is not met, a matrix organization is likely to fail.

12-1d The Process Structure

A relatively new logic for structuring organizations is to form multidisciplinary teams around core processes, such as product development, order fulfillment, sales generation, and customer support.[8] As shown in Figure 12.5, *process-based structures* emphasize lateral rather than vertical relationships.[9] All functions necessary to produce a product or service are placed in a common unit usually managed by a role labeled a "process owner." There are few hierarchical levels, and the senior executive team is relatively small, typically consisting of the chief executive officer, the chief operating officer, and the heads of a few key support services such as strategic planning, human resources, and finance.

Process structures eliminate many of the hierarchical and departmental boundaries that can impede task coordination and slow decision making and task performance. They reduce the enormous costs of managing across departments and up and down the hierarchy. Process-based structures enable organizations to focus most of their resources on serving customers, both inside and outside the firm.

The use of process-based structures is growing rapidly in a variety of manufacturing and service companies. Typically referred to as "horizontal," "boundaryless," or "team-based" organizations, they are used to enhance customer service at such firms as American Express Financial Advisors, Healthways, Johnson & Johnson, 3M, Xerox, and General Electric Capital Services. Although there is no one right way to design process-based structures, the following features characterize this new form of organizing:[10]

FIGURE 12.5

The Process Structure

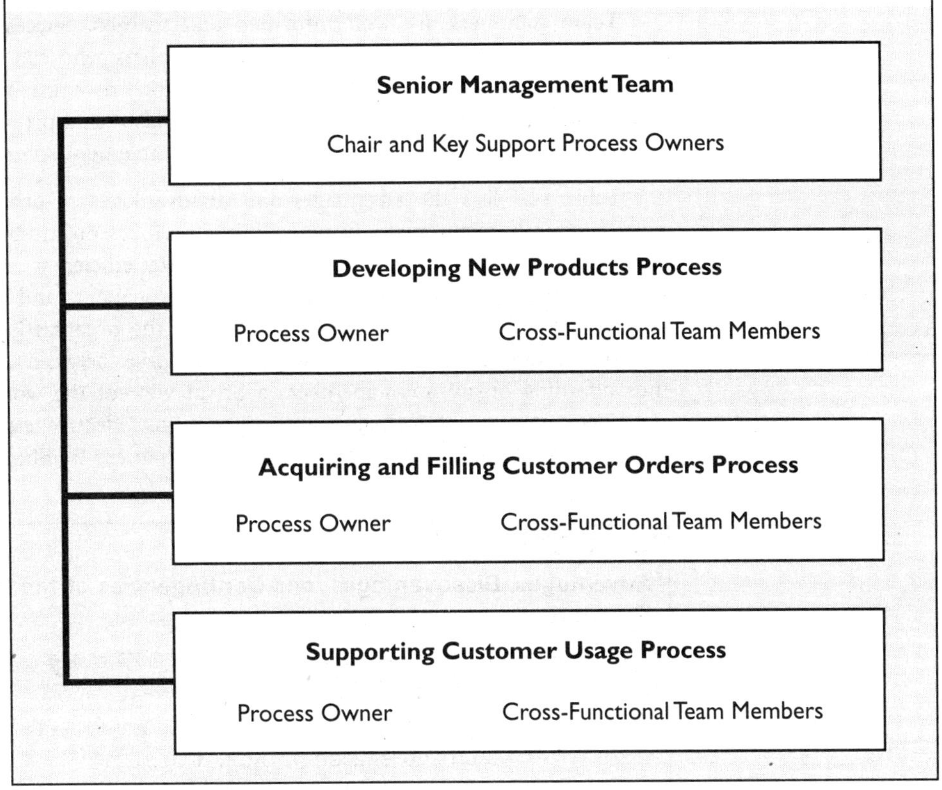

- **Processes drive structure.** Process-based structures are organized around the three to five key processes that define the work of the organization. Rather than products or functions, processes define the structure and are governed by a "process owner." Each process has clear performance goals that drive task execution.
- **Work adds value.** To increase efficiency, process-based structures simplify and enrich work processes. Work is simplified by eliminating nonessential tasks and reducing layers of management, and it is enriched by combining tasks so that teams perform whole processes.
- **Teams are fundamental.** Teams are the key organizing feature in a process-based structure. They manage everything from task execution to strategic planning, are typically self-managing, and are responsible for goal achievement.
- **Customers define performance.** The primary goal of any team in a process-based structure is customer satisfaction. Defining customer expectations and designing team functions to meet those expectations command much of the team's attention. The organization must value this orientation as the primary path to financial performance.
- **Teams are rewarded for performance.** Appraisal systems focus on measuring team performance against customer satisfaction and other goals, and then provide real recognition for achievement. Team-based rewards are given as much, if not more, weight than is individual recognition.

- **Teams are tightly linked to suppliers and customers.** Through designated members, teams have timely and direct relationships with vendors and customers to understand and respond to emerging concerns.
- **Team members are well informed and trained.** Successful implementation of a process-based structure requires team members who can work with a broad range of information, including customer and market data, financial information, and personnel and policy matters. Team members also need problem-solving and decision-making skills and abilities to address and implement solutions.

Table 12.4 lists the advantages and disadvantages of process-based structures. The most frequently mentioned advantage is intense focus on meeting customer needs, which can result in dramatic improvements in speed, efficiency, and customer satisfaction. Process-based structures remove layers of management, and consequently information flows more quickly and accurately throughout the organization. Because process teams comprise multiple functional specialties, boundaries between departments are removed, thus affording organization members a broad view of the workflow and a clear line of sight between team performance and organization effectiveness. Process-based structures also are more flexible and adaptable to change than are traditional structures.

TABLE 12.4

Advantages, Disadvantages, and Contingencies of the Process-Based Structure

ADVANTAGES
• Clear line of sight focuses resources on customer satisfaction
• Improves speed and efficiency, often dramatically
• Responds to environmental change and customer requests rapidly
• Strong cross-functional collaboration and integration
• Develops broad knowledge and increases ability to see total work flow
• Enhances employee involvement
• Lowers costs because of less overhead structure
DISADVANTAGES
• Changing to this structure can threaten middle managers and staff specialists
• Must learn to balance competing demands for fluidity and efficiency
• Can be difficult to supervise multiple functions, requires changes in command-and-control mindsets
• Duplicates scarce resources, sharing learnings can be difficult
• Requires new skills and knowledge to manage lateral relationships and teams
• May take longer to make decisions in teams and result in internal focus
• Can be ineffective if wrong processes are identified
CONTINGENCIES
• Uncertain and changing environments
• Moderate- to large-size
• Nonroutine and highly interdependent technologies
• Customer-oriented goals

A major disadvantage of process structures is the difficulty of changing to this new organizational form. These structures typically require radical shifts in mindsets, skills, and managerial roles—changes that involve considerable time and resources and can be resisted by functional managers and staff specialists. Managers must learn to balance competing demands for organization fluidity and efficiency.[11] Moreover, process-based structures may result in expensive duplication of scarce resources and, if teams are not skilled adequately, an overly internal focus and slower decision making as they struggle to define and reach consensus. Finally, implementing process-based structures relies on properly identifying key processes needed to satisfy customer needs. If critical processes are misidentified or ignored altogether, performance and customer satisfaction are likely to suffer.

Table 12.4 shows that process structures are particularly appropriate for highly uncertain environments where customer demands and market conditions are changing rapidly. They enable organizations to manage nonroutine technologies and coordinate workflows that are highly interdependent. Process-based structures generally appear in medium- to large-size organizations having several products or projects. They focus heavily on customer-oriented goals and are found in both domestic and global organizations.

Application 12.1 describes the process-based structure proposed as part of the structural change process at Healthways Corporation.

12-1e The Customer-Centric Structure

Closely related to the process-based structure, the *customer-centric structure* focuses subunits on the creation of solutions and the satisfaction of key customers or customer groups.[12] As shown in Figure 12.7, these customer or market-facing units are supported by other units that develop new products, manufacture components and products, and manage the supply chain. A variety of organizations, including the Lord Corporation, Dow, IBM, and Citibank, have implemented these complex structures. Also known as front–back organizations, these structures excel at putting customer needs at the top of an organization's agenda.

Galbraith notes that globalization, e-commerce, and the desire for solutions have greatly enhanced the power of the customer to demand organizational structures that service their needs. These new structures highlight the radical differences between product-focused organizations, like the function or divisional structure, and customer-centric organizations as shown in Table 12.5. In a product-centric organization, the goal is to provide customers with the best product possible and to create value by developing new products and innovative features. Product-centric structures have core structural features that include product groups and teams that are measured by product margins. The most central process is new-product development.

Customer-centric structures have a very different look and feel. In a customer-centric structure, the organization develops the best solution for the customer by offering a customized bundle of products, services, support, and education. Their core structures focus attention and resources on customers with market-facing units organized around large individual customers or customer segment teams that attempt to maximize customer profit and loss. These core units are supported by sophisticated customer relationship management processes and integrating mechanisms that link the market-facing units with the support units.

While any one of these differences may seem obvious, a careful look will show that the product-centric dimensions represent important and deeply rooted assumptions in

application 12.1

HEALTHWAYS' PROCESS STRUCTURE

Healthways Corporation (HC) (www.healthways.com) is a provider of specialized disease management services to health plans and hospitals. In fiscal year 2002, HC had revenues of $122 million. The company, founded in 1981 as American Healthcorp (AMHC), originally owned and managed hospitals. In 1984 it offered its first disease management service focused on diabetes. Under the name Diabetes Treatment Centers of America, it worked with hospitals to create "centers of excellence" to improve hospital volumes and lower costs. After going public in 1991, it offered in 1993 its first diabetes management program to health plans—an entirely new customer segment. This shift in customer base was a key event in the company's history, and two new disease management programs for cardiac and respiratory diseases were offered in 1998 and 1999, respectively. By 2000, hospital revenues, once 100% of the company's mix, had dropped to 38% as the health plan business grew.

The organization recognized that its current structure would not support the expected growth. As part of its structural change effort, the initial organization design and development task force (the ODD group) recommended a process-based organization structure to the senior leadership team. The organization was described in terms of five core processes: understand the market and plan the business, acquire and retain customers, build value solutions, deliver solutions and add value, and manage the business (Figure 12.6).

- The *understand-the-market process* was responsible for scanning AMHC's external environment for business opportunities, trends, regulatory changes, and competitive intelligence. The process also was responsible for generating new product ideas, based on their environmental scanning activities, and for developing and driving the strategic planning process of the organization.
- Based on the outputs of the understand-the-market process, the *build-value-solutions process* was responsible for translating business or product opportunities into reproducible products. This included more fully developing the business case initially identified by the understand-the-market process, devising performance metrics, developing new products and testing them, and creating marketing materials.
- The *acquire-and-retain-customers process* involved the sales and marketing organization. It was responsible for finalizing marketing materials, identifying new customers, selling and signing contracts, developing relationships with key stakeholders, implementing marketing plans, and responding to requests for proposals.
- The *deliver-solutions-and-add-value process* was responsible for delivering on contractual commitments, managing accounts and upselling, maintaining product integrity, and building delivery capacity.
- In the *manage-the-business process*, the small corporate headquarters was responsible for human resources, financial governance, information technology standards, medical leadership, and corporate image and branding. It was to act as a shared services organization supporting the value-adding process organizations.

Each process was to be staffed with an appropriate mix of functional experts. The operational basis of the new organization was a cross-functional team that could represent the different perspectives at each stage of the business. For example, the acquire-and-retain-customers process included not only sales and marketing expertise, but also functional expertise in account management, information technology, finance, medical and clinical specialties, and product development. In recommending that a core process be staffed with the appropriate mix of functional expertise, the task force also suggested that the structure within a core process be team-based. The acquire-and-retain-customers process could flexibly organize cross-functional teams to address a specific customer's requirements and then recombine resources to pursue a different customer.

FIGURE 12.6

HC's Proposed Process Structure

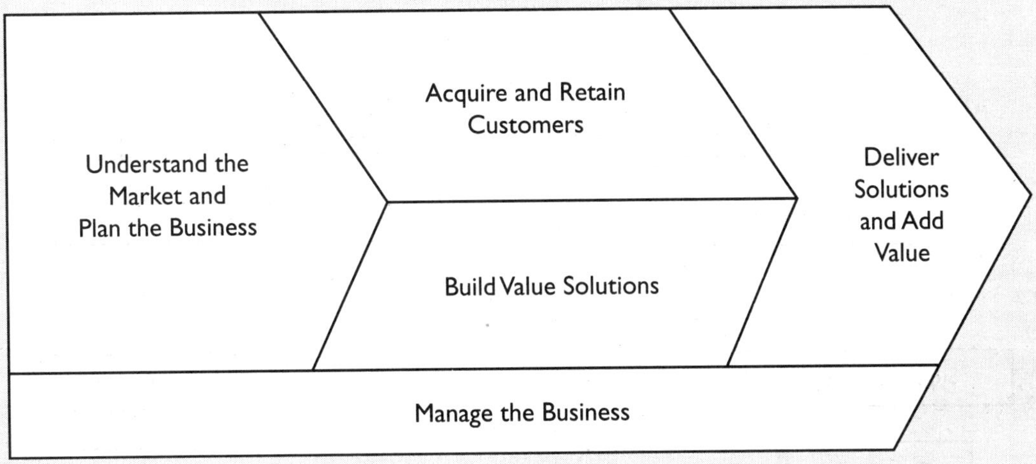

In addition, appropriate metrics for monitoring the effectiveness of each process as well as the relationships between any two processes in the organization were specified. In terms of effectiveness metrics, the key outcome for all processes was customer satisfaction. The acquire-customer process was judged primarily on the extent to which it acquired customers and contracts that the deliver-solutions-and-add-value process believed could be managed. In terms of relationships, any new business opportunities identified by the understand-the-market process required certain approvals by senior management before being handed off to the build-value-solutions process. This "go-no go" decision assured that the organization had sufficient investment resources to fund new business or product development and that good opportunities, not just a lot of opportunities, were being forwarded to the build-value-solutions process.

most organizations. Deciding to execute a customer-centric organization is a substantial undertaking.

As shown in Table 12.6, customer-centric structures have important strengths and weaknesses. Customer-centric structures present one face to the customer. Divisional structures, for example, can confuse customers when each division sends its own sales team. When one team is dedicated to a customer or customer group, it develops a deep understanding of the customer's needs, preferences, and industry trends. This knowledge supports the customization of solutions and helps to build a robust customer-satisfaction capability.

In terms of weaknesses, customer teams can become too inwardly focused and lose sight of the larger organization strategy. This can make it difficult to share learning from successful innovation or customization with the rest of the organization. One of the most important weaknesses of the customer-centric organization is its reliance on lateral

FIGURE 12.7

The Customer-Centric Structure

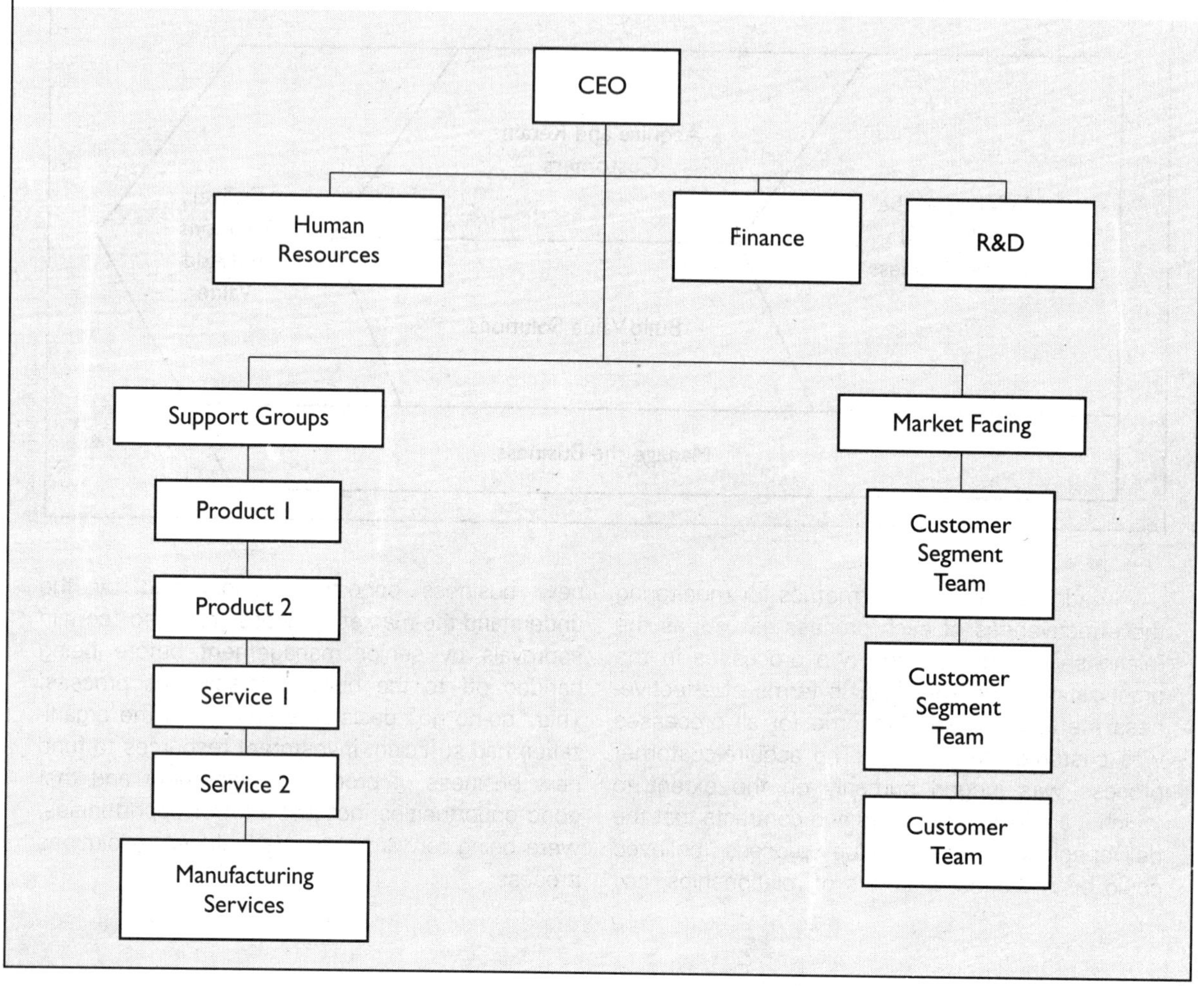

TABLE 12.5

Comparing Product-Centric with Customer-Centric Structures

Organizational Feature	Product-Centric	Customer-Centric
Goal	Best product for customer	Best solution for customer
Source of value	New products, new features	Customized bundles of products, services, support, education, and consulting
Core structures	Product teams, product reviews, product profit centers	Customer teams and segments, customer P&Ls
Core processes	New-product process	Customer relationship management processes and integration/solutions

SOURCE: Adapted from J. Galbraith, *Designing the Customer-centric Organization* (San Francisco: Jossey-Bass, 2005).

TABLE 12.6

Advantages, Disadvantages, and Contingencies of the Customer-Centric Structure

ADVANTAGES
• Presents one integrated face to the customer • Generates a deep understanding of customer requirements • Enables organization to customize and tailor solutions for customers • Builds a robust customer response capability
DISADVANTAGES
• Customer teams can be too inwardly focused • Sharing learnings and developing functional skills is difficult • Managing lateral relations between customer-facing and back office units is difficult because some processes are split apart • Developing common processes in the front and back is problematic • Clarifying the marketing function is problematic
CONTINGENCIES
• Highly complex and uncertain environments • Large organizations • Goals of customer focus and solutions orientation • Highly uncertain technologies

mechanisms and relationships. To be effective, a customer-centric organization must have strong lateral capabilities, including information systems, capital allocation processes, resource prioritization systems, and the like, to integrate the front and back end of the organization. Few organizations have developed this capability. Finally, customer-centric organizations must decide where to put the marketing function. Should marketing be done by the "front" or "back" of the organization? This is a question not easily answered.

Customer-centric organizations work best in large organizations, where there are strong and powerful customer forces in the industry and where technology and market changes are highly complex and uncertain. In addition, as noted above, the organization has to have a certain amount of maturity. It is unlikely that an organization can successfully implement a customer-centric structure without a strong lateral capability.

12-1f The Network Structure

A *network structure* manages the diverse, complex, and dynamic relationships among multiple organizations or units, each specializing in a particular business function or task.[13] Organizations that utilize network structures have been called shamrock organizations and virtual, modular, or cellular corporations.[14] Less formally, they have been described as pizza structures, spiderwebs, starbursts, and cluster organizations. Some of the confusion over the definition of a network can be clarified by a typology describing four basic types of networks.[15]

1. An *internal market network* exists when a single organization establishes each subunit as an independent profit center that is allowed to trade in services and resources with each other as well as with the external market. Asea Brown Boveri's (ABB) 50 worldwide businesses consist of 1,200 companies organized into 4,500 profit centers that conduct business with each other.
2. A *vertical market network* is composed of multiple organizations linked to a focal organization that coordinates the movement of resources from raw materials to end consumer. Nike, for example, has its shoes manufactured in different plants around the world and then organizes their distribution through retail outlets.
3. An *intermarket network* represents alliances among a variety of organizations in different markets and is exemplified by the Japanese *keiretsu*, the Korean *chaebol*, and the Mexican *grupos*.
4. An *opportunity network* is the most advanced form of network structure. It is a temporary constellation of organizations brought together to pursue a single purpose. Once accomplished, the network disbands. Li and Fung is a Hong Kong–based trading company that pulls together a variety of specialist supplier organizations to design and manufacture a wide range of products.

These types of networks can be distinguished from one another in terms of whether they are single or multiple organizations, single or multiple industries, and stable or temporary.[16] For example, an internal market network is a stable, single-organization, single-industry structure; an opportunity network is a temporary, multiple-organization structure that can span several different industries.

As shown in Figure 12.8, the network structure redraws organizational boundaries and links separate organizations or business units to facilitate task interaction. The essence of networks is the relationships among organizations that perform different aspects of work. In this way, organizations do the things that they do well. For example, a firm that is good at selling products might outsource manufacturing to other organizations that perform that task better than it does. Network organizations use strategic

FIGURE 12.8

The Network Structure

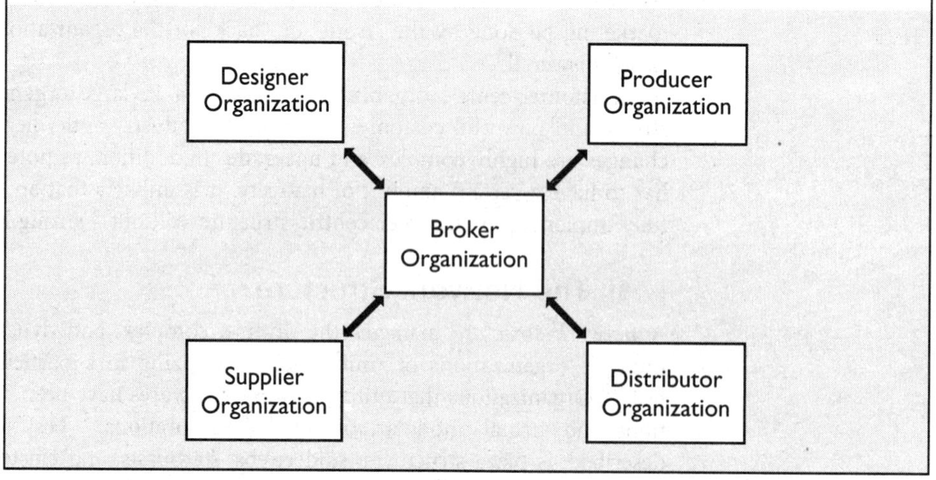

alliances, joint ventures, research and development consortia, licensing agreements, and wholly owned subsidiaries to design, manufacture, and market advanced products, enter new international markets, and develop new technologies. Companies such as Apple Computer, Benetton, Liz Claiborne, Nike, and Merck have implemented fairly sophisticated vertical market and intermarket network structures. Opportunity networks also are commonplace in the construction, fashion, and entertainment industries, as well as in the public sector.[17]

Network structures typically have the following characteristics:

- **Vertical disaggregation.** This refers to the breaking up of the organization's business functions, such as production, marketing, and distribution, into separate organizations performing specialized work. In the film industry, for example, separate organizations providing transportation, cinematography, special effects, set design, music, actors, and catering all work together under a broker organization, the studio. The particular organizations making up the opportunity network represent an important factor in determining its success.[18] Increasingly, disintermediation, or the replacement of whole steps in the value chain by information technology—specifically the Internet—has fueled the development and numbers of network structures.
- **Brokers.** Networks often are managed by broker organizations or "process orchestrators" that locate and assemble member organizations. The broker may play a central role and subcontract for needed products or services, or it may specialize in linking equal partners into a network. In the construction industry, the general contractor typically assembles and manages drywall, mechanical, electrical, plumbing, and other specialties to erect a building.
- **Coordinating mechanisms.** Network organizations generally are not controlled by hierarchical arrangements or plans. Rather, coordination of the work in a network falls into three categories: informal relationships, contracts, and market mechanisms. First, coordination patterns can depend heavily on interpersonal relationships among individuals who have a well-developed partnership. Conflicts are resolved through reciprocity; network members recognize that each likely will have to compromise at some point. Trust is built and nurtured over time by these reciprocal arrangements. Second, coordination can be achieved through formal contracts, such as ownership control, licensing arrangements, or purchase agreements. Finally, market mechanisms, such as spot payments, performance accountability, technology standards, and information systems, ensure that all parties are aware of each other's activities and can communicate with each other.

Network structures have a number of advantages and disadvantages, as shown in Table 12.7.[19] They are highly flexible and adaptable to changing conditions. The ability to form partnerships with different organizations permits the creation of a "best-of-the-best" company to exploit opportunities, often global in nature. They enable each member to exploit its distinctive competence. They can accumulate and apply sufficient resources and expertise to large, complex tasks that single organizations cannot perform. Perhaps most important, network organizations can have synergistic effects whereby members build on each other's strengths and competencies, creating a whole that exceeds the sum of its parts.

The major problems with network organizations are in managing such complex structures. Galbraith and Kazanjian describe network structures as matrix organizations extending beyond the boundaries of single firms but lacking the ability to appeal to a higher authority to resolve conflicts.[20] Thus, matrix skills of managing lateral relations across organizational boundaries are critical to administering network structures. Most organizations, because they are managed hierarchically, can be expected to have

TABLE 12.7

Advantages, Disadvantages, and Contingencies of the Network-Based Structure

ADVANTAGES
• Enables highly flexible and adaptive response to dynamic environments • Creates a "best-of-the-best" organization to focus resources on customer and market needs • Enables each organization to leverage a distinctive competency • Permits rapid global expansion • Can produce synergistic results
DISADVANTAGES
• Managing lateral relations across autonomous organizations is difficult • Motivating members to relinquish autonomy to join the network is troublesome • Sustaining membership and benefits can be problematic • May give partners access to proprietary knowledge/technology
CONTINGENCIES
• Highly complex and uncertain environments • Organizations of all sizes • Goals of organizational specialization and innovation • Highly uncertain technologies

difficulties managing lateral relations. Other disadvantages of network organizations include the difficulties of motivating organizations to join such structures and of sustaining commitment over time. Potential members may not want to give up their autonomy to link with other organizations and, once linked, they may have problems sustaining the benefits of joining together. This is especially true if the network consists of organizations that are not the "best of breed." Finally, joining a network may expose the organization's proprietary knowledge and skills to others.

As shown in Table 12.7, network organizations are best suited to highly complex and uncertain environments where multiple competencies and flexible responses are needed. They seem to apply to organizations of all sizes, and they deal with complex tasks or problems involving high interdependencies across organizations. Network structures fit with goals that emphasize organization specialization and innovation.

Application 12.2 describes how Amazon.com's network structure was configured to align with its strategy and how relationships are managed.[21]

12-2 Downsizing

Downsizing refers to interventions aimed at reducing the size of the organization.[22] This typically is accomplished by decreasing the number of employees through layoffs, attrition, redeployment, or early retirement or by reducing the number of organizational units or managerial levels through divestiture, outsourcing, reorganization, or delayering.

application 12.2

AMAZON.COM'S NETWORK STRUCTURE

Amazon.com (www.amazon.com) was launched in mid-1995 as the "Earth's Biggest Bookstore." It offered more than one million titles to online buyers, more than three times the number offered at traditional bookstores. Since then, it has evolved into a powerful network structure involving both other Internet retailers as well as more traditional retailers, including other bookstores. Amazon also has expanded into information services, offering a variety of network services to firms under the banner Amazon Web Services. At the center of it all is Amazon's massive website, Amazon.com. By pairing Amazon's state-of-the-art technology, built-in traffic, and industry-leading fulfillment and customer-service processes with its partners' products and their own strengths, a complex network of organizations is working together to make everyone more successful.

The company went public in the first quarter of 1997 riding the dot.com wave. Its revenue grew from $147.8 million in 1997 to over $61 billion in fiscal year 2012 and is predicted to exceed $100 billion in 2015. Despite this impressive sales growth, there has been increasing pressure to deliver profits, which occurred for the first time in fiscal year 2002. From at least one point of view, the development of Amazon's network structure is an important reason for this profitability.

From the beginning, Amazon operated as a virtual organization and leveraged its network structure. For example, it developed and operated the Amazon.com website to draw in customers and to learn about creating an effective online customer experience. However, the company owned little or no inventory, warehouses, distribution centers, or customer-service operations. Early on, order fulfillment was left to Ingram Book Distributors, one of the largest book wholesalers, who also contracted out delivery to third-party vendors, such as UPS.

In June of 1998, Amazon began selling CDs, and added DVDs and videos in November 1998. It added electronic products, toys, software, and video games in 1999, and tools, health and beauty products, kitchen products, and photo services in 2000. It also expanded internationally starting in 1999, opening up markets in Canada, Europe, and Asia over the next decade. Amazon's first West Coast distribution center was built in 1996 and an East Coast distribution center was added in 1997. In 1999, in anticipation of the Christmas rush, Amazon built five warehouse and distribution facilities and several customer-service centers to improve its order fulfillment capabilities.

Amazon's initial forays into a broader network began in 1999 but were compartmentalized on the website. Non-Amazon products, such as used books or individuals auctioning off different products, were not allowed to infiltrate Amazon's millions of book, CD, and DVD pages. Third-party products were put under "tabs" that roughly described the kind of commerce to be conducted, such as the "auction" tab or the "zShops" tab, which contained a variety of vendor products. Thus, traditional Amazon products were separated from products offered by others. Continued profit pressure, however, forced the organization to look at relationships differently.

Jeff Bezos, company founder and CEO, stated as follows:

> "We realized that what was most important to the marketplace sellers was demand—access to prospective buyers. So, the idea of the "single store" was to give them a level of access equal to our own—listing their goods right alongside ours."

With the "single store" strategy, Amazon.com transformed itself from an Internet retailer to a platform for commerce. Small businesses and individuals, which used to be in the Auctions or zShops sections, were given the opportunity to place their products on Amazon's most visited sites. In exchange for this visibility, Amazon developed a contract that included a fee schedule and described the responsibilities and activities that each organization would perform. Amazon quickly expanded its network to include partnerships with large companies as well as partially- and fully-owned affiliates, gaining over two million third-party sellers by 2013. It leveraged its state-of-the-art transaction-processing systems and networking capabilities to provide sellers with access to an immense customer base and rapid, low-cost sales and order fulfillment. Driven by a "culture of metrics," Amazon was able to provide its sellers with access to unprecedented amounts of real-time data on customer product preferences and purchasing behavior.

Amazon also engaged in more traditional marketing arrangements where the Amazon.com website served as a marketing vehicle for other companies. From the Amazon website, users were transferred over to the vendor's website and Amazon received a fee based on the number of customers exposed to the vendor's marketing message or on the number of customers referred. Amazon made its first set of partnerships with Drugstore.com, Living.com, and Wine.com among others. As Amazon affiliates, they paid Amazon placement and referral fees for advertising on the Amazon website. This was called the Amazon Commerce Network.

Given the vast scale of the information storage and computing infrastructure needed to run Amazon's marketplace, Amazon Web Services was launched in 2002 to sell excess infrastructure capacity as well as information services to other companies. This logical extension of Amazon's network grew rapidly into over 25 proprietary Web-based services that have attracted over 300,000 developer customers, making Amazon the market leader in cloud computing worldwide. Amazon Web Services is expected to have revenue of $3.8 billion in 2013 and could be worth up to $30 billion if it were a standalone company.

By excelling at particular aspects of retailing in the Internet environment, Amazon has been able to leverage those competencies into a powerful network of alliances and partnerships. It has been able to expand its business beyond the Internet marketplace to the information services arena. The network structure is one important reason Amazon has been one of the few Internet start-ups to actually post a profit.

In practice, downsizing generally involves layoffs where a certain number or class of organization members is no longer employed by the organization. Although traditionally associated with lower-level workers, downsizing increasingly has claimed the jobs of staff specialists, middle managers, and senior executives especially during the recent economic turndown.

An important consequence of downsizing has been the rise of the contingent workforce. In companies like Cisco or Motorola, less expensive temporary or permanent part-time workers often are hired by the same organizations that just laid off thousands of employees. A study by the American Management Association found that nearly a third of the 720 firms in the sample had rehired recently terminated employees as independent contractors or consultants because the downsizings had not been matched by an appropriate reduction in or redesign of the workload.[23] Overall cost reduction was achieved by replacing expensive permanent workers with a contingent workforce.

Few corporations or government agencies have escaped the massive downsizing brought on by the recent global recession. In the United States, for example, layoffs reached a yearly peak of over three million workers in 2009; although declining in subsequent years, almost 8% of the workforce was unemployed in 2012.[24] In addition to layoffs, organizations have downsized by redeploying workers from one function or job to another. When IBM's business shifted from hardware to software and services in the 1990s, more than 69,000 people were laid off, yet the size of the total workforce increased by 16,000 employees.[25]

Downsizing is generally a response to at least four major conditions. First, it is associated increasingly with mergers and acquisitions as redundant jobs are eliminated to gain labor efficiencies. Second, it can result from organization decline caused by loss of revenues and market share and by technological and industrial change. As a result of fuel oil prices, terrorism, and other changes, nearly a quarter of U.S. airline jobs were lost in the first decade of the twentieth century. Third, downsizing can occur when organizations implement one of the new organizational structures described previously. For example, creation of network-based structures often involves outsourcing work that is not essential to the organization's core competence. Fourth, downsizing can result from beliefs and social pressures that smaller is better.[26] In the United States, there is strong conviction that organizations should be leaner and more flexible. Hamel and Prahalad warned, however, that organizations must be careful that downsizing is not a symptom of "corporate anorexia."[27] Organizations may downsize for their own sake and not think about future growth. They may lose key employees who are necessary for future success, cutting into the organization's core competencies and leaving a legacy of mistrust among members. In such situations, it is questionable whether downsizing is developmental as defined in OD.

12-2a Application Stages

Successful downsizing interventions tend to proceed by the following steps:[28]

1. **Clarify the organization's strategy**. As a first step, organization leaders specify corporate strategy and communicate clearly how downsizing relates to it. They inform members that downsizing is not a goal in itself, but a restructuring process for achieving strategic objectives. Leaders need to provide visible and consistent support throughout the process. They can provide opportunities for members to voice their concerns, ask questions, and obtain career counseling if necessary.
2. **Assess downsizing options and make relevant choices.** Once the strategy is clear, the full range of downsizing options can be identified and assessed. Table 12.8 describes three primary downsizing methods: workforce reduction, organization redesign, and systemic change. A specific downsizing strategy may use elements of all three approaches. Workforce reduction is aimed at reducing the number of employees, usually in a relatively short timeframe. It can include attrition, retirement incentives, outplacement services, and layoffs. Organization redesign attempts to restructure the firm to prepare it for the next stage of growth. This is a medium-term approach that can be accomplished by merging organizational units, eliminating management layers, and redesigning tasks. Systemic change is a longer-term option aimed at changing the culture and strategic orientation of the organization. It can involve interventions that alter the responsibilities and work behaviors of everyone in the organization and that promote continual improvement as a way of life in the firm.

   Case Construction, a manufacturer of heavy construction equipment, used a variety of methods to downsize in the mid-1990s, including eliminating money-losing product lines; narrowing the breadth of remaining product lines; bringing customers to the company headquarters to get their opinions of new-product design (which surprisingly resulted in maintaining, rather than changing, certain preferred features, thus holding down redesign costs); shifting production to outside vendors; restructuring debt; and spinning off most of its 250 stores. Eventually, these changes led to closing five plants and to payroll reductions of almost 35%.[29] The number of

TABLE 12.8

Three Downsizing Tactics

Downsizing Tactic	Characteristics	Examples
Workforce reduction	Aimed at headcount reduction Short-term implementation Fosters a transition	Attrition Transfer and outplacement Retirement incentives Buyout packages Layoffs
Organization redesign	Aimed at organization change Moderate-term implementation Fosters transition and, potentially, transformation	Eliminate functions Merge units Eliminate layers Eliminate products Redesign tasks
Systemic redesign	Aimed at culture change Long-term implementation Fosters transformation	Change responsibility Involve all constituents Foster continuous improvement and innovation Simplification Downsizing: a way of life

SOURCE: K. Cameron, S. Freeman, and A. Mishra, "Best Practices in White-Collar Downsizing: Managing Contradictions," *Academy of Management Executive* 5 (1991), 62.

jobs lost would have been much greater, however, if Case had not implemented a variety of downsizing methods.

Unfortunately, organizations often choose obvious solutions for downsizing, such as layoffs, because they can be implemented quickly. This action produces a climate of fear and defensiveness as members focus on identifying who will be separated from the organization. Examining a broad range of options and considering the entire organization rather than only certain areas can help allay fears that favoritism and politics are the bases for downsizing decisions. Moreover, participation of organization members in such decisions can have positive benefits. It can create a sense of urgency for identifying and implementing options to downsizing other than layoffs. Participation can provide members with a clearer understanding of how downsizing will proceed and can increase the likelihood that whatever choices are made are perceived as reasonable and fair.

3. **Implement the changes.** This stage involves implementing methods for reducing the size of the organization. Several practices characterize successful implementation. First, downsizing is best controlled from the top down. Many difficult decisions are required, and a broad perspective helps to overcome people's natural instincts to protect their enterprise or function. Second, specific areas of inefficiency and high cost need to be identified and targeted. The morale of the organization can be hurt if areas commonly known to be redundant are left untouched. Third, specific actions should be linked to the organization's strategy. Organization members need to be

reminded consistently that restructuring activities are part of a plan to improve the organization's performance. Finally, communicate frequently using a variety of media. This keeps people informed, lowers their anxiety over the process, and makes it easier for them to focus on their work.

4. **Address the needs of survivors and those who leave.** Most downsizing eventually involves reduction in the size of the workforce, and it is important to support not only employees who remain with the organization but also those who leave. When layoffs occur, employees are generally asked to take on additional responsibilities and to learn new jobs, often with little or no increase in compensation. This added workload can be stressful, and when combined with anxiety over past layoffs and possible future ones, it can lead to what researchers have labeled the "survivor syndrome."[30] This involves a narrow set of self-absorbed and risk-averse behaviors that can threaten the organization's survival. Rather than working to ensure the organization's success, survivors often are preoccupied with whether additional layoffs will occur, with guilt over receiving pay and benefits while coworkers are struggling with termination, and with the uncertainty of career advancement.

   Organizations can address these survivor concerns with communication processes that increase the amount and frequency of information provided. Communication should shift from explanations about who left or why to clarification of where the company is going, including its visions, strategies, and goals. The linkage between employees' performance and strategic success is emphasized so that remaining members feel they are valued. Organizations also can support survivors through training and development activities that prepare them for the new work they are being asked to perform. Senior management can promote greater involvement in decision making, thus reinforcing the message that people are important to the future success and growth of the organization.

   Given the negative consequences typically associated with job loss, organizations have developed an array of methods to help employees who have been laid off. These include outplacement counseling, personal and family counseling, severance packages, office support for job searches, relocation services, and job retraining. Each service is intended to assist employees in their transition to another work situation.

5. **Follow through with growth plans.** This final stage of downsizing involves implementing an organization renewal and growth process. Failure to move quickly to implement growth plans is a key determinant of ineffective downsizing.[31] For example, a study of 1,020 human resource directors reported that only 44% of the companies that had downsized in the previous five years shared details of their growth plans with employees; only 34% told employees how they would fit into the company's new strategy.[32] Organizations must ensure that employees understand the renewal strategy and their new roles in it. Employees need credible expectations that, although the organization has been through a tough period, their renewed efforts can move it forward.

Application 12.3 describes how the City of Menlo Park, California, successfully responded to a serious fiscal downturn through effective downsizing initiatives.[33] It demonstrates how straightforward communication and active engagement with key stakeholders can inform downsizing decisions, gain commitment to implementing them, and mitigate their negative consequences. The application also shows the complexity of downsizing in the public sector where there are often multiple competing interests and that even a relatively small organization can mount a sophisticated and effective downsizing intervention.

DOWNSIZING IN MENLO PARK, CALIFORNIA

application 12.3

Menlo Park is a modest-sized city of around 32,000 residents located in the San Francisco Bay area. Like many California municipalities, Menlo Park experienced challenging fiscal problems well before the global economic crisis erupted in 2008. In 2004–2005, the city had an operating budget of $29.2 million and 230 full-time equivalent (FTE) employees. Over the previous four years, Menlo Park was forced to reduce spending in line with declining revenues. Sales-tax revenue had dropped about 50% in two years (from $12 million to $6 million) and the state of California had diverted local government revenue to help balance its budget. Worse yet, the city's costs had been rising significantly primarily because of retiree benefit expenses.

According to Audrey Seymour, the Assistant City Manager at the time, Menlo Park moved strategically to remedy these fiscal problems. It trimmed more than $4 million from its annual operating budget and reduced its workforce by about 13%, the equivalent of 30 FTEs. To minimize the negative impact of these changes on the city and its employees, Menlo Park's elected officials and administrators implemented the following downsizing initiatives:

- Involve employees early and often. All-employee forums were used to communicate to members and to listen to their reactions and suggestions. These meetings helped everyone clearly understand the magnitude and causes of the city's fiscal problem. Then, action teams were formed in each city department comprised of employees from all levels. The teams were given guidelines and support and asked to devise plans to streamline operations, cut costs, and enhance revenues. The city also used suggestion boxes and the intranet to solicit ideas from employees. To keep everyone abreast of what was occurring, the city manager used both personal and electronic forms of communication, frequently holding employee briefings and sending emails. After cuts were implemented, informal debriefing sessions were held and counselors from the city's employee assistance program helped employees deal with the impacts of the changes on their lives.
- Work with unions to achieve common goals. Cost cutting started with reducing expenses and eliminating vacant positions, and then moved to filled positions. The city worked closely with union representatives to find ways to avoid layoffs while still reducing the size of the workforce. The union offered several ideas and worked with the city to develop a voluntary separation process that offered employees in service areas targeted for reduction early retirement, enhanced severance, or shorter hours.
- Seek community input. Because the downsizing efforts would adversely affect city services, Menlo Park started an initiative called "YourCity/YourDecision." This program included sending a survey to community households asking residents to rank order the importance of city services. From a total of 15,500 households, more than 1,000 surveys were returned. As a follow-up to the survey, interactive community workshops were conducted across the city to gain further input into specific ideas residents would recommend to balance the budget in line with the priorities identified in the survey. In addition, each of the city's commissions was asked for suggestions to simplify policies and procedures to save money. The feedback from all of these outreach efforts helped the City Council make tough choices about which services to fund and at what level. The information also guided city staff in developing budget-balancing strategies.
- Keep elected officials in the loop. City administrators held a half-day retreat and a series of meetings with City Council members to discuss the details of the fiscal problems and to get guidance about high-priority service areas and possible cost reductions. Council members were asked to rate city services and these

data, along with the community survey results, were used to determine service-area cuts. Council members also spent time discussing which criteria were most important to consider when weighing potential budget cuts. Follow-up activities included periodic phone calls to Council members to update them on the downsizing process and to answer any questions. This kept members informed in case they had to respond to questions from employees, union leaders, or the press. The city also brought in a panel of experts to give projections on the regional economy, thus providing information about what the fiscal future might hold for Menlo Park. All of these activities made the difficult decision-making process and the adoption of the city budget easier.

As a result of these downsizing initiatives, Menlo Park was able to bring its operations and spending in line with tough fiscal realities. It did this in a way that mitigated damage to community services and to workplace morale. The city was better able to prioritize community services and to allocate funds accordingly. Because the downsizing process had wide involvement from the union, City Council, the community, and employees, the city gained the necessary guidance and commitment from these stakeholders to make tough decisions and to continue to deliver on core community priorities. In the end, Menlo Park was able to reduce the size of its workforce without having to make any layoffs. It was able to trim its operating budget without having to reduce essential community services.

12-2b Results of Downsizing

The empirical research on downsizing is mostly negative.[34] A review conducted by the National Research Council concluded, "From the research produced thus far, downsizing as a strategy for improvement has proven to be, by and large, a failure." A number of studies have documented the negative productivity and employee consequences. One survey of 1,005 companies that used downsizing to reduce costs reported that fewer than half of the firms actually met cost targets. Moreover, only 22% of the companies achieved expected productivity gains, and consequently about 80% of the firms needed to rehire some of the same people that they had previously terminated. Fewer than 33% of the companies surveyed reported that profits increased as much as expected, and only 21% achieved satisfactory improvements in shareholder return on investment. Another survey of 1,142 downsized firms found that only about a third achieved productivity goals. In addition, the research points to a number of problems at the individual level, including increased stress and illness, loss of self-esteem, reduced trust and loyalty, and marriage and family disruptions.[35]

Research on the effects of downsizing on financial performance also shows negative results.[36] One study examined an array of financial-performance measures, such as return on sales, assets, and equity, in 210 companies that announced layoffs. It found that increases in financial performance in the first year following the layoff announcements were not followed by performance improvements in the next year. In no case did a firm's financial performance after a layoff announcement match its maximum levels of performance in the year before the announcement. These results suggest that layoffs may result in initial improvements in financial performance, but such gains are temporary and not sustained at even prelayoff levels. In a similar study of 16 firms that wrote off more than 10% of their net worth in a five-year period, stock prices, which averaged 16% below the market average before the layoff announcements, increased on the day that the restructuring was announced but then began to decline steadily. Two years after the layoff announcements, 10 of the 16 stocks were trading below the market by 17–48%, and 12 of the 16 were below comparable firms in their industries by 5–45%.

These research findings paint a rather bleak picture of the success of downsizing. The results must be interpreted cautiously, however, for three reasons. First, many of the survey-oriented studies received responses from human resources specialists who might have been naturally inclined to view downsizing in a negative light. Second, the studies of financial performance may have included a biased sample of firms. If the companies selected for analysis had been poorly managed, then downsizing alone would have been unlikely to improve financial performance. There is some empirical support for this view because low-performing firms are more likely to engage in downsizing than are high-performing firms.[37] Third, disappointing results may be a function of the way downsizing was implemented. A number of organizations, such as Florida Power and Light, General Electric, Motorola, Texas Instruments, Boeing, and Hewlett-Packard, have posted solid financial returns following downsizing.[38] A study of 30 downsized firms in the automobile industry showed that those companies that implemented effectively the process described above scored significantly higher on several performance measures than did firms that had no downsizing strategy or that implemented the steps poorly.[39] Several studies have suggested that when downsizing programs adopt appropriate OD interventions or apply strategies similar to the process outlined above, they generate more positive individual and organizational results.[40] Thus, the success of downsizing efforts may depend as much on how effectively the intervention is applied as on the size of the layoffs or the amount of delayering.

12-3 Reengineering

The final restructuring intervention is *reengineering*—the fundamental rethinking and radical redesign of business processes to achieve dramatic improvements in performance.[41] Reengineering transforms how organizations traditionally produce and deliver goods and services. Beginning with the Industrial Revolution, organizations have increasingly fragmented work into specialized units, each focusing on a limited part of the overall production process. Although this division of labor has enabled organizations to mass-produce standardized products and services efficiently, it can be overly complicated, difficult to manage, and slow to respond to the rapid and unpredictable changes experienced by many organizations today. Reengineering addresses these problems by breaking down specialized work units into more integrated, cross-functional work processes. This streamlines work processes and makes them more efficient with faster cycle times and better information handling capabilities. Consequently, work processes are more responsive to changes in competitive conditions, customer demands, product life cycles, and technologies.[42] Reengineering has been applied to work processes in manufacturing and service industries, in business firms, not-for-profits, and government agencies; and in diverse global settings, such as Australia, India, Ireland, Turkey, and South Africa.

As might be expected, successful reengineering requires an almost revolutionary change in how organizations design their work structures. It identifies and questions the often-unexamined assumptions underlying how organizations perform work and why do they do it in a particular way. This effort typically results in major changes in thinking and work methods—a shift from specialized jobs, tasks, and structures to integrated processes that deliver value to customers. Such revolutionary change differs considerably from incremental approaches to performance improvement, such as continuous improvement and total quality management (Chapter 13), which emphasize small, yet constant, changes in existing work processes. Because reengineering radically alters the status quo, it seeks to produce dramatic increases in organization performance.

Reengineering seeks to leverage the latest developments in information technology to enable significant change in large-scale business processes, such as supply-chain logistics.[43] It can help organizations break out of traditional ways of thinking about work and embrace entirely new ways of producing and delivering products. For example, the most popular software systems, SAP and PeopleSoft, standardize information flows and help to integrate data on a range of tasks and to link work processes together. On the other hand, many existing information systems do not provide the data needed to operate integrated business processes.[44] Such legacy systems can make reengineering difficult if not impossible to implement because they do not allow interdependent departments to interface with each other; they often require new information to be entered manually into separate computer systems before people in different work areas can access it.

Reengineering has been associated with downsizing. Reengineering can result in production and delivery processes that require fewer people and fewer layers of management. Conversely, downsizing may require subsequent reengineering interventions. When downsizing occurs without fundamental changes in how work is performed, the same tasks simply are being performed with a smaller number of people. Thus, expected cost savings may not be realized because lower salaries and fewer benefits are offset by lower productivity.

Reengineering also can be linked to transformation of organization structures and work design. Its focus on work processes helps to break down the vertical orientation of functional and divisional organization structures. Reengineering identifies and assesses core business processes and redesigns work to account for key task interdependencies running through them. That typically results in new jobs or teams that emphasize multifunctional tasks, results-oriented feedback, and employee empowerment—characteristics associated with motivational and sociotechnical approaches to work design (Chapter 14). Regrettably, reengineering initially failed to apply these approaches' attention to individual differences in people's reactions to work to its own work-design prescriptions. It advocated enriched work and teams, without consideration for the wealth of research that shows that not all people are motivated to perform such work.[45]

12-3a Application Stages

Early reengineering interventions emphasized identifying which business processes to reengineer and technically assessing the workflow. Efforts that are more recent have extended reengineering practice to address issues of managing change, such as how to deal with resistance to change and how to manage the transition to new work processes.[46] The following application steps are included in most reengineering efforts, although the order may change slightly from one situation to another:[47]

1. **Prepare the organization.** Reengineering begins with clarification and assessment of the organization's competitive environment, strategy, and objectives. This effort establishes and communicates the need for reengineering and the strategic direction that the process should follow. For example, preparing for reengineering at the U.S. Veterans Administration (VA) health care system was made easier because everyone agreed the health care delivery process was broken. Veterans' groups were outspoken in their complaints of quality care, the system was publicly ridiculed in the movie *The Fourth of July* with Tom Cruise, and many patients were figuratively

"falling through the cracks." The old way of doing business, reinforced by years of government protection and a long period of peace, seriously saddled the organization with high costs, old systems, and siloed processes.[48] The VA's leadership, led by Kenneth Kizer, recognized that the keys to the health care system's success were low costs and customer satisfaction. Consequently, they set dramatic goals of increasing patient visits while holding annual cost per patient steady. Defining these objectives gave the reengineering effort a clear focus.

A final task in preparing the organization is to communicate clearly—through words and deeds—why reengineering is necessary and the direction it will take. The VA's preparation included not only traditional communications through speeches, newsletters, and meetings, but visible commitments such as reorganizing the pharmacy organization and making substantial technology commitments to an electronic medical record system. Thus, senior executives were careful to communicate, both verbally and behaviorally, that they were fully committed to the change effort. Demonstration of such unwavering support seems necessary if organization members are to challenge their traditional thinking about how business should be conducted.

2. **Fundamentally rethink the way work gets done.** This step lies at the heart of reengineering and involves these activities: identifying and analyzing core business processes, defining their key performance objectives, and designing new processes. These tasks are the real work of reengineering and typically are performed by a cross-functional design team that is given considerable time and resources to accomplish them.[49]

   a. **Identify and analyze core business processes.** Core processes are considered essential for strategic success. They include activities that transform inputs into valued outputs. Core processes typically are assessed through development of a process map that identifies the three to five activities required to deliver an organization's products or services. For a health care system, the core processes include the intake of patients through the primary care physician, inpatient and outpatient services, and medical records and billing.

   Analysis of core business processes can include assigning costs to each of the major phases of the workflow to help identify costs that may be hidden in the activities of the production process. Traditional cost-accounting systems do not store data in process terms; they identify costs according to categories of expense, such as salaries, fixed costs, and supplies.[50] This method of cost accounting can be misleading and can result in erroneous conclusions about how best to reduce costs. For example, most traditional accounting systems suggest that salaries and fringe benefits account for the largest percentage of total costs—an assessment that supports workforce downsizing as the most effective way to lower costs. An activity-based accounting system often reveals a different picture—that rework, errors, and delays during the workflow are major sources of unnecessary cost.

   Business processes also can be assessed in terms of value-added activities—the amount of value contributed to a product or service by a particular step in the process. For example, early in the VA's process, senior managers learned that only 10% of the patients covered by the VA had a primary care physician. By assigning a primary care physician to each veteran patient, the total cost of care was greatly reduced. Patients saw one physician who could address many issues rather than making multiple visits to a variety of specialists. Conversely, organizations often engage in a variety of process activities that have little or no added value.

b. **Define performance objectives.** Challenging performance goals are set in this step. The highest possible level of performance for any particular process is identified, and dramatic goals are set for speed, quality, cost, or other measures of performance. These standards can derive from customer requirements or from benchmarks of the best practices of industry leaders. For example, at Andersen Windows, the demand for unique window shapes pushed the number of different products from 28,000 to more than 86,000.[51] The pressure on the shop floor for a "batch of one" resulted in 20% of all shipments containing at least one order discrepancy. As part of its reengineering effort, Andersen set targets for ease of ordering, manufacturing, and delivery. Each retailer and distributor was sold an interactive, computerized version of Andersen's catalog that allowed customers to design their own windows. The resulting design is then given a unique "license plate number" and the specifications are sent directly to the factory. Four years later, new sales had tripled at some retail locations, the number of products had increased to 188,000, and fewer than 1 in 200 shipments had a discrepancy.

c. **Design new processes.** This task involves designing new business processes to achieve breakthrough goals. It often starts with a clean sheet of paper and addresses the question "If we were starting this company today, what is the most effective and efficient way to deliver this product or service?" Each essential process is then designed according to the following guidelines:[52]
   - Begin and end the process with the needs and wants of the customer.
   - Simplify the current process by combining and eliminating steps.
   - Use the "best of what is" in the current process.
   - Attend to both technical and social aspects of the process.
   - Do not be constrained by past practice.
   - Identify the critical information required at each step in the process.
   - Perform activities in their most natural order.
   - Assume the work gets done right the first time.
   - Listen to people who do the work.

   An important activity that appears in many successful reengineering efforts is implementing "early wins" or "quick hits." Analysis of existing processes often reveals obvious redundancies and inefficiencies for which appropriate changes may be authorized immediately. These early successes can help generate and sustain momentum in the reengineering effort.

3. **Restructure the organization around the new business processes.** This last step in reengineering involves changing the organization's structure to support the new business processes. This endeavor typically results in the kinds of process-based structures that were described earlier in this chapter. Reengineered organizations typically have the following characteristics:[53]
   - Work units change from functional departments to process teams.
   - Jobs change from simple tasks to multidimensional work.
   - People's roles change from controlled to empowered.
   - The focus of performance measures and compensation shifts from activities to results.
   - Organization structures change from hierarchical to flat.
   - Managers change from supervisors to coaches; executives change from scorekeepers to leaders.

The VA's experience reflects many of these features. As suggested earlier, the key to a reengineered organization is often its commitment to and development of an integrated information system. During the VA's reengineering, it was an electronic medical record system that integrated nearly every step in the patient care process. The following examples support how the information system radically transformed the way patient care was delivered:

- A physician gets a computerized reminder that one of his patients in the hospital, a 44-year-old diabetic, is due to have an eye exam. Through the system, the doctor asks the floor nurse to send the patient to the eye clinic on the second floor, where an ophthalmologist administers the test. An alert soon flashes on the doctor's monitor saying the exam has been completed.
- A nurse on a different floor uses the same computer network to make sure she's giving the right medication to a 60-year-old patient with high blood pressure. With a handheld device, she scans a bar-coded bracelet on her patient's wrist and then a bar code on the drug bottle. A nearby computer linked to the hospital pharmacy confirms that she's giving the right drug to the right patient.
- In the Tele-Health unit, a nurse reads the vital statistics of a 57-year-old patient that were sent to her computer via an electronic system that the VA has rigged at the patient's home. Today the news is worrisome: The patient, who is suffering from heart disease, has gained three pounds overnight, indicating that he's retaining fluids. After a few quick phone calls to the patient and his doctor, the nurse tells him to double his diuretic medication today. "We caught him before his condition got worse," she says with satisfaction.

Application 12.4 describes the reengineering efforts at Honeywell's Industrial Automation and Control business. It highlights the importance of mapping current processes and aligning the rest of the organization to support the change, especially information technology.[54]

12-3b Results from Reengineering

The results from reengineering vary widely. Industry journals and the business press regularly contain accounts of dramatic business outcomes attributable to reengineering. On the other hand, the best-selling book on reengineering reported that as many as 70% of the efforts failed to meet their cost, cycle time, or productivity objectives.[55] One study polled 497 companies in the United States and 1,245 companies in Europe, and found that 60% of U.S. firms and 75% of European firms had engaged in at least one reengineering project. Eighty-five percent of the firms reported little or no gain from the efforts.[56] Despite its popularity, reengineering is only beginning to be evaluated systematically, and there is little research to help unravel the disparate results.[57]

One evaluation of business process reengineering examined more than one hundred companies' efforts.[58] In-depth analyses of 20 reengineering projects found that 11 cases had total business-unit cost reductions of less than 5%, whereas six cases had total cost reductions averaging 18%. The primary difference was the scope of the business process selected. Reengineering broad value-added processes significantly affected total business-unit costs; reengineering narrow business processes did not.

Similarly, performance improvements in particular processes were associated strongly with changes in six key levers of behavior, including structure, skills, information systems, roles, incentives, and shared values. Efforts that addressed all six levers produced average cost reductions in specific processes by 35%; efforts that affected only one or two change levers reduced costs by 19%. Finally, the percentage reduction in total unit costs was associated with committed leadership. Similarly, a survey of 23 "successful"

application 12.4

HONEYWELL IAC'S TOTALPLANT™ REENGINEERING PROCESS

Honeywell (www.honeywell.com) is a diversified technology and manufacturing organization that serves customers worldwide with aerospace products and services; control technologies for buildings, homes, and industry; automotive products; and specialty materials. Its industrial automation and control (IAC) business unit in Phoenix, Arizona, is responsible for the design, manufacture, and configuration of world-class process control equipment marketed as the TDC 3000X family of systems. IAC's customer base includes refineries, chemical plants, and paper mills around the world.

In response to declining performance results, IAC management set out to implement an ISO 9000 certified quality program named TotalPlant™ as part of an effort to optimize global customer satisfaction. The objectives of this initiative were reducing defects, minimizing production cycles, and optimizing resource management. The TotalPlant™ initiative was a business process reengineering intervention based upon four principles: process mapping, fail-safing, teamwork, and communication. Cross-functional multiskilled teams were created and given responsibility for an entire module or product line. Each team member was then trained in each of the principles and empowered to enact them to create improvements within their work groups.

Process mapping is a methodology that converts any business activity into a graphical form. It creates a common visual language that can be used to enhance an employees' ability to see beyond the boundaries of their work process. It is also the basis of radical change in business processes. As part of the TotalPlant™ initiative, process mapping consisted of eight major stages.

- The first three stages were to select the process to be reviewed, identify all customers, and set the boundaries of the process. Through consensus decision making, these simple steps kept the participants focused on the process being mapped. In addition, the team reviewed its composition to ensure that all appropriate functions were represented.
- Fourth, the team developed an "as is" map. This required members to outline and document the existing process. By creating a visual map the team was able to identify the flow of both the product and the information related to the process. Cross-functional decision points and dependencies became visually apparent through the process. Fifth, the "as is" map was used by the team to calculate cycle times, the elapsed times between the start of a process and the conclusion of a process, as well as the distance the product travels during that cycle. Both the mean and the range were calculated for each process cycle time.
- Sixth, the team identified areas of improvement that did not require additional costs or resources. Non-value-added steps, extended approval processes, and processes with highly variant cycle times were analyzed and either streamlined or completely eliminated. Following this step, the seventh stage was to develop a "should be" map that described the improved process.
- Finally, the eighth step directed the team to develop a process implementation plan, establish confirmation from a steering committee, and then implement it. New goals were established and results tracked for each of the process steps.

The second major component of the TotalPlant™ process was the *fail-safing process*. Fail-safing is a five-step process intended to create a product that is defect free by identifying and analyzing defects, and understanding their root causes. A root cause has three characteristics: (1) it is defined as being the cause of the defect; (2) it is possible to change the cause; and (3) if eliminated, the defect will be removed or at least significantly reduced. Once the root cause is identified, a set of alternative solutions is developed to eliminate the defect in future products. Each alternative is evaluated for ease of implementation, cost, and time to implement.

Once a solution is agreed upon, the team implements the PDCA (Plan, Do, Check, Act) process to move the solution forward. Planning includes developing a full implementation plan, which includes areas impacted, timing, resource requirements, and costs. This becomes a living document outlining the action items needed to implement the change. "Doing" consists of executing against the implementation plan. Once the new process has been implemented, the results are "checked" to ensure that they are in line with the desired results. Finally, the team must "act" to determine the next steps for continuous improvement.

Teamwork was the critical third piece of the TotalPlant™ process. Honeywell realized that the transition to a team environment needed to happen gradually. Through the process mapping and fail-safing process, they gave people real problems to address and systematic tools with which to solve them. With the addition of education and training around teams, these "hard-skill" activities became the fertile soil for team development. As team members were asked to own the whole process, an environment that fosters teamwork was created. Creativity, innovation, and risk taking were rewarded and the values of the organization moved to trust, respect, and empowerment. Managers were trained to support the teams, not to run them, in order to further enrich the team environment.

The final and foundational element of the TotalPlant™ process was *communication*. Top management's successful communication of the TotalPlant™ paradigm shift was pivotal to the initiative's success. Through their everyday actions, top managers lived the values of open communication throughout the organization. In addition, teams were given training in conflict resolution, problem solving, and listening skills to enhance the overall effectiveness of communication within the teams. The creation of a positive, open environment became critical to the success of the change initiative. Top management understood that the environment needed to shift to consistently support teamwork, creativity, and "new thinking." The major challenges within the process took the form of middle-management resistance. The new team concepts made managers, who had been functional or process experts, move outside their comfort zone by requiring them to look at processes across functions and to broaden their view of success. Top management was required to move from command and control to a more facilitative and empowering approach to support this type of behavior change.

In addition to the four major components of the TotalPlant™ process, Honeywell made significant changes in the technology strategy to support the business strategy. The information systems group was converted into an information technology shop where all technology was developed in direct support of the ICA business unit and its operations. All systems were fully integrated to optimize the timeliness and accuracy of information.

After three years, performance results indicated a reduction in defects of 70%, customer rejects declined by 57%, and there was a 46% reduction in inventory investments. Honeywell's execution against its vision is what set this business process reengineering apart from others. Top managers did not just speak the vision, they lived and supported it through active participation in the entire change process. Another critical component was that the organizational structure was redesigned to align with the new processes and strategies. Top management at Honeywell understood that change of this magnitude takes time and therefore was able to set the organization's expectations accordingly. Additionally, it committed appropriate levels of training and financial resources to make the initiative a success.

The Honeywell case provides some excellent learning for making a reengineering initiative successful. First, people are the key enablers of change. They must be trained, developed, and rewarded to support the change process. Second, people must be able to question all of their assumptions. Nothing can be sacred as each process is deconstructed and then rebuilt. Third, process mapping provides people with a systematic process for analyzing and improving existing systems and processes. Next, management must be able to create dissatisfaction with the existing process and allow the teams to own the solution. An environment conducive to change must be created and supported by management's attitudes and behaviors. This includes active participation at all stages of the process.

However, while support and participation from the top is important, implementation should take place by empowering decision makers at the level where the work is being done. Honeywell also demonstrated that reengineering must be a business-driven and continuous process. Initiatives like fail-safing demonstrated the need to challenge the status quo continuously. Stretch goals must be set throughout the process to keep employees motivated. Finally, the most critical component of a successful reengineering initiative is the ability to actively implement and execute against the plan. By keeping its eye on the end goal, Honeywell was able to successfully optimize its customer satisfaction through this process.

reengineering cases found that they were characterized by a clear vision of the future, specific goals for change, use of information technology, top management's involvement and commitment, clear milestones and measurements, and the training of participants in process analysis and teamwork.[59]

SUMMARY

This chapter presented interventions aimed at restructuring organizations. Several basic structures, such as the functional, divisional, and matrix structures, dominate most organizations. Three newer forms, process-based, customer-centric, and network-based structures, were also described. Each of these structures has corresponding strengths and weaknesses, and supportive conditions must be assessed when determining which structure is an appropriate fit with the organization's environment, strategy, technology, and size.

Two restructuring interventions were described: downsizing and reengineering. Downsizing decreases the size of the organization through workforce reduction or organizational redesign. It generally is associated with layoffs where a certain number or class of organization member are no longer employed by the organization. Downsizing can contribute to organization development by focusing on the organization's strategy, using a variety of downsizing tactics, addressing the needs of all organization members, and following through with growth plans. Reengineering involves the fundamental rethinking and radical redesign of business processes to achieve dramatic improvements in performance. It seeks to transform how organizations traditionally produce and deliver goods and services. A typical reengineering project prepares the organization, rethinks the way work gets done, and restructures the organization around the newly designed core processes.

NOTES

1. P. Lawrence and J. Lorsch, *Organization and Environment: Managing Differentiation and Integration* (Cambridge, MA: Harvard Graduate School of Business, Administration Division of Research, 1967); J. R. Galbraith, *Designing Organizations* (San Francisco: Jossey-Bass, 2002); J. R. Galbraith, "Organization Design," in *Handbook of Organization Development*, ed. T. Cummings (Los Angeles, CA: Sage Publications, 2008), 325–52.

2. L. Gulick and L. Urwick, eds., *Papers on the Science of Administration* (New York: Institute of Public Administration,

Columbia University, 1937); M. Weber, *The Theory of Social and Economic Organization*, ed. A. Henderson and T. Parsons (Glencoe, IL: Free Press, 1947).

3. A. Chandler, *Strategy and Structure: Chapters in the History of the Industrial Enterprise* (Cambridge, MA: MIT Press, 1962).
4. S. Davis and P. Lawrence, *Matrix* (Reading, MA: Addison-Wesley, 1977); H. Kolodny, "Managing in a Matrix," *Business Horizons* 24 (March–April 1981): 17–35; J. Galbraith, *Designing Matrix Organizations that Actually Work* (San Francisco: Jossey-Bass, 2008).
5. Davis and Lawrence, *Matrix.*
6. W. Joyce, "Matrix Organization: A Social Experiment," *Academy of Management Journal* 29 (1986): 536–61; C. Worley and C. Teplitz, "The Use of 'Expert Power' as an Emerging Influence Style within Successful U.S. Matrix Organizations," *Project Management Journal* 24 (1993): 31–36.
7. Davis and Lawrence, *Matrix.*
8. J. Byrne, "The Horizontal Corporation," *BusinessWeek,* December 20, 1993, 76–81; S. Mohrman, S. Cohen, and A. Mohrman, *Designing Team-Based Organizations* (San Francisco: Jossey-Bass, 1995); R. Ashkenas, D. Ulrich, T. Jick, and S. Kerr, *The Boundaryless Organization* (San Francisco: Jossey-Bass, 1995).
9. J. Galbraith, E. Lawler, and Associates, *Organizing for the Future: The New Logic for Managing Complex Organizations* (San Francisco: Jossey-Bass, 1993).
10. Byrne, "Horizontal Corporation"; Mohrman, Cohen, and Mohrman, *Designing Team-Based Organization.*
11. G. Schreyögg and J. Sydow, "Organizing for Fluidity? Dilemmas of New Organizational Forms," *Organization Science* 21 (2010): 251–1262.
12. J. Galbraith, *Designing the Customer-Centric Organization* (San Francisco: Jossey-Bass, 2005).
13. C. Snow, R. Miles, and H. Coleman Jr., "Managing 21st Century Network Organizations," *Organizational Dynamics* 20 (1992): 5–19; R. Rycroft, "Managing Complex Networks: Key to 21st Century Innovation Success," *Research-Technology Management* (May–June 1999): 13–18; J. Brown, S. Durchslag, and J. Hagel, "Loosening Up: How Process Networks Unlock the Power of Specialization," *McKinsey Quarterly* (August 6, 2002) (downloaded from Dow Jones Interactive); M. Castells, *The Rise of the Network Society* (New York: John Wiley & Sons, 2010).
14. W. Davidow and M. Malone, *The Virtual Corporation: Structuring and Revitalizing the Corporation of the 21st Century* (New York: Harper Business, 1992); J. Bryne, R. Brandt, and O. Port, "The Virtual Corporation," *BusinessWeek,* February 8, 1993, 98–102; Tully, "The Modular Corporation"; R. Keidel, "Rethinking Organizational Design," *Academy of Management Executive* 8 (1994): 12–30; C. Handy, *The Age of Unreason* (Cambridge, MA: Harvard Business School Press, 1989); R. Miles, C. Snow, J. Mathews, G. Miles, and H. Coleman, "Organizing in the Knowledge Age: Anticipating the Cellular Form," *Academy of Management Executive* 11 (1997): 7–20.
15. R. Chisolm, *Developing Network Organizations: Learning from Theory and Practice* (Reading, MA: Addison-Wesley, 1998); R. Achrol, "Changes in the Theory of Interorganizational Relations in Marketing: Toward a Network Paradigm," *Journal of the Academy of Marketing Science* 25 (1997): 56–71.
16. C. Snow, "Twenty-First Century Organizations: Implications for a New Marketing Paradigm," *Journal of the Academy of Marketing Science* 25 (1997): 72–74.
17. W. Powell, "Neither Market Nor Hierarchy: Network Forms of Organization," in *Research in Organizational Behavior*, vol. 12, ed. B. Staw and L. Cummings (Greenwich, CT: JAI Press, 1990), 295–336; M. Lawless and R. Moore, "Interorganizational Systems in Public Service Delivery: A New Application of the Dynamic Network Framework," *Human Relations* 42 (1989): 1167–84; M. Gerstein, "From Machine Bureaucracies to Networked Organizations: An Architectural Journey," in *Organizational Architecture*, ed. D. Nadler, M. Gerstein, R. Shaw, and associates (San Francisco: Jossey-Bass, 1992), 11–38.
18. D. Tapscott, *The Digital Economy* (New York: McGraw-Hill, 1996); Bryne, Brandt, and Port, "Virtual Corporation."
19. Bryne, Brandt, and Port, "Virtual Corporation"; G. Dess, A. Rasheed, K. McLaughlin, and R. Priem, "The New Corporate Architecture," *Academy of Management Executive* 9 (1995): 7–20.
20. J. Galbraith and R. Kazanjian, *Strategy Implementation: Structure, Systems and Process*, 2nd ed. (St. Paul: West, 1986), 159–60.
21. "Amazon Alliances Create Next-gen E-tail Model," *DSN Retailing Today* 41 (2002): 47; T. Kemp, "Partnerships R Us—Toysrus.com is Building a Sustainable E-retail Business by Drawing on the Strengths of Its Two Giant Business Partners," *InternetWeek* 882 (October 15, 2001): 14, 15+; S. Leschly, M. Roberts, and W. Sahlman, "Amazon.com—2002," *Harvard Business School Case 9-803-098*, 2003; S. Kotha, "Amazon.com: Expanding Beyond Books," University of Washington Business School, 1998, accessed from http://us.badm.washington.edu/kotha/cases.htm on May 9, 2003.
22. C. L. Cooper, A. Pandey, and J. Quick, *Downsizing: Is Less Still More* (Cambridge, UK: 2012); W. Cascio, "Employment Downsizing: Causes, Costs, and Consequences," in *More Than Bricks in the Wall: Organizational Perspectives for Sustainable Success*, ed. L. Stadtler, A. Schmitt, P. Klarner, and T. Straub (New York: Springer, 2010): 87–96.

23. J. Laabs, "Has Downsizing Missed Its Mark?" *Workforce* (April 1999): 30–37.
24. Recent layoff statistics accessed from http://www.bls.gov/mls/home.htm on December 31, 2012.
25. Laabs, "Has Downsizing Missed Its Mark?"
26. W. McKinley, C. Sanchez, and A. Schick, "Organizational Downsizing: Constraining, Cloning, Learning," *Academy of Management Executive* 9 (1995): 32–44.
27. G. Hamel and C. Prahalad, *Competing for the Future* (Cambridge, MA: Harvard Business School Press, 1994).
28. K. Cameron, S. Freeman, and A. Mishra, "Best Practices in White-Collar Downsizing: Managing Contradictions," *Academy of Management Executive* 5 (1991): 57–73; K. Cameron, "Strategies for Successful Organizational Downsizing," *Human Resource Management* 33 (1994): 189–212; R. Marshall and L. Lyles, "Planning for a Restructured, Revitalized Organization," *Sloan Management Review* 35 (1994): 81–91; N. Polend, "Downsizing and Organization Development: An Opportunity Missed, but Not Lost" (unpublished senior project, The Union Institute, 1999); A. Mishra, K. Mishra, and G. Spreitzer, "Downsizing the Company without Downsizing Morale," *MIT Sloan Management Review* 50 (2009): 39–44.
29. K. Kelly, "Case Digs Out from Way Under," *BusinessWeek*, August 14, 1995.
30. J. Brockner, "The Effects of Work Layoffs on Survivors: Research, Theory and Practice," in *Research in Organizational Behavior*, vol. 10, ed. B. M. Staw and L. L. Cummings (Greenwich, CT: JAI Press, 1989), 213–55; J. Byrne, "The Pain of Downsizing," *BusinessWeek*, May 9, 1994.
31. Marshall and Lyles, "Planning for a Restructured, Revitalized Organization."
32. J. E. Rogdon, "Lack of Communication Burdens Restructurings," *Wall Street Journal*, November 2, 1992, B1.
33. This application was adapted from "Case Study: Downsizing Is Rough," *Public Management* 86 (December 2004): 10–16.
34. D. Druckman, J. Singer, and H. Van Cott, eds., *Enhancing Organizational Performance* (Washington, DC: National Academy Press, 1997); F. Gandolfi, "Where Did Downsizing Go? A Review of 30 Years of a Strategic Business Phenomenon," *Australasian Journal of Business and Social Inquiry* 7 (2009): 40–65; F. Gandolfi and P. Neck, "Consequences, Payoffs, and Fallout of Downsizing (A Literature Review of Corporate Downsizing: Part 3)," *Review of International Comparative Management* 9 (2008): 55–78.
35. A. Roan, G. Lafferty, and R. Loudoun, "Survivors and Victims: A Case Study of Organisational Restructuring in the Public Health Sector," *New Zealand Journal of Industrial Relations* (June 2002): 151; R. Cole, "Learning from Learning Theory: Implications for Quality Improvements of Turnover, Use of Contingent Workers, and Job Rotation Policies," *Quality Management Journal* 1 (1993): 1–25; K. Kozlowski, G. Chao, E. Smith, and J. Hedlund, "Organizational Downsizing: Strategies, Interventions, and Research Implications," in *International Review of Industrial and Organizational Psychology* (New York: John Wiley & Sons, 1993); Druckman, Singer, and Van Cott, eds., *Enhancing Organizational Performance*; B. Luthans and S. Sommer, "The Impact of Downsizing on Workplace Attitudes," *Group and Organization Management* (March 1999): 46–55.
36. W. Baumol, A. Blinder, and E. Wolf, *Downsizing in America: Reality, Causes and Consequences* (New York: Russell Sage, 2003); E. Love and N. Nohria, "Reducing Slack: The Performance Consequences of Downsizing by Large Industrial Firms, 1877–93," *Strategic Management Journal* 26 (2005): 1087–1108; J. Guthrie and D. Datta, "Dumb and Dumber: The Impact of Downsizing on Firm Performance as Moderated by Industry Condition," *Organization Science* 19 (2008): 108–23; C. Trevor and A. Nyberg, "Keeping Your Headcount When All About You Are Losing Theirs: Downsizing, Voluntary Turnover Rates, and the Moderating Role of HR Practice," *Academy of Management Journal* 51 (2008): 259–76.
37. Morris, Cascio, and Young, "Downsizing."
38. J. Byrne, "There Is an Upside to Downsizing," *BusinessWeek*, May 9, 1994.
39. Cameron, Freeman, and Mishra, "Best Practices."
40. Cameron, Freeman, and Mishra, "Best Practices"; Kozlowski et al., "Organizational Downsizing"; J. Davy, A. Kinicki, and C. Schreck, "Developing and Testing a Model of Survivor Responses to Layoffs," *Journal of Vocational Behavior* 38 (1991): 302–17; K. Labich, "How to Fire People and Still Sleep at Night," *Fortune*, June 10, 1996, 65–72; D. Feldman and C. Leana, "Better Practices in Managing Layoffs," *Human Resource Management Journal* 33 (1995): 239–60; J. Byrne, "Why Downsizing Looks Different These Days," *BusinessWeek*, October 10, 1994; Trevor and Nyberg, "Keeping Your Head."
41. T. Davenport and J. Short, "The New Industrial Engineering: Information Technology and Business Process Redesign," *Sloan Management Review* 31 (1990): 11–27; M. Hammer and J. Champy, *Reengineering the Corporation: A Manifesto for Business Revolution* (New York: HarperCollins, 1993, 2003); T. Stewart, "Reengineering: The Hot New Managing Tool," *Fortune*, August 23, 1993, 41–48; J. Champy, *Reengineering Management* (New York: HarperCollins, 1994).
42. R. Kaplan and L. Murdock, "Core Process Redesign," *McKinsey Quarterly* 2 (1991): 27–43.
43. M. Attaran, "Exploring the Relationship between Information Technology and Business Process Reengineering,"

Information & Management 41 (2004): 585–96; Y. Lee, P. Chu, and H. Tseng, "Exploring the Relationships between Information Technology Adoption and Business Process Reengineering," *Journal of Management & Organization* (2009): 170–85.

44. Tapscott, *Digital Economy.*
45. J. Moosbruker and R. Loftin, "Business Process Redesign and Organizational Development: Enhancing Success by Removing the Barriers," *Journal of Applied Behavioral Science* (September 1998): 286–97; T. Davenport, L. Prusak, and J. Wilson, "Reengineering Revisited," *Computerworld* 37 (2003): 48–49.
46. M. Miller, "Customer Service Drives Reengineering Effort," *Personnel Journal* 73 (1994): 87–93.
47. Kaplan and Murdock, "Core Process Redesign"; R. Manganelli and M. Klein, *The Reengineering Handbook* (New York: AMACOM, 1994); H. Reijers and S. Mansar, "Best Practices in Business Process Redesign: An Overview and Qualitative Evaluation of Successful Redesign Heuristics," *Omega: The International Journal of Management Science* 33 (2005): 283–306; N. Eftekhari and P. Akhavan, "Developing a Comprehensive Methodology for BPR Projects by Employing IT Tools," *Business Process Management Journal* 19 (2013): 4–29.
48. D. Stires, "Technology Has Transformed the VA," *Fortune*, May 15, 2006, accessed from http://www.fortune.com on August 28, 2007.
49. J. Katzenbach and D. Smith, "The Rules for Managing Cross-Functional Reengineering Teams," *Planning Review* (March–April 1993): 12–13; A. Nahavandi and E. Aranda, "Restructuring Teams for the Re-Engineered Organization," *Academy of Management Executive* 8 (1994): 58–68.
50. M. O'Guin, *The Complete Guide to Activity Based Costing* (Englewood Cliffs, NJ: Prentice Hall, 1991); H. Johnson and R. Kaplan, *Relevance Lost: The Rise and Fall of Management Accounting* (Cambridge, MA: Harvard Business School Press, 1987).
51. J. Martin, "Are You as Good as You Think You Are?" *Fortune*, September 30, 1996, 142–52.
52. Hammer and Champy, *Reengineering the Corporation.*
53. Ibid.
54. This application was written and submitted by Ann McCloskey based on information adapted from D. Paper, J. Rodger, and P. Pendharker, "A BPR Case Study at Honeywell," *Business Process Management Journal* 7 (2001): 85–99.
55. Hammer and Champy, *Reengineering the Corporation.*
56. CSC Index, "State of Reengineering Report, 1994," *Economist*, July 2, 1994, 6.
57. Champy, *Reengineering Management*; K. Jensen, "The Effects of Reengineering on Injury Frequency" (unpublished master's thesis, Pepperdine University, 1993); Druckman, Singer, and Van Cott, eds., *Enhancing Organizational Performance*; D. Rigby, "Management Tools and Techniques: A Survey," *California Management Review* 34 (2001): 139–60; M. Al-Mashari, Z. Irani, and M. Zairi, "Business Process Reengineering: A Survey of International Experience" *Business Process Management Journal* 7 (2001): 437–55.
58. G. Hall, J. Rosenthal, and J. Wade, "How to Make Reengineering Really Work," *Harvard Business Review* (November–December 1993): 119–31.
59. J. Dixon, "Business Process Reengineering: Improving in New Strategic Directions," *California Management Review* 36 (1994): 93–108.

13

Employee Involvement

learning objectives

Define the principles of employee involvement and describe its relationship to performance.

Compare three employee involvement interventions: parallel structures, total quality management, and high-involvement organizations.

Faced with competitive demands for lower costs, higher performance, and greater flexibility, organizations are increasingly turning to employee involvement (EI) to enhance the participation, commitment, and productivity of their members. This chapter presents organization development (OD) interventions aimed at moving decision making downward in the organization, closer to where the actual work takes place. This increased employee involvement can lead to quicker, more responsive decisions, continuous performance improvements, and greater employee flexibility, commitment, and satisfaction.

Employee involvement is a broad term that has been variously referred to as "empowerment," "participative management," "engagement," "work design," "high involvement," "industrial democracy," and "quality of work life." It covers diverse approaches to gaining greater participation in relevant workplace decisions. Organizations such as General Mills, The Hartford, and Intel have enhanced worker involvement through enriched forms of work; others, such as Verizon, Deutsche Telekom, Wells Fargo, and Boeing, have increased participation by forming EI teams that develop suggestions for improving productivity and quality; Southwest Airlines, Shell Oil, and Nucor Steel have sought greater participation through union–management cooperation on performance and quality-of-work-life issues; and still others, such as Texas Instruments, Kimberly-Clark, 3M, the IRS, and Motorola, have improved employee involvement by emphasizing participation in quality-improvement approaches.

As described in Chapter 1, current EI approaches evolved from earlier quality-of-work-life efforts in Europe, Scandinavia, and the United States. The terms "employee involvement" and "empowerment" gradually have replaced the designation "quality of work life," particularly in the United States. A current definition of EI includes four elements that can promote meaningful involvement in workplace decisions: power, information, knowledge and skills, and rewards. These components of EI combine to exert powerful effects on productivity and employee well-being.

Major EI applications discussed in this chapter are parallel structures, including cooperative union–management projects and quality circles; total quality management; and high-involvement organizations. Two additional approaches that include elements of EI, work design and reward-system interventions, are discussed in Chapters 14 and 15, respectively.

13-1 Employee Involvement: What Is It?

Employee involvement is the current label used to describe a set of practices and philosophies that started with the quality-of-work-life movement in the late 1950s. The phrase "quality of work life" (QWL) was used to stress the prevailing poor quality of life at the workplace.[1] As described in Chapter 1, both the term "QWL" and the meaning attributed to it have undergone considerable change and development. More recently, the term "engagement" has been popular, and a great deal of effort has been invested in differentiating the term. "Engagement" refers to organization members' work experience. Engaged employees are motivated, committed, and interested in their work.[2] Engagement, then, is the outcome of EI interventions. In this section, we provide a working definition of EI, document the growth of EI practices in the United States and abroad, and clarify the important and often misunderstood relationship between EI and productivity.

13-1a A Working Definition of Employee Involvement

Employee involvement seeks to increase members' input into decisions that affect organization performance and employee well-being.[3] It can be described in terms of four key elements that promote worker involvement:[4]

1. **Power.** This element of EI includes providing people with enough authority to make work-related decisions covering various issues such as work methods, task assignments, performance outcomes, customer service, and employee selection. The amount of power afforded employees can vary enormously, from simply asking them for input into decisions that managers subsequently make, to managers and workers jointly making decisions, to employees making decisions themselves.
2. **Information.** Timely access to relevant information is vital to making effective decisions. Organizations can promote EI by ensuring that the necessary information flows freely to those with decision authority. This can include data about operating results, business plans, competitive conditions, new technologies and work methods, and ideas for organizational improvement.
3. **Knowledge and skills.** Employee involvement contributes to organizational effectiveness only to the extent that employees have the requisite skills and knowledge to make good decisions. Organizations can facilitate EI by providing training and development programs for improving members' knowledge and skills. Such learning can cover an array of expertise having to do with performing tasks, making decisions, solving problems, and understanding how the business operates.
4. **Rewards.** Because people generally do those things for which they are recognized, rewards can have a powerful effect on getting people involved in the organization. Meaningful opportunities for involvement can provide employees with internal rewards, such as feelings of self-worth and accomplishment. External rewards, such as pay and promotions, can reinforce EI when they are linked directly to performance outcomes that result from participation in decision making. (Reward systems are discussed more fully in Chapter 15.)

Those four elements—power, information, knowledge and skills, and rewards—contribute to EI success by determining how much employee participation in decision making is possible in organizations. To the extent that all four elements are made available throughout, and especially in the lower levels of, the organization, the greater the employee involvement. Furthermore, because the four elements of EI are interdependent, they must be changed together to obtain positive results. For example, if organization members are given more power and authority to make decisions but do not have the information or knowledge and skill to make good decisions, then the value of involvement is likely to be negligible. Similarly, increasing employees' power, information, and knowledge and skills but not linking rewards to the performance consequences of these changes gives members little incentive to improve organizational performance. The EI methods that will be described in this chapter vary in how much involvement is afforded employees. Parallel structures, such as union–management cooperative efforts and quality circles, are limited in the degree that the four elements of EI are moved downward in the organization. Total quality management and high-involvement organizations provide far greater opportunities for involvement.

13-1b The Diffusion of Employee Involvement Practices

Employee involvement interventions are being used in organizations throughout the world. In addition to firms in the United States, organizations are applying EI in West European countries, including France, Germany, Denmark, Ireland, Sweden, Norway, Holland, Italy, and Great Britain.[5] EI efforts are among the tremendous changes currently taking place in countries such as Russia, Bulgaria, the Philippines, and the People's Republic of China.[6] Organizations in Canada, Mexico, India, Australia, New Zealand, Hong Kong, and Japan also are using EI. Internationally, EI may be considered a set of processes directed at changing the structure of the work situation within a particular economic and cultural environment and under the influence of particular values and philosophies. As a result, in some cases, EI has been promoted by unions; in others, by management; and in still others, by government. In some cases, it has been part of a pragmatic approach to increasing productivity; in other cases, it has been driven by socialist values.[7]

In a recent long-term study of EI applications, Lawler and his colleagues at the Center for Effective Organizations at the University of Southern California surveyed the *Fortune* 1000 and discovered positive trends in EI use among these firms, including both a growing number of firms applying EI and a greater percentage of the workforce included in such programs.[8] Despite these positive trends, however, this research revealed that the scope and depth of EI interventions were relatively modest. EI interventions that involved more than 20% of the workforce fell at the lower end of the EI scale, with low to moderate shifts in power, information, knowledge and skills, and rewards, such as might be found in suggestion systems and survey feedback. Interventions that included significant changes in these EI dimensions had more modest coverage, however, and were applied to fewer than 20% of the workforce in *Fortune* 1000 firms. Thus, although many large organizations are using EI practices, there is considerable room for their diffusion across organizations and throughout the workforce.

13-1c How Employee Involvement Affects Productivity

An assumption underlying much of the EI literature is that such interventions will lead to higher productivity. Although this premise was initially based on anecdotal evidence and a good deal of speculation, there is now a growing body of research findings to support that linkage.[9] Studies have found a consistent relationship between EI practices and such measures as productivity, financial performance, customer satisfaction, labor hours, and waste rates.

Attempts to explain this positive linkage traditionally have followed the idea that giving people more involvement in work decisions raises their job satisfaction and, in turn, their productivity. There is growing evidence that this satisfaction-causes-productivity premise is too simplistic and sometimes wrong.

A more realistic explanation for how EI interventions can affect productivity is shown in Figure 13.1. EI practices, such as participation in workplace decisions, can improve productivity in at least three ways.[10] First, they can improve communication and coordination among employees and organizational departments, and help integrate the different jobs or departments that contribute to an overall task.

Second, EI interventions can improve employee motivation, particularly when they satisfy important personal needs. Motivation is translated into improved performance when people have the necessary skills and knowledge to perform well and when the technology and work situation allow people to affect productivity. For example, some jobs are so rigidly controlled and specified that individual motivation can have little impact on productivity.

Third, EI practices can improve the capabilities of employees, thus enabling them to perform better. For example, attempts to increase employee participation in decision making generally include skill training in group problem solving and communication.

Figure 13.2 shows the secondary effects of EI. These practices increase employee well-being and satisfaction by providing a better work environment and a more fulfilling job. Improved productivity also can increase satisfaction, particularly when it leads to greater rewards. Increased employee satisfaction, deriving from EI interventions and increased productivity, ultimately can have a still greater impact on productivity by attracting talented employees to join and remain with the organization.

Recent research has identified an additional path for the performance effects of EI interventions—organizational citizenship behavior (OCB).[11] OCB involves a broad set of discretionary work behaviors that sustain and enhance the functioning of the organization, such as helping coworkers, sharing tacit task knowledge, and going beyond the call of duty to help customers. These behaviors are not prescribed by the organization but occur voluntarily at employees' discretion. There is growing evidence that EI practices promote OCB, and in turn, OB increases organization performance.

In sum, EI interventions can increase productivity by improving communication and coordination, employee motivation, and individual capabilities. They also can

FIGURE 13.1

How Employee Involvement Affects Productivity

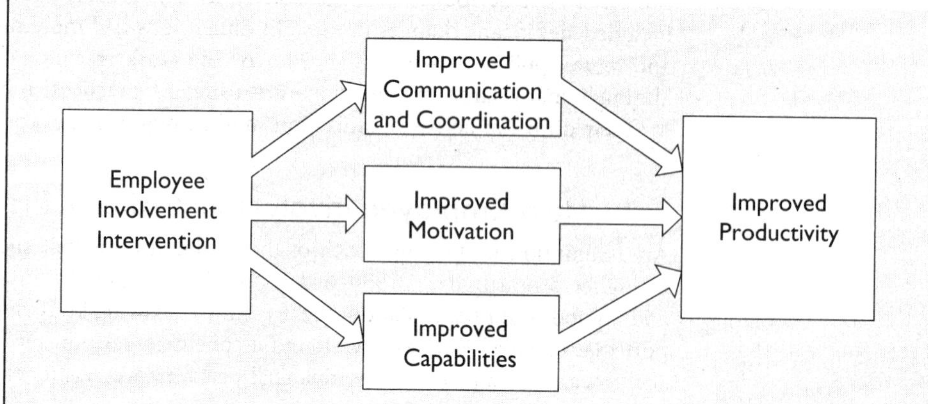

SOURCE: Lawler & Ledford, "Productivity and QWL," *National Productivity Review* 1, 1 (Winter 1981–82). © 1982 by Executive Enterprises, Inc. Reprinted by permission of John Wiley & Sons, Inc.

FIGURE 13.2

Secondary Effects on Productivity

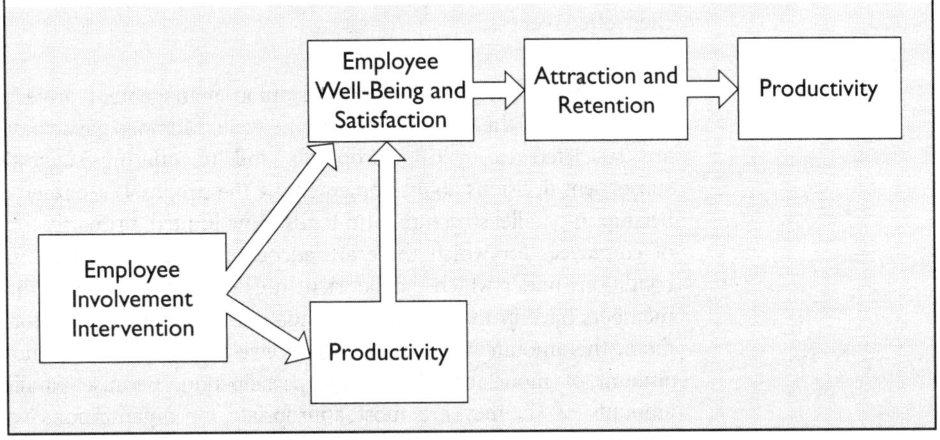

SOURCE: Lawler & Ledford, "Productivity and QWL," *National Productivity Review* 1, 1 (Winter 1981–82). © 1982 by Executive Enterprises, Inc. Reprinted by permission of John Wiley & Sons, Inc.

influence productivity by means of the secondary effects of increased employee well-being and satisfaction, and through employees' organizational citizenship behavior. Although a growing body of EI and engagement research supports these relationships, there is considerable debate over the strength of the association between EI and productivity.[12] Recent data support the conclusion that relatively modest levels of EI produce moderate improvements in performance and satisfaction, and that higher levels of EI produce correspondingly higher levels of performance.[13]

13-2 Employee Involvement Interventions

Described below are three major EI interventions that vary in the amounts of power, information, knowledge and skills, and rewards that are moved downward through the organization (from least to most involvement): parallel structures, including cooperative union–management projects and quality circles; total quality management; and high-involvement organizations.

13-2a Parallel Structures

Parallel structures involve employees in resolving ill-defined, complex problems and build adaptability into bureaucratic organizations.[14] Also known as "collateral structures," "dualistic structures," or "shadow structures,"[15] parallel structures operate in conjunction with the formal organization. They provide members with an alternative setting in which to address problems and to propose innovative solutions free from the existing, formal organization structure and culture. For example, members may attend periodic off-site meetings to explore new ways to improve quality in their work area or they may be temporarily assigned to a special project or facility to devise new products or solutions to organizational problems. Parallel structures facilitate problem solving and change by providing time and resources for members to think, talk, and act in completely new ways. Consequently, norms and procedures for working in parallel structures tend to be different from those of the formal organization. This section describes the application steps associated with the two most common parallel structures, cooperative union–management projects and quality circles, and reviews the research on their effectiveness.

Application Stages Cooperative union–management projects and quality circle interventions fall at the lower end of the EI scale. Member participation and influence typically are restricted to making proposals and to offering suggestions for change because subsequent decisions about implementing the proposals are reserved for management. Membership in parallel structures also tends to be limited, primarily to volunteers and to numbers of employees for which there are adequate resources. Management heavily influences the conditions under which parallel structures operate. It controls the amount of authority that members have in making recommendations, the amount of information that is shared with them, the amount of training they receive to increase their knowledge and skills, and the amount of monetary rewards for participation. Because parallel structures offer limited amounts of EI, they are most appropriate for organizations with little or no history of employee participation, top-down management styles, and bureaucratic cultures.

Cooperative union–management and quality circle programs typically are implemented in the following steps:[16]

1. **Define the purpose and scope.** This first step involves defining the purpose for the parallel structure and initial expectations about how it will function. Organizational diagnosis can help clarify which specific problems and issues to address, such as productivity, absenteeism, or service quality. In addition, management training in the use of parallel structures can include discussions about the commitment and resources necessary to implement them; the openness needed to examine organizational practices, operations, and policies; and the willingness to experiment and learn.
2. **Form a steering committee.** Parallel structures typically use a steering committee composed of acknowledged leaders of the various functions and constituencies within the formal organization. For example, in cooperative union–management projects, the steering committee would include key representatives from management, such as a president or chief operating officer, and each of the unions and employee groups involved in the project, such as local union presidents. This committee performs the following tasks:
   - Refining the scope and purpose of the parallel structure
   - Developing a vision for the effort
   - Guiding the creation and implementation of the structure
   - Establishing the linkage mechanisms between the parallel structure and the formal organization
   - Creating problem-solving groups and activities
   - Ensuring senior management support.

   OD practitioners can play an important role in forming the steering committee. First, they can help to establish the team and to select appropriate members. Second, they can assist in developing and maintaining group norms of learning and innovation. These norms set the tone for problem solving throughout the parallel structure. Third, they can help the committee create a vision statement that refines the structure's purpose and promotes ownership of it. Fourth, they can help committee members develop and specify objectives and strategies, organizational expectations and required resources, and potential rewards for participation in the parallel structure.

3. **Communicate with organization members.** The effectiveness of a parallel structure depends on a high level of participation from organization members. Communicating the purpose, procedures, and rewards of participation can promote that involvement. Moreover, employee participation in developing a structure's vision and purpose can increase ownership and visibly demonstrate the "new way" of working. Continued communication concerning parallel structure activities can ensure member awareness.
4. **Create forums for employee problem solving.** These forums are the primary means of accomplishing the purpose of the parallel learning structure. The most common forum is the employee problem-solving group. Its formation involves selecting and training group members, identifying problems for the group to work on, and providing appropriate facilitation. Selecting group members is important because success often is a function of group membership.[17] Members need to represent the appropriate hierarchical levels, expertise, functions, and constituencies that are relevant to the problems at hand. This allows the parallel structure to identify and communicate with the formal structure. It also provides the necessary resources to solve the problems. Ad hoc committees or task forces may also be formed, as when workers and managers initiate action to address an issue of interest to the parallel organization. Ad hoc teams are typically charged with a particular task and have a limited lifetime.

   Once formed, members of a problem-solving group need appropriate training. This may include discussions about the vision of the parallel structure, the specific problems to be addressed, and the way those problems will be solved. As in the steering committee, group norms promoting openness, creativity, and coordination need to be established.

   Another increasingly common forum is the large group intervention described in Chapter 11. Search conferences and appreciative inquiry (AI) summits can be used to generate a variety of ideas for change, innovation, and problem solving. Application 13.1 describes one example of such a process.[18] Roadway Express found the AI summit to be an effective way of engaging union members in solving organizational problems.

   Another key resource for parallel structures is facilitation support. Although this can be expensive, it can yield important benefits in problem-solving efficiency and quality. Small groups are asked to form quickly and to solve problems by cutting through traditional hierarchical and functional boundaries. Facilitation support can help charter and build the team as well as pay special attention to processes that encourage problem solving. They can help members identify and resolve issues within groups. Similarly, large group interventions require time, resources, and knowledge. They must be designed and facilitated well if they are to produce relevant results.
5. **Address the problems and issues.** Parallel structures solve problems by using an action research process. They diagnose specific problems, plan appropriate solutions, and, if empowered to do so, implement and evaluate them. Problem solving can be facilitated when the groups and the steering committee relate effectively to each other. This permits the steering committee to direct problem-solving efforts in an appropriate manner, to acquire the necessary resources and support, and to approve action plans. It also helps ensure that the solutions and changes are linked appropriately to the formal organization. In this manner, early attempts at change will have a better chance of succeeding.
6. **Implement and evaluate the changes.** This step involves implementing appropriate organizational changes and assessing the results. Change proposals need the support of the steering committee and the formal authority structure. As changes are implemented, the organization needs information about their effects. This lets members know how successful the changes have been and if they need to be modified. In addition, feedback on changes helps the organization learn to adapt and innovate.

application 13.1

USING THE AI SUMMIT TO BUILD UNION–MANAGEMENT RELATIONS AT ROADWAY EXPRESS

Roadway Express was the largest subsidiary of $2.9 billion (2001 revenues) Roadway Corp., based in Akron, Ohio (Roadway has since been acquired by Yellow Transit Co.). In the first three quarters of 2002, Roadway Express's operating income fell 14% to $130 million and revenue dropped 7% to $1.8 billion. In September 2002, Roadway's biggest competitor, Consolidated Freightways, filed for bankruptcy and 15,000 Teamsters lost their jobs. Nonunionized carriers like CNF Freight Services were gaining market share with lower costs and a more flexible workforce.

Roadway Express is a "less-than-truckload carrier," which means that its trucks deliver a variety of packages and freight to multiple locations for more than one customer at a time. This places tremendous pressure on the organization, its managers, and employees to effectively plan the delivery routes and loads in order to make a profit. Complicating the task, Roadway Express is heavily unionized: 20,000 of its 27,000 employees belong to the Teamsters or other unions. They are paid, on average and including benefits, 5% above nonunionized competitors.

To compete in an industry in which net profit margins are less than 5% in a good year—let alone in a year when business is contracting—every one of its 27,000 employees must be a leader. "Almost two-thirds of every revenue dollar is consumed by wages and benefits," says Roadway president and COO James Staley. In comparison, Conway Transportation, a division of nonunionized CNF, only pays out 53 cents of every dollar of revenue. "There's not a lot of new technology that's going to make us more efficient. So future opportunities are going to come from our people being more involved in the business."

Persuading the Teamsters and other union members to be more efficient and breaking down a long history of hostility between workers and management were no small tasks. Many of the programs Staley had seen had a way of producing a short-term glow and not much lasting change. Union bosses are naturally wary of such programs and assume that efficiency is just a fancy way of saying that some workers will be laid off and the rest made to work harder. The cooperative union–management program Staley adopted paired classroom efforts to educate union members on how the organization works with a series of Appreciative Inquiry (AI) summits to generate ideas and organize change efforts.

Part of the program involved teaching workers about the industry's economics, competition, and financial status, including Roadway's income statement and operating ratios. The classes encouraged employees to think and act like owners and emphasized the importance of cutting costs. The experience of one 36-year-old dockworker, a 13-year veteran and union representative, demonstrated how difficult change was going to be. The dockworker had been accused of instigating worker slowdowns and engaging in screaming matches with supervisors. At one of the business education seminars, a graph illustrating how unionized trucking companies' market share had slipped from 75% to 50% since 1990 made a powerful argument for change. "Suddenly my ability to support my wife and two children depended on the security of the company," he said. In response, he wrote a plan to improve service in his Greenville, South Carolina, facility that included teaching dockworkers to use computers to communicate with customer-service reps and keep them up-to-date on the status of freight. However, the plan and its implementation also resulted in many of his coworkers labeling him as a management "suck up."

The second part of the union–management program involved the use of AI summits. The first AI summit process began at the Akron terminal and then was extended to the Winston-Salem facility in North Carolina. A steering committee of workers from across the facility was created to plan an off-site meeting aimed at setting a course for the future. Its first task was to decide who among the terminal's employees would be invited to attend. The goal was to create a microcosm of the company, with workers from all departments and all functions and with varying degrees of empathy for Roadway's corporate objectives. A few weeks later, about 100 employees gathered at a local Holiday Inn for the three-day off-site summit. Using a collaborative process, the trucking firm began to engage its heavily unionized workforce in ways that hardly seemed possible just five years ago.

At the start of the AI summit, representatives from all parts of the system, workers from all functions who barely knew one another, participated. Having the whole system in the room allowed everyone to see each other, face-to-face, and increased the chances of building trust and of participants seeing their collective purpose. On the AI summit's first day, participants explored their organization's "positive change core." The opening question in a round of interviews among all the participants was, "Talk about a time when you felt the most alive, the most engaged, in your job at Roadway." The wording was intentional, a signal that this wasn't going to be the usual management–labor gripe session. The second question fed off the first: "Imagine that you've woken up after being asleep for five years. What would you want Roadway to look like?" When participants paired off to discuss their responses, they made a powerful discovery. "It didn't matter what your job was," said one worker who had been a Roadway driver for 24 years, "everyone wanted the same things"—things such as sustained growth, happy customers, and job security. In short, everyone wanted a successful company.

Over the next two days, the AI summit participants moved from mission to plan. On day two, participants broke into small groups and envisioned their organization's potential for positive influence and impact: What will the company look like in 2010? What will be happening in the world outside it? What is the best outcome we can imagine? The groups then reported back to the large group, and participants began to focus on creating an organization that incorporated the positive change core into every strategy, process, and system. The result was a set of action-oriented statements of how the organization would function. On the final day, participants distilled their organizational design into a list of "inspired actions." They drew an "opportunity map" of needs and priorities and voted on which ones were most urgent. Then they organized into seven action teams. One group addressed the trust gap between management and the union. Another devised strategies to turn drivers—the Roadway employees who have the most contact with the company's customers—into de facto sales reps. Other teams addressed employee communications, performance measurement and monitoring, and education. One team's efforts resulted in the distribution center saving $118,000 a year because the workers determined that trucks carrying more fuel than necessary were getting lower miles/gallon. If successful, these groups would sustain themselves long after the summit ended.

At another session in North Carolina, workers were asked to recall ideal work experience, a time when they were treated with respect, and when trucks were loaded to capacity or arrived on time. Assembled into nine groups, they were then encouraged to devise money-saving ideas. A team of short-haul drivers came up with 12 cost-cutting and revenue-generating ideas. Here is one of the most ambitious: Have each of the 32 drivers in Winston-Salem deliver just one more customer order each hour. Using management data, the drivers calculated the 288 additional daily shipments, at an average revenue of $212 each and with a 6% margin, would generate just about $1 million a year of operating profit.

The workers understood that their efforts to transform Roadway were just the beginning. As one local Teamsters boss put it, "Times have changed, if we don't work together, and smarter, we won't survive." AI summits held at Roadway over the next three years focused on designing structures, creating faster throughput, and recasting the roles of supervisors and leadership at every level. Each involved from 200 to 400 people, and Roadway planned five more AI Summits, convening dockworkers, truck drivers, Teamsters, senior leaders, customers, suppliers, and partners to do strategic planning at terminals throughout the country.

Roadway Corporation reported increased revenues for the fourth quarter of 2002, up 25.7% over that of the same period the year before. More importantly, operating ratios improved significantly and the union–management programs designed to create a more efficient delivery process had produced an estimated $35 million dollars in improvements for the quarter. Of the top terminals leading the bottom-line improvements, all were sites that had held AI Summits.

Results of Parallel Structure Approaches A large body of literature exists on the implementation and impact of parallel structure approaches to EI. The business and popular press generally report about the benefits of union–management cooperative projects, quality circles, and other parallel structure interventions. For many people, especially lower-level employees, this opportunity to influence the formal organization leads to increased work satisfaction and task effectiveness.[19] Several classic case studies support these conclusions: General Motors' central foundry division; the Harman plant in Bolivar, Tennessee; the Rockwell International plant in Battle Creek, Michigan (a joint UAW–GM effort); and the Rushton Mines in Pennsylvania.[20]

Early large-sample evaluations of parallel structures typically reported mixed results.[21] Over a period of at least three years, the University of Michigan's Institute for Social Research (ISR) studied eight major projects implemented during the 1970s. Although the projects showed some improvements in employee attitudes, only two projects showed improvements in productivity. The ISR researchers explained the meager productivity results in terms of the projects' mistakes. All of the projects were pioneering efforts and hardly could be expected to avoid mistakes during implementation.[22] Similarly, Ledford, Lawler, and Mohrman concluded that the existing research showed no clear positive or negative trend in the productivity effects of quality circles.[23] Although the evidence of attitudinal effects was more extensive than that of productivity effects, the studies reviewed still showed mixed results for attitudinal changes.

Data that are more recent suggest stronger relationships between employee participation and direct performance outcomes, such as productivity, customer satisfaction, quality, and speed; profitability; and employee satisfaction.[24] A study by the Commission on the Future of Worker–Management Relations supported that conclusion. It found that systematically implemented programs often improve productivity and almost always increase investment in employee skills and knowledge.[25] "The newer projects tend to be much better linked to the management and union hierarchies, receive better assistance from a widening circle of experienced consultants, have more realistic goals, and use more sharply focused organizational change strategies."[26]

Finally, court rulings in the early 1990s challenged the legality of some EI approaches under provisions of the National Labor Relations Act (NLRA). This law, passed by Congress in 1935, gives employees the right to form labor unions and decrees that employers must bargain in good faith with representatives of those organizations. In protecting employees' rights to collective bargaining, the NLRA precludes certain employer unfair labor practices, one of which is aimed at employer domination of a labor organization. Under the law, a committee or team of workers that meets to address issues related to wages, hours, or conditions of work can be considered a "labor organization." If management creates the team, provides it with resources, or influences it in any way, then management may be found to dominate this so-called labor organization. In two legal cases involving Electromation, Inc. and DuPont, the court ruled that in setting up employee teams or committees to address such issues as communication, cost cutting, and safety, the companies had created labor organizations and had dominated them unfairly. Although the NLRA does not outlaw EI teams per se, such interventions may be legally questionable in situations where teams address issues traditionally reserved for bargaining and where management influences or controls the teams. In response to these rulings, Congress passed legislation in 1996 to amend the NLRA. The Teamwork for Employees and Management Act of 1995 preserves legitimate EI programs without infringing on the rights of employees to bargain collectively.

13-2b Total Quality Management

Total quality management (TQM) is a more comprehensive approach to employee involvement than parallel structures. Also known as "business excellence," "continuous process improvement," "continuous quality," "lean," and "Six Sigma," TQM grew out of a manufacturing emphasis on quality control and represents a long-term effort to orient all of an organization's activities around the concept of quality. Quality is achieved when organizational processes reliably produce products and services that meet or exceed customer expectations. Although it is possible to implement TQM without employee involvement, member participation in the change process increases the likelihood of sustaining the results. Quality-improvement processes were popular in the 1990s, and many organizations, including Morton Salt, Weyerhaeuser, Xerox, Boeing's Airlift and Tanker Programs, Motorola, and Analog Devices, incorporated TQM interventions. Today, a capability for continuous quality improvement is essential for global competitiveness.

TQM increases workers' knowledge and skills through extensive training, provides relevant information to employees, pushes decision-making power downward in the organization, and ties rewards to performance. When implemented successfully, TQM also is aligned closely with a firm's overall strategy and attempts to direct the entire organization toward continuous quality improvement.[27]

The principles underlying TQM can be understood by examining the careers of W. Edwards Deming and Joseph M. Juran, the fathers of the modern quality movement. They initially applied statistical techniques to improve product quality at defense plants in the United States during World War II, but in an odd twist of fate, they found their ideas taking hold more in Japan than in the United States.[28] When the war ended, U.S. businesses turned to mass-production techniques and emphasized quantity over quality to satisfy postwar demand. Deming, known for his statistical and sampling expertise, was asked by General Douglas MacArthur to conduct a census of the Japanese population. During his discussions with Japanese officials and managers, he advocated a disciplined approach of "plan–do–check–adjust" to identify and improve manufacturing processes that affected product quality. With such an approach, the Japanese could produce world-class-quality products and restore their country economically. Deming's ideas eventually were codified into the "Fourteen Points" and the "Seven Deadly Sins" of quality summarized in Table 13.1. In honor of the ideas that helped to rejuvenate the Japanese economy, the Union of Japanese Scientists and Engineers created the Deming Prize to distinguish annually the best in quality manufacturing.

At about the same time, Juran's publication of the *Quality Control Handbook* in 1951 identified two sources of quality problems: avoidable and unavoidable costs. Avoidable costs included hours spent reworking defective products, processing complaints, and scrapping otherwise useful material. Unavoidable costs included work associated with inspection and other preventive measures. He suggested that when organizations focused on unavoidable costs to maintain quality, an important opportunity was being missed, and he advocated that an organization focus on avoidable costs that could be found in any process or activity, not just in manufacturing.

The popularity of TQM in the United States can be traced to a 1980 NBC television documentary titled, "If Japan Can … Why Can't We?" The documentary chronicled Deming's work with the Japanese and his concern that U.S. companies would not listen to him after the war. The documentary had a powerful impact on firms facing severe competition, particularly from the Japanese, and many companies, including Ford Motor Company, General Motors, Dow Chemical, and Hughes Aircraft, quickly sought Deming's advice. Another important influence on the TQM movement in the United

TABLE 13.1

Deming's Quality Guidelines

The Fourteen Points	The Seven Deadly Sins
1. Create a constancy of purpose	1. Lack of constancy of purpose
2. Adopt a new philosophy	2. Emphasizing short-term profits and immediate dividends
3. End the practice of purchasing at lowest prices	3. Evaluation of performance, merit rating, or annual review
4. Institute leadership	4. Mobility of top management
5. Eliminate empty slogans	5. Running a company only on visible figures
6. Eliminate numerical quotas	6. Excessive medical costs
7. Institute on-the-job training	7. Excessive costs of warranty
8. Drive out fear	
9. Break down barriers between departments	
10. Take action to accomplish the transformation	
11. Improve constantly and forever the process of production and service	
12. Cease dependence on mass inspection	
13. Remove barriers to pride in workmanship	
14. Retrain vigorously	

States was Philip Crosby's book *Quality Is Free*.[29] He showed that improved quality can lower overall costs, dispelling the popular belief that high quality means higher total costs for the organization. With fewer parts reworked, less material wasted, and less time spent inspecting finished goods, the organization's total costs actually can decline.

In 1987, Congress established the Malcolm Baldrige National Quality Award (www.nist.gov/baldrige). It recognizes large and small organizations in business, education, and health care for quality achievement along seven dimensions: leadership; strategic planning; customer and market focus; measurement, analysis, and knowledge management; human resources focus; process management; and business results. The 2012 award winners were Lockheed Martin Missiles and Fire Control, in manufacturing; MESA Products, in small business; Northern Mississippi Medical Center, in health care; and the City of Irving, Texas, in nonprofit. Competition for the award has grown enormously. Some large organizations spend large sums to prepare for the contest; others apply just to receive the extensive feedback from the board of examiners on how to improve quality; and still others feel compelled to apply because customers insist that they show progress in process improvement.

Another quality award is the Shingo Prize (www.shingoprize.org) for business and government organizations that achieve highly efficient production methods. The 2012 award in operational excellence went to Ethicon, Inc.'s plant in Juarez, Mexico. Numerous states have initiated their own quality awards. At the national level, the Carey Award is given to federal agencies and the Hammer Awards are given as part of the National Performance Review for innovation and quality improvement in the federal government.

TQM is a growing industry itself, with consulting firms, university courses, training programs, and professional associations related to quality improvement diffusing rapidly across industrialized nations. The quality approach is supported by at least three major associations: the American Society for Quality (ASQ; www.asq.org), the American Productivity and Quality Center (APQC; www.apqc.org), and the International Society of Six Sigma Professionals (ISSSP; www.isssp.com). These associations actively support TQM by sponsoring quality training workshops and conferences and serving as clearinghouses for important information on TQM programs. The International Organization for Standardization (ISO) also supports TQM. Its ISO 9000 standard applies to quality systems, and certification requires firms to document key goals and processes, to demonstrate compliance, and to create processes for improvement.

Application Stages TQM typically is implemented in five major steps. With the exception of gaining senior management commitment, most of the steps can occur somewhat concurrently.

1. **Gain long-term senior management commitment.** This stage involves helping senior executives understand the importance of long-term commitment to TQM. Without a solid understanding of TQM and the key success factors for implementation, managers often believe that workers are solely responsible for quality. Yet only senior executives have the authority and larger perspective to address the organization-wide, cross-functional issues that hold the greatest promise for TQM's success.

   Senior managers' role in TQM implementation includes giving direction and support throughout the change process. For example, establishing organization-wide TQM generally takes three or more years, although technical improvements to the workflow can be as quick as six to eight months. Senior managers need to clarify and communicate throughout the organization a totally new orientation to producing and delivering products and services.

   The longer-term and more difficult parts of implementation, however, involve changes in the organization's support systems, such as customer service, finance, sales, and human resources. Often these systems are frozen in place by old policies and norms that can interfere with the new approach. Senior managers have to confront those practices and create new ones that support TQM and the organization's strategic orientation.

   Top executives also must be willing to allocate significant resources to TQM implementation, particularly to make large investments in training. For example, as part of its Baldrige Award preparation, Motorola developed Motorola University, a training organization that teaches in 27 languages. Departments at Motorola allocate at least 1.5% of their budgets to education, and every employee must take a minimum of 40 hours of training a year. This effort supports Motorola's goal of six sigma process quality (a statistical measure of product quality that implies 99.9997% perfection) and of having a workforce that is able to read, write, solve problems, and do math at the seventh-grade level or above. When several business units within Motorola achieved the six sigma target, the company demonstrated its commitment to continuously improving quality with a new target of tenfold improvement in key goals.
2. **Train members in quality methods.** TQM implementation requires extensive training in the principles and tools of quality improvement. Depending on the organization's size and complexity, such training can be conducted in a few weeks to more than two years. Members typically learn problem-solving skills and simple statistical process control (SPC) techniques, usually referred to as the seven tools of quality.

At Cedar-Sinai Hospital in Los Angeles, all employees took a three-day course on the applicability of brainstorming, histograms, flowcharts, scatter diagrams, Pareto charts, cause-and-effect diagrams, control charts, and other problem-solving procedures. This training was the beginning of a long-term process in continuous improvement. The knowledge gained is used to understand variations in organizational processes, to identify sources of avoidable costs, to select and prioritize quality improvement projects, and to monitor the effects of changes on product and service quality. By learning to analyze the sources of variation systematically, members can improve the reliability of product manufacturing or service delivery. For example, HCA's West Paces Ferry Hospital used TQM methods to reduce direct costs attributable to antibiotic waste.[30] It used flowcharts, fishbone diagrams, and Pareto charts to determine the major causes of unused intravenous preparations. Changes in the antibiotic delivery process resulted in reduced costs of antibiotics to the hospital of 44.5% and to patients of 45%.

The recent interest in Six Sigma programs has produced an additional training issue. Many of the quality-improvement projects (described below) require considerable facilitation and support. To enable those projects, many organizations have committed to the development of "green belt" and "black belt" roles. These are internal consultants with specialized knowledge, skill, and experience in TQM methods that guide project team members through a specific program of process improvement.

3. **Start quality-improvement projects.** In this phase of TQM implementation, individuals and work groups apply the quality methods to identify the few projects that hold promise for the largest improvements in organizational processes. They identify output variations, intervene to minimize deviations from quality standards, monitor improvements, and repeat this quality-improvement cycle indefinitely. Identifying output variations is a key aspect of TQM. Such deviations from quality standards typically are measured by the percentage of defective products or, in the case of customer satisfaction, by on-time delivery percentages or customer survey ratings. For example, VF Corporation, a leading retail apparel firm, found that retailers were out of stock on 30% of their items 100% of the time. In response, VF revamped its systems to fill orders within 24 hours 95% of the time.

   TQM is concerned not only with variations in the quality of finished products and services but also with variations in the steps of a process that produce a product or service and the levels of internal customer satisfaction. For example, Eastman Chemical Company established a patent process improvement team to enhance the relationship between scientists and lawyers in applying for patent approvals. The team, made up of inventors, lab managers, and attorneys, doubled the number of patent attorneys and relocated their offices near the labs. Attorneys now meet with scientists during the experimental phase of research to discuss ways to increase the chances of yielding a patentable product or process. Patent submissions have increased by 60%, and the number of patents issued to the company has doubled.[31]

   Based on the measurement of output variations, each individual or work group systematically analyzes the cause of variations using SPC techniques. For example, product yields in a semiconductor manufacturing plant can go down for many reasons, including a high concentration of dust particles, small vibrations in the equipment, poor machine adjustments, and human error. Quality-improvement projects often must determine which of the possible causes is most responsible, and, using that information, run experiments and pilot programs to determine which adjustments will cause output variations to drop and quality to improve. Those adjustments that do reduce variations are implemented across the board. Members continue to monitor the quality process to verify improvement and then begin the problem-solving process again for continuous improvement.

4. **Measure progress.** This stage of TQM implementation involves measuring organizational processes against quality standards. Knowing and analyzing the competition's performance are essential for any TQM effort because it sets minimum standards of quality, cost, and service and ensures the organization's position in the industry over the short run. For the longer term, such analytical efforts concentrate on identifying world-class performance, regardless of industry, and creating stretch targets, also known as *benchmarks*. Benchmarks represent the best in organizational achievements and practices for different processes and generally are accepted as "world class." For example, Nordstrom is considered the benchmark of customer service in the retail industry, while Disney's customer-service orientation is considered a world-class benchmark.

   The implied goal in most TQM efforts is to meet or exceed a competitor's benchmark. Alcoa's former chairman Paul H. O'Neill charged all of the company's business units with closing the gap between Alcoa and its competitor's benchmarks by 80% within two years.[32] In aluminum sheet for beverage cans, for example, Japan's Kobe Steel, Ltd., was the benchmark, and Wall Street estimated that achieving O'Neill's goal would increase Alcoa's earnings by one dollar per share. The greatest leverage for change often is found in companies from unrelated industries, however. For example, Alcoa might look to Nordstrom or Disney to get innovative ideas about customer service. Understanding benchmarks from other industries challenges an organization's thinking about what is possible and promotes what is referred to as "out-of-the-box thinking."

5. **Rewarding accomplishment.** In this final stage of TQM implementation, the organization links rewards to improvements in quality. TQM does not monitor and reward outcomes that are normally tracked by traditional reward systems, such as the number of units produced. Such measures do not necessarily reflect product quality and can be difficult to replace because they are ingrained in the organization's traditional way of doing business. Rather, TQM rewards members for "process-oriented" improvements, such as increased on-time delivery, gains in customers' perceived satisfaction with product performance, and reductions in cycle time—the time it takes a product or service to be conceived, developed, produced, and sold. Rewards usually are designed initially to promote finding solutions to the organization's key problems. The linkage between rewards and process-oriented improvements reinforces the belief that continuous improvements, even small ones, are an important part of the new organizational culture associated with TQM. According to a survey of 500 firms in four countries, conducted by Ernst and Young and the American Quality Foundation, more than half of the U.S. companies studied linked executive pay to improving quality and achieving benchmarks.[33]

TQM has continued to evolve in most industrialized countries. It is increasingly associated with lean manufacturing and Six Sigma programs. Lean manufacturing derives from the Toyota Production System (TPS) and seeks to identify and eliminate wastes and inefficiencies from production process. Six Sigma programs, although based on the principles of TQM, attempt to drive out important sources of variation and achieve near perfection in the execution of critical processes in such large organizations as Samsung, SGL Carbon, Motorola, Starwood Hotels, Ford, and Xerox.

Results of Total Quality Management TQM's emergence globally and the variations in how it is applied across organizations have made rigorous evaluation of results difficult. A 1999 survey of the *Fortune* 1000 companies showed that about 75% have implemented some form of TQM.[34] Furthermore, 87% of the companies rated their TQM experience as either positive or very positive, up from 76% in 1993. The research also found that TQM is often associated with the implementation of other EI interventions. Finally, the study revealed that TQM was positively associated with performance outcomes, such as productivity, customer service, product/service quality, and profitability, as well as with human outcomes, such as employee satisfaction and quality of work life. Other TQM studies have shown that as organizations enact process improvements, they may need to make supporting changes in reward systems and work design.[35]

The U.S. Commerce Department's National Institute of Standards and Technology routinely tracks the stock performance of Baldrige Award winners compared to the Standard & Poor's 500 index. On the one hand, the Baldrige winners outperformed the S&P 500 significantly between 1994 and 1999.[36] More recently, however, of the 16 award recipients between 1994 and 2003, only one has outperformed the S&P 500. Another study of hospitals provided empirical support for the Baldrige framework.[37] Significant relationships were identified between hospitals' adherence to the Baldrige Criteria and their performance in the areas of patient and customer satisfaction, staff and work systems, and organization-specific results. However, the relationships between hospital quality systems and financial/market performance or health care outcomes were not significant. The authors recommend more longitudinal research because of the likely time lags between implementation and manifestation of financial or health outcomes.

One of the most rigorous longitudinal studies of the long-term outcomes of TQM found that in contrast to a matched control group, the 600 North American firms that had first won a prominent quality award between 1983 and 1993 scored significantly higher on operating income measures as well as on long-term stock performance.[38] A replication and extension of this study with over 700 European quality award winners found similar long-term TQM effects.[39] A study of Swedish quality award winners found that they consistently outperformed their competitors on measures of sales and profitability.[40]

A balanced picture of TQM effects is provided by a study of 54 firms of different sizes, both adopters and nonadopters of TQM. It found that TQM firms significantly outperformed non-TQM firms. The source of the performance advantage was not the tools and techniques of TQM, however, but the culture, empowerment, and commitment that came from successful implementation. The study concluded that "these tacit resources, and not TQM tools and techniques, drive TQM success," and that "organizations that acquire them can outperform competitors with or without the accompanying TQM ideology."[41] A good example is Boeing's Airlift and Tanker program, which won the Baldrige Award in 1998. Boeing's experience with TQM has suggested that the biggest organizational gains have come through the integration of TQM concepts with other business and strategic initiatives. TQM has helped Boeing be a better all-around company.

Application 13.2 describes how TQM is applied at the Ritz-Carlton Hotel Company.[42] It shows how the company's culture, senior leadership, and empowered work practices contribute to TQM success.

application 13.2

TQM AT THE RITZ-CARLTON

The Ritz-Carlton Hotel Company, the premier flagship of Marriott International, operates 81 luxury hotels in 27 countries. Employing about 38,000 staff, the firm has a venerable record of excellent service that is considered the benchmark by many in the hospitality industry. Ritz-Carlton has been involved in TQM for over 30 years and was the first hotel chain to win the coveted Malcolm Baldrige National Quality Award in 1992. Needless to say, Ritz-Carlton is passionate about quality guest care, from the president and chief operating officer, Herve Humler, to the maintenance, front desk, and housekeeping staff.

Ritz-Carlton's unique approach to TQM is embedded in its strong corporate culture, which is spelled out clearly in its "Gold Standards." These standards are the backbone of the company and include the values and philosophy that guide how it operates, including processes for solving problems and criteria for grooming, housekeeping, safety, and efficiency. The Gold Standards include Ritz-Carlton's credo, motto, three steps to service, service values, and other proprietary statements. All employees know the Gold Standards by heart and are well-trained in what they mean for daily work behavior. For example, Ritz-Carlton's motto, "We are Ladies and Gentlemen serving Ladies and Gentlemen," is closely tied to how guests are welcomed, with "a warm and sincere greeting," and depart with a "fond farewell."

Ritz-Carlton's TQM program begins at the top with senior executives who spend about a quarter of their time on quality issues. Because the company's service culture is built on trust, these leaders hold themselves accountable for behaving according to the values that they require of the organization. The senior executives comprise the corporate steering committee for TQM as well as the senior quality-management team. Each week the steering committee reviews various measures of service quality and performance. It engages in detailed planning by setting objectives, devising action plans, and assessing results.

This planning process is essential to Ritz-Carlton's TQM program. It extends to each level of the firm where teams in the individual work areas set objectives and create action plans that are reviewed by the corporate steering committee. This cross-level planning process helps to assure that quality goals and action plans are consistent across organizational levels and integrated with the firm's overall plan. In addition, each hotel has a designated quality leader, who serves as a resource and advocate as teams develop and implement their quality plans.

Teams play a key role in providing quality service. Each work area in a hotel includes teams responsible for problem solving, strategic planning, and setting quality-certification standards for each position. Employees meet as teams to spot problem patterns, prioritize problems, and develop measures to prevent their recurrence. These cross-functional teams require sufficient time and resources to learn how to function effectively. Managers are still responsible for objectives and solutions but rely on input and involvement from team members. A unique team tradition at Ritz-Carlton is the "lineup," drawn from early French restaurants where the chef got his whole team, including the waiters and waitresses, together at the same time each evening to communicate what they are going to be serving. At the Ritz-Carlton, teams on every shift use the lineup for about 15 minutes every day. This includes sharing up-to-the-minute information as well as talking about great things employees have done to deliver exceptional service.

An integral part of Ritz-Carlton's TQM program is empowering employees to solve guests' problems as quickly as possible. Employees are responsible for acting at first notice, regardless of the type of problem or guest complaint. They are expected to stop their normal routine and to take immediate positive action to discover what went wrong and resolve it. They are empowered to handle any customer complaint on the spot and can demand the immediate assistance of other employees and spend up to $2,000 if necessary. Employees can apply this rapid response not just to solve problems but to do something that creates an absolutely wonderful stay for a guest, such as surprising guests with champagne and cake in their room on their birthdays. Ritz-Carlton also works hard to avoid guest problems before they occur. Employees who detect a potential problem in service delivery are immediately expected to bring it to management's attention and a solution is found. Eliminating internal employee complaints can avoid external complaints that might come from guests.

A key to Ritz-Carlton's TQM success is the continuous collection and analysis of data on service quality and its comparison to predetermined customer expectations. Assisted by the latest information technology, the company gathers information on such quality measures as percentage of check-ins with no queuing, time spent to achieve industry-best clean-room appearance, time to service an occupied guest room, and guest room preventive-maintenance cycles. Data submitted from each of a hotel's 720 work areas provide daily quality production reports, which enable rapid identification of problems in achieving quality and customer-satisfaction goals.

Ritz-Carlton's human resource practices are tied closely to TQM. Selection, training, and performance appraisal are geared to talent acquisition, development, and retention. Only about 2% of the people who apply for jobs are hired. A key criterion is how well the applicant is likely to fit the company's culture including being a team member. Once on board, new employees are versed on the corporate culture through a two-day orientation, followed by extensive on-the-job training, then job certification. To obtain certification, employees are assessed on their mastery of skills associated with their particular job. They also are tested on how well they know the company's TQM philosophy and credo, which can qualify them as "quality engineers." Ritz-Carlton expects 100% compliance with skills testing, so that everyone is certified to do a particular job and is a quality engineer as well. The company's performance appraisal system is based on the Gold Standards and employees are held responsible only for those things under their control.

Ritz-Carlton also has extended TQM to its suppliers. To assure that suppliers can meet the firm's quantity and quality needs, it has developed a supplier certification process, which measures how often suppliers meet specifications on time and how well they improve their cycle time from order to delivery. The certification process also includes an internal audit of suppliers' capabilities and a quality survey of those who use their products and services, including purchasing agents, accounting personnel, sales persons, and hotel guests. Ritz-Carlton ranks suppliers based these data with the objective of getting them certified to become a fully integrated partner.

The fundamental aim of Ritz-Carlton's TQM process is not simply to meet the expectations of guests but to provide them with a visit that is unique, memorable, and personal. According to independent surveys, 92% to 97% of the guests leave with that impression. Ritz-Carlton's experience and success with TQM has spread worldwide to organizations in a variety of industries and regions. Started in 2000, its Leadership Center provides knowledge, information and benchmarking to organizations interested in learning many of the business practices that led to Ritz-Carlton becoming a two-time recipient of the Malcolm Baldrige National Quality Award.

13-2c High-Involvement Organizations

Over the past two decades, an increasing number of employee involvement projects have been aimed at using high-involvement work practices to create high-involvement organizations (HIOs). These interventions create organizational conditions that support high levels of employee participation. What makes HIOs unique is the comprehensive nature of their design process. Unlike parallel structures that do not alter the formal organization or TQM interventions that tend to focus on particular processes, HIOs address almost all features of an organization's design. Structure, work design, management processes, physical layout, personnel policies, and reward systems are designed jointly by management and workers to promote high levels of involvement and performance.

Features of High-Involvement Organizations High-involvement organizations are designed with features congruent with one another. For example, in HIOs employees have considerable influence over decisions. To support such a decentralized philosophy, members receive extensive training in problem-solving techniques, plant operation, and organizational policies. In addition, both operational and issue-oriented information is shared widely and is obtained easily by employees. Finally, rewards are tied closely to unit performance, as well as to knowledge and skill levels. These different aspects of the organization are mutually reinforcing and form a coherent pattern that contributes to employee involvement. Table 13.2 presents a list of compatible design elements characterizing HIOs,[43] and most such organizations include several if not all of the following features:

- **Flat, lean organization structures** contribute to involvement by pushing the scheduling, planning, and controlling functions typically performed by management and staff groups toward the shop floor. Similarly, mini-enterprise, team-based structures that are oriented to a common purpose or outcome help focus employee participation on a shared objective. Participative structures, such as work councils and union–management committees, create conditions in which workers can influence the direction and policies of the organization.
- **Job designs** that provide employees with high levels of discretion, task variety, and meaningful feedback can enhance involvement. They enable workers to influence day-to-day workplace decisions and to receive intrinsic satisfaction by performing work under enriched conditions. Self-managed teams encourage employee responsibility by providing cross-training and job rotation, which give people a chance to learn about the different functions contributing to organizational performance.
- **Open information systems** that are tied to jobs or work teams provide the necessary information for employees to participate meaningfully in decision making. Goals and standards of performance that are set participatively can provide employees with a sense of commitment and motivation for achieving those objectives.
- **Career systems** that provide different tracks for advancement and counseling to help people choose appropriate paths can help employees plan and prepare for long-term development in the organization. Open job posting, for example, makes employees aware of jobs that can further their development.
- **Selection** of employees for HIOs can be improved through a realistic job preview providing information about what it will be like to work in such situations. Team member involvement in a selection process oriented to potential and social skills of recruits can facilitate a participative climate.
- **Training** employees for the necessary knowledge and skills to participate effectively in decision making is a heavy commitment in HIOs. This effort includes education on the economic side of the enterprise, as well as interpersonal skill development. Peer training is emphasized as a valuable adjunct to formal, expert training.
- **Reward systems** can contribute to EI when information about them is open and the rewards are based on acquiring new skills, as well as on sharing gains from improved performance. Similarly, participation is enhanced when people can choose among different fringe benefits and when reward distinctions among people from different hierarchical levels are minimized.
- **Personnel policies** that are participatively set and encourage stability of employment provide employees with a strong sense of commitment to the organization. People

feel that the policies are reasonable and that the firm is committed to their long-term development.

- **Physical layouts** of organizations also can enhance EI. Physical designs that support team structures and reduce status differences among employees can reinforce the egalitarian climate needed for employee participation. Safe and pleasant working conditions provide a physical environment conducive to participation.

TABLE 13.2

Design Features for a Participation System

ORGANIZATIONAL STRUCTURE	TRAINING
1. Flat 2. Lean 3. Mini-enterprise-oriented 4. Team-based 5. Participative council or structure	1. Heavy commitment 2. Peer training 3. Economic education 4. Interpersonal skills
JOB DESIGN	**REWARD SYSTEM**
1. Individually enriched 2. Self-managing teams	1. Open 2. Skill-based 3. Gain sharing or ownership 4. Flexible benefits 5. All salaried workforce 6. Egalitarian perquisites
INFORMATION SYSTEM	**PERSONNEL POLICIES**
1. Open 2. Inclusive 3. Tied to jobs 4. Decentralized; team-based 5. Participatively set goals and standards	1. Stability of employment 2. Participatively established through representative group
CAREER SYSTEM	**PHYSICAL LAYOUT**
1. Tracks and counseling available 2. Open job posting	1. Around organizational structure 2. Egalitarian 3. Safe and pleasant
SELECTION	
1. Realistic job preview 2. Team-based 3. Potential and process-skill oriented	

SOURCE: Reproduced by permission of the publisher from Edward E. Lawler III, "Increasing Worker Involvement to Enhance Organizational Effectiveness: Design Features for a Participation System," in *Change in Organizations*, eds. P. S. Goodman and associates (San Francisco: Jossey-Bass, 1982), pp. 298–99.

These HIO design features are mutually reinforcing. "They all send a message to people in the organization that says they are important, respected, valued, capable of growing, and trusted and that their understanding of and involvement in the total organization is desirable and expected."[44] Moreover, these design components tend to motivate and focus organizational behavior in a strategic direction, and thus can lead to superior effectiveness and competitive advantage, particularly in contrast to more traditionally designed organizations.[45]

Application Factors At present, there is no universally accepted approach to implementing the high-involvement features described here. The actual implementation process often is specific to the situation, and little systematic research has been devoted to understanding the change process itself.[46] Nevertheless, at least two distinct factors seem to characterize how HIOs are implemented. First, implementation generally is guided by an explicit statement of values that members want the new organization to support. Typically, such values as teamwork, equity, quality, and empowerment guide the choice of specific design features. Values that are strongly held and widely shared by organization members can provide the energy, commitment, and direction needed to create HIOs. A second feature of the implementation process is its participative nature. Managers and employees take active roles in choosing and implementing the design features. They may be helped by OD practitioners, but the locus of control for the change process resides clearly within the organization. This participative change process is congruent with the high-involvement design being created. In essence, high-involvement design processes promote high-involvement organizations.

Results of High-Involvement Organizations Extensive research has been done on the HIO intervention and the results generally support its positive effects. An early study surveyed 98 HIOs and showed that about 75% of them perceived their performance relative to competitors as better than average on quality of work life, customer service, productivity, quality, and grievance rates.[47] Analyses of company records revealed that voluntary turnover was 2%, substantially below the national average; return on investment was almost four times greater than industry averages; and return on sales was more than five times greater. Recent studies have confirmed a positive relationship between applications of high-involvement practices and various measures of organizational effectiveness, including return on investment, turnover, job performance, and work stress.[48] Research also has identified conditions that can influence HIO outcomes. For example, in a study of 132 manufacturing firms, the strength of the relationship between high-involvement practices and labor productivity varied depending on the industry's capital intensity, R&D intensity, and growth.[49] Improving high-involvement practices by one standard deviation in a high-capital-intensive industry increased sales per employee by 1%, a nontrivial amount. In a study involving 17 industries in New Zealand, increased use of high-involvement practices was associated with enhanced employee well-being, as measured by job satisfaction, fatigue, and job stress.[50] The researchers warned, however, that these positive human effects might not be realized if HIO interventions lead to work intensification with greater pressures to work harder and longer.

Application 13.3 describes the implementation of a high-involvement organization at Air Chemicals and Products.[51] The case provides a good example of the broad approach to EI. Over time, power, information, knowledge and skill, and rewards were all addressed in an effective organization development process.

application 13.3

BUILDING A HIGH-INVOLVEMENT ORGANIZATION AT AIR PRODUCTS AND CHEMICALS, INC.

Chris Loyd, the vice president and general manager of the Process Systems Group Operations (OPS) division of Air Products and Chemicals, Inc. (APCI), a *Fortune* 200 company, believed there was too much variability in key performance metrics, such as quality, safety, and productivity, across the plants in his division. Despite communication and implementation of several quality-related initiatives, a subset of plants consistently outperformed all others. In response, Chris commissioned a diagnostic process to uncover the sources of exemplary performance in those high-performing facilities.

The OPS division was responsible for ensuring the manufacture and delivery of high-volume industrial gas products directly to customer facilities. The division provided oxygen, nitrogen, hydrogen, helium, argon, and specialty gas products in various states (e.g., liquid, gaseous) and purities to large industrial customers representing a variety of markets, including electronics, refining, pharmaceutical, steel-making, food, aerospace and many others.

The diagnosis identified four factors resulting in exceptional plant performance: employee involvement, information access, technical capability, and incentives. These four factors consistently differentiated between the high performing and comparison plants. In particular, the single greatest source of variance was the level of employee involvement—or the extent to which organization members at all levels participated in decision making—in a facility. With this learning, and working with Jim Byron, an internal OD consultant, a high-involvement strategy was established to broadcast and advance involvement across the entire division. Loyd was convinced that elevating his 900-person division's business effectiveness required pervasive employee involvement in plant management and operations.

HIGH-INVOLVEMENT STRATEGY

The high-involvement (HI) strategy was developed to influence each of the four factors contributing to exceptional plant performance. To address the employee involvement factor, the organization adopted the "working with others" (WWO) training process (described below) to model and educate organization members on how to solve problems in a group setting. In addition, and in an effort to symbolize shared decision making across the division, Loyd created an HI Advisory Team. The team's mandate was to carry forward the work of promoting employee involvement. Members of the advisory team represented all workforce levels, from hourly employees through top management. The WWO training also addressed the technical capability factor by improving and reinforcing the workforce's skills and knowledge related to quality-improvement processes.

The information-access factor was addressed by increasing the organization's capability to share information. The existing intranet was enhanced to provide all workers with access to business and division information (within any constraints imposed by legal or financial regulations).

Finally, the incentive factor was addressed by adjusting the reward system of the division. A gain-sharing system was designed and implemented to reward team performance at the local level and included incentives for plants that were serving similar customers and geographies to share information and best practices with one another.

THE ROLE OF TRAINING IN HIGH INVOLVEMENT

A central component of the HI strategy interventions was the WWO training sessions. Each session addressed the knowledge and skills needed to elevate involvement in the organization and used them immediately to engage employees in making improvements to the business. The WWO sessions not only provided information about employee involvement and the skills and knowledge required to be effective at it, the sessions immediately applied those competencies by engaging participants in an assessment of the current state of involvement in the workplace, and in identifying and resolving a quality-improvement challenge in the participants' respective plants. Action teams were spawned from these sessions to follow through on making changes that were not achievable within the WWO session itself.

Beginning with Loyd's team, Byron led the WWO training sessions during the first two years of the initiative and reached every member of the organization. Division and plant leadership demonstrated its commitment to the goal by participating in WWO sessions. As part of that work, a video was produced that displayed leaders' use of the WWO skills and explored their own personal insights into the benefits involvement offered employees and the business.

As the WWO sessions progressed, participants who had interest in becoming WWO trainers and coaches were identified. They who would train their plants in using teamed approaches to solving local problems and to uncovering and realizing business opportunities. Within two years, every member of OPS received training in these core skills and processes and participated in making quality improvements to their business. More than 100 trainer-coaches were developed to support teaming within local organizations.

These trainer-coaches had responsibility for implementing the second phase of the HI effort, which was to conduct a regular assessment of each plant's authority and power-sharing levels against goals, roles, relationships, and procedure dimensions. The assessments identified areas for improvement, and the trainer-coaches were expected to initiate changeover plans with the assistance of a team development tool kit and additional training that was specifically designed to lead them and their teams through an improvement process. The trainer-coaches documented best practices on a regular basis and broadcast these lessons electronically to all employees through the enhanced intranet and to the HI Advisory Team, as well as distributing hard copy to local plants. They also met regionally to promote best practices and to determine additional ways to increase the level of involvement and power sharing as a means of delegating more management of plant operations lower down the organization.

As the WWO and problem-solving processes unfolded, Loyd began communicating the results to the organization. For example, he included feedback on progress and accomplishment is his weekly telephone conferences with his North American subordinates and in all his other presentations to employees (e.g., face-to-face, in-house TV). Two other mechanisms were used to recycle the measured results: (1) a yearly planning function in which managers reviewed the status of employee involvement within their units and developed personal targets and plans for achieving them and (2) a similar planning session focusing on the organization as a whole completed by the HI Advisory Team. To stress the importance of HI progress, the results of measurement helped to determine the performance appraisal each leader received. Each manager's appraisal plan required yearly progress in increasing employee involvement within his or her plant. This strengthened the significance of the yearly management planning session, which included a half-day session in which managers worked together to analyze the results from their plant's HI assessment, uncover the causes of the results, target next year's improvement level, and generate actions they personally would take to realize their individual improvement targets.

SUSTAINING HIGH INVOLVEMENT

Subsequent to the rollout phase, the HI Advisory Team used the results of the HI assessments to uncover new activities that would further implementation of HI. One such activity was sponsorship of an HI Idea Book that brought together the best innovations employee involvement produced in each area of business function. The book was distributed in print and electronically. It was updated and used to transfer expertise and increase the business benefits each improvement generated.

WWO sessions continued for training new hires. In addition, WWO sessions were used to refresh OPS member skills, while involving participants in solving workplace problems, generating quality improvements, and uncovering and executing ways to accomplish yearly business drivers (e.g., safety improvements, cost reduction, improved customer satisfaction, reduced service interruptions). This sustained use of WWO sessions strengthened the commitment to good communications and simultaneously accomplished ever-broader use of employee involvement.

One highly significant special use of the sessions was to facilitate the integration of an entire new organization into OPS. This integration occurred fours years into the HI initiative. It required incorporating into OPS an organization that was larger (1,100 employees), performed very different work, and had a culture that was fully top-down in character.

EVALUATION

Over the course of its implementation, several evaluations were made of OPS's HI initiative. In particular, the organization tracked the movement of HI scores across plants in the division and performed a study of the return on the investment in the HI effort. Progress was calibrated by yearly measurement of involvement using an EI scale shown in the table below. Measurement was made in each OPS plant.

HI progress was assessed by plotting the year-to-year changes in the prevalence of employee involvement throughout the workplace. A chart depicted the percentage of plants and other operating groups that achieved HI scores of Level 3 or higher. For example, during the last four years, the percentage of units with aggregate HI scores of 3 or higher increased from 15% to over 85%. In addition, an evaluation of the benefits and costs of the program found that for every dollar invested, the organization received 9.7 dollars of benefit. Most of the benefits flowed from improved worker productivity and other workplace improvements that were generated by the WWO sessions.

When Chris Loyd retired, he commented, "When I think about the most significant changes over the last 20 years, I think HI was the most important change we made. The technology changes were not as critical and the organizational restructurings often had little effect, but the HI changes will stay with us forever. In fact, the HI training and its acceptance has been a foundation that has allowed us to make all other changes."

Levels of High Involvement

LEVEL OF HI ADOPTION	DESCRIPTION
I	Managers use a top-down approach and emphasize direction of the workforce. They are either unaware of the HI strategy or doubt its value. The employee's involvement is limited to doing assigned work, and workers see themselves as "hired hands." Employees have limited access to information.
II	Managers use a top-down approach, but employees are asked to provide input concerning business issues that are outside their immediate assignments. Managers are aware of HI and are willing to experiment with its use in accomplishing business objectives. Employees see themselves as having some say over the content of their work and workplace. They have some access to some organizational information as well as data that are relevant to their work.
III	Managers use a participative approach that engages employees in thinking through options, recommending actions, and assessing accomplishment. Management still makes the final decisions but is convinced of the importance of involving employees in addressing business issues. Employees see themselves as advising on the business through their participation in problem-solving teams and special task forces. The employee's knowledge about the workplace is expanded to provide an informed basis for team problem solving.
IV	Management delegates decision-making authority to work teams that are empowered to manage their assigned goals and are involved in every aspect of business management and operations. Management is convinced of the importance of HI for accomplishing business objectives and has begun to redefine its role as to enable personnel rather than to direct them. Employees feel they have a direct stake in the organization's success. Each employee has access to all information about the workplace so that they can participate fully in defining and accomplishing its objectives.
V	Management defines itself as partners with employees on one team dedicated to defining and achieving business goals. Managers position themselves to enable the free and collaborative enterprise of the team. Employees experience ownership for the business and a personal commitment to ensuring its success. Work unit personnel operate as a self-led team, configuring themselves as needed to define and achieve corporate purposes and to coordinate with other work teams. Each employee has access to all information about the workplace except that information restricted by law.

SUMMARY

This chapter described employee involvement interventions. These technostructural change programs are aimed at moving organization decision making downward to improve responsiveness and performance and to increase member flexibility, commitment, and satisfaction. Different approaches to EI can be described by the extent to which power, information, knowledge and skills, and rewards are shared with employees.

The relationship between EI and productivity can be oversimplified. Productivity can be increased through improved employee communication, motivation, and skills and abilities. It also can be affected through increased worker satisfaction, which in turn results in productive employees joining and remaining with the organization.

Major EI interventions are parallel structures, including cooperative union–management projects and quality circles, TQM, and high-involvement organizations. The results of these approaches generally are positive, and the quality of research supporting these interventions is increasing.

NOTES

1. L. Davis, "Enhancing the Quality of Work Life: Developments in the United States," *International Labour Review* 116 (July–August 1977): 53–65.
2. W. Macey, B. Schneider, K. Barbera, and S. Young, *Employee Engagement: Tools for Analysis, Practice, and Competitive Advantage* (Malden, MA: Wiley Blackwell, 2009); A. Konrad, "Engaging Employees Through High-Involvement Work Practices," *Ivey Business Journal* (March/April 2006) accessed from http://www.iveybusinessjournal.com/article.asp?intArticle_ID=617 on August 20, 2007; M. Buckingham and C. Coffman, *First, Break All the Rules: What the World's Greatest Managers Do Differently* (New York: Simon & Schuster, 1999).
3. D. Glew, A. O'Leary-Kelly, R. Griffin, and D. Van Fleet, "Participation in Organizations: A Preview of the Issues and Proposed Framework for Future Analysis," *Journal of Management* 21, no. 3 (1995): 395–421; J. Cotton, *Employee Involvement: Methods for Improving Performance and Work Attitudes* (Newbury Park: Sage Press, 1993).
4. E. Lawler III, *High-Involvement Management* (San Francisco: Jossey-Bass, 1986).
5. M. Marchington, A. Wilkinson, and P. Ackers, "Understanding the Meaning of Participation: Views from the Workplace," *Human Relations* 47, no. 8 (1994): 867–94; C. Goulden, "Supervisory Management and Quality Circle Performance: An Empirical Study," *Journal of Management Development* 14, no. 7 (1995): 15–27.
6. D. Welsh, F. Luthans, and S. Sommer, "Managing Russian Factory Workers: The Impact of U.S.-Based Behavioral and Participative Techniques," *Academy of Management Journal* 36, no. 1 (1993): 58–79; D. Jones, "Employee Participation During the Early Stages of Transition: Evidence from Bulgaria," *Economic and Industrial Democracy* 16, no. 1 (1995): 111–35.
7. E. Poutsma, J. Hendrickx, and F. Huijgen, "Employee Participation in Europe: In Search of the Participative Workplace," *Economic and Industrial Democracy* 24 (2003): 45–77; J. Wimalasiri and A. Kouzmin, "A Comparative Study of Employee Involvement Initiatives in Hong Kong and the USA," *International Journal of Manpower* 21 (2000): 614–32; C. Cooper and E. Mumford, *The Quality of Working Life in Western and Eastern Europe* (Westport, CT: Greenwood Press, 1979); Center for Effective Organizations, "Survey of Organization Improvement Efforts" (Los Angeles: Center for Effective Organizations, 2006).
8. E. Lawler, *Organizing for High Performance: Employee Involvement, TQM, Re-engineering, and Knowledge Management in the* Fortune *1000* (San Francisco: Jossey-Bass, 2001); E. Lawler III, S. Mohrman, and G. Ledford, *Strategies for High-Performance Organizations* (San Francisco: Jossey-Bass, 1998).
9. O. O'Neill, D. Feldman, R. Vandenberg, D. Dejoy, and M. Wilson, "Values, High-Involvement Work Practices, and Business Unit Performance," *Human Resource Management* 50 (2011): 541–58; K. Macky, and P. Boxall, "High-Involvement Work Processes, Work Intensification and Employee Well-Being: A Study of New Zealand Worker Experiences," *Asia Pacific Journal of Human Resources* 46 (2008): 38–55; C. Riordan, R. Vandenberg, and H. Richardson, "Employee Involvement Climate and Organizational Effectiveness," *Human Resource Management* 44 (2005): 471–88; D. Datta, J. Guthrie, and P. Wright, "Human Resource Management and Labor

Productivity: Does Industry Matter?" *Academy of Management Journal* 48 (2005): 135–45; E. Appelbaum, T. Bailey, and P. Berg, *Manufacturing Advantage: Why High-Performance Work Systems Pay Off* (Ithaca, NY: Cornell University Press, 2000).

10. E. Lawler III and G. Ledford, "Productivity and the Quality of Work Life," *National Productivity Review* 2 (Winter 1981–1982): 23–36.

11. M. Kizilos, L. Cummings, and T. Cummings, "How High Involvement Work Processes Increase Organization Performance: The Role of Organizational Citizenship Behavior," *Journal of Applied Behavioral Science*, in press; Y. Gong, S. Chang, and S. Cheung, "High Performance Work System and Collective OCB: A Collective Social Exchange Perspective," *Human Resource Management Journal* 20 (2010): 119–37; L. Sun, S. Aryee, and K. Law, "High-Performance Human Resource Practices, Citizenship Behavior, and Organizational Performance: A Relational Perspective," *Academy of Management Journal* 50 (2007). 558–77.

12. J. Coombs, J. Liu, A. Hall, and D. Kitchen, "How Much Do High-Performance Work Practices Matter? A Meta-Analysis of Their Effects on Organizational Performance," *Personnel Psychology* 59 (2006): 501–28; G. Ledford and E. Lawler, "Research on Employee Participation: Beating a Dead Horse?" *Academy of Management Review* 19 (1994): 633–36.

13. Lawler, Mohrman, and Ledford, *Strategies for High-Performance Organizations*, 150; Datta, Guthrie, and Wright, "Human Resource Management."

14. G. Bushe and A. Shani, "Parallel Learning Structure Interventions in Bureaucratic Organizations," in *Research in Organizational Change and Development*, vol. 4, ed. W. Pasmore and R. Woodman (Greenwich, CT: JAI Press, 1990), 167–94.

15. D. Zand, "Collateral Organization: A New Change Strategy," *Journal of Applied Behavioral Science* 10 (1974): 63–89; S. Goldstein, "Organizational Dualism and Quality Circles," *Academy of Management Review* 10 (1985): 504–17.

16. D. Zand, *Information, Organization, and Power: Effective Management in the Knowledge Society* (New York: McGraw-Hill, 1981), 57–88; G. Bushe and A. Shani, *Parallel Learning Structures: Increasing Innovation in Bureaucracies* (Reading, MA: Addison-Wesley, 1991).

17. C. Worley and G. Ledford, "The Relative Impact of Group Process and Group Structure on Group Effectiveness" (paper presented at the Western Academy of Management, Spokane, WA, April 1992).

18. This application was adapted from the following sources: K. Hammonds, "Leaders for the Long Haul," *Fast Company* 48 (2001): 56–57; J. Gordon, "Meet the Freight Fairy," *Forbes* 171 (January 20, 2003): 64–65; AI Commons Website, accessed from http://appreciativeinquiry.case.edu on August 18, 2007.

19. Zand, "Collateral Organization;" A. Honeycutt, "The Key to Effective Quality Circles," *Training and Development Journal* 43 (May 1989): 81–84; "A Quality Circle Nets a Nice Round Figure," *Supervisory Management* 40 (1995): 7; S. Mohrman and G. Ledford Jr., "The Design and Use of Effective Employee Participation Groups," *Human Resource Management* 24 (1985): 413–28; E. Lawler III and S. Mohrman, "Quality Circles after the Fad," *Harvard Business Review* 85 (1985): 64–71; D. Collins, "Self-Interests and Group Interests in Employee Involvement Programs: A Case Study," *Journal of Labor Research* 16 (1995): 57–79; C. Worley, "Implementing Participation Strategies in Hospitals: Correlates of Effective Problem-Solving Teams," *Public Administration and Management: An Interactive Journal* 5 (2000): 1–27.

20. E. Miller, "The Parallel Organization Structure at General Motors—An Interview with Howard C. Carlson," *Personnel* (September–October 1978): 64–69; M. Barrick and R. Alexander, "A Review of Quality Circle Efficacy and the Existence of Positive-Findings Bias," *Personnel Psychology* 40 (1987): 579–92; R. Steel and G. Shane, "Evaluation Research on Quality Circles: Technical and Analytical Implications," *Human Relations* 39 (1986): 449–68; M. Duckles, R. Duckles, and M. Maccoby, "The Process of Change at Bolivar," *Journal of Applied Behavioral Science* 13 (1977): 387–499.

21. G. Bushe, "Developing Cooperative Labor–Management Relations in Unionized Factories: A Multiple Case Study of Quality Circles and Parallel Organizations Within Joint Quality of Work Life Projects," *Journal of Applied Behavioral Science* 24 (1988): 129–50; H. Katz, T. Kochan, and M. Weber, "Assessing the Effects of Industrial Relations Systems and Efforts to Improve the Quality of Working Life on Organizational Effectiveness," *Academy of Management Journal* 28 (1985): 509–26.

22. Lawler and Ledford, "Productivity and the Quality of Work Life."

23. G. Ledford Jr., E. Lawler III, and S. Mohrman, "The Quality Circle and Its Variations," in *Enhancing Productivity: New Perspectives from Industrial and Organizational Psychology*, ed. J. P. Campbell and J. R. Campbell (San Francisco: Jossey-Bass, 1988), 225–94.

24. Lawler, Mohrman, and Ledford, *Strategies for High-Performance Organizations*, 112–13; D. Tjosvold, "Making Employee Involvement Work: Cooperative Goals and Controversy to Reduce Costs," *Human Relations* 51 (1998): 210–14.

25. "Employee Participation and Labor–Management Cooperation in American Workplaces," *Challenge* 38 (1995): 38–46.
26. Lawler and Ledford, "Productivity and the Quality of Work Life," 35.
27. Y. Shetty, "Product Quality and Competitive Strategy," *Business Horizons* (May–June 1987): 46–52; D. Garvin, *Managing Quality: The Strategic and Competitive Edge* (New York: Free Press, 1988); "The Quality Imperative," *BusinessWeek*, October 25, 1991, 34.
28. W. Deming, *Quality, Productivity, and Competitive Advantage* (Cambridge, MA: MIT Center for Advanced Engineering Study, 1982); W. Deming, *Out of the Crisis* (Cambridge, MA: MIT Press, 1986); J. Juran, *Quality Control Handbook* 3rd ed. (New York: McGraw-Hill, 1974); J. Juran, *Juran on the Leadership for Quality: An Executive Handbook* (New York: Free Press, 1989).
29. P. Crosby, *Quality Is Free* (New York: McGraw-Hill, 1979); P. Crosby, *Quality Without Tears* (New York: McGraw-Hill, 1984).
30. C. Caldwell, J. Mceachern, and V. Davis, "Measurement Tools Eliminate Guesswork," *Healthcare Forum Journal* (July–August 1990): 23–27.
31. "Quality Imperative," *BusinessWeek*, 152.
32. Ibid., 14.
33. Ibid.
34. Lawler, *Organizing for High Performance.*
35. T. Douglas and W. Judge Jr., "Total Quality Management Implementation and Competitive Advantage: The Role of Structural Control and Exploration," *Academy of Management Journal* 44 (2001): 158–70; R. Allen and R. Kilmann, "The Role of the Reward System for a Total Quality Management Based Strategy," *Journal of Organizational Change Management* 14 (2001): 110–32.
36. "Betting to Win on the Baldie Winners," *BusinessWeek*, October 18, 1993, 8; additional information about this study can be accessed from http://www.nist.gov/public_affairs/stockstudy.htm.
37. S. Goldstein and S. Schweikhart, "Empirical Support for the Baldrige Award Framework in U.S. Hospitals," *Health Care Management Review* 27 (2002): 62–75.
38. K. Hendricks, and V. Singhal, "Does Implementing an Effective TQM Program Actually Improve Operating Performance? Empirical Evidence from Firms That Have Won Quality Awards," *Management Science* 43 (1997): 1258–74; K. Hendricks and V. Singhal, "Firm Characteristics, Total Quality Management and Financial Performance," *Journal of Operations Management* 19 (2001): 269–85; K. Hendricks and V. Singhal, "The Long-Run Stock Price Performance of Firms with Effective TQM Programs," *Management Science* 47 (2001): 359–68.
39. L. Boulter, T. Bendell, and J. Dahlgaard, "Total Quality Beyond North America: A Comparative Analysis of the Performance of European Excellence Award Winners," *International Journal of Operations & Production Management* 33 (2013): 197–215.
40. J. Hansson and H. Eriksson, "The Impact of TQM on Financial Performance," *Measuring Business Excellence* 6 (2002): 44–54.
41. T. Powell, "Total Quality Management as a Competitive Advantage: A Review and Empirical Study," *Strategic Management Journal* 16 (1995): 15–37.
42. This application was adapted from material of the following sources: http://www.ritzcarlton.com; R. Reiss, "How Ritz-Carlton Stays on Top," *Forbes,* October 30, 2009; "How Ritz-Carlton Applies 'TQM'," *Cornell Hotel and Restaurant Administration Quarterly* 34 (August 1993): 16–25.
43. Lawler, *High-Involvement Management.*
44. E. Lawler III, "Increasing Worker Involvement to Enhance Organizational Effectiveness," in *Change in Organizations*, ed. P. Goodman (San Francisco: Jossey-Bass, 1982), 299; R. Walton, "From Control to Commitment in the Workplace," *Harvard Business Review* 63 (1985): 76–84.
45. M. Beer, *High Commitment-High Performance: How to Build a Resilient Organization* (San Francisco: Jossey-Bass, 2009); Lawler, *High-Involvement Management*; E. Lawler, *The Ultimate Advantage* (San Francisco: Jossey-Bass, 1992).
46. Glew et al., "Participation in Organizations."
47. G. Ledford, "High-Involvement Organizations" (working paper, Center for Effective Organizations, University of Southern California, 1992).
48. O. O'Neill, D. Feldman, R. Vandenberg, D. Dejoy, and M. Wilson, "Values, High-Involvement Work Practices, and Business Unit Performance," *Human Resource Management* 50 (2011): 541–58; C. Riordan, R. Vandenberg, and H. Richardson, "Employee Involvement Climate and Organizational Effectiveness," *Human Resource Management* 44 (2005): 471–88; J. Guthrie, "High-Involvement Work Practices, Turnover, and Productivity: Evidence from New Zealand," *Academy of Management Journal* 44 (2001): 180–91; R. Vandenberg, H. Richardson, and L. Eastman, "The Impact of High Involvement Work Processes on Organizational Effectiveness: A Second-Order Latent Variable Approach," *Group & Organization Management* 24 (1999): 300–39.

49. Datta, Guthrie, and Wright, "Human Resource Management."
50. K. Macky and P. Boxall, "High-Involvement Work Processes, Work Intensification and Employee Well-Being: A Study of New Zealand Worker Experiences," *Asia Pacific Journal of Human Resources* 46 (2008): 38–55.
51. This application was developed and submitted by James Byron based on the original study by J. S. Byron and R. L. Vitalo, documented in "Using Working with Others Training Sessions to Drive Employee Involvement" (Hope, ME: Vital Enterprises—http://vitalentusa.com/learn/drive_ei.php, 2003).

14

Work Design

learning objectives

- Describe the engineering approach to work design.
- Explore and evaluate the motivational approach to work design.
- Discuss and apply the principles of sociotechnical systems work design.
- Learn how to design work to meet technical and personal needs.

This chapter is concerned with work design—creating jobs and work groups that generate high levels of employee fulfillment and productivity. This technostructural intervention can be part of a larger employee involvement application, or it can be an independent change program. Work design has been applied and researched extensively in organizations. Recently, organizations have tended to combine work design with formal structure and supporting changes in goal setting, reward systems, work environment, and other performance management practices. These organizational factors can help structure and reinforce the kinds of work behaviors associated with specific work designs. (How performance management interventions can support work design is discussed in Chapter 15.)

This chapter examines three approaches to work design. First, the engineering approach focuses on efficiency and simplification, and results in traditional job and work-group designs. Traditional jobs involve relatively routine and repetitive forms of work, where little interaction among people is needed to produce a service or product. Call center operators, data-entry positions, and product support representatives are examples of this job design. Traditional work groups are composed of members performing routine yet interrelated tasks. Member interactions are typically controlled by supervisors, schedules, and rigid workflows, such as might be found on assembly lines.

A second approach to work design derives from motivational theories and attempts to enrich the work experience. Job enrichment involves designing jobs with high levels of meaning, discretion, and knowledge of results. A well-researched model focusing on job attributes has helped clear up methodological problems with this important intervention.

The third approach to work design derives from sociotechnical systems methods, and seeks to optimize both the social and the technical aspects of work systems. This method has led to a popular form of work design called "self-managed teams," which are composed of multiskilled members performing interrelated tasks. Members are given the knowledge, information, and power necessary to control their own task behaviors with relatively little external control. New support systems and supervisory styles are needed to manage them.

The chapter describes each of these perspectives on work design, and then presents a contingency framework for integrating the approaches based on personal and technical factors in the workplace. When work is designed to fit these factors, it is both satisfying and productive.

14-1 The Engineering Approach

The oldest and most prevalent approach to designing work is based on engineering concepts and methods. The engineering approach is less an organization development (OD) intervention than a benchmark in history. It proposes that the most efficient work designs can be determined by clearly specifying the tasks to be performed, the work methods to be used, and the workflow among individuals. The engineering approach is based on the pioneering work of Frederick Taylor, the father of scientific management, in the late 1800s. He developed methods for analyzing and designing work and laid the foundation for the professional field of industrial engineering.[1]

The engineering approach scientifically analyzes workers' tasks to discover those procedures that produce the maximum output with the minimum input of energies and resources.[2] This generally results in work designs with high levels of specialization and specification. Such designs have several benefits: They allow workers to learn tasks rapidly; they permit short work cycles so performance can take place with little or no mental effort; and they reduce costs because lower-skilled people can be hired and trained easily and paid relatively low wages.

The engineering approach produces two kinds of work design: traditional jobs and traditional work groups. When the work can be completed by one person, such as with bank tellers and telephone operators, traditional jobs are created. These jobs tend to be simplified, with routine and repetitive tasks having clear specifications concerning time and motion. When the work requires coordination among people, such as on automobile assembly lines, traditional work groups are developed. They are composed of members performing relatively routine, yet related, tasks. The overall group task is typically broken into simpler, discrete parts (often called jobs). The tasks and work methods are specified for each part, and the parts are assigned to group members. Each member performs a routine and repetitive part of the group task. Members' separate task contributions are coordinated for overall task achievement through such external controls as supervisors, schedules, and rigid workflows.[3] This method of work design, pioneered in the early 1900s by Henry Ford's assembly line, was popularized in the 1950s and 1960s by the mass-production methods of American automobile manufacturers and was an important reason for the growth of American industry following World War II.

Critics of the engineering approach to work design argue that the method ignores workers' social and psychological needs. They suggest that the rising educational level of the workforce and the substitution of automation for menial labor point to the need for more enriched forms of work in which people have greater discretion and are more challenged. Moreover, the growth of the service economy and work that involves information processing and decision making require work designs that do not readily conform to the traditional engineering approach. The current competitive climate requires a more committed and involved workforce able to make online decisions and to develop performance innovations. Work designed with the employee in mind is more humanly fulfilling and productive than that designed in traditional ways. However, it is important to recognize the strengths of the engineering approach. It remains an important work design intervention because its cost savings and efficiency can be measured readily, is well understood, and is easily implemented and managed.

14-2 The Motivational Approach

The motivational approach to work design views the effectiveness of organizational activities primarily as a function of member needs and satisfaction, and seeks to improve employee performance and satisfaction by enriching jobs. The motivational method provides people with opportunities for autonomy, responsibility, closure (that is, doing a complete job), and performance feedback. Enriched jobs are popular in the United States at such companies as Wells Fargo, The Hartford, and Hewlett-Packard.

The motivational approach usually is associated with the research of Herzberg and of Hackman and Oldham. Herzberg's two-factor theory of motivation proposed that certain attributes of work, such as meaningfulness, responsibility, and recognition, serve as "motivators" to increase job performance and satisfaction.[4] Other attributes, which Herzberg called "hygiene factors," such as company policies, working conditions, pay, and supervision, do not motivate people but rather prevent them from being dissatisfied with work. Successful job enrichment experiments at AT&T, Texas Instruments, and Imperial Chemical Industries helped to popularize job enrichment in the 1960s.[5]

Herzberg's motivation and hygiene factors are intuitively appealing. However, the validity of the two factors has been challenged based on the way that Herzberg measured them. Furthermore, important worker characteristics that can affect whether people will respond favorably to job enrichment were not included in his theory. Finally, Herzberg's failure to involve employees in the job enrichment process itself does not suit most OD practitioners today. Consequently, a second, well-researched approach to job enrichment has been favored. It focuses on the attributes of the work itself and has resulted in a more scientifically acceptable theory of job enrichment than Herzberg's model. The research of Hackman and Oldham represents this more recent trend in job enrichment.[6]

14-2a The Core Dimensions of Jobs

Considerable research has been devoted to defining and understanding core job dimensions.[7] Figure 14.1 summarizes the Hackman and Oldham model of job design. Five core dimensions of work affect three critical psychological states, which in turn produce personal and job outcomes. These outcomes include high internal work motivation, high-quality work performance, satisfaction with the work, and low absenteeism and turnover. The five core job dimensions—skill variety, task identity, task significance, autonomy, and feedback from the work itself—are described below and associated with the critical psychological states that they create.

Skill Variety, Task Identity, and Task Significance These three core job characteristics influence the extent to which work is perceived as meaningful. Skill variety refers to the number and types of skills used to perform a particular task. Nurses in an oncology unit must be able to interact successfully with patients, patient families, and physicians. They also must juggle a variety of medical procedures, understand and apply the latest treatment therapies, and perform a variety of charting tasks. The more tasks an individual performs, the more meaningful the job becomes. When skill variety is increased by moving a person from one job to another, a form of job enrichment called job rotation is accomplished. However, simply rotating a person from one boring job to another is not likely to produce the outcomes associated with a fully enriched job.

Task identity describes the extent to which an individual performs a whole piece of work. For example, an employee who completes an entire wheel assembly for an airplane, including the tire, chassis, brakes, and electrical and hydraulic systems, has more task identity and will perceive the work as more meaningful than someone who only assembles the

FIGURE 14.1

Relationships Among Core Job Dimensions, Critical Psychological States, and Personal and Work Outcomes

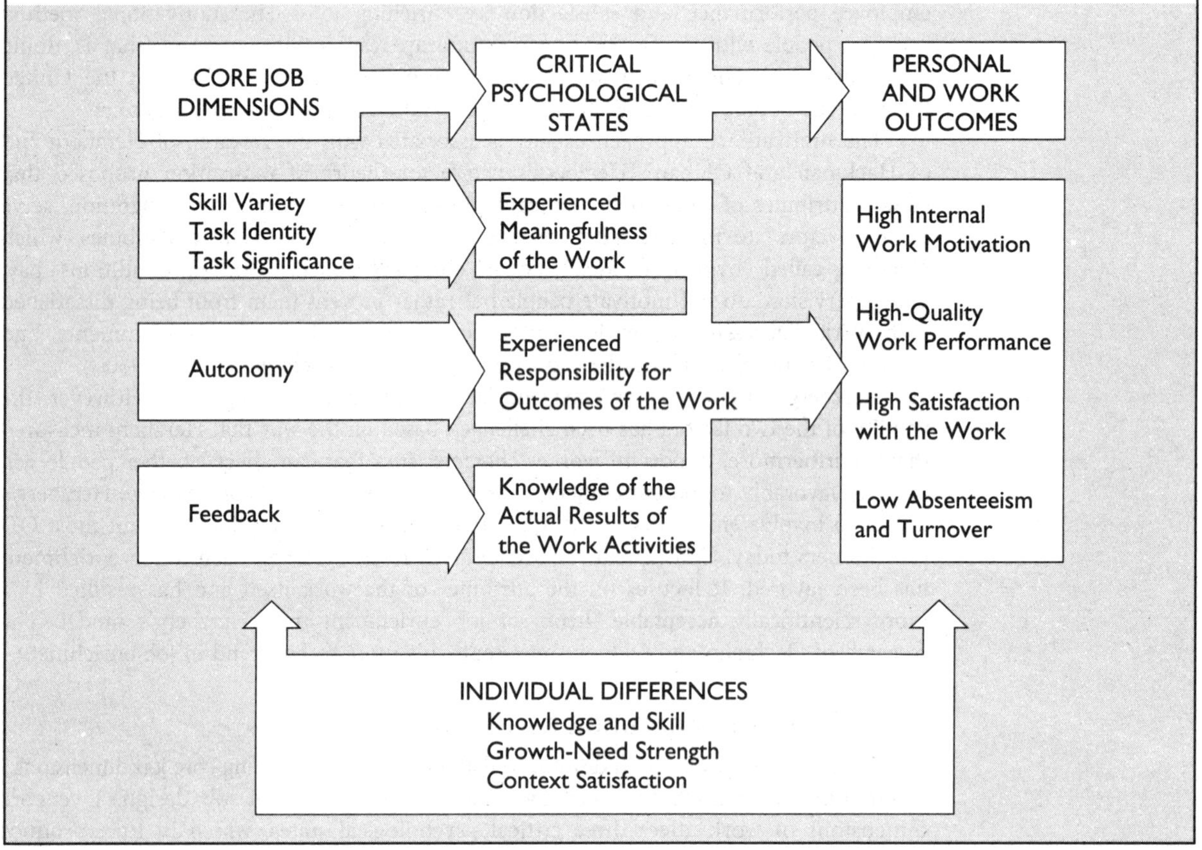

SOURCE: J. Richard Hackman & Greg R. Oldham, *Work Redesign*, 1st Edition, © 1980. Reprinted by permission of Pearson Education, Inc., Upper Saddle River, NJ.

braking subsystem. Job enlargement, another form of job enrichment that combines increases in skill variety with task identity, blends several narrow jobs into one larger, expanded job. For example, separate machine setup, machining, and inspection jobs might be combined into one. This method can increase meaningfulness, job satisfaction, and motivation when employees comprehend and like the greater task complexity.

Task significance represents the impact that the work has on others. In jobs with high task significance, such as nursing, consulting, or manufacturing something like sensitive parts for the space shuttle, the importance of successful task completion creates meaningfulness for the worker.

Experienced meaningfulness is expressed as an average of these three dimensions. Thus, although it is advantageous to have high amounts of skill variety, task identity, and task significance, a strong emphasis on any one of the three dimensions can, at least partially, make up for deficiencies in the other two.

Autonomy This refers to the amount of independence, freedom, and discretion that the employee has to schedule and perform tasks. Salespeople, for example, often have considerable autonomy in how they contact, develop, and close new accounts, whereas assembly-line workers often have to adhere to work specifications clearly detailed in a policy-and-procedure manual. Employees are more likely to experience responsibility for their work outcomes when high amounts of autonomy exist.

Feedback from the Work Itself This core dimension represents the information that workers receive about the effectiveness of their work. It can derive from the work itself, as when determining whether an assembled part functions properly, or it can come from such external sources as reports on defects, budget variances, customer satisfaction, and the like. Because feedback from the work itself is direct and generates intrinsic satisfaction, it is considered preferable to feedback from external sources.

14-2b Individual Differences

Not all people react in similar ways to job enrichment interventions. Individual differences—among them, a worker's knowledge and skill levels, growth needs strength, and satisfaction with contextual factors—moderate the relationships among core dimensions, psychological states, and outcomes. Worker knowledge and skill refers to the education and experience levels characterizing the workforce. If employees lack the appropriate skills, for example, increasing skill variety may not improve a job's meaningfulness. Similarly, if workers lack the intrinsic motivation to grow and develop personally, attempts to provide them with increased autonomy may be resisted. (We will discuss growth needs more fully in the last section of this chapter.) Finally, contextual factors include reward systems, supervisory style, and coworker satisfaction. When the employee is unhappy with the work context, attempts to enrich the work itself may be unsuccessful.

14-2c Application Stages

The basic steps for job enrichment, as described by Hackman and Oldham, include making a thorough diagnosis of the situation, forming natural work units, combining tasks, establishing client relationships, vertical loading, and opening feedback channels.[8]

Making a Thorough Diagnosis The most popular method of diagnosing a job is using the Job Diagnostic Survey (JDS) or one of its variations.[9] An important output of the JDS is the motivating potential score, which is a function of the three psychological states—experienced meaningfulness, autonomy, and feedback. The survey can be used to profile one or more jobs, to determine whether motivation and satisfaction are really problems or whether the job is low in motivating potential, and to isolate specific job aspects that are causing difficulties. Figure 14.2 shows two jobs. Job A in engineering maintenance is high on all of the core dimensions. Its motivating potential score is 260 (motivating potential scores average about 125). Job B, the routine and repetitive task of answering frequently asked questions in a call center, has a motivating potential score of 30. The score is well below average and would be even lower except for the job's relatively high task significance. This job could be enriched and improved.

The JDS also indicates how ready employees are to accept change. Employees who have high growth needs will respond more readily to job enrichment than will those with low or weak growth needs. A thorough diagnosis of the existing work system should be completed before implementing actual changes. The JDS measures satisfaction with pay, coworkers, and supervision. If there is high dissatisfaction with one or more of these areas, other interventions might be more helpful prior to work redesign.

FIGURE 14.2

The JDS Diagnostic Profile for a "Good" and a "Bad" Job

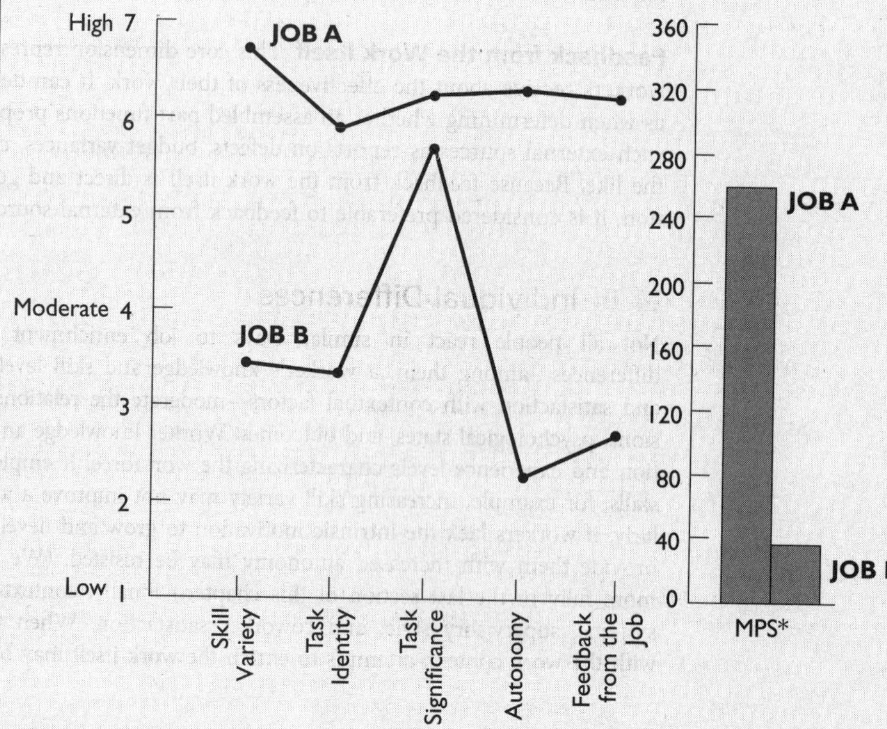

*MPS, Motivating Potential Score

Forming Natural Work Units As much as possible, natural work units should be formed. Although there may be a number of technological constraints, interrelated task activities should be grouped together. The basic question in forming natural work units is "How can one increase 'ownership' of the task?" Forming such natural units increases two of the core dimensions—task identity and task significance—that contribute to the meaningfulness of work.

Combining Tasks Frequently, divided jobs can be put back together to form a new and larger one. In a Corning Glass Works plant, the task of assembling laboratory hotplates was redesigned by combining a number of previously separate tasks. After the change, each hotplate was completely assembled, inspected, and shipped by one operator, resulting in an increased productivity of 84%. Controllable rejects dropped from 23 to less than 1%, and absenteeism dropped from 8% to less than 1%.[10] A later analysis indicated that the change in productivity was the result of the intervention.[11] Combining tasks increases task identity and allows a worker to use a greater variety of skills. The hotplate assembler can identify with a finished product ready for shipment, and self-inspection of his or her work adds greater task significance, autonomy, and feedback from the job itself.

Establishing Client Relationships When jobs are divided into small units, the typical worker has little or no contact with, or knowledge of, the ultimate user of the product or service. Improvements often can be realized simultaneously on three of the core dimensions by encouraging and helping workers to establish direct relationships with the clients of their work. For example, when an individual from a support pool is assigned to a particular department, feedback increases because of the additional opportunities for praise or criticism of his or her work. Because of the need to develop interpersonal skills in maintaining the client relationship, skill variety may increase. If the worker is given personal responsibility for deciding how to manage relationships with clients, autonomy is increased.

Three steps are needed to create client relationships: (1) The client must be identified; (2) the contact between the client and the worker needs to be established as directly as possible; and (3) criteria and procedures are needed by which the client can judge the quality of the product or service received and relay those judgments back to the worker. For example, even customer-service and data-entry operations can be set up so that people serve particular clients. In the hotplate department, personal nametags can be attached to each instrument. The Indiana Bell Telephone Company found substantial improvements in satisfaction and performance when telephone directory compilers were given accountability for a specific geographic area.[12]

Vertical Loading The intent of vertical loading is to decrease the gap between doing the job and controlling it. A vertically loaded job has responsibilities and controls that formerly were reserved for management. Vertical loading may well be the most crucial of the job-design principles. Autonomy is invariably increased. This approach should lead to greater feelings of personal accountability and responsibility for the work outcomes. For example, at an IBM plant that manufactures circuit boards for personal computers, assembly workers were trained to measure the accuracy and speed of production processes and to test the quality of finished products. Their work was more "whole," they were more autonomous, and the engineers who measure and test were free to design better products and more efficient ways to manufacture them.[13]

Loss of vertical loading usually occurs when someone has made a mistake. Once a supervisor steps in, the responsibility may be removed indefinitely. For example, many skilled machinists have to complete forms to have maintenance people work on a machine. The supervisor automatically signs the slip rather than allowing the machinist to either repair the machine or ask directly for maintenance support.

Opening Feedback Channels In almost all jobs, approaches exist to open feedback channels and help people learn whether their performance is remaining at a constant level, improving, or deteriorating. The most advantageous and least threatening feedback occurs when a worker learns about performance as the job is performed. In the hotplate department at Corning Glass Works, assembling the entire instrument and inspecting it dramatically increased the quantity and quality of performance information available to the operators. Data given to a manager or supervisor often can be given directly to the employee. Computers and other automated operations can be used to provide people with data not currently accessible to them. Many organizations simply have not realized the motivating impact of direct, immediate performance feedback.

Application 14.1 presents an example of job enrichment at the Hartford Insurance Group. The employee relations consulting services (ERCS) group provided a single, one-stop place for managers to get answers to employee relations questions, such as how to document employee discipline or how to advise employees on benefit changes, and allowed the human resource generalists to focus on the more strategic aspects of their work. The initial implementation of the ERCS produced jobs low in motivating potential and an internal organization effectiveness consultant helped to redesign the unit.[14]

application 14.1

ENRICHING JOBS AT THE HARTFORD'S EMPLOYEE RELATIONS CONSULTING SERVICES GROUP

Founded in 1810, The Hartford Financial Services Group, Inc. is one of the largest U.S.-based providers of investment products (e.g., annuities, mutual funds, college savings plans), life insurance, group and employee benefits, automobile and homeowners' insurance, and business insurance serving millions of customers worldwide—including individuals, institutions, and businesses—through independent agents, brokers, through financial institutions, and online. With 30,000 employees and approximately $26.5 billion in income in 2006, The Hartford was ranked 78th on the 2006 *Fortune* 100 list.

Hartford's corporate human resources (HR) organization included about 175 HR Generalists (HRGs) who were deployed throughout the organization's business units. It also included a centralized group known as "HR Source," which handled lower-level HR transactions such as basic policy, protocol, and benefit questions. The HRGs addressed the majority of HR-related issues that arose within their respective units, including workforce planning, change management, employee relations, and talent management. The range of responsibilities meant high levels of skill variety, the deployment to a business unit meant high levels of task identity and feedback, and the relevance of the work meant high levels of task significance. However, the HRGs also were in high demand; the number of requests often exceeded the number of important responsibilities, and this made autonomy difficult. HRGs reported a high level of stress in their work and there was some variation in their results depending on such factors as leadership expectations, the skill set of the HRG, geographic location, and so on.

In 2006, and in response to these data, the Employee Relations Consulting Services (ERCS) group was created. It centralized some HR functions so they would be more strategic, consistent, and efficient. ERCS was staffed with 12 Employee Relations Consultants (ERCs), who were prior HRGs with knowledge and expertise in employee relations. A business decision also was made to outsource the work of the HR Source to an outside vendor. The new ERCS group would handle all questions and requests related to HR matters that fell outside the expertise of the outsource vendor.

ERCS thus handled higher complexity HR issues. Initially, cases flowed into ERCS electronically and were assigned to the next available consultant, similar to a first-in, first-out method. This approach required each of the consultants to be well versed in all types of employee relations issues and maintain a high level of skill variety. However, since the initial face to the customer was through an 800 number and handled by a third-party service provider, the ERCS had the feel of a call center despite its higher-level service offering. As a result, customers expected their requests to be addressed right away or within a very short period of time, even though the calls related to complex HR matters that often required input from internal legal counsel and other staff functions. This system added to the complexity and turnaround time of each case. Coupled with the high volume of cases received each day, the ERCS became a very stressful work environment. While the ERCs believed they were doing everything possible to satisfy the customers, the customers seemed to keep demanding more and pushing for faster turnaround times.

An internal OD consultant was called in to help ERCS address these problems. The consultant worked closely with the Assistant Vice President, Employee Relations, and a small group of ERCS members to understand the current situation. To help frame the diagnosis, an organization design model and various Six Sigma tools were used to create a survey that was sent out to the customer base that consisted of managers (70%), employees (20%), and HRGs in the business units, recruiters, and other third-party customers (representing the remaining 10%).

The results suggested that most customers were satisfied with ERCS's service with some opportunities for improvement. Many of the comments complimented the ERCs for their professionalism, expert knowledge, and personal touches like the follow-up call after a case had been closed. Respondents also liked the centralized ERCS model and agreed that it was smoother, more consistent, and reduced the risk of litigation. However, customers did want faster case-closure times, less "phone-tag," and a single point of contact for cases like progressive discipline that required follow-up. Hartford employees wanted someone in ERCS they could talk with who would listen and empathize with them; while the HRGs felt disconnected from their centralized counterparts in ERCS and the pertinent information they were receiving about trends in the HRGs' business units.

The OD consultant also interviewed the ERCs and observed their processes while talking with others in the organization to better understand what was working and what was not. Although the ERCs' jobs could be characterized as "moderately enriched," the relative levels of skill variety, task identity, and feedback were declining. Instead of working on a broad array of HR issues and forming relationships, the ERCs were focused on a steady stream of individual HR cases. Unlike the HRGs, the ERCs were not working with a particular business, but rather the "first-in, first-out" work assignment process lowered overall task identity since the ERCs might work with the property and casualty business on one case and the life insurance business on another. Finally, unless managers or employees got back to the ERCS on the outcome of the case, there was little feedback available. The volume of calls was high enough that it was hard for the ERCs to know what had happened after they had counseled the customer. In fact, following up with a customer and determining the level of satisfaction was not one of the metrics for which they were held accountable, and typically only unsatisfied customers would provide them with feedback. In addition, the ERCs missed a sense of appreciation from their customers. Their work had devolved to transaction processing and concentrating on how quickly they could answer/resolve a question.

While the centralized ERCS model made perfect sense from a business and risk-mitigation perspective, there was something missing from it. Surprisingly, the HRGs had similar misgivings. Many of them missed being involved with some of the now centralized employee relations issues that formerly helped them understand the pulse of the organization. As a result, the HRGs also wanted a consistent point of contact in the ERCS who could provide data on organizational trends. Thus, the HRGs wanted a relationship with the ERCs as much as the ERCs wanted one with them.

Based on this diagnosis, and in collaboration with the Assistant Vice President and members of ERCS, a program of redesign and implementation was established. With respect to the workflow and organization design, the following changes were made:

- ERCS was reorganized by line of business and customer-type. This increased task identity and significance by associating an ERC with a particular business unit. As a result, the ERCs could develop a deeper-level expertise in and awareness of a particular business unit's operations while also monitoring trend data and proactively identifying potential problem areas with recommended solutions This had the benefit of addressing customers' request to have an ERC more closely aligned to their business, developing an intimate link between the ERCs, the unit business managers, and the HRGs deployed in the units, while increasing task significance and processing feedback. ERCs working with a particular business had more opportunity to understand how their work was affecting the organization and to hear about how their work was received while still being able to maintain a consistent approach and rationale for resolving cases. It is important to note that although ERCs appeared to be assigned to a particular line of business, due to tight capacity constraints, in case of a spike in volume, any of the ERCs could take on work from another line of business.
- ERCS also was reorganized by case complexity. This change created new roles (e.g., senior- and junior-level ERCs and subject-matter experts), increased skill variety, and identified a viable career path. ERCS could now leverage its consultants' skill set, knowledge, and capability based on the needs of the customer and the complexity of the case. For example, junior and senior ERCs could resolve a majority of the cases that came to ERCS. However, certain cases required a deep

level of knowledge or information that existed only in other departments of The Hartford. In these cases, additional research was needed. The subject-matter experts often had the experience to resolve an issue without having to go outside ERCS and/or the relationships necessary to acquire the information from other departments quickly. By capitalizing on subject-matter experts, such cases could be addressed immediately within ERCS. This deepened the skill variety and allowed subject-matter experts to have higher task significance and to add value to the process.

The ERCS created and enhanced a series of lateral linkages through governance and partnership councils. These forums were used to communicate the trends and other events transpiring within the business and/or within ERCS that were beneficial to the customer. Such sessions helped to close some of the communication gaps and allowed for a strengthened partnership between the ERCs and the HRGs, and provided another avenue to enhance skill variety and task identity.

In combination with other changes in structure, hiring, and metrics, the work of the ERCS was greatly enriched. In particular, the new organizational design aligned the internal workflow with the needs of the customer. It created appropriate lateral relationships and management practices to satisfy the task identity and task significance needs of the ERCs, the lines of business, and the HRGs. Overall, the changes improved the ERCs' job satisfaction and the quality and closure time of HR cases. Further monitoring of the effectiveness and efficiency of the new design continued to ensure its success or need for change.

14-2d Barriers to Job Enrichment

As the application of job enrichment has spread, a number of obstacles to significant job restructuring have been identified. Most of these barriers exist in the organizational context within which the job design is executed. Other organizational systems and practices, whether technical, managerial, or personnel, can affect both the implementation of job enrichment and the lifespan of whatever changes are made.

At least four organizational systems can constrain the implementation of job enrichment:[15]

1. **The technical system.** The technology of an organization can limit job enrichment by constraining the number of ways jobs can be changed. For example, long-linked technology like that found on an assembly line can be highly programmed and standardized, thus limiting the amount of employee discretion that is possible. Technology also may set an "enrichment ceiling." Some types of work, such as continuous-process production systems, may be naturally enriched so there is little more that can be gained from a job enrichment intervention.
2. **The human resource system.** Human resources systems can constrain job enrichment by creating formalized job descriptions that are rigidly defined and limit flexibility in changing people's job duties. For example, many union contracts include such narrowly defined job descriptions that major renegotiation between management and the union must occur before jobs can be significantly enriched.
3. **The control system.** Control systems, such as budgets, production reports, and accounting practices, can limit the complexity and challenge of jobs within the system. For example, a company working on a government contract may have such strict quality-control procedures that employee discretion is effectively curtailed.

4. **The supervisory system.** Supervisors determine to a large extent the amount of autonomy and feedback that subordinates can experience. To the extent that supervisors use autocratic methods and control work-related feedback, jobs will be difficult, if not impossible, to enrich.

Once these implementation constraints have been overcome, other factors determine whether the effects of job enrichment are strong and lasting.[16] Consistent with the contingency approach to OD, the staying power of job enrichment depends largely on how well it fits and is supported by other organizational practices, such as training, compensation, and supervision. These practices need to be congruent with jobs having high amounts of discretion, skill variety, and meaningful feedback.

14-2e Results of Job Enrichment

Hackman and Oldham reported data from the JDS on more than a thousand people in about a hundred different jobs in more than a dozen organizations.[17] In general, they found that employees whose jobs were high on the core dimensions were more satisfied and motivated than were those whose jobs were low on the dimensions. The core dimensions also were related to such behaviors as absenteeism and performance, although the relationship was not strong for performance. In addition, they found that responses were more positive for people with high growth needs than for those with weaker ones. Similarly, research has shown that enriched jobs are strongly related to mental ability.[18] Enriching the jobs of workers with low growth needs or with low knowledge and skills is more likely to produce frustration than satisfaction.

An impressive amount of research has been done on Hackman and Oldham's approach to job enrichment. In addition, a number of studies have extended and refined their approach, including a modification of the original JDS instrument to produce more reliable data[19] and the incorporation of other moderators such as the need for achievement and job longevity.[20] In general, research has supported the proposed relationships between job characteristics and outcomes, including the moderating effects of growth needs, knowledge and skills, and context satisfaction.[21] In regard to context satisfaction, for example, research indicates that employee turnover, dissatisfaction, and withdrawal are associated with dark offices, a lack of privacy, and high worker densities.[22]

Reviews of the job enrichment research also report positive effects. An analysis of 28 studies concluded that the job characteristics are positively related to job satisfaction, particularly for people with high growth needs.[23] Another review concluded that job enrichment is effective at reducing employee turnover.[24] A different examination of 28 job enrichment studies reported overwhelmingly positive results.[25] Improvements in quality and cost measures were reported slightly more frequently than improvements in employee attitudes and quantity of production. However, the studies suffered from methodological weaknesses that suggest that the positive findings should be viewed with some caution. Another review of 16 job enrichment studies showed mixed results; 13 of the programs were developed and implemented solely by management.[26] These 16 studies showed significant reduction in absenteeism, turnover, and grievances, and improvements in production quality in only about half of the cases where these variables were measured. The three studies with high levels of employee participation in the change program showed improvements in these variables in all cases where they were measured. Although it is difficult to generalize from such a small number of studies, employee participation in the job enrichment program appears to enhance the success of such interventions.

Finally, a comprehensive meta-analysis of more than 75 empirical studies of the Hackman and Oldham model found modest support for the overall model.[27] Although some modifications to the model appear warranted, the studies suggested that many of the more substantive criticisms were unfounded. For example, research supported the conclusion that the relationships between core job characteristics and psychological outcomes were stronger and more consistent than the relationships between core job dimensions and work performance, although these latter relationships did exist and were meaningful. The researchers also found support for the proposed linkages among core job dimensions, critical psychological states, and psychological outcomes. It is interesting that the job feedback dimension emerged as the strongest and most consistent predictor of both psychological and behavioral work outcomes. The researchers suggested that of all job characteristics, increasing feedback had the most potential for improving work productivity and satisfaction. The role of growth needs strength as a moderator was also supported, especially between core dimensions and work performance. Clearly, research supporting the job enrichment model is plentiful. Although the evidence suggests that the model is not perfect, it does appear to be a reasonable guide to improving the motivational outcomes of work.

14-3 The Sociotechnical Systems Approach

The sociotechnical systems (STS) approach is currently the most extensive body of scientific and applied work underlying employee involvement and innovative work designs. Its techniques and design principles derive from extensive action research in both public and private organizations across diverse national cultures. This section reviews the conceptual foundations of the STS approach and then describes its most popular application: self-managed work teams.

14-3a Conceptual Background

Sociotechnical systems theory was developed originally at the Tavistock Institute of Human Relations in London and has spread to most industrialized nations in a little more than 60 years.[28] In Europe and particularly Scandinavia, STS interventions are almost synonymous with work design and employee involvement. In Canada and the United States, STS concepts and methods underlie many of the innovative work designs and team-based structures that are so prevalent in contemporary organizations. Intel, United Technologies, General Mills, and Procter & Gamble are among the many organizations applying the STS approach to transforming how work is designed and performed.

STS theory is based on two fundamental premises: that an organization or work unit is a combined, social-plus-technical system (sociotechnical), and that this system is open in relation to its environment.[29]

Sociotechnical System The first assumption suggests that whenever human beings are organized to perform tasks, a joint system is operating—a sociotechnical system. This system consists of two independent but related parts: a social part, including the people performing the tasks and the relationships among them; and a technical part, including the tools, techniques, and methods for task performance. These two parts are independent of each other because each follows a different set of behavioral laws. The social part operates according to biological and psychosocial laws, whereas the technical part functions according to mechanical and physical laws. Nevertheless, the two parts are related because they must act together to accomplish tasks. Hence, the term "sociotechnical" signifies the joint relationship that must occur between the social and the technical parts, and the word "system" communicates that this connection results in a unified whole.

Because a sociotechnical system is composed of social and technical parts, it follows that it will produce two kinds of outcomes: products, such as goods and services; and social and psychological consequences, such as job satisfaction and commitment. The key issue is how to design the relationship between the two parts so that both outcomes are positive (referred to as "joint optimization"). Sociotechnical practitioners design work and organizations so that the social and technical parts work well together, producing high levels of product and human satisfaction. This effort contrasts with the engineering approach to designing work, which focuses on the technical component, worries about fitting in people later, and often leads to mediocre performance at high social costs. The STS approach also contrasts with the motivational approach, which views work design in terms of human fulfillment and that can lead to satisfied employees but inefficient work processes.

Environmental Relationship The second major premise underlying STS theory is that such systems are open to their environments. As discussed in Chapter 5, open systems must interact with their environments to survive and develop. The environment provides the STS with necessary inputs of energy, raw materials, and information, and the STS provides the environment with products and services. The key issue here is how to design the interface between the STS and its environment so that the system has sufficient freedom to function while exchanging effectively with the environment. In what is typically called "boundary management," STS practitioners structure environmental relationships both to protect the system from external disruptions and to facilitate the exchange of necessary resources and information. This enables the STS to adapt to changing conditions and to influence the environment in favorable directions.

In summary, STS theory suggests that effective work systems jointly optimize the relationship between their social and technical parts. Moreover, such systems effectively manage the boundary separating and relating them to the environment. This allows them to exchange with the environment while protecting themselves from external disruptions.

14-3b Self-Managed Work Teams

The most prevalent application of the STS approach is self-managed work teams. Alternatively referred to as self-directed, self-regulating, or high-performance work teams, these work designs consist of members performing interrelated tasks.[30] Self-managed teams typically are responsible for a complete product or service, or a major part of a larger production process. They control members' task behaviors and make decisions about task assignments and work methods. In many cases, the team sets its own production goals within broader organizational guides and may be responsible for support services, such as maintenance, purchasing, and quality control. Team members generally are expected to learn many if not all of the jobs within the team's control and frequently are paid on the basis of knowledge and skills rather than seniority. When pay is based on performance, team, rather than individual performance, is the standard.

Self-managed work teams are being implemented at a rapid rate across a range of industries and organizations, such as Intel, Boeing, General Mills, General Electric, and Motorola. A 2006 survey of *Fortune* 1000 companies found that 65% of these firms were using self-managed work teams, a small decrease compared to the 2001 data, but a 40% increase from 1987.[31] Although this work design typically does not cover a majority of the workforce, this represents an impressive increase in the use of self-managed teams.

FIGURE 14.3

Model of Self-Managed Work Teams

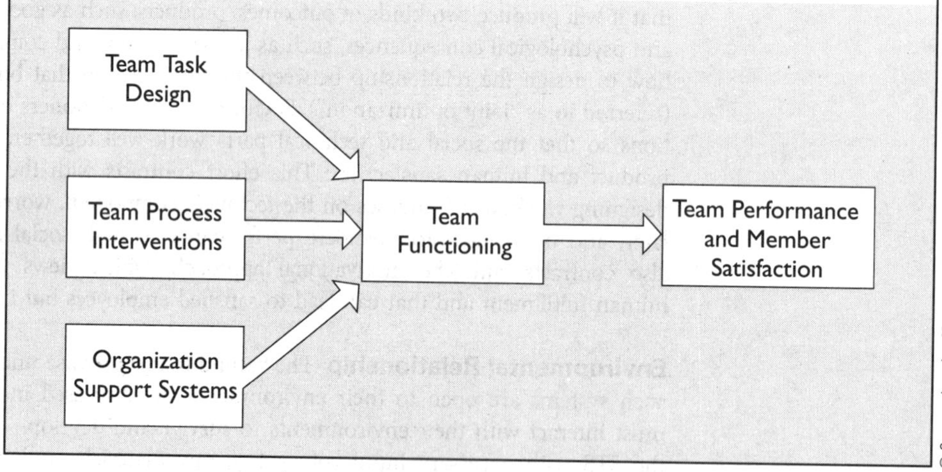

Figure 14.3 is a model explaining how self-managed work teams perform.[32] It summarizes current STS research and shows how teams can be designed for high performance. Although the model is based mainly on experience with teams that perform the daily work of the organization (work teams), it also has relevance to other team designs, such as problem-solving teams, management teams, cross-functional integrating teams, and employee involvement teams. The model shows that team performance and member satisfaction follow directly from how well the team functions: how well members communicate and coordinate with each other, resolve conflicts and problems, and make and implement task-relevant decisions. Team functioning, in turn, is influenced by three major inputs: team task design, team process interventions, and organization support systems. Because these inputs affect how well teams function and subsequently perform, they are key intervention targets for designing and implementing self-managed work teams.

Team Task Design Self-managed work teams are responsible for performing particular tasks; consequently, how the team is designed for task performance can have a powerful influence on how well it functions. Task design generally follows from the team's mission and goals that define the major purpose of the team and provide direction for task achievement. When a team's mission and goals are closely aligned with business strategy and objectives, members can see how team performance contributes to organization success. This can increase member commitment to team goals.

Team task design links members' behaviors to task requirements and to each other. It structures member interactions and performances. Three task-design elements are necessary for creating self-managed work teams: task differentiation, boundary control, and task control.[33] Task differentiation involves the extent to which the team's task is autonomous and forms a relatively self-completing whole. High levels of task differentiation provide an identifiable team boundary and a clearly defined area of team responsibility. At Johnsonville Sausage, for example, self-managed teams comprise 7–14 members each. Each team is large enough to accomplish a set of interrelated tasks but small enough to allow face-to-face meetings for coordination and decision making. In many hospitals, self-managed nursing teams are formed around interrelated tasks that together produce a relatively whole piece of work. Thus, nursing teams may be responsible for particular groups of patients, such as those in intensive care or undergoing cancer treatments, or they may be accountable for specific work processes, such as those in the laboratory, pharmacy, or admissions office.

Boundary control involves the extent to which team members can influence transactions with their task environment—the types and rates of inputs and outputs. Adequate boundary control includes a well-defined work area; group responsibility for boundary-control decisions, such as quality assurance (which reduces dependence on external boundary regulators, such as inspectors); and members sufficiently trained to perform tasks without relying heavily on external resources. Boundary control often requires deliberate cross-training of team members to take on a variety of tasks. This makes members highly flexible and adaptable to changing conditions. It also reduces the need for costly overhead because members can perform many of the tasks typically assigned to staff experts, such as those in quality control, planning, and maintenance.

Task control involves the degree to which team members can regulate their own behavior to provide services or to produce finished products. It includes the freedom to choose work methods, to schedule activities, and to influence production goals to match both environmental and task demands. Task control relies heavily on team members having the power and authority to manage equipment, materials, and other resources needed for task performance. This "work authority" is essential if members are to take responsibility for getting the work accomplished. Task control also requires that team members have accurate and timely information about team performance to enable them to detect performance problems and to make necessary adjustments.

Task control enables self-managed work teams to observe and control technical variances as quickly and as close to their source as possible. Technical variances arise from the production process and represent significant deviations from specific goals or standards. In manufacturing, for example, abnormalities in raw material, machine operation, and workflow are sources of variance that can adversely affect the quality and quantity of the finished product. In service work, out-of-the-ordinary requests, special favors or treatment, or unique demands create variances that can place stress on the work process. Technical variances traditionally are controlled by support staff and managers, but this can take time and add greatly to costs. Self-managed work teams, on the other hand, have the freedom, skills, and information needed to control technical variances online when they occur. This affords timely responses to production problems and reduces the amount of staff overhead needed.

Team Process Interventions A second key input to team functioning involves team process interventions. As described in Chapter 10, teams may develop ineffective social processes that impede functioning and performance, such as poor communication among members, dysfunctional roles and norms, and faulty problem solving and decision making. Team process interventions, such as process consultation and team building, can resolve such problems by helping members address process problems and moving the team to a more mature stage of development. Because self-managed work teams need to be self-reliant, members generally acquire their own team process skills. They may attend appropriate training programs and workshops or they may learn on the job by working with OD practitioners to conduct process interventions on their own teams. Although members' process skills generally are sufficient to resolve most of the team's process problems, OD experts occasionally may need to supplement the team's skills and help members address problems that they are unable to resolve.

Organization Support Systems The final input to team functioning is the extent to which the larger organization is designed to support self-managed work teams.

The success of such teams clearly depends on support systems that are quite different from traditional methods of managing.[34] For example, a bureaucratic, mechanistic organization is not highly conducive to self-managed teams. An organic structure, with flexibility among units, relatively few formal rules and procedures, and decentralized authority, is much more likely to support and enhance the development of self-managed work teams. This explains why such teams are so prevalent in high-involvement organizations (described in Chapter 13). Their different features, such as flat, lean structures, open information systems, and team-based selection and reward practices, all reinforce teamwork and responsible self-management.

A particularly important support system for self-managed work teams is the external leadership. Self-managed teams exist along a spectrum ranging from having only mild influence over their work to near-autonomy. In many circumstances, such teams take on a variety of functions traditionally handled by management. These can include assigning members to individual tasks, determining the methods of work, scheduling, setting production goals, and selecting and rewarding members. These activities do not make external supervision obsolete, however. That leadership role usually is changed to two major functions: working with and developing team members, and assisting the team in managing its boundaries.[35]

Working with and developing team members is a difficult process and requires a different style of managing than do traditional systems. The team leader (often called a team facilitator) helps team members organize themselves in a way that enables them to become more independent and responsible. He or she must be familiar with team-building approaches and must assist members in learning the skills to perform their jobs. Recent research suggests that the leader needs to provide expertise in self-management.[36] This may include encouraging team members to be self-reinforcing about high performance, to be self-critical of low performance, to set explicit performance goals, to evaluate goal achievement, and to rehearse different performance strategies before trying them.

If team members are to maintain sufficient autonomy to control variance from goal attainment, the leader may need to help them manage team boundaries. Where teams have limited control over their task environment, the leader may act as a buffer to reduce environmental uncertainty. This can include mediating and negotiating with other organizational units, such as higher management, staff experts, and related work teams. Research suggests that better managers spend more time in these lateral interfaces.[37]

These new leadership roles require new and different skills, including knowledge of sociotechnical principles and group dynamics, understanding of both the task environment and the team's technology, and ability to intervene in the team to help members increase their knowledge and skills. Leaders of self-managed teams also should have the ability to counsel members and to facilitate communication among them.

Many managers have experienced problems trying to fulfill the complex demands of leading self-managed work teams. The most typical complaints mention ambiguity about responsibilities and authority, lack of personal and technical skills and organizational support, insufficient attention from higher management, and feelings of frustration in the supervisory job.[38] Attempts to overcome these problems have been made in the following areas:[39]

1. **Recruitment and selection.** Recruitment has been directed at selecting team leaders with a balanced mixture of technical and social skills. Those with extensive technical experience have been paired with more socially adept leaders so that both can share skills and support each other.
2. **Training.** Extensive formal and on-the-job training in human relations, group dynamics, and leadership styles has been instituted for leaders of self-managed work teams. Such training is aimed at giving leaders concepts for understanding

their roles, as well as hands-on experience in team building, process consultation, and third-party intervention (see Chapter 10).

3. **Evaluation and reward systems.** Attempts have been made to tie team leader rewards to achievements in team development. Leaders prepare developmental plans for individual workers and the team as a whole, and set measurable benchmarks for progress. Performance appraisals of leaders are conducted within a group format, with feedback supplied by team members, peers, and higher-level management.
4. **Leadership support systems.** Leaders of self-managed work teams have been encouraged to develop peer support groups. Team leaders can meet off-site to share experiences and to address issues of personal and general concern.
5. **Use of freed-up time.** Team leaders have been provided with a mixture of strategies to apply their talents beyond the immediate work team. A team leader has more time when the team has matured and taken on many managerial functions. In those cases, team leaders have been encouraged to become involved in such areas as higher-level planning and budgeting, companywide training and development, and individual career development.

14-3c Application Stages

STS work designs have been implemented in a variety of settings, including manufacturing firms, hospitals, schools, and government agencies. Although the specific implementation strategy is tailored to the situation, a common method of change underlies many of these applications. It generally involves high employee participation in work design and implementation. Such participative work design enables employees to translate their special knowledge of the work situation into relevant designs, and employees with ownership over the design process are likely to be highly committed to implementing the outcomes.[40]

STS applications generally proceed in six steps:[41]

1. **Sanctioning the design effort.** At this step, workers receive the necessary sanction and support to diagnose their work system and to create an appropriate work design. In many unionized situations, top management and union officials jointly agree to suspend temporarily the existing work rules and job classifications so that employees have the freedom to explore new ways of working. Management also may provide workers with sufficient time and external help to diagnose their work system and to devise alternative work structures. In cases of redesigning existing work systems, normal production demands may be reduced during the redesign process. Also, workers may be given some job and wage security so that they feel free to try new designs without fear of losing their jobs or money.
2. **Diagnosing the work system.** This step includes analyzing the work system to discover how it is operating. Knowledge of existing operations (or of intended operations, in the case of a new work system) is the basis for creating an appropriate work design. STS practitioners have devised diagnostic models applicable to work systems that make products or deliver services. The models analyze a system's technical and social parts and assess how well the two fit each other. The task environment facing the system also is analyzed to see how well it is meeting external demands, such as customer quality requirements.
3. **Generating appropriate designs.** Based on the diagnosis, the work system is redesigned to fit the situation. Although this typically results in self-managed work teams, it is important to emphasize that the diagnosis may reveal that tasks are not very interdependent and that an individual-job work design, such as an enriched job, might be more appropriate. Two important STS principles guide the design process.

The first principle, compatibility, suggests that the process of designing work should fit the values and objectives underlying the approach. For example, the major goals of STS design are joint optimization and boundary management. A work-design process compatible with those objectives would be highly participative, involving those having a stake in the work design, such as employees, managers, engineers, and staff experts. They would jointly decide how to create the social and technical components of work, as well as the environmental exchanges. This participative process increases the likelihood that design choices will be based simultaneously on technical, social, and environmental criteria. How well the compatibility guideline is adhered to can determine how well the work design subsequently is implemented.[42]

The second design principle is called minimal critical specification. It suggests that STS designers should specify only those critical features needed to implement the work design. All other features of the design should be left free to vary with the circumstances. In most cases, minimal critical specification identifies what is to be done, not how it will be accomplished. This allows employees considerable freedom to choose work methods, task allocations, and job assignments to match changing conditions.

The output of this design step specifies the new work design. In the case of self-managed teams, this includes the team's mission and goals, an ideal work flow, the skills and knowledge required of team members, a plan for training members to meet those requirements, and a list of the decisions the team will make now as well as the ones it should make over time as members develop greater skills and knowledge.

4. **Specifying support systems.** As suggested above, organizational support systems may have to be changed to support new work designs. When self-managed teams are designed, for example, the basis for pay and measurement systems may need to change from individual to team performance to facilitate necessary task interaction among workers.
5. **Implementing and evaluating the work designs.** This stage involves making necessary changes to implement the work design and evaluating the results. For self-managing teams, implementation generally requires a great amount of training so that workers gain the necessary technical and social skills to perform multiple tasks and to control task behaviors. It also may entail developing the team through various team-building and process-consultation activities. OD practitioners often help team members carry out these tasks with a major emphasis on helping them gain competence in this area. Evaluation of the work design is necessary both to guide the implementation process and to assess the overall effectiveness of the design. In some cases, the evaluation information suggests the need for further diagnosis and redesign efforts.
6. **Continual change and improvement.** This last step points out that STS designing never is complete but rather continues as new things are learned and new conditions are encountered. Thus, the ability to design and redesign work continually needs to be built into existing work designs. Members must have the skills and knowledge to assess their work unit continually and to make necessary changes and improvements. From this view, STS designing rarely results in a stable work design but instead provides a process for modifying work continually to fit changing conditions and to make performance improvements.

Application 14.2 describes how WI, Inc. implemented self-managed teams.[43] It shows that a medium-sized company, with strong leadership and a progressive human resource function, can significantly improve its competitive position through workplace change. It clearly demonstrates the importance of aligning organizational systems to support self-management as well as the wisdom of including employees in the change process.

application 14.2

DEVELOPING SELF-MANAGED TEAMS AT WI, INC.

WI, Inc. is a privately owned, medium-sized manufacturer of audible, visual, and voice-action message products. It employs about 350 people called "associates," with about 220 working in manufacturing and the rest in sales, customer service, and administrative functions. WI is a global supplier of message products, which must meet high standards of performance, reliability, and quality. The company enjoyed a strong market niche in leading-edge products but faced stiff competition from much larger, more capitalized firms. To increase market share, improve performance, and lower costs, WI set out to redesign work and to create an organizational culture that promoted teamwork, participative decision making, and continuous improvement.

Spearheaded by a progressive People Services or human resources department, this team-based initiative, called "Partners in Perfection" (PIP), took about three years to complete. From the start, it had strong support and commitment from WI's CEO and major stockholder, the grandson of the firm's founder. Educated in business, engineering, and psychology, he saw the human resources function as a strategic partner and essential to achieving his vision of a "participatory, team-centered climate" at WI.

PIP started with a series of small-group sessions spread over several weeks. Led by the CEO and People Services, these sessions brought together manufacturing associates and asked them two questions: "What's happening?" and "How can we collectively continuously improve?" Associates expressed their answers in an open forum, and their feedback was summarized on flipcharts that were posted on the company cafeteria walls for several weeks. This enabled manufacturing associates to see the responses from all of the sessions and to add to them if they desired. People Services then summarized the feedback into common themes, which revealed associates' willingness to become involved in WI's growth and "become a part of the solution." Specifically, they wanted to be involved in decision making, to continuously improve products, processes, and customer service, to develop themselves, to better balance work and home life, and to decrease costs, especially the rising price of health care benefits.

Next, the PIP initiative turned to designing self-managed work teams. They were organized around natural work units, either assembly line or functional department, such as paint shop, maintenance, and warehouse. In total, 16 teams of between 5 and 16 associates were created across two shifts of operation. Each team created an operating charter spelling out its major tasks, responsibilities, and objectives. Teams met formally at least every two weeks to discuss PIP progress and emergent issues and to devise action plans with specific deliverables. Over time, teams took on more and more tasks, decisions, and responsibilities, as members gained skills and expertise and teams showed through their performance that they could function effectively. For example, manufacturing teams did their own work scheduling, job assignments, quality and product inspection, inventory and material control, and certain preventive-maintenance functions. All teams worked with management on manpower planning, recommended their own budgets, checked results, and made necessary adjustments. They identified training needs, monitored their own attendance, vacation time, illness-injury, and continuously improved work processes and methods in line with industry standards and codes.

To facilitate PIP implementation, People Services created a corporate Enrichment Center to train associates in the skills and knowledge needed to develop self-managed teams and to continually improve products and processes. Based on a preliminary skills assessment, it was determined that members had the expertise for task performance but lacked team facilitation skills. Thus, initial training involved a four-day team-building course that all associates were required to attend. Those who passed the course and showed interest in becoming a team facilitator could take an advanced, two-day team-building course. Eventually both courses were required for all new associates. The Enrichment Center gradually developed a variety of courses and associates were required to spend a minimum of 40 hours per year gaining new skills and knowledge. These courses ranged from technical skills, such as forklift operations and blueprint reading, to team skills related to goal setting and conflict resolution, to improvement skills, such as Six Sigma and quality improvement, to basic skills, such as math and English as a second language. Given the extensive training need for PIP, WI applied for and received over $2 million in training funds from State Department of Labor.

A major goal of PIP was to become an employer of choice and attract talented people who would fit into the participative, team-based culture. Teams had to be comfortable with new hires because they would be working closely with them. Thus, People Services developed a recruitment and selection process that involved team members. Associates attended job fairs, helped to create and hold open-house recruitment days, and learned job-interviewing skills. A team with an open job would review applications, choose those to interview, and with the help of People Services, prescreen applicants by telephone and interview in person those who matched certain criteria. Then, the team would send the paperwork for its recommended hire to its department coach or advisor and People Services. Final job offers were made by People Services and a team member who had been involved in the interview process.

WI's existing reward system was geared to contractual wage scales of individual jobs. Because it was not performance-driven and worked at cross-purposes to PIP's team orientation, People Services worked with associates to create a system that rewarded team performance as well as member contributions. One component of the system tied rewards to measures of team productivity, quality, customer satisfaction, and attendance. Teams were rated on these measures and the top three teams were financially rewarded monthly. A second part of the system involved a gain-sharing program in which associates' were rewarded bi-weekly for measurable gains above standards of productivity and quality. A third part of the incentive system recognized individual associates for outstanding contributions to performance, helpfulness, development, and coaching. Peers nominated associates, a cross-functional committee assessed nominees, and winners received small but meaningful gifts at a monthly recognition event.

Finally, People Services worked with associates to address problems that had plagued the company for years. One area concerned safety and the need to reduce workers' compensation costs. Associates attended training sessions on worker safety and a safety committee was formed to assess current safety practices, to recommend improvements, and to recognize teams that made significant progress. Another area involved work-life balance and the need to help associates better manage this interface. This led to a variety of programs, such as parenting and financial planning workshops, employee assistance activities, holiday events for families, a service award dinner, and flextime work hours. Still another area involved health and wellness with the need to reduce escalating health insurance premiums. A company survey revealed that associates' attention to their health and wellness was abysmal and an aggressive initiative was implemented to turn things around. It included a lunch and learn program, periodic health and wellness fairs, and regular screening for blood pressure, cholesterol, and the like, and assessment of work habits and conditions by health professional and recommendations for improvement.

In a little over three years, the PIP intervention produced significant results. Associates' productivity increased from 85% to 114%, based on company standards and excluding increases due to new equipment and machinery. Voluntary turnover went from 33% to less than 5%, while daily absenteeism dropped from 18% to 1%. On-time delivery rose from 78% to 93%, while quality prior to final inspection increased from approximately 86% to 99%. Health care premiums stayed steady in year 3 and decreased in year 4 saving the company more than $1 million. The incurred cost of worker's compensation was reduced by 4.68% and the loss ratio by 9.93%. The product development cycle decreased time from 76 process activities to 26. Global sales increased more than 35%.

Deservedly, WI, Inc. has received numerous national and statewide awards. Professional associations, such as the Society for Human Resource Management, the John J. Heldrich Center for Workforce Development, and the New Jersey Business and Industry Association, have publically recognized the company for innovative human resource practices, economic development, and workplace education.

14-3d Results of Self-Managed Teams

Research on STS design efforts is extensive. Over 20 years ago, a bibliography by researchers at Eindhoven University of Technology in The Netherlands found 3,082 English-language studies.[44] Today, we estimate the number of publications to be significantly higher. As with reports on job enrichment, most of the published reports on self-managed teams show favorable results.[45]

A series of famous case studies at General Foods' Gaines Pet Food/Topeka plant, the Saab-Scania engine assembly plant, and Volvo's Kalmar and Uddevalla plants provide one set of positive findings.[46] In each case, productivity and other technical measures of efficiency and quality improved significantly. In addition, measures of job satisfaction and other attitudes also improved. Perhaps most importantly, these improvements were sustained over time.

A second set of studies supporting the positive impact of sociotechnical design teams comes from research comparing self-managed teams with other interventions. For example, a longitudinal study of self-managed teams conducted in a Midwestern U.S. food-processing plant found that one year after start-up, production was 133% higher than originally planned, start-up costs were 7.7% lower than expected, and employee attitudes were extremely positive about the change.[47] This study also permitted a comparison of self-managed teams with job enrichment, which occurred in another department of the company. Both interventions included survey feedback. The self-managing project involved technological changes, whereas the job enrichment program did not. The results showed that the interventions had similar positive effects in terms of employee attitudes, but only the self-managing intervention had significant improvements in productivity and costs. Thus, the productivity improvements may not be attributed solely to the self-managed teams but might also be the result of the technological changes.

A third set of positive results comes from reviews, or meta-analyses, of self-managed team studies. One review examined 16 studies and showed that when productivity, costs, and quality were measured, improvements occurred in more than 85% of the cases.[48] Significant reductions in employee turnover and absenteeism rates and improvements in employee attitudes were reported in about 70% of the cases where these variables were measured. Certain methodological weaknesses in the studies suggest, however, that the positive results should be viewed carefully. Another review of 12 studies of self-managed teams showed improvements in hard performance measures in about 67% of the cases where such measures were taken.[49] Both of these reviews also included job enrichment studies, as reported earlier in this chapter. The relative impact of self-managing groups seems about equal to that of job enrichment, especially when the latter includes worker participation in the design process.

Three more recent meta-analyses also provide general support for self-managed teams. In a review of all STS work-design studies conducted in the 1970s, researchers found a strong positive relationship between the installation of self-managed teams and attitudinal and economic gains.[50] These work designs were found to increase employee satisfaction, to reduce production costs through group member innovations, and to decrease absenteeism, turnover, and accident rates. The researchers reported little evidence for claims of increased productivity primarily because of the lack of sufficient reported data. In a comprehensive meta-analysis, researchers concluded that self-managed teams do produce increases in productivity and reductions in escape behavior, such as absenteeism, but that these effects varied widely. Higher results were associated with high levels of work-group autonomy, supporting changes in the reward system, interventions that did not include technological changes, and applications outside of the United States.[51] Finally, a detailed and comprehensive meta-analysis of 131 North American field experiments reported that self-managed teams (called autonomous and semiautonomous work groups in the study) were more likely to have a positive impact on financial-performance measures, including costs, productivity, and quality, than on behavioral or attitudinal variables.[52] Considerable variation in the size of the positive effect, however, led the researchers to suggest that changes in other organization components may be needed to support the teams. Only when other organizational features, such as reward systems, information systems, and performance appraisal systems changed simultaneously, was the probability of positive results increased.

Although the majority of studies report positive effects of self-managing groups, some research suggests a more mixed assessment. A field experiment studying the long-term effects of self-managed teams showed improvements in job satisfaction but no effects on job motivation, work performance, organizational commitment, mental health, or voluntary turnover.[53] The company did lower indirect overhead costs, however, by reducing the number of supervisors. This study, which received an award from the Academy of Management for quality research, concluded that the major benefits of self-managed teams are economic, deriving from the need for less supervision. Another study found that the introduction of self-managed teams into an independent insurance agency threatened the personal control and autonomy of individual employees.[54] The teams, which were implemented without employee participation, exerted strong pressures on insurance agents to follow rigid procedures. Group leaders focused on the concerns of younger, inexperienced employees and ignored older workers' requests for less red tape and more freedom. The older employees felt that the groups undermined their individual discretion, autonomy, and initiative. The study concluded that unless self-managed teams are implemented and managed properly, individual members' autonomy and motivation can be constrained inadvertently.

A rigorous field experiment in a telecommunications company compared self-managed teams with traditionally designed work groups performing the same types of tasks.[55] The study found that self-managed teams scored significantly higher than traditional work groups in job satisfaction, growth-needs satisfaction, social-needs satisfaction, and group satisfaction. Self-managing group members and higher-level managers perceived group performance as superior to traditionally managed groups. In contrast to these attitudinal and perceptual findings, however, objective measures of service quality and customer satisfaction did not differ between the two types of groups. A similar study of 952 British firms across 12 industries found that team-based work designs, in contrast to nonteam forms of work, were associated with higher financial performance; however, there was no difference in financial performance between teams that were self-managed and those that were not.[56] This finding suggests that the team or coordination aspect of self-managed teams may contribute more to performance than the self-control part.

Finally, a growing number of studies are examining the mechanisms through which self-managed teams achieve positive outcomes. For example, one study showed how turnover among self-managed team members led to decreases in team learning behavior and task flexibility, which, in turn, led to decreases in team effectiveness.[57] Another study found that in self-managed teams performing stable tasks, greater team structure was related to more information sharing, less conflict, and more psychological safety among members, which, in turn, promoted team learning and improvement.[58] Another study of self-managed teams showed that peer-based rational control, in which members perceive the distribution of economic rewards as dependent on teammates' behavior, was related to higher performance of both individuals and of the collective team.[59] This effect was particularly strong when normative control or cohesion among team members was low, suggesting that peer-based rational control may substitute for low normative control.

14-4 Designing Work for Technical and Personal Needs

This chapter has described three approaches to work design: engineering, motivational, and sociotechnical. Trade-offs and conflicts among the approaches must be recognized. The engineering approach produces traditional jobs and work groups and focuses on efficient performance. It downplays employee needs and emphasizes economic outcomes. The motivational approach designs jobs that are stimulating and demanding and highlights the importance of employee need satisfaction. Research suggests, however, that increased satisfaction may not generate improvements in productivity. Finally, the STS approach integrates social and technical aspects, but it may not be practical or appropriate in all situations.

In this final section, we attempt to integrate the three perspectives by providing a contingency framework that suggests that any of the three approaches can be effective when applied in the appropriate situations. Work design involves creating jobs and work groups for high levels of employee satisfaction and productivity. A large body of research shows that achieving such results depends on designing work to match specific factors operating in the work setting, factors that involve the technology for producing goods and services and the personal needs of employees. When work is designed to fit or match these factors, it is most likely to be both productive and humanly satisfying.

The technical and personal factors affecting work-design success provide a contingency framework for choosing among the four different kinds of work designs discussed in the chapter: traditional jobs, traditional work groups, enriched jobs, and self-managed teams.

14-4a Technical Factors

Two key dimensions can affect change on the shop floor: technical interdependence, or the extent to which cooperation among workers is required to produce a product or service; and technical uncertainty, or the amount of information processing and decision-making employees must do to complete a task.[60] In general, the degree of technical interdependence determines whether work should be designed for individual jobs or for work groups. When interdependence is low and there is little need for worker coordination—as, for example, in field sales and call centers—work can be designed for individual jobs. Conversely, when interdependence is high and employees must coordinate their task activities—as in technical processes like oil refining, assembly lines, and major surgery—work should be designed for groups composed of people performing interacting tasks.

The second dimension, technical uncertainty, determines whether work should be designed for external forms of control, such as supervision, scheduling, and standardization, or for worker self-control. When technical uncertainty is low and little information has to be processed by employees during task performance, work can be designed for external control, such as might be found on assembly lines and in other forms of repetitive work. On the other hand, when technical uncertainty is high and people must process more information and make decisions, work should be designed for high levels of employee self-control, such as might be found in professional work and hospital emergency rooms.

Figure 14.4 shows the different types of work designs that are most effective, from a purely technical perspective, for different combinations of interdependence and uncertainty. In quadrant 1, where technical interdependence and uncertainty are both low, such as might be found in call centers, jobs should be designed traditionally with limited amounts of employee interaction and self-control. When task interdependence is high but uncertainty is low (quadrant 2), such as work occurring on assembly lines, work should be designed for traditional work groups in which employee interaction is scheduled and self-control is limited. When technical interdependence is low but uncertainty

FIGURE 14.4

Work Designs That Optimize Technology

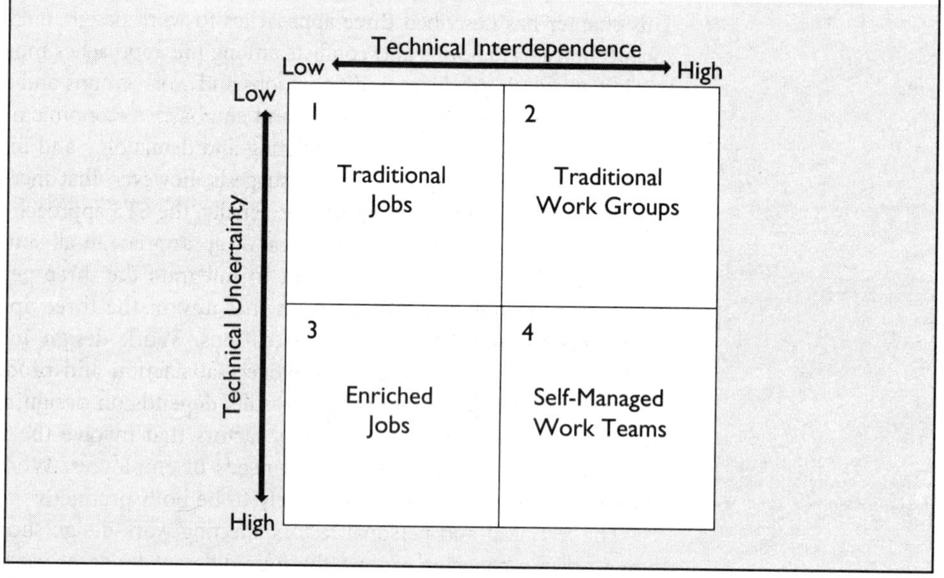

SOURCE: Reproduced by permission from T. Cummings, "Designing Work for Productivity and Quality of Work Life," *Outlook* 6 (1982): 39.

is high (quadrant 3), such as in field sales, work should be structured for individual jobs with internal forms of control, such as in enriched jobs. Finally, when both technical interdependence and uncertainty are high (quadrant 4), such as might be found in a continuous-process chemical plant, work should be designed for self-managed teams in which members have the multiple skills, discretion, and information necessary to control their interactions around the shared tasks.

These prescriptions for designing work to fit different technological conditions are rudimentary and more research is needed to refine them, especially since the nature of interdependence and uncertainty is likely to change, as work becomes more and more knowledge intense, information driven, and service oriented. A recent review and integration of work-design research identified two emergent perspectives that can help to extend work design to account for these changes in technology.[61] The relational perspective embeds work design in a social context and expands technical interdependence to include interactions across organizations, different forms of interdependence, and different methods for managing it. The proactive perspective grounds work design in opportunities for personal autonomy and initiative in changing work design. It expands uncertainty to include conditions that stimulate employees to proactively alter work design to meet changing conditions. We expect both streams of research gradually to inform how work-design interventions can be tailored to fit the organization's technology.

14-4b Personal-Need Factors

Most of the research identifying individual differences in work design has focused on selected personal traits. Two types of personal needs can influence the kinds of work designs that are most effective: social needs, or the desire for significant social relationships; and growth needs, or the desire for personal accomplishment, learning, and development.[62] In general, the degree of social needs determines whether work should be designed for individual jobs or work groups. People with low needs for social relationships are more likely to be satisfied working on individualized jobs than in interacting groups. Conversely, people with high social needs are more likely to be attracted to group forms of work than to individualized forms.

The second individual difference, growth needs, determines whether work designs should be routine and repetitive or complex and challenging. People with low growth needs generally are not attracted to jobs offering complexity and challenge (that is, enriched jobs) but are more satisfied performing routine forms of work that do not require high levels of decision making. On the other hand, people with high growth needs are satisfied with work offering high levels of discretion, skill variety, and meaningful feedback. Performing enriched jobs allows them to experience personal accomplishment and development.

It is often difficult for OD practitioners to accept that some people have low social and growth needs, particularly in light of the social and growth values underlying traditional OD practice. It is important to recognize, however, that individual differences do exist. Assuming that all people have high growth needs or want high levels of social interaction can lead to recommendations for enriched work or self-managed teams when they are not warranted.

It is important to emphasize that people who have low growth or social needs are not inferior to those placing a higher value on those factors; they simply are different. It is necessary also to recognize that people can change their needs through personal growth and experience. OD practitioners must be sensitive to individual differences in work design and careful not to force their own values on others. Many consultants, eager to be seen on the cutting edge of practice, recommend self-managed teams in all situations, without careful attention to technological and personal considerations.

Figure 14.5 shows the different types of work designs that are most effective for the various combinations of social and growth needs. When employees have relatively low social and growth needs (quadrant 1), traditional jobs are most effective. When employees

FIGURE 14.5

Work Designs That Optimize Personal Needs

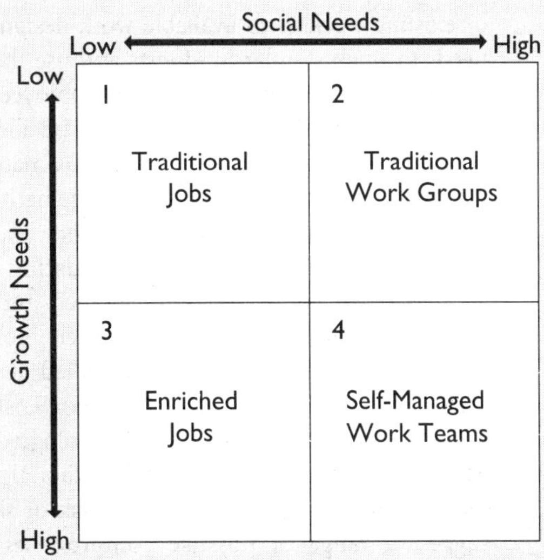

SOURCE: Reproduced by permission from T. Cummings, "Designing Work for Productivity and Quality of Work Life," *Outlook* 6 (1982): 40.

have high social needs but low growth (quadrant 2), traditional work groups, such as might be found on an assembly line, are most appropriate. These allow for some social interaction but limited amounts of challenge and discretion. When employees have low social needs but high growth needs (quadrant 3), enriched jobs are most satisfying. Here, work is designed for individual jobs that have high levels of task variety, discretion, and feedback about results. A research scientist's job is likely to be enriched, as is that of a skilled craftsperson. Finally, when employees have high social and growth needs (quadrant 4), work should be designed for self-managed teams that offer significant social interaction around complex and challenging tasks. A team of astronauts in a space shuttle resembles a self-managed work group, as does a group managing the control room of an oil refinery or a surgical team in a hospital unit.

14-4c Meeting Both Technical and Personal Needs

Jointly satisfying technical and human needs to achieve work-design success is likely to occur only in limited circumstances. When the technical conditions of a company's production processes (as shown in Figure 14.4) are compatible with the personal needs of its employees (as shown in Figure 14.5), the respective work designs combine readily and can satisfy both. On General Motors' assembly lines, for example, the technology is highly interdependent but low in uncertainty (quadrant 2 in Figure 14.4). Much of the production is designed around traditional work groups in which task behaviors are standardized and interactions among workers are scheduled. Such work is likely to be productive and fulfilling to the extent that General Motors' production workers have high social needs and low growth needs (quadrant 2 in Figure 14.5).

When technology and people are incompatible—for example, when an organization has quadrant 1 technology and quadrant 4 worker needs—at least two kinds of changes can be made to design work that satisfies both requirements.[63] One strategy is to change technology or people to bring them more into line with each other. This is a key point underlying STS approaches. For example, technical interdependence can be reduced by breaking long assembly lines into more discrete groups. In Sweden, Volvo redesigned the physical layout and technology for assembling automobiles and trucks to promote self-managed teams. Modifying people's needs is more complex and begins by matching new or existing workers to available work designs. For example, companies can assess workers' needs through standardized tests and use the information gleaned from them to select new employees or to counsel existing employees and help them locate jobs compatible with their needs. Similarly, employees can be allowed to volunteer for specific work designs—a common practice in STS projects. This matching process is likely to require high levels of trust and cooperation between management and workers, as well as a shared commitment to designing work for high performance and employee satisfaction.

A second strategy for accommodating both technical and human requirements is to leave the two components unchanged and create compromise work designs that only partially fulfill the demands of either component. The key issue is to decide to what extent one contingency will be satisfied at the expense of the other. For example, when capital costs are high relative to labor costs, such as in highly automated plants, work design is likely to favor the technology. Conversely, in many knowledge work jobs where labor is expensive relative to capital, organizations may design work for employee motivation and satisfaction at the risk of shortchanging the technology. These examples suggest a range of possible compromises based on different weightings of technical and human demands. Careful assessment of both types of contingencies and of the cost–benefit trade-offs is necessary to design an appropriate compromise work design.

Clearly, the strategy of designing work to bring technology and people more into line with each other is preferable to the compromise work-design strategy. Although the latter approach seems necessary when there are heavy constraints on changing the contingencies, in many cases those constraints are more imagined than real. The important thing is to understand the technical and personal factors existing in a particular situation and to design work accordingly. Traditional jobs and traditional work groups will be successful in certain situations (as shown in Figures 14.4 and 14.5); in other settings, enriched jobs and self-managed teams will be more effective.

SUMMARY

In this chapter, we discussed three different approaches to work design and described a contingency framework to determine the approach most likely to result in high productivity and worker satisfaction. The contingency framework reconciles the strengths and weaknesses of each approach. The engineering approach produces traditional jobs and traditional work groups. Traditional jobs are highly simplified and involve routine and repetitive forms of work with little coordination among people to produce a product or service. Traditional jobs achieve high productivity and worker satisfaction in situations characterized by low technical uncertainty and interdependence and low growth and social needs.

Traditional work groups are composed of members who perform routine yet interrelated tasks. Member interactions are controlled externally, usually supervisors, schedules, and rigid workflows. Traditional work groups are best suited to conditions of low technical uncertainty but high technical interdependence. They fit people with low growth needs but high social needs.

The motivational approach produces enriched jobs involving high levels of skill variety, task identity, task significance, autonomy, and feedback from the work itself. Enriched jobs achieve good results when the technology is uncertain but does not require high levels of coordination and when employees have high growth needs and low social needs.

Finally, the STS approach is associated with self-managed teams. These groups are composed of members performing interrelated tasks. Members are given the multiple skills, autonomy, and information necessary to control their own task behaviors with relatively little external control. Many OD practitioners argue that self-managed teams represent the work design of the 2000s because high levels of technical uncertainty and interdependence are prevalent in today's workplaces and because today's workers often have high growth and social needs.

NOTES

1. F. Taylor, *The Principles of Scientific Management* (New York: Harper & Row, 1911).
2. Ibid.
3. T. Cummings, "Self-Regulating Work Groups: A Socio-Technical Synthesis," *Academy of Management Review* 3 (1978): 625–34; G. Susman, *Autonomy at Work* (New York: Praeger, 1976); J. Slocum and H. Sims, "A Typology of Technology and Job Redesign," *Human Relations* 33 (1983): 193–212.
4. F. Herzberg, B. Mausner, and B. Snyderman, *The Motivation to Work* (New York: John Wiley & Sons, 1959); F. Herzberg and Z. Zautra, "Orthodox Job Enrichment: Measuring True Quality in Job Satisfaction," *Personnel* 53 (September–October 1976): 54–68.
5. R. Ford, *Motivation Through the Work Itself* (New York: American Management Association, 1969); W. Paul, K. Robertson, and F. Herzberg, "Job Enrichment Pays Off," *Harvard Business Review* 45 (March–April 1969): 61–78.
6. J. Hackman and G. Oldham, *Work Redesign* (Reading, MA: Addison-Wesley, 1980).
7. J. Hackman and G. Oldham, "Development of the Job Diagnostic Survey," *Journal of Applied Psychology* 60

(April 1975): 159–70; H. Sims, A. Szilagyi, and R. Keller, "The Measurement of Job Characteristics," *Academy of Management Journal* 19 (1976): 195–212.

8. Hackman and Oldham, *Work Redesign*; J. Hackman, G. Oldham, R. Janson, and K. Purdy, "A New Strategy for Job Enrichment," *California Management Review* 17 (Summer 1975): 57–71; R. Walters, *Job Enrichment for Results: Strategies for Successful Implementation* (Reading, MA: Addison-Wesley, 1975).
9. J. Hackman and G. Oldham, *The Diagnostic Survey: An Instrument for the Diagnosis of Jobs and the Evaluation of Job Redesign Projects*, Technical Report No. 4 (New Haven, CT: Yale University, Department of Administrative Sciences, 1974); Sims, Szilagyi, and Keller, "Measurement of Job Characteristics"; M. Campion, "The Multimethod Job Design Questionnaire," *Psychological Documents* 15 (1985): 1; J. Idaszak and F. Drasgow, "A Revision of the Job Diagnostic Survey: Elimination of a Measurement Artifact," *Journal of Applied Psychology* 72 (1987): 69–74.
10. E. Huse and M. Beer, "Eclectic Approach to Organizational Development," *Harvard Business Review* 49 (September–October 1971): 103–12.
11. A. Armenakis and H. Field, "Evaluation of Organizational Change Using Nonindependent Criterion Measures," *Personnel Psychology* 28 (Spring 1975): 39–44.
12. R. Ford, "Job Enrichment Lessons from AT&T," *Harvard Business Review* 51 (January–February 1973): 96–106.
13. R. Henkoff, "Make Your Office More Productive," *Fortune*, February 25, 1991, 84.
14. This application was developed and submitted by Darlene O'Connor. Her contribution is gratefully acknowledged.
15. G. Oldham and J. Hackman, "Work Design in the Organizational Context," in *Research in Organizational Behavior*, vol. 2, ed. B. Staw and L. Cummings (Greenwich, CT: JAI Press, 1980), 247–78; J. Cordery and T. Wall, "Work Design and Supervisory Practice: A Model," *Human Relations* 38 (1985): 425–41.
16. Hackman and Oldham, *Work Redesign*.
17. Ibid.
18. M. Campion, "Interdisciplinary Approaches to Job Design: A Constructive Replication with Extensions," *Journal of Applied Psychology* 73 (1988): 467–81.
19. C. Kulik, G. Oldham, and P. Langner, "Measurement of Job Characteristics: Comparison of the Original and the Revised Job Diagnostic Survey," *Journal of Applied Psychology* 73 (1988): 426–66; Idaszak and Drasgow, "Revision of the Job Diagnostic Survey."
20. R. Steers and D. Spencer, "The Role of Achievement Motivation in Job Design," *Journal of Applied Psychology* 62 (1977): 472–79; J. Champoux, "A Three-Sample Test of Some Extensions to the Job Characteristics Model," *Academy of Management Journal* 23 (1980): 466–78; R. Katz, "The Influence of Job Longevity on Employee Reactions to Task Characteristics," *Human Relations* 31 (1978): 703–25.
21. R. Zeffane, "Correlates of Job Satisfaction and Their Implications for Work Redesign," *Public Personnel Management* 23 (1994): 61–76.
22. G. Oldham and Y. Fried, "Employee Reactions to Workspace Characteristics," *Journal of Applied Psychology* 72 (1987): 75–80.
23. B. Loher, R. Noe, N. Moeller, and M. Fitzgerald, "A Meta-Analysis of the Relation of Job Characteristics to Job Satisfaction," *Journal of Applied Psychology* 70 (1985): 280–89.
24. B. McEvoy and W. Cascio, "Strategies for Reducing Employee Turnover: A Meta-Analysis," *Journal of Applied Psychology* 70 (1985): 342–53.
25. T. Cummings and E. Molloy, *Improving Productivity and the Quality of Work Life* (New York: Praeger, 1977).
26. J. Nicholas, "The Comparative Impact of Organization Development Interventions on Hard Criteria Measures," *Academy of Management Review* 7 (1982): 531–42.
27. Y. Fried and G. Ferris, "The Validity of the Job Characteristics Model: A Review and Meta-Analysis," *Personnel Psychology* 40 (1987): 287–322.
28. E. Trist and H. Murray, eds., *The Social Engagement of Social Science, Volume II: The Socio-Technical Perspective* (Philadelphia: University of Pennsylvania Press, 1993).
29. E. Trist, B. Higgin, H. Murray, and A. Pollock, *Organizational Choice* (London: Tavistock, 1963); T. Cummings and S. Srivastva, *Management of Work: A Socio-Technical Systems Approach* (San Diego: University Associates, 1977); W. Pasmore and J. Sherwood, eds., *Sociotechincal Systems: A Sourcebook* (San Diego: University Associates, 1978); A. Cherns, "Principles of Sociotechnical Design Revisited," *Human Relations* 40 (1987): 153–62.
30. Cummings, "Self-Regulating Work Groups"; Cummings and Srivastva, *Management of Work*; Susman, *Autonomy at Work*; H. Sims and C. Manz, "Conversations within Self-Managed Work Groups," *National Productivity Review* 1 (Summer 1982): 261–69; T. Cummings, "Designing Effective Work Groups," in *Handbook of Organizational Design: Remodeling Organizations and Their Environments*, vol. 2, ed. P. C. Nystrom and W. H. Starbuck (New York: Oxford University Press, 1981), 250–71; C. Manz, "Beyond Self-Managing Teams: Toward Self-Leading Teams in the Workplace," in *Research in Organizational Change and Development*, vol. 4, ed. W. Pasmore and R. Woodman (Greenwich, CT: JAI Press, 1990), 273–99; C. Manz and H. Sims Jr., "Leading Workers to Lead Themselves: The External Leadership of Self-Managed Work Teams," *Administrative Science Quarterly* 32 (1987): 106–28.

31. Center for Effective Organizations, "Survey of Organization Improvement Efforts" (Los Angeles: Center for Effective Organizations, 2006); E. Lawler, *Organizing for High Performance: Employee Involvement, TQM, Reengineering, and Knowledge Management in the Fortune 1000* (San Francisco: Jossey-Bass, 2001).
32. Cummings, "Self-Regulating Work Groups;" G. Stewart, C. Manz, and H. Sims, *Team Work and Group Dynamics* (New York: John Wiley, 1999); J. R. Hackman, "The Design of Work Teams," in *Handbook of Organizational Behavior*, ed. J. Lorsch (New York: Prentice Hall, 1986), 315–42; S. Cohen, G. Ledford, and G. Spreitzer, "A Predictive Model of Self-Managing Team Effectiveness," *Human Relations* 49 (1996): 643–76; P. Goodman, ed., *Designing Effective Work Groups* (San Francisco: Jossey-Bass, 1986); P. G. Herbst, *Autonomous Group Functioning* (London: Tavistock Publications, 1962).
33. Cummings, "Self-Regulating Work Groups."
34. Cummings, "Self-Regulating Work Groups"; J. Pearce II and E. Ravlin, "The Design Activation of Self-Regulating Work Groups," *Human Relations* 40 (1987): 751–82; J. R. Hackman, "The Design of Work Teams," in *Handbook of Organizational Behavior*, ed. J. Lorsch (Englewood Cliffs, NJ: Prentice Hall, 1987), 315–42.
35. Ibid.
36. C. Manz and H. Sims, "The Leadership of Self-Managed Work Groups: A Social Learning Theory Perspective" (paper delivered at meeting of National Academy of Management, New York, August 1982); C. Manz and H. Sims Jr., "Searching for the 'Unleader': Organizational Member Views on Leading Self-Managed Groups," *Human Relations* 37 (1984): 409–24.
37. H. Mintzberg, *The Nature of Managerial Work* (New York: Harper & Row, 1973); L. Sayles, *Managerial Behavior: Administration in Complex Organizations* (New York: McGraw-Hill, 1964).
38. R. Walton and L. Schlesinger, "Do Supervisors Thrive in Participative Work Systems?" *Organizational Dynamics* 8 (Winter 1979): 25–38.
39. C. Manz and H. Sims, "Leading Workers to Lead Themselves: The External Leadership of Self-Managing Teams," *Administrative Science Quarterly* 32 (1987): 106–28; Manz and Sims, "The Leadership of Self-Managed Work Groups"; Walton and Schlesinger, "So Supervisors Thrive."
40. M. Weisbord, "Participative Work Design: A Personal Odyssey," *Organizational Dynamics* (1984): 5–20.
41. T. Cummings, "Socio-Technical Systems: An Intervention Strategy," in *New Techniques in Organization Development*, ed. W. Burke (New York: Basic Books, 1975), 228–49; Cummings and Srivastva, *Management of Work*; Cummings and Molloy, *Improving Productivity*.
42. Cherns, "Sociotechnical Design Revisited."
43. This application was adapted from A. Fazzari and J. Mosca, "Partners in Perfection"; "Human Resources Facilitating Creation and Ongoing Implementation of Self-Managed Manufacturing Teams in a Small Medium Enterprise," *Human Resource Development Quarterly* 20 (2009): 353–76.
44. F. van Eijnatten, S. Eggermont, G. de Goffau, and I. Mankoe, *The Socio-Technical Systems Design Paradigm* (Eindhoven, The Netherlands: Eindhoven University of Technology, 1994).
45. P. Goodman, R. Devadas, and T. Hughson, "Groups and Productivity: Analyzing the Effectiveness of Self-Managing Teams," in *Productivity in Organizations*, ed. J. Campbell, R. Campbell, and Associates (San Francisco: Jossey-Bass, 1988), 295–325.
46. R. Walton, "How to Counter Alienation in the Plant," *Harvard Business Review* 12 (November–December 1972): 70–81; R. Schrank, "On Ending Worker Alienation: The Gaines Pet Food Plant," in *Humanizing the Workplace*, ed. R. Fairfield (Buffalo, NY: Prometheus Books, 1974), 119–20, 126; R. Walton, "Teaching an Old Dog Food New Tricks," *Wharton Magazine* 4 (Winter 1978): 42; L. Ketchum, "Innovating Plant Managers Are Talking About ..." (presentation at the International Conference on the Quality of Working Life, Toronto, August 30–September 3, 1981): 2–3; H. Simon et al., "General Foods Topeka: Ten Years Young" (presentation at the International Conference on the Quality of Working Life, Toronto, August 30–September 3, 1981): 5–7; J. Norsted and S. Aguren, *The Saab-Scania Report* (Stockholm: Swedish Employer's Confederation, 1975); P. Gyllenhammèr, *People at Work* (Reading, MA: Addison-Wesley, 1977), 15–17, 43, 52–53; B. Jünsson, "Corporate Strategy for People at Work—The Volvo Experience" (presentation at the International Conference on the Quality of Working Life, Toronto, August 30–September 3, 1981); N. Tichy and J. Nisberg, "When Does Work Restructuring Work? Organizational Innovations at Volvo and GM," *Organizational Dynamics* 5 (Summer 1976): 73; J. Kapstein and J. Hoerr, "Volvo's Radical New Plant: The Death of the Assembly Line?" *BusinessWeek* (August 28, 1989): 92–93.
47. W. Pasmore, "The Comparative Impacts of Sociotechnical System, Job-Redesign, and Survey-Feedback Interventions," in *Sociotechnical Systems: A Source Book*, ed. W. Pasmore and J. Sherwood (San Diego: University Associates, 1978), 291–300.
48. Cummings and Molloy, *Improving Productivity*.
49. Nicholas, "Comparative Impact."
50. Pearce and Ravlin, "Design and Activation."
51. R. Beekun, "Assessing the Effectiveness of Sociotechnical Interventions: Antidote or Fad?" *Human Relations* 42 (1989): 877–97.

52. B. Macy, P. Bliese, and J. Norton, "Organizational Change and Work Innovation: A Meta-Analysis of 131 North American Field Experiments—1961–1990," in *Research in Organizational Change and Development*, vol. 7, ed. R. Woodman and W. Pasmore (Greenwich, CT: JAI Press, 1994).
53. T. Wall, N. Kemp, P. Jackson, and C. Clegg, "Outcomes of Autonomous Workgroups: A Long-Term Field Experiment," *Academy of Management Journal* 29 (June 1986): 280–304.
54. C. Manz and H. Angle, "Can Group Self-Management Mean a Loss of Personal Control: Triangulating a Paradox," *Group and Organization Studies* 11 (December 1986), 309–34.
55. S. Cohen and G. Ledford Jr., "The Effectiveness of Self-Managing Teams: A Quasi-Experiment," *Human Relations* 47 (1994): 13–43.
56. J. DeVaro, "Teams, Autonomy, and the Financial Performance of Firms: New Evidence from Panel Data," in *Advances in the Economic Analysis of Participatory & Labor-Managed Firms*, vol. 12, ed. J. DeVaro (Bingley, UK: Emerald Group Publishing Limited 2011): 63–85.
57. G. van der Vegt, J. S. Bunderson, and B. Kuipers, "Why Turnover Matters in Self-Managing Work Teams: Learning, Social Integration, and Task Flexibility," *Journal of Management* 36 (2010): 1168–91.
58. J. S. Bunderson and P. Boumgarden, "Structure and Learning in Self-Managed Teams: Why 'Bureaucratic' Teams Can Be Better Learners," *Organization Science* 21 (2010): 609–24.
59. S. Greg, L. Courtright, S. Barrick, and R. Murray, "Peer-Based Control in Self-Managing Teams: Linking Rational and Normative Influence with Individual and Group Performance," *Journal of Applied Psychology* 97 (2012): 435–47.
60. Cummings, "Self-Regulating Work Groups"; Susman, *Autonomy at Work*; Slocum and Sims, "Typology of Technology"; M. Kiggundu, "Task Interdependence and Job Design: Test of a Theory," *Organizational Behavior and Human Performance* 31 (1983): 145–72.
61. A. Grant and S. Parker, "Redesigning Work Design Theories: The Rise of Relational and Proactive Perspectives," *Academy of Management Annals* 3 (2009): 317–75.
62. Hackman and Oldham, *Work Redesign*; K. Brousseau, "Toward a Dynamic Model of Job–Person Relationships: Findings, Research Questions, and Implications for Work System Design," *Academy of Management Review* 8 (1983): 33–45; G. Graen, T. Scandura, and M. Graen, "A Field Experimental Test of the Moderating Effects of Growth Needs Strength on Productivity," *Journal of Applied Psychology* 71 (1986): 484–91.
63. T. Cummings, "Designing Work for Productivity and Quality of Work Life," *Outlook* 6 (1982): 35–39.

CITY OF CARLSBAD, CALIFORNIA: RESTRUCTURING THE PUBLIC WORKS DEPARTMENT (A)

OVERVIEW

In 1995, the City of Carlsbad, California, an ocean-front community of about 75,000 people, was emerging from the worst recession in its history. In response to a call from the City Council and nationwide efforts to operate governments in a more businesslike manner, the City Manager led the organization through a comprehensive strategic planning process. Through highly participative methods, including focus groups and a large-group community visioning process, a new city mission and vision (Figure 1) and a set of values to guide decision making (Figure 2) were developed. In addition, several important strategic initiatives, including a new information system and a revised performance appraisal and incentive compensation process were started.

These strategic initiatives and the City Manager's assessment of the organization's design pointed to misalignments in the city's structure. He convened a small representative task force of managers to design a new structure. The result was a reorganization of the city into five major service areas (MSAs), such as community development, safety services (e.g., fire, police), and public works.

An evaluation of the entire strategic change effort suggested that a large majority of the internal and external stakeholders viewed the changes positively and believed that they had improved customer focus and employee commitment. The results also promised to reduce operating costs and to create an organization that could absorb the expected growth in demand for new and better services.

FIGURE 1

City of Carlsbad Mission and Vision Statement

Our mission is to provide top-quality services to our citizens and customers in a manner that enhances the quality of life for all who live, work, and play in Carlsbad.

The Public Works Department

The largest of the new MSAs, Public Works, consisted of six previously independent departments responsible for engineering services; parks, streets, facilities, and fleet maintenance; and a legally separate water district owned by the city (Figure 3). The new organization was expected to design, construct, and maintain the infrastructure for the growing city. The new Public

FIGURE 2

City of Carlsbad Values

We believe these values are important to achieve our desired future as employees for the City of Carlsbad. They are chosen freely, prized publicly, and acted upon again and again.
Integrity—An organization and workforce distinguished by sound moral and ethical character
Trust—A workplace characterized by widespread belief in the integrity, reliability, and ability of employees
Competence—A workplace characterized by employees who have the skills and training to do their jobs
Accountability—An environment characterized by employees who are willing to be responsible
Teamwork—A workplace that encourages the use of teams to accomplish organizational goals and objectives
Quality—An environment characterized by employees with passion for excellence
Empowerment—Employees who have the authority, responsibility and accountability to decide and act

FIGURE 3

Proposed Public Works Structure Immediately Following City Reorganization

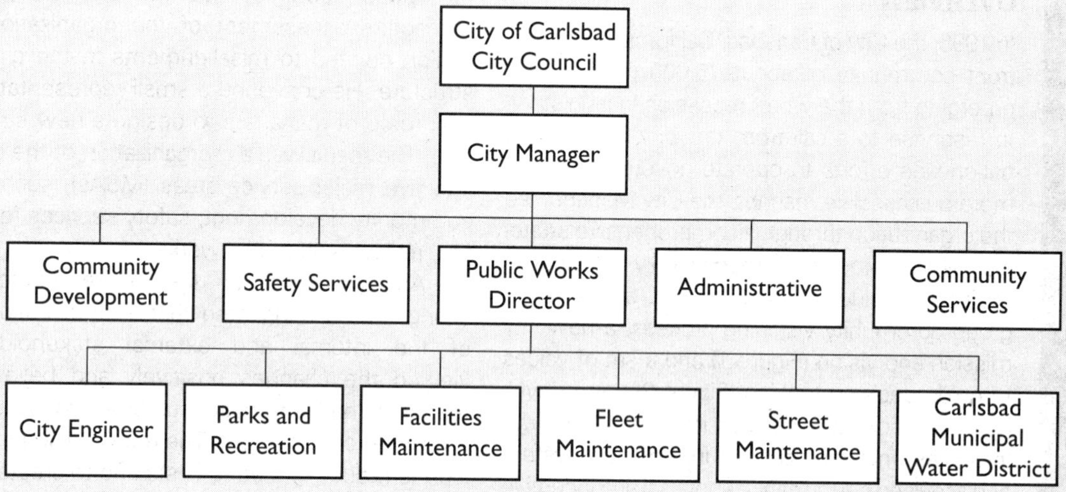

Works Director was excited about the prospect of designing his new MSA according to the vision and values created by the city during its strategic change efforts. In line with those values, he saw the opportunity to implement the new design in participative and empowering ways, and he wanted to take advantage of the city's general plan that called for new buildings to house the engineering staff and the public works yard.

In consultation with an OD consultant, diagnostic interviews and focus groups with a variety of employees and other stakeholders were commissioned. The data can be summarized as follows:

- *Each of the previously independent departments had their own way of doing things.* They were suspicious of the reasons for the structural change. The water district employees were particularly cohesive.
- *Many of the work processes in each department were similar.* For example, the buildings, parks, and street departments each had equipment and work assignments involving the maintenance of restrooms, painting, landscaping, and light construction. The engineering department for the water district was largely redundant with the engineering department in the City, and both the City and the water district owned several pieces of large and expensive equipment.
- *Each department had members with both long and short tenures.*
- *Most of the departments lacked formal goals and planning processes.*
- *The current Public Works Director was also acting as the City Engineer.*
- *The engineering department was anticipating an increased workload over the next ten years as the City continued growing.* Conversely, workloads in the maintenance groups were expected to grow over time but lag the growth rates in engineering.
- *Almost all of the employees enjoyed working for the City of Carlsbad and intended to stay.*
- Based on these data, the Public Works Director and the OD consultants worked together to understand the implications of the data and to design an action plan to describe and refine the new structure.

Questions

1. What is your diagnosis of the situation in the Public Works Department?
2. How would you proceed from this point?
3. What interventions would you recommend and why?
4. For your preferred intervention, develop an action plan for implementation.

THE SULLIVAN HOSPITAL SYSTEM

PART I

At the Sullivan Hospital System (SHS), CEO Ken Bonnet expressed concern over market share losses to other local hospitals over the past six to nine months and declines in patient satisfaction measures. To him and his senior administrators, the need to revise the SHS organization was clear. It was also clear that such a change would require the enthusiastic participation of all organizational members, including nurses, physicians, and managers.

At SHS, the senior team consisted of the top administrative teams from the two hospitals in the system. Bonnet, CEO of the system and president of the larger of the two hospitals, was joined by Sue Strasburg, president of the smaller hospital. Their two styles were considerably different. Whereas Bonnet was calm, confident, and mild-mannered, Strasburg was assertive, enthusiastic, and energetic. Despite these differences, both administrators demonstrated a willingness to lead the change effort. In addition, each of their direct reports was clearly excited about initiating a change process and was clearly taking whatever initiative Bonnet and Strasburg would allow or empower them to do.

You were contacted by Bonnet to conduct a three-day retreat with the combined management teams and kick off the change process. Based on conversations with administrators from other hospitals and industry conferences, the team believed that the system needed a major overhaul of its Total Quality Management (TQM) process for two primary reasons. First, they believed that an improved patient care process would give physicians a good reason to use the hospital, thus improving market share. Second, although the Joint Commission on Accreditation of Healthcare Organizations (JCAHO) had enacted policies some time ago encouraging hospitals to adopt continuous improvement principles, SHS's system was sorely behind the times. The team readily agreed that they lacked the adequate skills and knowledge associated with implementing a more sophisticated TQM process. This first meeting was to gather together to hear about how TQM, engagement, and other strategic change processes had advanced and the issues that would need to be addressed if more sophisticated processes were to be implemented. During the meeting, you guided them through several exercises to get the team to examine methods of decision making, how team-based problem solving had advanced, and explored their understanding of the hospital's current mission, goals, and strategies.

Although you were concerned about starting the process with a workshop that explored a solution rather than understanding the problem, you remembered Roger Harrison's consulting rule, "Start where your client is at," and agreed to conduct the workshop. You were assured by Bonnet that the hospital system was committed to making substantive changes and that this was only the first step. In addition, and in support of this commitment, Bonnet told you that he had already agreed in principle to begin a work redesign process in a few of the nursing units at each hospital and had begun to finalize a contract with a large consulting firm to do the work. The workshop was highly praised and you convinced the team to hold off on the work design implementation long enough to conduct a diagnosis of the system.

Following the retreat, your diagnosis of the SHS organization employed a variety of data collection activities including interviews with senior managers from both hospitals as well as a sampling of middle managers and staff (for example, nurses, ancillary professionals, and environmental services providers). Questions about the hospital's mission garnered the most consensus and passion. There was almost unanimous commitment to the breadth of services provided and the values that played a prominent role in the delivery of those services by a Catholic-sponsored health care organization, such as SHS. A mission and values statement was clearly posted throughout the hospital and many of the items in that statement were repeated almost verbatim in the interviews.

From there, however, answers about the organization's purpose and objectives became more diverse. With respect to goals and objectives, different stakeholder groups saw them differently. Senior administrators were fairly clear about the goals listed in the strategic plan. These goals included increasing measurements of patient satisfaction, decreasing the amount of overtime, and increasing market share. However, among middle managers and supervisors, there was little awareness of hospital goals or how people influenced their accomplishment. A question about the hospital's overall direction or how the goals were being achieved yielded a clear split in people's perceptions. Some believed the hospital achieved its objectives through its designation as the area's primary trauma center. They noted that if someone's life were in danger, the best chance of survival was to go to SHS. The problem, respondents joked, was that "after we save their life, we tend to forget about them." Many, however, held beliefs that could be labeled "low cost." That is, objectives were achieved by squeezing out every penny of cost no matter how that impacted patient care.

Opinions about the policies governing the hospital's operation supported a general belief that the organization was too centralized. People felt little empowerment to make decisions. There also were a number of financial policies that were seen as dictated from the corporate office, where "shared services" existed, including finance, marketing, information systems, and purchasing. Further, several policies limited a manager's ability to spend money, especially if it wasn't allocated in budgets.

In addition to the managerial sample, a variety of individual contributors and supervisors were interviewed either individually or in small groups to determine the status and characteristics of different organization design factors. The organization's policy and procedure manuals, annual reports, organization charts, and other archival information were also reviewed. This data collection effort revealed the following organization design features:

- **The hospitals' structures were more bureaucratic than organic.** Each hospital had a functional structure with a chief executive officer and from two to five direct reports. Both hospitals had directors of nursing services and professional services. The larger hospital had additional directors in special projects, pastoral care, and other staff functions that worked with both hospitals. Traditional staff functions, such as finance, procurement, human resources, and information services, were centralized at the corporate office. There were a number of formal policies regarding spending, patient care, and so on.
- **The basic work design of the hospitals could be characterized as traditional.** Tasks were narrowly defined (janitor, CCU nurse, admissions clerk, and so on). Further, despite the high levels of required interdependency and complexity involved in patient care, most jobs were individually based. That is, job descriptions detailed the skills, knowledge, and activities required of a particular position. Whenever any two departments needed to coordinate their activities, the work was controlled by standard operating procedures, formal paperwork, and tradition.
- **Information and control systems were old and inflexible.** From the staff's perspective, and to some extent even middle management's, little, if any, operational information (that is, about costs, productivity, or levels of patient satisfaction) was shared. Cost information in terms of budgeted versus actual spending was available to middle managers and their annual performance reviews were keyed to meeting budgeted targets. Unfortunately, managers knew the information in the system was grossly inaccurate. They felt helpless in affecting change, since the system was centralized in the corporate office. As a result, they devised elaborate methods for getting the "right" numbers from the system or duplicated the system by keeping their own records.
- **Human resource systems, also centralized in the corporate office, were relatively generic.** Internal job postings were updated weekly (there was a shortage of nurses at the time). There was little in the way of formal training opportunities beyond the required, technical educational requirements to maintain currency and certification. Reward systems consisted mainly of a merit-based pay system that awarded raises according to annual performance appraisal results. Raises over the previous few years, however, had barely kept pace with the cost of living. There also were various informal recognition systems administered by individual managers.

Questions

1. Assemble the diagnostic data into a framework and prepare feedback to the senior administrators of the hospitals. What's your sense of the organization's current structure and employee involvement issues?
2. What changes would you recommend? Is a total quality management intervention appropriate here? What alternatives would you propose?
3. Design an implementation plan for your preferred intervention.

PART II

This diagnostic data was discussed and debated among the senior team. A steering committee composed of physicians, managers, nurses, and other leaders from both hospitals was convened, and creating a vision for the system and the change effort became one of their first tasks.

The steering committee spent hours poring over vision statements from other organizations, discussing words and phrases that described what they thought would be an exciting outcome from interacting with the hospital, and trying to satisfy their own needs for something unique and creative. When the first draft of a statement emerged, they spent several months sharing and discussing it with a variety of stakeholders. To their dismay, the initial version was roundly rejected by almost everyone as boring, unimaginative, or unreal. The group discussed the input gathered during these discussions and set about the task of revising the vision. After several additional iterations and a lot of wordsmithing, a new and more powerful vision statement began to emerge. The centerpiece of the vision was the belief that the organization should work in such a way that the patient felt like they were the "center of attention." Such an orientation to the vision became a powerful rallying point since many of the hospitals' management teams readily understood that there was an existing perception of poor service that needed to be turned around.

The three months spent working and adapting the vision statement was well worth it. As it was presented to people in small meetings and workshops, each word and phrase took on special meaning to organizational members and generated commitment to change.

Questions

1. Critique SHS's visioning process.
2. What implications does the visioning process have for the intervention you want to implement? How can you take advantage of the process in your action plan?

PART 5

HUMAN RESOURCE INTERVENTIONS

15 Performance Management

16 Talent Management

17 Workforce Diversity and Wellness

SELECTED CASES

Employee Benefits at HealthCo

Designing and Implementing a Reward System at Disk Drives, Inc.

15

Performance Management

learning objectives

- Understand the components of a performance management system.
- Describe and evaluate the effectiveness of goal setting interventions in organizations.
- Understand the application of performance appraisal interventions.
- Discuss how reward systems interventions can be applied in organizations.

This is the first of three chapters devoted to human resources management interventions, including performance management, talent management, and diversity and wellness. It specifically addresses performance management, or how goal setting, performance appraisal, training and development, and reward systems can be used to manage individual and group performance. (How training and development can support performance management is discussed in Chapter 16.) This chapter also describes how to align performance management systems with business strategy, employee involvement, and workplace technology.

Goal setting describes the interaction between managers and employees in jointly defining member work behaviors and outcomes. Orienting employees to the appropriate kinds of work outcomes can reinforce the work designs described in Chapter 14 and support the organization's strategic objectives. Goal setting can clarify the duties and responsibilities associated with a particular job or work group. When applied to jobs, goal setting can focus on individual goals and can reinforce individual contributions and work outcomes. When applied to work groups, it can be directed at group objectives and can reinforce members' joint actions and overall group outcomes. One popular and classic approach to goal setting is called *management by objectives.*

The performance appraisal process involves collecting and feeding back data about individual or group performance and the way results were achieved. It is a systematic process that jointly assesses work-related achievements, strengths, and weaknesses. The purpose of this process is to improve work outcomes in the near term and over time. It also can facilitate career counseling, provide information about the strength and diversity of human resources in the company, and link employee performance with rewards. In worldwide organizations, the appraisal process must be sensitive to different cultural assumptions regarding openness, transparency, and relationships to authority.

Reward systems are concerned with eliciting and reinforcing desired behaviors and work outcomes through compensation and other forms of recognition. They can support goal setting and appraisal systems by acknowledging the kinds of behaviors required to implement a particular work design or support a business strategy. Like goal setting, rewards systems can be oriented to individual jobs and goals or to group functions and objectives. Moreover, they can be tailored to support traditional work designs as well as enriched, self-regulating designs. Developing innovative reward systems is an active area of change in many organizations today.

Performance management interventions traditionally are implemented by the human resources department within organizations, whose managers have special training in these areas. Because of the breadth and depth of knowledge required to carry out these kinds of change programs successfully, practitioners tend to specialize in one part of the human resources function, such as performance appraisal or compensation. Increasingly, however, the effectiveness of these interventions and processes rely on strong collaboration with line managers.

The interest in integrating human resources management with organization development (OD) continues unabated. OD practitioners involved in organization design and employee involvement interventions have realized the need to bring human resources practices more in line with the new designs and processes. Consequently, human resource specialists now frequently help initiate OD projects. For example, a large electronics firm expanded the role of compensation specialists to include initiation of work design projects. The compensation people at this firm, who traditionally were consulted by OD practitioners *after* the work design had taken place, were dissatisfied with this secondary role and wanted to be more proactive. In most cases, human resource practitioners continue to specialize in their respective areas, but they become more sensitive to and competent in organization development. Similarly, OD prac-titioners continue to focus on planned change while becoming more knowledgeable about human resources management.

We begin by describing a performance management model. It shows how goal setting, performance appraisal, training and development, and rewards are closely linked and difficult to separate in practice, but how each element is distinct and has its own dynamics. Following the model, goal setting, performance appraisal, and reward system interventions are discussed and their impact on organization effectiveness evaluated.

15-1 A Model of Performance Management

Performance management is an integrated process of defining, assessing, developing, and reinforcing employee work behaviors and outcomes.[1] Organizations with a well-developed performance management process often outperform those without this element of organization design.[2] As shown in Figure 15.1, performance management includes practices and methods for goal setting, performance appraisal, training and development, and reward systems. These practices jointly influence the performance of individuals and work groups. Goal setting specifies the kinds of performances that are desired; performance appraisal assesses those outcomes; training and development systems build individual competences; and reward systems provide the reinforcement to ensure that desired outcomes are repeated. Because performance management occurs in a larger organizational context, at least three contextual factors determine how these practices affect work performance: business strategy, workplace technology, and employee involvement.[3] High levels of work performance tend to occur when goal setting, performance appraisal, training and development, and reward systems are aligned jointly with these contextual factors.

Business strategy defines the goals and objectives, policies, and intended relationships between the organization and its environment to achieve effectiveness. Whether the organization is for-profit, nonprofit, or operates on a worldwide basis, the business strategy must account for the extent to which its activities have to be tailored to a local situation. Performance management focuses, assesses, develops, and reinforces member

FIGURE 15.1

A Performance Management Model

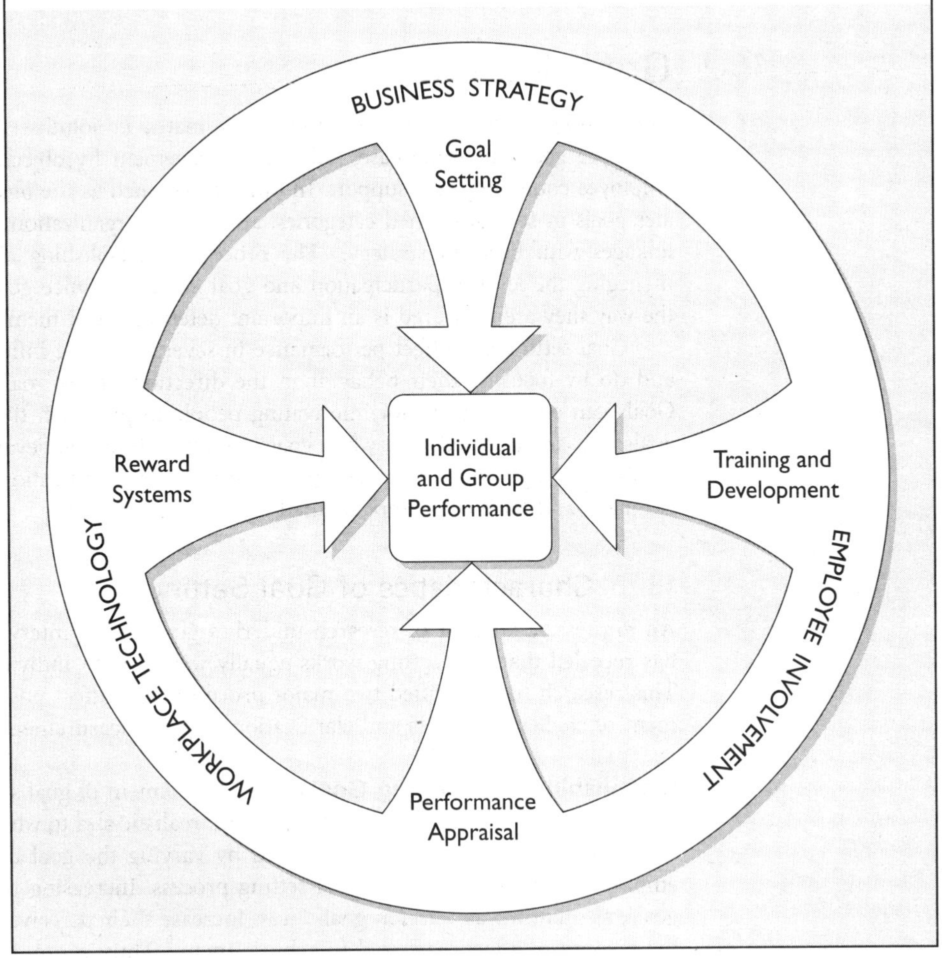

work behaviors toward those objectives and intentions. This ensures that work behaviors, both locally and globally, are strategically driven.

Workplace technology affects whether performance management practices should be based on the individual or the group. When the work processes are low in interdependence and work is designed for individual jobs, goal setting, performance appraisal, development, and reward systems should be aimed at individual work behaviors. Conversely, when work is highly interdependent and work is designed for groups, performance management should be aimed at group behaviors.[4]

Finally, the level of employee involvement in an organization should determine the nature of performance management practices. When organizations are highly bureaucratic, with low levels of participation, then goal setting, performance appraisal, development, and reward systems should be formalized and administered by management and staff personnel. In high-involvement situations, on the other hand, performance management should be heavily participative, with both managers and employees setting goals, determining appropriate development programs, and appraising and rewarding performance. In high-involvement organizations, for example, employees participate in all stages of performance management, and are heavily involved in both designing and administering its practices.

15-2 Goal Setting

Goal setting involves managers and subordinates in jointly establishing and clarifying employee goals. In some cases, such as management by objectives, it also can facilitate employee counseling and support. In other cases, such as the *balanced scorecard*, it generates goals in several defined categories, at different organizational levels, to establish clear linkages with business strategy.[5] The process of establishing challenging goals involves managing the level of participation and goal difficulty. Once goals have been established, the way they are measured is an important determinant of member performance.[6]

Goal setting can affect performance in several ways. It influences what people think and do by focusing their behavior in the direction of the goals, rather than elsewhere. Goals can energize behavior, motivating people to put forth the effort to reach difficult goals that are accepted, and when goals are difficult but achievable, goal setting prompts persistence over time. Goal-setting processes and interventions to improve them are common and have been implemented in most organizations.

15-2a Characteristics of Goal Setting

An impressive amount of research underlies goal-setting interventions and practices;[7] it has revealed that goal setting works equally well in both individual and group settings.[8] This research has identified two major processes that affect positive outcomes: establishment of challenging goals and clarification of goal measurement.

Establishing Challenging Goals The first element of goal setting concerns establishing goals that are perceived as challenging but realistic and to which there is a high level of commitment. This can be accomplished by varying the goal difficulty and the level of employee participation in the goal-setting process. Increasing the difficulty of employee goals, also known as "stretch goals," can increase their perceived challenge and enhance the amount of effort expended to achieve them.[9] Thus, more difficult goals tend to lead to increased effort and performance, as long as they are seen as feasible. If goals are set too high, however, they can lose their motivating potential and could even lead to unethical behavior.[10] One frequent method for increasing the acceptance of a challenging goal is to collect benchmarks or best-practice referents. When employees see that other people, groups, or organizations have achieved a specified level of performance, they are more motivated to achieve that level themselves.

Another aspect of establishing challenging goals is to vary the amount of participation in the goal-setting process. Having employees participate can increase motivation and performance, but only to the extent that members set higher goals than those typically assigned to them. Participation also can convince employees that the goals are achievable and can increase their commitment to achieving them.

All three contextual factors play an important role in establishing challenging goals. First, there must be a clear "line of sight" between the business strategy goals and the goals established for individuals or groups. This is a key strength of the balanced scorecard approach to goal setting. When the group is trying to achieve goals that are not aligned with the business strategy, performance can suffer and organization members can become frustrated. Second, employee participation in goal setting is more likely to be effective if employee involvement policies in the organization support it. Under such conditions, participation in goal setting is likely to be seen as legitimate, resulting in the desired commitment to challenging goals. Third, when tasks are highly interdependent and work is designed for groups, group-oriented participative goal setting tends to increase commitment.[11]

Clarifying Goal Measurement The second element in the goal-setting process involves specifying and clarifying the goals. When given specific goals, workers perform higher than when they are simply told to "do their best" or when they receive no guidance at all. Specific goals reduce ambiguity about expectations and focus the search for appropriate behaviors.

To clarify goal measurement, objectives should be operationally defined. For example, a group of employees may agree to increase productivity by 5%—a challenging and specific goal. But there are a variety of ways to measure productivity, and it is important to define the goal operationally to be sure that the measure can be influenced by employee or group behaviors. For example, a productivity goal defined by sales per employee may be inappropriate for a manufacturing group.

Clarifying goal measurement also requires that employees and supervisors negotiate the resources necessary to achieve the goals—for example, time, equipment, raw materials, and access to information. If employees cannot have appropriate resources, the targeted goal may have to be revised.

Contextual factors also play an important role in the clarifying process. Goal specification and clarity can be difficult in high-technology settings where the work often is uncertain and highly interdependent or in developing countries where the competitive situation is changing rapidly. Increasing employee participation in clarifying goal measurement can give employees ownership of a nonspecific but challenging goal. Employee involvement policies also can impact the way goals are clarified. The entire goal-setting process can be managed by employees and work teams when employee involvement policies and work designs favor it. Finally, the process of specifying and clarifying goals is extremely difficult if the business strategy is unclear. Under such conditions, attempting to gain consensus on the measurement and importance of goals can lead to frustration and resistance to change.

15-2b Application Stages

Based on these features of the goal-setting process, OD practitioners have developed specific approaches to goal setting. The following steps characterize those applications:

1. **Diagnosis.** The first step is a thorough diagnosis of the job or work group, of employee needs, and of the three context factors, business strategy, workplace technology, and level of employee involvement. This provides information about the nature and difficulty of specific goals, the appropriate types and levels of participation, and the necessary support systems.
2. **Preparation for goal setting.** This step prepares managers and employees to engage in goal setting, typically by increasing interaction and communication between managers and employees, and offering formal training in goal-setting methods. Specific action plans for implementing the program also are made at this time.
3. **Setting of goals.** In this step, challenging goals are established and methods for goal measurement are clarified. Employees participate in the process to the extent that contextual factors support such involvement and to the extent that they are likely to set higher goals than those assigned by management.

4. **Review.** At this final step, the goal-setting process is assessed so that modifications can be made, if necessary. The goal attributes are evaluated to see whether the goals are energizing and challenging and whether they support the business strategy and can be influenced by the employees.

15-2c Management by Objectives

A common form of goal setting used in organizations is *management by objectives (MBO).* This method is chiefly an attempt to align personal goals with business strategy by increasing communications and shared perceptions between the manager and subordinates, either individually or as a group, and by reconciling conflict where it exists.

All organizations have goals and objectives; all managers have goals and objectives. In many instances, however, the organizational goals are not stated clearly, and managers and subordinates have misunderstandings about what those objectives are. MBO is an approach to resolving these differences in perceptions and goals. It is characterized by systematic and periodic manager–subordinate meetings designed to accomplish organizational goals by joint planning of the work, periodic reviewing of accomplishments, and mutual solving of problems that arise in the course of getting the job done.

MBO has its origin in two different backgrounds: organizational and developmental. The organizational root of MBO was developed by Drucker, who emphasized that organizations need to establish objectives in eight key areas: "market standing; innovation; productivity; physical and financial resources; profitability; manager performance and development; worker performance and attitude; and public responsibility."[12] Drucker's work was expanded by Odiorne, whose first book on MBO stressed the need for quantitative measurement.[13]

According to Levinson,[14] MBO's second root is found in the work of McGregor, who stressed the qualitative nature of MBO and its use for development and growth on the job.[15] With respect to improving performance, McGregor attempted to shift the emphasis from identifying weaknesses to defining strengths and potentials. He believed that this shift could be accomplished by having subordinates reach agreement with their bosses on major job responsibilities. Then, individuals could develop short-term performance goals and action plans for achieving those goals, thus allowing them to appraise their own performance. Subordinates then would discuss the results of this self-appraisal with their supervisors and develop a new set of performance goals and plans. The emphasis on mutual understanding and performance rather than personality would shift the supervisor's role from judge to helper, thereby reducing both role conflict and ambiguity. The second root of MBO reduces role ambiguity by making goal setting more participative and transactional, by increasing communication between role incumbents, and by ensuring that both individual and organizational goals are identified and achieved.

An MBO program often goes beyond the one-on-one, manager–subordinate relationship to focus on problem-solving discussions involving work teams as well. Setting goals and reviewing individual performance are considered within the larger context of the job. In addition to organizational goals, the MBO process gives attention to individuals' personal and career goals and tries to make those and the organizational goals more complementary. The target-setting procedure allows real (rather than simulated) subordinate participation in goal setting, with open, problem-centered discussions among team members, supervisors, and subordinates.

There are five basic steps in implementing an MBO process.[16]

1. **Work group involvement.** In the first step of MBO, the members of the primary work group define overall group and individual goals and establish action plans for achieving them. If this step is omitted or if organizational goals and strategies are unclear, the effectiveness of an MBO approach may be greatly reduced over time.
2. **Joint manager–subordinate goal setting.** Once the work group's overall goals and responsibilities have been determined, attention is given to the job duties and responsibilities of individuals. Roles are carefully examined in light of their interdependence with the roles of others outside the work group.
3. **Establishment of action plans for goals.** The subordinate develops action plans for goal accomplishment, either in a group meeting or in a meeting with the immediate manager. The action plans reflect the individual style of the subordinate, not that of the supervisor.
4. **Establishment of criteria, or yardsticks, of success.** At this point, the manager and subordinate agree on the success criteria for the goals that have been established—criteria that are not limited to easily measurable or quantifiable data. A more important reason for jointly developing the success criteria is to ensure that the manager and subordinate have a common understanding of the task and what is expected of the subordinate. Frequently, the parties involved discover that they have not reached a mutual understanding. The subordinate and the manager may have agreed on a certain task, but in discussing how to measure its success, they find that they have not been communicating clearly. Arriving at a joint understanding and agreement on success criteria is the most important step in the entire MBO process.
5. **Review and recycle.** Periodically, the manager reviews work progress, either in the larger group or with the subordinate. There are three stages in this review process. First, the subordinate takes the lead, reviewing progress and discussing achievements and the obstacles faced. Next, the manager discusses work plans and objectives for the future. Last, after the action plans have been made, a more general discussion covers the subordinate's future ambitions and other factors of concern. In this final phase, a great deal of coaching and counseling usually takes place.

Application 15.1 describes how the Cambia Health Solutions organization changed their goal setting and broader performance management process. It shows how goal-setting processes are part of the larger performance management system and can be linked with business strategies.

15-2d Effects of Goal Setting and MBO

The impact of goal setting has been researched extensively and shown to be a particularly effective OD intervention and a key part of an overall performance management process. For example, a study by the Center for Effective Organizations at USC showed a strong correlation between perceptions of performance management effectiveness and goals that are jointly set by managers and workers and when those goals are tied to strategy.[17] The research results on MBO generally are positive but less consistent than are the findings on goal setting.

Goal setting appears to produce positive results over a wide range of jobs and organizations.[18] It has been tested on data-entry operators, logging crews, clerical workers, engineers, and truck drivers, and it has produced performance improvements of between 11% and 27%. Moreover, four meta-analyses of the extensive empirical evidence supporting goal setting concluded that the proposed effects of goal difficulty, goal specificity, and

application 15.1

CHANGING THE HUMAN CAPITAL MANAGEMENT PRACTICES AT CAMBIA HEALTH SOLUTIONS

Cambia Health Solutions (www.cambiahealth.com) is a nonprofit health care and insurance company dedicated to transforming the way people experience the health care system. Located in the Pacific Northwest of the United States, Cambia's portfolio of companies spans health care information technology and software development; retail health care; health insurance plans; pharmacy benefit management; life, disability, dental, vision and other lines of protection; alternative solutions to health care access; and free-standing health and wellness solutions. The largest business in the portfolio is Regence Health, a health insurance plan associated with the Blue Cross and Blue Shield brands. Regence Health is over 90 years old and operates in Washington, Oregon, Idaho, and Utah.

In 2010, Cambia convened a cross-functional design team to increase the organization's overall agility. As part of that effort, the design team initiated a change to its performance management system for leadership staff (approximately 750 people). The performance management system changes were based on diagnostic data that the organization was not focused on the critical areas required for success as well as feedback from organization members. The feedback suggested that (1) there were inconsistencies with respect to disciplined human capital management practices, (2) leaders were unclear about their individual objectives and how their objectives related to the organization's strategies, and (3) objectives were not clearly connected to professional development and career advancement.

The design team chartered a cross-functional task force to develop a new performance management process aimed at all leadership roles (supervisors and above), and supported the team with an external organization development and performance management consultant. At the highest level, the task force recommended a process that began with a requirement that all leaders establish annual objectives, conduct quarterly performance conversations, and enable a focused talent review twice a year. On an annual basis, the performance conversations would be linked to a revised compensation and reward process. At the center of the new process was a series of quarterly "performance conversations." Performance conversations established a dialogue where the leader and his/her direct reports could review past quarter performance on agreed upon objectives and prepare for the next quarter. The conversation was oriented around four questions:

- Did the employee accomplish what was committed to in the prior performance period?
- How could the employee have performed more effectively?
- What objectives should be continued into the next quarter, what should be stopped, and what new objectives should be established for the next quarter?
- How should the employee go about doing what needs to be done?

The cycle of quarterly performance conversations and semiannual talent reviews was initiated by an objective-setting process. The task force and design team were influenced by the timely processes established by some internal departments who had success with similar processes around quarterly conversations and regular talent reviews (this process was also validated to be a "best practice" by the external consultant). This entire process significantly simplified the existing performance appraisal process in which leaders were evaluated across seven categories. This new process focused on only two things: (1) the "what" (the established objectives) and (2) the "how" (the extent to which the company's values were carried out in achieving the objectives). The "what" conversation was intended to develop and establish a total of three to six objectives with at least one in each of three categories: (1) human capital management or how the leader was going to develop his/her people, (2) operational goals linked to the organization's strategic objectives, operational improvements, and/or regulatory/legislative mandates, and (3) the leader's own professional development. In addition, the "how" conversation was to focus on the way the leader achieved the "what" objectives (by demonstrating the company's values). Leaders were encouraged to—and their ultimate annual performance review was dependent on—getting work done through others, holding people accountable, and encouraging cross-functional, innovative, and problem-solving behaviors. These latter two issues—accountability and cross-functional problem solving—had been identified as important areas in the diagnosis.

To support the program, an on-line, on-demand training module was developed. In the module, leaders were helped to understand the importance of employing sound human capital management practices (with a particular focus on the quarterly conversations) as well as the importance of developing "SMART" objectives that were specific, measurable, achievable, relevant, and timely. This online training module was provided as a prerequisite to a series of more detailed webinars which were facilitated by senior leaders (not HR staff).

The new objective setting and performance conversation process was approved by the design team and supported by Cambia's leadership team. As part of that support, the leadership team accepted the recommendation of the task force and design team to have "coaches" oversee the early implementation of the new process—which included the CEO taking on the role of coach for his direct reports. He committed to monitoring and reviewing the development and establishment of objectives and to holding quarterly performance conversations. The members of the task force served as coaches to the other levels of management in the organization. The coaches were a visible means of championing the new system, holding leaders accountable for implementation, and raising the bar and expectations for human capital management at Cambia.

To reinforce the expected changes in behavior, the task force also included two reward-system-related recommendations. The first was to increase differentiation in the appraisal process by changing the performance categories from four to two. In the old system, leaders rated their direct reports according to a "top-key-core-low" scheme and then engaged in a calibration process that helped ensure the validity of those ratings. The task force recommended moving to a two-tier system of "performing and exceeding." They acknowledged that there may be situations where leaders were in a "performance improvement" scenario that was associated with correcting poor performance. In most cases, however, leaders were expected to be "performing" but the highest performers would be recognized for "exceeding" expectations. The existing calibration process was retained as many leaders indicated that it was a beneficial process for maintaining consistency in the system. The performing and exceeding performance categories were tied to recommendations for base-pay increases. The system was set up to reward "exceeders" at a rate 2.5 times that of "performers" to provide the differentiation.

The second reward system recommendation was to establish a unique "spot" awards program for all leadership staff. The spot awards program, entitled the "Excellence in Leadership Award," was designed to recognize leaders for exemplary performance in either human capital management or agile behaviors. The cash portion of the award was set at $1,000 and the awards were to be delivered personally by a member of Cambia's leadership team. Recipients of the award are highlighted in the company's newsletter—the goal being to reinforce among all leaders the kind of leadership behavior that is required for moving forward.

Although the new process had been developed with a broad range of inputs, it was kicked off with a presentation to senior leaders at Cambia's annual senior leadership summit. There, these senior leaders were able to ask questions, hear about the way the process worked, and understand the assumptions underlying its design. Following the presentation, these leaders were given a schedule to develop the initial quarterly "what" objectives for themselves and all other leadership staff across the company.

As the objectives were submitted, the task force members and performance coaches reviewed the objectives and provided feedback as appropriate. By the deadline, over 90% of all leadership staff (of the 750 supervisors and above) had submitted quarterly objectives and participated in the online training program and webinar. The organization has been through two cycles of quarterly conversations, had their initial talent reviews, and is anticipating the first cycle of the new reward system. To date, leadership staff have supported the objective setting process, the quarterly performance conversations, and the semiannual talent reviews. The importance of setting aligned objectives and using the performance management process to manage human capital in the organization has received increased emphasis and visibility in the organization.

participation in goal setting generally are substantiated across studies and with both groups and individuals.[19] Longitudinal analyses support the conclusion that the gains in performance are not short-lived.[20] A field study of the goal-setting process, however, failed to replicate the typical positive linear relationship between goal difficulty and performance, raising some concern about the generalizability of the method from the laboratory to practice.[21] Additional research has attempted to identify potential factors moderating the results of goal setting, including task uncertainty, amount and quality of planning, personal need for achievement, education, past goal successes, and supervisory style.[22] Some support for the moderators has been found. For example, when the technical context is uncertain, goals tend to be less specific and people need to engage in more search behavior to establish meaningful goals.

The existing research on MBO effectiveness is large but mixed.[23] However, it suggests that a properly designed MBO program can have positive organizational results. Carroll and Tosi conducted a long-term study of an MBO program at Black & Decker,[24] first evaluating the program and then using those data to help the company revise and improve it. This resulted in greater use of and satisfaction with the program. The researchers concluded that top-management support of MBO is the most important factor in implementing such programs. Many programs are short-lived, however, and wither on the vine because they have been installed without adequate diagnosis of the context factors. In particular, MBO can focus too much on *vertical alignment* of individual and organizational goals and not enough on the *horizontal issues* that exist when tasks or groups are interdependent.

15-3 Performance Appraisal

Performance appraisal is a feedback system that involves the direct evaluation of individual or work group performance by a supervisor, manager, or peers. Most organizations have some kind of evaluation system that is used for performance feedback, pay administration, and, in some cases, counseling and developing employees.[25] Thus, performance appraisal represents an important link between goal-setting processes and reward systems. A 2001 survey of over 300 North American companies, for example, found that 65% reported a link between performance ratings and rewards, 46% used the system equally for performance development and decision making, and 53% of the organizations believed the system was aligned with organizational values and priorities.[26] Abundant evidence, however, indicates that organizations do a poor job appraising employees.[27] As one study put it, "The appraisal of performance appraisals is not good.... In fact, our review indicates that, regardless of a program's stated purpose, few studies show positive effects."[28] Another study found that only 55% believed the appraisal process adequately distinguished between poor, average, and good performers.[29] Frustrated with the performance appraisal process, there have been calls for discontinuing it altogether,[30] however, a growing number of firms have sought ways to improve performance appraisal. Some innovations have been made in enhancing employee involvement, balancing organizational and employee needs, and increasing the number of raters.[31] These newer forms of appraisal are being used in such organizations as DaVita, Cambia Health Solutions, Alliant Energy, Microsoft, Intel, and Monsanto.

As demonstrated in Application 15.1, an important trend in goal setting and appraisal processes is the use and feedback of both the results achieved as well as the way those results were accomplished. Reflecting an increased interest in the economic and social value of ethics and integrity, many organizations are implementing performance management processes that establish, appraise, and reward *what* was achieved and *how* the objectives were achieved. Organization members that operate under these conditions are encouraged to think about achievement of relevant goals in ways that support the organization's values and beliefs.

15-3a The Performance Appraisal Process

Table 15.1 summarizes several common elements of performance appraisal systems.[32] For each element, two contrasting features are presented, representing traditional bureaucratic approaches and newer, high-involvement approaches. Performance appraisals are conducted for a variety of purposes, including affirmative action, pay and promotion decisions, and human resources planning and development. Because each purpose defines what performances are relevant and how they should be measured, separate appraisal systems are often used. For example, appraisal methods for pay purposes are often different from systems that assess employee development or promotability. Employees also have a variety of reasons for wanting appraisal, such as receiving feedback for career decisions, getting a raise, and being promoted. Rather than trying to meet these multiple purposes with a few standard appraisal systems, the new appraisal approaches are more tailored to balance the multiple organizational and employee needs. This is accomplished by actively involving the appraisee, coworkers, and managers in assessing the purposes of the appraisal at the time it takes place and adjusting the process to fit that purpose. Thus, at one

TABLE 15.1

Performance Appraisal Elements

Elements	Traditional Approaches	High-Involvement Approaches
Purpose	Organizational, legal Fragmented	Developmental Integrative
Appraiser	Supervisor, managers	Appraisee, co-workers, and others
Role of appraisee	Passive recipient	Active participant
Measurement	Subjective Concerned with validity	Objective and subjective
Timing	Periodic, fixed, administratively driven	Dynamic, timely, employee- or work-driven

time the appraisal process might focus on pay decisions, another time on employee development, and still another time on employee promotability. Actively involving all relevant participants can increase the chances that the purpose of the appraisal will be correctly identified and understood and that the appropriate appraisal methods will be applied.

The new methods tend to expand the appraiser role beyond managers to include multiple raters, such as the appraisee, peers or coworkers, and direct reports and others having direct exposure to the manager's or employee's performance. Also known as *360-degree feedback*, this broader approach is used more for member development than for compensation purposes.[33] This wider involvement provides a number of different views of the appraisee's performance. It can lead to a more comprehensive assessment of the employee's performance and can increase the likelihood that both organizational and personal needs will be taken into account. The key task is to form an overarching view of the employee's performance that incorporates all of the different appraisals. Thus, the process of working out differences and arriving at an overall assessment is an important aspect of the appraisal process. This improves the appraisal's acceptance, the accuracy of the information, and its focus on activities that are critical to the business strategy.

The newer methods also expand the role of the appraisee. Traditionally, the employee is simply a receiver of feedback. The supervisor unilaterally completes a form concerning performance on predetermined dimensions, usually personality traits, such as initiative or concern for quality, and presents its contents to the appraisee. The newer approaches actively involve appraisees in all phases of the appraisal process. The appraisee joins with superiors and staff personnel in gathering data on performance and identifying training needs. This active involvement increases the likelihood that the content of the performance appraisal will include the employee's views, needs, and criteria, along with those of the organization. This newer role for employees increases their acceptance and understanding of the feedback process.

Performance measurement is typically the source of many problems in appraisal because it is seen as subjective. Traditionally, performance evaluation focused on the consistent use of prespecified traits or behaviors. To improve consistency and validity of measurement, considerable training is used to help raters (supervisors) make valid assessments. This concern for validity stems largely from legal tests of performance appraisal systems and leads organizations to develop measurement approaches, such as the *behaviorally anchored rating scale (BARS)* and its variants. In newer approaches, validity is not only a legal or methodological issue but a social issue as well; all appropriate participants are involved in negotiating acceptable ways of measuring and assessing performance. Increased participation in goal setting is a part of this new approach. All participants are trained in methods of measuring and assessing performance. Because it focuses on both objective and subjective measures of performance, the appraisal process is more understood, accepted, and accurate.

The timing of performance appraisals traditionally is fixed by managers or staff personnel and is based on administrative criteria, such as yearly pay decisions. Newer approaches increase the frequency of feedback. In 1997, 78% of appraisals were performed annually; in 2003, over 40% of companies surveyed conducted appraisals two times per year.[34] Another study found that 63% of high growth companies reviewed performance more than once per year versus 22% of the low-growth companies.[35]

Although it may not be practical to increase the number of formal appraisals, the frequency of informal feedback can increase, especially when strategic objectives change or when the technology is highly uncertain. In those situations, frequent performance feedback is necessary for appropriate adaptations in work behavior. The newer approaches to appraisal increase the timeliness of feedback and give employees more control over their work.

15-3b Application Stages

The process of designing and implementing a performance appraisal system has received increasing attention. OD practitioners have recommended the following six steps:[36]

1. **Select the right people.** For political and legal reasons, the design process needs to include human resources staff, legal representatives, senior management, and system users. Failure to recognize performance appraisal as part of a complex performance management system is the single most important reason for design problems. Members representing a variety of functions need to be involved in the design process so that the essential strategic and organizational issues are addressed.
2. **Diagnose the current situation.** A clear picture of the current appraisal process is essential to designing a new one. Diagnosis involves assessing the contextual factors (business strategy, workplace technology, and employee involvement), current appraisal practices and satisfaction with them, work design, and the current goal-setting and reward system practices. This information is used to define the current system's strengths and weaknesses.
3. **Establish the system's purposes and objectives.** The ultimate purpose of an appraisal system is to help the organization achieve better performance. Managers, staff, and employees can have more specific views about how the appraisal process can be used. Potential purposes can include serving as a basis for rewards, career planning, human resources planning, and performance improvement or simply giving performance feedback.
4. **Design the performance appraisal system.** Given the agreed-upon purposes of the system and the contextual factors, the appropriate elements of an appraisal system can be established. These should include choices about who performs the appraisal, who is involved in determining performance, how performance is measured, and how often feedback is given. Criteria for designing an effective performance appraisal system include timeliness, accuracy, acceptance, understanding, focus on critical control points, and economic feasibility.

   First, the timeliness criterion recognizes the time value of information. Individuals and work groups need to get performance information before evaluation or review. When the information precedes performance evaluation, it can be used to engage in problem-solving behavior that improves performance and satisfaction. Second, the information contained in performance feedback needs to be accurate. Inaccurate data prevent employees from determining whether their performance is above or below the goal targets and discourage problem-solving behavior. Third, the performance feedback must be accepted and owned by the people who use it. Participation in the goal-setting process can help to ensure this commitment to the performance appraisal system. Fourth, information contained in the appraisal system needs to be understood if it is to have problem-solving value. Many organizations use training to help employees understand the operating, financial, and human resources data that will be fed back to them. Fifth, appraisal information should focus on critical control points. The information received by employees must be aligned with important elements of the business strategy, employee performance, and reward system. For example, if the business strategy requires cost reduction but workers are measured and rewarded on the basis of quality, the performance management system may produce the wrong kinds of behavior. Finally, the economic feasibility criterion suggests that an appraisal system should meet a simple cost–benefit test. If the costs associated with collecting and feeding back performance information exceed the benefits derived from using the information, then a simpler system should be installed.

5. **Experiment with implementation.** The complexity and potential problems associated with performance appraisal processes strongly suggest using a pilot test of the new process to spot, gauge, and correct any flaws in the design before it is implemented systemwide.
6. **Evaluate and monitor the system.** Although the experimentation step may have uncovered many initial design flaws, ongoing evaluation of the system once it is implemented is important. User satisfaction from human resources staff, manager, and employee viewpoints is an essential input. In addition, the legal defensibility of the system should be tracked by noting the distribution of appraisal scores against age, sex, and ethnic categories.

Application 15.2 describes evolution of the performance management system at Capital One. It demonstrates the importance of involvement and learning in the process, the importance of being responsive to the business situation, and how systems can be designed for flexibility.

15-3c Effects of Performance Appraisal

Despite the poor track record organizations have in implementing appraisal processes well, the research supports the linkage between feedback and performance.[37] Early studies concluded that objective feedback as a means for improving individual and group performance has been "impressively effective" and has been supported by a large number of literature reviews over the years.[38] Another researcher concluded that "objective feedback does not usually work, it virtually always works."[39] In field studies where performance feedback contained behavior-specific information, median performance improvements were over 47%; when the feedback concerned less-specific information, median performance improvements were over 33%. In a meta-analysis of performance appraisal interventions, feedback was found to have a consistently positive effect across studies.[40] In addition, although most appraisal research has focused on the relationship between performance and individuals, several studies have demonstrated a positive relationship between group performance and feedback.[41]

15-4 Reward Systems

Organizational rewards are powerful incentives for improving employee and work group performance. As pointed out in Chapter 13, rewards also can produce high levels of employee satisfaction. OD traditionally has relied on intrinsic rewards, such as enriched jobs and opportunities for decision making, to motivate employee performance. Early quality-of-work-life interventions were based mainly on the intrinsic satisfaction derived from performing challenging, meaningful types of work. More recently, OD practitioners have expanded their focus to include extrinsic rewards: base pay, stock options, bonuses, gain sharing, promotions, and benefits. They have discovered that both intrinsic and extrinsic rewards can enhance performance and satisfaction.[42]

OD practitioners increasingly are attending to the design and implementation of reward systems. This recent attention to rewards has derived partly from research in organization design and employee involvement. These perspectives treat rewards as an integral part of an organization.[43] They hold that rewards should be congruent with other organizational systems and practices, such as the organization's structure, top management's human relations philosophy, and work designs. Many reward system features contribute to both employee fulfillment and organizational effectiveness. In this section,

application 15.2

ADAPTING THE APPRAISAL PROCESS AT CAPITAL ONE FINANCIAL

Capital One is one of the largest financial services organizations in the United States. Its original credit card business began in 1993 when they were part of Signet Bank, and their success led to a spin-off and subsequent public offering in 1994. Since then, Capital One has expanded the credit card business, entered the auto loan and home mortgage businesses, grown internationally, and most recently acquired two traditional banks.

Capital One has always had a strong human resource management function and the organization has done a great job adapting a robust human resource strategy to shifting business conditions. Carol Anderson, who leads the performance management process, notes, "One overlay to the whole performance management strategy, and one of the reasons we've had some success in this area, is that the actual philosophy and core infrastructure of the program has not changed. For example, we've always had a system that included 360-degree feedback and well-grounded compensation models." Driven by the business situation and feedback about the performance management process, the organization has modified the appraisal process, the mix of reward components, and the specific issues that are appraised. In addition, they have learned from their experiences.

One of the early changes in the performance management system came in 2000. On the business front, Capital One was diversifying away from credit cards and into other financial services and needed to identify and develop talent for the future. The organization set up a performance management design team who initiated a benchmarking program as part of their review and revision process. To their surprise, most benchmark companies said, "we benchmark you." That is, most of the organizations they talked to noted that their appraisal system was based on the Capital One model. The notion of a full and detailed performance review, including 360-degree feedback, was the best in class. But the system wasn't delivering the results the organization wanted.

In particular, a relatively young and inexperienced group of managers and an ill-defined 7-point rating scale resulted in little differentiation in performance (e.g., there were a lot of 4, 5, and 6 ratings and very few 1, 2, or 3s), poor participation, and the largest proportion of complaints in the all-employee surveys. Initial attempts to address the lack of differentiation resulted in the announcement that a forced distribution system—where a percentage of employees had to be in high, medium, and low ratings—would be used. It wasn't a full GE-type model where the bottom 10% of the employees were let go, but it tried to impress upon managers the need to differentiate. Given the relative maturity of managers at the time and the lack of participation in the process, the change got little traction; it was poorly executed and had little effect on the number or type of complaints. In the context of the growth and diversification in the business and the need for talent, this was not the right process.

As the design team regrouped, it committed to preserving the high feedback culture, competencies model, and detailed written performance aspect of the model. The organization had always viewed performance management as an evaluation opportunity, and with that as a core, the design team set about looking at what could be changed.

One of the shifts they proposed was to lighten the administrative load. The team noted that the detailed evaluations, ratings, and feedback processes were forcing managers to spend about half the year in the performance management process. They recommended creating a system that would provide managers with the tools to manage associate performance without forcing the distribution. That principle led to the decision to automate the process, with the automation of the 360-degree feedback process leading the way.

The design team also recommended shifting the rating scale. Based on employee ratings of competencies and performance, managers computed a nonintuitive overall score that was more confusing than helpful. For example, although a -4 score was interpreted as "meeting expectations," that's not the way employees felt after receiving it. The design team recommended shifting from 7-point to a 5-point rating scale and adopting a simple interpretation scheme where low scores meant that action and development were required and moderate scores reflected strong (but not exceptional) performance. Learning from their prior implementation experiences, these revisions were supported by local champions in each business unit. Rather than announcing the changes, these local champions helped managers put the process in place with some consistency but not at the expense of driving business results.

In the 2003, a new set of business conditions resulted in additional adaptations to the system. First, changes in the regulations governing stock option recognition and expensing led the organization to shift its eligibility qualifications. In prior years, nearly all employees were eligible for salary increases, bonuses, and some equity compensation. With the regulation change, the organization tightened the pool of managers who were eligible for equity awards as well as the basis for awarding stock compensation.

Second, although Capital One maintained everyone's eligibility for bonus compensation, a corporate initiative to clarify the organization's values led the performance management design team to clarify what had always been an assumption in the system—that rewards were based on results as well as on competence. The list of values and behaviors reflecting the corporate values needed to be integrated with and aligned to the existing competency models. Moreover, the forecasted business growth and diversification suggested that the organization was going to need many new competencies. As a result, the team recommended specifying and rewarding competency development as 50% of the appraisal process, or that bonus compensation was tied to equal parts current results and the learning of new competencies. Managers' and associates' bonuses depended on achieving results set during goal setting meetings as well as learning and development activities. Such a system supported the development of a flexible workforce.

The organization's recognition that it needed to be more flexible and agile drove the first shift in organizational-level competencies. The effort to build a change capability (see Application 19.4) suggested that the competencies models reflect an emphasis on learning about and being capable of managing change. Based on the success of prior changes in the performance management system, formal, local champions in the form of senior VPs who represented their line of business, were made a part of the design team. This expanded design team increased the number of change-related behaviors in the competency models and asked Capital One University to highlight them in change-related training. This sent a clear message about the importance of these behaviors for the future. As a result, between 2003 and 2005, managers and associates were appraised not only on their current business results, but on the development of change management skills and knowledge. The champions were able to reinforce the importance of the new behaviors in the local implementation of the performance management process and provided important synergies for the change capability implementation.

As a result of these changes, Capital One managers came to believe that meeting aggressive but achievable goals required them to lead change and build new operational capabilities. Achieving results—50% of their appraisal score—was unlikely unless the manager actively drove change in their organizations. The other 50% of the appraisal score depended on the extent to which associates and managers were demonstrating the values and competencies of the corporation related to change. As one manager remarked, "if I lead change in the group but leave my people behind, I'm not doing my job and my bonus is at risk."

A new strategic imperative around "customer experience" has driven the most recent shift in the performance appraisal system. Senior managers asked Anderson's design team to ensure that the competency models, recruitment, selection, and performance management systems support the values and behaviors leading to outstanding customer experiences. "There's been a lot of interest in how the competencies are structured to reflect our increasing interest in customer experience.

One camp is advocating for adding a whole new and separate competency in customer experience that is populated with a set of behaviors. Another group is arguing that customer experience competencies should be integrated into the existing competencies, that customer experience should be as natural to everyone as the change-related competencies. As the competencies are decided, and in keeping with Capital One's overall performance management philosophy, achieving these competencies will continue to be 50% of the appraisal rating.

For the other 50% focused on results, executives were clear about how to orchestrate the reinforcement process. "We expect that customer experience metrics will be presented to associates during the 2007 round of appraisals. In the following year, objectives around customer experience will be a part of associate goal setting activities, but there will not be any rewards attached to achievement. Then in the third cycle, we expect that all associates will be held accountable for achievement of customer experience results." That is, compensation will be tied to the achievement of great customer experiences.

The Capital One performance management system has adapted with the times and has addressed a variety of issues, including process concerns, business needs, and human capital development. Its ongoing balance of rewarding results *and* the development of competencies allows Capital One to adjust the criteria for current performance but also encourage associates and managers to learn new skills for future success.

we describe the structural features of a reward system and how rewards affect individual and group performance; discuss four specific rewards, including skill-based pay, performance-based pay, gain sharing, and promotions; and review the process issues involved in establishing and administrating reward systems.

15-4a Structural and Motivational Features of Reward Systems

A reward system is an important part of an organization's design and must be aligned with the strategy, structure, employee involvement, and work. The design features of a reward system are summarized in Table 15.2.[44]

- **Person/job based versus performance based.** One of the first and most important design choices is the focus or basis of the reward system. The most prevalent system is the job-based system. Here, job descriptions are created for each position in the organization and a value is attached to the work performed. Pay is based on that valuation process. More recently, organizations challenged to be more agile and adaptable, such as Netflix and Nike, have crafted their reward systems around the person in the job and the value brought by their skills and knowledge. Skill-based pay and knowledge-based pay are important examples of this system. The other major alternative is to base rewards on the performance achieved by a job or person. In this system, pay is contingent on the outcomes produced.
- **Individual versus group rewards.** The interdependency among work tasks is another important reward system contingency. When work is complex and the performance of one task depends on prior tasks, the appropriate work design is team based because successfully adding value requires tight coordination. This tight coordination is reinforced by reward systems that recognize group level outputs. When work tasks are independent, individual reward systems incent individual behavior.
- **Internal and external equity.** Member satisfaction and motivation can be influenced by design features that ensure that the organization's pay policies are

TABLE 15.2

Reward System Design Features

Design Feature	Definition
Person/Job based vs. performance based	The extent to which rewards and incentives are based on the person in a job, the job itself, or the outcomes of the work
Market position (external equity)	The relationship between what an organization pays and what other organizations pay
Internal equity	The extent to which people doing similar work in an organization are rewarded the same
Hierarchy	The extent to which people in higher positions get more and varied types of rewards than people lower in the organization
Centralization	The extent to which reward system design features, decisions, and administration are standardized across an organization
Rewards mix	The extent to which different types of rewards are available and offered to people
Security	The extent to which work is guaranteed
Seniority	The extent to which rewards are based on length of service

equitable or fair. Internal equity concerns comparison of individual rewards to those holding similar jobs or performing similarly in the organization. Internal inequities typically occur when employees are paid a similar salary or hourly wage regardless of their position or level of performance. Many organizations work hard to establish practices to ensure that people who are doing similar kinds of activities have similar levels of compensation. Internal equity is often a challenge in worldwide organizations where cost-of-living and a country's level of economic development can imply different pay levels for the same work.

External equity involves comparing the organization's rewards with those of other organizations in the same labor market. Most human resources policies commit to a rewards and compensation system relative to the market. Organizations can decide to pay below, at, or above market rates. In their quest for attracting and retaining scarce human resource talent, many organizations have had to commit to above-market pay schemes. When an organization's reward level does not compare favorably with the level of other organizations, employees are likely to feel inequitably rewarded and may leave.

- **Hierarchy.** Although not often a formal policy, many organizations offer different types of rewards based on a position's level in the organization structure. The recent concerns over CEO pay reflect the increasing prevalence of hierarchical reward systems.[45] In hierarchical systems, senior managers have access to a variety of perquisites, such as corporate transportation, expense accounts, financial aid, or health benefits that others do not.

- **Rewards mix.** This design feature involves specifying the extent to which different types of rewards are included in the overall reward strategy. These rewards can include pay in various forms, including base salary, bonuses, commissions, and stock; benefits, such as health care, insurance, child care, leaves, and education; and perquisites, including preferred office space, cell phones, cars, or health club memberships. Recent changes in the laws governing the expensing of stock options are changing the way stock is viewed as part of the rewards mix. In addition, although pay receives most of the attention in reward systems, the contribution of other rewards, such as benefit programs and status incentives, should not be underestimated. For example, rising health care costs and increasing interest in retaining important skills and competencies have resulted in a variety of benefit innovations to increase the value of this reward.[46]
- **Security.** Organizations, such as IBM and AT&T, were once associated with the benefits of lifetime employment for organization members. Today, the rapid expansion and contraction of markets and the realities of downsizing have dramatically altered the psychological employment contract. Instead of job security, a more instrumental relationship has emerged. However, organizations can and do make commitments to people and job security and this remains an important feature of reward systems.
- **Seniority.** Many reward systems include an implicit or explicit policy concerning the value of longevity. Organizations, especially unionized companies covered by a collective bargaining agreement, often have built-in rewards for increasing lengths of service.

15-4b Reward System Design Features

The structural features of a reward system represent important design choices available to human resources and other senior managers. These features interact with work design and employee involvement practices to produce goal-directed behavior and task performance. Considerable research has been done on how different rewards and reward system features affect individual and group performance. The most popular model describing this relationship is value expectancy theory. In addition to explaining how performance and rewards are related, it suggests requirements for designing and evaluating reward systems.

The *value expectancy model*[47] posits that employees will expend effort to achieve performance goals that they believe will lead to outcomes that they value. This effort will result in the desired performance goals if the goals are realistic, if employees fully understand what is expected of them, and if they have the necessary skills and resources. Ongoing motivation depends on the extent to which attaining the desired performance goals actually results in valued outcomes. Consequently, key objectives of reward systems interventions are to identify the intrinsic and extrinsic outcomes (rewards) that are highly valued and to link them to the achievement of desired performance goals.

Based on value expectancy theory, the ability of rewards to motivate desired behavior depends on these five factors:[48]

1. **Availability.** For rewards to reinforce desired performance, they must be not only desired but also available. Too little of a desired reward is no reward at all. For example, pay increases are often highly desired but unavailable. Moreover, pay increases that are below minimally accepted standards may actually produce negative consequences.[49]

2. **Timeliness.** Like effective performance feedback, rewards should be given in a timely manner. A reward's motivating potential is reduced to the extent that it is separated in time from the performance it is intended to reinforce.
3. **Performance contingency.** Rewards should be closely linked with particular performances. If the goal is met, the reward is given; if the target is missed, the reward is reduced or not given. The clearer the linkage between performance and rewards, the better able rewards are to motivate desired behavior. Unfortunately, this criterion often is neglected in practice. Many, if not most, employees nationwide believe that there is no linkage between pay and performance.[50] If salary increases are concentrated at certain levels, almost everyone, regardless of performance level, is getting about the same raise.
4. **Durability.** Some rewards last longer than others. Intrinsic rewards, such as increased autonomy and pride in workmanship, tend to last longer than extrinsic rewards. Most people who have received a salary increase realize that it gets spent rather quickly.
5. **Visibility.** To leverage a reward system, it must be visible. Organization members must be able to see who is getting the rewards. Visible rewards, such as placement on a high-status project, promotion to a new job, and increased authority, send signals to employees that rewards are available, timely, and performance contingent.

Reward systems interventions are used to elicit and maintain desired levels of performance. To the extent that rewards are available, durable, timely, visible, and performance contingent, they can support and reinforce organizational goals, work designs, and employee involvement. The next sections describe four types of rewards. Skill-based pay, pay for performance, gain sharing, and promotions can be used to reward individual, team, or organization performance. Each system represents a flexible intervention that is effective in improving employee performance and satisfaction.

15-4c Skill- and Knowledge-Based Pay Systems

The most traditional reward system is individual and job based. The characteristics of a particular job are determined, and pay is made comparable to what other organizations pay for jobs with similar characteristics. Pay increases are primarily a function of cost-of-living adjustments (COLA) or small merit pools that are awarded with little relationship to performance. This job evaluation and reward method tends to result in pay systems with high external and internal equity. However, it fails to reward employees for all of the skills that they have, discourages people from learning new skills, and results in a view of pay as an entitlement.[51]

Some organizations, such as General Mills, United Technologies, Frito-Lay, Procter and Gamble, and General Foods, have worked to resolve these problems by designing pay systems according to people's skills and abilities. A 2006 survey found that almost 24% of the *Fortune* 1000 use skill or knowledge-based pay to at least some extent.[52] By focusing on the individual, rather than the job, skill-based pay systems reward learning and growth.

Skill-based pay systems must first establish the skills needed for effective operations, identify the optimal skill profile and number of employees needed with each skill, price each skill and skill set, develop rules to sequence and acquire skills, and develop methods to measure member skill acquisition.[53] Typically, employees are paid according to the number of different jobs that they can perform. For example, in the classic case of General Mill's Squeeze-It plant new employees were paid a starting wage at the low end of the skilled worker wage rate for premium employers in the community. They were then assigned to one of four skill blocks corresponding to a particular set of activities in the production process. For each skill block, there were three levels of skill. Pay was based on the level of skill in each of the skill blocks; the more proficient the skill in each block and the more blocks one was proficient at, the higher the pay. After all skill blocks were learned at the highest level, the top rate was given.[54] This progression in skills typically took two years to complete, and employees were given support and training to learn the new jobs.

Skill-based pay systems have a number of benefits. They contribute to organizational effectiveness by providing a more flexible workforce and by giving employees a broad perspective on how the entire plant operates. This flexibility can result in leaner staffing and fewer problems with absenteeism, turnover, and work disruptions. Skill-based pay can lead to durable employee satisfaction by reinforcing individual development and by producing an equitable wage rate.[55]

The three major drawbacks of skill-based pay schemes are the tendency to "top out," the expense, and the lack of performance contingency. Top-out occurs when employees learn all the skills there are to learn and then run up against the top end of the pay scale, with no higher levels to attain. Some organizations have resolved this topping-out effect by installing a gain-sharing plan after most employees have learned all relevant jobs. *Gain sharing*, discussed later in this section, ties pay to organizational effectiveness, allowing employees to push beyond previous pay ceilings. Other organizations have resolved this effect by making base skills obsolete and adding new ones, thus raising the standards of employee competence. Skill-based pay systems also require a heavy investment in training, as well as a measurement system capable of telling when employees have learned the new jobs. These systems typically increase direct labor costs, as employees are paid highly for learning multiple tasks. In addition, because pay is based on skill and not performance, the workforce could be highly paid and flexible but not productive.

Unfortunately, and despite their wide use, limited evaluative research exists on the effectiveness of these interventions. Long-term assessment of the Gaines Pet Food plant revealed that the skill-based pay plan contributed to both organizational effectiveness and employee satisfaction. Several years after the plant opened, workers' attitudes toward pay were significantly more positive than those of people working in other similar plants that did not have skill-based pay. Gaines workers reported much higher levels of pay satisfaction, as well as feelings that their pay system was fairly administered.[56] Similarly, a longitudinal study of skill-based pay focused on the design characteristics, supervisor and employee support, and facility characteristics to determine overall success as measured by workforce productivity and flexibility, cost-effectiveness, and survival. They found that skill-based pay plans were more successful and sustainable in manufacturing facilities than in service organizations, and that support among supervisors and employees for the innovative plans consistently predicted productivity and cost-effectiveness.[57]

A national survey of skill-based pay plans sponsored by the U.S. Department of Labor concluded that such systems increase workforce flexibility, employee growth and development, and product quality and quantity while reducing staffing needs, absenteeism, and turnover.[58] These results appear contingent on management commitment to the plan and having the right kind of people, particularly those with interpersonal skills, motivation, and a desire for growth and development. This study also showed that skill-based pay is applicable across a variety of situations, including both manufacturing and service industries, production and staff employees, new and old sites, and unionized and nonunionized settings. Finally, in a 1996 survey of *Fortune* 1000 companies, 42% indicated that skill-based pay systems were successful or very successful, down from 52% in 1993.[59]

15-4d Performance-Based Pay Systems

In addition to person- or job-based reward systems, organizations have devised many ways of linking pay to performance,[60] making it the fastest-growing and most popular segment of pay-based reward systems. Studies suggest that 60% to 70% of businesses have some form of performance-based or variable pay system.[61] They are used in such organizations as American Express, DaVita, Frito-Lay, and DOW. Pay-for-performance plans tend to vary along three dimensions: (1) the organizational unit by which performance is measured for reward purposes—an individual, group, or organization basis; (2) the way performance is measured—the subjective measures used in supervisors' ratings or objective measures of productivity, costs, or profits; and (3) what rewards are given for good performance—salary increases, stock, or cash bonuses. Table 15.3 lists different types of performance-based pay systems varying along these dimensions and rates them in terms of other relevant criteria.

In terms of linking pay to performance, individual pay plans are rated highest, followed by group plans and then organization plans. The last two plans score lower on this factor because pay is not a direct function of individual behavior. At the group and organization levels, an individual's pay is influenced by the behavior of others and by external market conditions. Generally, stock and bonus plans tie pay to performance better than do salary plans. The amount of awarded stock may vary sharply from year to year, whereas salary increases tend to be more stable because organizations seldom cut employees' salaries. Finally, objective measures of performance score higher than subjective measures. Objective measures, such as profit or costs, are more credible, and people are more likely to see the link between pay and objective measures.

Most of the pay plans in Table 15.3 do not produce negative side effects, such as workers falsifying data and restricting performance. The major exceptions are individual bonus plans. These plans, such as piece-rate systems, tend to result in negative effects, particularly when trust in the plan is low. For example, if people feel that piece-rate quotas are unfair, they may hide work improvements for fear that quotas may be adjusted higher.

As might be expected, group- and organization-based pay plans encourage cooperation among workers more than do individual plans. Under the former, it is generally to everyone's advantage to work well together because all share in the financial rewards of higher performance. The organization plans also tend to promote cooperation among functional departments. Because members from different departments feel that they can benefit from each others' performance, they encourage and help each other make positive contributions.

From an employee's perspective, Table 15.3 suggests that the least acceptable pay plans are individual bonus programs. Employees tend to dislike such plans because they encourage competition among individuals and because they are difficult to administer fairly. Such plans may be inappropriate in some technical contexts. For example, technical innovations typically lead engineers to adjust piece-rate quotas upward because employees should be able to produce more with the same effort. Workers, on the other hand, often feel that the performance worth of such innovations does not equal the incremental change in quotas, thus resulting in feelings of pay inequity. Table 15.3 suggests that employees tend to favor salary increases to bonuses. This follows from the simple fact that a salary increase becomes a permanent part of a person's pay, but a bonus does not.

The overall ratings in Table 15.3 suggest that no one pay-for-performance plan scores highest on all criteria. Rather, each plan has certain strengths and weaknesses

TABLE 15.3

Ratings of Various Pay-for-Performance Plans*

		Tie Pay to Performance	Produce Negative Side Effects	Encourage Cooperation	Employee Acceptance
Salary Reward					
Individual plan	Productivity	4	1	1	4
	Cost-effectiveness	3	1	1	4
	Superiors' rating	3	1	1	3
Group	Productivity	3	1	2	4
	Cost-effectiveness	3	3	2	4
	Superiors' rating	2	1	2	3
Organization-wide	Productivity	2	1	3	4
	Cost-effectiveness	2	1	2	4
Stock/Bonus Reward					
Individual plan	Productivity	5	3	1	2
	Cost-effectiveness	4	2	1	2
	Superiors' rating	4	2	1	2
Group	Productivity	4	1	3	3
	Cost-effectiveness	3	1	3	3
	Superiors' rating	3	1	3	3
Organization-wide	Productivity	3	1	3	4
	Cost-effectiveness	3	1	3	4
	Profit	2	1	3	3

*Ratings: 1 = lowest rating, 5 = highest rating.

SOURCE: Reproduced by permission of the publisher from E. Lawler III, "Reward Systems," in *Improving Life at Work*, eds. J. Hackman and J. Suttle (Santa Monica, Calif.: Goodyear, 1977), p. 195.

that depend on a variety of contingencies. As business strategies, organization performance, and other contingencies change, the pay-for-performance system also must change. At Lincoln Electric, a longtime proponent and model for incentive pay, growth into international markets, poor managerial decisions, and other factors have put pressure on the bonus plan. In one instance, a poor acquisition decision hurt earnings and left the organization short of cash for the bonus payout. The organization borrowed money rather than risk losing employees' trust. Financially weakened by the acquisition, and in combination with the other changes, Lincoln Electric has initiated a planned change effort to examine its pay-for-performance process and recommend a new approach.[62]

When all criteria are taken into account, however, the best performance-based pay systems seem to be group and organization bonus plans that are based on objective measures of performance and individual salary-increase plans. These plans are relatively good at linking pay to performance. They have few negative side effects and at least modest employee acceptance. The group and organization plans promote cooperation and should be used where there is high task interdependence among workers, such as might be found on assembly lines. The individual plan promotes competition and should be used where there is little required cooperation among employees, such as in field sales jobs.

15-4e Gain-Sharing Systems

As the name implies, *gain sharing* involves paying employees a bonus based on improvements in the operating results of an organization. Although not traditionally associated with employee involvement, gain sharing increasingly has been included in comprehensive employee involvement projects. Many organizations, such as Harley Davidson, General Dynamics, Gould Electronics, and Mondragon (Spain) are discovering that when designed correctly, gain-sharing plans can contribute to employee motivation, involvement, and performance.

Developing a gain-sharing plan requires making choices about the following design elements:[63]

- **Process of design.** The success of a gain-sharing system depends on employee acceptance and cooperation. Recommended is a participative approach that involves a cross section of employees to design the plan and be trained in gain-sharing concepts and practice. The task force should include people who are credible and represent both management and nonmanagement interests.
- **Organizational unit covered.** The size of the unit included in the plan can vary widely, from departments or plants with less than 50 employees to companies with several thousand people. A plan covering the entire plant would be ideal in situations where there is a freestanding plant with good performance measures and an employee size of less than 500. When the number of employees exceeds 500, multiple plans may be installed, each covering a relatively discrete part of the company.
- **Bonus formula.** Gain-sharing plans are based on a formula that generates a bonus pool, which is divided among those covered by the plan. Although most plans are custom-designed, there are two general considerations about the nature of the bonus formula. First, a standard of performance must be developed that can be used as a baseline for calculating improvements or losses. Some plans use past performance to form a historical standard, whereas others use engineered or estimated standards. When available, historical data provide a relatively fair standard of performance; engineer-determined data can work, however, if there is a high level of trust in the standard and how it is set. Second, the costs included in arriving at the bonus must be chosen. The key is to focus on those costs that are most controllable by employees. Some plans use labor costs as a proportion of total sales; others include a wider range of controllable costs, such as those for materials and utilities.
- **Sharing process.** Once the bonus formula is determined, it is necessary to decide how to share gains when they are obtained. This decision includes choices about what percentage of the bonus pool should go to the company and what percentage to employees. In general, the company should take a percentage low enough to ensure that the plan generates a realistic bonus for employees. Other decisions

about dividing the bonus pool include who will share in the bonus and how the money will be divided among employees. Typically, all employees included in the organizational unit covered by the plan share in the bonus. Most plans divide the money on the basis of a straight percentage of total salary payments.

- **Frequency of bonus.** Most plans calculate a bonus monthly. This typically fits with organizational recording needs and is frequent enough to spur employee motivation. Longer payout periods generally are used in seasonal businesses or where there is a long production or billing cycle for a product or service.
- **Change management.** Organizational changes, such as new technology and product mixes, can disrupt the bonus formula. Many plans include a steering committee to review the plan and to make necessary adjustments, especially in light of significant organizational changes.
- **The participative system.** Many gain-sharing plans include a participative system that helps to gather, assess, and implement employee suggestions and improvements. These systems generally include a procedure for formalizing suggestions and different levels of committees for assessing and implementing them.

Although gain-sharing plans are tailored to each situation, three major plans are used most often: the Scanlon plan, the Rucker plan, and Improshare. The most popular program is the Scanlon plan, and such organizations as Donnelly Corporation, De Soto, Midland-Ross, and Dana Corporation pioneered it. The incentive part of the Scanlon plan generally includes a bonus formula based on a ratio measure comparing total sales volume to total payroll expenses. This measure of labor cost efficiency is relatively responsive to employee behaviors and is used to construct a historical base rate at the beginning of the plan. Savings resulting from improvements over this base make up the bonus pool. The bonus is often split equally between the company and employees, with all members of the organization receiving bonuses of a percentage of their salaries. The Rucker plan and Improshare use different bonus formulas and place less emphasis on worker participation than does the Scanlon plan.[64]

Gain-sharing plans tie the goals of workers to the organization's goals. It is to the financial advantage of employees to work harder, to cooperate with each other, to make suggestions, and to implement improvements. Reviews of the empirical literature and individual studies suggest that when such plans are implemented properly, organizations can expect specific improvements.[65] A study sponsored by the General Accounting Office found that plans in place more than five years averaged annual savings of 29% in labor costs;[66] there also is evidence to suggest that they work in 50% to 80% of the reported cases.[67] A report on four case studies in manufacturing and service settings noted significant increases in productivity (32% in manufacturing and 11% in services), as well as in several other measures.[68] A longitudinal field study employing experimental and control groups supports gain sharing's positive effect over time and even after the group's bonus was discontinued.[69] Other reported results include enhanced coordination and teamwork; cost savings; acceptance of technical, market, and methods changes; demands for better planning and more efficient management; new ideas as well as effort; reductions in overtime; more flexible union–management relations; and greater employee satisfaction.[70]

Gain-sharing plans are better suited to certain situations than to others.[71] In general, gain sharing seems suited to small organizations with favorable market conditions, simple measures of historical performance, and production costs controllable by employees. Product and market demand should be relatively stable, and employee–management relations should be open and based on trust. Top management should support the plan, and support services should be willing and able to respond to increased demands. The workforce should be interested in and knowledgeable about gain sharing and should be technically proficient in its tasks.

Application 15.3 describes the reward system at Lands' End Direct Merchants.[72] It describes a variety of reward system design features as well as how a number of different types of rewards can be mixed together to produce an overall reward system.

15-4f Promotion Systems

Like decisions about pay increases, many decisions about promotions and job movements in organizations are made in a top-down, closed manner: Higher-level managers decide whether lower-level employees will be promoted. This process can be secretive, with people often not knowing that a position is open, that they are being considered for promotion, or the reasons why some people are promoted but others are not. Without such information, capable people who might be interested in a new job may be overlooked. Furthermore, because employees may fail to see the connection between good performance and promotions, the motivational potential of promotions is reduced. Finally, emphasizing promotions as a reward focuses attention on advancement instead of developing new skills and knowledge and can lead to reduced flexibility in the workforce.[73]

Fortunately, this is changing. Most organizations today have tried to reduce the secrecy surrounding promotions and job changes by openly posting the availability of new jobs and inviting people to nominate themselves.[74] Although open job posting entails extra administrative costs, it can lead to better promotion decisions. Open posting increases the pool of available personnel by ensuring that interested people will be considered for new jobs and that capable people will be identified. Open posting also can increase employee motivation by showing that a valued reward is available and contingent on performance.

Some organizations have increased the accuracy and equity of job-change decisions by including peers and subordinates in the decision-making process. Peer and subordinate judgments about a person's performance and promotability help bring all relevant data to bear on promotion decisions. Such participation can increase the accuracy of these decisions and can make people feel that the basis for promotions is equitable. In many self-regulating work teams, for example, the group interviews and helps select new members and supervisors. This helps ensure that new people will fit in and that the group is committed to making that happen. Evidence from high-involvement plants suggests that participation in selecting new members can lead to greater group cohesiveness and task effectiveness.[75]

15-4g Reward-System Process Issues

Thus far, we have discussed the different structural features of reward systems and assessed their strengths and weaknesses. Considerable research has been conducted on the process aspect of reward systems. Process refers to how pay and other rewards typically are administered in the organization. At least two process issues affect employees' perceptions of the reward system: who should be involved in designing and administering the reward system, and what kind of communication should exist with respect to rewards.[76]

application 15.3

REVISING THE REWARD SYSTEM AT LANDS' END

Lands' End Direct Merchants is an international catalog retailer employing a seasonal workforce that varies between 5,500 and 8,500 full- and part-time staff. It is widely recognized as one of the best companies to work for as a result of its participative culture, employment practices, and rewards. The company operates through a simple belief in employees "doing the right thing." This philosophy has helped to make the company an employer of choice.

The organization has been proactively rethinking and implementing specific aspects of its reward system over a four-year period to help Lands' End stay ahead of other companies. The reward system is composed of a mix of competitive pay, innovative benefits, work-life initiatives, and a variety of internal opportunities that encourage organization members to progress.

The firm's reward strategy is guided by principles such as maintaining direct and clear communication channels regarding any aspect of employment practice; encouraging the free exchange of information, ideas, and suggestions; and where possible, eliminating any causes and conditions that lead to inequities, complaints, or employee dissatisfaction. For example, an employee job-evaluation committee annually reviews and analyzes pay rates in different organizations and industries. This task force, composed of a variety of employees, then assigns specific wage levels to work positions. As a result, rates are perceived as fair by individuals while Lands' End itself learns more about how to value jobs and work based on predefined factors such as knowledge, skills, environment, and responsibility.

In the area of pay, one of the key changes has been a shift from rewarding a job population to rewarding the person. For example, under the old reward system, all salaried people used to receive a cash bonus based on sales volume and profits for the entire company. Now, each job is assigned an annual-incentive-plan target expressed as a percentage of base salary. Payouts on the plan are dependent on actual pretax profit performance for the whole company and the business-units-against-performance goals established each year by the board. Individual bonuses are based 50% on business-unit performance and 50% by corporate performance, thus linking individual effort to both local and organizational results.

In addition to the above changes in the pay system, the organization is piloting a gain-sharing-style bonus plan designed by a departmental task force for a small 20-person unit. It is being progressively deployed across the operations organization. Five operations departments have so far designed plans to link people's effort and knowledge to business-unit results—in both cost and quality terms. Each operations department has its own performance measures. For example, employees in the order-filling department are measured on a cost-per-piece and quality basis. These changes are being made to introduce group- or departmental-level performance rewards in addition to individual pay and annual-incentive-plan bonuses.

An individual reward system for the large hourly workforce supplements the bonus system. The inputs to the system are the employee job-evaluation committee's assignment of wage grades to jobs. Each grade has a minimum and maximum hourly rate, with six steps in between. Full- and part-time employees can progress through these six steps and increase their pay by completing a required number of hours in the job and satisfactorily meeting four generic performance standards that are specifically interpreted for each job and function. The four performance standards are:

- **Service:** helpfulness and support for customers and colleagues
- **Quality:** how well the job is done
- **Quantity:** a measure of individual productivity
- **Reliability:** a measure of dependability

These four performance standards are reviewed during performance reviews with immediate supervisors throughout the year.

An individual's ratings are based on achieving jointly set personal goals that are tied to:

- The four performance standards
- Job responsibilities and competencies
- Personal aspirations
- Business-unit objectives
- The spirit of Lands' End principles of doing business

Pay increases within a grade are given automatically until the maximum within grade rate is achieved. Then annual company increases only are received until the employee enters a new grade. The system is based on giving credit for hours worked in each grade, although individuals can be promoted to a higher grade and begin the process again. Hourly employees can also receive an annual performance bonus based on annual-incentive-plan computations that is typically between 2% and 4% of earnings.

Lands' End is also attempting to repackage work-life benefits to suit individual preferences, and so get greater value from its significant investments in this area. The main elements of the work-life benefits are:

- Plans for health care and additional retirement health care
- Child-care leave, summer camps, and provision of an on-site day-care center
- Health promotion and sports facilities
- A range of time-off-with-pay schemes, for matters ranging from family member illness to child adoption
- Employee-assistance programs to support life changes or crises
- Flexible working hours
- Education opportunities with financial support
- Job share and a six-week "try a job" work-experience scheme
- An emergency fund to help employees who suffer loss because of fire, tornado, or flood

Lands' End also offers between $35 and $1,000 to employees who recommend people who subsequently come to work for the company. More than half of job applicants from outside the company are usually referrals.

The guiding principle in Lands' End's thinking to pay the person rather than a given job population, repackage incentives and not reinvent them, and manage individuals rather than the compensation plan or system itself for best results has been simplicity. Through the reward system revision process, the organization has learned the importance of (1) involving and educating leaders and top managers to gain the confidence of business partners; (2) clearly stating the business case; (3) listening to others and inviting feedback on the basis of engagement and respect; (4) continually challenging yourself to stay abreast of new developments or options that are emerging in the areas of compensation and benefits; and (5) achieving a level of change with which people feel comfortable to encourage participation in ongoing dialogue.

Traditionally, reward systems are designed by top managers and compensation specialists and are simply imposed on employees. Although this top-down process may result in a consistent system, it cannot ensure that employees will understand and trust it, and more often than not, it results in a system that does not improve performance. In the absence of trust, workers are more likely to develop negative perceptions of the reward system. There is growing evidence that employee participation in the design and administration of a reward system can increase employee understanding and can contribute to feelings of control over and commitment to the plan. In fact, research supports that when managers "own" the performance management process and see it as a way to manage workforce performance, there are more positive attitudes toward the overall system as well as improved performance. In contrast, there is no relationship between attitudes about the system and the extent to which human resources "owns" the process.[77]

Lawler and Jenkins described a small manufacturing plant where a committee of workers and managers designed a pay system, after studying alternative plans and collecting salary survey data.[78] This resulted in a plan that gave control over salaries to members of work groups. Team members behaved responsibly in setting wage rates. They gave themselves 8% raises, which fell at the 50th percentile in the local labor market. Moreover, the results of a survey administered six months after the start of the new pay plan showed significant improvements in turnover, job satisfaction, and satisfaction with pay and its administration. Lawler attributed these improvements to employees having greater information about the pay system. Participation led to employee ownership of the plan and feelings that it was fair and trustworthy.

Communication about reward systems also can have a powerful impact on employee perceptions of pay equity and on motivation. Most organizations maintain secrecy about pay rates, especially in the managerial ranks. Managers typically argue that secrecy is preferred by employees. It also gives managers freedom in administering pay because they do not have to defend their judgments. There is evidence to suggest, however, that pay secrecy can lead to dissatisfaction with pay and to reduced motivation. Dissatisfaction derives mainly from people's misperceptions about their pay relative to the pay of others. Research shows that managers tend to overestimate the pay of peers and of people below them in the organization and that they tend to underestimate the pay of superiors. These misperceptions contribute to dissatisfaction with pay because regardless of a manager's pay level, it will seem small in comparison to the perceived pay level of subordinates and peers. Perhaps worse, potential promotions will appear less valuable than they actually are.

Secrecy can reduce motivation by obscuring the relationship between pay and performance. For organizations having a performance-based pay plan, secrecy prevents employees from testing whether the organization is actually paying for performance; employees come to mistrust the pay system, fearing that the company has something to hide. Secrecy can also reduce the beneficial impact of accurate performance feedback. Pay provides people with feedback about how they are performing in relation to some standard. Because managers overestimate the pay of peers and subordinates, they will consider their own pay low and thus perceive performance feedback more negatively than it really is. Such misperceptions about performance discourage those managers who are actually performing effectively.

Fortunately, more organizations are opening up their pay information. A recent study of *Fortune* 1000 companies found that 61% had some form of open pay policy covering at least a quarter of the workforce.[79] For organizations having a history of secrecy, initial steps toward an open reward system should be modest. For example, an organization could release information on pay ranges and median salaries for different jobs. Organizations with unions generally publish such data for lower-level jobs, and extending that information to all jobs would not be difficult. Once organizations have established higher levels of trust about pay, they might publicize information about the size of raises and who receives them. Finally, as organizations become more democratic, with high levels of trust among managers and workers, they can push toward complete openness about all forms of rewards.

It is important to emphasize that both the amount of participation in designing reward systems and the amount of frankness in communicating about rewards should fit the rest of the organization design and managerial philosophy. Clearly, high levels of participation and openness are congruent with democratic organizations. It is questionable whether authoritarian organizations would tolerate either one.

SUMMARY

This chapter presented three types of performance management interventions: goal setting, performance appraisal, and rewards systems. These three change programs offer powerful methods for managing employee and work group performance. They also help enhance worker satisfaction and support work design, business strategy, and employee involvement practices.

Principles contributing to the success of goal setting include establishing challenging goals and clarifying measurement. These are accomplished by setting difficult but feasible goals, managing participation in the goal-setting process, and being sure that the goals can be measured and influenced by the employee or work group. The most common form of goal setting—management by objectives—depends on top-management support and participative planning to be effective.

Performance appraisals represent an important link between goal setting and reward systems. As part of an organization's feedback and control system, they provide employees and work groups with information they can use to improve work outcomes. Appraisals are becoming more participative and developmental. An increasing number of people are involved in collecting performance data, evaluating an employee's performance, and determining how the appraisee can improve.

Reward systems interventions elicit, reinforce, and maintain desired performance. They can be oriented to individual jobs, work groups, or organizations and affect both performance and employee well-being. In addition to traditional job-based compensation systems, the major reward systems interventions in use today are skill-based pay, pay for performance, gain sharing, and promotions. Each of the plans has strengths and weaknesses when measured against criteria of performance contingency, equity, availability, timeliness, durability, and visibility. The critical process of implementing a reward system involves decisions about who should be involved in designing and administering it and how much information about pay should be communicated.

NOTES

1. E. Lawler and J. Boudreau, *Effective Human Resource Management: A Global Analysis* (Palo Alto: Stanford University Press, 2012); A. Mohrman, S. Mohrman, and C. Worley, "High-Technology Performance Management," in *Managing Complexity in High-Technology Organizations*, ed. M. Von Glinow and S. Mohrman (New York: Oxford University Press, 1990), 216–36; E. Lawler, *Talent: Making People Your Competitive Advantage* (San Francisco: Jossey-Bass, 2008).
2. E. Lawler and J. Boudreau, *Achieving Excellence in Human Resources Management: An Assessment of Human Resource Functions* (Palo Alto: Stanford University Press, 2009); D. McDonald and A. Smith, "A Proven Connection: Performance Management and Business Results," *Compensation and Benefits Review* 27 (1995): 59–64; P. Bernthal, R. Sumlin, P. Davis, and R. Rogers, *Performance Management Practices Survey Report* (New York: Development Dimensions International, 1997).
3. J. Riedel, D. Nebeker, and B. Cooper, "The Influence of Monetary Incentives on Goal Choice, Goal Commitment, and Task Performance," *Organizational Behavior and Human Decision Processes* 42 (1988): 155–80; P. Earley, T. Connolly, and G. Ekegren, "Goals, Strategy Development, and Task Performance: Some Limits on the Efficacy of Goal Setting," *Journal of Applied Psychology* 74 (1989): 24–33; N. Perry, "Here Come Richer, Riskier Pay Plans," *Fortune*, December 19, 1988, 50–58; E. Lawler III, *High-Involvement Management* (San Francisco: Jossey-Bass, 1986); A. Mohrman, S. Resnick-West, and E. Lawler III, *Designing Performance Appraisal Systems* (San Francisco: Jossey-Bass, 1990).
4. Mohrman, Mohrman, and Worley, "High-Technology Performance Management."

5. R. Kaplan and D. Norton, "Transforming the Balanced Scorecard from Performance Measurement to Strategic Management—Part II," *Accounting Horizons* 15 (2001): 147–61.

6. E. Locke and G. Latham, *A Theory of Goal Setting and Task Performance* (Englewood Cliffs, NJ: Prentice Hall, 1990).

7. Locke and Latham, *Theory of Goal Setting;* E. Locke, R. Shaw, L. Saari, and G. Latham, "Goal Setting and Task Performance: 1969–1980," *Psychological Bulletin* 97 (1981): 125–52; M. Tubbs, "Goal Setting: A Meta-Analytic Examination of the Empirical Evidence," *Journal of Applied Psychology* 71 (1986): 474–83.

8. A. O'Leary-Kelly, J. Martocchio, and D. Frink, "A Review of the Influence of Group Goals on Group Performance," *Academy of Management Journal* 37 (1994): 1285–1301.

9. S. Sherman, "Stretch Goals: The Dark Side of Asking for Miracles," *Fortune*, November 13, 1995, 231–32; S. Tully, "Why to Go for Stretch Targets," *Fortune*, November 14, 1994, 145–58.

10. D. Ackman, "Pay Madness at Enron," *Forbes*, March 22, 2002, accessed from http://www.forbes.com/2002/03/22/0322enronpay.html on August 9, 2012; R. Stevenson, "Sears Ducks, Then Tries to Cover," *New York Times*, June 17, 1992, D1.

11. D. Crown and J. Rosse, "Yours, Mine, and Ours: Facilitating Group Productivity Through the Integration of Individual and Group Goals," *Organizational Behavior and Human Decision Processes* 64, no. 2 (1995): 138–50.

12. P. Drucker, *The Practice of Management* (New York: Harper & Row, 1954), 63.

13. G. Odiorne, *Management by Objectives* (New York: Pittman, 1965).

14. H. Levinson, "Management by Objectives: A Critique," *Training and Development Journal* 26 (1972): 410–25.

15. D. McGregor, "An Uneasy Look at Performance Appraisal," *Harvard Business Review* 35 (May–June 1957): 89–94.

16. E. Huse and E. Kay, "Improving Employee Productivity Through Work Planning," in *The Personnel Job in a Changing World*, ed. J. Blood (New York: American Management Association, 1964), 301–15; R. Byrd and J. Cowan, "MBO: A Behavioral Science Approach," *Personnel* 51 (March–April 1974): 42–50.

17. E. Lawler, "Reward Practices and Performance Management System Effectiveness" *Organizational Dynamics* 32 (2003): 396–404.

18. G. Latham and E. Locke, "Enhancing the Benefits and Overcoming the Pitfalls of Goal Setting," *Organization Dynamics* 34 (2006): 332–48; Locke and Latham, *Theory of Goal Setting.*

19. Tubbs, "Goal Setting"; R. Guzzo, R. Jette, and R. Katzell, "The Effects of Psychologically Based Intervention Programs on Worker Productivity: A Meta-Analysis," *Personnel Psychology* 38 (1985): 275–91; A. Mento, R. Steel, and R. Karren, "A Meta-Analytic Study of the Effects of Goal Setting on Task Performance: 1966–1984," *Organizational Behavior and Human Decision Processes* 39 (1987): 52–83; O'Leary-Kelly, Martocchio, and Frink, "Influence of Group Goals."

20. C. Pearson, "Participative Goal Setting as a Strategy for Improving Performance and Job Satisfaction: A Longitudinal Evaluation with Railway Track Maintenance Gangs," *Human Relations* 40 (1987): 473–88; R. Pritchard, S. Jones, P. Roth, K. Stuebing, and S. Ekeberg, "Effects of Group Feedback, Goal Setting, and Incentives on Organizational Productivity," *Journal of Applied Psychology* 73 (1988): 337–58.

21. S. Yearta, S. Maitlis, and R. Briner, "An Exploratory Study of Goal Setting in Theory and Practice: A Motivational Technique That Works?" *Journal of Occupational and Organizational Psychology* 68 (1995): 237–52.

22. R. Steers, "Task-Goal Attributes: Achievement and Supervisory Performance," *Organizational Behavior and Human Performance* 13 (1975): 392–403; G. Latham and G. Yukl, "A Review of Research on the Application of Goal Setting in Organizations," *Academy of Management Journal* 18 (1975): 824–45; R. Steers and L. Porter, "The Role of Task-Goal Attributes in Employee Performance," *Psychological Bulletin* 81 (1974): 434–51; Earley, Connolly, and Ekegren, "Goals"; J. Hollenbeck and A. Brief, "The Effects of Individual Differences and Goal Origin on Goal Setting and Performance," *Organizational Behavior and Human Decision Processes* 40 (1987): 392–414.

23. Huse and Kay, "Improving Employee Productivity," 301–15; A. Raia, "Goal Setting and Self-Control: An Empirical Study," *Journal of Management Studies* 2 (1965): 34–53; A. Raia, "A Second Look at Management Goals and Controls," *California Management Review* 8 (1965): 49–58; D. Terpstra, P. Olson, and B. Lockeman, "The Effects of MBO on Levels of Performance and Satisfaction Among University Faculty," *Group and Organization Studies* 7 (1982): 353–66.

24. S. Carroll and W. Tosi Jr., *Management by Objectives* (New York: Macmillan, 1973), 23.

25. G. Latham and R. Wexley, *Increasing Productivity Through Performance Appraisal* (Reading, MA: Addison-Wesley, 1981).

26. L. Holsinger, *Effective Performance Management Practices* (New York: Mercer Human Resource Consulting, 2002).

27. Mohrman, Resnick-West, and Lawler, *Designing Performance Appraisal Systems*; "Employees Say Companies Must Improve Performance Management," *HR Focus* 80

(2003): 9; J. Smither, ed., *Performance Appraisal* (San Francisco: Jossey-Bass, 1998).

28. H. Bernardin, C. Hagan, J. Kane, and P. Villanova, "Effective Performance Management," in *Performance Appraisal*, ed. J. Smither (San Francisco: Jossey-Bass, 1998), 348–64.
29. "Companies Must Improve," *HR Focus*.
30. L. Kellaway, "My Appraisal of Job Appraisals: Get Rid of Them," *Financial Times*, July 12, 2010, p. 10; S. Culbert, *Get Rid of the Performance Review* (New York: Business Plus, 2010).
31. G. Yukl and R. Lepsinger, "How to Get the Most Out of 360-Degree Feedback," *Training* 32, no. 21 (1995): 45–50; G. Roberts, "Employee Performance Appraisal System Participation: A Technique That Works," *Public Personnel Management* 32 (2003): 89–97.
32. E. Lawler, "Creating an Effective Appraisal System," in *The Executive Guide to Integrated Talent Management*, ed. K. Oakes and P. Galagan (Alexandria, VA: American Society for Training & Development, 2011): 79–90; S. Scott and W. Einstein, "Strategic Performance Appraisal in Team-Based Organizations: One Size Does Not Fit All," *Academy of Management Executive* 15 (2001): 107–17.
33. W. Tornow and M. London, *Maximizing the Value of 360-Degree Feedback: A Process for Successful Individual and Organizational Development* (San Francisco: Jossey-Bass, 1998); B. O'Reilly, "360 Feedback Can Change Your Life," *Fortune*, October 17, 1994, 93–100.
34. "Performance Management Systems Are Quickly Becoming Popular," *HR Focus* 80 (2003): 8–10.
35. "More Evidence that Performance Management Yields Higher Profits," *HR Focus* 84 (February 2007): 8.
36. Mohrman, Resnick-West, and Lawler, *Designing Performance Appraisal Systems*; E. Lawler, "Performance Management: The Next Generation," *Compensation and Benefits Review* 26, no. 3 (1994): 16–19.
37. "Performance Management Delivers Double the Return," *HR Focus* 83 (2006): 8; L. Pettijohn, R. Parker, C. Pettijohn, and J. Kent, "Performance Appraisals: Usage, Criteria, and Observations," *Journal of Management Development* 20 (2001): 754–72.
38. B. Cawley, L. Keeping, and P. Levy, "Participation in the Performance Appraisal Process and Employee Reactions: A Meta-analytic Review of Field Investigations," *Journal of Applied Psychology* 83 (1998): 615–33; J. Fairbank and D. Prue, "Developing Performance Feedback Systems," in *Handbook of Organizational Behavior Management*, ed. L. Frederiksen (New York: John Wiley & Sons, 1982); J. Sassenrath, "Theory and Results on Feedback and Retention," *Journal of Educational Psychology* 67 (1975): 894–99.
39. R. Kopelman, *Managing Productivity in Organizations* (New York: McGraw-Hill, 1986).
40. Guzzo, Jette, and Katzell, "Psychologically Based Intervention Programs."
41. D. Nadler, "The Effects of Feedback on Task Group Behavior: A Review of the Experimental Research," *Organizational Behavior and Human Performance* 23 (1979): 309–38; D. Nadler, C. Cammann, and P. Mirvis, "Developing a Feedback System for Work Units: A Field Experiment in Structural Change," *Journal of Applied Behavioral Science* 16 (1980): 41–62; J. Chobbar and J. Wallin, "A Field Study on the Effect of Feedback Frequency on Performance," *Journal of Applied Psychology* 69 (1984): 524–30.
42. W. Scott, J. Farh, and P. Podsakoff, "The Effects of 'Intrinsic' and 'Extrinsic' Reinforcement Contingencies on Task Behavior," *Organizational Behavior and Human Decision Processes* 41 (1988): 405–25; E. Lawler III, *Strategic Pay* (San Francisco: Jossey-Bass, 1990); A. Stajkovic and F. Luthans, "Differential Effects of Incentive Motivators on Work Performance," *Academy of Management Journal* 44 (2001): 580–90.
43. J. Galbraith, *Designing Organizations* (San Francisco: Jossey-Bass, 2001); E. Lawler, *Rewarding Excellence: Pay Strategies for the New Economy* (San Francisco: Jossey-Bass, 2000).
44. Lawler, *Rewarding Excellence*.
45. M. Conyon, S. Peck, and G. Sadler, "Compensation Consultants and Executive Pay: Evidence from the United States and the United Kingdom," *Academy of Management Perspectives* 23, no. 1 (2009): 43–55; J. Useem, "Have They No Shame," *Fortune*, April 14, 2003, 57–63.
46. J. Bruner, "The Next Big Thing in Health Benefits: Consumer Choice," *Benefits Quarterly* 18 (2002): 49–53.
47. J. Campbell, M. Dunnette, E. Lawler III, and K. Weick, *Managerial Behavior, Performance, and Effectiveness* (New York: McGraw-Hill, 1970).
48. S. Kerr, "Risky Business: The New Pay Game," *Fortune*, July 22, 1996, 94–96.
49. C. Worley, D. Bowen, and E. Lawler III, "On the Relationship Between Objective Increases in Pay and Employees' Subjective Reactions," *Journal of Organization Behavior* 13 (1992): 559–71.
50. "Performance Management Systems Are Quickly Becoming Popular"; "Performance Management: Still a Long Way to Go for Many Companies," *HR Focus* 84 (2007): 8.
51. V. Gibson, "The New Employee Reward System," *Management Review* (February 1995): 13–18.
52. Center for Effective Organizations, "Survey of Organization Improvement Efforts" (Los Angeles: Center for Effective Organizations, 2006).

53. Lawler, *Rewarding Excellence.*
54. G. Ledford and G. Bergel, "Skill-Based Pay Case Number 1: General Mills" (Skill-based pay seminar materials, American Compensation Association, Scottsdale, AZ, 1990).
55. E. Lawler, *Pay and Organization Development* (Reading, MA: Addison-Wesley, 1981): 66; E. Lawler and G. Ledford Jr., "Skill-Based Pay," *Personnel* 62 (1985): 30–37; Lawler, *From the Ground Up.*
56. Lawler, *Pay and Organization Development*, 66.
57. J. Shaw, N. Gupta, A. Mitra, and G. Ledford, "Success and Survival of Skill-based Pay Plans," *Journal of Management* 31, no. 1 (2005): 28–49.
58. N. Gupta, G. D. Jenkins Jr., and W. Curington, "Paying for Knowledge: Myths and Realities," *National Productivity Review* (Spring 1986): 107–23.
59. E. Lawler III, S. Mohrman, and G. Ledford, *Strategies for High-Performance Organizations* (San Francisco: Jossey-Bass, 1998).
60. Lawler, *Rewarding Excellence.*
61. F. Lyons and D. Ben-Ora, "Total Rewards Strategy: The Best Foundation of Pay for Performance," *Compensation and Benefits Review* (March/April, 2002): 34–40; Center for Effective Organizations, "Survey of Organization Improvement Efforts."
62. Z. Schiller, "A Model Incentive Plan Gets Caught in a Vise," *BusinessWeek* (January 22, 1996): 89–90.
63. Lawler, *Pay and Organization Development*, 134–43; M. Schuster, J. Schuster, and M. Montague, "Excellence in Gainsharing: From the Start to Renewal," *Journal for Quality and Participation* 17, no. 3 (1994): 18–25; D. Band, G. Scanlon, and C. Tustin, "Beyond the Bottom Line: Gainsharing and Organization Development," *Personnel Review* 23, no. 8 (1994): 17–32; J. Belcher, "Gainsharing and Variable Pay: The State of the Art," *Compensation and Benefits Review* 26, no. 3 (1994): 50–60.
64. Lawler, *Pay and Organization Development*, 146–54.
65. J. Ramquist, "Labor–Management Cooperation: The Scanlon Plan at Work," *Sloan Management Review* (Spring 1982): 49–55; T. Cummings and E. Molloy, *Improving Productivity and the Quality of Work Life* (New York: Praeger, 1977), 249–60; R. J. Bullock and E. Lawler III, "Gainsharing: A Few Questions, and Fewer Answers," *Human Resource Management* 23 (1984): 23–40; C. Miller and M. Schuster, "A Decade's Experience with the Scanlon Plan: A Case Study," *Journal of Occupational Behavior* 8 (April 1987): 167–74; T. Welbourne and L. Gomez-Meija, "Gainsharing: A Critical Review and a Future Research Agenda," *Journal of Management* 21, no. 3 (1995): 559–609; W. Imberman, "Is Gainsharing the Wave of the Future," *Management Accounting* 77 (1977): 35–40; D. Collins, *Gainsharing and Power: Lessons from Six Scanlon Plans* (Ithaca, NY: ILR Press of Cornell University Press, 1998).
66. General Accounting Office, *Productivity Sharing Programs: Can They Contribute to Productivity Improvement?* (Washington, DC: Author, 1981).
67. Bullock and Lawler, "Gainsharing"; C. O'Dell, *People, Performance, and Pay* (Houston, TX: American Productivity Center, 1987).
68. E. Doherty, W. Nord, and J. McAdams, "Gainsharing and Organization Development: A Productive Synergy," *Journal of Applied Behavioral Science* 25 (1989): 209–29.
69. S. Hanlon, D. Meyer, and R. Taylor, "Consequences of Gainsharing: A Field Experiment Revisited," *Group and Organization Management* 19, no. 1 (1994): 87–111.
70. E. Lawler III, "Gainsharing Theory and Research: Findings and Future Directions," in *Organizational Change and Development*, vol. 2, ed. W. Pasmore and R. Woodman (Greenwich, CT: JAI Press, 1988), 323–44.
71. E. Lawler, *Pay and Organization Development* (Upper Saddle River, NJ: Pearson, 1981).
72. This application was adapted from C. Ashton, "Lands' End Rethinks Pay for Performance," *Human Resource Management International Digest* 8 (2000): 18–21.
73. E. Lawler and C. Worley, *Built to Change* (San Francisco: Jossey-Bass, 2006).
74. E. Lawler III, "Reward Systems," in *Improving Life at Work*, ed. J. Hackman and J. Suttle (Santa Monica, CA: Goodyear, 1977), 176.
75. R. Walton, "How to Counter Alienation in the Plant," *Harvard Business Review* 50 (November-December 1972): 70–81.
76. Lawler, *Rewarding Excellence*, 57–59.
77. Lawler, "Reward Practices and Performance Management System Effectiveness"; "Performance Management: Still a Long Way to Go for Many Companies," *HR Focus* 84 (2007): 8; "More Evidence That Performance Management Yields Higher Profits," *HR Focus* 84 (February 2007): 8.
78. E. Lawler III and G. Jenkins, *Employee Participation in Pay Plan Development* (unpublished technical report to U.S. Department of Labor, Ann Arbor; Institute for Social Research, University of Michigan, 1976).
79. Center for Effective Organizations, "Survey of Organization Improvement Efforts."

16

Talent Management

learning objectives

- Examine and evaluate the coaching and mentoring intervention.
- Describe the process of implementing management and leadership development interventions.
- Understand how career planning and development interventions improve the individual's personal competencies and enhance traditional human resource approaches.

This is the second chapter on human resource management interventions—planned change efforts intended to address the attraction, development, and retention of human capital in organizations. It presents three interventions concerned with talent management. First, coaching interventions attempt to improve an individual's ability to set and meet goals, lead change, improve interpersonal relations, handle conflict, or address style issues. These resource-intense interventions focus on the skills, knowledge, and capabilities of an organization member, usually a manager or executive but in the case of mentoring also can apply to individual contributors. Second, management and leadership development processes are the primary human resource interventions for transferring knowledge and skills to many individuals. They can include in-house training programs, external educational opportunities, action-learning projects, and other activities. Third, career planning and development interventions address different professional needs and concerns as organization members progress through their work lives. All three interventions can support the training and development aspects of performance management described in Chapter 15. In the following chapter, interventions that address workforce diversity, stress, and employee wellness are presented.

Boudreau argues that HR and organization development (OD) professionals need to increase the decision-making rigor regarding talent management.[1] He suggests that talent management investments are as critical to organization effectiveness as finance and marketing investments and warrant a more reasoned decision science in human resources thinking. In the absence of such an approach, human resource policies resemble a "one size fits all" point of view and lead to blanket human capital policy statements like "everyone should get 40 hours of training each year." In fact, some talent pools are more important to effectiveness than others are.

In times of scarce investment resources, organizations should determine which talent pools (e.g., customer contact positions, engineering positions, or leadership) are most "pivotal." Those talent pools where improvements in skills, knowledge, and competence are most likely to have the biggest impact on performance should get a disproportionate amount of investment. This perspective will likely conflict with OD's traditional egalitarian values, but reflects an important future trend in human resources management as the function matures and becomes more strategic in nature.[2]

16-1 Coaching and Mentoring

Coaching involves working with organizational members, typically managers and executives, on a regular basis to help them clarify their goals, address potentially limiting behavioral style issues, and improve their performance. This intervention is highly personal and generally involves a one-on-one relationship between the OD practitioner and the client. Almost every OD intervention involves some coaching. However, the intervention described here helps managers to gain perspective on their dilemmas and transfer their learning into organizational results; it increases their leadership skill and effectiveness.[3]

Similar to coaching, mentoring involves establishing a relationship between a manager or someone more experienced and another organization member who is less experienced. Unlike coaching, mentoring is often more directive, with the mentor intentionally transferring specific knowledge and skill and guiding the client's activities, perhaps as part of a career development process (see career planning and development processes below).[4]

Coaching can be seen as a specialized form of OD, one that is focused on using the principles of applied behavioral science to increase the capacity and effectiveness of individuals as opposed to groups or organizations. It is one of the fastest-growing areas of OD practice. The International Coach Federation (www.coachfederation.org), founded in 1995, grew to over 5,500 members in 2002 and to over 18,000 members in 2012. CoachVille (www.coachville.com), the largest professional network and trainer of coaches worldwide, has over 30,000 members in more than 175 countries. They both offer coaching certification programs and standards to professionalize the field.

Coaching is a skill that any OD practitioner or manager can develop.[5] It involves using guided inquiry, active listening, reframing, and other techniques to help individuals see new or different possibilities and to direct their efforts toward what matters most to them. When done well, coaching improves personal productivity and builds capacity in individuals to lead more effectively. Unfortunately, despite growing professionalism in the coaching field, the process can be technique driven, especially when practitioners substitute formulas, tools, and advice for experience, good judgment, facilitation, and compassion.

16-1a What Are the Goals?

Coaching typically addresses one or more of the following goals: assisting an executive to execute more effectively some transition, such as a merger integration or downsizing; addressing a performance problem; or developing new behavioral skills as part of a leadership development program. A Harvard Business Review study of 140 coaches identified the top three reasons for coaching: (1) developing high potentials or facilitating a transition, (2) acting as a "sounding board," and (3) addressing derailing behavior.[6] In any case, coaching is often confused with therapy.[7] Most coaching approaches acknowledge that coaching is not therapy. While both coaching and therapy can focus on personal development, coaching assumes that the client is healthy rather than suffering from some pathology. Coaching is also primarily future and action oriented rather than focused on the past, as are many therapeutic models. Coaching can involve helping clients understand how their behaviors are contributing to the current situation. Such understanding is often difficult to achieve and often deeply personal. Therefore, clients and client organizations must acknowledge the limits of a coach's skills and abilities. Many coaching failures have been attributed to working too far from the practical application of behavioral principles, or too close to the boundaries of therapy, and to the failure of the coach to understand the difference.

16-1b Application Stages

The coaching process closely follows the process of planned change outlined in Chapter 2, including entry and contracting, assessment, debriefing (feedback), action planning, intervention, and assessment.[8] The mentoring process is similar except that the assessment is generally presumed and the process moves straight to action planning.

1. **Establish the principles of the relationship.** The initial phases of a coaching intervention involve establishing the goals of the engagement; the parameters of the relationship, such as schedules, resources, and compensation; and ethical considerations, such as confidentiality and boundary issues.
2. **Conduct an assessment.** This process can be personal or systemic. In a personal assessment, the client is guided through an assessment framework.[9] It can involve a set of interview questions that elicit development opportunities or a more formal personal-style instrument, such as the Myers–Briggs Type Indicator, the FIRO-B, or DISC profile. Other instruments, including the Hogan's battery of tests, the Minnesota Multiphasic Personality Inventory (MMPI), or the "Big 5" instrument, are also used, but they require extensive training and certification. OD practitioners should carefully consider the ethics of using different instruments and their qualifications for administering and interpreting the results. In a systemic assessment, the client's team, peers, and relevant others are engaged in the process. The most common form of systemic assessment involves a 360-degree feedback process.
3. **Debrief the results.** The coach and client review the assessment data and agree on a diagnosis. The principles of data feedback outlined in Chapter 6 apply here. The purpose of the feedback session is to get the client to move to action. In light of the assessment data, intervention goals can be further refined and revised if necessary.
4. **Develop an action plan.** Together, the client and coach outline specific activities to engage in. These can include new actions that will lead to goal achievement, learning opportunities that build knowledge and skill, or projects to demonstrate competence. Developing an action plan can be the most difficult part of the process because the client must own the results of the assessment and begin to see new possibilities for action. The action plan should also include methods and milestones to monitor progress and to evaluate the effectiveness of the coaching process.
5. **Implement the action plan.** In addition to the elements of the action plan listed above, much of the coaching process involves one-on-one meetings between the coach and client. In these sessions, the coach supports and encourages the client to act on her/his intentions. A considerable amount of skill is required to confront, challenge, and facilitate learning.
6. **Assess the results.** At appropriate intervals, the coach and client review and evaluate the results of implementation. Based on this information, the goals or action plans can be revised, or the process can be terminated.

16-1c The Results of Coaching and Mentoring

Although coaching has been practiced for many years, there are only a small number of studies assessing its effectiveness. Most of the evidence remains anecdotal and case based although a few large sample studies have been conducted.[10] The case evidence cites diverse benefits depending on the nature of the client's objectives. For example, one found that coaching improved personal productivity, quality, working relationships, and job satisfaction. The return was estimated to be 5.7 times the initial investment.[11] Another study reported that managers found positive results with respect to their personal lives, social interactions with others, and the skills and knowledge that were important to their work.[12]

A prepost test design in a government organization found that the experimental group receiving coaching made significant improvements compared to the control group on two of six measures, including "acting in a balanced way" and in beliefs about their ability to set goals.[13] Similarly, a randomized control group design of 41 executives in a public health agency received 360-degree feedback, a one-half day leadership workshop, and four individual coaching sessions over ten weeks. The coaching group reported enhanced goal attainment, increased resilience and workplace wellbeing, and reduced depression and stress. Qualitative responses indicated participants found coaching helped increase self-confidence and personal insight, build management skills, and helped participants deal with organizational change.[14] Finally, a review of the empirical and case study research between 2001 and 2010 found only one meta-analysis of coaching cases. In the researchers' opinion, there were too few cases to conduct a meta-analysis and concluded that the wide range of reported results, while positive and supportive of an organizational impact, was primarily driven by the client's readiness for change and the nature of the coaching relationship.[15] Clearly, more rigorous studies are necessary to judge the effectiveness of coaching interventions.

The modest research on mentoring suggests that it is relatively prevalent in organizations, including Hewlett-Packard, Charles Schwab, Ford Motor Company, Ernst & Young, Quaker Oats Company, IBM, Georgia-Pacific, Ceridian, JCPenney, PriceWaterhouseCoopers, 3M, and General Mills. About two-thirds of top executives report having a mentor or sponsor during their early career stages, when learning, growth, and advancement were most prominent. Effective mentors were willing to share knowledge and experience, were knowledgeable about the company and the use of power, and were good counselors. Mentored executives, in contrast to executives who did not have mentors, received slightly more compensation, had more advanced college degrees, had engaged in career planning prior to mentoring, and were more satisfied with their careers and their work.[16]

Research also shows that mentoring is critical for minority and female employees. One recent study of mentoring minorities stresses that a strong network of mentors is critical to advancement, and that the mentor of minorities must understand the challenges that race presents to career development and advancement.[17] Similarly, women face unique challenges, and must address some of the same issues.

16-2 Management and Leadership Development Interventions

Management and leadership development programs are one of the most popular OD interventions aimed at developing talent and increasing employee retention. These programs build an individual's skills, socialize leaders in corporate values, and prepare executives for strategic leadership roles.[18] A wide-array of organizations offer leadership development programs, including Procter & Gamble, Teekay, Federal Express, PartnerRe, PepsiCo, Cisco Systems, IBM, Microsoft, and Hewlett-Packard.

Management and leadership development interventions can be differentiated from career development (described below). In management and leadership development, the focus is on developing the skills and knowledge the organization believes will be necessary to implement future strategies and manage the business. In career development, the focus in on building the skills and knowledge the individual believes will best equip them for the career they prefer. Ideally, there is considerable overlap between the two.

Executives agree that preparing leaders is an important top management team function. However, a recent survey of over 600 executives by the Center for Effective Organizations and Heidrick and Struggles also found that top management teams were "uncertain" about the extent to which they performed this function well.[19] This section describes the purpose and goals of leadership development interventions, the application steps and conditions for transfer, and the research support for this intervention.

16-2a What Are the Goals?

The term *training* is typically used when the goal is development of the workforce, while the terms *management development* or *leadership development* are normally applied when the goal is development of the organization's management and executive talent. There is a wide range of training and development interventions, and not all involve OD. For leadership development to be considered an OD intervention, it must focus on changing the skills and knowledge of a group of organization members to improve their effectiveness or to build the capabilities of an organization system.[20] For example, a leadership development program that provides information about the organization's strategy would not qualify as an OD intervention.

16-2b Application Stages

Management and leadership development interventions generally follow a process of needs assessment, setting instructional objectives and design, delivery, and evaluation.[21]

1. **Perform a needs assessment.** Similar to the diagnostic process in the general model of planned change, a needs assessment typically determines the competencies believed to characterize effective leaders in the organization. This can be done by interviewing well-respected executives or reviewing lists of published leadership competencies. The logic of this intervention assumes that if OD practitioners can identify the right leadership skills and knowledge, they can develop a program to educate and equip participants with these competencies. McCall has challenged this approach and suggested that good leaders develop competencies from experience, not training. As a result, a needs assessment must gather data on the strategy, the organization, and the individuals who might attend the leadership program.[22]

   The *strategy assessment* involves understanding the knowledge and experiences future leaders will need to execute the business strategy. It includes tasks, activities, and decisions that participants should perform better after training as well as the conceptual frameworks that guide these activities. This can be done by identifying the top three to five external and internal leadership challenges facing the business[23] and the experiences that might help build the competence to deal with them. For example, the Hartford Financial services group believed that its long history of success had created an internal culture that favored stability over change. In the face of increasingly aggressive competition and more demanding customers, its leadership development program included the analysis of a business situation and activities intended to create change readiness in a relevant portion of the organization.

The *organization assessment* focuses on the systems that may affect the ability to transfer learning and developmental experiences back to the organization. For transfer to occur, a leadership development program must provide participants with the opportunity and appropriate conditions to apply their new skills, knowledge, and abilities to the work situation. The organization assessment determines whether the necessary support exists in the organization to make leadership development worthwhile. For example, if executives were generally unwilling to send their managers to the program for fear of losing them to promotion, then the organization assessment would suggest addressing management's readiness for change before implementing the program.

The final element, *individual assessment*, aims to understand the existing pool of people who should be candidates for the program. Such an assessment would include their current level and ranges of skills, knowledge, and abilities. Recently, leadership development programs have begun to focus on the personal growth of the participants, and so an important part of the assessment would be to understand individuals' attitudes toward personal reflection and its role in leadership effectiveness.

2. **Develop the objectives and design of the training.** This step first establishes outcome objectives for the development intervention. These objectives should describe both the results expected from a competent leader and how those results were achieved. For a leadership development program, an appropriate objective might be "the ability to produce an acceptable strategic plan for a strategic business unit" or "to increase participants' commitment to the strategic direction of the corporation."

   The design of the training involves making choices from among a wide variety of techniques. The more traditional methods of classroom lectures, 360-degree feedback, simulations, case studies, or experiential exercises, have been augmented by more recent emphases on rotational assignments, on-the-job training, coaching, or action learning projects.
3. **Deliver the training.** This stage implements the development program. Participants are invited or apply to attend the program, complete the activities included in its design, and return to their normal work routines.
4. **Evaluate the training.** This final step assesses the training to determine whether it met its objectives. The four criteria most commonly used to evaluate training effectiveness are reaction, learning, behavior, and results.[24] *Reaction* is the most commonly used evaluation criterion and refers simply to the participants' initial judgment about the training's usefulness. It is often assessed via questionnaires completed immediately following the training activity. The *learning* criterion refers to whether or not participants acquired the knowledge that should have been transferred during the training; it stops short of assessing performance or behavior on the job. This can be assessed via interview or questionnaire. The *behavior* criterion assesses whether new skills and abilities gained in the training are actually applied to job activities. These data can be collected through observation or through interviews with the participant's manager. The final criterion, *results*, determines whether the training can be credited with improvements in the participant's or the system's effectiveness.

Application 16.1 describes a management development program at Microsoft Corporation. The company was interested in building the strategic competence of its middle managers and making the organization more capable at managing strategic change.

application 16.1

LEADING YOUR BUSINESS AT MICROSOFT CORPORATION

Microsoft is the largest software development organization and one of the most successful businesses in the world. In its relatively short history, growth has characterized almost every aspect of the company. Growth fueled not only Microsoft's reputation and no small number of millionaires, but it also demanded that the Microsoft organization mature. As technologies, products, markets, and revenues grew, so did the opportunities for professional advancement. Software development engineers that wanted to guide, shape, and manage the organization's growth found plenty of chances to become managers, directors, and vice presidents.

After years of double-digit growth, senior management at Microsoft worried that promotion of the young and brilliant technologists it had recruited was occurring too fast. While they understood technology, they were ill prepared to manage strategy, structure, people, and change. Interviews with successful and unsuccessful Microsoft managers about the competencies necessary to lead a business confirmed these suspicions. CEO Steve Ballmer believed that the speed of change in the software industry demanded leadership from the middle of the organization where people were closest to the technology and customers. He commissioned Microsoft's Management Development Group (MDG) to create a series of workshops aimed at developing the future leaders of the organization. Three courses were envisioned for the series, including one focused on strategic thinking and strategic change.

The MDG group contacted an OD practitioner with a background in educational interventions, strategy, and large-scale systems change. Together with internal OD practitioners and other members of the MDG organization, the OD practitioner interviewed additional managers, discussed program philosophy and company culture, shared strategy and strategic change concepts, and proposed a variety of methods to transfer the topics of strategic leadership to the participants.

After several weeks of discussions, a two-day workshop design began to emerge. It consisted of a variety of learning technologies and was based on a principle and philosophy of self-managed learning. That is, the OD practitioner and the MDG consultants assumed that the participants, already having achieved a middle-management position, would possess a broad range of experiences and knowledge. The purpose of the workshop would be to marry that experience with the concepts from strategy and change. A number of delivery methods, including lectures, videos, experiential exercises, and case studies, were used to expose the participants to certain topics, such as goals and goal setting, distinctive competencies, environmental scanning, strategy, and strategy implementation. At the beginning of the workshop, the participants would be allowed to form "peer consulting teams" and, following an input module, the teams would work individually and then in groups to apply the concepts to their own business. In this way, the participants actually left the workshop with a roughed-out strategic plan.

The design was "beta tested" with a group of about 20 middle managers and their comments, reactions, and suggestions were used to make adjustments in different parts of the workshop design. For example, the peer consulting groups turned out to be a very powerful idea and all of the groups wanted more time at the beginning of the workshop to explain their business so that the other members of the group had a good understanding of the competitive issues. After the beta workshop, the program was marketed to all middle managers at the Redmond, Washington, headquarters. Eventually, middle managers in Asia, Canada, and Europe were included. Over two years, about 500 of Microsoft's most important future leaders went through the workshop.

Ten days after the workshop, an evaluation was emailed to all participants for the reactions and feedback. This provided an ongoing database to ensure that the program continued to meet the needs of the middle managers. In addition, a qualitative study of the workshop's impact was conducted about a year into the program. A variety of information about how participants had used the workshop was gathered. Most participants rated the course highly, found the materials relevant and useful, had applied many of the frameworks and models in their day-to-day work, and appreciated the opportunity to stop and think about their business. The most highly rated feature of the class was the peer-to-peer learning and the business view the participants gained, there were few examples of direct impact on the organization. However, only a few cases of dramatic success were found, including a substantial increase in strategic focus, clarity, and profitability within one of the Microsoft Office groups; a merger between two groups that was conceived during the workshop and then executed successfully after the program; and the launching of a new strategy within groups of the MSN and Xbox organizations. In each of these cases, the managers reported taking the ideas and plans worked out in the workshop and involving their direct reports in additional discussions. These additional inputs along with the original plans became the basis for implementing changes.

16-2c The Results of Development Interventions

There are hundreds of self-reported case studies in industry magazines and a relatively equal number of evaluation case studies in the academic press. This is due mostly to the widespread application of management and leadership development interventions in the workplace. However, most of the evaluation research consists of only reactions, the weakest measure of effectiveness.[25]

A few of the more rigorous assessments provide some evidence about leadership development effects. For example, a leadership development program at Catholic Healthcare Partners that involved 360-degree feedback and action learning projects indicated both organizational and individual improvements. The greatest individual improvements occurred in self-awareness, setting and achieving goals, and working across boundaries. The greatest organization benefits were an increased focus on strategy and goal setting, more effective teams, and members feeling more empowered in their work.[26] Leadership development programs have reported increased organizational productivity, decreased turnover, and increased sales.[27]

In a book-length evaluation of a leadership development program for school superintendents in the state of Florida, the most common outcomes of the program included the development of strategies and competencies for continuous learning, personal change in specific areas, and progress on learning projects undertaken by groups of participants. However, the researchers note that less than 50% of the participants reported such outcomes and that the most participants reported no or very little change on a survey instrument. Relevant to the reported outcomes, the researchers found no particular element of the program was more or less effective. Finally, the researchers speculated that much of the variation in results was due to the participants themselves. Those superintendents who were in "fine tuning" mode had little to learn while those in a "role expansion" or "new perspectives" mode reported more positive outcomes.[28]

16-3 Career Planning and Development Interventions

Organizations are becoming more and more reliant on their "intellectual capital." The war for talent, the changing nature of the workforce, shifting social expectations about work and family, and increasingly knowledge-based strategies have pressured organizations to clarify their career planning and development strategies.[29] At the same time, the increasing volatility in the marketplace, the readiness of organizations to engage in downsizing initiatives, and the willingness of members to "job hop" have pressured organizations to think through the cost-benefit ratio of implementing such strategies. Providing career planning and development opportunities as well as management and leadership development programs can help to recruit and retain skilled and knowledgeable workers. Many talented job candidates, especially minorities and women, are showing preference and more loyalty for employers who offer career and leadership development opportunities.

Career planning and development interventions are an important tool in developing and retaining an effective workforce. Growing numbers of managers and professional staff are seeking more control over their work lives. Organization members, especially women, minorities, mid-career workers, and new college recruits, are not willing to have their careers "just happen" and are taking an active role in planning and managing them.[30] For example, a study by the Hay Group found that technology professionals were willing to leave their jobs for better career development opportunities.[31]

Many organizations—IBM, Booz-Allen-Hamilton, Aetna, British Telecommunications, Wipro Technologies, and the U.S. Naval Education and Training Command, among others—have adapted their career planning and development programs to meet the needs of their members. These programs have attempted to improve the quality of work life for managers and professionals, enhance their performance, increase employee retention, and respond to equal employment and affirmative action legislation. Companies have discovered that organizational growth and effectiveness require career development programs to ensure that needed talent will be available. Competent managers are often the scarcest resource. Many companies also have experienced the high costs of turnover among recent college graduates, including MBAs; the turnover can reach 50% after five years. Career planning and development interventions help attract and hold such highly talented people and can increase the chances that the organization will use their skills and knowledge.

16-3a What Are the Goals?

Career planning and development interventions provide the appropriate resources, tools, and processes necessary to help organization members plan and attain their career objectives. A career consists of a sequence of work-related positions occupied by a person during the course of a lifetime.[32] *Career planning* is concerned with individuals choosing jobs, occupations, and organizations at each stage of their careers. *Career development* involves helping employees attain career objectives.[33] Although both of these interventions generally are aimed at managerial and professional employees, a growing number of programs are including lower-level employees, particularly those in white-collar jobs.

Research suggests that employees progress through at least four distinct career stages as they mature and gain experience. Each stage has unique concerns, needs, and challenges.

1. **The establishment stage (ages 21–26).** This phase is the outset of a career when people are generally uncertain and may be stressed about their competence and potential. They are dependent on others, especially bosses and more experienced employees, for guidance, support, and feedback. At this stage, people are making initial choices about committing themselves to a specific career, organization, and job. They are exploring possibilities while learning about their own capabilities.

2. **The advancement stage (ages 26–40).** During this phase, employees become independent contributors who are concerned with achieving and advancing in their chosen careers. They have typically learned to perform autonomously and need less guidance from bosses and closer ties with colleagues. This settling-down period also is characterized by attempts to clarify the range of long-term career options.
3. **The maintenance stage (ages 40–60).** This phase involves leveling off and holding on to career successes. Many people at this stage have achieved their greatest advancements and are now concerned with helping less-experienced subordinates. For those who are dissatisfied with their career progress, this period can be conflictual and depressing, as characterized by the term "midlife crisis." People often reappraise their circumstances, search for alternatives, and redirect their career efforts. Success in these endeavors can lead to continuing growth, whereas failure can lead to early decline.
4. **The withdrawal stage (age 60 and above).** This final stage is concerned with leaving a career. It involves letting go of organizational attachments and getting ready for greater leisure time and retirement. The employee's major contributions are imparting knowledge and experience to others. For those people who are generally satisfied with their careers, this period can result in feelings of fulfillment and a willingness to leave the career behind.

The different career stages represent a broad developmental perspective on people's jobs. They provide insight about the personal and career issues that people are likely to face at different career phases. These issues can be potential sources of stress because employees are likely to go through the phases at different rates, and to experience personal and career issues differently at each stage. For example, one person may experience the maintenance stage as a positive opportunity to develop less-experienced employees; another person may experience the maintenance stage as a stressful leveling off of career success.

16-3b Application Stages

The two primary applications steps are to establish a mechanism for career planning and assemble an appropriate set of career development processes.

Establish a Career Planning Mechanism Career planning involves setting individual career objectives. It is a highly personalized process and generally includes assessing one's interests, capabilities, values, and goals; examining alternative careers; making decisions that may affect the current job; and planning how to progress in the desired direction. This process results in people choosing jobs, occupations, and organizations. It determines, for example, whether individuals will accept or decline promotions and transfers and whether they will stay or leave the company for another job or for retirement.

Individual responsibility for careers and career planning has increased significantly, and recent estimates project that an individual career beginning now will involve an average of eight major job and/or organization changes. The U.S. Department of Labor estimates that the average annual turnover in an organization is 20% although turnover rates have declined significantly in recent years reflecting the difficult economic climate. Such turnover rates are not confined to the United States. Turnover among professional employees in China was over 18% in 2006.[34] Further, as organizations downsize and restructure, there is less trust in the organization to provide job

TABLE 16.1

Career Stages and Career Planning Issues

Career Stage	Career Planning Issues
Establishment	What are alternative occupations, organizations, and jobs? What are my interests and capabilities? How do I get the work accomplished? Am I performing as expected? Am I developing the necessary skills for advancement?
Advancement	Am I advancing as expected? How can I advance more effectively? What long-term options are available? How do I get more exposure and visibility? How do I develop more effective peer relationships? How do I better integrate career choices with my personal life?
Maintenance	How do I help others become established and advance? Should I reassess myself and my career? Should I redirect my actions?
Withdrawal	What are my interests outside of work? What postretirement work options are available to me? How can I be financially secure? How can I continue to help others?

security. In the past, when employees more frequently spent their entire career in one organization, careers were judged in terms of advancement and promotion upward in the organizational hierarchy. Today, they are defined in more holistic ways to include a person's attitudes, experiences, and ability to perform. For example, individuals may make numerous job changes to acquire additional responsibilities, skills, and knowledge within or across organizations, or they can remain in the same job, acquiring and developing new skills, and have a successful career. Similarly, people may move horizontally through a series of jobs in different functional areas of the firm. Although they may not be promoted upward in the hierarchy, their broadened job experiences constitute a successful career.

The four career stages can be used to make career planning more effective. Table 16.1 shows the different career stages and the career planning issues relevant at each phase. Applying the table to a particular employee involves first diagnosing the person's existing career stage—establishment, advancement, maintenance, or withdrawal. Next, available career planning resources are used to help the employee address pertinent issues. Career planning programs include some or all of the following resources:

- Communication about career opportunities and resources, such as social networks and employee resource groups, available to employees within the organization
- Workshops to encourage employees to assess their interests, abilities, and job situations and to formulate career development plans
- Career counseling by managers or human resources personnel

- Self-development materials, such as books and articles, webinars and podcasts, and other media, directed toward identifying life and career issues
- Assessment programs that provide various tests of vocational interests, aptitudes, and abilities relevant to setting career goals

According to Table 16.1, the company should provide members in the establishment stage with considerable communication and counseling about available career paths and the skills and abilities needed to progress in them. Workshops, self-development materials, and assessment techniques should be aimed at helping employees assess their interests, aptitudes, and capabilities and at linking that information to possible careers and jobs. Considerable attention should be directed to giving employees continual feedback about job performance and to counseling them about how to improve it. The supervisor–subordinate relationship is especially important for these feedback and development activities.

In the advancement stage, organizations should provide members with communication and counseling about challenging assignments and possibilities for more exposure and demonstration of skills. This communication and counseling should help clarify the range of possible long-term career options and provide members with some idea about where they stand in achieving them. Workshops, developmental materials, and assessment methods should be aimed at helping employees develop wider collegial relationships, join with effective mentors and sponsors, and develop more creativity and innovation. These activities also should help people assess both career and personal life spheres and integrate them more successfully.

At the maintenance stage, the organization should provide information about its long-term vision and communicate with individuals about how they might fit into it. Workshops, developmental materials, counseling, and assessment techniques should be aimed at helping employees to assess and develop skills to train and coach others.

Organizations should provide members in the withdrawal stage with communications and counseling about options for postretirement work and financial security, and it should convey the message that the employee's experience in the organization is still valued. Retirement planning workshops and materials can help employees gain the skills and information necessary to make a successful transition from work to nonwork life. They can prepare people to shift their attention away from the organization to other interests and activities.[35]

Effective career planning and development requires a comprehensive program integrating both corporate business objectives and employee career needs. As shown in Figure 16.1, this is accomplished through human resources planning aimed at developing and maintaining a workforce to meet business objectives. It includes recruiting new talent, matching people to jobs, helping them develop careers and perform effectively, and preparing them for satisfactory retirement. Career planning activities feed into and support career development and human resources planning activities.

Assemble an Appropriate Set of Career Development Processes Career development interventions help individuals achieve their career objectives. Career development follows closely from career planning and includes organizational practices that help employees implement those plans. Career development can be integrated with people's career needs by linking it to different career stages. As described earlier, employees progress through distinct career stages, each with unique issues relevant to career planning. Career development interventions help members implement these plans. Table 16.2 identifies career development interventions, lists the career stages to

FIGURE 16.1

Individual Career Planning and Human Resources Planning

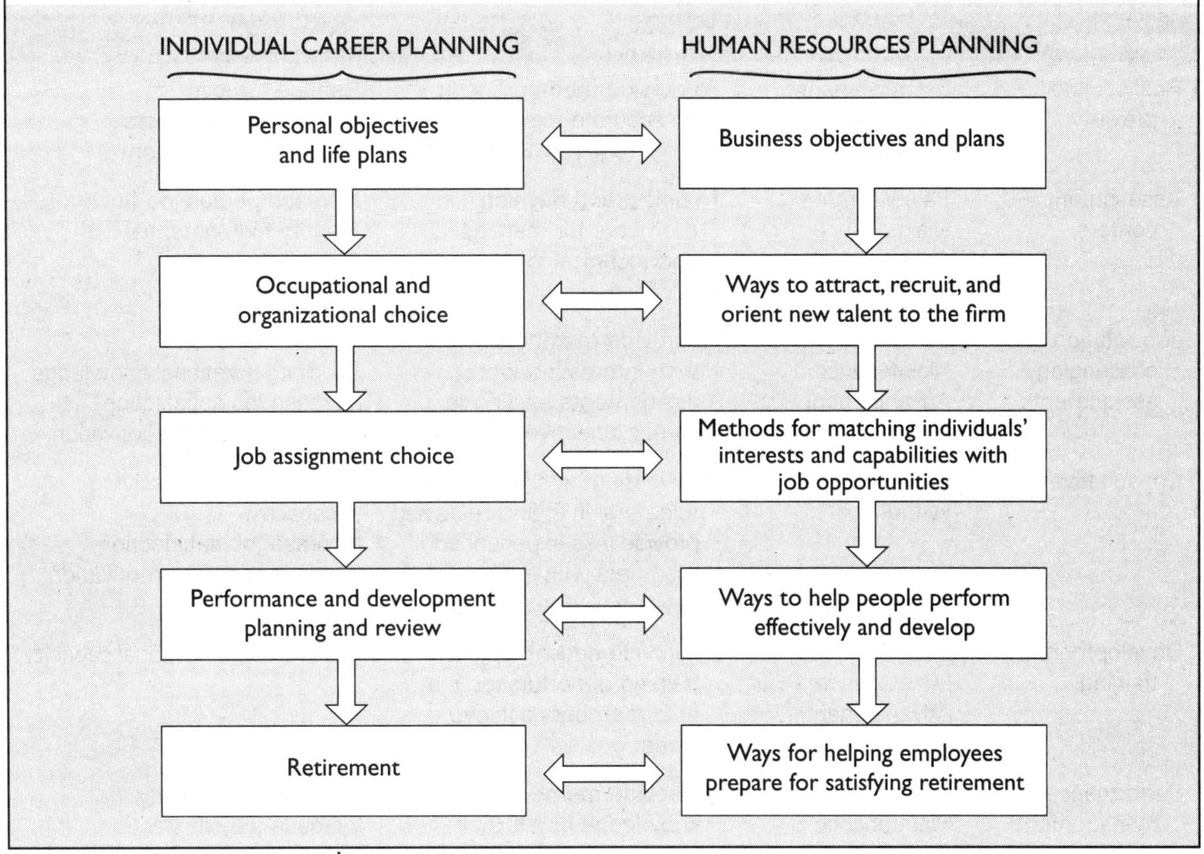

SOURCE: Reprinted with permission from *Business Horizons*, 16(1). © 1973 by The Trustees at Indiana University, Kelley School of Business.

which they are most relevant, and defines their key purposes and intended outcomes. It shows that career development practices may apply to one or more career stages and that many interventions double as both career development processes and interventions in their own right. Performance management, for example, is relevant to all stages, but especially in establishment and advancement stages. It is also an important independent intervention (see Chapter 15). Career development interventions also can contribute to different organizational outcomes such as lowering turnover and costs and enhancing member satisfaction.

Career development interventions traditionally have been applied to younger employees who have a longer time period to contribute to the organization than do older members. Managers often stereotype older employees as being less creative, alert, and productive than younger workers and consequently provide them with less career development support. However, the aging of the workforce has focused new attention on older workers, including a focus on the pace and organization of work, physical and psychological factors, and ergonomic factors.[36] Table 16.2 suggests that the OD field has kept pace with these trends: six of the eight interventions presented

TABLE 16.2

Career Development Interventions

Intervention	Career Stage	Purpose	Intended Outcome
Realistic job preview	Establishment Maintenance Advancement	To provide members with an accurate expectation of work requirements	Reduce turnover Reduce training costs Increase commitment
Assessment centers	Establishment Maintenance Advancement Withdrawal	To select and develop members for managerial and technical jobs	Increase person-job fit Identify high-potential candidates
Job rotation and challenging assignments	Establishment Maintenance Advancement	To provide members with interesting work assignments leading to career objective	Reduce turnover Build organizational knowledge Increase job satisfaction Maintain member motivation
Consultative roles	Maintenance Withdrawal	To help members fill productive roles later in their careers and provide less experienced members with exposure to key knowledge and skill	Increase problem-solving capacity Increase job satisfaction Increase member motivation
Developmental training	Establishment Maintenance Advancement Withdrawal	To provide education and training opportunities that help members achieve career goals	Increase organizational capacity
Performance management	Establishment Maintenance Advancement Withdrawal	To provide members with knowledge about their career progress and work effectiveness	Increase productivity Increase job satisfaction Monitor human resources development
Work life balance	Establishment Maintenance Advancement Withdrawal	To help members balance work and personal goals	Improve quality of life Increase productivity and morale Increase organizational commitment Decrease absenteeism Decrease turnover

there apply to the withdrawal stage. This emphasis is likely to remain as the U.S. workforce continues to gray. To sustain a highly committed and motivated workforce, organizations increasingly will have to address the career needs of older employees. They will have to recognize and reward the contributions that older workers make to the company. Workforce diversity interventions, discussed in the next chapter, are a positive step in that direction.

We present eight interventions that can be mixed and matched to meet the needs of a diverse workforce, including realistic job previews, assessment centers, job rotation and challenging assignments, consultative roles and mentoring, performance management, developmental training, work-life balance, and phased retirement.

Realistic Job Preview. This intervention provides applicants with credible expectations about the job during the recruitment process. It provides recruits with information about whether the job is likely to be consistent with their needs and career plans. Knowledge resulting from realistic job previews can be especially useful during the establishment stage, when people are most in need of full and balanced information about organizations and jobs. It also can help employees during the advancement stage, when job changes are likely to occur because of promotion. Research suggests that people may develop unrealistic expectations about the organization and job. They can suffer from "reality shock" when those expectations are not fulfilled and may leave the organization or stay and become disgruntled and unmotivated. To overcome these problems, organizations such as Bank of America, AON Consulting, the Transportation Security Administration, and Johnson & Johnson provide new recruits with information about both the positive and negative aspects of the company and the job. They furnish recruits with booklets, talks, videos, and site visits showing what organizational life is really like. Such information reduces the chances that employees will develop unrealistic job expectations, become disgruntled, and leave the company, especially when their tenure is viewed over the long term.[37]

Assessment Centers. This intervention was traditionally designed to help organizations select and develop employees with high potential for managerial jobs. More recently, assessment centers have been extended to career development and to selection of people to fit new work designs, such as self-managing teams, or organizational growth.[38] Assessment centers can be designed and operated "in house," but are often contracted out to consulting firms that specialize in selection and assessment psychology.

When used to evaluate managerial capability, assessment centers typically process 12 to 15 people at a time and require them to spend two to three days on site. Participants are given a comprehensive interview, take several tests of mental ability and knowledge, and participate in individual and group exercises intended to simulate managerial work. An assessment team consisting of experienced managers and human resources specialists observes the behaviors and performance of each candidate. This team arrives at an overall assessment of each participant's managerial potential, including a rating on several items believed to be relevant to managerial success in the organization, and pass the results to management for use in making promotion decisions.

Assessment centers have been applied to career development as well, where the emphasis is on feedback of results to participants. Trained staff help participants hear and understand feedback about their strong and weak points. They help participants become clearer about career advancement and identify training experiences and job assignments to promote that progress. When used for developmental purposes, assessment centers can provide employees with the support and direction needed for career development. They can demonstrate that the company is a partner rather than an adversary in that process. Although assessment centers can help people's careers at all stages of development, they seem particularly useful at the advancement stage, when employees need to assess their talents and capabilities in light of long-term career commitments.

Job Rotation and Challenging Assignments. The purpose of these interventions is to provide employees with the experience and visibility needed for career advancement or with the challenge needed to revitalize a stagnant career at the maintenance stage. A more formalized approach to job rotation is called *job pathing or career ladders*, which specify a sequence of jobs to reach a career objective, although the notion of a job path in the new economy is being challenged.[39] Job rotation and challenging assignments are less planned and may not be as oriented to promotion opportunities.

Job rotation during the establishment and advancement stages help members develop new skills, knowledge, and competencies in new jobs. Organization members in the advancement stage may be moved into new job areas after they have demonstrated competence in a particular work specialty. Research suggests that employees who receive challenging job assignments early in their careers do better in later jobs.[40] Companies such as General Electric, Intel, Campbells, Pirelli, and Fidelity Investments identify "comers" (managers under 40 years of age with potential for assuming top management positions) and "hipos" (high-potential candidates) and provide them with cross-divisional job experiences during the advancement stage. These job transfers provide managers with a broader range of skills and knowledge as well as opportunities to display their managerial talent to a wider audience of corporate executives. Such exposure helps the organization identify members who are capable of handling senior executive responsibilities; it helps the members decide whether to seek promotion to higher positions or to particular departments. Retaining "hipos" is seen as critical to success in today's highly competitive labor market.[41] To reduce the risk of transferring employees across divisions or functions, some firms create "fallback positions." These jobs are identified before the transfer, and employees are guaranteed that they can return to them without negative consequences if the transfers or promotions do not work out. Fallback positions reduce the risk that employees in the advancement stage will become trapped in a new job assignment that is neither challenging nor highly visible in the company.

In the maintenance stage, challenging assignments or job pathing can help revitalize veteran employees by providing them with new challenges and opportunities for learning and contribution. For example, enriched jobs are more likely to be seen as challenging and motivating during the first one to three years an individual is in the position.[42] People who have leveled off and remained in enriched jobs for three years or more may become unresponsive to their motivating features. One way to prevent this loss of job motivation—especially among mid-career employees who are likely to remain on jobs for longer periods of time than are people in the establishment and advancement phases—is to rotate workers to new, more challenging jobs at about three-year intervals, or to redesign their jobs at those times. Such job changes would keep employees responsive to challenging jobs and sustain motivation and satisfaction during the maintenance phase.[43]

Consultative Roles. This role involves opportunities to apply wisdom and knowledge to helping others develop in their careers and solve organizational problems, and is most frequently offered to employees in the maintenance and withdrawal stages. Such roles, which can be structured around specific projects or problems, involve offering advice and expertise to those responsible for resolving the issues, thus increasing the organization's problem-solving abilities. For example, a large aluminum-forging manufacturer was having problems developing accurate estimates of the cost of producing new products. The sales and estimating departments lacked the production experience to make accurate bids for potential new business, thus either losing customers or losing money on products. The company temporarily assigned a production manager who was nearing retirement to consult with the salespeople and estimators about bidding on new business. The consultant applied his years of forging experience to help the sales and estimating people make more accurate estimates. In about a year, the sales staff and estimators gained the skills and invaluable knowledge necessary to make more accurate bids. Perhaps equally important, the preretirement production manager felt that he had made a significant contribution to the company—something he had not experienced for years.

In contrast to coaching and mentoring, consultative roles are not necessarily focused directly on guiding or sponsoring younger employees' careers. They are directed at helping others deal with complex problems or projects. Similarly, in contrast to managerial positions, consultative roles do not include the performance evaluation and control inherent in being a manager. They are based more on wisdom and experience than on authority. Consequently, consultative roles provide an effective transition for moving preretirement managers into more support-staff positions. They free up managerial positions for younger employees while allowing older managers to apply their experience and skills in a more supportive and less threatening way than might be possible from a strictly managerial role.

Developmental Training. Training and development interventions are among the oldest strategies for organizational change.[44] They provide new or existing organization members with the skills and knowledge they need to perform work. The focus of training interventions has broadened from classroom methods aimed at hourly workers to varied methods, including simulations, action learning, computer-based or on-line training, and case studies, intended for all levels and types of organization members.

Training and development is a large practice area with growing importance in organizations. The American Society of Training and Development (ASTD) (www.astd.org), the largest professional organization, has over 38,000 members worldwide. According to its most recent state of the industry report, U.S. companies spent about $171.5 billion on learning and development in 2010.[45] Training and development represents an important organization investment accounting for between 2.2% and 2.7% of a company's payroll on average.

This intervention is applicable to all career stages and helps employees gain the skills and knowledge for successfully fulfilling current job responsibilities. It may include workshops and training materials oriented to communications or supervising others as well as technical aspects of work. It can also involve substantial investments in education, such as tuition reimbursement programs that assist members in achieving advanced degrees. Developmental training interventions generally are aimed at increasing the organization's reservoir of skills and knowledge, and can be related to increased retention and performance.[46] This enhances its capability to implement personal and organizational strategies.

Performance Management. One of the most effective interventions during the establishment and advancement phases is the integration of performance management systems with career development conversations. As suggested in the discussions of goal setting and performance appraisal interventions (Chapter 15), employees need continual feedback about goal achievement as well as the necessary support to improve their performances. Feedback and support, in the form of coaching, developmental training, or management development are particularly relevant when employees are establishing careers. They have concerns about how to perform the work, whether they are performing up to expectations, and whether they are gaining the necessary skills for advancement. A manager can facilitate career establishment by providing feedback on performance and on-the-job training. These activities can help employees get the job done while meeting their career development needs. Companies such as Steelcase, Wipro, and Intercontinental Hotels Group, for example, are effective at integrating performance management processes with employee career development. They separate the career development aspect of performance appraisal from the salary review component, thus ensuring that employees' career needs receive as much attention as salary issues. Feedback and support interventions can increase employee performance, satisfaction, and morale, and provide a systematic way to monitor the development of human resources in the firm, at little or no cost.[47]

Work–Life Balance Interventions. This OD intervention helps employees better integrate and balance work and home life. Restructuring, downsizing, and increased global competition have contributed to longer work hours and more stress. Generation X'ers and baby-boomers approaching the withdrawal career stage are rethinking their priorities and seeking to restore some balance in a work-dominated life. Organizations from a variety of industries, such as Wegmans and Whole Foods in grocery, The Container Store in retailing, and USAA in insurance were included in *Fortune*'s 2012 "100 Best Companies to Work For," are responding to these concerns so they can attract, retain, and motivate the best workforce.[48] In addition, many cities, such as Boston, San Francisco, Denver, and Birmingham, are identifying and publishing a "Best Companies" list.[49]

Early work–life balance programs started with a focus on women with young children in the workforce, but now these programs serve men and women, all ages, and all family and life situations. Work life programs continue to focus on dependent care of both children and elders, but they also focus on job scheduling and flexibility, paid and unpaid leaves, employee wellness, concierge services, and others. Work–life balance planning helps members better manage the interface between work or paid employment and all the work and responsibilities associated with a person's life.

Although these interventions can apply to all career stages, they are especially relevant during advancement. This is because of the increased number of dual career households. Transfer to another location—a common occurrence during the advancement stage—usually means that the working partner must also relocate. In many cases, the company employing the partner must either lose the employee or arrange a transfer to the same location. Dual careers also affect expatriate assignments, and being able to facilitate or accommodate a spouse or partner's wish to work may make the difference in terms of an employee accepting such an assignment. Similar problems can occur in recruiting employees. A recruit may not join an organization if its location does not provide career opportunities for the partner.

Phased Retirement. This intervention provides older employees with an effective way of withdrawing from the organization and establishing a productive leisure life by gradually reducing work hours and moving to full retirement.[50] A study of women over 35 indicates a strong interest for phased retirement plans, which may put new demands on related human resource management programs.[51] Employees gradually devote less of their time to the organization and more time to leisure pursuits (which to some might include developing a new career). For example, people may use the extra time off work to take courses, to gain new skills and knowledge, and to create opportunities for productive leisure. IBM, for example, once offered tuition rebates for courses on any topic taken within three years of retirement.[52] Many IBM preretirees used this program to prepare for second careers.

Equally important, phased retirement lessens the reality shock often experienced by those who retire all at once. It helps employees grow accustomed to leisure life and withdraw emotionally from the organization. A growing number of companies have some form of phased retirement. Pepperdine University and the University of Southern California, for example, implemented a phased retirement program for professors that allow them some choice about part-time employment starting at age 55. The program is intended to provide more promotional positions for younger academics and to give older professors greater opportunities to establish a leisure life and still enjoy many benefits of the university.

Application 16.2 describes how the HR organization within PepsiCo evolved its career planning and development processes.[53]

application 16.2

PEPSICO'S CAREER PLANNING AND DEVELOPMENT FRAMEWORK

PepsiCo has a long and well deserved history of innovative employee and leadership development practices. However, in the late 1990s, a significant number of strategic and organizational changes, including the spin-off of Tricon and the Pepsi Bottling Group and the acquisition of Tropicana and Quaker, had left employees feeling unsure about the requirements for success in the organization. In particular, employees wanted to know more about how to build a successful career within the new organization. Moreover, and because of Pepsi's traditionally entrepreneurial and autonomous culture, each business unit had set up its own way of developing employees. In this new organization, employees wanted more information about how to take advantage of cross-business unit and cross-functional opportunities.

In response, senior management tasked the internal OD group to partner with the HR organization and line managers to develop tools and processes to address these concerns. Their initial efforts resulted in:

- The *PepsiCo Leadership Model* that outlined leadership competencies and provided a framework for the 360-degree feedback process
- A career-development web resource called *MyDevelopNet* that provided assessment tools and development resources
- A cross-business unit job posting process called *MyCareerConnection* that listed open jobs in other functions and business units

Although these tools and processes became an important part of PepsiCo's career planning and development process, people continued to want more detail and support regarding what it took to build a successful career in a given function.

The interest in functional careers was somewhat at odds with Pepsi's strong division focused culture. To shift from a business unit-focused approach to broader and standardized enterprise view, the organization needed to explore the importance of consistency in language and processes across specialties but within functions. The HR function was selected to pilot the approach—to set the agenda, lead the initiative, and resolve any problems inherent in the design and implementation process. The task force, representing the ten specialties within global HR (e.g., compensation, benefits, diversity, staffing, OD), was established in 2003 to develop a fully integrated career solution within the HR function. It was chartered with the following objectives:

1. Provide employees access to *career information* that will allow greater ownership of their development and enhanced development planning discussions with their managers
2. Provide consistent language around *competencies, leadership skills, and the critical experiences* required for career progression in the HR function at PepsiCo
3. Provide greater clarity regarding *different opportunities* and choices rather than prescribed paths.

If properly designed and implemented, the intervention would result in a stronger and more capable HR function—one that spoke a consistent language across very different types of specialties, and had a greater emphasis on individual development and career growth. In addition, it would pave the way for similar efforts in other major functions such as sales, marketing, finance, operations, and R&D. Based on this diagnosis, the HR Careers Task Force adopted a five step, OD-related process that emphasized input from key stakeholders across the function as well as early involvement and participation in the process.

The first step was to develop an appropriate competency model for the HR function. The task force collected lists of HR competencies from internal and external sources, including business unit models, professional associations, and the literature. Importantly, although several business units had their own competency list, a successful intervention required a list that worked well with all employees in HR. The resulting model consisted of 12 competencies that were measured by 50 specific areas of applied knowledge and practice.

The second step was to identify the jobs that would be part of the solution. The task force believed that it was unrealistic to analyze and include every job in a function. Rather, the team identified key positions with multiple incumbents within each of the ten HR specialties. These jobs represented consistent, sustainable, long-term roles to which employees could aspire as part of their career planning. The final list of key jobs comprised the target for their work.

The third step was to validate and calibrate the competencies for each of these key jobs. To do that, the task force created a "job modeling" survey that sampled the incumbents in the key jobs across the entire HR function. The first 50 questions represented the key HR competencies identified in Step 1, and asked participants to rate the proficiency level required to do the job well. The next set of questions were drawn from the *PepsiCo Leadership Model* to understand the leadership emphasis required in the job, and the final section asked about the experiences the incumbents were gaining from the role. For example, did the job provide the opportunity to partner with other divisions, manage a merger or acquisition process, or apply organization design skills.

The fourth step required the task force to build the key job database so that it could be used by managers and employees. That is, whenever a manager, HR professional, or executive coach sat down with an employee to have a career conversation, the data base needed to be able to address at least three questions:

1. Where are the jobs (level, location, specialty area)?
2. What are the different accountabilities, experiences, and competencies required for the job?
3. How do I get to the next job from where I am?

The database was designed to provide information on each of these questions and to facilitate rich career discussions. Data elements in the profiles included: overall position description, key accountabilities, requisite functional and leadership competencies, experiences gained, typical next jobs within and across levels and functions, required education and experience, and interactions with other roles.

To facilitate the database's use, additional supporting tools were developed, including:

- an interactive online tool that allowed employees to view all of the key jobs in the function and their own division with typical next steps identified for each position
- the ability to initiate self-assessments against functional or leadership competencies and compare those with either the current job or any other job in the database
- the ability to request a manager's assessment on an employee against the same competencies for comparison and discussion
- a HR Resource Guide containing development tips, tactics, and resources to help employees build their functional competencies
- a behavioral interviewing guide to assist in job interviews and placements
- new training resources and modules to support deeper knowledge acquisition in key areas of need.

The database and tools were shared with managers, functional VPs, and senior leaders to ensure that the jobs were properly calibrated against others both within and across HR divisions. This data feedback stage was time consuming but ensured the product was of high quality and high validity, created additional buy-in on the part of leaders to actually use the tools, and allowed leaders to reevaluate the nature and accountabilities of the jobs in question.

The final step of the process involved implementing the system and evaluating its acceptance and use for areas in need of adjustment. Each HR specialty created their own integrated rollout strategy based on current initiatives and available resources. Certain key messages and tools supporting the framework and their relationship to existing HR processes were standardized to ensure a common language and approach to career development.

16-3c The Results of Career Planning and Development

As shown in this section, career planning and development is a broad field within organization development. A variety of studies have examined individual aspects of career development. For example:

- Realistic job previews have been associated with reduced turnover and training costs, and increased organization commitment and job satisfaction[54]
- Assessment centers have been associated with career advancement when the participant works on the recommended areas of improvement[55]
- Challenging assignments and job rotations have helped "plateaued employees" (those with little chance of further advancement) increase their work satisfaction and productivity if the organization supports lateral (as opposed to strictly vertical) job changes[56]
- General training programs in organizations have produced documented returns on investment from 16% to 492%[57]
- Work life balance interventions have led to beneficial outcomes for both employees and organizations, including increased creativity, morale, and effectiveness, and decreased absenteeism and turnover.[58]

This variety of career planning and development interventions also makes program evaluation very difficult, although the overall assessment of its impact on retention and motivation remains positive.

SUMMARY

This chapter presented three major human resources interventions: coaching and mentoring; leadership and management development interventions; and career planning and development interventions. Although human resources specialists generally carry out these kinds of change programs, OD practitioners are gaining competence in these areas and are increasingly involved in these interventions.

Coaching interventions are aimed at helping individuals. Although it can be an integral part of other OD interventions, it is intended to help individuals clarify their goals, deal with potential stumbling blocks, learn to lead change, and improve their performance.

Management and leadership development programs build leadership skills, often in alignment with a predetermined set of competencies, socialize managers and leadership in a set of values believed to be important to the success of the organization, and help execute strategic change agendas. Leadership development is one of the most popular OD interventions today.

Both management and leadership development and career planning and development interventions are intended to improve the organization's ability to develop and retain a valuable workforce. Career planning involves helping people choose jobs, occupations, and organizations at different stages of their careers. It is a highly personalized process that includes assessing one's interests, values, and capabilities; examining alternative careers; and making relevant decisions. Career development helps employees achieve career objectives. Effective efforts in that direction include linking corporate business objectives, human resources needs, and the personal needs of employees. Different career development needs and practices exist and are relevant to each of the four stages of people's careers.

NOTES

1. J. Boudreau and P. Ramstad, *Beyond HR* (Cambridge, MA: Harvard Business School Publishing, 2007).
2. J. Boudreau and I. Ziskin, "The Future of HR and Effective Organizations," *Organizational Dynamics* 20 (2011): 255–66; A. Myers and S. Edwards, "Educational Leave of Absence: Retaining High-Potential Employees Pursuing MBA Degrees," *Cornell HR Review* (June 2012), accessed from http://www.cornellhrreview.org/educational-leave-of-absence-retaining-high-potential-employees-pursuing-mba-degrees on January 15, 2013.
3. J. Passmore, "An Integrative Model for Executive Coaching," *Consulting Psychology Journal* 59 (2007): 68–78; M. O'Neill, *Executive Coaching with Backbone and Heart: A Systems Approach to Engaging Leaders with Their Challenges* (San Francisco: Jossey-Bass, 2000); M. Goldsmith, L. Lyons, A. Freas, and R. Witherspoon, eds., *Coaching for Leadership: How the World's Greatest Coaches Help Leaders Learn* (San Francisco: Jossey-Bass, 2000); C. Fitzgerald and J. Berger, eds., *Executive Coaching: Practices and Perspectives* (Palo Alto, CA: Davies-Black Publisher, 2002).
4. W. Evers, A. Brouwers, and W. Tomic, "A Quasi-experimental Study on Management Coaching Effectiveness," *Consulting Psychology Journal* 58 (2006): 174–82; B. Patwell and E. Seashore, *Triple Impact Coaching* (Columbia, MD: Bingham House Books, 2006); K. Kram, *Mentoring at Work* (Glenview, IL: Scott, Foresman, 1984); A. Geiger-DuMond and S. Boyle, "Mentoring: A Practitioner's Guide," *Training and Development* (March 1995): 51–54; E. Collins and P. Scott, "Everyone Who Makes It Has a Mentor," *Harvard Business Review* 56 (July–August 1978): 100; M. Murray, *Beyond the Myths and Magic of Mentoring* (San Francisco: Jossey-Bass, 1991).
5. R. Heckler, *The Anatomy of Change: A Way to Move Through Life's Transition* (Berkeley, CA: North Atlantic Books, 1993); L. Whitworth, H. House, P. Sandahl, and H. Kimsey-House, *Co-active Coaching: New Skills for Coaching People Toward Success in Work and Life* (Palo Alto, CA: Davies-Black Publishing, 1998); R. Hargrove, *Masterful Coaching: Extraordinary Results by Impacting People and the Way They Think and Work Together* (San Diego: Pfeiffer and Co., 1995).
6. D. Coutu and C. Kauffman, "What Can Coaches Do for You?" *Harvard Business Review* (January 2009): 91–97.
7. J. Gephardt, "From Therapist to Executive Coach," in *Consultation for Organizational Change*, vol. 1, ed. A. Buono and D. Jamieson (Charlotte, NC: Information Age Publishing, 2010): 155–80; V. Hart, J. Blattner, and S, Leipsic, "Coaching versus Therapy: A Perspective," *Consulting Psychology Journal* 53 (2001): 229–37.
8. M. O'Neill, *Executive Coaching with Backbone and Heart* (San Francisco: Jossey-Bass, 2000); C. Gegner, *Coaching: Theory and Practice* (San Francisco: University of San Francisco, 1997); S. Kampa-Kokesch and M. Anderson, "Executive Coaching: A Comprehensive Review of the Literature," *Consulting Psychology Journal* 53 (2001): 205–28; Patwell and Seashore, *Triple Impact Coaching*.
9. J. Flaherty, *Coaching: Evoking Excellence in Others* (Burlington, MA: Butterworth-Heinemann, 1998).
10. A. Grant, *Workplace, Executive and Life Coaching: An Annotated Bibliography from the Behavioural Science and Business Literature (May 2009)*, Coaching Psychology Unit, University of Sydney, Australia, 2009; Kampa-Kokesch and Anderson, "Executive Coaching"; Evers, Brouwers, and Tomic, "A Quasi-experimental Study on Management Coaching Effectiveness."
11. L. Miller, "Coaching Pays Off," *HR Magazine*, March 2001, 16.
12. Gegner, *Coaching: Theory and Practice*.
13. Evers, Brouwers, and Tomic, "A Quasi-experimental Study on Management Coaching Effectiveness."
14. A. Grant, L. Curtayne, and G. Burton, "Executive Coaching Enhances Goal Attainment, Resilience and Workplace Well-being: A Randomised Controlled Study," *Journal of Positive Psychology* 4, no. 5 (2009): 296–407.
15. J. Passmore and A. Fillery-Travis, "A Critical Review of Executive Coaching Research: A Decade of Progress and What's to Come," *Coaching: An International Journal of Theory, Research and Practice* 4, no. 2 (2011): 70–88.
16. G. Roche, "Much Ado About Mentors," *Harvard Business Review* 57 (January-February 1979): 14–28.
17. D. Thomas, "The Truth About Mentoring Minorities: Race Matters," *Harvard Business Review* 79 (April 2001): 98–107; E. Fagensen and G. Baugh, "Career Paths, Networking, and Mentoring," in *Women at Work*, ed. D. Smith (Saddle River, NJ: Prentice-Hall, 2000).
18. J. Conger and B. Benjamin, *Building Leaders: How Successful Companies Develop the Next Generation* (San Francisco: Jossey-Bass, 1999).
19. R. Rosen and F. Adair, "CEO's Misperceive Top Management Team Performance," *Harvard Business Review* (September 2007): 30.
20. C. Worley and A. Feyerherm, "Reflections on the Future of OD," *Journal of Applied Behavioral Science* 39 (2003): 97–115.

21. I. Goldstein, "Training in Work Organizations," in *Handbook of Industrial and Organizational Psychology*, ed. M. Dunnette (Chicago: Rand McNally, 1976), 507–619; G. Dessler, *Essentials of Human Resource Management* (Upper Saddle River, NJ: Prentice Hall, 1999); C. Greer, *Strategic Human Resource Management* (Upper Saddle River, NJ: Prentice Hall, 2001); Conger and Benjamin, *Building Leaders*; R. Fulmer and J. Conger, *Growing Your Company's Leaders* (New York: AMACOM, 2004).
22. Goldstein, "Training in Work Organizations"; M. McCall and G. Hollenbeck, "Getting Leadership Development Right," *Leadership Excellence* 24 (2007): 8–10, accessed from http://proquest.umi.com.lib.pepperdine.edu/pqdweb?RQT=572&VType=PQD&VName=PQD&VInst=PROD&pmid=14272&pcid=35414921&Srch Mode=3.
23. McCall and Hollenbeck, "Getting Leadership Development Right."
24. D. Kirkpatrick, "Techniques for Evaluating Training Programs," *Journal of the American Society of Training Directors* 13 (1959): 21–26.
25. L. Ralphs and E. Stephan, "HRD in the *Fortune* 500," *Training and Development Journal* 40 (1986): 69–76; A. Alliger and E. Janak, "Kirkpatrick's Levels of Training Criteria: Thirty Years Later," *Personnel Psychology* 42 (1989): 331–41.
26. C. McCauley and M. Hughes-James, *An Evaluation of the Outcomes of a Leadership Development Program* (Greensboro, NC: Center for Creative Leadership, 1994); Center for Creative Leadership, "Developing Next-Generation Leaders Within an Action-Learning Approach" (Greensboro, NC: Center for Creative Leadership, n.d.), accessed from http://www.ccl.org on August 22, 2007.
27. J. Porras and B. Anderson, "Improving Managerial Effectiveness Through Modeling-based Training," *Organizational Dynamics* 9 (1981): 60–77; J. Barling, T. Weber, and E. Kelloway, "Effects of Transformational Leadership Training on Attitudinal and Financial Outcomes," *Journal of Applied Psychology* 81 (1996): 827–32.
28. McCauley and Hughes-James, *An Evaluation of the Outcomes of a Leadership Development Program.*
29. E. Michaels, H. Handfield-Jones, and B. Axelrod, *The War for Talent* (Boston: Harvard Business School Press, 2001); J. Whitmore, *Coaching for Performance,* 3rd ed. (London: Nicholas Brealey Publishing, 2002).
30. J. Fierman, "Beating the Midlife Career Crisis," *Fortune,* September 6, 1993, 52–62; L. Richman, "How to Get Ahead in America," *Fortune,* May 16, 1994, 46–54; D. Hall, "Protean Careers of the 21st Century," *Academy of Management Journal* 10 (1996): 8–16;
31. "IT Workers Expect Career Development and Job Satisfaction," *HR Focus* (August 1, 1999): 4.
32. S. Niles and J. Harris-Bowlsbey, *Career Development Interventions in the 21st Century,* 4th ed. (New York: Pearson, 2013); D. Feldman, *Managing Careers in Organizations* (Glenview, Ill.: Scott, Foresman, 1988).
33. G. Bohlander and S. Snell, *Managing Human Resources* (Cincinnati, OH: South-Western College Publishing, 2004).
34. S. Derkach, "Exploring Retention of Chinese Employees in Western-based Multinationals," Unpublished Master's Thesis (Malibu, CA: Pepperdine University, 2007).
35. C. Thompson, E. Koon, W. Woodwell, and J. Beauvais, "Training for the Next Economy: An ASTD State of the Industry Report on Trends in Employer-provided Training in the U.S.," American Society of Training and Development, 2002.
36. N. Munk, "Finished at Forty," *Fortune,* February 1, 1999, 50–66; "How to Prepare for the Coming Older Workforce," *IOMA's Safety Director's Report* 1 (April 2001).
37. R. Finnegan, *Rethinking Retention in Good Times and Bad* (Boston: Davies-Black, 2010); J. Wanous, "Effects of a Realistic Job Preview on Job Acceptance, Job Attitudes, and Job Survival," *Journal of Applied Psychology* 58 (1973): 327–32; S. Premack and J. Wanous, "A Meta-Analysis of Realistic Job Preview Experiments," *Journal of Applied Psychology* 70 (1985): 706–19.
38. G. Thornton, *Assessment Centers* (Reading, MA: Addison-Wesley, 1992); A. Engelbrecht and H. Fischer, "The Managerial Performance Implications of a Developmental Assessment Center Process," *Human Relations* 48 (1995): 387–404; P. Griffiths and P. Goodge, "Development Centres: The Third Generation," *Personnel Management* 26, no. 6 (1994): 40–43; P. Geradus, W. Jansen, and F. DeJongh, *Assessment Centres: A Practical Handbook* (New York: John Wiley & Sons, 1998); R. Jones and M. Whitmore, "Evaluating Developmental Assessment Centers as Interventions," *Personnel Psychology* 48 (1995): 377–88; M. Lehman, J. Hudson Jr., G. Appley, E. Sheehan Jr., and D. Slevin, "Modified Assessment Center Approach Facilitates Organizational Change," *Journal of Management Development* 30 (2011): 893–913.
39. L. Thurow, "Building Wealth," *Atlantic Monthly,* June 1999, 57–69.
40. D. Bray, R. J. Campbell, and D. Grant, *Formative Years in Business: A Long Term AT&T Study of Managerial Lives* (New York: John Wiley & Sons, 1974).
41. J. Boudreau and P. Ramstad, *Beyond HR: The New Science of Human Capital* (Boston: Harvard Business School Press, 2007); B. Kaye and S. Jordan-Evans, "From Assets to Investors," *Training & Development* 57 (2003): 40–46.
42. R. Katz, "Time and Work: Towards an Integrative Perspective," in *Research in Organizational Behavior,* vol. 2, ed.

B. Staw and L. Cummings (New York: JAI Press, 1979), 81–127.

43. K. Brousseau, "Toward a Dynamic Model of Job-Person Relationships: Findings, Research Questions, and Implications for Work System Design," *Academy of Management Review* 8 (January 1983): 33–45.

44. R. Chin and K. Benne, "General Strategies for Effecting Changes in Human Systems," in *The Planning of Change*, 3rd ed., ed. W. Bennis, K. Benne, and R. Chin (New York: Holt, Rinehart and Winston, 1976).

45. R. Fulmer and M. Goldsmith, *The Leadership Investment: How the World's Best Organizations Gain Strategic Advantage Through Leadership Development* (New York: AMACOM, 2000).

46. S. Wager, "Retention Update," *Training & Development* 55 (2001): 63–66.

47. F. Balcazar, B. Hopkins, and Y. Suarez, "A Critical Objective Review of Performance Feedback," *Journal of Organizational Behavior Management* 7 (1986): 65–89; J. Chobbar and J. Wallin, "A Field Study on the Effect of Feedback Frequency on Performance," *Journal of Applied Psychology* 69 (1984): 524–30; R. Waldersee and F. Luthans, "A Theoretically Based Contingency Model of Feedback: Implications for Managing Service Employees," *Journal of Organizational Change Management* 3 (1990): 46–56; P. Swinburne, "How to Use Feedback to Improve Performance," *People Management* 7 (2001): 11.

48. CNNMoney, "*Fortune*'s 100 Best Companies to Work For," *Fortune*, January 30, 2012, accessed from http://jobs.aol.com/articles/2012/01/30/fortunes-100-best-companies-to-work-for on August 13, 2012.

49. For an example, see S. Merkner, ed., *Birmingham's Best Companies for Working Families 2000 Annual Report* (Birmingham: Child Times, Inc., 2003).

50. Allerton, "Trend Watch," *Training & Development* 54, no. 1 (January 2000): 11.

51. J. Gordon, L. Litchfield, and K. Whelan-Berry, *Women at Midlife and Beyond: A Glimpse into the Future* (Chestnut Hill, MA: Boston College Center for Work & Family, 2003).

52. J. Ivancevich and W. Glueck, *Foundations of Personnel/Human Resource Management*, 3rd ed. (Plano, TX: Business Publications, 1986), 541.

53. A. Church and M. Herena, "The PepsiCo HR Career Framework," *OD Practitioner* 35 (2003): 27–33.

54. B. Meglino, A. DeNisi, S. Youngblood, and K. Williams, "Effects of Realistic Job Previews: A Comparison Using an Enhancement and a Reduction Preview," *Journal of Applied Psychology* 73 (1988): 259–66; J. Vandenberg and V. Scarpello, "The Matching Method: An Examination of the Processes Underlying Realistic Job Previews," *Journal of Applied Psychology* 75 (1990): 60–67.

55. R. Jones and M. Whitmore, "Evaluating Developmental Assessment Centers as Interventions," *Personnel Psychology* 48 (1995): 377–88.

56. J. Carnazza, A. Korman, T. Ference, and J. Stoner, "Plateaued and Non-Plateaued Managers: Factors in Job Performance," *Journal of Management* 7 (1981): 7–27.

57. C. Morrow, M. Jarrett, and M. Rupinski, "An Investigation of the Effect and Economic Utility of Corporate-wide Training," *Personnel Psychology* 50 (1997): 91–119.

58. "Absence Makes the Business Run Slower," *Journal of Business Strategy* 22 (2001): 3.

17

Workforce Diversity and Wellness

learning objectives

Examine human resources management interventions related to workforce diversity.

Understand and evaluate the effectiveness of employee wellness interventions.

This chapter presents two additional human resources management interventions in organizations. Increasing workforce diversity provides an especially challenging environment for human resources management, and an attractive opportunity for line managers looking for a source of innovation. The mix of age, gender, race, sexual orientation, disabilities, and culture and value orientations in the modern workforce is increasingly varied. Management's perspectives, strategic responses, and implementation approaches can help address pressures posed by this diversity and leverage this resource for organization effectiveness. In addition, wellness interventions, such as stress management programs and employee assistance programs (EAPs), are addressing several important social trends, such as the relationship and interaction between professional and personal roles and lives, fitness and health consciousness, and drug and alcohol abuse.

17-1 Workforce Diversity Interventions

Several profound trends are shaping the labor markets of modern organizations. Researchers suggest and managers confirm that contemporary workforce characteristics are radically different from what they were just 20 years ago. Employees represent every ethnic background and color; range from highly educated to illiterate; vary in age from 18 to 80; may appear perfectly healthy or may have a terminal illness; may be single parents or part of dual-income, divorced, same-sex, or traditional families; and may be physically or mentally challenged.

Workforce diversity is more than a euphemism for cultural or racial differences. Such a definition is too narrow and focuses attention away from the broad range of issues that a diverse workforce poses. Diversity results from people who bring different resources and perspectives to the workplace and who have distinctive needs, preferences, expectations, and lifestyles.[1] Organizations must design human resources systems that account for these differences if they are to attract and retain a productive workforce and if they want to turn diversity into a competitive advantage.

17-1a What Are the Goals?

Figure 17.1 presents a general framework for managing diversity in organizations.[2] First, the model suggests that an organization's diversity approach is a function of *internal and external pressures* for and against diversity. Social norms and globalization support the belief that organization performance is enhanced when the workforce's diversity is embraced as an opportunity. But diversity is often discouraged by those who fear that too many perspectives, beliefs, values, and attitudes dilute concerted action. Second, management's *perspective and priorities* with respect to diversity can range from resistance to active learning and from marginal to strategic. For example, organizations can resist diversity by implementing only legally mandated policies such as affirmative action, equal employment opportunity (EEO), or Americans with Disabilities Act requirements. On the other hand, a learning and strategic perspective can lead management to view diversity as a source of competitive advantage. For example, a health care organization with a diverse customer base can not only improve perceptions of service quality by having a more diverse physician base, but it can also embrace diversity by tailoring the range of services to that market and building systems and processes that are flexible. Third, within management's priorities, the organization's *strategic responses* can range from reactive to proactive. Diversity efforts at Texaco and Denny's had little momentum until a series of embarrassing race-based

FIGURE 17.1

A General Framework for Managing Diversity

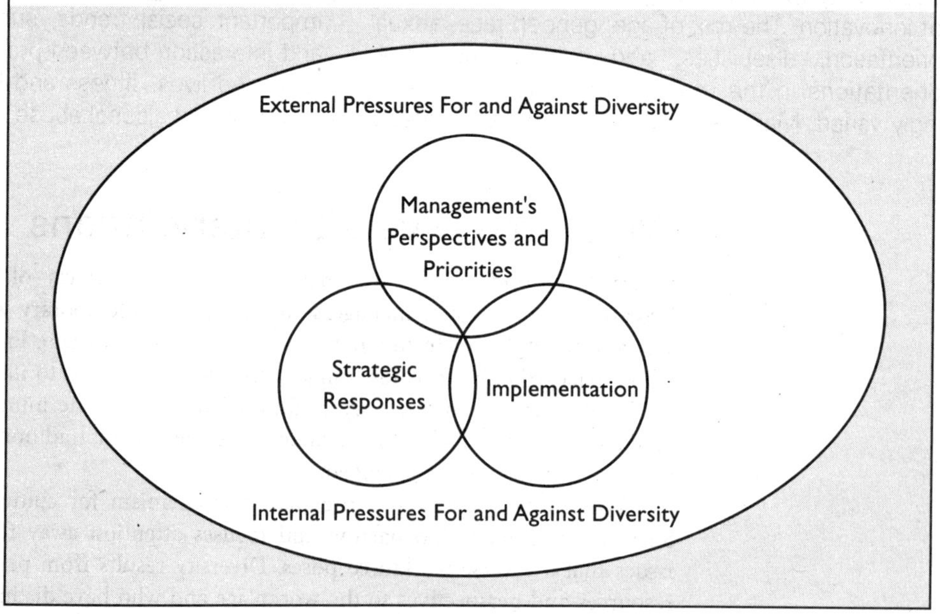

SOURCE: P. Dass, and B. Parker, "Strategies for Managing Human Resource Diversity: From Resistance to Learning," *Academy of Management Executive*, 13 (1999), p. 69. Permission conveyed via © Clearance Center.

events forced a response. Fourth, the organization's *implementation style* can range from episodic to systemic. A diversity approach will be most effective when the strategic responses and implementation style fit with management's intent and internal and external pressures.

Unfortunately, organizations have tended to address workforce diversity pressures in a piecemeal fashion; only 16% of companies surveyed in 2010 thought their diversity practices were "very effective."[3] As each trend makes itself felt, the organization reacts with appropriate but narrow responses. For example, as the percentage of women in the workforce increased, many organizations simply added maternity leaves to their benefits packages; as the number of physically challenged workers increased and when Congress passed the Americans with Disabilities Act in 1990, organizations changed their physical settings to accommodate wheelchairs. Demographers warn, however, that these trends are not only powerful by themselves but will likely interact with each other to force organizational change. Thus, a growing number of organizations, such as L'Oreal, PepsiCo, Procter & Gamble, American Airlines, and Carrefour, are taking bolder steps. They are not only adopting learning perspectives with respect to diversity, but systemically weaving diversity-friendly values and practices into the cultural fabric of the organization.

17-1b Application Stages

Many of the organization development (OD) interventions described in this book can be applied to the strategic responses and implementation of workforce diversity, as shown in Table 17.1. It summarizes several of the internal and external pressures facing organizations, including age, gender, race, disability, culture and values, and sexual orientation.[4] For example, the median age of the workforce is increasing, women make up a larger percentage of the workforce, and globalization is increasing the number of different cultural values present in the workplace. The table also reports the major trends characterizing those dimensions, organizational implications and workforce needs, and specific OD interventions that can address those implications.

Age To address age diversity, organization development interventions, such as work design, wellness programs (discussed below), career planning and development, and reward systems must be adapted to these different age groups and demographic cohorts.[5] For the older employee, work designs can reduce the physical components or increase the knowledge and experience components of a job. The governments in Singapore, Japan, and the European Union have implemented formal programs to encourage organizations to redesign jobs for elderly workers. The adjustments include more flexible arrangements regarding when and where work is performed, automating certain tasks, changing roles to allow for mentoring, and altering pay and benefit options to fit an older workers stage of life. Generation X employees, who are now in the age range from 32 to 52 years, will likely require more accommodations for work and life balance and for mid-career plateauing. The youngest workers, often called Generation Y or millennials, will likely need more challenge and autonomy. Wellness programs can be used to address the physical and mental health of employees from all generations. Career-planning and development programs will have to recognize the different career stages of each cohort and offer resources tailored to that stage. Finally, reward system interventions may offer increased health benefits, time off, and other perks for the older worker while using promotion, ownership, and pay to attract and motivate the scarcer, younger workforce.

TABLE 17.1

Work Diversity Dimensions and Interventions

Workforce Differences	Trends	Implications and Needs	Interventions
Age	Median age up Distribution of ages changing	Health care Mobility Security	Wellness program Job design Career planning and development Reward system
Gender	Percentage of women increasing Dual-income families	Child care Maternity/paternity leave Single parents	Job design Fringe benefit rewards
Disability	The number of people with disabilities entering the workforce is increasing	Job challenge Job skills Physical space Respect and dignity	Performance management Job design Career planning and development
Culture and values	Rising proportion of immigrant and minority-group workers Shift in rewards	Flexible organizational policies Autonomy Affirmation Respect	Career planning and development Employee involvement Reward systems
Sexual orientation	Number of single-sex households up More liberal attitudes toward sexual orientation	Discrimination	Equal employment opportunities Fringe benefits Education and training

Gender Work design, reward systems, and career development are among the more important interventions for addressing issues arising out of the gender trend. For example, jobs can be modified to accommodate the special demands of working mothers. A number of organizations, such as SAS, Oracle, Booz Allen Hamilton, and Hewlett-Packard, have instituted job sharing, by which two people perform the tasks associated with one job. The firms have done this to allow their female employees to pursue both family and work careers. Reward system interventions, especially fringe benefits, can be tailored to offer special leaves to mothers and fathers, child-care options, flexible working hours, and health and wellness benefits. The Container Store offers a family-friendly shift from 9 A.M. to 2 P.M. so that working mothers can easily drop off and pick up kids from school. Career development interventions help maintain, develop, and retain a competent and diverse workforce. Recent research on career development programs suggests that organizations consider the assumptions embedded in their career development programs to ensure programs are not biased toward masculine experiences and worldviews, especially those related to careers.[6]

Unfortunately, many programs over the last several years have tended to focus more on the symptoms, as opposed to sources of gender inequity.[7] Recent research suggests that once an organization recognizes the problem, diagnosis through interviews with employees is critical to addressing the sources of gender inequity. The research further suggests that using a strategy of small interventions, "small wins," or small initiatives that combine behavior and understanding and that target the organization's specific issues are more effective. For example, one European retail company discovered upon interviewing its employees that a key issue in turnover among female employees was the company's lack of discipline regarding time. Last-minute scheduling, meeting overruns, and tardiness wreaked havoc for female employees trying to manage work and home responsibilities. Company leadership began a more disciplined approach to time, resulting in greater efficiency and effectiveness. Resolving such issues requires careful and organization-specific diagnosis and intervention.

Race and Ethnicity Race continues to be an important issue in diversity interventions, especially as organizations globalize and endeavor to increase diversity among top leadership and board members. Training can increase the likelihood that effective diversity management programs are responsive to data (not impressions or perceptions), move beyond eliminating obvious racism to eradicating more subtle forms as well, eliminate vague selection and promotion criteria which can let discrimination persist, link diversity management to individual performance appraisals, and develop and enforce appropriate rules.[8] For example, 20% of Verizon's board of directors are African American; an increasing number of organizations are creating chief diversity officer positions reporting into the C-suite or directly to the CEO, and a more than 40 firms, including Yum! Brands, Credit Suisse, and General Mills work with nonprofit firm Minority Leadership Talent to identify, recruit, and retain black and Hispanic candidates. Mentoring programs can ensure that minorities in the advancement stage get the appropriate coaching and those successful minority managers and executives get the chance to share their wisdom and experience with others.

Sexual Orientation Diversity in sexual and affectional orientation, including gay, lesbian, bisexual, and transgender (GLBT) individuals and couples, increasingly is affecting the way that organizations think about human resources. The primary organizational implication of sexual orientation diversity is discrimination. Members of the GLBT community may be reticent to discuss how organizational policies can be less discriminatory because they fear their openness will lead to unfair treatment. People can have strong emotional reactions to sexual orientation. When these feelings interact with the gender, culture, and values trends described in this section, the likelihood of both overt and unconscious discrimination is high, especially around the often misperceived relationship between sexual orientation and AIDS/HIV. The good news is that the Corporate Equality Index—an annual report that grades U.S. companies on their practices related to the GLBT employees—is improving. In 2002, a total of 13 businesses achieved the top ranking of 100%; in its 2010 report, 305 companies made the 100% mark, an increase of 45 companies over 2009.[9]

Interventions aimed at this dimension of workforce diversity are relatively new in OD and are being developed as organizations encounter sexual orientation issues in the workplace. The most frequent response is education and training. This intervention increases members' awareness of the facts and decreases the likelihood of overt discrimination. In 2012, federal legislation and the Equal Employment Opportunity Council (EEOC) placed sexual orientation into a protected class supporting the many cities and states that had already passed such legislation. Human resources practices having to do with EEO and fringe benefits will help to address sexual orientation parity issues although most organizations have already modified their EEO statements to address sexual orientation, including 61% of *Fortune* 500 companies.[10] Firms such as Ben & Jerry's, Boeing, Northop Grumman, Hilton, and Google have communicated strongly to members and outsiders that decisions with respect to hiring, promotion, transfer, and so on cannot (and will not) be made with respect to a person's sexual orientation. Similarly, organizations are increasingly offering domestic-partner benefit plans, and now over 33% of firms polled in a 2012 Society of Human Resource Management survey offer health benefits to same sex domestic partners.[11] Companies, such as Shell Oil, Microsoft, and Apple, as well as governments and universities, have extended health care and other benefits to the same-sex partners of their members.

Disability The organizational implications of the disability trend represent both opportunity and adjustment. The productivity of physically and mentally disabled workers often surprises managers. Training is required to increase managers' awareness of this opportunity and to create a climate where accommodation requests can be made without fear.[12] Employing disabled workers, however, also means a need for more comprehensive health care, new physical workplace layouts, new attitudes toward working with the disabled, and challenging jobs that use a variety of skills.

OD interventions, including work design, career planning and development, and performance management, can be used to integrate the disabled into the workforce. For example, traditional approaches to job design can simplify work to permit physically handicapped workers to complete an assembly task. Career planning and development programs need to focus on making disabled workers aware of career opportunities. Too often these employees do not know that advancement is possible, and they are left feeling frustrated. Career paths need to be developed for these workers.

Performance management interventions, including goal setting, monitoring, and coaching performance, aligned with the workforce's characteristics are important. At Blue Cross and Blue Shield of Florida, for example, a supervisor learned sign language to communicate with a deaf employee whose productivity was low but whose quality of work was high. Two other deaf employees were transferred to that supervisor's department, and over a two-year period, the performance of the deaf workers improved 1,000% with no loss in quality.

Culture and Values Cultural diversity has broad organizational implications. Different cultures represent a variety of languages, values, work ethics, and norms of correct behavior. Not all cultures want the same things from work, and simple, piecemeal changes in specific organizational practices will be inadequate if the workforce is culturally diverse. Management practices will have to be designed with various cultural values in mind and support both career and family orientations. Take language as an example. Operating in multiple countries with multiple languages implies that jobs of all types (processing, customer contact, production, and so on) may need to be adjusted for non-native-speaking customers, but it also represents opportunity. If there are large non-native-speaking markets, the organization has an important resource for reaching those markets. Finally, the organization will be expected to satisfy both extrinsic and monetary needs, as well as intrinsic and personal growth needs.

Several planned change interventions, including employee involvement, reward systems, and career planning and development, can be used to adapt to cultural diversity. Employee involvement practices can be adapted to the needs for participation in decision making. People from certain cultures, such as Scandinavia, are more likely to expect and respond to high-involvement policies; other cultures, such as Latin America, view participation with reservation. Participation in an organization can take many forms, from suggestion systems and attitude surveys to high-involvement work designs and performance management systems. Organizations can maximize worker productivity by basing the amount of power and information workers have on cultural and value orientations.

Reward systems can focus on increasing flexibility. For example, flexible working hours enable employees to meet personal obligations without sacrificing organizational objectives. Many organizations have implemented this innovation, and most report that the positive benefits outweigh the costs. Work locations also can be varied. Many organizations, including Capital One, Oracle, and Gap, Inc., allow workers to spend part of their time telecommuting from home. Other flexible benefits, such as floating holidays, allow people from different cultures to match important religious and family occasions with work schedules.

Child-care and dependent-care assistance also support different lifestyles. For example, at Stride Rite Corporation (now a part of Collective Brands), the Stride Rite Intergenerational Day Care Center accommodates 55 children between the ages of 15 months and 6 years as well as 24 elders over 60 years old. The center was established after an organizational survey determined that 25% of employees provided some sort of elder care and that an additional 13% anticipated doing so within 5 years.

Finally, career planning and development programs can help workers identify advancement opportunities that are in line with their cultural values. Some cultures value technical skills over hierarchical advancement; others see promotions or titles as a prime indicator of self-worth and accomplishment. By matching programs with people, job satisfaction, productivity, and employee retention can be improved.

17-1c The Results for Diversity Interventions

Workforce diversity interventions have been growing rapidly in OD for more than three decades. Despite this growth, most evaluation efforts are survey oriented and somewhat cursory. A 2010 survey by the Society of Human Resource Management found that 68% of firms have diversity practices in place.[13] Research suggests that diversity interventions are especially prevalent in large organizations with diversity-friendly senior management and human resources policies,[14] and an internal evaluation of a diversity training program in a large manufacturing firm showed positive attitudinal changes over a three-month period with respect to emotional reactions, making judgments, behavioral reactions, and organizational impacts.[15] Although existing evidence shows that diversity interventions are growing in popularity, there is still ambiguity about the depth of organizational commitment to such practices and the contingencies that moderate the relationship between commitment and performance.[16]

Recently, however, two more complete evaluations of diversity management programs revealed positive results.[17] First, using data collected by the EEOC and survey data from organizations, researchers divided diversity programs into three categories: structures of responsibility, such as affirmative action plans, diversity committees and task forces, and diversity managers; educational programs, such as diversity training and diversity feedback for managers; and networking and mentoring programs. The data displayed a clear pattern. Structural programs were associated with significant increases in overall managerial diversity. Education and feedback programs were not followed by increases in managerial diversity. Finally, programs that attempted to increase the networking among different groups were associated with modest increases in management diversity. Importantly, the presence of structural interventions improved the effect of the other two interventions. In efforts to reduce inequality in the workplace, the researchers suggest that the popularity of individually based diversity interventions should be reviewed carefully. A great deal more research like this is needed to understand these newer interventions and their outcomes.

Second, a study by the Rand Corporation compared a *Fortune* "Best Places to Work for Minorities" company with a similar company from *Fortune*'s overall "Best Places to Work For" list. The results suggest that firms recognized as leaders in diversity management were much more likely than companies known for their superior HR practices to have leadership, structures, initiatives, and evaluation practices reflecting best practices in the diversity literature. These companies favored diversity for a variety of reasons, but primarily because they believed it would improve their business performance; as a result, top officials in these firms demonstrated strong support for diversity in word and deed. Similarly, best diversity companies implemented more diversity-related initiatives and established at least some means of measuring outcomes. Best HR firms pursued fewer kinds of diversity initiatives than best diversity firms (preferring to focus on basic recruiting, retention, and promotion programs) and had fewer means to evaluate company effectiveness with respect to diversity.

Application 17.1 describes the evolution of a workforce diversity intervention at L'Oreal, showing how diversity can be aligned with strategy on a global basis.[18]

17-2 Employee Stress and Wellness Interventions

In the past two decades, organizations have become increasingly aware of the relationship between employee wellness and productivity.[19] At the high end, the American Institue of Stress (AIS, www.stress.org) estimated that job stress costs U.S. business over $300 billion annually due to increased absenteeism, employee turnover, diminished productivity, medical, legal and insurance expenses, and Workers' Compensation payments. Stress management and wellness interventions, including employee assistance programs (EAPs), have grown because organizations are interested in retaining a skilled workforce and concerned for the welfare of their employees. Data also suggest that the greater emphasis on workforce health can vary significantly by region. In Asia, the focus is the need to compete for top talent, while in the United States, cost containment continues to be the primary concern. European multinationals are interested in reducing absenteeism and improving employees' health and safety.[20] Companies such as Johnson & Johnson, Weyerhaeuser, Federal Express, Quaker Oats, and Abbott Laboratories are sponsoring a wide range of fitness, wellness, and stress management programs.

17-2a What Are the Goals?

Individual well-being or wellness comprises "the various life/nonwork satisfactions enjoyed by individuals, work and job-related satisfactions, and general health."[21] Health is a subcomponent of well-being and includes both mental/psychological and physical/physiological factors. In addition, a person's work setting, personality

application 17.1

ALIGNING STRATEGY AND DIVERSITY AT L'ORÉAL

L'Oréal is the world's largest beauty products company. It creates cosmetics, perfume, and hair and skin care items in more than 130 countries under 23 brands, including L'Oréal Paris, Maybelline, Lancôme, SoftSheenCarson, and Redken. L'Oréal also owns the UK-based natural cosmetics retailer The Body Shop International, which operates about 2,550 stores worldwide. In 2006, L'Oréal had revenues of €15.8 billion and expected future growth to come more from its emerging markets rather than its traditionally large U.S. and European markets. The organization was highly decentralized with countries having full profit-and-loss responsibility. Local results were then rolled up to the group level to provide a picture of overall effectiveness.

L'Oréal's strategy was conducive to a diversity perspective; the very nature of its business makes diversity vital for success. With diverse customer from around the world, innovation must be based on understanding and respecting differences. In order to be global, the organization must be global from within, and their experience showed that variety breeds more creativity and innovation. As a mirror of the ever-changing world, a diverse workforce is better equipped to deal with change, be in tune with the environment, and a represent a key to L'Oréal being a "great place to work."

The organization's current efforts are built on a long history of diversity which began in 1974 with the "Schueller" leave, a maternity policy named after the company's founder that gives women an additional four weeks leave in addition to the statutory requirements and which can be taken, in full or in part, until the child is two years old. In 2000, L'Oréal adopted an Ethics Charter describing its values and practices as a global company and it implemented several other initiatives, such as the adoption of policies concerning diversity practices, the appointment of specific roles (a U.S. vice president of diversity was appointed in 2002), the inception of diversity training, and participation in career fairs.

Momentum for diversity efforts at L'Oréal increased in 2004 with the signing of the Diversity Charter, along with 35 other large French organizations, and the appointment of a global diversity director. The charter represented a national effort to promote pluralism and diversity as strategies for success. It visibly committed the organization to pursue a variety of initiatives, including raising awareness, incorporating diversity progress metrics in annual reports, and implementing policies that promoted diversity throughout the corporation. Diversity within L'Oréal came to be defined as "a mosaic of visible and invisible differences ... which influence attitudes, behaviors, values, and ways of working within the professional environment."

The new global diversity director assembled a team that developed an explicit diversity strategy. The strategy involved five action levers, including recruitment and integration, training, career management interventions, management and inclusion, and communication. These five levers were expected to drive results along six visible and invisible dimensions, including nationality, ethnic and cultural background, social promotion, gender, disability, and age. The team believed the biggest obstacle to implementation was the cultural differences between the countries and a low-level of awareness of the benefits that a diversity strategy could bring. For example, many of the workforces in the emerging market countries were quite homogenous relative to the United States and France, their economies were growing fast, and their leadership teams had little experience or understanding of diversity related practices. On the other hand, the diversity efforts in the United States were quite advanced. L'Oréal's U.S. diversity program was recognized with the 2004 Diversity Best Practices' Global Leadership Award for creating an environment of diversity and inclusion for employees, customers, and suppliers. The U.S. experience thus provided some important internal benchmarks for the global team.

For example, with respect to the recruiting strategy, the U.S. vice president of diversity had introduced the concept of "fishing in different ponds" to suggest that where the organization looked for diverse talent was as important as whom they were looking for. The organization identified seven different ponds and as a result, more than 60% of the general managers were women compared to a L'Oréal international average of about 33%. In addition, minority representation had increased from 13.9% in 2001 to 16% in 2004. Eventually, this led to the principle of sourcing diversification to be able to access a broader range of profiles.

In addition, the international organization began computerizing the application process in 2004. Through its website, they deleted request for certain kinds of information that might contribute to recruiting biases. Since its inception, the organization has deleted home addresses, a type of information that French studies believed was among the most discriminatory, as well as information related to gender, age, and nationality.

In terms of the training strategy, the U.S. vice president collaborated with the global training organization to make diversity and inclusion part of the core curriculum for all major leadership development training programs. One of the global diversity team's initial activities was a two-day diversity seminar that involved over 8,000 managers in 32 countries in Europe. The seminar explained the diversity strategy and created opportunities for managers to establish goals and action plans to make diversity practices a reality in their countries. In line with the global team's concerns, the managers' reactions were mixed, depending on their organizational role and the country they represented. Many wondered if this was a "flavor of the month" issue, believed they were already managing with diversity in mind, or had more important business issues to address. However, many of the managers also realized the potential of diversity and became aware of some personal biases. These managers were used to leverage the diversity effort as it rolled out globally.

The U.S. program also led with way in terms of implementing the strategy of management and inclusion. Diversity objectives were included as part of a manager's responsibilities in annual performance reviews. That practice was eventually expanded, and today diversity objectives are included on a worldwide basis.

To measure the progress of the programs, L'Oréal benchmarks the company against leading *Fortune* 500 companies that are recognized as "Best in Class" for women and people of color. A quarterly "State of Diversity Report" measures results and monitors progress in key areas; it is shared with senior leaders and human resources teams. In 2006, L'Oréal was recognized with the World Diversity Leadership Council's Diversity Innovation Award, and in 2007 *Ethisphere* magazine ranked the organization as one of the "world's most ethical companies."

traits, and stress coping skills affect overall well-being. In turn, well-being impacts personal and organizational outcomes, including absenteeism, productivity, and health insurance costs.[22]

Concern has been growing in organizations about managing the dysfunction caused by stress. According to a national APA survey of Stress in America, 39% said their stress had increased over the past year and even more said that their stress had increased over the past five years (44%).[23] The problem is not unique to the United States. In a Towers Watson global survey, 55% of firms responding reported that mental health and stress issues were a priority in all or most of the countries they were operating.[24] Of the six major economies making up 50% of the world's gross domestic product, the United Kingdom has the highest level of worker stress (35%), while China and India have the lowest (17%).[25]

A study by O'Toole and Lawler concluded that the price most U.S. workers and managers have paid to get more interesting and enriched jobs is an increased amount of stress.[26] Stress has been linked to hypertension, heart attacks, diabetes, asthma, chronic pain, allergies, headache, backache, various skin disorders, cancer, immune system weakness, and decreases in the number of white blood cells and changes in their function. It can also lead to alcoholism and drug abuse, two problems that are reaching epidemic proportions in organizations and society. For organizations, these personal effects can result in costly health benefits, absenteeism, turnover, and low performance. One study reported that one in three workers said they have thought about quitting because of stress; one in two workers said job stress reduced their productivity; and one in five workers said they took sick leave in the month preceding the survey because of stress.[27] Another study estimates that each employee who suffers from a stress-related illness loses an average of 16 days of work per year.[28]

17-2b Applications Stages

Stress and wellness interventions involve (1) diagnosing stress and being aware of its causes and (2) alleviating and coping with stress to improve wellness.

Diagnosing Stress and Becoming Aware of Its Causes Stress refers to the reaction of people to their environments. It involves both physiological and psychological responses to environmental conditions, causing people to change or adjust their behaviors. Stress is generally viewed in terms of the fit of people's needs, abilities, and expectations with environmental demands, changes, and opportunities.[29] A good person–environment fit results in positive reactions to stress; a poor fit leads to the negative consequences already described. Stress is generally positive when it occurs at moderate levels and contributes to effective motivation, innovation, and learning. For example, a promotion is a stressful event that is experienced positively by most employees. On the other hand, stress can be dysfunctional when it is excessively high (or low) or persists over a long period of time. It can overpower a person's coping abilities and cause physical and emotional exhaustion. For example, a boss who is excessively demanding and unsupportive can cause subordinates undue tension, anxiety, and dissatisfaction. Those factors, in turn, can lead to withdrawal behaviors, such as absenteeism and turnover; to ailments, such as headaches and high blood pressure; and to lowered performance. Situations in which there is a poor fit between employees and the organization produce negative stress consequences.

A tremendous amount of research has been conducted on the causes and consequences of work stress. Figure 17.2 identifies specific occupational stressors, potential dysfunctional consequences, and interventions to address stress. People's individual differences determine the extent to which the stressors are perceived negatively. For example, people with strong social support experience the stressors as less stressful than those who do not have such support. This greater perceived stress can lead to such negative consequences as anxiety, poor decision making, increased blood pressure, and low productivity.

The stress model shows that almost any dimension of the organization, including the physical environment, structure, roles, or relationships, can cause negative stress. This suggests that much of the material covered so far in this book provides knowledge about work-related stressors, and implies that virtually all of the OD interventions included in the book can play a role in stress management. Team

FIGURE 17.2

Stress Management: Diagnosis and Intervention

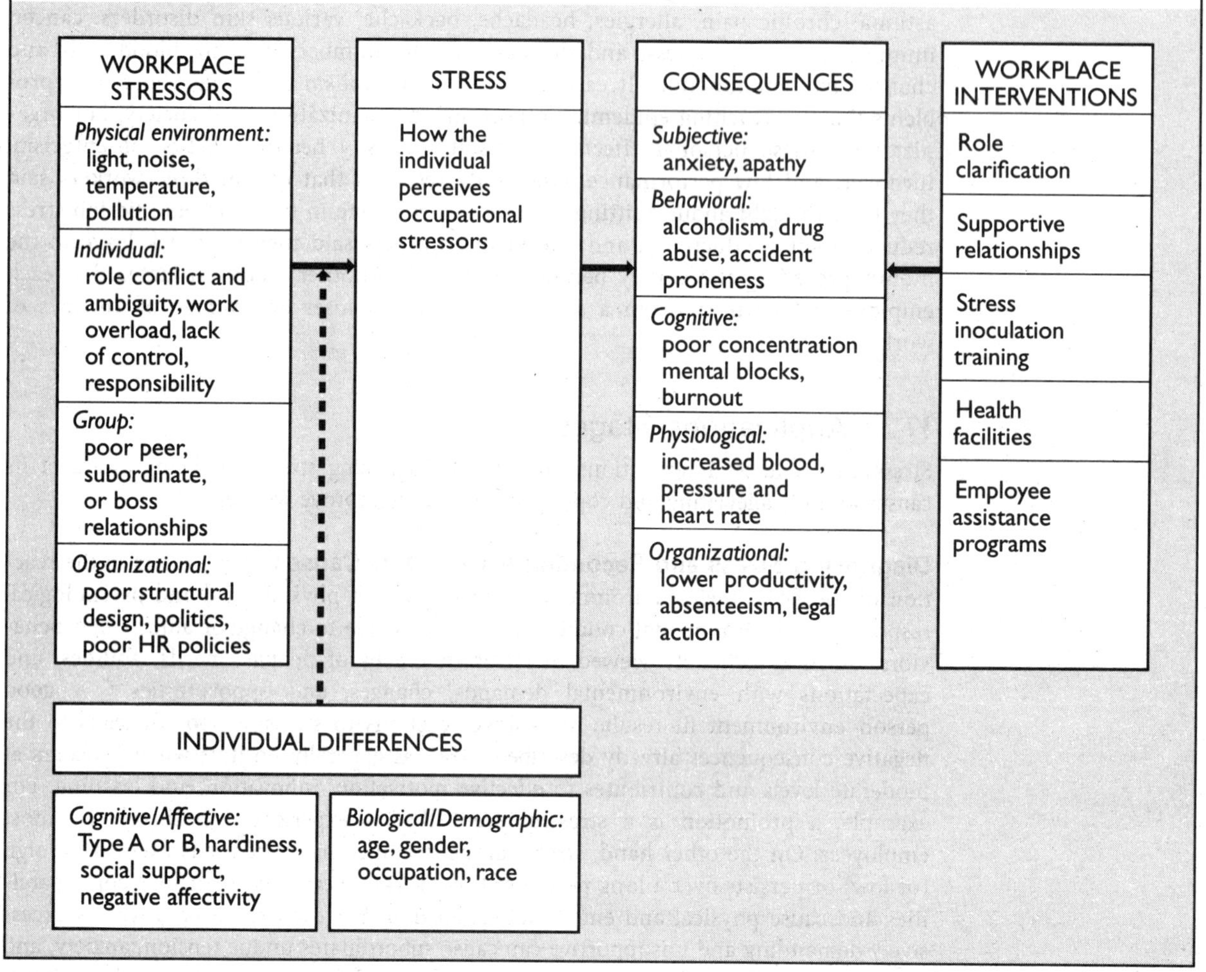

SOURCE: Adapted from J. Gibson, J. Ivancevich, and J. Donnelly Jr., *Organizations: Behaviors, Structure, Processes*, 8th ed. (Plano, Texas: Business Publications, 1994): 266. Reproduced with permission of The McGraw-Hill Companies.

building, employee involvement, reward systems, and career planning and development all can help alleviate stressful working conditions. Thus, to some degree stress management has been under discussion throughout this book. Here, the focus is on those occupational stressors and stress management techniques that are unique to the stress field and that have received the most systematic attention from stress researchers.

Workplace Stressors. Figure 17.2 identifies several organizational sources of stress, including the physical environment, individual situations, group pressures, and organizational conditions. Extensive research has been done on three key individual sources of stress: the individual items related to work overload, role conflict, and role ambiguity.

Research relating workload to stress outcomes reveals that both too much and too little work can have negative consequences. Apparently, when the amount of work is in balance with people's abilities and knowledge, stress has a positive impact on performance and satisfaction, but when workload either exceeds employees' abilities (overload) or fails to challenge them (underload), people experience stress negatively. This negative experience can lead to lowered self-esteem and job dissatisfaction, nervous symptoms, increased absenteeism, and reduced participation in organizational activities.[30]

People's roles at work also can be a source of stress. A role can be defined as the sum total of expectations that the individual and significant others have about how the person should perform a specific job. Problems arise when there is role ambiguity and the person does not clearly understand what others expect of him or her, or when there is role conflict and the employee receives contradictory expectations that cannot be satisfied at the same time.[31] Extensive studies of role ambiguity and conflict suggest that both conditions are prevalent in organizations, especially among managerial jobs where clarity often is lacking and job demands often are contradictory.[32] For example, managerial job descriptions typically are so general that it is difficult to know precisely what is expected on the job. Similarly, managers spend most of their time interacting with people from other departments, and opportunities for conflicting demands abound in these lateral relationships. Role ambiguity and conflict can cause severe stress, resulting in increased tension, dissatisfaction, and withdrawal, and reduced commitment and trust in others.

Individual Differences. Figure 17.2 identifies two classes of individual differences that can affect how people respond to workplace stressors: cognitive/affective characteristics and biological/demographic characteristics. Much research has been devoted to the cognitive/affective category, especially the Type A behavior pattern, which is characterized by impatience, competitiveness, and hostility. Type A personalities (in contrast to Type B's) invest long hours working under tight deadlines, and put themselves under extreme time pressure by trying to do more and more work in less and less time. Type A people are especially prone to stress. For example, a longitudinal study of 3,500 men found that Type A's had twice as much heart disease, five times as many second heart attacks, and twice as many fatal heart attacks as did Type B's.[33]

Stress management is directed at preventing negative stress outcomes either by changing the organizational conditions causing the stress or by enhancing employees' abilities to cope with them. This preventive approach starts from a diagnosis of the current situation, including employees' self-awareness of their own stress and its sources. This diagnosis provides the information needed to develop an appropriate stress management program. There are two methods for diagnosing stress.

Charting stressors involves identifying organizational and personal stressors operating in a particular situation. Guided by a conceptual model like that shown in Figure 17.2, data can be collected through questionnaires and interviews about environmental and personal stressors. For example, researchers at the University of Michigan's Institute for Social Research have developed standardized instruments for measuring most of the stressors shown in Figure 17.2. Similarly, there are specific instruments for measuring the individual differences, such as hardiness, social support, and Type A or B behavior pattern. In addition to perceptions of stressors, it is necessary to measure stress consequences, such as subjective moods, performance, job satisfaction, absenteeism, blood pressure, and cholesterol level. Various instruments and checklists have been developed for obtaining people's perceptions of negative consequences, and these can be supplemented with hard measures taken from company records, medical reports, and physical examinations.

Once measures of the stressors and consequences are obtained, the two sets of data must be related to reveal which stressors contribute most to negative stress in the situation under study. For example, an analysis might show that qualitative overload and role ambiguity are highly related to employee fatigue, absenteeism, and poor performance, especially for Type A employees. This kind of information points to specific organizational conditions that must be improved to reduce stress. Moreover, it identifies the kinds of employees who may need special counseling and training in stress management.

Health profiling is aimed at identifying stress symptoms so that corrective action can be taken. Many firms contract with local health care facilities to provide the service. It starts with a questionnaire asking people for their medical history; personal habits; current health; and vital signs, such as blood pressure and cholesterol levels. It also may include a physical examination if some of the information is not readily available. Information from the questionnaire and physical examination is then analyzed, usually by a computer that calculates the individual's health profile. This profile compares the individual's characteristics with those of an average person of the same gender, age, and race. The profile identifies the person's future health prospect, typically by placing him or her in a health-risk category with a known probability of fatal disease, such as cardiovascular risk. The health profile also indicates how the health risks can be reduced by making personal and environmental changes such as dieting, exercising, or traveling.

Alleviating and Coping with Stress to Improve Wellness After diagnosing the presence and causes of stress, the next step in stress management is to do something about it. OD interventions for reducing negative stress tend to fall into two groups: those aimed at changing the organizational conditions causing stress and those directed at helping people to cope better with stress. Because stress results from the interaction between people and the environment, both strategies are needed for effective stress management. Five such interventions are described below.

Role Clarification. This involves helping employees better understand the demands of their work roles. A manager's role is embedded in a network of relationships with other managers, each of whom has specific expectations about how the manager should perform the role. Role clarification is a systematic process for revealing others' expectations and arriving at a consensus about the activities constituting a particular role. There are several role clarification methods that follow a similar strategy.[34] First, the people relevant to defining a particular role are identified (e.g., members of a managerial team, a boss and subordinate, and members of other departments relating to the role holder) and brought together at a meeting, usually in a location away from the organization.

Second, the role holder discusses his or her perceived job duties and responsibilities and the other participants are encouraged to comment on and to agree or disagree with the role holder's perceptions. An OD practitioner may act as a process consultant to facilitate interaction and reduce defensiveness. Third, when everyone has reached consensus on defining the role, the role holder is responsible for writing a description of the activities that are seen now as constituting the role. A copy of the role description is distributed to all participants to ensure that they fully understand and agree with the role definition. Fourth, the participants periodically check to see whether the role is being performed as intended and make modifications if necessary.

Supportive Relationships. Building supportive relationships is aimed at helping employees cope with stress rather than at changing the stressors themselves. It involves establishing trusting and genuinely positive relationships among employees, including bosses, subordinates, and peers. Supportive relations have been a hallmark of organization development and are a major part of such interventions as team building, intergroup relations, employee involvement, work design, goal setting, and career planning and development. Considerable research shows that supportive relationships can buffer people from stress.[35] When people feel that relevant others really care about what happens to them and are willing to help, they can cope with stressful conditions.

Work Leaves. In the United States, employees work more hours and take less time off than in most other developed countries. For example, Americans worked an average of 1,878 hours per year while workers in the United Kingdom averaged 1,711, France averaged 1,532, and German workers averaged 1,467. Only Korean employees worked more than Americans. Similarly, other countries offer longer and more flexible work leave arrangements, with vacation minimums often subject to government mandate. The United States and Japan average ten days annual vacation, and the United Kingdom, France, and Germany average 22, 25, and 24 days, respectively.[36] While some differences can be explained by cultural values or government policies, the potential to affect wellness through work leaves should not be ignored.

As organizations struggle to minimize the effects of work stress, paid and unpaid work leaves are receiving increasing attention. Paid leaves include vacation, holidays, personal days, as well as maternity and paternity leaves. The comparative statistics suggest that globalization may increase pressure on vacation allowances. As with vacation time, the United States lags behind other countries in regards to maternity and paternity leave. Although the Family Medical Leave Act (FMLA) guarantees parents 12 weeks unpaid leave (and more people are taking advantage of FMLA unpaid leave), many employees cannot afford to take it, and firms at the top of *Fortune*'s "Best Companies to Work For" list have responded with paid maternity and paternity leave.[37] Another key work leave intervention is paid sabbaticals, typically received after a specified tenure of service. For example, Perkins Coie, a Seattle law firm with approximately 1,400 employees, offers eight-week paid sabbaticals. In another survey, 19% of companies, including Deloitte and Touche, Microsoft and Intel, offered sabbaticals, but only 5% with pay.[38] Sabbaticals are a way of avoiding burnout and renewing employee creativity and commitment.

Unpaid leaves, or leaves of absence, also offer employees a chance to renew and to bring new experiences to the organization, while guaranteeing a job for them upon their return. For example, personal growth leaves or social service leaves may allow an employee to explore an individual interest or cause. Such a leave is an exchange, offering the employee a chance for time off, renewal, and pursuit of a given interest, while retaining a valued employee for the organization.

Health Facilities. A growing number of organizations are providing facilities for helping employees cope with stress. Elaborate exercise facilities are maintained by such firms as Qualcomm, Xerox, Weyerhaeuser, Google, and PepsiCo, and a majority of the *Fortune* 500 operate corporate cardiovascular fitness programs. Employees at Aetna can earn a financial incentive for their involvement in weight management and fitness programs. Before starting such programs, employees must take an exercise tolerance test and have the approval of either a private or a company doctor. Each participant is then assigned a safe level of heart response to the various parts of the fitness program.

In addition to exercise facilities, some companies, such as McDonald's and Equitable Life Assurance Society, provide biofeedback facilities in which managers take relaxation breaks using biofeedback devices to monitor respiration and heart rate. Feedback of such data helps managers lower their respiration and heart rates. Some companies provide time for employees to meditate, and other firms have stay-well programs that encourage healthy diets and lifestyles.

Employee Assistance Programs. This final stress and wellness intervention is an organizational intervention and a method for helping individuals directly. EAPs help identify, refer, and treat workers whose personal problems affect their performance.[39] While some large companies still provide an in-house EAP, most outsource their EAPs. Initially started in the 1940s to combat alcoholism, these programs have expanded to deal with emotional, family, marital, and financial problems, and, more recently, drug abuse. For example, 2008 data from the federal Substance Abuse and Mental Health Services Administration, suggest that 10.2% of full-time employed adults and 11% of part-time working adults are substance-dependent. Of these, about 85% are dependent on alcohol alone or on alcohol and drugs; 15% abuse drugs only.[40]

Alcohol and drug use costs U.S. business an estimated $102 billion per year in lost productivity, accidents, and turnover.[41] Britain's Royal College of Psychiatrists suggested that up to 30% of employees in British companies would experience mental health problems and that 115 million workdays were lost each year as a result of depression.[42] Other factors, too, have contributed to increased problems: altered family structures, the growth of single-parent households, the increase in divorce, greater mobility, and changing modes of child rearing are all fairly recent phenomena that have added to the stress experienced by employees. These trends indicate that an increasing number of employees need assistance with personal problems, and the research suggests that EAP use increases during downsizing and restructuring.[43]

When other stress management interventions are not effective or when employees have particular types of wellness and or health issues, EAPs provide a means of responding to employee wellness problems including extreme or chronic stress, drug and alcohol abuse, problems with child and elder care, grief, and financial problems.[44] Central to the philosophy underlying EAPs is the belief that although the organization has no right to interfere in the private lives of its employees, it does have a right to impose certain standards of work performance and to establish sanctions when these are not met. Anyone whose work performance is impaired because of a personal problem is eligible for admission into an EAP. Successful EAPs have been implemented at Kimpton Hotels and Restaurants, Telemundo Network, Alcoa, Sprint-Nextel, Wells Fargo Bank, and Johnson & Johnson. Numerous websites, including that of the Employee Assistance Professionals Association, share or provide at minimal cost detailed guidelines on establishing an EAP. These steps include developing an appropriate EAP policy, deciding to insource or outsource the program, communicating the program to organization members, and providing training on EAP use. Recent changes in health care privacy as a result of the Health Insurance Portability and Privacy Act (HIPAA) impact EAPs, related health insurance benefits, data requirements, and how such data and information can be used and shared.[45]

17-2c The Results of Stress Management and Wellness Interventions

The variety of stress management and wellness interventions makes it difficult to provide overall conclusions, but the numerous studies about stress and any particular intervention do add up to a positive recommendation. For example, the research on role clarification supports this intervention. One study found that it reduced stress and role ambiguity and increased job satisfaction.[46] Another study reported that it improved interpersonal relationships among group members and contributed to improved production and quality.[47] Like many of the other studies in this area, the findings should be interpreted carefully because of weak research designs and perceptual measures.

The research on supportive relationships suggests that organizations must become more aware of their value in helping employees cope with stress. They may need to build supportive, cohesive work groups in situations that are particularly stressful, such as introducing new products, solving emergency problems, and handling customer complaints. For example, firms such as Procter & Gamble and the Hartford Financial Services Group have recognized that internal OD consultants bear a lot of the stress of organization change, and so they encouraged internal OD practitioners to form support teams to help each other cope with the demands of the role. Equally important, organizations need to direct more attention to ensuring that managers provide the support and encouragement necessary to help subordinates cope with stress. For example, Pepperdine University's executive programs often include a module on helping subordinates cope with stress, and firms are training managers to be more sensitive to stress and more supportive and helpful to subordinates.

Preliminary evidence suggests that fitness programs can reduce absenteeism and coronary risk factors, such as high blood pressure, body weight, percentage of body fat, and cholesterol levels.[48] A review of the research, however, suggests that fitness programs primarily result in better mental health and resistance to stress and that such organizational improvements as reduced absenteeism and turnover and improved performance are more uncertain.[49]

The amount of research on EAP-related issues is quite large, as a look through dedicated journals, such as the *Journal for Workplace Behavioral Health* or *Employee Assistance Quarterly*, will attest. Two studies reviewed the multinational EAP evaluation research for 39 studies between 1990 and 1999 and 42 studies between 2000 and 2009.[50] The research explored several aspects of EAP implementation including assessments of program success. For example, one study reported on a four-year, quasi-experimental design of Fairview Health Services' EAP and reported average per-employee savings of $230 in lost work days, $340 in medical costs, and $188 in workers compensation claims for a combined cost savings of $758 per employee accessing the EAP. Application 17.2 provides additional data regarding the benefit of EAP-related programs.[51] Johnson and Johnson's "Live for Life" program, among one of the most regarded in the world, has been studied extensively and demonstrates the long-term value of this approach. The author concludes: "To state it as simply as possible, EAPs are effective. They save organizations money. EAPs also increase the well-being of the majority of employees who actively participate in counseling offered through the auspices of the programs and as a result enhance the wellness of our communities."

application 17.2

JOHNSON & JOHNSON'S HEALTH AND WELLNESS PROGRAM

Johnson & Johnson (J&J) is the most diversified health care corporation in the world. It grosses more than $65 billion a year and employs approximately 117,900 people at 190 companies in 51 countries. The J&J companies are decentralized and directly responsible for their own operations. Corporate management is committed to this structure because of the many proven advantages to the businesses and people involved, such as the development of general managers, faster product development, and a closer connection with the customer. Its philosophy is embodied in a document called "Our Credo," a section of which makes a commitment to the welfare of its employees.

J&J has a long history of commitment to health, wellness, and stress management programs. For example, based on a successful pilot project in its Ethicon division during the 1970s, J&J top management decided to implement EAPs throughout the rest of the company. The J&J EAPs were in-house treatment programs that offered employees and family members confidential, professional assistance for problems related to alcohol and drug abuse, as well as marital, family, emotional, and mental health difficulties. The major goal was to help clients assume responsibility for their own behavior and, if it was destructive to themselves or others, to modify it. Employees could enter an EAP by self-referral or by counseling from their supervisor. The program emphasized the necessity of maintaining complete confidentiality when counseling the employee or family member to protect both the client's dignity and job.

The EAPs were implemented between 1980 and 1985 in three phases. The first phase consisted of contacting the managers and directors of personnel for each of the decentralized divisions and assessing their divisions' EAP needs. An educational process was initiated to inform managers and directors about the EAP. This EAP training then was conducted in each of the personnel departments of the divisions. The second phase included a formal presentation to the management board of each division. It included information about the EAP and about an alcohol and drug component for executives. In the third phase, cost estimates were developed for EAP use and for employment of an EAP administrator to implement the program in each division. In addition, the corporate director of assistance programs established a quality assurance program to review all EAP activities biennially.

Eventually, more than 90% of all domestic employees had direct access to an EAP, and the remaining employees had telephone access. There were EAPs at all major J&J locations throughout the United States, Puerto Rico, and Canada. Programs also operated in Brazil and England. A study of J&J's EAP in the New Jersey area showed that clients with drug abuse, emotional, or mental health problems who availed themselves of EAP services were treated at substantial savings to the company.

The EAPs were ultimately integrated with J&J's original wellness program known as Live for Life. This program was initiated by the chairman of the board in 1979, when he committed to provide all employees and their families with the opportunity to become the healthiest employees of any corporation in the world. The program brought together experts in health care education, behavior change, and disease management to create a program to improve the health and productivity of workers. The Live for Life program offered classes in nutrition, weight reduction, and smoking cessation. In addition, small gymnasiums with workout equipment, aerobics rooms, and swimming pools were made available. In the late 1980s and 1990s the combined programs became known as Live for Life

Assistance programs. Health, safety, benefits, wellness, and EAPs worked together to promote employee well-being in the workplace.

The current Johnson & Johnson Health and Wellness Program is an outgrowth of those early programs. It has undergone several transformations in the past three decades to respond to shifting business requirements and changing employee health needs. The Johnson & Johnson Health and Wellness Program includes disability management, occupational health, employee assistance, work–life programs, and wellness and fitness programs. The program is often studied by other corporations because of its integrated service deliveries.

In 1995, Johnson & Johnson's health and fitness group took a simple step that catapulted participation in the company's wellness program from 26% to 90%. Patricia Flynn, vice president of Johnson & Johnson's health care system, described how J&J offered every employee a $500 health-benefits credit in exchange for completing an annual health-risk assessment before enrolling in the plan. Although the company had offered the assessment optionally for years as part of its wellness program, it was not until the incentive was attached that employees flocked to it. "People think they are fit and might not want to bother with an assessment," Flynn says. "This incentive got them to do it."

In the past, organization members were given incentives for participating in various wellness programs, but the company's focus has shifted all of its incentive dollars toward risk assessment. "We are confident that once employees know what their risks are, then we can make a positive impact on their health," says Jennifer Bruno, director of business planning. Early studies conducted at the company showed that even those employees who took the assessment but had no follow-up support through wellness programs showed improvements in their health.

But for Johnson & Johnson, the assessment is just the beginning. The aggregate data helps the health care group choose the right wellness programs for the exact needs of the population, Bruno says. The program developers aren't guessing at employees' health interests or expecting them to know what programs they will benefit from, she says. They use the hard data to guide their wellness program choices. "We are making better use of our health care dollars, thanks to the assessment information."

For example, the initial assessment showed that the employees had three areas of risk: high cholesterol, high blood pressure, and inactivity. The company now regularly offers exercise and counseling programs to help employees reduce cholesterol and blood pressure and manage weight. Bruno says there are also subtle additions to the workplace environment that contribute to a healthy culture, such as nutritious choices in the cafeteria, scales in all of the bathrooms, and a non-smoking environment.

Johnson & Johnson's *Live for Life* program is one of the most emulated and evaluated programs of its kind. The most recent evaluation, which compared J&J's program against 16 other programs over time, found that their average annual growth in medical costs were 3.7% lower. That is, after accounting for inflation, J&J's average medical and drug costs increased 1% per year between 2002 and 2008 compared to the average increase of 4.8% in 16 other companies with EAPs. That translates to an average annual savings of $565 per employee, and a return on investment estimate of between $1.88 and $3.92 for every dollar spent. Further tests suggested that J&J employees were significantly less likely to be at risk for high blood pressure, high cholesterol, poor nutrition, obesity, physical inactivity, and tobacco use. The researchers conclude that the benefits from health promotion programs, especially those as comprehensive as J&Js, may be long lasting. Johnson & Johnson's Health and Wellness program demonstrates a long-term commitment to its strategy, its industry, and its people. The execution and coordination of the different wellness components has paid off handsomely for many stakeholders.

SUMMARY

This chapter presented two important human resources interventions: workforce diversity interventions and employee stress and wellness interventions. Like coaching, career planning and development, and leadership development presented in Chapter 18, these change programs generally are carried out by human resources specialists but have become an important part of OD's practice.

Workforce diversity interventions are designed to adapt human resources practices to an increasingly diverse workforce. Age, gender, race, sexual orientation, disability, and culture and values trends point to a more complex set of human resources demands. Within such a context, OD interventions (e.g., job design, performance management, and employee involvement practices) have to be adapted to a diverse set of personal preferences, needs, and lifestyles.

Employee stress and wellness interventions, such as work leaves and EAPs, recognize the important link between worker health and organizational productivity. A model for understanding work-related stress includes occupational stressors; individual differences, which affect how people respond to the stressors; stress outcomes; and interventions to increase wellness or decrease stress. The two main steps in stress management are diagnosing stress and its causes, and alleviating stressors and helping people to cope with stress. Two methods for diagnosing stress are charting stressors and health profiling. Techniques for alleviating stressful conditions include role clarification and supportive relationships. Means for helping workers cope with stress are developing supportive relationships and participation in activities at health and fitness facilities. Finally, EAPs identify, refer, and treat employees and their families for such problems as marital difficulties, drug and alcohol abuse, emotional disturbances, and financial crises. EAPs preserve the dignity of the individual but also recognize the organization's right to expect certain work behaviors.

NOTES

1. F. Miller and J. Katz, *The Inclusion Breakthrough* (San Francisco: Berrett-Koehler, 2002); R. Thomas, *Building on the Promise of Diversity* (New York: AMACOM Books, 2005); M. Bell, *Diversity in Organizations,* 2nd ed. (Mason, OH: South-Western College Publishing, 2011).
2. P. Dass and B. Parker, "Strategies for Managing Human Resource Diversity: From Resistance to Learning," *Academy of Management Executive* 13 (1999): 68–80.
3. Society for Human Resource Management, "Workplace Diversity Practices Poll" (Alexandria, VA: SHRM, 2010), accessed from http://www.shrm.org/Research/SurveyFindings/Articles/Pages/WorkplaceDiversityPractices.aspx on August 12, 2012.
4. This section has benefited greatly from the advice and assistance of Pat Pope, president of Pope and Associates, Cincinnati, OH. Much of the data and many examples cited in support of each trend can be found in the following references and websites: M. Galen, "Equal Opportunity Diversity: Beyond the Numbers Game," *BusinessWeek,* August 14, 1995, 60–61; K. Hammon and A. Palmer, "The Daddy Trap," *BusinessWeek,* September 21, 1998, 56–64; H. Kahan and D. Mulryan, "Out of the Closet," *American Demographics* (May 1995): 40–47; http://stats.bls.gov; http://nces.ed.gov; http://census.gov; http://cdc.gov.
5. "How to Prepare for the Coming Older Workforce," *IOMA's Safety Director's Report* 1, no. 3 (April 2001). See also World Health Organization information on aging of the workforce.
6. E. Cook, M. Heppner, and K. O'Brien, "Career Development of Women of Color and White Women: Assumptions, Conceptualizations, and Interventions from an Ecological Perspective," *Career Development Quarterly* 50 (2002): 291–305.
7. D. Meyerson and J. Fletcher, "A Modest Manifesto for Breaking the Glass Ceiling," *Harvard Business Review* (January-February 2000): 127–35.
8. A. Brief, R. Buttram, R. Reizenstein, D. Pugh, J. Callahan, R. McCline, and J. Vaslow, "Beyond Good Intentions: The Next Steps Toward Racial Equality in the American Workplace," *Academy of Management Executive* 11 (1997): 59–72.
9. H. Ernst, "Promoting Diversity and Equality," *Fortune,* June 14, 2010, 142.
10. "More Employers Cover Domestic Partners," *Employee Benefit News* 17, no. 8 (June 15, 2003): 30.

11. Society for Human Resource Management, "2012 Employee Benefits: The Employee Benefits Landscape in a Recovering Economy" (Alexandria, VA: SHRM, 2012), accessed from http://www.shrm.org/Research/SurveyFindings/Articles/Pages/2012EmployeeBenefitsResearchReport.aspx on August 14, 2012.
12. D. Baldrige and J. Veiga, "Toward a Greater Understanding of the Willingness to Request an Accommodation: Can Requesters' Beliefs Disable the Americans with Disabilities Act?" *Academy of Management Review* 26 (2001): 85–99.
13. Society for Human Resource Management, "Workplace Diversity Practices Poll" (Alexandria, VA: SHRM, 2010), accessed from http://www.shrm.org/Research /SurveyFindings/Articles/Pages/WorkplaceDiversityPractices.aspx on August 12, 2012.
14. S. Rynes and B. Rosen, "A Field Survey of Factors Affecting the Adoption and Perceived Success of Diversity Training," *Personnel Psychology* 48 (1995): 247–70; K. Labich, "Making Diversity Pay," *Fortune*, September 9, 1996, 177–80.
15. K. De Meuse, T. Hostager, and K. O'Neill, "A Longitudinal Evaluation of Senior Managers' Perceptions and Attitudes of a Workplace Diversity Training Program," *Human Resource Planning* 30 (2007): 38–47.
16. M. Kwak, "The Paradox of Effects of Diversity," *Sloan Management Review* 44 (Spring 2003): 7–8; M. Hamdani and M. Buckly, "Diversity Goals: Reframing the Debate and Enabling a Fair Evaluation," *Business Horizons* 54 (2011): 33–40.
17. A. Kalev, F. Dobbin, and E. Kelly, "Best Practices or Best Guesses? Assessing the Efficacy of Corporate Affirmative Action and Diversity Policies," *American Sociological Review* 71 (2006): 589–617; J. Marquis, N. Lim, L. Scott, M. Harrell, and J. Kavanagh, "Managing Diversity in Corporate America" (Santa Monica, CA: RAND Corporation, 2008), accessed from http://www.rand.org/pubs/occasional_papers/OP206 on August 13, 2012.
18. This application was adapted from the following sources: "L'Oréal Dedicated to Diversity," *Global Cosmetic Industry* 173 (February 2005): 80; K. Mark, "L'Oréal S.A.: Rolling Out the Global Diversity Strategy" (London, Ontario, Canada: Richard Ivey School of Business, 2010), #910C26; http://www.loreal.com.
19. L. Berry, A. Mirabito, and W. Baun, "What's the Hard Return on Employee Wellness Programs?" *Harvard Business Review* (December 2010): 104–12; "Cadbury's Runs Smoothly Under Pressure; Wellness Program Keeps IT Project on Track," *Human Resource Management International Digest* 15 (2007): 14; C. Haltom, "Health Risk Management: Well-Being for the Employee and the Bottom Line," *Benefits Quarterly* 21 (2005): 7–10; M. O'Rourke and L. Sullivan, "Corporate Wellness: A Healthy Return on Employee Investment," *Risk Management* 50 (2003): 34–36.
20. Towers Watson, "Multinational Workforce Health: Building a Sustainable Global Strategy" (New York: Towers Watson, 2012), accessed from http://www.towerswatson.com/en-ZA/Insights/IC-Types/Survey-Research-Results/2011/05/Multinational-Workforce-Health-Building-a-Sustainable-Global-Strategy-1 on June 3, 2013.
21. K. Danna and R. Griffin, "Health and Well-Being in the Workplace: A Review and Synthesis of the Literature," *Journal of Management* 25 (1999): 357–84.
22. These data were accessed from http://www.successunlimited.co.uk/costs.htm on January 14, 2000. The results have since been moved to http://www.bullyonline.org /workbully/costs.htm, accessed October 1, 2003.
23. American Psychological Association, "Stress in America" (Washington, DC, 2012), report accessed from http://www.apa.org/news/press/releases/stress/index.aspx on August 13, 2012.
24. Towers Watson, "Multinational Workforce Health: Building a Sustainable Global Strategy."
25. S. D'Mello, "Stress: The Global Economic Downturn Has Taken Its Toll on Employees. What's the Impact for Organizations?" Kenexa High Performance Institute, 2011, accessed from http://khpi.com/documents/KHPI-WorkTrends-Report-Stress on August 13, 2012.
26. J. O'Toole and E. Lawler, *The New American Workplace* (New York: Palgrave Macmillan, 2007).
27. T. O'Boyle, "Fear and Stress in the Office Take Toll," *Wall Street Journal*, November 6, 1990, B1, B3; A. Riecher, "Job Stress: What It Can Do to You," *Bryan-College Station Eagle*, August 15, 1993, D1.
28. D. Allen, "Less Stress, Less Litigation," *Personnel* (January 1990): 32–35; D. Hollis and J. Goodson, "Stress: The Legal and Organizational Implications," *Employee Responsibilities and Rights Journal* 2 (1989): 255–62.
29. T. Cummings and C. Cooper, "A Cybernetic Framework for Studying Occupational Stress," *Human Relations* 32 (1979): 395–418.
30. J. French and R. Caplan, "Organization Stress and Individual Strain," in *The Failure of Success*, ed. A. Morrow (New York: AMACOM, 1972).
31. C. Cooper and R. Payne, *Stress at Work* (New York: John Wiley & Sons, 1978).
32. C. Cooper and J. Marshall, "Occupational Sources of Stress: A Review of the Literature Relating to Coronary Heart Disease and Mental Ill Health," *Journal of Occupational Psychology* 49 (1976): 11–28; Cooper and Payne, *Stress at Work*.
33. R. Rosenman and M. Friedman, "The Central Nervous System and Coronary Heart Disease," *Hospital Practice* 6 (1971): 87–97.

34. E. Huse and C. Barebo, "Beyond the T-Group: Increasing Organizational Effectiveness," *California Management Review* 23 (1980): 104–17; I. Dayal and J. Thomas, "Operation KPE: Developing a New Organization," *Journal of Applied Behavioral Science* 4 (1968): 473–506.

35. J. House, *Work Stress and Social Support* (Reading, MA: Addison-Wesley, 1982).

36. M. Peak, "I Think I'll Go to Work in France," *Management Review* 84 (1995): 7; U.S. Department of Labor, "Annual Hours Worked per Employed Person 1990 and 2001," Chart 19.

37. R. Levering and M. Moskowitz, "100 Best Companies to Work For," *Fortune*, January 20, 2003, 127–52.

38. T. Gunter, "The Pause That Refreshes," *BusinessWeek*, November 19, 2001, 138.

39. G. Bohlander and S. Snell, *Managing Human Resources* (Cincinnati, OH: South-Western College Publishing, 2004).

40. R. Grossman, "What to Do About Substance Abuse?" *HR Magazine* 55 (2010): 32–38.

41. S. Savitz, "Mental Health Plans Help Employees, Reduce Costs," *Best's Review* 96, no. 3 (1995): 60–62.

42. C. Hodges, "Growing Problem of Stress at Work Alarms Business," *People Management* 1 (1995): 14–15.

43. W. Lissy and M. Morgenstern, "Employees Turn to EAPs During Downsizing," *Compensation and Benefits Review* 27, no. 3 (1995): 16.

44. K. Blassingame, "Providers Offer Bereaved Employees Counseling Options," *BenefitNews.com*, September 1, 2003, 51.

45. K. Bakich and K. Pestaina, "HIPAA Mean Changes for Human Resources," *Employee Relations Law Journal* 28 (2002): 29–54; K. Bakich and K. Pestaina, "HIPAA Mean Changes for Human Resources—Part II: Addressing the Most Challenging HR Issues," *Employee Relations Law Journal* 28 (2003): 47–64.

46. Huse and Barebo, "Beyond the T-Group."

47. Dayal and Thomas, "Operation KPE."

48. J. Zuckerman, "Keeping Managers in Good Health," *International Management* 34 (January 1979): 40.

49. L. Falkenberg, "Employee Fitness Programs: Their Impact on the Employee and the Organization," *Academy of Management Review* 12 (1987): 511–22.

50. R. Csiernik, "A Review of EAP Evaluation in the 1990s," *Employee Assistance Quarterly* 19 (2004): 21–37; R. Csiernik, "The Glass Is Filling: An Examination of Employee Assistance Program Evaluations in the First Decade of the New Millennium," *Journal of Workplace Behavioral Health* 26 (2011): 334–55.

51. Adapted from T. Desmond, "An Internal Broadbrush Program: J & J's Live for Life Assistance Program," in *The EAP Solution*, ed. J. Spicer (Center City, MN: Hazelden, 1987), 148–56; L. Paetsch, "Wellness Program Saves Johnson and Johnson $8.5 Million in Health Care Costs," *Employee Benefit Plan Review* 56 (2002): 31–32; S. Gale, "Selling Health to High-Risk Workers," *Workforce* 81 (2002): 74–76; R. Henke, R. Goetzel, J. McHugh, and F. Isaac, "Recent Experience in Health Promotion at Johnson & Johnson: Lower Health Spending, Strong Return on Investment," *Health Affairs* 30 (2011): 490–99; the company's website http://www.jnj.com.

EMPLOYEE BENEFITS AT HEALTHCO*

Scenario #1

"Pat, I just can't do it. I know you want me to go to New York tonight, but I can't make a trip like this at the last minute."

"Chris, you are the best attorney we have for these negotiations—we need you."

"I appreciate the compliment, but I can't arrange the care for my mother and my daughter on four hours notice. I told you during my performance appraisal about the demands I am under—in terms of carrying my own workload and part of Sidney's [a coworker] during this parental leave time. In addition, like I said, I have two elderly parents, one needing daily care, my toddler daughter, and I am moving next week. I know you want me to progress and I appreciate it, but you know I work hard—I work overtime every week—but I can't do what you want this time. I'm sorry. I'll talk to you later."

Pat hangs up the phone and thinks, "Okay, I know I am asking a lot, but how do I resolve these issues? It's frustrating that Sidney is out on 12 weeks leave—geez!!!—and it's only going to get worse. Chris is my best person ... why isn't Chris more committed? And doesn't Sidney know that 12 weeks off creates hardships for everyone else? How can I get them to do more?"

Chris walks to the parking lot thinking, "Boy, I thought I made a good move in coming here. But Pat is worse than the partners I used to work for. What am I going to do? Oh well, at least the job market for attorneys is good."

Scenario #2

"Francis, I appreciate your help these last few weeks. I never could have exceeded all my goals or facilitated my team exceeding its goal if you hadn't connected me with Kyle's Elder Care Referral Service. I feel like I would have had to take at least five to seven days off to gather the same information that Kyle had immediately available. And then I would have spent another week or two—not two days—getting my dad settled. I don't know why he decided to retire to Ireland, but he is delighted with the arrangements, and is doing well."

"That's okay, Blair, I'm happy to help. Thank you for the excellent job you've been doing. I really appreciate it. Let's talk about next month's key goals."

Blair had been the project lead during the implementation of a new quality process in the laboratory, and despite an above-average workload the last month, had successfully met the project's objectives. Francis thought, "It was touch and go when Blair's dad suddenly wanted to retire to Ireland, and wanted to move immediately. Thank heaven I remembered reading about Kyle and the Elder Care Referral Service."

Blair left Francis' office with a smile, thinking, "Francis is great to work for ... I can't even consider any of the calls I'm getting from other hospitals or headhunters. It's just great to work for someone who understands that work is just one part of life."

Scenario #3

Robin, department head for pediatrics at HealthCo's second largest hospital, had asked to meet with Mercer, the director of pediatrics for HealthCo.

"Mercer, thanks for your time. As you know I'm 56 this year, and I want to talk to you about my retirement. I have many interests beyond my medical practice, and also want more time with my family and community. What I would like to do is begin working part-time after this first year. What I'm thinking is that I would work 30 hours a week for two years, still holding clinic hours two days week. Then the next three to five years I would like to transition to full-time retirement. What I would like is to work 20 or so hours per week for those years, working with medical school students and on research projects."

"Well, Robin, as you know, we don't have any formal retirement policy except to fully

---

*This case was prepared by Professor Karen Whelan-Berry of Utah Valley State College for classroom discussion. It is published with permission of the author.

retire. I'm going to have to talk to HR about this. You have extensive experience and expertise, and I don't want to lose that. I'm just not sure what HR or the Physicians' Council will say."

"I understand. My first choice is to remain with HealthCo, but I know there are organizations that would be interested in my working part-time. When can you get back to me?"

"Give me a couple of weeks, Robin."

"Okay."

Mercer began to think about Robin's request, already hearing HR raise issues like benefits, ongoing participation in retirement funding, and precedents being set. But Mercer didn't want to lose Robin's expertise. And Robin's idea of working with the medical students might let HealthCo create a unique internship and residency experience, which would let HealthCo attract the top students.

BACKGROUND

The people in these three scenarios work for HealthCo, a fully integrated, nonprofit health care organization with nine major medical centers and 36 affiliated clinics, rehabilitation units, therapy facilities, hospice and geriatric units, and other highly specialized centers. Located in the eastern United States, HealthCo has about 6,700 employees. Like other health care companies, it employs a disproportionate number of women, especially in nursing and patient care, allied health services, and support staff. The backgrounds of Pat, Francis, and Mercer, all managers at HealthCo, are provided below.

Pat is the chief counsel of HealthCo's internal legal department. Pat has worked for HealthCo for five years, after 15 years in a major law firm in Washington, D.C. It has been a difficult transition from the "do-anything, 24/7" pace of the firm to the "slower, less professional" pace of HealthCo. Pat is married and has three kids. Pat's spouse is also an attorney. Pat's staff is primarily full-time and works "nine to five." The department is very busy, often with a workload that significantly exceeds the day-to-day capacity of the staff.

Francis serves as the director of laboratory services for the largest hospital. The laboratory is staffed around the clock and can be called on to perform routine and emergency procedures at any time. The new quality process that Blair helped to implement was critical to the lab supporting the hospital's status as the primary emergency and critical-care facility in the region. Francis, who had started in a research lab prior to joining HealthCo, felt the pressure of staffing a 24/7 lab. Having never married, Francis could not imagine juggling marriage and children in addition to the demands of having two parents and five siblings and their families living nearby. Francis tried to help the lab's employees with family or life demands, but did so on a personal basis, and not because the hospital had many such benefits available.

Mercer is a nationally known pediatrician with 15 years experience, and was recently hired to head HealthCo's pediatrics organization. Mercer's expertise and management capabilities were stretched in a positive way by the demands of such a large and comprehensive pediatric practice. Thriving on that challenge, Mercer had been very successful since taking over the organization. Marrying after medical school to another physician, Mercer felt grateful for being able to work the hours required to fully learn and understand this new position. Mercer knew a number of people on the pediatric staff, including a number of the pediatricians. Many of them felt Mercer worked way too much, and moreover, worried Mercer expected the same of them. Mercer knew that younger physicians weren't as keen on the 24/7 doctor lifestyle that Mercer's father had lived.

RECENT EVENTS

A couple of weeks after Pat's conversation with Chris, Francis' with Blair, and Mercer's with Robin, a senior staff meeting was called to discuss current issues and the coming year's strategic initiatives. The CEO, Dr. Palmer, recently had become focused on employee retention, after Human Resources reported that HealthCo's turnover was 1.5 times the industry average. While HealthCo was competitive about salary, benefits seemed to be an area needing improvement. Further, the recent issue of *Fortune*, which identified the "Best Companies to Work For," raised Dr. Palmer's awareness of the growing importance of work–life programs and policies.

Dr. Palmer realized that HealthCo did not provide many of the benefits offered by these "best companies." In fact, very few health care

TABLE 1

Rank-Order Importance of Work–Life Benefits for Female Employees at HealthCo

Benefit	Rank	Currently Offered by Healthco
Maternity/Paternity and Family Leave Includes paid maternity and paternity leave, extended paid leave for family issues, and unpaid leave for family issues with the ability to return to work.	1	HealthCo pays six weeks maternity and paternity leave, after the employees has been with the company for one year. Employees can take another six weeks unpaid. No extended leave.
Sabbatical/Extended Leave Paid extended leave after working for a specified time with the company.	2	Not offered by HealthCo.
Fitness Includes on-site fitness facilities, and/or paid health club memberships.	3	Not offered by HealthCo.
Flextime Includes part-time work schedules, flextime, and telecommuting.	4	Flextime, with two-hour flex offered in some departments.
Work–Life Task Force Employee committee that oversees work–life issues.	5	Currently overseen by HR.
Concierge Services Includes services such as on-site takeout, dry cleaning, auto service, and other similar services.	6	Not offered except at corporate headquarters.
Child Care Includes on-site child care, vacation programs, and before and after school care.	7	Sick-child care offered at some of the medical centers.
Referral Services Includes child care, elder care, and other referral services.	8	Not offered by HealthCo.
Paid Health Insurance Premiums	*	HealthCo pays the employee's premium.

*Payment of health insurance premium not rank-ordered, but included in survey information.

companies made the list. Palmer conceded that the 24/7 nature of health care organizations probably complicated the provision of work–life benefits. However, Palmer also saw a potential competitive advantage in being a leader in providing such benefits, especially when combined with the competitive salary and merit structure HealthCo offered. Dr. Palmer remembered that a survey had been done of HealthCo female employees by an outside research team, and that one area of the survey was work–life issues. A review of the data revealed a number of benefits seen as important to the female employees of HealthCo (see Table 1). The research also had suggested that the immediate supervisor played a vital role in the employee's ability to successfully balance work and life, and the employee's satisfaction with her work–life balance. An immediate supervisor's direct support of work–life balance was significantly linked to other important outcomes, such as job satisfaction, organizational commitment, and intent to leave the organization.

Dr. Palmer raised the question of offering work–life benefits at the senior staff meeting. Dr. Palmer noted that while funding was not unlimited, of course, HealthCo's recent financial performance would permit budget allocations to such benefits, and might also be offset by reduced turnover costs or improved productivity.

Pat immediately stated, "I can barely get my staff together now with all the work we have going on. And, I certainly can't hold their hands. They would never be coddled this way in a law firm. People work the hours needed, no questions asked." Francis said, "I can see the difference such benefits would make, but how do I make this work in a 24/7 department? While Legal might see it as difficult, I see it as impossible, especially any movement away from traditional shifts." A nursing director commented thoughtfully, "Some hospitals are considering shorter, split shifts, and longer shifts to create flexibility—there might be something to that." A number of departments immediately argued such scheduling was a leader's nightmare, and that the company's existing two hours of flextime in a number of departments created serious issues. The V.P. of finance for the hospital spoke up, "I don't see why people with children should be treated differently—it's their choice to have children. I have a life, too, and you don't see me asking for special arrangements. I have employees asking me to work from home—how do I appraise their performance if they primarily work at home?" Mercer thought about Robin's request, wondering if other baby-boomer employees would soon be making similar requests.

Dr. Palmer listened to what was quickly becoming a heated discussion, noting the varied and complicated reactions of the different directors, vice presidents, and other top leaders of the organization. Dr. Palmer commented, "We say in our recruiting materials that our employees *are* HealthCo, that it is individual care in all areas of the company—from nursing to accounting—that makes us different. How can we expect our employees to give individual care if we, as an organization, don't care about them and their lives?"

"I'd like a team of four to six volunteers to put together a plan for becoming a top company in terms of work–life benefits. Please identify the key issues in serving all employees with such a set of benefits, and any related issues."

Questions

1. How would you conduct a diagnosis of the situation at HealthCo?
2. Based on the information provided in the scenarios and the case, what is your own diagnosis of the situation?
3. What do you see as the key issues in HealthCo becoming a top company in terms of work–life benefits?

DESIGNING AND IMPLEMENTING A REWARD SYSTEM AT DISK DRIVES, INC.*

Disk Drives, Inc. (DDI) is a specialty electronics firm that designs, markets, and distributes disk drives for the computer industry. DDI began in 1980 by manufacturing and marketing large-format disk drives for minicomputer firms, such as Digital Equipment Corporate (DEC) and Data General, as well as for complex, large-scale word-processing systems offered by Xerox and Wang. DDI's first products were quite successful and the company grew to revenues of $119 million by 1985. A strategic decision to integrate different technologies inside the disk drive for a different type of customer resulted in a newer and smaller product line with lower costs and lower prices. Unfortunately, DDI was late to market and its products did not have the performance features these customers wanted or needed. Thus, despite the new customers and higher product volumes, sales and profits plummeted as its original products faded and its new products faltered.

One of DDI's subsidiaries, however, was designing and selling different and even smaller disk drives to personal computer original equipment manufacturers (OEMs). Following a different business model, they had outsourced their manufacturing capacity to a Japanese plant. The subsidiary—over the 1985–1989 time frame—saved DDI from failure. By 1988, DDI announced it would stop developing and manufacturing all of its larger disk drives and focus on the smaller ones for PCs. It also phased out its domestic manufacturing operations and began sourcing its drives exclusively from the Japanese plant. Whereas two-thirds of DDI's 1988 revenues had come from large drives manufactured domestically, by the end of 1989, 100% of its revenues were from the small drives manufactured in Japan. The question facing DDI management was how to maintain the momentum. It required a careful look at the existing organization and determining its fitness for the future.

The head of HR at DDI, who was quite knowledgeable in organization change and development, convinced the executive team to go through a systematic process of diagnosing the organization's current operating model and redesigning the company to handle the projected growth and the increased complexity it was facing.

THE CURRENT DDI ORGANIZATION

At the macro level, competition in the disk drive market was characterized by fast-paced technology change and product evolution as well as a number of equally sized competitors. First, customers—the OEM manufacturers of PCs, such as IBM, Dell, Toshiba, and HP—were not only designing newer, faster, and more sophisticated computers, they were demanding and expecting newer, faster, and more sophisticated disk drives. Although management was confident in the firm's technical ability to offer the best price/performance products in the industry, they realized that the period during which a new DDI drive could retain a performance edge before being leapfrogged by a competitor was getting shorter and shorter. Second, when an OEM announced a new computer model, all of the disk drive manufacturers competed aggressively to get the business. The disk drive firms had a limited amount of time—usually less than a few months—to make their bid, and it was often based on yet untried technological capabilities. Moreover, the sales process had a "gold rush" or "winner take all" feel. If a disk drive manufacturer could win a contract with an OEM manufacturer, it usually meant that a *whole line* of disk drives, including follow-on models, would be part of the deal. As a result, quality, speed of customer response, and cost were increasingly important

*This case was derived and adapted from materials found in C. Christensen, "Quantum Corporation—Business and Product Teams," *Harvard Business School Case 9-692-023* (Boston: Harvard Business School, 1992); S. Mohrman, "Computer Components," Center for Effective Organizations (Los Angeles: University of Southern California, 2012).

FIGURE 1

The DDI Value Chain

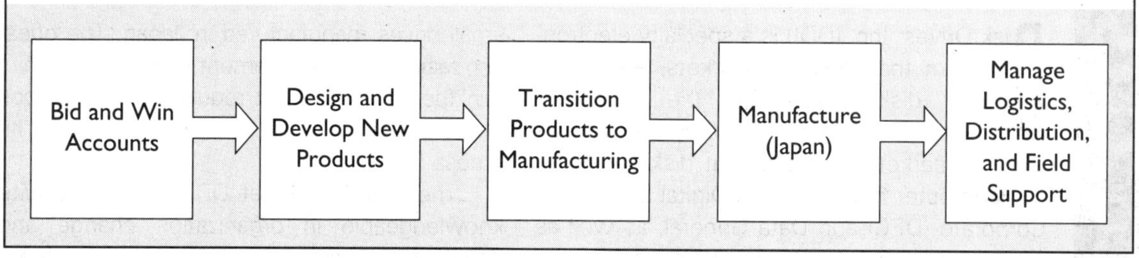

dimensions to be managed. Quality was necessary to win the confidence of the OEMs and increase the chances of winning follow-on business, speed of response was necessary given the narrow timeframe, and cost vigilance was necessary to produce a profit.

In this environment, the company was clear about the processes for adding value (Figure 1). The key work processes included:

1. Working with appropriate technical support, it was important to bid and win on new accounts. A Request for Proposal (RFP) provided by the OEM detailed the technical specifications for the disk drive in its new computer model.
2. The disk drive was then designed to fit the technical specifications and to meet quality and cost targets.
3. The resulting design was then prepared for transfer to the manufacturing facility.
4. The drive was manufactured in Japan.
5. The drive was then released to the OEM to be incorporated into the computer, and support issues were handled.

DDI was growing fast and new models were being continually released that embodied technology advances, new capabilities, and enhanced designs. The life cycle for a disk drive (once a contract was signed with the OEM) was about six to eight months for development, first-run production, and field distribution and service. Even including a second release (follow-on) product, the entire life cycle for the model was generally about 12 to 16 months. The company was handling about five to six disk drive designs at any particular time and that number was expected to increase significantly.

As described above, DDI had signed a long-term, exclusive contract to outsource manufacturing to a Japanese company that promised, in turn, to continually retool and upgrade its manufacturing capabilities as DDI grew. To manage this process, DDI had experienced manufacturing engineers, quality assurance, process optimization, and distribution staff to plan the movement of the disks into the contracted factory and to manage its introduction into the field.

In line with this functional structure and work process, the organization was governed by the executive committee, composed of the CEO and trusted colleagues who had "grown up" together in the industry. Each took responsibility for certain functional tasks (Figure 2). Each hired people to carry out the functions they managed as the company achieved success and grew rapidly.

The executive team was also responsible for the planning, coordination, and integration of the activities of marketing and sales, technical development, and managing operations and field distribution and support. That is, decision making, goal setting, and strategic direction were centralized to this group. Similarly, the organization's performance management system was centralized and traditional. Managers and functional employees were given overall company targets for revenue and each function was expected to translate those goals into specific objectives for their group. Functional supervisors gave annual performance appraisals that provided the basis for merit pay increases. In addition, all DDI employees were eligible for a profit sharing bonus that had been running at about 5% of salary. Executives were eligible for stock options as well.

FIGURE 2

DDI's Functional Organization

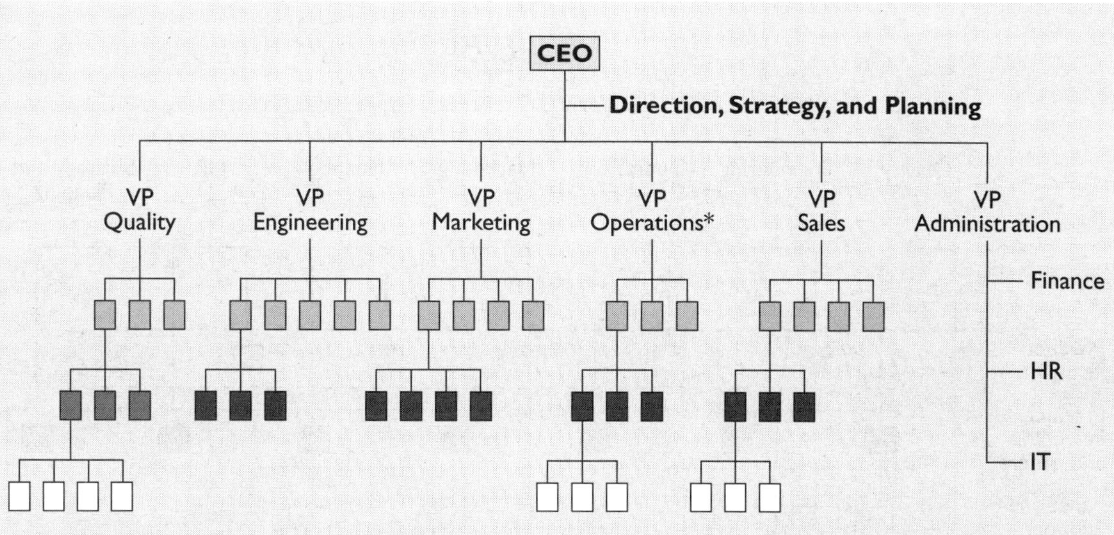

ENGAGING IN A REDESIGN OF DDI

Although happy with the recent success of the company, the executive team realized that it could not continue to grow and be successful as it was currently designed. It was not effectively coordinating the complexity that came with rapid growth, and it was having trouble keeping up with demand. It had experienced several delays and quality incidents, including one major field warranty problem due to a disk drive failure. The executive team was highly involved in ongoing operational issues, and the CEO was concerned that they did not have time to attend to the strategic decisions required in the rapidly developing computer industry. He also believed that the executive team had become a bottleneck and was slowing product decision making. The CEO recalled being in an executive committee meeting and asking about why a particular product had not yet shipped to the customer. After collecting a variety of data and information about component inventories, capacity planning, forecasts, and other details, he realized that management—in particular, the executive committee—was part of the problem. "We were trying to manage details we weren't knowledgeable about. We had a bandwidth problem—the executive staff just didn't have enough time or brain capacity to keep making all the key decisions."

The executive team decided that they needed to assume a more strategic role in the organization and decentralize cross-functional integration and operational decision making about new product development, manufacturing, and field support. Although they wanted insight into product development progress and milestone achievement, they also understood that to decentralize this integration and decision making, they needed to be clear about the roles, responsibilities, and accountabilities for success. They believed such a change would create and build a cadre of future leaders for the organization.

Based on the diagnostic data and the executive team's requirements, the head of HR led the team through a systematic redesign of the organization.

Commitment to Strategic Direction

The executive team first recommitted itself to the basic strategy of rapidly advancing the technology through aggressively bidding on and delivering disk drives to computers that required increasing operating speed, flawless quality, and continual new functionalities.

Structure Modification

The executive team believed that the existing functional structure provided important advantages.

FIGURE 3

The Proposed Product Team Structure

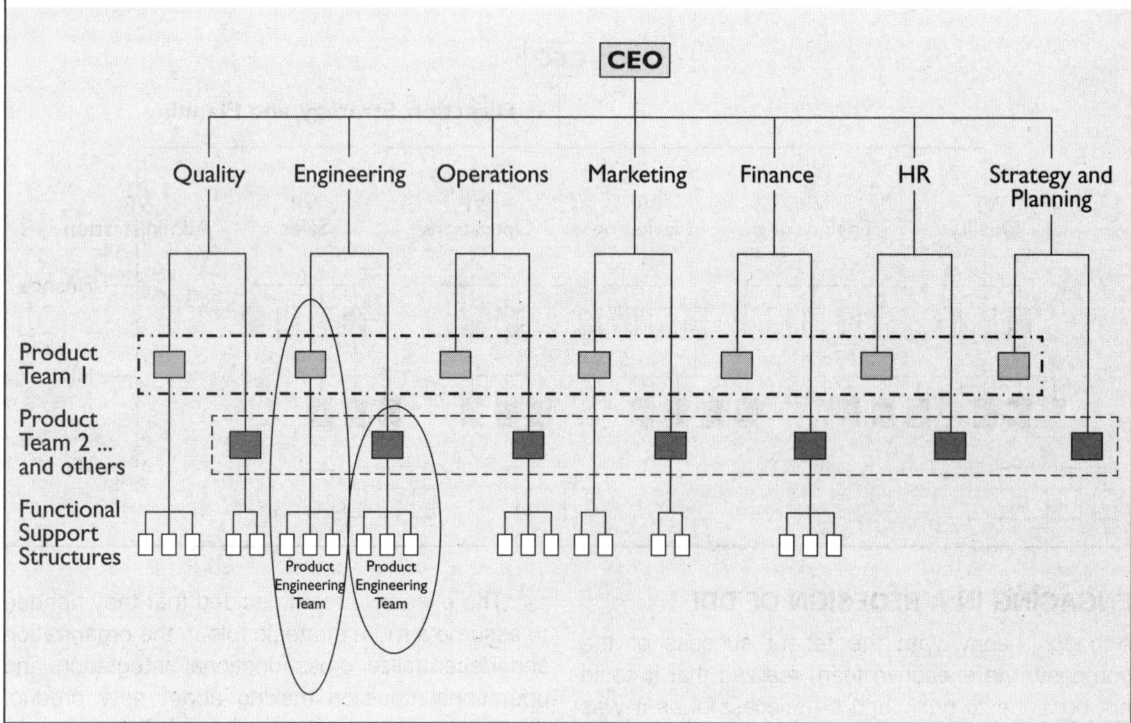

There was a clear focus on technical excellence and clear technical career paths. However, to achieve the cross-functional integration and speed objectives and to begin building leadership skills, they decided to implement cross-functional product teams as a lateral structure to coordinate the development of each disk drive. Functions would remain the core units of the company, but the management of each disk drive model would be carried out by a team, established as soon as a contract was signed, to manage the product over its life cycle (see the dotted horizontal lines in Figure 3).

The members of each product team would be functional managers at the director or senior manager level—moving the operational cross-functional coordination and management lower in the organization and freeing up the executive team to concentrate on more strategic issues.

The teams were to consist of seven members, one from each function (although there was no member from the sales organization). They were to be *collectively* responsible for the general management of their product and not just represent their functional point of view. In general, the engineering team member was to be the leader during the initial phases of the program, but as the product approached commercial launch, the marketing member would assume more leadership responsibilities. The engineering team member would also lead a dedicated group of engineers assigned to develop the drive and to work through any product design problems encountered during manufacturing and in the field (see the solid vertical lines in Figure 3). The engineering member was the only person with a functional group dedicated to the product; all other functions would allocate personnel to a product team based on the project's stage of development and need. Each team member would continue to have management responsibilities within their function. In other words, working on a team was considered an "overload" responsibility in addition to their regular functional responsibilities.

Management Processes

The executive team was careful to delineate which issues were the responsibility of the product teams,

TABLE 1

Product Team and Functional Organization Responsibilities

Product Team Mission: To work in a coordinated way to address market needs	Functional Organization Mission: To ensure high quality technical support services
• Define, develop, and introduce new products • Manage cycle time, cost, and quality objectives • Manage the inventories required to support revenues • Manage product revenues and gross margins	• Provide career path and skill development • Support team projects and provide specialized services • Allocate engineering and manufacturing personnel to product team projects • Execute plans and staffing programs initiated by product teams

the functional organizations, and the executive staff. The product team would be empowered to make all decisions relating to developing and bringing a specific product into the field—and it would be incented to bring the product to market on time, within cost, and with high levels of quality and customer satisfaction. Teams were responsible for the revenues and gross margins generated by the product and for the inventories required to support the revenues. The product teams were responsible for achieving faster and faster development cycle times. Each product team was given clearly defined milestones that were derived from the contract, including cost, quality, and profitability targets.

Functional groups, on the other hand, were charged with managing ongoing functional activities and expenses, providing effective career paths and skill-building programs, executing the plans, and staffing the programs initiated by the product teams. For example, the engineering organization was responsible for maintaining DDIs overall technical edge, dedicating a group of engineers to a specific product, and defining professional development. In addition, each function was divided into discipline groups that carried out specialty tasks. For example, the quality function had a group that specialized in design quality, prototype testing, and manufacturing quality specifications and monitoring (the latter working closely with the contract manufacturing facility). The responsibilities of the product teams and the functional organizations are summarized in Table 1.

Finally, the executive team controlled milestone reviews for each product, including prototype design completion, design completion/release to manufacturing, release to customer, and the three-week release to field.

Performance Management

The executive team next considered the question of performance management and incentives.

Questions

1. Does DDI need a new performance system to account for the structural and management process changes they are contemplating? Why or why not?
2. Assuming a modification to the performance management system is necessary, describe the features of a system you would recommend. What changes need to be made in the goal setting, feedback/appraisal, and reward systems at DDI? Be specific about the features of the system(s) you believe need to be changed and the characteristics of the system itself. That is, do not describe the process for designing the system (see Question 3) but focus on the characteristics of the reward system that are required to fit or align with the strategy, structure, and management processes.
3. Describe the change management process you would use to design and implement the new system. What roles and responsibilities should the executive team take on? How fast should the system be implemented?

PART 6

STRATEGIC CHANGE INTERVENTIONS

18 Transformational Change
19 Continuous Change
20 Transorganization Change

SELECTED CASES

Global Mobile Corporation
Leading Strategic Change at DaVita: The Integration of the Gambro Acquisition

18

Transformational Change

learning objectives

- Describe the characteristics of transformational change.
- Explain the organization design intervention for both domestic and worldwide situations.
- Learn about the integrated strategic change intervention and understand how it represents the revolutionary and systemic characteristics of transformational change.
- Discuss the process and key success factors associated with culture change.

This is the first of three chapters describing strategic change interventions. In prior chapters of this text, *organizational* development processes aimed at improving specific parts of an organization were described. For example, third-party interventions addressed conflict between two individuals, team-building interventions improved group functioning, employee involvement interventions increased member engagement, and reward system interventions aligned individual and team incentives with business strategy. In every case, the intervention focused on one particular organizational subsystem and placed other subsystems in the background. That is, diagnostic data pointed to one specific aspect of the organization, such as a structure, system, or process, as needing development. More importantly, there was an implicit or explicit assumption that the organization's culture was part of that background and that the interventions were unlikely to influence the culture in any significant way.

The focus of the interventions in Part 6 is on the whole system—on *organization* development. These change programs are "strategic" in that they are intended to alter the relationship between an organization and its environment, and they are intended to affect outcomes at the organization level, including sales, profitability, and culture. These interventions involve changing the strategy and/or design of a single organization or combining or orchestrating the activities of multiple organizations.

This chapter describes transformational interventions. These change processes bring about important alignments between the organization and its competitive environment and among the organization's strategy, design elements, and culture. They are initiated in response to or in anticipation of major changes in the organization's environment or technology. As a result, these changes often trigger significant revisions in business strategy, which, in turn, may require modifying internal structures and processes to support the new direction. Such fundamental change entails a new paradigm for organizing and managing the organization; it requires qualitatively different ways of perceiving, thinking, and behaving. Movement toward this new way of operating requires senior executives to take an active leadership role. The change process is characterized by considerable innovation as members discover new ways of improving the organization and adapting it to changing conditions.

Transformational change is an emerging part of organization development, and there is some confusion about its meaning and definition. This chapter starts with a description of several major features of transformational change. For example, transformational change is triggered by internal or external disruptions; initiated by line managers and executives; influenced by multiple stakeholders, systemic and revolutionary; and characterized by significant learning and a new paradigm.

Organization design interventions address the different elements that comprise the "architecture" of the organization, including structure, work design, human resources practices, and management processes. In either domestic or worldwide settings, organization design interventions seek to fit or align these components with each other so they direct members' behaviors in support of a strategic direction. Integrated strategic change is a comprehensive OD intervention that builds on the systemic and revolutionary nature of transformational change. It leverages traditional change management frameworks and aims to transform a single organization or business unit. It suggests that business strategy and organization design must be aligned and changed together to respond to external and internal disruptions. A strategic change plan helps members manage the transition between the current strategic orientation and the desired future strategic orientation.

Organizational culture is the pattern of assumptions, values, and norms regarding correct behavior that is shared, more or less, by organization members. A growing body of research confirms that culture can affect strategy formulation and implementation as well as the firm's ability to achieve high levels of performance.[1] Culture change involves helping senior executives and administrators diagnose the existing culture and make necessary alterations in the basic assumptions and values underlying organizational behaviors.

18-1 Characteristics of Transformational Change

Organization transformation implies radical changes in how members perceive, think, and behave at work. These changes go far beyond making the existing organization better or fine-tuning the status quo. They are concerned with fundamentally altering the prevailing assumptions about how the organization functions and relates to its environment. Changing these assumptions entails significant shifts in corporate values and norms and in the structures and organizational arrangements that shape members' behaviors. Not only is the magnitude of change greater, but it can fundamentally alter the qualitative nature of the organization.

18-1a Change Is Triggered by Environmental and Internal Disruptions

Increased global competition and the lingering economic recession are forcing many organizations to engage in radical changes to their operating strategies and structures, downsize or consolidate, or become leaner, more efficient, and flexible.[2] Global warming, social unrest, and the rise of watchdog nongovernmental organizations are pushing firms to implement a variety of corporate social responsibility and sustainability initiatives. Public demand for less government intervention and lower deficits conflicts with expectations of support during hard times. Public sector agencies must try to expand services, streamline operations, and deliver more for less. Rapid changes in technologies render many organizational practices obsolete, pushing firms to be continually innovative and agile.

However, research suggests that traditional organizations are unlikely to undertake transformational change without significant reasons to do so.[3] Power, emotion, and expertise are vested in the existing organizational arrangements, and when faced with problems, organizations are more likely to fine-tune those structures than to alter them drastically. Thus, in most cases, organizations must experience or anticipate a severe threat to survival before they will be motivated to undertake large-scale, transformational change.[4] Such threats arise when environmental and internal changes render existing organizational strategies and designs obsolete. These disruptions threaten the existence of the organization's current design and the likelihood of continuing to perform at a high level.

In studying a large number of organization transformations, researchers suggest that large-scale change occurs in response to at least three kinds of disruption:[5]

1. Industry discontinuities—sharp changes in legal, political, economic, and technological conditions that shift the basis for competition within an industry.
2. Product life cycle shifts—changes in product life cycle that require different business strategies or business models.
3. Internal company dynamics—changes in size, corporate portfolio strategy, or executive turnover.

In each case, the organization's current or future performance is threatened in substantive ways. These disruptions severely jolt organizations and push them to question their business strategy and, in turn, their organization's design.

18-1b Change Is Initiated by Senior Executives and Line Managers

Senior executives and line managers usually initiate transformational change.[6] They are responsible for maintaining the organization's character and performance. As a result, senior managers decide when to initiate large-scale change, what the change should be, how it should be implemented, and who should be responsible for directing it. Because existing executives may lack the talent, energy, or commitment to undertake these tasks, the organization may recruit outsiders to lead the change. Externally recruited executives are three times more likely to initiate such change than are existing executives.[7]

Executive leadership in large-scale and transformational change is critical, especially when the change must happen quickly. Lucid accounts of transformational change describe how executives, such as Ray Anderson at Interface Carpet, Lou Gerstner at IBM, and Victor Fung at Li and Fung, actively managed both the organizational and personal dynamics of transformational change. Researchers have identified four key roles for executive leadership during transformational change:[8]

- **Envisioning**. Executives must articulate a clear, credible, compelling, and consistent vision of the new strategic orientation. During changes of this magnitude, it is imperative that leaders throughout the organization maintain the message and their commitment to a desired future state that is fundamentally better than the current one. In periods of change, when anxiety is elevated, people need to know that everyone in the organization is committed to the new organization and its purpose. Creating and discussing the organization's future configuration is a leadership behavior that helps to meet this need.

- **Energizing**. Executives must demonstrate personal excitement for the changes and model the behaviors that are expected of others. Behavioral integrity, credibility, and "walking the talk" are important ingredients.[9] Christening initiatives and allocating resources to key transformation tasks in line with the vision demonstrates that commitment. Change is accelerated when organization members see important and scarce resources being devoted to large-scale change tasks. Executives must provide the resources necessary for undertaking significant change and use rewards to reinforce new behaviors.
- **Enabling**. The third leadership behavior that contributes to large-scale change is communication that helps people make sense of transformation. They must communicate examples of early success to mobilize energy for change. By "connecting the dots"—showing people how certain accomplishments, results, milestones, and other activities are working together to achieve the transformation—leaders help organization members understand that change can happen and is happening.
- **Engaging**. Executives also must set new and difficult standards for performance, and hold people accountable to those new standards. During transformational change, the organization explicitly or implicitly voids prior employment relationship understandings and all of its implied behaviors and incentives. Managers must lay out the new expectations and incentives. Sending clear signals in conversations with people about the values and behaviors that will be supported in the new organization—and those values and behaviors that will not be supported—is an important contributor to transformational change. While there must be an appropriate recognition for past performance and pride in past accomplishments, there must also be enthusiastic support for the new strategy.

18-1c Change Involves Multiple Stakeholders

Transformational change invariably affects many organization stakeholders, including owners, managers, employees, vendors, regulators, and most importantly, customers. An organization's current performance is the result of tacit and explicit coordination among a variety of stakeholders. As performance declines due to the internal or external disruptions described above, these different stakeholders are likely to have different goals and interests related to the change process. Unless the differences are revealed and reconciled, enthusiastic support for change may be difficult to achieve. Consequently, the change process must attend to the interests of multiple stakeholders.[10]

The creation of a "stakeholder map" or open systems plan, such as that described in Chapter 11, facilitates transformational change.[11] It helps to document the current demands of relevant stakeholders, the current organizational responses to each stakeholder, how each stakeholder's demands are changing or likely to change, and the implications of those changes on the organization's mission and strategy. Involving a variety of organization stakeholders creates an accurate view of the environment, organization, and the change challenges.

18-1d Change Is Systemic and Revolutionary

Transformational change involves reshaping the organization's strategy and design elements to affect culture and performance. These changes can be characterized as systemic and revolutionary because the focus is on the realignment of the entire organization in a relatively short period of time.

An organization's design includes the structure, work design, human resources practices, and management processes that support the business strategy. Because each of these features significantly affects member behavior, they need to be designed and changed together to reinforce their mutual support of a new strategic direction and its desired behaviors.[12] This comprehensive and systemic view of transformational change contrasts sharply with piecemeal approaches that address the design elements separately. A fragmented approach risks misaligning design elements and sending mixed signals about desired behaviors.[13] For example, many organizations have experienced problems implementing team-based structures because their existing human resource systems emphasize individual-based performance.

Longitudinal change studies also underscore the revolutionary nature of transformational change and point to the benefits of implementing change as rapidly as possible.[14] Organizations often move through relatively long periods of smooth growth, operational improvements, and incremental changes. At times, however, they experience severe external or internal disruptions that render existing organizational arrangements ineffective. Successful firms respond to these survival threats by transforming themselves to fit the new conditions. Examples of successful transformational change include IBM, Harley Davidson, and DaVita. These periods of total system and quantum change represent abrupt shifts in the organization's strategy, structure, and processes. Also, the majority of the people in the organization change their behavior.[15] Typically driven by senior executives, change occurs rapidly so that it does not get mired in politics, individual resistance, and other forms of organizational inertia.[16] The faster the organization can respond to disruptions, the quicker it can attain the benefits of operating in a new way. If successful, the shift enables the organization to experience another long period of smooth functioning until the next disruption signals the need for drastic change.[17]

18-1e Change Involves Significant Learning and a New Paradigm

Organizations undertaking transformational change are, by definition, involved in second-order or gamma types of change.[18] *Gamma change* involves discontinuous shifts in mental or organizational frameworks[19] and therefore requires much learning and innovation.[20] Organizational members must learn how to enact the new behaviors required to implement new strategic directions. This typically involves trying new behaviors, assessing their consequences, and modifying them if necessary. Because members usually must learn qualitatively different ways of perceiving, thinking, and behaving, the learning process is likely to be substantial and to involve a considerable amount of "unlearning."

Creative metaphors, such as "organization learning" or "continuous improvement," are often used to help members visualize the new paradigm.[21] Increases in technological change, changes in climate patterns, concern for quality, and worker participation have led many organizations to shift their organizing paradigm. This transformation has been characterized as the transition from a "command and control-based" paradigm to a "commitment-based" or "sustainability-based" paradigm.[22] The features of the new paradigm include broader, more inclusive organizational goals; leaner, more flexible structures; information and decision making pushed down to the lowest levels; decentralized teams and business units accountable for specific products, services, or customers; and participative management and teamwork. This new organizing paradigm is well suited to changing conditions. Thus, a compelling vision of the future organization and the values and norms needed to support it also encourage the learning process. Because the environment itself is likely to be changing during the change process, transformational change often has no clear beginning or ending point but is likely to persist as long as the firm needs to adapt to change. Learning how to manage change continuously can help the organization keep pace with a dynamic environment. It can provide the built-in capacity to fit the organization continually to its environment. Chapter 19 presents OD interventions for helping organizations gain this capability for continuous change and learning.

18-2 Organization Design

Organization design configures the organization's structure, work design, human resources practices, and management processes to guide members' behaviors in a strategic direction. This intervention typically occurs in response to a major change in the organization's strategy that requires fundamentally new ways for the organization to function and members to behave. It involves many of the organizational features discussed in previous chapters such as restructuring organizations (Chapter 12), work design (Chapter 14), and performance management (Chapter 15).

18-2a Conceptual Framework

A key notion in organization design is "fit," "congruence," or "alignment" among the organizational elements.[23] Figure 18.1 presents a systems model similar to the one presented in Chapter 5 showing the different components of organization design and the interdependencies among them. It highlights the idea that the organization is designed

FIGURE 18.1

A Systems Model of Organization Design

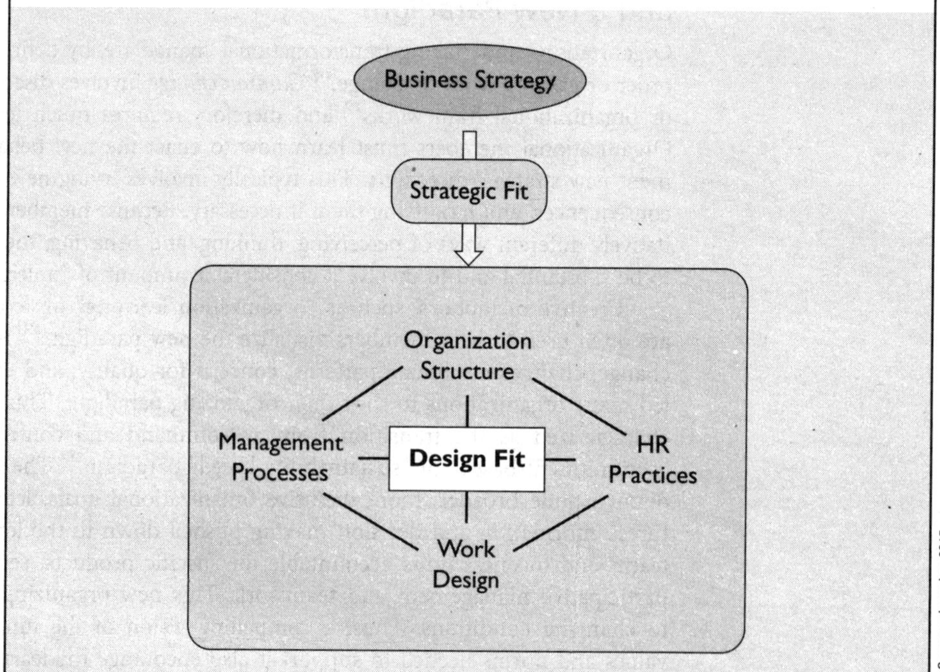

to support a particular strategy (strategic fit) and that the different design elements must be aligned with each other and all work together to guide members' behavior in that strategic direction (design fit). Research shows that the better these fits, the more effective the organization is likely to be.[24] These design components have been described previously in this book, so they are reviewed briefly below.

- Business strategy determines how the organization will use its resources to gain competitive advantage and achieve its objectives in the short to medium term. It may change, for example, the degrees of breadth, aggressiveness, and differentiation to focus on introducing new products and services (innovation strategy) or controlling costs and reducing prices (cost-minimization strategy). Strategy sets the direction for organization design by identifying the organizational capabilities needed to make the strategy happen.
- Structure describes how the organization divides tasks, assigns them to departments, and coordinates across them. It generally appears on an organization chart showing the chain of command—where formal power and authority reside and how departments relate to each other. Structures can be highly formal and promote control and efficiency, such as a functional structure; or they can be loosely defined, flexible, and favor change and innovation, such as a matrix, process, or network structure.
- Work design specifies how tasks are performed and assigned to individual or groups to add value. That is, work and organization design must be aware of the underlying processes that transform inputs into valued outputs. Work design can create traditional jobs and groups that involve standard tasks with little task variety and decision making or enriched jobs and self-managed teams that involve highly variable, challenging, and discretionary work.
- Human resource practices involve recruiting, selecting, developing, and rewarding people. These methods can be oriented to hiring and paying people for specific jobs, training them when necessary, and rewarding their individual performance. Conversely, human resource practices can also select people to fit the organization's culture, continually develop them, and pay them for learning multiple skills and contributing to business success.
- Management processes describe how goals are set, how decisions are made, how resources are allocated, and how information and knowledge is stored and communicated. Managers can set direction, allocate resources, or make decisions using a command and control style that relies on hierarchical authority and the chain of command; or they can utilize highly participative methods that facilitate employee involvement. Information can be tightly controlled and centralized, with limited access and data sharing; or it can be transparent and shared freely throughout the organization.

18-2b Basic Design Alternatives

Table 18.1 shows how these design components can be configured into two radically different organization designs: *mechanistic*, supporting efficiency and control, and *organic*, promoting innovation and change.[25] Mechanistic designs have been prevalent in organizations for over a century; they propelled organizations into the industrial age. Today, competitive conditions require many organizations to be more flexible, fast, and inventive.[26] Thus, organization design is aimed more and more at creating organic designs, both in entirely new start-ups and in existing firms that reconfigure mechanistic designs

TABLE 18.1

Organization Designs

	Mechanistic Design	Organic Design
Strategy	• Cost minimization	• Innovation
Structure	• Formal/hierarchical • Functional	• Flat, lean, and flexible • Matrix, process, and network
Work design	• Traditional jobs • Traditional work groups	• Enriched jobs • Self-managed teams
Human resources practices	• Selection to fit job • Up-front training • Standard reward mix • Pay for performance and individual merit • Job-based pay	• Selection to fit organization • Continuous training and development • Individual choice rewards • Pay for performance and business success • Skill-based pay
Management processes	• Centralized decision making • Top down goal setting and communication	• Employee involvement • Transparent information

to make them more organic. Designing a new organization is much easier than redesigning an existing one in which multiple sources of inertia and resistance to change are likely embedded.

As shown in Table 18.1, a mechanistic design supports an organization-strategy emphasizing cost minimization, such as might be found at Carrefour and McDonalds or other firms competing on price. The organization tends to be structured into functional departments, with employees performing similar tasks grouped together for maximum efficiency. The managerial hierarchy is the main source of coordination and control. Accordingly, work design follows traditional principles, with jobs and work groups being highly standardized with minimal decision making and skill variety. Human resources practices are geared toward selecting people to fit specific jobs and training them periodically when the need arises. Employees are paid on the basis of the job they perform, share a standard set of fringe benefits, and achieve merit raises based on their individual performance. Management processes stress centralized decision making, with power concentrated at the top of the organization and orders flowing downward through the chain of command. Similarly, communication and goal setting systems are driven from the top. Information is not widely shared. When taken together, all of these design elements direct organizational behavior toward efficiency and cost minimization.

Table 18.1 shows that an organic design supports an organization strategy aimed at innovation, such as might be found at 3M, Google, and Unilever or other firms competing on new products and services. All the design elements are geared to getting employees directly involved in the innovation process, facilitating interaction among them, developing and rewarding their knowledge and expertise, and providing them with relevant and timely information. Consequently, the organization's structure tends to be flat, lean, and flexible like the matrix, process, and network structures described in Chapter 12. Work design is aimed at employee motivation and decision making with enriched jobs and self-managed teams. Human resources practices focus on attracting, motivating, and retaining talented employees. They send a strong signal that employees' knowledge and expertise are key sources of competitive advantage. Members are selected to fit an organization culture valuing participation, teamwork, and invention. Training and development are intense and continuous. Members are rewarded for learning multiple skills, have choices about fringe benefits, and gain merit pay based on the business success of their work unit. Management processes are highly participative and promote employee involvement. Communication systems are highly open, inclusive, and transparent providing relevant and timely information throughout the organization. In sum, these design choices guide members' behaviors toward change and innovation.

Application 18.1 describes organization design at Deere & Company.[27] It illustrates how the different design elements must fit together and reinforce each other to promote a high-performance organization.

18-2c Worldwide Organization Design Alternatives

An important trend facing many business firms is the emergence of a global marketplace. Driven by competitive pressures, lowered trade barriers, increased knowledge work, and advances in information technologies, the number of companies developing or offering products and services in multiple countries continues to rise. Worldwide organizations[28] offer products or services and actively manage direct investments in more than one country; must balance product and functional concerns with geographic issues of distance, time, and culture; and must carry out coordinated activities across cultural boundaries using expatriates, short-term and extended business travelers, and local employees. They must relate to a variety of demands, such as unique product requirements, tariffs, value-added taxes, governmental and environmental regulations, labor practices, transportation laws, and trade agreements, and adapt their human resources policies and procedures to fit different cultures. Tobacco companies, for example, face technological, moral, and organizational issues in determining whether to market cigarettes in less-developed countries, and if they do, they must decide how to integrate manufacturing and distribution operations on a global scale. The organizational complexity associated with managing these organizations is challenging.

How these firms choose to arrange their products/services, organization, and personnel enable them to compete in the global marketplace.[29] Despite the many possible combinations, researchers have found that two dimensions are useful in guiding managerial decisions about these choices.

As shown in Figure 18.2, managers need to assess two key success factors: the degrees to which there is a need for global integration or for local responsiveness.[30] *Global integration* refers to whether or not business success requires tight coordination of people, plants, equipment, products, or service delivery on a worldwide basis. For example, Intel's "global factory" designs semiconductors in multiple countries, manufactures them in a variety of locations around the world, assembles and tests the finished products in different countries, and then ships the final product to customers. All of this activity must be coordinated carefully to maintain an integrated flow of goods. *Local responsiveness*, on the other hand, is the extent to which business success is dependent on customizing products,

ORGANIZATION DESIGN AT DEERE & COMPANY

application 18.1

Deere & Company, one of the world's leading producers of agricultural, construction, forestry, and turf care equipment, has a rich history of dedicated employees, quality products, and loyal customers. When Robert W. Lane, an 18-year veteran of Deere, became Chairman and CEO in August of 2000, however, economic and organizational problems were threatening this tradition. The company's operations were capital intensive, extremely decentralized, and spread across a diversity of products with highly cyclical business cycles. This meant that overall company profitability required constant vigilance and comparison of profit margins across products with an eye to reducing cyclical swings and to optimizing the whole business and not just a particular business unit. Unfortunately, Deere focused too loosely on managing assets and profit margins and was too decentralized to do business this way, often wasting economic value. Lane described the firm as "asset heavy and margin lean." Moreover, Deere was having problems keeping pace with a rapidly changing and demanding global business environment.

With the support of a unified senior team, Lane immediately created a plan to manage assets more efficiently, to make a new generation of products geared to emerging market demands, and to reduce the firm's vulnerability to cyclical swings and uncertain agriculture and construction markets which together accounted for about 70% of Deere's sales. To make the plan work over the next several months, Lane made a number of related changes in the company's management and information systems, structure, and human resources practices.

Deere's redesign effort started with a simple yet powerful approach to measuring firm performance: shareholder value added (SVA), which is net operating profit after taxes minus cost of capital. Because this value-based metric is straightforward and intuitive, it was easily understood and embraced by operating people throughout the firm. SVA became the central tool for managing the company's business. It provided a common performance measure that could be applied to every product; it addressed the fundamental question: What value does this product add to Deere's shareholders?

Consistent with this new performance measure, Deere restructured its largest division, agriculture, into two business units: worldwide harvesting and tractors/implements. This enabled each new unit to focus more diligently on the underlying economics of its products. It also provided for a far more integrated business than the previous structure allowed. Thus, for example, worldwide harvesting could now get its combine harvester factories in Asia, Europe, and North America to all work together as one global product team with common metrics. It could also do the same for its factories that made cotton pickers and so on.

Next, Lane introduced an online performance management system to align goals and rewards with SVA. All 18,000 salaried employees now had to develop goals that were explicitly linked to the firm's goals. Specific SVA targets were set for each product line at various points in the business cycle. High expectations for improvements in operating performance and SVA growth were set and widely communicated. Then, rewards were tied directly to progress on meeting those objectives. The simplicity and consistency of this system focused employee behaviors on the economics of the business and reinforced the need to continuously improve performance and raise SVA.

Finally, Lane made significant changes in Deere's talent mix to better meet the higher performance standards and the increasing demands of global competition. Employee selection and training practices were oriented to acquiring and developing a workforce with a strong customer orientation and collaborative skills. Employees needed to understand customer needs fully so they could respond with appropriate technological solutions and product innovations. They needed to be able to work together in teams on a worldwide basis.

Six years into Deere's organization redesign, financial results were remarkable. In contrast to 2003, the firm's 2006 net income more than doubled and revenues were up almost 50%. In 2006, SVA was near $1 billion. Perhaps more important, Deere's culture had shifted from mainly family values to those promoting a high-performance organization.

FIGURE 18.2

Worldwide Success Factors

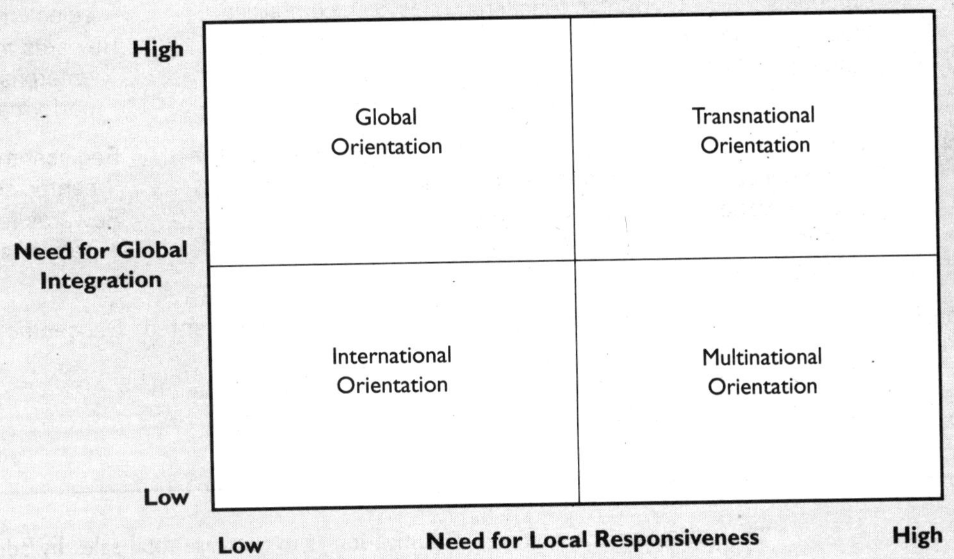

services, support, packaging, and other aspects of operations to local conditions. Intel has to do very little customization; a microprocessor is a microprocessor everywhere in the world.

Based on that information, worldwide organization development involves one of four designs: international, global, multinational, or transnational. Table 18.2 presents these designs in terms of the features described above. Each design is geared to specific market, technological, and organizational requirements.

The International Design The international design exists when the key success factors of global integration and local responsiveness are low. This is the most common label given to organizations making their first attempts at operating outside their own country's markets. Success requires coordination between the parent company and the small number of foreign sales and marketing offices in chosen countries. Similarly, local responsiveness is low because the organization typically exports the same products and services offered domestically.

TABLE 18.2

Design Characteristics for Worldwide Strategic Orientations

Worldwide Strategic Orientation	Business Strategy	Structure	Management Processes	Human Resources
International	Existing products Goals of increased foreign revenues	International division	Loose but centralized Learning orientation	Volunteer recruitment Retain existing performance management processes
Global	Standardized products Goals of efficiency through volume	Global product divisions Global functions	Formal and centralized	Ethnocentric selection Rewards for enterprise performance
Multinational	Tailored products Goals of local responsiveness through specialization	Decentralized operations; centralized planning Global geographic divisions	Profit centers	Regiocentric or polycentric selection Rewards for regional performance
Transnational	Tailored products Goals of learning and responsiveness through integration	Decentralized, worldwide coordination Global matrix or network	Subtle, clan-oriented controls Learning orientation	Geocentric selection

The goal of an international organization is to increase total sales by adding revenues from nondomestic markets. By using existing products/services, domestic operating capacity is extended and leveraged. As a result, most domestic companies will enter international markets by extending their product lines first into nearby countries and then expanding to more remote areas. For example, most U.S.-based companies first offer their products in Canada or Mexico. If a certain period of successful performance and learning occur, they may begin to set up operations in other countries.

To support this goal and operations strategy, an "international division" is given responsibility for marketing, sales, and distribution, although it may be able to set up joint ventures, licensing agreements, distribution territories/franchises, and in some cases, manufacturing plants. The organization retains its original structure and operating practices. The management processes governing the division are typically looser, however. While expecting returns on its investment, the organization recognizes the newness of the venture and gives the international division some "free rein" to learn about operating in a foreign context.

Finally, roles in the new international division are staffed with volunteers from the parent company, often with someone who has appropriate foreign language skills, experience living overseas, or eagerness for an international assignment. Little training or orientation for the position is offered as the organization is generally unaware of the requirements for being successful in international business.

The Global Design This design is appropriate when the need for global integration is high but the need for local responsiveness is low. The decision to favor global integration over local responsiveness must be rooted in a strong belief that the worldwide market is relatively homogenous in character. That is, products and services, support, distribution, or marketing activities can be standardized without negatively affecting sales or customer loyalty. This decision should not be made lightly, and OD practitioners can help to structure rigorous debate and analysis of this key success factor.

The global organization is characterized by a strategy of marketing standardized products in different countries. It is an appropriate orientation when there is little economic reason to offer products or services with special features or locally available options. Manufacturers of heavy equipment (Caterpillar and Komatsu), bathroom fixtures (American Standard, Toto), computers (Dell, HP, Lenovo), and tires (Michelin and Goodyear), for example, can offer the same basic product in almost any country.

The goal of efficiency dominates the design choices for this orientation. Production efficiency is gained through volume sales and a small number of large manufacturing plants, and managerial efficiency is achieved by centralizing product design, manufacturing, distribution, and marketing decisions. The close physical proximity of major functional groups and formal control systems that balance inputs, production, and distribution with worldwide demand supports global integration. Many Japanese firms, such as Honda, Sony, NEC, and Matsushita, used this strategy in the 1970s and early 1980s to grow in the international economy. In Europe, Nestlé exploits economies of scale in marketing by advertising well-known brand names around the world. The increased number of microwave and two-income families, for example, allowed Nestlé to push its Nescafé coffee and Lean Cuisine low-calorie frozen dinners to dominant market-share positions in Europe, North America, Latin America, and Asia.

In the global design, the organization tends to be centralized with a global product structure. Presidents of each major product group report to the CEO and form the line organization. Each of these product groups is responsible for worldwide operations. Management processes in global organizations tend to be quite formal with local units reporting sales, costs, and other data directly to the product president. The predominant human resources policy integrates people into the organization through ethnocentric selection and staffing practices. These methods seek to fill key foreign positions with personnel from the home country where the corporation headquarters is located.[31] Key managerial jobs at Emerson, Siemens, Nissan, and Michelin, for example, are often occupied by American, German, Japanese, and French citizens, respectively. Ethnocentric policies support the global orientation; expatriate managers are more likely than host-country nationals to recognize and comply with the need to centralize decision making and to standardize processes, decisions, and relationships with the parent company. Although many Japanese automobile manufacturers have decentralized production, Nissan's global strategy has been to retain tight, centralized control of design and manufacturing, ensure that almost all of its senior foreign managers are Japanese, and have even low-level decisions emerge from face-to-face meetings in Tokyo.

Application 18.2 describes how one organization faced the challenges of implementing a global strategy.[32] They tried to find the right balance between strong headquarters control and local responsiveness. The OD practitioner in the case describes her data, actions, and results.

The Multinational Design This design is appropriate when the need for global integration is low, but the need for local responsiveness is high. The decision to favor local responsiveness over global integration must be made with the same analytic rigor

application 18.2

IMPLEMENTING THE GLOBAL STRATEGY: CHANGING THE CULTURE OF WORK IN WESTERN CHINA

China has a strong culture, but one that allows it, paradoxically, to assimilate other ideas and philosophies. For example, Buddhism was added to Confucianism during the heydays of the Silk Road, and China has adapted to globalization quickly since it began market reforms in the early 1990s. For many firms entering China, the question is, "Will China assimilate Western cultural ways from the multinational corporations that enter, or will they insist on a Chinese cultural process of doing business?" This application describes the process one American technology company utilizing a global worldwide strategy used in opening a manufacturing plant in a western Chinese province. The story is told from the perspective of the internal OD consultant who was charged with plant start-up support.

In 2003, a major U.S. multinational broke ground for a new set of factories in the "second tier" Chinese city of Chengdu. A city of more than ten million people in Western China, Chengdu is correctly considered the heartland of Chinese culture with a strong tradition of Taoism and a relaxed, friendly culture. In contrast, the multinational technology company came to western China with a strong business-centered, "just get results," U.S. culture. While the organization had facilities all over the world, and several in China, it had not started-up a true greenfield plant as the first MNC in a city in more than ten years. In keeping with the firm's global strategy, the corporate headquarters expected each plant to integrate seamlessly with other plants in the supply chain. Low costs and meeting the technical specifications of the product were the key measures of performance.

The first time I saw the factory site in Chengdu it was bare dirt with the wind blowing dust over what had been a farmer's field. Even as the buildings came out of the ground—an office building, one factory and then another, a large warehouse, and a training center—the local culture of Chengdu was being challenged in the way it thought about safety. In China, construction projects have a traditional algorithm for safety: the millions of Yuan (the local currency) spent in construction was proportionate to the number of deaths resulting from it. This project was different. There was a clear expectation that no deaths would occur, and that no injuries more serious than cut fingers were going to be tolerated. Subcontractors were required to wear hard hats, steel-toed shoes, goggles, and the like, and not everyone liked it. One subcontractor walked off the job believing the safety equipment was too burdensome.

About 30 expatriates were brought in to manage the site. They were experienced company employees from four different cultures: Malaysia, Philippines, Costa Rica, and the United States. Most were Malaysian; very few were American. The first local employees hired were support personnel in human resources, accounting, and purchasing. They were trained in their jobs in the way that the company expected them to work. The first Chinese factory workers were part of the Early Involvement Team (EIT), and they were sent to another of the company's factories to learn the correct processes and behaviors necessary to run the production lines. When the EIT returned, they were to teach the next generation of employees. While this training could be considered just learning the job, it was also a culture change for people who had never worked in a Western high-tech factory. Ramping up this factory to production required that we hire and integrate 100 to 200 people per month; 70% of those hired were recent college graduates.

As the OD manager, my job was to set up systems to transmit the culture and develop leaders, managers, and teams. I began with the site's Vision, Mission, and Guiding Principles. To help the team begin the process, I defined the Vision as "the best we could be," the Mission as "our marching orders—what the corporation expected of us" and Guiding

Principles as "how we make decisions and treat each other." We utilized two off-site sessions with the "whole system in the room." Inclusive processes employing exercises and conversations about what was important to people were used to formulate beginning statements. After we had a set of draft statements, I formed small teams of Chinese leaders who debated the elements of Vision, Mission, and Guiding Principles. The teams came to consensus for each statement to ensure that both the English and Chinese words we used reflected Chinese culture and spoke in a way that fit the Chinese thought processes. We unpacked each statement using Chinese metaphors to provide depth of meaning. Essentially, we were defining the site's specific culture, which while congruent with the corporation, was specific to this site and its chosen values. When completed, these statements went back to the site leadership for ratification. To disseminate the Vision, Mission, and Guiding Principles, each leader, whether expatriate or local Chinese, took responsibility to waterfall the message to their team using dialogues to explore the meaning of the statements for the team. It was not enough to have posters on the wall, or simply tell people what they were. People needed to talk through the meaning and come to some conclusion for themselves as to their own belief. Additionally, people needed to see that leadership practiced what they espoused. So, when an important site decision was made, its fit with the Guiding Principles was publicly communicated. When certain initiatives were begun, such as management training, it was tied to the site Vision. Only because people could see the Vision, Mission, and Guiding Principles in practice did they become real.

Before the first building was under construction, I came to Chengdu to do the initial cultural research for the site. I interviewed university students, business leaders, and Chinese cultural experts in Chengdu. I found a disparity between how the middle managers viewed management and leadership and what the young, university students wanted in a manager. As this was the first multinational organization in Chengdu, most of the middle managers we hired were from state-owned enterprises with a very top-down, hierarchical culture. The university students expected Western-style, consensual decision making—a clear mismatch even within the Chinese culture. Management training and coaching would be required to help middle managers learn to work in a consensual way.

To accomplish that, we engaged the expatriate site leaders as teachers and mentors in a nine-month management development program that included two outdoor "adventure-style" sessions. The first program placed the initial outdoor session after four months of activities. I found that in the classroom, Chinese managers could "talk the talk," but when we put them in the team decision-making situations of the outdoor sessions, they were unable to make productive decisions. In the second management development program, I placed the outdoor session earlier so that the Chinese managers would understand the required managerial behaviors right away. We eventually graduated more than 50 managers with two-thirds of them receiving promotions within a year of completion.

The corporation had a number of key espoused values in its culture, including quality, safety, and business practice excellence. These were primary and nonnegotiable values. While that may seem the arbitrary hubris of a foreign multinational, I found that the Chinese employees appreciated these three values, especially safety. As mentioned above, China has a poor record of workplace safety. When asked about this value, many people responded that "the company cares for my life." Rather than seeing it as an imposition of a foreign cultural value, they found it fit the Chinese value of *renqing* or human heartedness.

The company also employed six values as basic to its culture. However, these values were really expected behaviors, such as discipline, risk taking, and being open and direct. In my work in Chengdu, I designed and implemented a process to develop those values as part of the expected behaviors of the site. I had learned that "telling-teaching," or putting posters on the wall, was not very effective in this culture, so I engaged a cadre of volunteer "ambassadors" for each value. They used a positive approach of catching people "doing it right" and rewarding them in a public ceremony with a "Star of Chengdu Culture" award. To create a common understanding of each value, we again used an interactive and participative process. We provided materials that allowed and encouraged every manager to have a conversation with their team as to the meaning of that particular value. We endeavored to make the materials relevant to a Chinese audience using Chinese stories and situations to illustrate the meaning of the value.

However, not all these values fit within Chinese culture, and this created cultural dilemmas for Chinese employees. Being open and direct was one example of a value that did not fit. Generally, the organization talked about being open and direct in terms of "constructive confrontation," which the Chinese employees shortened to "con con." In my interviews, I found that this value was both the most difficult and the least practiced. The Chinese employees related con con to a lack of harmony rather than a method of solving problems directly and easily. It was antithetical to Chinese culture. Chinese employees who learned to practice con con in the workplace found themselves out of step when those behaviors were used with their family and friends outside of the factory. Essentially they had to bifurcate their life, learning to be one way inside the organization and another way outside. When I asked people what they lost by coming to work at the factory, employees often noted that they had lost some friends because they were now different from the Chinese culture at large. Practicing con con was a big part of that. They also told me of many instances in which they appeared to the expatriates as though they were practicing con con, when in fact they were practicing harmony. They felt that harmony was a better long-term solution to the problem at hand than creating a situation in which fellow workers lost "face." They talked about finding a "middle way" to do business that allowed problem solving while still maintaining harmonious relationships.

If real cultural differences can keep people from assimilating into an organization, the question becomes, "Did these skilled Chinese workers actually assimilate into the factory culture, or did they simply appear to apply the organization's value system while maintaining traditional Chinese values?" While much of the work on Values, Mission, and Guiding Principles was well accepted and understood, the Chinese workers in this situation had difficulty placing con con into a usable framework that worked in their social setting because it did not align with the Chinese value of harmony. Since con con was a foundational behavior/value for the company, such a misfit reveals a lack of real assimilation into the corporate culture.

Some Chinese lament that China is losing her cultural traditions as the country becomes part of the global economy. At least in Chengdu, I did not find that to be true. People described themselves as traditional Chinese who practiced their own culture and struggled with those organizational processes that did not fit Chinese culture. They continued to look for the middle way that allows them to maintain their Chinese cultural values while moving into a capitalistic future. Just as China assimilated Buddhism into their Confucian practices millenniums ago, they see the value of assimilating some Western practices into their way of doing business, but it will still be capitalism with a Chinese face—a middle way.

described earlier. In this case, the analysis must support the belief that worldwide markets are relatively heterogeneous in character. That is, success requires customized and localized products and services, support, distribution, or marketing activities. It represents a strategy that is conceptually quite different from the global strategic orientation.

A multinational organization is characterized by a product line that is tailored to local conditions and is best suited to markets that vary significantly from region to region or country to country. At American Express, for example, charge card marketing aligns to local values and tastes. The "Don't leave home without it" and "Membership has its privileges" brand messages that were popular in the United States had to be translated to "Peace of mind only for members" in Japan because of the negative connotations of "leaving home" and "privilege."[33]

The multinational design emphasizes a decentralized, global division structure. Each regional or country division reports to headquarters but operates autonomously and mostly controls its own resources. This results in a highly differentiated and loosely coordinated corporate structure. Operational decisions, such as product design, manufacturing, and distribution, are decentralized and tightly integrated at the local level. For example, laundry soap manufacturers offer product formulas, packaging, and marketing strategies that conform to the different environmental regulations, types of washing machines, water hardness, and distribution channels in each country. On the other hand, planning activities are often centralized at corporate headquarters to achieve important efficiencies necessary for worldwide coordination of emerging technologies and of resource allocation. A profit-center control system allows local autonomy as long as profitability is maintained. Examples of multinational corporations include Hoechst and BASF of Germany, MTV and Procter & Gamble of the United States, and Fuji Xerox of Japan. Each of these organizations encourages local subsidiaries to maximize effectiveness within their geographic region.

People are integrated into multinational firms through polycentric or regiocentric personnel policies because these firms believe that host-country nationals can understand native cultures most clearly.[34] By filling positions with local citizens who appoint and develop their own staffs, the organization aligns the needs of the market with the ability of its subsidiaries to produce customized products and services. The distinction between a polycentric and a regiocentric selection process is one of focus. In a polycentric selection policy, a subsidiary represents only one country; in the regiocentric selection policy, the organization takes a slightly broader perspective and regional citizens (that is, people who might be called Europeans, as opposed to Belgians or Italians) fill key positions.

The Transnational Design This orientation exists when the need for global integration and local responsiveness are both high. It represents the most complex and ambitious worldwide strategic orientation and reflects the belief that products or services should be developed, produced, or distributed in the places where it makes the most sense but customized to sell anywhere.[35]

The transnational design combines customized products with both efficient and responsive operations; the key goal is learning. This is the most complex worldwide strategic orientation because transnationals can manufacture products, conduct research, raise capital, buy supplies, and perform many other functions wherever in the world the job can be done optimally. They can move skills, resources, and knowledge to regions where they are needed.

Transnational organizations combine the best of global and multinational design and add a third capability—the ability to transfer resources both within the firm and across national and cultural boundaries. Otis Elevator, a division of United Technologies, developed a new programmable elevator using six research centers in five countries: a U.S. group handled the systems integration; Japan designed the special motor drives that make the elevators ride smoothly; France perfected the door systems; Germany created the electronics; and Spain produced the small-geared components.[36] In addition, Otis has the production capability to ensure that all the parts made in different places all fit together perfectly as well as the logistics capability to guarantee that all the parts will arrive at a specific job site on the right day. Other examples of transnational firms include General Electric, Asea Brown Boveri (ABB), Unilever, Electrolux, HP, and most worldwide professional services firms.

Transnational firms organize themselves into global matrix and network structures especially suited for moving information and resources to their best use. In the matrix structure, local sales and marketing divisions are crossed with product groups at the headquarters office, engineering groups in different countries, and other dimensions as required. The network structure treats each local office, including headquarters, product groups, functions, call centers, and production facilities, as self-sufficient nodes that coordinate with each other to move knowledge and resources to their most valued place. Because of the heavy communication and logistic demands needed to operate these structures, transnationals have sophisticated information systems. State-of-the-art information technology stores and moves strategic and operational information and knowledge throughout the system rapidly and efficiently. Organizational learning practices (see Chapter 19) gather, organize, and disseminate the knowledge and skills of members who are located around the world.

People are integrated into transnational firms through a geocentric selection policy that staffs key positions with the best people, regardless of nationality.[37] This staffing practice recognizes that the unique capability of a transnational firm is its capacity to optimize resource allocation on a worldwide basis. Unlike global and multinational firms, which spend more time training and developing managers to fit the strategy, the transnational firm attempts to hire the right person from the beginning. Recruits at any of HP's foreign locations, for example, are screened not only for technical qualifications but for personality traits that match the company's cultural values.

18-2d Application Stages

Organization design can be applied to the whole organization or to a major subpart, such as a large department or stand-alone unit. It can start from a clean slate in a new organization or more commonly, reconfigure an existing organization design. To construct the different design elements appropriately requires broad content knowledge of them. Thus, organization design interventions typically involve a team of OD practitioners with expertise in business strategy, organization structure, work design, human resources practices, and management processes. This team works closely with senior executives who are responsible for determining the organization's strategic direction and leading the organization design intervention. The design process itself can be highly participative, involving stakeholders from throughout the organization. This can increase the design's quality and stakeholders' commitment to implementing it.[38]

Organization design interventions generally follows the three broad steps outlined below.[39] Although they are presented sequentially, in practice they are highly interactive, often feeding back on each other and requiring continual revision as the process unfolds.

1. **Diagnosing the current design.** This preliminary stage, following the processes outlined in Chapter 5, involves assessing the organization's current performance and alignment of design features. It starts with a description of current effectiveness and the extent to which changes in the strategy and organization design elements are required. The organization's new strategy and objectives are examined to determine what organization capabilities are needed to achieve them. For worldwide designs, this involves a careful analysis of the required levels of global integration and local responsiveness. Then, the organization is assessed against these capabilities and requirements to uncover gaps between how it is currently designed and the necessary design changes. This gap analysis identifies current problems the design intervention should address. It provides information for determining which design

elements will receive the most attention and the likely magnitude and timeframe of the design process.

2. **Designing the organization.** This step involves describing and configuring the design components to support the business strategy and objectives. The most effective design sequence is to first identify the work processes and work designs that will best add value to customers and other key stakeholders according to the strategy. Based on these work processes, alternative structures, such as functional, matrix, or customer-centric, should be described and debated among the design team and senior executives. The core structure that best supports the work and strategy should be chosen, although no structure is perfect. Managers need to be aware of the strengths and weaknesses of each structural alternative and be conscious about the tradeoffs. OD practitioners can help managers work through this difficult decision.

    Once the strategy-structure-work design decisions are made, the next step is to specify the management processes and human resource practices that will compliment and support them. These two design features are well suited to address any weaknesses in the chosen structure. For example, functional structures are good at promoting technical excellence but weaker with respect to coordination. Management processes can be designed to increase the flow of cross-functional information exchange and human resource practices can be designed to reward cross-functional decision making. The resulting design usually falls somewhere along the continuum from mechanistic to organic.

    A broader set of organizational members often participates in these decisions, relying on its own as well as experts' experience and know-how, knowledge of best practices, and information gained from visits to other organizations willing to share design experience. This stage results in an overall design for the organization, detailed designs for the components, and preliminary plans for how they will fit together and be implemented.

3. **Implementing the design.** The final step involves making the new design happen by putting into place the new structures, practices, and systems. In all cases, implementation draws heavily on the methods for leading and managing change discussed in Chapter 8 and applies them to the entire organization or subunit, and not just limited parts. Because organization design generally involves large amounts of transformational change, this intervention can place heavy demands on the organization's resources and leadership expertise. Members from throughout the organization must be motivated to implement the new design; all relevant stakeholders must support it politically. Organization designs usually cannot be implemented in a single step but must proceed in phases that involve considerable transition management. They often entail significant new work behaviors and relationships that require extensive and continuous organization learning.

The transition from domestic to global or multinational designs is an important period in an organization's development. It represents a significant shift in strategic breadth even though many firms approach it as a simple and incremental extension of the existing strategy into new markets. Despite the logic of such thinking, the shift is neither incremental nor simple. OD practitioners can play an important role in making the transition smoother and more productive by maintaining a focus on the systemic nature of the change and applying the appropriate human process, technostructural, and human resource interventions. For example, team-building interventions are appropriate in almost every implementation of a worldwide design. The centralized policies of the global design make the organization highly dependent on the top management team, and team building with this group can help to improve the speed and quality of decision making and improve interpersonal relationships. Team building remains an important intervention for the multinational design, but unlike team building in global designs, the local management teams require attention in multinational firms. This presents a challenge for OD practitioners because polycentric selection policies can produce management teams with different cultures at each subsidiary. Thus, a program developed for one subsidiary may not work with a different team at another subsidiary, given the different cultures that might be represented.

Similarly, managers can apply technostructural interventions to design organization structures that clarify new tasks, work roles, and reporting relationships between corporate headquarters and foreign-based units. Finally, managers and staff can apply human resource interventions to train and prepare managers and their families for international assignments and to develop selection methods and reward systems relevant to operating internationally.[40]

The evolution from a global or multinational to a transnational design is a particularly complex strategic change effort because it requires the acquisition of two additional capabilities. First, global organizations, which are good at centrally coordinating far-flung operations, need to learn to trust local management teams, and multinational organizations, which are good at decentralized decision making, need to become better at coordination. Second, both types of organizations need to acquire the ability to transfer resources efficiently around the world. Much of the difficulty in evolving to a transnational strategy lies in developing these additional capabilities.

In the transition from a global to a transnational design, the administrative challenge is to encourage creative over centralized thinking and to let each functional area contribute and operate in a way that best suits its context. For example, if international markets require specialized products, then operations must configure manufacturing or service capacity to minimize costs but optimize customization. OD interventions that can help this transition include training efforts that increase the tolerance for differences in management practices, control systems, performance appraisals, and policies and procedures; reward systems that encourage entrepreneurship, coordination, and performance at each location; and structural changes at both the corporate office and local levels.

In moving from a multinational to a transnational design, products, technologies, and regulatory constraints can become more homogeneous and require more efficient operations. The competencies required to compete on a transnational basis, however, may be located in different geographic areas. The need to balance local responsiveness against the need for coordination among organizational units is new to multinational firms. They must create interdependencies among organizational units through the flow of parts, components, and finished goods; the flow of funds, skills, and other scarce resources; or the flow of intelligence, ideas, and knowledge. For example, prior to Alan Mulally's appointment as CEO, Ford was operating as a multinational with different divisions in different parts of the world acting independently. Mulally's "One Ford" strategy recognized that its operational assets were not being leveraged. As a result of the strategy, ten different car models now use the same platform and share about 80 of the parts which can be sourced anywhere in the world. The strategy has allowed Ford to offer different looking cars in different markets but to have similar platforms and parts that lower costs.[41]

18-3 Integrated Strategic Change

As described above, transformational change is systemic and revolutionary in nature. *Integrated strategic change* (ISC) is an OD intervention that extends traditional OD processes into the content-oriented discipline of strategic management and describes how to conduct a systemic and revolutionary change program. It is an intentional process that leads an organization through a realignment between the environment and a firm's strategic orientation, and that results in improvement in performance and effectiveness.[42]

The ISC process was initially developed by Worley, Hitchin, and Ross in response to managers' complaints that good business strategies often are not implemented.[43] Research suggested that managers and executives were overly concerned with the financial and economic aspects of strategic management.[44] The predominant paradigm in strategic management—formulation and implementation—artificially separates strategic thinking from operational and tactical actions; it ignores the contributions that planned change processes can make to implementation.[45] In the traditional process, senior managers and strategic planning staff prepare economic forecasts, competitor analyses, and market studies. They discuss these studies and rationally align the firm's strengths and weaknesses with environmental opportunities and threats to form the organization's strategy.[46] Then, implementation occurs as middle managers, supervisors, and employees hear about the new strategy through memos, restructuring announcements, changes in job responsibilities, or new departmental objectives. Consequently, because participation has been limited to top management, there is little understanding of the need for change and little ownership of the new behaviors, initiatives, and tactics required to achieve the announced objectives.

18-3a Key Features

ISC, in contrast to the traditional strategic management process, is more integrated, comprehensive, and participative. It has three key features:[47]

1. The relevant unit of analysis is the organization's *strategic orientation* comprising its strategy and organization design. An organization's business strategy and the design features that support it must be considered as an integrated whole.
2. Creating a strategic plan, gaining commitment and support for it, planning its implementation, and executing it are treated as one integrated process. The ability to repeat such a process quickly and effectively when conditions warrant is valuable, rare, and difficult to imitate. Thus, a strategic change capability represents a sustainable competitive advantage.[48]
3. Individuals and groups throughout the organization are integrated into the analysis, planning, and implementation process to create a more achievable plan, to maintain the firm's strategic focus, to direct attention and resources on the organization's key competencies, to improve coordination and integration within the organization, and to create higher levels of shared ownership and commitment.

18-3b Implementing the ISC Process

The ISC process is applied in four phases: performing a strategic analysis, exercising strategic choice, designing a strategic change plan, and implementing the plan. The four steps are discussed sequentially but actually unfold in overlapping and integrated ways. Figure 18.3 displays the steps in the ISC process and its change components. An organization's existing strategic orientation, identified as its current strategy (S_1) and organization design (O_1), is linked to its future strategic orientation (S_2/O_2) by the strategic change plan.

FIGURE 18.3

The Integrated Strategic Change Process

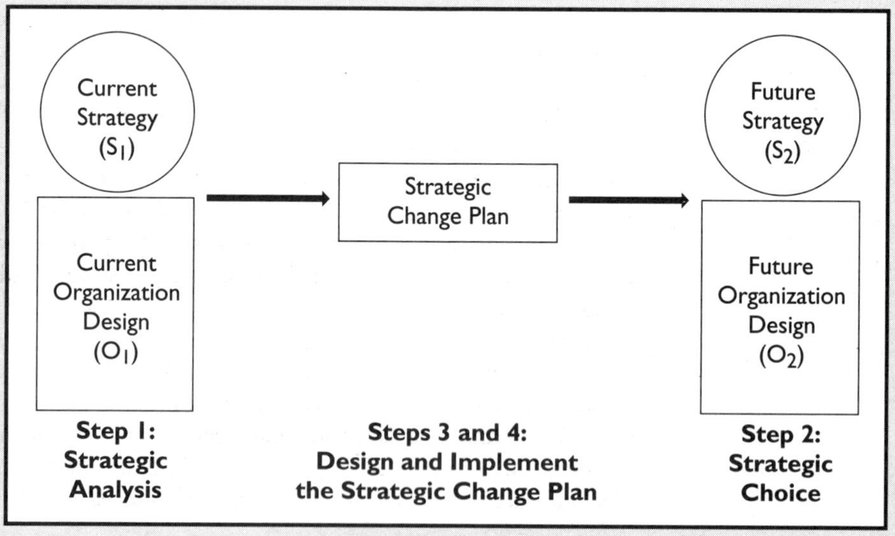

1. **Performing the strategic analysis.** The ISC process begins with a diagnosis of the organization's readiness for change and its current strategy and organization design (S_1/O_1). The most important indicator of readiness is senior management's willingness and ability to carry out strategic change. Greiner and Schein suggest that the two key dimensions in this analysis are (1) the leader's willingness and commitment to change and (2) the senior team's willingness and ability to follow the leader's initiative.[49] Organizations whose leaders are not willing to lead and whose senior managers are not willing and able to support the new strategic direction when necessary should consider team-building or coaching interventions to align their commitment.

   The second stage in strategic analysis is to understand the current strategy and organization design. The diagnostic process begins with an examination of the organization's industry and current performance. This information provides the necessary context to assess the current strategic orientation's viability. Porter's industry attractiveness model[50] and the environmental frameworks introduced in Chapter 5 should be used to look at both the current and likely future environments. Next, the current strategic orientation is described to explain current levels of performance and human outcomes. Several models for guiding this diagnosis exist.[51] For example, the organization's current strategy, structure, and processes can be assessed according to the model and methods introduced in Chapter 5. A metaphor or other label that describes how the organization's mission, objectives, and business policies lead to improved performance can be used to represent strategy. 3M's traditional strategy of "differentiation" aptly summarizes its mission to solve unsolved problems innovatively, its goal of having a large percentage of current revenues come from products developed in the last five years, and its policies that support innovation, such as encouraging engineers to spend up to 15%

of their time on new projects. An organization's objectives, policies, and budgets signal which parts of the environment are important, and allocate and direct resources to particular environmental relationships.[52] Intel's new-product development objectives and allocation of more than 20% of revenues to research and development signal the importance of its linkage to the technological environment.

The structure, work design, management processes, and human resources system describe the organization's design. These descriptions should be used to assess the likely sources of customer dissatisfaction, product and service offering problems, financial issues, employee disengagement, or other outcomes. The strategic analysis process actively involves organization members. Large group conferences, employee focus groups, interviews with salespeople, customers, and purchasing agents, and other methods allow a variety of employees and managers to participate in the diagnosis and increase the amount and relevance of the data collected. This builds commitment to and ownership of the analysis; should a strategic change effort result, members are more likely to understand why and be supportive of it.

2. **Exercising strategic choice**. Once the strengths and weaknesses of the existing strategic orientation are understood, a new one must be designed. For example, the strategic analysis might reveal misfits among the organization's environment, strategic orientation, and performance. These misfits can be used as inputs for crafting the future strategy and organization design. Based on this analysis, senior management formulates visions for the future and broadly defines two or three alternative sets of strategies and objectives for achieving those visions. Market forecasts, employees' readiness and willingness to change, competitor analyses, and other projections can be used to develop the alternative future scenarios.[53] The different sets of strategies and objectives also include projections about the organization design changes that will be necessary to support each alternative. It is important to involve other organizational stakeholders in the alternative generation phase, but the choice of strategic orientation ultimately rests with top management and cannot easily be delegated. Senior executives are in the unique position of viewing a strategy from a general management position. When major strategic decisions are given to lower-level managers, the risk of focusing too narrowly on a product, market, or technology increases.

   This step determines the content or "what" of strategic change. The desired strategy (S_2) defines the ideal breadth of products or services to be offered and the markets to be served. It also describes the aggressiveness with which these outputs will be pursued and the differentiators to be employed. The desired organization design (O_2) specifies the structures and processes necessary to support the new strategy. Aligning an organization's design with a particular strategy can be a major source of superior performance and competitive advantage.[54]

3. **Designing the strategic change plan**. The strategic change plan is a comprehensive agenda for moving the organization from its current strategy and organization design to the desired future strategic orientation. It represents the process or "how" of strategic change. The change plan describes the types, magnitude, and schedule of change activities, as well as the costs associated with them. In line with the research on transformational change, the change plan should be aggressive and attempt to complete the required change activities in as short a time frame as possible. As a result, the change plan also specifies how the changes will be implemented, given

power and political issues, the nature of the organizational culture, and the current ability of the organization to implement change.[55]

4. **Implementing the plan**. The final step in the ISC process is the actual implementation of the strategic change plan. This draws heavily on knowledge of motivation, group dynamics, and change processes. It deals continuously with such issues as alignment, adaptability, teamwork, and organizational and personal learning. Implementation requires senior managers to champion the different elements of the change plan to effect change quickly. They can, for example, initiate action and allocate resources to particular activities, set high but achievable goals, and provide feedback on accomplishments. In addition, leaders must hold people accountable to the change objectives, institutionalize the changes that occur, and be prepared to solve problems as they arise. This final point recognizes that no strategic change plan can account for all of the contingencies that emerge. There must be a willingness to adjust the plan as implementation unfolds to address unforeseen and unpredictable events and to take advantage of new opportunities.

Application 18.3 describes an ISC process at Microsoft Canada and demonstrates how the process was refined over time as the organization built its capability in strategic management.

18-4 Culture Change

The topic of organization culture is again becoming an important one to companies. Originally spurred by a number of best-selling management books in the 1980s, including *Theory Z, The Art of Japanese Management*, and *In Search of Excellence*, culture is re-emerging as an important concern as organizations look for competitive advantage beyond the traditional sources, such as products, technologies, and markets. Culture has remained a focus of research, with books such as *Built to Last* and *Corporate Culture and Performance*,[56] demonstrating why culture is seen as a major strength in such companies as Herman Miller, Intel, PepsiCo, and Southwest Airlines. A growing number of managers appreciate the power of corporate culture in shaping employee beliefs and actions. A well-conceived and well-managed organization culture, closely linked to an effective business strategy, can mean the difference between success and failure in today's demanding environments.

18-4a Defining and Diagnosing Organization Culture

OD practitioners have developed a variety of culture definitions[57] and number of culture change interventions.[58] There is good agreement about the elements or features of culture that are typically measured. As shown in Figure 18.4, they include artifacts, norms, values, and basic assumptions.[59] The meanings attached to these elements help members make sense out of everyday life in the organization. The meanings signal how work is performed and evaluated, and how employees are to relate to each other and to significant others, such as customers, suppliers, and government agencies.

Diagnosing organization culture poses at least three difficult problems for collecting pertinent information.[60] First, to the extent culture reflects the more or less shared assumptions about what is important, how things are done, and how people should behave in organizations, organization members generally take cultural

application 18.3

MANAGING STRATEGIC CHANGE AT MICROSOFT CANADA

Microsoft Canada is a subsidiary of the Microsoft Corporation responsible for the marketing, sales, and service of the full range of software products, including the Windows operating systems and Microsoft Office, enterprise solutions, and the Xbox video game console. The organization marketed to a variety of segments, such as software application developers, small and medium business, and large enterprises, through a broad range of partners that worked directly with the client organizations to install and optimize the software's use. A small service organization, along with the partners, provided consulting support to clients.

Prior to 2001, Microsoft Canada had been part of the North American subsidiary. Under this structure, the large U.S. market was clearly the focus of attention for Microsoft's server, desktop, and other software products. However, the President of Microsoft Canada argued that the Canadian market was different and underdeveloped. It had a different mix of customers than did the United States, different competitors, and different growth opportunities. Moreover, software sales and personal computer shipments as a percentage of the market's size and growth were below worldwide averages. These differences, he argued, warranted a specialized strategy.

As the fiscal year ended, the president and his newly appointed Director of Strategic Planning wanted to seize the opportunity to define a uniquely Canadian strategy. The strategic planning director's prior position had been as Director of Marketing and Corporate Communications in Microsoft Canada. Together with her senior marketing manager, they had crafted and implemented a participative process of strategic planning. The strategic planning director contacted the OD practitioner who had worked with them and contracted to design and implement a strategic planning process for the Canadian organization. Over a two-month period, the strategic planning director conceived of a series of workshops involving the Canadian Leadership Team (CLT). This team represented a broad cross section of the organization, including representatives from the legal staff, human resources, Microsoft's consulting and service business, marketing managers, customer support, and managers responsible for different segments of Microsoft's business, including enterprise customers, small and medium business, Xbox, and the Microsoft Network (MSN).

The strategic analysis phase consisted of preliminary work by several members of the CLT as well as initial exercises during the first workshop. Members of the CLT each prepared an analysis of their respective area of responsibility. For example, the enterprise sales manager provided historical growth rates in revenues, developed forecasts for market growth and Microsoft's share, described current levels of customer satisfaction, and a technology road map of products being developed by the Redmond headquarters organization. In addition to these specific analyses, the strategic planning director contracted with a market-research firm to provide overall descriptions of the Canadian information technology market. Finally, a competitor analysis was performed to develop an understanding of likely strategies, goals, and initiatives from key competitors such as IBM, Oracle, and (at the time) Sun Microsystems, as well as the competitive threat posed by alternative operating systems software.

During the first workshop, the CLT used the prework data to perform an environmental scan. They discussed, debated, and ultimately came to some agreements about the trends affecting the organization. Based on that scan, the group engaged in a vision and value formulation exercise and set out an initial list of short- and long-term goals. These activities led to several important decisions for the new marketing organization. For example, the vision and values exercise produced important insights about what the Canadian organization stood for, its uniqueness compared to other marketing subsidiaries within the Microsoft organization, and its strengths in competing as a Canadian organization. The values also informed discussions about future goals and the strategy for achieving them. Importantly, the Canadian leadership realized that customer loyalty would and should become a driving force for the organization. This realization led to passionate discussions about the relative emphasis in the organization on revenues versus customer satisfaction and loyalty. It also led to the development of a Big Hairy Audacious Goal (BHAG) that the members of the CLT believed would be challenging but achievable.

The first workshop ended with a number of assignments, unresolved issues, and excitement about the future. In between the first and second workshops, members of the CLT worked with their own organizations. Issues, decisions, and questions that were addressed within the CLT were discussed throughout the organization. The most important discussion concerned the BHAG and the relative emphasis of revenues and customer loyalty over the short and the long term. A consensus began to emerge that the right and proper strategy for Microsoft Canada was to argue for a slower growth rate in revenues in the short term, invest in customer satisfaction and loyalty, and then leverage that loyalty for a more secure stream of revenues in the future.

The president took this idea to the executives in Redmond and discussed the implications of this strategy, including revenue projections, budget implications, the risks involved, and how the strategy aligned with corporate and other marketing organizations' initiatives. The results of these conversations became the subject of opening discussions at the second workshop.

The cautious but positive support from the corporate organization allowed the CLT to move forward on its strategic intent. In the second workshop, the organization's mission and values were finalized, year-by-year revenue goals were agreed upon to achieve the BHAG, and these goals were broken down and assigned to specific groups and managers. Finally, key customer and partner-loyalty programs were established and outlined. Ownership for the different initiatives was assigned and a strategic change plan emerged. The president pressed the group on its decision to emphasize customer loyalty and challenged the group with several scenarios that tempted them to trade off satisfaction for revenue. These scenarios helped cement the CLT's commitment to their strategy.

An important part of the strategic change plan that emerged was a discussion and decision to tie the individual performance appraisals of CLT members to the achievement of both revenue and customer satisfaction goals. The CLT as a whole also staked their end-of-fiscal-year bonuses to the achievement of customer satisfaction, rather than revenue goals.

The strategic change efforts at Microsoft Canada are important for several reasons. First, the Canadian organization's realization of the importance of customer satisfaction and loyalty was influential in moving the larger Microsoft Corporation to examine its values in this area. A *BusinessWeek* article reported on the changes Steve Ballmer was making in the organization; they reflected the increased importance of customer loyalty in Microsoft's strategy and structure changes. Second, the organization learned how to organize a strategic planning effort. In the two years since this effort began, the strategic planning director has built a stronger strategic planning organization and has taken more and more responsibility for driving the strategic planning process. Even as the corporate Microsoft organization was making important changes in its reporting structure, financial systems, and business processes, the Canadian organization was able to adapt using its own resources and knowledge. Finally, the BHAG has become an institutionalized part of the organization that drives thinking and decision making in the organization.

FIGURE 18.4

Culture Components

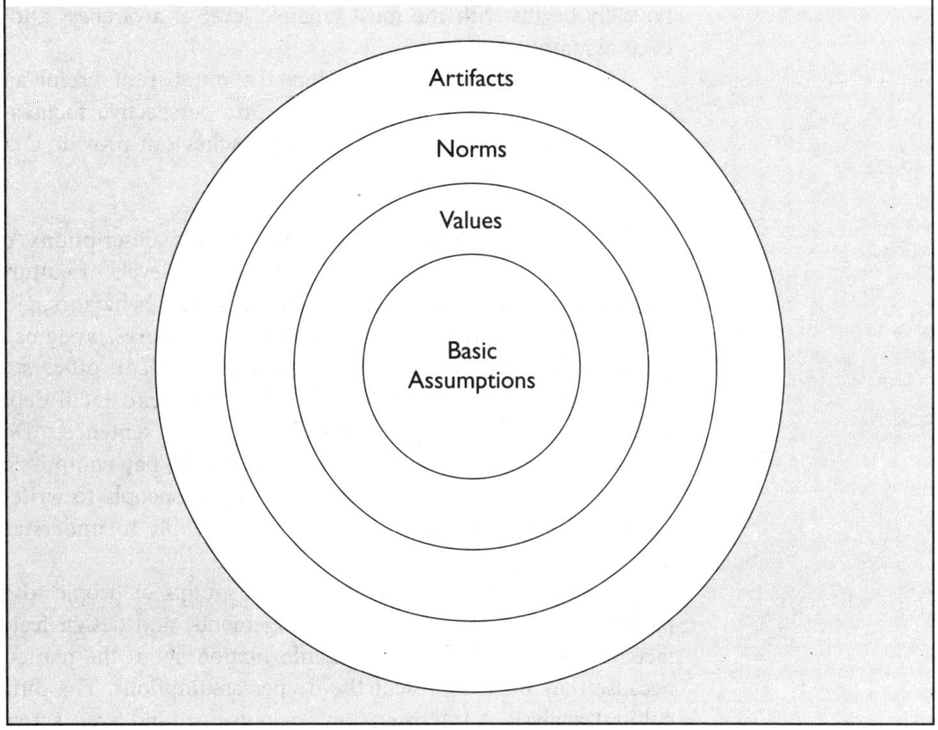

assumptions for granted and rarely speak of them directly. This means that considerable time and effort must be spent observing, sifting through, and asking people about these cultural outcroppings, such as daily routines, stories, rituals, and language, to understand their deeper significance for organization members.

Second, values and beliefs come in two forms: espoused values and values-in-use. Espoused values are the beliefs organizations declare openly as important. Organizations often post their espoused values on plaques in the office or on corporate websites. Values-in-use are those beliefs that actually drive behaviors. People sometimes espouse values that have little to do with the ones they really hold and follow. People are reluctant to admit this discrepancy, yet somehow the real assumptions underlying idealized portrayals of culture must be discovered.

Third, large, diverse, or global organizations are likely to have several subcultures, which Martin called "differentiated" cultures,[61] including countercultures going against the grain of the wider organization culture. Assumptions may not be shared widely and may differ across groups in the organization. This can be a very real issue in worldwide organizations, and it means that focusing on limited parts of the organization or on a few select individuals may provide a distorted view of the organization's culture and subcultures. All relevant groups in the organization must be identified and their cultural assumptions sampled. Only then can practitioners judge the extent to which assumptions are shared widely.

Transformational change interventions generally include diagnosing the organization's existing culture to assess its fit with current or proposed business strategies. A comprehensive approach to describing and diagnosing culture emphasizes all four levels of organization culture—artifacts, norms and values, as well as the generally unexamined, but tacit and shared assumptions that guide member behavior and that often have a powerful impact on organization effectiveness. A comprehensive diagnosis typically begins with the most tangible level of awareness and then works down to the deep assumptions.

OD practitioners have developed a number of useful approaches for diagnosing organization culture, and each diagnostic perspective focuses on particular aspects of organization culture. Together the approaches can provide a comprehensive assessment of this complex phenomenon.

Artifacts Most cultural assessments include descriptions of surface-level artifacts. Artifacts are the visible symbols of the deeper levels of culture, such as norms, values, and basic assumptions. They include members' behaviors, clothing, and language; the organization's design features, including structures, systems, and processes; and the organization's physical arrangements, such as décor, office space layouts and appointments, and noise levels. At Nordstrom, a high-end retail department store, the policy and procedure manual is rumored to be one sentence, "Do whatever you think is right." In addition, stores promote from within; pay commissions on sales to link effort and compensation; provide stationery for salespeople to write personal notes to customers; and expect buyers to work as salespeople to understand better the customer's expectations.

One diagnostic method simply asks groups of people to generate lists of language patterns, clothing norms, office arrangements, and design features. By themselves, artifacts can provide a great deal of information about the real culture of the organization because they often represent the deeper assumptions. The difficulty in their use during cultural analysis is interpretation; an outsider (and even some insiders) has no way of knowing what the artifacts represent, if anything.

A second method emphasizes the pattern of behaviors that produce business results.[62] It is among the more practical approaches to culture diagnosis because it assesses key work behaviors that can be observed. It provides specific descriptions about how organizations perform tasks and manage relationships. For example, a series of individual and group interviews can ask managers to describe "the way the game is played," as if they were coaching a new organization member, in regard to four key relationships—companywide, boss–subordinate, peer, and interdepartmental—and in terms of six managerial tasks—innovating, decision making, communicating, organizing, monitoring, and appraising or rewarding. These perceptions can reveal a number of common behaviors that describe how tasks are performed and relationships managed.

Norms and Values A deeper level of cultural diagnosis can occur by focusing on the norms and values level of culture. Just below the artifact level of cultural awareness are norms guiding how members should behave in particular situations. These represent unwritten rules of behavior. Norms generally are inferred from observing how members behave and interact with each other. At Nordstrom, norms dictate that it is okay for members to go the extra mile to satisfy customer requests, and it is not okay for salespeople to process customers who were working with another salesperson.

Values are the next-deeper level of awareness and include beliefs about what ought to be in organizations. Values in use, as opposed to espoused values, tell members what is important in the organization and what deserves their attention. Because Nordstrom values customer service, the sales representatives pay strong attention to how well the customer is treated. Obviously, the norms and artifacts support this value.

One popular method of cultural diagnosis at the values level looks specifically at how the organization resolves a set of value dilemmas.[63] A value dilemma consists of contradictory values placed at opposite ends of a continuum, as shown in Figure 18.5. The two value dilemmas are (1) internal focus and integration versus external focus and differentiation and (2) flexibility and discretion versus stability and control. Organizations continually struggle to satisfy the conflicting demands placed on them by these competing values. For example, when faced with the competing values of internal versus external focus, organizations must choose between attending to the integration problems of internal operations and the competitive issues in the external environment. Too much emphasis on the environment can result in neglect of internal efficiencies. Conversely, too much attention to the internal aspects of organizations can result in missing important changes in the competitive environment.

This "competing values" approach commonly collects diagnostic data about the competing values with a survey designed specifically for that purpose.[64] It provides measures of where an organization's existing values fall along each of the dimensions. When taken together, these data identify an organization's culture as falling into one of the four quadrants shown in Figure 18.5: clan culture, adhocracy culture, hierarchical culture, and market culture. For example, if an organization's values emphasize internal integration as well as innovation and flexibility, it manifests a clan culture. On the other hand, a market culture reflects values that emphasize an external focus as well as stability and control.

Deep Assumptions of Culture Finally, OD practitioners have a couple of options for understanding the deep assumptions level of culture.[65] The deepest level of cultural

FIGURE 18.5

The Competing Values Approach to Culture

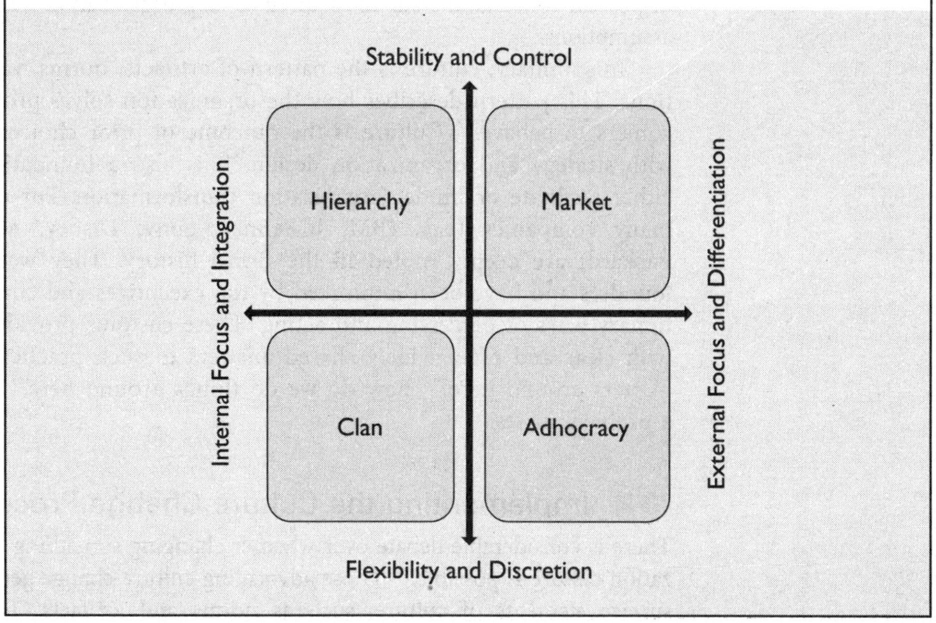

SOURCE: Adapted from K. Cameron and R. Quinn. *Diagnosing and Changing Organizational Culture. Based on the Competing Values Framework*, p. 32 © 1999 Addison-Wesley Publishing Co., Inc.

awareness are the taken-for-granted assumptions about how organizational problems should be solved. These basic assumptions tell members how to perceive, think, and feel about things. They are nonconfrontable and nondebatable assumptions about relating to the environment and about human nature, human activity, and human relationships. For example, a basic assumption at Nordstrom is the belief in the fundamental dignity of people; it is morally right to treat customers with extraordinary service so that they will become loyal and frequent shoppers.

One OD method involves an iterative interviewing process involving both outsiders and insiders.[66] Outsiders help members uncover cultural elements through joint exploration. The outsider enters the organization and experiences surprises and puzzles that are different from what was expected. The outsider shares these observations with insiders, and the two parties jointly explore their meaning. This process involves several iterations of experiencing surprises, checking for meaning, and formulating hypotheses about the culture. It results in a formal written description of the assumptions underlying an organizational culture.

A second method for identifying the organization's basic assumptions brings together a group of people for a culture workshop—for example, a senior management team or a cross section of managers, old and new members, labor leaders, and staff.[67] The group first brainstorms a large number of the organization's artifacts, such as behaviors, symbols, language, and physical space arrangements. From this list, the values and norms that would produce such artifacts are deduced. In addition, the values espoused in formal planning documents are listed. Finally, a facilitator asks the group to identify the assumptions that would explain the constellation of often conflicting values, norms, and artifacts. For example, some employees challenged Nordstrom's to reconcile its espoused value of respect for people with the practice of encouraging salespeople to conduct customer support activities "off the clock" in order to save costs. Nordstrom has had to work hard to make sure its actions aligned with its words. Because these basic assumptions generally are taken for granted, they can be very difficult to articulate. A great deal of process consultation skill is required to help organization members see the underlying assumptions.

In summary, culture is the pattern of artifacts, norms, values, and basic assumptions. This pattern describes how the organization solves problems and teaches newcomers to behave.[68] Culture is the outcome of prior choices about and experiences with strategy and organization design. It is also a foundation for change that can either facilitate or hinder organization transformation. For example, the cultures of many companies (e.g., IBM, JCPenney, Sony, Disney, Microsoft, and Hewlett-Packard) are deeply rooted in the firm's history. They were laid down by strong founders and have been reinforced by top executives and corporate success into customary ways of perceiving and acting. These customs provide organization members with clear and often widely shared answers to such practical issues as "what really matters around here," "how do we do things around here," and "what we do when a problem arises."

18-4b Implementing the Culture Change Process

There is considerable debate over whether changing something as deep-seated as organization culture is possible.[69] Those advocating culture change generally focus on the more surface elements of culture, such as norms and artifacts. These elements are more changeable than the deeper elements of values and basic assumptions. They offer OD practitioners a more manageable set of action levers for changing organizational behaviors. Some would argue, however, that unless the deeper values and assumptions are changed, organizations have not really changed their culture.

The people who argue that culture change is extremely difficult, if not impossible, typically focus on the deeper elements of culture (values and basic assumptions). Because these deeper elements represent assumptions about organizational life, members do not question them and have a difficult time envisioning anything else. Moreover, members may not want to change their cultural assumptions. The culture provides a strong defense against external uncertainties and threats.[70] It represents past solutions to difficult problems. Members also may have vested interests in maintaining the culture. They may have developed personal stakes, pride, and power in the culture and may strongly resist attempts to change it. Finally, cultures that provide firms with a competitive advantage may be difficult to imitate, thus making it hard for less successful firms to change their cultures to approximate the more successful ones.[71] However, given the problems with cultural change, most practitioners in this area suggest that changes in corporate culture should be considered only after other, less difficult and less costly solutions have been applied or ruled out.[72]

Despite problems in changing corporate culture, large-scale cultural change may be necessary in certain situations: if the firm's culture does not fit a changing environment; if the industry is extremely competitive and changes rapidly; if the company is mediocre or worse; if the firm is about to become a very large company; or if the company is smaller and growing rapidly.[73] Organizations facing these conditions need to change their cultures to adapt to the situation or to operate at higher levels of effectiveness. They may have to supplement attempts at cultural change with other approaches, such as modifying strategy or making organization design changes.

A large amount of research and experience provides the following practical advice with respect to interventions intended to bring about cultural change:[74]

1. **Formulate a clear strategic vision.** Effective cultural change should start from a clear vision of the firm's new strategy and of the shared values and behaviors needed to make it work.[75] This vision provides the purpose and direction for cultural change. It serves as a yardstick for defining the firm's existing culture and for deciding whether proposed changes are consistent with the core values of the organization. A useful approach to providing clear strategic vision is development of a statement of corporate purpose, listing in straightforward terms the firm's core values. For example, Johnson & Johnson calls its guiding principles "Our Credo." It describes several basic values that guide the firm, including, "We believe our first responsibility is to the doctors, nurses and patients, to mothers and all others who use our products and services"; "Our suppliers and distributors must have an opportunity to make a fair profit"; "We must respect [employees'] dignity and recognize their merit"; and "We must maintain in good order the property we are privileged to use, protecting the environment and natural resources."[76]
2. **Display top-management commitment.** Cultural change must be managed from the top of the organization. Senior executives and administrators have to be strongly committed to the new values, need to create constant pressures for change, and must have the staying power to see the changes through.[77] For example, when Jack Welch was CEO at General Electric, he enthusiastically pushed a policy of cost cutting, improved productivity, customer focus, and bureaucracy

busting for more than ten years to every plant, division, group, and sector in his organization. His efforts were rewarded with a *Fortune* cover story lauding his organization for creating more than $52 billion in shareholder value during his tenure.[78]

3. **Model culture change at the highest levels.** Senior executives must communicate the new culture through their own actions. Their behaviors need to symbolize the kinds of values and behaviors being sought. In the few publicized cases of successful culture change, corporate leaders have shown an almost missionary zeal for the new values; their actions have symbolized the values forcefully.[79] For example, when the Four Seasons hotel chain agreed to operate the George V hotel in Paris, it not only remodeled the hotel; it had to implement a culture consistent with its corporate brand and strategy, which were both "North American" in nature. Didier Le Calvez, General Manager of the Four Seasons George V, made a number of controversial decisions, including agreeing to the 35-hour work week, hiring an executive chef, and implementing a performance appraisal process. The nature of these decisions symbolized his understanding of French culture on the one hand and the importance of the Four Seasons' standards on the other. In addition, Le Calvez was very visible on the property, meeting the French union officials for lunch, finding constructive ways to correct behavior in line with the Four Seasons' service expectations, and participating in the interview and selection of all employees.[80]
4. **Modify the organization to support organizational change.** Cultural change generally requires supporting modifications in organization structure, human resources systems, work design, and management processes. These organizational features can help to orient people's behaviors to the new culture.[81] They can make people aware of the behaviors required to get things done in the new culture and can encourage performance of those behaviors. For example, to support the culture change at Cambia Health Solutions, a Blue Cross-Blue Shield provider, the leadership team sponsored a variety of large and small reorganizations, changes in the reward system, and changes in the goal setting process. The leadership team monitored each of these changes, and the internal OD function and HR business partners supported them.
5. **Select and socialize newcomers and terminate deviants.** One of the most effective methods for changing corporate culture is to change organizational membership. People can be selected and terminated in terms of their fit with the new culture. This is especially important in key leadership positions, where people's actions can significantly promote or hinder new values and behaviors. For example, a midterm evaluation of the culture change effort at Cambia Health Solutions found that many people believed the effort was working because of several leadership changes, including the movement or replacement of key executives as well as the hiring of new executives that behaved in line with the new values.

   Another approach is to socialize newly hired people into the new culture. People are most open to organizational influences during the entry stage, when they can be effectively indoctrinated into the culture. For example, companies with strong cultures like Samsung, Procter & Gamble, and 3M attach great importance to socializing new members into the company's values.

Application 18.4 presents an example of culture change at IBM. It illustrates how important cultural principles are used to shape behavior during a period of organizational growth and how culture can be used to facilitate merger and acquisition integration processes.[82]

application 18.4

CULTURE CHANGE AT IBM

IBM began in 1914 as a maker of cheese slicers, scales, and tabulating machines. Thomas Watson, its founder who became famous for the "Think" watchword, created the company on three values called "Basic Beliefs:" "respect for the individual," "the best customer service," and "the pursuit of excellence." Based on these values, IBM grew into one of the great industrial giants of the world, routinely hailed as a "best managed company."

By the late 1980s and the early 1990s, however, IBM's enormous success had an unintended consequence. The firm became complacent; its basic beliefs provided a rationale for stability. "Respect for the individual" had morphed into an entitlement mentality where lifetime employment was reinforced by cultural norms. The "pursuit of excellence" gave way to corporate arrogance and a failure to listen to customers or the marketplace because IBM knew what was right. Finally, its devotion to large, centralized computer systems rather than PC-based distributed architectures led to its downfall. IBM's stock price dropped 75% between August 1987 and September 1993.

To turn things around, IBM appointed Lou Gerstner CEO in 1991. When asked how he would lead IBM, this former GE executive retorted: "The last thing IBM needs right now is a vision." Over the next few years, Gerstner cut IBM's workforce in half, abolished lifetime employment, and refocused business strategy from hardware to software and services. The spectacular success that followed is regarded as one of the great turnarounds in business history.

So what would you do as the CEO who followed Gerstner? Sam Palmisano, a lifetime IBM employee, was appointed CEO in 2002. He strongly believed that IBM's continued success depended on re-laying its foundation. "We couldn't be casual about tinkering with the DNA of a company like IBM. We had to come up with a way to get the employees to create the value system, to determine the company's principles. Watson's Basic Beliefs, however distorted they might have become over the years, had to be the starting point."

To clarify and shift IBM's culture, Palmisano orchestrated a process that began with the corporation's top 300 executives. Together, they generated the basic categories for the new values, including respect, customer, excellence, and innovation. These categories were tested in focus groups and broad surveys with more than 1,000 employees across levels, locations, and functions. Based on this input, three proposed values—commitment to the customer, excellence through innovation, and integrity that earns trust—were submitted to "ValuesJam," a 72-hour process where all employees at IBM were invited to comment on the proposed values via IBM's intranet. ValuesJam organized employee discussion around four forums. A company values forum asked general questions about the importance of values. A "first draft" discussion forum asked for reactions to the three proposed values. A third forum asked about IBM's value in society, and a fourth asked people to describe IBM when it was at its best. Including Palmisano, 50,000 employees made over 10,000 comments about the company's culture and identity. The following were some early-on comments:

- "The only value in IBM today is the stock price."
- "Company values (ya right)."
- "I feel we talk a lot about trust and taking risks, but at the same time, we have endless audits, mistakes are punished and not seen as a welcome part of learning, and managers (and others) are consistently checked."
- "There appears to be great reluctance among our junior executive community to challenge the view of our senior execs."
- "Many times I have heard expressions like 'Would you tell Sam that his strategy is wrong?'"

However, after initial feedback about why things weren't working or wouldn't work, the debate turned more positive. Eventually, a small design team took all the comments, looked for themes, and revised the proposed values into "dedication to every client's success," "innovation that matters—for our company and for the world," and "trust and personal responsibility in all relationships." Palmisano announced them in November 2003. The feedback, in the form of postings on the intranet and more than a thousand emails sent directly to Palmisano, was "these are fine… show me."

In the final stage of the culture intervention, Palmisano sponsored a series of change projects to demonstrate how the values would be used to make decisions and manage the company. One project was dubbed, the "$100 million bet on trust." It was in response to a story that Palmisano heard about an IBM employee prototyping software for a client in Tokyo who immediately needed a software engineer based in Austin to help configure a server. The employee couldn't get the help right away because a charge code was first needed so there would be a way to account for the software engineer's time. In effect, employees were unable to respond quickly to client needs because financial control processes required several levels of management approval. Although the money would usually be approved, it was often too late to be responsive. To address these issues, the $100 million bet on trust gave each manger in a pilot group up to $5,000 annually to spend, no questions asked, to respond to extraordinary situations that would help generate business, to develop client relationships, or to respond to an IBMer's emergency need. Subsequent evaluation showed that the money was being spent wisely. There were several examples of teams winning deals and delighting clients with a small amount of immediately available cash. Consequently, the program was extended to all 22,000 first-line managers. Palmisano was convinced that allowing line managers to take some reasonable risk and trusting them with those decisions would pay off. More importantly, the program symbolized living the IBM values.

Another important change to reflect the values better involved setting prices. ValuesJam surfaced many stories about the difficulty of pricing a customer solution that involved a variety of products and services from multiple IBM groups. Since each brand and business unit had its own P&L, an across-IBM bid was usually pulled apart by each unit and run through the financial accounting system as separate bids for individual products and services. This made it extremely difficult to come up with an all-inclusive price, which ran counter to IBM's value of client success and the strategy of being able to offer a total solution—hardware, software, services, and financing. In one classic case, IBM's CFO was putting together a deal for his partnership account that involved hardware, software, and services. He was told by the finance function that he couldn't price it as an integrated solution. In other words, IBM's CFO was told he couldn't offer the deal he was proposing!

In response, IBM developed an integrated bid system to better reflect its values. All of the people who set prices for clients were brought together and told, "You work for IBM. When there's a cross-IBM bid with multiple products, you price it on the IBM income statement, not on the income statements of each product." This led to a series of intense meetings with senior executives about allocating integrated bids to business-unit P&Ls. IBM made it work because it was the right thing to do in aligning the organization to its values.

The IBM culture change was led by senior executives and involved the whole organization in discussing and debating the firm's values and identity. There was remarkable agreement on what the values should be. The debate, as it turned out, wasn't over the values themselves but on whether IBM would be willing and able to live with them. To make this happen, specific organization changes were made that symbolized the values in use.

SUMMARY

In this chapter, interventions were presented for helping organizations initiate and implement transformational change. Transformational changes typically happen in response to or in anticipation of significant environmental, technological, or internal changes; senior line managers initiate them; they involve multiple stakeholders; they are systemic and revolutionary; and they involve considerable learning to implement a new paradigm.

Organization design involves the organization's structure, work design, human resources practices, and management processes. It aligns these components with the organization's strategy and with each other so they mutually direct behavior to execute the strategy. In domestic settings, this usually results in organization designs that vary along a continuum from mechanistic to organic depending on the requirements of the firm's strategy. In worldwide settings, organization designs need to address the requirements for global integration and local responsiveness. Organization design interventions typically start with assessing the organization to clarify the current design's fitness and the changes required. Then the design components are configured to support the organization's strategy. Finally, implementation involves putting the new structures, practices, and systems into place using many of the methods for leading and managing change described in Chapter 8.

Integrated strategic change (ISC) is a comprehensive intervention for responding to complex and uncertain environmental pressures. It gives equal weight to the strategic and organizational factors affecting organization performance and effectiveness. In addition, these factors are highly integrated during the process of assessing the current strategy and organization design, selecting the desired strategic orientation, developing a strategic change plan, and implementing it.

Transformational change as well as other large-scale organizational changes may require modifications of organization culture. Organization culture includes the pattern of basic assumptions, values, norms, and artifacts shared by organization members. It influences how members perceive, think, and behave at work. Culture affects whether firms can implement new strategies and whether they can operate at high levels of excellence. Culture change interventions start with diagnosing the organization's existing culture. Changing corporate culture can be extremely difficult and requires clear strategic vision, top-management commitment, symbolic leadership, supporting organizational changes, and selection and socialization of newcomers and termination of deviants.

NOTES

1. E. Abrahamson and C. J. Fombrun, "Macrocultures: Determinants and Consequences," *Academy of Management Journal* 19 (1994): 728–55; C. Bernick, "When Your Culture Needs a Makeover," *Harvard Business Review* (June 2001): 5–11; J. Ryan and J. Hurley, "An Empirical Examination of the Relationship Between Scientists' Work Environment and Research Performance," *R&D Management* 37 (2007): 345–54; D. Denison, "The Climate, Culture, and Effectiveness of Work Organizations: A Study of Organizational Behavior and Financial Performance" (Ph.D. diss., University of Michigan, 1982); J. Collins and J. Porras, *Built to Last* (New York: Harper Business, 1994); J. Kotter and J. Heskett, *Corporate Culture and Performance* (New York: Free Press, 1992); A. Xenikou and M. Simosi, "Organizational Culture and Transformational Leadership as Predictors of Business Unit Performance," *Journal of Managerial Psychology* 21 (2006): 566–79.
2. F. Hesselbein and M. Goldsmith, eds., *The Organization of the Future* (San Francisco: Jossey-Bass, 2009); L. Bryan and C. Joyce, "The 21st Century Organization," *The McKinsey Quarterly* (2005): 24–33.
3. M. Tushman and E. Romanelli, "Organizational Evolution: A Metamorphosis Model of Convergence and Reorientation," in *Research in Organizational Behavior*, vol. 7, ed. L. Cummings and B. Staw (Greenwich, CT: JAI Press, 1985), 171–222.
4. F. Suarez and R. Oliva, "Environmental Change and Organizational Transformation," *Industrial and Corporate Change* 14 (2005): 1017–41; J. Sorensen, "The Strength of Corporate Culture and the Reliability of

Firm Performance," *Administrative Science Quarterly* 47 (2002): 70–91.

5. M. Tushman, W. Newman, and E. Romanelli, "Managing the Unsteady Pace of Organizational Evolution," *California Management Review* (Fall 1986): 29–44; C. Christensen, *The Innovator's Dilemma: When New Technologies Cause Great Firms to Fail* (Cambridge: Harvard Business School Press, 1997); J. Balogun and S. Floyd, "Breaking Out of Strategy Vectors: Reintroducing Culture," in *Research in Organizational Change and Development*, vol. 18, ed. W. Pasmore, A. Shani, and R. Woodman (Bingley, UK: Emerald Group Publishing, 2010), 51–76.
6. R. Eisenbach, K. Watson, and R. Pillai, "Transformational Leadership in the Context of Organization Change," *Journal of Organizational Change Management* 12 (1999): 80–89; R. Waldersee, "Becoming a Learning Organization: The Transformation of the Workplace," *Journal of Management Development* 16 (1997): 262–74; A. Pettigrew, "Context and Action in the Transformation of the Firm," *Journal of Management Studies* 24 (1987): 649–70; Tushman and Romanelli, "Organizational Evolution."
7. M. Tushman and B. Virany, "Changing Characteristics of Executive Teams in an Emerging Industry," *Journal of Business Venturing* 2 (1986): 37–49; L. Greiner and A. Bhambri, "New CEO Intervention and Dynamics of Deliberate Strategic Change," *Strategic Management Journal* 10 (Summer 1989): 67–86.
8. T. Hutzschenreuter, I. Kleindienst, and C. Greger, "How New Leaders Affect Strategic Change Following a Succession Event: A Critical Review of the Literature," *Leadership Quarterly* 23 (2012): 729–55; P. Nutt and R. Backoff, "Facilitating Transformational Change," *Journal of Applied Behavioral Science* 33 (1997): 490–508; M. Tushman, W. Newman, and D. Nadler, "Executive Leadership and Organizational Evolution: Managing Incremental and Discontinuous Change," in *Corporate Transformation: Revitalizing Organizations for a Competitive World*, ed. R. Kilmann and T. Covin (San Francisco: Jossey-Bass, 1988): 102–30; W. Bennis and B. Nanus, *Leaders: The Strategies for Taking Charge* (New York: Harper & Row, 1985); Pettigrew, "Context and Action"; R. Tenkasi, S. Mohrman, and A. Mohrman, "Accelerated Learning During Organizational Transition," in *Tomorrow's Organization*, ed. S. Mohrman, J. Galbraith, E. Lawler, and Associates (San Francisco: Jossey-Bass, 1998).
9. J. Kouzes and B. Posner, *The Leadership Challenge*, 3rd ed. (San Francisco: Jossey-Bass, 2002); T. Simons, "Behavioral Integrity as a Critical Ingredient for Transformational Leadership," *Journal of Organizational Change Management* 12 (1999): 89–105.
10. M. Weisbord, *Productive Workplaces* (San Francisco: Jossey-Bass, 1987); R. Freeman, *Strategic Management* (Boston: Ballinger, 1984).
11. G. Jayaram, "Open Systems Planning," in *The Planning of Change*, 3rd ed., ed. W. Bennis, K. Benne, R. Chin, and K. Corey (New York: Holt, Rinehart, & Winston, 1976): 275–83.
12. D. Miller and P. Friesen, *Organizations: A Quantum View* (Englewood Cliffs, NJ: Prentice-Hall, 1984).
13. A. Meyer, A. Tsui, and C. Hinings, "Guest Co-Editors Introduction: Configurational Approaches to Organizational Analysis," *Academy of Management Journal* 36 (1993): 1175–95.
14. Tushman, Newman, and Romanelli, "Managing the Unsteady Pace"; L. Greiner, "Evolution and Revolution as Organizations Grow," *Harvard Business Review* (July–August 1972): 37–46; B. Lamont, R. Williams, and J. Hoffman, "Performance During 'M-form' Reorganization and Recovery Time: The Effects of Prior Strategy and Implementation Speed," *Academy of Management Journal* 37 (1994): 153–66; D. Miller and P. Friesen "Structural Change and Performance: Quantum Versus Piecemeal-Incremental Approaches," *Academy of Management Journal* 25 (1982): 867–92.
15. B. Blumenthal and P. Haspeslagh, "Toward a Definition of Corporate Transformation," *Sloan Management Review* 35 (1994): 101–7.
16. Tushman, Newman, and Romanelli, "Managing the Unsteady Pace."
17. Tushman and Romanelli, "Organizational Evolution."
18. J. Bartunek and M. Louis, "Organization Development and Organizational Transformation," in *Research in Organizational Change and Development*, vol. 2, ed. W. Pasmore and R. Woodman (Greenwich, CT: JAI Press, 1988), 97–134.
19. R. Golembiewski, K. Billingsley, and S. Yeager, "Measuring Change and Persistence in Human Affairs: Types of Changes Generated by OD Designs," *Journal of Applied Behavioral Science* 12 (1975): 133–57.
20. T. Cummings and S. Mohrman, "Self-Designing Organizations: Towards Implementing Quality-of-Work-Life Innovations," in *Research in Organizational Change and Development*, vol. 1, ed. R. Woodman and W. Pasmore (Greenwich, CT: JAI Press, 1987), 275–310.
21. J. Sackmann, "The Role of Metaphors in Organization Transformation," *Human Relations* 42 (1989): 463–85.
22. E. Lawler and C. Worley, *Management Reset* (San Francisco, CA: Jossey Bass, 2011).
23. J. Galbraith, *Organization Design* (Reading, MA: Addison Wesley, 1977); D. Nadler, M. Tushman, and M. Nadler, *Competing by Design: The Power of Organizational Architecture* (New York: Oxford University Press, 1997); R. Burton, B. Eriksen, D. Håkonsson, and C. Snow, *Organization Design: The Evolving State-of-the-Art* (New York: Springer, 2006); A. Kates and J. Galbraith, *Designing Your*

Organization: Using the STAR Model to Solve 5 Critical Design Challenges (San Francisco: Jossey-Bass, 2007); J. Galbraith, "Organization Design," in *Handbook of Organization Development*, ed. T. Cummings (Thousand Oaks, CA: Sage Publications, 2008), 325–52.

24. P. Lawrence and J. Lorsch, *Organization and Environment: Managing Differentiation and Integration* (Harvard University, 1967).
25. T. Burns and G. Stalker, *The Management of Innovation* (London: Social Science Paperbacks, 1961).
26. S. Mohrman, J. Galbraith, and E. Lawler, eds., *Tomorrow's Organization: Crafting Winning Capabilities in a Dynamic World* (San Francisco: Jossey-Bass, 1998); J. Galbraith, D. Downey, and A. Kates, *Designing Dynamic Organizations: A Hands-on Guide for Leaders at All Levels* (New York: AMACOM, 2001); E. Beinhocker, "The Adaptable Corporation," *The McKinsey Quarterly* 2 (2006): 76–87.
27. R. Boehm, "Leading Change: An Interview with the CEO of Deer & Company," *McKinsey Quarterly* (December 2006): 1–7.
28. C. Bartlett and P. Beamish, *Transnational Management*, 6th ed. (New York: McGraw-Hill, 2010); M. Peng. *Global Strategy* (Mason, OH: South-Western College Publishing, 2008).
29. Bartlett and Beamish, *Transnational Management*; D. Heenan and H. Perlmutter, *Multinational Organization Development* (Reading, MA: Addison-Wesley, 1979); P. Evans, "Organization Development in the Transnational Enterprise," in *Research in Organizational Change and Development*, vol. 3, ed. R. Woodman and W. Pasmore (Greenwich, CT: JAI Press, 1989); C. Bartlett, Y. Doz, and G. Hedlund, *Managing the Global Firm* (London: Routledge, 1990).
30. C. Prahalad and Y. Doz. *The Multinational Mission: Balancing Local Demands and Global Vision* (New York: The Free Press, 1987).
31. Heenan and Perlmutter, *Multinational Organization Development*, 13.
32. This application was developed and submitted by Dr. Nora L. Hughes, and is based on her doctoral dissertation. See N. Hughes, "Changing Faces: Adaptation of Highly Skilled Chinese Workers to a High-Tech Multinational Corporation," *Journal of Applied Behavioral Science* 45 (2009): 212–38.
33. J. Main, "How to Go Global—And Why," *Fortune*, August 28, 1989, 76.
34. Heenan and Perlmutter, *Multinational Organization Development*, 20.
35. L. Thurow, *The Future of Capitalism* (New York: Morrow, 1996).
36. A. Borrus, "The Stateless Corporation," *BusinessWeek*, May 14, 1990, 101–3.
37. Heenan and Perlmutter, *Multinational Organization Development*, 20.
38. S. Mohrman and T. Cummings, *Self-designing Organizations: Learning How to Create High Performance* (Reading, MA: Addison Wesley, 1989); N. Stanford, *Organization Design: The Collaborative Approach* (Burlington, MA: Elsevier Butterworth-Heinemann, 2005).
39. J. Galbraith et al., *Designing Dynamic Organizations*; Kates and Galbraith, *Designing Your Organization*; Stanford, *Organization Design*.
40. H. Lee, "Factors That Influence Expatriate Failure: An Interview Study," *International Journal of Management* 24 (2007): 403–15; L. Littrell, E. Salas, K. Hess, M. Paley, and S. Riedel, "Expatriate Preparation: A Critical Analysis of 25 Years of Cross-Cultural Training Research," *Human Resource Development Review* 5 (September 2006): 355–89; R. Tung, "Expatriate Assignments: Enhancing Success and Minimizing Failure," *Academy of Management Executive* (Summer 1987): 117–26; A. Mamman, "Expatriate Adjustment: Dealing with Hosts' Attitudes in a Foreign Assignment," *Journal of Transitional Management Development* 1 (1995).
41. J. Henry, "Engineering a Comeback." *Success*, accessed from http://www.success.com/articles/1479-engineering-a-comeback on December 1, 2012.
42. C. Worley, D. Hitchin, and W. Ross, *Integrated Strategic Change: How Organization Development Builds Competitive Advantage* (Reading, MA: Addison-Wesley, 1996).
43. Worley, Hitchin, and Ross, *Integrated Strategic Change*.
44. M. Jelinek and J. Litterer, "Why OD Must Become Strategic," *Organizational Change and Development*, vol. 2, ed. W. Pasmore and R. Woodman (Greenwich, CT: JAI Press, 1988), 135–62; A. Bhambri and L. Pate, "Introduction—The Strategic Change Agenda: Stimuli, Processes, and Outcomes," *Journal of Organization Change Management* 4 (1991): 4–6; D. Nadler, M. Gerstein, R. Shaw, and Associates, eds., *Organizational Architecture* (San Francisco: Jossey-Bass, 1992); Worley, Hitchin, and Ross, *Integrated Strategic Change*.
45. C. Worley, D. Hitchin, R. Patchett, R. Barnett, and J. Moss, "Unburn the Bridge, Get to Bedrock, and Put Legs on the Dream: Looking at Strategy Implementation with Fresh Eyes" (paper presented to the Western Academy of Management, Redondo Beach, CA, March 1999).
46. H. Mintzberg, *The Rise and Fall of Strategic Planning* (New York: Free Press, 1994).
47. Worley, Hitchin, and Ross, *Integrated Strategic Change*.
48. P. Senge, *The Fifth Discipline* (New York: Doubleday, 1990); E. Lawler, *The Ultimate Advantage* (San Francisco: Jossey-Bass, 1992); Worley, Hitchin, and Ross, *Integrated Strategic Change*.

49. L. Greiner and V. Schein, *Power and Organization Development* (Reading, MA: Addison-Wesley, 1988).
50. M. Porter, *Competitive Strategy* (New York: Free Press, 1980).
51. R. Grant, *Contemporary Strategy Analysis*, 7th ed. (New York: Wiley, 2010).
52. C. Hofer and D. Schendel, *Strategy Formulation: Analytic Concepts* (St. Paul, MN: West Publishing, 1978).
53. K. van der Heijden, *Scenarios: The Art of Strategic Conversation* (New York: Wiley, 2007); M. Lindgren and H. Bandhold, *Scenario Planning* (New York: Palgrave Macmillan, 2009); M. Weisbord, *Productive Workplaces* (San Francisco: Jossey-Bass, 1987).
54. E. Lawler, *The Ultimate Advantage* (San Francisco: Jossey-Bass, 1992); Tushman, Newman, and Romanelli, "Convergence and Upheaval"; R. Buzzell and B. Gale, *The PIMS Principles* (New York: Free Press, 1987).
55. L. Hrebiniak and W. Joyce, *Implementing Strategy* (New York: Macmillan, 1984); J. Galbraith and R. Kazanjian, *Strategy Implementation: Structure, Systems, and Process*, 2nd ed. (St. Paul, MN: West Publishing, 1986).
56. J. Collins and J. Porras, *Built to Last* (New York: Harper Business, 1994); J. Kotter and J. Heskett, *Corporate Culture and Performance* (New York: Free Press, 1992); J. Barney, "Organizational Culture: Can It Be a Source of Sustained Competitive Advantage?" *Academy of Management Review* 11 (1986): 656–65.
57. J. Martin, *Organization Culture* (Newbury Park, CA: Sage Publications, 2002); D. Meyerson and J. Martin, "Cultural Change: An Integration of Three Different Views," *Journal of Management Studies* 24 (1987): 623–47; K. Cameron and R. Quinn, *Diagnosing and Changing Organizational Culture*, 2nd ed. (San Francisco: Jossey-Bass, 2011); E. Schein, *Organizational Culture and Leadership*, 4th ed. (San Francisco: Jossey-Bass, 2010).
58. C. M. Lau, L. Kilbourne, and R. Woodman, "A Shared Schema Approach to Understanding Organizational Culture Change," in *Research on Organizational Change and Development*, vol. 14, ed. W. Pasmore and R. Woodman (Greenwich, CT: JAI Press, 2003), 225–56; J. Sorensen, "The Strength of Corporate Culture and the Reliability of Firm Performance," *Administrative Science Quarterly* 47 (2002): 70–91; T. Deal and A. Kennedy, *Corporate Cultures* (Reading, MA: Addison-Wesley, 1982); T. Peters and R. Waterman, *In Search of Excellence* (New York: Harper & Row, 1982); J. Pfeffer, *Competitive Advantage Through People* (Cambridge, MA: Harvard Business School, 1994); J. Collins and J. Porras, *Built to Last* (New York: Harper Business, 1994); J. Collins, *Good to Great* (New York: Harper-Collins, 2001); J. Kotter and J. Heskett, *Corporate Culture and Performance* (New York: Free Press, 1992); P. Frost, L. Moore, M. Louis, C. Lundberg, and J. Martin, eds., *Organizational Culture* (Beverly Hills, CA: Sage, 1985), 95–196; Martin, *Organizational Culture*.
59. Schein, *Organizational Culture*; R. Kilmann, M. Saxton, and R. Serpa, eds., *Gaining Control of the Corporate Culture* (San Francisco: Jossey-Bass, 1985).
60. Schein, *Organizational Culture*.
61. Martin, *Organization Culture*.
62. H. Schwartz and S. Davis, "Matching Corporate Culture and Business Strategy," *Organizational Dynamics* (Summer 1981): 30–48; S. Davis, *Managing Corporate Culture* (Cambridge, MA: Ballinger, 1984).
63. R. E. Quinn, *Beyond Rational Management: Mastering the Paradoxes and Competing Demands of High Performance* (San Francisco: Jossey-Bass, 1988); Cameron and Quinn, *Diagnosing and Changing Organizational Culture*.
64. R. Quinn and G. Spreitzer, "The Psychometrics of the Competing Values Culture Instrument and an Analysis of the Impact of Organizational Culture on Quality of Life," in *Research in Organizational Change and Development*, vol. 5, ed. R. Woodman and W. Pasmore (Greenwich, CT: JAI Press, 1991), 115–42.
65. R. Zammuto and J. Krakower, "Quantitative and Qualitative Studies of Organizational Culture," in *Research in Organizational Change and Development*, vol. 5, ed. R. Woodman and W. Pasmore (Greenwich, CT: JAI Press, 1991), 83–114; Quinn and Spreitzer, "Psychometrics."
66. Schein, *Organizational Culture*.
67. E. Schein, *The Corporate Culture Survival Guide* (San Francisco: Jossey-Bass, 1999).
68. Schein, *Organizational Culture*.
69. Frost, Moore, Louis, Lundberg, and Martin, eds., *Organizational Culture*; Martin, *Organizational Culture*.
70. Meyerson and Martin, "Cultural Change."
71. J. Barney, "Organizational Culture: Can It Be a Source of Sustained Competitive Advantage?" *Academy of Management Review* 11 (1986): 656–65.
72. B. Uttal, "The Corporate Culture Vultures," *Fortune*, October 17, 1983, 66–72.
73. Ibid., 70.
74. Schein, *Corporate Culture Survival Guide*; H. Schwartz and S. Davis, "Matching Corporate Culture and Business Strategy," *Organizational Dynamics* (Summer 1981): 30–48; Uttal, "Corporate Culture Vultures"; Frost et al., *Organizational Culture*; V. Sathe, "Implications of Corporate Culture: A Manager's Guide to Action," *Organizational Dynamics* (Autumn 1983): 5–23; B. Drake and E. Drake, "Ethical and Legal Aspects of Managing Corporate Cultures," *California Management Review* (Winter 1988): 107–23; K. Cameron, "A Process for Changing Organization Culture," in *Handbook of Organization*

Development, ed. T. Cummings (Thousand Oaks, CA: Sage Publications, 2008), 429–45.

75. Worley, Hitchin, and Ross, *Integrated Strategic Change*; R. Beckhard and W. Pritchard, *Changing the Essence* (San Francisco: Jossey-Bass, 1992).
76. F. Aguilar and A. Bhambri, *Johnson and Johnson (A)* (Boston: HBS Case Services, 1983).
77. B. Dumaine, "Creating a New Company Culture," *Fortune*, January 15, 1990, 127–31; C. O'Reilly, "Corporations, Culture, and Commitment: Motivation and Social Control in Organizations," *California Management Review* 31 (Summer 1989): 9–25; Pettigrew, "Context and Action."
78. N. Tichy and S. Sherman, *Control Your Destiny or Someone Else Will* (New York: Doubleday, 1993); B. Morris, "The Wealth Builders," *Fortune*, December 11, 1995, 80–96.
79. Dumaine, "Creating a New Company Culture."
80. R. Hallowell, D. Bowen, and C. Knoop, "Four Seasons Goes to Paris," *Academy of Management Executive* 16 (2002): 7–24.
81. Tichy and Sherman, *Control Your Destiny*.
82. This application was based on material found in L. Applegate, C. Heckscher, B. Michael, and E. Collins, "IBM's Decade of Transformation: Uniting Vision and Values," Harvard Business School Case 9-807-030, Harvard Business School, 2006; O. Bjelland and R. Wood, "An Inside View of IBM's 'Innovation Jam,'" *Sloan Management Review* (2008), accessed from http://sloanreview.mit.edu/the-magazine/2008-fall/50101/an-inside-view-of-ibms-innovation-jam on November 30, 2012; P. Hemp and T. Stewart, "Leading Change When Business Is Good," *Harvard Business Review* 82 (2004): 60–70.

19

Continuous Change

learning objectives

- Compare and contrast four continuous change organization development (OD) interventions.
- Describe the elements and processes associated with the dynamic strategy-making intervention.
- Define the demands of turbulent environments and describe the self-design intervention.
- Outline the definition and application of organization learning interventions.
- Explain the logic and process of developing built-to-change organizations.

This chapter describes interventions that enable organizations to change themselves continually. These change processes are increasingly common in organizations, but are still being developed and refined. They are aimed at the growing number of organizations facing highly turbulent environments, such as firms in high-technology, entertainment and fashion, and biotechnology industries, where timing is critical, technological change is rapid, and competitive pressures are unrelenting and difficult to predict. In these situations, standard sources of competitive advantage—strategic positioning and core competencies—erode quickly and provide only temporary advantage.[1] What is needed are *dynamic capabilities*[2] built into the organization that enable it to renew forms of competitive advantage constantly to adapt to a rapidly shifting environment.

Continuous change interventions extend transformational change into a nonstop process of strategizing, designing, and implementing.[3] Rather than focus on creating and implementing a particular strategy and organization design, continuous change addresses the underlying structures, processes, and activities for generating new forms of competitive advantage. Thus, the focus is on learning, changing, and adapting—on how to produce a constant flow of new strategies and designs and not just on how to transform existing ones.

Dynamic strategy making uses a process of "guided involvement" to help organizations implement a *strategic system*.[4] A statement of strategic direction—the organization's competitive logic, goals, organization design, and action plan—and a repeatable strategic process define the strategic system. OD practitioners work with managers and key stakeholders to build a system that continually adapts. Dynamic strategy making addresses both the content (the "what") of strategy formulation and the process (the "how" and "who") of strategy implementation.

Self-designing organizations have the capability to alter themselves fundamentally and continuously. Creating them is a highly participative process in which multiple stakeholders set strategic direction, design appropriate structures and processes, and implement them. This intervention includes considerable innovation and learning as organizations gain the capacity to design and implement significant changes continually.

Learning organizations are those with the ability to learn how to change and improve themselves constantly. Distinct from individual learning, this intervention helps organizations move beyond solving existing problems to gain the capability to improve constantly. It results in the development of a learning organization where empowered members take responsibility for changing the organization and learning how to do this better and better.

Built-to-change organizations include strategizing processes, design elements, and managerial practices that support change as the primary driver of effectiveness. This intervention provides design and implementation guidelines for building change capabilities into the structures, processes, and behaviors of the organization so that it can respond continually to a rapidly changing environment.

19-1 Dynamic Strategy Making

Dynamic strategy making represents a new type of OD intervention that combines OD's traditional human process focus on relationships among organization members with strategic management's customary emphasis on strategy and organization design to help organizations manage strategic change. Similar to integrated strategic change (ISC) (Chapter 18), dynamic strategy making is a deliberate, coordinated process that leads to continuous realignments between an organization and its environment. Whereas ISC focuses on making a systemic and revolutionary change, dynamic strategy making creates a continuous strategic change process intended to improve performance and effectiveness over time.[5]

Greiner and Cummings developed the dynamic strategy-making process based on their research and practice in strategy implementation.[6] They found that managers consistently underestimated the impact of change and human process issues during strategy execution.[7] Greiner and Cummings' analysis of the history and practice of strategy formulation and implementation, along with the increasing pace of change in complex environments, led them to propose several criteria for an effective strategic change process:[8]

- **Speed over delay**. New opportunities and threats need immediate strategic action, but organizations are often slow to react, gathering more information and assessing more solutions instead of acting.
- **Breadth over narrowness.** Unpredictable and complex conditions require expansive thinking and openness to innovative ideas, but organizations tend to be discipline focused and take input from select stakeholders.
- **Flexibility over rigidity.** Organizations must discover new solutions, adjust priorities, and reallocate resources constantly, but they are often ruled by rigid policies and annual budgets.
- **Empowerment over autocracy.** Strategy making must permeate the entire organization and give members the freedom to respond to local changes; it cannot remain the sole domain of top management.
- **Simplicity over complexity.** Complexity threatens to overwhelm organization members; strategy needs to be concrete and specific enough to be acted on but not so detailed that members cannot respond and improvise as situations change.
- **Unity over fragmentation.** Strategy must promote consistent and integrated action, because organizations spread out across countries, markets, and businesses tend to fragment, lose coordination, and deviate from the intended strategy.

19-1a Conceptual Framework

Dynamic strategy making is a comprehensive and pragmatic approach to strategic change. It views strategy as a central concept that permeates the organization rather than being another element to align with other parts. It treats the process of creating and implementing strategy and the content of strategy interactively and seeks strategies that are executable and flexible. Figure 19.1 broadly outlines the framework. The *strategic system* is the core of dynamic strategy making. It includes strategy content in the form of a statement of strategic direction and a strategic process for developing and executing the strategy. When designed effectively, the strategic system continually matches the firm's resources and capabilities to changing environmental opportunities and demands.

The specific issues addressed in the strategic system come from senior managers' situational assessments about the organization and its environment. The organization is examined to identify core capabilities, resources, know-how, and all potential strengths needed to succeed in the marketplace. Because neither the organization nor its environment is static, this assessment is not a one-shot event and so the strategic process is ongoing and built into the organization. In fast-moving environments, the results of strategic analysis have a short shelf life, so data collection and assessment need to be continuous and keep pace with change.

Statement of Strategic Direction A written statement of strategic direction is the primary outcome from the situational assessment—it makes strategic information about the organization and environment concrete and permits revision over time. It provides a way to record, communicate, and implement the strategy. A written statement avoids misunderstandings in the future and provides a clearer way to articulate the content with organization members and other stakeholders about the journey ahead.[9]

FIGURE 19.1

A Dynamic Strategy System

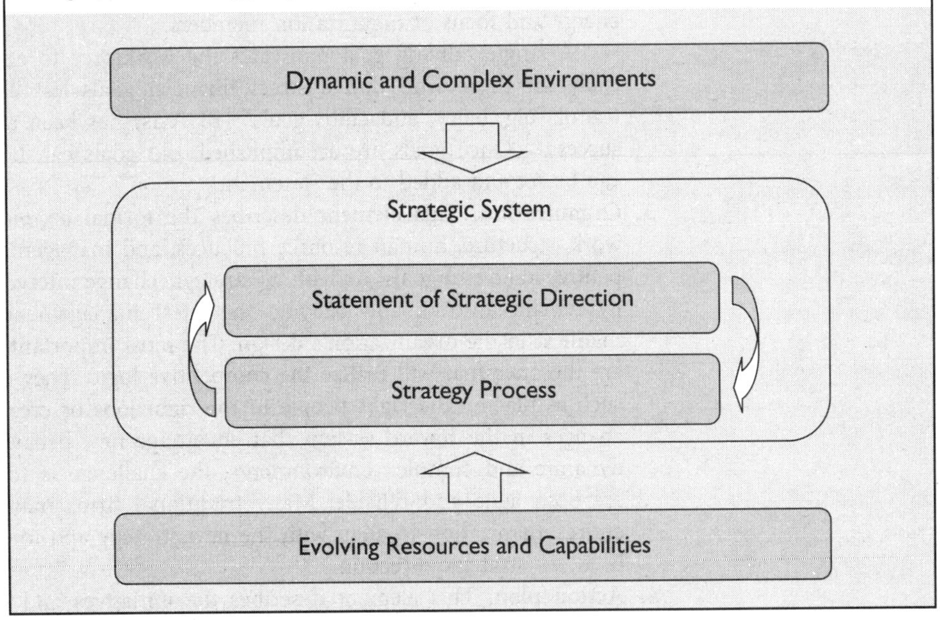

SOURCE: Adapted from Greiner and Cummings, 2009.

The statement of strategic direction includes four elements: (1) the competitive logic that describes the organization's market position and customer tiebreakers, or the business model for gaining competitive advantage; (2) the financial and rallying goals that will direct and motivate members' behavior; (3) the organization design that will structure and link members to work activities, each other, and company values; and (4) the action plan that includes strategic initiatives and specific steps for implementing the strategic system. The four elements are described below:

1. **Competitive logic**. An effective strategy centers on a value proposition that connects the firm's capabilities to market opportunities. This value proposition is the *competitive logic*, or how the firm will compete in the marketplace, and includes statements about the organization's *market position* and *customer tiebreakers*. The best market position is one where the organization has the capabilities to deliver value to specific customers in ways that competitors cannot easily match. Finding and describing this position is more creative than deductive, but is assisted by such traditional strategy tools as strengths, weaknesses, opportunities, and threats (SWOT) analyses or Porter's competitive strategy model.[10] More recent methods, such as value migration techniques, the resource-based view of strategy, or "blue ocean" models, can also be used.[11] The organization's customer tiebreakers are the differentiators that attract and retain customers. Tiebreakers are the product, service, after-sales support, or brand characteristics that customers use to make purchase decisions. The organization's capabilities must be able to deliver on these tiebreakers for a competitive logic to be effective.
2. **Goals**. Greiner and Cummings suggest that *goals* represent the unifying target for achievement, and should be separated into financial goals and a single rallying goal. Financial goals direct effort and measure progress. Research suggests that when top management teams agree on the financial goals and their importance, the firm's performance is higher than it would have been otherwise.[12] A few specific and clear goals help to unify and motivate employees to make the strategy happen. Unfortunately, too many organizations set too many goals that diffuse and dilute the energy and focus of organization members.

   A single rallying goal motivates the workforce to embrace the strategy, especially for those who find abstract financial goals less exciting. For example, the use of "big, hairy, audacious goals" (BHAGs) has been associated with short-term success.[13] Once goals are accomplished, old goals can be dropped, and new ones can be set and added to the statement.
3. **Organization**. This element describes the formal *organization* design that aligns work, structure, human resource practices, and management processes to the competitive logic and goals. As with all strategic change interventions, a strategy can easily remain abstract and become the latest management fad unless its intent is manifest in the organization's design. The most important design features to change are the ones that will realize the competitive logic. They can be structural changes, such as placing the right people in the right jobs or creating new departments, or changes in the reward system that encourage new behaviors. For organizations in dynamic and complex environments, the challenge is to build organizations that are both agile and reliable. Many traditional firms may have to transform their entire organization to align with the new strategy and to direct employees to move in a new strategic direction.
4. **Action plan**. This element describes the initiatives and specific steps required to implement the strategy and to ensure that everyone's daily behavior reflects the

strategy. The *action plan* sets priorities and spells out what things need to happen over a specific time frame to move forward. Action plans are generally organized around four to six broad initiatives that take their cue directly from the other three elements of the statement of strategic direction. Each initiative usually requires three or four specific steps to cause implementation. These steps should specify responsibilities, accountabilities, and deadlines and include a realistic evaluation of the costs, benefits, and feasibility of moving the competitive logic forward. Managers revise the action plan continuously, when initiatives are accomplished, or when real-time events make changes necessary. Initiatives that divert energy from key goals or organization design changes, make accountability vague, or cause employees to lose focus should be eliminated.

The four elements of the statement of strategic direction are straightforward and easy for organization members to understand and remember. In a world that frequently requires spontaneous responses, this simplicity is important. It makes it easier for people to make adjustments in line with the strategic direction.

Strategic Process While the statement of strategic direction captures the content of an organization's strategy and design, Greiner and Cummings suggest that the second part of the strategic system shown in Figure 19.1, strategic process, is equally important to successful strategy making. Strategic process has to do with the "who" and "how" of developing the statement and subsequently implementing it. It involves identifying the relevant stakeholders who should be involved directly in the strategy-making process and engaging them in a highly interactive set of conversations and debates about the organization's strategic direction and how to move forward. As described below in the application stages, strategic process is informed by the philosophy of "guided involvement,"[14] which includes a repeatable series of retreats and activities for developing and executing strategic direction. Guided involvement speaks to the nature of the dialogue expected among organization members and to the role OD practitioners can play in building the required organization capabilities. It bridges the learning and applied behavioral science aspects of OD with the technical aspects of strategic management and organization design by holding organization participants to a high standard of direct, open, and concrete engagement.

In uncertain environments, a strategic process must promote both quickness and participation. Guided involvement helps participants rapidly assess the organization and its environment, share their knowledge and experience, and agree on strategic direction. As a result, politics—the way power and influence are managed in organizations—is made more constructive through guided involvement. It reaches out to all organization members to encourage their relevant participation in strategy making and facilitates their understanding and commitment to the strategic direction.

19-1b Application Stages

Making the statement of strategic direction actionable requires integrated content and a supporting process. Dynamic strategy making helps organizations construct content and process together into a strategic system. The following tools and concepts in the form of building blocks support this construction process.

1. **Choosing relevant stakeholders**. The dynamic strategy-making process is kicked off by identifying and recruiting the relevant stakeholders. Getting the right stakeholders involved from the start ensures that the strategic system results in a more

realistic formulation of the strategy and has the commitment necessary to support its implementation. The process is driven by senior executives or the top management team and they can employ a variety of techniques, including open system planning or stakeholder mapping processes (Chapter 11), to systematically identify stakeholders. Typical stakeholders include the board of directors, union officials, customers, managers and organization members, regulators, and community representatives, among others. The balance of the application stages describe how the stakeholders are organized for meaningful interaction and decision making.

2. **Holding the first retreat**. The purpose of the first retreat is to create an initial draft of the statement of strategic direction, especially the competitive logic and goal elements. Before the session, participants provide information about their perceptions of strengths, weaknesses, opportunities, and threats through personal interviews or other methods. These interviews are important because they will be the primary input to conversations about strategy. Although many organizations are full of data about customers, regulations, competitor actions, and market forces—and these should be available to the group—much of dynamic strategy making is about gaining consensus regarding the implications of these data and about the actions to be taken. Interview summaries must not ignore data points only mentioned by one or a few members. OD practitioners should be careful to present all the data and not over-consolidate it; "small noises" often can turn into a "big signal."

   Based on these data, three primary discussions define the first retreat: understanding the data, formulating competitive logic and goals, and preparing for broader organizational involvement. Following introductions, agenda setting, and any educational inputs, the group discusses the prework data. This is best done as a total group where everyone can hear about all of the data. The philosophy of guided involvement suggests that inquiry—understanding what is known and what it means—is the most appropriate behavior during this discussion.

   The second conversation is the most difficult. After hearing and discussing the data, the total group is then split into smaller breakout groups to develop a competitive logic for the organization. This creative assignment asks small groups to explore the organization and its environment and to discover or invent the best match between existing market opportunities and internal strengths. It allows participants to use their common knowledge and individual experiences to create content and develop a consensus strategy.

   This small group dialogue is likely to be complex and uncertain; it represents an opportunity for guided involvement by the OD practitioner. Finding the right fit between the organization and its environment is a creative act. Companies have many internal strengths and external opportunities to consider, not all of which will match up. Participants should be encouraged to be broad enough in their thinking to see a variety of possibilities, but focused enough to come to some agreement about the best opportunities.

   Initial ideas for a rough draft of the competitive logic and goals from the small groups are reviewed in the total group and depending on the length of time available, a second round of small group discussions can be conducted. While desirable, it is not necessary to come to consensus. Some teams are able to complete a draft of the entire strategy statement at the first retreat, but this is rare, and the remaining elements, organization and action plans, are typically addressed in the second retreat.

   The last discussion involves establishing procedures and timelines for gathering feedback on the draft logic and goals before the next retreat.

3. **Engaging stakeholders between the first and second retreats.** Between the first and second retreats, senior managers reflect on their work and perform reality tests on the validity of assumptions in the statement. The primary method for this testing is through feedback on the draft statement from other stakeholders. During interim meetings, senior executives from the first retreat lead reviews of the draft on competitive logic and goals. Middle managers, frontline employees, and other relevant stakeholders provide feedback and comments. These meetings can be in person or virtual and extend the strategy-making process out to the larger workforce. In general, the meetings address four questions:
   - Is the draft statement sufficiently realistic in its assumptions about the market?
   - Do we have the capabilities to pull it off?
   - Is it sufficiently inspirational, and will it win commitment?
   - What suggestions would improve it?

   The reactions from these meetings are fed back to a designated member of the retreat team, who incorporates them into a redraft of the competitive logic and goals statement. These are presented at the second off-site retreat.
4. **Holding the second retreat.** The purpose of the second retreat is to review the feedback, finalize the competitive logic and goal statements, and complete the statement of strategic direction. Initially, the total group reviews and discusses the input from stakeholders and builds consensus regarding the competitive logic and goals.

   Then, subgroups are asked to identify alternative organization designs with pros and cons for each, keeping in mind the need to ensure a close fit between the proposed design and the competitive logic and goals. This involves specifying the design components at a high level first, and then describing specifics of the design through participation and involvement of organization members. Politics is inherent in any organization design discussion, especially if names are attached to positions, and OD practitioners must be careful that discussions do not derail. Best practice here suggests defining the design logic and recommending preferred alternatives to the CEO or senior manager. Following the second retreat or during a third retreat, the final organization design can be discussed.

   The outcome of the second retreat is an outline and action plan for implementing the new strategy. At this time, only the key strategic initiatives are outlined; specific steps are postponed until a team is charted to own the initiative or a third off-site retreat is convened. Initiatives appear rather logically after reflecting back on the logic, goals, and high level design. They typically answer the following questions:
   - What are the few priorities stemming from the competitive logic that will help us to move forward?
   - What resources are needed for what goals?
   - Who will do what, when, and where?
5. **Implementing actions.** Following the second retreat, organizations have several options for moving forward. All of them involve putting effort into pursuing the statement of strategic direction. For example, a third retreat could finalize organization design changes, or provide details about initiative resources and action steps. Alternatively, the organization could establish task forces with charters to develop action plans and implement the initiatives and to report progress to the senior team.

   In any case, it is important for the senior team to arrange for the statement of strategic direction to be communicated and to be built into the organization's performance management system. Dynamic strategy making requires exceptional leadership from all managers (not just senior executives). Strategic leaders must step forward and support the creation, execution, and refinement of the organization's strategy. They must model the behaviors implied by the strategic statement and hold themselves accountable for it. It is also important to create systems to hold other managers accountable for results. This takes a good deal of vision, personal insight, and social acumen. Strategic leadership must ensure that strategy is enacted effectively at all levels on a daily basis. This often requires change, leaving behind traditional habits and replacing them with new strategy-oriented behavior.[15] A good leader must assure that the dynamic strategy making process continues over time by periodically reassessing the statement of strategic direction and making changes in the statement and organization as needed. This might involve recycling through the application stages at periodic intervals to keep pace with a changing environment.

Application 19.1 describes a dynamic strategy-making intervention at Whitbread PLC. The organization leveraged a written statement of strategic intent to gather feedback from the larger organization and to clarify and focus its strategy and organization. In using a deliberate, guided process, it also built a process for continuing to make strategic changes over time.[16]

19-2 Self-Designing Organizations

A growing number of researchers and practitioners have called for organizations with a built-in capacity to transform continually and to achieve high levels of performance in today's competitive and changing environments.[17] Mohrman and Cummings developed the self-design intervention in response to a number of demands facing organizations in turbulent environments. It involves cycles of diagnosing, designing, and implementing activities that managers and employees at all levels of the firm can carry out.[18] This section begins with a discussion of the demands of a turbulent environment and then describes the application stages of self-design.

19-2a The Demands of Turbulent Environments

Turbulent environments are both complex and changing rapidly. To be effective in these situations requires a coordinated organization response. As a result, large-scale change needs to occur at multiple levels of the organization if new strategies are to result in changed behaviors throughout the system. Top executives must formulate a strategy and clarify a vision of what the organization needs to look like to support it. Middle and lower levels of the organization need to put those broad parameters into operation by creating structures, procedures, and behaviors to implement the strategy.[19] Self-design processes help members change the organization systemically.

In turbulent environments, change is constant. Therefore, organization change is never totally finished, as new structures and processes will continually have to be modified to fit new conditions. Thus, the change process needs to be dynamic and iterative, with organizations continually changing themselves.

In turbulent environments, the direction of change is unclear. Organizations need to learn how to translate general prescriptions of change, such as "be more nimble" and "go global," into specific structures, processes, and behaviors appropriate to their situations. This generally requires considerable on-site innovation and learning by doing—trying out new structures and behaviors, assessing their effectiveness, and modifying them if necessary. Large-scale change in turbulent environments calls for constant organizational learning.[20]

application 19.1

DYNAMIC STRATEGY MAKING AT WHITBREAD PLC

Whitbread PLC is one of Britain's leading organizations, a member of the FTSE 100 with a strong brand presence in hotels (Premier Hotels) and restaurants (Costa Coffee, Beefeater Grill). It also has a long history of change and transformation, starting out in 1742 as a brewer and pub owner/operator. In 1800, it was arguably the largest brewer in Britain, and for most of its history operated as a vertically integrated brewer, owning the brewery, transportation, and retail outlets. But regulatory changes in the early 1990s—specifically the "Beer Orders"—restricted pub ownership by brewers and greatly changed the industry's dynamics. Whitbread diversified by entering into restaurants, hotels, and health clubs.

In June 1997, David Thomas was named CEO largely because of his success in building and growing these new ventures and he wanted to accelerate Whitbread's changes. But in 1999, a large and public failure to acquire a number of pubs destroyed confidence in the company both internally and externally. The proposed acquisition painted a confusing picture of corporate strategy. Was brewing a core part of the portfolio or not? The expansion into hotels, restaurants, and health clubs followed by the failed pub acquisitions left people wondering, "What *is* the strategy at Whitbread?" Stock price plummeted and Whitbread fell out of the FTSE 100.

The company thought long and hard about this issue, and Thomas wondered if he had been clear enough or done enough to build an organization that could sustain the growth he thought was possible. In October 2000, he announced the "Future Whitbread" strategy, clarifying that the organization would focus on "lodging, eating out, and active leisure," areas that were forecasted to grow more than 30% between 2001 and 2006. His group executive team had decided that brewing could no longer be its core business and Whitbread sold the beer operations, representing almost half of the workforce, in 2000.

At this time, Whitbread was best described as a multibrand, multidivisional organization. Reporting to the CEO were the managing directors of the different brands and divisions (e.g., hotels, restaurants, health clubs) and corporate functional heads (e.g., finance, human resources, legal counsel). To encourage organic growth and operational efficiency, traditional hallmarks of the Whitbread organization, each division had a full complement of functions reporting directly to the managing directors, and only "dotted line" responsibility to the corporate function. Corporate functions were expected to formulate and implement cross-business initiatives that would bring synergies to the brands and make Whitbread more than the sum of its parts. In reality, the managing directors acted like and were referred to as "barons." There was little room for collaboration. Career paths and loyalty were clearly associated with a particular division; there were few stories of cross-division transfers. As a result, Whitbread found it difficult to balance brand building and brand identity with corporate identity and coordination, and a "nice" culture emerged. Reflecting to some extent the larger British culture, there was little confronting of people or holding them accountable for results. This description applied well to Thomas. He was seen generally as easy and good to work for.

The "Future Whitbread" strategy challenged this organization. It clearly implied that correct executive behavior involved putting shareholders ahead of management empire building, shifted the organization from an operations-driven to a brand-driven orientation, and would hold executives more accountable for their performance. To this last point, Thomas announced increased transparency of Whitbread's results to the financial community. No longer could a managing director hide from scrutiny in results that were buried in corporate statements.

To back up these commitments, Thomas held a series of workshops with his executive team. The hotel group managing director had read Collins' *Good to Great* and suggested it would be good basis for discussions about how to change and manage Whitbread. Initial meetings among the executive team, facilitated by OD practitioners, were later expanded to include the top 40 managers. They discussed and debated their core purpose and values, the things the organization was passionate about, the economic engine of the corporation, and how success should be measured. At the end of the process, the hotel group managing director thought it would be important to get feedback from the rest of the organization: "What do other people at Whitbread think of our work?"

Despite some resistance from the executives, including Thomas himself, the idea was eventually endorsed. To get the process started, Thomas and Whitbread's corporate human resources officer drafted a "statement of strategic and organizational intent." It was a two-page summary of the Good to Great sessions and listed out Whitbread's intended core and enduring purpose, passions, ambitions, values, measures, and economic engine. The group executive team also commissioned a "strategic fitness" task force that consisted of eight upper level managers. With the OD consultant's support, the task force's mandate was to interview 100 managers from different functions, businesses, and levels around three questions: "What do you think of the statement of strategic intent?" and "What are the organizational strengths and weaknesses with respect to implementing this intent?"

Prior to a two-day meeting of Thomas' group executive team, the task force members gathered to prepare their feedback and presentation. The members were generally struck by the level of disappointment in the data. Most managers expressed a great amount of loyalty to the organization but were concerned that it was not achieving everything that it could. The task force members tried to figure out how to convey that feeling. Ultimately, they decided to present the data along five themes:

- **Why Whitbread?** Managers were confused about the overall purpose of the organization. Why, for example, were they better off as one organization rather than independent businesses? What was the role of the corporate functions? Why were executives not pursuing obvious synergies, such as selling Costa Coffee in Whitbread hotels or locating Whitbread health clubs in Whitbread hotels?
- **Brand management.** If Whitbread was going to focus on brands, then a lot of attention needed to be paid to building brand management skills and processes into the organization.
- **Culture.** The task force members captured this category by describing Whitbread's culture as "institutionalized underperformance."
- **Leadership.** The interviews suggested that many people talked about the "New Whitbread, Old Executives." Nearly every executive had been with the company more than ten years. To a person, and despite large and obvious mistakes, they were never held accountable. They received a sizeable bonus, visibly announced every year in the annual report. Moreover, the team noted consistent agreement among the interviewees that the group executive team did not work well together, did not speak with one voice, and could not articulate a consistent corporate direction.
- **Statement of intent.** The overall feeling was that the statement, as written, was "motherhood and apple pie."

The task force presented its findings to the group executive team. Although anxious about the content of the feedback, the task force described the meeting as direct, professional, and businesslike. The day after the feedback, the group executive team discussed and reflected on the data, discussed and debated the organization's business and corporate strategy, and addressed the role of the corporate center in response to the feedback about "Why Whitbread."

In the weeks following the feedback meeting, Thomas and the human resources officer, supported by input from other members of the group executive team, developed an action plan to address the feedback. They also called the task force back to a meeting to present their plan.

During the combined group executive/task force meeting, Thomas presented the plan. Following the presentation, the group executives left and the task force prepared a response. The task force members believed that the executives had not heard them and failed to grasp the depth of the problems facing the organization. They debated whether it was because the executives weren't listening, whether they had sugarcoated the information, and what they were going to do about it. They decided to confront the very culture they were trying to change.

When the two groups reconvened, the task force made a short but powerful statement. After restating the themes of their findings, they made several bold recommendations for inclusion in the action plan, including reorganization of the divisions into brands with a direct reporting relationship to the CEO, a radical overhaul of the leadership group by identifying who was "on the bus" and who wasn't, and the need to invest in the capabilities required to build and manage brands. The task force went so far as to say they wondered whether the group executives were the able to lead the change.

Although the group executive response was polite at the time, Thomas later reflected what was obvious to everyone: The plan and the strategic intent it was built on was "crap." The task force was clearly saying that they were not being bold and not taking risks. It was clear that just being more transparent to the financial market was not leadership.

Thomas and his group executive team were finally feeling the urgency and met numerous times to develop a new plan. Eventually dubbed the "11-point plan," it spelled out specific initiatives and the executive who would be responsible and accountable for its execution. The 11-point plan included significant commitments to restructuring the organization, in particular the restaurant and hotel divisions; the development of a "master class" in brand management and the commitment to build brand skills; and a personal development program for the top 100 leaders in the organization.

The 11-point plan received a positive response from the task force and was presented to the organization. By 2004, much of the 11-point plan had been implemented. An outside firm had implemented a rigorous personal development program and helped the organization manage a radical change in its talent management policies. Following the implementation of the program, it was announced that the top 100 managers were to be "owned" by the CEO and not the brands. Their development and assignments were to be handled by the group executive team. Similarly, the brand management capability building initiatives had begun. Finally, there was some movement in reorganizing the brands, but the process was less than complete. The hotel division successfully split into two groups with each director reporting to the president. The restaurant division, however, had not reorganized even though the managing director was seen as a potential successor to Thomas. Eventually, the hotel managing director was named CEO.

These demands strongly suggest the need for a self-design process. In contrast, more traditional and programmed approaches to large-scale change emphasize rigid timelines, see change as a periodic event, and rely on consulting expertise. That is, traditional change management practices are often guided by the values of control and certainty and do not emphasize the OD values of learning and participation. The self-design process suggests that the way the organization thinks about and prepares for change determines, to a large extent, whether the change will be implemented expediently and successfully.

19-2b Application Stages

The self-design intervention focuses on all features of the organization (for example, structure, human resources practices, and work design) and designs them to support the strategy. It is a dynamic and an iterative process aimed at providing organizations with the built-in capacity to change and redesign themselves continually as the circumstances demand. The approach promotes organizational learning among multiple stakeholders at all levels of the firm, providing them with the knowledge and skills needed to continuously change and improve the organization.

FIGURE 19.2

The Self-Design Change Process

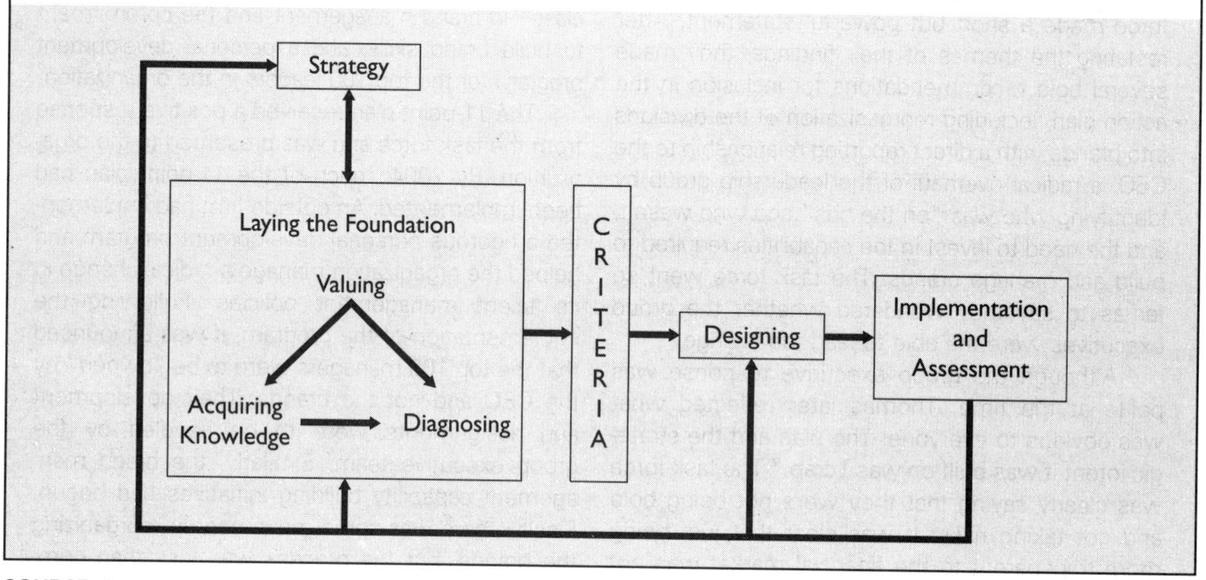

SOURCE: Adapted from Mohrman and Cummings, 1989.

Figure 19.2 outlines the self-design approach. In the typical case, a "design team" (Chapter 10, microcosm groups) guides the intervention. It can be the top management team or a cross-functional or cross-level group made up of formal and informal leaders, high-potential managers, or selected employees and staff. Experience suggests that if the top management team is not the design team, then at least one to two members from the top management team should be on the design team, represent senior management's perspectives, and serve as liaisons between the two groups.

Although the process is described in five stages, in practice the stages merge and interact iteratively over time. Each stage is described below:

1. **Clarifying the strategy.** This initial stage involves making the organization's strategy clear. Most organizations have a strategy but often do not share or write it in ways that are clear to members. This stage clarifies the organization's strategic objectives, translates the strategy into descriptions of breadth, aggressiveness, and differentiation, and explains how they are changing. The self-design process assumes that an unclear strategy will result in an unfocused organization design. As one OD practitioner put it, "if the strategy is unclear, then any organization design will work."
2. **Laying the foundation.** This stage provides the design team with the basic knowledge and information needed to get large-scale change started. It involves three kinds of activities. The first activity involves *valuing*—determining the beliefs and values that will guide the change process. These values represent those performance outcomes and organizational conditions that will be needed to implement the strategy. They are typically written in a values statement that is discussed and negotiated among multiple stakeholders at all levels of the organization. For example, the valuing process might result in statements that emphasize "delivering value to the customer," "employee engagement," or "maintaining gross margins."

The second activity is *acquiring knowledge* about how organizations function, about organizing principles for achieving high performance, and about the self-design process. This information is generally gained through reading relevant material, attending in-house workshops, and visiting other organizations with a history of successful continuous change. This learning typically starts with senior executives or with the design team but can cascade to lower organizational levels as the change process unfolds. The third activity is *diagnosing* the current organization to determine what needs to be changed to enact the strategy and values. The design team generally assesses the different features of the organization's design, describes the organization's culture, and draws linkages to the current levels of performance. They look for incongruities between its functioning and its valued performances and conditions.

3. **Creating design criteria.** In this stage, the design team develops the principles and standards that will guide the new organization design. While the valuing process in the laying the foundation stage specifies what is important to the organization, the design criteria are more concrete. They describe any new organization capabilities required by the strategy, what the new organization will need to be able to do to support the strategy, and how the organization is expected to operate. Organization design criteria do not specify particular features or solutions, however. Design criteria would not specify that the organization needed to implement a matrix structure or suggest that 5% of the workforce needed to be laid off. Rather, design criteria are action oriented, specific and measureable, future oriented, and linked to creating a strategic advantage. Examples of design criteria include the following:
   - Facilitate fast reaction to market changes.
   - Increase coordination across the organization around key customers.
   - Move decision making out to those interfacing with customers.
   - Enable and encourage process efficiencies and repeatable processes.
   - Optimize resource leverage and utilization—people and systems.
   - Eliminate redundant work.

   Design criteria are an important milestone in the self-design process. As the process moves to the designing stage, design criteria are an effective and objective standard for evaluating alternative design options. Moreover, clearly stated and agreed to design criteria reduce the likelihood of covert political processes derailing the change.
4. **Designing**. In this fourth stage of self-design, the design team generates alternative organization designs and innovations to reflect the strategy, values, and design criteria. Members of the design team describe the work design, structures, HR practices, and management processes that will support the strategy. This process usually starts with a broad outline of how the organization should be designed at the highest level and how the design components should fit together. Senior executives responsible for the overall direction of the organization typically participate in creating this overarching design.

   Only the broad parameters of the new organization are specified. This enables the design team to assess the extent to which alternative designs meet the strategy and design criteria, to test the design criteria for completeness, and to build commitment to a design approach before getting into specifics. This also allows other groups and levels in the organization to detail and tailor the design according to local conditions. This process recognizes that designs need to be refined and modified as they are implemented throughout the firm.

   Next, the design process addresses the specific details of the organization design components, which involve generating alternatives and making specific design choices. A broader set of organizational members often participates in these decisions, relying on its own as well as experts' experience and know-how, knowledge of best practices, and information gained from visits to other organizations willing to share design experience. This stage results in an overall design for the organization, detailed designs for the components, and preliminary implementation plans for how everything will fit together.

5. **Implementing and assessing**. This last stage involves making the new design happen by putting into place the new structures, practices, and systems. It draws heavily on the methods for leading and managing change discussed in Chapter 8 and applies them to the entire organization or subunit, and not just limited parts. It also includes an ongoing cycle of action learning: changing structures and behaviors, assessing progress, and making necessary modifications. Information about how well implementation is progressing and how well the new organizational design is working is collected and used to clarify design and implementation issues and to make necessary adjustments. This learning process continues not only during implementation but also indefinitely as members periodically assess and improve the design and alter it to fit changing conditions. The feedback loops shown in Figure 19.2 suggest that the implementing and assessing activities may lead back to affect subsequent activities of designing, diagnosing, valuing, and acquiring knowledge. This iterative sequence of activities provides organizations with the capacity to transform and improve continually.

The self-design intervention has been applied successfully to whole organizations or major subunits in a wide variety of situations. Experience suggests that organizations may not always work through the process as described above but that attending to all of the parts and stages increases the effectiveness of the change and the quality of the learning. The self-design approach is quite flexible and can be used in both evolutionary and revolutionary change contexts. For example, the process can be accelerated with the use of large-group interventions at any stage of the process or by dedicating a design team to work on the project full time. Application 19.2 describes how Healthways used the self-design process to design and implement a new structure.

19-3 Learning Organizations

The third continuous change intervention is aimed at helping organizations develop and use knowledge to change and improve themselves constantly. Like self-design, organization learning (OL) enhances an organization's capability to acquire and develop new knowledge. It differs from self-design in its attention to the cognitive aspects of learning and how members can become more effective learners. Whereas self-design changes behaviors by changing organization design, OL focuses on changing behaviors by changing the way people solve problems and address opportunities.

OL is crucial in today's complex, rapidly changing environments. It can be a source of strategic renewal, and it can enable organizations to acquire and apply knowledge more quickly and effectively than competitors, thus establishing a potentially long term competitive advantage.[21] Moreover, when learning and knowledge are translated into new products and services, they can become a key source of wealth creation for organizations.[22] OL remains one of the most widespread interventions in OD. It is the focus of an expanding body of research and practice, and has been applied in such diverse firms as McKinsey, L.L. Bean, Saudi Aramco, Shell, the Canadian Broadcasting Corporation, Wells Fargo, Telefonica, Boeing, Microsoft, and the U.S. Army.

application 19.2

SELF-DESIGN AT HEALTHWAYS CORPORATION

The senior leaders at Healthways (HMC) clearly sensed a need to look at the organization's design in the context of the expected rapid growth of its health plan business. HMC had identified an important and growing niche (proactive disease management) in the growing health care industry. They had crafted an impressive strategy but recognized that the current structure was insufficient to the task.

A university-based OD practitioner initially recommended a task force and a series of workshops to choose an appropriate organization design for the company. The task force and workshop idea was guided by a self-design philosophy. The organization knew its structure was inadequate and that it needed a new way of operating, but it did not have a broad range of skills or experience in operating a large organization. This led the OD practitioner to believe that the self-design model would be the best approach. As the organization considered what structure to implement, it also needed to learn and build the capacity to change itself.

Three organization design and development (ODD) task forces were guided by the self-design strategy. The first ODD task force was dedicated to laying the foundation; their output was the recommendation to pursue a process-based structure. The second ODD task force was responsible for designing; they were charged with putting "meat on the bones" of the approved structure. The third ODD task force began implementing the new design as well as developing more sophisticated long-term implementation templates.

"Laying the foundation" activities dominated the first ODD task force. Members of the task force, representing most of the organization's key functional areas, read extensively on organization design, interviewed other organizations who had adopted different structures, and studied alternative change processes. As a result of the knowledge acquired through this process, the task force became aware that the organization lacked a clear vision and "big hairy audacious goal" (BHAG) that most change management frameworks listed as a key success factor. This insight led the task force to instigate a vision and strategy effort to clarify the organization's purpose, to forecast revenues, and to understand the organization's strategic intent. Within the context of a clearer strategy, the task force was able to examine the pros and cons of alternative structures and to ground their recommendation in business terms. The first ODD task force also engaged in diagnostic activities. This process allowed the group to better understand the current organization's strengths and weaknesses, to test the initial draft of the BHAG, to alert the organization to the task force's activities, and to ensure that the new organization aligned with the organization's culture. Finally, the task force spent a considerable amount of time discussing and debating the values that would guide the new organization. A culture initiative was proceeding concomitantly with the ODD task force and the outputs of their work were an important input to these discussions.

The first ODD task force used the knowledge and information generated in the laying-the-foundation phase to design three alternative structures that they believed would meet the needs of the future organization. Each of the alternative structures was formalized with high-level charts, pros and cons, and a business case rationale. The group discussed the structures and debated their relative strengths and weaknesses in the context of the diagnostic information, values, and strategy of the organization. The design phase concluded with a recommendation to senior management to adopt the process-based structure. The recommendation of the first ODD task force was debated and approved by members of HMC's senior management team, several of whom had been on the task force. The senior team recommended that another task force be created to expand on the recommended structure.

Design phase activities dominated the second ODD task force. In addition to a few original task force members, the second task force consisted of organization members representing a broader range of functions and levels in the organization. This ensured that knowledge and understanding of the process-based structure generated in the first task force would be passed along to a larger set of managers in the organization. More importantly, the second task force was expected to model the type of cross-functional team that would be the centerpiece of the new structure. As a result, the laying-the-foundation phase of the second task force included acquiring knowledge about cross-functional and self-managed teams and continuous improvement processes. The team reviewed the rationale for the process-based structure and discussed the values guiding the structural choice. However, the primary work of the second ODD task force was to add detail to each of the core processes, conceptualize and define the corporate office organization, create design principles to aid managers in understanding why functions and processes were assigned in certain ways, create financial statements reflecting expected operating expenses in the new design, and create additional timelines and implementation templates to guide execution of the new structure. The second task force ended with a presentation of roles, reporting relationships, metrics, and control and reward mechanisms to the senior management team.

The organization applied what they learned from the first two task forces as they debated how to implement the structure. That is, both groups had developed important insights about the operation of a process-based organization and recommended that the next group to manage the change process had to be the senior management team itself. As a result, the COO appointed the senior management team to be the third ODD task force. The primary focus of this group would be implementation, the third phase of the self-design strategy. Despite several senior managers' participation on the first two task forces, the entire senior management team was not intimately familiar with the logic and operation of the process-based organization, nor had this group operated as a cross-functional team. By having the COO's direct reports operate as a cross-functional team, ownership for the new structure would be placed squarely on the shoulders of those who would guide its implementation and an important symbol of the new organization structure would be established. Early in the life of the third task force, and based on its recommendation, the COO and CEO renamed and replaced the old senior management team with the executive leadership group structure that would be responsible for operating the new organization. In addition, several key process owners were named to begin the implementation. The third ODD task force also developed more detailed implementation guidelines, including a variety of measures to monitor the success of the structure's implementation and methods to keep the organization's focus on meeting customer needs during the transition.

The logic of the self-design intervention drove the development and implementation of the process-based structure at HMC. It produced important insights and changes in the way managers at the organization viewed its strategy, culture, and operations. Most importantly, the process itself built capacity and knowledge into the system. A variety of managers in different organizational functions and levels gained a deeper understanding of the structure's rationale and valuable experience working on cross-functional teams. This knowledge and experience served the organization well as it implemented the process-based structure.

19-3a Conceptual Framework

Like many new interventions in OD, there is some ambiguity about the concepts underlying OL.[23] For example, practitioners often use the term "organization learning" synonymously with "knowledge management" to describe the broad set of activities through which organizations learn and organize knowledge. Other times, they are used separately to emphasize different aspects of learning and managing knowledge. This confusion derives in part from the different disciplines and applications traditionally associated with OL and knowledge management.[24]

OL interventions emphasize the organizational structures and social processes that enable organization members and teams to learn and to share knowledge. They draw heavily on the social sciences for conceptual grounding and on OD interventions, such as team building, structural design, and employee involvement, for practical guidance. In organizations, OL change processes are typically associated with the human resources function and may be assigned to a special leadership role, such as chief learning officer.

Knowledge management, on the other hand, focuses on the tools and techniques that enable organizations to collect, organize, and translate information into useful knowledge. They are rooted conceptually in the information and computer sciences and, in practice, emphasize electronic forms of knowledge storage and transmission, such as intranets, data warehousing, and knowledge repositories. As a result, knowledge management applications often are located in the information systems function, may be under the direction of a chief information or technology officer, and are rightly seen as a part of the management processes component of organization design. Nevertheless, knowledge management is an important part of OL.

There is also confusion about the concept of organization learning itself, about whether it is an individual- or organization-level process. Some researchers and practitioners describe OL as individual learning that occurs within an organization context; thus, it is the aggregate of individual learning processes occurring within an organization.[25] Others characterize it in terms of organization processes and structures; they emphasize how learning is embedded in structures, routines, policies, and organization cultures.[26] Snyder has proposed an integration of the two perspectives that treats organization learning as a relative concept.[27] Individuals do learn in organizations but that learning may or may not contribute to OL. Learning is organizational to the extent that

- It is done to achieve organization purposes.
- It is shared or distributed among members of the organization.
- Learning outcomes are embedded in the organization's systems, structures, and culture.

To the extent that these criteria are met, organization learning is distinct from individual learning. It is possible for individual members to learn while the organization does not. For example, a member may learn to serve the customer better without ever sharing such learning with other members. Conversely, it is possible for the organization to learn without individual members learning. Improvements in equipment design or work procedures, for example, reflect OL, even if these changes are not understood by individual members. Moreover, because OL serves the organization's purposes and is embedded in its structures, it stays with the organization, even if members leave.

A key premise underlying much of the literature on OL is that such interventions will lead to higher organization performance, and there is some evidence to support that view.[28] However, the mechanisms through which OL and knowledge management translate into performance improvements are rarely identified or explained. Successfully applying OD interventions in organizations requires a better understanding of those mechanisms.

Based on existing research and practice, Figure 19.3 provides an integrative framework for understanding OL and knowledge management interventions,[29] summarizing the elements of these change processes and showing how they combine to affect organization performance. This framework suggests that specific organization characteristics, such as structure and human resources systems, influence how well organization learning

FIGURE 19.3

How Organization Learning Affects Performance

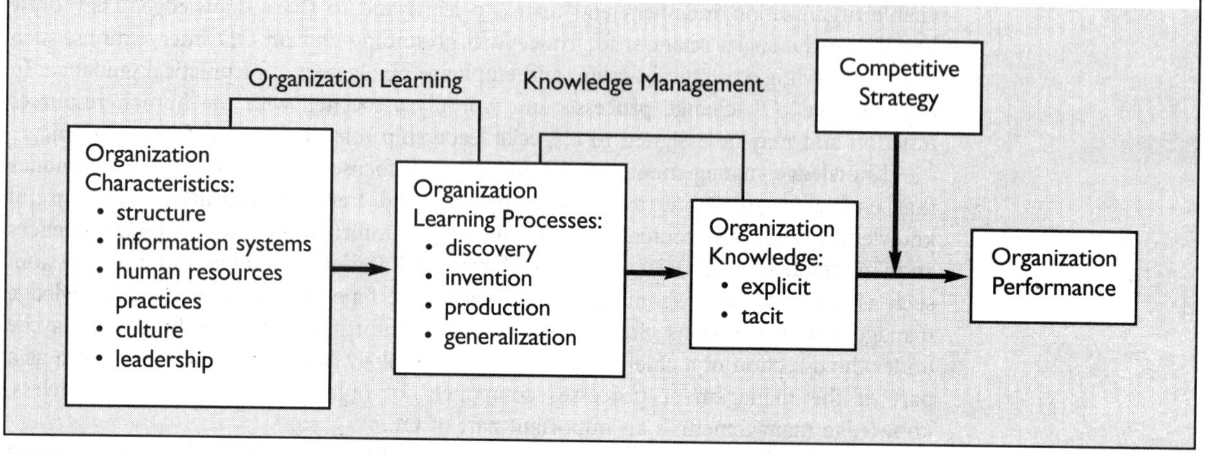

SOURCE: Reprinted with permission of Sage Publications Ltd. From W. Snyder and T. Cummings, "Organization Learning Disorders: Conceptual Model and Intervention Hypotheses," *Human Relations* 51 (1998): 873–95. © The Tavistock Institute, 1998.

processes are carried out. These learning processes affect the amount and kind of knowledge that an organization possesses; that knowledge, in turn, directly influences performance outcomes, such as product quality and customer service. As depicted in Figure 19.3, the linkage between organization knowledge and performance depends on the organization's competitive strategy. Organization knowledge will lead to high performance to the extent that it is both relevant and applied effectively to the strategy. For example, customer-driven organizations require timely and relevant information about customer needs. Their success relies heavily on members having that knowledge and applying it effectively in their work with customers.

Figure 19.3 also shows how OL and knowledge management are interrelated. OL interventions address how organizations can be designed to promote effective learning processes, and how those learning processes themselves can be improved. Knowledge management practices operate on the outcomes of learning processes; on how strategically relevant knowledge can be effectively organized and used throughout the organization. Each of the key elements of OL—organization characteristics and organization learning processes—are described below along with the interventions typically associated with them.

19-3b Organization Learning Interventions

As shown in Figure 19.3, OL interventions consist of change programs designed to alter organization design features and OL processes. Changes in organization design are intended to create a learning organization that promotes effective OL processes. In turn, these processes can affect the organization's knowledge management and performance.

Learning Organizations The designs of most traditional organizations are ineffective at learning and may even intensify errors. Referred to as *Model I learning*, it includes structures and management processes as well as values and norms that emphasize unilateral control of environments and tasks, and protection of oneself and others from information that may be hurtful.[30] These structures and norms result in a variety of defensive routines that inhibit learning, such as withholding information and feelings, competition and rivalry, and little public testing of norms and the assumptions underlying them. Model I is limited to learning that improves the status quo.

A more effective approach to learning, called *Model II learning*, is based on values promoting valid information, free and informed choice, internal commitment and ownership to courses of action, and continuous improvement of learning processes.[31] These values provide the underlying social support needed for successful learning. They result in an organization characterized by minimal defensiveness, greater openness to information and feedback, personal mastery and collaboration with others, and public testing of norms. Model II learning enables organizations to significantly change themselves and to improve the learning process itself. It encourages members to acquire, process, and share information, to nurture innovation and provide the freedom to try new things, and to risk failure and learn from mistakes.

OL practitioners have linked the characteristics of Model II learning to the features of organization design. The "learning organization" is "skilled at creating, acquiring, interpreting, transferring, and retaining knowledge, and at purposefully modifying its behavior to reflect new knowledge and insights."[32] Much of the literature on the learning organization is prescriptive and proposes how organizations should be designed and managed to promote effective learning. Although relatively little systematic research supports these premises, there is growing consensus among researchers and practitioners about specific organizational features that characterize the learning organization.[33] These qualities are mutually reinforcing and fall into the four categories of organization design:

- **Structure**. Organization structures emphasize teamwork, fewer layers, strong lateral relations, and networking across organizational boundaries both internal and external to the firm.
- **Work design**. Learning organizations tend to favor enriched jobs and self-managed teams. These work designs support the sharing of information and the continuous development of new skills, knowledge, and competencies.
- **Human resources practices**. Recruitment practices in learning organizations favor people with high needs for achievement, expectations for change, and relative comfort with ambiguity. Performance appraisal, rewards, and training are designed to account for long-term performance and knowledge development; they reinforce the acquisition and sharing of new skills and knowledge. Finally, like most large-scale change interventions, the leaders of learning organizations must actively model the openness, risk taking, and reflection necessary for learning. They must communicate a compelling vision of the learning organization and provide the empathy, support, and personal advocacy needed to lead others in that direction.
- **Management processes**. Organization learning involves gathering and processing information, and consequently, the information systems of learning organizations provide an infrastructure for OL. These systems facilitate rapid acquisition, processing, and sharing of rich, complex information and enable people to manage knowledge for competitive advantage. Together, these organization design features promote information sharing, involvement in decision making, systems thinking, and empowerment.

Learning organizations generally are designed and implemented using organization design interventions like those described in Chapter 18. OD practitioners help members diagnose how well their organization's current design promotes learning. Then, necessary changes are made to bring the organization's design components more in line with those just described.

Organization Learning Processes Figure 19.3 suggests that OL processes consist of four interrelated activities: discovery, invention, production, and generalization.[34] Learning starts with *discovery* when errors or gaps between desired and actual conditions are detected. For example, sales managers may discover that revenues are falling below projected levels and set out to solve the problem. *Invention* is aimed at devising solutions to close the gap between desired and current conditions; it includes diagnosing the causes of the gap and creating appropriate solutions to reduce it. The sales managers may learn that poor advertising is contributing to the revenue problem and may devise a new campaign to improve sales. *Production* processes involve implementing solutions, and *generalization* includes drawing conclusions about the effects of the solutions and extending that knowledge to other relevant situations. For instance, if the new advertising program is implemented and successful, the managers might use variations of it with other product lines. Thus, these four learning processes enable members to generate the knowledge necessary to change and improve the organization.

Organizations can apply the learning processes described above to three types of learning.[35] First, *single-loop learning* or *adaptive learning* is focused on improving the status quo. Consistent with Model I learning, it is the most prevalent learning process in organizations and enables members to reduce errors or gaps between desired and existing conditions. It can produce incremental change in how organizations function. The sales managers described above engaged in single-loop learning when they looked for ways to reduce the difference between current and desired levels of sales.

Second, *double-loop learning* or *generative learning* is aimed at changing the status quo. More in line with Model II learning, it operates at a more abstract level than single-loop learning because members learn how to change the existing assumptions and conditions within which single-loop learning operates. This level of learning can lead to transformational change, where the status quo itself is radically altered. For example, the sales managers may learn that sales projections are based on faulty assumptions and models about future market conditions. This knowledge may result in an entirely new conception of future markets, with corresponding changes in sales projections and product development plans. It may lead the managers to drop some products that had previously appeared promising, develop new ones that were not considered before, and alter advertising and promotional campaigns to fit the new conditions.

The third type of learning is called *deutero-learning*, which involves learning how to learn. It is the highest form of Model II learning; it is directed at the learning process itself and seeks to improve how organizations perform single- and double-loop learning. For example, the sales managers might periodically examine how well they perform the processes of discovery, invention, production, and generalization. This could lead to improvements and efficiencies in how learning is conducted throughout the organization. Most OL interventions are intended to initiate this type of learning.

OD practitioners have developed interventions specifically for organization learning processes. In describing these change strategies, we draw heavily on the work of Argyris and Schön and of Senge and his colleagues because it is the most developed and articulated work in OL practice.[36]

From this perspective, organization learning is not concerned with the organization as a static entity but as an active process of sense making and organizing. Based on the interpretive model of change (Chapter 2), members socially construct the organization as they continually act and interact with each other and learn from those actions how to organize themselves for productive achievement. This active learning process enables members to develop, test, and modify mental models or maps of organizational reality. Called *theories in use*, these cognitive maps inform member behavior and organizing.[37] They guide how members make decisions, perform work, and organize themselves. Unfortunately, members' theories in use can be faulty, resulting in ineffective behaviors and organizing efforts. They can be too narrow and fail to account for important aspects of the environment; they can include erroneous assumptions that lead to unexpected negative consequences. Effective OL can help members resolve these problems. It can provide them with the skills and tools to detect and correct errors in their mental maps, and thus promote more effective organizing efforts.

OL interventions help organization members change from Model I to Model II learning and become more capable of single-loop learning, double-loop learning, and deutero-learning. Like all learning, this change approach includes discovery, invention, production, and generalization processes. Although the application phases are described linearly below, in practice they form a recurrent cycle of four overlapping learning activities:

1. **Discover theories in use and their consequences.** This first step involves uncovering members' mental models or theories in use and the consequences that follow from behaving and organizing according to them. Depending on the size of the client system, this may involve the executive team, a microcosm group that includes representatives from the system, or all members through a large-group intervention (Chapter 10).

   OL practitioners have developed a variety of techniques to help members identify their theories in use. Similar to the deep assumptions of organization culture, these theories generally are taken for granted and rarely examined; members need to generate and analyze data to infer the theories' underlying assumptions. One approach is called *dialogue*, a variant of the human process interventions described in Chapter 10.[38] It involves members in exchanges about how they currently address problems, make decisions, and interact with each other and relevant stakeholders, such as suppliers, customers, and competitors. By asking members to suspend assumptions about what is "right," OD practitioners encourage participants to inquire into their own and others' ways of thinking, to advocate for certain beliefs, and to reflect on the assumptions that lead to those beliefs. Dialogue can result in a clearer understanding of existing theories in use and their behavioral consequences and enable members to uncover faulty assumptions that lead to ineffective behaviors and organizing efforts.

   A second method of identifying theories in use involves the application of *systems thinking.*[39] It is a set of concepts and tools for detecting subtle but powerful structures that underlie complex situations. Learning to see such structures can help members understand previously unknown forces operating in the organization and their behavioral consequences.[40] This information is essential for developing effective theories for organizing, particularly in today's complex, changing world. OL practitioners typically interview members about recurrent problems in the organization, why they are occurring, actions that are taken to resolve them, and outcomes of those behaviors. Based on this information, a map is constructed showing interrelationships among the values underlying theories in use, the action strategies that follow from them, and the results of those actions. Such information is fed back to members so that they can test the validity of the map, assess the effectiveness of their theories in use, and identify factors that contribute to functional and dysfunctional learning in the organization.[41] Systems thinking helps members make radical shifts in their view of the world: from seeing parts to seeing wholes; from seeing linear cause–effect chains to seeing interrelationships; and from seeing static entities to seeing processes of change.

A third technique for identifying theories in use and revealing assumptions is called the *left-hand, right-hand column*.[42] It starts with a member selecting a specific situation where he or she was interacting with others in a way that produced ineffective results. The situation is described in the form of a screenplay or movie script and is written on the right side of a page. For instance, the story might begin with a statement such as, "I told Joyce that I was offering her a special assignment." Then the rest of the conversation would be written down: "Joyce said to me that she did not want to take the assignment because her workload was too heavy," and "I responded that it was a real chance to get some extra and useful skills," and so on. After the example is finished, the left-hand side of the page is used to write down what he or she was thinking but not saying at each phase of the exchange. For example, "When I told Joyce about the assignment, what I was really thinking is that she is always taking long lunch breaks and seems overly concerned with busy work. I thought she should help out the group by pitching in more." "When Joyce said she didn't want to take the assignment because her workload is too heavy, that just proved my suspicion." This simple yet powerful exercise reveals hidden assumptions that guide behavior and can make members aware of how erroneous or untested assumptions can undermine work relationships.

A fourth method that helps members discover their mental models and theories in use is called the *ladder of inference*, as shown in Figure 19.4.[43] It is a tool that aids in understanding how concrete experiences are connected to the assumptions and beliefs that guide behavior. The ladder shows vividly how members' theories in use can be faulty and lead to ineffective actions. People may draw invalid conclusions from limited experience; their cultural and personal biases may distort meaning attributed to selected data. The ladder of inference can help members understand why their theories in use may be invalid and why their behaviors and organizing efforts are ineffective. Members can start with descriptions of actions that are not producing intended results and then work back down the ladder to discover the reasons underlying those ineffective behaviors. For example, a service technician might withhold from management valuable yet negative customer feedback about product quality, resulting in eventual loss of business. Backing down the ladder, the technician could discover an untested belief that upper management does not react favorably to negative information and may even "shoot the messenger." This belief may have resulted from assumptions and conclusions that the technician drew from observing periodic layoffs and from hearing widespread rumors that the company is out to get troublemakers and people who speak up too much. The ladder of inference can help members understand the underlying reasons for their behaviors and help them confront the possibility that erroneous assumptions are contributing to ineffective actions.

2. **Invent and produce more effective theories in use**. Based on what is discovered in the first step of the change process, members invent and produce theories in use that lead to more effective actions and that are more closely aligned with Model II learning. Many of the interventions described in this book can help to support more effective learning capabilities. Human resource management interventions—performance appraisal, reward systems, and career planning and development—can reinforce members' motivation to gain new skills and knowledge. Technostructural interventions, such as process-based and network structures, self-managing work

FIGURE 19.4

The Ladder of Inference

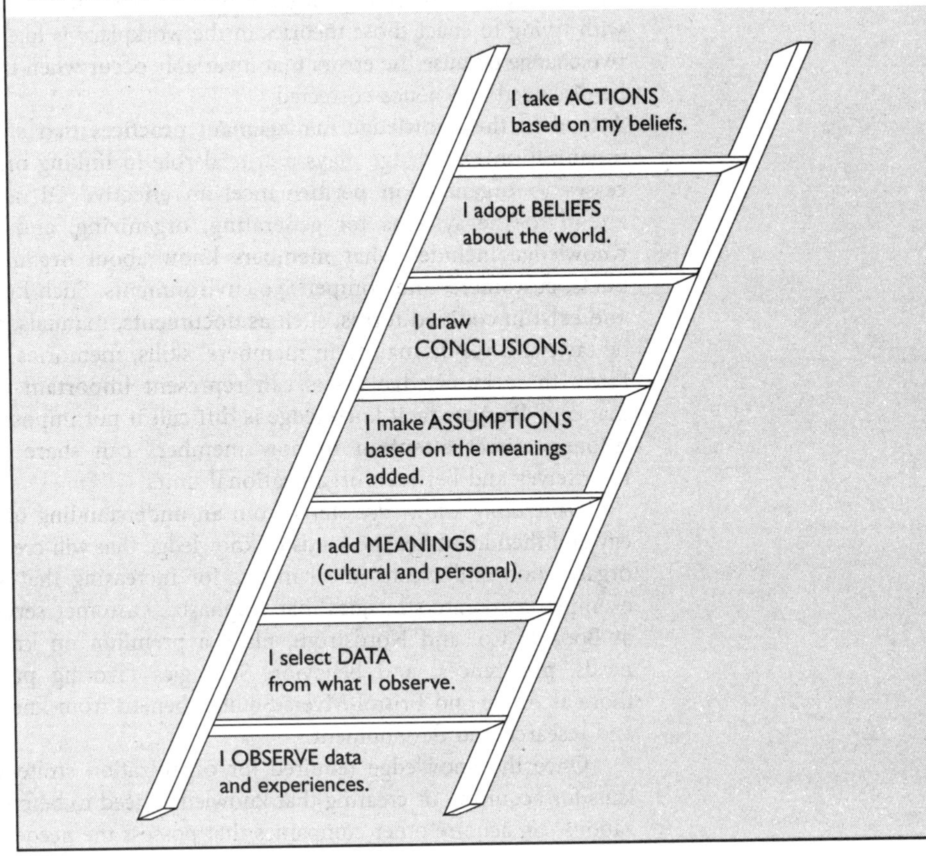

teams, and reengineering, can provide the kinds of lateral linkages and teamwork needed to process, develop, and share diverse information and knowledge. Human process changes, including team building, search conferences, and intergroup relations interventions, can help members develop the kinds of healthy interpersonal relationships that underlie effective OL. Strategic interventions, such as dynamic strategy making and alliances, can help organizations gain knowledge about their environments and develop values and norms that promote OL.

Making changes in organization learning processes involves double-loop learning as members try to create and enact new theories in use. In essence, members learn by doing; they learn from their invention and production actions how to invent and produce more effective theories in use. As might be expected, learning how to change theories in use can be extremely difficult. There is a strong tendency for members to revert to habitual behaviors and modes of learning. They may have trouble breaking out of existing mindsets and seeing new realities and possibilities.

OD practitioners can help members apply the values underlying Model II learning—valid information, free choice, and internal commitment—to question their experience of trying to behave more consistently with Model II.[44] They can encourage members to confront and talk openly about how habitual actions and learning methods prevent them from creating and enacting more effective theories.

Once these barriers to change are discussed openly, members typically discover that they are changeable. This shared insight often leads to the invention of more effective theories for behaving, organizing, and learning. Subsequent experimentation with trying to enact those theories in the workplace is likely to produce more effective change because the errors that invariably occur when trying new things now can be discussed and hence corrected.

3. **Attend to the knowledge management practices that support learning**. Because organization knowledge plays a crucial role in linking organization learning processes to organization performance, an effective OL application process must attend to the systems for generating, organizing, and distributing knowledge. Knowledge includes what members know about organizational processes, products, customers, and competitive environments. Such knowledge may be explicit and exist in codified forms, such as documents, manuals, and databases, or it may be tacit and reside mainly in members' skills, memories, and intuitions.[45] In any form, these knowledge assets can represent important contributions to performance.[46] Because tacit knowledge is difficult if not impossible to codify, OD practitioners direct attention to how members can share such knowledge among themselves and between organizational units.

   Generating knowledge starts from an understanding of the organization's strategy and then identifies the kinds of knowledge that will create the most value for the organization and creates mechanisms for increasing that stock of knowledge. For example, corporate strategies that emphasize customer service, such as those found at Booz & Co. and Nordstrom, place a premium on knowledge about customer needs, preferences, and behavior. Strategies favoring product development, like those at Apple and Bristol-Myers-Squibb, benefit from knowledge about technology and research and development.

   Once the knowledge required for organization strategy is identified, mechanisms for acquiring or creating that knowledge need to be created. Externally, organizations can acquire other companies that possess the needed knowledge, or they can rent it from knowledge sources, such as consultants and university researchers.[47] Internally, organizations can facilitate *communities of practice*—informal networks among employees performing similar work to share expertise and to solve problems together.[48] They can also create more formal groups for knowledge generation, such as R&D departments, corporate universities, and centers of excellence. Organizations can bring together people with different skills, ideas, and values to generate new products or services.

   Organizing knowledge involves putting it into a form that organizational members can use readily. Two broad strategies for organizing knowledge include codification and personalization.[49] *Codification* relies on information technology and the development of databases where knowledge can be accessed and used by appropriate members. This strategy works best for explicit forms of knowledge that can be extracted from people, reports, and other data sources, and then organized into meaningful categories called "knowledge objects" that can be reused for various purposes. *Personalization* strategies for organizing knowledge focus on the people who develop knowledge and on how they can share it person-to-person. Tacit knowledge is typically accessed through personal conversations, direct contact, and ongoing dialogue with the people who possess it. For example, most professional service firms foster networking among their employees by transferring people across offices, encouraging the prompt return of phone calls from colleagues, and using cross-functional project teams.

Distributing knowledge involves developing mechanisms that enable members to gain access to needed knowledge. It overlaps with the previous phase of knowledge management and involves making knowledge easy for people to find and encouraging its use and reuse. For example, organizations can develop databases for storing articles, reports, customer data, best practices, or other knowledge as well as locator systems for helping members find what they want. Databases can include such diverse information as articles, analytical reports, customer data, and best practices. Organizations can also create knowledge services (e.g., help desks or specific organization units) and networks (e.g., intranet portals, informal "brown bag" presentations) to promote knowledge transfer. Finally, organizations can create specific roles to facilitate the transfer of organization knowledge and encourage knowledge distribution. For example, Britain's Collaboration for Leadership in Applied Health Research and Care for Nottinghamshire, Derbyshire, and Lincolnshire (CLAHRC-NDL) uses "Diffusion Fellows," senior managers, and clinicians assigned from the National Health Service to provide best-practice, evidence-based clinical practice to physicians and nurses in the system.[50]

4. **Continuously monitor and improve the learning process.** This final stage involves deutero-learning—learning how to learn. It includes assessing OL strategies and the organizational structures and processes that contribute to them. Members assess periodically how well these elements facilitate single- and double-loop learning. They generalize positive findings to new or changing situations and make appropriate modifications to improve OL. Because these activities reflect the highest and most difficult level of OL, they depend heavily on members' willingness to question openly their theories in use about OL and to test publicly the effectiveness of both their learning strategies and those of the wider organization.

Application 19.3 describes a long-term, comprehensive organization learning intervention.[51] The initial intervention was primarily a dialogue process among senior managers but was extended to the larger organizational community. The application also demonstrates how systemic many OL and strategic change interventions can be.

19-4 Built-to-Change Organizations

One of the newest continuous change interventions involves intentionally designing an entire organization for change and not stability. Lawler and Worley's built-to-change (B2C) approach to designing organizations is based on the simple fact that most organizations are designed for stability and dependable operations.[52] Traditional organization design components and managerial practices aim to reinforce predictable behaviors for sustaining a particular competitive advantage. Lawler and Worley argue that many change efforts are unsuccessful, not because of human resistance or lack of visionary leadership, but because most organization design features assume that stability leads to effectiveness. Such built-in assumptions can be a recipe for failure in rapidly changing environments, where the ability to change constantly is the best sustainable source of competitive advantage. The B2C intervention helps organizations design themselves for change.

19-4a Design Guidelines

As shown in Table 19.1, the B2C intervention includes the following design guidelines and challenges the assumption of stability in the specification of design components.

application 19.3

DIALOGUE AND ORGANIZATION LEARNING AT DMT

DMT is a small but global business that designs, builds, and installs sophisticated food processing systems. It has a global market share of over 50% and employs about 800 people. Roughly two-thirds of the employees are in the primary office and manufacturing plant in the Netherlands while the other third, consisting of sales and engineering, works in the field to market and install the systems.

In the late 1980s, DMT adopted a socio-technical systems philosophy and introduced self-managing teams and other empowering structures into most of the operations function. After ten years, and despite continued success in both market share and profitability, the socio-tech initiatives had lost focus.

The heir apparent to the founder of DMT had been reading and thinking about the concepts of complexity and learning. He asked an OD consultant familiar with these ideas for help in translating them into action. The future CEO and consultant handpicked a set of managers in the company to be on a change leadership team and the initial intervention focused on the transformation of DMT's leaders through dialogue.

Facilitated by the OD consultant, the change leadership team spent significant time over an 18-month period in heavy dialogue sessions. Early sessions were spent learning about the dialogue process while later sessions explored assumptions about the market, DMT's current and future strategies, and most importantly, the predominant styles of communicating, leading, and operating.

The result was a close-knit team that had explored and confronted their theories of action. However, none of the rest of the organization knew what was happening. The OD consultant described a variety of emergent "water cooler" conversations among organization members with respect to: "What's happened to them?" and "Why are they acting so strange?"

The change leadership team and the OD consultant worked together to craft a series of organization learning interventions that would involve a broader and broader segment of the population. These interventions, like the overall change strategy, sound more complete and thought out than they were. In general, the organization tried some things out and if they worked, they were refined. If they didn't work, they moved onto another idea. Eventually, however, nearly two-thirds of the organization members participated in the following learning activities:

Complexity Concepts Workshop. This intensive one-day workshop represented an introduction to the concepts and organizing principles associated with complexity, learning, and dialogue. It offered the participant an opportunity to look at themselves, their organization, and their world. The workshop compared the assumptions of a "scientific" worldview with the assumptions of complexity. The session ended with an introduction to dialogue and a facilitated conversation to help participants apply the concepts in their work. Overall, the session was designed to help members become aware of an alternative way of organizing that held the possibility of changing the entire organization by an order of magnitude.

Dialogue Training. After completing the Complexity workshop, groups of 10 to 15 people were introduced to dialogue as a communication process that supported the principles of complexity and the practice of organization learning. Through mostly applied experiences in dialogue, participants were shown how this form of communication differed from hierarchically constrained and competitive discussion. In contrast, dialogue allowed meaning and influence to flow freely and emerge. The workshop also tried to integrate concepts from the complexity workshop and to prepare participants for "dolphin training."

"Dolphin" Training. A leadership metaphor based on the "strategy of the dolphin" (e.g., do what works and forget the rest) was introduced as a set of empowerment guidelines for action and decision making. The goal of this workshop was to enable every member of DMT to step forward and assume responsibility for the greater whole. That is, when the situation demands it, DMTers are to be ready.

The Visioning Conference. The final intervention was the visioning conference and involved as many as 50 people at a time. Building on the principles of a learning organization and personal mastery, a one-day dialogue-based workshop suggested that a company's true "vision" incorporates the personal visions of each member. This approach was contrasted with the standard visioning process where senior leaders formulate and then impose a vision on the system. The workshop asked individuals to elaborate on their personal visions through statements, actions, or drawings and to specify what they needed from the organization and their fellow participants. As a result of the visioning conferences, groups of DMT members representing a cross-section of the company spent entire days engaged in deep dialogue around the question: "How must DMT be in order to realize the collective vision of all its members?"

In addition to these formal workshops, DMT's transformation also involved a great many "hallway dialogues" about the meaning and/or applicability of a complexity principle and "retreats" to think about the implications of the emerging culture. Moreover, the change leadership team that had catalyzed the entire process continued to meet and dialogue on the transformation. The researchers found the DMT process interesting because its essential activities were more likely to emerge from the interaction of its members than to be planned or organized for them. Although the change leadership team had a vested interest in this process, the transformation of DMT was never "owned" by them exclusively but by every member of the firm—the essence of emergent leadership.

As the transformation progressed, the change leadership team recognized that the internal changes in communicating, thinking, and leading would need to be reflected in and embedded in the structure of the system. An evaluation of DMT's design suggested that its long history of success had resulted in structures, systems, and processes that were increasingly fixed and resistant to change. Managers who had been receptive to, if not enthusiastic about, the effort to bring about change in the culture suddenly balked at the notion of design changes. The change leadership team, however, remained resolute in seeing the change through.

More than two years into the change process, the change leadership team issued a call for people to participate in a "blank slate" design process; a whole-system architecture capable of realizing the visions of all its members and for thriving, not merely surviving, in the company's increasingly complex and turbulent marketplace. Interesting, the change leadership team excluded managers and supervisors from the call. Even so, more than 50 individuals stepped forward to self-organize into an active network intent on producing the "New DMT."

Only three constraints were placed on the newly formed design team: (1) the design had to follow the principles of complexity, learning, and dialogue, (2) each design team member had to act as a representative of every one of their colleagues, and (3) the resulting design had to enable the personal visions of every member of the organization. The design team was supported with time, financial resources, the OD consultant, and any other expertise they needed.

The OD consultant kicked off the "New DMT" process with a workshop on organization design and whole system transformation. Following the training, the group, recognizing the scope and complexity of their task, self-organized into a configuration they dubbed the Design Network (DN). The DN revolved around a "hub" of nine people who were responsible for creating an architectural model for the New DMT based on "intelligence" relayed to it by the remaining members. These would comprise the "network" whose job it was to reach out into the system and involve more and more people as time passed. They were to convey information to and from the hub.

After nearly a year of effort, the DN announced its D(esign)-Day and invited the entire company, all 600-plus people, to join them for the "unveiling" of the architecture for the New DMT. Following the presentation, the team organized a process to allow people to translate the multiple dimensions of its design into reality. DMT's transformation is well on its way.

The organization learning process and each of the interventions represented a significant departure from the way DMT had operated in the past. The consistency and persistence of the interventions over a two-year period of time and the inclusiveness with which the interventions involved people in the organization led to important behavioral changes. In particular, members began to see the organization in more systemic and complex terms rather than hierarchical and linear; dialogue replaced discussion as the primary communication process in the organization; and members engaged in emergent, shared leadership rather than viewing leadership as something only senior managers did.

TABLE 19.1

Design Guidelines for B2C Organizations

From Traditional Principles...	To Dynamic Principles
Strategy	**Strategizing**
Short-term, static environmental scans and industry analyses	Long-term, alternative scenarios and contingency planning
Pursuit of a sustainable competitive advantage	Pursuit of a series of momentary advantages
Design	**Designing**
Focus on efficiency over effectiveness	Focus on effectiveness over efficiency
What do we do well?	What do we need to learn?
Alignment as the key to performance	Change as the key to performance

From Strategy to Strategizing The stability assumption first shows up in the way organizations formulate strategy. Most strategy processes rely on relatively static and short-term views of the environment. Most environmental scanning tools, such as SWOT and industry attractiveness models, implicitly assume that the forces operating today will operate tomorrow and reinforce the pursuit of a single sustainable competitive advantage. Although most managers and organizations describe the environment as changing, they act and decide *as if* it is not. As a result, strategies are formulated, budgets and goals are set, and any successful competitive advantage is expected to last.

B2C organizations move from static to dynamic views of strategy, using interventions like dynamic strategy making described previously in this chapter. Instead of believing that any competitive advantage will last, they recognize that any particular advantage is fleeting. The development and reliance on strong and robust "futuring" processes supports this dynamic view of strategy.[53] Managers in B2C organizations spend a lot of time thinking about alternative future environments and scenarios. Using these scenarios to sharpen their strategic thinking, they explore options, think about the capabilities that might be needed, and formulate the next likely competitive advantage they will have to pursue. Importantly, senior managers spend less time worrying about the execution of the current strategy; they see their role as worrying about the future strategy.

From Design to Designing Traditional organizations view organization design as a set of relatively stable features that only get better through continuous improvement. Rather than thinking about how structure, work, management processes, and HR systems need to change to increase effectiveness, traditional organizations become enamored with short-term efficiency and reliability initiatives. Such a focus tends to lock the organization into a way of operating that is very difficult to change.

B2C organizations recognize that change is never over and so focus more on effectiveness than efficiency. B2C organizations do work to improve existing systems and processes, but using change processes like self-designing organizations, they allocate significant resources to thinking about how organization design elements need to be changed. In fact, B2C organizations are wary of too much alignment that can result in rigidity. Instead, they focus on being able to change as the key to long-term performance. B2C organizations shift the conversation from "what do we do well?" to "what do we need to learn?" This orientation and mindset always keeps them open to changing organization design features as described below.

19-4b Application Stages

Lawler and Worley stress that not all organizations should be built to change, though most could benefit from applying some B2C principles. This intervention is mainly for organizations having problems adapting to complex and rapidly changing environments. They require a change capability for success in the future. For them, and following a thorough diagnosis,[54] the following three initiatives can help the transition to a B2C organization:

1. **Reframe culture as a facilitator of change.** This first stage addresses the organization's culture—the established set of core values, norms, and beliefs shared by organization members. Culture is the most stable part of an organization—it is deep-seated, taken for granted, and guides decisions and behaviors like an invisible hand—but it does not need to be a constraint to changing. As described in Chapter 18, organization culture can promote or hinder organization change depending on whether it supports change or stability.[55] In many traditionally designed organizations, values and norms reinforce stability and predictability, thus making change difficult. To move toward a change-friendly culture requires surfacing existing values and norms, assessing their relevance to change, and making appropriate adjustments. This typically involves highly interactive sessions where relevant stakeholders openly discuss and debate questions about the organization's culture and how it can be "reframed" to be more change friendly. Attention is directed at creating or redefining values and norms that focus behavior on the organization's environment and help members see change as necessary and natural. To enhance member commitment to a new change-friendly culture, these new or reframed values and norms are placed in the context of important external pressures facing the organization and what these mean for its effectiveness. The organization's existing design is also assessed in relation to the culture, and plans are made for changing specific components using the B2C guidelines outlined above.
2. **Redefine organization design components for flexibility.** Each feature of an organization's design can be created under an assumption of stability or flexibility. The second step in moving to a B2C organization is to design and implement these components with flexibility in mind.

   B2C designs emphasize a flat, lean, and flexible organization *structure*, such as process, matrix, and network designs. These structures can be reconfigured quickly when the circumstances demand. The key objective in most B2C structures is establishing what Lawler and Worley call "maximum surface area."[56] That is, as many roles in the organization as possible should be defined to include interaction with the external environment. Organization members are more likely to support change if they are in direct contact with customers, regulators, markets, and the community.

B2C *human resource practices* are geared to selecting, developing, and managing the right talent for change. Selection practices seek quick learners who want to take initiative, desire professional growth, and thrive on change. Employment contracts specify clearly that change is to be expected and support for change is a condition of employment and a path to success. Rather than specific job descriptions, members are encouraged to discover what needs to be done by frequent goal-setting reviews where tasks are constantly assessed and revised. Training and development are continuous and aimed at supporting change and gaining value-added skills and knowledge.

Because rewards play a key role in motivating and reinforcing change in B2C organizations, individual or team bonuses are tied directly to change goals, learning new things, and performing new tasks well.[57] This establishes a clear line of sight between rewards and change activities. Bonuses can include one-time rewards given at the end of a particular change effort, or rewards targeted to different phases of the change process. B2C designs also shift the basis of rewards from jobs to people. Members are rewarded for what they can do, not for the particular job they perform. Jobs and tasks are continually changing, and rewards can motivate people to learn new skills and knowledge, thus keeping pace with change and enhancing their long-term value to the organization.

In B2C organizations, *management processes* are moved throughout the organization to wherever they are needed. This ensures that information is transparent and current and provides a clear picture of how the organization is performing relative to its competitors. It enables organizations to make timely and relevant decisions to keep pace with changing conditions.

3. **Build an orchestration capability.** This stage helps the organization leverage the flexibility built into the organization's strategy and design. An orchestration capability enables the organization to implement changes in strategy and to execute design changes effectively over and over again.[58] It first specifies the events and decisions necessary to make the strategy happen, including how new competencies will be developed, if necessary. Then, based on the B2C belief that the ability to change is the key to competitive advantage, attention is directed at building this change capability into the organization. This involves three related activities. First, change management skills are developed widely in the organization by hiring people with those skills and by training existing managers and employees to acquire those skills. Second, an organization effectiveness function is created with competencies in strategic planning, organization design, and change management. This center of excellence is usually staffed by professionals from the strategic planning and human resources functions; they provide advice and facilitation for planning and executing change in the organization. Third, organization members learn how to apply their change capability by engaging in organizational changes and reflecting on that experience. This so-called "learning by doing" is essential for building an orchestration capability. It provides members with the hands-on experience and reflective learning necessary to hone their change skills in action.

   An important part of the orchestration capability is a redefinition of leadership. B2C designs stress the importance of shared leadership throughout the organization.

application 19.4

CREATING A BUILT-TO-CHANGE ORGANIZATION AT CAPITAL ONE FINANCIAL

Capital One, a leading financial services firm and a top issuer of credit cards in the United States, has built an organization that does not view change as an unwanted intruder or as an afterthought to get resistors to buy into a new initiative. Rather, change capability is integrated into every aspect of Capital One's strategy, structure, and culture. This enables the firm to execute change routinely.

Capital One treats strategic planning as a continuous process of exploring alternative futures and gaining momentary advantages in a fast-paced competitive environment. According to Mike McDermott, former Director of Organization Effectiveness, "Strategic thinking goes pretty deep on two levels. On one level, the strategic planning department runs a variety of scenarios that look several years out." As described by CEO and Founder Rich Fairbank, "Eighty percent of strategy is figuring out where the world is going, and 20% is figuring out what you are going to do in response. If you can figure out where the world is going, what you need to do usually becomes obvious." For example, Capital One might explore the broader forces affecting interest rates or the impact of changes in China's monetary policy. Each business line, in turn, would consider how these future trends might affect its particular business. "On another level," notes McDermott, "the executive committee meets regularly to discuss and debate a set of annual 'imperatives' or bold challenges. The imperatives are just that ... they are things that *must* be done if we are to achieve our long-term vision." They are intended to provide Capital One with a series of temporary competitive advantages.

This robust strategizing enables Capital One to "test and learn" how best to compete in a constantly changing environment. It combines educated guesses about how the environment is changing with rigorous analysis of consumer behaviors to produce testable propositions about what credit services to offer specific consumer groups. When a consumer group and its associated service reach a certain threshold of business, a potential competitive advantage exists. The service is then broadened to a larger customer base. Because consumer profiles, competitor behaviors, and other market forces are constantly changing, however, any current advantage is fleeting and new ones must be identified to grow revenues. Moreover, to monetize a competitive advantage even in the short run, Capital One must often modify its human capital, resources, systems, and structures. Thus, it constantly renews itself as it moves from one competitive advantage to the next.

To adapt quickly to gain new competitive advantages, Capital One has developed a highly agile organization design. It begins with hiring people who have a passion for excellence, collaborate well with others, and thrive in a changing environment. Once hired, associates are given challenging work assignments and opportunities to develop new skills as business needs change. Complimenting the selection process is a decentralized and fluid organization structure, with few layers of management and decision making pushed downward in the organization. Associates are allowed to take on a variety of tasks without having to worry about job descriptions and pay grades. An adaptable performance management system completes Capital One's flexible design. It focuses on both performance and development. Rewards are tied directly to current results as well as to developing competencies the organization believes are important for its future.

The final feature of Capital One's built-to-change organization involves change capability.

In the past, the firm's aggressive growth often left associates feeling overwhelmed by the rapidly changing product/service offerings. Adding to the stress were frequent updates in associates' knowledge base, reorganizations that tested their ability to remain flexible and to take on new assignments, and modifications in work processes and methods to maintain customer satisfaction. To make change manageable and even routine, Capital One charged McDermott with developing the firm's change capability. With the help of a design team composed of HR generalists and line managers, he created a unique approach to change management.

Most organizations develop change capability by deploying HR generalists to facilitate change in business units or by creating a center of excellence in change management staffed mainly by OD professionals. Capital One created a more embedded strategy. It rooted change skills and responsibilities directly into the roles of line managers. This promised to radically shorten the cycle time of change because managers would have the expertise needed to carry out most changes on their own. But tasking managers with change management responsibilities raised important questions about Capital One's commitment to change capability as a source of competitive advantage. Critics argued, "Shouldn't the focus of line managers be on getting business results?" The design team answered affirmatively, of course, but then added that in fast changing environments, this was not enough to succeed. Managers needed to be able to combine their business expertise with knowledge about change so that strategies to acquire new competitive advantages could be implemented faster and their benefits gained sooner.

Capital One's embedded approach was based on a standardized change methodology that everyone shared and learned. Called ADKAR, it proposed that successful change followed a process of (1) creating *awareness* of the need for change, (2) having the *desire* to change, (3) possessing the *knowledge* to change, (4) having the *ability* to change, and (5) being *reinforced* for change. The change model included a common language and mindset for thinking and communicating about organizational change; it afforded Capital One a highly efficient approach to change management. For example, service changes often required cooperation among the credit card business, IT services, and the regulatory compliance and HR departments. Because all parties were familiar and comfortable with the same change model, coordination costs and change cycle times were significantly reduced. This contrasted to earlier times when Capital One employed over 17 different change models and more than 160 different change tools throughout the firm.

To implement the new change method, McDermott's team applied three action levers: knowledge/skill acquisition, visible demonstrations, and alignment with performance management. First, Capital One's corporate university offered two courses to build people's change knowledge and skill. One course, attended by both managers and staff, went deep into the change methodology and provided the opportunity to apply it to existing change projects. This helped participants learn by doing, while driving change in the organization. The second course was a one-day program designed for line managers. It provided an overview of the methodology and linked it to the organization's values and leadership competencies. This helped managers see the connection between change capability and performance management.

Second, McDermott's team targeted several large-scale change projects as visible demonstrations of the change model. This created an internal "buzz" for the methodology and encouraged people to learn how to apply it. For example, McDermott's team highlighted change initiatives coming out of a strategic imperative called ACE (Achieving Corporate Excellence): a large-scale systems conversion project, an HR reengineering effort, and a workplace redesign process called the Future of Work.

Third, McDermott's team worked closely with a group revising Capital One's performance management system to ensure that it measured and rewarded change management competencies. Together, the two groups increased the number of change-related behaviors that were rated, assessed, and rewarded. This sent a clear message about the importance of these behaviors for the future.

Capital One's built-to-change organization is widely accepted and firmly entrenched in the firm's culture. Change capability is treated like a muscle that gets better with exercise. Not surprisingly, Capital One engages in lots of change and is getting better and better at it. Its change capability is a key source of sustained competitive advantage. As one executive put it, "We can take on more change because with this new muscle, it doesn't seem like we are changing all that much. It feels like we are changing less because we are capable of handling more change than our competitors."

Rather than having the organization rely on individuals and centralized sources of power and control, these designs spread leadership across multiple levels of the organization. Leadership shifts from an individual trait to an organization capacity. This speeds decision making and response rates because those lower in the organization understand how to change and need not wait for top-down direction. It provides leadership experience and skills to a broad array of members, thus developing a strong cadre of leadership talent. Shared leadership supports continuous change by spreading change expertise and commitment across the organization. It increases the chances that competent leaders will be there to keep the change process moving forward.

Application 19.4 describes how Capital One Financial created a B2C organization.[59] It shows how change capability is built into the firm's strategy, design features, and culture.

SUMMARY

In this chapter, we presented increasingly sophisticated interventions for helping organizations conduct strategic change. These change processes are particularly applicable for organizations facing turbulent environments where traditional sources of competitive advantage erode quickly. Building change capabilities directly into the organization is essential to constantly renew forms of competitive advantage to keep pace with a rapidly shifting environment.

Dynamic strategy making involves specifying and implementing the four elements that comprise the backbone of a new strategic system, thereby charting an organization's direction forward. It begins with defining a competitive logic, which derives from an analysis about how fitting the firm's capabilities can be used to exploit environmental opportunities. Then the other three elements—goals, organization, and action plan—are aligned closely with the competitive logic so as to support its implementation. They spell out exactly what is to be achieved, how the organization will be structured to accomplish it, and what steps are needed to make it happen. The combined effect is to position the firm in the market and tightly link its objectives, structure, and action to that strategy.

A self-design change strategy helps a firm gain the capacity to design and implement its own continuous change. Self-design involves multiple levels of the firm and multiple stakeholders and includes an iterative series of activities: acquiring knowledge, valuing, diagnosing, designing, implementing, and assessing.

Organization learning interventions help organizations develop and use knowledge to change and improve themselves continually. Organization learning interventions address how organizations can be designed to promote effective learning processes and how those learning processes themselves can be improved. An organization designed to promote learning can create a continuous stream of valuable knowledge. Knowledge management focuses on how that knowledge can be organized and used to improve organization performance.

Built-to-change organizations are designed for change, not stability. They are based on design guidelines that promote change capability in the firm's strategy, design, and leadership. In a rapidly changing environment, this change capability can help the organization transition from one competitive advantage to another.

NOTES

1. R. Wiggins and T. Ruefli, "Schumpeter's Ghost: Is Hypercompetition Making the Best of Times Shorter?" *Strategic Management Journal* 26 (2005): 887–911.
2. I. Barreto, "Dynamic Capabilities: A Review of Past Research and an Agenda for the Future," *Journal of Management* 36 (2010): 256–80; D. Teece, G. Pisano, and A. Shuen, "Dynamic Capabilities and Strategic Management," *Strategic Management Journal* 18 (1997): 509–33.
3. T. Lawrence, B. Dyck, S. Maitlis, and M. Mauws, "The Underlying Structure of Continuous Change," *Sloan Management Review* 47 (2006): 59–66; E. Lawler and C. Worley, *Built to Change* (San Francisco: Jossey-Bass, 2006).
4. L. Greiner and T. Cummings, *Dynamic Strategy Making: A Real-Time Approach for the 21st Century Leader* (San Francisco: Jossey-Bass, 2009).
5. L. Greiner and A. Bhambri, "New CEO Intervention and the Dynamics of Strategic Change," *Strategic Management Journal* 10 (1989): 67–87; M. Beer, "Transforming Organizations: Embrace the Paradox of E and O," in *Handbook of Organization Development*, ed. T. Cummings (Thousand Oaks, CA: Sage Publications, 2008); M. Beer, "Developing an Effective Organization: Intervention Method, Empirical Evidence, and Theory," in *Research in Organizational Change and Development*, vol. 19, ed. W. Pasmore, A. Shani, and R. Woodman (Bingley, UK: Emerald Group Publishing, 2011), 1–54.
6. Greiner and Cummings, *Dynamic Strategy Making*.
7. C. Worley, D. Hitchin, and W. Ross, *Integrated Strategic Change: How Organization Development Builds Competitive Advantage* (Reading, MA: Addison-Wesley, 1996); M. Jelinek and J. Litterer, "Why OD Must Become Strategic," *Organizational Change and Development*, vol. 2, ed. W. Pasmore and R. Woodman (Greenwich, CT: JAI Press, 1988), 135–62; A. Bhambri and L. Pate, "Introduction—The Strategic Change Agenda: Stimuli, Processes, and Outcomes," *Journal of Organization Change Management* 4 (1991): 4–6.
8. Greiner and Cummings, *Dynamic Strategy Making*.
9. D. Collis and M. Rukstad, "Can You Say What Your Strategy Is?" *Harvard Business Review* (April 2008): 1–11.
10. M. Porter, *Competitive Strategy* (New York: The Free Press, 1980).
11. A. Slywotsky, *Value Migration: How to Think Several Moves Ahead of the Competition* (Cambridge, MA: Harvard Business School Press, 1995); J. Barney, *Gaining and Sustaining Competitive Advantage*, 4th ed. (New York: Prentice Hall, 2010); W. Kim and R. Mauborgne, *Blue Ocean Strategy* (Cambridge, MA: Harvard Business School Press, 2005).
12. A. Colbert, A. Kirstof-Brown, B. Bradley, and M. Barrick, "CEO Transformational Leadership: The Role of Goal Importance Congruence in Top Management Teams," *Academy of Management Journal* 51 (2008): 81–96.
13. J. Collins and J. Porras, *Built to Last* (New York: HarperCollins, 1996).
14. Greiner and Cummings, *Dynamic Strategy Making*.
15. D. Ready and J. Conger, "Make Your Company a Talent Factory," *Harvard Business Review* (June 2007): 1–12.
16. This application was adapted from material found in M. Beer and J. Weber, "Whitbread PLC (A)," Case 9-406-007, Harvard Business School, 2005; M. Beer and J. Weber, "Whitbread PLC (B)," Case 9-406-008, Harvard Business School, 2005; Whitbread's corporate website, http://www.whitbread.co.uk/whitbread/aboutus.html.
17. B. Hedberg, P. Nystrom, and W. Starbuck, "Camping on Seesaws: Prescriptions for a Self-Designing Organization," *Administrative Science Quarterly* 21 (1976): 41–65; K. Weick, "Organization Design: Organizations as Self-Designing Systems," *Organizational Dynamics* 6 (1977): 30–46.
18. S. Mohrman and T. Cummings, *Self-Designing Organizations: Learning How to Create High Performance* (Reading, MA: Addison-Wesley, 1989); T. Cummings and S. Mohrman, "Self-Designing Organizations: Towards Implementing Quality-of-Work-Life Innovations," in *Research in Organizational Change and Development*,

vol. 1, ed. R. Woodman and W. Pasmore (Greenwich, CT: JAI Press, 1987), 275–310.

19. D. Miller and P. Friesen, *Organizations: A Quantum View* (Englewood Cliffs, NJ: Prentice Hall, 1984).

20. C. Argyris, R. Putnam, and D. Smith, *Action Science* (San Francisco: Jossey-Bass, 1985); C. Lundberg, "On Organizational Learning: Implications and Opportunities for Expanding Organizational Development," in *Research on Organizational Change and Development*, vol. 3, ed. R. Woodman and W. Pasmore (Greenwich, CT: JAI Press, 1989), 61–82; P. Senge, *The Fifth Discipline* (New York: Doubleday, 1990).

21. T. Lant, "Organization Learning: Creating, Retaining, and Transferring Knowledge," *Administrative Science Quarterly* (Winter, 2000): 622–43; M. Crossan, H. Lane, and R. White, "An Organizational Learning Framework: From Intuition to Institution," *Academy of Management Review* 24 (1999): 522–37; J. C. Spender, "Making Knowledge the Basis of a Dynamic Theory of the Firm," *Strategic Management Journal* 17 (1996): 45–62; R. Strata, "Organizational Learning: The Key to Management Innovation," *Sloan Management Review* 30 (1989): 63–74.

22. D. Teece, "Capturing Value from Knowledge Assets: The New Economy, Market for Know-How, and Intangible Assets," *California Management Review* 40 (Spring 1998): 55–79.

23. G. Roth, "The Order and Chaos of the Learning Organization," in *Handbook of Organization Development*, ed. T. Cummings (Thousand Oaks, CA: Sage Publications, 2008), 475–97; B. Sugarman, "Organizational Learning–Dynamic, Integrative: A Concept Returns, Older and Wiser," in *Research in Organizational Change and Development*, vol. 20, ed. W. Pasmore, A. Shani, and R. Woodman (Bingley, UK: Emerald Group Publishing, 2012), 91–143.

24. D. Bray, "Literature Review—Knowledge Management Research at the Organizational Level" (May 2007), accessed from http://ssrn.com/abstract=991169.

25. C. Argyris and D. Schon, *Organizational Learning: A Theory of Action Perspective* (Reading, MA: Addison-Wesley, 1978); C. Argyris and D. Schon, *Organizational Learning II: Theory, Method, and Practice* (Reading, MA: Addison-Wesley, 1996); Senge, *Fifth Discipline*.

26. P. Adler and R. Cole, "Designed for Learning: A Tale of Two Auto Plants," *Sloan Management Review* 34 (1993): 85–94; S. Cook and D. Yanow, "Culture and Organizational Learning," *Journal of Management Inquiry* 2 (1993): 373–90; G. Huber, "The Nontraditional Quality of Organizational Learning," *Organization Science* 2 (1991): 88–115.

27. W. Snyder, "Organization Learning and Performance: An Exploration of the Linkages Between Organizational Learning, Knowledge, and Performance" (unpublished Ph.D. diss., University of Southern California, Los Angeles, 1996).

28. A. B. Shani and P. Docherty, *Learning by Design: Building Sustainable Organizations* (London: Blackwell, 2003); A. B. Shani and P. Docherty, "Learning by Design: Key Mechanisms in Organization Development," in *Handbook of Organization Development*, ed. T. Cummings (Thousand Oaks, CA: Sage Publications, 2008), 499–518; S. Hauschild, T. Licht, and W. Stein, "Creating a Knowledge Culture," *McKinsey Quarterly* 1 (2001): 74–81; B. Choi, S. Poon, and J. Davis, "Effects of Knowledge Management Strategy on Organizational Performance: A Complementarity Theory-Based Approach," *Omega* 36 (2008): 235–51; B. Ya-Hui Lien, R. Hung, and G. McLean, "Organizational Learning as an Organization Development Intervention in Six High-Technology Firms in Taiwan: An Exploratory Case Study," *Human Resource Development Quarterly* 18 (2007): 211–28.

29. This framework draws heavily on the work of W. Snyder and T. Cummings, "Organization Learning Disorders: Conceptual Model and Intervention Hypotheses," *Human Relations* 51 (1998): 873–95.

30. Argyris and Schon, *Organizational Learning II*.

31. Argyris and Schon, *Organizational Learning II*; C. Argyris, *Intervention Theory and Method* (Reading, MA: Addison-Wesley, 1970).

32. D. Garvin, *Learning in Action* (Cambridge, MA: Harvard Business School Press, 2000).

33. M. McGill, J. Slocum, and D. Lei, "Management Practices in Learning Organizations," *Organizational Dynamics* (Autumn 1993): 5–17; E. Nevis, A. DiBella, and J. Gould, "Understanding Organizations as Learning Systems," *Sloan Management Review* (Winter 1995): 73–85.

34. J. Dewey, *How We Think* (Boston: D.C. Heath, 1933).

35. Argyris and Schon, *Organizational Learning;* Argyris and Schon, *Organizational Learning II*; Senge, *Fifth Discipline*.

36. Argyris and Schon, *Organizational Learning II*; Senge, *Fifth Discipline*; P. Senge, C. Roberts, R. Ross, B. Smith, and A. Kleiner, *The Fifth Discipline Fieldbook: Strategies for Building a Learning Organization* (New York: Doubleday, 1995).

37. Argyris and Schon, *Organizational Learning II*.

38. Senge, *Fifth Discipline*.

39. Ibid.

40. Argyris and Schon, *Organizational Learning II*.

41. Senge, *Fifth Discipline*.

42. Argyris and Schon, *Organizational Learning II*; Senge et al., *Fifth Discipline Fieldbook*; B. Dumaine, "Mr. Learning Organization," *Fortune*, October 17, 1994, 147–57.

43. Senge et al., *Fifth Discipline Fieldbook*.

44. Argyris and Schon, *Organizational Learning II*; Argyris, *Intervention Theory and Method.*
45. M. Polanyi, *The Tacit Dimension* (New York: Doubleday, 1966); I. Nonaka and H. Takeuchi, *The Knowledge-Creating Company: How Japanese Companies Foster Creativity and Innovation for Competitive Advantage* (New York: Oxford University Press, 1995).
46. D. Leonard-Barton, *Wellsprings of Knowledge: Building and Sustaining the Sources of Innovation* (Boston: Harvard Business School Press, 1995); Nonaka and Takeuchi, *Knowledge Creating*; C. Prahalad and G. Hamel, "The Core Competencies of the Corporation," *Harvard Business Review* 68 (1990): 79–91; H. Itami, *Mobilizing for Invisible Assets* (Cambridge, MA: Harvard University Press, 1987); L. Edvinsson and M. Malone, *Intellectual Capital: Realizing Your Company's True Value by Finding Its Hidden Brainpower* (New York: Harper Business, 1997); T. Stewart, *Intellectual Capital: The New Wealth of Organizations* (New York: Doubleday, 1997); J. Nahapiet and S. Ghoshal, "Social Capital, Intellectual Capital, and the Organizational Advantage," *Academy of Management Review* 23 (1998): 242–66.
47. V. Anand, C. Manz, and W. Glick, "An Organizational Memory Approach to Information Management," *Academy of Management Review* 23 (1998): 796–809.
48. E. Wenger, *Communities of Practice: Learning, Meaning, and Identity* (Cambridge: Cambridge University Press, 1999); J. Brown and P. Duguid, "Organizational Learning and Communities of Practice: Towards a Unified View of Working, Learning, and Innovation," *Organization Science* 2 (1991): 40–57.
49. M. Hansen, N. Nohria, and T. Tierney, "What's Your Strategy for Managing Knowledge?" *Harvard Business Review* (March–April 1999): 106–16; C. O'Dell and C. Grayson, *If Only We Knew What We Know* (New York: Free Press, 1998).
50. L. Thomson, J. Schneider, and N. Wright, "Developing Communities of Practice to Support the Implementation of Research into Clinical Practice," *Leadership in Health Services* 26 (2013), date online September 29, 2012, accessed December 5, 2012.
51. This application was adapted from the case study and evaluation of dialogue and organization learning presented in F. van Eijnatten, M. van Galen, and L. Fitzgerald, "Learning Dialogically: The Art of Chaos-Informed Transformation," *Learning Organization* 10 (2003): 36–367.
52. E. Lawler and C. Worley, *Built to Change: How to Achieve Sustained Organizational Effectiveness* (San Francisco: Jossey-Bass, 2006); C. Worley and E. Lawler, "Designing Organizations That Are Built to Change," *Sloane Management Review* 48 (2006): 19–23.
53. K. van der Heijden, *Scenarios: The Art of Strategic Conversation* (New York: Wiley, 2007); M. Lindgren and H. Bandhold, *Scenario Planning* (New York: Palgrave Macmillan, 2009); M. Weisbord, *Productive Workplaces* (San Francisco: Jossey-Bass, 1987).
54. C. Worley and E. Lawler, "Agility and Organization Design: A Diagnostic Framework," *Organizational Dynamics* 39 (2010): 194–204.
55. J. Kotter and J. Heskett, *Corporate Culture and Performance* (New York: Free Press, 1992); J. Amis, T. Slack, and C. Hinings, "Values and Organizational Change," *Journal of Applied Behavioral Science* 38 (2002): 436–465.
56. Lawler and Worley, *Built to Change.*
57. E. Lawler and C. Worley, "Winning Support for Organizational Change: Designing Employee Reward Systems That Keep on Working," *Ivey Business Journal* (March–April 2006): 1–5.
58. C. Worley and E. Lawler, "Building a Change Capability at Capital One Financial," *Organizational Dynamics* 38 (2009): 245–51; T. Fredberg, F. Norrgren, and A. Shani, "Developing and Sustaining Change Capability via Learning Mechanisms: A Longitudinal Perspective on Transformation," in *Research in Organizational Change and Development*, vol. 19, ed. W. Pasmore, A. Shani, and R. Woodman (Bingley, UK: Emerald Group Publishing, 2011), 117–61; M. Beer and R. Eisenstat, "Developing an Organization Capable of Implementing Strategy and Learning," *Human Relations* 49 (1996): 597–619.
59. Worley and Lawler, "Building a Change Capability."

20

Transorganizational Change

learning objectives

- Explain the rationale and logic behind organization collaboration.
- Describe and apply organization development (OD) interventions that enable mergers and acquisitions.
- Discuss and apply the OD process to alliance formation and development.
- Describe the process of network formation and transorganizational development as well as how networks change.

The focus of this chapter is OD interventions that move beyond the single organization to include merging, allying, or networking with other organizations. These multiorganizational change programs are becoming more prevalent in OD as organizations extend their boundaries to keep pace with highly complex and rapidly changing environments. Under these conditions, organizations may merge with or acquire other firms to gain essential capabilities and resources, to operate at a larger scale, and to enter new markets. They may form strategic alliances with other organizations to share costs and expertise and to manage their exchanges more efficiently. They may join with other organizations to tackle complex problems and projects that single organizations cannot accomplish.

Mergers, alliances, and transorganizational change helps organizations create and sustain such multiorganizational linkages. It helps them transcend the perspective of a single organization and address the needs and concerns of all involved stakeholders. This represents a fundamental shift in strategic orientation because the strategies, goals, structures, and processes of two or more organizations become interdependent and must be coordinated and aligned. This raises the scope and complexity of change processes; it increases the chances that conflicts and misunderstandings will occur. Multiorganizational change calls for OD practitioners to move to a higher diagnostic and intervention level to straddle the boundaries of different organizations, attend to their unique and often conflicting needs, and bring structure to what is frequently an underorganized and highly uncertain process. Practitioners must develop new concepts, skills, and expertise for implementing these change interventions.

Because transorganizational change is relatively new to OD, this chapter starts with an explanation of the rationale underlying multiorganizational arrangements. Then, three kinds of interventions are described: mergers and acquisitions (M&As), strategic alliances, and networks.

M&As leverage the strengths (or shore up the weaknesses) of one organization by combining with another organization. This transorganizational change involves integrating many of the interventions previously discussed in this text, including human process, technostructural, and human resources management interventions. Research and practice in M&As strongly suggest that OD practices can contribute to implementation success.

Alliance interventions, including joint ventures, franchising, and long-term contracts, help to develop the relationship between two organizations that believe the benefits of cooperation outweigh the costs of lowered autonomy and control. These increasingly common arrangements require each organization to understand its goals and strategy in the relationship, build and leverage trust, and ensure that it is receiving the expected benefits.

Finally—and building on the knowledge of alliances—network interventions are concerned with helping a group or system of organizations to engage in relationships that perform tasks or solve problems that are too complex and multifaceted for a single organization to resolve. These multiorganizational systems abound in today's environment and include research and development consortia, public–private partnerships, nonprofit coalitions, and constellations of profit-seeking organizations. They tend to be loosely coupled and nonhierarchical, and consequently they require methods different from most traditional OD interventions that are geared to single organizations. These methods help organizations recognize the need for transorganizational partnerships and develop coordinating structures to support their networks.

20-1 Transorganizational Rationale

More and more, organizations are linking with other organizations to achieve their objectives. These transorganizational strategies can provide additional resources for large-scale research and development; spread the risks of innovation; apply diverse expertise to complex problems and tasks; make information or technology available to learn and develop new capabilities; position the organization to achieve economies of scale or scope; build collaborative relationships to advance social or environmental issues; and gain access to new, especially international, marketplaces.[1] For example, pharmaceutical firms form strategic alliances to distribute noncompeting medications and to avoid the high costs of establishing sales organizations; firms from different countries form joint ventures to overcome restrictive trade barriers; and high-technology firms form research consortia to undertake significant and costly research and development for their industries.

More generally, however, transorganizational strategies allow organizations to perform tasks that are too costly and complicated for single organizations to perform.[2] These tasks include the full range of organizational activities, including purchasing raw materials, hiring and compensating organization members, manufacturing and service delivery, obtaining investment capital, marketing and distribution, and strategic planning. The key to understanding transorganizational strategies is recognizing that these individual tasks must be coordinated with each other. Whenever a good or service from one of these tasks is exchanged between two units (individuals, departments, or organizations), a *transaction* occurs. Transactions can be designed and managed internally within the organization's structure, or externally between organizations. For example, organizations can acquire a raw materials provider and operate these tasks as part of internal operations or they can collaborate with a raw material supplier through long-term contracts in an alliance.

Economists and organization theorists have spent considerable effort investigating when transorganizational strategies work best. They have developed frameworks, primarily transaction cost theory and agency theory, that are useful for understanding these interventions.[3] As a rule, transorganizational strategies work well when transactions occur frequently and are well understood. Many organizations, for example, outsource their payroll tasks because the inputs, such as hours worked, pay rates, and employment status; the throughputs, such as tax rates and withholdings; and the outputs, such as issuing paychecks, occur regularly and are governed by well-known laws and regulations. Moreover, if transactions involve people, equipment, or other assets that are unique to the task, then transorganizational linkage is the preferred approach. For example, Microsoft works with a variety of value-added resellers, independent software vendors, and small and large consulting businesses to bring their products to customers ranging in size from individual consumers to the largest business enterprises in the world. An internal sales and service department to handle the unique demands of each customer segment would be much more expensive to implement and would not deliver the same level of quality as the partner organizations. In general, relationships between and among organizations become more formalized as the frequency of interaction increases, the type of information and other resources that are exchanged become more proprietary, and the number of different types of exchanges increases.[4]

Cummings has referred to groups of organizations that have joined together for a common purpose as *transorganizational systems* (TSs).[5] TSs are functional social systems existing intermediately between single organizations on the one hand and societal systems on the other. These multiorganizational systems can make decisions and perform tasks on behalf of their member organizations, although members maintain their separate organizational identities and goals. This separation distinguishes TSs from M&As.

In contrast to most organizational systems, TSs tend to be underorganized. Relationships among member organizations are loosely coupled; leadership and power are dispersed among autonomous organizations, rather than hierarchically centralized; and commitment and membership are constantly being assessed as member organizations act to maintain their autonomy while jointly performing. These characteristics make creating and managing TSs difficult.[6] Potential member organizations may not perceive the need to join with other organizations. They may be concerned with maintaining their autonomy or have trouble identifying potential partners. U.S. firms, for example, are traditionally "rugged individualists" preferring to work alone rather than to join with other organizations. Even if organizations decide to join together, they may have problems managing their relationships and controlling joint operations and decisions. Because members typically are accustomed to hierarchical forms of control, they may have difficulty managing lateral relations among independent organizations. They also may have difficulty managing different levels of commitment and motivation among members and sustaining membership over time. The network interventions described in this chapter can help TSs understand and address these problems.

20-2 Mergers and Acquisitions

M&As involve the combination of two organizations. The term *merger* refers to the integration of two previously independent organizations into a completely new organization; *acquisition* involves the purchase of one organization by another for integration into the acquiring organization. M&As are distinct from the interventions described later in this chapter because at least one of the organizations ceases to exist. The stressful dynamics associated with M&As led one researcher to call them the "ultimate change management challenge."[7]

Organizations have a number of reasons for wanting to acquire or merge with other firms, including diversification or vertical integration; gaining access to global markets, technology, or other resources; and achieving operational efficiencies, improved innovation, or resource sharing.[8] As a result, M&As have become a preferred method for rapid growth and strategic change. In 2011, for example, the announced value of M&As worldwide reached $3.1 trillion, a 7% increase over 2010 but far below the all-time high of $6.4 trillion in 2007.[9] Recent large transactions include financial integrations resulting from the economic crisis in 2008 (e.g., Wells Fargo and Wachovia, Bank of America and Countrywide Financial) and other industries (e.g., Microsoft-Skype, United-Continental, Sanofi-Genzyme, Southwest-AirTran, and Oracle and Sun Microsystems). There have been more than a few failed announcements as well, including AT&T and T-Mobile, Microsoft and Yahoo, and BEA and EADs.

Despite the popularity of M&As, they have a questionable record of success.[10] Among the reasons commonly cited for merger failure are inadequate due diligence processes, lack of a compelling strategic rationale, unrealistic expectations of synergy, paying too much for the transaction, conflicting corporate cultures, and failure to move quickly.

M&A interventions typically are preceded by an examination of the organization's strategy. Executives must decide whether their strategic goals should be achieved by either an internal change or a multiorganizational arrangement, such as an M&A, strategic alliance, or network. M&As are preferred when internal development is considered too slow or when strategic alliances or networks do not offer sufficient control over key resources to meet the firm's objectives.

In addition to the OD issues described here, M&As are complex changes that involve legal and financial knowledge beyond the scope of this text. OD practitioners are encouraged to seek out and work with specialists in these other relevant disciplines. The focus here is on how OD can contribute to M&A success.

20-2a Application Stages

M&As involve three major phases as shown in Table 20.1: precombination, legal combination, and operational combination.[11] OD practitioners can make substantive contributions to the precombination and operational combination phases as described below.

Precombination Phase This first phase consists of planning activities designed to ensure the success of the combined organization. Organizations pursuing the M&A option must identify a candidate organization, gather and reveal information about each other, and plan the implementation and integration activities. Research shows that precombination activities are critical to M&A success.[12] These include the following:

1. **Search for and select candidate.** This involves developing screening criteria to assess and narrow the field of candidate organizations, agreeing on a first-choice candidate, assessing regulatory compliance, establishing initial contacts, and formulating a letter of intent. Criteria for choosing an M&A partner can include leadership and management characteristics, market access resources, technical or financial capabilities, physical facilities, and so on. OD practitioners can add value at this stage of the process by encouraging screening criteria that include managerial, organizational, and cultural components as well as technical and financial aspects. In practice, financial issues tend to receive greater attention at this stage, with the goal of maximizing shareholder value. Failure to attend to cultural and organizational issues, however, can result in diminished shareholder value during the operational combination phase.[13]

   Identifying potential candidates, narrowing the field, agreeing on a first choice, and checking regulatory compliance are relatively straightforward activities. They generally involve investment brokers and other outside parties who have access to databases of organizational, financial, and technical information. The final two

TABLE 20.1

Major Phases and Activities in Mergers and Acquisitions

Major M&A Phases	Key Steps	OD and Change Management Issues
Precombination	Search for and select candidate Create M&A team Establish business case Perform due diligence assessment Develop merger integration plans	Ensure that candidates are screened for cultural as well as financial, technical, and physical asset criteria Define a clear leadership structure Establish a clear strategic vision, competitive strategy, and systems integration potential Specify the desirable organization design features Specify an integration action plan
Legal combination	Complete financial negotiations Close the deal Announce the combination	
Operational combination	Day 1 activities Organizational and technical integration activities Cultural integration activities	Implement changes quickly Communicate Solve problems together and focus on the customer Conduct an evaluation to learn and identify further areas of integration planning

activities, making initial contacts and creating a letter of intent, are aimed at determining the candidate's interest in the proposed merger or acquisition.

2. **Create an M&A team.** Once there is initial agreement between the two organizations to pursue a merger or acquisition, senior leaders from the respective organizations appoint an M&A team to establish the business case, to oversee the due diligence process, and to develop a merger integration plan.[14] This team typically comprises senior executives and experts in such areas as business valuation, technology, organization, and marketing. OD practitioners can facilitate formation of this team through human process interventions, such as team building and process consultation, and help the team establish clear goals and action strategies. They can also help members define a leadership structure, apply relevant skills and knowledge, and ensure that both organizations are represented appropriately. The group's leadership structure, or who will be accountable for the team's accomplishments, is especially critical. In an acquisition, an executive from the acquiring firm is typically the team's leader. In a merger of equals, the choice of a single individual to lead the team is more difficult, but essential. The outcome of this decision and the process used to make it are the first outward symbols of how this transorganizational change will be conducted.
3. **Establish the business case.** The purpose of this activity is to develop a *prima facie* case that combining the two organizations will result in a competitive advantage that exceeds their separate advantages.[15] It includes specifying the strategic vision,

competitive strategy, and systems integration potential for the M&A. OD practitioners can facilitate this discussion to ensure that each issue is fully explored. If the business case cannot be justified on strategic, financial, or operational grounds, the M&A should be revisited, terminated, or another candidate should be considered.

A strategic vision or goal represents a description of the organizations' combined capabilities. It synthesizes the strengths of the two organizations into a viable new organization. For example, AT&T had a clear picture of its intentions in acquiring T-Mobile. They believed that their common network equipment provider and Global Mobile System (GSM) operating system and the difficulty in acquiring additional spectrum would bring better coverage, better quality, and better functionality to its more than 250 million customers.

Competitive strategy describes how the combined organization will add value in a particular product market or segment of the value chain, how the value proposition is best performed by the combined organization (compared with competitors), and how it will be difficult to imitate. The purpose of this activity is to force the two organizations to go beyond the rhetoric of "these two organizations should merge because it's a good fit." AT&T's acquisition of T-Mobile eventually failed, in part, because their competitive strategy arguments could not dispel regulatory concerns of monopoly power.

Systems integration specifies how the two organizations will be combined. It addresses how and if they can work together. It includes such key questions as: Will one firm be acquired and operated as a wholly owned subsidiary? Does the transaction imply a merger of equals? Are layoffs implied, and if so, where? On what basis can promised synergies or cost savings be achieved?

4. **Perform a due diligence assessment.** This involves evaluating whether the two organizations actually have the managerial, technical, and financial resources that each assumes the other possesses. It includes a comprehensive review of each organization's articles of incorporation, stock option plans, organization charts, and so on. Financial, operational, technical, logistical, and human resources inventories are evaluated along with other legally binding issues. The discovery of previously unknown or unfavorable information can halt the M&A process.

   Although due diligence assessment traditionally emphasizes the financial aspects of M&As, this focus is increasingly being challenged by evidence that culture clashes between two organizations can ruin expected financial gains.[16] Thus, attention to the cultural features of M&As is becoming more prevalent in due diligence assessment. For example, Microsoft's venture integration team applies cultural and talent screens as part of its due diligence activities along with financial and operational criteria. The process identifies the fit between Microsoft's values and those of possible merger candidates. Human resource assessments like these contribute heavily to the success of the merger. OD expertise can contribute significantly to M&A cultural assessment; it can help organizations carry out cultural due diligence systematically and objectively.

   The scope and detail of due diligence assessment depend on knowledge of the candidate's business, the complexity of its industry, the relative size and risk of the transaction, and the available resources. Due diligence activities must reflect symbolically the vision and values of the combined organizations. An overly zealous assessment, for example, can contradict promises of openness and trust made earlier in the transaction. Missteps at this stage can lower or destroy opportunities for synergy, cost savings, and improved shareholder value.[17]

5. **Develop merger integration plans.** This stage specifies how the two organizations will be combined. It defines integration objectives; the scope and timing of

integration activities; organization design criteria; Day 1 requirements; and who does what, where, and when. The scope of these plans depends on how integrated the organizations will be. If the candidate organization will operate as an independent subsidiary with an "arm's-length" relationship to the parent, such as Microsoft's initial decision with Skype, merger integration planning need only specify those systems that will be common to both organizations. A full integration of the two organizations requires a more extensive plan.

Merger integration planning starts with the business case conducted earlier and involves more detailed analyses of the strategic vision, competitive strategy, and systems integration for the M&A. For example, assessment of the organizations' markets and suppliers can reveal opportunities to serve customers better and to capture purchasing economies of scale. Examination of business processes can identify best operating practices; which physical facilities should be combined, left alone, or shut down; and which systems and procedures are redundant. Capital budgeting processes can show which investments should be continued or dropped. Typically, the M&A team charters subgroups composed of members from both organizations to perform these analyses. OD practitioners can conduct team-building and process-consultation interventions to improve how those groups function.

Next, plans for designing the combined organization are developed. They include the organization's structure, reporting relationships, human resources policies, information and control systems, operating logistics, work designs, and customer-focused activities. Applying large-scale change interventions are most appropriate here.

The final task of integration planning involves developing an action plan for implementing the M&A. This specifies tasks to be performed, decision-making authority and responsibility, and timelines for achievement. It also includes a process for addressing conflicts and problems that will invariably arise during the implementation process.

Legal Combination Phase This phase of the M&A process involves the legal and financial aspects of the transaction. The two organizations settle on the terms of the deal, register the transaction with and gain approval from appropriate regulatory agencies, communicate with and gain approval from shareholders, and file appropriate legal documents. In some cases, an OD practitioner can provide advice on negotiating a fair agreement, but this phase generally requires knowledge and expertise beyond that typically found in OD practice.

Operational Combination Phase This final phase involves implementing the merger integration plan. In practice, it begins during due diligence assessment and may continue for months or years following the legal combination phase. M&A implementation includes the three kinds of activities described below.

1. **Day 1 activities.** These include communications and actions that officially start the implementation process. For example, announcements may be made about key executives of the combined organization, the location of corporate headquarters, the structure of tasks, and areas and functions where layoffs will occur. Special attention is paid to sending important symbolic messages to organization members, investors, and regulators about the soundness of the merger plans and the changes that are critical to accomplishing strategic and operational objectives.[18]
2. **Operational and technical integration activities.** These involve the physical moves, structural changes, work designs, and procedures that will be implemented to

accomplish the strategic objectives and expected cost savings of the M&A. The merger integration plan lists these activities, which can be large in number and range in scope from seemingly trivial to quite critical. For example, United Airlines's acquisition of Continental involved changing employee uniforms, the signage at all airports, marketing and public relations campaigns, repainting airplanes, and integrating the route structures, among others. When these integration activities are not executed properly, the M&A process can be set back.

Application 20.1 describes some of the operational, technical, and cultural integration activities associated with the United–Continental merger.[19]

3. **Cultural integration activities.** These tasks are aimed at building new values and norms in the combined organization. Successful implementation melds both the technical and cultural aspects of the combined organization. For example, members from both organizations can be encouraged to solve business problems together, thus addressing operational and cultural integration issues simultaneously.[20]

The M&A literature contains several practical suggestions for managing the operational combination phase.[21] First, the merger integration plan should be implemented sooner rather than later, and quickly rather than slowly. Integration of two organizations generally involves aggressive financial targets, short timelines, and intense public scrutiny. Moreover, the change process is often plagued by culture clashes and political fighting. Consequently, organizations need to make as many changes as possible in the first hundred days following the legal combination phase. Quick movement in key areas has several advantages. It preempts unanticipated organization changes that might thwart momentum in the desired direction; it reduces organization members' uncertainty about when things will happen; and it lessens members' anxiety about the M&A's impact on their personal situation. All three of these conditions work against desired collaboration and other benefits.

Second, integration activities must be communicated clearly and promptly to a variety of stakeholders, including shareholders, regulators, customers, and organization members. M&As can increase uncertainty and anxiety about the future, especially for members of the involved organizations who often inquire: Will I have a job? Will my job change? Will I have a new boss? These kinds of questions can dominate conversations, reduce productive work, and spoil opportunities for collaboration. To reduce ambiguity, organizations can provide concrete answers through a variety of channels including company newsletters, email and intranet postings, press releases, video, podcasts, and in-person presentations, one-on-one interaction with managers, and so on.

Third, members from both organizations need to work together to solve implementation problems and to address customer needs. Such coordinated tasks can clarify work roles and relationships and contribute to member commitment and motivation. Moreover, when coordinated activity is directed at customer service, it can assure customers that their interests will be considered and satisfied during the merger.

Fourth, organizations need to assess the implementation process continually to identify integration problems and needs. The following questions can guide the assessment process:[22]

- Have savings estimated during precombination planning been confirmed or exceeded?
- Has the new entity identified and implemented shared strategies or opportunities?
- Has the new organization been implemented without loss of key personnel?
- Was the merger and integration process seen as fair and objective?
- Is the combined company operating efficiently?

application 20.1

PLANNING THE UNITED–CONTINENTAL MERGER

United Airlines is one of the oldest and most recognized brands in the world. But like most of the older airlines, it has struggled over the years. Beset by a weak industry structure—overcapacity, easy entry, and a perishable product (empty seats can never be resold)—few airlines make money. Financial analysts have, for years, called on the airlines to restructure, lower costs, and consolidate. Following the widespread bankruptcies in the wake of 9/11, consolidation has slowly set in, leading to the mergers of US Airways and America West; Delta and Northwest; Southwest and AirTran; and, most recently, United and Continental. With consolidation comes an opportunity for organization development.

The announcement of the United and Continental merger in May 2010 was the ultimate event in a long string of strategic decisions by both organizations. Before actually coming together as merger partners, United and Continental had discussed the possibility of a formal merger. But United's merger talks with US Airways, United's and Continental's own journeys through bankruptcies, their "virtual" merger through the Star Alliance, and Continental's equity relationship with Northwest prevented consummation of the deal.

When the path to a merger opened up, the rationale for the deal went beyond simple economics. Important organizational reasons included Continental's superior management capabilities and reputation as well as United's scale and scope. These issues were apparent even as the deal was announced: Former Continental head, Jeff Smisek, was named CEO of the new company and many if not most top management positions were to be filled with former Continental executives, but the company would be called United and its headquarters would be in Chicago.

Combining two airlines is tremendously difficult, largely because of the number of things they can do differently. For example, choices have to be made on boarding processes (Continental's traditional back to front process or United's window, middle, then aisle seat process); baggage and loading policies (should all dog crates be loaded backwards into the cargo hold so frightened dogs don't tip the crate off the conveyor belt); uniforms (male Continental employees could choose from three different shirts and a few ties, United only has the one); how to identify unaccompanied minors (bracelet or a button); and whether to serve nuts in a bag or a heated dish in first class.

The planning and integration efforts utilized "functional integration teams"—Continental employees working alongside United employees in months of meetings—to make things happen. For example, 33 functional integration teams in the fourth quarter of 2011 spent $170 million on everything from technology training and severance to repainting airplanes in an attempt to balance safety, cost, space, style, reliability, convenience, speed, and comfort.

Simple choices could become incredibly complicated. For example, a 14-member functional integration beverage team composed of members from procurement, flight operations, finance, food services, and marketing was chartered with, among other things, choosing a coffee supplier. Continental and United had different coffee providers, and it made no sense to have two contracts. Buying from one source offered the possibility of bigger volume discounts and the kinds of savings Wall Street was expecting. The taste test winner was cheaper and it was approved by colleagues outside the beverage committee, the new CEO, and company officers at a general meeting. Just to be sure, the new blend was tested on flight attendants in Washington Dulles, Chicago O'Hare, Denver, Los Angeles, and San Francisco. Out of the 1,100 who did, all but eight approved.

On July 1, the new United introduced its new coffee, and the protests came flying in. Flight attendants reported a barrage of complaints, and the beverage committee and the CEO received angry emails from customers. The coffee was "watery." When the beverage committee looked into it, they discovered that it wasn't the coffee: The coffee makers on United aircraft were different from Continental's, and the differences—the height of the brew basket above the pot—determined whether excess water flowed into the pot (watering down the coffee) or not.

One of the biggest challenges was planning the integration of the flight information and passenger information systems. As CEO Smisek put it, "It's akin to changing the engine while the airplane's in flight." The flight information system tracks everything related to a particular flight, including the type of plane, departure and arrival times, flight number, air speed, altitude, and current location. The system is monitored by employees in the network operations center. Merging Continental's and United's operations centers was handled by the operations center's functional integration team and took more than 18 months. The team had to determine the hardware and software platforms that would best handle the volume and complexity of activity as well as the system's operation. For example, every airline has a set of rules to determine when a plane will go faster to make up for a late departure and when it will not—the so-called "speedup-slowdown calculation." Flying faster is costly because more fuel is used, but being late costs money in terms of missed connections, rebooking costs, putting stranded customers up in hotels, and paying extra time for flight crews and ground crews. United's and Continental's calculations didn't always agree and the functional integration team had to marry the best of both.

Moreover, the functional integration team had to plan the exhaustive list of tests and contingency plans to ensure that the data could be combined without breaking the system. When the team thought it had an integration solution in place, they tested the system by flying an empty Continental 737 from Houston to El Paso and back just to make sure the operations center could track it. Then they had the pilots pretend to have a mechanical problem and return to the gate, and then they had the pilots change the flight number and reroute the plane to Austin to see if that showed up.

Integrating the flight information system involved more than 500 employees reducing 440 manuals down to 260. When the new system came online, the only glitch was that the few planes that had crossed the international dateline had an extra 24 hours added to their arrival times. The FAA awarded the new United a single operating certificate on November 30, 2011.

The second technical integration challenge, the passenger information system, proved more troublesome. The system hosts the website and reservation system, tracks schedules and schedule changes, records frequent flyer information, connects ticket counters to airport kiosks to gates, and prints boarding passes. Until the passenger information system is integrated, the organization looks to customers and really acts like separate airlines, with separate websites, gates, ticketing processes, and so on. United customers who want help from a Continental agent cannot get it.

As with the flight system integration, there are technical issues to address but the real layer of complexity is that this system is used by customers and employees alike. The new United adopted Continental's passenger services system, a Hewlett-Packard program called Shares that is more flexible than United's old Apollo system. Although it provides a more customizable customer experience, it is also less intuitive and therefore required a lot of training. There was some fear among the agents. "It's a little challenging at the moment. We just get this on-the-job training a couple hours here and there," said a 20-year United employee.

Although United began planning this integration early on, the complexity of the data interactions—and an independent and unrelated decision to change a few of the elements of the frequent flyer programs at the same time—was too much to handle. The lack of training, the inevitable technical glitches, and the increased call loads from frequent flyers asking questions overwhelmed the system and employees. Initially, the system operated poorly and there were loud complaints from both customers and employees.

Integrating labor practices, talent, and culture is one of the biggest issues in most mergers, and integrating United's and Continental's human capital practices and culture was expected to be a particular challenge. Continental had a strong reputation as an employee- and customer-focused organization. Like other carriers, it had to deal with high fuel prices, natural disasters (such as the volcanic eruption in Iceland), and the recession, but it had managed to retain its positive culture.

Continental was consistently at the top of customer satisfaction surveys and the country's 100 best employers. Labor relations and customer service reputations at United, however, were just the opposite. Its 2002–2006 bankruptcy involved layoffs and salary cuts, increased customer complaints, and pilot "sick outs." Although these were the most proximate causes of mistrust, there was a legacy of hostility.

Like the technical processes, United adopted the functional integration team idea to address its human capital and culture strategies. All of them had to work together to build a coordinated workforce. For example, getting alignment among the labor agreements was as much a social issue as a financial one. Looking like one airline to consumers means that employees have to feel like one airline. Integrating contracts meant reconciling rules regarding schedules, routes, seniority, and pay. Despite its importance, this was a difficult process because United and Continental had similar groups of employees that were represented by different collective bargaining agreements, as well as employee groups that were covered by a union in one organization that were not covered by a union in the other. Sequencing union votes, talent selection processes, and HR systems integration were a big part of the HR functional integration of team's responsibilities.

Fortunately, the team had a lot of help from the top. The new United management saw the merger as a rare opportunity to get things right. CEO Smisek noted, "My management team and I are spending a lot of time on developing the new culture. It won't be precisely Continental's culture, and it sure won't be United's old culture. It'll be something that takes what I hope to be the best of both. We're very focused on that because you do run the risk in any integration of ending up with mediocrity."

In the first days after the merger was closed, Smisek did 16 "CEO exchanges" in the United States. Standing up in front of employees, he answered any question they wanted. This was something the Continental employees understood, but the United workers had never seen. The tough questions came quickly. "When are you going to snap me back to the wages I had in the year 2000?" The answer was "never," and Smisek had to explain that today's airline industry was different than it was in 2000; that the business had changed because low-cost carriers were now an important part of the way business was done. The exchanges were continued in Europe, Asia, and Latin America before more were conducted in the United States

The new management team was also hoping to use the new strategy to align people to the business. The new United adopted the "Go Forward Plan" process from Continental. Once a year, the Go Forward Plan was a short, simple, and easy to understand statement, no more than one-page long, of marketing, finance, operations, and employee objectives. As a pilot, ticket agent, or operations person, it focused everybody on the things that mattered most. Smisek tells people that "if you're doing something and you can't trace it back to the Go Forward Plan, stop what you're doing and do something else."

Although there were some bumps along the way and the culture and labor integration processes continue, the use of functional integration teams to address the important operational challenges and senior management's visible commitment to the merger have helped United manage the change.

- Have major problems with stakeholders been avoided?
- Did the process proceed according to schedule?
- Were substantive integration issues resolved?
- Are people highly motivated (more so than before)?

M&As are among the most complex and challenging interventions facing organizations and OD practitioners.

20-3 Strategic Alliance Interventions

A strategic alliance is a formal agreement between two or more organizations to pursue a set of private and common goals through the sharing, exchange, or codevelopment of resources, including intellectual property, people, capital, technology, capabilities, or physical assets.[23] It is an important strategy for such organizations as Microsoft, Eli Lilly, Corning Glass, DOW, Federal Express, IBM, Starbucks, Cisco Systems, and Oracle. The term *strategic alliance* generally refers to any collaborative effort between two or more organizations, including licensing agreements, franchises, long-term contracts, and joint ventures. Franchising is a common collaborative strategy.[24] Companies such as McDonald's, Subway, or Holiday Inn license their name and know-how to independent organizations that deliver the service and leverage the brand name for marketing. A *joint venture* is a special type of strategic alliance where a third organization, jointly owned and operated by two (or more) organizations, is created.[25] Joint ventures between domestic and foreign firms, such as Equate, a joint venture between DOW and Petrochemical Industries Companies KSC to produce value-added chemicals and plastics, or Fuji–Xerox, a long-term collaboration that began with Fuji selling Xerox copying machines in Japan, can help overcome trade barriers and facilitate technology transfer across nations. The New United Motor Manufacturing, Inc., in Fremont, California, for example, was a successful, long-term joint venture between General Motors and Toyota to produce automobiles using Japanese teamwork methods that was just recently dissolved.

20-3a Application Stages

The development of effective strategic alliances generally follows a process of strategy formulation, partner selection, alliance structuring and start-up, and alliance operation and adjustment.

1. **Alliance strategy formulation.** The first step in developing strategic alliances is to clarify the business strategy and understand why an alliance is an appropriate method to implement it. About one-half to two-thirds of alliances fail to meet their financial objectives, and the number one reason for that failure is the lack of a clear strategy.[26] For example, Collins found that alliance success was heavily influenced by the alignment of the partner to the company's "hedgehog concept" or what it is best at doing.[27] If the organization understood its passion, distinctive capabilities, and economic drivers, it was more likely to develop alliances that supported its strategy. Thus, it is important to pursue alliances according to a "collaboration logic."[28] The alliance must be seen as a more effective way of organizing and operating than developing new capabilities to perform the work in-house; acquiring or merging with another organization; or buying the capabilities from another organization in a transactional relationship.
2. **Partner selection.** Once the reasons for a strategic alliance are clear, the search for an appropriate partner or partners begins. Alliances always involve a cost–benefit trade-off; while the organization typically gains access to new markets or new capabilities, it does so at the cost of yielding some autonomy and control over its activities.

   Similar to identifying merger and acquisition candidates discussed previously, this step involves developing screening criteria, agreeing on candidates, establishing initial contacts, and formulating a letter of intent. A good alliance partnership will leverage both similarities and differences to create competitive advantage. Compatible commitment levels, management styles, cultures, goals, information technologies, or operations are important similarities that can smooth alliance formation and implementation.[29] However, different perspectives, technologies, capabilities, and other resources can complement existing ones and be good sources of learning and value in the partnership. These differences can also be a source of frustration for the alliance.

OD practitioners can add value at this stage of the process by helping potential alliance partners explore and understand their similarities and differences. In addition, the way the alliance begins and proceeds is an important ingredient in building trust, a characteristic of successful alliances explored more fully in the next step.

3. **Alliance structuring and start-up.** Following agreement to enter into an alliance, the focus shifts to how to structure the partnership and build and leverage trust in the relationship. First, an appropriate governance structure must be chosen and can include medium- to long-term contracts, minority equity investments, equal equity partnerships, or majority equity investments. As the proportion of equity investment increases, the costs, risk, and amount of required management attention also increase.[30] In general, partners need to know how expenses, profits, risk, and knowledge will be shared.

   Second, research increasingly points to "relational quality" as a key success factor of long-term alliances.[31] Strategic alliances shift the nature of the relationship from the simple exchange of goods, services, or resources with no necessary expectation of a future relationship to one where there is a clear expectation of future exchange. The organizations in the relationship must act in good faith to ensure the future. This requires trust, "a psychological state comprising the intention to accept vulnerability based upon positive expectations of the intentions or behavior" of another firm or individual representing the organization. It implies an expectation that the organization will subordinate its self-interest to the "joint interest" of the alliance under most conditions.[32]

   Trust can increase or decrease over the life of the alliance. Early in the alliance formation process, it can serve as an initial reservoir of comfort and confidence based on perceptions of the organizations' reputation, prior success, and other sources. These same factors can also contribute to a lack of initial trust. Trust can be increased or decreased by new assessments of the others' capabilities, competence, and ethical behavior. OD practitioners can assist in this initial start-up phase by making implicit perceptions of trust explicit and getting the involved parties to set appropriate expectations.[33] During the structuring and start-up phase, trust can increase through direct activities as a function of the number, frequency, and importance of interactions; differences between expectations and reality; the nature of mistakes and how they are resolved; and attributions made about partners' behavior.

4. **Alliance operation and adjustment.** Once the strategic alliance is functioning, the full range of OD interventions described in this text can be applied. Team building, conflict resolution, large-group interventions, work design, employee involvement, dynamic strategy making, and culture change efforts have all been reported in alliance work.[34] OD practitioners should pay particular attention to helping each partner in the alliance clarify the capabilities contributed, the lessons learned, and the benefits received.

   Diagnosing the state of the strategic alliance and making the appropriate adjustments is a function of understanding whether the environment has changed in ways that make transorganizational linkage unnecessary, whether partner goals and capabilities have changed the nature of the relationship and interdependence, and whether the alliance is successfully generating outcomes. The long-term success of the Fuji-Xerox joint venture, for example, has been due to the willingness and ability of the two organizations to adjust the relationship in terms of ownership, profit sharing, new product development responsibilities, and market access.[35]

Application 20.2 describes an alliance-building intervention between two firms in India.[36] It shows how, despite good intentions, OD projects can encounter vexing problems, especially in cross-cultural alliance contexts.

application 20.2

BUILDING ALLIANCE RELATIONSHIPS

Maharashtra Hybrid Seeds Company Limited (MAHYCO), the leading producer and marketer of hybrid seeds in India, formed a strategic alliance with Monsanto to expand and extend its business. Founded in 1964 by B. R. Barwale, the father of the Green Revolution in India, MAHYCO was family owned and run. Mr. Barwale's son was the firm's managing director (MD) and several family members played critical roles in its daily management. In 1998, the company opened a state-of-the-art research and development complex, the same year that B. R. Barwale received the World Food Prize for his work on hybrid seed development.

In the early 1990s, MAHYCO first made contact with Monsanto India Private Limited as a potential business partner with complementary capabilities. Monsanto India was part of the Monsanto Company, a publicly held multinational corporation based in the United States, and a leading global developer of transgenic plants using biotechnology. Monsanto's focus on biotechnology, part of the firm's larger transformation from chemicals to biotechnology, gave it the lead in introducing insect- and herbicide-resistant genetic traits in plants. With a presence in India since 1947, Monsanto India had a sales and marketing organization with a research facility and formulation plant.

During the next few years, the two companies explored a strategic alliance primarily through personal relationships among MAHYCO's MD and two key executives from Monsanto India, an Indian operations manager and an expatriate from the United States. The MD had strong interest in progressive business practices; the Monsanto operations manager possessed a keen business savvy and local knowledge; and the expatriate had tremendous technical knowledge and cultural sensitivity. These qualities helped the three executives forge a strong personal bond based on respect, friendship, and trust.

In 1998, Monsanto made an equity investment in MAHYCO. The two companies believed that their complementary resources and capabilities could be leveraged to develop competitive advantage for the alliance. For example, MAHYCO could apply Monsanto's biotechnological know-how to its vast germ plasma inventory to create plants that would support the food production and fiber needs of South Asia. Even with Monsanto's long-term presence in India, MAHYCO could provide it with better access to India's markets, government officials, and regulatory agencies.

In moving the alliance forward, however, both firms recognized that their different corporate cultures posed a special challenge. MAHYCO's culture was characterized by high levels of loyalty and commitment, owing to its family background and close connection to the noble effort of bringing biotechnology to India. The firm's management–employee relationship was highly formal, with little employee involvement in decisions and low comfort with change. Monsanto, on the other hand, was nearly opposite on all of these dimensions. It was a large fast-paced organization undergoing considerable change. Its people were in constant flux as its business models and plans were changing. Many were new to the organization and just learning their positions, while the experienced people were leading the company's conversion from chemicals to biotechnology.

Given these organizational differences and the fact that neither partner could know in advance how long the alliance would last, MAHYCO employees were fearful that Monsanto would buy out or consume MAHYCO and thereby threaten their careers. Adding to the ambiguity and stress, MAHYCO's MD openly expressed hope that the alliance would help the firm become more professionally managed and malleable, and less patriarchal and rigid.

Building on the strong personal bond between the three executives at the top of the two firms, an alliance-building intervention was considered to develop trust and collaboration at lower organizational levels. In preparing for the change program, an OD team interviewed

44 people from Monsanto India and MAHYCO. Numerous opportunities and obstacles to alliance success were identified. Members of both organizations wanted to learn more about their partner's business and culture. They expressed excitement about combining their resources in the alliance and cited the importance of collaboration and mutual understanding to make it work. Four critical success factors emerged from the interviews: clear vision and mission for the alliance, key initiatives and goals, mutual trust and operating norms, and support for each firm's internal change plans.

The OD team then met with the top leaders at MAHYCO and Monsanto India and proposed an appreciative inquiry (AI) process for the alliance-building program. It would involve multiple organizational levels and include all relevant alliance stakeholders. AI would help participants create common ground, discover each other's capabilities, and envision the alliance's future. The proposed intervention was approved by Monsanto India but surprisingly rejected by MAHYCO, which was uncomfortable with the AI process. Specifically, MAHYCO's leaders believed they did not know enough about Monsanto India to engage in an open, loosely structured process for developing relationships and setting alliance direction and strategy. Moreover, they felt that AI would give too much decision-making power to middle managers, take too much time, and be seen as too childish for grown men with many years of experience. As a compromise, MAHYCO agreed that its R&D people would engage in AI with their Monsanto India counterparts, but the MAHYCO executive team would only participate in a more formal management education session to learn more about the alliance and their partner. Thus, two different alliance-building interventions were conducted in late 1998.

The AI session was attended by 32 participants representing four cross-alliance R&D teams. One of those teams—the Cotton team—had already been formed and was actively working on a joint project. An opening exercise encouraged participants to build relationships that go beyond name tags. It was followed by an information session where participants learned about the alliance partners and the purpose for the alliance. They gained insight about each firm's core strengths and the synergies that could be derived from the alliance. In fact, this exercise had such a strong impact that the design of the subsequent management education session was modified to include it. The AI session then moved from learning to envisioning. Participants were asked to imagine how the alliance would be publicly recognized by the year 2005. They imagined an alliance that would increase the nutrient content of pulse crops, create nitrogen-fixating plants, develop new insect-resistant crops, and spawn a "gene revolution" (a playful allusion to the Green Revolution). Moreover, the alliance would create plants that produce hydrocarbons and new color fibers and ensure the Asian food supply. Many participants experienced the envisioning process as energizing; others, mostly from the Cotton team, however, were skeptical and viewed it as "waste of our time." Despite this criticism, the subsequent dialogue revealed productive ways to address the alliance vision and to create action plans. For example, one R&D team that had not met prior to the session developed several recommendations on how to improve information sharing between the two companies.

The management education session was conducted in a more traditional presentation format than the AI session and included MAHYCO's top-30 managers and Monsanto India's top 10. It was geared to providing participants with better understanding of the alliance partners—their history, current business, future opportunities, and expectations for the alliance. After formal introductions, the session involved presentations on alliance management and Monsanto's biotechnology strategy. The latter was mainly for the benefit of MAHYCO's executives. Then, participants learned about each firm's core competencies and how they translated into alliance benefits. Interestingly, this part of the session evolved into a somewhat awkward discussion about "professionalism" in the MAHYCO organization. The ensuing dialogue about changing from a family business to a more professional firm raised issues of trust, loyalty, respect, and so on, all topics difficult to address in this formal setting.

With facilitation from the OD team, the education session shifted to question-and-answer discussions geared to increase cross-firm communication and understanding. The session ended with discussion of the top executives' role in making the alliance successful. Participants generated ideas for the next steps in developing the alliance and positioning it and biotechnology in India. They assumed no further responsibility, however, for implementing them, leaving it up to the Director of Monsanto India and the MAHYCO MD to determine the next steps and to make them happen.

In sum, the AI and ME alliance-building interventions differed considerably in their respective purposes, participants, processes, and outcomes. The AI session encouraged learning, relationship building, and cocreation of future alliance plans, whereas the management education session was intended to convey information about the alliance and its partner organizations. To assess intervention results, the OD team administered questionnaires to all participants at the beginning and end of both sessions. In addition, a follow-up survey was administered to all participants via email four months later to explore any longitudinal effects of the interventions. Seventy-two percent of AI participants returned the email survey, while only half of the management education participants did. Participants in the AI session reported significantly greater levels of relationship building, collaboration, and follow-through in alliance project development than did the education session participants. Management education participants indicated that they missed the opportunity to build relationships. Participants in both sessions reported increased levels of mutual understanding, thereby laying the foundation for future alliance development.

Over the next six years, many of the same issues that showed up in the alliance-building sessions still persisted, to the dismay of the OD team. These included concerns over trust and collaboration, unwillingness to change, and inequalities in compensation and available equipment between the two partners. People who were roadblocks in 1998 were still roadblocks in 2003. Aspects of corporate control and decision making were still frustrating the alliance, making it difficult to chart its own future and success. The inherent differences between the two partner organizations continued to challenge alliance leadership.

On reflection, members of the OD team learned from their alliance experience. They realized that their original views about the AI and education interventions were overly optimistic, even naive. What they observed during the AI session was only surface-level dialogue, the result of a design that minimized tension and fostered collaboration. They concluded that alliance partners as well as OD professionals need to enhance their business and cultural knowledge prior to participating in a cross-cultural alliance intervention. From a business perspective, for example, it would be helpful for participants to diagnose their own organization prior to the alliance-building activities. This would provide valuable insight into the firm's collaborative orientation and alliance capability, providing a realistic basis for determining how best to create and develop the alliance. From a cultural perspective, it would be helpful to appreciate the diverse ways in which people from different cultures are likely to react to alliance interventions such as AI and management education. In intergroup encounters, for example, people from more implicit cultures (such as India) tend to share only a shade of what they believe and feel. In contrast, people from more explicit cultures (such as the United States) tend to be more open and forward in such interactions. Such understanding would be invaluable in designing how best to build alliance relationships. Finally, the OD team concluded that alliance building is not a one-time event but an ongoing process. It needs continuous organizational support and attention to the structures and processes that sustain optimal levels of collaboration and trust among alliance partners.

20-4 Network Interventions

Network interventions help organizations join together for a common purpose; their use is growing rapidly in today's highly competitive, global environment.[37] In the private sector, research and development consortia, for example, allow companies to share resources and risks associated with large-scale research efforts. Networks among airlines with regional specializations combine to provide worldwide coverage; Japanese *keiretsu,* Korean *chaeobols,* or Mexican *grupos* enable different organizations to take advantage of complementary capabilities among them. In the public sector, partnerships between government and business provide the resources and initiative to undertake complex urban renewal projects, such as Cleveland's Cuyahoga River, Baltimore's Inner Harbor Project, and Lyon's *zones de redynamisation urbaines* (urban renewal zones), or improve health care, including Sweden's "Bring a Friend" program that increases cancer screenings or Britain's National Health Service (NHS) sustainability project. Other networks of business, labor, government, education, finance, community organizations, and economic development agencies, such as China's Low Carbon City Initiative, are helping to identify exemplary efforts related to building and energy efficiency, public awareness, and low carbon development that can help coordinate services and promote more responsible growth.[38]

Managing the development of multiorganizational networks involves two types of change: (1) creating the initial network and (2) managing change within an established network. Both change processes are complex and not well understood. First, the initial creation of networks recognizes their underorganized nature. Forming them into a more coherent, operating whole involves understanding the relationships among the participating organizations and their roles in the system, as well as the implications and consequences of organizations leaving the network, changing roles, or increasing their influence. Second, change within existing networks must account for the relationships among member organizations as a whole system.[39] The multiple and complex relationships involved in networks produce emergent phenomena that cannot be fully explained by simply knowing the parts. Each organization in the network has goals that are partly related to the good of the network and partly focused on self-interest. How the network reacts over time is even more difficult to capture and is part of the emerging science of complexity.[40]

20-4a Creating the Network

OD practitioners have evolved a unique form of planned change aimed at creating networks and improving their effectiveness.[41] In laying out the conceptual boundaries of network development, also known as *transorganizational development*, Cummings described the practice as following the phases of planned change appropriate for underorganized systems (Chapter 2).[42] The four stages are shown in Figure 20.1 along with key issues that need to be addressed at each stage. The stages and issues are described below.

1. **Identification stage.** This initial stage of network development involves identifying existing and potential member organizations best suited to achieving their collective objectives. Identifying potential members can be difficult because organizations may not perceive the need to join together or may not know enough about each other to make membership choices. These problems are typical when trying to create a new network. Relationships among potential members may be loosely coupled or nonexistent; thus, even if organizations see the need to form a network, they may be unsure about who should be included.

   The identification stage is generally carried out by one or a few organizations interested in exploring the possibility of creating a network. OD practitioners work with these initiating organizations to clarify their own goals, such as product or technology exchange, learning, or market access, and to understand the trade-off between the loss of autonomy and the value of collaboration. Change agents also help specify criteria for network membership and identify organizations meeting those standards. Because networks are intended to address particular problems or opportunities, a practical criterion for membership is how much organizations can contribute to this work. Potential members can be identified and judged in terms of the skills, knowledge, and resources that they bring to bear on the network task. Practitioners warn, however, that identifying potential members also should take

FIGURE 20.1

Application Stages for Transorganizational Development

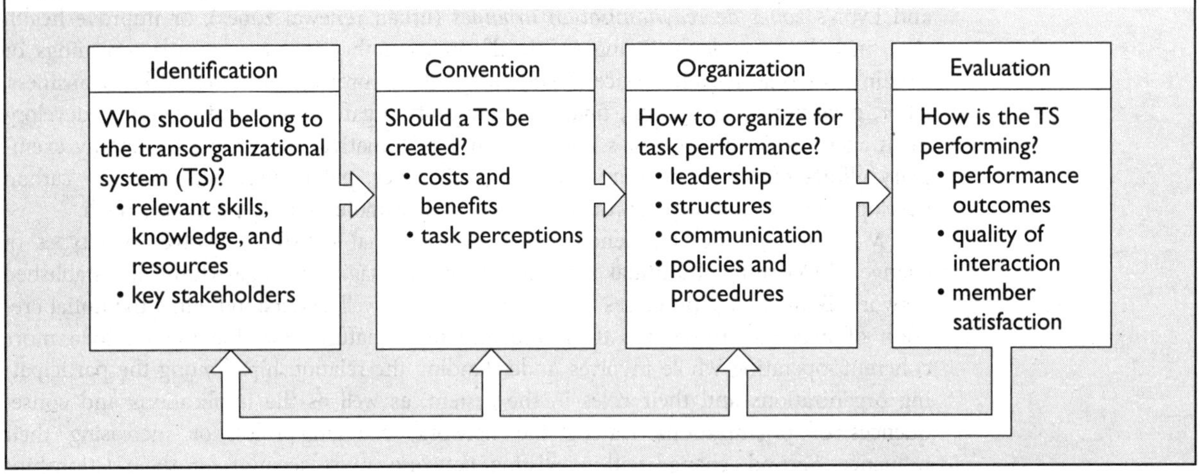

into account the political realities of the situation.[43] Consequently, key stakeholders who can affect the creation and subsequent performance of the network are identified as possible members.

An important difficulty at this stage can be insufficient leadership and cohesion among participants to choose potential members. In these situations, OD practitioners may need to play a more activist role in creating the network.[44] They may need to bring structure to a group of autonomous organizations that do not see the need to join together or may not know how to form relationships. In several cases of network development, change agents helped members create a special leadership group that could make decisions on behalf of the participating organizations.[45] This leadership group comprised a small cadre of committed members and was able to develop enough cohesion among members to carry out the identification stage. The OD activist role requires a good deal of leadership and direction. For example, change agents may need to educate potential network members about the benefits of joining together. They may need to structure face-to-face encounters aimed at sharing information and exploring interaction possibilities.

2. **Convention stage.** Once potential network members are identified, the convention stage is concerned with bringing them together to assess whether formalizing the network is desirable and feasible. This face-to-face meeting enables potential members to explore mutually their motivations for joining and their perceptions of the activities they might have to perform together. They work to establish sufficient levels of motivation and task consensus to form the network.

   Like the identification stage, this phase of network creation generally requires considerable direction and facilitation by OD practitioners. Existing stakeholders may not have the legitimacy or skills to perform the convening function, and practitioners can serve as conveners if they are perceived as legitimate and credible by the attending organizations. This necessitates that change agents maintain a neutral role, treating all members alike.[46] They need to be seen by members as working on behalf of the total system, rather than as being aligned with particular organizations or views. When practitioners are perceived as neutral, network members are more likely to share information with them and to listen to their inputs. Such neutrality can enhance change agents' ability to mediate conflicts among members. It can help them uncover diverse views and interests and forge agreements among stakeholders. OD practitioners, for example, can act as mediators, ensuring that members' views receive a fair hearing and that disputes are equitably resolved. They can help to bridge the different views and interests and achieve integrative solutions. In many cases, practitioners come from research centers or universities with reputations for neutrality and expertise in networks. Because participating organizations tend to have diverse motives and views and limited means for resolving differences, change agents may need to structure and manage interactions to facilitate airing of differences and arriving at consensus about forming the network. They may need to help organizations work through differences and reconcile self-interests with those of the larger network.

Research and practice suggest that the movement from convention into organization is facilitated by agreement among TS members as to the problem/opportunity to be address, the interdependence of network members required to address the issue, and the likelihood that concerted effort will result in positive outcomes.[47] Known as a "negotiated order," TS members' realization of the potential power of a network is key to the network moving forward. Nathan and Mitroff demonstrated how a negotiated order among business, government, and nonprofit organizations concerned with crisis management emerged and facilitated action.[48] Worley and Parker's study of the Cuyahoga River Valley's government-led initiative showed how the lack of a clear negotiated order can hinder network development.[49]

3. **Organization stage.** When the convention stage results in a decision to create a network, members then begin to organize themselves for task performance. This involves developing the structures and mechanisms that promote communication and interaction among members and that direct joint efforts on the activities required to achieve TS objectives.[50] It includes the organizations to be involved in the network and the roles each will play; the communication and relationships among them; and the control system that will guide decision making and provide a mechanism for monitoring performance. For example, members may create a coordinating council to manage the network and a powerful leader to head it.[51] They might choose to formalize exchanges among members by developing rules, policies, and formal operating procedures. When members are required to invest large amounts of resources in the network, such as might occur in an industry-based research consortium, the organizing stage typically includes voluminous contracting and negotiating about members' contributions and returns. Here, corporate lawyers and financial analysts play key roles in specifying the network structure. They determine how costs and benefits will be allocated among member organizations as well as the legal obligations, decision-making responsibilities, and contractual rights of members. OD practitioners can help members define competitive advantage for the network as well as the structural requirements necessary to support achievement of its goals.
4. **Evaluation stage.** This final stage of creating a network involves assessing how the network is performing. Members need feedback so they can identify problems and begin to resolve them. This generally includes information about performance outcomes and member satisfaction, as well as indicators of how well members are interacting jointly. Change agents can periodically interview or survey member organizations about various outcomes and features of the network and feed that data back to network leaders. Such information enables network leaders to make necessary operational modifications and adjustments. It may signal the need to return to previous stages in the process to make necessary corrections, as shown by the feedback arrows in Figure 20.1.

20-4b Managing Network Change

In addition to developing new networks, OD practitioners may need to facilitate change within established networks. Planned change in existing networks derives from an understanding of the "new sciences," including complexity, nonlinear systems, catastrophe, and chaos theories. From these perspectives, organization networks are viewed as complex systems displaying the following properties:[52]

1. The behavior of a network is sensitive to small differences in its initial conditions. How the network was established and formed—the depth and nature of trust among the partners, who was selected (and not selected) to be in the network, and how the network was organized—play a key role in its willingness and ability to change.
2. Networks display "emergent" properties or characteristics that cannot be explained through an analysis of the parts: "Given the properties of the parts and the laws of their interaction, it is not a trivial matter to infer the properties of the whole."[53] The tools of systems thinking and the understanding of emergence in complex systems are still being developed and applied.[54]
3. A variety of network behaviors and patterns, both expected and unexpected, can emerge from members performing tasks and making decisions according to simple rules to which everyone agreed. This is amply demonstrated in Senge's "beer game" simulation where a retailer, a wholesaler, and a brewery each acts according to the simple rule of maximizing its own profit. Participants in the simulation routinely end up with enormous inventories of poor-selling beer, delayed deliveries, excess capacity, and other problems. Without an understanding of the "whole" system, the nature of interdependencies within the system, and timely and complete information, each part, acting in its own self-interest, destroys itself.[55] Apparently random changes in networks may simply be chaotic patterns that are not understood. These patterns cannot be known in advance but represent potential paths of change that are the result of the complex interactions among members in the network.

The process of change in complex systems such as networks involves creating instability, managing the tipping point, and relying on self-organization. These phases roughly follow Lewin's model of planned change described in Chapter 2. Change in a network requires an unfreezing process where the system becomes unstable. Movement in the system is described by the metaphor of a "tipping point" where changes occur rapidly as a result of information processing. Finally, refreezing involves self-organization. The descriptions below represent rudimentary applications of these concepts to networks; research and practice in changing networks are still in a formative stage.

1. **Create instability in the network.** Before change in a network can occur, relationships among member organizations must become unstable. A network's susceptibility to instability is a function of members' motivations for structure versus agency.[56] *Structure* refers to the organization's expected role in the network and represents a source of stability. All things being equal, network members tend to behave and perform according to their agreed-upon roles. For example, most routine communications among the network members are geared toward increasing stability and working together. A manufacturing plant in Nike's network is expected to produce a certain number of shoes at a certain cost with certain features. Nike headquarters in Beaverton, Oregon, plans on the plant behaving this way. On the other hand, *agency* involves self-interest which can create instability in the network. Each member of the network is trying to maximize its own performance in the context of the network. Changes in member goals and strategies, the ratio of costs and benefits in network membership, and so on, can affect the willingness and ability of members to contribute to network performance. When a plant in Nike's network grows to

a sufficient size or develops a sufficient range of capabilities, it may consider altering its role in the network to perform a broader set of activities or dedicate capacity to its own products. As the ratio of agency to structure increases, the instability of the network rises, thus enabling change to occur.

OD practitioners can facilitate instability in a network by changing the pattern of communication among members. They can, for example, encourage organizations to share information. Technology breakthroughs, new product introductions, changes in network membership, or changes in the strategy or capability of a network member all represent fluctuations that can increase the susceptibility of the network to change. Another important aspect of changing the pattern of information is to ask who should get the information. Understanding and creating instability is difficult because the nature of members' connectedness also influences the system's susceptibility. Some organizations are more connected than others; most organizations are closely connected to several others, but relatively unconnected to many. This makes creating a sense of urgency for change difficult. Diagnosis of the relationships among member organizations can provide important information about organizations that are central to network communications.[57]

2. **Manage the tipping point.** Although instability provides the impetus and opportunity for change, the direction, type, and process of change are yet to be determined. An unstable network can move to a new state of organization and performance, return to its old condition, or simply cease to exist. At this point, network members, individually and collectively, make choices about what to do. OD practitioners can help them through this change period. Recent studies suggest the following guides for facilitating network change:[58]
   a. *The law of the few.* A new idea, practice, or other change spreads because of a relatively few but important roles in the network. Connectors, mavens, and salespeople help an innovation achieve sufficient awareness and credibility throughout the network to be considered viable. *Connectors* are individuals who occupy central positions in the network and are able to tap into many different network audiences. They have "Rolodex" power; they are quickly able to alert and connect with a wide variety of people in many organizations. *Mavens* are "information sinks." They passionately pursue knowledge about a particular subject and are altruistically willing to tell anyone who is interested everything they know about it. The key to the maven's role is trust. People who speak to mavens know that they are getting unbiased information—that there is no "hidden agenda," just good data. Finally, *salespeople* are the champions of change and are able to influence others to try new ideas, do new things, or consider new options. Thus, the first key factor in changing a network is the presence of communication channels occupied by connectors, mavens, and salespeople.

      OD practitioners can fill any of these roles. They can, if appropriate, be mavens on a particular subject and act as a source of unbiased information about a new network practice, aspects of interpersonal relationships that network members agree is slowing network response, or ideas about information systems that can speed communication. Less frequently, OD practitioners can be connectors, ensuring that any given message is seeded throughout the network. This is especially true if the change agent was part of the network's formation. In this case, the practitioner might have extensive relationships with organizations in the network. Thus, networking skills, such as the ability to manage lateral relations among autonomous organizations in the relative absence of hierarchical control, are indispensable to practitioners of network change. Change agents must be able to span the boundaries of diverse organizations, link them together, and facilitate exchanges among them.[59] OD practitioners can also play the role of salesperson. Although it is in line with the "activist" role described earlier in the practice of network creation, it is not a traditional aspect of OD practice. The wisdom of having a change agent as the champion of an idea rather than a key player in the organization network is debatable. The change agent and network members must understand the trade-offs in sacrificing the OD practitioner's neutrality for influence. If that trade-off is made, the change agent will need the political competence to understand and resolve the conflicts of interest and value dilemmas inherent in systems made up of multiple organizations, each seeking to maintain autonomy while jointly interacting. Political savvy can help change agents manage their own roles and values in respect to those power dynamics.

b. *Stickiness.* The second ingredient in network change is stickiness. For a new idea or practice to take hold, the message communicated by the connectors, mavens, and salespeople must be memorable. A memorable or sticky message is not a function of typical communication variables, such as frequency of the message, loudness, or saliency. Stickiness is often a function of small and seemingly insignificant characteristics of the message, such as its structure, format, and syntax, as well as its emotional content, practicality, or sequencing with other messages. OD practitioners can help network members develop sticky messages for communicating about network change. Brainstorming alternative phrases, using metaphors to symbolize meaning, or enlisting the help of marketing and communications specialists can increase the chance of developing a sticky message. Since the ingredients of stickiness are often not obvious, several iterations of a message's structure may be necessary to create memorable communication about network change.

c. *The power of context.* Finally, a message must be meaningful and relevant to network members. Meaning derives from the context of the network. When network members are feeling pressure to innovate or move quickly in response to external demands, for example, messages about new cost-cutting initiatives or a new financial reporting system may be uninteresting and easily neglected. On the other hand, a message linking these changes to expected improvements in network performance may be seen as relevant. OD practitioners can help members understand the network's current climate or "conversation"; they can help members determine the appropriate timing and relevance of proposed communications about network change.[60]

When the right people communicate a network change, present and package it appropriately, and distribute it in a timely fashion, implementation is likely to move forward swiftly. When there is insufficient information, interest, or relevance, network change is likely to stall.

3. **Rely on self-organization.** Networks tend to exhibit "self-organizing" behavior. Network members seek to reduce uncertainty in their environment, while the network as a whole drives to establish more order in how it functions. OD practitioners can rely on this self-organizing feature to refreeze change. Once change has occurred in the network, a variety of controls can be leveraged to institutionalize it. For example, communication systems can spread stories about how the change is affecting different members, diffusing throughout the network, or contributing to network effectiveness. This increases the forces for stability in the network. Individual organizations can communicate their commitment to the change in an effort to lower agency forces that can contribute to instability. Each of these messages signifies constraint and shows that the different parts of the network are not independent of each other.

Application 20.3 describes the formation of the Alaskan Workforce Coalition.[61] The shortage of adequate health care workers in Alaska became a critical issue that only a network of organizations could address. The case reflects the complex issues of identifying, convening, and organizing a TS.

application 20.3

THE ALASKA WORKFORCE COALITION

The low supply of health care workers in Alaska was constraining the industry's ability to deliver care. In addition to the usual forces driving change in the industry, including health care reform, aging workforces, rapidly changing technologies, and new delivery models, Alaska's remoteness, harsh climates, vast geography, and small population complicated the challenges of developing, recruiting, and retaining an adequate and qualified health care workforce.

As an industry, health care accounted for 8% of total employment and around 16% of the state's economy. Moreover, health and social service jobs in Alaska were projected to increase 31% between 2010 and 2020, driven in large part by a projected 89% increase for the population age 65 and older over the same time period. But the lack of health care workers left many rural communities without access to health care services and resulted in health care costs that were among the highest in the nation.

Most health care organizations felt the pinch of too few workers, but had limited experience working in a coordinated manner to address them. For more than a decade, individual health care organizations worked on solutions they could advance on their own. Some of these efforts worked, such as the University of Alaska's initiative to double the number of nurses educated in state; but the breadth and depth of health care industry demands vastly outpaced such efforts. While other industries, such as construction, were gaining statewide visibility and investments, the health care industry was making only incremental gains.

Individual solutions might have helped individual firms, but it did little to help the state's problems. Although various surveys had provided episodic data describing point in time needs, sometimes for a subset of health care workers, data sources were typically used in isolation and were difficult to assess holistically due to inconsistent terminology. Integrated and accurate health care workforce data was not available to focus industry efforts. In the early 2000s, a promising coalition emerged among three public sector entities to build a behavioral health workforce, however no one had ever developed an industry wide projection with occupational priorities that would enable greater focus of efforts. Absent a collective effort, policy makers and funders lacked a complete understanding of health care workforce issues, resulting in limited investment and influence.

One catalyst for change occurred in 2009 with the passage of the American Recovery and Reinvestment Act (ARRA). This federal program included funding opportunities to states for workforce development in high-demand industries. However, without a statewide plan, a coordinated set of priorities, and an appropriate entity to guide the work, access to such funds was unlikely. The ARRA funding opportunity served as a trigger that brought individual groups together quickly.

At the same time, the Alaska Workforce Investment Board (AWIB) had long recognized health care as an important and growing industry, and they called for a statewide health care workforce plan. The AWIB's call was motivated by its prior involvement with industry coalitions. For example, the oil, gas, and mining industry's Alaska Process Industry Careers Consortium (APICC) had addressed a variety cross-industry needs and attracted new investments. A workforce plan specifically for the development of a natural gas pipeline was an important complement to their work. The construction industry also formed a nonprofit foundation, implemented new programs, and attracted additional resources from the state. These industries modeled the value of partnering to define industry workforce priorities, identifying skill standards, and attracting targeted investments in selected workforce development programs and strategies to meet their needs. Similarly, a joint effort by public sector partners had been established to build a qualified behavioral health workforce, led by the Alaska Mental Health Trust Authority (AMHTA), the Alaska Department of Health and Social Services (DHSS), and the University of Alaska.

The Alaska Health Workforce Coalition (AHWC) was formed in 2009 to ensure an adequate and qualified health care workforce for hospitals, nursing homes, clinics, and public health service throughout Alaska.

THE COALITION'S BEGINNINGS

In response to these triggers, a leader at Providence, the state's largest health care system, who had previous experience leading Alaska's workforce development through roles in both industry and key state agencies, invited several key stakeholders to exploratory conversations about collaboration. Her experience suggested that industry needed to take a lead role and she had existing relationships with many of the stakeholders. Thanks to corporate support, personal experience, and reputation, initial meeting invitations were well received.

She targeted these invitations at the formal organizational leaders representing health care employers, educators, policy makers, and funders. They included the Alaska State Hospital and Nursing Home Association (ASHNHA), representing the state's largest private sector health employers; AWIB, through its private sector chair who happened to also be the Chief Financial Officer for Fairbanks Memorial Hospital; the University of Alaska as the state's leading health educator; and Alaska's DHSS, which served a dual role as a significant public sector health employer and a key player in shaping state health policy. Each of these organizations had worked together in the past. In the relatively small population of Alaska, individuals can readily identify the key partners required to move quickly into action.

The initial meetings and conversations explored the opportunity and confirmed interest in creating a statewide health care workforce plan. The concept of an organization to sustain the work was acknowledged, but the general feeling was that the first priorities should be to use the existing people and resources to develop a plan and to submit a proposal for funding to an ARRA grant opportunity.

Additional partners were soon engaged based on their ability to enhance the plan's development. New partners included the AMHTA, the Alaska Native Tribal Health Consortium, and the Alaska Primary Care Association. The group also increased its level of commitment by shifting from teleconferences to face-to-face meetings every month or two. This required partners to travel at their own expense and commit to full days of work to guide development of the plan and proposal.

Early meetings benefited from good cross-sector attendance and rich, respectful conversations that deepened collective understandings of current issues as well as specific opportunities that interested individual partners. However, with so many needs in the industry, there were too many options and it was clear the participants had to prioritize to gain traction. They elected to focus on strategies and actions that could be best achieved *because* a coalition existed versus actions that individual entities could accomplish under the status quo. The term "net new" emerged in the dialogue to distinguish new or expanded value-added strategies and actions that were unlikely to be achieved without a collaborative effort *and* which benefited multiple partners.

Still, some topics were inherently more difficult to advance due to the innate competitive issues among employers. Collaboration on statewide recruiting was seen as an opportunity, but had been a challenge to implement. Each employer invested a great deal to attract potential employees from outside Alaska to fill critical vacancies, but large employers with more resources could leverage their relative advantage in recruiting. However, partners knew from the success of the Alaska Seafood Marketing Institute and the Alaska tourism industry that they could be more effective and efficient in marketing a concept versus a company. For example, the Alaskan quality of life is appealing to many medical professionals and the coalition saw the merits of a statewide, coordinated campaign that could be more impactful than what individual firms could achieve. This approach is gradually gaining momentum with a shared website, www.alaskaphysicianjobs.net. In addition, one of the coalition's key successes in the first two years was the funding of a new loan reimbursement and incentive program that benefited multiple employers in their most critical shortages.

FORMATION

To guide, reflect, and reinforce the positive group norms that began to emerge, an organizational charter was developed to ensure clarity for its diverse members on the purpose, principles, and intended outcomes of the coalition. For example, the group's operating style did not involve formal leadership roles, such as a chair or officers. At the heart of the coalition's success was an adaptive process guided by six principles: *inclusive, coordinated, cooperative, strategic, adaptive,* and *results focused.*

A core team emerged consisting of roughly 15 people from nine organizations. This group developed an overarching four-part framework to organize and develop the workforce plan: engage, train, recruit, and retain. For each theme, a set of potential strategies was identified, although they lacked specificity in the early stages. Occupational priorities were also developed with available data. They were organized into three tiers representing the relative priorities. The upper tier included more than 15 occupations, and the coalition worked to define the top six occupational priorities. They included primary care providers, nurses, direct care workers, behavioral health clinicians, physical therapists, and pharmacists. The occupations were both highly needed *and* there were pertinent strategies that the coalition could advance.

BUILDING THE COALITION

A significant opportunity to engage more stakeholders in prioritizing and organizing the plan was offered by ASHNHA. They had begun to plan a workforce summit for their hospital and nursing home members. With the plan framework and high-level set of strategies and priorities established, the summit was an ideal time and place for the core group to share information and gather input from a much wider audience. It was also a good place to begin discussions about the kind of organization needed to sustain efforts in the future.

More than 60 participants at the summit heard plenary presentations about similar efforts and entities working on health care workforce issues in others states, and from other industries in Alaska. They provided tangible evidence of what was possible. The core group members shared the plan's framework and initial data about workforce gaps. Participants contributed to the development of initial strategies through small group and round table discussions. Core group members aligned the topics with the framework and then used a modified Open Space approach that allowed people to refine ideas in strategies about which they were most passionate. Core team members facilitated each table, gathered information and insights, and presented the results in a plenary session using simple planning templates. The overall feedback from the summit was very positive and supported the idea of continuing the effort to develop a statewide plan and a new corresponding entity/organization to guide the efforts.

Following the summit, the core team worked diligently on outreach. Over several months, they engaged as many stakeholders as possible from the health care industry, policy makers, and funders as well as education and training providers. Nearly a dozen presentations were made, always by at least two members from the core team to demonstrate shared ownership. A subteam led by the University of Alaska worked closely with the Research & Analysis Section of the Department of Labor and Workforce Development to refine occupational priorities through presentations with diverse audiences and with an online survey. The core team created a website and a contact list to communicate with the wider coalition of interested stakeholders.

In parallel with the outreach process, core team members continued to meet monthly. They discussed and integrated what they were learning from stakeholders, and strengthened their resolve to produce a well-written strategic plan summarizing the compelling and complex workforce needs of the health care industry focusing not only on occupational priorities but also on systems change and capacity-building strategies. Funding offered by three of the larger partners was pooled to hire contract resources to assist with writing and printing the plan. The AWIB endorsed the Health Workforce Plan in early 2010—making it the first significant product from the AHWC.

The plan was well received and helped to achieve significant visibility for health care industry issues, priorities, and possible actions. However, it was not specific enough to drive collective action. The group's logical next step was to follow up the plan with a targeted, four-year Action Agenda. They also recognized the need to address organization development and sustainability issues. The founding individuals and organizations had developed the initial plan through informal processes and volunteer contributions of time and resources. To sustain the effort and reap the benefits of the plan would require a more formal approach and organization.

CONTINUED COALITION DEVELOPMENT

Over the next year, the AHWC became larger and more formal. In part, this was enabled by a planning grant from the Health Resources and Services Administration (HRSA). This grant provided one year's worth of funding to support the research and development of a four-year Action Agenda, greater alignment of health care workforce data, and contractual support for staff, organization development, and sustainability efforts. During this time, the AHWC welcomed the opportunity to join forces with related groups where their goals were aligned and they could support one another's efforts to go further together than either might achieve alone. For example, the Alaska Health Care Commission (HCC) recognized workforce shortages as a priority when they were initially formed, and rather than conducting independent research and developing their own recommendations, the HCC aligned their direction with the AHWC, endorsing the work of the coalition as their own. Similarly, the AMHTA had several years of experience advancing their Workforce Focus Area focused on home and community based behavioral health services. They realized that sustaining their efforts and participation in the AHWC could be aligned with the Focus Area to create a single, unified approach. As a result, the two efforts merged in 2011 to unite health care workforce planning and action for Alaska, inclusive of the distinct needs of the AMHTA and its beneficiaries.

The coalition researched alternative approaches to forming a sustainable organization to advance their goals around health care workforce issues. A number of models were identified and explored using the principles from the initial charter to guide the process. The core group determined that continuing their loose collaboration without formally establishing a new nonprofit entity was preferred. The individual who provided support to the Workforce Focus Area on behalf of the AMTHA, DHSS, and the University, had her scope of work extended to include AHWC activities in late 2011, bridging the staff needs from the planning grant to full operations. Organization development consulting support has continued to provide additional resource and continuity with coalition and core meetings and activities.

EVALUATION

The creation of the Alaska Health Workforce Coalition has resulted in several benefits to its members and to the Alaskan health care system as a whole. These include:

- An industry-led workforce plan with tangible actions, accountabilities, and committed resources
- The use and integration of data to establish occupational priorities
- Actions focused on occupational and systems change priorities that drive health care workforce activities and investments by members and other stakeholders
- A unified approach to advocacy for policy changes and funding opportunities
- Increased resource commitments, actions, and emerging results that all serve to build the Alaska health care workforce

In 2012, the coalition documented a retrospective of early achievements by AHWC in response to requests by other industry groups. The coalition also elected to undergo a "strategic refresh" process in recognition of the completion of several Action Agenda objectives and the actual or planned transition of several leaders. The AHWC coordinator and OD consultant interviewed each core team member to gather feedback on the greatest achievements to date, alignment with each organization's priorities, update to occupational and systems change priorities given the changes to the health care industry, and suggestions that would enhance the effectiveness, relevance, and impact of the coalition going forward.

The data suggested that success has been achieved through the attention and balance of two equally important aspects:

- **Content, action, and results.** The coalition convened on the premise of shared need and the desire to take collective action. This was achieved through a strategic plan that defined the workforce goals to engage, train, recruit, and retain a qualified health care workforce for Alaska. The coalition developed a corresponding Action Agenda with objectives to drive action in six occupational priorities and six systems change and capacity-building efforts.
- **Process, relationships, and respect.** The coalition emerged through relationships and shared need. Individuals with loose relationships agreed to begin exploring the merits of common-goals and collaborative action. The processes have been thoughtfully guided and intentionally nurtured throughout the first three years to build respect and strengthen relationships across the organizations and individual leaders.

The results also helped the core team to update the Action Agenda priorities as well as refine their processes of engaging with one another. The process of evaluation and continuous improvement confirmed the need to retain and nurture strong relationships among key partners—particularly when decisions and direction are needed. It also confirmed the need for dynamic strategy and priority setting processes given the uncertainty faced by the health care industry and the resulting changes in care models that lead to new demands for the health care workforce of the future.

SUMMARY

In this chapter, we describe merger, alliance, and transorganizational change interventions that move beyond the single organization. These multiorganizational change programs enable organizations to extend their boundaries to keep pace with highly complex and rapidly changing environments. They help organizations create and sustain multiorganizational linkages. Because transorganizational interventions transcend a single organization, attention is directed at the strategies, objectives, structures, and processes of two or more interdependent organizations. This raises the scope and complexity of change and requires OD practitioners to develop new concepts, skills, and expertise.

M&As interventions involve combining two or more organizations to achieve strategic and financial objectives. They generally involve three phases: precombination, legal combination, and operational combination. The M&A process has been dominated by financial and technical concerns, but experience and research strongly support the contribution that OD practitioners can make to M&A success.

Strategic alliance interventions help organizations create partnerships with other organizations to share resources and capabilities for competitive advantage. They include licensing agreements, franchises, long-term contracts, and joint ventures. The development of strategic alliances generally follows a process of strategy formulation, partner selection, alliance structuring and start-up, and alliance operation and adjustment.

Network interventions must address two types of change. First, because multiorganizational systems tend to be underorganized, the initial development of the network follows the stages of planned change relevant to underorganized systems: identification, convention, organization, and evaluation. Second, the management of change within a network also must acknowledge the distributed nature of influence and adopt methods of change that rely on the Law of the Few, the power of context, and the stickiness factor.

NOTES

1. R. Gulati, D. Lavie, and R. Madhavan, "How Do Networks Matter? The Performanace Effects of Interorganizational Networks," in *Research in Organizational Behavior*, vol. 31, ed. B. Staw and A. Brief (Kidlington, Oxford, UK: Elsevier, 2011), 207–24; A. Inkpen and E. Tsang, "Social Capital, Networks, and Knowledge Transfer," *Academy of Management Review* 30 (2005): 146–65; B. Teng, "Corporate Entrepreneurship Activities Through Strategic Alliances: A Resource-Based Approach Toward Competitive Advantage," *Journal of Management Studies* 44 (2007): 119–42; F. Kuglin with J. Hook, *Building, Leading, and Managing Strategic Alliances* (New York: Amacom, 2006).
2. H. Aldrich, *Organizations and Environments* (New York: Prentice-Hall, 1979).
3. O. Williamson, *Markets and Hierarchies* (New York: Free Press, 1975); M. Jensen and W. Meckling, "A Theory of Firm: Managerial Behavior, Agency Costs and Ownership Structure," *Journal of Financial Economics* 3 (1976): 305–60; O. Williamson, *The Economic Institutions of Capitalism* (New York: Free Press, 1985); J. Barney and W. Ouchi, *Organizational Economics* (San Francisco: Jossey-Bass, 1986); K. Eisenhardt, "Agency Theory: An Assessment and Review," *Academy of Management Review* 14 (1989): 57–74.
4. P. Kenis and D. Knoke, "How Organizational Field Networks Shape Interorganizational Tie-Formation Rates," *Academy of Management Review* 27 (2002): 275–93.
5. T. Cummings, "Transorganizational Development," in *Research in Organizational Behavior*, vol. 6, ed. B. Staw and L. Cummings (Greenwich, CT: JAI Press, 1984), 367–422.
6. B. Gray, "Conditions Facilitating Interorganizational Collaboration," *Human Relations* 38 (1985): 911–36; K. Harrigan and W. Newman, "Bases of Interorganization Co-operation: Propensity, Power, Persistence," *Journal of Management Studies* 27 (1990): 417–34; Cummings, "Transorganizational Development"; R. Chisholm, *Developing Network Organizations: Learning from Practice and Theory* (Reading, MA: Addison-Wesley, 1998).
7. T. Galpin and D. Robinson, "Merger Integration: The Ultimate Change Management Challenge," *Mergers and Acquisitions* 31 (1997): 24–29.
8. M. Marks and P. Mirvis, *Joining Forces: Making One Plus One Equal Three in Mergers, Acquisitions, and Alliances*, 2nd ed. (San Francisco: Jossey-Bass, 2010); A. Sherman and M. Hart, *Mergers and Acquisitions from A to Z*, 2nd ed. (New York: Amacom, 2006).
9. Data on M&A value accessed from http://www.imaa-institute.org/statistics-mergers-acquisitions.html#MergersAcquisitions_Worldwide on October 22, 2012.
10. A variety of studies have questioned whether merger and acquisition activity actually generates benefits to the organization or its shareholders, including M. Porter, "From Competitive Advantage to Corporate Strategy," *Harvard Business Review* (May–June 1978): 43–59; T. Brush, "Predicted Change in Operational Synergy and Post-Acquisition Performance of Acquired Businesses," *Strategic Management Journal* 17 (1996): 1–24; P. Zweig with J.Perlman, S. Anderson, and K. Gudridge, "The Case Against Mergers," *BusinessWeek*, October 30, 1995, 122–30. The research includes an A. T. Kearney study of 115 multibillion-dollar global mergers between 1993 and 1996 where 58% failed to create "substantial returns for shareholders," measured by tangible returns in the form of dividends and stock price appreciation; a Mercer Management Consulting study of all mergers from 1990 to 1996 where nearly half "destroyed" shareholder value; a PriceWaterhouseCoopers study of 97 acquirers that completed deals worth $500 million or more from 1994 to 1997 and where two-thirds of the buyer's stocks dropped on announcement of the transaction and "a year later" a third of the losers still were lagging the levels of peer-company shares or the stock market in general; and a European study of 300 companies that found that planning for restructuring was poorly thought out and underfunded. Similarly, despite the large amount of writing on the subject, a large proportion of firms involved in mergers have not gotten the message that postmerger integration is the key to success. For example, in the A. T. Kearny study, only 39% of the cases had set up a management team in the first hundred days and only 28% had a clear vision of corporate goals when the acquisition began.
11. T. Galpin and M. Herndon, *The Complete Guide to Mergers and Acquisitions: Process Tools to Support M&A Integration*

at Every Level (San Francisco: Jossey-Bass, 2007); Sherman and Hart, *Mergers and Acquisitions*; Marks and Mirvis, *Joining Forces*; R. Ashkenas, L. DeMonaco, and S. Francis, "Making the Deal Real: How GE Capital Integrates Acquisitions," *Harvard Business Review* (January–February 1998); D. Jemison and S. Sitkin, "Corporate Acquisitions: A Process Perspective," *Academy of Management Review* 11 (1986): 145–63.

12. R. Palter and D. Srinivasan, "Habits of the Busiest Acquirers," *McKinsey on Finance* 20 (Summer 2006): 8–13; Ashkenas, DeMonaco, and Francis, "Making the Deal Real."
13. M. Epstein, "The Drivers of Success in Post-merger Integration," *Organizational Dynamics* 33 (2004): 174–89; J. Perry and T. Herd, "Mergers and Acquisitions: Reducing M&A Risk Through Improved Due Diligence," *Strategy and Leadership* 32 (2004): 12–19; A. Buono, J. Bowditch, and J. Lewis, "When Cultures Collide: The Anatomy of a Merger," *Human Relations* 38 (1985): 477–500; D. Tipton, "Understanding Employee Views Regarding Impending Mergers to Minimize Integration Turmoil" (unpublished master's thesis, Pepperdine University, 1998).
14. Palter and Srinivasan, "Habits of the Busiest Acquirers"; Marks and Mirvis, *Joining Forces*; Ashkenas, DeMonaco, and Francis, "Making the Deal Real."
15. D. Harding and S. Rovit, "Building Deal on Bedrock," *Harvard Business Review* (September 2004): 1–8; B. Brunsman, S. Sanderson, and M. Van de Voorde, "How to Achieve Value Behind the Deal During Merger Integration," *Oil and Gas Journal* 96 (1998): 21–30; M. Sirower, "Constructing a Synergistic Base for Premier Deals," *Mergers and Acquisitions* 32 (1998): 42–50.
16. Perry and Herd, "Mergers and Acquisitions."
17. S. Elias, "Due Diligence," 1998.
18. Ashkenas, DeMonaco, and Francis, "Making the Deal Real"; Brunsman, Sanderson, and Van de Voorde, "How to Achieve Value."
19. This application was developed from information found in G. Colvin, "Jeff Smisek: United-Continental's King of the Skies," *Fortune*, April 21, 2011; D. Bennett, "Making the World's Largest Airline Fly," *BusinessWeek*, February 2, 2012; "United Airlines Merger Integration: 10 Questions," June 2012, accessed from http://www.towerswatson.com/en/Insights/Newsletters/Global/strategy-at-work/2012/10-questions-for-doug-rose-vice-president-human-resources-united-airlines on October 24, 2012; United and Continental's website, http://www.united.com.
20. Galpin and Robinson, "Merger Integration."
21. R. Chanmugam, W. Schill, and D. Mann, "Mastering the Art of Value-Capture in Mergers and Acquisitions," *Outlook Journal* (February 2005): 1–4; D. Harding, S. Romit, and A. Corbett, "Avoid Merger Meltdown: Lessons from Mergers and Acquisitions Leaders," *Strategy and Innovation* (2004): 3–5; A. Burt, T. MacDonald, and T. Herd, "Two Merger Integration Imperatives: Urgency and Execution," *Strategy and Leadership* 31 (2003): 42–49; Galpin and Robinson, "Merger Integration"; Galpin and Herndon, *The Complete Guide*; Sherman and Hart, *Mergers and Acquisitions*; Vantrappan and Kilefors, "A Users Guide"; Ashkenas, DeMonaco, and Francis, "Making the Deal Real"; K. Kostuch, R. Malchione, and I. Marten, "Post-Merger Integration: Creating or Destroying Value?" *Corporate Board* 19 (1998): 7–11.
22. Kostuch, Malchione, and Marten, "Post-Merger Integration."
23. J. Child, D. Faulkner, and S. Tallman, *Strategies of Cooperation: Managing Alliances, Networks, and Joint Ventures*, 2nd ed. (New York: Oxford University Press, 2005); O. Shenkar and J. Reuer, eds., *Handbook of Strategic Alliances* (Thousand Oaks, CA: Sage Publications, 2005); J. Reuer, ed., *Strategic Alliances: Theory and Evidence* (New York: Oxford University Press, 2004); A. Arino, J. de la Torre, and P. Ring, "Relational Quality: Managing Trust in Corporate Alliances," *California Management Review* 44 (2001): 109–31; M. Hitt, R. Ireland, and R. Hoskisson, *Strategic Management* (Cincinnati, OH: South-Western College Publishing, 1999).
24. R. Blair and F. Lafontaine, *The Economics of Franchising* (New York: Oxford University Press, 2005).
25. K. Harrigan, *Joint Ventures, Alliances, and Corporate Strategy* (New York: Beard Books, 2003).
26. J. Bamford, B. Gomes-Casseres, and M. Robinson, *Mastering Alliance Strategy* (New York: John Wiley and Sons, 2002).
27. J. Collins, *Good to Great* (New York: Harper-Collins, 2001).
28. B. Gomes-Casseres, *Managing International Alliances: Conceptual Framework*, Case 9-793-133 (Harvard Business School, 1993); J. Child and D. Faulkner, *Strategies of Cooperation: Managing Alliances, Networks, and Joint Ventures* (New York: Oxford University Press, 1998).
29. R. Shah and V. Swaminathan, "Factors Influencing Partner Selection in Strategic Alliances: The Moderating Role of Alliance Context," *Strategic Management Journal* 42 (2008): 471–94.
30. Bamford, Gomes-Casseres, and Robinson, *Mastering Alliance Strategy*.
31. Arino, de la Torre, and Ring, "Relational Quality"; Y. Zhang and C. Huxham, "Identity Construction and Trust Building in Developing International Collaborations," *Journal of Applied Behavioral Science* 45 (2009): 186–211.

32. C. Rousseau, S. Sitkin, R. Burt, and C. Camerer, "Not So Different After All: A Cross-Discipline View of Trust," *Academy of Management Review* 23 (1998): 395; P. Kale and H. Singh, "Managing Strategic Alliances: What Do We Know Now and Where Do We Go from Here?" *Academy of Management Perspectives* 23 (2009): 45–62.
33. M. Hutt, E. Stafford, B. Walker, and P. Reingen, "Case Study Defining the Social Network of a Strategic Alliance," *Sloan Management Review* 41 (Winter 2000): 51–62.
34. Marks and Mirvis, *Joining Forces*; Child and Faulkner, *Strategies of Cooperation.*
35. K. McQuade and B. Gomes-Casseres, "Xerox and Fuji-Xerox," Case 9-391-156 (Harvard Business School, 1991).
36. This application was adapted from M. Miller, S. Fitzgerald, K. Murrell, J. Preston, and R. Ambekar, "Appreciative Inquiry in Building a Transcultural Strategic Alliance: The Case of a Biotech Alliance Between a U.S. Multinational and an Indian Family Business," *Journal of Applied Behavioral Science* 41 (2005): 91–111.
37. C. Huxham and S. Vangen, *Managing to Collaborate: The Theory and Practice of Collaborative Advantage* (London: Routledge, 2005); R. Chisholm, "Developing Interorganizational Networks," in *Handbook of Organization Development*, ed. T. Cummings (Thousand Oaks, CA: Sage Publication, 2008), 629–50; S. Klein and A. Poulymenakou, eds., *Managing Dynamic Networks: Organizational Perspectives of Technology Enabled Inter-Firm Collaboration* (New York: Springer, 2006).
38. Information on the Low Carbon City Initiative accessed from http://en.wwfchina.org/en/what_we_do/climate___energy/mitigation/lcci.
39. D. Watts, *Six Degrees* (New York: W. W. Norton and Co., 2003).
40. S. Strogatz, "Exploring Complex Networks," *Nature* 410 (March 2001): 268–76.
41. Cummings, "Transorganizational Development"; C. Raben, "Building Strategic Partnerships: Creating and Managing Effective Joint Ventures," in *Organizational Architecture*, ed. Nadler et al. (San Francisco: Jossey-Bass, 1992), 81–109; B. Gray, *Collaborating: Finding Common Ground for Multiparty Problems* (San Francisco: Jossey-Bass, 1989); Harrigan and Newman, "Bases of Interorganization Co-operation"; P. Lorange and J. Roos, "Analytical Steps in the Formation of Strategic Alliances," *Journal of Organizational Change Management* 4 (1991): 60–72; Gomes-Casseres, "Managing International Alliances"; D. Boje and M. Hillon, "Transorganizational Development," in *Handbook of Organization Development*, ed. T. Cummings (Thousand Oaks, CA: Sage Publication, 2008), 651–63.
42. Cummings, "Transorganizational Development."
43. T. Williams, "The Search Conference in Active Adaptive Planning," *Journal of Applied Behavioral Science* 16 (1980): 470–83; B. Gray and T. Hay, "Political Limits to Interorganizational Consensus and Change," *Journal of Applied Behavioral Science* 22 (1986): 95–112.
44. Cummings, "Transorganizational Development."
45. E. Trist, "Referent Organizations and the Development of Inter-organizational Domains," *Human Relations*, 36 (1983): 269–85.
46. Cummings, "Transorganizational Development."
47. M. Nathan and I. Mitroff, "The Use of Negotiated Order Theory as a Tool for Analysis and Development of an Inter-organizational Field," *Journal of Applied Behavioral Science* 27 (1991): 163–80; H. Bradbury, B. Lichtenstein, J. Carroll, and P. Senge, "Relational Space and Learning Experiments: The Heart of Sustainability Collaborations," in *Research in Organizational Change and Development*, vol. 18, ed. W. Pasmore, A. Shani, and R. Woodman (Bingley, UK: Emerald Group Publishing, 2010), 109–48.
48. Nathan and Mitroff, "The Use of Negotiated Order Theory."
49. C. Worley and S. Parker, "Building Multi-stakeholder Sustainability Networks: The Cuyahoga River Valley Initiative," *Organizing for Sustainable Effectiveness*, vol. 1., ed. S. Mohrman, A. Shani, and P. Docherty (East Sussex, UK: Emerald Group Publishing, 2011), 187–214.
50. Raben, "Building Strategic Partnerships"; C. Baldwin and K. Clark, "Managing in an Age of Modularity," in *Managing in the Modular Age*, ed. R. Garud, A. Kumaraswamy, and R. Langlois (Malden, MA: Blackwell Publishing Ltd., 2003), 149–60.
51. Trist, "Referent Organizations."
52. P. Anderson, "Complexity Theory and Organization Science," *Organization Science* 10 (1999): 216–32.
53. H. Simon, "The Architecture of Complexity," in *Managing in the Modular Age*, ed. R. Garud, A. Kumaraswamy, and R. Langlois (Malden, MA: Blackwell Publishing Ltd., 2003), 15–37.
54. P. Senge, *The Fifth Discipline* (New York: Doubleday, 1990); B. Lichtenstein, "Emergence as a Process of Self-Organizing: New Assumptions and Insights from the Study of Non-Linear Dynamic Systems," *Journal of Organizational Change Management* 13 (2000): 526–46.
55. Senge, *The Fifth Discipline.*
56. Watts, *Six Degrees.*
57. P. Monge and N. Contractor, *Theories of Communication Networks* (New York: Oxford University Press, 2003).
58. This section relies on information in M. Gladwell, *The Tipping Point* (Boston: Little, Brown, 2000).

59. B. Gricar and D. Brown, "Conflict, Power, and Organization in a Changing Community," *Human Relations* 34 (1981): 877–93.

60. P. Shaw, *Changing Conversations in Organizations: A Complexity Approach to Change* (London: Routledge, 2002).

61. This application was developed and written by Kitty Farnham, Owner, Catalyst Consulting in Fairbanks, Alaska. Her contribution to this chapter and to the state of Alaska is greatly appreciated.

GLOBAL MOBILE CORPORATION*

"Damn it, he's done it again!"

Charlie Newburg had to get up and walk around his office, he was so frustrated. He had been reviewing the most recent design, parts, and assembly specifications for Global Mobile's latest smart phone (code named: Nonphixhun) that had been released for production the previous Thursday. The files had just come back to Charlie's engineering services department with a caustic note that began, "This one can't be produced, either..." It was the fourth time production had returned the design.

Newburg, director of engineering for the Global Mobile Corporation, was normally a quiet person. But the Nonphixhun project was stretching his patience; it was beginning to appear like several other new products that had hit delays and problems in the transition from design to production during the eight months Charlie had worked for Global Mobile. These problems were nothing new at Global Mobile's Asian factory; Charlie's predecessor in the engineering job had run afoul of them, too, and had finally been fired for protesting too vehemently about the other departments. But the Nonphixhun phone should have been different. Charlie and the firm's president, Hannah Hoover, had video-conferenced two months earlier (on July 3, 2006) with the factory superintendent, Tyson Wang, to smooth the way for the new phone's design. He thought back to the meeting ...

> "Now, we all know there's a tight deadline on the Nonphixhun," Hannah Hoover said, "and Charlie's done well to ask us to talk about its introduction. I'm counting on both of you to find any snags in the system, and to work together to get that first production run out by October 2. Can you do it?"
>
> "We can do it in production if we get a clean design two weeks from now, as scheduled," answered Tyson Wang, the factory manager. "Charlie and I have already talked about that, of course. I've spoken with our circuit board and other parts suppliers and scheduled assembly capacity, and we'll be ready. If the design goes over schedule, though, I'll have to fill in with other runs, and it will cost us a bundle to break in for the Nonphixhun. How does it look in engineering, Charlie?"
>
> "I've just reviewed the design for the second time," Charlie replied. "If Marianne Price can keep the salespeople out of our hair, and avoid any more last minute changes, we've got a shot. I've pulled my technical support people off of three other overdue jobs to get this one out. But, Tyson, that means we can't spring engineers loose to confer with your production people on other manufacturing problems."
>
> "Well Charlie, most of those problems are caused by the engineers, and we need them to resolve the difficulties. We've all agreed that production problems come from both of us bowing to sales pressure, and putting equipment into production before the designs are really ready. That's just what we're trying to avoid on the Nonphixhun. But I can't have 500 people sitting on their hands waiting for an answer from your people. We'll have to have *some* engineering support."
>
> Hannah Hoover broke in, "So long as you two can talk calmly about the problem I'm confident you can resolve it. What a relief it is, Charlie, to hear the way you're approaching this. With Brady (the previous director of engineering), this conversation would have been a shouting match. Right, Tyson?" Tyson nodded and smiled.
>
> "Now there's one other thing you should both be aware of," Hoover continued. "Doc Brown and I talked last night about a new battery-charging technique, one that might reduce the charging time of the Nonphixhun by 25%. There's a chance Doc can come up with it before the Nonphixhun reaches production, and if it's possible, I'd like to use the new process. That would give us a real jump on the competition and quiet the environmentalists."

---

*This case is an adaptation and revision of Rondell Data Corporation, by John A. Seeger, Professor of Management at Bentley College, Waltham, MA, 1981.

Four days after that meeting, Charlie found that two of his key people on the Nonphixhun project had been called to an emergency video consultation about a problem in final assembly: The two halves of the new smartphone interface wouldn't fit together because recent changes in the face required a different chassis design for the rear end.

One week later, Doc Brown proudly walked into Charlie's office with the new battery casing. "This won't affect the other modules of the Nonphixhun much," Doc had said. "Look, it takes three new pins, a new connector, and some new shielding, and that's all."

Charlie had tried to resist the last-minute design changes, but Hannah Hoover had stood firm. With considerable overtime by the engineers and technical support staff, engineering services should still be able to finish documenting the parts and specifications in time.

Two hardware engineers and three support staff went into 12-hour days to get the Nonphixhun ready, but the specifications were still five days late reaching Tyson Wang. Two days later, the files came back to Charlie, heavily commented in red. Wang worked all day Saturday to review the job and found more than a dozen discrepancies in the specifications—most of them caused by the new battery-charging process and insufficient checking time before release. Correction of these design faults gave rise to a new generation of discrepancies: Wang's cover note on the second return of the prints indicated that he had had to release the assembly capacity reserved for the Nonphixhun. On the third iteration, Wang committed other production capacity to another rush job. The Nonphixhun would be at least one month late getting into production. Marianne Price, the vice-president for sales, was furious. Her customer needed units *now*. Global Mobile was the customer's only supplier not to come out with a new model this quarter.

"Here we go again," thought Newburg.

COMPANY HISTORY

Global Mobile Corporation traced its lineage through several generations of electronics technology. Its original founder, Bob Murray, launched the firm in 1960 as Global Electronics & Equipment Co. to manufacture several electronic testing devices he had invented as an engineering faculty member at a large university. The firm entered communications equipment in 1980. A well-established corps of direct sales representatives, mostly engineers, called on industrial, scientific, and government accounts but concentrated heavily on original equipment manufacturers. Using their technical know-how, they entered the mobile phone market in the mid-to-late 1980s and changed their name to Global Mobile Corporation. In this market, Global Mobile had developed a reputation as a source of high-quality, innovative designs. The firm's salespeople fed a continual stream of challenging problems into the engineering department, where the creative genius of Doc Brown and several dozen other engineers "converted problems to solutions" (as the sales brochure bragged). Product design, especially hardware and structural design, formed the spearhead of Global Mobile's growth.

By 2010, Global Mobile offered a wide range of products in two major lines. Mobile phone sales had benefited from the phenomenal growth of cell phones. However, the shift from analog to digital technology and the emergence of smart phones mean that mobile phones only accounted for 35% of company sales. Smart phone sales, on the other hand, had blossomed and, with the rapid technological changes and Global Mobile's reputation, there was an increasing demand for phones with unique features, ranging from specialized screen displays, functions, applications, and novel form factors.

The company had grown from 100 employees in 1980 to more than 2,000 in 2010. (Figure 1 shows the current organization chart.) Hannah Hoover, who had been a student of the company's founder, had presided over most of that growth and took great pride in preserving the family spirit of the old organization. Informal relationships between Global Mobile's veteran employees formed the backbone of the firm's day-to-day operations; all managers relied on personal contact, and Hoover often insisted that the absence of bureaucratic red tape was a key factor in recruiting outstanding engineering talent. This personal approach to management extended throughout the organization. All exempt employees were paid a straight salary and a share of the profits. Global Mobile boasted an extremely loyal group of senior

FIGURE 1

Global Mobil Corporation—Organizational Chart (Partial), 2006

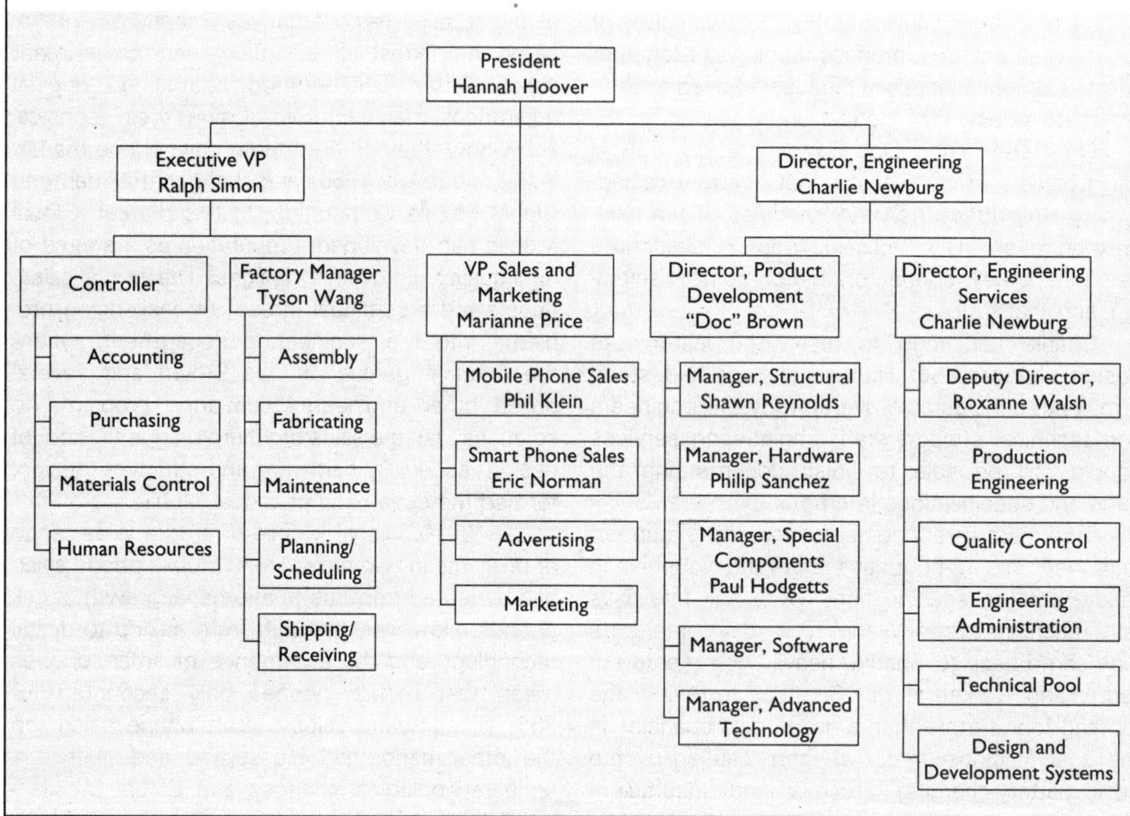

employees, and very low turnover in nearly all areas of the company.

The highest turnover job in the firm was director of engineering services. Newburg had joined Global Mobile in January 2010, replacing Jim Brady, who had lasted only ten months. Brady, in turn, had replaced Tom Swanson, a talented engineer who had made a promising start but had taken to drinking after a year in the job. Swanson's predecessor had been a genial old-timer, who retired at 70 after 25 years in charge of engineering. (Doc Brown had refused the directorship in each of the recent changes, saying, "Hell, that's no promotion for a bench man like me. I'm no administrator.")

For several years, the firm had experienced a steadily increasing number of disputes between product development, engineering, sales, and production people that generally centered on the problem of new-product introduction. Quarrels between departments became more numerous under Swanson, Brady, and Newburg. Some managers associated these disputes with the company's recent decline in profitability—a decline that, despite higher sales and gross revenues, was beginning to bother people. Hoover commented:

> Better cooperation, I'm sure, could increase our output by 5 to 10%. I'd hoped Brady could solve the problems, but pretty obviously he was too young—too arrogant. People like him—that conflict type of personality—bother me. I don't like strife, and with him it seemed I spent all my time smoothing out arguments. Brady tried to tell everyone else how to run their departments, without having his own house in order. That approach just wouldn't

work, here at Global Mobile. Charlie Newburg, now, seems much more in tune with our style of organization. I'm really hopeful now.

Still, we have just as many problems now as we did last year. Maybe even more. I hope Charlie can get a handle on engineering services soon.

ENGINEERING DEPARTMENT: PRODUCT DEVELOPMENT

According to the organization chart Newburg was in charge of both product development (the applied research and design function) and engineering services (engineering support). To Newburg, however, the relationship with design was not so clear-cut:

> Doc Brown is one of the world's unique people, and none of us would have it any other way. He's a creative genius. Sure, the chart says he works for me, but we all know Doc does his own thing. He's not the least bit interested in management routines, and I can't count on him to take any responsibility in scheduling projects, or checking budgets, or what-have you. But as long as Doc is director of product development, you can bet this company will keep on leading the field. He has more ideas per hour than most people have per year, and he keeps the whole engineering staff fired up. Everybody loves Doc—and you can count me in on that, too. In a way, he works for me, sure. But that's not what's important.

Doc Brown—unhurried, contemplative, casual, and candid—tipped his stool back against the wall of his research cubicle and talked about what *was* important:

> Hardware and structural design engineering. That's where the company's future rests. Either we have it there, or we don't have it.
>
> There's no kidding ourselves that we're anything but a bunch of Rube Goldbergs here. But that's where the biggest kicks come from—from solving development problems and dreaming up new ways of doing things. That's why I so look forward to the new designs we get involved in. We accept them not for the revenue they represent but because they subsidize the basic development work that goes into all our basic mobile phone products.
>
> This is a fantastic place to work. I have a great crew and they can really deliver when the chips are down. Why, Hannah Hoover and I (he gestured toward the neighboring cubicle, where the president's name hung over the door) are likely to find as many people here at work at 10 P.M. as at 3 P.M. The important thing here is the relationships between people; they're based on mutual respect, not on policies and procedures. Administrative red tape is a pain. It takes away from development time.
>
> Problems? Sure, there are problems now and then. There are power interests in production, where they sometimes resist change. But I'm not a fighting man you know. I suppose if I were, I might go in there and push my weight around a little. But I'm an engineer, and can do more for Global Mobile sitting right here, or working with my own people. That's what brings results.

Other members of the product development department echoed these views and added additional sources of satisfaction from their work. They were proud of the personal contacts built with customers' technical staffs—contacts that increasingly involved project work as expert advisors in thinking through operational problems like international compatibility, interoperability issues between carriers, next generation technologies, and so on. The engineers were also delighted with the department's encouragement of their personal development, continuing education, and independence on the job.

But there were problems, too. Shawn Reynolds, of the structural design group, noted:

> In the old days I really enjoyed the work—and the people I worked with. But now there's a lot of irritation. I don't like someone breathing down my neck. You can be hurried into jeopardizing the design.

Philip Sanchez, head of the hardware design section, was another designer with definite views:

> Production engineering is almost nonexistent in this company. Very little is done by the preproduction section in engineering services.

> Charlie Newburg has been trying to get preproduction into the picture, but he won't succeed because you can't start from such an ambiguous position. There have been three directors of engineering in three years. Charlie can't hold his own against the others in the company. Brady was too aggressive. Perhaps no amount of tact would have succeeded.

Paul Hodgetts was head of special components in the R&D department. Like the rest of the department, he valued engineering design work. But he complained of engineering services:

> The services don't do things we want them to do. Instead, they tell *us* what they're going to do. I should probably go to Charlie, but I don't get any decisions there. I know I should go through Charlie, but this holds things up, so I often go direct.

ENGINEERING SERVICES DEPARTMENT

The engineering services department (ESD) provided ancillary and support services to R&D and served as liaison between engineering and the other Global Mobile departments. Among its main functions were the maintenance of the design systems, simple and advanced prototyping, management of the central technicians' pool, scheduling and expediting engineering products, documentation and publication of parts lists and engineering orders, preproduction engineering (consisting of the final integration of individual design components into mechanically compatible packages), and quality control (including inspection of incoming parts and materials, and final inspection of subassemblies and finished equipment). The original description of the department included the line, "ESD is responsible for maintaining cooperation with other departments, providing services to the design engineers, and freeing the more valuable people in R&D from essential activities that are diversions from their main focus."

Many of the 75 ESD employees were located in other departments and locations. Quality control people, for example, were scattered through the manufacturing and receiving areas of the Asian plant, and technicians worked primarily in the research area or the prototype fabrication room. The remaining ESD personnel were assigned to leftover nooks and crannies near the engineering sections. Newburg described his position:

> My biggest problem is getting acceptance from the people I work with. I've moved slowly rather than risk antagonism. I saw what happened to Brady, and I want to avoid that. But although his decisiveness had won over a few of the younger R&D people, he certainly didn't have the department's backing. Of course, it was the resentment of other departments that eventually caused his discharge. People have been slow accepting me here. There's nothing really overt, but I get a negative reaction to my ideas.
>
> My role in the company has never been well-defined, really. It's complicated by Doc's unique position, of course, and also by the fact that ESD sort of grew by itself over the years, as the design engineers concentrated more and more on the creative parts of product development. I wish I could be more involved in the technical side. That's been my training, and it's a lot of fun. But in our setup, the technical side is the least necessary for me to be involved in.
>
> Wang is hard to get along with. Before I came and after Brady left, there were six months when no one was really doing any scheduling. No work loads were figured, and unrealistic promises were made about releases. This puts us in an awkward position. We've been scheduling way beyond our capacity to manufacture or engineer.
>
> Certain people within R&D, for instance Philip Sanchez, understand scheduling well and meet project deadlines, but this is not generally true of the rest of the R&D department, especially the design engineers, who won't commit themselves. Most of the complaints come from sales and production department heads because new products, such as the Nonphixhun, are going to production before they are fully developed, under pressure from sales to get out the unit, and this snags the whole process. Somehow, engineering services should be able to intervene and resolve these complaints, but I haven't made much headway so far.

I should be able to go to Hoover for help, but she's too busy most of the time, and her major interest is the design side of engineering, where she got her own start. Sometimes she talks as though she's the engineering director as well as president. I have to put my foot down; there are problems here that the front office just doesn't understand.

Salespeople were often observed taking their problems directly to designers, while production frequently threw designs back at R&D, claiming they could not be produced and demanding the prompt attention of particular design engineers. The latter were frequently observed in video conference with production supervisors from the assembly floor. Charlie continued:

> The designers seem to feel they're losing something when one of us tries to help. They feel it's a reflection on them to have someone take over what they've been doing. They seem to want to carry a project right through to the final stages. Consequently, engineering services people are used below their capacity to contribute, and our department is denied functions it should be performing. There's not as much use made of engineering services as there should be.

An ESD technician supervisor added his comments:

> Production picks out the engineer who'll be the "bum of the month." They pick on every little detail instead of using their heads and making the minor changes that have to be made. The people with 15 to 20 years of experience shouldn't have to prove their ability any more, but they spend four hours defending themselves and four hours getting the job done. I have no one to go to when I need help. Charlie Newburg is afraid. I'm trying to help him but he can't help me at this time. I'm responsible for 25 people and I've got to support them.

Roxanne Walsh, who Newburg had brought with him to the company as an assistant, gave another view of the situation:

> I try to get our people in preproduction to take responsibility but they're not used to it, and people in other departments don't usually see them as best qualified to solve the problem. There's a real barrier for a newcomer here. Gaining people's confidence is hard. More and more, I'm wondering whether there really is a job for me here. [Walsh left Global Mobile a month later.]

Another subordinate of Newburg gave his view:

> If Doc gets a new product idea, you can't argue. But he's too optimistic. He judges that others can do what he does—but there's only one Doc Brown. We've had over 500 production change orders this year—they changed 2,500 documents. If I were in Charlie's shoes, I'd put my foot down on all this new development. I'd look at the reworking we're doing and get production set up the way I wanted it. Brady was fired when he was doing a good job. He was getting some system in the company's operations. Of course, it hurt some people. There is no denying that Doc is the most important person in the company. What gets overlooked is that Hoover is a close second, not just politically but in terms of what she contributes technically and in customer relations.

Production personnel said that Brady had failed to show respect for old-timers and was always meddling in other departments' business. This was the reason for his being fired, they contended. Taylor Flores, in charge of quality control, commented:

> I am now much more concerned with administration and less with work. It is one of the evils you get into. There is tremendous detail in this job. I listen to everyone's opinion. Everybody is important. There shouldn't be distinctions—distinctions between people. I'm not sure whether Charlie has to be a fireball like Brady. I think the real question is whether Charlie is getting the job done. I know my job is essential, I want to supply service to the more talented people and give them information so they can do their jobs better.

SALES DEPARTMENT

Marianne Price was angry. Her job was supposed to be selling, but instead it had turned into settling disputes and making excuses to waiting customers. She pointed a finger toward her desk:

> You see that telephone? I'm actually afraid nowadays to hear it ring. Three times out of five, it will be a customer who's hurting because we've failed to deliver on schedule. The other two calls will be from production or ESD, telling me some schedule has slipped again.
>
> The Nonphixhun is typical. Absolutely typical. We padded the delivery date by six weeks to allow for contingencies. Within two months, the slack had evaporated. Now it looks like we'll be lucky to ship it before Christmas. (It was now November 28.) We're *ruining* our reputation in the market. Why, just last week one of our best customers—people we've worked with for 15 years—tried to hang a penalty clause on their latest order.
>
> We shouldn't have to be after the engineers all the time. They should be able to see what problems they create without our telling them.

Phil Klein, head of mobile phone sales under Price, noted that many sales decisions were made by top management. He thought that sales was understaffed and had never really been able to get on top of the job.

> We have grown further and further away from engineering. The director of engineering does not pass on the information that we give him. We need better relationships there. It is very difficult for us to talk to customers about development problems without technical help. We need each other. The whole of engineering is now too isolated from the outside world. The morale of ESD is very low. They're in a bad spot—they're not well-organized.
>
> People don't take much to outsiders here. Much of this is because the expectation is built by top management that jobs will be filled from the bottom. So it's really tough when an outsider like Charlie comes in.

Eric Norman, order and pricing coordinator for smart phones, talked about his relationships with the production department:

> Actually, I get along with them fairly well. Oh, things could be better, of course, if they were more cooperative generally. They always seem to say, "It's my bat and my ball, and we're playing by my rules." People are afraid to make production mad; there's a lot of power in there.
>
> But you've got to understand that production has its own set of problems. And nobody in Global Mobile is working any harder than Tyson Wang to try to straighten things out.

PRODUCTION DEPARTMENT

Wang had joined Global Mobile just after the Iraq War where he had seen some combat and worked a stint in the intelligence organization. Both experiences had been useful in his first year of civilian employment at Global Mobile. The former factory superintendent and several middle managers had apparently been engaging in highly questionable side deals with Global Mobile's suppliers. Wang gathered the evidence, revealed the situation to Hoover, and stood by the president as the accusations and terminations ensued. Seven months after joining the company, Wang was named factory manager.

Wang's first move had been to rebuild the factory team with new people from outside the corporation. This group did not share the traditional Global Mobile emphasis on informality and friendly personal relationships and had worked long and hard to install systematic manufacturing methods and procedures. Before the reorganization, production had controlled purchasing, stock control, and final quality control. Because of the scandal, management decided on a check-and-balance system of organization and moved these three departments from production to ESD. The new production managers felt they had been unjustly penalized by this reorganization, particularly since they had uncovered the behavior that was detrimental to the company in the first place.

By 2007, the production department had grown to 500 employees, of whom 60% worked in the assembly area—an unusually pleasant environment that had been commended by *Factory* magazine for its colorful decoration, cleanliness, and low noise level. Another 30% of the work force, mostly skilled technicians, staffed various production support departments. The remaining employees performed scheduling, supervisory, and maintenance duties. Production workers were not union members, were paid by the hour, and participated in both the liberal profit-sharing program and the stock purchase plan. Morale in production was traditionally high and turnover was extremely low.

Wang commented:

> To be efficient, production has to be a self-contained department. We have to control what comes into the department and what goes out. That's why purchasing, inventory control, and quality ought to run out of this office. We'd eliminate a lot of problems with better control there. Why, even Taylor Flores of QC would rather work for me than for ESD; he's said so himself. We understand his problems better.
>
> The other departments should be self-contained, too. That's why I always avoid the underlings, and go straight to the department heads with any questions. I always go down the line.
>
> I have to protect my people from outside disturbances. Look what would happen if I let unfinished half-baked designs in here—there'd be chaos. The bugs have to be found before the designs go to parts manufacturers and into assembly, and it seems I'm the one who has to find them. Look at the Nonphixhun, for example. [Tyson had spent most of Thanksgiving Day (it was now November 28) reviewing the latest set of specifications from the system.] ESD should have found every one of those discrepancies. They just don't check the files properly. They change most of the things I flag, but then they fail to trace through the impact of those changes on the rest of the design. I shouldn't have to do that.
>
> And those engineers are tolerance crazy. They want everything manufactured and assembled to a thousandth of an inch. I'm the only one in the company who's had any experience at that level. We make sure that the things that engineers say on their drawings actually have to be that way and whether they're obtainable from the kind of raw materials and parts we use.
>
> That shouldn't be production's responsibility, but I have to do it. Accepting bad designs and documentation wouldn't let us ship the order any quicker. We'd only make a lot of junk that had to be reworked. And that would take even longer.
>
> This way, I get to be known as the bad guy, but I guess that's just part of the job. [Wang paused and smiled wryly.] Of course, what really gets them is that I don't even have a degree.

Wang had fewer bones to pick with the sales department, because he said that they trusted him.

> When *we* give Marianne Price a shipping date, she knows the equipment will be shipped *then*.
>
> You've got to recognize, though, that all of our new product problems stem from sales making absurd commitments on equipment that hasn't been fully developed. That *always* means trouble. Unfortunately, Hoover always backs sales up, even when they're wrong. She always favors them over us.

Ralph Simon, executive vice-president of the company, had direct responsibility for Global Mobile's production department. He said:

> There shouldn't really be a dividing of departments among top management in the company. The president should be czar over all. The production people ask me to do something for them, and I really can't do it. It creates bad feelings between engineering and production, this special attention that they [R&D] get from Hannah. But then Hoover likes to dabble in design. Wang feels that production is treated like a poor relation.

PRODUCT RELEASE

At the executive committee meeting of December 6, it was duly recorded that Wang had accepted the prints and specifications for the Nonphixhun smart phone and had set December 29 as the shipping date for the first 100 phones. Hoover, as chairperson, shook her head and changed the subject quickly when Newburg tried to initiate a discussion of interdepartmental coordination.

About a week later, Hoover called Newburg into her office.

> Charlie, I didn't know whether to tell you now, or after the holiday. But I figured you'd work right through Christmas Day if we didn't have this talk, and that just wouldn't have been fair to you. I can't understand why we have such poor luck in the engineering director's job lately. And I don't think it's entirely your fault. But....

Charlie only heard half of Hoover's words, and said nothing in response. He'd be paid through June 30.... He should use the time for searching.... Hoover would help all she could.... Jim Brady was supposed to be doing well at his own new job, and might need more help.

Charlie cleaned out his desk and numbly started home. The electronic carillon near his house was playing a Christmas carol. Charlie thought again of Hoover's rationale: conflict still plagued Global Mobile—and Charlie had not made it go away. Maybe somebody else could do it.

Questions

1. What is your diagnosis of the strategy and organization design at Global Mobile? How well does Global Mobile's strategic intent fit with its external environment?
2. How would you work with Hannah Hoover and the executive committee to bring about strategic change at Global Mobile?

Selected Cases

LEADING STRATEGIC CHANGE AT DAVITA: THE INTEGRATION OF THE GAMBRO ACQUISITION

In the summer of 2005, Kent Thiry, a 49-year-old Harvard MBA, ex-Bain consultant, and now the CEO of DaVita, thought about how he and his management team should address a set of emerging and important challenges. DaVita (publicly traded on the New York Stock Exchange under the symbol DVA) was a $2.2 billion annual revenue operator of free-standing and in-hospital kidney dialysis centers.

Thiry and his senior team were meeting to discuss the next steps the company should take to continue its organizational development and strategic evolution. They were especially focused on how to manage several looming challenges. DaVita was just in the process of completing a $3.1 billion purchase of Gambro, a large competitor. The acquisition would nearly double its size, from 700 to more than 1,200 dialysis centers and from 13,000 to 25,000 people. As such, it would cement its position as the second largest operator of kidney dialysis centers in the United States.

When Thiry came to lead the company in October 1999, the organization had been beset with financial, operational, regulatory, and morale difficulties. "The company was technically bankrupt," he said. "It was being investigated by the SEC, sued by shareholders, had turnover at over twice our current levels, was almost out of cash, and, in general, wasn't the happiest of places."[1] By 2005, the new management team had achieved a complete turnaround. The company's market capitalization had grown from $200 million to more than $5 billion, the clinical outcomes had become the best in the industry, the company's organic growth was the highest in the industry, and employee retention had improved dramatically, with a 50% reduction in turnover.

However, this had not been a typical turnaround. Instead, a closer look at DaVita's culture and leadership showed that the DaVita management team's focus had been on creating a strong and positive values-based organization where all levels of the organization had an emotional commitment to its success. The foundation was the Mission and Values, first created by 700 of the company's managers in 2000 and now widely practiced throughout the company. To the management team, the company's rebirth strategy was based on the belief that they had to create something larger than themselves in order to be successful. Thiry commented:

> At Vivra [another kidney dialysis company where many of DaVita's senior leaders had worked together], we implemented many people, team, and culture-friendly policies. They were consistent with my basic values, but the extra energy I brought to them was because they were a means to the end of having a successful company. This time it is different. This time the building of a successful company is a means to the end of building a healthy community. Because humans spend more waking hours at work than anywhere else, if you are a leader who purports to care about your team, it makes no sense to create a paradigm which concedes all that time needs to be spent in [a] relatively vanilla values or sterile emotional commitment environment.[2]

Because of this, Thiry and his team flagged several important challenges they believed needed to be addressed if DaVita was to continue its successful evolution of both operations *and* culture. The question was, How could they use the culture to achieve even greater operational excellence?

THE GAMBRO INTEGRATION

One immediate task entailed integrating Gambro into the DaVita way of managing and its culture. Gambro was significantly more hierarchical and formal than DaVita, and did not have a strong people-oriented culture. Prior to the

[1] http://www.redcoatpublishing.com.

[2] Kent Thiry, email, November 27, 2005.

merger, DaVita had been disparaged inside Gambro, with Thiry described as "a compliance maverick, reckless, and egotistical." Ironically, Gambro had itself purchased Vivra in 1997, then a smaller, publicly traded dialysis company led and transformed by Thiry during the 1990s. As the leader of the combined organization, Thiry's goal was to be respectful of Gambro, its people, and its capabilities, while maintaining DaVita's unique culture and way of management.

PERSONAL TOUCH IN A GROWING ORGANIZATION

Prior to the Gambro integration, DaVita operated in 37 states. Its growth, size, and diverse locations made it increasingly difficult for Thiry to personally touch the many teammates on a regular basis. This presented a key challenge: How to personally impact teammates as he had during his first five years at the helm? Affectionately called "KT" by many teammates in the company, Thiry was, by everyone's estimation, extremely charismatic and energetic. More than that, Thiry was the primary architect of and cheerleader for DaVita's unique culture and values. The company reflected the vision shared by Thiry, Joe Mello, and a few others such as Doug Vlchek. Mello, DaVita's COO, and Vlchek, DaVita's chief wisdom officer, had worked with Thiry before and had joined DaVita in 1999 to help drive the organizational change initiative.

TEAMMATE MORALE AND COMPENSATION

Maintaining the culture and sense of community within DaVita was not easy, even before the acquisition of Gambro. Taking care of dialysis patients is a difficult job. One out of every five dialysis patients dies each year, creating not only a difficult work environment but also a lot of emotional strain. With the company's turnaround receding into the past, numerous employees—or "teammates" as all are called at DaVita—had rising expectations for wages and working conditions. The company's ability to raise salaries was constrained by the high volume of patients—about 79%[3]—who were covered by government programs such as Medicare and Medicaid but whose reimbursement rate did not cover the cost of treatment.

Because of financial constraints, dialysis providers could not afford to pay high overtime rates. As a result, many of DaVita's patient care technicians, who typically earned between $11 and $14 per hour, worked two jobs in order to generate sufficient income. One manifestation of the pay challenge was the barrage of questions that Thiry and Mello would get as they traveled the country conducting "town hall meetings." Town hall meetings were an opportunity for teammates to ask questions of senior leadership, in person. It was quite common for teammates to ask why their wages were not higher and why productivity expectations were so high and always rising. Moreover, DaVita competed for nurses in labor markets with nursing shortages. Many other organizations had chosen to just throw money at the problem of attracting and keeping nurses, something DaVita could not afford to do.

OPERATIONAL EFFICIENCIES AND PRODUCTIVITY IMPROVEMENT

The fifth challenge was to continue to drive productivity improvement and to think about ways to fundamentally reengineer the business. As Mello noted, the company had made great strides in enhancing labor productivity over the past several years. But there was always the looming threat of reduced reimbursement from the government for dialysis services. This revenue stream represented approximately 60% of total company revenue.[4] Mello talked about the challenge of doing things that would materially and fundamentally enhance the company's cost structure so DaVita could be largely impervious to what might happen in its environment.

As Thiry prepared for the meeting with his executive team, he thought about what the company should do about these challenges and maintaining the culture his senior team had worked so hard to build. He wanted the team to come up with some ideas about how to address the challenges facing the company, and of course, to do so in a way that was consistent with its values and culture.

[3]From 2004 DaVita Annual Report, p. 4.

[4]From 2004 DaVita Annual Report, p. 4.

A BRIEF HISTORY OF DAVITA (1994–1999)

DaVita was the new name given in 2000 to Total Renal Care (TRC), a company originally founded by Victor Chaltiel. Chaltiel had sold a former company for a good profit, with the business model of leveraging cost savings obtained through large-scale purchasing and distribution systems for drugs in the Medicare reimbursement program. Based on his success, he planned to do the same thing in the domain of kidney dialysis centers through roll-ups of smaller chains and individual centers. One of Chaltiel's strategies was to apply strict business principles and reap their rewards upon entering the traditionally not-for-profit domain of kidney dialysis centers (run by hospitals and physician specialists). He focused on growth through acquisition through the 1990s. The Internet bubble focused many analysts on top-line revenue growth, which provided TRC with a high stock price that allowed it to continue making acquisitions at a fast pace.

Unfortunately, Chaltiel and his team failed to integrate their acquisitions, leading to some operational incoherence in TRC. One example noted by Harlan Cleaver, DaVita's chief information officer, was that there was no uniformity in a critical patient data form used to record and monitor patient care during dialysis, and little standardization in reporting and work methods across centers. This absence of standardization made routine management activities, such as transferring personnel and patients across centers, much more difficult if not impossible.

Cash flow issues created serious problems. Mello commented that another operational weakness of TRC was insurance reimburse-ment—a critical problem for a company whose revenue was entirely dependent on it. Insurers and the government would frequently question charges and demand additional documentation. They would occasionally unilaterally reduce the reimbursement amount, and delay payment until they received answers to queries and requested documentation. Medical service providers such as DaVita needed to pay close attention to billing and collections to avoid a cash crunch.

Finally, senior executives paid scant attention to the dialysis centers themselves, which were seen more as an avenue of corporate growth where patients and caregivers were economic units in a bigger financial structure. This head-quarter-centric, financially oriented operating culture did not win friends among the health care practitioners who worked hard in the field to deliver quality care.

In 1999, Total Renal Care ran into severe financial difficulties, having just recently merged with another large competitor that had also been built in a rapid fashion. The board of directors turned to Thiry, who was in the process of leaving a private-equity–funded managed care company where he had been for two years post-Vivra in 1997. He was eagerly anticipating time off with his family. When headhunters called to see if he wanted to interview for another CEO position, he always replied, "No." Thiry was within 90 days of his "retirement" when TRC called:

> I still remember the call. After my assistant told me who was on the phone, I picked it up with the intention of giving the same 'no' answer. As I started to listen, all the positive memories of my first time in dialysis, at Vivra, came flooding back. It had been the most powerfully positive time of my professional life. I have no idea what I said in that phone conversation. All I know is I went home that night and asked my wife Denise if it was okay to interview. She was livid. What about my alleged interest in more time with the family? What about the fact that this was a turnaround located in another city [Thiry lived near San Francisco and TRC was headquartered in the Los Angeles area]? The difficulty of the decision felt like a terrible burden at the time. It turned out to be a gift. Never before did I have to think so deeply about why I wanted to do something. After agonizing for a few weeks, we decided I would give it a try. There is a saying I love—we use it at DaVita all the time: 'Begin with the end in mind.' I started at DaVita with more of an end in mind than any other beginning in my professional life.

Before accepting the job offer, Thiry reached out to a set of people who had been with him in his previous dialysis venture, people whom he trusted, liked, and respected. He recruited Harlan Cleaver, who was now living in Denver, to be the chief technology officer and David Barry to be COO. He reached out to Doug Vlchek, whom he had hired into Vivra, to lead the organizational change and culture-building efforts. Thiry recalled, in reference to the musketeer imagery he loves, asking them something like, "Will you ride again?" They all accepted. When Barry left in the first year for personal reasons, Thiry brought in Joe Mello, who had also been with him at Vivra.

When Thiry arrived at TRC in October 1999, the company was a mess. It could barely make payroll, was in default on its loan covenants, and was paying penalties to the banks. Highly leveraged from its many acquisitions, it was essentially on the verge of bankruptcy. The stock had fallen from nearly $50 to $2 a share. Systems were nonexistent or in chaos, and the organization's employees were dispirited and unhappy. It was not at all clear that financial survival was possible.

KEY SUCCESS FACTORS FOR A DIALYSIS COMPANY LIKE DAVITA

There were four critical factors for organizational success along both financial and clinical outcome dimensions.

Attention to Detail

The first factor was painstaking attention to operational details and compliance with government regulations. For instance, a company that charged the government, through the Medicare program, for services that were not actually delivered and/or were not documented could face accusations of fraud and suffer financial penalties as well as delays in payment. Legal problems could also arise from actually delivering care or medicines that patients did not need, as well as for improper relationships with drug companies or physicians that might entail kickbacks for patient referrals or purchases of pharmaceutical supplies. Proper record keeping and ethical behavior were vital to the ongoing success of dialysis companies.

Managing Financial Outcomes

The opportunity to make a financial difference in operational results rested largely on small but important behaviors and decisions. One such activity was carefully using supplies to avoid waste and maintaining appropriate stock levels so that inventory costs were not unnecessarily high, yet avoiding emergency ordering. Another activity was the reuse of dialysis filters and maintenance of the dialysis machines to ensure both long life of the equipment and lower cost per treatment.

Possibly even more important was the activity of efficient labor-hour management, given that the proportion of labor costs in the total cost structure equaled one-third to one-half of the treatment cost. As Mello pointed out, in 2005 DaVita would do about 7,000,000 dialysis treatments. Each 0.01 savings in labor hours per treatment achieved across the company was worth about $1.8 million; this savings went directly to the bottom line.

Achieving Good Clinical Outcomes

Attention to detail during the dialysis visit and strong personal relationships among the DaVita staff and patients drove the achievement of good clinical outcomes. First, attention to detail also mattered a lot for obtaining good clinical outcomes. For example, it was important to take care while putting the patient on the machine, monitoring the treatment as it was occurring, and taking the patient off the machine at the end of the session. It was also critical to monitor the patient's health status generally so that treatment issues could be foreseen and addressed. Good clinical outcomes also enabled DaVita teammates to take pride in working in a company that provided the best care in the industry, an advantage in recruiting and retention.

Second, achieving good clinical outcomes depended not only on the patient's commitment to treatment but on the emotional tone and bond between the center's teammates and the patients. Patients sometimes missed their dialysis appointments because they found the treatment unpleasant, the logistics of setting up appointments too difficult, or they became depressed by the likelihood of success. However, according to various DaVita clinic teammates, one important factor affecting patient compliance was the extent to which patients trusted and felt comfortable with the dialysis center and its staff. Emotions are contagious, and to the extent that DaVita could create positive, genuine emotions on the part of its workforce, those positive emotions might influence the attitude of patients. This could thereby improve the patients' survival, not only through their positive mental attitudes but also by affecting their compliance with the difficult regimen of living with late-stage kidney disease. As one administrator said, "It's important that the teammates like their jobs and smile and relate in a compassionate way to patients, because that makes the patients feel better about being here."

Employee Attraction and Retention

The final critical success factor was the attraction and retention of teammates. DaVita competed for nurses with hospitals, doctors' offices, other health care providers, and, of course, with other dialysis companies, and the chronic nursing shortage in the United States meant there were always unfilled positions. Hospitals typically paid more per hour than DaVita or its competitors.

Patient care technicians (PCTs), the largest category of employees, typically earned less than $15 an hour. Many worked two jobs, with their second job often being for another provider of dialysis services. PCTs were often tempted to leave for better-paying opportunities, either with other health care providers or to find different occupations.

Retention of teammates was important because turnover was costly, entailing finding and training replacement people, and possibly paying overtime labor rates if a center was temporarily short-staffed. High turnover could also impair clinical outcomes, because a nurse's or PCT's experience in doing dialysis and working in a team enhanced patient care outcomes. Being an employer of choice was not just part of DaVita's mission, but was also important for business success and better patient care.

THE TURNAROUND (1999–2005)

With an acute awareness of these critical success factors, Thiry and his colleagues set about the task of turning the organization around. The first order of business was the business itself. Over the next four years, the organization worked to fix billing and cash flow problems, restructure outstanding debt, bring the information systems up to speed, hire people who could "get stuff done" ("GSD" remained a popular acronym in the company, and being "good at GSD" was a high compliment), and invest in continuous improvement projects and training.

It was a difficult time for the company. For a time, the government stopped paying DaVita for laboratory tests because of issues in record maintenance and documentation. The company had to decide what to do with the patients whose lab tests were not being reimbursed. The team decided to continue performing tests that it felt were essential in delivery of care and to appeal the decision to an administrative law judge to attempt to obtain the denied funds. Four years later, after winning six successive judgments, the government paid DaVita over $90 million. Harlan Cleaver, the chief information officer, described the process of bringing order to the system and establishing common practices, measures, and information systems across the centers. His first step was to standardize the paper-based system used to keep track of patient care in the various centers. As he pointed out, it made sense to start with that patient record system because the issues were of standardization, common practices, and alignment; without the added complication of computers on top of everything else.

The second order of business was getting the philosophy right. Thiry and his colleagues recognized that what they said and did in those first months would set the tone for the ensuing years at the company, so close attention to building the kind of culture and organization they wanted proceeded in parallel with the business turnaround efforts. Thiry described early meetings of the executive team in which they would spend time discussing basic issues, such as whether they could make payroll and their ongoing negotiations with the banks, and then they would turn to talk about the core values, culture, and operating philosophy they wanted to instill. When Thiry and Vlchek would start talking about Mission and Values, many of the executives were very skeptical about the value and intent of this activity when the company was in such dire straits. Thiry believed that without a clear statement of Mission and Values, the operational turnaround could not be sustained.

A big part of the new philosophy was to recognize that the centers, where patient care was delivered and where most DaVita teammates worked, were key to the company's success. To emphasize the importance of the centers, Thiry had all senior managers, himself included, "adopt" a center and drop by occasionally. Thiry's center was in Hayward, California, and long after his last visit, people in the center were still commenting on his attention to them.

The company later replaced the adopt-a-center program with the practice of having everyone hired in or promoted to the vice president level or above go through "Reality 101," which entailed spending a week in a center helping to do the day-to-day work. Executives participated in activities such as machine set-up prior to dialysis, machine teardown and disinfection post treatment, helping with blood pressure monitoring, or whatever tasks they felt comfortable

FIGURE 1

DaVita's Mission Statement and Core Values

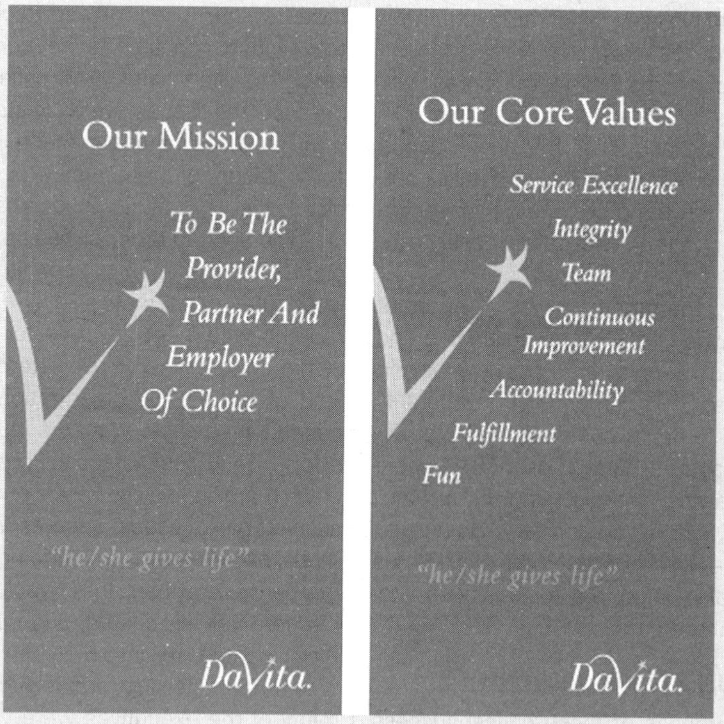

in actually performing. As Thiry explained, it was important not to push people to do things they felt uncomfortable or unskilled at doing, but it was also important for people to experience what it was like to get up at 4 A.M. to get to a center at 5 A.M. so it could be open for the first patients at 6 A.M., and to see what life in a center was about.

Thiry and the senior management group understood they needed the involvement, cooperation, energy, and ideas of the clinic managers, the front-line supervisors who make the centers work. In May of 2000, more than 400 clinic managers, plus people from corporate headquarters assembled in Phoenix, Arizona, for the first of what has now become annual corporate-wide meetings. The choice of location, Phoenix, was intentional, as the phoenix is a bird that rose from the ashes, just as the company was seeking to rise from its precarious condition. At this first meeting, suggestions for a new name for the company were presented. It was the company's teammates, not the board or just the senior management, collectively assembled at this off-site, who voted on and thereby chose the new name, DaVita, which is an approximate translation of the Italian phrases "to give life" or "he/she gives life."[5] Also at that meeting, groups discussed, debated, and voted on proposals for the core values. Figure 1 shows the mission statement that Thiry presented at the meeting and the core values decided upon by the Phoenix delegation. Over the years, the seventh value, "fun," was added by another election.

For much of the first 18 months, Thiry and Mello would hold frequent conference calls with the top 800 or so people in the company to update them on progress. As part of each call, Thiry would say, "What is the incremental evidence that we are serious about our Mission and Values?" And then he would provide an answer to that question.

[5]"Total Renal Care Announces New Company Name," Investor Relations–DaVita, June 5, 2000.

Thiry commented, "There were many periods where, absent the pressure of knowing I had to ask and answer that simple question out loud in front of 800 people, in many instances I would not have launched another program, or policy, or communication. They would have been squeezed out by the harsh realities of normal business—like they normally are."

With increased focus and attention to operational details, the commitment of the company's teammates, and the bank negotiations behind it, DaVita embarked on a remarkable transformation in its performance, achieving not only great financial results, as shown in Figure 2, but also consistent, year-over-year improvements in clinical outcomes and reductions in turnover.

THE DAVITA WAY: VALUES AND ORGANIZATIONAL CULTURE

DaVita did not develop its culture by accident. The culture was a result of what Thiry calls "purposeful actions" that "articulated and demonstrated" what a company could be. First, Thiry created a clear, concise, easy-to-remember mission that was quickly turned into a song still sung today. Then, he asked 700 colleagues to come to a consensus on the core values. They also used the following question as a benchmark for their own development: What did

FIGURE 2

DaVita Financial Results

	1999	2000	2001	2002	2003	2004
Revenues ($millions)	1,445.4	1,486.3	1,650.8	1,854.6	2,016.4	2,298.6
Operating margin	13.0%	19.6%	25.6%	24.6%	28.3%	27.8%
Net profit ($millions)	<56.4>	17.0	98.1	147.8	163.2	217.3
Earnings per share	<0.46>	0.13	0.76	1.23	1.69	2.11
Cash flow per share	0.46	1.06	1.59	2.33	2.46	3.08

SOURCE: Value Line Investment Survey.

DaVita Split-Adjusted Stock Price

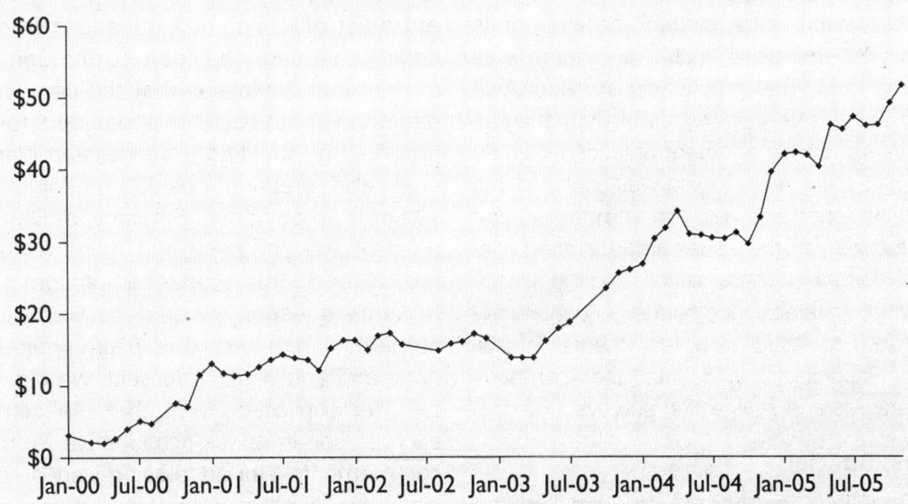

other great companies do to cultivate cultures—companies like Southwest and Disney?

Employees became teammates, and, if they "crossed the bridge" of believing the company could be special, they became "citizens" of the "village" (not a company), with Thiry as "mayor." Hugs were common, as were high-fives and laughter, even among the intense ex-consultants and MBAs who populated the business offices. Through what are called "tradi tions and symbols," DaVita executives brought organizational change concepts to life and made them real.

Cathy Gelb, who ran the DaVita Academies as part of DaVita University and who had been with the company since 2001, commented that one of the things that distinguished DaVita from the *Fortune* 1000 companies where she had worked as a freelance training consultant was the tremendous amount of strategic thought and intentionality that went into every single action and decision. She noted that, for instance, all meetings were carefully planned, even to thinking about the particular music that would be used, the sequencing of materials, seating arrangements (for instance, at Academies, should guests be put in the back?), and the specific words and terms that would be employed during presentations. All of this planning was an effort to create the right message and feelings and provide an optimal experience for those in attendance.

Evaluation data were collected about everything, including every meeting and class, and used to make educational activities and meetings more effective over time. Gelb also commented that Thiry did not like the word "culture" because of its association with the word "cult," and there was already some joking about "drinking the Kool Aid" because of DaVita's very strong, carefully managed, and inclusive set of management practices.

The DaVita Way of Managing was captured in a set of phrases—short and easily remembered—that encapsulated many of the values and operating principles of the company. These values, and the associated behaviors, were also incorporated into interview schedules used to select new teammates, into all performance appraisals, and into the company employee attitude and satisfaction surveys.

New, Ours, Special

At DaVita meetings, executives always asked the assembled people to respond to three questions: "What is this company? Whose company is it? What could it be?" The answers, literally shouted back, were "New," "Ours," and "Special." The idea of "new" was not just that DaVita was a different organization after the 2000 turnaround, but with its ongoing acquisitions and new business ventures it was always a new place reinventing itself. "Ours" means that the company is the responsibility and under the control of the teammates who work for it, who have the opportunity to make the company what they would like it to be. This leads to the last question. Note that the executives do not ask what "is" the company, but rather, "What could it be?" The answer, "special," captures in a word the aspirations for building an organization that is truly unique in its culture and its results for its patients, while "could" reflects the fact that the deve lopment of the organization is a journey, and although it has achieved great things, its aspirations are for more, and that being special is something yet to be fully achieved.

We Said, We Did

Accountability is an important value at DaVita. So is measurement—the company measured not just clinical outcomes, costs, and labor utilization, but almost everything that was related to dimensions of performance. In addition, there is an emphasis on systematic, planned thinking and actions. All of this came together in the idea of follow-up, something that began at the very top of the organization. As Richard Fontaine, one of the directors on the com pany's board, explained, at virtually every board meeting Thiry would present a list of issues and questions from the preceding meeting, and then go through them one at a time and explain what the company and he had done about each. This included, for instance, progress on building a succession planning process and preparing back-up people ready for senior-level positions. Similarly, at DaVita Academies, if the company had made assurances or pro mises to the workforce—to get an answer to some question, to address some concern or problem—Thiry would explain what had been done and end with, "We said, we did."

The implication was that the company and each person in it was accountable for meeting its commitments—for addressing issues and explaining how another important value, continuous improvement, was occurring. As several people noted, if someone was in a position of often having to say, "We said, but we didn't do," that person would probably not last long at an organization that stressed accountability and getting stuff done.

One for All, All for One

This idea, from the *Three Musketeers* books and movies, was a prominent theme in the company. Thiry's office at corporate headquarters in El Segundo, California, near the Los Angeles airport, had a movie poster from *The Man with the Iron Mask*, and has hanging in it the sword that Thiry brandishes—in full Musketeer uniform—at DaVita Academies and other meetings. The phrase represents one way of understanding the idea of community and shared obligations and responsibility. "One for all" means that it is the obligation of every DaVita teammate to contribute what they can to the whole, to expend their best efforts on behalf of the collective, and to take responsibility for the company and each of its members. "All for one" means that just as the individual should devote himself or herself to the group, the group has a responsibility to help that individual develop and succeed and surmount difficult setbacks and transitions.

An example of this care and community was a fund called the DaVita Village Network, to which DaVita teammates contributed to help others out with, for example, unexpected medical expenses or other financial needs. Teammate contributions to the DaVita Village Network were matched by contributions made by the company out of its profits.

The Village—Not Just a Company, But a Community

Related to the idea of "one for all, all for one" was the idea of DaVita as a community—represented in the word "village." Corporate headquarters in El Segundo was referred to as "Casa DaVita" (the house of DaVita), and village language and imagery were used in many ways. Joe Mello would tell a story from one of his favorite books about a man living on a hillside who sees other members of his village below in danger from an onrushing flood, and sets his own house on fire, so that when the people rush up the hill to put out the fire, they are saved from the flood. The word "worker" was never used and seldom was the word "employee"—instead, people were referred to as "teammates" or "citizens" and, consistent with the village imagery, language that evoked the idea of "citizenship" and the mutual obligations of citizens and their community was emphasized. In the words of Gina Randolph, a group vice president, "We think of ourselves as a village where each facility is a neighborhood." When pressed on how important these distinctions were, she responded, "From the viewpoint of a career that spans several decades, this is the first time I have had the privilege of working for a company whose Mission and Values are so completely alive and not hanging on the wall."[6]

No Brag, Just Facts

DaVita was committed to a fact-based approach to management and decision making, to talking to people about the facts, and to using facts and evidence as much as possible for every decision and statement. So, when Thiry stood up at a DaVita Academy meeting and stated that DaVita provides the best care for dialysis patients in the industry—a statement that, on its surface, was not unlike the typical corporate claim about its quality, service, or leading edge technology—he then provided quantitative data showing how DaVita was doing on specific clinical outcome measures, ending with the phrase, "No brag, just facts." It was a way of cementing the idea that people at the company should attempt to anchor their judgments, their statements, and their claims in quantitative data, not in hyperbole or wishes.

Fact-based decision making was reinforced in the company's measurement system. Clinic managers received monthly, multipage reports showing how their performance compared to goals or budgets, to their own prior results, and to other facilities in their region, in their division, and in DaVita as a whole. Annual surveys of employees provided information on satisfaction and engagement, as well as perceptions about the extent to which people felt the company was living up to its Mission and Values.

But what was most interesting, and what really reinforced the commitment to a fact-based, measurement-rich culture, was what happened when the company was unable to measure something of importance. Patients who did not show up for dialysis because they were in the hospital or on

[6]David Robbins, http://srarchitects.com/health%20care.htm.

vacation made scheduling labor more difficult and affected labor productivity. But this indicator could not be captured systematically given current management information systems. Therefore, the measure was included in the monthly reports as a blank graph with the notation, "Not Available." As Joe Mello explained, if there were some important critical data that could not yet be assessed, the company included them anyway on the reports, showing they were not available. This presentation of a missing measure, month after month, encouraged people to figure out ways to measure what might have first been viewed and dismissed as "unmeasurable," and therefore the availability of data useful for making decisions kept improving.

We Are Here

DaVita wanted to encourage its teammates to be fully involved and present in the company, not just physically but also emotionally. There were "We Are Here Awards," which were $1,000 in vacation expenses given to randomly selected nonexempt (hourly paid) teammates who had perfect attendance (no unplanned absences) during a 90-day period. At DaVita meetings, teams would be asked if they were here, and would respond with a cheer, or chant, or yell, or some combination that indicated not only physical presence but also involvement and commitment. In Thiry's office, painted on the wall was the saying, "This is not a dress rehearsal, this is my Life." There was an emphasis on having people fully engaged in their work and with the company, so they could find meaning and fulfillment in their jobs and in their associations with teammates.

The Shining Star

The "i" in DaVita was dotted as a star, referred to as a "shining star." Thiry would say that the star lived in a lush green valley and only came out to sit on top of the "i" when a DaVita teammate did something special for a patient or a fellow teammate. Because at any given moment there was always someone doing something special in the company, the star was always "out." At the national awards ceremony, the highest awards were called "Shining Star Awards," for people who not only performed their jobs with exceptional proficiency, but who also exemplified the DaVita values and who contributed to the well-being of the team.

DAVITA MANAGEMENT PRACTICES

Values and beliefs, ways of being, and the organizational culture had to be produced and reproduced every day to be real and meaningful. DaVita did a number of things to ensure that its Mission and Values would infuse the day-to-day behavior of its teammates and to help ensure that it operated in ways consistent with its aspirations. Many of its management practices seemed (and were) like common sense. All were products of extensive discussion by people inside the company, and all were talked about regularly, practiced, and were embedded in everything the company did.

The DaVita Way and the DaVita Way of Managing

DaVita thought that it was beliefs that drove behaviors that, in turn, produced performance. As Thiry explained it, the "DaVita Way" was "what (who) we are: our Beliefs (which have been introduced and articulated over the past few years), as well as the consistently practiced Behaviors (which are derived from those beliefs)." The company articulated and lived its beliefs through talking about its history, its symbols and traditions, the idea of the village, communication, talking about the future, and caring and sharing for members of the community. The DaVita Way of Managing defined a set of behaviors and competencies that the company sought to promote and produce, and which formed the basis of all of its selection and performance management practices, and were reinforced in its educational activities. There were four behaviors critical to the DaVita Way of Managing: It (1) gets the right stuff done, (2) fosters team, (3) stewards resources, and (4) builds relationships.

There was one other aspect to the DaVita management approach—an emphasis on execution. When the leadership, including Mello, Vlchek, and Thiry, had been together at Vivra, they had noticed that even though they had an extremely talented executive team of about nine people who were all working hard, things were not happening. They went to an off-site meeting and concluded that there were four elements critical for effective execution: (1) absolute clarity of purpose, (2) absolute accountability, (3) relentless follow-up, and (4) celebrating successes. These principles and practices helped build operational excellence and an ability to get things done at

DaVita, where they were very much a part of the fabric of the management approach.

DaVita University

DaVita had many employees in a large number of centers, and although turnover had been reduced, it was still high enough that—coupled with corporate growth—a large number of new people were entering the company each year. The Gambro acquisition would bring 12,000 new people into the organization. To achieve a higher level of uniformity in understanding, communication, and management practice, a lot of the DaVita way of managing was transmitted through DaVita University. This activity was started within a year of Thiry's arrival in the company, even as the financial recovery was proceeding, and the programming has expanded significantly over time.

DaVita University was run out of the Wisdom Department, and the head of the department, who had been Doug Vlchek until mid-2005, was called the chief wisdom officer. Vlchek's nickname was "Yoda," after the *Star Wars* character, an appellation he had been given by Thiry shortly after they first met almost 12 years previously. The name for the department came from Joe Mello. At Vivra, they had a chief knowledge officer, but that was too conventional a name for the department and its head at DaVita. Wisdom seemed to be what the company was trying to impart to its teammates and to continually develop.

DaVita University offered programs in continuous quality improvement (a two-day program required for newly hired facility administrators, managers, and vice presidents who had not taken the class previously), presentation skills, leadership development, team skills, and programs for vice presidents. There were also numerous courses on clinical subjects. But two of the most important programs that reached the most people either directly or indirectly were the DaVita Academy (and more recently, a program called Academy II) and a program called FAST, which stood for Facility Administrator Survival Training.

FAST. FAST was a five-day program taken by all new clinic managers. The program consisted of training in managerial skills such as time management, communication, providing coaching and feedback to team members, and interviewing, as well as material on the DaVita culture (the DaVita Way and One for All). On Thursday afternoons there was a town-hall meeting with Thiry or Mello so that participants could express their opinions, ask questions, and interact in an informal way with senior executives. The course also consisted of specific technical knowledge and skills necessary for administrators of dialysis centers. Evenings were, with one exception, devoted to organized social interaction, including group dinners and bowling, to help build friendships and a feeling of team spirit among the 25 to 30 people who typically took this class together.

DaVita Academy. DaVita Academy was a two-day program for all front-line teammates (for instance, patient care technicians, nurses, social workers, and the people who serviced the dialysis machines). Originally offered on a voluntary basis to people who were interested in attending, the Academy was evolving to become an activity that facility administrators were encouraged to send new teammates to, preferably within the first 90 days of joining DaVita. Data showed that people who attended an Academy had a turnover rate of about 12% compared to 28% for those who had not, so attending an Academy was critical for both retention and also for engaging people fully in the DaVita spirit and way of relating to each other.

A typical Academy session consisted of a combination of lecture and experiential sessions on subjects such as communications, team dynamics, and conflict resolution. The evening activity between the first and second day was always the DaVita Olympics, where teams competed with each other in various indoor light physical activities and performed skits with songs and music that they developed. This informal social interaction, singing together, acting silly together, and working together to compete against other teams, helped break down barriers and build energy and spirit.

Academy II

Academy II was a newer program attended by all teammates from a specific region, designed to "take facility performance to the next level by fostering mutual accountability amongst the team."[7] Because the program involved all teammates from a region, centers were completely closed on that day, requiring that dialysis treatments be rescheduled. By emphasizing how to hold difficult and

[7]DVU Course Catalog, p. 3.

honest conversations among the teammates to resolve interpersonal issues, the course fostered better and more productive interactions. The course also contained numerous activities designed to impart skills for team building and joint planning for operational improvement at the facilities.

There was every indication that the commitment to training and development at DaVita was increasing in scope and reach. Evaluation of all DaVita University activities was taken very seriously and the programs and materials were constantly being tweaked to make them better. In June 2005, *Training* (now *Training & Coaching Today*) awarded DaVita the "*Training* Top 100 Award," which recognized the company's commitment to learning and performance improvement.

Recognition and Communications

Another way in which people learned about the DaVita way, felt attached to the company, and learned what was going on was through communications and recognition. There were bimonthly conference calls with all of the facility administrators; more than ten different newsletters including *DaVita News and Views*, the overall company publication; an intranet and email system, and voice mails and emails to celebrate special events and company milestones. Thiry personally answered every email he received from anyone in the company, and he received a number of them, particularly following his appearance at an Academy or training program or a visit to a facility. Facility administrators were encouraged to hold informal meetings with their teams on a regular basis to check in with each other, engage in joint problem solving, and to share information about the facility and the company. It was a company-wide policy that a "town-hall meeting" had to be held whenever an executive at the level of vice president or director or higher visited with a group of teammates at a facility or business office. These meetings gave teammates the opportunity to interact informally with the executive and to ask questions about whatever was on their mind about the company.

Recruitment and Career Development

Although there were obviously a number of people who had been with the company prior to late 1999, at least some of those who had joined since its "rebirth" in Phoenix had been attracted by its reputation and unique style. For example, Cathy Gelb recalled,

> In 2001, my husband was doing consulting with DaVita and he would come home and just rave about this company and they were so unique and the different things they were doing. I said, "Well find out if they need any trainers." Lo and behold, they were running this two-day program called The Academy that they had just started in 2001 and they were looking for someone to run it for them. So, in November of 2001 I joined DaVita to be associate dean of the Academy.

Many, although not all, of the regional directors and the vice presidents (the people the regional directors reported to) had been nurses and then nurse administrators—they had worked their way up in administration. Of course, people in finance and some of the other staff functions had MBAs and other backgrounds. Recently, DaVita had expanded its recruiting efforts at business schools, including Harvard and Stanford. The intention was to hire people with MBAs who would go fairly quickly into general manager roles such as regional directors, overseeing a number of facilities. Thiry noted that it was important to get general management talent into the company from numerous sources.

Benefits and Pay

DaVita offered a comprehensive benefits and pay package that was somewhat unusual for a company that had a reasonably large number of relatively low-paid, hourly employees. Pay was pegged against competitive benchmarks. At each Academy, Thiry would say, "With respect to wages and healthcare benefits, we intend to be fair and competitive. We must be consistent with the market. With respect to everything else, we want to be superior." There was a broad-based profit-sharing program that covered virtually all team members, based on the idea of sharing the village's good times and success with all of its citizens. These cash bonuses meant a lot to those receiving them. One email to Thiry is reflective of the sentiments expressed:

> Good Morning and Happy Holidays! I would like to say THANK YOU for the check I received this morning in homeroom. This was an unexpected gift from the Village. This will help with Christmas for my family. We have many to help and feed that day. I am almost in tears right now writing this to you thinking of the extra things

that I will be able to get for my daughter and husband and the extended family that is living with me. This thank you comes from the heart and [I] wanted to express my gratitude for it.

There were also benefits that provided people an opportunity to invest in professional and personal growth. The brochure listing the benefits for teammates was called "Because We Care: Davita Teammate Benefits." Inside it said, "The strength of our team is the foundation of our company.... In our quest to be the Employer of Choice in the healthcare industry, we have developed a comprehensive program of benefits that are focused on your health and welfare, investing in your future and special programs that are unique to the DaVita Village." In describing this investment, Thiry noted that "it is not only in education for their jobs, but also in helping everyone advance their leadership skills and their own sense of self."[8]

Health and welfare benefits included a comprehensive package of medical, dental, and vision benefits, extended illness leave, both short-term and long-term disability insurance, life insurance, and a flexible spending account to set aside pre-tax dollars for health or child-care expenses, and an employee assistance program. Investing in the teammates' future included a 401(k) retirement program, a teammate stock purchase program, profit sharing, the internal training the company provided, and various forms of educational assistance, including tuition reimbursement up to $3,000 per year, and an RN scholarship program that permitted people to work for DaVita while attending nursing school, with all tuition and fees paid up to a maximum of $5,000 per year.

Unique to the village were also two programs that provided tuition assistance for the children and grandchildren of teammates. The DaVita Children's Foundation provided some college scholarships for children and grandchildren of teammates, selected on a competitive basis. And the KT Family Foundation, funded by Thiry and others, provided money to be used for educational expenses for the children and grandchildren of DaVita teammates attending grades 6 to 11, again selected on a competitive basis.

[8]http://redcoatpublishing.com/spotlights/sl.

NEXT STEPS

Thiry was a person incapable of being complacent. If you talked to him about what DaVita was doing right, he seemed almost disengaged.

It was only when you brought out problems that he seemed really interested in the conversation. Although DaVita had enjoyed a remarkable transformation and success along multiple dimensions since he and his colleagues had arrived in late 1999, he wondered what *else* he and the company could be doing to make it even more successful and special. For instance, the team's goal had been to make DaVita "The Greatest Dialysis Company the World Has Ever Seen," an objective that it mentioned on its Website and repeated in virtually every gathering of DaVita people, whether executives or front-line caregivers.

It was clear that DaVita had gone a long way toward that goal in six years and was a unique organization with a distinct style and approach. DaVita had been largely successful in a quest to, at least for a time, eliminate the apparent conflicts between the interests of shareholders, teammates, and patients. The company had created a management system in which the interests of each were coincident. Led by Thiry, Mello, Vlceck, and others, the company's deliberate culture-building efforts had paid dividends in terms of reduced turnover and improved performance.

However, challenges remained, including integrating Gambro teammates, continuing to improve operating performance, ensuring continuity and growth into the future, managing governmental relations, and maintaining the commitment and passion of teammates doing difficult work in a very competitive labor market. At the top of Thiry's "to do" list was the integration of Gambro's 500 centers and 12,000 people.

Questions

1. How would you characterize DaVita's strategy?
2. What advice would you give Kent Thiry in terms of leading and managing the integration of the Gambro organization?
3. What would be included in your "first 100 days" action plan?
4. How could you preserve DaVita's culture in the face of an acquisition that includes Thiry's former organization, Vivra.

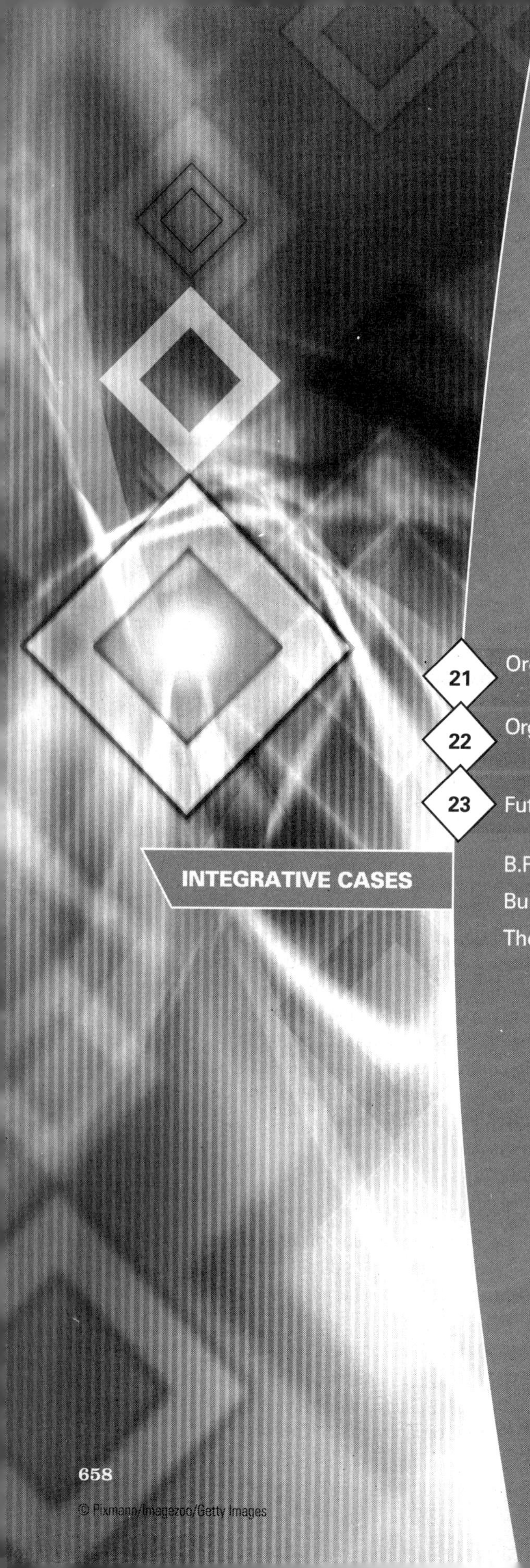

PART 7

SPECIAL APPLICATIONS OF ORGANIZATION DEVELOPMENT

21 Organization Development for Economic, Ecological, and Social Outcomes

22 Organization Development in Nonindustrial Settings: Health Care, School Systems, the Public Sector, and Family-Owned

23 Future Directions in Organization Development

INTEGRATIVE CASES

B.R. Richardson Timber Products Corporation

Building the Cuyahoga River Valley Organization

The Transformation of MECK Insurance

© Pixmann/Imagezoo/Getty Images

21

Organization Development for Economic, Ecological, and Social Outcomes

learning objectives

Describe organization development (OD) interventions that help organizations balance economic, social, and environmental objectives.

Describe sustainable management organizations (SMOs) and how OD can assist in their design and development.

Describe global social change organizations and how to adopt OD practices to develop them.

This chapter describes two relatively new interventions in organization development (OD) aimed at enabling organizations to pursue "sustainable effectiveness."[1] They are still being developed and refined but are intended for the growing number of organizations seeking balance in the achievement of economic, social, and environmental outcomes.

The first intervention—sustainable management organizations (SMOs)—proposes that the central purpose of human systems should be *sustainable effectiveness*. These organizations are built to change and adapt in the service of positive economic, social, and environmental results. This intervention describes the elements of a sustainable strategy and provides design and implementation guidelines for building these capabilities into the structures, processes, and behaviors of the organization.

Global social change organizations engage in activities that increase the social and environmental outcomes of predominantly economically oriented organizations. OD practitioners are using this intervention to facilitate the development of evolving countries, to change the practices of for-profit entities, to provide a voice to underrepresented social classes, and to bridge the gap between cultures facing similar social issues. The application of planned change processes in these settings requires a new set of OD practitioner skills.

21-1 Sustainable Management Organizations

A recent, global survey found that 93% of CEOs believe sustainability issues are critical to the future success of their firms,[2] and there is evidence they are acting on this belief. The second annual Sustainability and Innovation Global Executive study found that, despite the economic downturn in 2010, 59% of companies increased their investments in sustainability.[3] Sustainability initiatives focus on the environmental impact of business operations, including travel reductions, two-sided printing, more environmentally sensitive product packaging, and recycling programs. Corporate social responsibility programs also are increasingly common. More and more, however, firms are recognizing that these positive actions are relatively short sighted; they are taking bigger steps to build financial, social, and environmental performance into their organization.[4] Loblaws, Canada's largest grocery chain, not only has packaging initiatives and energy-saving programs, they are also developing policies, including a sustainable seafood policy, that extend their organization into supply chain relationships, coordinate with environmentally-concerned nongovernmental organizations, educate consumers, and contribute to financial performance.

A variety of OD-related approaches that promote sustainability are being developed, including the Coalition for Environmentally Responsible Economics principles, the Natural Step, ISO 14000, and natural and climate capitalism.[5] These frameworks represent opportunities to make sustainability, especially ecological sustainability, a more deliberate and intentional value of OD. The SMO intervention asks a fundamentally different question about how to develop organizations compared to the strategic change interventions in Chapters 18–20. Those change programs asked, how can we develop organizations to improve their economic effectiveness—domestically or globally? SMO interventions ask, how can we develop organizations to achieve sustainable effectiveness? Based on action research at the University of Southern California's Center for Effective Organizations, Mohrman, Lawler, and Worley have developed the features and processes for creating SMOs.[6]

SMOs are designed to achieve sustainable effectiveness. They can perform in three areas—people, planet, and profit—and are agile enough to remain effective over time. This capability follows closely from the United Nations World Commission on Environment and Development's description of sustainability: "meeting the needs of the present without compromising the ability of future generations to meet their own needs."[7] There are two important implications of this definition:

- First, the organization should generate sustainable outcomes. This means achieving a triple-bottom-line objective—positive economic, social, and ecological results.[8] The organization must be clear about its purpose and consider the needs of all stakeholders—shareholders, customers, employees, business partners, governments, the ecology, local communities, and the public. The triple-bottom-line objective is also a normative value that guides how organizations should go about minimizing harm or maximizing benefits through their decisions and actions. This value is manifest in the day-to-day decisions that give social and ecological outcomes equal standing with economic concerns. SMOs are designed to do consistently well in all three of these areas.
- Second, SMOs should be able to sustain effectiveness over time. They must be adaptable, innovative, and agile. Traditional organizations equate stability and reliability with effectiveness[9] and, in a world that is changing rapidly, they often find it difficult to maintain adequate levels of performance. SMOs assume that little about their environment will be stable even in the midterm. They are committed to having execution, innovation, and implementation capabilities that support change.

21-1a Design Guidelines

Consistent with the definition of sustainable effectiveness, the design of SMOs follows broad guidelines that are still being developed and refined. These guides have to do with setting strategies that support sustainability, determining sustainable objectives, establishing an organization identity that is sustainability-friendly, and creating an agile organization.

Strategies That Support Sustainable Effectiveness Sustainable effectiveness—being effective along financial, social, and environmental dimensions over a long period of time—requires an appropriately defined strategic intent. As described in Chapters 5, a strategic intent consists of resource allocations that reflect choices of breadth, aggressiveness, and differentiation. Each of these dimensions can support sustainable effectiveness.

- **Breadth**. Participation in multiple countries, markets, technologies, or products and services increases the complexity of an organization's carbon footprint and social impact. It makes it difficult to understand the impact of the organization on ecological and social outcomes. Over the years, Starbucks' scope of domestic and international operations, its product mix, and ancillary services (e.g., music, Internet hot spots, food) have broadened dramatically. As it grew, the complexity of its operations required responses in its fair trade, water conservation, energy, and recycling policies and systems to maintain an appropriate balance. On the other hand, some breadth and diversification makes it easier to make strategic changes that insure reasonable profits over a long time frame. SMOs think hard about this balance.
- **Aggressiveness**. In fast-changing markets, there are many appropriate opportunities to pursue objectives aggressively, but in general SMOs are wary of too much aggressiveness too often. While SMOs are effective competitors, their growth objectives are reasonable and reasoned. Tartan Yachts, a high-quality manufacturer of sailboats, faced this dilemma in the early 2000s. Its success resulted in more orders than its single plant could produce in a timely fashion, and the growing overall economy provided a tempting opportunity to support the increased demand with increased production capacity. In the end, Tartan Yachts decided not to increase capacity. The organization realized that a key differentiator was the special relationships it had built with customers and that quality was partly a function of keeping capacity sized appropriately. The wisdom of its conservative growth approach paid off handsomely during the 2008–2010 economic downturn. Tartan Yachts did not have to go through the painful and disruptive downsizing that many of its competitors did, and it maintained its reputation for quality.
- **Differentiation**. Understanding why customers make purchasing decisions and how the organization's product and service features align with those choices is critical to success. SMOs build features into their offerings that reflect all three outcomes. For example, Microsoft's Windows 7 made big improvements over the ill-fated Vista operating system that were important for economic objectives, but its sustainability-friendly identity encouraged the firm to also incorporate a variety of power-saving features that contributed to energy conservation.

Objectives That Support Sustainable Effectiveness In SMOs, social and ecological outcomes have equal standing with economic results. This is easier said than done. Greenpeace revealed that Nestlé, a well-respected and responsible company, was purchasing large quantities of low-priced palm oil from firms that were destroying rain forests to build even larger palm plantations. The news that Nestlé may have favored economic over environmental objectives damaged its reputation and provoked a boycott of its products. SMOs deliberately integrate economic, social, and ecological objectives.

First, SMOs must create positive *economic* outcomes to survive. Organizations that cannot operate in a way that leads to revenues meeting or exceeding expenses cannot survive, let alone create other types of valued outcomes. The difference between SMOs and traditional organizations is how much profit they make, how they make a profit, and toward what end that profit is used.

SMOs reject the goal of maximizing profit or shareholder returns and set sustainable goals for profitability and growth. Achieving social and environmental goals requires investment dollars that are unavailable under a profit maximizing philosophy. Former Johnson & Johnson CEO, William Weldon, argued that the firm had responsibilities to patients, customers, staff, and the community that may prevent it from providing the best possible return, at least in the short term. Organizations are increasingly realizing that maximizing profits by leveraging debt, incenting sales forces and executives to achieve "big hairy audacious goals," or pursuing acquisitions to "gain important synergies" that rarely materialize is a distraction from sustainable effectiveness.

As suggested above, SMOs take a less aggressive approach to growth.[10] Business strategies, in general, try to grow the organization along some dimension, including size, profits, revenues, market share, or influence. Aggressiveness that takes advantage of a short-term market opportunity is different from aggressiveness that consistently pursues organizational growth rates that greatly exceed the rate of market growth, the market's capacity to sustain growth, or the organization's capacity to support growth.

Align Technologies, for example, is the maker of Invisalign orthodontics, a series of customized mouthpieces that achieve the same results as metallic braces without the wires. Its technology challenges existing orthodontic suppliers as well as the skill sets and status of orthodontists. For Align Technologies to be successful, it must move aggressively to establish its position and technology as the incumbents defend their franchises. Nevertheless, Align Technologies must be careful to ensure that an aggressive growth strategy does not become its corporate identity. Expecting the firm to grow at the same rates after it has established its position in the market may not be reasonable.

Reasonable and sustainable profit and growth expectations mean that SMOs may never be the best performers in their industries at any particular point in time. Setting high, difficult-to-achieve economic goals requires dedicated resources and focus that can distract employees' attention from other goals and the creation of other kinds of value. SMOs recognize that the cost of sustainable profit and growth is a lower return on immediate financial performance but a more stable, long-term profitability with the ability to pursue social and environmental objectives.

Second, SMOs create positive *ecological* outcomes. They are keenly aware of their carbon footprint and their overall contribution to the planet's ecology. SMOs accept the logic of the Natural Step, i.e., that current economic models of growth cannot reconcile the increasing demand for and decreasing supply of finite and fundamental natural resources.[11] This incompatibility is a central source of SMO strategies; how the organization generates economic and social value without compromising the natural environment differentiates SMO strategies from those of other organizations. Creating ecological value suggests that business strategies built around the productive use of natural resources can solve environmental problems at a profit.

Most organizations pursuing sustainable effectiveness start by setting an initial goal of not destroying the environment. When profit maximizing and growth-oriented worldwide organizations attempt to lower costs by placing activities in geographic areas with the lowest wage rates, such as Asia, large, complex sourcing and distribution supply chains are created. By some estimates, each of the largest tanker ships used in these supply chains can emit as much as 5,000 tons of sulfur a year, the equivalent of 50 million typical automobiles.[12] As regulatory changes are being sought by environmental groups, these operating costs will likely increase. Thus, when the cost of pollution is factored into the cost of manufacturing and supply chain activities, SMOs begin to rethink the low wage rate decision. Instead, they seek ways to not only lower overall costs but to reduce environmental damage as well.

Third, SMOs create positive *social* outcomes. This goal mandates that organizations contribute to human and cultural well-being and recognizes the role social issues play in innovation and long-term adaptability. Social value includes the way an organization treats its workforce and the communities, cultures, governments, and countries in which it operates.

Organizations without a clear perspective on social issues are vulnerable to the profit maximization motive. McDonalds noted the growing numbers of automobiles in Beijing, the attendant increase in driving times and stresses on family life, and concluded that opening drive-thru restaurants would be a good idea. The initial drive-thru's struggled because the concept was unfamiliar to the Chinese. If someone actually found the drive-thru lane, they didn't know what to do at the ordering station, didn't know they had to drive up to the next window to pay, and didn't know they needed to drive to the next window to pick up their food. After they picked up their food, they usually drove to a parking space, got out of the car, and went into the restaurant to have their meal. In response, McDonalds made it easier to find the drive-thru lane and trained the workers to point cars to the next window, including holding the bag of food out of the last window to encourage drivers to move forward to get their meal.

When profit maximization overrides the creation—or even the maintenance—of social and cultural values, organizations can unwittingly contribute to cultural homogenization. McDonalds' pursuit of economic growth may come at the expense of Chinese behaviors and culture. Does teaching them to behave like Westerners enhance cultural diversity?

Identities That Are Sustainability-Friendly SMOs' long-term success derives from their organizational identity.[13] Identity represents the "central and enduring attributes of an organization that distinguish it from other organizations" and answers the question, "Who are we as an organization?"[14] SMO identities are closely aligned with sustainable effectiveness, with balancing economic, ecological, and social outcomes.

As shown in Figure 21.1, identity both flows from and helps to create an organization's culture. Identity emerges from the values in use that define an organization's culture, and in turn identity gives meaning to culture through the stories told to members. Figure 21.1 also suggests that identity flows from and helps to create an organization's brand, image, and reputation. Identity drives the brand promises and messages that organizations make to customers and the market. Because all organizations must compete for resources, they must proactively communicate their mission and brand—what they offer, what markets they serve, and what they stand for—to the marketplace. For example, Philips' tag line in all of its media content, "Sense and Simplicity," reflects a commitment to products that are easy to use and designed well for the task.

FIGURE 21.1

The Components of Organization Identity

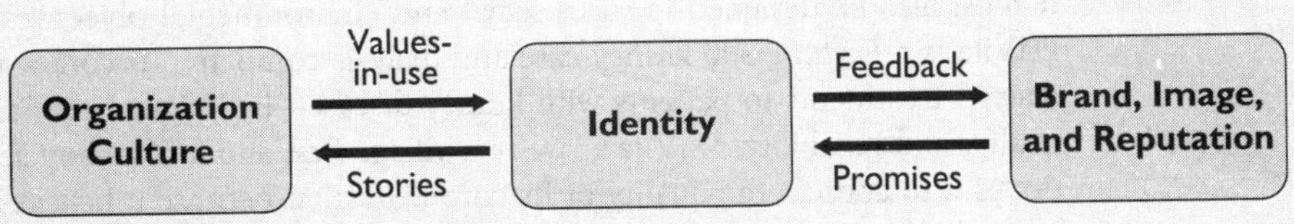

SOURCE: Adapted from Hatch and Schultz, 2002.

However, the image and reputation that external stakeholders hold about the organization also influence identity. Customers and other stakeholders get to experience whether the organization generally lives up to its brand promises. Experiences using the product or service, encounters with after-sales support services, stories from the business press or websites, and other sources of information provide feedback about the alignment between message and behaviors. For example, Citibank displayed advertisements in its offices that it was proud to be a part of programs that created jobs in America—and then announced it would cut 11,000 jobs. Over time, the organization builds up a reputation as reliable or unreliable, aggressive and litigious or relatively passive, a defender of human rights or a polluter, or a firm that stands behind its products or avoids publicity. Analysts, for example, have been skeptical about Philips' ability to manage its complex business portfolio. It dropped from #5 to #7 among the world's most admired electronics firms (and did not make the Top 350 overall), but generally has a positive image among consumers (#41 among best global brands).

An SMO's identity should meet the standard of "sustainability friendly." A sustainability-friendly identity embraces the continuous pursuit of financial, social, and environmental values as a core part of who the organization believes it is. Thus, environmental initiatives and corporate social responsibility programs would not be "in addition to," but rather central to strategic and operational decisions. When decisions and actions are oriented toward integrating financial, social, and environmental outcomes without the use of special incentives or projects, the organization makes important contributions to sustainable effectiveness as a matter of course. For example, Nokia and Unilever do not emphasize efforts to market and produce a particular "sustainable" product; rather they are developing product portfolios that are financially successful, environmentally friendly, and socially beneficial.

Agile Organization Designs That Support Sustainable Effectiveness The final design guideline for SMOs is the need to create an organization that can change and adapt routinely—an organization that is "built to change" (Chapter 19).[15] Agility represents a *dynamic capability*[16] that enables timely and effective responses to changing environments and multiple stakeholder demands. Here we discuss the features of an agile organization, including work systems, structures, management processes, and human resource systems.

- **Work systems.** An SMO's sustainability-friendly strategy and triple-bottom-line objectives are manifest in its work systems and processes. These work processes directly account for a large percentage of the organization's economic, social, and environmental impact. To achieve current and long-term economic performance, the organization must design two types of work: (1) core and exploitive and (2) creative and exploratory.[17]

  Core work in SMOs supports the current strategic intent and must be reliable, predictable, and as efficient as practicable. Since the organization's strategic intent can be subject to change, SMO core work may never be 100% efficient, but it must be reliable enough to support the differentiators, meet demand, and generate profit. It must also be designed to meet social and environmental objectives. For example, DaVita is a *Fortune* 500 kidney care and dialysis company. Its core work—delivering dialysis treatments to patients with kidney disease—is designed primarily for clinical quality and reliability. DaVita's "we're a village first and a company second" identity drives it to address the quality of its core work first because it believes that will generate the best economic and social outcomes. Thus, work efficiency is not at the expense of workforce, customer, or community outcomes. Work processes are designed to generate positive work experiences for organization members and DaVita's organization identity encourages members to build strong personal relationships with patients and the local community through its "wall of fame." Moreover, a well-understood continuous improvement process works to increase efficiency and reduce the negative environmental by-products of dialysis.

Creative work in SMOs is designed to generate new projects, services, and other disruptive innovations; it can obsolete the current strategic intent and is fundamentally different than core work. Creative work is temporary and iterative; it is based on initiatives and activities not jobs, driven by shared goals, and performed by cross-functional teams. In addition to its core work, DaVita must also build future leaders, understand the likely changes and implications of health care reform, identify potential acquisitions or perform due diligence activities, develop new business opportunities, and other nonroutine and innovative activities.

For any activity that warrants attention, DaVita leaders create teams consisting of multiple functions and often including external stakeholders, such as regulators, legislators, customers, physicians, and community representatives. These teams have clear goals and appropriate decision authority. Early in the team's work, members are expected to report out frequently on progress or obstacles. This creative work system enables DaVita to develop its members, to gather and charter resources quickly, and to make resources available for other projects when a project is over.

Both core and creative work involve innovation. Core work must innovate to improve efficiency and effectiveness; creative work must innovate to develop future opportunities. Moreover, to achieve social and environmental outcomes, both types of work processes must carefully consider and adapt their input and throughput processes to insure appropriate output characteristics.

- **Structures.** Structures focus member attention and organization resources on the most important aspects of getting core and creative work accomplished. The unique feature of SMO structures is their external focus and "maximum surface area."[18] As described in Chapter 19, maximum surface area structures support core and creative work with roles that are directly connected to some aspect of the external environment. To the extent possible, every role in an SMO should be a "boundary spanning" role.[19] Externally focused roles enable organization members to experience what is happening in professional, business, competitive, and regulatory environments as well as community and environmental sectors and bring that information into the organization as meaningful inputs to strategy and operations.

  The surface area of almost any structure can be increased. For example, IBM and Cisco have different structures but both have good external focus and surface area. In IBM's case, a "front-back" structure puts cross-functional solution teams into direct contact with customers, and the back office groups must stay current in their technical expertise to support the requested solutions. Both the front and back of the organization work to support IBM's "smarter planet" strategic intent. Cisco increases the surface area of its functional structure by creating cross-functional "councils and boards" that address specific segments. Organization members must stay connected to their own professional communities in addition to working with other functions to build and implement strategies for enterprise customers, emerging markets, or some other important business segment. For example, Cisco created its "eco-board" to achieve the "if it can be connected, it can be green" objective across the organization.
- **Management processes.** SMOs use flexible decision-making and resource allocation processes to leverage information gathered by the externally focused roles. An important feature here is transparency. In SMOs, information is transparent and

moved throughout the organization to wherever it is needed and decision-making rights are assigned to the appropriate level and role in the organization. This ensures that the right information is available and provides a clear picture of how the organization is performing relative to triple-bottom-line objectives. It enables organizations to make timely and relevant decisions to keep pace with changing conditions.

- **Human resource systems.** SMOs rethink the way that people are attracted, retained, developed, motivated, and led. To attract the right kind of diverse workforce for the right period of time, SMOs use multiple employment deals and offer a wide variety of work arrangements, including contract labor, outsourcing, and longer term commitments to create the ability to treat employees as individuals. Individual treatment is necessary to match the skills, motives, and lifestyles of individuals with the work that needs to be done. Accenture and Deloitte have career customization programs that attract employees who want to choose and shape their own career tracks, lifestyles, work hours, and work locations. Such systems mean that not everyone in the organization is a career employee, has job security, and can expect the organization to provide them with stable employment. While stable employment might seem like a reasonable social sustainability practice, it may not be cost effective or even desired by individuals who prefer the flexibility of contract employment.

  SMOs assess the skills and competencies that individuals have, develop particular skills in employees, and pay for the effective deployment of those skills in the service of triple-bottom-line objectives. IBM has developed a corporation-wide talent information system that helps make this possible. It provides information on open positions, career paths, and on the skills and competencies of employees. When IBM launched its "smarter planet" strategy, the talent information system helped to identify who had the skills and experiences that would support the strategy and assisted in reallocating important talent.

  Aligning financial and nonfinancial reward systems to support sustainable effectiveness is critical. In general, financial and nonfinancial rewards should be given based on the individual's triple-bottom-line performance. Executives, for example, need to be rewarded and recognized for achieving reasonable profit levels, corporate social responsibility targets, lower carbon footprints, and healthy relationships with the communities and countries in which they operate. In many cases, it makes sense to stress group or team performance because of the interdependencies that exist in organizations committed to sustainable effectiveness. For organization members, SMOs shift the basis of rewards from jobs to people. Members are rewarded for what they can do with regard to sustainable effectiveness, not for the particular job they perform. Because jobs and tasks are continually changing, people are motivated to learn new skills and knowledge, thus keeping pace with change and enhancing their long-term value to the organization.

  Rewards also play a role in motivating and reinforcing change in SMOs. Individual or team bonuses are tied directly to change goals, learning new things, and performing new tasks well. This establishes a clear line of sight between rewards and change activities. Bonuses can include one-time rewards given at the end of a particular change effort, or rewards targeted to different phases of the change process.

  Finally, development and reward systems support the importance of a shared leadership philosophy; leadership in SMOs does not rest with jobs and is not restricted to executives. Rather than relying on centralized sources of power and control, SMOs spread leadership across multiple levels of the organization. This approach speeds decision making and response rates because those lower in the organization need not have to wait for top–down direction. It provides leadership experience and skills to a broad array of members, thus developing a strong cadre of leadership talent. Shared leadership supports continuous change by spreading change expertise and commitment across the organization. It increases the chances that competent leaders will be there to keep the change process moving forward.

21-1b Application Stages

Sustainable management design principles are being implemented in a growing number of organizations. Patagonia, The Body Shop, and Ben & Jerry's are good examples of companies that were built from the ground up using SMO principles. UPS, Unilever, Gap Inc., GE, PepsiCo, and P&G are in the midst of making sustainable management an integral part of their identities. These companies are challenging long-held assumptions and making significant changes in their strategies and organization designs. Like other strategic change interventions, SMO applications tend to involve systemic and revolutionary change processes driven by senior executives. Because these changes tend to be radical—they generally alter every feature of the organization's design and challenge many of its long-held assumptions—they usually proceed at a quick pace, taking at least three years to implement. The following SMO application stages are broadly described; as OD practitioners gain more experience with this OD intervention, we can expect more detailed knowledge of how it works and produces results.

Identifying and Redefining Organization Identity Probably the biggest distinction between an SMO intervention and other strategic changes is the development of a new organization identity. Change initiatives are directed at redefining or changing the organization's identity to support sustainable effectiveness and agility. Identity change is both an outcome of the transformation process and a key measure of the change's effectiveness. It indicates that the organization is applying new strategies and organization principles to achieving triple-bottom-line results. Once identity redefinition is underway, continuous change interventions, such as those described in Chapter 19, can facilitate the change process.

Redefining organization identity typically starts from a diagnosis of the organization's existing identity. This involves assessing how well the organization's values-in-use and brand promise and reputation support sustainable effectiveness and agility. OD practitioners can help organization members conduct a cultural diagnosis (Chapter 18) along with an analysis of the firm's brand promises and reputation in the market. Then, change processes are directed at leveraging organization values and reputational elements that already support sustained effectiveness rather than trying to "fix" those values and brand images that are not aligned with it.

Repurposing the Board of Directors In contrast to boards of directors in traditional organizations, SMO boards face more demanding roles, more complicated decision making, and more intense discussions. Most U.S. and European boards are designed and staffed to serve investors, and this leads to a singular focus on economic performance. This also tends to be the case for nonprofit boards that are dominated by fundraising interests. OD practitioners can help boards address key issues that invariably arise when moving toward sustainable effectiveness.[20]

- The board may need to assess whether its membership reflects the most important stakeholders, including investors and representatives of the community, workforce, and environment. This stakeholder approach to board membership differs significantly from the classic financial accountability-driven membership model. For example, less than 10% of large U.S. corporate boards have someone with an HR background,[21] and it is unreasonable to expect boards to pursue sustainable effectiveness if they lack expertise with respect to the social and environmental impact of their business model. Membership diversity enables decisions that balance financial, social, and environmental outcomes.

- The board also may need to consider changing its committee structure. In addition to traditional audit and compensation committees, the board may need to establish committees for human capital, social responsibility, and environmental impact. Developing effective strategies and addressing the right set of decisions requires a committee structure that reflects the organization's sustainable effectiveness objectives.
- Board members may need to create new goal-setting processes. These might include addressing how social and ecological goals can be integrated with economic objectives. It may involve adopting the Global Reporting Initiative (GRI), an effort to improve the measurement of the environmental impact of organizations that is supported by Shell, Kimberly-Clark, and Cemex among others.[22] The board may choose to highlight such traditional indicators as turnover rates and employee attitude data, and other measures such as job creation and charitable contributions, to increase awareness of social and human capital performance. In some cases, the board may explore reregistering the organization as a "benefit corporation," which would allow the firm to pursue other objectives without fear of legal action by shareholders looking for a maximized return.[23] Patagonia's board pursued this approach to enable the company to set integrated triple-bottom-line goals.
- The board of directors needs to have effective decision-making skills and clear guidelines to make tough choices about sustainability, such as taking actions that may have a significant negative impact on financial performance but a significant positive impact on social and environmental outcomes, or holding executives accountable for triple-bottom-line achievements. For example, boards face problems promoting sustainable effectiveness when they consistently reward executives for financial performance at the expense of environmental and social performance. Human process interventions, such as team building and process consultation, can help boards become effective decision makers.

Building Capabilities Becoming an SMO involves identifying which existing organization capabilities support sustainable effectiveness and determining which new abilities need to be built. Most organizations do not have sufficient resources to create all the necessary capabilities at once, so tough choices need to be made. These decisions are symbolically important; they signal to employees, owners, communities, and NGOs how much the organization actually supports a sustainability-friendly identity. Two capabilities that are essential to sustainability involve multistakeholder decision making and change management.

SMOs need to be good at multistakeholder decision making and take into account diverse perspectives in making choices.[24] Organizations like Gap, Inc., GE, Social Accountability International, Loblaw's, Unilever, and the World Wildlife Fund are working hard to develop this capability. It may require making changes in both the organization and its external alliances and partnerships. First, training and development interventions can help organization members learn collaborative decision making and "systems thinking" skills that acknowledge the interdependencies and trade-offs necessary to meet triple-bottom-line objectives. Next, decision-making processes may need to be expanded to include nontraditional stakeholders, such as community and environmentally related NGOs. Team-building processes for developing trust, exploring alternatives, and integrating perspectives among diverse participants can be helpful.[25] Lastly, organizational learning interventions can help the organization apply its new skills and decision processes. Early experiences in trying to apply multistakeholder decision skills and systems are likely to be awkward and inefficient.[26] Organization learning interventions can help members learn how to improve their multistakeholder decision-making capabilities.

SMOs also need to develop a change capability, which involves three related activities.[27] First, change management skills can be developed widely in the organization by hiring people with those skills and by training existing managers and employees to acquire them. Most organization members have a good understanding of technical and operational issues but are less familiar with managing change. Second, an organization effectiveness function can be designed with competencies in strategic planning, organization design, and change management. Some SMOs have created a center of excellence staffed by professionals from the strategic planning and human resources functions; they provide advice and facilitation for planning and executing change in the organization. Third, organization members can learn how to apply their change capability by engaging in organizational changes and reflecting on that experience. This so-called "learning by doing" is essential for building a change capability. It provides members with the hands-on experience and reflective learning necessary to hone their change skills in action. Developing these change capabilities is likely to involve a significant investment in training and development.[28]

Sequencing the Changes Repurposing boards and building capabilities to support a sustainability-friendly identity are extensive and complex changes. The change to an SMO has to account for this complexity to positively move the organization's identity. This involves a particular sequence of changes, starting with work system redesign. Then the strategy needs to be clarified and the organization redesigned to promote agility. Large-group intervention (LGI) techniques, described in Chapter 11, are particularly helpful to accelerate the transformation process because they can support the organization's development of multistakeholder and change capabilities.

Work Systems Redesign. Work is the primary driver of an organization's carbon footprint; it directly affects the workforce's well-being and is most connected to the creation of economic value. Thus, redesigning work systems can have the most payoff to an SMO. Assessing how both standard and creative work get done and designing them for sustainable effectiveness will likely make the biggest advance toward becoming an SMO. Redesigning work to add economic value in environmentally and socially acceptable ways can provide a solid foundation for further change.

Focusing on work redesign first ensures that the organization's future aspirations are aligned with its past and current behaviors. It shows concretely that the organization's commitment to sustainability is real not just window-dressing. In many organizations today, there is growing pressure to "do something" about sustainability. Organizations that develop marketing campaigns proclaiming support for green issues and social concerns before thinking through how their work processes affect those outcomes run a serious risk. If intentions of sustainable effectiveness are announced too early and with too much fanfare, an organization's reputation can be damaged if marketing promises are not backed up by tangible actions. The organization's efforts will be seen as "greenwashing," and its ability to change identity is set back, perhaps permanently. It may take the firm a long time to rebuild trust in corporate sustainability promises.

Clarifying the Strategy. Early in the change process, the organization needs to meet with key stakeholders to clarify goals and to explore the implications of becoming an SMO on its capabilities and resources. This can be accomplished through a series of large-group interventions (LGIs) with key stakeholders. LGIs are well suited for this part of the SMO change process. They enable organization members to interact with multiple stakeholders, to learn new ways of behaving and deciding, and to gain clarity and commitment to becoming an SMO. The first LGI, typically led by the board and the executive team, is concerned with fleshing out the organization's sustainability strategy and future state. The focus is on gaining stakeholder support, determining how the different stakeholders will work together, and clarifying the organization's vision, mission, and values. Subsequent LGIs address the design and implementation of particular aspects of strategy and organization design.

Building an Agile Design. To move further toward being an SMO, an organization needs to build an agile organization design that supports and reinforces the new sustainable-friendly work processes. Agile organization designs have a "maximum surface area" to support an external focus, strong collaboration capabilities, flexible resource allocation systems, and transparent decision-making processes. They also include a talent management system with goals, performance appraisals, and rewards that promote flexibility and sustainable effectiveness outcomes. In particular, people are retained or hired for their compatibility with an SMO; they are appraised and rewarded for sustainable behaviors. Performance management interventions (Chapter 15), talent management changes (Chapter 16), and organization design interventions (Chapter 18) can help the organization build an agile design.

Application 21.1 describes Interface Carpets, one of the most referenced cases of a transformation to an SMO.

21-2 Global Social Change

Organization development applied to global social change is one of the boldest and most exciting developments in the field.[29] This form of OD is generally practiced in global social change organizations (GSCOs), not-for-profit and nongovernmental entities that are created at the grassroots level to help communities and societies address such important problems as unemployment, race relations, sustainable development, homelessness, hunger, disease, water quality and conservation, and political instability. Globally, GSCOs are heavily involved in the developing nations. Examples include the World Conservation Union (IUCN), the Kids Global Outreach Foundation (United States–Africa), the Society of Entrepreneurs and Ecology (China), the Nature Conservancy (International), the Mountain Forum (Peru), International Physicians for the Prevention of Nuclear War, and the Asian Coalition for Agrarian Reform and Rural Development (ANGOC-Philippines). Many practitioners who help create and develop GSCOs come from OD backgrounds and have adapted their expertise to fit highly complex, political situations. This section describes GSCOs and how OD is used for social change.

21-2a Global Social Change Organizations

GSCOs are part of a social innovation movement to foster the emergence of a global civilization.[30] They exist under a variety of names, including development organizations (DOs), nongovernmental organizations (NGOs), social movement organizations, international private voluntary organizations, and bridging organizations. They address complex

application 21.1

INTERFACE CARPET'S TRANSFORMATION TO SUSTAINABILITY

Interface Flooring Systems was founded by Ray Anderson as a joint venture with Britain's Carpets International in 1973 to make carpet tiles. Carpet tiles, an alternative to long rolls of carpet, can be replaced piece by piece rather than all at once. Between 1978 and 1983, revenues grew from $11 million to $80 million as a result of building close relationships with commercial customers. Interface went public in 1983 and through 2008 grew revenues at an average annual rate of 11.5%.

Interface's transformation to sustainable management began in 1994 when Anderson received a memo from a research division task force to speak about Interface's environmental vision. The group had been formed in response to questions from customers, architects, and interior designers about Interface's environmental efforts. The task force's operational review suggested that, in fact, Interface had very few environmental initiatives and was not doing much to be environmentally friendly. The memo made Anderson anxious over what he would say since there was no environmental policy other than "comply, comply, comply." At the same time, Anderson received Paul Hawkin's book, *The Ecology of Commerce*. The book's message confronted his sense of responsibility and changed his attitudes about what a business should achieve.

In his speech to the task force, he declared that Interface would become a company that "could grow and prosper without doing harm to the earth." He later said that he didn't want his legacy to be that he dug up the earth, turned petroleum and other materials into polluting products, and dumped them in landfills. At the time, Interface was part of an industry that extracted and processed 1.2 billion pounds of material from the earth to produce $802 billion worth of products. Of the 1.2 billion pounds, 800 million pounds was petroleum based and two-thirds of that was burned to convert the remaining third into product. As an industry, carpeting firms were depositing 4.5 billion pounds of material into landfills that would degrade over 20,000 years.

In January 1995, Interface convened a "green supply chain" conference with its suppliers to discuss its goals and to gain commitments from its business partners. The eventual sustainability strategy outlined seven goals, including eliminate waste (any measureable input that did not create value), limit toxic emissions from manufacturing plants, switch to renewable sources of energy, "close the loop" which meant using any waste or discarded carpet as inputs to new products, achieve resource-efficient transportation, and educate customers, suppliers, and even competitors. The seventh goal, to redesign commerce, eventually resulted in what was called the "evergreen service agreement." It was a radical innovation that attempted to shift Interface's business model from "selling carpet" to "renting flooring systems."

In 1996, Interface held its first "Eco Dream Team" conference of outside environmental experts and organization members to explore the strategy and organizational requirements necessary to achieve its sustainability goals. The conference recommendations led to changes in Interface's product design and manufacturing, supply chain, and operations. Implementing the changes required the organization to address a variety of issues.

First, as the new strategy was communicated, organization members expressed a variety of concerns and resistance, including questions about what sustainability meant and how the organization was going to change. The depth of misunderstanding was particularly troublesome. After hearing about the sustainability goal, one employee asked "How many sheep are we planning to have, and where are they going to graze?" In particular, few people in the organization understood how ecologically unfriendly existing operations were. As a result, a large commitment to employee training about the environment and operations led to Interface being named one of the Best 100 Companies to Work for by *Fortune* magazine in 1997.

Second, figuring out *where* to eliminate waste and toxicity or to use clean technology was a straightforward process of total quality management that was implemented under the acronym QUEST (Quality Utilizing Employee Suggestions and Teamwork). However, figuring out *how* to do these things was a giant technical problem. The organization's research group and its engineers had to redesign (or reinvent) almost every production process and product, including how to recycle nylon and how to make carpet using less petroleum.

Third, creating the evergreen services agreement required Interface to develop a leasing contract that would make financial sense in the context of existing rules and regulations. The idea of moving funds from capital expense (sale of carpet) to operating expense (lease of carpet) was an easy sell, but getting a lease agreement written that met current tax and accounting standards was a lot more difficult. In addition, Interface had to work with customers because the price of the lease seemed very high to customers. Few customers actually knew the full cost of their flooring because the amounts associated with carpet purchase, maintenance, and other services were separated into different accounts.

By 2000, a variety of market and economy changes, including the Y2K threat, the dot.com bust, and other changes that reduced customer budgets, were hurting the industry. In January 2001, Interface held a leaders conference to address a 30% workforce reduction and other organization changes in response to business declines. At the conference, managers affirmed their commitment to sustainability saying that it was part of the organization's DNA.

Interface's transformation to sustainability is both remarkable and cautionary. The organization clearly made a radical change in its carbon footprint, established clear benchmark and best practice standards, and redefined the business model in carpet manufacturing, distribution, and sales. Economically, however, its stock price and profitability have varied considerably since the transformation, although its annual growth rate is impressive. Socially, it has not been a stable employer, meeting most economic challenges with layoffs. Nonetheless, its tremendous accomplishments in environmental matters represent an important social benefit. These highs and lows of effectiveness vis-à-vis the triple bottom line testify to the difficulties of the transformation to an SMO.

social problems, including overpopulation, ecological degradation, the increasing concentration of wealth and power, the lack of management infrastructures to facilitate growth, and the lack of fundamental human rights. The early efforts of many GSCOs to raise awareness and mobilize resources toward solving these problems culminated in the United Nations' Conference on Environment and Development in Rio de Janeiro in June 1992, where leaders from both industrialized and less-developed countries met to discuss sustainable development.[31] Since then, a number of conferences and agreements have occurred. The most notable are the 1997 Kyoto Protocol that attempted to gain commitment from countries around the world to reduce greenhouse gas emissions and the Global Compact, a strategic policy initiative that asks businesses to align their operations with ten universally accepted principles related to human rights, labor, environment, and corruption. The Doha Climate Conference in December 2012 successfully extended the Kyoto protocol agreements to 2020 despite continued debates. The work of GSCO's can be aided or constrained by these larger, governmental accords.

GSCOs have the following characteristics:[32]

- They assert, as their primary task, a commitment to serve as an agent of change in creating environmentally and socially sustainable world futures; their transformational missions are articulated around the real needs of people and the earth.

- They have discovered and mobilized innovative social-organizational architectures that make possible human cooperation across previously polarizing or arbitrarily constraining boundaries.
- They hold values of empowerment, or people-centered forms of action, in the accomplishment of their global change mission, emphasizing the central role of people as both means and ends in any development process.
- They are globally and locally linked in structure, membership, or partnership and thereby exist, at least in identity and practice (maybe not yet legally), as entities beyond the nation-state.
- They are multiorganizational and often cross-sectorial. They can be business, government, or not-for-profit organizations. Indeed, many of the most significant global change entities involve multiorganization partnerships bridging sectorial boundaries in new hybrid forms of business, government, and volunteerism.

GSCOs therefore differ from traditional for-profit firms on six dimensions.[33] First, they typically advocate a mission of social change—the formation and development of better societies and communities. "Better" typically means more just (Amnesty International, the Hunger Project, World Vision), peaceful (Peace Direct, International Physicians for the Prevention of Nuclear War), or ecologically conscious (Nature Conservancy, the Global Village of Beijing, the Mountain Forum, IUCN, World Wildlife Fund, Friends of the Earth).

Second, the mission is supported by a network structure. Most GSCO activity occurs at the boundary or periphery between two or more organizations.[34] Unlike most industrial firms that focus on internal effectiveness, GSCOs are directed at changing their environmental context. For example, World Vision (www.worldvision.org) operates microfinance institutions in 43 countries to boost the economic status of entrepreneurs, create jobs, and develop local economies.

Third, GSCOs generally have strong values and ideologies that justify and motivate organization behavior. These "causes" provide intrinsic rewards to GSCO members and a blueprint for action.[35] For example, the ideological position that basic human rights include shelter has directed Habitat for Humanity to erect low-cost homes in a wide variety of underdeveloped communities.

Fourth, GSCOs interact with a broad range of external and often conflicting constituencies. To help the poor, GSCOs often must work with the rich; to save the ecology, they must work with the polluters; and to empower the masses, they must work with the powerful few. This places a great deal of pressure on GSCOs to reconcile pursuit of a noble cause with the political reality of power and wealth.

Fifth, managing these diverse external constituencies often creates significant organizational conflict. On the one hand, GSCOs often need to be organized into departments to serve and represent particular stakeholders; on the other, they are strongly averse to bureaucracy and desire collegial and consensus-seeking cultures. The conflicting perspectives of the stakeholders, the differentiated departments, and the ideological basis of the organization's mission can produce a contentious internal environment. For example, the International Relief and Development Agency promotes grassroots development projects in developing countries using resources donated from developed countries. As the agency grew, departments were created to represent different stakeholders: a fundraising group handled donors, a projects department worked in the local offices, a public relations department directed media exposure, and a policy information department lobbied the government. Each department adapted to fit its role. Fundraisers and lobbyists dressed more formally, took more moderate political positions, and managed less participatively than did the projects departments. These differences were often interpreted in political and ideological terms, creating considerable internal conflict. OD practitioners designed a series of feedback meetings to increase the understanding and relevance of the different groups[36] Finally, GSCO membership often is transitory. Many people are volunteers, and the extent and depth of their involvement varies over time and by issue. Turnover can be quite high.

21-2b Application Stages

GSCOs are concerned with creating sustainable change in communities and societies. This requires a form of planned change in which the practitioner is heavily involved, many stakeholders are encouraged and expected to participate, and "technologies of empowerment" are used. Often referred to as "participatory action research,"[37] planned change in GSCOs typically involves three types of activities: building local organization effectiveness, creating bridges and linkages with other relevant organizations, and developing vertical linkages with policymakers.

Building the Local Organization Although GSCOs are concerned primarily with changing their environments, a critical issue in development projects is recognizing the potential problems inherent in the GSCO itself. Because the focus of change is their environment, members of GSCOs are often oblivious to the need for internal development. Moreover, the complex organizational arrangements of a network make planned change in GSCOs particularly challenging.

OD practitioners focus on three activities in helping GSCOs build themselves into viable organizations: using values to create the vision, recognizing that internal conflict is often a function of external conditions, and understanding the problems of success.

- **Values to create vision**. For leadership to function effectively, the broad purposes of the GSCO must be clear and closely aligned with the ideologies of its members. Singleness of purpose can be gained from tapping into the compelling aspects of the values and principles that the GSCO represents. For example, the Latin American Division of the Nature Conservancy held annual two-day retreats. Each participant prepared a white paper concerning his or her area of responsibility: the issues, challenges, major dilemmas or problems, and ideas for directions the division could take. Over the course of the retreat, participants actively discussed each paper. They had broad freedom to challenge the status quo and to question previous decisions. By the end of the retreat, discussions produced a clear statement about the course that the division would take for the following year. People left with increased clarity about and commitment to the purpose and vision of the division.[38]

  Developing a shared vision can align individual and organizational values. Because most activities occur at the boundary of the organization, members are often spread out geographically and are not in communication with each other. A clearly crafted vision allows people in disparate regions and positions to coordinate their activities. For example, ACDI/VOCA (www.acdivoca.org) is a "nonprofit that means business." The organization provides sustainable solutions that integrate approaches from agribusiness, community and enterprise development, financial services, and food security perspectives. Its vision, "A world in which people are empowered to succeed in the global economy," helps to coordinate the work of the people throughout the organization. "Our mission and a vision grow out of the farmer cooperative movement in the U.S. going back 45 years. We know something about how you bring food from the farm to the table." As one member put it, "I'm part of helping a small farmer in a small village somewhere in the world be able to put food on their table and send their kids to school or to buy a net to protect themselves from malaria. I don't know how that couldn't impact you." Another staff member noted, "It's a privilege to have a job that is making a difference, and as a mom you feel that more. When I hear a story of a woman who's saying, 'I couldn't feed my children,' I think, oh my goodness. And now, because they got a loan, they got their business going, and they're connected with people who wanted to buy their stuff, you can just see it in their eyes and their voices. They have hope for the future. It's a fantastic thing."

- **Recognizing conflict.** Because of the diverse perspectives of the different stakeholders, GSCOs often face multiple conflicts. In working through them, the organizational vision can be used as an important rallying point for discovering how each person's role contributes to the GSCO's purpose. The affective component of a GSCO vision gives purpose to members' lives and work. Another way to manage conflict is to prevent its occurrence. At the Hunger Project, the "committed listener" and "breakthrough" processes give GSCO members an opportunity to seek help before conflict becomes dysfunctional. Every member of the organization has a designated person who acts as a committed listener. When things are not going well, or someone is feeling frustrated in their ability to accomplish a goal, they can talk it out with this colleague. The role of the committed listener is to listen intently, to help the individual understand the issues, and to think about framing or approaching the problem in new ways. This new perspective is called a "breakthrough"—a creative solution to a potentially conflictual situation.[39]
- **Problem of success**. Finally, a GSCO's success can create a number of problems. The very accomplishment of its mission can take away its reason for existence, thus causing an identity crisis. For example, a GSCO that succeeds in creating jobs for underprivileged youth can be dissolved because its funding is redirected toward organizations that have not yet met their goals, because its goals change, or simply because it has accomplished its purpose. During these times, the vital social role that these organizations play needs to be emphasized. GSCOs often represent bridges between the powerful and powerless, between the rich and poor, and between the elite and oppressed, and as such may need to be maintained as legitimate parts of the community.

  Another problem can occur when GSCO success produces additional demands for greater formalization. New people must be hired and acculturated; greater control over income and expenditures has to be developed; new skills and behaviors have to be learned. The need for more formal systems often runs counter to ideological principles of autonomy and freedom and can produce a profound resistance to change. Employees' participation during diagnosis and implementation can help them commit to the new systems. In addition, new employment opportunities, increased job responsibilities, and improved capabilities to carry out the GSCO's mission can be used to encourage commitment and reduce resistance to the changes.

  Supported by sponsors in industrialized countries, the International Child Sponsorship Agency (ICSA) delivers services that enhance children's welfare in developing countries. For many years, entrepreneurial leadership in the field led to growth in the number of programs and activities that were difficult to coordinate and monitor. The organization brought in a new "business-oriented" CEO to improve resource and program efficiencies. While everyone agreed that better coordination was necessary, they also believed that the new CEO's implementation of new accounting and information systems was too top-down. Tensions between headquarters and the field increased and turnover among key staff members led to an OD intervention. It started with a diagnosis that showed that the focus on control and efficiency conflicted with ICSA's traditional, entrepreneurial values. Changes were implemented to increase the involvement of the field in strategic planning, to increase and clarify the decisions that could be made in the field, and to reinforce the leadership and cultural styles that best represented the vision. The changes were viewed as a rebalancing of the organization's priorities, giving fundraising and program development relatively equal influence over strategy and operations.[40]

Alternatively, a GSCO can maintain its autonomy through structural arrangements. The Savings Development Movement (SDM) of Zimbabwe was a grassroots effort to organize savings clubs, the proceeds of which helped farmers buy seed in volume. Its success in creating clubs and helping farmers lower their costs caused the organization to grow very rapidly. Leaders chose to expand SDM not by adding staff but by working with the Ministry of Agriculture to provide technical support to the clubs and with the Ministry of Community Development and Women's Affairs to provide training. The savings clubs remained autonomous and locally managed. This reduced the need for formal systems to coordinate the clubs with government agencies. The SDM office staff did not grow, but the organization remained a catalyst, committed to expanding participation rather than providing direct services.[41]

Creating Horizontal Linkages Successful social change projects often require a network of local organizations with similar views and objectives. Such projects as creating a civil society in China, turning responsibility for maintenance and control over small irrigation systems to local water users in Indonesia, or teaching leadership skills in South Africa require that multiple organizations interact. Consequently, an important planned change activity in GSCOs is creating strong horizontal linkages to organizations in the community or society where the development project is taking place. The formation of "support" organizations—value-added agencies that provide services to NGOs for their development—are an important part of these linkages.[42] For example, CANGO, the China Association for NGOs (www.cango.org), is a government-sponsored NGO that provides capacity-building and project-execution services to support the emergence of a civil society in China. CANGO sponsors conferences and programs where like-minded NGOs can connect with each other and support common interests. Similarly, GSCOs aimed at job development not only must recruit, train, and market potential job applicants but also must develop relationships with local job providers and government authorities. The GSCO must help these organizations commit to the GSCO's vision, mobilize resources, and create policies to support development efforts.

The ability of GSCOs to sustain themselves depends on establishing linkages with other organizations whose cooperation is essential to preserving and expanding their efforts. Unfortunately, members of GSCOs often view local government officials, community leaders, or for-profit organizations as part of the problem. Rather than interacting with these stakeholders, GSCOs often "protect" themselves and their ideologies from contamination by these outsiders. Planned change efforts to overcome this myopia are similar to the transorganizational development interventions discussed in Chapter 20. GSCO members are helped to identify, convene, and organize these key external organizations. For example, hurricane Katrina in 2005 devastated many of New Orleans' oldest, poorest, and culturally rich neighborhoods. The rebuilding of neighborhoods, such as Tremé or Holycross, was usually overseen by local NGOs, such as Esplanade Ridge/Tremé Neighborhood Association or Holy Cross Neighborhood Association. These groups connected with other NGOs, local and state government departments (other than Federal Emergency Management Agency [FEMA], which had lost credibility during the initial response), funding agencies, and volunteers. Local coordination of the NGO activities allowed each neighborhood to pursue locally relevant strategies for rehabilitation, to bring the right resources to the right places, and to maintain local cultural and historical traditions.[43]

Developing Vertical Linkages GSCOs also must create channels of communication and influence upward to governmental and policy-level decision-making processes. These higher-level decisions often affect the creation and eventual success of GSCO activities. For example, the Global Village of Beijing (GVB) is a nongovernmental organization that raises the environmental consciousness of people in China. GVB leveraged its relationships with journalists and the government to produce a weekly television series on government channels to discuss and promote environmentally friendly practices, such as recycling, and to expose the Chinese people to environmental projects in different countries. When the Chinese government proposed new environmental regulations and policies as part of the World Trade Organization admission process, GVB helped assess the proposals.[44] GVB's success and visibility also contributed to its founder, Liao Xiaoyi, being invited to participate in Beijing's successful 2008 summer Olympics bid and the inclusion of a "green Olympics movement" proposal that addressed concerns about Beijing's pollution.

Vertical linkages also can be developed by building on a strong record of success. The Institute of Cultural Affairs (ICA) is concerned with the "application of methods of human development to communities and organizations all around the world." With more than 100 offices in 39 nations, ICA trains and consults with small groups, communities, organizations, and voluntary associations, in addition to providing leadership training for village leaders, conducting community education programs, and running ecological preservation projects. Its reputation has led to recognition and credibility. It was given consultative status by the United Nations in 1985, and it has category II status with the Food and Agriculture Organization, working relation status with the World Health Organization, and consultative status with UNICEF.

For decades in Mali, a centralized one-party government that neglected teachers, schools, books, and materials, especially in the rural areas, had dominated the country's educational system. When a new reformist government took control, a variety of GSCOs helped to organize grassroots groups to improve the schools. Supported by the GSCOs, local parent-teacher associations (PTAs) were organized, local members were elected, and the groups were given training on how to manage the school. Although there was local improvement, the overall educational system remained fragmented. In response, GSCO-organized conferences brought PTAs from different villages together for dialogue and decision making. As regional PTA federations were formed, the GSCOs provided policy analysis and advocacy training to help them speak with one voice in negotiations over policy formulation with the Ministry of Education. These collective efforts have resulted in increased attention, influence, and expenditures to rural schools.[45]

Application 21.2 describes how OD has contributed to the work of LDI Africa.[46] The opening of its program provides important clues about the development of vertical and horizontal linkages and how GSCOs work within a clear vision.

21-2c Change-Agent Roles and Skills

Planned global social change is a relatively new application of organization development. The number of practitioners is small but growing, and the skills and knowledge necessary to carry out OD in these situations are being developed. The grassroots, political,

application 21.2

SOCIAL AND ENVIRONMENTAL CHANGE AT LDI AFRICA

Landmark Development Initiative Africa (LDI Africa) is a nonprofit social enterprise based in the United States. It builds the capacity of African corporations, small businesses, and nonprofits to compete in the global marketplace by recruiting skilled volunteers, especially young African professionals from outside of the continent. Through LDI Africa's partnerships with the Foundation Center in Nigeria and investors in five countries, African nonprofits and businesses can access funding and business development services. LDI Africa also plans to send young professionals in Africa to the United States and around the world for overseas fellowships with nonprofits and businesses seeking an international perspective on the challenges they face.

As a young professional in Nigeria, Gbenga Ogunjimi, LDI Africa's founder and CEO, had limited access to international management principles and professional development opportunities. Gbenga saw an opportunity to address development challenges facing his country and other parts of the African continent while working in the Washington, DC, headquarters of Atlas Corps, a nonprofit organization that sponsors international fellowships. He believed that by matching organizational needs for globally competitive expertise with a rapidly growing local workforce, he could create a virtuous cycle of social and economic development. He was motivated to establish a social enterprise based on his own experiences and developed the initial concept for LDI Africa.

Through volunteer placement services administered by LDI Africa, young professionals gain hands-on international experience helping African organizations launch and expand their operations. The youth fellows are able to hone their skills in a challenging work environment characterized by resource constraints, limited infrastructure, and uncertain policies. The African organizations benefit from access to international business practices and skills, such as business planning, finance, marketing, and management. When the 3 to 12 month fellowship ends, LDI Africa also offers recruitment services for host organizations interested in hiring fellows. Thus, what separates LDI Africa from other nonprofits is the fundamental goal of altering a status quo where African youth and organizations are struggling to obtain the capabilities needed to effectively compete in a global marketplace.

The organization development process at LDI Africa started with a chance meeting between Gbenga and an OD practitioner, Kimberley Jutze. Kimberley, a graduate of Pepperdine University's Master of Science in Organization Development Program, was working to establish a consulting practice that addressed the resource and organization development needs of social enterprises. After exchanging contact information, Gbenga and Kimberley met to discuss opportunities to work together on securing start-up capital, setting up an office in Washington, DC, and developing partnerships with organizations involved in work abroad programs.

Once the consulting relationship was formalized, Kimberley conducted an informal assessment, which revealed that the planning documents in place were insufficiently detailed to prepare LDI Africa for a successful launch. Thus, before any of the initial requests for support could be addressed, LDI Africa needed a strategic plan to clearly define its mission, programs, and operations. A business planning approach pioneered by the nonprofit consulting firm Root Cause guided the development of a three-year strategy for launching and expanding LDI Africa. The plan described the social and financial returns that social impact investors could expect.

Over the next five months, Kimberley worked closely with Gbenga to facilitate the development of a social impact strategy. The strategy development process consisted of a series of meetings where each section of the social impact strategy outline (Need and Opportunity, Social Impact

Model, Implementation Strategy, and Action Plan) was reviewed and ideas were discussed. In between meetings, Gbenga prepared drafts of the social impact strategy.

Despite having a mutually agreed upon scope of work, differences in communication styles between Kimberley and Gbenga and expectations that were not clearly defined upfront posed challenges to the consulting relationship. For example, both parties had different assumptions about what level of detail was sufficient for addressing each section of the social impact strategy. Gbenga, who wanted to make the most of his limited time in the United States to launch LDI Africa as soon as possible, preferred a moderately detailed plan where he could address questions from social impact investors as they came up. In contrast, Kimberley believed that investing more time up front in addressing anticipated questions in the plan itself would facilitate smoother implementation later on. A final agreement was reached through ongoing feedback on drafts of the plan and open discussions about the quality and quantity of information needed to complete it. Attention also was given to establishing a collaborative relationship characterized by open and honest communication between Kimberley and Gbenga. This greatly improved communication between them as well as their working relationship.

By the time the social impact strategy was completed, Gbenga gained greater insight into the essential steps needed to transition LDI Africa from a concept to an operational organization. He was better prepared to meet with prospective financial supporters and refer to details captured in the social impact strategy to fully explain LDI Africa's model.

After the social impact strategy was completed and LDI Africa was registered as a nonprofit organization, Gbenga asked Kimberley to help obtain seed funding. As a first step, they agreed to prepare a strategy to guide LDI Africa's resource development efforts. This consisted of meetings to review each section of the strategy outline and discuss ideas. Gbenga also drafted the strategy with support from Kimberley. After agreeing upon a funding target based on the organization's annual operating budget, Kimberley used a strengths-based approach to assess LDI Africa's fundraising assets. She worked closely with Gbenga to determine which sources of funding the organization was best prepared to cultivate as well as best and worst case scenarios for the amount of funding that LDI Africa could anticipate receiving from each source. A contingency plan was also developed that explained how LDI Africa would continue to operate in the event that the funding target was not fully reached during its first year of operation. The strategy also included an action plan with specific tasks, timeline, and targets. Gbenga's active participation in the strategic planning process led him to appreciate the importance of thinking through different options to obtain funding and deploy LDI Africa's resources expediently rather than just pursuing whatever opportunities happened to come along. With an action plan in place, Gbenga was also better prepared to begin seeking start-up capital.

Most recently, Gbenga began forming a board of directors for LDI Africa and invited Kimberley to join as an advisor for resource and organization development. Recognizing the importance of an effective board, Kimberley coached Gbenga on board development issues, such as defining member roles and responsibilities, enlisting their support for fundraising activities, and facilitating board meetings. Through this informal consultation process, Gbenga is learning how to provide overall direction to the board and to obtain its support for LDI Africa's work. He is also addressing the challenge of board member engagement by managing expectations around each board member's role and time commitments.

As LDI Africa prepares to launch its pilot fellowship program in June 2013, it has recognized the need to develop partnerships with African organizations that have expressed interest in hosting young professionals, but are unable to cover fellowship costs, such as housing, transportation, and insurance. Gbenga and Kimberley worked together to prepare a teaming agreement with an African foundation that provides micro investments and mentorship to start-up enterprises. Their initial conversations with the African foundation involved explaining how the teaming process would work for preparing consortium grant applications to foundations, examining the pros and cons of joint fundraising before entering into an agreement, and drafting a teaming agreement for both parties to sign. As a result, Gbenga was better prepared to lead the partnership negotiation process. If LDI Africa is successful in obtaining grants for its pilot fellowship program, both organizations will benefit from the opportunity to contribute to the professional development of fellows and to the sustainability of newly formed African companies.

Throughout the process, Kimberley "led from behind" by working one-on-one with Gbenga to enhance his leadership capabilities and serving as an observer in meetings so that he was consistently seen as leading LDI Africa's partnership and resource development efforts. Over the past 18 months, LDI Africa has made tremendous strides in its internal development. It has grown from a concept to a registered nonprofit, hired four people to staff positions in Nigeria and the United States, and established an international board of directors. LDI Africa has also succeeded in obtaining an initial round of start-up capital that can help position the social enterprise to attract additional funding for its pilot program. Gbenga's strong personal commitment to LDI Africa and his dedication to developing it in a systematic way has poised the organization for success within Nigeria and across Africa.

and ideological natures of many GSCOs require change-agent roles and skills that are quite different from those in more formal, for-profit settings.[47] GSCO change agents typically occupy stewardship and bridging roles. The *steward* role derives from the ideological and grassroots activities associated with GSCOs. It asks the change agent to be a colearner or coparticipant in achieving global social change. This type of change is "sustainable," or ecologically, politically, culturally, and economically balanced. Change agents must, therefore, work from an explicit value base that is aligned with GSCO activities. For example, change agents are not usually asked, "What are your credentials to carry out this project?" Instead, practitioners are asked, "Do you share our values?" or "What do you think of the plight of the people we are serving?" Stewardship implies an orientation toward the development of sustainable solutions to local and global problems.

The second role, *bridging*, derives from the grassroots and political activities of many GSCOs. Bridging is an appropriate title for this role because it metaphorically reflects the core activities of GSCOs and the change agents who work with them. Both are mainly concerned with connecting and integrating diverse elements of societies and communities toward sustainable change, and with transferring ideas among individuals, groups, organizations, and societies.

Carrying out the steward and the bridging roles requires communication, negotiation, and networking skills. Communication and negotiation skills are essential for GSCO change agents because of the asymmetrical power bases that exist in grassroots development efforts. GSCOs are relatively powerless compared with governments, wealthy upper classes, and formal organizations. Given the diverse social systems involved, there often is only a loose consensus about a GSCO's objectives. Moreover, different constituencies may have different interests, and there may be histories of antagonism among groups that make promulgation of the development project difficult. The steward and the bridging roles require persuasive articulation of the GSCO's ideology and purpose at all times, under many conditions, and to everyone involved.

The change agent must also be adept at political compromise and negotiation.[48] Asymmetrical power contexts represent strong challenges for stewardship and bridging. To accomplish sustainable change, important trade-offs often are necessary. The effective change agent needs to understand the elements of the ideology that can and cannot be sacrificed and when to fight or walk away from a situation.

Networking skills represent a significant part of the action research process as applied in GSCO settings. Networking takes place at two levels. First, in the steward role, practitioners bring to the GSCO specific knowledge of problem solving, technologies of empowerment using processes that socially construct and make sense of the surrounding conditions, and organization design.[49] The participants bring local knowledge of political players, history, culture, and ecology. A "cogenerative dialogue" or "collective reflection" process emerges when these two frames of reference interact to produce new ideas, possibilities, and insights.[50] When both the practitioner and the participants contribute to sustainable solutions, the stewardship role is satisfied.

Second, in the bridging role, networking skills create conditions that enable diverse stakeholders to interact and solve common problems or address common issues. Change agents must be able to find common ground so that different constituencies can work together. Networking requires the capability to tap multiple sources of information and perspective, often located in very different constituencies. Action becomes possible through these networks.

But bridging also implies making linkages among individual, group, GSCO, and social levels of thought. Ideas are powerful fuel in global grassroots development projects. Breakthrough thinking by individuals to see things in new ways can provide the impetus for change at the group, GSCO, social, and global levels. This was demonstrated by U2's Bono and U.S. Treasury secretary Paul O'Neill during their 2002 visit to understand and develop solutions to poverty in Africa. The change agent in international GSCO settings must play a variety of roles and use many skills. Clearly, stewardship and bridging roles are important in facilitating GSCO accomplishment. Other roles and skills will likely emerge over time. Change agents, for example, are finding it increasingly important to develop "imaginal literacy" skills—the ability to see the possibilities, rather than the constraints, and the ability to develop sustainable solutions by going outside the boxes to create new ideas.[51]

SUMMARY

In this chapter, we presented two interventions designed to help organizations generate positive social, environmental, and economic outcomes. These change processes are fundamentally different from other OD interventions that focus primarily on the achievement of economic objectives.

Sustainable management organization interventions are intended to achieve sustainable effectiveness. Organizations must be agile enough to sustain high levels of economic, social, and environmental performance. Achieving these triple-bottom-line objectives relies on design guidelines that promote capabilities in change and multistakeholder decision making. The organization's strategy must be realigned and clarified to support sustainability and the work systems, structure, management and information systems, and human resource systems must be oriented appropriately.

Finally, applications of OD to global social change were discussed. Typically carried out in global social change organizations, these interventions promote the establishment of a global civilization. Strong ideological positions regarding the fair and just distribution of wealth, resources, and power fuel this movement. By strengthening local organizations, building horizontal linkages with other like-minded GSCOs, and developing vertical linkages with policy-making organizations, a change agent can help GSCOs become more effective and alter their external context. To support roles of stewardship and bridging, change agents need communication, negotiation, and networking skills.

NOTES

1. S. Mohrman and A. Shani, "Organizing for Sustainable Effectiveness: Taking Stock and Moving Forward," in *Organizing for Sustainability*, vol. 1, ed. S. Mohrman and A. Shani (Bingley, UK: Emerald Group Publishing, 2011): 1–40.
2. P. Lacy, T. Cooper, R. Hayward, and L. Neuberger, "A New Era of Sustainability: UN Global Compact-Accenture CEO Study 2010," accessed from http://www.unglobalcompact.org/news/42-06-22-2010, on October 4, 2012.
3. K. Haanaes, B. Balagopal, D. Arthur, M. T. Kong, I. Velken, N. Kruschwitz, and M. Hopkins, "First Look: The Second Annual Sustainability and Innovation Survey," *MIT Sloan Management Review* 52, no. 2 (2010): 77–83.
4. E. Lawler and C. Worley, *Management Reset* (San Francisco: Jossey-Bass, 2011), J. Ludema, C. Laszlo, and K. Lynch, "Embedding Sustainability: How the Field of Organization Development and Change Can Help Companies Harness the Next Big Competitive Advantage," in *Research in Organizational Change and Development*, vol. 20, ed. A. Shani, W. Pasmore, and R. Woodman (Bingley, UK: Emerald Group Publishing, 2012), 265–99.
5. A. Lovins, L. Lovins, and P. Hawken, "A Road Map for Natural Capitalism," *Harvard Business Review* (May–June, 1999): 145–58; L. Lovins and B. Cohen, *Climate Capitalism* (New York: Farrar, Straus, and Giroux, 2011); information on the Natural Step can be found at http://www.naturalstep.org and in H. Bradbury and J. Clair, "Promoting Sustainable Organizations with Sweden's Natural Step," *Academy of Management Executive* 13 (1999): 63–74; information on CERES principles can be found at http://www.ceres.org.
6. Lawler and Worley, *Management Reset*; E. Lawler and C. Worley, *Built to Change: How to Achieve Sustained Organizational Effectiveness* (San Francisco: Jossey-Bass, 2006); C. Worley and E. Lawler, "Designing Organizations That Are Built to Change," *Sloan Management Review* 48 (2006): 19–23; Mohrman and Shani, "Organizing for Sustainable Effectiveness."
7. G. Brundtland, ed., *Our Common Future: The World Commission on Environment and Development* (Oxford: Oxford University Press, 1987).
8. J. Elkington, "Towards the Sustainable Corporation: Win-Win-Win Business Strategies for Sustainable Development," *California Management Review* 36, no. 2 (1994): 90–100.
9. D. Katz and R. Kahn. *The Social Psychology of Organizations* (San Francisco: Wiley, 1978); M. Weber, *The Theory of Social and Economic Organization*, trans. A. M. Henderson and T. Parsons (London: Collier Macmillan Publishers, 1947).
10. A. De Geus, *The Living Company* (Cambridge, MA: Harvard Business School Press, 1997).
11. Bradbury and Clair, "Promoting Sustainable Organizations with Sweden's Natural Step."
12. Data accessed from http://www.viewzone.com/sixteenships.html on January 10, 2013; International Maritime Organization, http://www.imo.org, accessed on January 10, 2013.
13. M. Hatch and S. Majken, "The Dynamics of Organizational Identity," *Human Relations* 55 (2002): 989–1018; J. Dutton and J. Dukerich, "Keeping an Eye on the Mirror: Image and Identity in Organizational Adaptation," *Academy of Management Journal* 34 (1991): 517–54; D. Whetten, "Albert and Whetten Revisited: Strengthening the Concept of Organizational Identity," *Journal of Management Inquiry* 15 (2006): 219–34.
14. Whetten, "Albert and Whetten Revisited."
15. Lawler and Worley, *Built to Change*.
16. K. Eisenhardt and J. Martin. "Dynamic Capabilities: What Are They?" *Strategic Management Journal* 21 (2000): 1105–21; S. Winter, "Understanding Dynamic Capabilities," *Strategic Management Journal* 24 (2003): 991–96.
17. C. O'Reilly and M. Tushman, "Organizational Ambidexterity in Action: How Managers Explore and Exploit," *California Management Review* 53 (2011): 5–22.
18. Lawler and Worley, *Built to Change*.
19. H. Aldrich and D. Herker, "Boundary Spanning Roles and Organization Structure," *Academy of Management Review* 2 (1977): 217–30.
20. E. Lawler and C. Worley, "Why Boards Need to Change," *Sloan Management Review* 54 (2012): 10–12.
21. E. Lawler, "CHROs and Boards: A Missing Link," in *The Chief HR Officer: Defining the New Role of Human*

Resource Leaders, ed. P. Wright, P. Boudreau, D. Pace, E. Sartain, P. McKinnon, and R. Antoine (San Francisco: Jossey-Bass, 2011), 183–92.

22. Information about the Global Reporting Initiative can be found at http://www.globalreporting.org.
23. J. Raskin, "The Rise of Benefit Corporations," *Nation*, June 8, 2011, accessed from http://www.thenation.com/article/161261/rise-benefit-corporations on October 4, 2012.
24. C. Worley, A. Feyerherm, and D. Knudsen, "Building a Collaboration Capability for Sustainability," *Organizational Dynamics* 39 (2010): 325–34.
25. Ibid.
26. P. Kale and H. Singh, "Managing Strategic Alliances: What Do We Know Now and Where Do We Go from Here?" *Academy of Management Perspectives* (August 2009): 45–62.
27. C. Worley and E. Lawler, "Building a Change Capability at Capital One Financial," *Organizational Dynamics* 38 (2009): 245–51.
28. A. Hoffman, "Climate Change as a Cultural and Behavioral Issue: Addressing Barriers and Implementing Solutions," *Organizational Dynamics* 39 (2010): 295–305.
29. P. McMichael, *Development and Social Change: A Global Perspective* (Thousand Oaks, CA: Pine Forge Press, 2007); L. Brown and J. Covey, "Development Organizations and Organization Development: Toward an Expanded Paradigm for Organization Development," in *Research in Organizational Change and Development*, vol. 1, ed. R. Woodman and W. Pasmore (Greenwich, CT: JAI Press, 1987), 59–88.
30. P. Freire, *Pedagogy of the Oppressed* (Harmondsworth, England: Penguin, 1972); D. Bornstein, *How to Change the World: Social Entrepreneurs and the Power of New Ideas* (New York: Oxford, 2004); T. Kidder, *Mountains Beyond Mountains* (New York: Random House, 2003); H. Perlmutter and E. Trist, "Paradigms for Societal Transition," *Human Relations* 39 (1986): 1–27; F. Westley, "Bob Geldof and Live Aid: The Affective Side of Global Social Innovation," *Human Relations* 44 (1991): 1011–36; D. Cooperrider and W. Pasmore, "Global Social Change: A New Agenda for Social Science," *Human Relations* 44 (1991): 1037–55; H. Perlmutter, "On the Rocky Road to the First Global Civilization," *Human Relations* 44 (1991): 897–920; E. Boulding, "The Old and New Transnationalism: An Evolutionary Perspective," *Human Relations* 44 (1991): 789–805; P. Johnson and D. Cooperrider, "Finding a Path with a Heart: Global Social Change Organizations and Their Challenge for the Field of Organizational Development," in *Research in Organizational Change and Development*, vol. 5, ed. R. Woodman and W. Pasmore (Greenwich, CT: JAI Press, 1991), 223–84; D. Cooperrider and T. Thachankary, "Building the Global Civic Culture: Making Our Lives Count," in Sorensen et al., eds., *Global and International Organization Development*, 282–306.
31. E. Smith, "Growth vs. Environment," *BusinessWeek*, May 11, 1992, 66–75.
32. D. Cooperrider and J. Dutton, eds., *Organizational Dimensions of Global Change* (Newbury Park, CA: Sage Publications, 1999), 12.
33. L. Brown, "Bridging Organizations and Sustainable Development," *Human Relations* 44 (1991): 807–31; Johnson and Cooperrider, "Finding a Path"; Cooperrider and Thachankary, "Building the Global Civil Culture"; L. D. Brown, M. Leach, and J. Covey, "Organization Development for Social Change," in *Handbook of Organization Development*, ed. T. Cummings (Thousand Oaks, CA: Sage Publications, 2008).
34. L. D. Brown and D. Ashman, "Social Capital, Mutual Influence, and Social Learning in Intersectoral Problem Solving in Africa and Asia," in *Organizational Dimensions of Global Change*, ed. Cooperrider and Dutton, 139–67.
35. F. Westley, "Not on Our Watch," in *Organizational Dimensions of Global Change*, ed. Cooperrider and Dutton, 88–113.
36. Brown and Covey, "Development Organizations"; Brown, Leach, and Covey, "Organization Development for Social Change."
37. P. Reason and H. Bradbury, eds., *The SAGE Handbook of Action Research*, 2nd ed. (Newbury Park, CA: Sage Publications, 2007).
38. Johnson and Cooperrider, "Finding a Path," 240–41.
39. Ibid, 237.
40. Brown, Leach, and Covey, "Organization Development for Social Change."
41. M. Bratton, "Non-Governmental Organizations in Africa: Can They Influence Public Policy?" *Development and Change* 21 (1989): 81–118.
42. L. D. Brown and A. Kalegaonkar, "Support Organizations and the Evolution of the NGO Sector," *Nonprofit and Voluntary Sector Quarterly* 31 (2002): 231–58.
43. R. Beech and B. Allen, *Dynamics of Disaster* (New York: Routledge, 2011).
44. Personal communication with members of the Global Village of Beijing, March 28, 2000.
45. Brown, Leach, and Covey, "Organization Development for Social Change."
46. This application was developed with the kind assistance of Kimberley Jutze. Her contribution is gratefully acknowledged.
47. Bornstein, *Change the World*; L. Brown and J. Covey, "Action Research for Grassroots Development: Collective

Reflection and Development NGOS in Asia" (presentation at the Academy of Management, Miami, 1990).

48. R. Saner and L. Yiu, "Porous Boundary and Power Politics: Contextual Constraints of Organization Development Change Projects in the United Nations Organizations," *Gestalt Review* 6 (2002): 84–94.

49. D. Cooperrider and S. Srivastva, "Appreciative Inquiry in Organizational Life," in *Research in Organizational Change and Development*, vol. 1, ed. R. Woodman and W. Pasmore (Greenwich, CT: JAI Press, 1987), 129–69; Cooperrider and Dutton, *Organizational Dimensions of Global Change.*

50. Brown and Covey, "Action Research"; M. Elden and M. Levin, "Cogenerative Learning: Bringing Participation into Action Research," in *Participatory Action Research*, ed. W. Whyte (Newbury Park, CA: Sage Publications, 1991), 127–42.

51. E. Boulding, *Building a Global Civic Culture: Education for an Interdependent World* (Syracuse, NY: Syracuse University Press, 1988).

22

Organization Development in Nonindustrial Settings: Health Care, School Systems, the Public Sector, and Family–Owned

learning objectives

- Understand how organization development (OD) in nonindustrial settings (health care, school systems, the public sector, and family-owned businesses) differs from traditional practice contexts.
- Describe the changes in the health care industry and how OD is practiced in this industry.
- Understand how OD can support educational reform.
- Explain the role of OD in government organizations.
- Discuss the components of family firms and how to apply OD in those settings.

Organization development is practiced in private and public organizations, service and manufacturing firms, and in domestic and international settings. Historically, however, most published material on organization development (OD) focused on applications in industrial and manufacturing organizations. As OD practitioners have applied processes of planned change outside of this narrow industrial model, they have modified and extended the traditional interventions to better fit the unique organizational setting or situation.

This chapter presents broad applications of OD in nonindustrial settings. As in previous editions of this text, a person with knowledge and experience in OD in a particular kind of organization was asked to contribute a section for this chapter. For this edition, we asked Foster Mobley, Erin Mobley, and Jennifer Perry from The Foster Mobley Group to examine OD in health care. Linda Purrington and Paul Sparks from Pepperdine University's Graduate School of Education and Psychology agreed to describe how educational systems are changing and the role OD can play in this transformation. Ray Patchett, the retired City Manager of Carlsbad, California, discusses OD applications in the public sector, and Otis Baskin, professor of management at Pepperdine University's Graziadio School of Business and Management, reports on OD in family businesses. Each author stresses the similarities and differences between traditional OD in industrial organizations and its application in these nonindustrial settings. Their conclusions suggest the need for a greater diversity of diagnostic methods, interventions, and values when using OD in nonindustrial environments.

22-1 Organization Development in Health Care*

Health care is a dynamic and complex industry facing significant growth, regulatory demands, and change. As such, significant opportunities exist for OD. This section highlights the current state of the health care industry, outlines the important trends driving change, and presents OD practices that are most likely to support the industry's transformation.

22-1a The Health Care Industry—A Snapshot

In 2010, health care expenditures accounted for 17.9% of the gross domestic product (GDP) in the United States, up from 13.8% in the year 2000.[1] In fact, the United States spends more on health care than the GDP of more than 170 nations.[2] This places annual national health expenditures at approximately $8,200 per person.[3] Although the rate of increase has been dropping since 2002, expenditures still grew at a rate of 4% in 2010.[4] At the same time, the number of uninsured people rose to 49.9 million, or 16.3% of the U.S. population[5] with more than three-quarters of uninsured in working families.[6] The amount of health care costs shouldered by the individual is also growing. Out of pocket payments for national health care expenditures grew from just under $200 billion in 2000 to $280 billion in 2010.[7]

The financial platform on which U.S. health care rests is unsustainable. These trends cited above, along with the need to reduce the federal budget deficit, will drive the transformation of America's health care system. Indeed, the debate over the delivery, financing, structure, and access to care continues vigorously in the halls of Congress, the boardrooms of large and small employers, and in the countless daily interactions between care providers (hospitals, physicians, and others who provide health care) and those they serve. The intensity of these debates has increased since the passage of the Patient Protection and Affordable Care Act (ACA) in 2012, which is intended to reduce costs, improve quality and access, and bring over 40 million previously uninsured people into the health care system.

Regardless of current trends, the health care industry represents a challenging context within which to practice OD. Compared to other industries, such as software development, manufacturing, or retail, health care differs along several dimensions.

Though it is beginning to change, consumers are often insulated from the economic consequences of their major health care decisions, including lifestyle choices, health habits, which hospital to go to, and where to get outpatient services. Access to the health care system and the cost of care are mostly determined by insurance provided through Medicare (a federally funded program for the elderly and disabled), Medicaid (a combined federal/state-funded program for the poor), or private insurance, typically provided through employers with some cost-sharing.

The key providers of care are not connected through an employment agreement. The hospital or other setting where care is delivered does not typically employ the physician. Rather, most physicians, with the exception of certain specialties, such as radiology, clinical pathology, or emergency medicine, have to apply for "privileges" to work at a hospital or other care setting. A single episode of care can involve multiple providers and health care settings, including hospitals, physicians, skilled nursing/rehabilitation centers, or home health agencies, many of them independent from one another.

Hospitals, a key component of the health care system, are primarily not-for-profit and face several challenges related to their ability to create sustainable revenue to support

---

*Written by Foster Mobley, Erin Mobley, and Jennifer Perry from The Foster Mobley Group in Southern California.

operations. For example, the government heavily regulates operations and influences much of a hospital's revenue base. Medicare accounts for an average of 39% of hospital revenues, while Medicaid accounts for an additional 16%, more than half of total revenues.[8]

In addition, the law requires hospitals to care for all patients regardless of their ability to pay, prompting the need to grow revenue in other areas. Hospitals are subject to fines if they do not serve these patients, and are either paid nothing or a set fee, if the patient qualifies for government funding, regardless of the costs incurred in treating the patients. Hospital uncompensated care costs rose from $21.5 billion in 2001 to $34 billion in 2007, likely due to the rising number of uninsured and underinsured.[9]

These factors have resulted in a fragmented industry focused on curing illness and providing more services to cover the costs, rather than creating efficiency or promoting wellness. This has created ethical dilemmas and increased complexity.

22-1b Trends in Health Care

Health care practitioners and leaders acknowledge several important trends in the industry. These trends include changes in the incentives and reimbursement models of health care reform; quality and cost as strategic and regulatory imperatives; a blurring of traditional industry segment lines and integration across different segments of health care; the rise of informatics and e-health; and an aging workforce and changing demographics of patients. Providers and leaders within the industry are scrambling to position themselves to respond to these trends and the resulting implications, many of which are uncertain and require significant human and capital investments, as well as fundamental restructuring. A more detailed description of each of these trends follows.

Responding to Health Care Reform, Changing Incentives, and Reimbursement Models The ACA's passage in 2012 served as the "shot over the bow" in terms of changing health care's historical business model. The ACA represents the most significant of many regulatory acts that have been enacted to control costs, and improve quality and connectivity within the complex and fragmented health care delivery system. The ACA legislation, which goes into effect over several years, shifts Medicare reimbursement from an activity-based model to a value-based model. Providers will be paid based on performance metrics, including quality outcomes and patient experience ratings, rather than the number of tests or number of visits. Further, providers will be paid a fixed rate or "bundled payment" for an episode of care, regardless of the services provided. The purpose is to encourage the coordination and delivery of appropriate, cost-effective care, risk sharing, and reimbursement across the full range of services and care providers. Different types of health care organizations, including hospitals, medical groups, or consortiums of different providers, may apply to set up an Accountable Care Organization (ACO), which will be paid a set amount per person and be responsible for providing all of the health care for those people who are assigned to or select that ACO.[10] In addition, the American Recovery and Reinvestment Act of 2009 (ARRA) requires all health care providers to implement electronic health records (EHR) and transition from paper-based to electronic medical record systems by 2014 or incur Medicare payment penalties.[11]

Quality and Cost as Strategic and Regulatory Imperatives The confluence of economic pressures, consumer and business demands, unsustainable cost structures, and looming regulatory requirements have led to the dual imperative to improve quality and reduce costs. Many leading health care organizations are employing approaches used for decades in other industries to standardize care and reduce costs, such as Lean performance improvement. The National Academy of Sciences' Institute of Medicine (IOM), known for its galvanizing reports on quality (e.g., *Crossing the Quality Chasm*) and safety (e.g., *To Err is Human*), recently published a report on how best to impact the cost curve in health care. The IOM's report, *Best Care at Lower Cost*, asserts that "achieving higher quality care at lower cost will require fundamental commitments to the incentives, culture, and leadership that foster continuous 'learning' and translating that into reliable care."[12]

The need to control costs is also being driven by the Budget Control Act of 2011 (BCA), which mandates a 2% reduction of Medicare spending between 2013 and 2021 to help reduce the deficit. Based on the Congressional Budget Office's (CBO) Medicare baseline analysis, the Medicare cuts that will occur from this reduction will grow from an estimated $10.7 billion in 2013 to $16.4 billion in 2021.[13] This reduction comes on top of the reductions in rate increases to Medicare that are included in the ACA, estimated to remove $550 billion in federal support for Medicaid and Medicare. To prepare for lower reimbursement and the transformation required, leading health systems have established goals and initiatives to take anywhere from 10% to 20% out of their cost structures.

The belief that improving quality, in the form of reduced waste and improved efficiency and coordination, also reduces costs is a driving factor in the Center for Medicare & Medicaid Services's (CMS) inclusion of 12 clinical process measures and mandatory patient experience survey scores in the reimbursement model of the ACA.[14] Beginning in 2015, when these metrics will be published online, a 300-bed hospital with poor quality metrics could be penalized by more than $1.3 million per year and suffer reputational damage.[15] As a result of these trends, hospitals are spending significant time and resources on programs and training around quality improvement and service excellence, in hopes of improving these areas.

Blurring of Traditional Industry Segment Lines and Integration Across Different Segments of Health Care A wave of consolidation is occurring across the health care industry in response to economic pressures, the need for capital, and attempts to compete through size and scale. More creative and different partnerships can be expected, as organizations strive to build broader networks of services to better manage care and risk for value-based payments. This includes consolidation within the hospital sector, but also a further blurring of the boundaries between insurers, hospitals and physicians, and between for-profit and nonprofit organizations. In the last year, health insurers have committed more than $2 billion to acquire or align with physician groups, clinics, and hospitals according to PwC Health Research estimates.[16]

Recent examples include the 2011 acquisition of West Penn Allegheny Health System by Highmark/Blue Cross Plan; UnitedHealth Group's acquisition of Monarch Health care, a 2,300-member physician group in Southern California; DaVita's (a medical dialysis company) purchase of a major medical group (HealthPartners); the for-profit Catholic health care venture created in 2011 by Ascension Health; and the private equity firm Oak Hill Partners.[17] Despite this consolidation, the ten largest hospitals and health systems only control 22% of all beds, in contrast to consolidation in other industries, like airlines where the ten largest airlines control 84% of all passenger seats or the ten largest retail pharmacy companies that control 68% of all prescriptions.[18] There is clearly more room for consolidation, which is expected to continue given the forces impacting the industry.

Health systems are also employing physicians, in all specialties, more than any time in history. Some estimates indicate that hospitals now employ more than 50% of the country's total practicing physicians.[19] Many physicians and groups are joining hospitals to gain access to capital for expensive information technology and care management tools, to reduce private practice overhead, and to use these expanded care management tools. Hospitals are looking to better integrate care, ensure access to a primary care physician base, and align financial incentives.

In the past, the view of "bigger is bad" prevailed and many organizational attempts at integrated models to manage a population's health failed in the 1990s. The landscape has changed with the advent of electronic medical records, physician alignment, and new Medicare reimbursement models. In a recent survey of individuals by the PwC Health Research Institute, nearly 75% of respondents indicated a preference for health care organizations that encompass a wide range of integrated health-related activities and services.[20]

The Rise of Informatics and E-Health Data is becoming increasingly important and available in managing health care, driven by both regulatory requirements for the use of EHRs and the advancement of computer and mobile technology. Investments in health informatics, the practice of identifying and translating valuable data into information to improve patient care, are growing across all segments of health care. Kaiser, Aetna, Humana, and UnitedHealthcare recently formed the Health Care Cost Institute, which will make data in more than 5 billion anonymous claims available to researchers.[21] McKinsey & Co. estimates that making data more transparent, usable, and connected for patient care could create $300 billion in value by reducing health care spending by 8%.[22]

Mobile health has also been shown to reduce the need for hospital admissions and physician visits. Forty percent of physicians surveyed said they could eliminate 11% to 30% of office visits through the use of mobile health technologies, like remote monitoring, email, or text messages with patients.[23] Smartphones and tablet computers are now in use in 80% of health care organizations.[24] The introduction and use of EHRs and other mobile and e-devices have major implications for organizations, including the training and process of integrating these tools into the culture.

An Aging Workforce and Changing Demographics of Patients Demographic changes and technological advances are leading to increased health care use. The baby boomer wave is reaching age 65, with the number of people over age 65 expecting to more than double from 40 million in 2010 to more than 88 million in 2050.[25] This segment of the population utilizes three times more health care in terms of cost. Nearly half of Medicare beneficiaries have three or more chronic conditions, which are growing in prevalence across all age groups.[26] The rising incidence of obesity will likely lead to a further increase in chronic conditions as well.

The diversity of population across the United States also continues to rise. The Hispanic population is projected to more than double between 2000 and 2050, while the size of the Asian population is projected to increase by 79%.[27] These trends imply that the prevalence of certain diseases, which vary by ethnic background, will increase and that the cultural needs of diverse populations will have to be accounted for in service delivery.

At the same time that the number of elderly and diverse populations grow, so do the health care professionals working within the industry. The current U.S. health care system is powered by baby boomers. The average age of registered nurses in the United States is 47[28] and 38% of physicians are over 50.[29] The entire senior management cadre of most hospitals and health systems are older boomers. A 2008 Institute of Medicine report projects a shortage of 868,000 registered nurses and 284,000 physicians in 2030, given the needs of the aging population.[30]

A nationwide shortage of faculty will only exacerbate these projections, as the average age of nursing faculty is about 57.[31] More than 75% of nursing schools in one survey identified lack of faculty as a main barrier to admitting more nursing students.[32] Shortages will only serve to drive up salary costs and force employers to bring more creative approaches to job roles and work environments.

22-1c Opportunities for Organization Development Practice

Despite the uncertainty and difficult trends facing the industry today, OD practitioners can significantly influence the process and outcomes of change in the health care environment. Such an influence will require two critical competencies that have not necessarily been required in the past. Effective OD practitioners in health care will need to possess robust expertise in managing large-scale change and maintain a keen awareness of the environmental and industry trends affecting their client organizations. In combination with traditional OD practices, such as visioning and goal setting, future search conferences, small- and large-group facilitation, process improvement, team development, and conflict mediation, practitioners should support their clients' needs for comprehensive approaches that strategically align people, systems, and cultures. There are five primary areas of opportunity for OD practitioners. These include: developing leaders and teams' strategic and emotional intelligence; shifting organizational systems to a new paradigm; designing aligned cultures; delivering comprehensive learning programs; and finally, creating engaged employees.

Developing Strategic, Emotionally Intelligent Leaders and Teams In an industry fraught with uncertainty, health care leaders will need to develop competencies that fall under the banner of emotional intelligence (EI).[33] This behavioral science model embraces four key domains: self-awareness, self-management, social awareness, and relationship management. EI is described as "how leaders handle themselves and their relationships."[34] Said another way, "leaders' emotional states and actions do affect how the people they lead will feel and therefore perform. How well leaders manage their moods and affect everyone else's moods, then, become not just a private matter, but a factor in how well a business will do."[35] Thus, this ability allows leaders to expand their capacity to adapt to change, maintain calm in a constant state of ambiguity, all the while maintaining their core values, sense of purpose, and vision. EI also enables leaders to relate to their partners and stakeholders with intentionality, candor, and transparency so that they can more consistently meet their needs. Not only will future leaders need to know how to bring forth their best under these challenging conditions of change and high stakes, they will also need to bring out the best of those around them. This new environment inherently demands more awareness of self and others than ever before.

In terms of transparency, leaders must be emphatic about truth-telling. Paul Craig, Assistant Vice Chancellor of Human Resources & Risk Management for University of California, San Diego Health System, underscores that the system will require more accountability than in the past: "Ten years ago, hospitals could keep their outcome data fairly private. Now, the public recording of outcome data is being used by payers and employers to make choices about which providers to select." Thus, leaders who proactively share information with patients and partners will go far in building the public's confidence in this vital industry.

Moreover, emotionally intelligent leaders and teams tend to be higher functioning: "When people feel good, they work at their best. Feeling good lubricates mental efficiency, making people better at understanding information and using decision rules in complex judgments, as well as more flexible in their thinking."[36] Leaders and groups that embody this self and social awareness manage themselves more effectively through challenge, leaving them with more energy to spend on broader, strategic needs of the business, another key requirement of leaders in this shifting landscape. No longer is tactical execution the sole differentiator between good leaders and great ones. Leaders must be self-aware, knowledgeable of environmental trends, and strategically oriented to ensure their organization is at the forefront of change, not reacting to it. Cindra Syverson, Senior

Vice President of Human Resources for Providence Health System, emphasizes this growing leadership need: "Given the nature of the acute care environment, it is often difficult for leaders to focus their time externally. Given the future environment, it will be essential for leaders to scan the horizon in order to link their strategies to the scenarios playing out with competitors, insurers, consumers, employers and in the political environment." OD practitioners' expertise in executive leader and team development, and strategic change has a vital role to play in transforming organizational health. OD practitioners can also add value by sharing best practices from industries outside health care that leverage successful change management and development practices.

Shifting Organizational Systems to a New Paradigm Recent legislation mandates a new paradigm of partnership and adaptability across all ends of the care spectrum, creating a substantial opportunity for OD practitioners to thoughtfully codesign organizational structures, management systems, and industry relationships that reflect this focus on collaboration. Unlike other sectors of the marketplace, health care has traditionally been slower to adopt cutting-edge management processes. Instead, silos, division, and hierarchy characterize the sector and make innovation and/or communication difficult to initiate and sustain. Now, management processes and delivery of care methods between providers will need to be much more coordinated and open, suggesting that how organizations are designed and operated needs to reflect a similar degree of openness and flexibility. One example may include shifting to a decentralized corporate support structure, reducing waste and increasing consistency in standards across an organization. Another example might include a greater role for OD in supporting mergers, acquisitions, and partnerships so that systems are organized to maximize the speed of learning and are aligned on mutual, strategic goals of coordinated patient care. Ed Tyson, former VP of Process Improvement for Sun Health care Group, emphasizes: "Health care needs to stop fundamentally treating itself as isolated from the business world at-large in terms of recruitment, selection, and retention; leadership and management; education and training; workplace and workflow design; organizational structure; etc. We need to know, understand, and deploy what is possible given today's human and industrial technologies, regardless of service, sector, or continent."

Supporting Aligned Cultures With a new paradigm for how the health care system manages and delivers patient care, the need to create effective cultures that align the new incentive/reward systems, new roles, and more efficient work processes with this evolved strategic focus is greater than ever. These new incentive structures will emphasize customer service, collaboration, and adaptability, so health care organizations whose cultures match those characteristics will likely see more positive returns in terms of talent attraction, retention, and performance. In addition, organizations that can effectively cultivate a culture of openness and learning, as opposed to hierarchy and control, will be most proficient at addressing the shift in focus to integrated patient care. Kim Martinez, VP of New Market Operations for DaVita Rx, suggests: "There is this concept emerging in the medical field of 'team sport.' Physicians have traditionally been seen as all-knowing, having all of the information they need and generally working autonomously. The world is changing. There is much more information available now, making it unrealistic to expect a physician to know everything all of the time. Bringing in a more collaborative, cross-functional approach will be critical for the medical field going forward. However, making this transition may be difficult. It will require physicians and other caregivers to work in new ways, embracing the concept of 'team sport' vs. autonomous 'all-knowing physicians' who are expected to know everything all of the time."

OD practitioners can contribute to the intentional creation and maintenance of such cultures. In addition, with the advent of new technological advances, such as EHRs, and innovative care delivery methods, new roles are being created every day to support the influx of data (e.g., informatics analysts) and higher coordination of care (e.g., hospitalists). Organizations that adapt to changing roles, data systems, and new reward structures will be notably more successful in creating competitive advantage. Moreover, OD practitioners can share process improvement and work redesign insights and methodologies, such as lean performance improvement or Six Sigma. Operating in a more efficient, connected manner can help ensure that the entire system reduces costs and achieves highest quality outcomes for patients.

Delivering Comprehensive Learning Programs Building a variety of skills and competencies deeper within health care provider systems will be another imperative in the new environment. OD can build on its traditional role of supporting training and development functions by addressing organizational learning needs related to customer service, clinical and technical skills, change management, lean performance improvement, and leadership training. First, as the incentive/reward system changes to focus on a value-based model, where patient satisfaction and quality metrics drive reimbursements to providers, all employees of health care organizations—from the front-line to the C-suite—must become increasingly adept at serving their customer/patient/partner needs or face dire consequences. Second, education programs will also need to develop employees' knowledge and skills to support new processes and roles, especially around new clinical practices and technologies. Third, organizations that teach and enforce process improvement methods throughout all levels will be well-served as they attempt to meet mandates to reduce cost while improving overall care quality. Fourth, the emerging health care environment requires the adoption of both management and leadership best practices to ensure that all health care organization members are applying effective management processes and emotionally intelligent leadership behaviors. Dr. J.D. Fitz of Sound Physicians reiterates the importance of leadership education within the physician population: "Training doctors around leadership is a huge need. Most doctors can talk to patients, but not each other to improve performance. It's about optimization of physician leadership."

Creating Engaged Employees The massive transformation of the industry in terms of operational design, cultural and leadership requirements, skill and role expectations, and a rapidly aging workforce, will challenge employee retention in the years to come. Sally Haslett, Global Head of Human Resources, Oncology Translational Medicine at Novartis, explains: "[Health care] is a competitive space with a war on talent." Recent OD research underscores the pertinent value in measuring and nurturing employee engagement, which can be defined to include "involvement and a heightened ownership of work, consisting of pride, identity, and connection to a work role in which the employee is energized, dedicated, and engrossed in their job."[37] It also involves "passion for work, in which an employee actively contributes to the improvement of the organization (activation)." During times of significant change, employee engagement is more critical than ever in long-term performance. Paul Craig explains: "The tendency during times of great change is for leaders to put their heads down and work harder. I've seen a fair number of health care leaders get tense and adopt narrow views, reducing their 'heart and soul' engagement. I sense a lot of people pulling back, getting disengaged, and overwhelmed."

Health care leaders can find tremendous value in partnering with OD practitioners with expertise in this arena to ensure they are cultivating an organizational environment in which their employees, physicians, and other partners feel connected, highly supported, and eager to shape the future of their companies for the next generation. An engaged workforce will be the competitive advantage for organizations looking to lead the reshaping of this uncertain, yet fundamental landscape.

22-1d Conclusions

The health care industry offers unprecedented challenges and opportunities. OD practitioners can influence growth and development by linking their efforts to the strategies of the organization, demonstrating competence and integrity, and being able to facilitate the integration of people and processes across traditional departmental and organizational boundaries.

This opportunity comes with a challenge. At a time when each dollar and every resource in health care is being closely scrutinized, the inherent value of the OD approach is being tested for validity. Clients, under increasing pressure to demonstrate the added-value of key activities will, in turn, subject OD practitioners and their change interventions to the same testing. The practitioner must seek a balance between responsiveness and relevance while maintaining a commitment to the core values that have defined OD, namely the equal importance of human needs and the creation of a work environment that allows growth, fulfillment, and performance.[38]

22-2 Organization Development in Public School Systems**

> At the present time, public education is in peril. Efforts to reform public education are, ironically, diminishing its quality and endangering its survival. We must turn our attention to improving the schools, infusing them with the substance of genuine learning and reviving the conditions that make learning possible.[39]

This section frames the complexity and evolutionary changes taking place in U.S. public schools, identifies the forces pushing for changes in the traditional models of schooling, and discusses the causes of failed large-scale reform efforts. It also describes the emerging concept of professional learning communities (PLCs) as a model for schools and suggests that OD practitioners are in a unique position to support this reform.

22-2a A Complex, Diverse, and Evolving K-12 Educational System

Great debate continues as to which purposes should be prioritized in modern education. A number of change forces are stressing the current system and many educational institutions in the United States are being criticized for continuing to serve purposes that no longer exist in ways that are no longer relevant. Rooted in the industrial age, assembly-line concepts of education are still deeply embedded in many schools even though the circumstances upon which these concepts were based have disappeared or changed dramatically. In fact, educational delivery systems and their related outcomes are undergoing tremendous societal scrutiny. Dissatisfaction with the status quo has resulted in unprecedented competition, such as charter schools, private schools, and home schooling. In response to the stress of changing circumstances and increased competition, "the system has turned up the speed on the assembly line—doing what it has always done only faster and harder.

**Written by Dr. Linda Purrington and Dr. Paul Sparks from Pepperdine University's Graduate School of Education and Psychology.

While this might produce a bit more output, all of us—students, teachers, and parents—should be asking whether or not it produces more learning."[40]

The United States does not have a national school system. Each state's own laws regulate education, and standards and curriculum are determined at the state and local levels. The federal government provides guidance and funding for federal educational programs in which public and private schools participate and the U.S. Department of Education oversees these programs. U.S. schools rank high globally in expenditures per student, but low in percentage of GDP. Almost 90% of K-12 American students attend public elementary and secondary schools that receive 92% of their funding from state and local taxes. Students who do not attend public elementary and secondary schools typically attend tuition-funded private schools and four out of five private schools are run by religious groups. In these schools, traditional academic courses as well as religious instruction are part of the curriculum. In addition, a growing number of parents homeschool their children themselves.[41]

This means of governance and finance makes for a very complex system of American education. Individual schools can draw upon a number of resources from different public and private institutions and must be accountable to multiple agencies. For example, a student may attend a public or private school whose curriculum must meet standards set by the state, some of whose programs or specific courses may be financed by federal funds or local foundation monies, and whose sports teams may play on local, publicly owned fields.[42]

Public schools are monitored for quality by local school boards and by state accrediting agencies. Charter schools are public but have fewer restrictions than traditional schools. Private schools are not subject to the same controls as public schools. For example, not all private schools have credential requirements for their teachers and administrators. Student performance is typically the most important measure of school quality and is determined by state and local formulas and assessments. In addition to norm-referenced, criterion-referenced, and locally developed assessments, school systems utilize other accountability data for determining student performance, including but not limited to college promotion rates, high school graduation and retention rates, suspension and expulsion rates, grades and grade point averages, and English Learner proficiency and re-classification rates.

School systems thus present a uniquely challenging environment for the application of OD. Schools differ in their structure, purpose, and process from most other organizations. Schools cannot be characterized simply as organizations or communities. They have characteristics of both. The degree to which one or the other of these characterizations dominates has been influenced by societal transformations and shifting purposes and values. Pink drew on three metaphors to describe societal progression in the United States from the 18th to the 21st centuries: "We have moved from an economy built on people's backs to an economy built on people's left brains to what is emerging today: an economy and society built more and more on people's right brains."[43] Butts categorized the purposes of education that have "been in play" throughout the progression as: academic discipline, social efficiency, individual development, vocational competence, freedom, equality, and community. He further described these purposes as "intersecting, competing, overlapping, fuzzy around the edges, if not in the center ..."[44]

22-2b Change Forces

A number of forces are challenging traditional models of schooling, including the changing nature of communication and learning, the evolution of the workplace and required skills, increased diversity, increased competition, and tough economic times.

The Changing Nature of Communication and Learning Internet scholar Clay Shirky suggests that changes in communication equate to changes in society itself. The explosion of communication technology at the end of the 20th century has forced a rethinking of teaching and student competencies.[45] Global access to information, collaborative virtual spaces, mobile technologies, participatory media, and multiplayer online games offer rich new learning opportunities independent of traditional school settings. Students have as much access to information as their parents and teachers. New educational technologies provide a mix of fun and learning in ways that schoolrooms are unable to match. Moreover, these learning technologies are student-centric. They can access them when they are ready and allow them to interact with their peers in mutually interesting ways. Innovative educators now work with students online. Emailed homework, discussion topics in newsgroups, dialogue using chat or IM, posting group work on blogs, and sharing video in real time are a few examples. Homeschooling is another fast growing, nontraditional educational option that is greatly facilitated by new technology.[46]

Evolution of the Workplace and Required Skills Global competition for jobs is a pressing national issue and new skills will be required for the future, not all of which are entirely known. In 2003, the Partnership for 21st Century Skills, in collaboration with business leaders, proposed a new set of competencies necessary for the success of students.[47] These competencies reflect the complexities of today's workplace and include Global Awareness, Creativity and Innovation Skills, Media Literacy, and Leadership/ Responsibility. While these 21st Century Skills have been widely praised, they have still not been adopted nationally.

Also, the assumption of a captive female labor market for teachers has disappeared as women have pursued a broader range of careers. Expectations for teacher certification have increased, teaching conditions have become more demanding (particularly in urban settings), and pay has not kept pace with other professions—circumstances that have resulted in more than half of new teachers leaving the profession within their first three years and raising serious concerns about teacher quality.

Increased Diversity Today's students are more diverse ethnically, culturally, and linguistically than ever before. Their learning needs, interests, and well-being require culturally responsive instructional practices and outreach to parents. Educators need to be sophisticated in their understanding of how culture and language influence identity and learning, well-versed in first and second language acquisition pedagogy, and equitable in their beliefs and actions in order to promote high levels of achievement for all students.

Increased Competition The weakened traditional educational system is manifested in discontentment on the part of students, administrators, and parents and has resulted in unprecedented competition. Strong political, economic, and religious forces have given rise to a plethora of options. Public schools, private schools, charter schools, and home schooling each has its own unique ideology, curriculum, and practices. Some options are not available to families who lack resources. Indeed learning has moved out of schools and classrooms altogether into cyberspace aided by new collaborative communication tools. New formats including serious games, online museums, and global learning communities are challenging the status quo.

Tough Economic Times The economic divide between students with resources and those without is widening. Children represent a disproportionate share of the poor in the United States; they are 24% of the total population, but 36% of the poor population. In 2010, 16.4 million children, or 22%, were poor.[48]

Poverty can impede children's ability to learn and contribute to social, emotional, and behavioral problems. Poverty also can contribute to poor health and mental health. Risks are greatest for children who experience poverty when they are young and/or experience deep and persistent poverty. Students in poverty are at great risk of failing and dropping out of school when they do not receive the additional resources they need to succeed academically.[49] Many public school districts are very challenged in the current economic times to provide the resources that these students need.

22-2c Disappointing Reform Efforts

In response to the stress of changing circumstances and increased competition, three large-scale school reform efforts have been launched over the past 30 years: the Excellence Movement; the Restructuring Movement; and the High Standards, Testing, and Accountability Movement. All three have been criticized for focusing on issues marginal to teaching and learning, and producing few if any positive outcomes. Each of these efforts are described and the reasons for their failure considered. Understanding these movements can inform better OD practice and intervention design.

The Excellence Movement The Excellence Movement was a response to the April 1983 National Commission on Excellence in Education's assessment of education report, *A Nation at Risk*. The Commission linked concerns over national security to substandard education in American public schools and generated considerable debate. In response to the report, hundreds of state and national task forces sprang into action to investigate the condition of U.S. public education. However, the Excellence Movement offered no new direction. Initiatives associated with this movement were described as "more of the same," including longer school days and longer school years. Roland Barth aptly described some of these efforts as nothing more than moving the same furniture around in the same room.[50] Within five years, the Excellence Movement had come and gone.

The Restructuring Movement In 1989, President George H.W. Bush convened the nation's governors for a summit meeting on education. Governors had convened only three times before in the nation's history to consider a single topic. A two-part strategy emerged from the summit: (1) a call for national educational goals and standards and (2) a national exam system. The result of the summit was the identification of national educational goals, Goals 2000, and a new emphasis on site-based reform. Ensuing efforts came to be known as the Restructuring Movement and included some common features: site-based management with meaningful authority over staffing, program, and budget; shared decision making; staff teams with frequent, shared planning time and shared responsibility for student instruction; multiyear instructional or advisory groups; and heterogeneous grouping in core subjects.

Great optimism was associated with the Restructuring Movement. The term suggested a comprehensive redesign and systemic transformation of the schools. Simplistic, more-of-the-same approaches were replaced by the mindset that fundamental changes were necessary if schools were to develop the capacity to successfully address the significant challenges with which they were presented. Roland Barth wrote, "The advent of the restructuring movement brought a sudden confidence that teachers and principals, with the help of parents and students, can get their own schoolhouse in order."[51] However, research on the Restructuring Movement suggested that most schools focused on nonacademic issues, such as student discipline and parent involvement, rather than on core issues of teaching and learning. This left the teaching and learning process largely unchanged.[52] Newmann and Wehlage suggested that the term restructuring was used so widely and ambiguously that it soon lost any specific, universally understood meaning.[53]

The High Standards, Testing, and Accountability Movement: NCLB and Race to the Top President George W. Bush signed the No Child Left Behind (NCLB) Act in January 2002, prompting what has been dubbed as the High Standards, Testing, and Accountability Movement. The purpose of NCLB was to improve public schools across the United States. NCLB reauthorized the Elementary and Secondary Education Act of 1965 (ESEA) to provide all students with a fair and equal opportunity to have a high-quality education. NCLB required annual testing in grades three through eight and imposed sanctions on schools that failed to make Adequate Yearly Progress (AYP). Under NCLB, every state was required to set grade-level standards and create a system to determine how students are meeting those standards. The system had to be based on challenging benchmarks in English language arts and mathematics. The intent of NCLB was to hold schools and school districts accountable for results and to ensure that all students were learning. School districts and schools that failed to meet AYP were required to undergo improvement, corrective action, and restructuring procedures designed to get them back on track and meet standards.

The remedies and sanctions imposed by NCLB were ineffective and did not result in high standards or high accomplishment.[54] The NCLB legislation proved to be punitive and based on flawed assumptions about how to improve schools. For example, it assumed that higher test scores on standardized tests of basic skills were synonymous with good education. As one evaluation stated, "Testing is not a substitute for curriculum and instruction. Good education cannot be achieved by a strategy of testing children, shaming educators, and closing schools."[55]

More recently, the Race to the Top reform initiative is being implemented. Race to the Top is a $4.35 billion United States Department of Education contest created to spur innovation and reforms in state and local district K-12 education. It is funded by the ED Recovery Act as part of the American Recovery and Reinvestment Act of 2009 and was announced by President Barack Obama and Secretary of Education Arnie Duncan in July 2009. To be eligible, states had to use value-added assessment measures, including student test scores in teacher evaluations. States were awarded points for satisfying certain educational policies, such as implementing performance-based standards (often referred to as an annual professional performance review) for teachers and principals, complying with nationwide standards, promoting charter schools and privatization of education, and computerizing the curriculum. In addition, the White House announced a $350 million federal grant funding the development of assessments aligned to the common standards. The common standards were developed by the National Governors Association and the Council of Chief State School Officers with funds from the Bill and Melinda Gates Foundation, the Charles Steward Mott Foundation, and others. Forty-eight states have since adopted these standards.[56]

Although many states have competed to win the grants, politicians, policy analysts, thought leaders, and educators have criticized Race to the Top as highly politicized. Teachers' unions and educators have complained that the tests are an inaccurate way to measure teachers, and have not worked in the past. Conservatives have complained that it imposes federal control on state schools. Critics say that high-stakes testing is unreliable, that charter schools weaken public education, or that the federal government should not influence local schools. Critics further contend that the reforms being promoted are unproven or have been unsuccessful in the past.[57] However, there are no definitive evaluative results on this initiative at the present time.

Reasons for Failed Reform Dufour and Eaker offer five reasons why these large-scale reform efforts have failed to produce meaningful change in schools: (1) the complexity of the task, (2) misplaced focus, (3) lack of clarity on intended results, (4) failure to appreciate and attend to the change process, and (5) lack of perseverance. Change is difficult in any organization, but changing something as complex as the fragmented system of education in the United States is an especially challenging task.[58] Fifty states operate over thousands of relatively autonomous school districts. These districts serve millions of students and are governed by local school board members. Constituents may agree that education is a national problem, but disagree about the quality of schools in their communities. While some teachers, students, and parents are disenchanted with their local schools, others staunchly defend their schools as serving their neighborhoods well.

Prior reform efforts have not directly addressed the quality of student learning. They have instead focused on peripheral issues outside of the classroom. Although there seems to be general agreement that the educational system needs improvement, there is little consensus around goals for improvement, what constitutes success, and how success should be measured. A need exists to shift the focus of reform efforts from marginal changes to core issues of teaching and learning and strategies that have proven to be effective. Subsequently, a need exists to clarify and articulate desired results in meaningful terms.

Failure to appreciate and attend to the change processes associated with organizational and system reform has resulted in superficial, short-lived, and failed efforts. As this text has explained, the change process requires skillful planning from beginning efforts to "sustaining" desired outcomes. Top down and bottom up initiated changes are likely to meet with resistance when not fully supported. Practitioners in schools who experience an endless array of reform "du jour" initiated one moment and abandoned the next are reluctant to persevere and devote the time and energy to what may be perceived as yet another fad. "This too will pass" becomes the pervasive thinking and teachers close their doors and go about their business as usual. Even changes that are believed to be important by a majority of persons are likely to be "stopped in their tracks" if they are not carefully supported with guidance, time, resources, opportunity to collaborate, opportunity to problem-solve, encouragement, celebration, and a plan for sustaining the change over time.

In addition to the five reasons for failure identified by Dufour and Eaker, inattention to the features that distinguish schools from other businesses has also contributed to failed reform efforts. Business in the schoolhouse is different than business elsewhere.[59] Education is a more purely industrial-age institution than is business. Although business borrowed and implemented industrial-age ideas, it was not created with these ideas. The modern school, on the other hand was conceived with the factory model in mind and has evolved into the school system we know today. School systems are far more tightly embedded in larger social systems than are businesses. Individual schools are nested within local districts, which in turn are nested within state departments that set policy and standards. As a result, schools are directly and immediately affected by changes in policy. Schools are part of communities in different ways than are businesses. Parents play an important role in school governance. They not only have goals for what and how their children learn, but they also influence school operations as a whole.

Senge suggests that the degree to which the industrial-age school lives in each of us can be a sobering realization from a standpoint of innovation and adaptation. He suggests that we begin by challenging industrial-age assumptions about learning such as: children are deficient and schools fix them; learning takes place in the head, not in the body as a whole; everyone learns or should learn in the same way; learning takes place in the classroom, not in the world; and there are smart kids and dumb kids. Senge also recommends that we challenge the following industrial-age assumptions about schooling in order to create conditions and foundations for change: schools are run by specialists who maintain control, knowledge is inherently fragmented, schools communicate the truth, learning is primarily individualistic, and competition accelerates learning.[60]

22-2d Considerations for OD Practitioners

Change forces and emerging models of schooling, such as PLCs, suggest challenges and opportunities for OD practitioners to consider. These challenges demand thoughtful and strategic application of OD principles. School transformation is a difficult and evolving process. Growing authentic learner-centric communities requires deep changes in theory and culture for traditional schools. Embracing the concept of school as a center for inquiry in which children and adults construct their own understandings of the world in which they live, calls for a significant shift in mindscape.[61] OD principles can inspire the most promising of school improvement practices—those that place emphasis on the teacher, the classroom, and the patterns of interaction that exist among teachers and between administrators in the school.[62] Several of the most promising applications follow.

Developing Professional Learning Communities PLCs provide a promising opportunity for OD practitioners. PLCs have been replacing the old model of schools as knowledge factories or organizations. The concept of schools as a learner-centered communities emerged in the 1990s and has continued to evolve. Peter Senge described schools as learning organizations in his book, *The Fifth Discipline*, and the term made its way from business literature to educational literature. In 1992, Sergiovanni translated one of Senge's five principles—team learning—to an educational context: the idea of school as a learning community, suggesting a family-like, close-knit connectedness among members.[63] A variety of authors have proposed characteristics and practices that reflect a learning community, including action and results-oriented focus; continuous improvement; supportive and shared leadership; shared purpose, mission, vision, values and goals; reflective dialogue and collective inquiry; and shared responsibility for students' learning.[64]

Rather than emphasizing externally imposed rules, regulations, monitoring, supervision, and evaluation systems to maintain control over teachers, PLCs are built around relationships and shared ideas. Relationships in communities are close, informal, cooperative, and trusting—similar to relationships found in families and other groups of people with close ties. Shared values, sentiments, and beliefs unite people in communities around common causes. Leadership in communities emerges from moral roots and is servant in nature. Leadership is initiated from "many different chairs," including leadership on the part of students, parents, and community members.[65] This in turn builds the leadership capacity of the school as a whole. Teams are formed with community needs and individual talents and strengths in mind. Efforts are made to distribute the work among those who are best suited. Building strength-based communities is a mindscape that replaces the deficit notion of fixing individuals and weaknesses. Learning communities are regularly engaged in learning and inquiry with a focus on results and continuous improvement.

Cultivating Trust and Learning Relationships An important first step in schools becoming authentic learning communities is the building of relational trust. A ten-year study of achievement in math and literacy in 12 Chicago public schools by the Center for School Improvement at the University of Chicago revealed that schools reporting strong positive trust levels were three times more likely to improve in reading and math than those with poor trust reports. OD values (respect, inclusion, collaboration, authenticity, self-awareness, and empowerment) are aligned with four components of relational trust associated with PLCs: respect for the importance of person's role and viewpoint, competence to administer one's role, personal regard for others, and integrity in words, actions, and ethics.[66] OD practitioners can help schools identify, acknowledge, and support learning relationships between peers, family members, and the community by promoting the values of self-awareness and empowerment. Family and community involvement are fundamental to student achievement in schools. OD practices can assist schools in gaining active engagement from family and community through the building of positive family and community relationships, effectively involving families in the school, and reaching out to family and community members. The National Parent Teacher Association offers six national standards for family involvement programs, along with practices that can provide a framework for OD support.[67] Standard areas include communication, parenting, student learning, volunteering, school decision making and advocacy, and collaborating with community. These are useful resources under most circumstances, but assume the local community and school district can provide family and community engagement. If the local socioeconomic conditions are inadequate to support the formation of a PTA or other outreach organizations, OD practitioners may need to consider alternative interventions, such as developing social change organizations as described in Chapter 21.

Creating a Collaborative Vision Four building blocks form the foundations of PLCs: mission, vision, values, and goals.[68] OD practices can support schools in the development of effective mission and vision statements. OD practices can also guide school efforts with regard to clarifying values and goal setting. Eaker, DuFour, and Burnette recommend that four critical questions be addressed in professional learning community mission statements: (1) If we expect students to learn, what is it we expect them to learn? (2) How will we know if they are learning it? (3) What will we do when they don't? and (4) How will we engage students in their own learning?[69] OD practices can also help PLCs develop effective vision statements through collaborative processes that promote ownership and unity. These processes can ensure that vision statements are based on relevant background information and research and that they clarify direction and priorities.

OD supported vision development can result in statements that are desirable, feasible, credible, and easy to communicate. OD practices can challenge members of the professional learning community to identify the specific attitudes, behaviors, and commitments they must demonstrate to translate vision into reality. They can also help communities to set goals, determine which steps need to be taken first, establish timelines, and identify measures of success. Interestingly, a common feature of these emerging learning strategies is the OD principle of community involvement. David Cavallo, director of the Center for the Future of Learning at MIT, has pushed for a new learning model called "emergent design." The design requires community development of learning goals similar to building design. He says, "the design and implementation of technology-enabled organizational change has not played a significant role in guiding educational thinking."[70] Perhaps it is time.

Improving Teaching Practice with Action Research A founding practice of OD, action research, has recently become an emergent practice among teachers seeking to improve their professional practice. The overarching goals of action research are to increase practitioner and community knowledge about the topic under study and to show results through improvements in education that have resulted from study. Methodological outcomes of action research for educators are to build professional capacity through critical reflection, promote focus and long-term engagement with issues that "matter most," develop local expertise, and leave practitioners more motivated and energized about their work. Participatory Action Research is based on five principles: (a) belief in human capacity, (b) unyielding commitment to social justice and equity, (c) value of collaborative work to individual educators and to their schools, (d) norms of professional and public accountability, and (e) mutual inquiry as a means to honor others, empower ourselves, and adapt to a changing educational environment.[71]

Whereas the effectiveness of traditional professional development practices are shown to be nominal, action research is growing as a strategy for honing skills and solving challenging learning problems. Teachers engaging in action research report greater control and satisfaction in their practices. Action researchers Jean McNiff and Jack Whitehead encourage educators to use the practice as a more effective approach to professional development.[72] Ravitch asks, "Can teachers successfully educate children to think for themselves if teachers are not treated as professionals who think for themselves?"[73]

Grounding Practice in Theory Theory should drive practice and specific methodologies used in the classroom. However, outdated and unsupported methods are still practiced in many classrooms. Social constructivism is the current most widely accepted learning theory. It suggests that students learn best by constructing meaning in social settings where ideas can be discussed. Social constructivism puts students at the center of learning. Each student is responsible for constructing their model of the world in community with peers and led by an inspired teacher. OD professionals adept at applying theory to practice can guide educators in the same process. Action research provides a powerful tool for helping teachers transform their practice and explore new methods grounded in the theory. Additionally, PLCs provide the motivation and the support to update methods.

Growing Leaders and Leadership Locally Traditional leadership models have largely failed public schools because they have ignored or marginalized the leaders already in the schools. Growing sustainable leadership capacity requires robust learning communities. In PLCs, common purpose, commitment, and action bonds members together in trusting and caring relationships and binds them to important values, purposes, and responsibilities. Leadership is a group activity linked to a practice rather than an individual activity linked to a person. Wenger's ongoing study of various communities of practice shows that communities naturally grow their own experts and leaders and internally negotiate responsibility in dynamic ways.[74] Consideration for situation and ability determines who assumes leadership for which responsibilities.[75] This approach is very different from imposed top down leadership styles of past. Lambert convincingly draws a parallel between the development of leadership and learning theory and sees leadership more organically. She observes and champions "acts of leadership" among teachers and parents who have been overlooked as leaders which amount to simple conversations.[76] OD practitioners should seek to discover, honor, and empower the local leaders of the learning community who are far more aware of the issues and solutions but have softer voices. In addition, they should seek to discover methods for developing that nascent leadership for the future good of the school and community.

Utilizing Technology as Catalyst for Innovation In *Disrupting Class*, innovation expert, Clayton Christensen, observes, "schools have done what all organizations are inclined to do when instituting a new technology. They have 'crammed' the new technologies into their existing structure, rather than allowing the disruptive technology to take root in a new model." He suggests a different focus on empowering students and teachers by providing a rich set of learner-centric tools to empower and access to a global content network to engage communities of learners.[77]

Mimi Ito, a cultural anthropologist, has discovered another approach in research done for the MacArthur Foundation. She observed how students use social media independent of school and found that new technologies have altered the way young people learn and interact. Her findings show how students actively and successfully use these new spaces for a new kind of self-directed, peer-based learning and that educators need to be encouraged to be more open to these spaces and platforms for learning.[78]

The story of Khan Academy is another great example of outside innovation. Video explanations intended for a family member now assist the understanding of a half a million online subscribers becoming a powerful social learning platform. Other popular media such as Twitter and Facebook support global social networks independent of schools where learning is shared. Games are another innovation with implications for education. It has been suggested that games are good for learning because they inherently teach many 21st century skills such as, systems thinking, leadership, accountability, adaptability, interpersonal skills, self-direction, and social responsibility.[79] Game systems can track interactions and deliver real time data on progress toward personal learning goals and even provide appropriate support information.[80]

These tools and innovations provide new opportunities to measure what matters, shifting from basic literacy to real-time assessment of 21st century skills called for in the National Educational Technology Plan.[81] OD practitioners can assist by applying the recent outside innovations and envisioning new platforms that will support learners rather than enforce teaching and testing.

22-2e Conclusions

Education in the United States is a complex, diverse, and continually evolving system. Schools differ in their structure, mission, and process from most other organizations and the purpose of education and best practices continue to be hotly debated. A number of forces, including changes in communication and learning, changes in the workplace and required new skills, increased diversity, increased competition, and tough economic times, are stressing traditional models of education and prompting change. Large-scale efforts to reform the system have been disappointing and criticized as focusing on issues marginal to teaching and learning and producing few if any results. Failed large-scale reform efforts have given rise to a new strategy for school improvement—PLCs. Considerations for OD practitioners with regards to supporting the transformation of schools to becoming PLCs include: developing trust and learning relationships, creating a collaborative vision, improving teaching practice through action research, grounding practice in research, growing leaders and leadership locally, and utilizing technology as a catalyst for innovation.

PLCs, however promising on a local level, may only result in pockets of success. Christensen suggests, "If we persist in believing that the problems of our schools can be solved by simply improving schools, we will never succeed."[82] He portrays education as a much larger ecosystem in which learning occurs as much and maybe even more outside of the schoolhouse than inside the schoolhouse. Based on his work with school districts and systems in the United States, United Kingdom, and Canada, Michael Fullan proposes a framework for what he describes as "whole system" and reform involving reciprocal partnerships across and within schools and communities, districts, and states. "Individual capacity is part of the development, but at the end of the day only collective capacity counts.

Coordination, focus, easy access to best ideas, the press of collaborative competitions and ultimately win–win outcomes are the drivers. There is simply and flatly no other way to get whole-system reform."[83] Christensen, Fullan, and others suggest a major paradigm shift in terms of understanding where and how learning occurs and how to improve learning through change efforts, adding to the complexities that educators and OD practitioners need to consider in order to be effective and relevant.[84]

22-3 Organization Development in the Public Sector***

Public-sector organizations in the United States, such as federal, state, and local governments, operate in a complex environment of competing political, social, and economic forces. Calls for the government to operate more efficiently, effectively, and accountably and to become more responsive and citizen focused are common. Legislation and programs aimed at improving government accountability, quality, and effectiveness are being introduced and adopted at all levels of government.[85] For example, Congress passed and President Obama signed the Government Performance and Results Modernization Act of 2010, updating the original Government Performance and Results Act that required federal agencies to create multiyear strategic plans, annual performance plans, and annual performance reports.[86] The new legislation creates a more defined performance framework and institutes quarterly reporting and reviews instead of annual ones.[87] In addition, states across the land are adopting legislation to reduce the cost of government and make it operate more effectively. For example, California Governor Brown signed public employee pension roll-back legislation aimed at reducing pension costs and discontinuing abuses such as "spiking."[88] The reform legislation intends to make the state's retirement system economically sustainable. Colorado is another example of more effective government. The state's new human resource system increases flexibility in hiring, improves the employee compensation structure, and better rewards employees through performance and tenure. Cast as the "Talent Agenda," a goal of the legislation is to attract top talent to its workforce.[89]

In addition, public-sector organizations face increasingly complex challenges in responding to citizens, crafting public policy, and providing public services. Conflicting public policy at the federal, state, and local level, coupled with unfunded mandates and restricted revenue further complicate their environment. Government's record of successfully responding has been spotty at best, with trust in government falling dramatically. In 2002, 60% of Americans said that they trust the government in Washington to do what is right "just about always" or "most of the time." By 2010, that percentage had dropped to 19%.[90] The Gallup organization has conducted similar polls about trust and satisfaction in government since 1972. In a recent poll, Gallup found that dissatisfaction rose from 39% in 2002 to 81% in 2011.[91] Less than half of Americans, 43%, down from 65% in 2001, now have a "great deal" or a "fair amount" of trust in the federal government to handle domestic problems.[92] Tragically, and at a time when political leadership is most needed, trust and confidence in the people who either hold or are running for public office is at historic lows.[93] In contrast, 2011 polling finds that 57% of Americans have a "great deal" or a "fair amount" of trust and confidence in state government to handle problems and just over two-thirds (68%) express even greater trust in their local governments."[94]

***Written by Raymond R. Patchett, city manager, City of Carlsbad, California, and Val Brown, Communications Department, City of Carlsbad.

In the face of the lingering Great Recession, terrorism, war, and social turbulence, these numbers at the federal level are unlikely to improve. Public participation, once the hallmark of the American democratic process, is suffering. Voter turnout in presidential elections has dropped from more than 62.77% in 1960 to 57.48% in 2008.[95] Nonpresidential elections find voter turnout dropping down to 38.5% in 2010 and similar low-levels for the prior nine elections.[96] As a result, public-sector organizations are engaging in a variety of efforts to increase citizen participation and involvement in hopes of developing greater public trust and confidence, making government more effective, and cutting the costs of government as they move further into the 21st century.

For example, on his first day in office, President Obama signed the Memorandum on Transparency and Open Government to build public trust and promote transparency, public participation, and collaboration.[97] To operationalize the initiative, he issued the Open Government Directive. It directed agencies to formulate an Open Government Plan, including the development of a strategic action plan for transparency, the creation of more opportunities for the public to collaborate and participate throughout the decision-making process, and the establishment of at least one specific, new initiative for implementation.[98]

At the local level, governments are supporting community building and neighborhood involvement initiatives such as the Connecting Community, Place & Spirit learning conference in Carlsbad, California, and the Block by Block neighborhood engagement program in Clearwater, Florida. At the same time, they are attempting to be more productive, efficient, and effective by downsizing and privatizing public services and introducing technology to increase effectiveness and productivity.[99] For example, the demand for certain public services on a 7/24 basis is making it necessary for government agencies to adapt and innovate. A report issued by the National Performance Management Advisory Commission proposed a Performance Management Framework to help governments measure results within resource constraints.[100] Similarly, The Alliance for Innovation (www.transformgov.org) has introduced nationwide initiatives to foster innovation at all levels of local government that also results in a culture of continuous improvement and learning. City governments, such as Phoenix, Arizona, and San Diego, California, are competing with the private sector through managed competition programs. Other cities, such as Carlsbad and Irvine, California, implemented performance management compensation systems that reward employees based on selected core competencies and the achievement of goals. All of these changes are being introduced to translate legislative mandates into measurable results and outcomes, such as citizen satisfaction and service quality.

These types of changes suggest a vital and important OD role in the public sector. Planned organization change efforts in this context can be as successful as those in private organizations,[101] and OD interventions are becoming more common and accepted in government. For example, the Great Recession is requiring that governments cut costs and find alternative methods to provide public services. As a result, state and local governments are outsourcing and privatizing the provision of many programs and services. At the same time, they are downsizing operations, implementing hiring freezes, pay freezes, and furloughs, and laying off employees to stem the rising cost of government.[102] Yet others are conducting community-visioning processes to engage citizens with their government; technology and social media has become an indispensable foundation for helping governments connect with citizens and operate more effectively; team building is being conducted for elected officials and staff at all levels of the organization; and performance management and compensation programs are being updated and implemented. Culture change initiatives are also finding their way into public-sector programs as a means to strengthen a shared knowledge of the values, mission, and vision of the organization. These OD interventions, and others included in this book, are helping public-sector organizations respond to the citizenry and transform themselves into citizen-focused, customer-driven, and results-oriented public-sector organizations.

Although public-sector OD applications are becoming more common, they face a unique set of circumstances, including a complex political and operational environment. Interventions often are conducted in the public arena among a number of stakeholders, each of whom has legitimate standing in the policy-making process—and often in the decision-making process. The climate and support for OD is complicated further by the structure of public-sector organizations. Although the legislative and political arena is interdependent with the administrative and staff domain, it is highly unlikely that both will be involved in the same OD intervention. If they are, each domain has a different role and operates based on different and sometimes competing values. To conduct planned change initiatives effectively, OD practitioners must recognize and appreciate these differences. This section highlights some key differences between the public and private sectors and discusses some of the implications for applying OD in public-sector organizations.

22-3a Comparing Public- and Private-Sector Organizations

Public- and private-sector organizations differ along four key dimensions: values and structure, the multiplicity of decision makers, stakeholder diversity and access, and the extent of intergovernmental relationships. Each of these differences is discussed along with its implications for OD practice. The discussion draws on the writing and research of John Nalbandian, H. George Frederickson, Bob Golembiewski, and John Bryson.[103]

Values and Structures Public- and private-sector organizations differ in important ways with respect to their values and structures. In private-sector companies, the key values are profitability and the creation of competitive advantage. The board of directors, who represent the shareholders, and the management team, who are tasked with implementing a strategy, share these values. Although public-sector organizations share a similar structural arrangement of representation and implementation, there are crucial differences in purpose and role that hold important implications for OD practice.

In contrast to the private sector, the overarching purpose of public-sector organizations is to govern toward greater public good and demonstrate responsiveness to public wants and needs. The public good is addressed through the adoption of laws and policies and the establishment of public services and programs that support a broad array of citizen needs that must, by law, be discussed and adopted in an open public meeting. Responsiveness is reflected in demands for representation, efficiency, individual rights, and social equity.[104] In service of these values and purposes, public-sector organizations also adopt a representation–implementation structural form. The representative function is known as the political or legislative domain, and the implementation function is known as the administrative domain.

The public sector political–administrative structure reflects the values and roles inherent in government organizations. In the classic theory of public administration, the political domain is led by elected representatives who pass legislation and enabling statutes in service of the public good. In turn, they delegate implementation of programs and statutes to administrative agencies.[105] The political domain includes both elected and politically appointed officials, and the administrative group includes the merit-based civil service and certain executives, such as city managers, who are appointed on the basis of professional rather than political criteria.[106] This structure mirrors the private sector's distinction between a board of directors and management.

Unlike private-sector organizations, however, the purposes and values within public-sector organizations are not shared necessarily by the political and administrative functions. For example, politicians serve at the pleasure of the public. Although private-sector board members are elected representatives of the shareholders, their elections are not as open and public as are those of political officeholders. Politicians must compete to get elected and continue to posture and compete to get reelected. As a result, political values of responsiveness, representation, social equity, and efficiency, and the ever present political survival value are reflected in an open and public process where the particular interests and values of a diverse set of constituencies are brought together to produce a common view of the public good. Clearly, politics is the art and science of government.[107]

Moreover, the political function is responsible for the establishment and oversight of an administrative organization that is designed to implement the outcomes of the legislative process. Generally, the mission of the administrative function is implementation and enforcement of the laws and delivery of public services or goods. The legislative mandates, rules, and procedures established to address public wants and needs make public-sector organizations less flexible than most private-sector organizations and constrain their ability to act outside of their legislative framework. Thus, the administrative function values partisan neutrality; selection and promotion on the basis of merit, specialization, and expertise; the use of information for analyzing public policy issues; recordkeeping for purposes of continuity; application of the work ethic; and the justification of decisions based on efficiency (achieving the most productivity for the money available) or economy (achieving a given level of productivity for as little money as possible) or both.[108] When elected officials are responding to the citizenry or setting policy, the political domain's values of responsiveness and representation may override the administrative values of functional expertise and economy. When such value conflicts occur, administrators are often caught in the tension between politics and their mandate to run an efficient organization.

These value differences, along with government's regulatory and taxation role, have contributed to the perception of government as a bureaucracy, which simply refers to the administration of a government through bureaus staffed with nonelected officials. Perceptions of bureaucracy are often negative, however, and include indifferent people exercising power through strict adherence to inflexible policies, rules, and procedures. In addition, government appetite for risk is extremely low, resulting in a plethora of rules and regulations fostered to minimize any possibility of something going wrong.

Although public- and private-sector organizations can take on the characteristics of a bureaucracy, such as departmentalization, vertical decision-making processes, and many formal rules and procedures, the characteristics are more pronounced in government organizations. A critical reason for this phenomenon is that government organizations are legislated into existence, giving the organization or agency life until it is legislated out of existence. As a result, the organization receives funding that sustains its existence regardless of performance. Although budgets at all levels of government are reviewed and adopted annually, the complete elimination of a public-sector agency or organization is rare. The effect is that public-sector organizations, despite their purpose, can be much less responsive to citizens and customers than private-sector organizations because they aren't directly reliant on the customer for funding to sustain their existence.

The political nature of the legislative and representation process and the functional expert and efficiency orientation of the administrative process produce important tensions in a public-sector organization. OD practitioners must be aware of these tensions and of the implications they have for OD practice. First, OD practitioners must understand that a public-sector organization's primary mission, unlike private-sector organizations, is set by law, and major changes can only occur through additional legislative action. Even so, appointed officials and staff have much flexibility and discretion on how to implement government services and programs. The implication for OD is that many of the interventions used to help private-sector organizations, such as strategic goal setting, performance management, succession planning, staff development and organization learning, culture change, and team building, can be used successfully in the public sector.

Second, public-sector interventions often require approval and funding from an elected board. This increases the probability that the design, especially one for citizen- and neighborhood-focused initiatives, will be scrutinized and challenged to ensure its efficacy. OD practitioners need to be ready to provide evidence of success for particular interventions in public-sector organizations.

Third, OD processes that support elected officials in citizen-focused initiatives or in enacting policy must consider the public environment in which they are being conducted. Public-sector organizations are subject to greater direct public access, media coverage, and a much broader array of responsibilities and more distributed power than are most private-sector organizations. As a result, most policy-level OD and citizen-focused applications will be conducted in public. OD practitioners must select processes that create a constructive environment on the one hand and allow for public participation and review on the other. In addition, OD interventions must account for the vulnerability that elected officials, and sometimes public administrators, experience. For example, the results of a community-visioning process may serve as the political platform for candidates seeking the same public office that the incumbents leading the visioning process currently hold. OD practitioners need to be aware of this possibility as interventions are designed and implemented.

Fourth, the values of the political domain may differ from traditional OD values. The win–lose dynamics associated with passing legislation, mediating competing interests and political trade-offs, and balancing scarce resources can conflict with OD values of collaboration, teamwork, and efficiency. Improving organization effectiveness is an OD value often at odds with the political process. Last, administrative values and OD values are more likely to be aligned than with the political domain. To be effective, an OD practitioner must appreciate the tensions found in these differences.

Multiplicity of Decision Makers The public sector operates in an environment of largely unlimited access to multiple authoritative decision makers, a phenomenon designed to ensure that "public business gets looked at from a variety of perspectives."[109] The public expectation of government is full and legitimate access to all decision makers at every level. As a result, access to the decision-making process is broader and accountability is more dispersed than in private-sector organizations, where such access is uncommon and responsibility is more clear-cut.[110] Further, government fragmentation complicates the public-sector decision-making process where it is common for different public agencies or even different departments within the same agency to be responsible for different steps in governmental processes. Such fragmentation often makes it confusing and difficult for citizens, clients, customers, and even public officials and staff to understand who is responsible for what decision and accountable for what service or product.

In addition, Golembiewski noted that decision making by public officials, "tends to favor patterns of delegation that maximize their sources of information and minimize the control exercised by subordinates."[111] Specifically, the goal was to have all decisions brought to their level for action and review. While this may have been the case in the past, most public-sector organizations today are just as embroiled as the private sector in the task of evolving from a command-and-control decision-making structure to one of empowered workers. Within the constraints of the legal mandates and regulations governing the organization, public officials can delegate decision-making responsibility and accountability to the public worker closest to the citizen and customer if they want to and if it is in alignment with their leadership philosophy. The implication is that OD values that seek to expand worker self-direction and move decision making closest to the point of service are consistent with many government transformation efforts currently underway.

This multiplicity of decision makers and government fragmentation results in additional implications for OD interventions. First, multiple decision makers make it difficult to determine the identity of the client and the expected results. For example, a legislative body may adopt a policy, such as pay-for-performance, and direct staff to design and implement the program. In this example, both the legislative body and the staff are accountable and responsible for different parts of the intervention. Because the policy and administrative decision-making process are interdependent, the OD practitioner may be unable to gain the same level of clarity about who is the client, their authority, and an understanding of their responsibilities that is possible in the private sector.

Second, support and funding approval for OD interventions may be more difficult to obtain than in the private sector. The implication for OD practitioners, when operating across multiple departmental lines within the same organization, is most direct when entering and contracting. The project may require staff support for the intervention and legislative approval and funding for the project. As a result of the public approval process, OD practitioners must be able to explain the process and outcomes that will result and must expect that the public or politicians resisting the project may challenge the efficacy of the intervention(s).

Stakeholder Access As described earlier, a stakeholder is any group or individual who is affected by or who can affect the policies and operations of the public-sector organization—citizens, customers, political parties, corporations, employees, other governments, interest groups, critics, and so forth.[112] In contrast to private industry, the public sector conducts business in open public meetings and involves a "greater variety of individuals and groups with different and often mutually exclusive sets of interests, reward structures, and values."[113] In addition, citizens and interest groups have full access to public reports, documents, plans, and other background information via public records, public notices, all of which are archived and can be easily accessed on the Internet. OD practitioners must recognize that all stakeholders, most of whom bring different values, goals, or proposed solutions to public issues, have legitimate entry into the public policy and administrative processes. For example, stakeholders supporting the goals inherent in the Americans with Disabilities Act must compete for funding with stakeholders supporting the objectives inherent in the Endangered Species Act and its programs. Such conflicting interests and access creates a broad array of challenges for OD. Foremost among the challenges is helping diverse groups of people with different and competing interests to collaborate with each other in developing a common goal, or set of goals, to meet their respective interests that may represent an unpopular compromise to the demands of any individual group.

Anyone who wants to, citizens and even nonresidents (legal or not), may influence the policy-making process. Such broad access may exist in the private sector with respect to certain types of information, but the ability to influence corporate decisions and activities is much more restricted. What this level of public access does to the policy-making process is complicate and politicize the roles and responsibilities of politicians and administrators. Thus, the role demands of an elected official are much broader than the role demands of a private-sector board member. In addition, public-sector administrators, who are responsible for implementing public policy, have a duty to respond to the citizens, elected officials, and the staff that work for them. Everyone must be listened to and no one can be ignored. The implications of this network of roles and responsibilities for OD practitioners is that, in reality, anybody can make a demand for full disclosure about the OD initiative and in some instances ask to be involved in the process at virtually any level of a public organization. The likelihood is high that the individual or group will have legitimate standing to do so.

In addition, public-sector employees are stakeholders as a result of their legal right to form unions to represent them on matters concerning wages, hours, and working conditions. Because collective bargaining laws are structured for managing disagreement, a challenge for OD practitioners, if involved, is to help facilitate the process in a way where all parties perceive their interests have been considered and they feel heard. A poor labor relations environment and poor employee morale will make it difficult, if not impossible, to implement OD interventions successfully. It also becomes especially difficult because most public-sector unions get involved politically in supporting or opposing the reelection or election of a candidate. This involvement can create a "shadow effect" on the intervention, sometimes helpful and at other times negative, depending on whether or not the union supported the candidate who was elected. Importantly, OD practitioners must understand that, in contrast to the private sector, it is difficult to arrange stakeholder interests and expectations behind a common goal. Even so, practitioners must appreciate that "attention to stakeholder concerns is crucial because the key to success in public and nonprofit organizations is the satisfaction of key stakeholders."[114]

Intergovernmental Relations Governments are designed to both focus functions and power, and paradoxically, to disperse power and functions so that no one government or agency is all powerful. As a result, "government" comprises a latticework of independent agencies or departments providing different public services to the same citizens and customers. The result is an intergovernmental relations environment where federal, state, and local government share power, responsibility and, in some cases, resources.[115] These intergovernmental relationships, amplified by the multitude of special purpose public agencies and districts, such as water and sewer districts, raise several considerations for public-sector OD applications.

First, issues of coordination and power may emerge out of the sharing of responsibility across public-sector organizations in the provision of public services. Although the services may appear to be provided by "the government," the reality is that a number of public organizations often are responsible for different aspects of the same public service. For example, providing an integrated transportation system requires federal, state, special district, private developer, and local government participation. The federal government and special districts work together to provide train and bus service. The state works with federal and local governments to provide interstate and state highways. Local governments provide the local road system with financial assistance from development, federal, and state agencies. OD practitioners working on intergovernmental relations projects must utilize a network perspective that makes explicit these differences with the intention of reaching agreement about overarching outcomes, responsibility, and shared resources.

Second, local governments must implement federal and state laws and policies that often conflict with each other. In such cases, it is common to find that federal policies, such as the Clean Water Act and the Endangered Species Act, set goals and objectives for state and local government organizations, the federal policy objectives of which are in direct conflict with each other. As a result, it often falls to local government to balance out the competing policies to comply with all of the mandates. The resulting questions about which agency has the most power, who is responsible for what services or programs, and what level of government pays for those services or programs have important OD implications. For example, a network development intervention would recognize the existing transorganizational system and help all agencies, each with a different degree of power, achieve reasonable agreement in addressing legislative goals and implementation issues. As with the private sector, however, reaching agreement often involves contentious negotiations where differing positions are addressed, acceptable tradeoffs are found, and conflict is managed and resolved. Since different levels of government have different degrees of power, the OD practitioner could facilitate a positive result to the process by getting early agreement between the organizations on the overarching desired outcomes, and how decision making and conflict will be managed. Such an intervention is complex, however, because government agencies tend to preserve their power and protect their interests at virtually all costs while limiting their financial and resource responsibility. Appreciation for the mission and power relationships among agencies is critical in designing effective network development interventions.

Clearly, there are important differences between public and private organizations, and in many instances, the public-sector organization is more complex. In addition, one must appreciate the distinctions between the political domain and the administrative domain to consult or work in public organizations. With this understanding and an appreciation of the political arena in which public organizations operate, application of OD programs and techniques can be successful.

22-3b Recent Research and Innovations in Public-Sector Organization Development

The comparisons between the public and private sectors described above suggest that OD has a role in government and not-for-profit organizations. OD practitioners need to appreciate the inherent differences and understand that OD applications in the public sector are conducted in a complex political and organizational environment. Moreover, the unique features of public organizations—the values and structures, the multiplicity of decision makers, stakeholder diversity, and the intergovernmental relations environment—make OD applications challenging but not impossible.

Despite these challenges to OD practice in the public sector, there is growing evidence that OD interventions in government are successful, even when compared with change efforts in private industry. One review of 574 OD applications across the two sectors showed a similar pattern of predominantly positive results in both government and private industry.[116] Another study of 154 quality circle interventions in public and private organizations concluded that, although the highest levels of success occurred in private firms, overall success rates were substantial in both sectors.[117] A particularly rigorous review of 52 OD interventions in government and industry confirmed these conclusions. The findings suggested that OD interventions were similarly successful in the two sectors, and led the researchers to conclude that the results "serve to contradict the common notion that planned change is likely to be less successful in the public sector."[118] Finally, a recent review of the impact, over a 30-year period, of a four-year OD intervention in the Metro County Sheriff's Department concluded results improved organization climate and leader effectiveness; decreased employee turnover, jail breaks, and citizen complaints; increased resources allocated to the organization; and improved organizational effectiveness.[119]

These results have been achieved through a variety of OD interventions, including strategic change organization learning programs (Chapter 19), high-involvement approaches (Chapter 13), and restructuring processes often brought on by outsourcing and reengineering projects aimed at streamlining work flows and response times (Chapter 12). They also have been achieved by perhaps the most difficult of all processes in government, performance management and human resource interventions to change the civil service system so that the workforce is more flexible, development-oriented, and performance-driven. For example, a national survey of 987 state agencies found that 60% of them were using some type of strategic planning.[120] Another national survey found that all but three states have performance-based budgeting requirements,[121] and almost every state has enacted quality awards based on the Hammer Award and Malcolm Baldrige National Quality Award criteria.[122] In addition, local governments have conducted a variety of OD activities, such as team building, leadership development, large-group interventions, and total quality management programs, to become more effective.[123] Many local governments, like Carlsbad, California, are conducting Citizens Academies to "tell their story" and help citizens become more involved in their community. Finally, nongovernmental organizations are working to help improve government.

The National Innovations in American Government Awards, cosponsored by the Ford Foundation, the John F. Kennedy School of Government at Harvard University, and the Council for Excellence in Government, recognize examples of creative problem solving in the public sector. The National Civic League's All-America City Award recognizes exemplary community problem solving and is given to communities that cooperatively tackle challenges and achieve results. The recently announced Mayor's Challenge, sponsored by New York City Mayor Michael Bloomberg will award a $5M prize and four $1M secondary prizes to innovative ideas that improve urban life across the country.[124] The Alliance for Redesigning Government of the National Academy of Public Administration is a national network for all levels of government that advocate performance-based, results-driven governance. The Alliance for Innovation is a national network and clearinghouse of local government organizations with the mission of innovation in the provision of public services, sustaining meaningful connections, and renewing passion for public service.

22-3c Conclusions

OD applications have proven to be effective in public-sector organizations. Faced with many of the same pressures as private industry and some that are unique to government, public organizations will continue to use OD applications and interventions to transform themselves into citizen- and customer-driven, more effective and responsive, results-oriented organizations. But to be effective, practitioners helping government must appreciate the differences incumbent in public-sector values and organization structure; the differences in public and private organizations; and the mindsets of elected officials and government workers. OD practitioners need to understand public-sector organizations and tailor interventions to fit highly diverse, politicized situations where elected officials and bureaucrats struggle with moving toward a greater emphasis on reorganizing and outsourcing, continuous improvement, teamwork, customer focus, employee development, and learning. Although public-sector OD is difficult and challenging, the successes cited in this chapter illustrate that OD is an invaluable tool in helping public-sector organizations provide top-quality services.

22-4 Organization Development in Family-Owned Businesses****

Family businesses, such as Levi Strauss, Cargill, and Kikkoman (founded in 1630), are at once the most common and least understood types of business organizations. Often thought of as "mom and pop" operations, more than one-third of the *Fortune* 500

****Written by Dr. Otis W. Baskin, professor of management, Pepperdine University's Graziadio School of Business and Management.

companies are owned or controlled by families. Moreover, family businesses comprise the single largest demographic segment (between 65% and 80% of all worldwide businesses), generate half of the U.S. domestic product, employ 50% of the workforce.[125] One recent study showed that one-third of S&P 500 firms are family controlled and that they outperform the publicly controlled companies.[126]

While professional advisors, such as accountants, lawyers, and financial planners, have been serving this market for years, they are frequently puzzled by the complexity of relationships in these organizations. OD practitioners have recently begun to recognize that their ability to understand the dynamics of human and family relationships can address many needs within this context. This section explores the definition and model of the family business system, outlines critical issues facing family firms, and describes a typical planned change process.

22-4a The Family Business System

The most common definition of a family business is an organization where ownership and/or management control rests with a family (or families).[127] This definition covers a wide range from small owner-managed businesses to the Ford Motor Company where the Ford family owns a minority of the stock but retains voting control through a complex system of voting shares. Some families retain 100% of the ownership while employing "professional management" to run their business. Cargill, for example, is a globally dominant agri-business with more than $133 billion in annual sales and employing about 142,000 people in 65 countries according to its 2012 annual report. Its ownership is held by some 80 family members.[128] Even when founding families no longer have managerial or voting control they may still be a significant force in the decision making process of the firm. Many believe that the principal reason the board of Hewlett-Packard failed to ultimately support CEO Carly Fiorina in her strategy for the HP–Compaq merger was because she did not recognize the influence of the Hewlett and Packard families beyond their votes on the board. Finally, even in companies that have long since lost all current family involvement, values and vision from founding families can be powerful forces. The ability of Johnson & Johnson to survive the poisoning of Tylenol capsules is generally attributed to the application of the company's "CREDO" originally written when it was family-owned. OD practitioners can help firms understand these "soft" decision factors in governance and management decision processes.

Generally, family firms are understood to have several potential competitive advantages that public- or private-equity-owned organizations do not (see Table 22.1). These include higher employee loyalty (family and nonfamily), the ability to quickly move in and out of market niches due to their flexible form of organization, their long-term (versus short-term) orientation and the ability to keep information about the business out of view of the public and their competitors. A comparison of the ways Ford, General Motors, and Chrysler survived the 2008–2009 recession illustrates this point. With the Ford family still owning controlling interest, Alan Mullaly, an industry outsider, was able to bring transformative change while being the only "Big 3" CEO not to accept federal bail-out funds.[129] Such unity between owners and management in support of sweeping change is virtually impossible in a purely public company. When a controlling family owns a business, even if family members are not active in management, their "patient capital," interest in their communities, and unity of purpose can result in distinctive capabilities that competitors are unable to match.[130]

A family business system model is shown in Figure 22.1 that defines the three basic components of family business organizations. It helps to understand the differences

TABLE 22.1

Comparing the Uniqueness of Resources and Attributes of Family Firms

Resource	Definition	Positive	Negative	Nonfamily Firms
Human capital	Acquired knowledge, skills, and capabilities of a person	Extraordinary commitment; warm, friendly, and intimate relationships; potential for deep firm-specific tacit knowledge	Difficult to attract and retain highly qualified managers; path dependencies	Not characterized by the positives but have fewer limitations
Social capital	Resources embedded in a network, accessed through relationships	Components embedded in family; legitimacy with constituencies enhanced; development of human capital	Limited number of networks accessed; often excluded from elite networks (i.e., *Fortune 500* CEOs)	Networks can be more diverse; may be opportunistic in accessing and leveraging; sometimes used for managers' benefit–agency costs
Patient financial capital	Invested financial capital without threat of liquidation	Generational outlook; not accountable to strict short-term results; effective management of capital; allows pursuit of creative and innovative strategies	Nonfamily investors excluded; limited to availability of family's financial capital	Largely do not have the benefits or limitations
Survivability capital	Pooled personal resources family members loan, contribute, and share with business	Helps sustain the business during poor economic times or redevelopment of the business; safety net	Not all family firms have it	Do not enjoy due to lack of commitment by employees and stakeholders
Governance structure and costs	Costs associated with control of firm: examples include incentives, monitoring, and controls	Family-owned and operated firms' structures, trust, and family bonds reduce governance costs	Some family firms may not have an effective structure, trust, and strong family bonds, thereby producing greater governance costs	Professional management and capital diversification often increase governance costs

SOURCE: D. Simon and M. Hitt, "Managing Resources: Linking Unique Resources, Management, and Wealth Creation in Family Firms," *Entrepreneurship Theory and Practice* 27 (2003): 339–358.

between family firms and traditional businesses, and how OD practice must be modified. The family business system is composed of three different subsystems: the business, the owners, and the family with varying boundary strengths.[131] For each subsystem, there is an implicit understanding and, in the best practices, an explicit plan that determines how

FIGURE 22.1

Three Systems in Family Business

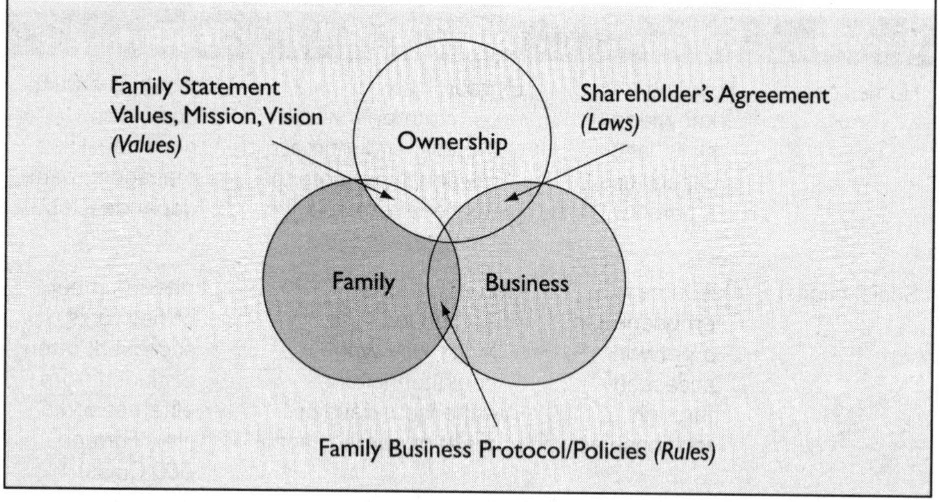

SOURCE: Adapted from Tagiuri and Davis, 1196. R. Tagiuri and J. Davis, "Bivalent Attributions of the Family Firm." Working Paper, Harvard Business School, Cambridge, MA. Reprinted *Family Business Review*, 9 (Summer, 1196): 49.

the objectives will be achieved with a governance structure that represents the people in that system. In the case of the founding generation of an owner-managed business, all three of these systems may completely overlap with a married couple both working in the business and sharing ownership. As the business and the family grow and ownership extends to subsequent generations these systems continue to move apart allowing for more variation in roles and creating more complexity in the system.

22-4b Business, Ownership, and Family Systems

One of the principal advantages of family businesses is the increased potential for unity of purpose and action between owners and management as described in the Ford example above.[132] The lack of this unity in publicly owned businesses is termed "agency cost" and was first described by Adam Smith in *The Wealth of Nations*: "(B)eing the managers of other people's money than of their own, it cannot well be expected that (the managers of public corporations) should watch over (public investors' wealth) with the same anxious vigilance with which partners in a private co-partnery frequently watch over their own."[133]

The business system may consist (depending upon the stage of development) of family and nonfamily managers, the strategic business plan, and a governance structure that included a board of directors and sometimes nonfamily directors or an advisory board. The strategic plan should outline the business goals, objectives, strategies, and organization design. The board of directors and advisors counsel the business's leader(s) on strategy implementation, organization form, and other key business policy decisions. There are potentially many reasons a family business may lack what is generally perceived as "professional" business systems.[134] It is not unusual to find family businesses with nonfunctioning boards made up of the founder and spouse and sometimes including a trusted attorney and accountant. These "nominal" boards often do not have meetings and only sign the required legal documents. One recent study of family firms found that only 54% of respondents rated their board as effective when only family members served as directors. However, when at least two independent directors served on a board where family members were in the majority, the effectiveness rating improved to 83%, and where independent directors were a majority board effectiveness was rated at 96%.[135] When siblings or cousins own a business where some owners are managers and others do not work in the business, a more functional and independent board of directors can help to preserve unity between management and owners. Independent directors can serve as objective observers and representatives of all owners through leadership of key board functions, such as succession planning, along with key roles on audit and compensation committees.

The ownership system consists of the business's owners (family and nonfamily), a shareholder's agreement (preferably a legal document), and a governance structure that may be represented in a formal shareholder meeting. The shareholder agreement should outline the owners' business goals and objectives, including risk tolerance, expected return on investment, liquidity goals, and a buy–sell mechanism. A shareholder meeting can provide a structure for owners to meet to develop and oversee their mutual interests in the business. Shareholder assumptions, including the buy–sell agreement, ownership succession, dividend policies, and investment options for business proceeds are relevant topics for this forum. Shareholders are responsible for reviewing the family enterprise plan (discussed below) and determining the relevant goals and policies to communicate to the board of directors/advisors. This is a critical step that sets family businesses apart from public companies: the ability of owners, directors, and management to be aligned in a vision for the business. It must be understood that more than equity is at stake in a family business; an unmistakable emotional component must be taken into account.[136]

Finally, the family system may consist of all family members (including those who have married into the family), their enterprise plan, and often a governance structure frequently referred to as the Family Council. The family enterprise plan outlines the family's philosophy, goals, and objectives for the business as well as other related family functions, such as community service, family gatherings, and philanthropy. The Family Council is often the body that represents the relevant groups of family members (those who work in the business and those who do not) and plans for discussions on such topics as educating family members on responsible ownership, developing policies on family participation in the business, communications and conflict resolution, and the financial education necessary to understand the performance of the business. Depending upon size and generation of ownership, business-owning families may have various degrees of structure. A "Family Assembly" consisting of the business founders, their direct descendants, and spouses may suffice in early transition planning for a first to second generation of ownership family. As the family and its business grows and becomes more complex it may form a "Family Association" consisting of family members who meet certain qualifications to vote on matters affecting the family. Large families with geographical diversity often move to a representative "Family Council" to serve as an executive decision-making body for issues that impact the family as a whole.[137] While this type of formal structure may seem overly complex in the context of family relationships, it can be a strong force in holding together a family with significant mutual assets.

22-4c Family Business Developmental Stages

The conventional wisdom of family business around the world is often summarized as "Wealth doesn't go beyond the third generation." This can be demonstrated with research that shows fewer than one-third of family businesses are able to make the transition of ownership into the second generation and only 12% of all family businesses survive into the third generation of ownership.[138] While some have pointed to these statistics as proof of the dangers of family business, they need to be understood in the broader context of business in general. For example, the expected life of a company on the S&P 500 list is only 10 years.[139] In fact, the survival rate of companies listed on the Dow Jones Industrial Average from its founding in 1886 through 1996 is about the same as the statistics for family businesses with one-third of the original firms disappearing every 25 years.[140] However, it cannot be denied that family businesses face some unique challenges as the business and the family change over time.

The challenge of generational transition in family business is complicated by the separation of the principal roles of *business, ownership*, and *family*. In the founding generation where one or both parents own and manage the business, these roles are embodied in the same people. However, as parents begin to make plans to retire and do estate planning, they often leave their children equal ownership of the business they have created. Usually one of the siblings (traditionally the oldest male) will be selected to become the next CEO. In such cases, the expectation often is that the successor will run the business "like dad" because that has been a successful model. If in fact the ownership of the business has transitioned from the founder(s) to their children, conflict can arise if the next generation attempts to lead the way the founder did. Siblings can be very quick to let a brother or sister know that they do not have the same rights their parents did. Second generation CEOs must learn that they have something mom and dad never had—shareholders.

When a sibling group owns a business together, they need decision-making and governance processes that the founders would have only found cumbersome and wasteful. This is especially true when the business does not employ all of the owners. Issues will arise about the amount of voice an owner who is not managing the business should have in the way their assets are being deployed. Also, questions of return on investment (ROI), shareholders dividends, or distributions versus bonuses to management and reinvestment in the business may become heated topics. When a business attempts to transition to a third generation of ownership (cousins), the issues of representation and voice in decision making can become even more explosive without well-designed governance processes in place.[141] The potential for conflict about the business can also create lasting divisions in a family unless sufficient planning takes place to maintain and build upon the trust relationships inherent in the family system.

22-4d A Parallel Planning Process

When a family owns a valuable asset, such as a business, their relationships can become much more complex. Deliberate planning is required to preserve the natural bond that exists in families and to make it possible for them to develop a shared vision for their mutual enterprise. Carlock and Ward describe a parallel planning process where "viable business strategy is still the outcome, but it is an outcome shaped by the concerns of the family."[142] Figure 22.2 illustrates the parallel processes leading to the simultaneous development of a family enterprise plan and a business strategy plan.

22-4e Values

At the center of the family business system model is a set of core values held by the family. Research shows that family members internalize family values, such as long-term reciprocity, filial obligation, and hard work for one's family.[143] They represent a key integration point for aligning the three subsystems listed above. However, values also best illustrate the

FIGURE 22.2

The Parallel Planning Processes

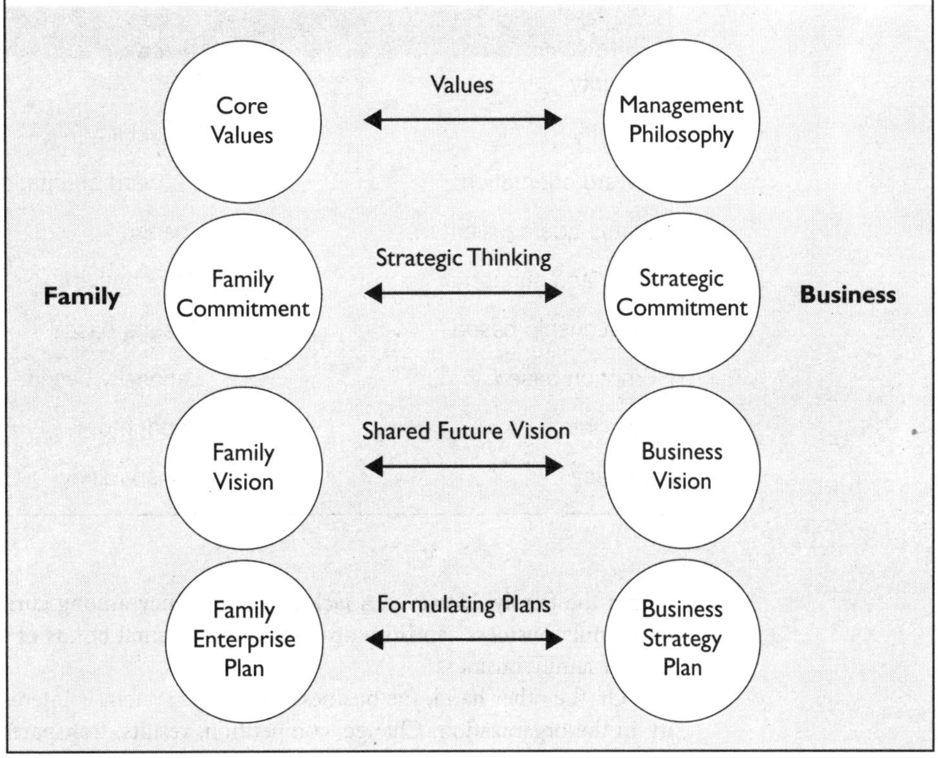

SOURCE: Carlock, Randel, S., and John I. Ward, *Strategic Planning for the Family Business*, Palgrave, 2001.

differences between family and nonfamily firms.[144] The complexity of the family business is a function of not only the interplay among the family, business, and shareholder systems, but the different (and often opposing) values that lie at the core of each system. For example, family and business system values are shown in Table 22.2. Based upon the values a family employs in making decisions about the business and the family they can be classified as either "Family First" or "Business First."[145] A family-first value system will place family above the business and may suboptimize business opportunity to benefit the family. A business-first value system is based upon the belief that a well-managed business will produce the most benefit for the family now and in the future.

Values of security and equality dominate the family-first approach. There is a strong inward focus on the family's dynamics, strong goals of keeping the system in equilibrium (even if it is an unhealthy equilibrium), and strong interest in maintaining unity and support. The family's continuity, even if the business does not prosper, produces a preference for stability and risk aversion. Relationships are most important, there is a great deal of emotion built into decisions, and one can only be born into (or married into) this system. Businesses typically hire the person that best fits the organization's needs based on knowledge, skills, and abilities; however, there is no job description to be a good family member. The family system places high import on family and business privacy. Families tend to hold very close financial information, family dynamics, and business information; often they do not want business and financial information shared even

TABLE 22.2

Family versus Business System Values

Family	Business
Security	Risk
Equality	Equitability
Inward orientation	Outward orientation
Status quo/equilibrium	Change
Unity and support	Competitive
Relationship based	Results based
Emotion based	Rationally based
Born into	Hired into
Secrecy	Transparency

within the family. However, a lack of transparency among current and intended owners of a family business can breakdown the fundamental bonds of trust that are the foundation of family business.

On the other hand, the business-first value system is interested in risk and equitability in the organization. Change, competition, results, transparency, and an outward orientation characterize business system values. Ideally, decisions are made rationally and objectively, and the system is composed of an often-changing mix of people who are hired into (or severed from) the organization. While 85% of those family firms who have identified a successor say they want it to be a family member,[146] the number of those family successors who would objectively fit the profile of the kind of leader the company needs based on its goals and strategy may be very different.

Thus, value dilemmas lie at the heart of how family businesses work. A family involved in a business can pursue its own objectives even when these are at odds with generally accepted business practices. Compensation, dividends, treatment of family and business expenses, performance evaluation and promotion, and the budget process are practices that can be influenced by family factors. Similarly, tensions in the business can be the result of the emotional relations in the family. Family relations are personal, often complex, and the result of a lifetime of positive and negative experiences. These relations influence business decisions overtly and covertly, as every family member is, in part, defined by their relationship to the business. Moreover, families often structure their business relationships in ways that fill a void in their family relationship outside of the business.[147] OD practitioners often have to consider such issues as:

- Should the chronic underperforming son or daughter be kept on in their business role and for how long?
- How much conflict should the family (and nonfamily) business members have to endure between two siblings in rivalry?
- When the business is suffering, will the family member's significantly higher compensation be addressed?

In sum, the family business system model provides an effective diagnostic tool and helps to explain some of the reasons why OD in family firms can be difficult.

22-4f Critical Issues in Family Business

The interaction of the family, ownership, and business subsystems, particularly at generational transition points, can be problematic.[148] Where these systems overlap as family members come together as owners both inside and outside of the business, there are potential interface issues, potential conflicts, and always dilemmas to be faced.

Transitions, particularly those from first to second generation and second to third generation can present even the most successful families and businesses with monumental changes. The change from an owner-managed business to a small group of sibling owners to a larger group of cousins can challenge the basic assumptions that have been the basis of trust and unity in decision making. It is instructive to consider each of these major inflection points from the perspective of three states of change:[149]

- The present or current state—identify the key elements of the organization and family that will be impacted by the change.
- The transition state—make the decision about where to begin the change process in each subsystem (family, business, ownership) from the present state to the desired state.
- The future state—a specific statement of the goal of the change process within a mid-range horizon of one to three years.

Some of the critical change triggers common to family businesses as they grow and develop are the following.

Entering or Leaving the Business as a Family Member Family members often report choosing the family business as a place to work with comments like "It just happened" or "I fell into it." Family members are a convenient workforce and may be the only option in the start-up phase of the founding generation but businesses that successfully integrate family members over the long-run do not base selection practices only on genetics. Policies on entering the family business, options for career paths, and multiple points of exposure to the family firm are a few of the best practices.[150]

There must be clear roles, recruiting processes, training, and development to give every family member who chooses to be part of the business a clear sense that they have earned their place. Moreover, the business strategy and organization structure should influence selection, although only 37% of family firms report having a written strategic plan.[151] Most importantly, every family member should feel they have the opportunity to "opt out" of the family business, without the risk of losing the unconditional love of the family. To that point, many founders find it impossible to leave;[152] close to 88% of family business respondents said that the family will continue to control the firm in five years.[153] Too often a founder's identity is largely derived from the family business they began, and many strive to keep the status quo at all costs instead of welcoming change, a values dilemma for an entrepreneurial business.

Conflicts and Rivalry in the Business Conflicts and rivalries are common in family firms and are often the result of values dilemmas.[154] If a family is relationship based and a business is results based, how is the family member to be evaluated? If equality is valued in the family system, how do you choose a business successor? Family member compensation, roles and responsibilities, authority, and opportunity are some of the critical issues that ignite conflict between family members. The family system is an emotional one, and when placed together in a business setting, family members often revert back to the family roles they played growing up. Another source of conflict lies in the secret nature of families. Substance abuse problems, for example, are much more likely to be kept quiet in the family business[155] and only 62% of significant shareholders report knowing the senior generation's share transfer intentions.[156] The complexity of the family business system requires additional structures, practices, and processes to ensure open communications, conflict resolution, and business performance.

Ownership Transfer and Estate Planning In addition to distinguishing between family and business roles, members of the family system may have a third role to play, that of "owner" or "shareholder." Owners' rights and responsibilities are different from family and business ones. Ownership rights typically include electing directors, creating bylaws, voting on specified major business decisions, and realizing a fair return on investment. Typical responsibilities include making informed decisions, creating and keeping agreements, respecting limits of authority, and developing business competencies to adequately fulfill their role as a shareholder.[157]

One value dilemma evidenced in the owner arena has to do with "equal vs. equitable." When ownership transfer issues arise, members of the shareholder group often struggle between transferring family business stock to members of the entire family versus only those family members who are active in the business. The former option can create challenges between inside-owners who work in the business and outside-owners who do not. Owners who earn their living from the business and are responsible for the success of the business often feel that outside-owners do not deserve any return for their investment because they inherited their shares.

Sometimes families attempt to resolve this dilemma by "equalizing" the total estate. For example, a family with two active and two inactive business members of the next generation all receive an equal share of the total estate, yet the two active members receive 100% of the business assets and the estate is "equalized" by transferring more of the nonbusiness assets to the inactive siblings. While this may seem equal at the time of the transfer, it can lead to future disputes if either the business or the other assets significantly outperform the other. Moreover, most business founders tend to reinvest everything in their business and may not be able to match the value of the business with other assets. Others attempt to avoid conflict over the business by establishing two classes of stock and leaving voting shares only to heirs who are working in the business. However, the long-term prospects for a family business where owners of a significant portion of the business have no voice in how their assets are utilized are not good.

No amount of planning by the previous generation can replace the need for the current owners to develop trust through a common vision for their business and an appreciation of the interest and needs of each other.

Selecting a New Leader The vast majority of family firms (85% according to one survey) choose successors that are family members.[158] However, a 2007–2008 survey conducted by PriceWaterhouseCoopers found that 25% of the family businesses surveyed were expecting a transition within the next five years but only about half of them had a succession plan in place.[159] Many families avoid the topic altogether due to its emotional intensity.[160] Some of the key reasons include a founder/owner who won't "let go" of the business, a reluctance to discuss the mortality of the current generation, the lack of competency in the next generation, rivalry among siblings for key leadership positions, succession timing, incongruent business visions of the current and successor generation, and pressures from various family branches.

Forward-thinking family business leaders spend the time to identify the optimum type of leader needed to take the business into the future. This can only happen after creating a shared business vision and strategy and then identifying the best leadership candidates. Once the current leaders have accepted the need for change, decisions can to be made as to where the potential candidates will come from. Will the next leader be a family or nonfamily member? If the choice is the former (and it typically is), what mentoring and development will ensure the family candidate is successful? Business is about risk and change, yet family is about stability and status quo, which explains part of the reason why choosing a new leader creates difficulties. Succession is marked by a shift of power and influence, followed by a period of shared power[161] and for many leaders, the proposed transition is met with great resistance.

Business Growth and Family Wealth As noted earlier, most family businesses struggle to transition the generations. Absence of successors, family assets too concentrated in the business, family conflict, passive versus active owners, empire building, lack of professional management, or the absence of a shared vision and sustainable business model can all contribute to a family business's demise. When the business fails, there is little chance for the family's wealth to grow.

To grow the business and the family's wealth requires careful thought and strategic planning.[162] The company must move from an entrepreneurial business to a professionally managed firm, develop governance structures, formalize systems and processes, and recruit talent (from inside and outside of the family). Owners must continually develop assets independent of the business. As the business grows, so do liquidity options such as venture capital, debt or equity financing, internal stock sale, sale of the company, or employee stock ownership plans (ESOPs).[163]

OD Interventions in Family Business System While research shows that advisors play a key role working with family businesses, complexity is the norm, a result of the interconnectedness of the family, business, and shareholder systems.[164] Necessarily addressing the entire family business system is a key difference from the work of a nonfamily business practitioner. The skill set required for a family business advisor is comprehensive and includes OD competencies (e.g., behavioral sciences, systems thinking, strategy, and organization design), family systems knowledge (e.g., life cycle development, birth order issues, family dynamics), conflict resolution skills, and family meeting facilitation. In addition, the family business consultant should acquire working knowledge in the areas of estate and financial planning, legal forms of organization, exit strategies, family philanthropy, family offices, financial analysis, and multidisciplinary (professional) teaming.

Perhaps the key to the success of a family business consultant is the ability to establish a trusting, caring relationship with the client system, to accurately surface the issues and dynamics at the heart of the family business dilemmas, and to effect positive, sustainable change. Consultants must know their own values, ethics, goals, and personal development areas, including their beliefs about families and families in business and insight into their own family system issues and dynamics. Such awareness increases the family business OD practitioner's ability to handle issues that arise in a family firm engagement.

In addition, given the many demands and diversity of the family business system, it can be beneficial to use a team consulting approach in certain cases. For example, a 60-year-old founder may relate best to a senior advisor perceived as an "equal," while younger next-generation leaders may connect better with someone closer to their age who has worked with other clients with similar experiences. If significant conflicts exist in the family, including an advisor with expertise and qualifications in individual and family therapy may be a valuable asset to the team.

Entering and Contracting The special entry and contracting issues involved in family businesses include the need to create quickly a safe emotional environment, to ask sensitive questions related to the family systems early in the engagement, to get permission to re-contract as issues emerge, to get permission to work with other family members, and to be clear about the requirements of collaboration. Unlike nonfamily firms, the "client" in a family business is the entire family business system. The mission of an OD practitioner dictates a systems approach, so any relationships begun in this phase must integrate family issues around the business issues. The contract will typically be with the major shareholders of the family firm; therefore, additional efforts are required up front to ensure buy-in and collaboration in the process. Establishing trust early increases the chance of moving forward successfully.

Diagnosing the Organization Diagnosing the family-run organization requires the particular tasks and skills necessary to understand the family system in addition to the business system. "Presenting" issues and problems that appear to be business related often require careful probing and unbundling to get an accurate picture of "what is." Trust building, begun in the entry phase, continues in the diagnosis stage by bringing the family together for an orientation meeting. This meeting, often the first time the family has congregated around business issues, helps them to understand they are not alone in the dilemmas they face, affords time for establishing trust within the family and between family members and the OD practitioner, and builds communications skills. Tools to help gather data include confidential interviews of a range of stakeholders, individual and business profiles, and a genogram, which is a visual representation of the family history, similar to an organization chart.[165] The genogram enables the practitioner to understand the intergenerational dynamics and to analyze how the family came to be who they are by identifying the patterns and issues that have been passed down. The individual, confidential interview is perhaps the most powerful tool for gathering data and intervening in the system. It is critical to assess not only the pressing business issues, but those that are in the family system and the shareholder arena, as well as determining what boundaries exist between the subsystems, including how communications flow.

Key questions for understanding the family business system include:

1. Describe what long-term "personal success" means to you and your own personal vision of the future.
2. What is most important to your family?
3. Tell me about the best time that you've had with the family. Looking at the entire experience, recall a time when you felt most alive, most involved, most excited. What made it a great experience? Describe the event in detail.
4. Describe what "business success" for your company means to you. For example, what would your company look like if it was operating at its very best? What is getting in the way of that success? What is your role?
5. As a shareholder in this business, what do you want most from your investment?
6. How much agreement (alignment) exists between the family, the business leaders, and the shareholders about the vision, values, policies, goals, and strategy for the family business?

Feedback and Planning Providing feedback to family business members often includes a one- to two-day offsite session to review a "discussion guide" (as opposed to a completed document) that summarizes key issues, priorities, and recommendations. This session should be the second time the group has come together and can be viewed as an opportunity to facilitate the practices of good communications, group decision making, and conflict resolution. The more the practitioner can help those in the system build competency in these areas, the stronger and more sustainable the family business system will be. Among the typical issues found in diagnostic results and the discussion guides are lack of role clarity; lack of shared vision for the family, the shareholders, and the business; a dearth of communications; conflict between family members; and systems, processes, and structure deficiencies. The goal for the meeting is for the family to identify and agree on key issues, priorities, and next steps. Building good communication practices (e.g., regular family meetings) and resolving conflict are two common starting points for work with family firms. These interventions are good places to begin to "name" the particular value dilemmas inherent in the particular system. Table 22.3 identifies the most common interventions in family business systems today.

1. **Strategic**. Strategic interventions, including mission and vision development, capability identification, and goal setting, are an appropriate place to begin work with a family business system as many family business issues stem from a lack of alignment around shared vision and values. Members of each subsystem—the business, family, and shareholders—need to dialogue and create a shared view of the future and an appropriate set of goals. In reality, there is a good amount of overlap between members of each subsystem so the family business OD practitioner must continually clarify roles, responsibilities, and boundaries. Strategic business planning is appropriate only after the family and shareholder subsystems have aligned on a set of values, goals, and shared vision for the family business. In addition, the process should be an iterative one with open communications between the appropriate family and shareholder governance structures.
2. **Systems**. System interventions include traditional OD approaches in the business, such as human resource policies and procedures, technical operations, information/management systems, and organization culture. Many family firms can benefit from formalizing their business systems, including performance management, succession planning, leadership development, rewards, core process improvement, information technology implementation, and recruiting. Family and shareholder systems tend to be less formal. Interventions in the family subsystem can focus on communications, education, family succession, compensation, and philanthropy while shareholder agreements, estate planning, ownership succession, and communications are appropriate in the shareholder subsystem.
3. **Structure**. Governance structures are necessary for all three subsystems so that effective communications and coordination can occur among these complex systems. The business system benefits from a professional management team, led by a qualified CEO who reports to a board of advisors or board of directors. Outside board members should be roughly balanced with inside board members; the former should be skilled at earning the trust of the family and working with members of the both the senior and junior generation.[166] The shareholders' subsystem requires its own governance structure—a shareholders' forum. Here, active and inactive shareholders can meet to develop their goals, review the performance of their investment and make important decisions about family ownership. Finally, the governance structure for the family—the Family Council—is a place for the family to plan for their future,

TABLE 22.3

Typical Family Business Intervention Areas

Type of Intervention	Business	Family	Shareholder
Strategy	Vision, mission, values Goals and strategic initiatives Organization capabilities	Mission, values, goals Policies Activities	Values, goals Policies regarding Risk tolerance Dividends Exit strategies Investment and ROI Liquidity
Systems	Human resource Technical Information/management Culture	Communications Education Social Succession Compensation Philanthropy	Shareholder agreement Estate plan Ownership succession Communications
Structure	Management team Board of advisors or directors	Family council	Shareholder forum
Process	Coaching founder/current leader Coaching next generation leaders/leadership teams Management team building Conflict resolution Role clarity Board development Board policies	Conflict resolution Communication planning Family business education Family/business roles, responsibilities, and boundaries Meeting management Family charter	Family policies Forum development Forum policies Communication planning Shareholders' roles, responsibilities, and boundaries Conflict resolution

to nurture and develop its members, and to continually determine to what extent the business will be able to fulfill their needs.

4. **Process**. Process interventions can be very effective with family firms. This is especially true if the source or resolution of the client's problem is unknown and the nature of the problem is such that the client would benefit from involvement in its diagnosis.[167] Process interventions in the business system include coaching both the founder/current leader and the next generation leader, team building, conflict resolution, and board development. Typical family process interventions include conflict resolution, communications and family meeting facilitation, and family charter development. The shareholder subsystem requires process interventions in the areas of forum development, communications/boundary management, and conflict resolution.

Implementing and Evaluating Change There are various levels of consultant involvement in implementation. It is important to understand where involvement will support intervention success, where organization members can be "coached," and where members can take primary responsibility for implementation. High involvement is almost always needed in the first stages of implementation, where activities typically include establishing goals and milestones, creating a shared vision, establishing boundaries for family and business roles, and facilitating productive communications. Also in the early stages, the OD practitioner can communicate the importance of establishing and keeping to an implementation timetable and meeting regularly to resolve the many family business–interface issues that arise. Once the implementation phase is well underway, a six-month or annual retreat can help to assess change process and effectiveness, reconnect with the family, and create plans around new family, business, and/or ownership transitions. The continual transitions that occur in a family business provide a unique opportunity for an OD practitioner to become a long-term, trusted advisor.

SUMMARY

Traditionally, the published material in OD has focused on applications in industrial organizations. This chapter presented broad applications of OD in nonindustrial organizations, such as health care, schools, government agencies, and family firms. The results of these change programs to date suggest that OD is being applied successfully but also needs a greater range of customized diagnostic methods and interventions, and it must be clear about the values in use when it is applied to nonindustrial settings.

Foster Mobley and his colleagues pointed out how dramatic changes in the health care industry are affecting the practice of OD in that setting. They noted how changes in the nature of the health care product and the way it is delivered, how technology is being adapted, and how health care is paid for are altering fundamentally the industry's structure and making it more difficult to identify the target of change. To be effective under these new conditions, OD practitioners will be under considerable pressure to demonstrate their competence in areas, such as culture, alliances and networks, and organization design. Change projects likely will be focused on integrating a diverse set of previously uncoordinated stakeholders. They will be more reactive than proactive; more solution-oriented than people-oriented.

Linda Purrington and Paul Sparks described the decline of the traditional model of education, one that had been based on principles of industrial organization. They suggested that close public scrutiny from multiple stakeholders and shifts in technology and society are demanding a new model, one that leverages technology and shifts the goals of the system to learning. Despite recent failed attempts at reform, a variety of OD programs hold great promise to shift the focus of education to the development of learning communities.

Ray Patchett's section suggested that the public sector is more bureaucratic and adheres more strongly to bureaucratic norms than does the private sector. Thus, differences between the two sectors stem largely from differences in underlying value structures that encourage people to behave in different ways. He indicated that many of the differences between the public and the private sectors may be a matter of degree, rather than kind. Further, the public sector has multiple access by multiple decision makers, which can make it difficult to know who is really at the top of the organization. Thus, OD interventions in the public sector focus more on technostructural interventions, such as workflow design and structure, than on process-oriented interventions, such as team building or performance management. Despite these differences, OD interventions in the public sector have an admirable track record of success, nearly equal to the success rate in industrial settings.

Otis Baskin presented a family business system model to underscore the important differences between traditional organizations and family businesses. The family, business, and ownership subsystems hold distinct and often conflicting values that make diagnosis and intervention in family businesses complex. The model also served as a diagnostic framework to guide inquiry into a family business. Effective OD interventions must account for these three subsystems, the relationships among them, and be sensitive to the family interpersonal dynamics that are likely to pervade the entire effort.

NOTES

1. American Hospital Association, "Trends in the Overall Health Care Market," chap. 1 in *TrendWatch Chartbook* (2012), Chart 1.4, accessed from http://www.aha.org on September 19, 2012.
2. Center for Health Transformation, 2/2010 American People's Online Health Summit, accessed from http://cht.typepad.com/hbhr/cost on April 4, 2013.
3. American Hospital Association, "Trends in the Overall Health Care Market," Chart 1.3.
4. Ibid., Chart 1.2.
5. U.S. Census Bureau, accessed from http://www.census.gov/hhes/www/hlthins/data/incpovhlth/2010/fig07.pdf on April 10, 2013.
6. Kaiser Family Foundation, *The Uninsured: A Primer-Key Facts About Americans Without Health Insurance* (October 2012), accessed from http://www.kff.org/uninsured/upload/7451-08.pdf on April 4, 2013.
7. American Hospital Association, "Trends in the Overall Health Care Market," Chart 1.9.
8. Ibid., Chart 1.13.
9. American Hospital Association, "The Cost of Caring: Drivers of Spending on Hospital Care," *AHA TrendWatch* (March 2012), accessed from http://www.aha.org on October 5, 2012.
10. Kaiser Family Foundation, *Focus on Health Reform: Summary of New Health Reform Law*, April 15, 2011, accessed from http://www.kff.org/healthreform/upload/8061.pdf on April 10, 2013.
11. American Hospital Association, "The Cost of Caring."
12. Institute of Medicine, *Better Care at Lower Cost: The Path to Continuously Learning in Health Care in America*, September 2012, accessed from http://www.iom.edu/Reports/2012/Best-Care-at-Lower-Cost-The-Path-to-Continuously-Learning-Health-Care-in-America.aspx on April 14, 2013.
13. Tripp Umbach Research, *The Negative Employment Impacts of the Budget Cuts in the Budget Control Act of 2011*, September 2012, accessed from http://www.ama-assn.org on October 9, 2012.
14. N. Schlichting, "Hospitals Challenged to Lead with Quality to Reduce Cost," in *FutureScan 2012 Health Care Trends and Implications, 2012–2017* (Society for Health Care Strategy and Market Development, 2012), 33.
15. American Hospital Association, *2013 AHA Environmental Scan*, 2013, accessed from http://www.hhnmag.com on October 5, 2012.
16. PwC Health Research Institute, "Top Health Industry Issues: Connecting in Uncertainty," November 2011, accessed from http://www.pwc.com/us/en/health-industries/health-research-institute on September 19, 2012.
17. K. Kaufman and M. E. Grube, "Health Care Reform: The Transformation of America's Hospitals: Economics Drives a New Business Model," in *FutureScan 2012 Health Care Trends and Implications, 2012–2017* (Society for Health Care Strategy and Market Development, 2012), 8.
18. Ibid., 9.
19. N. Fabrizio, "Employing Physicians: The Future Is Now," in *FutureScan 2012 Health Care Trends and Implications, 2012–2017* (Society for Health Care Strategy and Market Development, 2012), 43.
20. PwC Health Research Institute, "Top Health Industry Issues: Connecting in Uncertainty."
21. Ibid.
22. American Hospital Association, *2013 AHA Environmental Scan*, 2013, accessed from http://www.ama-assn.org on October 9, 2012.
23. Ibid.
24. Ibid.
25. U.S. Census Bureau, *Statistical Abstract of the United States*, 2012, accessed from http://www.census.gov/compendia/statab on October 17, 2012.
26. American Hospital Association, "The Cost of Caring."
27. U.S. Census Bureau, *Statistical Abstract of the United States.*
28. U.S. Department of Health and Human Services, Health Resources and Services Administration, Bureau of Health Professions, 2006.
29. Merritt Hawkins & Associates, *2004 Survey of Physicians 50–65 Years Old.*
30. American Hospital Association, "The Cost of Caring."
31. J. Lavelle, "Nursing Needs Teachers," *San Diego Union Tribune*, September 12, 2012.
32. Ibid.
33. D. Goleman, *Working with Emotional Intelligence* (New York: Bantam 1998).
34. D. Goleman, R. Boyatzis, and A. McKee, *Primal Leadership: Learning to Lead with Emotional Intelligence* (Cambridge, MA: Harvard Business School Press, 2002).
35. Ibid.
36. Ibid.
37. The Foster Mobley Group, Inc., 2012.

38. The authors of the OD in Healthcare section would like to extend our deep gratitude to the numerous health care leaders and OD practitioners whose perspectives

provided us significant direction for this chapter. They include: Matthew Auron, Director of Wisdom DVU, DaVita; Paul Craig, Assistant Vice Chancellor of Human Resources & Risk Management, UCSD Health System; J. D. Fitz, M.D., Senior Vice President of Physician Development, Sound Physicians; Josh Golomb, President & General Manager, DaVita Rx; Sally Haslett, Global Head of Human Resources, Oncology Translational Medicine, Novartis; Andrew Hayek, Chief Executive Officer, Surgical Care Affiliates; David Hoerman, Director of Leadership Development, DaVita; Debra Krupa, Vice President of Client Solutions, Morehead Associates; Linda Lansing, Senior Vice President of Clinical Services & Training, Surgical Care Affiliates; Kim Martinez, Vice President of New Market Operations, DaVita Rx; Deb Rodriguez, Senior Vice President of Human Resources, Alliance Health Care Services; Chris Rucker, President, DaVita Clinical Research & Central Labs; Rich Statuto, Chief Executive Officer, Bon Secours Health System; Cindra Syverson, Senior Vice President of Human Resources, Providence Health System; Ed Tyson, Vice President of Process Improvement, Sun Health Care Group.

39. D. Ravitch, *The Death and Life of the Great American School System: How Testing and Choice Are Undermining Education* (New York, NY: Basic Books, 2010).
40. P. Senge, *Schools That Learn* (New York, NY: Doubleday, 2000), 32.
41. Education spending statistics accessed from http://www.nationmaster.com/graph/edu_edu_spe-education-spending-of-gdp on October 25, 2012.
42. Ibid.
43. D. Pink, *Drive: The Surprising Truth About What Motivates Us* (New York: Riverhead Books, 2009).
44. R. Butts and R. Freeman, "The Search for Purpose in American Education," *College Board Review* 98 (1976): 386.
45. C. Shirky, *Here Comes Everybody: The Power of Organizing Without Organizations* (New York: Penguin Group USA, 2009).
46. P. Basham, J. Merrifield, and C. Hepburn, *Home Schooling: From the Extreme to the Mainstream*, 2nd ed. (Vancouver, BC: Fraser Institute, 2007).
47. Partnership for 21st Century Skills, *Learning for the 21st Century 2003* (Washington, DC), accessed from http://www.21centuryskills.org/default.asp on November 1, 2012.
48. U.S. Bureau of the Census, *Income, Poverty, and Health Insurance Coverage in the United States: 2010*, Report P60: 68–73.
49. Child Poverty data accessed from http://www.nccp.org/topics/childpoverty.html on December 3, 2012.
50. R. Barth, *Improving Schools from Within* (San Francisco: Jossey-Bass, 1990).
51. Ibid., 126.
52. J. Murphy, C. Evertson, and M. Radnofsky, "Restructuring Schools: Fourteen Elementary and Secondary Teachers' Perspectives on School Reform," *Elementary School Journal* 92, no. 2 (1991): 135–48.
53. F. M. Newmann and G. Wehlage, *Successful School Restructuring* (Madison: Center on Organization and Restructuring of Schools, School of Education, University of Wisconsin-Madison, 1995).
54. R. Rothstein, "A Bet Over No Child Left Behind" (September 2011), *The Economic Policy Institute Blog*, accessed from http://www.epi.org/blog/rothstein-ravitch-no-child-left-behind on December 3, 2012.
55. D. Ravitch, "The Big Idea—It's Bad Education Policy," *Los Angeles Times*, March 14, 2010, accessed from http://articles.latimes.com/2010/mar/14/opinion/la-oe-ravitch14-2010mar14 on November 15, 2012.
56. "Race to the Top Fund," U.S. Department of Eduction, accessed from http://www2.ed.gov/programs/racetothetop/index.html on October 25, 2012.
57. D. Ravitch, *The Death and Life of the Great American School System: How Testing and Choice Are Undermining Education* (New York: Basic Books, 2010).
58. R. DuFour and R. Eaker, *Professional Learning Communities at Work: Best Practices for Enhancing Student Achievement* (Bloomington, IN: National Educational Service, 1998).
59. Senge, *Schools That Learn.*
60. Ibid.
61. L. Purrington, "Creating Successful Learning Communities," *Thrust for Educational Leadership* (October 1996): 4–5.
62. A. Lieberman and L. Miller, "School Improvement: Themes and Variations," in *Rethinking School Improvement: Research Craft and Concept*, ed. A. Lieberman (New York, NY: Teachers College Press, 1986).
63. A. Blankstein, *Failure Is Not an Option* (Thousand Oaks, CA: Corwin Press, 2004).
64. S. Kruse, K. S. Louis, and A. S. Bryk, *Building Professional Communities in Schools* (Madison, WI: Center on Organization and Restructuring of Schools, 1994); F. M. Newmann and G. Wehlage, *Successful School Restructuring* (Madison, WI: Center on Organization and Restructuring of Schools, School of Education, University of Wisconsin-Madison, 1995); S. M. Hord, *Professional Learning Communities: Communities of Continuous Inquiry and Improvement* (Austin, TX: Southwest Educational Development Library, 1997); R. DuFour and R. Eaker, *Professional Learning Communities at Work: Best Practices for Enhancing Student Achievement* (Bloomington, IN: National Educational Service, 1998).

65. R. Zander and B. Zander, *The Art of Possibility* (Cambridge, MA: Harvard Business School Press, 2000).
66. A. S. Bryk and B. Schneider, *Trust in Schools: A Core Resource for Improvement* (New York: Russell Sage Foundation, 2002).
67. National Parent Teacher Association, accessed from http://www.pta.org on June 18, 2003.
68. DuFour and Eaker, *Professional Learning Communities at Work.*
69. R. Eaker, R. DuFour, and R. Burnette, *Getting Started: Reculturing Schools to Become Professional Learning Communities* (Bloomington, IN: National Educational Service, 2002).
70. D. Cavallo, "Leveraging Learning Through Technological Fluency" (master's thesis, MIT, 1996).
71. J. E. Milenkiewicz and A. Bucknam, *Participatory Action Research for Educational Leadership: Using Data-Driven Decision Making to Improve Schools* (Thousand Oaks, CA: Sage Publications, 2008).
72. J. McNiff and J. Whitehead, *Action Research for Teachers: A Practical Guide* (London: David Fulton, 2005).
73. Ravitch, *The Death and Life of the Great American School System.*
74. E. Wenger, *Communities of Practice: Learning, Meaning, and Identity* (Cambridge: Cambridge University Press, 1999).
75. T. Sergiovanni, *Rethinking Leadership: A Collection of Articles* (Thousand Oaks, CA: Corwin Press, 2007).
76. L. Lambert, *The Constructivist Leader* (New York: Teachers College Press, 2002).
77. C. M. Christensen and M. Horn, *Disrupting Class: How Disruptive Innovation Will Change the Way the World Learns* (New York: McGraw-Hill, 2008).
78. M. Ito, et al. *Living and Learning with New Media: Summary of Findings from the Digital Youth Project* (Cambridge, MA: MIT Press, 2008).
79. J. P. Gee, "What Video Games Have to Teach Us About Learning and Literacy," *Computers in Entertainment* 1 (2003): 20.
80. Department of Education, "National Education Technology Plan 2010," accessed from http://www.ed.gov/technology/netp-2010 on October 22, 2012.
81. Ibid.
82. Christensen and Horn, *Disrupting Class.*
83. M. Fullan, *All Systems Go: The Change Imperative for Whole System Reform* (Thousand Oaks, CA: Corwin, 2010).
84. Christensen and Horn, *Disrupting Class*; Fullan, *All Systems Go*; Kruse et al., *Building Professional Communities in Schools*; Hord, *Professional Learning Communities.*
85. M. G. Popovich, *Creating High-Performance Government Organizations* (San Francisco: Jossey-Bass, 1998).
86. Public Law 111-352—January 4, 2011, GPRA Modernization Act of 2010.
87. The Business of Government, accessed from http://www.businessofgovernment.org on November 3, 2012.
88. California Faculty Association, accessed from http://www.calfac.org/headline-special-edition/gov-brown-signs-pernsion-roll-back-legislation on November 3, 2012.
89. The Business of Government, accessed from http://www.businessofgovernment.org on November 3, 2012; "Gov. Hickenlooper signs legislation to improve the state personnel system," June 6, 2012, accessed from http://www.colorado.gov on November 3, 2012.
90. Gallup, "Trust in Government," accessed from http://www.gallup.com/poll/5392/Trust-Government.aspx on October 30, 2012.
91. Gallup, "Americans Express Historic Negativity Toward U.S. Government," September 26, 2011, accessed from http://www.gallup.com/poll/149678/americans-express-historic-negativity-toward-government.aspx on October 30, 2012.
92. Ibid.
93. Ibid.
94. Gallup, "In U.S., Local and State Governments Retain Positive Ratings," October 3, 2011, accessed from http//www.gallup.com/poll/149888/Local-State-Governments-Retain-Positive-Ratings.aspx on November 3, 2012.
95. The American Presidency Project, "Voter Turnout in Presidential Elections: 1828–2008," accessed from http://www.presidency.ucsb.edu/data/turnout.php on October 30, 2012.
96. IDEA, "Voter turnout by country," accessed from http://www.idea.int/vt/countryview.cfm on November 3, 2012.
97. White House, "Memorandum on Transparency and Open Government," accessed from http://www.whitehouse.gov/the_press_office/TransparencyandOpenGovernment on June 4, 2013.
98. White House, "Open Government Directive," December 8, 2009, accessed from http://www.whitehouse.gov/open/documents/open-government-directive on November 4, 2012.
99. R. Dilger, R. Moffett, and L. Struyk, "Privatization of Municipal Services in America's Largest Cities," *Public Administration Review* 57 (1997): 21–26.
100. National Performance Management Advisory Commission, "A Performance Management Framework for State and Local Government: From Measurement and Reporting to Management and Improving," 2010.
101. P. Robertson and S. Seneviratne, "Outcomes of Planned Organizational Change in the Public Sector: A

Meta-Analytic Comparison to the Private Sector," *Public Administration Review* 55 (1995): 547–58.

102. Center for State and Local Government Excellence, "Survey Findings: The Great Recession and the State and Local Government Workforce" (January 2010).

103. John Nalbandian introduces the legislative-administrative values and roles conflicts inherent in government; H. George Frederickson emphasizes that political and administrative values differ significantly and highlights that politics is the art and science of government; Bob Golembiewski notes that access to a multiplicity of decision makers looking at the public's business from a variety of perspectives is broad and accountability is dispersed; John Bryson emphasizes that stakeholder access, whether an individual or group, is broad and attention to and care to stakeholder concerns must be exercised.

104. J. Nalbandian, "City Council–City Manager Partnerships" (presentation to the California City Managers Conference, 1998).

105. H. G. Frederickson, *The Spirit of Public Administration* (San Francisco: Jossey-Bass, 1997).

106. Ibid., 164.

107. Frederickson, *The Spirit of Public Administration*; W. Morris, *The American Heritage Dictionary of the English Language* (Boston: Houghton-Mifflin, 1981); P. Appleby, "Government Is Different," in *Classics of Public Administration*, ed. J. Shafritz and A. Hyde (Oak Park, IL: Moore, 1978), 101–7.

108. Frederickson, *The Spirit of Public Administration.*

109. R. Golembiewski, "Organization Development in Public Agencies: Perspectives on Theory and Practice," *Public Administration Review* 29 (July–August 1969): 370.

110. Popovich, *Creating High-Performance Government Organizations*, 29; Golembiewski, "Organization Development in Public Agencies."

111. Golembiewski, "Organization Development in Public Agencies."

112. Bryson, *Strategic Planning*; T. Cummings and C. Worley, *Organization Development and Change*, 6th ed. (Cincinnati, OH: South-Western College Publishing, 1997), 163; Golembiewski, "Organization Development," 370.

113. Golembiewski, "Organization Development," 370.

114. J. Bryson, *Strategic Planning for Public and Nonprofit organizations: A Guide to Strengthening and Sustaining Organizational Achievement* (San Francisco, CA: Jossey Bass, 1995).

115. Ibid., 246.

116. R. Golembiewski, C. Proehl, and D. Sink, "Success of OD Applications in the Public Sector: Toting Up the Score for a Decade, More or Less," *Public Administration Review* 41 (1981): 679–82; R. Golembiewski, C. Proehl, and D. Sink, "Estimating the Success of OD Applications," *Training and Development Journal* 72 (April 1982): 86–95.

117. S. Park, "Estimating Success Rates of Quality Circle Programs: Public and Private Experiences," *Public Administration Quarterly* 15 (1991): 133–46.

118. P. J. Robertson and S. J. Seneviratne, "Outcomes of Planned Organizational Change in the Public Sector: A Meta-Analytic Comparison to the Private Sector," *Public Administration Review* 55 (1995): 547–58.

119. R. Boss, B. Dunford, A. Boss, and L. McConkie, "Sustainable Change in the Public Sector: The Longitudinal Benefits of Organization Development," *Journal of Applied Behavioral Science* (2010): 436–72.

120. F. Berry and B. Wechsler, "State Agencies' Experience with Strategic Planning: Findings from a National Survey," *Public Administration Review* 55 (1995): 159–68.

121. J. Melkers and K. Willoughby, "The State of the States: Performance-Based Budgeting Requirements in 47 out of 50," *Public Administration Review* 58 (1998): 66–73.

122. H. Hill and K. Shook, "Virginia's Results Manager," *New Public Innovator* (1998): 30–33.

123. Robertson and Seneviratne, "Outcomes"; E. M. Berman and J. P. West, "Municipal Commitment to Total Quality Management: A Survey of Recent Progress," *Public Administration Review* 55 (1995): 57–66; K. Parry, "Enhancing Adaptability: Leadership Strategies to Accommodate Change in Local Government Settings," *Journal of Organizational Change Management* 12 (1999): 134–48; L. White, "Changing the 'Whole System' in the Public Sector," *Journal of Organizational Change Management* 13 (2000): 162–78.

124. Mayors Challenge, accessed from http://mayorschallenge.bloomberg.org on November 17, 2012.

125. K. Gersick, J. Davis, M. Hampton, and I. Lansberg, *Generation to Generation* (Cambridge: Harvard Business School Press, 1997).

126. R. Anderson and D. Reeb, "Founding-Family Ownership and Firm Performance: Evidence from the S&P 500," *Journal of Finance* 58 (2003): 1301.

127. J. Ward and C. Aronoff, "Just What Is a Family Business?" in *Family Business Sourcebook II*, ed. C. E. Aronoff, J. H. Astrachan, and J. L. Ward (Atlanta: Business Owners Resources, 1996), 2–3.

128. S. Kilman, "Bountiful Harvest: Giant Cargill Resists Pressure to Go Public As It Pursues Growth—Largest Private Firm in U.S. Has Quietly Succeeded As a Global Presence—Some Heirs Want to Cash In," *Wall Street Journal*, January 9, 1997, A1.

129. D. Kiley, "Alan Mullaly: The Outsider at Ford," *Bloomberg Businessweek*, March 4, 2009.
130. J. Ward, "Strategic Planning Starts with the Family," in *Unconventional Wisdom: Counterintuitive Insights for Family Business Success*, ed. J. Ward (New York: Wiley, 2005), 35–55.
131. B. J. Distelberg and A. Blow, "Variations in Family System Boundaries," *Family Business Review* (March 2011): 28–46.
132. R. Schulz, M. Lubatkin, R. Dino, and A. Buchholtz, "Agency Relationships in Family Firms: Theory and Evidence," *Organization Science* 12 (2001): 99–116.
133. Quoted in R. Morck and B. Yeung, "Agency Problems in Large Family Business Groups," *Entrepreneurship Theory and Practice* 27 (2003): 367–82.
134. A. Stewart and M. A. Hitt, "Why Can't a Family Business Be More Like a Nonfamily Business?" *Family Business Review* (March 2012): 58–86.
135. J. M. Pendergast, J. L. Ward, and S. Brun de Pontet, *Building a Successful Family Business Board: A Guide for Leaders, Directors, and Families* (New York: Palgrave Macmillan, 2011).
136. A. Bjornberg and N. Nicholson "Emotional Ownership: The Next Generation's Relationship with the Family Firm," *Family Business Review* (December 2012): 374–90.
137. C. J. Eckrich and S. L. McClure, *The Family Council Handbook: How to Create, Run, and Maintain a Successful Family Business Council* (New York: Palgrave Macmillan, 2012).
138. J. Hilburt-Davis and W. G. Dyer Jr., *Consulting to Family Business: A Practical Guide to Contracting, Assessment, and Implementation* (San Francisco: Jossey-Bass/Pfeiffer, 2003).
139. R. Foster and S. Kaplan, *Creative Destruction* (New York: Currency/Doubleday, 2001).
140. C. E. Aronoff, "Family Business Survival: Understanding the Statistics," *Family Business Advisor* (1999), accessed from http://www.efamilybusiness.com/fep_articles_view.php on December 10, 2007.
141. C. E. Aronoff and O. W. Baskin, *Effective Leadership in the Family Business* (New York: Palgrave Macmillan, 2011).
142. R. Carlock and J. Ward, *Strategic Planning for the Family Business* (London: Palgrave, 2001), 12.
143. A. Steward, "Help One Another, Use One Another: Toward an Anthropology of Family Business," *Entrepreneurship Theory and Practice* 27 (2003): 383–96.
144. C. Aronoff and J. Ward, *Family Business Values: How to Assure a Legacy of Continuity and Success* (Marietta, GA: Family Enterprise Publisher, 2001).
145. Carlock and Ward, *Strategic Planning for the Family Business.*
146. Raymond Institute, "American Family Business Survey" (Alfred, NY: Raymond Institute/Mass Mutual Financial, 2003). The report can be downloaded at http://www.raymondinstitute.org.
147. I. Lansberg, *Succeeding Generations: Realizing the Dream of Families in Business* (Cambridge, MA: Harvard Business School Press, 1999).
148. E. Poza, S. Hanlon, and R. Kishida "Does the Family-Business Interaction Factor Represent a Resource or a Cost?" *Family Business Review* 17 (2004): 99–118.
149. R. Beckhard and W. Pritchard, *Changing the Essence: The Art of Creating and Leading Fundamental Change in Organizations* (San Francisco: Jossey-Bass, 1992).
150. Lansberg, *Succeeding Generations.*
151. Raymond Institute, "American Family Business Survey."
152. M. Gagne, C. Wrosch, and S. Brun de Pontet, "Retiring From the Family Business: The Role of Goal Adjustment Capacities," *Family Business Review* (December 2011): 292–304.
153. Raymond Institute, "American Family Business Survey."
154. J. Ward, *Keeping the Family Business Healthy: How to Plan for Continuing Growth, Profitability, and Family Leadership* (San Francisco: Jossey-Bass, 1987).
155. D. Bork, D. Jaffe, S. Lane, L. Dashew, and Q. Heisler, *Working with Family Businesses* (San Francisco: Jossey-Bass, 1996).
156. Raymond Report, "American Family Business Survey."
157. E. Doud Jr. and L. Hausner, *Hats Off to You: Balancing Roles and Creating Success in Family Business* (Los Angeles: DHV Family Business Advisors, 2000).
158. Raymond Report, "American Family Business Survey."
159. Pendergast et al., *Building a Successful Family Business Board.*
160. Ward, *Keeping the Family Business Healthy.*
161. Bork et al., *Working with Family Businesses.*
162. R. Mickelson and C. Worley, "M&As: A Strategic Choice for Family-Owned Firms," *Family Business Journal* 16 (2003): 251–68.
163. E. Doud Jr., *Evolution of Family Business and Wealth* (Los Angeles: DHV Family Business Advisors, 2003).
164. V. M. Strike, "Advising the Family Firm: Reviewing the Past to Build the Future," *Family Business Review* (June 2012): 156–77.
165. Bork et al., *Working with Family Businesses.*
166. Lansberg, *Succeeding Generations.*
167. E. Schein, *Process Consultation Revisited* (Reading, MA: Addison-Wesley, 1999); T. Cummings and C. Worley, *Organization Development and Change*, 7th ed. (Cincinnati, OH: South-Western College Publishing, 2001).

Future Directions in Organization Development

learning objectives

Explore the trends occurring within organization development (OD) and the different futures they suggest for the field's progress.

Explore the trends occurring in the larger context within which OD operates and how they are likely to influence future OD practice.

Many OD practitioners, including internal and external consultants, executives, and researchers, believe OD faces important crossroads in its evolution. On the one hand, OD is growing rapidly on a global basis. Organizations within emerging countries and economies are becoming more complex and seeking methods to adapt and grow. Most of these organizations initially applied Western bureaucratic models that helped them be efficient but now must address whether such models align with their cultural values. This is driving demand for OD services in a variety of economies, and OD conferences in Asia, Africa, and South America are increasingly popular and well attended. On the other hand, U.S. organization development conferences are less popular and the founding professional associations of the field, such as the National Training Laboratories and the Organization Development Network, are struggling to maintain memberships and financial viability. Although new methods and interventions are being applied, more complex and rigorous research is being conducted, and organizations from diverse countries and cultures are becoming involved, there are some challenges to the field's coherence and relevance. In this final chapter, we will step back and explore where organization development is headed.

Because so much change has occurred in a relatively brief period, predicting the future of OD is risky, if not foolhardy. The field is maturing and it is useful to look at the forces influencing how OD is likely to evolve. This knowledge can enable OD practitioners, researchers, and managers to more readily affect a relevant OD future. This chapter first identifies the primary internal trends pushing the field toward different futures and discusses their implications. The chapter then describes trends in the larger context within which OD operates, including economic, workforce, technology, and organization trends. It concludes with a discussion of how these trends are likely to influence future OD practice.

23-1 Trends Within Organization Development

Researchers note that many of the recent writings in OD have focused more on the status of the field than on evaluations of practice or improvements in the processes of change.[1] In support of that observation, reviews of the literature and the diversity in OD education and training opportunities suggest three trends within OD—traditional, pragmatic, and scholarly.[2] While they all agree on some issues, such as the increasing likelihood of international practice, each trend has a different vision of what OD can and should be. Moreover, although the trends are presented separately, they are not mutually exclusive or independent. On the contrary, the future of OD will no doubt emerge from their integration. Figure 23.1 summarizes the trends and their likely implications.

23-1a Traditional Trend

The first trend calls for a return to OD's traditional values and practices. OD practitioners from such organizations as the National Training Laboratories (NTL) and others argue that OD should be driven by long-established values of human potential, equality, trust, and collaboration. The major objective of OD should be to promulgate these root values through interventions that humanize work, organizations, and society; help employees balance work and family life; promote diversity and spirituality at the workplace; and champion the self-actualization of organization members.[3] Thus, traditionalists propose

FIGURE 23.1

Trends Within OD and Their Impacts on OD's Future

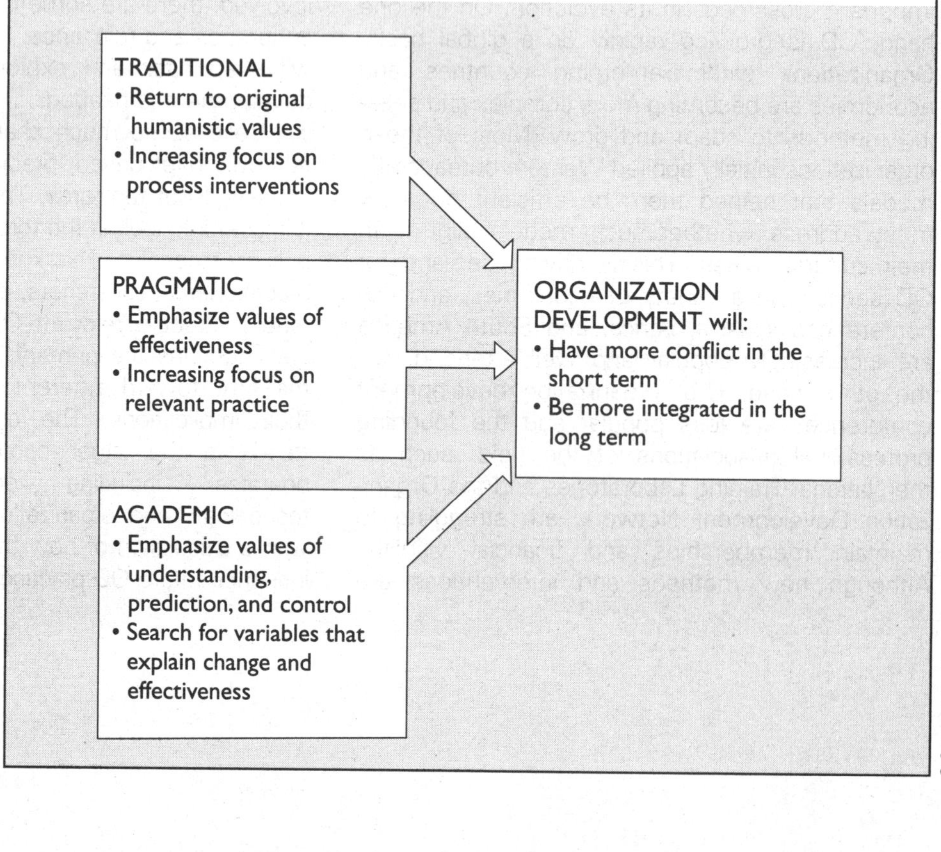

that OD should do what is "right" by assuring that organizations promote positive social change and corporate citizenship.

A strong focus on process interventions characterizes the traditional trend. OD's key purpose, according to this view, is to ensure that organizational processes are transparent, possess integrity, treat people with dignity, and serve diverse stakeholders. OD's primary goal should be to help organizations create such processes. By implication, these processes should lead to greater organization effectiveness.

23-1b Pragmatic Trend

The second trend within OD calls for increasing attention to professionalization of the field and an emphasis on relevance. Championed by the change-management practices at large consulting firms and some OD professional associations, pragmatists argue that OD practitioners should be certified like most other professionals.[4] This drive to professionalize OD is in response to a growing number of people marketing themselves as OD practitioners without any formal training or education in the field, as well as a lack of consistency in applying OD's core theories, skills, and interventions. As a result, distinguishing between qualified and unqualified OD practitioners can be a difficult challenge for organizations, and professionalization of the field can help to remedy that problem.[5]

To become a profession, according to pragmatists, OD should require certification of members, create a common body of knowledge, define minimum levels of competencies, and institute other regulatory infrastructure. Certification would create boundaries between who is (and is not) an OD professional and what is (and is not) good OD practice.

The pragmatic trend is distinguished by an emphasis on change technologies, typically under the banner of "change management." In contrast to OD's "soft" reputation, change management is viewed as a highly relevant and applied practice, much like medicine, engineering, or accounting.[6] It focuses on helping organizations implement change and adapt to turbulent environments. Relevance, a minor chord among traditionalists, is a major theme among pragmatists, who value the performance outcomes of OD work. Thus, process interventions are not seen as ends in themselves but as means for implementing change and achieving the desired results.

23-1c Scholarly Trend

The third trend is connected with the increasing number of people making research contributions to our understanding of change and development. Championed by universities and applied research centers, such as USC's Center for Effective Organizations (http://ceo.usc.edu), MIT's Society of Organization Learning (www.solonline.org), the Tavistock Institute (www.tavinstitute.org), and the Institut de Socio-Economie des Enterprises et des Organizations (Institute for Socio-Economic Enterprises and Organizations [ISEOR], www.iseor.com), scholars propose a "research agenda" for OD that includes (1) the inclusion of time, history, process, and action in theories of change; (2) the link between change processes and organization performance; (3) the comparative analysis of international and cross-cultural OD interventions; (4) the relational and social effects of networks on change; (5) the study of episodic versus continuous change processes; (6) the role of individual and organizational identity in change; and (7) the applications of complexity theory concepts to OD.[7] The scholarly perspective focuses on understanding, predicting, and controlling change. It is less concerned about how OD is defined, what its values are, how it is practiced, or whether an OD practitioner is involved except as potential explanations for change success. OD is just one of several ways organizations can be changed. Unlike traditionalists and pragmatists, scholars are concerned with creating valid knowledge, and with generalizing conclusions about how change occurs, how it is triggered, under what conditions it works well, and so on. In fact, the preferred method among OD scholars, action research, is thriving.[8]

23-1d Implications for OD's Future

Those three trends are likely to affect OD's future. In the short term, advocates of each view will likely continue on their separate paths with periodic and perhaps intense conflicts among them. In the longer term, however, there should be increasing attempts at reconciling these differences and generating a more integrative view of OD.

OD Will Continue to Experience Internal Conflicts in the Short Term Current views and debates about OD values and professionalization are likely to continue at least in the near term. The traditional and pragmatic trends hold different and often conflicting views of how the field should evolve. Traditionalists fear that OD is becoming too corporate and may unwittingly collude with powerful stakeholders to promote goals that are inconsistent with OD's social responsibility and humanistic values. For example, corporate strategies can concentrate wealth and ignore cultural diversity. Technology can isolate people and alienate them. The traditionalists, therefore, advocate for a stronger focus on the central values of the field. Pragmatists, on the other hand, worry that relying too heavily on traditional values will reinforce OD's "touchy-feely" reputation. They argue that focusing on human potential exclusively will doom OD to irrelevance in today's highly competitive organizations. Thus, in the short term, the battle over values within the field is likely to continue.

Symbolic of the struggle, in 2008, no fewer than three formal projects were under way at the same time to clarify OD's values. Each effort was championed by a different institutional sponsor, relied on a different set of OD practitioners, and argued that their results would clarify this important issue for the field. Today, each of the professional associations list the values under which their members practice and, despite some overlap, they do not have the same focus. NTL focuses more on diversity and social change; the OD Network focuses more on practice. The ongoing conflict in the field is therefore likely to continue and may become even more intense as additional values, such as ecological sustainability and economic equality, enter the debate.[9] OD is also likely to face more disagreement over professionalization. The debate over values discussed above demonstrates how difficult it will be to gain agreement about standards, competencies, enforcement mechanisms, and oversight. Unless a groundswell of support for a common set of OD values emerges, judgments about qualifications will likely become caught up in conflicts between the traditional and the pragmatic perspectives. Several prior attempts to professionalize the field or to accredit practitioners have had limited success, and provide ample evidence of the difficulty of resolving such differences.

OD Will Become More Integrated in the Long Term Despite the conflicts likely to continue in the short run, there is considerable common ground among the diverse trends within OD, and the emergence of a more integrated view of the field seems likely in the long term. For example, both the traditional and the pragmatic trends agree that applying behavioral science to organizations can improve effectiveness, increase member satisfaction, and build capability. Both trends believe that knowledge and skill should be transferred to a client system, and all three trends believe that a body of theory and practice underlie the process of change in organizations.

Given OD's history, its long-term future is likely to be some blend of practitioner values-in-use (traditional trend), professional change practice (pragmatic trend), and change theory (scholarly trend). The field is not likely to be completely pragmatic and ignore its values base: There is little sense in a purely process-oriented approach that has low relevance to business outcomes, and the subject of change is too important and personal to be left to research alone. A more limited integration is also problematic. A pragmatic and research-driven OD would be cold and impersonal; a traditional and research-driven field would be naïve and irrelevant to economic realities; and a traditional and pragmatic-driven OD would be intuitive and noncumulative. An integration of the three trends, on the other hand, will assure that OD has moral purpose, drives sustainable bottom lines, and represents a healthy balance of art and science.

A set of integrated values, including participation and effectiveness but recognizing the tension between them, will drive the traditional and pragmatic trends to exploit the common ground in theory and practice. For example, the theories of change underlying traditional action research; positive scholarship and practice; contemporary approaches to change, such as network models, complexity, and chaos theories; and the evolution of underorganized systems can be integrated. The practical benefits of traditional objective approaches and the traditional values reflected in a social constructionist view hold promise for a new view of OD.

This integrated view will challenge the field to redefine existing views of work, competition, culture, and organizations. OD cannot view systems only as objects with inertia, structure, resistance, and permanence, but as social processes produced, maintained, and changed through conversations that are flexible, aspirational, and changeable.[10] A positive view of organizations and their members' potential aligns well with the traditional trend, and it supports values of basic human rights, social responsibility, democracy, and ecological sustainability. This view of organizations also supports the pragmatic trend; it recognizes the importance of economic viability, the time value of activity, and the opportunities that growth conveys. If carefully applied, an integrated objective and socially constructed perspective can be an influential voice in OD's future.

23-2 Trends in the Context of Organization Development

The field of OD is evolving, but so too is the context within which OD is applied. As summarized in Figure 23.2, several interrelated trends are affecting the context within which OD will be applied in the near future. They concern various aspects of the economy, the workforce, technology, and organizations. In some cases, the trends will directly affect OD practice. Technology trends, such as voice-over-Internet protocols (VoIP), videoconferencing, mobile technology and wireless networks, and three-dimensional video will no doubt influence how OD practitioners communicate with organization members, facilitate teams, and manage change. Other trends, such as the increasing concentration of wealth, represent important contextual forces that will indirectly affect OD through their interaction with other trends.[11]

23-2a The Economy

Researchers and futurists have described a variety of economic scenarios, and there is substantial agreement that the world's economy is in the midst of a transition from the industrial age that characterized much of the twentieth century.[12] Although these

FIGURE 23.2

Contextual Trends and Their Effects on OD's Future

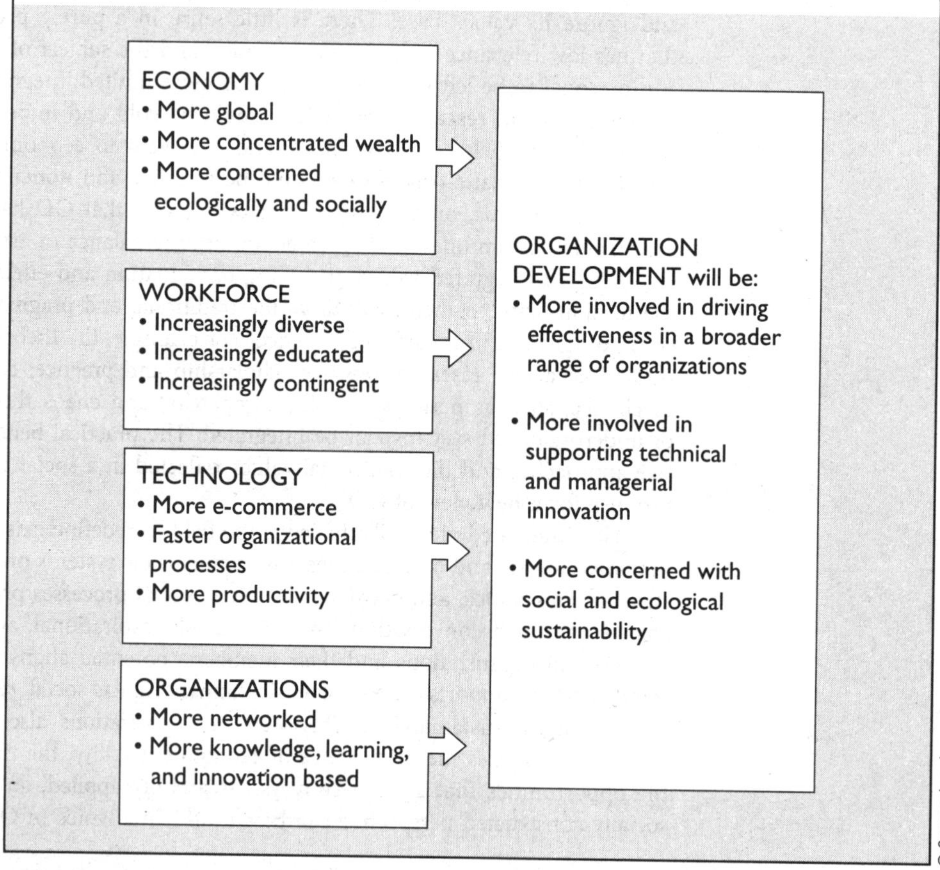

scenarios differ in their particulars, they all fit under the rubric of *globalization*, and many of the same trends are identified as drivers, including technology, workforce, and organization, which will be discussed separately.

The "Arab Spring," orchestrated bailouts of U.S. and European governments and organizations that are "too big to fail," an extended drug war in Mexico, the Occupy movement, and the closely watched leadership transition in China are the latest signals to the emergence of a complex and global economy. Organizations from around the world that increasingly shifted their manufacturing low-labor-cost countries are rethinking that strategy as wage rates increase relative to quality. Today, almost any product or service can be designed, made, transported, and bought anywhere in the world.

The emergence of a global economy may well be under way, but its promise and rationalization is far from complete.[13] The initial steps toward globalization have fueled real price decreases in many consumer products, provided employment for people in less-developed nations, and driven revenue growth in a variety of industries. However, the transition to a global economy is for the most part unmanaged, and there is increasing concern over its social and ecological consequences.[14] This raises troublesome questions about three key issues: *cultural diversity*, *income distribution*, and *ecological sustainability*.

First, globalization is a complex and daunting process that involves organizations, technology, people, and governments. There are few generally accepted principles to follow, and the role and function of these actors and their influence on cultural diversity is not well understood. Some economists argue that globalization is good for countries and cultures.[15] They cite numerous examples of how music, art, political thought, technology, and other artifacts of culture have crossed boundaries and enriched people's experiences.

Others argue that governments must balance the difficult choice of cultural preservation at the expense of participation in the global economy or economic success that sacrifices cultural values.[16] For example, the Chinese government is trying diligently to preserve its cultural and political underpinnings while facing a rapid influx of capitalist goods and services,[17] and many other developing nations face pressures to move to a Western capitalism model despite questions as to whether it is appropriate for their cultures.[18] Organizations implementing worldwide strategies (Chapter 18), for example, often prefer the standardized approaches of a global orientation because the economic logic of this strategy admits to little practical incentive to account for cultural or governmental differences. Pursuing both cultural preservation and economic participation is possible, but it is a complex task. The short-term financial benefits often appear much larger than the long-term social consequences and the required leadership and management capabilities are not widely available. The decisions governments make to resolve this dilemma will dramatically shape the character of the global economy.

Second, globalization of the economy is closely related to an increasing concentration of income and wealth in relatively few individuals, corporations, and nations. In the years following World War II and into the 1970s, incomes for the U.S. population grew at about the same rate for all income classes. However, since the early 1970s, income growth for the top end of the distribution has been significantly higher.[19] Today, the upper 1% of Americans account for 25% of the nation's income and 40% of the wealth, up from 12% and 33% a quarter century ago.[20] A study by the Economic Policy Institute estimates that CEO pay has increased 725% between 1978 and 2011 compared to an increase of 5.7% for workers, or 127 times faster.[21]

The pattern is the same when viewed on a global basis. Of the 1,210 billionaires in 2011 (up from 793 in 2006), there are 413 in the United States (34%). However, the 115 (9.5%) billionaires from China is up from 64 in 2010, and measured on the basis of the "gini" index, China and South Africa are among highest income inequality countries in the world.[22] The CIA's report, *Global Trends, 2015*, concluded that globalization is creating "an even wider gap between regional winners and losers than exists today. [Its] evolution will be rocky, marked by chronic volatility and a widening economic divide … deepening economic stagnation, political instability, and cultural alienation. [It] will foster political, ethnic, ideological, and religious extremism, along with the violence that often accompanies it."[23]

The concentration of wealth may be a natural outcome of fast growth in emerging economies or capitalism facing imperfectly competitive markets, but it can contribute to misallocation of resources, environmental degradation, and short-term thinking.[24] For example, the financial markets' focus (and the executives that work in them) on short-term results were the proximate cause of the 2009–2010 recession.[25] Similarly, Toyota's drive to become the biggest automaker and BP's aggressive profit objectives resulted in embarrassing lawsuits, substantial fines, and damaged reputations. The Occupy Movement's demonstrations also confirm that the concentration of wealth can contribute to social conflict driven by fears that the wealthy will act in their own self-interest at the expense of those who are financially less fortunate. As Joseph Stiglitz writes, "The more divided a society becomes in terms of wealth, the more reluctant the wealthy become to spend money on common needs."[26]

Third, there are increasingly clear warnings that the ecosystem can no longer be treated as a factor of production, and that success cannot be defined as the accumulation of wealth and material goods at the expense of the environment. There are strong pressures to fuel economic growth and create jobs in the United States, for example, by building the Keystone pipeline from Canada to Texas even as environmental reports warn against this project. By holding off on the enforcement of environmental reform, much of China's water and air continue to be polluted in service of maintaining growth rates. Electronic waste—mostly mobile phones—piles up in landfills so we can enjoy the status and benefits of possessing the latest technology. These concerns arise in part from the proliferation of short-term capitalism, but also from the growing realization that free and open markets can have negative unintended consequences for the global ecosystem.

The conclusions from the Intergovernmental Panel on Climate Change and several follow-on studies suggest that industrialization is not a controversial but a probable cause of global warming.[27] Several traditional organizations, such as Interface Carpet, BHP Billiton, and Royal Dutch/Shell, reversed long-held opinions about their contribution to environmental decay and set aggressive goals to reduce greenhouse gases.[28] Unfortunately, many developing economies, including China, the Philippines, and Mexico, continue to operate with loose environmental controls. As a result, there are more calls for change in the values underlying capitalism—from consumption to investment, from open to mindful markets, and from wealth accumulation as an end in itself to an examination of the return on living capital.[29] Some observers note that such value shifts are already under way in many nations and organizations. For example, traditional business models that assume labor scarcity and natural resource abundance are being tempered by models that emphasize the abundance of knowledge and the scarcity of natural resources. A handful of companies, including Ikea, Interface, Honda, Gap Inc., Unilever, and Suzuki, have altered their operations and practices radically to reduce emissions, waste, and environmental degradation and to increase sustainability, profits, and customer satisfaction.

23-2b The Workforce

The workforce is becoming more diverse, educated, and contingent. Chapter 17 documented the diversity trend and suggested that organizations, whether they operate primarily in their home country or abroad, will need to develop policies and operating styles that embrace the changing cultural, ethnic, gender, and age diversity of the workforce.

The workforce is also becoming more educated. The 2011 U.S. Census data, for example, report that 87.8% of adults over 25 years of age have completed high school and that 30% have a bachelor's or higher degree.[30] Both numbers represent a 2–3% increase over 2006 but significant increases compared to 2000. A more educated workforce is likely to demand higher wages, more involvement in the decision-making process, and continued investment in knowledge and skills. For example, the rate of change in information systems technology requires IT professionals to continually update their knowledge and skills to remain competent. In response, organizations are increasing their training and management development budgets significantly.[31] Many organizations, such as Motorola, Capital One, Boeing, and Harley-Davidson, have invested in corporate universities and corporate–university partnerships, and many others have policies outlining the minimum hours of technical and managerial training that each employee will receive yearly.

Finally, the continued high rate of downsizings, reengineering efforts, and mergers and acquisitions described in Chapters 12 and 20 is forcing the workforce to become more contingent and less loyal. The Bureau of Labor Statistics reports that contingent and "alternative arrangement" workers, including temporary and contract employees, freelancers, independent professionals, and consultants, made up about 11% of the workforce in 2005.[32] That number has no doubt shifted upwards since the 2009–2010 recession. In addition, much of the economic recovery in 2011 and 2012 is fueled by temporary workers, part of a risk management strategy by organizations that are uncertain about the future economy.[33]

The increasing dependence on contingent workers may be part of a long-coming trend. However, the implicit psychological contract that governs relationships between employers and contingent employees likely is being rewritten with new assumptions about long-term employment and rewards in exchange for commitment and loyalty. For example, it is estimated that 90% of companies use temporary help and that the personnel supply services industry, about 90% of which is involved in providing contingent employees, will be among the top five fastest-growing industries.[34]

23-2c Technology

By almost any measure, information technology is a significant and increasingly pervasive fact of life. There were 5.98 billion mobile/smartphone subscriptions in 2011, up from 4.7 billion in 2009, and projected to grow to 8 billion by 2016.[35] An estimated 360.9 million worldwide Internet users in 2000 grew to 2.4 billion in 2012.[36] The growth rates continue to boggle the mind, with Africa's usage growing 3,607% between 2000 and 2012 and an overall growth rate of 566% over the same time period. The Internet is the backbone of a global economy, and mobile use is expected to outpace desktop use over the next couple of years.

At the core of information technology is e-commerce, an economy that knows no boundaries.[37] The business-to-consumer market garners much attention and awareness because it is how the public participates in e-commerce. This market, which includes e-tailers such as Amazon.com, eBay.com, and Fandango.com, is expected to grow in the United States from $165.4 billion in 2010 to over $269.8 billion by 2015.[38] In these businesses, OD must help to create and implement novel business models. Dell Computer and Hewlett-Packard, for instance, are the leading sellers of desktop and laptop computers and rely on the Internet for much of their consumer business. However, both companies started out in different business—Dell as a mail-order company and HP as a small instruments business—and had to transform their business models. Today, they are again facing radical challenges to their business models as consumers opt for tablets and smartphones. The complexity of the transformation required to shift into a business that heavily depends on e-commerce represents the kind of change that many organizations will face and the challenges OD practitioners must meet.

The organizational issues in the business-to-business market are even more complex. A good example of the implications and OD challenges in this market is the evolution of Covisint. The global automobile industry created Covisint in 2000 as an online parts and supply store to jointly address the escalating costs and gross inefficiencies of their supply chains. Covisint leveraged the power and potential of the Internet to solve industry-specific business problems in real time. By 2007, Covisint not only supported more than 30,000 organizations in over 96 countries in the global automotive industry, it had moved into the health care industry to help more than 450 North American health systems, commercial payers, physician groups/practices, home health agencies, third-party administrators, extended care facilities, and home medical equipment providers. Covisint helped to migrate an entire industry's supply chain onto the Internet and radically reengineered the way businesses interact with each other. Web-based transactions are replacing the phone, mail, and face-to-face sales call processes that dominated these industries. Today, Covisint has moved their business model into "cloud" computing and serves the automotive, health care, and employee services industries to provide energy efficient, low-cost services.

In addition to providing the infrastructure for e-commerce, technology is also changing and enabling a variety of organizational processes. Enterprise resource planning technologies, such as SAP or PeopleSoft, are changing how information and work processes are coordinated and managed. They also require modification in the way productivity is measured. For example, UPS works with organizations to integrate their logistics and supply-chain technologies and capabilities with existing work processes and the competencies of organization members. UPS provides customers the metrics and measures of supply-chain efficiency using its own processes. This investment in technology is expected to have a bottom-line impact. The relationship between technology and productivity, however, has proven difficult to measure. The available evidence suggests that productivity improvements are a function of both the technology itself but also the organization adjustments to work skills and the entire sociotechnical system.[39] For example, UK bookmaker William Hill's investment in new electronic point-of-sale technologies didn't pay off until it addressed the retail managers and customer-service advisors work processes in its 1,630 betting offices.[40]

23-2d Organizations

The final trend likely to shape OD's future involves the increasingly networked and knowledge-based nature of organizations. The interventions described in this book help organizations become more streamlined and flexible, more capable of improving themselves continuously in response to economic and other trends, and more effective. A large proportion of organizations are not aware of these practices, however, and still others resist applying them.[41] Despite the attention to them in the business press, only a small percentage of organizations use self-managed work teams, are organized into networks, successfully manage strategic alliances, or have organization learning programs. But these organizations are harbingers of the future, and they will invent entirely new, entrepreneurial structures capable of exploiting new ideas and technologies quickly.

Clearly, organizations are becoming more networked. As explained in Chapters 12 and 20, network structures rely on collaborative strategies and allow single organizations to partner with other organizations to develop, manufacture, and distribute goods and services.[42] More than any other organization form, networks hold the promise of realizing the economic opportunities presented by globalization without the negative social consequences of large multinational corporations.[43] Large organizations that gain economies of scale in manufacturing, distribution, and marketing can become rigid and slow, and indifferent to unintended social and ecological consequences.[44] These latter outcomes can be disastrous in today's rapidly changing environments and cannot be easily remedied in the future. Networks, on the other hand, enable small organizations to access the advantages of scale and scope traditionally reserved for large firms. Small, focused firms that perform particular tasks with excellence can align with organizations that have complementary resources and expertise. These networks are highly adaptable and can disband and reform along different task or market lines as the circumstances demand. To succeed, organizations are learning how to assess quickly whether they are compatible with network partners and whether the joint product/service is successful. They are gaining competence to form and end networks swiftly, thus enabling them to exploit product/market opportunities rapidly and to "fail fast" when the network is unproductive. Because each network node (organization) is small and local, resident cultures and ecosystems are more likely to be preserved.

Finally, in an organizational world that is technically enabled, fast-paced, and networked, there will be a premium placed on learning and knowledge management. This increasingly important source of organizational capability and competitive advantage will require unprecedented amounts of innovation and coordination. Multiple stakeholders representing a diversity of interests will come together to envision a shared future and to learn how to enact it.

Because this process typically leads into uncharted waters, both organizational members and OD practitioners will be joint learners, exploring new territory together. Moreover, implementing new organizational innovations will require significant amounts of experimentation as members try out new ways of operating, assess progress, and make necessary adjustments. In essence, they will learn from their actions how to create a new strategy, organization, or product/service. Such collaborative learning is capable of implementing radically new possibilities and ways of functioning that could not be envisioned beforehand. It is a process of *innovation*, not of detection and correction of errors. In turn, the new structures and systems will increase feedback and information flow to the organization, thereby improving its capacity to learn and adapt to a rapidly changing environment. They will transcend both internal and external organizational boundaries, remove barriers to learning, and facilitate how employees acquire, organize, and disseminate knowledge assets.

23-2e Implications for OD's Future

The definition and practice of OD in the future will depend on the forces within OD as well as the economic, workforce, technology, and organization trends outlined above. Although a variety of scenarios is possible, the future alternative presented below is based on the powerful role OD played in organization and social change in the 1960s and 1970s. A set of widely-shared values, including involvement and participation, and a complementary set of practices, such as team building and survey feedback, shaped the way leaders and managers designed and operated organizations. Together, these integrated values and practices had a significant influence on both human and economic outcomes.[45] Figure 23.2 summarized this positive view.[46]

OD in the future will support a policy of "responsible progress."[47] Responsible progress begins with an economist's definition of an effective system, integrates traditional OD and more recent effectiveness values, and promotes a set of practices to actualize those values. Economists traditionally define progress and economic health in terms of the development of products and services that make society better off, the ability to put scarce resources to their most efficient use, the capacity to support full employment, and the equitable distribution of rewards in relation to the risks people take in productive enterprise. Although few people would argue with these criteria, the trends discussed above suggest that there have been important unintended consequences of promoting those goals. For example, global warming and the concentration of wealth cannot be the metrics by which society is judged as "better off." The traditional criteria of progress either ignore the ecology and cultural diversity or make untenable assumptions about the market's ability to account for them.

Responsible progress addresses that gap by defining a policy that supports economic success and innovation, promotes efficiency and progress, but incorporates cultural diversity and ecological sustainability to produce a more balanced view of effectiveness. It supports a set of traditional and effectiveness-related values as well as practices that reflect today's and tomorrow's organizations. The responsible progress policy asserts that individuals, organizations, and countries can pursue economic and personal success through open innovation that leverages and nurtures cultural diversity and the ecology.[48] It defines a vision, strategy, and future path for OD.

OD will work to shape a global economy populated with flexible, innovative, networked, and ecologically responsible organizations that thrive on cultural diversity. As an important influence of this world vision, OD is more likely to develop interventions that drive effectiveness in a broader range of organizations, support technological and managerial innovation, and advocate for ecologically sustainable and socially diverse practices.

OD Will Be More Involved in Driving Effectiveness in a Broader Range of Organizations Responsible progress affirms that all forms of organizations should pursue economic success. It suggests, however, that organizations should not achieve that success at the expense of cultural diversity and the ecology. When OD lacks the shared values and applied focus of responsible progress, success can lead to cultural assimilation and ecological damage. The changing context of OD, in particular the economic and organizational trends, suggest that planned change in the future should be as concerned with effectiveness as it is with traditional values of participation and workplace democracy. It will also be applied to a more diverse client base.

Traditionally, OD focused on large business organizations, but three other types of organizations increasingly will become targets of planned change: *small entrepreneurial start-ups*, *government organizations*, and *global social change organizations.* Small, entrepreneurial start-ups are an important and underserved market for OD. Many of these organizations are at the forefront of the technology trends cited earlier. Because they are often funded by expensive and finite venture capital, time is their scarcest asset and the one most critical to their success. As a result, entrepreneurial firms generally have a clear action orientation, little perceived need to reflect and learn, and few structures and systems to guide behaviors and decisions.[49] This is a context that can be well-served by fast, flexible change processes orienting new people quickly to the business strategy, integrating them rapidly into new work roles, increasing the efficiency of work processes, and helping founders and key managers think about how the market, competitors, and technology are changing. Entrepreneurs are not inclined to think about nor are they trained to examine these issues. OD can help them gain the needed competence to address such matters.

Chapter 22 described the differences between public- and private-sector organizations and the implications of those differences for the practice of OD. The economic, workforce, technology, and organization trends are pushing government organizations to become more efficient, flexible, and networked. Consequently, government is increasingly applying OD interventions such as strategic planning, employee involvement, and performance management, and we expect that the demand for change-management expertise in the public sector will grow. Moreover, governments will become more proactive in managing the effects of global economic development. Public–private partnerships, a form of collaborative strategy, are also likely to flourish. They will require the assistance of OD practitioners who are sensitive to the differences between these two types of organizations and to the demands the partnerships will be under, such as environmental protection, corporate citizenship, and taxation.

Similarly, Chapter 21 described the application of OD in global social change organizations. The increasing concentration of wealth and globalization of the economy will create a plethora of opportunities for OD to assist developing countries, disadvantaged citizens, and the ecology. In China, for example, as the government breaks up the old "work unit" structure and creates market-facing enterprises, the need for NGOs to take over delivery of social services is likely to increase. For example, the Global Village of

Beijing has begun campaigns to involve the Chinese people in pro-environment practices; the China Association for NGOs (CANGO) provides capacity-building services to develop leaders for other NGOs; and the World Wildlife Fund (WWF) is partnering with corporations to initiate environmentally friendly policies. OD can help these organizations achieve their objectives, manage their resources, and improve their functioning through such interventions as team building, strategic planning, and alliance building.

Not only will OD be applied to a broader range of organizations, it will also be more concerned with effectiveness than in the past. A large portion of the interventions described in this text were developed in the 1950s and 1960s with the primary aim of increasing participation in organizational processes. As the global economy and information technology enable and push for faster, more flexible organizations, the ability to manage change continuously will become a key source of competitive advantage in all types of organizations. This suggests that OD practices will become more embedded in the organization's normal operating routines. OD skills, knowledge, and competencies can and should become part of the daily work of managers and employees.[50] This will diffuse change capabilities throughout the organization rather than limit them to a special function or role. It will permit faster and more flexible reactions to challenges faced by the organization. In addition to embedding OD skills in managerial roles, OD interventions themselves will be integrated into core business processes, such as product development, strategic planning, and supply-chain management. This should provide a closer linkage between OD and business results.

This does not mean that the role of the professional OD practitioner will go away. Professionals will be needed to help organization members gain change-management competencies. Small, entrepreneurial firms will need specialized assistance in bringing on new members rapidly and organizing their efforts. Organizations involved in strategic alliances, mergers, and acquisitions will need professional help managing interorganizational interfaces, integrating diverse corporate cultures, and coordinating business practices. OD professionals will also be needed to assist in the implementation of new technologies, particularly knowledge management practices. As supported by the contingent workforce trends, the demand for skilled OD practitioners is likely to increase rather than decrease. For example, there is some anecdotal evidence to suggest that as line and senior managers learn more about the knowledge and skills associated with OD practice, their requests for assistance in formulating change processes increase. Managers will look more frequently for help in leading and facilitating organization change.

OD's ability to influence responsible progress will grow as it becomes more concerned with effectiveness and more embedded in a broader range of organizations. As OD demonstrates its ability to solve problems or help the organization to be more agile and responsive to opportunities, it will become easier to suggest that leaders consider the ecological and cultural implications of their innovations. The promise and purpose of responsible progress encourages such a balanced view of success. Moreover, OD practitioners could begin influencing leaders to consider leveraging cultural and ecological resources to accelerate innovation and effectiveness. OD practitioners can help leaders make policy and implement actions that drive performance by leveraging cultural diversity and recognizing how the ecology can improve the long-term health of the organization, its people, and the planet.

OD Processes Will Be More Involved in Supporting Technological and Managerial Innovation According to the responsible progress policy, innovation is the primary driver of economic success. Innovation helps to create new products and services, the processes to manufacture and distribute them (technological innovation), and the methods and activities necessary to govern and organize systems toward some goal (managerial innovation). Although technological innovation gets most of the attention in the research and business press, Hamel has argued that managerial innovation may be more important.[51] He argued that organizations are still managed and operated according to rules and principles laid down before World War I. If the future of organization effectiveness hinges more on managerial innovation than technological innovation, there is a clear opportunity for OD. The "open innovation" models of Chesbrough and the "built-to-change" (B2C) principles from Lawler and Worley (described in Chapter 19) represent two such sets of new management principles.[52] But there is much more that can be done. In the future, OD will be more involved in shaping technological and managerial innovation according to the principles of responsible progress.

There is little doubt about the pervasive influence of technological innovation on organizations. Increases in the speed with which data and information can be manipulated will drive the rate of new product and service development and the organizational changes needed to support those developments. The extent to which technology allows information to be shared within and between organizations will increase the speed and complexity of innovation, coordination, and other decision-making processes. The amount of information that can be stored and accessed greatly enhances the potential quality of decisions and actions, and the sheer amount of information that research, practice, and experience generates threatens to overwhelm our ability to make sense of it.

In general, these trends will shorten product, organization, and industry life cycles. Pressures to reduce the cycle time of innovation and the OD activities that support them are also likely to increase. OD practitioners must be mindful of opportunities to quicken the pace of innovation and to simultaneously remain aware of the practices and processes that cannot be hurried.

For example, innovation is likely to be more synchronous (anytime, anywhere) as well as more virtual and less face-to-face. In global organizations, innovation occurs in a variety of locations, cultures, and time zones. OD interventions that support innovation, such as team building, employee involvement, and organization learning, will have to be planned and implemented in ways that encourage contributions from a variety of stakeholders at times that are convenient or at times when creative ideas emerge. Social networking technology and knowledge management systems can enable organization members to make these contributions at any time they are ready. In addition, groupware technologies allow members to discuss issues in chat rooms and portals, in Web and video conferences, and in the more traditional telephone conference. IBM's CEO Lou Gerstner used these technologies to lead a vigorous discussion of corporate values, a process they called Values Jam, that involved organization members from around the world.

Using these technologies to exchange ideas, develop technologies, or discuss implementation will produce different types of group dynamics from those found in face-to-face meetings. OD practitioners will need to be comfortable with this technology and to develop virtual facilitation skills that recognize these dynamics. In many cases, a more structured and assertive approach will be necessary to ensure that all members have an opportunity to share their ideas. The effect of these technically mediated exchanges on work satisfaction, productivity, and quality is only beginning to emerge. In addition, processes of visioning, diagnosis, data feedback, and action planning will have to be reengineered to leverage new information technologies.

Innovation processes need to be adapted to ensure that members have more information at their fingertips. For example, organization intranets provide members with an information channel that is richer, more efficient, more interactive, and more dynamic than such traditional channels as newsletters and memos. Thus, intranets can provide a timely method to collect data on emerging technologies, to monitor progress on a development project or organization change, and to involve members in key decisions. Processes of "Extreme Strategizing" or "fast HR" can leverage internal communication channels and external linkages.[53] These same technologies can also support increased innovation speed by processing a wide variety of inputs in as little as a few hours. In coming years, technological advances in groupware and Web conferencing will increasingly be used to bring more people together faster than ever before. In short, there is real potential to reduce dramatically the time required to perform many OD practices.

Despite the enablement of increased innovation speed, there are physical, psychological, cultural, and ecological limits to reductions in the innovation and change cycle. It is not realistic to expect new product development and other forms of innovation to be instantaneous.[54] For example, managers often want product development to occur more rapidly or managerial innovations to be implemented more quickly. Announcing a technological breakthrough, drug formulation, or new method of operating is one thing, but its implementation often takes longer than expected because of cultural values, ecological concerns, or other unforeseen obstacles. A new organization chart or a new vision and values statement hung on members' office walls often gives the illusion that change has occurred, but the working relationships, process improvements, and other aspects of fully implementing new technologies or organizations often take longer than expected. Similarly, most organization members are not capable of dropping a well-known and understood set of behaviors one day and picking up a new set of behaviors the next with the same level of efficiency. Members can face a steep learning curve when they are asked to change their routines, and thus there are likely minimums with respect to the speed of change in individual behavior.

The impact that technical and managerial innovation can have on an organization's effectiveness is immense. They are key drivers in economic and social progress. Without the invisible hand of responsible progress to guide OD practitioners and the organizations they serve, however, they also contain the possibility of great harm to cultures and the ecology. To fulfill the promise of responsible progress, innovation must not only support economic success, but must do so in ways that do not standardize or homogenize world cultures. Innovation must also unfold in ways that do not harm the ecology. OD practitioners can help organizations increase their innovative activity and raise the questions of diversity and ecology as the process unfolds.

OD Will Become More Concerned with Social and Ecological Sustainability As described in Chapter 21, OD will become increasingly oriented to supporting social diversity and ecological health. Most sustainability models go beyond ecological concerns to promote a multidimensional view called the *triple bottom line.*[55] In line with responsible progress, the triple bottom line proposes that organization change and globalization should be guided by the economic, social, and ecological value that is added or destroyed. These three values provide a framework for measuring and reporting corporate performance. They also guide how organizations should go about minimizing harm or maximizing benefits through their decisions and actions to achieve innovation and effectiveness. Organizations must be clear about their purpose in order to take into consideration the needs of all stakeholders—shareholders, customers, employees, business partners, governments, the ecology, local communities, and the public.

Responsible progress assumes that the practice of OD is capable of working effectively across cultures. However, we know relatively little about planned change processes in cross-cultural settings. Traditionally, OD has been practiced in organizations within specific cultures: British-trained OD practitioners helped British organizations in Great Britain; Mexican OD practitioners helped Latin American organizations; and so on. But the current trends clearly point to the need for OD practitioners and OD applications that can work well across cultures. Team-building interventions cannot assume open and direct communication is appropriate for a team composed of Americans, Indians, Chinese, Koreans, and Ukrainians who have never met face-to-face but are charged with developing a new product in a short period of time. Merger-and-acquisition processes need to be adapted to help a Japanese and a U.S. firm implement a new organization structure that honors both cultures. Because the number of organizations operating in multiple countries is growing rapidly, opportunities for OD in these situations seem endless: interorganizational and network relationships among subsidiaries, operating units, and headquarters organizations; team building across cultural boundaries; working out global logistic and supply-chain processes; and implementing diversity-centric values in ethnocentric cultures. Moreover, OD is likely to find increased opportunities in GSCO organizations that are often part of an international network. Alliance development processes and network structure interventions adapted for cross-cultural contexts have yet to be developed and will have important applications in the future.

However, working across cultures or with multiple cultures is not the same as pursuing progress and innovation that preserves the environment or leverages cultural diversity. Organizations today and in the future will operate in multiple countries, governments, and cultures but under one ecological system. The deep connection between economy and ecology was aptly demonstrated by Eyjafjallajökull's eruption and the transportation snarls it created in Europe, or the Japanese earthquake that sent a tsunami and the attendant debris throughout the Pacific. A single-minded pursuit of economic progress can—consciously or unconsciously—undermine local cultures and the ecology in service of greater efficiency, increased speed, or higher market shares. Developing and implementing business models and organization designs that operate globally but support local cultures and repair the environment will require significant managerial innovation. This is the promise and challenge of responsible progress.

Responsible progress does not suggest that preserving cultural diversity and contributing to ecological health are ends in themselves. If OD truly believes in diversity, then diversity must be a strategy that fuels innovation and economic progress. If OD truly believes in environmental sustainability, then it cannot only support recycling but must help organizations see sustainability as a source of competitive advantage. Biological diversity has always been the source of adaptation in nature, and the seeds of organizational responsiveness and successful change are in the innovative possibilities that exist when multiple viewpoints, values, and beliefs are heard and nurtured over time.

In the short run, ecological sustainability is likely to be a constraint on economic success and innovation. Most organization leaders and members hold assumptions about management and innovation that do not account for the ecology in decision making. Responsible progress challenges these beliefs and the largely uncontested value of organization and economic growth. This represents an important challenge for OD practitioners. As demonstrated by models of natural capitalism, the trick will be to see sustainability not as a cost or constraint, but as an ingredient and opportunity. OD practitioners in the future will become well versed in helping organization members see what Ikea, Unilever, and Nokia see—the possibility that honoring the ecology can be a source of innovation and success.

SUMMARY

In this concluding chapter, we described three trends within OD and four trends driving change in OD's context. OD's future is likely to be the result of the interactions among the traditional, pragmatic, and scholarly trends as well as how the global economy evolves, technology develops, workforces engage, and organizations structure themselves. To be relevant, OD practitioners and the field as a whole must act together to influence the future they prefer or adjust to the future that is coming. Moving OD toward rigor and relevance requires more than simple extensions of existing theory and practice. OD's ability to contribute to an organization's success, to shape globalization, or unite the trends within OD will depend on its ability to generate new and more powerful interventions that draw on new models and integrated values in pursuit of responsible progress. Our hope is that this text will be able to inform and equip the reader with the skills, knowledge, and value awareness necessary to shape the future.

NOTES

1. D. Bradford and W. Burke, *Reinventing Organization Development: New Approaches to Change in Organizations* (San Francisco: Wiley, 2005); A. Feyerherm and C. Worley, "Forward to the Past: Reclaiming OD's Influence in the World," *OD Practitioner* 40 (2008): 2–8; C. Worley, "Toward a Relevant and Influential OD," *OD Practitioner* 44 (2012): 5–6.
2. C. Worley and A. Feyerherm, "Reflections on the Future of Organization Development," *Journal of Applied Behavioral Science* 39 (2003): 97–115; F. Korten, L. DeCaluwé, and J. Geurt, "The Future of Organization Development: A Delphi Study Among Dutch Experts," *Journal of Change Management* 10 (2010): 393–405; B. Burnes and B. Cooke, "The Past, Present and Future of Organization Development: Taking the Long View," *Human Relations* 65 (2012): 1395–1429.
3. J. Milliman, J. Ferguson, D. Trickett, and B. Condemi, "Spirit and Community at Southwest Airlines: An Investigation of a Spiritual Values-Based Model," *Journal of Organizational Change Management* 12 (1999): 221–33; W. Gellerman, M. Frankel, and R. Ladenson, *Values and Ethics in Human Systems Development* (San Francisco: Jossey-Bass, 1990); D. Jamieson and W. Gellerman, "Values, Ethics, and OD Practice," in *The NTL Handbook of Organization Development and Change*, ed. B. Jones and M. Brazzel (San Francisco: Pfeiffer, 2006).
4. C. Weidner and O. Kulick, "The Professionalization of Organization Development: A Status Report and Look to the Future," in *Organizational Change and Development*, vol. 12, ed. W. Pasmore and R. Woodman (Oxford, England: JAI Press, 1999); A. Church, "The Professionalization of Organization Development: The Next Step in an Evolving Field," in *Organizational Change and Development*, vol. 13, ed. R. Woodman and W. Pasmore (Oxford, England: JAI Press, 2001), 1–42.
5. L. Forcella, "Marketing Competency and Consulting Competency for External OD Practitioners" (unpublished master's thesis, Pepperdine University, 2003).
6. N. Worren, K. Ruddle, and K. Moore, "From Organizational Development to Change Management: The Emergence of a New Profession," *Journal of Applied Behavioral Science* 35 (1999): 273–86; H. Hornstein, "Organizational Development and Change Management: Don't Throw the Baby Out with the Bath Water," *Journal of Applied Behavioral Science* 37 (2001): 223–26; M. Davis, "OD and Change Management Consultants: An Empirical Examination and Comparison of their Values and Interventions" (unpublished doctoral dissertation, George Washington University, 2002).
7. A. Pettigrew, R. Woodman, and K. Cameron, "Studying Organizational Change and Development: Challenges for Future Research," *Academy of Management Journal* 44 (2001): 697–714; L. Martins, "Organizational Change and Development," in *APA Handbook of Industrial and Organizational Psychology*, vol. 3 (Washington, DC: American Psychological Association, 2011).
8. A. Shani, D. Coghlan, and P. Coughlan, *Handbook of Collaborative Management Research* (Thousand Oaks, CA: Sage Publications, 2008); D. Coghlan, "Seeking Common Ground in the Diversity and Diffusion of Action Research and Collaborative Management Research Action Modalities: Toward a General Empirical Method," in *Research in Organization Change and Development*, vol. 18, ed. W. Pasmore, A. Shani, and R. Woodman (Emerald Group Publishing Limited, 2010); S. Mohrman and E. Lawler, "Generating Knowledge That Drives Change," *Academy of Management Perspectives* 26 (2012): 41–51.

9. T. Yaeger and P. Sorensen, "The Heritage, the Future, and the Role of Values in the Field of Organization Development," *Revue Sciences de Gestion* 65 (2008): 119–37.
10. P. Berger and T. Luckman, *The Social Construction of Reality* (New York: Anchor Books, 1967); K. Gergen, "The Social Constructionist Movement in Modern Psychology," *American Psychologist* 40 (1985): 266–75; D. Cooperrider, "Positive Image, Positive Action: The Affirmative Basis for Organizing," in *Appreciative Management and Leadership*, ed. S. Srivastva, D. Cooperrider, and Associates (San Francisco: Jossey-Bass, 1990).
11. C. Worley and A. McCloskey, "A Positive Vision of OD's Future," in *The NTL Handbook of Organization Development and Change*, ed. B. Jones and M. Brazzel (San Francisco: Pfeiffer, 2006); B. Nixon, "The Big Issues—The Challenge for OD Practitioners," *OD Practitioner* 34 (2002): 16–19.
12. A. Toffler, *The Third Wave* (New York: William Morrow, 1980); D. Korten, *When Corporations Rule the World* (West Hartford, CT: Kumarian Press; San Francisco: Berrett-Koehler, 1995); L. Thurow, *The Future of Capitalism* (New York: William Morrow, 1996); T. Friedman, *The World Is Flat* (New York: Farrar, Straus and Giroux, 2006); E. Lawler and C. Worley, *Management Reset* (San Francisco: Jossey-Bass, 2011).
13. Friedman, *The World Is Flat.*
14. A. Chua, *World on Fire* (New York: Anchor Books, 2003); The International Forum on Globalization, *Alternatives to Economic Globalization* (San Francisco: Berrett-Koehler, 2002); D. Cooperrider and J. Dutton, eds., *Organizational Dimensions of Global Change: No Limits to Cooperation* (Thousand Oaks, CA: Sage Publications, 1999); J. Perkins, *Confessions of an Economic Hit Man* (San Francisco: Berrett-Koehler Publishers, 2004); J. Stiglitz, *The Price of Inequality* (New York: W. W. Norton, 2012).
15. J. Bhagwati, *In Defense of Globalization* (New York: Oxford University Press, 2004); T. Cowen, *Creative Destruction* (Princeton, NJ: Princeton University Press, 2002).
16. T. Friedman, *Lexus and the Olive Tree* (New York: Anchor Books, 2000).
17. "America's Fear of China," *Economist*, May 19, 2007, 9–10; T. Carrel, "Beijing: New Face for the Ancient Capital," *National Geographic* 197 (2000): 116–37.
18. International Forum on Globalization, *Alternatives to Economic Globalization.*
19. C. Stone, D. Trisi, and A. Sherman, "A Guide to Statistics on Historical Trends in Income Inequality," Center on Budget and Policy Priorities, October 23, 2012, accessed from http://www.cbpp.org/cms/index.cfm?fa=view&id=3629 on December 16, 2012.
20. J. Stiglitz, "Of the 1%, By the 1%, for the 1%," *Vanity Fair*, May 2011, accessed from http://www.vanityfair.com/society/features/2011/05/top-one-percent-201105 on December 15, 2012.
21. L. Mishel and N. Sabadish, "CEO Pay and the Top 1%," *Economic Policy Institute Brief* no. 331, May 2, 2012, accessed from http://www.epi.org/publication/ib331-ceo-pay-top-1-percent on December 12, 2012.
22. Data accessed from http://www.forbes.com/billionaires on December 15, 2012; M. Fisher, "Study: Income Inequality Skyrockets in China, Now Among World's Highest," *Washington Post*, December 11, 2012, accessed from http://www.washingtonpost.com/blogs/worldviews/wp/2012/12/11/study-income-inequality-skyrockets-in-china-now-among-worlds-highest on December 16, 2012; "Inequality in China: To each, not according to his needs," *The Economist*, December 15, 2012, accessed from http://www.economist.com/news/finance-and-economics/21568423-new-survey-illuminates-extent-chinese-income-inequality-each-not on December 16, 2012.
23. Central Intelligence Agency, *Global Trends*, 2015 (Langley, VA: Central Intelligence Agency, 2000) as cited in The International Forum on Globalization, *Alternatives to Economic Globalization* (San Francisco: Berrett-Koehler, 2002).
24. Thurow, *Future of Capitalism*; Korten, *When Corporations Rule*; N. Mankiw, *Principles of Economics* (Fort Worth, TX: Dryden Press, 1997).
25. S. Chan, "Financial Crisis Was Avoidable, Inquiry Finds," *New York Times*, January 25, 2011, accessed from http://www.nytimes.com/2011/01/26/business/economy/26inquiry.html?_r=0 on December 15, 2012.
26. Stiglitz, "Of the 1%, By the 1%, For the 1%."
27. IPCC, "Summary for Policymakers," in *Climate Change 2007: The Physical Science Basis. Contribution of Working Group I to the Fourth Assessment Report of the Intergovernmental Panel on Climate Change*, ed. S. Solomon, D. Qin, M. Manning, Z. Chen, M. Marquis, K. B. Avery, M. Tignor, and H. L. Miller (Cambridge: Cambridge University Press, 2007); U. McFarling, "Climate Is Warming at Steep Rate Study Says," *Los Angeles Times*, February 23, 2000, A1.
28. J. Guyon, "A Big Oil Man Gets Religion," *Fortune*, March 6, 2000, F87–89; Sustainability Asset Management, "The Sustainability Yearbook – 2012," accessed from http://www.sustainability-indexes.com/review/annual-review-2012.jsp on December 17, 2012.
29. Thurow, *Future of Capitalism*; Korten, *When Corporations Rule.*
30. Data for these statistics accessed from http://www.census.gov/hhes/socdemo/education/data/cps/2011/tables.html on December 15, 2012.
31. R. Rivera and A. Paradise, "State of the Industry Report," American Society of Training and Development, 2006.
32. Data from the Department of Labor accessed from http://www.bls.gov/news.release/conemp.t05.htm on December 15, 2012.

33. B. Baden, "Larger Temporary Workforce Could be New Normal," November 17, 2011, accessed from http://money.usnews.com/money/careers/articles/2011/11/17/larger-temporary-workforce-could-be-new-normal on December 15, 2012; Y. Mui, "Surge in Temp Workers Reflects Fundamental Change in American Workplace," February 17, 2012, accessed from http://articles.washingtonpost.com/2012-02-17/news/35444268_1_temporary-workers-unemployment-rate-carl-camden on December 15, 2012.

34. R. Melchionno, "The Changing Temporary Work Force," *Occupational Outlook Quarterly* (Spring 1999), accessed from http://www.bls.gov/opub/ooq/1999/Spring/art03.pdf on November 13, 2003; M. Goldsmith, "The contingent workforce," *BusinessWeek*, May 23, 2007, accessed from http://www.businessweek.com/print/careers/content/may2007/ca20070523_580432.htm on October 5, 2007.

35. Statistics accessed from http://mobithinking.com/mobile-marketing-tools/latest-mobile-stats/a#subscribers on December 17, 2012.

36. Statistics accessed from http://www.internetworldstats.com/stats.htm on December 16, 2012. Internet users were for June 30, 2012.

37. P. Drucker, "Beyond the Information Revolution," *Atlantic Monthly*, October 1999, 47–57.

38. A. Enright, "E-commerce will Grow 13.7% this Year, eMarketer Predicts," March 17, 2011, accessed from http://www.internetretailer.com/2011/03/17/e-commerce-will-grow-137-year-emarketer-predicts on December 16, 2012.

39. E. Sanders, "Tech-Driven Efficiency Spurs Economic Boom," *Los Angeles Times*, February 22, 2000, A-1; T. Kretschmer, "Information and Communication Technologies and Productivity Growth: A Survey of the Literature," *OECD Digital Economy Papers*, No. 195, OECD Publishing (2012), accessed from http://dx.doi.org/10.1787/5k9bh3jllgs7-en on December 15, 2012.

40. D. Pollitt, "William Hill Backs a Winner with EPoS Training: Employees Embrace Culture Change and New Working Practices," *Human Resource Management International Digest* 17 (2009): 18–20.

41. G. Colvin, "Managing in the Info Era," *Fortune*, March 6, 2000, F6–F9.

42. R. Beckstrom and O. Brafman, *The Starfish and the Spider: The Unstoppable Power of Leaderless Organizations*: (New York: Portfolio, 2006); J. Child and D. Faulkner, *Strategies of Cooperation: Managing Alliances, Networks, and Joint Ventures* (New York: Oxford University Press, 1998); J. Bamford, B. Gomes-Casseres, and M. Robinson, *Mastering Alliance Strategy* (New York: John Wiley & Sons, 2002).

43. M. Piore and C. Sabel, *The Second Industrial Divide* (New York: Basic Books, 1984); D. Watts, *Six Degrees* (New York: W.W. Norton and Co., 2003); C. Huxham, *Managing to Collaborate* (Oxford: Routledge, 2005).

44. E. Lawler and C. Worley, *Management Reset* (San Francisco: Jossey-Bass).

45. A. Kleiner, *The Age of Heretics*, 2nd ed. (San Francisco: Jossey-Bass, 2008).

46. This section draws heavily from Worley and McCloskey, "A Positive Vision," but we were also influenced by J. Wirtenberg, L. Abrams, and C. Ott, "Assessing the Field of Organization Development," *Journal of Applied Behavioral Science* 40 (2004): 465–79; J. Wirtenberg, D. Lipsky, L. Abrams, M. Conway, and J. Slepian, "The Future of Organization Development: Enabling Sustainable Business Performance Through People," *Organization Development Journal* 25 (2007): 11–27; R. Marshak, "Organization Development as a Profession and a Field," in *The NTL Handbook of Organization Development and Change*, ed. B. Jones and M. Brazzel (San Francisco: Pfeiffer, 2006).

47. C. Worley and E. Lawler, "Built to Change Organizations and Responsible Progress: Twin Pillars of Sustainable Success," in *Research in Organization Change and Development*, ed. W. Pasmore, A. Shani, and R. Woodman (Howard House, UK: Emerald Group Publishing, 2010).

48. H. Chesbrough, *Open Innovation* (Boston: Harvard Business School Press, 2005); Lawler and Worley, *Management Reset.*

49. K. Chee, "Strategic and Organization Development Challenges Faced by High-Technology Startup Chief Executive Officers" (unpublished master's thesis, Pepperdine University, 1999).

50. C. Worley and E. Lawler, "Building a Change Capability at Capital One Financial," *Organizational Dynamics* 38 (2009): 245–251; N. Tichy, "The Death and Rebirth of Organizational Development," in *Organization 21C*, ed. S. Chowdhury (Upper Saddle River, NJ: Financial Times Prentice Hall, 2002), 155–74.

51. G. Hamel, *The Future of Management* (Boston: Harvard Business School Press, 2007).

52. Chesbrough, *Open Innovation*; E. Lawler and C. Worley, *Built to Change* (San Francisco: Jossey-Bass, 2006).

53. T. Welbourne, "Extreme Strategizing," *Leader to Leader* (Spring 2009): 42–48; T. Welbourne, "Fast HR–Enhancing Service Excellence," *Organizational Dynamics* 40 (2011): 292–301.

54. C. Worley and R. Patchett, "Myth and Hope Meet Reality: The Fallacy of and Opportunities for Reducing Cycle Time in Strategic Change," in *Fast Cycle Organization Development*, ed. M. Anderson (Cincinnati, OH: South-Western College Publishing, 2000); C. Worley, T. Cummings, and P. Monge, "A Critique, Test, and Refinement of the Punctuated Equilibrium Model of Strategic Change" (working paper, Pepperdine University, 1999).

55. J. Elkington, "Towards the Sustainable Corporation: Win-Win-Win Business Strategies for Sustainable Development," *California Management Review* 36, no. 2 (1994): 90–100.

Integrative Cases

B. R. Richardson Timber Products Corporation*

Jack Lawler returned to his desk with a fresh cup of coffee. In front of him was a file of his notes from his two visits to the B. R. Richardson Timber Products Corporation. As Lawler took a sip and opened the file, he was acutely aware that he had two tasks. In a week, he was to meet with the company president, B. R. Richardson, and the industrial relations officer, Richard Bowman, to make a presentation on his findings with regard to the lamination plant and his recommendations for what might be done. Lawler knew he had a lot of preparation to do, starting with a diagnosis of the situation. It wouldn't be easy. Taking another sip from his mug, he leaned back in his chair and recalled how this project had begun.

MAKING A PROPOSAL

It was about 2:30 P.M. when the office intercom buzzed. Lawler's secretary said there was a Richard Bowman calling from Papoose, Oregon. Lawler knew that Papoose was a small community about 150 miles south, a town with three or four lumber mills lying in the mountain range of western Oregon. When Lawler picked up his telephone, Bowman introduced himself as being in charge of industrial relations for the B. R. Richardson Timber Products Corporation. He was calling because a friend of his in a regional association for training and development persons had recommended Lawler, and Bowman had heard of Lawler's management training and consulting reputation. Bowman said he was searching for someone to conduct a "motivation course" for the blue-collar employees of the lamination plant. Morale in the plant was very low, there had been a fatality in the plant a few months before, and the plant manager was "a bit authoritative." Given the gravity of the plant situation, Bowman wanted to conduct the course within the next few months.

Lawler asked if the plant manager was supportive of the course idea. Bowman replied that he hadn't asked him but had gotten approval from B. R. Richardson, the founder and president of the firm. Lawler then stated that he really didn't have enough information on which to design such a course nor enough information to determine whether such a course was appropriate. He suggested a meeting with Bowman and Richardson the next week; he would be able to stop by Papoose in the late afternoon on his way home from another engagement. Bowman immediately accepted his proposal and gave Lawler directions.

Taking another sip of coffee, Jack Lawler continued to reminisce, visualizing the road winding past two very large lumber and plywood plants and over a small hill, and recalling his first sight of the company. It was much smaller than its neighbors, consisting of a one-story office building, a medium-size lumber mill, open storage yards, an oblong, hangarlike structure, dirt connecting roads, lumber and log piles seemingly scattered around, and cars and pickup trucks parked at random. The office building entryway was paneled with photographs showing the company buildings as they had changed over many years.

Bowman greeted Lawler, led him to a carpeted and paneled conference room, and introduced him to Ben Richardson. "BR" was a man in his late fifties, dressed in western apparel. The subsequent conversation was one in which the company as a whole was outlined and information was presented about the plant workers. Lawler described his preferred ways of working (essentially, diagnosis before training or other action). BR and Bowman shared their concerns that the plant manager, Joe Bamford, was getting out the work but wasn't sensitive to the workers. Bowman then took Lawler on a tour of the lamination plant.

*Printed by permission of Craig C. Lundberg, Cornell University. Events described are not intended to illustrate either effective or ineffective managerial behavior.

The meeting ended cordially, with Lawler promising to write a letter in a few days in which he would outline his thoughts on going forward.

Lawler opened the file in front of him on his desk and smiled as he found the copy of the letter he had sent:

Mr. Richard Bowman
B. R. Richardson Timber Corporation
P.O. Box 66
Papoose, Oregon

Dear Mr. Bowman:

When I departed from your office about a week ago, I promised a letter outlining my thoughts on some next steps regarding the laminating plant. Let me sketch some alternatives:

1. One is for me to put you in touch with someone in your immediate region who could design and/or present the "motivation" course for the laminating workers that you originally had in mind.
2. Second is for me to be engaged as a consultant. Recall the experience I described with the plywood plant in northern California in which I facilitated an approach called "action research." You'll remember that it basically involved a process wherein the concerned parties were helped to identify noncontrolled problems and plan to overcome them. This would begin with a diagnosis conducted by myself.
3. Third, you'll also recall that I teach part-time at State University. This relationship leads to two ways graduate students might become involved:

   I believe I could get a colleague in personnel management training to create a student team to design and conduct the motivation course.

   I can have a student team in my change seminar do a diagnosis of the laminating plant and provide you with their analyses and recommendations.

I believe I was clear during my visit that I think a diagnosis is needed first, regardless of next steps. When you and Mr. Richardson have thought about these alternatives, give me a call. I'll be prepared to outline what I see as the costs of alternatives 2 and 3.

Thanks for the opportunity to visit. I enjoyed meeting you and beginning to learn about your company.

Sincerely,
Jack Lawler
Partner
Oregon Consulting Associates

VISITING THE PLANT

Lawler remembered that six weeks went by before Bowman called. He had shown Lawler's letter to BR and they agreed that a more adequate diagnosis was probably a useful first step. Bowman was quite clear that BR did not want to invest much money but also wanted Lawler's expertise. In the ensuing conversation, Bowman and Lawler worked out an initial plan in which he would utilize several of his graduate students in a one-day visit to the company to gather information. Lawler would then analyze it and make a presentation to BR and Bowman. The use of the graduate students would substantially reduce his time as well as provide the students with some useful experience. They agreed that he would bill for three days of his time plus the expenses incurred when he and the students visited.

The next week when Lawler went to campus to teach his evening seminar called "The Management of Change" at the Graduate School of Business, he shared with the class the opportunity for some relevant fieldwork experience. He and four students could do the observing and interviewing in one day by leaving very early in the morning to drive to Papoose and arriving home by midevening. The information gained would be the focus of a subsequent class in which all seminar participants performed the diagnosis. When he asked his seminar who was interested in the information-gathering day, six students volunteered. When particular dates for the trip to Papoose were discussed, however, most of the six had conflicting schedules. Only Mitch and Mike, two second-year MBA students, were available on one of the days that Lawler's schedule permitted.

Having constituted the field team, Lawler suggested that the seminar invest some time that evening in two ways. He wanted to share with the class some information he had gained on his first visit to Richardson Timber and suggested that the class could help prepare Mitch and Mike for the experience in the field. He then drew an organization chart on the blackboard that showed the various segments of the corporation and the lamination business, including the personnel and main work groups. He further drew a layout of the laminating plant on the board. (Figures 1 and 2 show these sketches.) While doing this, Lawler spoke of his understanding of the technology, work flow, and product of the laminating plant as follows:

> It's a family-held corporation. It's composed of four small companies, divisions really, three in Papoose—a logging operation, a lumber mill, and

FIGURE 1

Organizational Chart

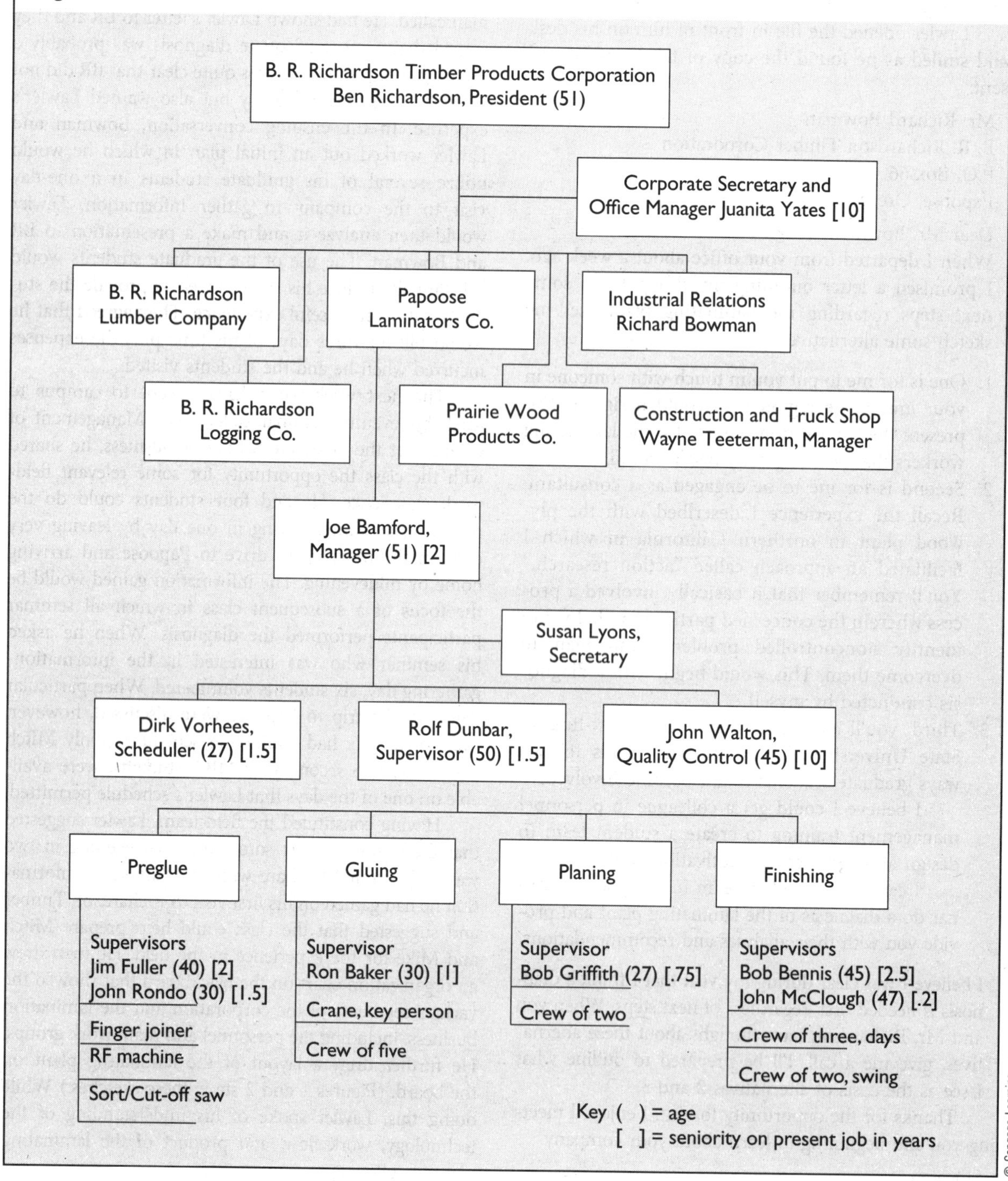

the laminating plant—and a mill over in eastern Oregon. The head office, the mill, and the lam plant are on the edge of Papoose, which is a very small logging town about six or seven miles from the interstate highway. The lam plant looks like a long airplane hangar, the type with a curved roof. Rich Bowman took me on a tour, safety helmet on, and explained the activities as we went along.

FIGURE 2

Laminating Plant

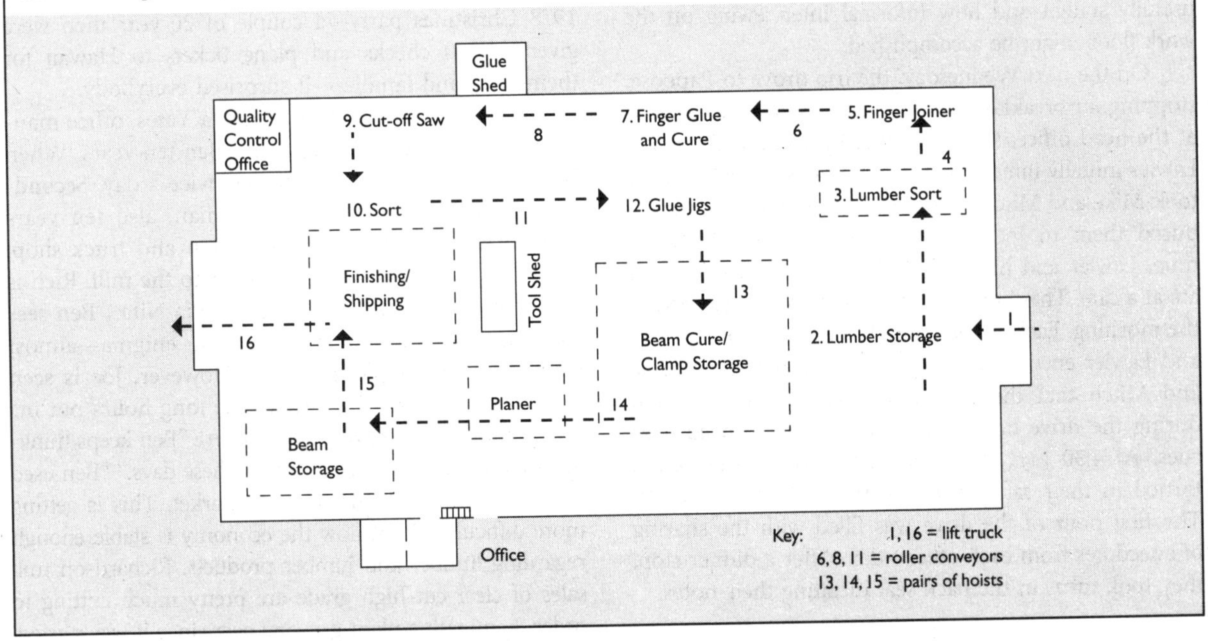

Now, the end products are long, laminated wood roof trusses or beams like you sometimes see in supermarkets and arenas. These are built up out of many layers of two-by-fours, two-by-sixes, and two-by-eights glued together end to end and then side to side. So in one end of the plant come lift trucks of lumber, which is stacked up to a height of 12 to 15 feet. According to orders—and all beams are made to customer order—the lumber is sorted and then hand-placed on a machine that cuts deep notches in the ends of the lumber. These go along one wall of the plant where the notched ends, called fingers, are glued together to make really long pieces.

These then go on along the roller conveyor, to the other end of the plant almost, where they are cut to the correct length, and sets of these long pieces are grouped together—the right number of the right length to make up a beam. This set then goes to a work station where there is a metal jig. The pieces are put in the jig one at a time, the glue is applied, and they are tapped down by hand. When the beam is fully assembled, clamps are put on every little way. This rough, clamped beam, running anywhere from 20 to, say, 78 feet in length and from one to three-plus feet high, obviously very, very heavy, is marked, then picked out of the jig by two small hoists and stacked up to cure (dry). The curing piles have cross sticks and must be 15 to 18 feet high in some places.

These beams cure and eventually are picked out of the stack with the hoists and maneuvered so that they are fed into the planer, which is set to plane the rough beam to exact thickness dimensions. After planing, the beam is stored until the finishing crew gets to it. This crew cuts the beam to length, patches minor surface blemishes, and wraps plastic around it for shipping. These beams then sometimes go directly onto a truck for shipment or into the yard until a load is ready.

The plant is noisy from saws, conveyors and hoists, and especially the planer. There are glue drippings, sawdust, and ends everywhere. The aisles tend to disappear in tools and piles. Above the plant offices of the manager, supervisor, and secretary is a lunchroom and another office for the scheduler. The company's head office is about fifty yards away in one direction and the mill about the same distance in another. The yard is graveled, with lumber of all kinds piled up and cars parked around the edges.

The class was encouraged to visualize the laminating plant and its working conditions. Lawler then divided the class into two groups around Mike and Mitch for the task of preparing for their visit to Richardson Timber. It was important to clarify what information might be usefully sought and how informal interviewing on the work floor might be accomplished.

On the next Wednesday, the trio drove to Papoose, stopping for breakfast along the way. When they arrived at the head office, they were met by Richard Bowman. Lawler initially interviewed Juanita Yates while Bowman took Mike and Mitch to the lamination plant and introduced them to Joe Bamford, the manager. At lunch time, Lawler and his students drove into Papoose and ate at a cafe. They summarized what they had learned in the morning. Each of them had been jotting some notes, and Lawler encouraged even more. He reminded Mike and Mitch that they would dictate their information during the drive home but that notes were needed as cues. At 4:30 P.M., the three met at Bowman's office, turned in their safety helmets, thanked him, and left. The first hour of the drive was filled with the sharing of anecdotes from each other's day. After a dinner stop, they took turns in the back seat dictating their notes.

REVIEWING THE NOTES

Jack Lawler's reverie was broken by the office intercom. His secretary announced a long-distance telephone call from a potential client. After the call, Jack turned his attention to the Richardson file. He realized that his forthcoming meeting with Ben Richardson and Richard Bowman would take place before his graduate seminar met to diagnose the laminating plant situation, and so he had best get to work himself. He decided to review the notes he and his students had created.

Jack's Notes

Current Lam schedule: Breakout crew 2:00 A.M. to 12:00 noon. Finish end 3:30 A.M. on. Joe typically works 7:00 A.M. to 6:00 P.M.

Ben Richardson (Juanita): "In the beginning he was very authoritarian, still is somewhat. Seen as a perfectionist." "Not quite a workaholic." "Has been, for several years, politically active—that is to say, locally." "When there is a cause, he throws his energies and resources behind it." Example, workers' compensation is currently a thorn in his side, and he has encouraged Rich to fight. "In the last few years, Ben has listened a little more and seems slightly more open." The last couple of years has had consultant Chuck Byron from Eugene, who has pushed the idea of a management team. Rich is the first real outsider hired as a professional. Ben has a "conservative philosophy." Will not have safety meetings on company time. Appreciates and rewards loyalty and dedication. Example, December 1978 Christmas party—a couple of 20-year men were given $1,000 checks and plane tickets to Hawaii for themselves and families—it surprised everybody.

Who's influential (Rich): Juanita Yates, office manager and secretary, has been with Ben ten years. When Ben is away, he calls her once or twice a day. Second-most influential is Wayne Teeterman, also ten years with Richardson. Heads construction and truck shop. Formerly ran the sawmill. Ben's ear to the mill. Rich is a distant third in influence. Mostly via Nita. "Ben sees Joe, manager of lam plant, as an enigma—almost canned him a couple of times." However, Joe is seen as dedicated, mostly because of the long hours put in.

Overall business pretty good (Rich): "Ben keeps thinking the other shoe will drop one of these days." "Ben used to be able to predict the lumber market. This is getting more difficult." Right now the economy is stable enough regarding lumber and lumber products. Richardson mill sales of clear-cut high grade are pretty much cutting to order. Laminating plant growing ever since it was started. It's very profitable, busy, and active—probably has the largest margin of all Richardson companies.

Laminating plant (Rich): Laminating plant has six- to seven-week delivery dates now.

Timber purchases (Rich): Timber purchases from Forest Service and BLM. One to two year's cutting is now available. Last year needed to cut only half of year's sales because of fortunate other purchases. Last year, half of timber requirements were from private ground. "Costs of cutting, however, go up, and it makes Ben nervous."

Laminating plant lumber (Rich): "Approximately 70% of laminating plant lumber purchased outside—30% from Richardson mill." This material is in the middle of the quality range. Outside purchases are primarily from Oregon companies—Weyerhaeuser, Bohemia, Georgia-Pacific, and smaller ones. Joe does the purchasing for lam plant. "He likes to do this."

Recent changes (Juanita): "Turnover has consistently been high and continues. For the company as a whole it is around 72 to 76%. In the lam plant there was 100% turnover last year" (among operators). "Right now this year it is down 50%."

Rolf (Juanita): Rolf was formerly industrial relations manager. A year ago April, he was appointed supervisor in the lam plant. Rolf's predecessor in lam plant ineffectual; gone from company. Rolf did not do a good job with personnel. Fatality in lam plant happened two months before Rolf went down there. It was in the breakdown area—several people quit at that time. There has been a constant concern for the height of stacking in the lam plant. "Joe has had a positive impact on morale—started a softball team in a community league."

Reward system (Juanita): "Nine paid holidays, hourly wage, liberal vacation plan, life insurance, no pension, no bonus except for those people who report directly to Ben (Nita, Wayne, Joe, and Rich). Joe has not had a bonus yet."

Incentives for safety: Joe and Rolf have introduced incentives for safety. Competition for groups about lost time. Joe gave a fishing outfit last month for the first time that a safety target was met.

Hiring (Rich): Hiring was traditionally done by division managers. At present, Rich has taken over that. He now goes into background more deeply.

Interaction with middle management (Rich): Normally when Ben is in Papoose, he and Joe interact a couple times a week, which is about the same as Ben interacts with other division or company managers.

Ben's style (Juanita): "He focuses on a problem. He will write a list and go over it with the manager item by item. Pretty much forcing his way. Later, he will pull out that list to check up with." He often wants Rich to play intermediary between top management and the lam plant. Rich tries to resist.

Rolf (Rich): "Fairly introverted, basically a nice guy. He finds it hard to be tough. Doesn't think he could do Joe's job." His folks were missionaries.

Dirk (Rich): "His goal is to get into sales. Ben has given okay, and he is supposed to look into local sales. Joe has agreed but has not given Dirk time to do any of this. Dirk probably has no long-run commitment to the company." He has a degree in forestry.

John Walton (Juanita): In charge of quality control. "Very loyal to the company. Very dedicated to quality. Member of national organization. Never gets very distressed. Seems well liked by crews. Not afraid to pitch in when they are a man short or behind."

Jim Fuller (Rich): "Ben doesn't like him." Had EMT training recently sponsored by the companies. Ben questions Jim's commitment. Jim gets into lots of community activities, has been a disc jockey on Sunday mornings, and is very active in community organizations with youth. "Not perceived as a real strong leadership type, but knowledgeable and pretty well liked in the lam plant."

John Rondo (Rich): "Dedicated, works hard. Pushes the men, too. Ben sees him as having future management promise." From an old logging family in the area. "Much more leadership oriented."

Ron Baker (Rich): Gluing supervisor. "Business-like, could be sour. Likes to impress others."

John McClough (Rich): "Failing as a finishing supervisor. Originally from California. Worked in Roseburg area as carpenter; does excellent work by himself. He is a flop and probably won't last much longer."

Bob Bennis (Rich): Finishing supervisor. "Not really a pusher." "Time has made him knowledgeable about the work." "Willing to be directed." He has had a number of family conflicts and has been in financial trouble. "Overall, a nice guy."

Bob Griffith (Rich): Planer. Came to Richardson out of the service. Started in gluing, then in breakdown, then gluing. Finally, planer's job opened up, and he took it. "Still learning the job. Generally a good worker; some question about his leadership."

Supervisors summary (Rich): "In general, the supervisors all kind of plod along."

Jim Fuller (Juanita): Is lam plant safety committee representative.

General reputation in community (Rich): "Not good from employees' point of view. Matter of turnover, accidents, and the fatality. Seems to be turning around somewhat over the last year. The company, as a whole economically, has a successful image. It's made money, survived downturns, and so forth."

Summer: During summer, fill-ins are hired for vacationers—sometimes college or high school students. The supervisor spots are filled in by key men on the crew.

Communication: Bulletin board outside of lam office has safety information, vacation schedule, and production information. Blackboard in lunchroom has jokes, congratulations, etc.

Reports: Daily production is scheduled by Dirk. Daily report from lam plant to office is compared against that. Production and lam's information reported daily. Joe keeps records on productivity by lam plant area. This duplicates Susan's records. Quality control turns in three sheets a day: on finger-joint testing, glue spread and temperature, and finished-product tests. Also Walton keeps cumulative information on block shear (where a core is drilled and stressed) and delamination tests made (where product is soaked and then stressed).

Records: A few years ago, 18,000 board feet was the high for preglue. May 9, daily was 16,406 board feet. Swing shift is consistently higher than the day shift preglue. Gluing, Ben expects 30,000 feet. On May 9, it was 27,815 feet.

Overtime (Juanita): "Is approximately 6% over the year. Right now lam plant is higher than that."

April (Juanita): Bids for the month were $8,166,000. Orders received for the month were $648,600. Shipped in April: $324,400. When $400,000 is shipped, that is an excellent month, according to Nita. Joe does all the bidding. Sue actually may do the calls, however. "The margin is significantly higher than the sawmill or planing mill."

History of lam plant (Juanita): "In 1968 Wayne Lauder started it. He had lots of prior experience." "The property that Richardson stands on had just been purchased. Wayne came to Joe with a proposition. Ended up with Wayne having stock in the Papoose Laminators Company." Original crew was eight to ten men. "In fact Wayne taught Ben all Ben knows about the laminating plant." "Got into lamination business at a very good time." "In the early days, there were no accidents and no turnover." "Wayne had hired old friends, largely married family types." "Walton is the only one left from those days." In the spring of 1973, Wayne went to South Africa on a missionary call. Between then and Joe, there have been four managers and four or five supervisors. Ben has an image of Wayne that successive managers cannot live up to. Joe, in Ben's eyes, has done better than anyone since Wayne. The supervisor's job was started under Wayne; since then it is not clear what they do. At one time, there was an experiment to move the lam office up to the main office so that the supervisor was forced to see the manager up there. This did not work. With Joe, the office moved back to the plant.

Sue (Juanita): Secretary in lam plant. Now hand-extending the data. Could use a computer. It is programmed; she has computer skills. "Computer never used for lam bidding since Sue came two years ago." Phone coverage is awkward. To get copies of things means Sue has to come to the office.

Market conditions: Market conditions have been good since Joe became manager.

Joe's ability (Juanita): Highly questioned around planning. Example: "Sue away; he knew it beforehand; it was a day he wanted to be away. This left the head office trying to get someone to cover for the phone." "Clearly sales is Joe's strong area. Get excellent reports back from customers. But Joe doesn't follow up, so payables are very weak. We still haven't got a 90-day payment and are likely to ship the next load to the customer anyway."

Lack of communication (Juanita): "Lack of communication with us about cash flow is another weak spot of Joe's. Lack of supervision over key people like Sue and Rolf. Seems to just let them go. Certainly doesn't supervise them. Sue gets to set her own hours." Example offered by Nita of misbidding because Sue didn't get the bid back to the customer. "Joe just wasn't aware of the timing—hadn't planned for it." Another example: "Sue runs out of invoice paper, which means we have to scurry around."

Sue's wages (Juanita): "At one time, Sue was all riled up about wages and upset the secretaries in the main office. She got no pay increase last year. Ben upset. Joe went to bat for her. Joe almost put his job on the line for her."

Sue's performance (Juanita): "Sue does sloppy work. Not very efficient. Poor letters; late; missing deadlines. Joe allows or accepts, or perhaps doesn't know." Nita is supposed to be responsible for Sue on quality matters. In general, to make sure that her backup is there. "Sue now works 10 to 15 hours a week overtime." Nita cannot see the reason for this.

Rolf's attitude (Rich/Juanita): Rolf's attitude changing. Seems more cooperative to both Rich and Nita. Nita thinks Rolf is a very intelligent man. Neither are clear exactly on what Rolf does. Company policy is to send out invoices each workday and that invoices should be sent and dated on the day shipped. Sue doesn't send them.

After Wayne, a lot of lam workers were hippies, had long hair, etc. Part of that is the reason why Rich now hires. Why is Ben down on Jim Fuller? Nita says because of time lost with accidents. "Ben knows his family and all about the radio station. Doesn't think he is committed to the lumber company. There have been financial problems, too. There were garnishments in the past. He's quit or been laid off, or was fired about three years ago. Some things stick in Ben's throat. Now Jim is out of debt; they sold the home and moved; his wife works; they do an awful lot of volunteer work at the school. Ben sees this and wonders why he can't give that energy to the company."

John Rondo (Juanita): From a local logging family. He is a nephew of Butch (someone from a logging company). "Notorious redneck." Once called Ben from a bar when he was drunk and swore to Ben about his paycheck. "Ben doesn't forget those things."

Sue hired by Joe: Does all the paperwork in the lam plant. Doesn't really have to interact with any of the men except Joe. Takes care of the purchase orders, invoices, and daily records.

Glue used in lam plant: Twenty-two thousand pounds at 60 cents per pound; that's nearly $10,000 a month.

Maintenance man: Leon replacing rails and turning chair at preglue. "Had help until noon. Don't know where they took off to." It's really a two-person job. Also said that they're probably six to eight months overdue with this job.

Hoists: Planer and helper talking at break that it is awkward and sometimes have to wait either on the finish end or breakdown side of planing because of competition for hoists. Believe the roof could hold more hoists. Can't understand why Ben won't spring for a couple of more hoists on each side. In the lunchroom, the planer was coaching a breakdown/finish helper on how to undo clamps efficiently. Says that the "whole operation has to be speeded up." 1:05 P.M.—lunchroom. The planer approaches Joe: "Can we get off a little early? We've been working lots of ten-hour days." Joe responds, "If you get that 57 job done, maybe we'll see." As Joe turns to leave, the other finish man, who helps the planer, says, "Hey, Joe, I want to talk to you later." Joe says, "Okay." The man turns to me and says, "He thinks we should be working harder. I want to tell him what's what."

Rolf put in lam plant by Ben: Probably consulted with Joe, but still he did it.

Goals for lam plant (Rich): Joe and Ben both have some goals in their heads, of course, and talk on occasion. "Probably not very systematically written down."

Jim Fuller, preglue supervisor: Swing shift now. Three men work directly under him. First work position is a lumber grading cut-off saw. A 19- to 20-year-old tends to work here. "You need a big reach." Then there is a cut-off saw that feeds a finger-joiner cut. Then the ends are glued. "Young men tend to be in this position, too. Need to have a lot of manual dexterity and a sense of rhythm." Then there is the radio frequency curing machine. It gives an eight- to ten-second jolt at 109; then the hardest job comes along. The lumber is stopped, set to length, and cut three inches longer than order and then put in stacks on rollers. "You need to visually check ahead, grade lumber, and everything else." This position has to be communicated back up to preglue line for amount.

Production scheduling (Rich/Jim): "Rolf is so-called production supervisor. However, if Joe has his druthers, he'd do that, too." Supposed to have orders from Joe to Dirk to Jim. Needs to be scheduling. This mostly happens, but sometimes he gets a message from Joe himself. Actually Jim says, "Both Rolf and Joe more or less equally give me orders." Jim confirms that the majority of materials come from external sources and suppliers. He thinks Joe is a "sharp bargainer." "If he can save $100 per thousand on eight- or ten-footers, he may buy them. Of course, this means they have to do a lot more cutting and gluing." Somehow it's known that 30,000 feet a day per shift is what the lam plant is to produce. It takes two preglue shifts to get that. A few years ago, Jim reports, a production quota for the plant was 18,000–20,000 feet per day. "Joe is really production-minded, a real pusher."

Asking about problems (Jim): He quickly responds with "confusion" and elaborates that it has to do with scheduling. "Sometimes Dirk has to work on the line and get inaccurate figures, or we don't get them in time." Nonetheless, he thinks Dirk is a good man and tries hard. Another problem has to do with stacking. There is not enough room to handle items where beams are curing, particularly in the finishing area. He makes a big point about the difference between architectural and other grades. There are 15% of the former in general, but it takes more layout space in the finish end to handle it.

The most inexperienced crew, in Jim's opinion, is in the breakdown area (unclamping beams for planing). There seems to be a bottleneck around the planer. "The crew tries hard but is somewhat inexperienced. His helpers couldn't care a damn." Planing is to a tolerance of plus or minus 1/16-inch. He gives an example of large beams for Los Angeles that were overplaned, and those beams now sit in the yard until they can be worked into some later order for someone.

Another problem, according to Fuller, has to do with Paul, an electrician who works under Wayne. Has strong sawmill preference. Can never find him. For example, the RF machine is only half rebuilt. "People who do this work for Wayne will probably never get it done."

Age of workers (Jim): Mostly young—"means that they don't really care about working, aren't very responsible. They take off when they feel like it; hence, there is a lot of personnel being shuffled around. Both Walton and Dirk, and even Joe, pitch in sometimes, not that this makes it really more efficient." "Personnel is shuffled too much." Fuller gives an example. He was hit by a beam and was off for seven weeks. Jay replaced him. There was stacking in the breakdown area on the main two. Jay tried to move a ceiling air hose; it came back; two top beams fell and "snuffed him out just like that." Maintenance men have to fill in on lines, too. This cuts into maintenance being done on time. The whole program is behind. It's sort of down to what Fuller calls "band-aid work." Also, major replacements are done poorly. Example: glue area where pipes come right down in the middle of the preglue line when they should have been run down the wall. Bruce did this.

Ben's approach (Jim): "Ben used to visit the laminating plant twice a week a few years ago. I haven't seen Ben through here for more than a month now. Ben likes to use a big-stick approach." He gives example of Ben looking at maintenance work in gluing shop and insisting that the millwright come in on Saturday to get it done, "or else."

Those who report to Ben: Rich, industrial relations; Wayne, construction; Juanita, who is secretary and office manager; and managers of three companies. Richardson Lumber, which has 110 employees, was founded in 1951. Papoose Laminators started in 1968, and Prairie Wood Products started in about 1976, with 45 employees. There is a logging company, too, which is for buying.

Mitch's Notes

Jack, Mike, and I arrive at B. R. Richardson. We enter through the main building into the office and are seated in a conference room located at the back of the main office, which is located up on a hill overlooking the rest of the plant.

Rich enters; after formal introductions, proceeds to talk about Joe, or I should say, describes Joe.

Describes Joe in the following way. Says that Joe is aware the training program was a possibility. Stated that Joe had had military experience, that he (Joe) believes he knows about management, that there are some possible resentful feelings toward our intrusion upon the plant, that he is aware of us and the fact that we are from State University.

Rich, Mike, and I leave the main office and go down to the plant to be introduced to Joe.

Rich introduces us to Joe by saying that we are with Jack and that we are down looking around at the plant, etc.—seemed awkward. Communication not straightforward. Not a lot of eye-to-eye contact. Rich is leaning up against the wall; he looks uncomfortable and leaves rather abruptly.

Joe immediately questions us as to what we are doing, why we are here, and what we are looking for. My perception is that he is resentful. In talking to Joe, I perceive that he felt the workers were good, that with the proper knowledge of the task they could lead themselves. He also stated they were "multicapacity"—that "they had many functions which they performed," and that it wasn't that specialized down on the floor. He mentioned that his functions were bidding, managing, and engineering. He made a comment toward work team functions ("work team crap"), and then he corrected himself. He also remarked that "theories come and theories go."

At one point, Joe stressed the use of communication as a tool in management. He showed Mike and me a little exercise and seemed to be impressed with it.

In looking on the walls of his office, he had approximately five awards or merits for leadership or worker participation.

His assistant Rolf had a desk right next to his, which was in an office off the side of the secretarial room serving as the entrance to his building.

Joe's background included working in many plants, primarily in forestry—that is my understanding. He said he preferred working at B. R. Richardson's mainly because it was a "small and nonpolitical plant." He likes leadership, and he enjoys working there. He stated, as we were walking through the plant, that he felt a high degree of frustration about the plant because the size was too small at times and the seasonal rush (which is beginning right now as of May) for summer building puts a crunch on things. He stated that production is up 10% from last year; that there have been scheduling problems—they received some wood in February, and it wasn't until May that they could use it and laminate it and get it out the other side, so it's been stacked taking up space. He stated that if they fall behind, they have no chance to catch up and that they are working at full capacity right now.

Later on that afternoon, I went back and talked to Joe. I asked him what his specific duties were. He replied in the following way: His duties were to take orders, to plan the shipping, to make bids on orders, and to manage the plant. His typical day was to arrive about 7:00 to 7:15 A.M., to look over the plant, to look at the new orders of the day, and to take care of any emergencies. Lately, he stated that he was making engineering drawings. When asked if this was common, he said it usually was done by the customers, but he felt it was a service he could render them. He stated, "It's foolishness because it takes too much time." However, he continued to work on that project. He stated that he liked the work, that he didn't mind long hours. When asked about the scheduling, he said that after he makes a bid and fills the order, it goes to Dirk, who schedules the work to be done, which goes to Ron, who is either in preglue or the gluing operation. I'm not sure, but I felt he was talking about the gluing operation. And he stated that Ron's job was very specific, that he had to coordinate the people to get the wood clamped up, to get the glue on, and to get it organized in a rather specified manner. (I think it is interesting to check Ron's description that I include later on.)

My personal comment on Joe is that he seemed very friendly with the workers, that it was a buddy-buddy relationship. At one time, we were in the lunchroom with Joe, and he was talking openly about the problems of the shop; it was kind of like "we all suffer through this too, don't we?" He seemed to enjoy his work, he likes to work hard, he was proud of the fact that production was up, he was supportive of the men down there, and he was also apprehensive of Mike's and my presence. I think it is interesting to note the roles that Mike and I took. Mike took the role of a person interested in design, more or less, and I took the role, as I stated to Joe, that I was interested in seeing what it was like to be a manager in this situation and to learn any knowledge he might have to offer. Many times during our encounter, he asked me what my background was and also about what I wanted to do when I got through school. He seemed very interested in my studies and my goals.

Joe's secretary, while I did not talk to her, seemed to play an important role in the organization. At one point, I was talking to Joe when the secretary answered the phone and interrupted our conversation to tell Joe about a possible bid. Joe then made the bid based on the board footage, and the secretary questioned him on this bid, at which point Joe thought a minute and said, "Yeah, I want to keep the bid the way it is." The secretary then asked him, "Are you sure?" and Joe said, "Yes," at which point the secretary completed the preliminary parts of the bid over the phone.

At one point when we were walking through the plant with Joe, I made mental notes on safety aspects of the plant—this was something in question. Some of the things I noted are as follows.

There seemed to be many metal spacers or clamps by the glue section. This section wasn't in use, so I don't know if this was normal or not. It was very crowded and difficult to walk around. As we walked through the plant, I saw at least two different types of band saws with no guarding whatsoever—a very dangerous situation in my opinion. There were no safety signs around the plant—at least not outside the lunchroom. One worker did not have a safety helmet on. I also noticed that the safety helmets that they gave us were of very low quality. I base this on past experience in wearing them; they were the cheapest I have seen. I did see a safety insignia on one gentleman's lunch box. (I wonder how they meet OSHA standards.) Also because of the crowdedness of the facility, it was very difficult to move around, and with things going on, I could see how it would be difficult not to get hurt. The workers at one point asked Joe about another worker (I think his name was Bob). It seems that Bob was going down the highway and was reaching for a speaker wire and hit the center rail on Highway I-5 and totaled his truck. He seemed to be okay with a mild concussion. The workers were very concerned. A group of about three of them asked Joe how Bob was doing.

I had a chance to talk to Ron, the team leader in gluing. His comment about his job was that there were long hours, that these were typically ten or more per day, and that he received overtime for the long hours provided that in total they were over 40 hours per week. Each hour over the 40 minimum would be paid at 1.5 times the normal rate. For Ron, the normal rate was about $8 an hour, $12 an hour overtime. His comments about his job and his attitude toward the plant were "sweatshop," "Richardson won't spend money," and "everyone's worked at BR's at one time or another before." "They have plans for expansion of the plant, but they don't want to spend the money on it." At one point, he said he didn't really know what he was doing in terms of how to be a supervisor, how to be a leader. When I questioned him some more, he really didn't know what the supervisor did, in this case Rolf. He had just finished his first year, as far as experience on the job.

Ron had a major complaint about his job in that the glue person also had to prepare the glue and was responsible for getting all the boards and clamps in the right direction. He seemed to think maybe an extra glue prepare person would help. It seems to be a major job for him. There seemed to be quite a bit of dissatisfaction about Rolf in his mind. He stated that when overtime or a certain amount of board footage was needed to meet a quota, this created work unrest, which led to accidents. He said that Rolf was always the one who initiated or told the workers that they had to work overtime. When asked about the death that had occurred, he stated that everybody was pretty upset about it, that it was bound to happen. I asked him what happened that day. He said that a guy got hurt, and yet management still wanted them to work even after the guy died. This seemed to upset Ron.

Ron mentioned that they (the workers) had a softball team; that he felt frustrated about it because he couldn't always play because the games were at six or seven o'clock and many times they were working until late in the evening trying to make a quota. He also stated that accidents were very high around here, that it was not uncommon to get a finger smashed or something, and that management didn't seem to care too much. He stated that he liked Joe, the manager, that he was okay but that he was maybe more production-oriented than necessary. He stated that the work is very hard and the need for better methods is evident. He stated that most men had bad backs, hernias, and broken fingers or toes, and he seemed to be kind of embarrassed. He did state that they had medical insurance.

Ron stated that one of the biggest causes of unrest, he felt, was due to overtime, and his own personal frustration was that in a year he had obtained probably the highest vertical level on the management structure, that of supervisor. He stated that the next job would probably be to take Joe's job. He said that wouldn't happen, so there seems to be a lack of job mobility in his eyes. He stated that workers do almost anything, any task at any time; that what needs to be done, needs to be done, and they do it. He also stated that in the summertime, when it is warmer, the metal building that they work in gets really hot, and it's not uncommon for men to lose five or more pounds in one shift, which would be in an eight-hour period. When asked if it was possible to ventilate the building a little bit more, he said it would be hard, that even if they could, management wouldn't spend the money to do it.

Ron said he didn't have enough time for his home life. He also stated that Rolf and Joe, who were the supervisor and manager, would come out and help when they had the time. He said they would actually end up losing a half-hour of production time that way and would be better off if they would just stay in their offices. Ron seemed to express a great amount of displeasure with Rolf, and he said most of the workers agreed that Rolf was a "thorn." When Rolf would give orders, men would get upset and throw things around, and this would cause accidents. When asked about new members, he said they don't last more than a couple of days, and very rarely do they last over a year. Ron stated that one of the jobs they gave new workers was to bang beams in the gluing job with a weight that was on a pole that is picked up and bounced up and down off the wood. It weighed anywhere from forty-five to one hundred pounds; very grueling work. He laughed a little bit and said that they usually hurt their back the first day, and it takes them a couple of weeks to learn how to do it, to learn the right technique, but he said "there is no other way to learn the job, other than just jumping up there and doing it."

My own personal opinion of Ron was that while somewhat upset at the conditions down there, he was dedicated, he did enjoy his role as a leader, and he was looked up to by the fellow workers. He mentioned at one time that the record of total board footage was broken by his crew, and he seemed very proud of that fact. He did not seem to think that any of our suggestions would make any waves around there, that "I would not be listened to." He was enjoyable to talk to, and he was more than willing to help me obtain the information I needed.

Marty, who like Ron has been there for over a year, was "key person" of the glue team. However, Ron acted as the leader. They seemed to be good friends and went home together that afternoon. Marty had been there the longest. He had stated that the work is hard, that there are long hours, and that he had been right next to the man who was killed. He stated that he was no more than three to six feet from his friend (I guess he was his friend) when it happened. He was the one to fill out the accident report for the police and insurance people. He stated that they wanted to stop work and that the plant, and he didn't say specifically who, didn't want to shut down but wanted to complete the work that was started. It seemed that most of the workers there did not want to work that day. That was the extent of my talking to Marty.

When the workers were leaving, it seems they had set up a bet for a keg of beer if the planer Griffith could plane all the beams that were set out in front of him, which from the comments of the men, was quite a chore. But Griffith seemed pretty confident that he could get the work out. He did say that he was looking to go to pharmacy school as soon as he got his hernia fixed, and when asked about the hernia, he said he got it some time ago. He said he got it working while picking up some stuff in the plant. Again, this seemed to be common.

I had a chance to talk to a couple of the preglue persons; there is a total of three. I believe Jack had talked to the leader, and I talked to the two workers. They pretty much agreed that a union would be nice; however, BR, the owner, would not allow one to come in. He said, "Work long hours, or you get fired." There seemed to be a lot of stress as far as meeting their quota, and they could not go home until they met the quota for the day. They stated that the job was okay, but that they didn't have much time for their families. One said, "I go home, I sleep, I get up, I go to work, and I go back home and go to sleep again." When asked about their salary, he stated that they're paying, in his opinion, 60 cents per hour lower than the unions around here, and he said further, "The unions will get a 65-cent-per-hour raise, and we'll get a 45-cent-per-hour raise."

I also had a chance to talk to some of the guys in the finish area. This seemed to be a typical eight-hour shift that consisted primarily of watching the beams run through the planer. They go back and clean it up so that it can be packaged and shipped out. One man's biggest complaint was that he was upset about the lunch-break change, which he stated was initiated by Rolf. It consisted of taking their one-hour lunch break and cutting it down to a half-hour. He stated that Rolf felt production would be increased by cutting down the lunch break. He seemed upset about this. I don't know his name. He lived five blocks away from the plant and didn't have time to go home to eat and then come back (on a half-hour break). He seemed to have a high degree of resentment toward Rolf, and he had no knowledge of what Rolf does.

I had an opportunity to meet with John, the quality-control man. He seemed like a very nice man. No real quotes. He was just there for a few minutes. He had had an eye operated on: I guess a new lens was put in. He seemed to talk with Joe very well. When I asked Joe about John, Joe stated John was officially to report to him; however, John reported to Rich, and that worked out for the best because quality control should really be removed from production somewhat. Joe seemed to see no conflict in that.

Mike's Notes

Mitch and I had a morning interview with Joe. Some of the quotes on management style were: "I don't know about this work team crap, oops, stuff," "Theories come and theories go," "I believe in giving my workers explicit instructions; perceptions differ, and you have to be sure they understand," and "I didn't like the politics of larger plants I've worked in." Also, Joe mentioned frustration over the lack of plant space. To a worker he mentioned, "You are frustrated, aren't you, Bill?"

During our tour, Joe set a brisk pace. He seemed to have quite a competent manner.

When Rich approached Joe about taking Mitch and me under his wing for a tour, I think Rich was intimidated by Joe. Rich had his back against the wall sideways to Joe, and he shifted his eyes from Joe to Mitch and me during the conversation.

Joe was more than a bit curious in regard to our plant visit objective. I said it was for a class project. Joe replied, "Oh, then it's theory." I explained we covered all the theories equally. Another quote from Joe: "A day's production lost is a day lost," delivered with a hint of frustration and impatience.

Joe's office contained numerous good-worker awards. One prominent sign contained a message roughly to the effect that "I am right in the end." My impression of the plant—there were no safety glasses on the workers. One worker had no helmet; there were no band-saw safety devices. Seemed pretty lackadaisical. During our initial interview with Joe, Darrell, a truck driver, was in the office. He talked good-naturedly with Joe, and he seemed to like Joe in general. Later on in the day I had an interview alone with Dirk. Dirk is the scheduler. Dirk has a master's in forestry from the University of Washington. Dirk mentioned that he spends half his time filling in various positions. He says one of the major problems is the transition between shifts. This is in regard to mistakes. One of Dirk's quotes: "There is no communication between shifts. Mainly people don't want to take the blame for mistakes." During the course of the interview, Dirk's manner was fidgety; he moved around a bit, but he seemed fairly open. A quote from Dirk: "The men change jobs so much that it is hard to train them. Everyone has to know what is needed in beams." This implies that workers weren't really trained well enough to know what was needed in beams. "Production people go home after the quota." That was his perception of the amount of overtime worked. "Repairs after gluing are costly and difficult. Double checking is needed before they are glued together. Average beam is 6,000 board feet, or approximately $840. I currently have 75 bastard beams I have to find a home for." Then Dirk went on to an example of mistakes made. A tapecloth shrunk two inches. They used this tape for quite some time before they finally found the mistake. He also mentioned there were frequent mixups between the 1 3/16-inch and 1 1/4-inch strips for laminated beams. Dirk's quote on the workers: "A few are incompetent; they just get soft warnings. Management should be harder on them."

Item on bidding or posting for jobs: seniority or ability (whoever they think will do best) decides who gets the job. On the workers: Morale is low. Safety and overtime are the main causes. On Rich, industrial relations: "The only contact I've had with him is when he came down and asked about people." I asked, "Who, what people?" and Dirk said, "I'd rather not say." On safety, he mentioned there are no physicals required. Later on in the interview, I asked why he didn't try to change things, seeing as he has a master's and seems to have his head together. Dirk mentioned, "Go up the line. Joe would listen." I said, "Listen?" and Dirk said, "Yeah, Joe would listen." At this point, Bruce, a bubbling and brassy guy who is a millwright in charge of special-projects maintenance, came in. The interview with Dirk was about thirty minutes under way; the next twenty minutes I spent with Dirk, he mentioned Ben Richardson, the president. I asked, "Do men like to see BR?" Dirk responded, "No, BR is bad news in the laminating plant." He also mentioned that in the year he has been there, BR had been down to the laminating plant only five times.

Item from Bruce: "I've had 30 projects in the year I've been here; I only finished one. Joe keeps jerking me around. As I get something operating but not all the kinks out, I'm on to something else." Bruce also mentioned that he is on emergency call every other week. He splits it with the other maintenance person.

The beam stacks before and after planing were mentioned as being in terrible disarray. Bruce mentioned that the Roseburg plants had a computer and a big yard with designated areas to organize their stacks. He said that this company should take a bulldozer and knock out the field to expand the outside stack area.

Item from Bruce: "Antiquated machinery. Maintenance is costly and time-consuming." Bruce commented on BR: "Joe thinks labor is cheap; we don't have that many benefits. An example of BR's attitude: one of his right-hand men got in a flap over the 3:30 A.M. shift parking down here instead of in the muddy, rutted parking lot an eighth of a mile up the road. Christ, they had a caterpillar running up there, and they didn't even smooth it out. Anyway, this guy tells Rolf, the super, if these guys are too lazy to walk down from the workers' parking lot, they can go work somewhere else." This was mentioned right in front of some of the men. Bruce went on to say, "It really makes us feel wanted." I then asked who was this guy, BR's right-hand man, and Bruce said, "I don't want to say…. What the hell, I'm quitting this heap in a while anyway. It was Wayne Teeterman, BR's special-projects director." During most of Bruce's spiel, Dirk appeared to be quite happy with what Bruce was saying; I'm sure he was glad he didn't have to say it himself.

It was mentioned that the sawmill didn't have a lunchroom, so the laminated plant felt favored. Also, Rolf mentioned that the bathroom was one of the best in BR's operations.

Bruce on Rolf: "He, Rolf, is a nice guy. Nobody respects him, though."

Dirk and Bruce mentioned that there are only six or seven men who have made it ten years in all of BR's five companies.

Dirk on Joe: "Joe does too much. He keeps it all in his head. He is efficient. It would take two people to replace him. He's overworked, he doesn't like the hours, and he's just trying to keep his job." Bruce concurred on the above points.

Bruce: "Stacks of beams are too high. Two of them fell last week. Damned near got me and another guy." I noted that the accidental death last year and its details were repeated to me three times during the day.

Bruce mentioned that he recently organized a softball team. "The first thing this plant has ever had. It's hard practicing and playing games with all the overtime. We went to BR to ask him for $700 to start it up. He gave us $250. There's fourteen teams in our league, and the minimum anyone else has gotten is $700."

Dirk mentioned that the workers peak out at $8 an hour after one year. He seemed to think that money was a big motivating factor.

In response to my query why there was no union, Bruce and Dirk mentioned that hearsay has it that when union representatives came, BR said, "Fine, if you want a union, I'll just close the place down."

Dirk: "Communication is the main problem. Joe schedules some changes, and I never hear about them."

Bruce, on the foremen meetings with BR: "Hell, the foremen will have their say, and in the end BR will stand up and say, 'This is the way it's going to be because I pay the checks.'"

About five minutes before the session ended, Joe came in and with a friendly greeting said, "There you are," to Bruce and indirectly to Dirk. Dirk got up as if getting ready to go back to work. Bruce stalled. Bruce then said that he didn't know how BR made any money on the operation. Dirk giggled lightly and nodded his head.

In the afternoon, I spent an hour and a half to two hours with Rolf, the superintendent. About an hour of this talking was Rolf trying to prove his competence by divulging intricate, technical, and totally useless details of the plant. I got some tasty stuff anyway, and here it is:

Me: "What does Joe do?"

Rolf: "So doggone many things, I don't know." Then he went on to mention he is a general manager in charge of scheduling and raw materials procurement and to rattle off two or three more. I said, "What's your working relationship with Joe?" Rolf said, "I implement his schedules. Dirk, the head of the finishing and planing department, and I get Joe's schedules. Joe will skip me whenever he wants to make changes—goes right to planing and finishing. Then I have to go see what's going on." I asked him if he thought it would be more efficient if Joe went through him. Rolf said, "No, we get along well. Joe saves time by going directly to the workers. We spend a lot of time after the shift going over and discussing what happened and planning for the next day and weeks ahead."

Rolf mentioned that there are often schedule changes when customers' trucks pick up their orders. I wondered if maybe they could get tougher with the customers, and Rolf said, "No, we'd lose them."

Rolf mentioned that the company deals with brokers, not contractors. He said that customers sometimes cancel their orders.

On Bruce's idea of bulldozing a pasture to expand finish-beam storage, Rolf said that in the winter it was tough enough to keep the field clear with the current area.

Rolf on equipment: "BR gives us the junkiest stuff to work with." He went on to mention one particular piece of machinery that has four wheels and five feet of clearance (I don't know what it is called): "It has no brakes and no shut-off; you have to idle it to kill it."

On Joe: "Joe's good; he and I go to bat for the guys."

Me: "You must have a pretty little bat; I hear BR is a tough guy to get through to."

Rolf: "Yeah, he picks his battles."

On Dirk: "Effective, will improve with time; he doesn't always see the opportunities for utilizing stock beams. He has his master's degree in glue technology."

On John: "Quality control marginal." That's all he said.

On Nita, BR's secretary: "She doesn't always use her power right."

On Sue, Joe's secretary: "She does the work of two people. Has lots of customer respect; they often comment on her."

On Joe: "He's too intelligent for the job. I don't know why he does not get something better. I guess he likes to work."

On Rich: "Rich does his job well."

On the workforce: "There are three types of guys. One is eight to five and a paycheck—never volunteers or does anything extra—50% of the workforce. Second are the ones who use workers' compensation to get time off all the time; this is 20%. Workers' compensation is the biggest deterrent to an effective workforce," he went on to comment. "And third, the ones who try, 30%."

Rolf mentioned that 15 to 20% of the work hours were spent trying to unsort the beam piles, pre- and postplaner.

Rolf mentioned that architectural beams, 7 to 12% of the output, took three times as long to process as the plain beams.

On Joe again: "Joe does a good job of scheduling and customer relations."

On BR: "BR is secretive; he should keep the guys informed."

Rolf often has to juggle men around on their tasks and catches a lot of flack for this. I asked his criteria for deciding which men would go on which jobs. They were (1) how well the man will do the job and (2) how easy it is to replace him at his original task.

Rolf said overtime is a big problem. It's necessary to go through the jobs in order. Men never know how long they'll have to work. Lock-ups have to be finished. He mentioned that a good lock-up will take an hour, a bad one, one and a half to two hours. (A lock-up is essentially gluing and clamping the beam into a form.)

Rolf said he used to spend three hours a day on the glue crew. He doesn't do this anymore; he has a good crew. Eighty percent of the glue crew are good workers, in Rolf's opinion. He mentioned that two of the bad ones quit because they didn't want overtime. Also, Rolf noted that it was possible to avoid overtime by scheduling good or easy lock-ups. This was done when the glue crew had been putting in too much overtime.

Rolf stated that the overall problem with the operation was that everyone knows that "BR doesn't give a shit about them." I asked him if there was anything he liked about working for the company, and he said, "I like working for Joe." We ended the interview with Rolf saying, "Overall, it's not a bad place to work; the checks don't bounce."

PREPARING THE DIAGNOSIS

Jack Lawler leaned back in his chair and stretched. It had all come back. Now he needed a plan for working. It seemed that the first step was to determine what ideas, models, or theories would be useful in ordering and understanding the information he had. Then he would have to do a diagnosis and, finally, think about what to say to Ben Richardson and Richard Bowman. After buzzing his secretary to say that he didn't want to be interrupted, Lawler rolled up his sleeves and began to work.

Questions

1. How would you assess Jack Lawler's entry and contracting process at B. R. Richardson? Would you have done anything differently?
2. What theories or models would you use to make sense out of the diagnostic data? How would you organize the information for feedback to Ben Richardson and Richard Bowman? How would you carry out the feedback process?
3. What additional information would you have liked Jack Lawler and his team to collect? Discuss.

Integrative Cases

Building the Cuyahoga River Valley Organization*

Sally Parker was heady with excitement. As the president and founder of the OD consulting firm, Currere, many of the ideas she had worked for over the past three years, in fact, many of the ideals she was passionate about, were coming to fruition. The Cuyahoga River Valley Organization (CRVO), an organization to be charged with carrying out the Cuyahoga Valley Initiative (CVI) through projects to restore the health and vitality of the region, was still not off the ground. There were lots of thinking to do and actions to take, but momentum was building for the transorganizational system that held the promise of not only rejuvenating the economic basis of the Cuyahoga River Valley but perhaps even restoring what was once a beautiful example of nature. As Sally pondered her next moves, she reflected on the history of the project, her involvement, and how the CRVO might be organized.

It had all started in November of 2000 with a series of articles in the *Cleveland Plain Dealer* entitled "The Forgotten Valley." Authored by Steven Litt, art and architecture critic for the local newspaper, the articles traced the history of the Cuyahoga River Valley and highlighted its "natural beauty and full-throated industry." As Litt concluded the series, he issued a challenge to the community to recognize and embrace the Valley as a place for "enjoyment, exploration, reinvestment, and renewal." In December, Cuyahoga County commissioner Timothy McCormick took up the challenge and the CVI was born.

*This case was developed and written by Sally Parker, with the assistance of Chris Worley. The case draws on several written documents and materials, including the Cuyahoga Valley Initiative website, the information on the Cuyahoga Valley in the Wikipedia site, the Cuyahoga Valley National Park site, and numerous documents prepared by the Cuyahoga County Planning Commission. The case was prepared for the purposes of class discussion and is not intended to illustrate either effective or ineffective handling of an administrative situation.

THE CUYAHOGA VALLEY

To understand the CVI, one must first understand the place—northeast Ohio and the Cuyahoga River Valley. As the transition point between the Allegheny Plateau and the Great Plains, the Cuyahoga Valley was the western frontier for the emerging American nation. The area of the valley is extensive, following the river as it flows south through Akron and Cleveland into Lake Erie, the 12th largest body of fresh water on the planet. The valley is home to the historic Ohio & Erie Canal and towpath system, once a prime contributor to Northeast Ohio's preeminence as an economic leader and now an integral part of the region's recreation system.

Deriving its name from the Iroquois word meaning "crooked," the Cuyahoga (or "Crooked") River Valley is the setting for one of the most significant examples of industrialization, urbanization, degradation, and preservation in America. Located midway between extensive deposits of natural resources and with access to land and water transportation networks, the Cuyahoga River Valley positioned northeast Ohio as an early center of industry. Cleveland and Akron gained reputations as trade centers thanks to a superhighway of canals and railroads that transported everything from cotton and coal, to coffee and window glass. Made possible by the technological advances of the Industrial Revolution, Cleveland, already a port on Lake Erie, became a center for steel mills because of its proximity both to the high quality iron ore from the upper Great Lakes region and to Ohio's bituminous coal. Shortly afterwards, John D. Rockefeller brought the oil industry to Cleveland in the form of refineries. Akron became home to the Quaker Oats Company and emerged as the "Rubber Capital of the World" when Benjamin F. Goodrich opened his factory to manufacture carriage and bicycle tires. Miller, Seiberling, Goodyear, and Firestone companies soon followed suit and thrived as the popularity of the automobile grew.

Industrial progress, however, also was associated with increases in industrial waste, and the lower Cuyahoga River became a "flowing dump." In fact, the Cuyahoga River has caught fire at least three times since 1936. The third and final fire in 1969 gained worldwide attention and initiated the passage of the Clean Water Act in 1972.

The Clean Water Act greatly reduced the waste that went into the river, and the Cuyahoga River slowly began to heal itself. By 1998, the Environmental Protection Agency designated the Cuyahoga one of 14 American Heritage Rivers. However, and despite great strides forward, the Cuyahoga River is far from healthy. Environmental issues continue to plague the health of the river valley driven by urban sprawl, poor land use, and unsustainable development practices. Storm water runoff, flooding, and erosion continue to degrade the Valley. In fact, in addition to its designation as an American Heritage River, the Environmental Protection Agency has also classified portions of the Cuyahoga River Watershed as one of 43 Great Lakes Areas of Concerns. Thus, remediation of the Cuyahoga River continues.

Similar to the environmental plight of the river, northeast Ohio struggles economically as jobs, population, and personal income decline at a rate above that of the rest of the country (Figure 1). Middle-class households have fled older urban areas for outlying suburbs, and once thriving, working-class neighborhoods have fallen into decline. Individual communities often find themselves in a "shell game," competing with neighboring communities and municipalities for the businesses, development, and residents that they hope will jump-start their economies. Meanwhile, there are a growing number of initiatives and organizations advocating regional approaches to address shared economic challenges, leverage regional assets, and market northeast Ohio as a great place for new businesses, leisure travelers, conventions, and meetings.

The Cuyahoga River Valley is home to many of these physical, economic, and regional assets. Over its course, the river offers numerous experiences connecting nature, recreation, entertainment, history, neighborhoods, and industry. In one week, without a car, an adventuresome explorer could sail on Lake Erie, hike or bike on the towpath trail for hours through great scenery, visit a zoo, ride a scenic train, tour a steel mill, shop at a farmer's market, experience the Rock "n" Roll Hall of Fame, hike in a National Park, and sleep in luxury accommodations.

The Cuyahoga River Valley is an invaluable regional asset, which happens to encapsulate a microcosm of the world's environmental, economic, and social challenges. If approached with thoughtful action, these challenges could catalyze creative, innovative solutions for the region. The CVI provided a framework for leveraging this asset.

FIGURE 1

Greater Cleveland's Economic Growth (Compared to the U.S. Baseline)

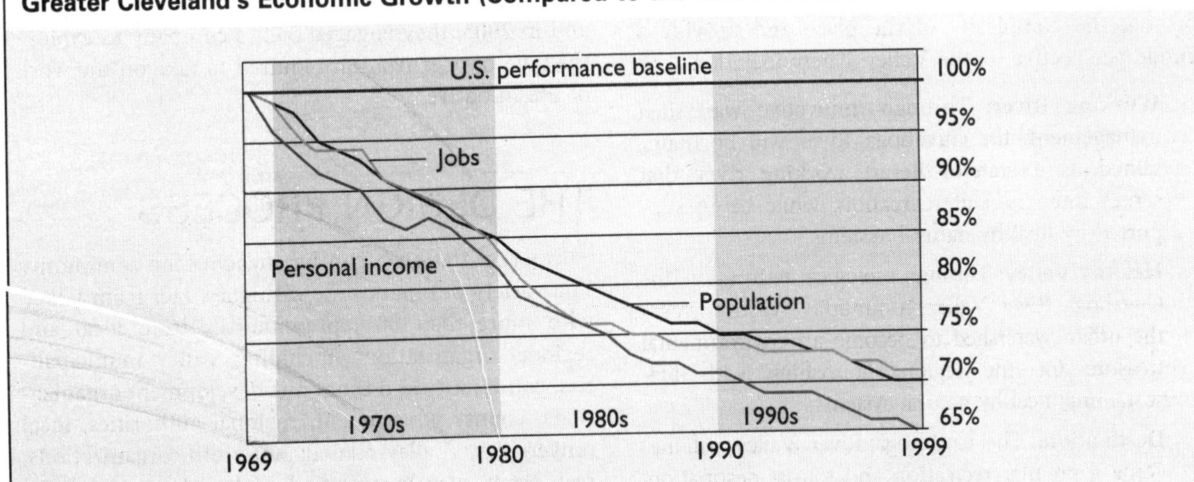

SOURCE: Bureau of Economic Analysis, U.S. Department of Commerce.

THE CUYAHOGA VALLEY INITIATIVE

The CVI began in 2001 as a Cuyahoga County–funded project under the direction of the Cuyahoga County Planning Commission and at the request of the county commissioners. Since 2001, the slate of elected commissioners has changed, yet the county has continued to budget funding for the CVI so that work on the Valley can continue.

The initial objective of the project was to create codes, guidelines, and other tools that municipalities in Cuyahoga County would use to direct redevelopment. Driven by the vision of the County Planning Commission Director Paul Alsenas, the project soon became known as the Cuyahoga Valley Initiative, a regional initiative for sustainable transformation and regeneration. Under Paul's leadership and the commitment and vision of a small team of county planners, the CVI expanded to a multicounty effort to create a culture of sustainability, using the Valley as a laboratory. During this time, local and national consultants, including Sally Parker's firm, Currere, joined Paul's team to engage hundreds of individuals and organizations that were part of the Valley.

Through Paul and the CVI team's efforts, the CVI developed a framework to guide action grounded upon the social, ecological, and financial principles of sustainability. Four principles and six organizing ideas formed the basic structure. The four principles were Build Connections, Renew the Economy, Create a Sustainable Urban Ecology, and Appreciate Our Shared Heritage. The six organizing ideas, or goals, helped to sort out the complexity of the place and provide a unique perspective on the Valley. These included:

Working River: Through innovative watershed management, the Cuyahoga River will be maintained as a state-of-the-art working river that serves industry and recreation, while being supported by healthy natural systems.

Healthy Valley: Through ecological restoration, the Cuyahoga River Valley community will transform the urban watershed to become an environmental treasure for the region, flourishing with life-sustaining, healthy natural systems.

Destination: The Cuyahoga River Valley will become a popular recreation and tourist destination. Residents and visitors alike will enjoy the Valley's cultural, historical, and ecological amenities.

Art and Design: The Valley will be a place of experimentation and creativity where new design paradigms that join artistic expression with purpose are tested.

Business Innovation: The Cuyahoga River Valley will become known for industry and thought models in economic development through environmentally friendly development and business practices.

Community Capacity: Every community will combine its diverse assets and talents with global best practices in a way that increases individual and community wealth, encourages the development of existing and new businesses, and brings about environmental health.

As work on the Initiative advanced, it quickly became evident to Paul and the team that the Valley's transformation, as envisioned by the Cuyahoga Valley Initiative, would require more capacity than the County Planning Commission could commit. Collaboration and cooperation amongst many different individuals and organizations with many different agendas over a long time period was required to accomplish the CVI mission. County and municipal governments; a wide variety of governmental agencies and authorities; environmental, social service, and economic development non-profits; for-profit businesses (large and small, local and global); and Valley residents were among the stake-holders to be involved in meaningful action. The team realized that the CVI needed to move beyond the walls of County Planning, and in 2005, they engaged Sally's company to explore the type of organization required to take on the work of the initiative.

THE DESIGN PROCESS

Sally's exploration began by engaging the community in a variety of one-on-one dialogues. Her team talked with more than 80 representatives from local and regional organizations, including Valley municipalities, community and economic development organizations, county government, regional authorities, local universities, Valley-related nonprofit organizations, real estate developers, and Valley businesses and landowners. Through these conversations, the team learned that:

- The Cuyahoga Valley is seen as an asset for the northeast Ohio region. Although many did not experience the Valley as a cohesive place, they felt that the area could sustain a rich range of experiences for businesses, leisure travelers, conventions, and meetings that could brand the region.
- In a region that tends to be fragmented and divided, the Cuyahoga Valley was universally perceived as a place of "connection and joining." In fact, many saw the Valley as a natural and nonthreatening "venue for regionalism"—as a way to leverage the region's sustainability efforts and other agendas, such as improving racial inclusion and income equity, attracting and growing businesses, reducing government fragmentation and inefficiency, and reducing sprawl and improving regional connectivity.
- The Cuyahoga Valley Initiative was not widely understood and in fact was a source of confusion and suspicion for some members of the community. Those with knowledge of the CVI were generally optimistic and intrigued with its approach and were eager to see results.
- If the Cuyahoga Valley Initiative was to have any chance of realizing its vision, it had to expand beyond the borders of Cuyahoga County and include Summit County to the south (Figure 2). This meant taking on a significantly larger area, including 25 local governments, three special government districts, numerous State of Ohio departments, over 40 nonprofit organizations, and thousands of private businesses and residents whose work and property management practices influence the Cuyahoga Valley—each entity having its own priorities and ways of operating.
- Any organization charged with the mission of the CVI would need to provide overall coordination and a cohesive context—or vision—for the many organizations working in the Valley. It would need to facilitate new kinds of collaborations whose work would benefit both the Valley and the members of the collaboration.

Participants in these conversations also shared a sense of reluctance about forming any kind of new organization. They warned Sally's team to "think long and hard" before recommending the creation of a new organization in a region that is saturated with nonprofits and governmental entities already competing for an insufficient and shrinking pool of resources—and where funders are looking at consolidations and collaborations to reduce redundancies.

As Sally's team considered all of this, they drew three primary conclusions:

- The Cuyahoga Valley is an asset worth leveraging and the CVI appears to be an adequate, if not inspiring, framework for its regeneration.
- To accomplish its objectives, the Cuyahoga Valley Initiative needs organizational capacity beyond that currently present in the community. It needs an organization able to work with a wide variety of organizations and agendas and able to provide context and a course and model for collaborative action.
- The formation of any new organization will be scrutinized by the community regardless of how "needed" it might be. From the get-go, its existence will have to be "justified" in the eyes of the community as an organization that is essential, non redundant, and legitimate.

Developing the Design

Armed with these conclusions, Currere worked with the County Planning Commission to secure supplemental funding through a grant from The Gund Foundation. With this funding, they decided that the next step was to think about the required design to deliver this additional capacity. Their design process was grounded on four key principles:

1. **Place Based:** The people of the community should design the organization to serve the needs of the place as a physical ecology, human community, and economy.
2. **Experiential, Participatory, Collaborative:** The organization design experience should expand thinking and perception and demonstrate how neutral space is created to support cross-organizational and cross-sectoral work.
3. **Task and Capacity Focused:** The process should accomplish specific results, while expanding individual and group capacity to accomplish additional results.
4. **Transparent:** Participants need to represent the mission and capabilities of their organizations, remaining transparent about their organization's interests or agendas.

FIGURE 2

The Cuyahoga River Valley

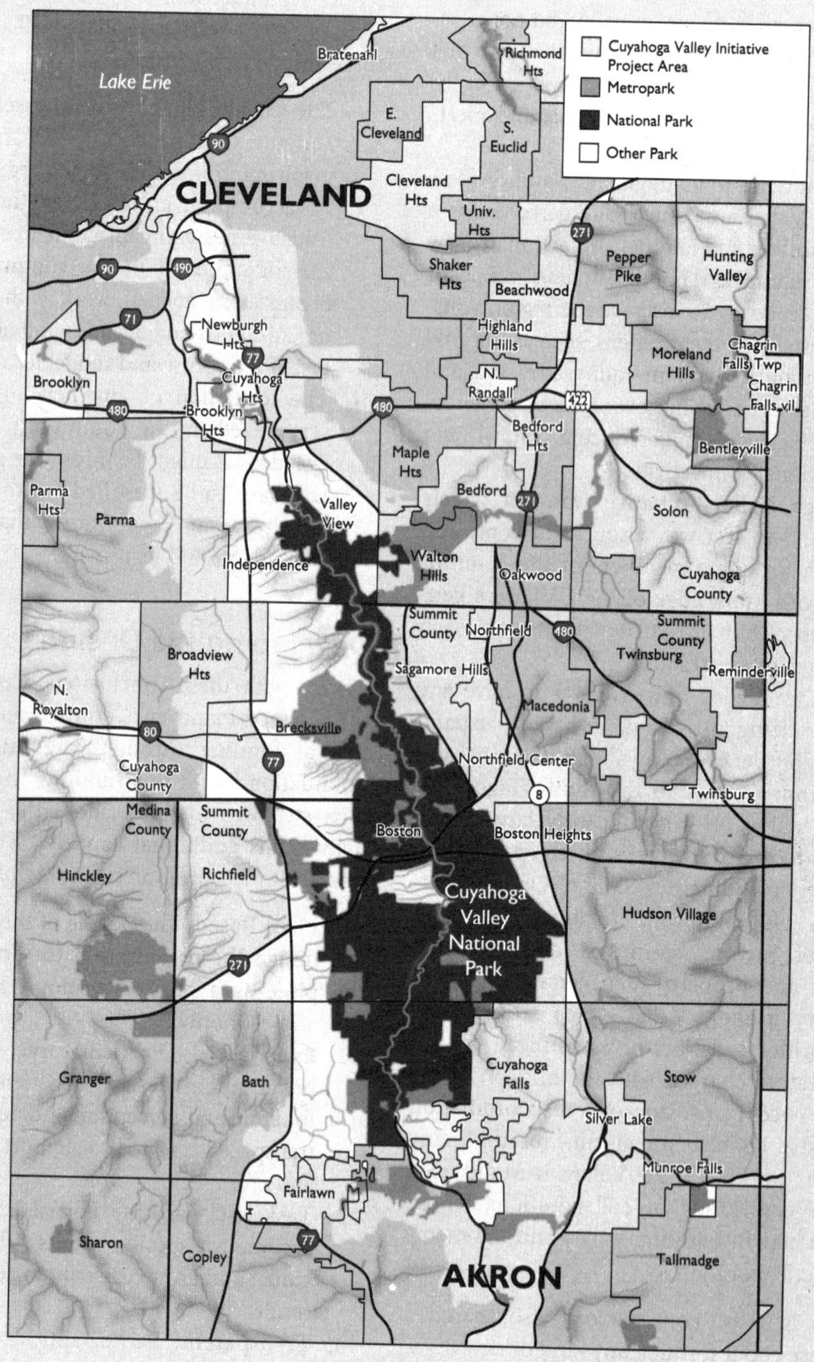

Following the above principles, Currere and the CVI team formed an ad hoc group of "usual and unusual suspects"—14 individuals representing different organizations and initiatives throughout Cuyahoga and Summit County. Pulling this ad hoc group together was a critical part of the process. The team created a matrix of the characteristics, expertise, experience, and perspectives they felt were important within this ad hoc group and brainstormed a list of prospects. They sought broad and systemic thinkers, civic champions, innovators, and leaders. They looked for individuals not afraid to speak the truth yet willing to listen to others. They wanted vision and passion about northeast Ohio and the Cuyahoga River Valley; they needed commitments of time and energy.

Paul and Sally began to meet with each of the prospects. Armed with information about the value and importance of the CVI, they prepared for a challenging "sell," expecting to be delegated to less powerful people in the chain of command. They were wrong. In fact, they were met with a great deal of interest. Whether they were meeting with the general manager of one of the world's largest steel companies, busy and successful entrepreneurs, the leader of the County library system, a mayor, a city councilman, or the head of strategy for a national developer, the most common response they got was, "How can I not do this? How can I not take this on?"

So, having met with an overwhelmingly positive response from this group of prospects, the task was to narrow the group down to 14. Together, this final ad hoc group, Currere, and the Planning Commission comprised the design team.

Under Currere's leadership, the design team immersed themselves into the Valley as place—a physical ecology, human community, and economy. Over a period of five months, the design team met about every three weeks for half-day sessions that were held in different locations throughout the Valley. In addition, three full-day sessions were conducted to provide the design team an opportunity to "try on" organization design criteria and principles with real Valley projects and the people and organizations working on them. For example, several Valley-related projects, such as the East Bank Flats Redevelopment and the City of Cleveland's industrial brownfield land-bank initiatives, were already underway, and the day-long sessions allowed the design team to think about how projects, sponsors, governments, and organizations might fit together into an organization model.

These meetings resulted in the design team grasping the complexity of a place that was the size and scale of the Valley and that hosted such a diversity of ecological, economic, and social issues. They realized how many organizations—large and small from different sectors—were already working to advance their agendas and affect the Valley. They also wrestled with questions about the essential "DNA" of an organization whose function was the transformation of such a place. They talked about the Valley as a whole system and wondered where attention and energy should be focused to catalyze and accelerate transformation and regeneration—to achieve results and create value. The design team had an epiphany as they struggled to define the physical boundaries of the Valley and to prioritize the places where work should be focused. *The primary point of leverage for effecting change in the Valley was not a project or a physical place—the primary point of leverage for transformation was people and the human network they formed.*

With this insight, the group's focus shifted to looking at the Valley as a networked system of people and organizations.

The Essential Components of the Network

With Sally's help, the design team pieced together the essential elements of the system that required coordination. Rather than a singular organizational form, the Valley's transformation called for four different networks of organizational capacity working together in *partnership* to effect change (Figure 3). Central to the partnership was the Cuyahoga River Valley Organization (CRVO), acting as an orchestrator for the other three: the triad, network partners, and projects.

- ***The Triad*** refers to a group of individuals representing three key stakeholders—government, business, and foundations within the two counties—that can collectively legitimatize and support the system of activity. This means legitimizing the Valley and the CVI as a top regional priority and the CRVO as the organization charged with the CVI mission. For the CRVO to be able to work through a network of other organizations, it must

FIGURE 3

The Cuyahoga River Valley Partnership

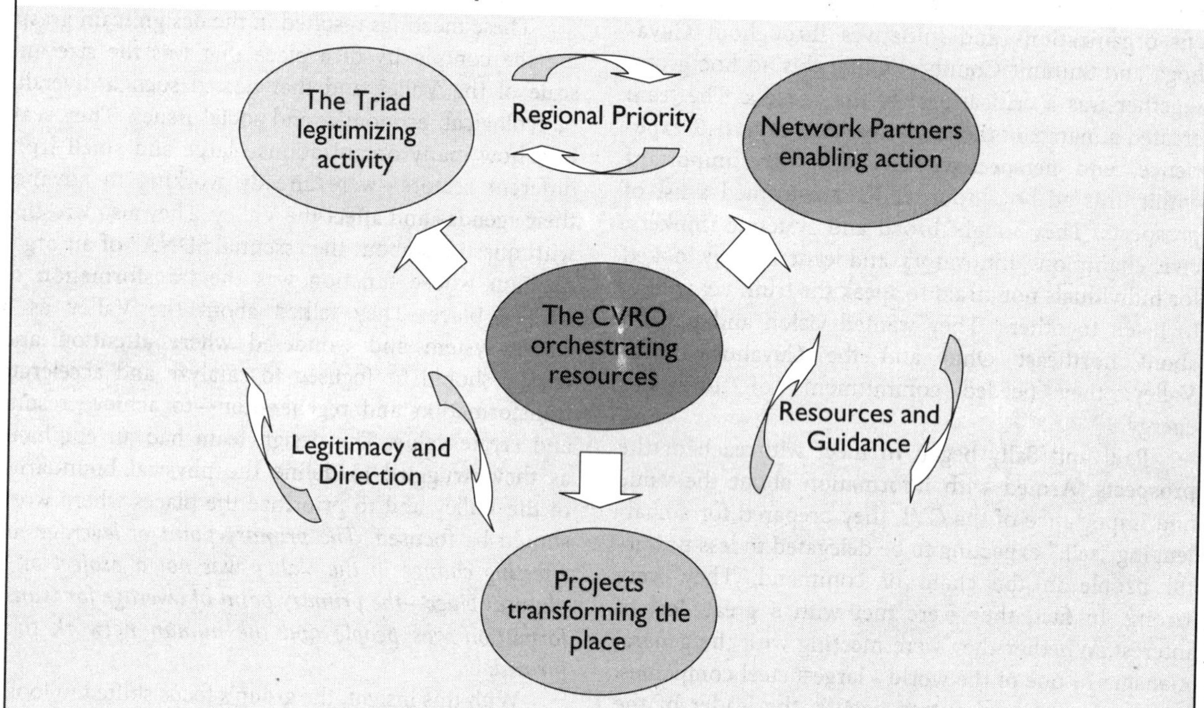

be seen by those organizations and the community as the legitimate entity to carry out this work. This legitimacy can be afforded through an articulated agreement between the governments, foundations, and business communities to:

- Legitimize and fund the transformation of the Valley as a top regional priority
- Authorize and fund the CRVO as leader and orchestrator of the Valley's transformation
- Ensure the CRVO's autonomy to operate as a neutral body that can develop the multiple agendas essential for regional transformation

It is through the Triad that the CRVO can be positioned in the community with the authority, autonomy, and resources necessary to accomplish its mission.

- ***Network Partners*** are organizations and individuals committed to doing and enabling the work of transformation in the Valley. There are a number of these organizations and individuals, some of them networks in their own right, who are currently working on a wide variety of interests in the Valley and the number seems to grow daily. The challenge is that these networks tend to be fragmented and focused on projects that advance specific objectives. The Valley transformation will require the emergence of a more robust and integrated "action" network of people and organizations working on the kinds of projects that will achieve positive impact at scale in the Valley. A network partner, like one of the park districts, would be motivated to be a part of this network because they would see it as a way to facilitate the accomplishment of their own objectives and also the larger regional objectives. The network would represent a means to accomplish more with less—provided each player is able to satisfy their own organizational interests.
- ***Valley Projects*** are where the rubber meets the road—where the Valley transformation will take shape. Many Valley projects and initiatives are already underway, engaging numerous organizations. For the CRVO, the priority would be initiating and supporting projects that address the most pressing needs of the Valley, can have an impact at scale, and will help build the Valley network.

- ***The CVRO***, as the fourth element, is the orchestrator of the larger network and serves as a champion of the Valley's transformation and regeneration as a whole place. Working with a clear and compelling identity and vision, it would provide thought and action leadership, inspiration, context, direction, and coordination. As a hub or orchestrator, it would assemble resources and projects with legitimacy to maintain a robust network of individuals and organizations willing and able to advance the Valley's overall health and effect change at scale. Since there was no single entity whose scope and focus was the transformation of the Valley as a whole, the CRVO is the only organizational form in the partnership that may in fact require the incorporation of a new entity.

A Process to Operate the System

In addition to the different forms of organizational capacity, the design team realized that the Valley's transformation would require a new "protocol" or process for working together within an expanded set of values that integrates economic, environmental, and social benefit. The protocol would support a process of exploration and discovery through trial and error and would have to be created from scratch. There were no time-tested models to draw on. In essence, the CRVO would be asking individuals and organizations to step into action, trust an exploratory process, and collaborate with others for mutual value in a region historically characterized as risk averse, fragmented, and distrustful. Even though northeast Ohioans were expressing a growing interest in regionalism, there were very few examples of collaborative regional initiatives and fewer, if any, at the CVI's scale and level of complexity.

The protocol would require working in ways that probably felt counter to conventional wisdom and often seem paradoxical. For instance, teams would need to be encouraged to "slow down to speed up"—to spend time building a foundation for intelligent and more aligned action. The protocol would help to identify how the Triad, network partners, and the CVRO contributed to such a process. In addition, participants of divergent groups would be asked to put their individual and corporate agendas on the back burner and be curious about the agendas of others—all in the interest of mutual benefit. The protocol would provide a decision process that would encourage the integration of divergent views without paralyzing action.

Currere and the CVI knew that this would be a core challenge for the Cuyahoga Valley Initiative in general and the CRVO in particular. The CRVO, the Triad, and the Network Partners would need to live with the reality that individuals and organizations working in the Valley would be under constant pressure to default to traditional, known ways of working—particularly when tensions and stakes are high.

Implementing the Design

As Sally and the CVI team thought about the tasks ahead, their biggest challenge was how to operationalize the network system and in particular, how to design and implement the CRVO. They knew that the reason for the CRVO's existence had to be clear and compelling and the design easily understood. Sally emphasized that the CRVO could be fully grasped only in the context of the Valley partnership as a collaborative system, even though the partnership concept was complex and might be confusing. She knew that the role of each of the four elements of the partnership needed to be articulated—keeping in mind the need for a protocol or system-wide decision-making process. Sally and the CVI team needed to think about (a) the detail of the design and operating practices of the CRVO and (b) how the CRVO would develop the protocol. She began to consider the following.

Purpose, Value Proposition, and Strategy From the beginning, the team heeded the community's caution about creating "yet another organization." They knew that for CRVO to have value in the Valley, it would need to provide tangible benefit to individual stakeholders and the broader regional community. It could not appear to create redundancies or compete with the organizations and initiatives already at work in the Valley. It had to provide a unique capacity that did not exist elsewhere and was essential and desired by the community.

They realized that at its core, the ***purpose*** of a CRVO would be to promote and leverage the Cuyahoga River Valley for the benefit of the region and to do that it would need to:

- Provide strategic thought leadership and direction;
- Establish a sense of identity and coherence for the Valley;
- Set and coordinate a course for aligned and collaborative action;
- Invite and engage the Cuyahoga River Valley community (organizations and individuals within the network partners) to work together in the Valley;

- Identify, facilitate, and launch projects responsible for revitalizing the Valley.

It would need to take on the following most pressing needs of the Valley:

- Healthy ecology, particularly of the water and air sheds;
- Industrial regeneration to leverage the assets in the industrial valley;
- A robust infrastructure system to link places, people, and experiences;
- Healthy place-making to create and re-create great neighborhoods and economies.

It would need to demonstrate its ***value proposition*** to its stakeholders by:

- Acting on behalf of county and municipal governments, the business community, and foundations, helping them to accomplish their objectives for sustainability within the Valley, while mitigating the risk associated with their direct leadership and/or involvement;
- Assembling and organizing regional and global expertise essential for transformation toward place-based sustainability and organize capacity for impact at scale;
- Promoting the Cuyahoga River Valley experience as a core component of the region's branded identity;
- Maintaining focus on the Cuyahoga River Valley as a top regional priority and be a constant force for focused and effective action;
- Leveraging the capacity of the Valley network for maximum effectiveness; nurturing/ managing relationships throughout the network; and gaining community support.

Assembling—or aggregating—people, places, and experiences to create mutual value would be CRVO's core ***strategy***. By integrating and organizing the many resources and experiences of the Valley, the CRVO increases the value of the Valley to visitors, residents, developers, business, etc.

Stakeholders and Customers In very general terms, CRVO's stakeholders and their related interests include the following:

- The Place—The Cuyahoga River Valley is an ecological, economic, and human community and the CRVO is its representative. The Place demands representation in the decisions of governments, the community, businesses, and nonprofits.
- The Triad—The shared agreement of Summit and Cuyahoga County governments, business community chambers, and foundations should support, legitimize, and authorize the CRVO as the leader and orchestrator of the Valley's transformation. As a collective, these organizations want to see that the Valley is leveraged for the good of the region—economically, socially, and environmentally. Individually, each organization wants to build goodwill amongst its constituents and stakeholders, demonstrating collaboration and sound investment in the Valley.
- The Network Partners—These are the core organizations of an emerging Valley action network whose support and collaborative efforts will transform the Valley. These organizations want to demonstrate an ability to work with others for the good of the region while advancing their own objectives. They want their work in the Valley to demonstrate their value as an individual organization and as an essential component of the Valley network. Finally, they want to be able to strengthen their own capacity and expand their reach and visibility.
- The Regional Community—The broader community served by the Valley's transformation wants to enjoy the Valley and be able to benefit from it.

Core Work Ultimately, the design team saw the work of the CRVO in five primary categories—leadership, network development and management, marketing/branding, knowledge creation and management, and funding—all in service to the Valley. In the early stages, however, the focus of the organization would need to be narrowed to include securing and coordinating financial and human resources for initiating, leading, and/or managing projects and activities that:

1. Restore air, water, and land quality in the Cuyahoga Valley;
2. Improve the performance of businesses already sited in the Valley with respect to sustainable ecological practices, and create an attractive market for new sustainable businesses in the Valley;
3. Promote and advocate for investments in high-performance infrastructure throughout the Valley watershed;

4. Advocate for a regulatory and legislative environment that supports "healthy place-making" in the Valley;
5. Build a robust Valley network.

Getting the CRVO Off the Ground For Sally and the team, this was perhaps the biggest concern. The Valley has so many players, is large and complex, and is not perceived as a cohesive place—like the Napa Valley or Silicon Valley. Although there are networks of individuals and organizations interested in the Valley, they tend to be localized and project focused, often burdened with competing agendas.

From the beginning, the CRVO needs to be legitimized as the "face of the Valley," yet it will need to launch before the Triad is fully formed. In fact, its existence will help the Triad develop, and while it needs the Triad to legitimize it, the CRVO will also need to maintain its autonomy because it needs to be able to work in ways that are nontraditional and may appear "risky."

What gave life to the CVI was the vision and tenacious focus of Paul Alsenas. Finding that kind of champion to continue to drive the CRVO forward is perhaps the next greatest challenge. The organization needs to be able to start small, and stay small, honing its skills as an initiator and orchestrator. It cannot represent redundant capacity. The CRVO can accomplish its vision only by working with and through the expertise and capacity of a Valley network. From the inception, it will need to inspire other organizations to follow its lead—and trust its process. It will need to keep its eye on the prize—which is the Valley *in service to the region*—and continually evolve to best meet the Valley's needs, remain adaptive, inventive, resourceful, and stealth-like.

Questions

1. Assuming you are Sally Parker, describe the process you will initiate to form the CVRO and the protocol for decision making in the network.
2. Describe the organization design features—structure, human resource processes, leadership—that you think should characterize the CVRO.
3. What do you think are the obstacles and facilitators to your process? What are your personal hopes and fears in conducting this task?

Integrative Cases

The Transformation of MECK Insurance*

The internal Organization Development (OD) team at MECK Insurance had just completed a full-day session with the Customer Service Organization (CSO) leadership team. Together, they were leading the journey to shift the culture and drive performance in one of MECK's largest business areas—and the hard part was just beginning. Customer, client relationship, and employee engagement measures had improved in the first 18 months of the transformation. However, the OD team knew from experience that the project was at an exciting and daunting moment in the journey. Their interventions could either accelerate the change or allow the customer service organization to slide back towards the status quo.

This was not the first time the OD team had collaborated with a MECK business area to create cultural transformation. Two other business areas, Customer & Enterprise Services and Technology, had been on similar journeys beginning in 2008. Through the highs, lows, and lessons learned, the OD team has adapted methods based on the business area's structure, the leader's objectives, and the unit's particular culture. Additionally, the OD team shared a continued belief that bringing the employees and their culture into alignment with the business strategy was a critical lever for performance.

There has been visible success along the way, but this time it felt different. Given the size of the CSO, success could represent the tipping point for the whole company. The task ahead of the OD team was to partner with the clients to determine the next steps in the change process, accelerate the change, and ensure the shifts were sustainable.

THE CULTURAL TRANSFORMATION METHODOLOGY

The CSO was the third business area to engage in large-scale transformation at MECK Insurance, a large, broad line provider of property, casualty, and life insurance sold through a multichannel business model that included call centers, the web and an agency force. Together with Customer & Enterprise Services and Technology, these three areas represented approximately 70% of the company's workforce.

While the three business areas served very different functions for the company, the motivation for change was similar: to improve business performance and to respond to feedback from the business areas' internal clients and external customers. A differentiated client and customer experience was critical to being competitive in the future. In addition, these business areas recognized that the desired impact on financial performance and customer experience could not be achieved through a single-solution approach, such as restructuring the organization, reducing expenses, or hiring a few new leaders. Instead, the leader of each business area knew change needed to be holistic to achieve better and sustainable levels of performance.

In each case, the OD team worked with the leaders of the business areas and their leadership teams to define clear and supported strategies as the first phase of work. With this foundation, the OD team leveraged several design and change tools, including Galbraith's Star Model, Sullivan's Whole System Transformation process, and Beckhard's change formula, to frame the change process across all three business areas. For example, Beckhard's change formula, $C = R < D^*V^*F$, suggests that change occurs when resistance is less than the product of dissatisfaction with the current state, a vision

*Anonymous members of the MECK Insurance OD team.

TABLE 1

Core Transformation Principles

Core Transformation Principles
Create real strategic business results
Ensure shared ownership by leaders
Think holistically about how to create and sustain change with a *common purpose* that drives everything
Engage diverse groups to leverage different perspectives, understand their needs, and create change—the wisdom is in the system
Build shared aspiration, understanding, and meaning that leads to committed and aligned action—combine head and heart
Measure and reward what you want and take action on what you don't want
Leverage the organization's strengths—honor what is already working
Build an organization that creates its own solutions to ensure sustainability

of the future, and clear first steps. These tools resulted in core "Transformation Principles" (Table 1).

These transformation principles focused on engaging the head and heart of organization members to create real, sustainable change. The deep transformation of an individual's experience was necessary to create space for new and different levels of engagement. Deep individual change at *all levels* of the organization was core to *how* organization change was created. The principles also recognized that design changes drove culture change. It was important to redesign structures, systems, and processes to support the new behaviors.

Although the transformation principles were leveraged in all three business areas, the way they were applied looked different based on the specific business area's context, leaders, culture, and business challenges.

WHERE IT ALL STARTED—CUSTOMER AND ENTERPRISES SERVICES

The Customer and Enterprise Services (CES) organization operated most of the company's call centers and back office functions. CES's employees engaged in hundreds of millions of customer interactions each year, were spread across the country, and delivered crucial services to policy holders as well as internal business units. Unfortunately, in 2008, CES customer loyalty and satisfaction scores had been stagnant at best, and feedback suggested significant improvements were needed in sales, service quality, and product support. In addition, internal business clients were demanding significant cost reductions and more support to help them meet their business goals.

CES's challenges stemmed largely from an internally focused, shared-service structure and culture that had been in place for two decades. Locations and functions were isolated from each other and tolerated the creation of "kingdoms." The result was little to no collaboration across locations, functions, or top leadership as well as lost efficiencies, lack of shared purpose, inconsistent practices to serve customer needs, and subcultures that varied widely across CES. CES also faced additional complexities: their recent merger with the Technology area formed a larger Technology & Operations organization under a single leader, and the appointment of a new CES leader resulted in a lack of clarity and focus on what was most important and how to best drive business performance.

The CES Transformation Process—Launches and Waves

The new CES leader initiated the change process. Leveraging both internal and external OD resources, the transformation process consisted of four phases or "launches." Within two years, CES saw most every business metric move in a positive direction, including enhanced cost effectiveness and increased customer service.

- **Launch 1: Ensuring Clear Sponsorship and Leadership Alignment.** Launch 1 began with ensuring that the CES leadership team was ready to support transformation and was willing to make the changes needed to impact business performance. The leadership team needed to be aligned and committed to the CES strategy, the need for change, and their role and accountability for the change before the OD team engaged others in the effort. The modeling of transformation by the leadership team was paramount in inspiring the remainder of the CES organization.

  This was no small task as the CES leadership team had a long history of competition and distrust, and lacked any shared commitment to a collective vision. The conversations and dialogue over multiple sessions shaped the direction of the team and the organization. The tipping point in the team's transformation came at one of those sessions. Following a period of continued questioning by the CES leader about how best to operate the function, the whole team—without the leader—stood up, walked over to the easel pad, and designed their ideal service delivery model. The team took full ownership of that future vision and operated collaboratively to design it. They left that session with a common purpose, guiding principles, operating norms, and a new paradigm about their value to the company. Based on the new delivery model, the leadership team was able to articulate a business goal to become more innovative, cost effective, and value added as perceived by customers. They eventually shortened everything into two key sentiments: *Thrill the Customer* and *Get Different.*

  Following these sessions, the leadership team spoke openly and publicly of their fears and perceptions, took ownership of the barriers and challenges they had created through their past leadership decisions and behaviors, listened to the organization, and accepted critical feedback. Later, when qualitative data was gathered about the role of leaders in the CES transformation effort, employees noted that it was the first time in years that everyone, at all levels, felt heard. Employees had a renewed sense of trust in and commitment to the leadership and the company.

  As part of the transformation, the leadership team agreed to engage people from across CES together in large-group events and formed a design team to plan and execute the Launch 2 phase. The design team was a microcosm of the organization and ensured that the large-group event agendas would meet the needs, concerns, and reality of the people who would attend them. The design team's responsibilities included:
  - Building relationships with each other as a way to learn about the experiences that people were having in different parts of CES;
  - Understanding the current state of the business;
  - Completing a scan of the internal environment;
  - Reviewing the organizational vision and all the work that was underway to help achieve it;
  - Identifying and aligning on a clear purpose and the outcomes for the large-group sessions;
  - Designing all the activities and conversations that would occur in the large-group sessions.

- **Launch 2: Engaging the Organization.** Launch 2 activities engaged CES members in a series of four two-and-a-half-day, large-group events or "waves" of about 200 people to understand the case for change, create the vision for the future, identify how to make the change happen at an organization and individual level, and consider ways to sustain the change. Wave I focused on understanding the current state and the sources of dissatisfaction (the "D" in Beckhard's change formula). Wave II focused on identifying a future vision (the "V" in Beckhard's formula). Wave III developed action plans or "first steps," and Wave IV focused on sustainability and system-wide transformation issues.

  Although the focus of each wave was different, there were a significant number of similarities in the way in which the waves were designed to ensure that the transformation principles were reflected. For example:
  - The first day of a session involved context setting, group connections, and a sharing of dissatisfactions with the current state.
  - The second day connected people to aspirations and visions of what was possible. For CES, this meant that the leadership team's common purpose—Thrill Our Customer—was embedded in every activity so that employees began to make a meaningful connection to what was possible given their customer facing roles.

- The third day generated confidence and enthusiasm as they developed actions to take at the individual, group, and organization levels as they walked out of the wave and returned to their day-to-day jobs.
- Small-group discussions always took place among a "max mix" of CES members—every table had a mixture of people representing different levels, geographies, and functions so that there was a microcosm of the organization—much like the make-up of the design team.
- The design of each day addressed both organization transformation *and* personal transformation. To change the organization, each individual also needed to make the commitment to change.

Together, the four waves engaged about 20% of the CES workforce, and generated visible alignment and excitement around the common purpose. The waves also formed relationships across locations, business functions and people, and brought collaboration and innovation to life. The experience shifted individual beliefs about the organization, their role, and how they could work differently to truly thrill the customer.

Participants took the shared sense of excitement and unity back to their work locations and became catalysts for the change. Individuals brought new ideas and business solutions to their leaders and people began to work differently across boundaries. This collective excitement and action from the participants after the sessions, combined with the broader sustainability efforts across CES (described below), shifted the organization and began to translate into business results. Importantly, the investment in leadership's transformation as a part of Launch 1 paid off when, about midway through the effort, it became clear that not all CES leaders were supporting the change or were taking steps to create an environment where employees could be heard and empowered. The CES leader held those leaders accountable for their actions—and eventually moved some out of their positions if they did not change. This action was a critical sign to the rest of the organization of the CES leader's commitment to move the organization into its vision.

- **Launch 3: Evaluation and Sustainability.** The output of Wave IV was a CES-wide action plan with "Six Bold Steps" to address the organization's design. The Six Bold Steps were to introduce a 360-degree feedback process for all employees, create a new online recognition program, design a business results dashboard, develop business acumen training, host a one-day wave event at every geographic office location, and document best practice process flows. These "bold steps" served as the basis of a sustainability plan to monitor and measure progress across CES. While CES made progress in achieving the "bold steps," sustainability efforts monitored overall progress and action to ensure that change was systemic and purposeful in bringing the CES common purpose and vision to life.

The CES senior leadership team worked with the design team and the OD team to hold review sessions at 6 and 14 month intervals after the completion of the four waves. These sessions assessed the leadership team's development, created an organizational strategy for the next two years, and established an elaborate ongoing measurement process, structure, and planning system to ensure long term sustainability.

CES—Results and Impact of the Transformation

The inclusiveness and depth of the CES transformation generated near-immediate business improvements. For example, after years of no movement, the satisfaction survey that customers take following a call center transaction began improved for seven months in a row, from 77% to 84%, and has been maintained by the organization. A variety of other expense and operations improvements were made as well. For example, half way through the fiscal year, there was concern about whether the CES organization would meet their sales goals, but after the four waves, the numbers rose and CES eventually exceeded their sales objectives.

BUILDING MOMENTUM—TRANSFORMATION IN TECHNOLOGY

CES's success convinced MECK's Chief Information Officer (CIO) to expand the work to the Technology organization—the remaining part of the overall Technology & Operations function. Services provided by the Technology organization play a critical role in supporting agencies and serving customers. They build and deliver applications and infrastructure that enable a wide range of business transactions. For example, technology allows the agencies to sell and service customers, supports the claims process in catastrophe situations, and provides customers with the ability to quote and buy policies on the Web. At the time the transformation effort began in 2009, the availability and stability of these services had room for improvement and the pressure from internal clients, agencies, and customers to make a change was growing.

Prior to 2009, the technology organization had restructured and changed leaders several times. The most significant of these was a merger between the application development and infrastructure development areas. It brought two leadership teams under one CIO and aligned the organization to the different enterprise functions. Unfortunately, people were unclear about whether Technology's true objective was to be a world class center of excellence or a low-cost service provider. Additionally, increasing amounts of work were being outsourced to both domestic and foreign locations and contributed to confusion about individual and organization purpose, value, and future direction.

The Technology Transformation Process

Building on the experience from CES, the Technology leadership team was similarly engaged in working sessions to ensure strategic clarity, an articulated case for change, and a commitment to how they led and supported the transformation. Similar to CES, improved customer service, affordability, and innovation were cornerstones for business performance. Additionally, the leadership team wanted increased employee engagement across the Technology organization.

- **Launch 1: Building an Aligned Senior Leadership Team.** During the Launch 1 sessions, the leadership team reviewed diagnostic data about the current state of the organization—its challenges, concerns, strengths, and opportunities. They noticed that the word "customer" was completely missing from their discussions. This was not surprising because, unlike CES, most of Technology employees did not have daily interactions with policy-holding customers. Without this direct connection, the line of sight between their work and how it directly impacted customers was more difficult to see. The data also highlighted another gap—most of Technology's success metrics were internally focused. The leadership team realized they had strayed from a focus on the needs of their core stakeholder—the bill-paying customer.

  A clear and common purpose had been a key success factor for the CES transformation. As a result, the Technology leadership team also spent time defining a common purpose. Because of the insight around their lost focus on the customer, the leadership team believed that they should share the same common purpose as CES, which was to Thrill Our Customer. The leadership team knew that, going forward, it was important to refocus themselves and the organization on this stakeholder. They also recognized that they needed to lead differently to bring the common purpose to life.
- **Launch 2: Engaging Employees.** Like CES, Launch 2 activities were to engage the organization beyond the leadership team. However, a "mini-wave" of only 40 individuals was designed and delivered by the OD team to help gauge the pulse of the Technology organization and to confirm the need for the larger group events or "waves. The participants in the mini-wave were unanimous: similar conversations needed to occur in the entire Technology organization. The executive sponsor and leadership team agreed.

  With this direction, the OD team used the case for change and the common purpose as the basis for designing the wave events. The Technology waves used similar design assumptions:
  - Each wave was two and a half days to allow the time for organizational and personal transformation.
  - Small groups applied the "max mix" concept to bring together leaders and employees from all levels on the design teams and at the tables in the events.
  - The first large-group event focused on unleashing individuals and getting a clear understanding of the current state, while Waves II and III focused on the future state and specific actions, in addition to continuing to provide feedback on organization initiatives and centering on personal transformation.
  - Eventually, approximately 30% of the Technology organization attended one of these large-group sessions.

While the OD team was leading the wave events, the leadership team was simultaneously defining objectives and priorities related to the organization's structure and work processes. These priorities were brought into the wave events for input and feedback from people across the Technology organization.

- **Launch 3: Broadening the Involvement of the Organization and Sustainability**. The final wave event produced four bold actions to support sustainability and engagement across the technology organization. One of these actions, similar to CES, was to create one-day large-group sessions for all Technology employees who had not attended a wave. These one-day sessions engaged employees in the common purpose of "Thrill Our Customer," connected their work to the purpose, and asked them to reflect on what they needed to do differently to bring the common purpose to life. A design team created and facilitated the one-day sessions. The other three bold actions focused on organizational design, including changes to rewards and performance management systems, continued capability building of inclusive behaviors, and leadership development.

The OD team took similar approaches to sustain the change, including:

- Continuing work with the leadership team to support their development in leading the transformation efforts;
- Building their own capabilities in whole system transformation and inclusive diversity by working with external partners;
- Forming an Operating Team—a "max mix" of employees and leaders from across Technology—to lead the sustainability work and provide input to the leadership team on the overall strategy.

Technology—Results and Impact of the Transformation

Following the wave events, the Technology organization faced increasing business pressure on overall performance, availability, and "up time." Despite initial momentum for the four bold actions, these pressures and several large-scale, corporate-sponsored organizational initiatives influenced Technology to re-define priorities. As a result, limited to no progress was made on three of the four bold actions. Only the one-day engagement sessions were fully executed. In addition, evidence emerged that some leaders were not shifting the way they led. This cast a shadow over parts of the organization; people began to believe, in pockets, that there was little commitment to change.

Shortly after the completion of the waves and one-day engagement sessions in 2010, the CIO moved to another position. A new leader took over the Technology and Operations organization, made several leadership changes and articulated clear priorities and focus areas. At the same time, the internal OD team that had been dedicated to the Technology and Operations organization was centralized into the Human Resources function to support the enterprise.

While there was a substantial increase in Technology employees' evaluation of their line of sight to the customer as measured by an organization-wide survey (which was one of the success measures for the effort), there was no clear measurable business impact, and no additional formal interventions were conducted during the transition period of the new leadership and the OD team. The progress that had been made up to that point in Technology became the backdrop for the new leader as he refocused the organization to address the mounting business demands and lead them into the next chapter of transformation.

CREATING SUSTAINABLE CHANGE IN THE CUSTOMER SERVICE ORGANIZATION

The Customer Service Organization (CSO) represents more than half of the company's total population. It is spread across the country as a primary customer contact point, is critical to satisfying and retaining customers, and holds the line on the company's operating expenses.

Historically, field offices across CSO had authoritative cultures that were created and dominated by leaders telling employees what to do and supported by processes and structures that left little room for deviation. According to this operating model, technological and work system changes were implemented to increase automation, maximize efficiency, and minimize error. This operating model and change process had served the company well. Process efficiency and cost reduction, two business measures for which the leadership team was held accountable, were consistently high.

At the same time that the OD team was transitioning to its new role, the CSO leadership team was discussing what they needed to do to compete in the future, including how to stay on top of emerging technology trends, changing demographics, and increasing customer experience expectations as part of their annual strategic planning process. The leadership team knew they were operating from a position of strength. However, they also acknowledged that the highly authoritative style of leadership would no longer work and that they did not have much insight or visibility into the geographically dispersed field offices given their location in the corporate office. They recognized the need to change not only how they operated but also how their culture would support the changing competitive landscape. The leadership team conducted an organization-wide survey, employee focus groups, and executive partner interviews to better understand the current state. The OD team began work with the CSO in 2011, after the current state data was collected and a series of conversations with the CSO leader were held, in which he made his commitment to leading the change clear.

The leaders used the diagnostic data to validate their assumptions. The data not only highlighted the leadership issue but brought into focus the barriers they faced if they wanted to shift the CSO culture. To be competitive in the future, they needed to maintain their efficiency and expense management strengths but build capabilities in customer service, innovation, and collaboration. This became the platform for the transformation effort. The leadership team also understood that engaging everyone in the organization was necessary if they were to believe that making this change was not a "nice to do," but a business need and a competitive differentiator.

The CSO Transformation Process

The OD team believed that changing the CSO operating model and culture required modifying the transformation process. If each of the field offices had its own culture and leadership style, the OD team and leadership team believed that the transformation's initial focus should be on all leaders of the organization before employees were engaged. They believed this would best leverage the transformation principles and would ensure leadership support and commitment to the desired culture.

As a result, the CSO transformation process proceeded as follows. Launch 1 involved setting direction and aligning leadership at *all levels* in the organization rather than just the senior leadership team. Launch 2 would broaden the engagement to help employees understand the current state, develop a vision for the future, and identify the change initiatives. Launch 3 would be about sustaining the change through implementation, tracking progress, and measuring success. Sustaining the change also had to include efforts to build leadership and employee capability for change.

- **Launch 1: Set Direction and Align Leadership.** Based on the CSO leadership team's progress to date, the OD team's initial conversation focused on the question: *if nothing changes, what will happen?* What emerged from the discussion was an affirmation that a focus only on process efficiency and expense management and without a focus on employee engagement and ownership would not be competitive in the future. The conversation confirmed the current state data; now the leadership team was aligned and committed to the change. It was one thing to see the data, but it was another thing for the leadership team to *believe* the data.

  The CSO leadership team then focused on articulating its vision for the future. This resulted in a document called *The Compass,* and included:

  1. **Purpose and mission**. We restore customers' lives after the unexpected happens.
  2. **Balanced objectives**. Two traditional performance measures, including customer satisfaction, and two objectives focused on leadership and employee engagement. The two people-oriented objectives made a strong statement that this was a departure from the past.
  3. **Cultural focus areas**. The cultural focus areas represented the tenets or values that needed to be strengthened to achieve The Compass. The cultural focus areas were:
     - *People First:* This focus area included guiding statements such as "*we trust employees to use good judgment*" and "*we hire and develop people with a passion for restoring lives.*"
     - *Customer Centricity:* This focus area included statements such as "*we value service behaviors*" and "*we are known as a service company.*"
     - *Collaboration and Innovation:* This area included statements such as "*employees who are comfortable and inspired to share their thoughts and ideas are more engaged and productive*" and "*trial and error is a measure of success.*"

The final leadership team conversation linked The Compass to required leader behaviors. For this conversation, the OD team introduced a "beliefs-behavior-results" framework. The framework suggests that shifting personal beliefs drives different behaviors and those different behaviors can lead to achieving the desired results. Said another way, to achieve the results described in The Compass, the senior leadership team needed to behave in a way that enabled those results. Those behaviors were a reflection of the beliefs (or mindsets) they hold true.

The OD team gathered input on how leadership team members "showed up" as leaders and collected input from other CSO leaders about their perceptions of the leadership team. Based on that data, leaders were asked to identify three new behaviors that would enable the achievement of the Compass, show their commitment to the transformation effort, and reflect the type of leadership team for which they wanted to be known. The leadership team took the extra step to explore more specifically the beliefs that would drive those three key behaviors.

At this time, the CSO leader made two changes in the leadership team. An external hire and an internal promotion visibly symbolized a culture shift and emphasized the commitment to achieving The Compass—from the balanced objectives to the cultural focus areas.

With The Compass and leadership team in place, the Launch 1 process extended to the field office leaders across the United States. Working with the CSO leadership team and a "max mix" design team from the leadership population, a leadership engagement session was designed to prepare the field leaders to support the transformation.

The design team shaped the agenda and facilitated the leadership engagement sessions. The leadership engagement sessions were to be a day and a half in length, based on the assumption that front-line leaders could not be away from their offices any longer. The design challenge became how to reflect fully the transformation principles while being flexible in the structure and flow of the leadership engagement sessions. The design team ended up with the following overall flow for the leadership engagement sessions:

1. Begin with discussions about The Compass and the case for change. Using data from the organizational survey and focus groups, the leaders engaged in conversations about the organization's purpose and future vision.
2. Illustrate the concepts by asking leaders to identify the most important organizational barriers to The Compass (aligned with each area of Galbraith's Star Model). To make the conversation more personal, the discussion also focused on what the vision meant for them and the possibilities for the organization if this vision was a reality.
3. Focus on what needed to change in the organization but also on what needed to change in the participants as leaders *and* as individuals. Using the Beliefs-Behaviors-Results framework, the leaders focused on increasing their self-awareness. They also built capability on their feedback skills and used real time examples to help them experience and apply what they were learning.
4. Identify two to three new behaviors to adopt. The intent was to focus their efforts on a few things to help support The Compass and the cultural focus areas. In turn, they identified beliefs or mindsets they needed to change or replace to embody the behaviors they identified in the session. The intent of all of this capability building was to focus their efforts on the critical few and to help sustain real, personal change after the sessions.

The leadership team stayed engaged and involved with the design team through the design and implementation of the sessions. This level of involvement was a significant symbol of the transformation; the leadership team had traditionally made the decisions about meeting design and then assigned roles and parts.

The leadership engagement sessions brought together all leaders, from front line to top management, in 15 sessions across the country. They debated the case for change, the business imperative, the organization's vision for the future, and what it meant for them as leaders. Just like the leadership team, the rest of the leaders spent time identifying the two to three new behaviors they would commit to in support of the Compass vision. These sessions also focused on building their capability as leaders in areas such as giving feedback.

- **Launch 2: Identify Actions and Engage the Organization in the Change.** As Launch 1 began to merge into Launch 2, the CSO leaders throughout the organization had identified specific actions to align with The Compass. They began to initiate efforts to address the top barriers to achieving The Compass and to sustain the momentum that had started in the leadership engagement sessions. Specifically, work was launched to create more customer centric processes, to shift metric-only individual performance documents to become more outcome-focused, and to more fully integrate behaviors into performance evaluation. These changes, along with the increased engagement of leaders in driving and supporting the change, began to symbolize that the organization was going to work differently.

In addition, and following the leadership engagement sessions, the leadership team and the OD team began partnerships with talent management, leadership development, and workforce measurement groups within the human resources function. Specific CSO resources were assigned full-time to the transformation effort to focus on and drive work that would continue the progress towards achieving the vision of The Compass. Although the transformation effort was only 18 months old, early business results indicated that a positive shift was occurring in the organization. There were measurable improvements in customer satisfaction, agency satisfaction, and employee engagement at the end of one full year of the effort.

But a large number of people—the ones who were actually delivering customer service on the frontlines—had not yet been engaged in the change process in a formal way. The OD team had to define how to engage the frontline employees in the progress and journey to date and to allow them to experience and take ownership of the transformation that was occurring in the organization. As the OD team contemplated future guidance for the CSO leadership team, it reflected on the lessons learned to date. How might these lessons (see Table 2) inform and illuminate the design of Launch 2 and Launch 3 in Customer Service?

TABLE 2

Lessons Learned from Three Transformation Efforts

Lessons and Explanation
Methodologies are effective only if they are adopted by and transferred to the organization—methods, models and tools must fit with the client's reality and be owned by them. All three business areas used many of the same methodologies, with differences in application. For example, the transformation principles have been the foundation for all of the efforts to date. However, each process was adjusted to meet the needs of a particular business area. The OD team transferred change competencies to the organization through design teams, executive working sessions, and the creation of change agent groups. Not fully achieving the Technology outcomes was partly the result of the OD team owning more of the transformation's design and delivery.
A clear and straightforward mission sets direction and drives effective and sustainable change. The transformation efforts in all three business areas were strategy driven. For CES and Technology, Thrill Our Customers represented their strategy to become a more innovative, cost-effective, value-added service provider. However, the Technology organization did not have a history of customer focus and so the strategy was seen as unclear and broad. It was difficult for many employees to see their line of sight to the company's customers and how their day-to-day work impacted the overall mission. The Customer Service organization's language in The Compass included a level of specificity that enabled individuals to better understand what it meant in practice. How can the OD team ensure that people understand the key initiatives to advance the achievement of The Compass? Also, how can the OD team engage frontline employees in understanding The Compass and the impact on their day-to-day work?

TABLE 2

Lessons Learned from Three Transformation Efforts (*continued*)

Lessons and Explanation
Leaders must understand the required behavior changes, commit to and model them, and be held accountable to them. An aligned and committed senior leadership team is at the core of any transformative change. Each leader must identify the mindset and behavior changes, and then model them for others. They must be held accountable was well. Leaders who did not attend a CES or Technology wave event often did not understand their role and the reason their employees were behaving differently. At best, they did nothing to encourage and support change; at worst, they acted as a strong opposing force, holding on to the status quo, and actively preventing change from occurring. The CES senior leader made it clear that not supporting the desired culture was unacceptable. This did not happen in Technology in the same way and probably contributed to slower and less impactful progress. Without accountability in this change, organization members will be hesitant to trust in the change and make their own transformative leap.
Sustainable transformation requires a whole systems approach; it's not just a people process. All of the cases used organization design elements to drive the purpose and desired culture. While the CES transformation involved all levels of the organization to identify and implement necessary changes, the Technology organization's senior leaders identified design changes concurrently with the large-group events. The integration of design changes and behavior changes after the fact was difficult. Some significant design changes appeared to be unrelated to, or even in conflict with, culture and behavior changes. The OD team knew that, in order to produce sustained change within CSO, design changes to reinforce the new culture would be required.
Measurement, using concrete data, is an intervention; not just a data-gathering process. In both the CES and Technology cases, the dual focus on business results and culture change, and the specific measurements attached to them, sent the message that both were equally important to the overall transformation effort.
Until a tangible shift is experienced in terms of day-to-day work, the change is not perceived to be real. While transformation begins with leaders and their behaviors, it is not enough to drive an effective change. Organization members need to feel and see changes in their day-to-day work. In CES, it was not until barriers at the local level were removed that people experienced the change. In the Technology case, members did not always see structure and process changes as cohesive and integrated with the overall transformation effort. As the OD team considered the CSO Launch 2 design phase, they wondered about how to make changes in the field offices real. The OD team had data from frontline employees that leadership behavior changes had been effective. However, employees also noted a sense of waiting for processes and structures to shift to prove that the change was real and to see more tangibly the connection between the cultural changes and business results.

Questions

The OD team must design the CSO Launch 2 phase activities with an eye toward Launch 3 of the transformation process.

1. What is your analysis of the MECK transformation to date? What has worked, what has not worked, and do the OD team's learnings seem complete?
2. Keeping in mind the lessons learned to date, propose a design (interventions, roles and responsibilities, timing, agendas, and other aspects) for Launch 2. Be sure to include or consider the following:

   - Continued work with leadership team
   - Building capability of leaders
   - Starting to engage rest of organization using core principles
   - Continuing to leverage organization design features, such as systems, structures, and rewards, to align behavior to The Compass

Glossary

This glossary was prepared to help the reader to understand some of the more frequently used terms in OD. Not all the terms in the glossary appear in the text, but they are frequently used in the field. Conversely, the glossary does not attempt to define every term used in the text. Nevertheless, knowledge of the terms in the glossary can be useful in understanding what at times appears to be an overly specialized language.

Accountability Responsibility to produce a promised result within a specific time.

Achievement needs A phrase applied to an individual, referring to the desire to perform work successfully and to advance in one's career.

Achievement orientation In cross-cultural analysis, the extent to which a culture favors the acquisition of power and resources.

Acquisition The purchase of one organization by another. (See *Merger.*)

Action learning A form of action research in which the focus is helping organizations to learn from their actions how to create entirely new structures, processes, and behaviors. Also called *action science, self-design*, or *appreciative inquiry*, this process involves considerable trial-and-error learning as participants try out new ways of operating, assess progress, and make necessary adjustments. (See *Action research.*)

Action research A cyclical process of diagnosis-change-research-diagnosis-change-research. The results of diagnosis produce ideas for changes, the changes are introduced into the same system, and their effects noted through further research and diagnosis. The number of cycles may be infinite.

Active listening Reflecting back to the other person not only what the person has said but also the perceived emotional tone of the message.

Adaptive A term used to describe the behavior of many kinds of systems. Originally used mainly to describe individuals (for example, adaptive behavior), it is now applied to groups and organizations vis-à-vis their environment.

Alliance A partnership between two organizations where their resources and capabilities are combined to pursue mutual goals in developing, manufacturing, or distributing goods and services.

Appreciative inquiry A contemporary approach to planned change. Contrary to typical approaches that assume organizations are like problems to be solved, appreciative inquiry works under the assumption that organizations are like mysteries to be understood. A focus on the "best of what is" in an organization provides the necessary vision for change.

Authenticity A term synonymous with the colloquial phrase "to be straight with another person." It refers to one's openness and honesty.

Balanced scorecard A control and information system that balances traditional financial measures with operational measures relating to an organization's critical success factors.

Behavioral science A phrase for the various disciplines that study human behavior. As such, all of the traditional social sciences are included.

Benchmarking A process where companies find out how other companies do something better than they do and then try to imitate or improve on the activity.

Body language An important part of nonverbal communications that involves the transmittal of thoughts, actions, and feelings through bodily movements and how other people interpret them.

Boundary A term used to describe systems or fields of interacting forces. Boundaries can be physical, such as a wall between two departments in an organization. More subtly, boundaries can be social processes, such as the boundaries between ethnic groups. Boundaries can be temporal: Things done at different times are said to be *bounded* from each other. Any set of forces or factors that tend to differentiate parts of the system can be said to have a boundary effect.

Breakthrough A sudden and significant advance, especially in knowledge, technique, or results.

Career The sequence of behaviors and attitudes associated with past, present, and anticipated future work-related experiences and role activities. A career is work related and lifelong.

Career development Activities directed at helping people to attain career objectives. These may include skill training, performance feedback and coaching, job rotation, mentoring roles, and challenging and visible job assignments.

Career planning Activities aimed at helping people to choose occupations, organizations, and jobs. It involves setting individual career goals.

Change management The tools, techniques, and processes that scope, resource, and direct activities to implement a change. Change management is less concerned about the transfer of knowledge, skill, and capacity to manage change in the future than organization development.

Client system The person, group, or organization that is the object of diagnosis or change efforts. Often shortened to the client. The client may be in the same organization as the consultant, as in the case of a line manager who is the client of a staff group, or the client and consultant may be in different organizations.

Closed system The tendency to disregard relations between a system and its environment. This is often an unwitting simplification and, as such, can lead to error.

Closure, need for A commonly felt need to see something finished or brought to a logical end point. Sometimes it is used to describe a person who is uncomfortable with ambiguity and uncertainty.

Coaching An intervention designed to improve the competencies of individual organization members through committed support, feedback, new views of work, new visions of the organization, and new ways of relating to people.

Collateral organization A parallel, coexisting structure that can be used to supplement the existing formal organization. It is generally used to solve ill-defined problems that do not fit neatly into the formal organizational structure.

Communication, one-way and two-way One-way communication describes an interaction in which one or both parties are paying little attention to what the other is saying or doing. In two-way communication, presumably both parties are engaging and responding to each other.

Competency The skills and knowledge necessary to carry out some specific activity or task.

Conflict management Management's task is to manage conflict by reducing or stimulating it, depending upon the situation, in order to develop the highest level of organizational performance.

Conformance The outputs produced as a part of work and passed on or delivered to the customer that will meet all the requirements to which the producer and the customer have agreed.

Confront The process by which one person attempts to make another person aware of aspects of behavior of which he or she seems unaware. It is used increasingly in the phrase *a confronting style* to describe a person who habitually gives such feedback to others.

Confrontation meeting A structured intervention that helps two (or more) groups resolve interdepartmental misunderstandings or conflict.

Consultant An individual (change agent) who is assisting an organization (client system) to become more effective. An external consultant is not a member of the system. An internal consultant is a member of the organization being assisted but may or may not have a job title that identifies the individual as such.

Content analysis A data analysis technique that derives themes from qualitative data such as interview responses.

Contingency approach This approach suggests that there is no universal best way to design an organization, that the design instead depends upon the situation.

Continuous improvement A philosophy of designing and managing all aspects of an organization in a never-ending quest for quality. The notion is that no matter how well things are going, there are always opportunities to make them better, and hundreds of small improvements can make a big difference in overall functioning. Also known as *kaizen*.

Contract A formal or informal agreement between the change agent and the client system to perform certain work. The contract typically identifies roles, expectations, resources, and other information required to successfully carry out the consultation process.

Core job dimensions These are the five basic dimensions of work, including skill variety, task identity, task significance, autonomy, and feedback.

Corporate culture This is the pattern of values, beliefs, and expectations shared by organization members. It represents the taken-for-granted and shared assumptions that people make about how work is to be done and evaluated and how employees relate to one another and to significant others, such as suppliers, customers, and government agencies.

Cost of quality The financial impact of poor quality. The cost of quality consists of the cost of conformance, nonconformance, and lost opportunity. The cost of conformance includes expenses associated with prevention measures, inspection, and appraisal. The cost of nonconformance is the dollar impact of not meeting customer expectations. The cost of lost opportunity is the revenue forgone when a customer leaves or does not renew a relationship with the organization.

Customer The person who receives the product of work. A customer may be either internal or external.

Data-based intervention A specific technique in action research. It follows some data collection phase and is an input into the system using the data that have been collected. Alternatively, it can be the act of presenting the data to members of the system, thus initiating a process of system self-analysis.

Defensive A term widely used to describe any kind of resistant behavior.

Development organizations See *Global social change organizations.*

Diagnosis The process of collecting information about a client system and working collaboratively with it to understand the system's current functioning. Diagnosis follows entry and contracting, and precedes action planning and implementation. Diagnosis is expected to point to possible interventions to address system effectiveness.

Differentiation The extent to which individual organizational units are different from each other along a variety of dimensions, such as time, technology, or formality. High uncertainty leads to the need for more differentiation, and low uncertainty leads to the need for less.

Dissonance A term reflecting the behavioral consequences of knowing two or more incompatible things at one time. Dissonance may be used to describe incompatibility in a person's point of view.

Diversity The mix of gender, age, disabilities, cultures, ethnic backgrounds, and lifestyles that characterize the organization's workforce and potential labor pool.

Dominant coalition That minimum group of cooperating employees who control the basic policymaking and oversee the operation of the organization as a whole.

Double-loop learning Organizational behaviors directed at changing existing valued states or goals. This is concerned with radically transforming an organization's structure, culture, and operating procedures. (See *Single-loop learning* and *Organization transformation.*)

Downsizing Interventions aimed at reducing the size of the organization. Although typically associated with layoffs and reductions in force, downsizing also includes attrition, early retirement, selling businesses or divisions, outsourcing, and delayering.

Dyad Two people and their dynamic interrelations; more informally, two people. Its usage has been extended recently to triad, or three people.

Dysfunctional Those aspects of systems that work against the goals. The term is meant to be objective but is often used subjectively to refer to the bad parts of systems. (See *Functional.*)

Empathic From empathy; to be able to project oneself into another's feelings and hence to understand the other person. It is used relatively interchangeably with *sensitive* and *understanding.*

Employee involvement Any set of technostructural interventions, such as quality circles, high involvement organizations, or total quality management, that adjust the power, information flows, rewards, and knowledge and skills in an organization. Also known as *quality of work life.*

Encounter An entire collection of interventions or techniques that aim to bring people into close and more intimate relations.

Enterprise resource planning (ERP) An information system that collects, processes, and provides data and information about a company, including order processing, product design, purchasing inventory, manufacturing distribution, human resources, procurement, and forecasting.

Entry The process that describes how an OD practitioner first encounters and establishes a relationship with a client system.

Environment The physical and social context within which any client system (a person, group, or organization) is functioning.

Ethics Standards of acceptable behavior for professional practicing in a particular field, such as law, medicine, or OD. In OD, it concerns how practitioners perform their helping relationship with organization members.

Evaluation feedback Information about the overall effects of a change program. It is generally used for making decisions about whether resources should continue to be allocated to the program.

Expectancy The belief, expressed as a subjective estimate or odds, that a particular act will be successful.

Expectancy model A model of motivation suggesting that people are motivated to choose among different behaviors or intensities of effort if they believe that their efforts will be rewarded in a meaningful fashion.

Experiential A kind of learning process in which the content is experienced as directly as possible, in contrast to being simply read or talked about. The term applies to a wide variety of training techniques. It is often used in the phrase experiential level, in contrast to cognitive level.

Expert power The power and influence that a person has in a situation by virtue of technical or professional expertise. (See *Power.*)

External validity A research term concerned with assessing the general applicability of interventions. This helps to identify contingencies upon which the success of change programs depend. (See *Internal validity.*)

Facilitate A process by which events are "helped to happen." Facilitating is a kind of influence role that is neither authoritarian nor abdicative.

Feedback Information regarding the actual performance or the results of the activities of a system. In communications, it concerns looking for and using helpful responses from others.

Filtering A barrier to communication that occurs when the sender intentionally shifts or modifies the message so that it will be seen more favorably by the receiver.

Fishbowl An experiential training technique in which some members of a group sit in a small inner circle and work the issue while other members sit in an outer circle and observe.

Force-field analysis A qualitative tool that analyzes the forces for and the forces resisting change. It implies two change strategies, increasing the forces for change or decreasing the resistance to change.

Formal (leader, organization, system) A term introduced originally in the Hawthorne studies to designate the set of organizational relationships that were explicitly established in policy and procedure (for example, the *formal organization*). The term has been prefixed to many types of organizational phenomena.

Functional The term describes those parts of a system that promote the attainment of its goals. It comes from a mode of systems analysis that seeks to explain systems by understanding the effects that parts of the system have on one another and the mutual effects between the system and its environment.

Gain sharing This involves paying employees a bonus based upon improvements in the operating results of an organization or department. It generally covers all employees working in a particular department, plant, or company and includes both a bonus scheme and a participative structure for eliciting employees' suggestions and improvements.

Gatekeeping A term from group dynamics that describes a person in a group who regulates interaction patterns by asking people for their ideas or suggesting to others that they should talk less.

Global social change organizations Not-for-profit and nongovernmental organizations whose primary purpose is to bring about change, such as ecological awareness, hunger relief, children's rights, or political stability in a community or society.

Global strategy A worldwide strategy characterized by goals of efficiency and volume; this strategy views the world as one homogenous market.

Goal setting Activities involving managers and subordinates in jointly setting subordinates' goals, monitoring them, and providing counseling and support when necessary.

Group dynamics A set of variables, including power and influence, norms, conflict, communication, decision making, or trust, that individually and collectively describe the functioning of a group.

Group maintenance Those behaviors exhibited by members of a group that are functional for holding the group together, increasing members' liking for each other, and differentiating the group from its environment.

Group task activities Activities that are directed at helping the group accomplish its goals. Successful groups are more able to properly combine group maintenance and group task activities than are less successful groups.

Groupthink A form of decision making that occurs when the members' striving for unanimity and closeness overcomes their motivation to realistically appraise alternative courses of action.

Growth A term reflecting theorists' and practitioners' concern for improvement in personal, group, and organizational behavior. Identification of growth stages, rates, and directions is a major focus of contemporary theory and research.

Growth needs The desire for personal accomplishment, learning, and development. An important contingency affecting work design successes; for example the greater people's growth needs, the more responsive they are to enriched forms of work.

Hawthorne effect When workers' behavior changes and productivity increases because the workers are aware that persons important in their lives are taking an interest in them.

Hidden agenda An undisclosed motive for doing or failing to do something. For example, a plant manager began to use team-building sessions, not because he wanted them but because he knew that his boss was in favor of such sessions.

Human resource systems These comprise mechanisms and procedures for selecting, training, and developing employees. They may include reward systems, goal setting, career planning and development, and stress management.

Ideal future state An articulated vision of the ideal state of the organization; the desired culture, infrastructure, and operation. What does it look like, sound like, feel like? What are people doing, with whom, and how? An ideal future state serves as the direction for present-day change efforts; it serves to bring the future into the present.

Implementation feedback Refers to information about whether an intervention is being implemented as intended. It is generally used to gain a clearer understanding of the behaviors and procedures required to implement a change program and to plan for the next implementation steps. (See *Evaluation feedback.*)

Individualism In cross-cultural analysis, the extent to which a country's culture supports individual growth, development, and achievement.

Industry structure The overall attractiveness of an industry as determined by the power of buyers, power of suppliers, threat of entry, threat of substitute products/services, and rivalry among firms.

Informal (leader, group, organization, system) A term introduced in the Hawthorne studies to designate the set of organizational relationships that emerge over time from the day-to-day experiences that people have with one another. Informal relationships are expressive of the needs that people actually feel in situations, in contrast to needs their leaders think they should feel.

Inputs Human or other resources, such as information, energy, and materials, coming into the system or subsystem. Also, more informally, used to describe people's contributions to a system, particularly their ideas.

Institutionalization Refers to making organizational changes a permanent part of the organization's normal functioning.

Integrated strategic change A model of large-scale organization change that integrates principles of strategic management with processes of planned change. It involves strategic analysis, strategic choice, strategic change plan design, and strategic change plan implementation.

Integration The state of collaboration that exists among departments that are required to achieve unity of effort by the demands of the environment. The term is used primarily for contingency approaches to organizational design. (See *Differentiation.*)

Interaction Almost any behavior resulting from interpersonal relationships. In human relations, it includes all forms of communication, verbal and nonverbal, conscious and unconscious.

Internal validity A research term concerned with assessing whether an intervention is responsible for producing observed results, such as improvements in job satisfaction, productivity, and absenteeism. (See *External validity.*)

Intervention Any action on the part of a change agent. Intervention carries the implication that the action is planned and deliberate and presumably functional. Many suggest that an OD intervention requires valid information, free choice, and a high degree of ownership by the client system of the course of action.

Jargon Overly specialized or technical language.

Job diagnostic survey (JDS) A questionnaire designed to measure job characteristics on such core dimensions as skill variety, task identity, task significance, autonomy, and feedback.

Job enrichment A way of making jobs more satisfying by increasing the skill variety, task identity, significance of the task, autonomy, and feedback from the work itself.

Joint optimization The goal of the sociotechnical system theory approach to work design that states that an organization will function best only if its social and technical systems are designed to fit the needs of one another and the environment.

Joint venture A separate entity for sharing development and production costs and penetrating new markets that is created by two or more firms.

Knowledge management (KM) A process that focuses on how knowledge can be organized and used to improve organization performance. KM tends to focus on the tools and techniques that enable organizations to collect, organize, and translate information into useful knowledge. Organizationally, KM applications are often located in the information systems function and may be under the direction of a chief information officer. (See *Organization learning.*)

Lab A shorthand term for a wide variety of programs that derive from the laboratory method of training, or T-group, an approach that is primarily experiential.

Large-group interventions Any of several techniques, such as search conferences and open space, designed to work with a whole system, including organization members, suppliers, customers, and other stakeholders.

Leadership A process of influence exercised when institutional, political, psychological, and other resources are used to arouse, engage, and satisfy the motives of followers.

Leadership development A training and education intervention aimed at improving the competencies of managers and executives of an organization.

Learning organization An organization where everyone is involved in identifying and solving problems, enabling the organization to continuously experiment, improve, and increase its capability.

Management by objectives (MBO) A process of periodic manager–subordinate or group meetings designed to accomplish organizational goals by mutual planning of the work, review of accomplishments, and mutual solving of problems that arise in the course of getting the job done.

Management development Training or other processes to increase managers' knowledge and skills in order to improve performance in present jobs or prepare them for promotion. Increasingly tied to career planning and development.

Marginality The degree to which an individual or role must straddle the boundary between two or more groups with differing goals, values systems, and behavioral patterns.

Matrix organization An approach for integrating the activities of different specialists while maintaining specialized organizational units.

Mechanistic organization This type of organization is highly bureaucratic. Tasks are specialized and clearly defined. This is suitable when markets and technology are well established and show little change over time.

Merger The formal and legal integration of two or more organizations into a single entity. (See *Acquisition.*)

Microcosm group A small, representative group selected from the organization at large to address important organizational issues. The key feature of the group is that it is a microcosm or representation of the issue itself.

Mission A statement of the organization's purpose, range of activities, character, and uniqueness.

Model A simplification of some phenomenon for purposes of study and understanding. The concrete embodiment of a theory. To behave in an idealized way so that others might learn or change their behavior by identifying with and adopting those behaviors displayed.

Motivation The conditions responsible for variation in the intensity, quality, and direction of ongoing behavior.

Motivation-hygiene model Originally developed by Frederick Herzberg and associates, the model describes factors in the workplace that dissatisfy people and factors that motivate them.

Multinational strategy A worldwide strategy with goals of local responsiveness and specialization; views the worldwide market as heterogeneous and requiring product and service customization.

Need A central concept in psychology, referring to a biological or psychological requirement for the maintenance and growth of the human animal. It is used among practitioners chiefly to refer to a psychological demand not met in organizational life, with the emphasis on the search for ways in which more such wants can be satisfied.

Need hierarchy A particular theory about the operation of human needs introduced by Abraham Maslow. The model of motivation describes a hierarchy of needs existing within people. The five need levels are physiological, safety, social, ego, and self-actualization. The theory says that higher needs cannot be activated until lower needs are relatively satisfied. This particular theory also was the basis for McGregor's Theory X Theory Y formulation.

Network organization A newly emerging organization structure that involves managing an interrelated set of organizations, each specializing in a particular business function or task. This structure extends beyond the boundaries of any single organization and involves linking different organizations to facilitate interorganizational exchange and task coordination. (See *Transorganizational development.*)

Norms Rules regulating behavior in any social system. They are usually unwritten and are more specific and pointed than values in that deviations from norms are followed by such punishments as kidding, silent disapproval, or in the extreme, banishment.

Off-site Away from the regular place of work, as an off-site lab or conference.

Openness Accepting the communications and confrontations of others and expressing oneself honestly, with authenticity.

Open space meeting See *Large-group interventions.*

Open system The need to take into account relations between a system and its environment. This concept in systems theory is borrowed from the biological sciences. It refers to the nature and functions of transactions that take place between a system and its environment.

Open-systems planning A method for helping organizations or groups to systematically assess their task environment and develop a strategic response to it.

Organic organization This type of organization is relatively flexible and relaxed. The organic style is most appropriate to unstable environmental conditions in which novel problems continually occur. (See *Mechanistic organization.*)

Organization design Involves bringing about a coherence or fit among organizational choices about strategy, organizing mode, and mechanisms for integrating people into the organization. The greater the fit among these organizational dimensions, the greater will be the organizational effectiveness.

Organization development (OD) The system-wide application and transfer of behavioral science knowledge to the planned development, improvement, and reinforcement of the strategies, structures, and processes that lead to organization effectiveness.

Organization development practitioner A generic term for people practicing organization development. These individuals may include managers responsible for developing their organizations or departments, people specializing in OD as a profession, and people specializing in a field currently being integrated with OD (for example, strategy or human resource management) who have gained some familiarity with and competence in OD.

Organization effectiveness An overall term that refers to the outputs of organization strategy and design. Typically includes financial performance, such as profits and costs; stakeholder satisfaction, such as employee and customer satisfaction; and measures of internal productivity, such as cycle times.

Organization learning (OL) A change process that seeks to enhance an organization's capability to acquire and develop new knowledge. It is aimed at helping organizations use knowledge and information to change and improve continually. It involves discovery, invention, production, and generalization. In organizations, OL change processes are typically associated with the human resource function and may be assigned to a special leadership role, such as chief learning officer. (See *Knowledge management.*)

Organization transformation A process of radically altering the organization's strategic direction, including fundamental changes in structures, processes, and behaviors. (See *Double-loop learning.*)

Parallel learning structure See *Collateral organization.*

Participative A term used to describe techniques used by a power figure that aim to involve subordinate, lower-power persons in the decision-making process of an organization (for example, participative management). One aim is to increase the sense of commitment to organizational goals.

Performance appraisal A human resource system designed to provide feedback to an individual or group about its performance and its developmental opportunities. The performance appraisal process may or may not be closely linked to the reward system.

Performance management A constellation of processes that involve goal setting, performance appraisal, and reward systems that guide, develop, reinforce, and control member behavior toward desired organizational outcomes.

Planned change A generic phrase for all systematic efforts to improve the functioning of some human system. It is a change process in which power is usually roughly equal between consultants and clients and in which goals are mutually and deliberately set.

Power The ability to influence others so that one's values are satisfied. It may derive from several sources, including organizational position, expertise, access to important resources, and ability to reward and punish others.

Power distance In cross-cultural analysis, the extent to which people in a country accept large differences in status, income, authority, and equality.

Presenting problem The most salient reason the client system has asked for help from a change agent. For example, a conflict between two people can be a presenting problem or symptom that is caused by structural problems. The presenting problem is often a symptom of the true underlying problem that diagnosis is expected to uncover.

Problem-solving process A systematic, disciplined approach to identifying and solving work-related problems.

Process The way any system is going about doing whatever it is doing. Social process is the way persons are relating to one another as they perform some activity. Organizational process is the way different elements of the organization interact or how different organizational functions are handled.

Process-based organizations A type of organization structure that uses teams focused on the accomplishment of core work processes.

Process consultation A set of activities on the part of the consultant that helps the client to perceive, understand, and act upon the process events that occur in the client's environment.

Process observation A method of helping a group to improve its functioning, usually by having an individual watch the group in action and then feeding back the results. Interviews may also be used. The group (or individuals) then use the data to improve its functioning.

Production group A work group that is separated (by a boundary) from other work groups so that they can operate with relative independence.

Profit An accounting term that measures total revenues minus total costs.

Quality (outcome) Meeting and exceeding customer needs for both internal and external customers.

Quality (process) The continuing commitment by everyone in the organization to understand, meet, and exceed the needs of its customers.

Quality circles Small groups of workers who meet voluntarily to identify and solve productivity problems. These are typically associated with Japanese methods of participative management.

Quality of work life (QWL) A way of thinking about people, work, and organization involving a concern for employee well-being and organizational effectiveness. It generally results in employee participation in important work-related problems and decisions.

Quasi-experimental research designs These designs enable OD evaluators to rule out many rival explanations for OD results other than the intervention itself. They involve choices about what to measure and when to measure; they are most powerful when they include longitudinal measurement, a comparison unit, and statistical analysis.

Re-engineering An intervention that focuses on dramatically redesigning core business processes. Successful re-engineering is often closely related to changes in an organization's information systems.

Refreezing The stabilization of change at a new state of equilibrium.

Return on assets (ROA) An accounting measure formed by the ratio of profits to total assets.

Reward power The present or potential ability to award something for worthy behavior. (See *Power.*)

Rewards, extrinsic Rewards given by the organization, such as pay, promotion, praise, tenure, and status symbols.

Rewards, intrinsic Rewards that must originate and be felt within the person. Intrinsic rewards include feelings of accomplishment, achievement, and self-esteem.

Role A set of systematically interrelated and observable behaviors that belong to an identifiable job or position. Role behavior may be either required or discretionary.

Role ambiguity A result of inadequate information regarding role-related expectation and understanding. This occurs when the individual does not clearly understand all the expectations of a particular role.

Role conflict A result of a conflict between managerial or individual expectations and managerial or individual experiences with regard to performance of the role.

Search conference A 1- to 3-day meeting involving as many organizational stakeholders as possible to reflect on the past, appreciate the present, and envision the future. The search conference specifically avoids a problem-solving approach in an effort to energize the organization toward a new way of working. (See also *Large-group interventions.*)

Selective perception The tendency to perceive only a part of a message, to screen out other information.

Self-awareness A positive goal of most training techniques that aim at behavior changes. Self-awareness means becoming aware of one's existing patterns of behavior in a way that permits a relatively nondefensive comparison of those patterns with potential new ones.

Self-designing organizations A change program aimed at helping organizations to gain the capacity to fundamentally change themselves. It is a highly participative process, involving multiple stakeholders in setting strategic direction, designing appropriate structures and processes, and implementing them. This process helps organizations to learn how to design and implement their own strategic changes.

Self-regulating work group A work group that has a clearly defined series of tasks and a clear boundary so that the group can be generally responsible for its own output, quality, and work space. Also known as a *self-managing team.*

Self-serving activities Activities that satisfy individual needs at the expense of the group.

Sensitivity training A method of helping individuals to develop greater self-awareness and become more sensitive to their effect on others. Individuals learn by interaction with other members of their group.

Single-loop learning Organizational behaviors directed at detecting and correcting deviations from valued states or goals. This is concerned with fine-tuning how an organization currently functions. (See *Double-loop learning.*)

Six sigma A quality standard that specifies a goal of no more than 3.4 defects per million occurrences of an activity or process. Also refers to a management initiative emphasizing the pursuit of higher quality and lower costs.

Skill training Training that is more concerned with improving effectiveness on the job than with abstract learning concepts.

Smoothing Dealing with conflict by denying or avoiding it.

Social construction of reality An approach concerned with the processes by which people, their values, and common-sense and scientific knowledge produce meaning and reality.

Sociotechnical system A term that refers to simultaneously considering both the social system (human) and the technical system in order to best match the technology and the people involved.

Stakeholder A person or group having a vested interest in the organization's functioning and objectives.

Strategic change An approach to bringing about an alignment or congruence among an organization's strategy, structure, and human resource systems, as well as a fit between them and the larger environment. It includes attention to the technical, political, and cultural aspects of organizations.

Strategy A plan of action defining how an organization will use its resources to gain a competitive advantage in the larger environment. It typically includes choices about the functions an organization will perform, the products or services it will provide, and the markets and populations it will serve.

Stress management Activities aimed at coping with the dysfunctional consequences of work-related stress. These generally include diagnosing the causes and symptoms of stress and taking action to alleviate the causes and to improve one's ability to deal with stress.

Structure The structure of a system is the arrangement of its parts. Also, jargon for a change strategy that focuses on the formal organization. This is a particularly important class of interventions when the target for change is an entire organization.

Subsystem A part of a system. A change in any subsystem has an effect on the total system.

Survey feedback A type of data-based intervention that flows from surveys of the members of a system on some subject and reports the results of the surveys to the client system for whatever action appears appropriate.

System A set of interdependent parts that together make up a whole; each contributes something and receives something from the whole, which in turn is interdependent with the larger environment.

T-groups A method of helping individuals to develop greater self-awareness and become more sensitive to their effect on others. Individuals learn by interaction with other members of their group.

Task control The degree to which employees can regulate their own behavior to convert incoming materials into finished (or semifinished) products or other outputs.

Task force A group established to solve a particular problem (it may be disbanded when its work is accomplished).

Team building The process of helping a work group to become more effective in accomplishing its tasks and in satisfying the needs of group members.

Technology Consists of the major techniques (together with their underlying assumptions about cause and effect) that an organization's employees use while engaging in organizational processes or that are programmed into the machines and other equipment.

Theory X Typical Theory X managers believe that people dislike work and will avoid it whenever possible. Such managers feel that they themselves are a small, elite group of individuals who want to lead and take responsibility but that the larger mass of people want to be directed and avoid responsibility.

Theory Y Typical Theory Y managers usually assume that workers will accept responsibility provided they can satisfy personal needs and organizational goals at the same time.

Third-party intervention Activities aimed at helping two or more people within the same organization to resolve interpersonal conflicts.

Total quality management (TQM) A comprehensive and large-scale intervention that aims to focus all organization systems on the continuous improvement of quality.

Training An educational intervention typically focused on supervisors and individual contributors that is intended to increase the skills and knowledge of the workforce.

Transition state A condition that exists when the organization is moving from its current state to a desired future state. During the transition state, the organization learns how to implement the conditions needed to reach the desired future; it typically requires special structures and activities to manage this process.

Transformational change A radical change in how members perceive, think, and behave at work.

Transnational strategy A worldwide strategy with goals of customized products/services and efficient and responsive operations. Attempts to integrate operations on a worldwide basis.

Transorganizational development An intervention concerned with helping organizations to join into partnerships with other organizations to perform tasks or solve problems that are too complex and multifaceted for single organizations to resolve. Includes the following cyclical stages: identification, convention, organization, and evaluation.

Trust level The degree of mutual trust among a set of persons. Raising the trust level is usually a major goal of team building.

Uncertainty avoidance In cross-cultural analysis, the extent to which people in a culture avoid risk taking and prefer routine, knowable situations.

Unfreezing A reduction in the strength of old values, attitudes, or behaviors.

Value judgment Statement or belief based on or reflecting the individual's personal or class values.

Values Relatively permanent ideals (or ideas) that influence and shape the general nature of people's behavior.

Visioning A process typically initiated by key executives to define the mission of the organization and to clarify desired values for the organization, including valued outcomes and valued organizational conditions.

Work design The arrangement of tasks, people, and technology to produce both psychological outcomes and work performance.

Some of the terms used in this glossary were taken or adapted from *Reference Book: Organizational Effectiveness* (Fort Leavenworth, Kan.: U.S. Army Command and General Staff College, 1979).

Name Index

A

Abbott Laboratories, 504
Academy of Management, 14, 48, 424
Accountable Care Organization (ACO), 687
Adhikar, 257–261
Aetna Inc., 689
Airbus ICT Organization, 329–337
Air New Zealand, 14
Air Products and Chemicals, Inc., 396–398
Akzo Nobel, 14
Alaska Department of Health and Social Services (DHSS), 627
Alaska Health Care Commission (HCC), 630
Alaska Health Workforce Coalition (AHWC), 626, 627–631
Alaska Mental Health Trust Authority (AMHTA), 627
Alaska Native Tribal Health Consortium, 628
Alaska Primary Care Association, 628
Alaska Process Industry Careers Consortium (APICC), 627
Alaska State Hospital and Nursing Home Association (ASHNHA), 628, 629
Alaska Workforce Investment Board (AWIB), 627
Alcoa, 389, 512
Alderfer, C., 302, 304
Alegent Health, 136–137, 219–221, 314–316
All-American University, 238
Alliance for Innovation, 704, 711
Alliance for Redesigning Government, 711
Alliant Energy, 449
Allstate Insurance, 318
Alonso, Fernando, 334
Amazon.com, 5, 356, 357–358, 739
American Airlines, 14, 499
American Express, 460
American Express Financial Advisors, 346
American Healthcorp (AMHC), 350
American Management Association, 358
American Productivity and Quality Center (APQC), 387
American Psychological Association, 14
American Quality Foundation, 389
American Society for Quality (ASQ), 387
American Society of Training and Development (ASTD), 489
American Standard, 541
American University, 59
America West Airlines, 613
Analog Devices, 385
Andersen Windows, 367
Anderson, Carol, 453–454
Anderson, Ray, 531
AON Consulting, 487
Apple, 100, 187, 355, 592
Argyris, Chris, 64
Arizona State University, 37
Ascension Health, 688
Asea Brown Boveri (ABB), 34, 354, 545
Assistance Professionals Association, 512
AT&T, 405, 457, 608, 610

B

B. R. Richardson Timber Products Corporation,751–765
Ballmer, Steve, 479
Bank of America, 487, 608
Barth, Roland, 696
Barwale, B. R., 618
BASF, 545
Baskin, Otis, 685
Beckhard, R., 2, 8, 13, 298, 301, 305
Beer, Michael, 2
Bekey, George, 37
Bell, C. H., Jr., 292
Ben and Jerry's, 187
Benedictine University, 59
Benetton, 355
Ben & Jerry's, 502
Berkshire Hathaway, 187
Bezos, Jeff, 357
BHP Billiton, 738
Bill and Melinda Gates Foundation, 697
Black & Decker, 448
Blake, Robert, 7, 9–11, 304
Block, Peter, 81
Bloomberg, Michael, 711
Blue Cross and Blue Shield of Florida, 502
The Body Shop, 187
Boeing, 14, 52, 318, 364, 375, 385, 390, 415, 502, 582, 738
Booz Allen Hamilton, 500
Booz & Co., 592
Boss, R. W., 291, 293
Boston Orchestra, 102
Bowen, Thella, 31–33
Bowling Green State University, 14, 59
BP, 737
Bristol-Myers-Squibb, 592
Bruno, Jennifer, 515
Bryson, John, 705
Buller, R., 292
Bureau of Labor Statistics, 738
Burke, Warner, 2
Bush, George H. W., 184, 696
Bush, George W., 697
Byron, Jim, 396–398

C

Caltech, 37
Calvez, Didier Le, 560
Cambia Health Solutions, 149–152, 302, 449, 560
Cameron, K., 127
Campbells, 488
Canadian Broadcasting Corporation, 582
Capital One, 163, 503, 599–601, 738
Care for Nottinghamshire, Derbyshire, and Lincolnshire (CLAHRCNDL), 593
Cargill, 711, 712
Carlock, R., 716
Carnegie Foundation, 8
Carrefour, 499, 536
Carroll, S., 448
Case Construction, 359–360
Case Western Reserve University, 14, 59
Caterpillar, 541
Cavallo, David, 700
CBS, 102
Cedar-Sinai Hospital, 388
Center for Effective Organizations (USC), 85, 377, 445, 733
Center for Manufacturing andAutomation Research (CMAR), 37, 38
Center for Medicare & Medicaid Services (CMS), 688
Ceridian, 476
Cerrano, John, 240, 247
Charles Schwab, 476
Charles Steward Mott Foundation, 697
Chicago Orchestra, 102
China Association for NGOs (CANGO), 743
Christensen, Clayton, 701, 702
Christian Caring Homes, 271–273
Chrysler, 712
Cisco Systems, 358, 477, 616
Citibank, 349
Citigroup, 52
City of Carlsbad, California, 318, 433
Clarke, Jeff, 198
Clarkson, Beth, 240
CNF Freight Service, 382
CoachVille, 474
Colgate-Palmolive, 342
Collaboration for Leadership in Applied Health Research, 593
Columbia University, 59
Committee on Community Interrelations (American Jewish Congress), 8
Communications Workers of America, 12
Compaq, 197, 198–199, 227
Connecticut Interracial Commission, 8
Consolidated Freightway, 382
Container Store, 490, 500
Continental Airlines, 613–615
Copperfield, Matt, 240, 247
Corning Glass Works, 408, 409, 616
Costco, 96

Council of Chief State School Officers, 697
Countrywide Financial, 608
Covisint, 739–740
Craig, Paul, 690, 692
Crosby, Philip, 386
Cruise, Tom, 365
Cummings, T., 128, 129, 570–573
Cuyahoga River Valley Organization (CRVO), 766–775

D

Dana Corporation, 463
DaVita, 449, 460, 533, 645–657, 688
Dekkers, Guus, 329–337
Dell Computer, 187, 541, 739
Deloitte, 511
Deming, W. Edwards, 385–386
Denny's, 498
Denton, Bob, 235, 236
Denton, Robert, 234
De Soto, 463
Deutsche Telekom, 375
Digital Equipment Corporation, 198
Direct Health Solutions, 149
Disk Drives, Inc., 523–527
Disney, 47, 52, 389, 558
DMT, 594–596
Donnan, Susan, 329–337
Donnelly Corporation, 463
Dow Chemical Company, 349, 385, 460, 616
Drucker, P., 444
Drugstore.com, 358
Dufour, R., 698, 700
Duncan, Arnie, 697
DuPont, 14, 342, 384
Dyer, W., 127, 282

E

Eaker, R., 698, 700
Eastman Chemical Company, 388
eBay, 5, 739
Eindhoven University of Technology, 423
Electrolux, 545
Electromation, Inc., 384
Eli Lilly, 616
Emerson, 541
Equate, 616
Equitable Life Assurance Society, 512
Ernst & Young, 389, 476
Eskom, 169
Esso Standard Oil, 8
Ethicon, Inc., 386
European Union, 499
ExxonMobil, 8, 342

F

Fadem, Joel, 314
Fairbank, Rich, 599
Fandango.com, 739
Federal Express, 477, 504, 616
Federal Mediation and Conciliation Service, 274
Feyerherm, A., 2
Fiat, 184
Fidelity Investments, 488
Fielding Institute, 59
Fiorina, Carleton S., 199
Fiorina, Carly, 198, 228, 712
Fitz, J. D., 692
Florida Power and Light, 364
Flynn, Patricia, 515
Ford, Henry, 187
Ford Foundation, 711
Ford Motor Company, 187, 385, 390, 476, 712
Fordyce, J., 306
Fortune, 377, 390, 410, 415, 458, 459, 467, 502, 506, 511
Foster Mobley Group, 685
Four Seasons, 560
Frederickson, H. George, 705
French, Wendell, 2
Frito-Lay, 458, 460
Fujitsu, 170
Fuji-Xerox, 545, 616
Fullan, Michael, 702, 703
Fungi, Victor, 531

G

Gaines Pet Food, 12, 423, 459
Galbraith, J., 96, 349, 355
Gambro, 645–657
Gap Inc., 503, 738
Gellerman, Bill, 70
General Accounting Office, 463
General Dynamics, 462
General Electric, 6, 14, 34, 46, 298, 300–301, 342, 346, 364, 415, 488, 545
General Electric Capital Services, 346
General Electric Medical Systems (GEMS), 299, 300–301
General Foods, 14, 423, 458
General Mills, 8, 375, 414, 415, 458, 501
General Motors, 12, 342, 384, 385, 428, 616, 712
George Washington University, 59
Georgia-Pacific, 476
Gerstner, Louis, 184, 531
Gestalt Institute, 47
Global Mobile Corporation, 636–644
Golembiewski, Bob, 705, 707
Goodyear, 541
Google, 502, 511, 536
Gould Academy, 8
Gould Electronics, 462
Greiner, Larry, 550, 570, 572, 573, 576

H

Hackman, J., 106, 113, 127, 215, 282, 292, 405, 407, 413, 414
Hamel, G., 359
Harley-Davidson, 182, 462, 533, 738
Harrison, R., 435
Hartford, 163, 200, 375
Hartman, Dale, 37, 39
Haslett, Sally, 692
Hay Group, 481
Health Care Cost Institute, 689
HealthPartners, 688
Healthways Corporation ((HMC), 346, 350–351, 583–584
Herman Miller, 552
Herzberg, F., 112, 405
Hewlett-Packard (HP), 14, 46, 197, 198–199, 227–228, 314, 318, 364, 405, 476, 477, 500, 541, 545, 546, 558, 712, 739
Highmark/Blue Cross Plan, 688
Hilton, 502
Hoechst, 545
Holiday Inn, 383, 616
Honda, 541, 738
Honeywell, 12, 368, 369–371
HP-Compaq, 314
Hughes Aircraft, 36, 385
Humana Inc., 689
Human Systems Development Consortium (HSDC), 70
Humler, Herve, 391
Huse, E., 308
Hyundai, 170

I

IBM, 6, 14, 36, 182, 184, 349, 358, 409, 457, 476, 477, 531, 533, 553, 558, 560, 561–562
Ikea, 738, 746
Illinois Institute of Technology, 61
Imperial Chemical Industries, 14, 405
Indiana Bell Telephone Company, 409
Industry–University Cooperative Research Center Program (IUCRCP), 37
Institut de Socio-Economie des Enterprises et des Organizations. *See* Institute for Socio-Economic Enterprises and Organizations (ISEOR)
Institute for Manufacturing and Automation Research (IMAR), 36–39
Institute for Social Research (ISR), 384, 509
Institute for Socio-Economic Enterprises and Organizations (ISEOR), 733
Intel Corporation, 14, 98, 375, 414, 415, 449, 488, 511, 537, 551, 552
Interface Carpet, 531, 738
International Coach Federation, 474
International Organization for Standardization (ISO), 369, 387
International Society of Six-Sigma Professionals (ISSSP), 387
IRS (Internal Revenue Service), 375

J

Janssen Research Foundation, 307
JCDecaux, 262
JCPenney, 476, 558
Jenkins, G., 467
Johnson & Johnson, 96, 307–308, 346, 487, 504, 512, 514–515, 559, 712
Johnsonville Sausage, 416
Joint Commission on Accreditation of Health Care Organizations, 322
Juran, Joseph M., 385

K

Kaiser Family Foundation, 689
Kaiser Permanente, 200
Kanter, R., 46
Kaplan, R., 274
Kawai, 102
Kazanjian, R., 355

Kelman, H., 63
Kenworth Motors, 234–237
Kikkoman Corporation, 711
Kimberly-Clark, 34, 375
Kimpton Hotels and Restaurants, 512
Kizer, Kenneth, 366
Kobe Steel, Ltd., 389
Kodak, 182
Komatsu, 541
Kotter, J., 22, 96

L

Lands' End Direct Merchants, 464
Lawler, Edward, 106, 128, 129, 377, 384, 467, 507, 593, 597–598, 744
Lawrence, Nancy, 247
Ledford, G., 384
Lenovo, 541
Levinson, H., 444
Levi Strauss, 711
Lewin, Kurt, 8, 22–23, 25, 27, 134
Li and Fung, 531
Likert, Rensis, 9, 10
Limited Brands, 163
Lincoln Electric, 461
Lincoln Hospital, 322–328
Lippitt, Gordon, 64, 78
Lippitt, R., 22
Living.com, 358
Liz Claiborne, 355
L.L. Bean, 582
Lord Corporation, 349
L'Oreal, 499, 504, 505–506
Loyd, Chris, 396–398
Loyola University, 59
Luft, J., 268

M

MacArthur, Douglas, 385
MacArthur Foundation, 702
Macy, B., 212, 213
Maharashtra Hybrid Seeds Company Limited (MAHYCO), 618–620
Mandela, Nelson, 169
Mann, Floyd, 9
Marchionne, Sergio, 184
Marconi Commerce Systems, 182
Marczak, Ann, 38
Marriott, 318, 391
Martin, J., 555
Martinez, Kim, 691
Matsushita, 170, 541
McCaskey, M., 106
McConkie, M., 291
McDermott, Mike, 599–600
McDonald's, 94, 99, 512, 616
McGregor, Douglas, 8, 444
McKesson, 201
McKinney, Webb, 198
McKinsey & Co., 582, 689
McNiff, Jean, 701
MECK Insurance, 776–785
Melkanoff, Michel, 37
Menlo Park, 362–363
Merck, 355
Michelin, 541
Microsoft Canada, 552, 553–554
Microsoft Corporation, 163, 187, 318, 449, 477, 478, 479–480, 511, 553, 558, 582, 608, 611, 616
Midland-Ross, 463
Mirvis, P., 212, 213
Mishra, Pia, 257, 260
Mishra, Rajan, 257
MIT (Massachusetts Institute of Technology), 8
Mitroff, I., 623
Mobley, Erin, 685
Mobley, Foster, 685
Mohrman, S., 106, 128, 129, 319, 384, 576
Monarch Health Care, 688
Mondragon, 462
Monsanto Company, 449, 618–620
Morris, C., 52, 106
Morton Salt, 385
Motorola, 318, 358, 364, 375, 385, 387, 390, 415, 738
Mouton, J., 7, 10
MTV, 545
Mullaly, Alan, 712

N

Nadler, D., 96
Nalbandian, John, 705
Nathan, M., 623
National Academy of Public Administration, 711
National Academy of Sciences' Institute of Medicine (IOM), 687
National Civic League, 711
National Education Association, 8
National Governors Association, 697
National Health Service (NHS), 621
National Parent Teacher Association, 700
National Performance Management Advisory Commission, 704
National Performance Review, 386
National Research Council, 363
National Science Foundation (NSF), 37–39
National Training Laboratories (NTL), 7, 8, 47, 732, 734
NATO, 60
NBC, 385
NEC, 170, 541
Nestlé, 541
Neusoft Corporation, 14
Nevitt, J., 319
New United Motor Manufacturing, Inc., 616
Nike, 354, 355, 624
Nissan, 170, 541
Nokia, 98, 746
Nordstrom, 389, 558, 592
Norling, Richard, 189
Northrop Grumman, 36, 502
Northwest Airlines, 182
Novartis, 692
Nucor Steel, 375

O

Oak Hill Partners, 688
Obama, Barack, 697, 703–704
OD Network, 14
Office of Naval Research, 8
Oil, Chemical, and Atomic Workers, 12
Oldham, G., 112, 127, 215, 405–407, 413–414
O'Malley, Stan, 240
O'Neill, Paul H., 389
Oracle, 100, 500, 503, 553, 608, 616
Orrefors, 14
Ortiv Glass Corporation, 109, 110
Otis Elevator, 545
O'Toole, J., 507
Ouchi, W., 12

P

Participative Management Program, 10
PartnerRe, 477
Patchett, Ray, 685
PeopleSoft, 365
Pepperdine University, 8, 14, 59, 115–116, 490, 490
PepsiCo, 477, 490, 491–492, 499, 511, 513, 552
Perkins Coie, 511
Perry, Jennifer, 685
Philadelphia Orchestra, 102
Philip Morris, 52
Pirelli, 488
Platt, Lewis, 228
Polaroid, 182
Porras, Jerry, 40
Porter, Michael, 96, 550
Port of San Diego, 31–32
Prahalad, C., 359
Premier Health Alliance, 187
PriceWaterhouseCoopers, 476, 720
Procter & Gamble, 14, 47, 52, 96, 200, 414, 458, 477, 499, 545
Purrington, Linda, 685
PwC Health Research Institute, 688, 689

Q

Quaker Oats, 476, 504
Qualcomm, 511
Quinn, R., 127

R

Randall, Drew, 238, 250
Regence Insurance Holding Company, 149
Research Center for Group Dynamics (MIT), 7, 9
Ritz-Carlton Hotel, 182, 391–392
RMIT University, 201, 202–204
Roadway Express, 382–383
Robertson, P., 40–41
Robert Wood Johnson Pharmaceutical Research Institute, 307
Rockport, 318
Rockwell International, 36, 384
Ross and Sherwin (R&S), 278–281
Royal College of Psychiatrists (Great Britain), 512
Royal Dutch/Shell, 738
Rushton Mines, 384

S

Saab, 14, 171
Saab-Scania, 423
Samick, 102
Samsung, 390, 560
San Diego-based American Healthcare Systems, 187

San Diego County Regional Airport Authority (SDCRAA), 31–33
Sanofi-Genzyme, 608
Saudi Aramco, 582
Schein, Edgar, 86, 267, 270
Schein, V., 550
Schwab, Ted, 314
Sears, 182, 342
Selmer Instruments, 102
Semco S/A, 169
Semler, Ricardo, 169
Senge, Peter, 699
Sensor, Wayne, 314
Seymour, Audrey, 362
SGL Carbon, 390
Shafer-Payne, Angela, 31, 44
Shell Oil Company, 375, 582
Shepard, Herbert, 8
Shingo Prize, 386
Shirky, Clay, 695
Siemens, 541
Smisek, Jeff, 613–615
Smith, Adam, 714
Society of Organization Learning (MIT), 733
Sondheim, Stephen, 102
Sony, 187, 541, 558
Southwest Airlines, 375, 552
Southwest-AirTran, 608
Sparks, Paul, 685
Spoornet, 169
Sprint-Nextel, 512
Staley, James, 382
Standard Oil of New Jersey, 342
Standard & Poor's, 390
Stanford University, 59
Starbucks, 616
Starwood Hotels, 390
Steinway Musical Instruments Company, 102
Steinway & Son, 102–104
Stiglitz, Joseph, 737
Stride Rite Corporation, 503
Subway, 616
Sullivan, Roland, 330–337
Sunflower Incorporated, 232–233
The SunHealth Alliance, 187
Sun Health care Group, 691
Sun Microsystems Inc., 198, 553, 608
Survey Research Center, 9
Suzuki, 738
Syverson, Cindra, 690

T

Tannenbaum, Robert, 8, 48
Tata Corporation, 187
Tavistock Institute of Human Relations (London), 11, 414, 733
Taylor, Frederick, 404
Teekay, 477
Telefonica, 582
Telemundo Network, 512
Telkom, 169
Texaco, 498
Texas Instruments, 14, 364, 375, 405
Thomas, David, 577–579
3M, 47, 187, 346, 375, 536, 550, 560
T-Mobile, 608, 610
Tosi, W., Jr., 448
Total Renal Care (TRC), 647–648
Toto, 541
Touche, 511
Toyota, 6, 170, 187, 318, 616, 737
Transportation Security Administration, 487
Tremont Hotel (Chicago), 9
Trist, Eric, 11
TRW Space Systems, 8, 36, 306
Tushman, M., 96
Tyson, Ed, 691

U

UNICEF, 677
Unilever, 536, 545, 738, 746
Union Carbide, 8
Union of Japanese Scientists and Engineers (JUSE), 385
United Airlines, 613–615
United Auto Workers (UAW), 12, 384
United-Continental, 608
UnitedHealthcare, 689
UnitedHealth Group, 688
United Technologies, 414, 458
University Associates, 59
University Cooperative Research Center Program (IUCRCP), 37
University of California, Los Angeles (UCLA), 8, 36, 37, 47, 59, 314
University of Michigan, 59, 127, 384, 509
University of Southern California (USC), 36, 47, 59, 80, 127, 377, 490
U.S. Army, 582
U.S. Commerce Department, 390
U.S. Department of Labor, 459, 482
US Airways, 613

V

Vaycot Product, 287–291
Verizon, 41, 375
Vitro, 14
Volvo, 171, 423, 428

W

Wachovia, 608
Walmart, 96
Walton, R., 276
Ward, J., 716, 717
Watson, J., 22
Wegmans, 490
Weil, R., 306
Weisbord, M., 96, 127
Welch, Jack, 300
Wells Fargo Bank, 375, 512, 582, 608
Westley, B., 22
West Paces Ferry Hospital, 388
West Penn Allegheny Health System, 688
Weyerhaeuser, 52, 385, 504, 511
Whitbread PLC, 576, 577–579
Whitehead, Jack, 701
Whole Foods, 187, 490
Whyte, William, 8
William Hill, 740
Winby, Stu, 314
Wine.com, 358
Women's and Children's (W&C), 314, 316
World Health Organization, 677
World Trade Organization, 677
World Vision, 318
World Wildlife Fund (WWF), 743
Worley, C., 2, 47, 319, 593, 597–598, 744
Wurlitzer, 102

X

Xerox, 36, 346, 385, 390, 511

Y

Yahoo, 608
Yamaha, 101, 102, 103, 104
Yellow Transit Co., 382
Young, John, 227, 228
Young Chang, 102

Subject Index

A

Absenteeism
  effect of skill-based pay on, 458
  positive effect of EAPs on, 513
Accountability, 433
Accountable Care Organization (ACO), 687
Achievement needs, 285, 413, 448
Achievement orientation, in global OD, 166
Acquisition, 162, 607–615. *See also* Mergers and acquisitions (M&As)
Action learning, 26, 480
Action map, in organization learning, 589
Action planning, 90, 157, 292, 572–573
  for coaching, 475
  for Vélo V project, 262–263
Action research, 8–9, 25–26, 681
  model, 24–26, 27
  process, used by groups in parallel structures, 379–381
  trends in application of, 25
Action research model, 24–26, 27
Action science, 26
Active listening, 183
Adaptive learning, 588. *See also* Single-loop learning
After-implementation evaluation, 208
Age
  average, of U.S. workforce, 484–486
  in workforce diversity, 484–486
Agency, 624, 706, 707, 709
Agency cost, 714
Aggressiveness, as sustainable effectiveness strategy, 661
Agile organization designs, 664–667
  building, 670
  features of, 664–667
    human resource systems, 666–667
    management processes, 665–666
    structures, 665
    work systems, 664–665
Alignment
  individual-level diagnosis, 114
  in organization system, 94
Alliance interventions, 606
  cross-cultural, 620
  strategic, 616–620
Alliances, 162
  defined, 616
  operation and adjustment, 617
  partner selection, 616–617
  strategy formulation for, 616
  structuring and start-up, 617
Alpha change, 218
Alternative dispute resolution (ADR), 274–275
American Recovery and Reinvestment Act (ARRA), 627–628, 687, 697
Americans with Disabilities Act (ADA), 498, 499, 708
Analysis
  of applying individual-level diagnosis to job design, 91, 95, 114
  content, 133–134
  force-field, 134–135
  group-level diagnosis, 109–112
  organization-level, Steinway & Sons, 103–104
Applications
  adapting the appraisal process at capital one financial, 453–455
  Alaska Health Workforce Coalition (AHWC), 627–631
  aligning strategy and diversity at L'oréal, 505–506
  aligning senior team at Vaycot Products, 287–291
  Amazon.com's network structure, 357–358
  American Healthways' process structure, 350–351
  in an underorganized system, 36–39
  approaching employee orientation as a cultural experience, 302–303
  building alliance relationships, 618–620
  changing the human capital management practices at cambia health solutions, 446–448
  conflict management at Ross and Sherwin (R&S), 278–281
  contracting at American Healthways Corporation, 350–351
  creating a built-to-change organization at Capital One Financial, 599–601
  creating a vision at Premier, 189–191
  culture of work in Western China, 542–544
  developing self-managed teams at WI, inc., 421–422
  dialogue and organization learning at DMT, 594–596
  dynamic strategy making at Whitbread PLC, 577–579
  employee involvement, 376–377, 379–381, 384, 392–393, 398, 403
  enriching jobs at the Hartford's employee relations consulting services group, 410–412
  ethics of OD, 62–66
  Honeywell IAC's TotalPlant reengineering process, 369–371
  implementing the global strategy, 542–544
  institutionalizing structural change at Hewlett-Packard, 227–228
  Interface Carpets transformation to sustainability, 671–672
  job design at Pepperdine University, 115–116
  in Johnson & Johnson's drug evaluation department, 307–308
  Johnson & Johnson's health and wellness program, 514–515
  leading your business at Microsoft Corporation, 479–480
  managing strategic change at Microsoft Canada, 553–554
  Pepsico's career planning and development framework, 491–493
  personal views of the internal and external consulting positions, 55–56
  and planned change at Cambia health solutions, 149–152
  planned change at the San Diego County Regional Airport Authority (SDCRAA), 31–33
  planning United and Continental merger, 613–615
  process consultation at Christian Caring Homes, Inc., 271–273
  revising the reward system at Lands' End, 465–466
  self-design at Healthways Corporation, 583–584
  social and environmental change at LDI Africa, 678–680
  Steinway's strategic orientation, 102–104
  top-management team at Ortiv Glass Corporation, 110
  training OD practitioners in data feedback, 146–147
  a work-out meeting at General Electric Medical Systems (GEMS), 300–301
Appraisal, performance. *See* Performance appraisal
Appreciative inquiry (AI), 26
"Arab Spring," 736
Arthik siksha, 257
Artifacts, of organization culture, 556
The Art of Japanese Management (Pascale and Athos), 552
Assessment, 475. *See also* Evaluation, OD intervention
  in coaching, 474–476
  performing needs, 481
Assessment centers, 487
Authenticity, 700
Autonomy
  employee, 406–407
  increase of, in vertical loading, 409
  team, 416–417
  of team members, maintaining sufficient, 418

B

Balanced scorecard, 442
Basic assumptions, of organization culture, 558

Basic design alternatives, 535–537
Behaviorally anchored rating scale (BARS), 450
Behavioral sciences, 2, 4, 734
  coaching, using principles of applied, 475
  consultation with experts from field of, 24
Behaviors
  changes in, required by OD interventions, 208
  goal setting, to jointly define member work, 442
  network, 624
  strategically driven work, 441
  team, 201
Benchmarks, 389, 419, 442
Benevolent authoritative systems, 10
Beta change, 218
Big, Hairy, Audacious Goals (BHAG), 187, 572, 583
"Big 5" instrument, 475
Biofeedback, 512
Bonus plans, 460. *See also* Gain sharing
  individual, 460
Boundary control, 416
Boundary management, 415, 420, 724
Bowling Green State University, 14
Brainstorming, 626
Breadth, as sustainable effectiveness strategy, 661
Bridging organizations, 670
Bridging role, of GSCO change agents, 680, 681
Brokers, 355
Budget Control Act of 2011 (BCA), 688
Built-to-change organizations, 593–601
  application stages, 597–601
    orchestration capability, building, 598–601
    redefining organization design components for flexibility, 597–598
    reframing culture as a facilitator of change, 597
  creating at Capital One Financial, 599–601
  design guidelines, 593–597
    for B2C organizations, 596
    from design to designing, 596
    from strategy to strategizing, 596
  design guidelines for B2C organizations, 596
  dialogue and organization learning at DMT, 594–596
  human resource practices, 598
Built to Last (Collins and Porras), 552
Burke, Warner, 2
Burnout, 45, 60
  steps to cope with, 60
  use of sabbaticals to avoid, 511
Business-to-business market, organizational issues in, 739–740
Business Week, 554

C

California Senate Bill AB93, 32
Capital budgeting, 611
Career development, 480. *See also* Career planning and development
  appropriate set of processes, 484–486
  interventions, 484
Career planning, 174, 476
  application stages, 482–493
    appropriate set of career development processes, 484–490
    mechanism, 482–484
  and development, 161
  and development interventions, 480
  goals, 481–482
  individual and human resources, 485 (figure 16.1)
  PepsiCo's framework, 491–492
  results, 477
Career planning and development, 480–493
  individual employee development intervention, 484
  performance feedback and coaching interventions, 489
  role and structure interventions, 488
  work-life balance interventions, 490
Career stages, 481–482
  and career planning issues, 483 (figure 16.1)
Career systems, in HIOs, 393
Carey Award, 386
Carnegie Foundation, 8
Case studies. *See also* Integrative case studies
  City of Carlsbad, California, restructuring the Public Works Department, 433–434
  diagnosis and feedback at Adhikar, 257–161
  Disk Drives, inc., 523–527
  employee benefits at HealthCo, 519–522
    background, 520
    recent events, 520–522
    three scenarios, 519–520
  managing change in the manufacturing and distribution division of PolyProd, 262–263
  preliminary diagnosis, in conjunction with OD practitioner, 24
  Sullivan Hospital System, 435–437
Cause-and-effect diagrams, 388
Chaeobols, 354, 620
Change. *See also* Resistance, to change
  consultant-dominated, 25–26
  contingencies related to target of, 164–171
  creating readiness for, 181–183
  culture, 161
  guides for facilitating network, 625–626
  implementing and evaluating, in family businesses, 724–725
  managing network, 624–626
  methods for generating sufficient dissatisfaction to produce, 181–184
  motivating, 181–184
  organization development (OD) and, 158
  practical advice for managing (figure 8.1), 180
  programmability and, 223
  situation, contingencies related to, 164–171
  target, level of, 223–224
Change, leading and managing
  developing political support for strategic planning project in sexual violence prevention unit, 195
  managing transition learning processes, 196–197
Change agents
  activities of, 200, 201
  attention to power and political activity by, 192
  building support system for, 180, 200
  employee involvement and, 200
  identification of powerful individuals and groups with interest in changes, by, 192–193
  OD practitioners and, 625–626
  sexual violence prevention unit of Minnesota's health department, 185–186
  specification of criteria for network membership by, 621
  trade-offs involving, 219
  use of power strategy by, 193–197
Change management, 3, 46, 179–201
  activities contributing to effective (figure 8.1), 180
  distinguishing between organization development and, 4
  need for competence in, 163
  overview of, 179–181
Change process, 81, 83
  time element of, 197
China
  China Association for NGOs (CANGO), 743
  environmental controls and, 738
  income inequality in, 737
China Association for NGOs (CANGO), 743
Choice, free and informed choice, 163
Clean Water Act, 709
Client
  determining relevant, 77
  relationships, in job enrichment, 407, 409
Closed system, 93
Coaching, 160, 174, 474–476
  application stages, 475
  goals, 474–475
  individual, interpersonal, and group process approaches, 265–293
  interventions, performance feedback and, 489
  organization process approaches, 297–319
  results of, 476
  training and development, 146
Codification, in organizing knowledge, 592
Collaborative strategies, 616, 740, 742
Collateral structures, 379
Collecting and analyzing diagnostic and feeding back information, 123–154. *See also* Data gathering
  data analysis techniques, 133–142
    qualitative tools, 133–135
    quantitative tools, 135–142
  diagnostic relationship/contract, 123–126
  methods for, 126–132
    interviews, 129–130
    observations, 130–131
    questionnaires, 127–129
    sampling, 132–133
    unobtrusive measures, 131–132
Commission on the Future of Worker-Management Relations, 384
Commitment
  internal, 163
  to intervention, 224–225
Communication, 361
  about reward systems, importance of, 455–453
  building good, in family businesses, 723
  changing nature of, 695
  in different types of organizations, 35
  effective, about changes, 174
  process consultation and, 157–158, 267–268
  and resistance to change, 183
  structure activities, 381

Communities of practice, 592
Comparison unit, 217
Compatibility, in work design, 420
Compensation specialists, 440, 466
Competing values approach, 557–558
  to diagnosing organization culture, 534–535
Competition
  strategies for, 610–611
  stress related to increased global, 504, 530
Competitive advantage
  ability to manage change as key source of, 743
  diversity as source of, 497–498
  sustainability as a source of, 746
Competitive logic, 572
Competitive strategies, 561–562, 572, 586
  integrated strategic change, 548–552
  mergers and acquisitions, 162, 610–611
Confidentiality, 71
  issues of, 82
  OD practitioners and, 125
Conflict management, 278–281
Conflict resolution, 169
  process, facilitating, 276–277
Conflict resolution cyclical model of interpersonal (figure 10.2), 275
Conflict(s). *See also* Conflict resolution
  episodic model of, 275–276
  informal procedures for resolving intergroup, 306–309
  management at Ross and Sherwin (R&S), 278–281
  mediation, 690
  ongoing, in OD field, 734
  relationship between change orders and (table 6.5), 140
  and rivalry in family businesses, 719–720
  social, 737
  value and goal, 64
Congress, 384, 386, 686
  establishment of Malcolm Baldrige National Quality Award by, 386
Congruence, 222–223
Connectedness (OD practitioners), 625
Connectors, in networks, 625, 626
Consultants, 26, 52–54, 82. *See also* Third-party interventions
  differences between external and internal (table 3.2), 53
  quick solutions and, 41
  resolution of dependency issues by, 64
  team-building meeting, 286
  third-party, 274–275
Consultative roles, in career development, 488–489
Consultative systems, 10
Content analysis, 133–134
Content interventions, 270
Content validity, 215, 216
Context orientation, in global OD, 165–166
Continuous change, 569–604
  built-to-change organizations, 593–601
    application stages, 597–601
    design guidelines, 593–597
  dynamic strategy making, 570–576
    application stages, 573–576
    conceptual framework, 571–573
  dynamic strategy making at Whitbread PLC, 577–579
  ladder of inference, 590, 591
  learning organizations, 582–593
    conceptual framework, 584–586
    Healthways Corporation (HMC), 583–584
    knowledge management interventions, 585, 586
    organization learning interventions, 586–593
    outcomes of OL and KM, 586
  organization learning affects organization performance, 586
  self-design at Healthways Corporation, 583–584
  self-design change process, 580
  self-designing organizations, 576–582
    application stages, 579–582
    self-design change process, 580
    turbulent environments, demands of, 576–579
Continuous quality improvement (CQI), 65
Contract, 79, 238–239
Control charts, 388
Control system. *See also* Diagnosing organizations
  as job enrichment constraint, 412
  of work system, 419
Convention stage in network development, 622–623
Convergent validity, 216
Coordinating mechanisms, in networks, 355
Core job dimensions, 405–407
Core purpose, 186–187
  example of, 190
Core values, 186–187
  example of, 190
Corporate Culture and Performance (Kotter and Heskett), 552
Cost/benefit trade-off, of alliances, 428
Cost-minimization strategy, 535
Cost-of-living adjustments (COLA), 458
Cross-cultural issues, 281
Cultural context, organization development, 167–171
  achievement orientation, 166
  context orientation, 165–166
  individualism, 166
  power distance, 166
  uncertainty avoidance, 166
Cultural diversity, 734, 736–737, 742, 746
Cultural resistance, 183
Cultural values and organization customs, 165
Culture change, 161, 187, 552
  application stages, 597
  competing values approach, 557
  deep assumptions approach, 557–558
  defining and diagnosing, 552, 555–558
  guidelines for, 559–560
  at IBM, 561–562
  national, 164
  organization culture and organization effectiveness
    four major elements, 556–558
Culture components, 555
Culture(s)
  approaching employee orientation as a cultural experience, 746
  change, 187. *See also* Culture change
  corporate, 608
  creating effective, in health care industry, 691–692
  ethnocentric, 746
  features of M&As, 610, 612
  globalization and, 737
  interaction between different, due to globalization, 281
  lack of success in establishing common, 189–191
  melding corporate, 199
  organization, 49, 99
    inferred, 105
    integration activities for M&As, 612
  supporting aligned, 691–692
  technical and managerial innovation and, 745
  value and organization customs, 165
  and values, in workforce diversity intervention, 497–498
Customer satisfaction, 347
Customer tiebreakers, 572

D

Data
  misuse of, 63
  unobtrusive, 131–132
Data gathering. *See also* Collecting and analyzing diagnostic and feeding back information
  after action, 24
  in conjunction with OD practitioner, 24
  and feedback cycle (figure 6.1), 124
  methods, 123
  preliminary, 76
Decision accelerators, 319
Decision making
  authority, of self-managed work teams, 415
  group, 277
  improving, 285
  including peers and subordinates in process of, 464
  in public-sector organizations, 704, 707–708
Deep assumptions approach, to diagnosing organization culture, 557–558
Defensive behavior, 144
Deming Prize, 385
Dependency, 63, 64, 86
  survey feedback and organizational, 148
Deutero-learning, 588
Developmental training, 489
Development organizations (DOs), 670. *See also* Global social change organizations (GSCOs)
Diagnosing organizations, 89–96. *See also* Diagnosis
  of current organization structure, 90
  need for diagnostic models, 91–92
  open-systems model, 92–96
  organization-level diagnosis, 96–98
Diagnosis, 48, 50. *See also* Diagnosing organizations
  components of, 94
  of family-run organizations, 722
  group-level, 109–112
    analysis (Ortiv Glass Corporation), 109–112
  groups and jobs, 109–112
  individual-level, 112–114

Diagnosis *(continued)*
joint, 24–25
linking interventions to, 208
in OD, 90–91
organization, 123
of organizational systems, 94–96
organization-level, 96–101
alignment, 100
analysis, 101–106
design components, 98–99
inputs, 93
in planned change, 29
preliminary, in conjunction with OD practitioner, 24
of state of alliance, 617
of team's design components (Ortiv Glass Corporation), 110
Dialogue approach, in organization learning, 589
Difference tests, 140–142
Differentiation, 98, 104
as sustainable effectiveness strategy, 661
Diffusion, 225
Disabilities, as workplace diversity factor, 502
DISC profile, 475
Discriminant validity, 216
Disintermediation, 355
Disk Drives, inc., 523–527
Diversity, 497–504
general framework for managing (figure 17.1), 498
increased, in health care industry, 695
as source of competitive advantage, 497–498
Divisional structure, 342–344
advantages and disadvantages of, 342–344
table, 12.2, 343
Domestic-partner benefit plans, 502
Double-loop learning, 588. *See also* Generative learning
Downsizing, 159, 174, 339, 356–359, 704
application stages, 359–361
coaching, used in, 474
increase of EAP use during, 512
in Menlo Park, 362–363
results of, 363–364
stress related to, 490
tactics (table 12.8), 360
Dual career employees, 490
Due diligence
assessment, performing, 610
processes, inadequate, 608
During-implementation assessment, 208
Dynamic capabilities, 569
of agile organization designs, 664

E

EAP. *See* Employee assistance programs (EAP)
Ecological sustainability, 736, 745–746
E-commerce, 5, 739–740
Economic development
as contingency affecting OD success, 166–167
organization development
industrial economies, 167
industrializing economies, 167
subsistence economies, 167
Economy
cost of stress-related disorders to U.S., 504
globalization of, 735–737
ED Recovery Act, 697
Elementary and Secondary Education Act of 1965 (ESEA), 697
Emergence, of global economy, 736
Emotional intelligence, 57, 87
Empathy, 183
Employee assistance programs (EAP), 161, 466, 504, 512
Employee involvement (EI), 12, 16, 171, 277, 375–398
applications, 380–381
and change agents, 200. *See also* Change agents
current definition, 376
effects on productivity of, 377–379
figure, 13.1, 378
generation of ideas for, 381
high-involvement organizations, 159, 393–395
key elements that promote, 376
parallel structures, 159, 380–384
practices, diffusion of, 377
secondary (figure 13.2), 379
total quality management (TQM), 159, 375, 385–390
using AI summit to build union-management relations at roadway express, 382–383
working definition of, 376
Employee stock ownership plans (ESOPs), 721
Employee stress and wellness intervention, 504–513
applications stages, 507–512
alleviating and coping with stress to improve wellness, 510–512
diagnosing stress and becoming aware of its causes, 507–510
DDI, 523–527
employee benefits at HealthCo, 519–522
goals, 504, 506–507
Johnson & Johnson's health and wellness program, 514–515
results of stress management and wellness interventions, 513
Employee stress and wellness interventions, 161
Enacted environment, 97
Endangered Species Act, 708, 709
Engineering approach, to work design, 404, 425
Entering and contracting, 75–87
clarifying the organizational issue, 76–77
contracting with Alegent health, 83–87
description and scope, 75
determining the relevant client, 77
issues involved in family businesses, 722
in planned change, 28–29
selecting an OD practitioner, 78–79
Enterprise resource planning technologies, 740
Environmental concerns
dilemmas involving, 62
effect on OD of, 61, 62
misuse of data, 63
Environmental expectations, 312
Environment(s), 102–103
design of interface between STS and its, 415
dimensions of, 97–98
information uncertainty, 97
external, for piano market, 101
framework of, 534–535
misfits among organization's, 551
relation of, to transformational change, 530–531
relation of structural design to organization, 339–356
responses to, 507
stability of organization, 238
task, of self-managed work teams, 415–419
types of, 96–97
Envisioned future, 187–188
bold and valued outcomes, 187–188
desired future state, 188
Equal employment opportunity council (EEOC), 501
Ethics, 61
coercion, 63–64
guidelines for organization development/human systems development (OD/HSD) professionals, 8
misrepresentation, 6
of organizational development, 61–66
technical ineptness, 64
value and goal conflict, 64
Evaluation. *See also* Evaluation feedback
key aspects of effective, 189–193, 207–210
measurement, 211–216, 217, 218
OD intervention, 207–221, 229
designing good measures, 212–216, 221, 229
implementation and evaluation feedback, 207–210
research design, 216–221
processes, 207
Evaluation feedback, 208–210
implementation and (figure 9.1), 209
selecting variables, 211–212
Evaluation stage in network development, 623
Expectancy model, 457–458
Expectations
mutual, of client and OD practitioner, 81
role of, in generating motivation, 182–183
Exploitive authoritative systems, 10
External consultants, 52–56, 59, 66, 224
differences between external and (table 3.2), 55–56
differences between internal and (table 3.2), 53
personal view of, 55–56
External validity, 216. *See also* Internal validity

F

Face validity, 215
Fallback positions, 488
Family business system
business, ownership, and family systems, 714–715
critical issues in, 719–725
conflicts and rivalry in, 719–720
entering and contracting, 722
entering or leaving the business as a family member, 719
family-run organization, diagnosing, 722
family wealth and growth of, 721
feedback and planning, 723–724

implementing and evaluating change, 724–725
new leader, selecting, 720–721
OD interventions in, 721–722, 725
ownership transfer and estate planning, 720
developmental stages, 715–716
key questions for understanding, 722
OD interventions in, 721–722, 725
most common (table 22.3), 723–724
organization development in, 711–725
parallel planning process, 716
typical family business intervention areas, 724
values at center of, 716–719
family *versus* business system values, 718
Family Medical Leave Act (FMLA), 511
employee benefits at HealthCo, 519–522
Feedback
about progress of OD relationship, 76
channels, in job enrichment, 405, 406
characteristics of effective, 142–143
data
in network creation, 623
ownership of, 144
training OD practitioners in, 164
of diagnostic information, 145–154. *See also* Survey feedback
implementation and evaluation, 208–210
performance, and coaching interventions, 493
possible effects of (figure 6.5), 148
process
characteristics of, 144–145
in organizations, 94
in performance appraisal, 439
providing, to family business members, 723
step, in change process, 27–28
success of data, 142
survey, 407
The Fifth Discipline (Senge), 699
FIRO-B profile, 475
Focus groups, 434
Force-field analysis, 134–135
Formal (leader, organization, system), 193, 380, 403, 680
"Four Principles," in open-space method, 313
Free choice, and informed choice, 163
Frequency distributions, 135–138
Functional structure, 159, 340–342
advantages and disadvantages of, 340–342
figure 12.2, table 12.1, 341
Futuring, 317

G

Gain sharing, 396, 459, 463
bonus formula, 462
change management, 463
frequency of bonus, 463
importance of design process for, 462
participative system, 463
sharing process, 462–463
unit coverage, 463
Gamma change, 218, 533
Gay, lesbian, bisexual, and transgender (GLBT), 501
Gender
inequity, 500–501
in workforce diversity, 501–502
General consultation skills, needed in OD, 51–52
General environment, 96
Generative learning, 588. *See also* Double-loop learning
Genogram, 722
Global design, 541
Global integration, 537
Globalization, 5, 13, 530. *See also* Global social change organizations (GSCOs); Organization development, outside the United States
of the economy,735–737
stress related to competition caused by, 490
of work and organizations, 281
Global recession, 4
Global Reporting Initiative (GRI), 668
Global social change, 670
application stages, 674–677
change agent roles and skills, 677, 680–681
Global social change organizations (GSCOs), 670–681, 742
application stages of, 674–677
building the local organization, 674–676
effects of success on, 675–676
horizontal linkages, creating, 676–677
vertical linkages, creating, 677
change agent roles and skills, 677, 680–681
characteristics, 672–673
conflicts in, 675
dimensions of, 673–674
increased opportunities for OD in, 742
problem of success, 675–676
social and environmental change at LDI Africa, 678–680
Global Trends, 2015 (CIA's report), 737
Goal setting, 160, 174, 403, 442–448
application stages, 443–444
balanced scorecard approach to, 442
characteristics, 442–443
clarifying goal measurement, 443
establishing challenging goals, 442–443
increased participation in, 450
joint manager-subordinate, 445
management by objectives (MBO), 444–445
and MBO, effects of, 445, 448
principles contributing to success of, 468
processes, performance appraisal as link between reward systems and, 452
Government organizations, 742
Government Performance and Results Act, 703
Government Performance and Results Modernization Act of 2010, 703
Great Recession, 704
GRI. *See* Global Reporting Initiative
Grid Organization Development, 10
Group design, 111
components, diagnosis of, 109–111
and individual-level diagnosis, 112–114
Group interventions, 270
diagnostic issues in, 266–267
Group-level diagnosis, 109–112
analysis, 114, 116–119
design components, 113
inputs, 112–113
Group(s). *See also* Team building; Teams
communication, 266
composition, 111
effectiveness, dimensions of, 104
functional roles in, 266
functioning, 111
goals, 109
interventions, 270
interviews, 129
leadership and authority, use of, 267
-level diagnosis, 112–114
design components, 109–111
norms, 111–112, 267
problem solving and decision making, process consultation and, 267–274
process consultation and, 157–158
task structure, 109
Group's performance norms, diagnosis of, 111
Groupthink, 312
Growth needs, 426–427
Grupos, 354, 620

H

Hammer Award, 386, 711
Health care industry
aging workforce and changing demographics of patients, 689–690
aligned cultures, supporting, 691–692
comprehensive learning programs, delivering, 692
engaged employees, creating, 692–693
environmental trends in, 691
health care reform, changing incentives, and reimbursement models, responding to, 687
informatics and e-health, rise of, 689
integration across different segments of health care, 688–689
opportunities for OD practice, 690–693
organization development in, 686–693
quality and cost as strategic and regulatory imperatives, 687–688
shifting organizational systems to a new paradigm, 691
a snapshot of, 686–687
strategic, emotionally intelligent leaders and teams, developing, 690–691
traditional industry segment lines, blurring of, 688–689
trends in, 687–690
Health care reform, 687
Health facilities, employee, 511–512
Health Insurance Portability and Privacy Act (HIPAA), 512
Health profiling, 510
Heroism, 187
Hidden agenda, 86
High-involvement organizations (HIOs), 159, 392–398
at Air Products and Chemicals, Inc., 396–398
application factors, 395
features of, 393–395
improving selection of employees for, 393
prevalence of teams in, 398
study results of, 395
HIV, 501
Horizontal issues, in MBO process, 444–445
Horizontal linkages, GSCOS and, 676–677
Human Development Index, 167
Humanism, 60

Human processes, improving, 157–158, 267. *See also* Process consultation (PC)
process consultation, 158
team building, 158
Human process interventions, 29, 171, 668. *See also* Intervention
third-party intervention: Lincoln Hospital, 322–328
Human resource practices, 535
Human resources department, 440
Human resources management
employee stress and wellness, 161
interventions, 160–161, 171, 439–440, 473. *See also* Goal setting; Intervention; Performance appraisal; Reward systems; Reward systems
managing workforce diversity, 161
performance appraisal, 160
reward systems, 160
Human resource systems, 98, 412
as features of agile organization, 666–667
Hurricane Katrina, 676
Hygiene factors, 405

I

Identification stage in network development, 621–622
"If Japan Can ... Why Can't We?", 385
Immigrants, entering workforce, 497. *See also* Workforce diversity interventions
Implementation, initial, 84
Implementation feedback, 208. *See also* Evaluation feedback
data for, 208
evaluation and (figure 9.1), 209
outcome measures of, 209
selecting variables, 229
Improshare, 463
Incentives, in health care industry, 687
Income distribution, 736
Individual, interpersonal, and group process approaches, 265–293
coaching, 160, 474
diagnostic issues in, 266–267
process consultation, 267–274
team building, 265, 277–286
third-party interventions, 274–277
Individual assessment, 478
Individual interventions, 268–270
Individual interviews, 276
Individualism, in global OD, 166
Individual-level diagnosis, 112–114
alignment, 114
analysis, 114
design components, 113
inputs, 112–113
Industrial economies, 167
Industrializing economies, 167
Industrial Revolution, 364
Industry discontinuities, 531
Industry structure, 96
Informatics and e-health, rise of, 689
Information
flows, environments as, 97
and promotion of EI, 376
uncertainty, 97
Information technology, 5, 13, 159–160, 339
effects on future OD practice, 739, 743
use of, for reengineering, 159, 364–365
and use of codification approaches for KM, 592
Informed choice, and free choice, 163
Innovation, 741
achieving awareness of, in networks, 625
employee, 46
managerial, 5–6, 743–745
need for, in transformational change, 530
strategy, 535
technological,743–745
Inputs, 93
individual-level diagnosis, 112–113
into strategic orientation, 96–98
In Search of Excellence (Peters and Waterman), 552
Instability, creation in network, 624–625
Institutionalization, of OD interventions, 208–225
defined, 208
framework, 222
(figure 11.2), 222
indicators of institutionalization, 226–229
institutionalization processes, 224–225
intervention characteristics, 223–224
organization characteristics, 222–223
indicators to assess level of, 226
Insurance, private, 686
Integrated strategic change (ISC), 161, 548–552, 570
application stages, 546–548
key features, 549
managing strategic change at Microsoft Canada, 553–554
performing strategic analysis, 549, 550–551
Integration, 99. *See also* Differentiation
Integrative case studies. *See also* Case studies
managing strategy at Vaycot Products, 287–291
overview of competitive environment, 284
Intergovernmental Panel on Climate Change, 738
Intergroup relations, 174
combining survey feedback with, 145
purpose of, 158
Intergroup relations interventions, 158, 174, 301–309, 591
at Johnson & Johnson, 307–308
microcosm groups, 301–304
purpose of, 309
resolving intergroup conflict application stages, 310–312
results of, 312
Intermarket network, 354
Internal commitment, 163
Internal company dynamics, 531
Internal consultants, 52–56, 388
clarification of sensitivity issues for, 81
differences between external and (table 3.2), 53
personal view of, 55–56
Internal market network, 354
Internal validity, 216. *See also* External validity
International design, 539–540
International private voluntary organizations, 670
Internet, 5, 355
as backbone of global economy, 739
influence on OD of,739–740
Interpersonal skills, needed in OD, 51
Intervention design. *See also* Intervention
consideration of contingencies related to change situation for, 164–171
cultural context and, 165–166
designing effective, 163–164
and effect on rate of success of contingencies related to target of change, 171
organizational issues of, 171
Interventions. *See also* Human process interventions; Human resources management, interventions; Intervention design; Strategic interventions; Technostructural interventions
alliance, 606
attitudinal change, 306
behavioral, 306
career planning and development, 161, 480–481
coercion and, 63–64
criteria defining effective, 162–163
defined, 173
designing effective, 164–171
contingencies related to change situation, 180
and employee assistance programs (EAPs), 161
employee stress and wellness, 161, 504–513
in family business system, 721–722, 725
features of, that can affect institutionalization processes, 224–225
human process, 29, 171
impact of accurate, 439
individual, 268–270
employee development, 450
institutionalizing, 208–210
intergroup relations, 158, 301–309
key targets of OD, 171
large-group
combining survey feedback with, 141–142
linking, to diagnosis, 208
major types of, 29
management and leadership development, 161
network, 620–631
and organizational levels (table 7.2), 174
and organization culture, 161
and organization design, 161
overview of, 157–162
and parallel structures, 159
performance feedback and coaching, 467
recent proliferation of OD, 58
selecting, 64
shaping competitive and collaborative strategies of organizations, 162
skills needed by OD practitioners for design and execution of, 50
specificity of goals in, 223
sponsors of, 224
strategic change, 161–162
sustainable management, 659–681
design guidelines of, 660–667
implications of, 660
third-party, 158. *See also* Third-party interventions
training and development, 146
types of, 29
and organizational issues (figure 7.2), 172
workforce diversity, 497–504
Interviews, 129–130, 286

Intranets, 744–745
Intrapersonal skills, needed in OD, 48, 51
Involvement, in planning changes, 184

J

Japan, 385
Jargon, 127
JDS. *See* Job Diagnostic Survey (JDS)
Job design
  applying individual-level diagnosis to, 112, 114
  in HIOs, 159, 393
  at Pepperdine University, 115–116
Job Diagnostic Survey (JDS), 127, 215, 407
  modification of, 413
  profile for "good" and "bad" jobs (figure 16.2), 408
Job enlargement, 406
Job enrichment, 160, 403, 405, 406, 409, 412–414
  application stages, 405–407
    combining tasks, 408
    establishing client relationships, 408–409
    forming natural work units, 408
    making thorough diagnosis, 407
    opening feedback channels, 409
    vertical loading, 409
  barriers to
    control system, 412
    human resource system, 412
    personnel system, 412
    supervisory system, 413
    technical system, 412
  core dimensions of jobs
    autonomy, 406–407
    feedback from work itself, 407
    human resource system, 405–407
    skill variety, task identity, and task significance, 406–407
  experiments, 405
  individual differences affecting reactions to, 407
  results of, 413–414
Job pathing, 487
Job rotation, 405
  and challenging assignments, 486, 487–488
Jobs
  autonomy, 113
  diagnosing groups and, 106–119
  feedback, 115
  key dimensions of individual, 113
  skill variety, 113
  task significance, 113
Job sharing, 500
Johari Window, 268–270
  diagram (figure 10.1), 269
Joint ventures, 616
Just-in-time inventory systems, 281

K

Keiretsu, 354, 620
Knowledge. *See also* Knowledge and experience; Knowledge management (KM)
  acquiring, 581
  distributing, 593
  generating, 592
  organization, 586, 592–593
  of organization members regarding behaviors connected to intervention, 224
  organizing, 592
  and skills, contributing to EI success, 376
  tacit, 592
Knowledge and experience
  use of, by OD practitioners, 59–60
  use of consultant's *versus* client's (figure 3.1), 58
Knowledge management (KM), 161, 584–586
  conceptual framework, 584–586
  knowledge services and networks, 593
  organization knowledge
    facilitated transfer of, 593
    as link to performance, 586, 592
  outcomes of, 586
Knowledge management interventions, 585, 586
  outcomes of OL and KM, 586
Knowledge objects, 592
Kyoto Protocol, 672

L

Ladder of inference, in organization learning, 590, 591
Large-group interventions, 141–142, 145, 158, 174, 309–310
  at Airbus ICT Organization, 329–337
  application stages conducting the meeting, 310–312
  following up on meeting outcomes, 318
  open-space methods in, 313, 317
  open-systems methods in, 313–317
  preparing for the large-group meeting, 310–311
  results of, 318–319
Large-group interventions (LGI), 669, 670
"Law of Two Feet," in open-space method, 313
Leader(s)
  developing strategic, emotionally intelligent, 690–691
  forward-thinking family business, 721
  growing locally, 701
  selecting new, 720–721
Leadership, 598, 601, 607, 608, 622, 688, 691–692, 695, 699, 701, 703
  growing locally, 701
  political, 703
Leadership development, 161, 476–478
Leadership development programs, 478, 480, 481
Leading and managing change
  motivating change
    at Johnsonville Sausage, 416
Learning organizations, 582–593, 699
  human resources practices, 587
  management processes, 587
  Model II learning, 587
  Model I learning, 586
  structure, 587
  work design, 587
Learnings, 83
Left-hand, right-hand column technique, in organization learning, 590
Legal combination phase (M&A), 611
Lewin's change model, 22–23, 28
Life stages, 481–482
Likert Scale, 9
Local representatives, 537
Longitudinal measurement, 217

M

Malcolm Baldrige National Quality Award, 386, 391–392, 711
Management and leadership development interventions, 161, 476–480
  application stages, 477–478
  goals, 477
  results, 480
Management by objectives (MBO), 444–445. *See also* Goal setting
  description and purpose, 449–450
  effects of goal setting and, 445, 480
  establishing action plans for goals, 445
  establishing criteria of success, 445
  joint manager-subordinate goal setting, 445
  origin, 444
  review process, 445
  work group involvement, 445
Management consulting, 46
Management development, 477
Management processes
  as features of agile organization, 665–666
  transformational change and, 535
Managerial Grid, 10
Managerial innovation, 5–6
Managing change, 169–201
  conveying credible positive expectations, 182–183
  creating a vision, 184–188, 189–191
    constructing envisioned future, 187–188
  creating readiness for change, 181–183
  describing core ideology, 186–187
  developing political support, 180, 188–193, 194–195, 201
    assessing change agent power, 192
  empathy and support, 183
  identifying key stakeholders, 192–193
  influencing stakeholders, 192–193
  managing the transition, 180, 193–197
    activity planning, 196
    change-management structures, 196
    commitment planning, 196
  motivating change, 181–184, 185–186
    communication, 183, 194
    empathy and support, 183
    overcoming resistance, 183–184
    participation and involvement, 184
  overview of change activities, 179–201
  revealing discrepancies between current and desired states, 182
  sustaining momentum, 180, 197–200
    building support system for change agents, 200
    developing new competencies and skills, 200–201
    providing resources for change, 200
    reinforcing new behaviors, 201
    staying the course, 201
Managing workforce diversity, 161
Marginality, and professional OD role, 54–57
Market position, of organization, 572
Matrix organization, 344–346
Matrix structure, 344–346
  advantages and disadvantages of, 345–346
  chart (figure 12.4), 344
  table 12.3, 345

Mavens, in networks, 625–626
Means, 135–138
Measurement, for OD evaluation, 211–216
  criterion, 211
  definitions and recording categories (table 9.3), 213
  designing good measures, 212–216
    operational definition, 212
    reliability, 212–215
    validity, 215–216
  measures and computational formulae (table 9.1), 213
  selecting variables, 211–212
Measurement systems, 99
Medicaid, 686–687, 688
Medicare, 686–688, 689
Mentoring, 474–476
Mentoring, and coaching. *See* Coaching
Merger integration plans, developing, 610–611
Mergers and acquisitions (M&As), 162, 607–615
  application stages, 608–615
    legal combination phase, 611
    operational combination phase, 611–615
    precombination phase, 608–611
  business case, establishing, 609–610
  choosing partner for, 608–609
  coaching, used in, 474–476
  cultural integration activities, 612, 615
  developing integration plans for, 610–611
  due diligence assessment for, 610
  major phases and activities in, 500, 609
  operational and technical integration activities, 611–612
  rationale for, 607
  team, creating, 609
  United and Continental merger, 613–615
Michigan Organizational Assessment Questionnaire, 127
Microcosm group, 301–304
  application stages, 302–303
  components of, 301–302
  results of, 304
Middle East, 5
Minimal critical specification, in work design, 420
Minnesota Coalition Against Sexual Violence (MNCASA), 185
Minnesota Multiphasic Personality Inventory (MMPI), 475
Minorities
  career development preferences of, 481
  use of mentoring with, 72
Misrepresentation, 62–63
MNCASA. *See* Minnesota Coalition Against Sexual Violence (MNCASA)
Model II learning, 587
  deutero-learning, 588
  values underlying, 587, 591
Model I learning, 586–587
Momentum, sustaining, 197–200
  building support system for, 200
  developing new competencies and skills, 200–201
  reinforcing new behaviors, 201
  staying the course, 201
Motivation. *See also* Reward systems
  for change, 181–184
  increase of, through employee participation in goal-setting process, 443–444. *See also* Goal setting
  reduction of, due to secrecy, 464
Motivational approach, to work design, 405–414, 415, 428
Motivators, 405
Moving step, in change process, 22
Multinational design, 541, 545
Myers-Briggs Type Indicator, 475

N

National culture, 164–165
National Innovations in American Government Awards, 711
National Labor Relations Act (NLRA), 384
Natural work units, in job enrichment, 407, 408
Network change, managing, 624–626
  creating instability in network, 624–625
  managing tipping point, 625–626
    law of the few, 625–626
    power of context, 626
    stickiness, 626
  self-organization, relying on, 626
Network interventions, 620–631
  creating network, 621–623
    convention stage, 622–623
    evaluation stage, 623
    identification stage, 621–622
    organization stage, 623
    stages and issues, 621–623
  managing network change, 624–626
    creation of instability in, 624–625
    law of the few, 625–626
    managing tipping point, 625–626
    power of context, 626
    self-organization, relying on, 626
    stickiness, 626
Networks, 162
  chaeobols, 620
  convention stage, 622–623
  creating, 621–623
  creation of instability in, 624–625
  creation of interdependence through, 623
  evaluation stage, 623
  grupos, 620
  identification stage, 621–622
  keiretsu, 620
  managing change in, 624–626
  multiorganizational, 621
  organization, 624
  organization stage, 623
  self-organizing behavior of, 626
Network structure, 159, 339, 353–356, 740. *See also* Networks
  advantages and disadvantages of, 353
    table, 12.5, 352
  Amazon.com's, 357–358
  chart (figure 12.7), 352
No Child Left Behind (NCLB) Act, 697
  purpose of, 697
Normative consensus, 225, 226
Norms, 556–557
  group's performance, 111
  in Model I learning, 586–587
  of organization culture, 530

O

Observations, 130–131
  core values and purpose of, 186–187
  stability of environment and technology, 223
Occupy Movement, 737
Off-site, 419
Open information systems, in HIOs, 393
Openness, 63
Open-space methods, 312, 313
Open system, 92–96, 312
Open-systems model, 92–96
  alignment, 94
  boundaries, 93–94
  diagnosing organizational systems, 94–96
  feedback, 94
  inputs, transformations, and outputs, 90–91
  in large-group approaches, 312–313
  organizations as open systems, 92–96
Open-systems planning, 312
Operational combination phase (M&A), 611–615
  day 1 activities, 611
  operational and technical integration activities, 611–612, 615
Opportunity network, 354
Orchestration capability, building, 598–601
Organizational changes, institutionalizing, 221–229
Organizational Culture Assessment Instrument, 127
Organizational development
  global social change
    change agent roles and skills, 677, 680–681
  sustainable management interventions, 659–681
Organizational identity, 663–664
  building capabilities of, 668–669
  identifying and redefining, 667
  repurposing boards of directors, 667–668
Organization assessment, 478
Organization capabilities, building, 668–669
Organization change, 3
  distinguishing between organization development and, 4
Organization confrontation meeting, 158, 298–301, 319
  application stages, 299
  results of, 301
Organization culture. *See also* Organizations, culture of
  changing, 161, 552
    application stages of, 559–560
    practical guidelines for, 559–560
  competing values approach, 557
  deep assumptions approach, 557–558
  defining and diagnosing, 552, 555–558
  implementing cultural change process, 558–560
  major elements of, 556–558
Organization design(s), 161, 534–548
  basic design alternatives, 535–537
  characteristics, 540
  conceptual framework, 534–535
  culture of work in Western China, 542–544
  at Deere & Company, 538–539
  implementing the global strategy, 542–544

and individual-level diagnosis, 112
model, 534
table 18.1, 536
three steps of, 546–547
worldwide organization design alternatives, 537, 539–541, 545–546
Organization development, 157
action research and survey feedback background, 8–9
and change programs, 158
contract development, 79–82
ground rules, 82
mutual expectations, 81
time and resources, 81–82
cultural context and economic development affect, 167–171
cultural values and organization customs, 165
defined, 1–4
diagnosis in, 89–90. *See also* Diagnosing organizations; Diagnosis
effect of cultural context and economic development on, 165–166
evolution in, 13–14
in family-owned businesses, 711–725
general introduction to, 1–19
global social change, 670–681
application stages, 674–677
organizations, 670, 672–674
growth and relevance of, 4–7
in health care industry, 686–693
history of, 7–13
integration of human resources management with, 440–442
interpersonal process issues, 82
interventions. *See* Interventions
laboratory training background, 8
major types of interventions in, 29
normative background, 9–11
outside the United States
cultural context approach, 165–166
economic development contingency, 166–167
high cultural fit, high industrialization, 169
high cultural fit, moderate industrialization, 169
low cultural fit, high industrialization, 169–170
low cultural fit, moderate industrialization, 168–169
overview, 15–17
personal process issues in, 82, 84
presenting problem, 76
process of
emergent nature of, 76–77
Kenworth Motors, 234–237
Peppercorn Dining, 238–257
Sunflower Incorporated, 232–233
procurement regulations for government agencies, 79
productivity and quality-of-life background, 11–13
in public school systems, 693–703
in public-sector organizations, 703–711
relationship, entering into, 76–79
social and environmental change at LDI Africa, 678–680
theory, needed by OD practitioners, 52
in the United States, cultural values tha guide, 39
Organization development practitioners, 34–35, 45–73. *See also* Collecting and analyzing diagnostic and feeding back information
careers, 59–60
competencies of effective, 47–52
data-gathering role of, 123
defining characteristics of term, 46–47
emotional demands on, 51, 57
ethical guidelines for
and human development professionals, 70–73
GSCOs and, 674–676
importance of ability to diagnose and understand intergroup relations by, 301
in international settings, 35, 39
and job enrichment, 160
knowledge and skill requirements of, 47–52
table, 3.1, 49–51
major criteria, 162–163
marginality and, 54–57
need for political skills by, 60
positions, 52–54
as process consultant for role clarification, 511
professional, 52, 66
role of, 52–59, 60–61
in role of salesperson, 556
selecting, 78–79
self-managed work teams, 160
SMO and, 667–668
training, in data feedback, 146–147
types of, 48
use of knowledge and experience, 57–59
use of power strategies by, 192–193
use of "shadow consultants" by, 200
Organization development trends, 731–747
B. R. Richardson Timber Products Corporation, 753–767
building Cuyahoga River Valley Organization (CRVO), 768–777
contextual, 735–746
economy, 735–738
effects on OD's future, 736
implications for future of OD, 741–746
organizations, 740–741
technology, 739–740
workforce, 738–739
impacts on OD's future, 732
and implications for future of OD, 734–735
application to more diverse organizations, 742–743
cross-cultural aspects, 746
experiencing internal conflicts in the short term, 734
increased focus on social and ecological sustainability, 745–746
increased integration in long term, 734–735
more involvement in supporting technological and managerial innovation, 743–745
increased focus on social and ecological sustainability, 745–746
pragmatic, 733
"research agenda" proposed by scholars for, 733–734
scholarly, 733–734
traditional, 732–733
transformation of Meck Insurance, 778–787
Organization learning (OL), 533, 582–593. *See also* Knowledge management (KM)
characteristics, 585–586
conceptual framework, 584–586
outcomes of, 586
performance affected by, 586
phases in, 589–593
processes, 586, 588–593
key outcome of, 586
Organization learning processes, 588–593
adaptive learning, 588
deutero-learning, 588
discovery, 588
double-loop learning (generative learning), 588
generalization process, 588
invention, 588
production processes, 588
single-loop learning, 588
Organization process approaches, 297–319
diagnostic issues in, 298
innovative strategies in Alegent's Women's and Children's Service Line, 314–316
intergroup relations interventions, 158, 301–309
large-group interventions, 158, 309–310
organization confrontation meeting, 158, 298–301, 319
Organizations, 171, 173
congruence, 222–223
culture of, 47, 99, 530. *See also* Culture change
diagnosing current structure of, 89–119
facing problems, steps for planned change in, 35
government, 742
high-involvement, 159, 393–395
human process issues in, 171
human resources issues in, 171
increasingly networked and knowledge-based nature of, 740–741
lack of success in establishing common, 183
levels of function in, 173
as open systems, 92–96
figure, 5.1, 92
physical layouts of, to enhance EI, 394–395
profit-seeking, 606
relative to M&As, 162, 607–615
sensitizing, to pressures for change, 182
strategic issues in, 171
technology and structure issues in, 171
transorganizational systems (TSs), 607
trends shaping change in, 5
unionization, 223
value issues within, 60
Organization stage in network development, 623
Organization transformation, 530
"Out-of-the-box thinking," 389
Outputs, of strategic orientation, 100
Outsourcing, 159, 339

P

Parallel processes, 302, 304
Parallel structures, 159, 174, 379–380
application stages, 379–384
EI and, 380
results of approaches to, 403

Pareto charts, 388
Participative group systems, 10
Participative Management Program, 10
Participatory action research, 26
Patient Protection and Affordable Care Act (ACA), 686
Pay
  negative effects of misperceptions about, 467
  performance-based systems, 460–462
  plans, least acceptable, 460
  skill-based systems, 458–459
Peer review panels, 32
Performance
  appraisal. *See* Performance appraisal
  effect of goal setting on, 160, 442
  feedback and coaching interventions, 478
  goals, in process-based structure, 347
  of intervention behaviors, 226
  job, positive effect of EAPs on, 445
  objective and subjective measures of, 450
  and reward systems, 160
Performance appraisal, 160, 174, 439–440, 448–452, 468
  application stages, 451–452
    criteria for design of system, 451
    diagnosing current situation, 451
    establishing system's purposes and objectives, 451
    evaluation and monitoring system, 452
    selecting right people, 451
    use of pilot tests, 452
  effects of, 452, 468
  elements (table 15.1), 449
  as link between goal-setting processes and reward system, 445
  process, 449–450
Performance-based pay systems, 460–462
  ratings of various (table 15.3), 461
Performance management, 489–490
  adapting appraisal process at Capital One Financial, 453–455
  components of, 453–455 (check the level)
  goal setting, 41
  model of, 440–442
  performance appraisal, 448–452, 468
  reward systems, 440, 441, 452–468
Performance management interventions, 502
Performance norms, in group-level diagnosis, 111–112
Personal characteristics, and individuallevel diagnosis, 113
Personalization, in organizing knowledge, 592
Personal management interview (PMI), 293
Personnel policies, in HIOs, 393
Phased retirement, 490
Piece-rate quotas, 460
Planned change
  action research model, 24–26
  in an underorganized system, 36–39
  comparisons of change models, 27–28
  conceptualization of, 40–41
  critique of, 40–42
  degree of organization, 34–35
  diagnosing, 29
  different types of, 30–39
  domestic *vs.* international settings, 35, 39
  entering and contracting, 28–29
  evaluating and institutionalizing change, 30
  general model of, 28
  in GSCOs, 681
  magnitude of change, 30, 33–34
  nature of, 22–42
  planning and implementing change, 29–30
  positive model, 26–27
  practice of, 41–42
  at the San Diego County Regional Airport Authority (SDCRAA), 31–33
  theories of, 22–28, 42
Plateaued employees, 493
Polarization, 304
Political resistance, 183
Political support development, 188–193, 194–195, 196, 201
  assessing change agent power, 192
  identifying key stakeholders, 192
  influencing stakeholders, 192–193
Porter's competitive strategy model, 572
Positive model of planned change, 21, 26–27, 91
  five phases of, 23, 26–27
Power, reinforcement of EI with, 376
Power distance, in global OD, 166
Power strategies
  attention being paid to, 191, 194–195
  widely used, 193
Precombination phase (M&A), 608–611
  business case, establishing, 609–610
  candidates, search and selection of, 608–609
  due diligence assessment, performing, 610
  M&A team, creation of, 609
  merger integration plans, developing, 610–611
Predictive validity, 216
Preferences, 226
Problem, joint diagnosis of, 24–25
Problem identification, 24
Problem solving
  formation of employee, 381
  groups, 267
  procedures, 388
  use of organization confrontation meeting for, 158, 298–299
Process consultation (PC), 174, 267–268
  at Christian Caring Homes, Inc., 271–273
  group interventions, 270
  group process, 158, 266–267
  individual interventions, 268–270
  principles to guide actions in, 267–268
  results of, 273–274
Process interventions, 270
Process mapping, 369
Process structure, 346–349
  advantages and disadvantages of, 348–349
  chart (figure 12.5), 347
Productivity, 10, 11–13
Product life cycle shifts, 531
Profile of Organizational Characteristics, 10
Proposal(s)
  elements of an effective (table 4.1), 78
  requests for submission of, 78
  sample process, 83
Psychometric tests, 215
Public school systems, 693–703
  collaborative vision, creating, 700
  communication and learning, changing nature of, 695
  complex, diverse, and evolving K-12 educational system, 693–694
  Excellence Movement, 696
  failed reform, reasons for, 698–699
  grounding practice in theory, 701
  growing leaders and leadership locally, 701
  High Standards, Testing, and Accountability Movement, 697
  improving teaching practice with action research, 700–701
  increased competition, 695
  increased diversity, 695
  learning relationships, cultivating, 700
  OD practitioners, considerations for, 699–702
  organization development in, 693–703
  professional learning communities (PLCs), developing, 699
  reform efforts, disappointing, 696–699
  Restructuring Movement, 696–697
  tough economic times and, 695–696
  trust, cultivating, 699–700
  utilizing technology as catalyst for innovation, 701–702
  workplace and required skills, evolution of, 695
Public-sector organizations
  comparing private- and, 705–710
    intergovernmental relations, 709–710
    multiplicity of decision makers, 707–708
    stakeholder access, 708–709
    values and structures, 705–707
  organization development in, 703–711
    recent research and innovations in, 710–711

Q

Qualitative tools, data analysis, 133–135
  content analysis, 133–134
  force-field analysis, 134–135
Quality, 195
  Fourteen Points and Seven Deadly Sins of, 385
  philosophy, need for managerial commitment to, 201
  seven tools of, 387–388
Quality circles, 11–13
Quality control, 385
Quality Control Handbook (Juran), 385
Quality Is Free (Crosby), 386
Quality of work life (QWL), 7, 11–13, 376
Quantitative tools, data analysis, 135–142
  difference tests, 140–142
  means, standard deviations, and frequency distributions, 135
  scattergrams and correlation coefficients, 135–138
Quasi-experimental research designs, 217

R

Random sample, 133
Reaction, as evaluation criterion, 478
Realistic job preview, 487
Recession, global, 4
Redesigning work system, SMO and, 669
Reengineering, 159, 174, 364–371
  application stages, 365–368
  process, Honeywell IAC's TotalPlant, 369–371
  results from, 368–371

Refreezing step, in change process, 22
Reimbursement models, in health care industry, 687
Relevant client, determining, 77
Research designs, 216–221
  alpha change, 218
  beta change, 218
  comparison unit, 217
  gamma change, 218
  longitudinal measurement, 217
  quasi-experimental (table 9.3), 217
  statistical analysis, 217
Resistance, to change, 183–184
  strategies for dealing with, 183–184
  types of, 183–184
Restructuring, 159, 339
  Carlsbad, California, Public Works Department (case study), 433–434
  increase of EAP use during, 512
  stress related to, 490
Retirement, phased, 490
Rewards, intrinsic, 225
Reward systems, 174, 440, 441, 452–468
  availability, 457
  centralized, 456
  design features (table 15.2), 456
  durability, 458
  focusing on increasing employee flexibility, 503
  gain sharing systems, 462–464
  hierarchical, 456–457
  in HIOs, 393
  internal and external equity, 455–456
  job-based *vs.* performance-based, 455
  at Lands' End, revising, 465–466
  performance
    appraisal, as link between goal setting processes and, 442
    based pay systems, 460–462
    contingency, 455, 458
  performance appraisal, as link between goal setting processes and, 160
  process issues regarding, 466–467
  promotion systems, 464
  as reinforcement for new behaviors, 201, 225
  reinforcement of EI with, 376
  rewards mix feature, 457
  security, 457
  seniority, 457
  skill-based pay systems, 458–459
  structural and motivational features of, 455–457
  timeliness, 458
  value expectancy model, 457–458
  visibility, 458
Role clarification, 510
Role conflict, 62
Roles, 510
  ambiguity, reducing, 444
  of network members, 624
  work, as source of stress, 509
Rucker plan, 463
Rumors, 183

S

Sabbaticals, paid, 511
Salespeople, in networks, 625, 626
Sample selection, 133
Sample size, 132
Sampling, 132–133
Scanlon plan, 463
Scattergrams, 138–140
  samples (figures 6.3 and 6.4), 138, 139
Search conferences, 6, 309, 312, 313, 381, 591. *See also* Large-group interventions
Self-design, 26
  change strategy, 580–582
  at Healthways Corporation, 583–584
Self-designing organizations, 576–582
  application stages, 579–582
  application stages of strategy for, 579–582
  design criteria, creating, 581
  designing, 581–582
  Healthways Corporation, 583–584
  implementing and assessing, 582
  laying foundation, 580–581
  self-design strategy, 580
  turbulent environments, demands of, 576–579
Self-managed teams, 415–419
  application stages, 419–420
  developing self-managed teams at WI, inc, 421–422
  model of (figure 14.3), 416
  organization support systems, 417–419
  problems between managers and, 418–419
  results of, 423–424
  team process interventions, 417
  team task design, 416–417
Self-managed work teams, 160
  assessment centers and, 487
Self-management competence, needed in OD, 48, 51
Self-organization, 624, 626
Sensing and calibration, 225
Sensing meetings, 129
Sensitivity training, 7
September 11, 2001 attacks, 104. *See also* Terrorism
Service orientation, 151
Service quality concepts, 281
Sexual orientation, and workplace diversity, 501–502
"Shining Star Awards," 654
Single-loop learning, 588. *See also* Adaptive learning; Double-loop learning
Site-based management, 696
Six sigma, 385, 387–388, 389
Six-sigma programs, 12
Skill-based pay systems, 458–459
Skill training, 378
Skill variety, 113, 405–406
Small entrepreneurial start-ups, 742
"Smarter planet" strategy, 666
Social construction of reality, 26, 309
Social constructivism, 701
Socialization, effect on intervention of, 224
Social movement organizations (SMOs), 670
Social needs, 426–428
Social turbulence, 704
Sociotechnical systems (STS)
  conceptual background, 414–415
    environmental relationship premise, 415
    sociotechnical system premise, 414–415
  outcomes of, 415
  self-managed work teams, 415–419
Sony, 187
Stakeholders
  access of, in public-sector organizations, 708–709
  choosing relevant, 573–574
  effect of transformational change on organization, 547
  engaging between the first and second retreats, 575
  in health care industry, restoring trust in and among, 723
  identifying key, 192
  influencing, 192–193
  steps in, 29
Standard deviations, 135
"A Statement of Values and Ethics for Professionals in Organization and Human System Development," 70–73
Statistical analyses, 215, 217
Statistical process control (SPC) techniques, 387
Status quo, preserving, 181
Steelworkers, 12
Steering committees, use of, in parallel structures, 380
Steinway's strategic orientation, 102–104
Stewardship, 681
Strategic alliance, 6, 616
Strategic alliance interventions, 616–620
  alliance-building intervention between Maharashtra Hybrid Seeds Company Limited (MAHYCO) and Monsanto, 618–620
  application stages, 616–617
    alliance operation and adjustment, 617
    alliance strategy formulation, 616
    alliance structuring and start-up, 617
    partner selection, 616–617
Strategic change, 281
  Carlsbad, California, Public Works Department (case study), 433–434
  difference between transformational change and other types of, 529–530. *See also* Transformational change
  managing, at Microsoft Canada, 553–554
Strategic change interventions, 161–162
  and integrated strategic change, 161
Strategic change process, criteria for an effective, 570
Strategic direction
  statement of, 571–573
    action plan, 572–573
    competitive logic, 572
    four elements of, 572–573
    goals of, 572
    organization, 572
Strategic interventions, 29, 171. *See also* Interventions
  in family businesses, 723
Strategic management
  application changes
    exercising strategic choice, 551
    implementing plan, 552
    performing strategic analysis, 550–551
  predominant paradigm in, 549

Strategic orientation
  alignment, 101
  design component, 98–99
  inputs, 93
  in integrated strategic change (ISC), 161
  outputs of, 100
  of Steinway & Sons, 102–104
Strategic plan, 549
Strategies, 592
  clarifying, 670
  codification, for organizing knowledge, 592
  personalization, 592
  sustainable effectiveness, 661–663
Stratified sample, 133
Strengths, weaknesses, opportunities, and threats (SWOT) analyses, 572
Stress inoculation training, 508
Stress management, 497, 504, 507–510, 512, 513, 514
  alleviating stressors and coping with stress, 510–512
    employee assistance programs (EAPs), 512
    health facilities, 511–512
    role clarification, 510
    supportive relationships, 511
    work leaves, 511
  diagnosis and awareness of stress and its causes, 507–510
    charting stressors, 509
    health profiling, 510
    individual differences, 509–510
    workplace stressors, 508–509
Stretch goals, 442. *See also* Goal setting
Structural change
  combining survey feedback with, 145
  institutionalizing, at Hewlett-Packard, 227–228
Structural design, 159, 174, 184, 339–340
  contingencies influencing (figure 12.1), 340
  customer-centric Structure, 349–353
  divisional structure, 342–344
  effects of, 183
  functional structure, 340–342
  matrix structure, 344–346
  network structure, 353–356
  process structure, 346–349
Structural interventions, 270
Structure, defined, 624
Structures, as features of agile organization, 665
Subsistence economies, 167
Substance abuse, 720
  costs to businesses of, 719–720
Success factors, worldwide, 539
Supervisory system, as job enrichment constraint, 413
Supportive relationships, to alleviate stress, 511
Survey feedback, 7. *See also* Feedback
  data, problem solving with, 142–143
  five steps of, 145–148, 147
  limitations of, 152
  and organizational dependencies, 148
  and planned change at Cambia health solutions, 149–152
  results of, 148, 152–154
  session, planning for, 146
Survey of Organizations, 127
Sustainability friendly, 664
Sustainable effectiveness, 659
  Agile organization designs, 664
    features, 664–667
  identities, 663–664
  objectives, 661–663
  organizational identity, 663–664
    figure 21.1, 663
  strategies supporting, 661
Sustainable management organizations (SMOs), 659–681. *See also* Interventions
  Agile organization designs, 664–667
    features of, 664–667
  application stages, 667–670, 673–674
  changes, sequencing, 669–670
    redesigning work system, 669
  design guidelines of, 660–667
  goals of, 661–663
  implications of, 660
  Interface Carpets transformation to sustainability, 671–672
  objectives, 661–663
  organizational identity, 663–664
    building capabilities of, 668–669
    identifying and redefining, 667
    repurposing boards of directors, 667–668
  strategies supporting, 661
    aggressiveness, 661
    breadth, 661
    differentiation, 661
Synergies
  looking for, 610
  unrealistic expectations of, 63
System, 10
System interventions, 723
Systems thinking, 589

T

Tacit knowledge, 592
Talent development
  career planning and development interventions, 480–493
    application stages, 482–490
    goals, 481–482
    results, 493
  coaching and mentoring, 160, 474–476
    application stages, 475
    coaching and mentoring, results, 476
    goals, 474–475
Task control, 416–417
Task differentiation, 416
Task environment, 96–97
Task force, 492, 503, 578–579, 583–584
Task identity, 127, 405–406
Tasks. *See also* Jobs
  combining, in job enrichment, 408
  differentiation of, in self-managed work team, 416–417
  identity of, in job enrichment, 408
  skill variety, 405–406
Task significance, 113, 405–406
Task structure, in group-level diagnosis, 109
Team building, 8, 153, 158, 159, 174, 277–278, 292–293
  activities, 281, 292
  affecting group's relationship with rest of organization, 286
  applicability of, 282
  categories (table 10.2), 285
  checklist (table 10.1), 283–284
  facilitation of other OD interventions by, 278–281
  manager's role in, 291–292
  oriented to group's operation and behavior, 285–286
  relevant to one or more individuals, 285
  results of, 292–293
Team design components, diagnosis of, 109–111
Team Development Survey, 127
Team functioning in groups, 111
Team leaders
  evaluation and reward systems for, 419
  leadership support systems, 419
  recruitment and selection, 418
  responsibilities of, 418
  support systems for, 420
  training, 418–419
  use of freed-up time by, 419
Team process interventions, 417
Teams. *See also* Self-managed work teams
  behaviors of, 201
  multidisciplinary, in process structure, 346
  group interviews by self regulating work, 464
  peer consulting, 479
  prevalence of, in high involvement organizations, 398
  problem-solving, 146
  in process-based structure, 346, 347–349
  top-management (at Ortiv Glass Corporation), 110
Team's task structure, 109
Teamwork, 187, 201, 370, 371
  cross-functional, 347
Teamwork for Employees and Management Act, 384
Technical interdependence, 425–426
Technical resistance, 183
Technical system, as job enrichment constraint, 412
Technical uncertainty, 425
Technology
  effect on workforce of, 738
  rapid changes in, 531
  trends influencing OD, 735,739–740
Technostructural interventions, 159–160, 339–371, 590–591. *See also* Work design
  downsizing, 356–363, 366
  reengineering, 159, 364–371
  structural design, 159, 339–356
Telecommuting, 5, 503
Terrorism, 5, 359, 704
Texas Instruments, 14
T-groups, 7
Theories in use, 589
  consequences of, 589–590
  dialogue approach, 589
  discovering, 589–590
  invent and produce more effective, 590–592
  ladder of inference, 590, 591
  left-hand, right-hand column technique, 590
Theory Z (Ouchi), 12, 552

Therapy, confusion of coaching with, 474
Third-party interventions, 158, 174, 274–277
 episodic model of conflict, 275–276
 facilitating conflict resolution process, 276–277
360-degree feedback, 450
Top management, 110
Total quality management (TQM), 12, 159, 174, 375, 385–390, 711
 application stages, 387–390
 awards for, 386
 evolution of, 390
 historical background, 385–387
 implementation senior managers' role in, 387
 measurement of output variations using, 388
 popularity in United States of, 385
 of progress of, 389
 results of, 390
 rewards for accomplishments using, 412–413
 at Ritz-Carlton, 391–392
 in state government agencies, 386
 training requirements for, 412–413
Trade-offs
 cost-benefit, of alliances, 616
 involving change agents, 681
 in networks, 621, 626
Traditional jobs, 425, 429
 defined, 403
 defined, 403
Traditional work groups, 425, 429
 comparison between self-managed teams and, 424
 defined, 403
 defined, 403
Training
 in HIOs, 393
 for managers dealing with workplace disability factors, 502
 sensitivity, 7
Transformational change, 529–530
 characteristics of, 530
 competing values approach, 557
 components of, 555
 culture change, 161, 552
  deep assumptions approach, 557–558
  defining and diagnosing, 552, 555–558
  at IBM, 561–562
 disruptions causing, 530–531
 environmental and internal disruptions, 530–531
 executive leadership of, 531
 integrated strategic change, 548–552
  process, 549–550
 management processes and, 535
 managing strategic change at Microsoft Canada, 553–554
 multiple stakeholders and, 532
 new organizing paradigm, 533–534
 new organizing paradigm demanded by, 533
 organization design(s), 161, 534–548
  basic design alternatives, 535–537
  characteristics, 540
  conceptual framework, 534–535
  at Deere & Company, 538–539
  model, 534
  worldwide organization design, 537, 539–541, 545–546
 role of envisioning, energizing, and enabling in, 531–532
 role of executives and line management in, 531–532
 senior executives and line management, 531–532
 significant learning, 533–534
 systemic and revolutionary, 532–533
 triggered by environmental and internal disruptions, 530–531
Transition management, 1, 193–197, 198–199
 activity planning, 196
 change-management structures, 196
 commitment planning, 196
 in the HP-Compaq acquisition, 198–199
Transition state, 195, 719
Transnational design, 545–546
Transorganizational change, 605–635
 building alliance relationships, 618–620
 mergers and acquisitions, 162, 607–615
 network interventions, 620–631
  creating network, 621–623
  managing network change, 624–626
 planning the United-continental merger, 613–615
 strategic alliance interventions, 616–620
  application stages, 616–617
  alliance operation and adjustment, 617
  alliance strategy formulation, 616
  alliance structuring and start-up, 617
  partner selection, 616–617
 transorganizational rationale, 606–607
Transorganizational development, 676
Transorganizational rationale, 606–607
Transorganizational systems (TSs), 607
Transorganization development, 621
 Alaska Health Workforce Coalition (AHWC), 627–631
 application stages for (figure 20.1), 622
Triple bottom line, 745
Trust
 alliances and, 617
 establishing, 129
 restoring, in and among stakeholders in health care industry, 723
Trust level, 700
Turbulent environments, demands of, 576–579
Turnover rates
 effect of skill-based pay on, 458–459
 high costs of, 481
 positive effect of EAPs on, 512
Type A behavior patterns, 509
Type B behavior patterns, 509

U

"The Undercover Change Agent," 62
Unfreezing step, in change process, 22
Union Carbide, 8
Union-management
 cooperative projects, 384. *See also* Quality circles
Unions, 77, 310. *See also* Union-management
 cooperative projects involving, 376–377, 379
 as force for change promotion, 224
 organizations with, handling of salary data at, 467
United Nations
 Conference on Environment and Development, 672
 Food and Agriculture Organization, 677
The United Nations' Human Development Programs, 167
Unobtrusive measures, 131–132

V

Valid information, 163
Value consensus, 226
Value expectancy model, of reward system, 457–458
Values, 60–61
 building GSCO, 674–675
 conference used in change process, 189–191
 core, 186–187
 culture and, in workforce diversity, 502–503
 differences of, in public- and private sector organizations, 705–707
 dilemmas caused by competing, 557
 of family business system model, 716–719
 in Model I learning, 586–587
 of organization culture, 556–557
 organization customs and cultural, 165
 underlying Model II learning, 587, 591
Vertical alignment, in MBO process, 448
Vertical disaggregation, 355
Vertical linakages, GSCOS and, 674–676
Vertical loading, in job enrichment, 407, 409
Vertical market network, 354
Vision
 formulation of clear strategic, for effective cultural change, 559
Vision creation, 181, 184–186
 for building GSCO values, 674–675
 exercises, 317
 for M&As, 609–610
 of preferred future, 23
 at Premier, 189–191
 as purpose and reason for change, 181

W

Wealth
 corporate strategies and concentration of, 734
 emerging economies and concentration of, 737
 globalization and increasing concentration of, 737
"We Are Here Awards," 654
Web sites, 357–385
Women, career development preferences of, 481
Work councils, 393
Work design, 174, 277, 403–429. *See also* Employee Involvement (EI)
 combining survey feedback with, 145
 effort, sanctioning, 419
 engineering approach, 404, 425
 generating appropriate, 419
 implementing and evaluating, 420
 meeting both technical and personal needs, 428–429
 motivational approach, 405–414
 need for continual change and improvement, 420
 personal-need factors, 426–428

Work design *(continued)*
- sociotechnical systems (STS) approach, 414–424
- specifying support systems, 420
- technical and personal factors affecting, 425–429
- technical factors, 425–426
- that optimizes personal needs (figure 14.5), 427
- that optimizes technology (figure 14.4), 426
- transformational change and, 535

Workforce
- aging of U.S., 485, 689–690
- changes affecting, 738–739
- downsizing, and rise of contingent, 358
- effect of technology on, 738
- flexibility, skill-based pay and, 458–459
- goal, 477
- immigrants entering, 499
- need for committed and involved, 404
- need for involvement of, for change, 418
- reduction in airline industry, 359
- shortages, in health care industry, 689–690

Workforce diversity and wellness, managing, 407
- aligning strategy and diversity at L'oréal, 505–506
- dimensions and interventions, 407
- employee stress and wellness intervention
  - applications stages, 507–512
  - goals, 504, 506–507
  - results of stress management and wellness interventions, 513
- employee stress and wellness interventions, 161, 504
- Johnson & Johnson's health and wellness program, 514–515
- managing diversity, framework for, 498
- workforce diversity interventions, 407
  - application stages, 499–503
  - goals, 498–499
  - results for diversity interventions, 503–504

Workforce diversity interventions, 497–504
- age factors, 499
- aligning strategy and diversity at L'oréal, 505–506
- culture and values factors, 502–503
- disability factors, 502
- gender factors, 500–501
- race and ethnicity factors, 501
- results for, 503–504
- sexual orientation factors, 501–502

Working with others (WWO), 370–372, 396–398

Work leaves, 511

Work-life balance
- desire for, 486
- employee benefits at HealthCo (case study), 519–522
- interventions, 490

Work systems
- as features of agile organization, 664–665
- redesigning, 669

World War II, 385
- use of engineering approach to job design following, 404

Worldwide organization design alternatives, 537, 539–541, 545–546
- design characteristics, 540
- figure 18.2, 539
- global design, 541
- international design, 539–540
- multinational design, 541, 545
- table 18.2, 540
- transnational design, 545–546

Worldwide success factors, 539